Human Exceptionality

Society, School, and Family

Sixth Edition

Michael L. Hardman
UNIVERSITY OF UTAH

Clifford J. Drew
UNIVERSITY OF UTAH

M. Winston Egan
BRIGHAM YOUNG UNIVERSITY

Allyn and Bacon

Boston   London   Toronto   Sydney   Tokyo   Singapore

Senior Editor: Ray Short

Developmental Editor: Alicia Reilly

Editorial Assistant: Karin Huang

Marketing Managers: Brad Parkins and Ellen Mann Dolberg

Composition Buyer: Linda Cox

Manufacturing Buyer: Megan Cochran

Production Administrator: Deborah Brown

Editorial-Production Service: Barbara Gracia

Textbook Designer: Seventeenth Street Studios

Electronic Composition: Karen Mason

Photo Researcher: Susan Duane

Cover Administrator: Linda Knowles

Copyright 1999, 1996, 1993, 1990, 1987, 1984 by Allyn and Bacon
A Viacom Company
160 Gould Street
Needham Heights, MA 02194

Internet: www.abacon.com
America Online: Keyword: College Online

Library of Congress Cataloging-in-Publication Data

Hardman, Michael L.
    Human exceptionality: society, school, and family / Michael L.
Hardman, Clifford J. Drew, M. Winston Egan.—6th ed.
      p.   cm.
    Includes bibliographical references and index.
    ISBN 0–205–28039–0
    1. Handicapped. 2. Exceptional children. 3. Handicapped—
Services for. 4. Learning disabilities.   I. Drew, Clifford J.,
1943– . II. Egan, M. Winston.   III. Title.
    HV1568.H37   1999
    362—dc21   98–15540
                                                                         CIP

Printed in the United States of America

10 9 8 7 6 5 4 3 2 1   VHP   03 02 01 00 99 98

Photo credits appear on page 616, which constitutes an extension of the copyright page.

Brief Contents

105939

Contents

PART II

Through the Lifespan

PART III

High-Incidence Disabilities

PART IV

Low-Incidence Disabilities

PART VI

Extraordinary Abilities

Selected Features

TODAY'S TECHNOLOGY

Preface

If we are to achieve a richer culture . . . we must weave one in which each diverse human gift will find a fitting place.

Margaret Mead

As you begin your study of the sixth edition of *Human Exceptionality: Society, School, and Family,* we would like to provide some perspective on those features that continue from our fifth edition of this text as well as on what is new and different. It is important to remember that this text is about people—people with diverse needs, characteristics, and lifestyles—people who for one reason or another are called exceptional. What does the word *exceptional* mean to you? For that matter what do the words, *disordered, deviant, disabled, challenged, different,* or *handicapped* mean to you? Who or what influenced your knowledge and attitudes about these terms and the people behind them? Up to this point in your life, you were probably most influenced by life experiences and not by any formal training. You may have a family member, friend, or casual acquaintance who is exceptional in some way. It may be that you are a person with exceptional characteristics. Then again, you may be approaching a study of human exceptionality with little or no background on the topic. You will find that the study of human exceptionality is the study of being human. Perhaps you will come to understand yourself better in the process.

Organizational Features

In addition to providing you with current and informative content, we are committed to making your first formal experience with exceptionality informative, interesting, enjoyable, and productive. To this end, we have incorporated features within the sixth edition text that should greatly enhance your desire to learn more and become acquainted with human exceptionality.

■ TO BEGIN WITH . . .

"To Begin With . . ." excerpts, found at the beginning of each chapter, are designed to introduce and stimulate interest in topics. They offer a variety of fascinating and current quotes, facts, and figures related to each subject area.

■ SNAPSHOTS

Snapshots is a series of personal statements found throughout the text that focus directly on individuals with differences. The purpose of this feature is to share with you some personal insights into the lives of these people. These insights may come from the teachers, family members, friends, peers, and professionals, as well as from the individual who is exceptional. All chapters of this sixth edition open with at least one Snapshot of an individual who is exceptional. In no way are these Snapshots representative of the range of characteristics associated with a given area of exceptionality. At best, they simply provide you with a frame of reference for your reading, and they let you know we are talking about real people who deal with life in many of the same ways. We believe you will find the Snapshots to be one of the most enriching aspects of your introduction to exceptionality.

■ INTERACTING IN NATURAL SETTINGS

Another feature in this new edition is Interacting in Natural Settings, which is intended to provide the reader with some brief tips on ways to communicate, teach, or just socialize with people who are exceptional across a variety of settings (home, school, and community) and age spans (early childhood through the adult years). The tips provided are certainly not inclusive of the many possible ideas on how to interact more effectively with people who are exceptional, but hopefully they provide some stimulus for further thinking on how to include these individuals as family members, school peers, friends, or neighbors.

REFLECT ON THIS

Every chapter includes Reflect on This boxes. Each one highlights a piece of interesting and relevant information that will add to your learning and enjoyment of the chapter content. These features offer a temporary diversion from the chapter narrative while providing some engaging facts about a variety of subjects. For example, Chapter 6 features a Reflect on This that focuses on the use of an innovative strategy to help students with learning disabilities develop writing skills in a general education classroom.

TODAY'S TECHNOLOGY

The sixth edition of this text features *new* information on the expanding use of technology for people who are exceptional. Today's Technology features highlight some of the innovations in computers, biomedical engineering, assistive technology, and instructional systems. These boxes focus on such topics as learning language skills through devices that synthesize speech, electronic readers for people with vision loss, and word processing programs with specialized features that assist students with learning disabilities in developing writing skills.

DEBATE FORUM

Every chapter in this sixth edition concludes with a Debate Forum. The purpose of these forums is to broaden your view of the issues concerning people with differences. The Debate Forums focus on issues about which there are some philosophical differences of opinion, such as federal involvement in education, inclusive education for students with disabilities, and the appropriateness of an intervention strategy. For each issue discussed, a position taken (*point*) and an alternative to that position (*counterpoint*) are given. The purpose of the Debate Forum is not to establish right or wrong answers, but to help you better understand the diversity of issues concerning individuals who are exceptional.

Improving Your Study Skills

Each chapter in this text is organized in a systematic fashion. Here are some brief suggestions that will increase your learning effectiveness.

PREVIEW THE CHAPTER

In the margins of each chapter you will find a series of Focus questions that highlight important information to be learned. Survey the Focus questions before reading the chapter to guide your reading. Then examine key chapter headings to further familiarize yourself with chapter organization.

ASK QUESTIONS

Using the Focus questions as a guide, ask yourself what you want to learn from the chapter material. After reviewing chapter headings and the Focus questions, write down any additional questions you may have and use them as a supplement to guide your reading. Now organize your thoughts and schedule time to actively read the chapter.

READ

Again using the Focus questions as your guide, actively read the chapter.

RECITE

After reading the chapter, turn back to the Focus questions and respond orally and in writing to each question. Develop a written outline of the key points to remember.

REVIEW

Each chapter in this text concludes with a section entitled Review. Each Focus question for the chapter is repeated in this section along with key points to remember from the material presented. Compare your memory of the material and your written outline to the key points addressed in the Review section. If you forgot or misunderstood any of the important points, return to the Focus question in the chapter and reread the material. Follow this process for each chapter in the book. You may also consider developing your own short-answer essay tests to further enhance your understanding of the material in each chapter.

A Study Guide is available to help you master the information included in this sixth edition of *Human Exceptionality*. Each chapter of the Study Guide is organized around effective methods for studying. Students are provided with information on what to preview, questions to ask, keys to effective reading, and how to recite, review, and reflect on the most important concepts in each chapter of the book. Exercises for mastering key terms, multiple-choice practice tests, fill-in-the-blank study sections, and activities that encourage further exploration into various topics of interest are included.

The study of human exceptionality is relatively young and unexplored. Those of you who may be seeking careers in fields concerned with exceptional people will be part of the exploration. If after reading this book you are excited and encouraged to study further in this area, then we have met our primary goal. We would be unrealistic and unfair if we said this book will provide you with everything you ever wanted to know about people who are exceptional. What it does provide, however, is an overview on the lives of these people within their own communities, at school, and as family members.

Acknowledgments

We begin with a very big thank you to our colleagues from around the country who provided in-depth and constructive feedback on various chapters within both the fifth and *sixth* editions of *Human Exceptionality*. We extend our gratitude to the following national reviewers: Robert S. Ristow, St. Ambrose University; Keith Storey, Chapman University; Mike Jakupcak, University of Montana; William A. Myers, University of Texas at Austin; David S. Katims, University of Texas at San Antonio; Judith Reymond, Loyola University Chicago; Sandra Alper, University of Northern Iowa; William N. Bender, University of Georgia; Sherwood J. Best, California State University–Los Angeles; Candace Bos, University of Arizona; Margaret Coleman, University of Texas at Austin; Gary A. Davis, University of Wisconsin-Madison; William E. Davis, University of Maine; Amy P. Dietrich, Memphis State University; Anne Y. Gallegos, New Mexico State University; Barbara C. Gartin, University of Arkansas; Cheryl Hanley-Maxwell, University of Wisconsin-Madison; Judith J. Ivarie, Eastern Illinois University; Michelle L. Kelley, Old Dominion University; Jennifer L. Kilgo, Virginia Commonwealth University; Earl Knowlton, University of Kansas; S. J. Kuder, Rowan College of New Jersey; Sheldon Maron, Portland State University; Donald F. Morres, Gallaudet University; Cathy Pratt, Indiana University; Joseph Renzulli, University of Connecticut; Rhia Roberts, University of Arizona; Ramon M. Rocha, State University of New York College at Geneseo; Ernest Rose, Montana State University; Robert Rutherford, Arizona State University; Barbara P. Sirvis, State University of New York College at Brockport; Corinne Smith, Syracuse University; Maureen Smith, Buffalo State College; Vicki D. Stayton, Western Kentucky University; Shari Stokes, Fitchburg State College; and Kathleen S. Quinn, Eastern Michigan University.

Special thanks to the people with disabilities and their families who participated in the Snapshot videos and case studies for this text. These are the people who make up the heart of what this book is all about. Throughout the writing and production of this book, they made us keenly aware that this book is first and foremost about people.

For a job exceptionally well done, we extend our gratitude to Loxi Calmes, currently the Director of Curriculum and Instruction in the Lunenburg School District in Massachusetts for her first-rate effort in taking the lead in writing the annotated instructor's manual of this text. Loxi spent untold hours developing and editing lecture notes, creating related activities, and locating the most current and informative media available in the area of exceptionality. Loxi was always on time with a high quality product.

We also extend our thanks to the faculty and students at the University of Utah and Brigham Young University who continue to teach us a great deal about writing textbooks. Many of the changes incorporated into this sixth edition are a direct result of critiques from university colleagues and students in our classes.

As authors, we are certainly grateful for the strong commitment of the Allyn and Bacon editorial and production team in bringing to fruition the highest quality text possible. As is true with other editions, the team has sought to consistently improve the readability, utility, and appearance of this book. Thanks to Nancy Forsyth, Editor-in-Chief of the Education Division, for her leadership in promoting an atmosphere of professionalism that supported the cooperative efforts of the A & B team and yours truly—the authors. We are indebted to our Senior Editor Ray Short and his editorial assistant Karin Huang. Ray has now provided leadership and support for us through four editions of the book, each time providing invaluable advice on keeping the book at the forefront of the topical issues in the field. Ray's knowledge of the needs and interests of professors and students in the field of education and psychology helped us to cast this edition into a comprehensive text for the next century and beyond. We genuinely appreciated the opportunity to once again work with Alicia Reilly as our developmental editor. Alicia has been a major force in shaping this edition from the very beginning, attending not only to the quality of the content but also ensuring that the book maintains its strong user-friendly approach to instruction. Her careful and indepth editing of the manuscript has been a crucial factor in presenting a product of which we are all very proud. We also thank Barbara Gracia, Editorial-Production Service, for her unwavering attention to the important details related to text figures, tables, sentence and paragraph structure, typographical errors, and APA style that can make or break a text. As was true in the last edition, Barbara showed considerable patience as we all sought perfection in the galleys and final page proofs. The photo researcher for this book was Susan Duane who did an outstanding job of locating photos that brought to life the text's printed word. Under Susan's direction, we have included the most recent photographs from Allyn and Bacon's photo shoots in general education classes including school systems that work with the inclusion model around the country. This photo resource also contains families with children and/or adults with disabilities. We are also especially pleased with the anatomical line art rendered by Jay Alexander that makes this edition particularly current and precise in delineating the physical effects that injury and disease can inflict. Last, but certainly not least, many thanks to Deborah Brown, Production Administrator, for her leadership in bringing this new edition home. It continues to amaze us how production quality, which is so good to begin with, can continue to get better and better with

each new edition. From where we sit, Deborah's leadership is a big reason why we keep improving.

To Chris Clark at the University of Utah, we express our appreciation for the painstaking keyboarding, copying, and mailing of the manuscript. Chris is also responsible for the layout of the Test Bank which now contains well over 1,000 questions, feedback, quizzes, and exams. Chris, we thank you for caring so much about the calibre of the finished product.

To those professors who have chosen this book for adoption, and to those students who will be using this book as their first information source on people with differences, we hope our sixth edition of *Human Exceptionality* meets your expectations.

A loving thank you to our families who have always been there during the past 20 years of writing and re-writing this text. We have strived to do our best.

Michael L. Hardman
Clifford J. Drew
M. Winston Egan

Human Exceptionality

1

A Multidisciplinary View of Exceptionality

To begin with . . .

 Disability used to signal the end of active life. Now it is a common characteristic of a normal lifespan. Sooner or later it will occur in the lives of most people, surely in the life of every family. (Dart, 1995)

 Nondisabled Americans do not understand disabled ones. That was clear at the memorial service for Timothy Cook, when longtime friends got up to pay tribute to him. "He never seemed disabled to me," said one. He was the least disabled person I ever met," pronounced another. It was the highest praise these nondisabled friends could think to give a disabled attorney who, at 38 years old, had won landmark disability rights cases, including one to force public transit systems to equip buses with wheelchair lifts. But more than a few heads in the crowded chapel bowed with embarrassment at the supposed compliments. It was as if someone had tried to compliment a black man by saying, "You're the least black person I ever met," as false as telling a Jew, "I never think of you as Jewish," as clumsy as flattering a woman with "You don't act like a woman." (Shapiro, 1994, p. 3)

 When people with and without disabilities live, work, play and go to school side-by-side, people with disabilities get noticed and accepted for their contributions just like everyone else. They don't get singled out for their disabilities. With this acceptance, the barriers to inclusion begin to disappear. ("Inclusion Works Here," 1993)

Truly, including all students in standards-based reform is not simple. All students represent an extraordinary range of ability, learning styles, and interests. State standards must encompass the needs of a full range of students, from those whose post-secondary plans include attending a college or university to those enrolling in vocational training programs, to students who plan to move directly into the work place. And the intricate interplay of policies will determine the extent to which students with disabilities are included in the reform. (Center for Policy Research on the Impact of General and Special Education Reform, 1996, p. 12)

Snapshot

Stephen Hawking

Stephen Hawking has been described as the most *gifted* physicist since Albert Einstein and one of the great minds of this century. He is currently the Lucasian Professor of Mathematics at Cambridge University, a post once held by Sir Isaac Newton. Professor Hawking is internationally known for his seminal research attempting to answer Einstein's question about whether God had any choice in creat-

ing the universe. His theory on the origin of black holes has provided new clues on the possible moment when the universe was born. His book, *A Brief History of Time: From the Big Bang to Black Holes*, became a worldwide best-seller and moved theoretical physics to the mainstream of public discussion. It was later made into a major motion picture.

Stephen Hawking spent the first 17 years of his life leading a relatively normal existence, although he described himself as somewhat bored with life in general and uncoordinated when it came to physical activities. At age 21, while working on his Ph.D. in physics at Cambridge University in England, he was diagnosed with amyotrophic lateral sclerosis (ALS—Lou Gehrig's Disease).

Over the next decade, his condition worsened and he became more and more *disabled*. The ALS resulted in slurred speech that very few people could understand. Initially, he communicated in public through an interpreter, until he discovered the world of technology. Using a computer program called Living Center, Professor Hawking began to communicate by selecting words from a screen that are then expressed orally through a speech synthesizer. The progressive nature of the disease also affected his voluntary motor functions, forcing him to use a wheelchair. Eventually he required round-the-clock nursing care but still lived at home. In the midst of dealing with an incurable and degenerative disease, he maintained

what he described as a fairly *normal* lifestyle that involved marriage and raising a family. Stephen Hawking is the father of Robert, Lucy, and Timmy Hawking. Throughout his adult years Stephen Hawking has maintained an optimistic view of his life and what he is capable of accomplishing. He is proud of his family and the success he has achieved in his career. His perspective on life is clear: "I was again fortunate that I chose theoretical physics, because it is all in the mind. *So my disability has not been a serious handicap.*"

Source: Information contained in this snapshot was adapted from S. Hawking (1988). *A brief history of time: From the big bang to black holes*, New York: Bantam Books.

Labeling People with Differences

IN THE OPENING SNAPSHOT, we met Stephen Hawking, an individual who throughout his life has received myriad labels attempting to describe, identify, and distinguish him from others. These labels have included terms such as *disabled, handicapped*, and *gifted*. Is Stephen Hawking a person with a disability or a handicap? If he is disabled, does he have a communication disorder or a physical disability? Or both? Is he gifted? Is it possible that he is both disabled and gifted?

Everyone differs from everyone else in some way. The issue is not merely *difference,* but rather the type and extent of the difference. To address differences, every society creates descriptors to identify people who vary significantly from the norm. This process is called *labeling.* Sociologists use labels to describe people who are socially deviant; educators and psychologists use labels to identify students with learning, physical, and behavioral differences; and physicians use labels to distinguish the sick from the healthy.

Common labels used by professionals to describe physical and behavioral differences include *disorder, disability,* and *handicap.* These terms are not synonymous.

focus 1

Why do we label people according to their differences?

A person described as exceptional is not necessarily a person with a handicap. At the University of Connecticut, Professor Dorean Simons-Margues, who does not speak or hear, teaches ASL to hearing students. In her class the students use sign language exclusively to communicate with her and with each other.

Disorder, the broadest of the three terms, refers to a general malfunction of mental, physical, or psychological processes. It is defined as a disturbance in normal functioning. A **disability** is more specific than a disorder and results from a loss of physical functioning (e.g., loss of sight, hearing, or mobility) or from difficulty in learning and social adjustment that significantly interferes with normal growth and development. A **handicap** is a limitation imposed on the individual by environmental demands and is related to the individual's ability to adapt or adjust to those demands. For example, Stephen Hawking uses a wheelchair because of a physical disability—the inability to walk. He is dependent on the wheelchair for mobility. When the physical environment does not accommodate his wheelchair (e.g., a building without ramps, accessible only by stairs), his disability becomes a handicap.

When applied as an educational label, *handicapped* has a narrow focus and a negative connotation. The word *handicapped* literally means "cap in hand"; it originates from a time when people with disabilities were forced to beg in the streets merely to survive. This term may be used to describe only those individuals who are deficient in or lack ability.

Exceptional is a much more comprehensive term. It may be used to describe any individual whose physical, mental, or behavioral performance deviates substantially from the norm, either higher or lower. A person with exceptional characteristics is not necessarily an individual with a handicap. People with exceptional characteristics may need additional educational, social, or medical services to compensate for physical and behavioral characteristics that differ substantially from what is considered normal. These differences can be **learning disorders, behavior disorders, speech and language disorders, sensory disorders, physical disorders, health disorders**, or **gifts and talents.**

Labels are only rough approximations of characteristics. Some labels, such as **deaf**, might describe permanent qualities; others, such as *overweight*, might describe temporary qualities. Some labels are positive, and others are negative.

Labels communicate whether a person meets the expectations of the culture. A society establishes criteria that are easily exceeded by some but are unreachable for others. For example, a society may value creativity, innovation, and imagination and will value and reward those with these attributes with positive labels, such as *bright, intelligent,* or *gifted.* A society, however, may brand anyone whose ideas drastically exceed the limits of conformity with negative labels, such as *radical, extremist,* or *rebel.* Moreover, the same label may have different connotations for different groups, depending on each group's viewpoint. For example, a high school student may be labeled a *conformist.* From the school administration's point of view, this is probably considered a positive characteristic, but to the student's peer group, it may have strong negative connotations.

What are the ramifications of using labels to describe people? Reynolds (1991) contended that the use of labels has produced mixed results at best: "At the extremes, human classification can be a demeaning process, causing stigma and leading to the isolation and neglect of those in unfavored classes; it, conversely, can be the basis on which extraordinary services and favors are rallied in support of selected groups" (p. 29). Labels are based on ideas, not facts. "When we create or construct them [labels], we do so within particular cultural contexts. That is, someone observes particular behaviors or ways of being and then describes these as a classification with a label (Kliewer & Biklen, 1996, pp. 83–84). Thus, even though labels have been the basis for developing and providing services to people, they can also promote stereotyping, discrimination, and exclusion. This view is shared by several professionals who indicate that the practice of labeling children in order to provide appropriate services has perpetuated and reinforced both the label and the behaviors it implies (Lipsky & Gartner, 1991, 1996; Minow, 1991; Reynolds, 1994; Stainback, Stainback, & Ayres, 1996).

If the use of labels can have negative consequences, why is labeling used so extensively? One reason is that many social services and educational programs for exceptional individuals require the use of labels to distinguish who is eligible for services and who is not. Funding may even be contingent on the numbers and types of individuals who are deemed eligible. To illustrate, Maria, a child with a hearing problem, by federal and state law must be assessed and labeled as having a hearing loss before specialized educational or social services can be made available to her. A second reason for the use of labels is that they assist professionals in communicating effectively with one another and provide a common ground for evaluating research findings. A third reason is that labeling helps identify the specific needs of a particular group of people. Labeling can help in determining degrees of needs or in setting priorities for service when societal resources are limited.

■ FORMAL VERSUS INFORMAL LABELING

Labels may be applied by both formal and informal labelers (Kammeyer, Ritzer, & Yetman, 1997). Formal labelers are sanctioned by society. For example, members of the criminal justice system—including the arresting officer, jury, and court judge—label the person who commits a crime a *criminal.* A criminal may be incarcerated in a penal institution and consequently be labeled a *convict.* Formal labelers speak for their society, as when a court judge pronounces sentence on a convicted felon on behalf of all who live in the community. Additional examples of formal labelers include doctors, educators, and psychologists. They use formal labels including *gifted and talented, mentally ill, mentally retarded, blind,* and so forth. Formal labels affect our perception of the individual and in turn may change the individual's self-concept.

An informal labeler is usually some significant other—such as a family member, friend, or peer—and the applied label is meaningful only to this person or to a restricted group. Informal labels may be expressed in a number of ways. They can be derogatory slang terms, such as *stupid, cripple, fat,* and *crazy.* Some informal labels, such as *witty, smart,* and *cool,* reflect more favorably on the individual. Other informal labels, such as *ambitious* and *conformist,* are open to individual interpretation.

■ APPROACHES TO LABELING

Significant physical and behavioral differences are found infrequently in every society. Most people in any given culture conform to its established standards. *Conformity*—people doing what they are supposed to do—is the rule for most of us most of the time (Baron & Byrne, 1994). Usually, we look the way we are expected to look, behave the way we are expected to behave, and learn the way we are expected to learn. When someone does deviate substantially from the norm, a number of approaches can be used to describe the nature and extent of the differences (see Figure 1.1).

focus 2
Identify three approaches that can be used to describe the nature and extent of human differences.

■ THE DEVELOPMENTAL APPROACH The **developmental approach to labeling** is based on deviations from what is considered normal physical, social, or intellectual growth. To understand these human differences, which result from an interaction of biological and environmental factors, we must first establish what is normal development.

According to the developmental view, normal development can be described statistically, by observing in large numbers of individuals those characteristics that occur most frequently at a specific age. For example, when stating that the average 3-month-old infant is able to follow a moving object visually, *average* is a statistical term based on observations of the behavior of 3-month-old infants. When comparing an individual child's growth pattern to that group average, differences in development (either advanced or delayed) are labeled accordingly.

■ THE CULTURAL APPROACH The **cultural approach to labeling** defines what is normal according to the standards established by a given culture. Whereas a developmental approach considers only the frequency of behaviors to define differences, a cultural approach suggests that differences can be explained partly by examining the values inherent within a culture. What constitutes a significant difference changes over time, from culture to culture, and among the various social classes within a culture. As Kammeyer et al. (1997) suggested, deviance begins when a person does something that is disapproved of by other members within the dominant culture. For example, in some cultures, intelligence is described in terms of how well someone scores on a test measuring a broad range of abilities, and in other cultures, intelligence relates much more to how skillful someone is at hunting or fishing. The idea that human beings are the products of their cultures has received its greatest thrust from anthropology, which emphasizes the diversity and arbitrary nature of cultural rules regarding dress, eating habits, sexual habits, politics, and religion. The human infant is believed to be so flexible that the child can adjust to nearly any environment.

■ THE INDIVIDUAL APPROACH The **individual approach to labeling** asserts that all people engage in a self-labeling process that others may not recognize. Thus self-imposed labels reflect how we perceive ourselves, not how others see us. Conversely, the culture uses a given label to identify a person, but that label may not be accepted by that person. Such was the case with Thomas Edison. Although the schools labeled Edison as an intellectually incapable child, he eventually recognized that he was an

FIGURE 1.1

Approaches to labeling: What is normal?

Developmental
Approach

Cultural Approach

Individual Approach

individualist. He proved himself by identifying his individual abilities and pursuing his own interests as an inventor.

■ THE EFFECTS OF LABELING

Reactions to a label differ greatly from one person to another but can often be negative (Dotter & Roebuck, 1988; Graham & Dwyer, 1987; Hastings, 1994; Van Bourgondien, 1987). Smith, Osborne, Crim, and Rho (1986) surveyed special education teachers, school officials, and parents to determine their perceptions of the label *learning disabilities*, and they found that these individuals attached multiple and sometimes conflicting meanings to the term. In two studies of college students' reactions to various labels used to describe people with **mental retardation** and learning disabilities, researchers found that older terms, such as *mental subnormality* and *mental handicap*, generate a more negative reaction than newer terms, such as *learning difficulty* or *learning disability* (Hastings & Remington, 1993; Hastings, Songua-Barke, & Remington, 1993). However, only one term, *exceptional*, received a positive rating from the college students studied. The authors attributed this positive reaction to the students defining *exceptional* as meaning "much above average."

■ SEPARATING THE PERSON AND THE LABEL Once a label has been affixed to an individual, the two may become inseparable. For example, instead of saying that Becky does not possess age-appropriate intellectual or socialization abilities, we may refer to her simply as retarded, losing sight of the fact that she is first and foremost a human being, and her exceptional characteristics are only part of who she is. To treat Becky as a label rather than as a person with special needs is an injustice, not only to Becky but to everyone else as well.

■ ENVIRONMENTAL BIAS The environment in which we view someone can clearly influence our perceptions of that person. For example, it can be said that, if you are in a mental hospital, you must be insane. Rosenhan (1973) investigated this premise by having himself and seven other sane individuals admitted to a number of state mental hospitals across the United States. Once in the mental hospitals, these subjects behaved normally.

The question was whether the staff would perceive them as people who were healthy instead of as patients who were mentally ill. Rosenhan reported that the pseudopatients were never detected by the hospital staff but were recognized as imposters by several of the real patients. Throughout their hospital stays, the pseudopatients were incorrectly labeled and treated as schizophrenics. In fact, when a staff nurse observed one experimenter writing, she noted, "Patient engages in writing behavior." Rosenhan's investigation showed that the perception of what is normal can be biased by the environment in which the observations are made.

Bringing About Social Change

■ A HISTORY OF DISCRIMINATION AND ISOLATION

Throughout recorded history, people perceived as different have been vulnerable to practices such as infanticide, slavery, physical abuse, and abandonment. These practices reflect a common societal fear that the so-called mentally and morally defective would defile the human race. It has been widely believed that most deviance is caused by hereditary factors that, if left unchecked, would result in widespread social problems (Gelb, 1995).

Humanitarian reform finally began in the last half of the 18th century, bringing with it optimism concerning the treatment and eventual cure of people described as deviant. However, when deviance wasn't cured and continued to be a major social problem well into the 19th century, many professionals became convinced that it was necessary to sterilize and segregate large numbers of these *mental and social degenerates*.

focus 3
Identify four indicators of quality supports and services for persons with disabilities.

Legal measures were undertaken to prohibit these people from marrying. Eventually, legislation was expanded to include compulsory **sterilization** of such individuals, and soon laws were passed in an effort to reduce the number of so-called deviates. Laws in some countries contained provisions for sterilizing people with mental retardation, individuals with epilepsy, the sexually promiscuous, and criminals. In addition to marriage and sterilization laws, measures were passed to move large numbers of individuals from the communities in which they lived to isolated special-care facilities whose sole purpose was maintenance. These facilities became widely known as **institutions.** Institutions have had many different labels: school, hospital, colony, prison, and asylum.

The institutions of the early 20th century became more and more concerned with social control as they grew in size and as financial resources diminished. To manage large numbers of individuals on a limited financial base, these facilities had to establish rigid rules and regulations, stripping away individuals' identities and forcing them into group regimentation. For example, individuals could not have personal possessions, were forced to wear institutional clothing, and were given identification tags and numbers. Institutions were characterized by locked living units, barred windows, and high walls enclosing the grounds. Organized treatment programs declined, and the number of "terminal," uncured patients grew, resulting in institutional expansion and the erection of new buildings. Given the public and professional pessimism concerning the value of treatment programs, this growth meant diminishing funds for mental health care. This alarming situation remained unchanged for nearly five decades and declined even further during the Depression years of the 1930s. By the early 1950s, more than 500,000 persons were committed to mental hospitals throughout the United States, and comparable numbers of persons with mental retardation lived in segregated institutions referred to as colonies, hospitals, or training schools. Several attempts to reform institutions were initiated. The American Psychiatric Association led efforts to inspect and rate the nation's 300 mental hospitals and called attention to the lack of therapeutic intervention and deplorable living conditions.

■ FROM ISOLATION TO INCLUSION: SUPPORTING PEOPLE WITH DISABILITIES IN FAMILY AND COMMUNITY SETTINGS

In spite of the growth of segregated institutions in the 20th century, the vast majority of people with disabilities remained at home within their families. For families, the choice to keep the child at home meant they were on their own, receiving little or no outside support. Government resources were very limited, and available funding was directed to support services outside of the family, often even beyond the community in which they resided (Bradley, Knoll, & Agosta, 1992). For the better part of this century, many families who had a child with a disability were unable to get help for basic needs, such as medical and dental care, social services, or education.

In response to the lack of government support and coinciding with the civil rights movement in the United States, parents of children with disabilities began to organize in about 1950. The United Cerebral Palsy Organization (UCP) was founded in 1949, and the National Association for Retarded children[1] (NARC) began in 1950. The UCP

---

[1] The National Association for Retarded Children became the Association for Retarded Citizens in 1974. It is now known as the ARC—A National Organization on Mental Retardation.

Social inclusion creates opportunities for children with disabilities to participate in a heterogeneous community group.

and NARC joined other professional organizations already in existence, such as the National Association for the Deaf, the American Association on Mental Deficiency,[2] the Council for Exceptional Children, and the American Federation for the Blind, to advocate for the rights of persons with disabilities. The purpose of these national organizations was to get accurate information to families with disabilities, professionals, policy makers, and the general public. Each organization focused on the rights of people with disabilities to be included in family and community life and have access to medical treatment, social services, and education (Berry & Hardman, 1998). Other parent groups followed, including those of the National Society for Autistic Children (1961) and the Association for Children with Learning Disabilities[3] (1964).

The inclusion of people with disabilities into community settings—such as schools, places of employment, and neighborhood homes—is based on a philosophy that recognizes and accepts the range of human differences within a culture. One way to evaluate the success of community services for any individual is to look at whether and how such supports make a difference in his or her life. As such, the quality of community services for people with disabilities can be viewed in terms of four indicators:

1. Do services promote personal autonomy?
2. Do opportunities for social interaction and **integration** exist?
3. Does the individual have a choice of lifestyle?
4. Do opportunities for economic self-sufficiency exist?

Each of these questions relates to different outcomes, depending on the age of the individual. For the preschool-age child, the world is defined primarily through the family and a small, same-age peer group. As the child grows older, the world expands to include the neighborhood, the school, and eventually a larger heterogeneous group called the community. The questions for professionals then change: How can services be structured to foster full participation as the individual's world expands? What barriers obstruct full participation, and how do we break them down?

We will now examine some of the ways in which society supports as well as limits the participation of people with disabilities in community settings.

---

[2] It is now called the American Association on Mental Retardation.
[3] It is now called the Learning Disabilities Association (LDA).

The Americans with Disabilities Act of 1990 (ADA)

focus 4

What is the purpose of the Americans with Disabilities Act?

In 1973, the U.S. Congress passed an amendment to the Vocational Rehabilitation Act that included a provision prohibiting discrimination against persons with disabilities in federally assisted programs and activities. **Section 504 of the Vocational Rehabilitation Act** (herein referred to as Section 504) set the stage for passage of the most sweeping civil rights legislation in the United States since the Civil Rights Act of 1964: the **Americans with Disabilities Act of 1990 (ADA).** The purpose of ADA is to provide a national mandate to end discrimination against individuals with disabilities in private-sector employment, all public services, and public accommodations, transportation, and telecommunications. ADA charged the federal government with the task of ensuring that these provisions be enforced on behalf of all people with disabilities (West, 1991). (See nearby Reflect on This feature.)

Reflect on This

THIS WOULDN'T HAVE HAPPENED WITHOUT THE ADA

At precisely 1:25 P.M. on Hayes Street near Franklin in San Francisco, Mary Lou Breslin's motorized wheelchair spat out a shower of sparks and died. Breslin, 50, disabled by polio since childhood, had been shopping with her friend, Kathy Martinez, 36, who is blind. "I haven't been dead in the water for years," Breslin muttered angrily. With that, she and Martinez began to "strategize," their term for improvising in the face of emergencies. As able-bodied pedestrians moved past in a hurried blur, Breslin pulled out her cellular phone and started making calls.

Despite Breslin's wheelchair breakdown, a day with them on the streets of the San Francisco area shows that commonplace life has improved dramatically for them since the advent of the Americans with Disabilities Act. Several years ago, for example, Breslin stopped at a drugstore near her home in Berkeley. The tight turnstiles at the entrance made access difficult, the checkout aisles were too narrow for her wheelchair, and Breslin had to wheel backward against the flow of other shoppers after she paid her bill. On a recent visit, she found that the store, now run by a different retailer, was much easier to deal with. There were no turnstiles to negotiate, and a wide checkout counter had been installed. "Without the ADA," Breslin said, "this wouldn't have happened."

Yet annoyances remain. An assistant manager seemed vaguely huffy when Martinez asked for help finding cough drops. The clerk assigned to the task was polite but, Martinez confided, "Sometimes they just take my [walking] stick and pull me along."

Later, at a Bay Area Rapid Transit station in Berkeley, Breslin had to wheel backward into a small, smelly elevator, while other people used escalators. Martinez, who also rides BART, feels safe there, thanks to bumps, or "edge detection strips," that warn the blind away from the edge of the platforms. Despite the tight elevator problem, BART is regarded as a disability-rights pioneer. "It was such a treat to take this train when I came to California years ago," says Breslin, who was raised in the Midwest. "I'd never lived anywhere where there was access."

But when the train pulled into the San Francisco Shopping Center, a mall on Market Street admired for its accessibility, the wheelchair lift refused to work. Breslin tinkered and finally made it move by asking a bystander to hold the bottom gate tightly shut while she pushed buttons inside. Later she spoke of the frustrations of "the Blanche DuBois life," a reference to the lonely, high-strung character in *A Streetcar Named Desire* who relies on "the kindness of strangers."

When Breslin's chair broke down an hour later, she was once again at the mercy of others. After telephoning a disabled-access taxi service, she had to wait nearly two hours. The driver charged $90 to transport her and Martinez to a wheelchair-repair shop across the bay. Strapped in her chair like furniture, Breslin rocked uncomfortably in the rear of the van with each high-speed freeway turn. A technician fixed her electric motor, and soon a friend arrived to help her get home. Such is the life of the disabled: determined, resourceful, and, all too often, reliant on the kindness of strangers.

Source: From "Under Their Own Power," by J. Willwerth, July 31, 1995, *Time,* p. 55. Reprinted by permission.

■ THE ADA DEFINITION OF DISABILITY

ADA uses a functional definition of disability that was originally established in federal law under Section 504. A person with a disability is defined as (1) having a physical or mental impairment that substantially limits him or her in some major life activity and (2) having experienced discrimination resulting from this physical or mental impairment. The following is a purely illustrative list from the U.S. Congress of what constitutes a physical impairment:

any physiological disorder or condition, cosmetic disfigurements, or anatomical loss affecting one or more of the following body systems: neurological; musculoskeletal; special sense organs; respiratory, including speech organs, cardiovascular; reproductive; digestive; genito-urinary; hemic and lymphatic; skin; and endocrine.

An illustrative list of what constitutes a mental impairment includes:

any mental or psychological disorder, such as mental retardation, organic brain syndrome, emotional or mental illness, and specific learning disabilities (House Report, 1990; Senate Report, 1989)

■ REASONABLE ACCOMMODATIONS

The intent of ADA is to create a "fair and level playing field" for eligible persons with disabilities. To do so, the law specifies that **reasonable accommodations** need to be made that take into account each person's needs resulting from his or her disability. The accommodations differ, depending on whether they are in the area of employment, transportation, or telecommunications. (See the Reflect on This feature on page 12.)

In the past, individuals with disabilities have had to contend with the reality that learning to live independently did not guarantee access to all that society had to offer in terms of services and jobs. Although several states have long had laws that promised otherwise, access to places such as public restrooms and restaurants and success in mainstream corporate America have often eluded those with disabilities, primarily because of architectural and attitudinal barriers. ADA is intended to change these circumstances, affirming the rights of 43 million Americans with disabilities to participate in the life of their community. Much as the **Civil Rights Act of 1964** gave clout to the African American struggle for equality, the ADA has promised to do the same for those with disabilities. Its success in eliminating the fears and prejudices of the general community remains to be seen, but the reasons for such legislation were obvious. First, it was clear that people with disabilities faced discrimination in employment, access to public and private accommodations (e.g., hotels, theaters, restaurants, grocery stores), and services offered through state and local governments (Harris & Associates, 1989, 1994, 1995). Second, because the historic Civil Rights Act of 1964 did not even mention people with disabilities, they had no federal protection against discrimination except through the somewhat limited provisions in Section 504. As stated by the National Council on Disability,

ADA is the most comprehensive policy statement ever made in American law about how the nation should address individuals with disabilities. Built on principles of equal opportunity, full participation, independent living and economic self-sufficiency, the law reflects the disability community's convictions and determination to participate as first class American citizens and to direct their own futures. (1996, p. 23)

Did you know that, in public and private employment . . . ?

- Employers cannot discriminate against an individual with a disability in hiring or promotion if the person is otherwise qualified for the job.
- Employers can ask about someone's ability to perform a job but cannot inquire if he or she has a disability or subject him or her to tests that tend to screen out people with disabilities.
- Employers need to provide reasonable accommodation to people with disabilities, such as job restructuring and modification of equipment.

Did you know that, in public transportation . . . ?

- New public transit buses, bus and train stations, and rail systems must be accessible to individuals with disabilities.
- Transit authorities must provide transportation services to individuals with disabilities who cannot use fixed-route bus services.
- All Amtrak stations must be accessible to people with disabilities by the year 2010.

Did you know that, in public accommodations . . . ?

- Restaurants, hotels, and retail stores may not discriminate against individuals with disabilities.
- Physical barriers in existing facilities must be removed, if removal is readily achievable. If not, alternative methods of providing the services must be offered.
- All new construction and alterations of facilities must be accessible.

Did you know that, in government . . . ?

- State and local agencies may not discriminate against qualified individuals with disabilities.
- All government facilities, services, and communications must be accessible to people with disabilities.

Did you know that, in telecommunications . . . ?

- Companies offering telephone service to the general public must offer telephone relay services to individuals with hearing loss who use telecommunication devices or similar devices.

On the fifth anniversary of the passage of ADA, Harris and Associates (1995) conducted a survey to see how the new law has been accepted by America's corporate employers. The survey found that

- 70% of these employers believe that ADA should not be changed. It is working as intended.
- 81% indicated that accommodations have been made in the workplace for people with disabilities.
- 64% have hired people with disabilities.
- only 2% indicated that ADA posed a threat to take jobs from people who are not disabled.
- 75% said they are likely to make greater efforts to hire people with disabilities in the future.

Living and Learning in Community Settings

Legislating against discrimination is one thing; enforcing laws against it is another. The purpose of ADA was to ensure that comprehensive services (e.g., employment, housing, educational programs, public transportation, restaurant access, and religious activities) be available to all individuals within or as close as possible to their family and community lives. Individuals should also be able to purchase additional services at will: dental examinations, medical treatment, life insurance, and so forth. Access to these services allows people the opportunity to be included in community life. Successful integration is based on two factors: (1) the individual's ability, with appropriate education and training, to adapt to societal expectations, and (2) the willingness of society to adapt to and accommodate individuals with differences.

Access to adequate housing and **barrier-free facilities** is essential for people with physical disabilities. A barrier-free environment may be created by renovating existing facilities and requiring that new buildings and public transportation incorporate barrier-free designs. People in wheelchairs or on crutches need entrance ramps to and within public buildings; accessibility to public telephones, vending machines, and restrooms; and lifts for public transportation vehicles. Available community living environments could include private homes, specialized boarding homes, supervised apartments, group homes, and foster homes.

Recreation and leisure opportunities within the community vary substantially according to the individual's age and the severity of his or her disability, and the availability of such opportunities also varies from community to community. Thus many persons with disabilities may not have access to dance and music lessons, gymnastics training, swimming lessons, and scouting—activities that are generally available to others within the community. Similar problems exist for children, adolescents, and adults with exceptional characteristics, many of whom may do little with their leisure time beyond watching television.

Recreational programs must be developed to assist individuals in developing worthwhile leisure activities and more satisfying lifestyles. Therapeutic recreation is a profession concerned specifically with this goal: using recreation to help people adapt their physical, emotional, or social characteristics to take advantage of leisure activities more independently in a community setting.

Work is essential to the creation of successful lifestyles for all adults, including those with disabilities. Yet many individuals with disabilities are unable to gain employment during their adult years. Harris polls have found that two thirds of people with disabilities between the ages of 16 and 64 were not working, but that two thirds of that group indicated that they would like to. A comparison of working and nonworking disabled individuals revealed that working individuals were more satisfied with life, had more money, and were less likely to blame their disability for preventing them from reaching their potential (Harris & Associates, 1987, 1989, 1994).

focus 5
What services must be available to ensure that an individual with a disability is able to live and learn successfully in a community setting?

Medical, Psychological, and Sociological Understandings of People with Disabilities

To gain a broader understanding of the nature and extent of human differences, we will briefly examine several disciplines concerned with individuals who are exceptional. These disciplines include medicine, psychology, and sociology. Each is unique in its approach to exceptionality, as reflected in the labels it uses to describe a person with exceptional characteristics. Figure 1.2 provides the common terminology associated with each field.

focus 6
How did the work of 19th-century physicians and philosophers contribute to our understanding of people with differences?

FIGURE 1.2

Common terminology of fields of
study concerned with individuals
who are exceptional

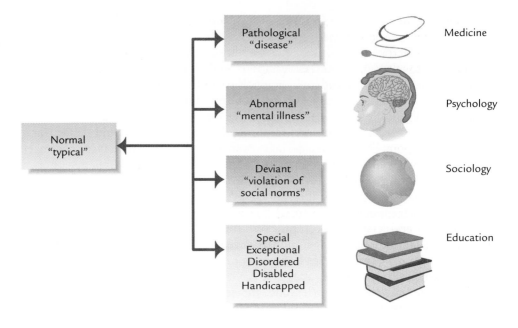

Normal "typical" → Pathological "disease" — Medicine

Abnormal "mental illness" — Psychology

Deviant "violation of social norms" — Sociology

Special Exceptional Disordered Disabled Handicapped — Education

▪ MEDICINE

The **medical model** has two dimensions: normalcy and pathology. *Normalcy* is defined as the absence of a biological problem. **Pathology** is defined as alterations in an organism caused by disease, resulting in a state of ill health that interferes with or destroys the integrity of the organism. The medical model, often referred to as the *disease model*, focuses primarily on biological problems and on defining the nature of the disease and its pathological effects on the individual. The model is universal and does not have values that are culturally relative. It is based on the premise that being healthy is better than being sick, regardless of the culture in which one lives.

When diagnosing a problem, a physician carefully follows a definite pattern of procedures that includes questioning the patient to obtain a history of the problem, conducting a physical examination and laboratory studies, and in some cases, performing surgical exploration. The person who has a biological problem is labeled the *patient*, and the deficits are then described as the *patient's disease*.

We must go back more than 200 years to find the first documented attempts to personalize medical treatment programs to the needs of people with differences. During the 16th and 17th centuries, people with mental or emotional disturbance were viewed as mad persons, fools, and public threats to be removed from society. This view changed during the 18th and 19th centuries, when many physicians contributed to expanding our understanding of human differences. Jean-Marc Itard (1775–1838) epitomized the orientation of professionals during this period, and his work is reflected in our modern medical, psychological, social, and educational intervention models.

In 1799, as a young physician and authority on diseases of the ear and education of those with hearing loss, Itard worked for the National Institute of Deaf-Mutes in Paris. He believed that the environment, in conjunction with physiological stimulation, could contribute to the learning potential of any human being. Itard was influenced by the earlier work of Philippe Pinel (1742–1826), a French physician concerned with mental illness, and John Locke (1632–1704), an English philosopher. Pinel advocated that people characterized as insane or idiots needed to be treated humanely, but his teachings emphasized that they were essentially incurable and that any treatment to remedy their disabilities would be fruitless. Locke, in contrast, described the mind as a "blank slate" that could be opened to all kinds of new stimuli. The positions of Pinel and Locke represent the classic controversy of **nature versus nurture:** What are the roles of heredity and environment in determining a person's capabilities?

Itard tested the theories of Pinel and Locke in his work with Victor, the so-called wild boy of Aveyron. Victor was 12 years old when found in the woods by hunters. He had not developed any language, and his behavior was virtually uncontrollable, described as savage or animal-like. Ignoring Pinel's diagnosis that the child was an incurable idiot, Itard took responsibility for Victor and put him through a program of sensory stimulation that was intended to cure his condition. After five years, Victor developed some verbal language and became more socialized as he grew accustomed to his new environment. Itard's work with Victor documented for the first time that learning is possible even for individuals described by most professionals as totally helpless.

Following Itard's ground-breaking work in the early 19th century, some European countries began establishing special schools and segregated living facilities for people with disabilities (such as mental illness, retardation, or hearing or sight loss). As explained by McCleary, Hardman, and Thomas (1990), expertise and knowledge about people with disabilities were extremely limited during this period. Most programs focused on care and management rather than treatment and education. Although many professionals had demonstrated that positive changes in individual development were possible, they had not been able to cure conditions such as insanity and idiocy.

Medical services for people with disabilities have evolved considerably. The typical course in the early part of the 20th century involved treatment primarily in a hospital or institutional setting. The focus today is directly on the individual in family and community settings. In many cases, the physician is the first professional with whom parents have contact concerning their child's disability, particularly when the child's problem is identifiable immediately after birth or during early childhood. The physician is the family adviser and communicates with parents regarding the medical prognosis and recommendations for treatment. However, too often, physicians assume that they are the family's only counseling resource (Drew, Hardman, & Logan, 1996). Physicians should be aware of additional resources within the community, including other parents, social workers, mental health professionals, and educators.

Medical services are often taken for granted simply because they are readily available to most people. This is not true, however, for many people with disabilities. It is not uncommon for a pediatrician to suggest that parents seek treatment elsewhere for their child with a disability, even when the problem is a common illness such as a cold or a sore throat.

It would be unfair to stereotype medical professionals as unresponsive to the needs of exceptional people. On the contrary, medical technology has prevented many disabilities from occurring and has enhanced the quality of life for many people. However, to ensure that people with disabilities receive comprehensive medical services in a community setting, several factors must be considered. The physician in community practice (e.g., the general practitioner, pediatrician) must receive more medical training in the medical, psychological, and educational aspects of disability conditions. This training could include instruction regarding developmental milestones; attitudes toward children with disabilities; disabling conditions; prevention;

screening, diagnosis, and assessment; interdisciplinary collaboration; effective communication with parents; long-term medical and social treatment programs; and community resources.

Physicians must also be willing to treat patients with disabilities for common illnesses when the treatment is irrelevant to the patient's disability. Physicians need not become disability specialists, but they must have enough knowledge to refer patients to appropriate specialists when necessary. For instance, physicians must be aware of and willing to refer patients to other nonmedical community resources, such as social workers, educators, and psychologists. The medical profession must continue to support physician specialists and other allied health personnel who are well equipped to work with people with disabilities. These specialized health professionals include **geneticists** and **genetic counselors, physical therapists** and **occupational therapists,** public health nurses, and nutritional and dietary consultants.

■ PSYCHOLOGY

focus 7
Distinguish between abnormal behavior and social deviance.

Psychology and sociology are similar in that both fields are concerned with the study of human behavior. Sociology is the science of social behavior, whereas psychology studies the person as a separate being.

Modern psychology is the science of human and animal behavior, the study of the overt acts and mental events of an organism that can be observed and evaluated. Broadly viewed, psychology is concerned with every detectable action of an individual. Behavior is the focus of psychology, and when the behavior of an individual does not meet the criteria of normalcy, it is labeled *abnormal.*

Psychology, as we know it today, is more than 100 years old. In 1879, Wilhelm Wundt (1832–1920) defined psychology as the science of conscious experience. His definition was based on the *principle of introspection*—looking into oneself to analyze experiences. William James (1842–1910) expanded Wundt's conception of conscious experience in his treatise *The Principles of Psychology* (1890) to include learning, motivation, and emotions. In 1913, John B. Watson (1878–1958) shifted the focus of psychology from conscious experience to observable behavior and mental events.

In 1920, Watson conducted an experiment with an 11-month-old child named Albert. Albert showed no fear of a white rat when initially exposed to the animal, seeing it as a toy and playing with it freely. Watson then introduced a loud, terrifying noise directly behind Albert each time the rat was presented. After a period of time, the boy became frightened by the sight of any furry white object, even though the loud noise was no longer present. Albert had learned to fear rats through **conditioning**, the process in which new objects or situations elicit responses that were previously elicited by other stimuli. Watson thus demonstrated that abnormal behavior could be learned through the interaction of the individual with environmental stimuli (Watson & Rayner, 1920).

In spite of Watson's work, most theorists during the first half of the 20th century considered the medical model to be the most logical and scientific approach to understanding abnormal behavior. The public was more accepting of the view that people with psychological disturbances were sick and not fully responsible for their problems.

The **ecological approach**, emerging in the latter half of the 20th century, supported Watson's theories. This approach views abnormal behavior more as a result of an individual's interaction with the environment than as a disease. The approach theorizes that social and environmental stress, in combination with the individual's inability to cope, lead to psychological disturbances.

We cannot live in today's society without encountering the dynamics of abnormal behavior. The media are replete with stories of murder, suicide, sexual aberration, burglary, robbery, embezzlement, child abuse, and other incidents that display abnormal behavior. Each case represents a point on the continuum of personal maladjustment that exists in society. Levels of maladjustment range from behaviors that are slightly deviant or eccentric (but still within the confines of normal human experience) to **neurotic disorders** (partial disorganization characterized by combinations of anxieties, compulsions, obsessions, and phobias) to **psychotic disorders** (severe disorganization resulting in loss of contact with reality and characterized by delusions, hallucinations, and illusions).

The study of abnormal behavior historically has been based in philosophy and religion in Western culture. Until the Middle Ages, the disturbed or mad person was thought to have "made a pact with the devil," and the psychological affliction was believed to be a result of divine punishment, the work of devils, witches, or demons residing within the person. The earliest known treatment for mental disorders, called *trephining*, involved drilling holes in a person's skull to permit evil spirits to leave (Carlson, 1997).

Today's psychologists use myriad approaches in the treatment of mental disorders, including **behavior therapy, rational-emotive therapy, group psychotherapy, family therapy,** or **client-centered therapy.** According to Carlson (1997), the majority of psychologists describe their therapeutic philosophy as eclectic. They choose from many different approaches in determining the best way to work with an individual in need of psychological help.

■ SOCIOLOGY

Whereas psychology focuses primarily on the behavior of the individual, sociology is concerned with modern cultures, group behaviors, societal institutions, and intergroup relationships. Sociology examines individuals in relation to their physical and social environment. When individuals meet the social norms of the group, they are considered normal. When individuals are unable to adapt to social roles or to establish appropriate interpersonal relationships, their behaviors are labeled **deviant**. Unlike medical pathology, social deviance cannot be defined in universal terms. Instead, it is defined within the context of the culture, in any way the culture chooses to define it.

Even within the same society, different social groups often define deviance differently. Groups of people who share the same norms and values will develop their own rules about what is and what is not deviant behavior. Their views may not be shared by members of the larger society, but the definitions of deviance will apply to group members (Kammeyer et al., 1997).

Four principles serve as guidelines in determining who will be labeled socially deviant:

1. Normal behavior must meet societal, cultural, or group expectations. Deviance is defined as a violation of social norms.
2. Social deviance is not necessarily an illness. Failure to conform to societal norms does not imply that the individual has pathological or biological deficits.
3. Each culture determines the range of behaviors that are defined as normal or deviant and then enforces these norms. Those people with the greatest power

within the culture can impose their criteria for normalcy on those who are less powerful.

4. Social deviance may be caused by the interaction of several factors, including genetic makeup and individual experiences within the social environment.

Today, many different kinds of sociologists specialize across more than 50 subfields and specialties. Within each specialty area, sociologists undertake a systematic study of the workings and influence of social groups, organizations, cultures, and societies on individual and group behavior. The sociologist accumulates and disseminates information about social behavior (including disability) in the context of the society as a whole (Kammeyer et al., 1997). The following are just a few examples of specialties within sociology that may include an emphasis on disability: deviant behavior and social disorganization, aging, criminology and criminal justice, family and marriage, medicine, and education.

Bringing About Educational Change

■ ACCESS TO EDUCATION

As children progress through formal schooling, their parents, teachers, peers, and others expect that they will learn and behave according to established patterns. Most students move through their educational programs in about the same way, requiring the same level of service and progressing within similar time frames. Students who do not meet educational expectations of normal growth and development may be labeled according to the type and extent of their deviation. They may also be provided with services and resources that differ from those provided for typical students.

focus 8

What educational services were available for students with disabilities during most of the 20h century?

Access to education is a basic American value, reflecting the expectation that each individual should have an opportunity to learn and develop to the best of his or her ability. From this value emerges some of the most fundamental goals of education. Schools exist to promote literacy, personal autonomy, economic self-sufficiency, personal fulfillment, and citizenship. McLaughlin, Shepard, and O'Day (1995) suggested that schools must prepare all students, not just the academically capable, to gain knowledge and apply what they learn in order to be productive workers and citizens. Full participation for everyone, regardless of race, cultural background, socioeconomic status, physical disability, or mental limitation, is the goal. Unfortunately, in the United States, it has taken more than two centuries to translate this value into actual practice in educating students with disabilities.

■ SPECIAL EDUCATION: 1900–1975

In the United States, education of children with exceptionalities began in the early 1900s with the efforts of many dedicated professionals. Those efforts consisted of programs that were usually separate from the public schools, the majority for children who were slow learners or had hearing or sight loss. These students were usually placed in segregated classrooms in a public school building or in separate schools. Special education meant segregated education. Moreover, students with substantial differences were excluded from public education entirely.

Because the schools needed to have some way of determining who would receive a public education, an assessment device was developed to determine who was intellectually capable of attending school. The result was an individual test of intelligence developed by Alfred Binet and Theodore Simon (1905). It was first used in France to predict how well students would function in school, and in 1908, it was translated into English. The Binet-Simon Scales, revised and standardized by Lewis Terman at Stanford University, were published in 1916 as the **Stanford-Binet Intelligence Scale.** This test provided a means of identifying children who deviated significantly from the average in intellectual capability, at least in terms of what the test actually measured.

From 1920 to 1960, the availability of public school programs for exceptional children continued to be sporadic and selective. Most states merely allowed for special education; they did not mandate it. Services to children with mild emotional disorders (discipline problems) were initiated in the early 1930s, but mental hospitals continued to be the only alternative for most individuals with severe emotional problems. Special classes for children with physical disabilities were also started in the 1930s, primarily for those with crippling conditions, heart defects, and other health-related problems that interfered with participation in general education programs. Separate schools for these children, very popular during the late 1950s, were specially equipped with elevators, ramps, modified doors, toilets, and desks.

During the 1940s, the appropriateness of placing students with disabilities in special versus general schools emerged as an important policy issue. Polloway (1984) asserted that, during this period, educators became determined to find the most effective placement for students with disabilities and to ensure that they had the opportunity for normal social interaction.

By the 1950s, many countries began to expand educational opportunities for students with disabilities in special schools and classes funded through public education. Two separate events had a significant impact on the evolution of education for students with disabilities. First, in many countries, parents of children with disabilities organized as a constituent group to lobby policy makers for more appropriate social and educational services for their children. Second, professionals from both the behavioral and medical sciences became more interested in services for individuals with disabilities, thus enriching knowledge through research, which could then be integrated into effective practice.

These events provided the setting for the current period, during which significant departures from past practice have been initiated (McCleary et al., 1990). The late 1950s brought an increase in the number of public school classes for students with mild mental retardation and those with behavior disorders. For the most part, these children continued to be educated in an environment that isolated them from nondisabled peers. The validity of segregation continued to be an important issue in the field of education. Several studies in the 1950s and 1960s (e.g., Cassidy & Stanton, 1959; Johnson, 1961; Jordan & deCharms, 1959; Thurstone, 1959) examined the efficacy of special classes for children with mild mental retardation. Johnson (1962), summarizing this research, suggested that the academic achievement of learners with mental retardation was consistent regardless of whether they were placed in special or general education classes, although the child's social adjustment was not harmed by the special program. Although numerous criticisms regarding the design of efficacy studies have been made over the years, they did result in a movement toward expanding services beyond special classes in public schools. An example of this outcome was the development of a model whereby a child could remain in the general class program for the majority, if not all, of the school day, receiving special education when and where it was needed.

The 1960s brought other major changes in the field of special education as well. The federal government took on an expanded role in the education of children who were exceptional. University programs for teacher preparation received federal financial support and initiated programs to train special education teachers throughout the United States. The Bureau of Education for the Handicapped (BEH) in the Office of Education (presently the Office of Special Education and Rehabilitative Services in the U.S. Department of Education) was created as a clearinghouse for information at the federal level. Demonstration projects were funded nationwide to establish a research base for the education of students with disabilities in the public schools.

■ LEGAL REFORMS[4] AND SPECIAL EDUCATION

focus 9

Identify the principal issues in the right-to-education cases that led to eventual passage of Public Law 94–142 (now referred to as IDEA).

The 1970s have often been described as a decade of revolution in the field of special education. Many of the landmark cases addressing the right to education for students with disabilities were brought before the courts during this period. In addition, major pieces of state and federal legislation were enacted to reaffirm the right of individuals with disabilities to a free public education.

It is often overlooked that the rights of individuals with disabilities came to the public forum as a part of a larger social issue: the civil rights of all minority populations in the United States. The civil rights movement of the 1950s and 1960s awakened the public to the issues of discrimination in employment, housing, access to public facilities (e.g., restaurants and transportation), and public education.

Education was reaffirmed as a right and not a privilege by the U.S. Supreme Court in the landmark case of *Brown* v. *Topeka, Kansas, Board of Education* (1954). In its decision, the court ruled that education must be made available to everyone on an equal basis. A unanimous Supreme Court stated, "In these days, it is doubtful that any child may reasonably be expected to succeed in life if he is denied the opportunity of an education. Such an opportunity, where the state has undertaken to provide it, is a right which must be made available to all on equal terms" (*Brown* v. *Topeka, Kansas, Board of Education,* 1954).

Although usually heralded for striking down racial segregation, this decision also set a major precedent for the education of students with disabilities in the United States. Unfortunately, it was nearly 20 years before federal courts were confronted with the issue of a free and appropriate education for these students.

In 1971, the Pennsylvania Association for Retarded Citizens filed a class-action suit on behalf of children with mental retardation who were excluded from public education on the basis of intellectual deficiency (*Pennsylvania Association for Retarded Citizens* v. *Commonwealth of Pennsylvania,* 1971). The suit charged that these children were being denied their right to a free public education. The plaintiffs claimed that children with mental retardation can learn if the educational program is adjusted to meet their individual needs. The issue was whether public school programs should be required to accommodate children who were intellectually different. The court ordered Pennsylvania schools to provide a free public education to all children with mental retardation of ages 6 to 21, commensurate with their individual learning needs. In addition, preschool education was to be provided for children with mental retardation if the local school district provided it for children who were not disabled.

The case of *Mills* v. *District of Columbia Board of Education* (1972) expanded the Pennsylvania decision to include all children with disabilities. District of Columbia schools were ordered to provide a free and appropriate education to every school-age

---

[4] Because the legal reforms discussed in this section exclude students who are gifted and talented, the more narrowly defined term *disability* has been used.

child with a disability. The court further ordered that, when general public school assignment was not appropriate, alternative educational services had to be made available. Thus, the right of students with disabilities to an education was reaffirmed. The *Pennsylvania* and *Mills* cases served as catalysts for several court cases and pieces of legislation in the years that followed. Table 1.1 summarizes precedents regarding the right to education for students with disabilities.

The Individuals with Disabilities Education Act (IDEA)

In 1975, the U.S. Congress saw the need to bring together the various pieces of state and federal legislation into one comprehensive national law. **Public Law 94-142** (PL 94-142) made available a free and appropriate public education to nearly 4 million school-age students with disabilities in the United States between the ages of 6 and 21. The law was renamed the **Individuals with Disabilities Education Act** in 1990 and is referred to throughout this text as **IDEA.**

In 1986, Congress amended IDEA to include provisions for preschool-age students. **Public Law 99-457** (PL 99-457), established a new mandate extending all the rights and protections of school-age children (ages 5 through 21) to preschoolers ages 3 through 5. This law required that states receiving federal funds ensure that all 3- to 5-year-old children with disabilities receive a free and appropriate public education. Another provision of PL 99-457 was the establishment of a state grant program for infants and toddlers up to 2 years old. Infants and toddlers who are developmentally delayed, as defined by each state, are eligible for services that include

focus 10

Identify five major provisions of the Individuals with Disabilities Education Act.

Preschool children with disabilities receive a free and appropriate education as mandated in a federal law passed by Congress in 1986.

TABLE 1.1	Major court cases and federal legislation focusing on the right to education for individuals with disabilities (1954–1997)

COURT CASES AND FEDERAL LEGISLATION	PRECEDENTS ESTABLISHED
Brown v. *Topeka, Kansas, Board of Education* (1954)	Segregation of students by race is held unconstitutional. Education is a right that must be available to all on equal terms.
Hobsen v. *Hansen* (1969)	The doctrine of equal educational opportunity is a part of the law of due process, and denying an equal educational opportunity is a violation of the Constitution. Placement of children in educational tracks based on performance on standardized tests is unconstitutional and discriminates against poor and minority children.
Diana v. *California State Board of Education* (1970)	Children tested for potential placement in a special education program must be assessed in their native or primary language. Children cannot be placed in special classes on the basis of culturally biased tests.
Pennsylvania Association for Retarded Citizens v. *Commonwealth of Pennsylvania* (1971)	Pennsylvania schools must provide a free public education to all school-age children with mental retardation.
Mills v. *Board of Education of the District of Columbia* (1972)	Declared exclusion of individuals with disabilities from free, appropriate public education is a violation of the due-process and equal protection clauses of the 14th Amendment to the Constitution. Public schools in the District of Columbia must provide a free education to all children with disabilities regardless of their functional level or ability to adapt to the present educational system
Public Law 93-112, Vocational Rehabilitation Act of 1973, Section 504 (1973)	Individuals with disabilities cannot be excluded from participation in, denied benefits of, or subjected to discrimination under any program or activity receiving federal financial assistance.
Public Law 93-380, Educational Amendments Act (1974)	Financial aid is provided to the states for implementation of programs for children who are exceptional, including the gifted and talented. Due-process requirements (procedural safeguards) are established to protect the rights of children with disabilities and their families in special education placement decisions.

a multidisciplinary assessment and an **Individualized Family Service Plan (IFSP).** Although this provision did not mandate that states provide services to all infants and toddlers who were developmentally delayed, it did establish financial incentives for state participation. (The IFSP and other provisions of PL 99-457 are discussed in more depth in Chapter 4 of this text.)

■ WHAT IS SPECIAL EDUCATION?

IDEA requires that all eligible students, regardless of the extent or type of their disability, are to receive at public expense the special education services necessary to meet their individual needs. Special education means specially designed instruction provided at no cost to parents in all settings (such as the classroom, physical education facilities, the home, and hospitals or institutions). IDEA also stipulates that students with disabilities are to receive any related services necessary to ensure that they benefit from their educational experience. **Related services** include:

TABLE 1.1   *(continued)*

COURT CASES AND FEDERAL LEGISLATION	PRECEDENTS ESTABLISHED
Public Law 94-142, Part B of the Education of the Handicapped Act (1975)	A free and appropriate public education must be provided for all children with disabilities in the United States. (Those up to 5 years old may be excluded in some states.)
Hendrick Hudson District Board of Education v. Rowley (1982)	The U.S. Supreme Court held that in order for special education and related services to be appropriate, they must be reasonably calculated to enable the student to receive educational benefits.
Public Law 99-457, Education of the Handicapped Act amendments (1986)	A new authority extends free and appropriate education to all children with disabilities ages 3 to 5 and provides a new early intervention program for infants and toddlers.
Public Law 99-372, Handicapped Children's Protection Act (1986)	Reimbursement of attorneys' fees and expenses is given to parents who prevail in administrative proceedings or court actions.
Public Law 101-336, Americans with Disabilities Act (1990)	Civil rights protections are provided for people with disabilities in private sector employment, all public services, and public accommodations, transportation, and telecommunications.
Public Law 101-476, Individuals with Disabilities Education Act (1990)	The Education of the Handicapped Act amendments are renamed the Individuals with Disabilities Education Act (IDEA). Two new categories of disability are added: autism and traumatic brain injury. IDEA requires that an individualized transition plan be developed no later than age 16 as a component of the IEP process. Rehabilitation and social work services are included as related services.
Public Law 105-17, Amendments to the Individuals with Disabilities Education Act (1997) (Commonly referred to as IDEA 97)	IDEA 97 expands the emphasis for students with disabilities from public school access to improving individual outcomes (results). The 1997 amendments modify eligibility requirements, IEP requirements, public and private placements, disciplining of students, and procedural safeguards.

transportation, and such developmental, corrective, and other supportive services (including speech–language pathology and audiology services, psychological services, physical and occupational therapy, recreation, including therapeutic recreation, social work services, counseling services, including rehabilitation counseling, orientation and mobility services, and medical services, except that such medical services shall be for diagnostic and evaluation purposes only) as may be required to assist a child with a disability to benefit from special education, and includes the early identification and assessment of disabling conditions in children. (Amendments to IDEA, PL 105-17, Sec. 602[22], 1997)

■ WHO IS ELIGIBLE FOR SPECIAL EDUCATION?

In order for an individual to receive the specialized services available under IDEA, two criteria must be met. First, the individual must be identified as having 1 of the 12 disability conditions identified in federal law or their counterparts in a state's special education law. These conditions include mental retardation, specific learning disabilities, serious emotional disturbances (behavior disorders), speech or language impairments, vision loss (including blindness), hearing loss (including deafness), **orthopedic impairments**, other health impairments, deafness–blindness, multiple disabilities, **autism**, and **traumatic brain injury**. Each condition will be defined and described in depth in subsequent chapters of this text.

In 1997 the Congress amended IDEA[5] and gave states and local education agencies (LEA) the option of eliminating categories of disability (such as mental retardation or specific learning disabilities) for children ages 3 to 9. For this age group, a state or LEA may define a child with a disability as

(i) experiencing developmental delays, as defined by the State and as measured by appropriate diagnostic instruments and procedures, in one or more of the following areas: physical development, cognitive development, communication development, social or emotional development, or adaptive development; and (ii) who, by reason thereof, needs special education and related services. (PL 105-17, Sec. 602[3][B])

The second criterion on eligibility is the student's demonstrated need for specialized instruction and related services in order to receive an appropriate education. This need is determined by a multidisciplinary team of professionals and parents. Both criteria for eligibility must be met. If this is not the case, it is possible for a student to be identified as disabled but not eligible to receive special education services under federal law. These students may still be entitled to accommodations or modifications in their educational program under Section 504 and the Americans with Disabilities Act (see the later section on Section 504, ADA, and students with disabilities).

Five basic tenets of IDEA drive the determination of eligibility for services, design of an instructional program, and educational placement:

1. **Nondiscriminatory and multidisciplinary assessment** of educational needs
2. Parental safeguards and involvement in developing each child's educational program
3. A **free and appropriate public education (FAPE)**
4. An **individualized education program (IEP)**
5. Education in the **least restrictive environment (LRE)**

■ NONDISCRIMINATORY AND MULTIDISCIPLINARY ASSESSMENT

IDEA incorporated several provisions related to the use of nondiscriminatory testing procedures in labeling and placement of students for special education services. Among those provisions are the following:

- ■ The testing of students in their native or primary language, whenever possible
- ■ The use of evaluation procedures selected and administered to prevent cultural or racial discrimination
- ■ Validation of assessment tools for the purpose for which they are being used
- ■ Assessment by a **multidisciplinary team,** utilizing several pieces of information to formulate a placement decision

Students with disabilities were too often placed in special education programs on the basis of inadequate or invalid assessment information. One result of such over-

---

[5] The 1997 Amendments to IDEA are herein referred to as IDEA 97.

sights was the placement of a disproportionate number of ethnic minority children and children from low socioeconomic backgrounds in special education programs.

■ PARENTAL SAFEGUARDS AND INVOLVEMENT

IDEA granted parents the following rights in the education of their children:

- To give consent in writing before the child is initially evaluated
- To give consent in writing before the child is initially placed in a special education program
- To request an independent education evaluation if they feel the school's evaluation is inappropriate
- To request an evaluation at public expense if a due-process hearing finds that the public agency's evaluation was inappropriate
- To participate on the committee that considers the evaluation, placement, and programming of the child
- To inspect and review educational records and challenge information believed to be inaccurate, misleading, or in violation of the privacy or other rights of the child
- To request a copy of information from the child's educational record
- To request a hearing concerning the school's proposal or refusal to initiate or change the identification, evaluation, or placement of the child or the provision of a free and appropriate public education

The intent of these safeguards is twofold: first, to create an opportunity for parents to be more involved in decisions regarding their child's education program; and second, to protect the student and family from decisions that could adversely affect their lives. Families thus can be secure in the knowledge that every reasonable attempt is being made to educate their child appropriately.

Some professionals and parents have argued that IDEA's provision for a parent and professional partnership has never been fully realized. Powell and Graham (1996) suggested that many barriers exist between the school and the home, such as "a lack of understanding, mistrust, a decrease in services as the child ages, and limited coordination of services" (p. 603). These authors further indicated a need to prevent the adversarial relationships that often result from due-process hearings. Such hearings may lead to mistrust and long-term problems.

IDEA 97 (PL 105-17) responded to the need for a mediation process to resolve any conflict between parents and school personnel and to prevent long-term adversarial relationships. This new law requires states to establish a mediation system in which parents and schools voluntarily participate. In such a system, an impartial individual would listen to parents and school personnel and attempt to work out a mutually agreeable arrangement in the best interest of the student with a disability. But although mediation is intended to facilitate the parent and professional partnership, it must not be used to deny or delay the parents' right to a due-process hearing.

■ A FREE AND APPROPRIATE PUBLIC EDUCATION (FAPE)

IDEA is based on the value that every student can learn. As such, all students with disabilities are entitled to a free and appropriate public education (FAPE) based upon individual ability and need. The IDEA provisions related to FAPE are based on the 14th Amendment to the U.S. Constitution guaranteeing equal protection of the law. No student with a disability can be excluded from a public education based on a disability. A major interpretation of FAPE was handed down by the U.S. Supreme

Court in *Hendrick Hudson District Board of Education* v. *Rowley* (1982). The Supreme Court declared that an appropriate education consists of "specially designed instruction and related services" that are "individually designed" to provide "educational benefit." Often referred to as the "some educational benefit" standard, the ruling mandates that a state need not provide an ideal education but must provide a beneficial one for students with disabilities.

■ THE INDIVIDUALIZED EDUCATION PROGRAM (IEP)

The vehicle for delivering a free and appropriate public education to every eligible student with a disability is a written statement referred to as an IEP. The IEP provides an opportunity for parents and professionals to join together in developing and delivering specially designed instruction to meet student needs.

■ THE IEP TEAM According to IDEA 97, the team responsible for developing the IEP should consist of the student's parents; at least one special education teacher; at least one regular (general) education teacher if the child is, or may be, participating in the regular (general) education environment; and a representative of the local education agency (LEA). The LEA representative must be qualified to provide, or supervise the provision of, specially designed instruction to meet the unique needs of children with disabilities. This individual must also be knowledgeable about the general curriculum and the availability of resources within the LEA.

At the discretion of the parents or the LEA, the IEP team may also include an individual who can interpret the instructional implications of evaluation results; other individuals who have knowledge or special expertise regarding the child, including related services personnel as appropriate; and whenever appropriate, the student with disability.

■ IEP REQUIREMENTS The intended result of the IEP process is more continuity in the delivery of educational services for students on a daily as well as an

A parent joins with professionals to develop a child's IEP.

annual basis. The IEP also promotes more effective communication between school personnel and the home.

IDEA 97 requires that each child's IEP must include

- a statement of the child's present levels of educational performance, including how the child's disability affects involvement and progress in the general curriculum. For preschool children the statement must describe how the disability affects the child's participation in appropriate activities.
- a statement of measurable annual goals, including benchmarks or short-term objectives related to meeting the child's needs that result from the disability. The annual goals should enable the child to be involved and make progress in the general curriculum and meet each of the child's other educational needs that result from the disability.
- a statement of the special education and related services and supplementary aids or services to be provided to, or on behalf of, the child. The statement must include (1) any program modifications or supports for school personnel that will be provided for the child to advance appropriately toward attaining the annual goals, (2) how the child will be involved and progress in the general curriculum and participate in extracurricular and other nonacademic activities, (3) how the child will be educated and participate with other children with disabilities and nondisabled children, and (4) an explanation of the extent, if any, to which the child will not participate with nondisabled children in the regular [general education] class and in the activities described above.
- a statement of any individual modifications in the administration of State or district-wide assessments of student achievement that are needed in order for the child to participate in such assessment. If the IEP Team determines that the child will not participate in a particular State or district-wide assessment of student achievement (or part of such an assessment), there must be a statement of why that assessment is not appropriate for the child and how the child will be assessed.
- the projected date for the beginning of the services and modifications, and the anticipated frequency, location, and duration of those services and modifications.
- a statement of how the child's progress toward the annual goals will be measured and how the child's parents will be regularly informed (by means such as periodic report cards), at least as often as parents are informed of their nondisabled children's progress, of their child's progress toward the annual goals. The statement should include the extent to which that progress is sufficient to enable the child to achieve the goals by the end of the year. (PL 105-17, Sec. 614[d])

See Chapter 4 for further discussion of the IEP process and a sample IEP form.

■ EDUCATION IN THE LEAST RESTRICTIVE ENVIRONMENT

All students have the right to learn in an environment consistent with their academic, social, and physical needs. Such a setting constitutes the least restrictive environment (LRE). IDEA mandated that students with disabilities receive their education with nondisabled peers to the maximum extent appropriate. To meet this mandate, federal regulations required schools to develop a continuum of placements, ranging from general classrooms with support services to homebound and hospital programs. About 95% of students with disabilities receive their education in a general education school building with the remaining 5% in a separate day

FIGURE 1.3

Educational service options for students with disabilities

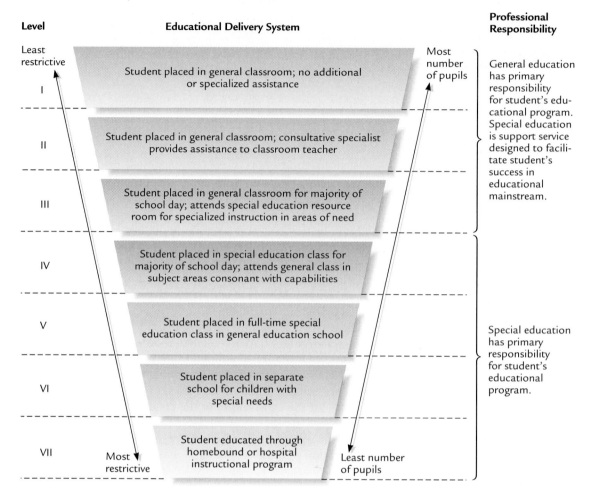

Level	Educational Delivery System	Professional Responsibility

Least restrictive

I — Student placed in general classroom; no additional or specialized assistance — Most number of pupils

II — Student placed in general classroom; consultative specialist provides assistance to classroom teacher

III — Student placed in general classroom for majority of school day; attends special education resource room for specialized instruction in areas of need

General education has primary responsibility for student's educational program. Special education is support service designed to facilitate student's success in educational mainstream.

IV — Student placed in special education class for majority of school day; attends general class in subject areas consonant with capabilities

V — Student placed in full-time special education class in general education school

VI — Student placed in separate school for children with special needs

VII — Student educated through homebound or hospital instructional program — Least number of pupils

Most restrictive

Special education has primary responsibility for student's educational program.

school, residential facility, or hospital/homebound program (U.S. Department of Education, 1997). An educational services model is presented in Figure 1.3.

At Level I in this continuum, a student remains in the general education classroom and receives no additional support services. Adaptations necessary for a given student are handled by the classroom teacher. Consequently, a student's success depends on whether his or her general education teacher has skills in developing and adapting programs to meet individual needs.

A student placed at Level II also remains in the general education classroom, but **consultative services** are available to both the teacher and the student. These services may be provided by a variety of professionals, including special educators, speech and language specialists, behavior specialists, physical education specialists, occupational therapists, physical therapists, school psychologists, and social workers. Services may range from assisting a teacher in the use of tests or modification of curriculum to direct instruction with students in the classroom setting.

The student placed at Level III continues in the general education classroom for the majority of the school day but also attends a **resource room** for specialized instruction in deficit areas. A resource room program is directed by a qualified special educator. The amount of time a student spends there varies according to his or her needs; it may range from as short as 30 minutes to as long as 3 hours a day. Instruction in a resource room is intended to reinforce or supplement the student's work in the general education classroom and includes the assistance necessary to help him or her keep pace with general education peers. The resource room is the most widely used public school setting for students with disabilities, serving about 6% of all school-age children.

At Levels I, II, and III, the primary responsibility for the student's education lies with the general education classroom teacher. Consultative services, including special education, are intended to support the student's general education class placement. At Levels IV and beyond, the primary responsibility shifts to special education professionals.

The student placed at Level IV is in a **special education classroom** for the majority of the school day. At this level, provisions are made to include him or her with general education peers whenever possible and consistent with his or her learning capabilities. For students with moderate to severe disabilities, inclusion is usually recommended for nonacademic subject areas.

Level V placement involves full-time participation in a special education class. Although still in a general education school, the student is not included with general education students for formal instructional activities. However, some level of social inclusion may take place during recess periods, lunch assemblies, field trips, and tutoring.

Placement at Level VI involves transferring the student from the general education facility to a classroom in a separate facility specifically for students with disabilities. These facilities include **special day schools**, where the education program is one aspect of a comprehensive treatment program.

Those students who, because of the severity of their disabilities, are unable to attend any school program must receive services through a homebound or hospital program. Placement at Level VII generally indicates a need for an **itinerant teacher** to visit an incapacitated student on a regular basis to provide tutorial assistance. Some students with chronic conditions, such as certain types of cancer, may be placed at this level indefinitely, whereas others are served while recuperating from short-term illnesses.

The issue of placement in the LRE continues to be a matter of public and private debate. Clearly, IDEA favors educating students in general education settings, mandating that students with disabilities be educated with their nondisabled peers to the maximum extent appropriate. An examination of the placement of students in segregated environments (Danielsen & Bellamy, 1989) suggested that about 6% of all students with disabilities receive their education in segregated schools. Approximately 24% of all students with disabilities are educated in separate special education classes. These authors also reported that, in spite of the law's strong preference for integrated placements, the use of "separate educational environments has been relatively stable over the 10 years in which the Department of Education has collected national data" (p. 452). Similar results were reported by Sawyer, McLaughlin, and Winglee in 1994. These authors found only a slight increase in the number of students served in a regular school building between 1977 and 1993. For a closer look at who is being served in special education programs, and where, see Figure 1.4.

FIGURE 1.4

A profile of special education in the United States (school year 1995–1996): (a) disabilities of students ages 6–21 receiving special education as a percentage of all students ages 6–21;* (b) number of students with disabilities receiving special education services by age under IDEA (5,619,099 children served); (c) percentage of special education students in the school building and other sites

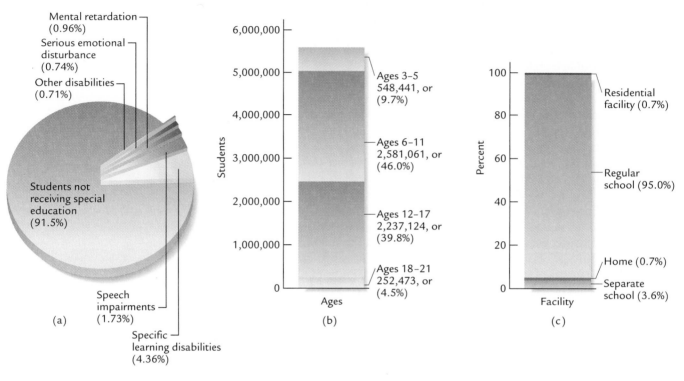

Source: The 19th annual report to Congress on the implementation of the Education for All Handicapped Children Act, by the U.S. Department of Education, 1997, Washington, DC: U.S. Government Printing Office.

* Based on estimated resident population

■ DISCIPLINING STUDENTS AND IDEA 97

focus 11

Describe two differing viewpoints on disciplining students with disabilities who represent a danger to others and themselves.

A major issue arose in Congress during discussions on the recent amendments to IDEA, regarding whether education services could be terminated and a student with a disability expelled because of dangerous or violent behavior. The concern was focused on incidents in which a student with a disability (1) brings a dangerous weapon to school or to a school function, (2) knowingly possesses or distributes illicit drugs or sells or solicits the sale of a controlled substance while at school or a school function, (3) is substantially likely to cause injury to self or others, and (4) exhibits any other behaviors that violate the school's written code of conduct.

Many professionals and parents of students with disabilities were concerned that if Congress allowed a cessation of services, it would undermine IDEA's **zero-exclusion principle**. This fundamental premise of IDEA states that, regardless of the nature or extent of a disability, the student must receive a free and appropriate public education (FAPE). Others argue that students with a disability should be treated no differently than nondisabled students when the individual is likely to cause injury to others and themselves. (See the Debate Forum for Chapter 7 for more information.)

In dealing with this controversial issue, IDEA 97 reiterated that a free and appropriate public education must be available to all students with disabilities and that there can be no cessation of services under any circumstances. The law provides, however, that schools may implement the following actions when a student with a disability brings a dangerous weapon to school or buys, sells, or possesses illicit drugs:

- Change the student's placement (such as a general education classroom) to an interim alternative educational setting or another setting outside of the school system as determined by the IEP team, or suspend the student from school for no more than 10 school days (to the extent such alternatives would be applied to students without disabilities).
- Change the student's placement to an appropriate interim alternative educational setting as determined by the IEP team for the same amount of time that a student without a disability would be subject to discipline, but for not more than 45 days.
- Any interim alternative educational setting in which a student is placed shall be selected so as to enable the child to continue to participate in the general curriculum. The setting must also allow the student to continue to receive those services and modifications, including those described in the current IEP, that will enable the student to meet the goals set out in that IEP. Any services and modifications must be designed to address the problem behavior that resulted in the change of placement.
- Within 10 days after taking a disciplinary action, convene an IEP meeting to conduct a behavioral assessment and implement a behavioral intervention plan. If the student already has a behavioral intervention plan, the school shall review the plan and modify it as necessary to address the problem behavior.
- In reviewing the disciplinary action taken by the school, the IEP team must determine that the problem behavior was not a manifestation of the student's

Surrounded by lawmakers, citizens, and children with disabilities, President Clinton signs into law the 1997 amendments to IDEA.

disability. The team must determine that the student's disability did not impair his or her ability to understand the impact and consequences, or control the problem behavior. If the IEP team determines that the problem behavior was not a manifestation of the student's disability, the relevant disciplinary procedures applicable to students without disabilities may be applied to the student with a disability. If the student's parents disagree with a determination that the problem behavior was not a manifestation of the student's disability, the parent may request a hearing.

- If parents disagree with the student's alternative educational placement, they may request a hearing. A hearing officer may order a change in the placement of a student with a disability to an appropriate interim alternative educational setting for not more than 45 days if the hearing officer determines that the school has demonstrated by substantial evidence that maintaining the current placement of such student is substantially likely to result in injury to the student or to others. The hearing officer must consider the appropriateness of the student's current placement in making the decision and determine whether the public agency has made reasonable efforts to minimize the risk of harm in the child's current placement, including the use of supplementary aids and services. (PL 105-17, Sec. 614[K][1–6])

Section 504, ADA, and Students with Disabilities

Today's schools must provide supports and services to two groups of students with disabilities. One group qualifies for special education services under IDEA, based upon educational need. Another group, while not eligible for special education, meets the definition of disability under Section 504 of the Vocational Rehabilitation Act (now incorporated into the Americans with Disabilities Act [ADA]).

Students eligible under Section 504 are entitled to reasonable accommodations or modifications as a means to "create a fair and level playing field" in their educational program. A plan for individually designed instruction must be developed for each student qualified under Section 504. Numerous accommodations or modifications can be made for students qualified under Section 504, depending on identified need. Some examples include untimed tests, extra time to complete assignments, change in seating arrangement to accommodate vision or hearing loss or distractibility, opportunity to respond orally on assignments and tests, taped textbooks, access to peer tutoring, access to study carrel for independent work, use of supplementary materials such as visual or auditory aids, and so on. A comparison of IDEA and the provisions of Section 504 can be found in Table 1.2. The Section 504 definition of disability (incorporated into ADA) encompasses a broader group of students than those eligible under IDEA. This definition may include individuals with conditions such as HIV infection, heart disease, drug addiction, or alcoholism, in addition to the disability conditions identified in IDEA. The actual number of students covered under Section 504/ADA is unknown.

School Reform and Inclusive Education

▪ STUDENTS WITH DISABILITIES AND SCHOOL REFORM

issue a challenge to the nation. Every state should adopt high national standards, and by 1999, every state should test every fourth grader in reading and every eighth grader in math to make sure these standards are met. Raising standards will not be easy, and some of our children will not be able to meet them at first. The point is not to put our children down, but to lift them up. (President Bill Clinton, State of the Union Address, February 5, 1997)

The current wave of school reform in the United States began with a report by the National Commission on Excellence in Education (1983), entitled *A Nation at Risk: The Imperative for Educational Reform. A Nation at Risk* is considered by many to be the basis for the current educational restructuring movement, which is centered on finding new and better ways to enhance student achievement. The rallying cry in today's schools is "higher expectations for all students." The call for high expectations has resulted in a standards-based approach to reforming schools—set high standards for what should be taught and how student performance should be measured. Four common elements characterize **standards-based reform** in America's schools:

1. A focus on student achievement as the primary measure of school success
2. An emphasis on challenging academic standards that specify the knowledge and skills students should acquire and the levels at which they should demonstrate mastery of that knowledge
3. A desire to extend the standards to *all* students, including those for whom expectations have been traditionally low
4. Heavy reliance on achievement testing to spur the reforms and to monitor their impact (National Research Council, 1997)

Some advocates for standards-based reform have strongly emphasized the importance of acknowledging student diversity both in terms of ability and needs. O'Day and Smith (1993), for example, argue that the standards movement must respond to student differences.

Not to accommodate student differences . . . could effectively deny access to large numbers of students. . . . For the reform to be successful, the approaches taken by all schools must be based on common curriculum frameworks and all students must be expected and given the opportunity to perform at the same high standards on a common assessment." (p. 265)

Hehir (1994) suggested that we should

seek nothing less than an education system that supports all *children and youth with disabilities in achieving the outcome of full participation in all aspects of community life. As reform efforts are carried out at the local and state levels, we should emphasize that special education has much to offer state and local personnel engaged in restructuring efforts. (p. 10)*

Yet, in spite of the call to include *all* students in school reform initiatives, concerns have arisen that students with disabilities and other disadvantaged students are being left out. Research suggests that the participation of students with disabilities in the general education curriculum and statewide assessments of student performance vary considerably from state to state and district to district (Erickson,

	IDEA	SECTION 504
General purpose	This federal funding statute provides financial aid to states in their efforts to ensure adequate and appropriate services for children and youth with disabilities.	This broad civil rights law protects the rights of individuals with disabilities in programs and activities that receive federal financial assistance (such as funds from the U.S. Department of Education).
Eligibility	IDEA identifies 12 categories of qualifying conditions. IDEA 97 allows states and school districts the option of eliminating categories for children age 3 through 9. The child may be defined as having developmental delays.	Section 504 identifies students as disabled if they meet the definition of qualified handicapped [disabled] person (i.e., student has or has had a physical or mental impairment that substantially limits a major life activity, or student is regarded as disabled by others).
Responsibility to provide a free and appropriate public education (FAPE)	Both require the provision of a free and appropriate education, including individually designed instruction, to students covered under specific eligibility criteria.	
	IDEA requires a written and specific IEP document.	Section 504 does not require a written IEP document, but does require a written plan.
	"Appropriate education" means a program designed to provide "educational benefit."	"Appropriate" means an education comparable to the education provided to students who are not disabled.
Special education or general education	A student is eligible to receive IDEA services only if the multidisciplinary team determines that the student is disabled under 1 of the 12 qualifying conditions and requires special education.	An eligible student meets the definition of qualified person with a disability: one who currently has or has had a physical or mental impairment that substantially limits a major life activity or who is regarded as disabled by others. The student is not required to need special education in order to be protected.
Funding	IDEA provides additional funding, if a student is eligible under the IDEA.	Section 504 does not provide additional funds.
Accessibility	IDEA requires that modifications be made, if necessary, to provide access to a free and appropriate education.	Section 504 includes regulations regarding building and program accessibility.

Thurlow, & Thor, 1995; Shriner & Thurlow, 1992). The National Research Council (1997) indicates anecdotal evidence that states and local school districts are keeping students with disabilities out of their accountability systems because of fears that they pull down scores.

In response to these concerns, IDEA 97 requires that a student's IEP must describe how the disability affects the child's involvement and progress in the general education curriculum. In addition, the IEP goals must enable the child to access the general education curriculum when appropriate. The new law requires an explanation of any individual modifications in the administration of state- or districtwide assessment of student achievement that are needed in order for the child to participate.

TABLE 1.2 *(continued)*

	IDEA	SECTION 504
Procedural safeguards	Both require notice to the parent or guardian with respect to identification, evaluation, and/or placement.	
	IDEA requires written notice.	Section 504 does not require written notice, but a district would be wise to do so.
	It delineates required components of written notice.	Particular components are not delineated.
	It requires written notices prior to *any* change in placement.	It requires notice only before a "significant change" in placement.
Evaluations	IDEA requires consent before an initial evaluation is conducted.	Section 504 does not require consent, but does require notice.
	It requires reevaluations at least every 3 years.	It requires periodic reevaluations.
	It requires an update and/or review before any change in placement.	Reevaluation is required before a significant change in placement.
	It provides for independent educational evaluations.	Independent educational evaluations are not required.
Due process	Both statutes require districts to provide impartial hearings for parents or guardians who disagree with the identification, evaluation, or placement of a student with disabilities.	
	Specific requirements are detailed in IDEA.	Section 504 requires that the parent have an opportunity to participate and be represented by counsel. Other details are left to the discretion of the local school district. These should be covered in school district policy.
Enforcement	IDEA is enforced by the Office of Special Education Programs.	Section 504 is enforced by the Office of Civil Rights.

As the movement to a standards-based system moves forward and students with disabilities gain more access to the general education curriculum, several questions are yet to be answered:

- How will reform efforts deal with the diverse needs of students with disabilities, given such a strong emphasis on ameliorating academic achievement?
- How will student competency in particular subject areas be measured?
- Will a variety of student performance measures be used, or will criteria be based solely on standardized achievement tests? If the criteria are standardized tests, will schools continue to exclude students with disabilities in the testing program to avoid lowering the school's overall achievement scores?

TABLE 1.3	Evolving terminology: From mainstreaming to inclusive education
Mainstreaming	The temporal, instructional, and social integration of eligible exceptional children with normal peers based on an on-going, individually determined educational planning and programming process . . . (Kaufman et al., 1975, pp. 40–41).
The Least Restrictive Environment	Educating students with disabilities with their nondisabled peers to the maximum extent appropriate . . . (Public Law 94-142 [renamed the Individuals with Disabilities Education Act]).
Educational Integration	The physical placement of students with extensive needs on regular [general] education campuses . . . (Sailor et al., 1989, p. 4).
Inclusion	Students attend their home school with their age and grade peers. It requires that the proportion of students labeled for special services is relatively uniform for all of the schools within a particular district . . . Included students are not isolated into special classes or wings within the school . . . (National Association of State Boards of Education, 1992, p. 12).
Full Inclusion	Students who are disabled or at risk receive all their instruction in a general education setting; support services come to the student.
Partial Inclusion	Students receive most of their instruction in general education settings, but students may be "pulled out" to another instructional setting when it is deemed appropriate to their individual needs.

■ INCLUDING STUDENTS WITH DISABILITIES IN GENERAL EDUCATION CLASSROOMS AND SCHOOLS

A discussion on perspectives for educational change as we enter the 21st century would not be complete without addressing the topic of **inclusive education**. Over the years, four terms have emerged as standards for describing the placement of students with disabilities in general education settings. In order of their evolutionary appearance and usage, these terms are **mainstreaming,** *the least restrictive environment*, **educational integration,** and **inclusion** (see Table 1.3). We have already discussed the least restrictive environment in the context of IDEA; we will now take a more in-depth look at this term as it relates to other terminology associated with the placement of students with disabilities in general education settings. We will then move into the terminology of the 1990s, whereby inclusive education has become the vernacular of choice to describe educating students with disabilities side by side with their nondisabled peers and friends.

■ MAINSTREAMING The expression "mainstreaming students with disabilities" dates back to the very beginnings of the field of special education. It didn't come into widespread use until the 1960s, however, with the growth of classes for children with disabilities in the public schools, most of which segregated students with disabilities from their nondisabled peers. The validity of segregated programs was called into question by some professionals. Dunn (1968) charged that classes for children with mild retardation could not be justified: "Let us stop being pressured into continuing and expanding a special education program that we know now to be undesirable for many of the children we are dedicated to serve" (p. 5). Dunn, among others, called for a placement model whereby students with disabilities could remain in the general education class program for at least some portion of the school day and receive special education when and where needed. This model became widely known as mainstreaming. One definition of mainstreaming was published in 1975:

[The] temporal, instructional, and social integration of eligible exceptional children with normal peers based on an ongoing, individually determined educational planning and programming process. . . . [Mainstreaming] requires classification of responsibility among regular and special education administrative, instructional and supportive personnel. (Kaufman, Gotlieb, Agard, & Kukic, 1975 pp. 40–41)

Although this definition strongly implies that mainstreaming students with disabilities requires ongoing individual planning and support from both general and special educators, this did not always happen in actual practice. In fact, the term *mainstreaming* fell from favor when it became associated with placing students with disabilities in general education classes without providing additional support, as a means to save money and limit the number of students who could receive additional specialized services. Such practices gave rise to the term *maindumping* as an alternative to *mainstreaming*.

The concept of least restrictive environment allows a student with disabilities, when appropriate, to participate in a general education class.

The term *mainstreaming* still remains in use today as one way to describe educating students with disabilities in general education settings. However, with the advent of the Education for All Handicapped Children's Act (now the Individuals with Disabilities Education Act) in 1975, a new term was defined in law: *the least restrictive environment.*

■ THE LEAST RESTRICTIVE ENVIRONMENT   Over the past 20 years, *least restrictive environment (LRE)* has become the term most often used in the United States to describe a process by which students with disabilities are to be placed in educational settings consistent with their individual educational needs. As defined in IDEA, the intent of LRE is to educate students with disabilities with their nondisabled peers to the maximum extent appropriate. Federal regulations require that the removal of a child from the general education setting is to occur only when the nature and severity of the child's disability is such that education in general education classes with supplementary aids or services cannot be achieved satisfactorily (34 C.F.R. Sec. 300.550[b]). But although the concept of the LRE suggests a strong preference for students with disabilities to be educated alongside their nondisabled peers, it also states that this should occur only when appropriate. As such, *LRE and mainstreaming are not synonymous*. The LRE may be any one of a "continuum of alternative placements," ranging from the general education classroom to separate educational environments exclusively for students with disabilities. School districts are required to provide such a continuum for students who cannot be satisfactorily educated in general education classes. Whenever possible, however, students should be educated in or close to the school they would attend if not disabled (see 34 C.F.R. Sec. 300.552[a][3] & 330.552[c]).

The concept of LRE as described in IDEA has been criticized in recent years. The concern is that, despite LRE's strong preference that students be educated with their nondisabled peers, it also has legitimized and supported the need for more restrictive, segregated settings. Additionally, LRE has created the perception that students with disabilities must "go to" services, rather than having services come to them. In other words, as students move farther from the general education class, the resources available to meet their needs increase concomitantly.

■ EDUCATIONAL INTEGRATION Whereas *LRE* is most often associated with the United States, *integration* is the term most often used to describe programs and services in several other countries throughout the world. For example, Italy mandates by law the integration of students with disabilities into general education classes. Australia may be described as moving toward full integration of these students, while to a lesser extent France, the United Kingdom, and Germany all have major initiatives promoting the integration of students with disabilities in general education settings.

In the United States, the term *integration* is most closely associated with social policy to end separate education for ethnic minority children, specifically students of color. In the landmark *Brown vs. Topeka, Kansas, Board of Education* in 1954, the U.S. Supreme Court ruled that education must be made available to everyone on an equal basis. Separate education for African American students was ruled as inherently unequal to that of white students. The increasing use of the term *integration* by many professionals and parents to describe the value of educating students with disabilities alongside their nondisabled peers coincided with the U.S. civil rights movement for people with disabilities of the 1980s, a movement that culminated in the passage of the Americans with Disabilities Act (ADA) in 1990. In fact, ADA moved away from the concept of the least restrictive environment as defined in IDEA, mandating that people with disabilities be placed in integrated settings appropriate to their individual needs.

Educational integration is most often defined quite simply as "the physical placement of students with extensive needs on regular [general] school campuses" (Sailor et al., 1989, p. 4). Some definitions may further expound on the need to ensure that appropriate supports and services are in place, and others may emphasize the need for collaboration between general and special educators. Regardless of the specific definition used, it is clear that integration is most commonly associated with the concept of mainstreaming. Its evolution as educational nomenclature in the United States parallels the civil rights movement in promoting access and opportunities for all people with disabilities in the natural settings of the home, community, and school.

■ INCLUSIVE EDUCATION Definitions of inclusion, while similar to those of integration, go beyond the rhetoric of educating students with disabilities side by side with their nondisabled peers. First, it promotes the value of acceptance and belonging. Landers and Weaver (1997) indicated that "inclusion is an attitude of unqualified acceptance and the fostering of student growth, at any level, on the part of all adults involved in a student's education" (p. 7). These authors further suggested that the responsibility for ensuring a successful inclusive program lies with adults. "Adults must be able to design appropriate educational opportunities that foster the individual student's growth within the context of the student's talents and interests among age-appropriate peers" (p. 7).

focus 13

Define *inclusive education*.

Another approach to defining inclusion is a call for specific changes in the education system. For example, both the National Association of State Boards of Education (NASBE) and the National Center on Educational Restructuring and Inclusion (NCERI) define inclusive education as **home school placement,** with the supports necessary to ensure an appropriate educational experience for the student. Home school placement occurs at the school the child would attend if he or she was not disabled. NASBE (1992) indicates that

inclusion . . . means that students attend their home school with their age and grade peers. It requires that the proportion of students labeled for special services is relatively uniform for all of the schools within a particular school district, and that this ratio reflects the proportion of people with disabilities in society at large. Included students are not isolated into special classes or wings within the school. To the maximum extent possible, included students receive their in-school educational services in the general education classroom with appropriate in-class support. (p. 12)

NCERI (1994), in its working definition, describes inclusive education as

providing to all students, including those with severe handicaps, equitable opportunities to receive effective educational services, with the needed supplementary aids and support services, in age-appropriate classes in their neighborhood schools, in order to prepare students for productive lives as full members of society. (p. 4)

Kukic (1993) (though not addressing the issue of home school placement) did advocate a *single educational system* that includes all students: "Inclusion is a shared value which promotes a single system of education dedicated to insuring that all students are empowered to become caring, competent, and contributing citizens in an integrated, changing, and diverse society" (p. 3).

Putnam (1993) and Nisbet (1992) addressed inclusion as a *support network* or *circle of friends*: "An inclusive classroom setting is one in which the members recognize each other's individual differences and strive to support one another's efforts" (Putnam, p. xiii). "This supportive network can comprise family, friends, classmates, coworkers, neighbors, and others who care. This network has been described as the individual's circle of support, circle of friends, or personal board of directors" (Nisbet, p. 4).

Inclusion also stipulates a distinct level of participation and support the individual receives in the educational setting. Two terms are used to describe this level of participation: *full inclusion* and *partial inclusion*. **Full inclusion** is an approach whereby students with disabilities or at risk receive all instruction in a general education classroom setting; support services come to the student. **Partial inclusion** involves students with disabilities receiving most of their instruction in general education settings but being "pulled out" to another instructional setting when appropriate to their individual needs.

The success of both full and partial inclusion programs depends on the availability of both formal and natural supports in the general education setting. **Formal supports** are those provided by, and funded through, the public school system. They include qualified teachers, paraprofessionals, appropriate curriculum materials, and technology aids. **Natural supports** in an educational setting most often consist of the individual's family and classmates. As described by Jorgensen (1992), "Natural supports bring children closer together as friends and learning partners rather than isolating them" (p. 183).

A more in-depth discussion of inclusive education and the characteristics of inclusive schools and classrooms can be found in Chapter 4.

Students at Risk but Not Disabled

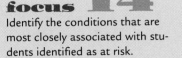
Although most of our discussion on education has focused on students who have been identified as having disabilities, a growing number of children in schools do not necessarily meet the definitions of disability but are at considerable risk for academic and social failure. Definitions of **students at risk** are very broad and vague. As suggested by Montgomery and Rossi (1994), there is a great deal of confusion and disagreement about "which children are at risk, why they are at risk, and what can be done to improve their chances for success in school and adult life" (p. v).

For the purposes of our discussion, we will address students at risk from the perspective that the individual is not identified as disabled but, due to myriad factors, needs specialized instruction and/or support to succeed in a school setting. As described by Manning and Baruth (1995), specific conditions associated with at-risk students include but are not limited to the following:

- *Lower achievement.* Students at risk for lower achievement develop a pattern of failure that is compounded through the school years. Once a lower achiever falls behind, the pattern of failure increases with each succeeding grade level. Lower achievers have poor self-concepts, are less ambitious about career aspirations, and are more likely to drop out of school.
- *Dropping out of school.* About 1 million children drop out of school each year (Davis & McCaul, 1991). More males drop out than females, and inner-city students have the highest dropout rates (nearly twice as high as those in small cities and towns). Approximately 25% of all school dropouts are unemployed, and two thirds of those employed are earning minimum wage.
- *Teenage pregnancy.* This condition is the major reason that students leave school. More than half of all high school students are sexually active, but do not use contraceptives consistently. Nearly 20% of all sexually active teens have an unintended pregnancy. Pregnant teenagers are more likely to withdraw from school (40%) and become welfare recipients (73% within four years of becoming pregnant).
- *Use of tobacco, alcohol, and other drugs.* By the age of 16, 23% of American teenagers report that they are using marijuana, 45% indicate they are consuming alcohol, and 30% smoke cigarettes. The use of tobacco, alcohol, and other drugs increases the probability of teenage pregnancy, health problems, and dropping out of school.
- *Involvement in delinquency, hate crimes, gangs, and criminal behavior.* Violence in American schools is at a critical level. Nearly 30,000 American high school students are attacked in school each month. One out of every 12 secondary-age students misses school each month because of fear. Approximately one third of these violent crimes are against teenagers and more than 80% of all thefts occur during school hours. Eight out of 10 high school students report that they have engaged in some form of delinquent behavior, ranging from drinking, theft, and truancy to destruction of property, assault, and gang fighting (Seifert & Hoffnung, 1991). Today's gangs are well organized and prone to violence, extortion, and the illegal trafficking of drugs and weapons. Hate crimes, caused by a number of factors, are on the increase.
- *Poverty and lower socioeconomic conditions.* About 25% of children in the United States live below the poverty line; 100,000 children are homeless; 10 million

children have no access to regular and appropriate medical care; and 7 million children below age 10 are latchkey kids with no after-school support (Davis & McCaul, 1991). Poverty and lower socioeconomic status (SES) are correlated with low ability, lack of motivation, and poor health. Poor children are more likely to go to school hungry, fall behind in school, have below-average basic academic skills, and drop out of school than teenagers above the poverty line (Children's Defense Fund, 1991).

- *Teenage suicide.* Teen suicide has tripled in the past 30 years and now accounts for more than 5,000 deaths each year (20% of all deaths among teenagers).
- *Health problems.* Adolescents are more likely to have health problems than either younger children or adults. Students who exhibit delinquent behavior are at greater risk for automobile accidents, alcohol and drug abuse, unwanted pregnancy, inadequate health care, and eating disorders. Poor health contributes to higher school absences, falling behind in school, and the inability to concentrate when in school (Seifert & Hoffnung, 1991).

Students at risk are often described as **educationally disadvantaged**, because they enter school with "two strikes" against them. By the time they get to high school, many of these students have not mastered even the basic level of skills necessary to complete school or succeed in adult living. Levin (cited in National School Boards Association, 1989) suggested that "because of poverty, cultural obstacles, or linguistic differences, these children tend to have low academic achievement and high drop out rates. Such students are heavily concentrated among minority groups, immigrants, non–English speaking families, and economically disadvantaged populations" (p. 6).

Although schools are often taken to task for their inability to meet the needs of students at risk, clearly at-risk students are the products of conditions that go far beyond the educational system. It will take the cooperation of many agencies—including those involved in health, social services, and education—to even begin to understand the extent of the challenges, let alone find the solutions. Conservative estimates have suggested that at least 40% of the nation's school-age children are at risk of failure because of living in poverty, being of ethnic or minority status, living in a single-parent family, having a poorly educated mother, and having limited English proficiency (Natriello, McDill, & Pallas, 1990).

What can be done to meet the needs of students at risk? Given the complexity of factors associated with failure in the schools, short-term solutions obviously will not suffice. Davis and McCaul (1991) have suggested that, first and foremost, the full extent of the problem must be recognized and then successful solutions must be identified and incorporated into the system. We know, for example, that early intervention programs benefit children who are both disadvantaged and disabled. We also know that

- early and frequent prenatal care can significantly reduce the risk of bearing low-birthweight babies.
- quality child-care programs and parenting classes held in schools allow many young teenage women to complete their education.
- appropriate sex education courses are effective in reducing the risks of sexually transmitted diseases (e.g., AIDS) and unwanted pregnancies.
- early health care, including necessary immunizations along with proper nutrition, can prevent the occurrence of serious and even fatal diseases in children.
- intensive instructional programs, conducted in school climates that are safe and conducive to both learning and promoting positive self-esteem, can remarkably

enhance the chances of disadvantaged children to become literate, self-assured, and eventually productive adults. (Davis & McCaul, 1991, pp. 130–131)

Montgomery and Rossi (1994) emphasized the need to enhance the living conditions of low-income families, to strengthen the family and prevent abuse, to expand youth programs (before and after school), and to increase parent–teacher collaboration. These authors pointed out that the schools must be ready and willing to teach students from "diverse backgrounds," and they suggested some strategies for enhancing the school environment:

- *Improvement in school administrative and support services.* Examples include improved psychological and guidance counseling, flexible schedules for teen mothers and working students, and support for highly mobile and homeless students.
- *Enhanced relevance and rigor of instruction.* Examples include use of the cultural knowledge that children bring to the classroom as "scaffolding" to build their skill acquisition, culturally relevant curriculum, high academic expectations, sensitivity to differences in learning styles, and heterogeneous instructional groupings.
- *Equitable and efficient use of resources.* Examples include increased funding for needy schools and targeting of resources to attract better school staff and teaching materials. (p. vii)

As we move into subsequent chapters on multicultural education, the family, education through the lifespan, categories of people with disabilities, and people who are gifted and talented, we will focus on effective practices for working with all students with exceptional characteristics, including those defined as at risk.

Case Study

STEVE

Over the past several years, many changes have occurred in Steve's life. After spending most of his life in a large institution, Steve is now in his late 30s, living in an apartment with two other individuals with disabilities and receiving ongoing training and assistance from a local supported living program. Over the years, Steve has had many labels describing his disability, including mental retardation, epilepsy, autism, physical disability, chronic health problems, and serious emotional disturbance. He is very much challenged both mentally and physically. Medical problems associated with epilepsy ne-

cessitate the use of medications that affect his behavior (motivation, attitude, etc.) and his physical well-being. During his early 20s, while walking up a long flight of stairs, Steve had a seizure that resulted in a fall and a broken neck. The long-term impact from the fall was a paralyzed right hand and limited use of his left leg.

A life-long goal for Steve has been to be able to work in a real job, make money, and have choices about how he spends it. For most of his life, the goal has been out of reach. His only jobs have been in sheltered workshops, where he worked for next to nothing doing piecemeal work such as

sorting envelopes, putting together cardboard boxes, or folding laundry. While most of the focus in the past has been on what he "can't do" (can't read, can't get along with supervisors, can't handle the physical requirements of a job), his family and the professionals on his team are looking more at his very strong desire to succeed in a job.

A job has opened up for a stock clerk at a local video store about 3 miles from Steve's apartment. The store manager is willing to pay minimum wage for someone to work 4 to 6 hours a day stocking the shelves with videos and handling some basic custodial tasks (such as

cleaning floors, washing windows, and dusting furniture). Steve loves movies and is really interested in this job. With the support of family and his professional team, he has applied for the position.

■ APPLICATION
As Steve's potential employer, what are some of the issues you would raise about Steve's capability as a person with a disability to meet the essential functions of the job?

What would you see as the "reasonable accommodations" necessary to help Steve succeed at this job if he were to be hired?

Debate Forum

GOVERNMENT'S INTRUSION IN THE EDUCATION OF STUDENTS WITH DISABILITIES

The debate over the federal government's role in the education of this nation's children continues as we move into the 21st century. The Individuals with Disabilities Act (IDEA) has fanned the fires of this debate, once again raising the issue of whether the federal government should have such an extensive role in the education of students with disabilities.

■ **POINT**

Prior to the passage of a national mandate to educate students with disabilities (IDEA), the vast majority of students with disabilities were not receiving an appropriate education in our nation's schools, if they were receiving any education at all. This vital legislation created a long overdue entitlement that afforded these students a free appropriate public education, one that would greatly enhance their opportunities of becoming contributors within society and end their role as consumers of society's resources. IDEA represents an investment in children that results in positive outcomes for everyone. Without this strong federal role, little change would have taken place in many states or local schools. In *A Nation at Risk,* the National Commission on Excellence indicated the need for the federal government to take primary responsibility in identifying the national interest in education. The continued support and expansion of IDEA are clearly within the framework of our national interest.

■ **COUNTERPOINT**

Federal intrusion into education violates the intent of the Constitution. Education is the responsibility of the states. The federal government's role should not extend beyond limited support to individual states as they attempt to meet the diverse needs of children throughout the country. Certainly, this supportive role doesn't extend into the type of intrusion imposed by IDEA, including the exhaustive procedural requirements such as IEPs, multidisciplinary teams, parent consent, related services, and so on. Without question, this law drains resources needed for other equally needy students while continuing the unnecessary process of labeling children in order to provide specialized instruction to them. All this, and the federal government has never fully met its obligation to provide states and local school districts with the funding necessary to meet the intent of this law. IDEA is an example of good intentions gone awry. It is an "unfunded federal mandate" that at best is a misguided effort, and at worst a fiscal nightmare.

Review

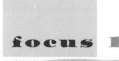

focus 1

Why do we label people according to their differences?

- Labels are an attempt to describe, identify, and distinguish one person from another.
- Many medical, psychological, social, and educational services require that an individual be labeled in order to determine who is eligible to receive special services.
- Labels help professionals communicate more effectively with one another and provide a common ground for evaluating research findings.
- Labels enable professionals to differentiate more clearly the needs of one group of people from those of another.

focus 2

Identify three approaches that can be used to describe the nature and extent of human differences.

- The developmental approach is based on differences that occur in the course of human development from what is considered normal physical, social, and intellectual growth. Human differences are the result of interaction between biological and environmental factors. Normal growth can be explained by observing large numbers of individuals and looking for characteristics that occur most frequently at any given age.
- The cultural approach to describing human differences defines *normal* according to established cultural standards. Human differences can be explained by examining the values of any given society. What is considered normal will change over time and from culture to culture.
- The individual approach to labeling suggests that labels may be self-imposed. Such labels reflect how we perceive ourselves, although those perceptions may not be consistent with how others see us.

focus 3

Identify four indicators of quality supports and services for persons with disabilities.

- They promote autonomy.
- They create opportunities for social interaction and inclusion.

- They give the individual a lifestyle choice.
- They create opportunities for economic self-sufficiency.

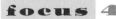 **focus 4**

What is the purpose of the Americans with Disabilities Act?

- ADA provides a national mandate to end discrimination against individuals with disabilities in private sector employment, all public services, and public accommodations, transportation, and telecommunications.

 **focus 5**

What services must be available to ensure that an individual with a disability is able to live and learn successfully in a community setting?

- Comprehensive community services must be available, including access to housing, employment, public transportation, recreation, and religious activities.
- The individual should be able to purchase services such as medical and dental care as well as adequate life insurance.

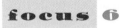 **focus 6**

How did the work of 19th-century physicians and philosophers contribute to our understanding of people with differences?

- Early 19th-century physicians emphasized that peo-

ple with disabilities should be treated humanely.
- Jean-Marc Itard demonstrated that an individual with a severe disability could learn new skills through physiological stimulation.

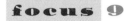 **focus 7**

Distinguish between abnormal behavior and social deviance.

- Human behavior is the focus of psychology. When the behavior of an individual does not meet the criteria of *normal,* it is labeled *abnormal.*
- Sociology is concerned with modern cultures, group behaviors, societal institutions, and intergroup relationships. When people are unable to adapt to social roles or establish interpersonal relationships, their behaviors are labeled *deviant.*

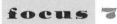 **focus 8**

What educational services were available for students with disabilities during most of the 20h century?

- Educational programs at the beginning of the 20th century were provided primarily in separate, special schools.
- For the first 75 years of this century, the availability of educational programs for special students was sporadic and selective. Special education was allowed in many states but required in only a few.
- Research on the efficacy of special classes for students with mild disabilities sug-

gested that there was little or no benefit in removing students from general education classrooms.

focus 9

Identify the principal issues in the right-to-education cases that led to eventual passage of Public Law 94–142 (now referred to as IDEA).

- Education was reaffirmed as a right and not a privilege by the U.S. Supreme Court.
- In Pennsylvania, the court ordered the schools to provide a free public education to all children with mental retardation of ages 6 to 21.
- The *Mills* case extended the right to a free public education to all school-age children with disabilities.

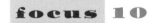 **focus 10**

Identify five major provisions of the Individuals with Disabilities Education Act.

- The labeling and placement of students with disabilities in educational programs required the use of nondiscriminatory and multidisciplinary assessment.
- Parental safeguards and involvement in the educational process included consent for testing and placement and participation as a team member in the development of an IEP. Procedural safeguards (e.g., due process) were included to protect the child and family from decisions that could adversely affect their lives.

- Every student with a disability is entitled to a free and appropriate public education.
- The delivery of an appropriate education occurs through an individualized education program (IEP).
- All children were given the right to learn in an environment consistent with their academic, social, and physical needs. The law mandated that children with disabilities receive their education with nondisabled peers to the maximum extent appropriate.

focus 11

Describe two differing viewpoints on disciplining students with disabilities who represent a danger to others and themselves.

- According to one view, terminating services and expelling a student with a disability violates the basic tenet of a free and appropriate public education.
- Others argue that students with a disability should be treated no differently than nondisabled students.

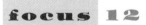 **focus 12**

Distinguish between students with disabilities eligible for services under Section 504 and those eligible under IDEA.

- Students eligible under Section 504 are entitled to accommodations and/or modifications to their educational program that will ensure that they receive an appropriate education com-

parable to their nondis-
abled peers.
- Students eligible under
IDEA are entitled to special
education and related
services to ensure they
receive a free and
appropriate education.

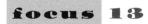

Define *inclusive education*.

- Inclusive education may be
defined as placing students
with a disability in a general
education setting while
making available the
necessary supports (or
support networks) to
ensure an appropriate
educational experience.
- Inclusive education may be
defined as both full (all instruction received in the
general education class-
room) or partial (students
pulled out for part of their
instructional program).

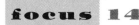

Identify the conditions that
are most closely associated
with students identified as at
risk.

- Low achievement
- Dropping out of school
- Teenage pregnancy
- Use of tobacco, alcohol,
and other drugs

- Involvement in delinquency,
hate crimes, gangs, and
criminal behavior
- Poverty and lower socioeconomic conditions
- Teenage suicide
- Health problems

2 Multicultural and Diversity Issues

 Taken as a group, minority children are comprising an ever larger percentage of public school students. . . . More minority children continue to be served in special education than would be expected from the percentage of minority students in the general school population. Poor African-American children are 2.3 times more likely to be identified by their teacher as having mental retardation than their white counterparts. Although African-Americans represent 16 percent of elementary and secondary enrollments, they constitute 21 percent of total enrollments in special education. (The 1997 Amendments to the Individuals with Disabilities Education Act [Sec. 687 (c) (7–8)])

 In New York City, poor and minority children are increasing as a percentage of total student growth. The social welfare index for children continues to decline; children are currently about 42 percent worse off than they were in 1974, and their welfare is likely to get even worse in the next five years. (U.S. Department of Education, 1996, p. 81)

 Beginning teachers in the induction program of a large metropolitan district in the West "attend a series of presentations entitled Multicultural Week" at the end of their initial year in the training program. "The presentations appeared to have little effect on how teachers think about these issues." (McDiarmid, 1992, p. 83)

Snapshot

Raphael

Ten-year-old Raphael lives with his adoptive parents. He is proud of his deafness—he accepts it and is comfortable with it. His mother is very aware of using sign language whenever Raphael is in the room, even if she is speaking to someone else. "If Raphael is watching, then I will sign. He deserves it."

Raphael does very well integrating with his hearing peers at recess. There are a group of guys—little boys—10 or 11 years old who are always coming around, "Can Raphael come out? Can Raphael do this? . . . Just ask him if he'll play with me." A lot of them are picking up the basic signs. So there's a lot of interaction going on.

"He's one of the most popular kids in the neighborhood, and he can play with anybody. He knows how to get his point of view across to the others and the others—they make up their own little signs that are not really sign language or anything, but they know what they're talking about. When we first moved to this neighborhood, the responses we got from our neighbors, that we have a deaf kid is, 'Wow. That's neat,' and then they'd kind of

go, 'Alright, now let's hold back. But when he goes out there, they see that he can play basketball with any kid in his neighborhood, that he can play street hockey, he can rollerblade, he can ride bikes, and he's not a problem to anybody. In fact, he's the most popular kid in the neighborhood.

"I see Raphael's future as . . . I'm really not sure yet. He's really getting involved in his computers at school. And I'd like to see him continue that way. His working with computers has made a whole new person out of him."

Denise

"Denise is a 9-year-old African American girl in the fourth grade. Her elementary school is in a midsize city in the southeastern United States. Denise lives with her parents and two older brothers in an apartment complex in a working-class African American neighborhood. Because of recent redistricting, Denise is being bused from an all-black school in her neighborhood to a predominantly middle-class white elementary school across town. This is her first year in the school and Denise is one of only five African American girls in the fourth grade.

Denise has always been a good student with no social problems. This had been the case when she started the year at her new school. Recently,

however, Denise has gotten into fights with several of her classmates. She has also been failing to complete her classwork and has been talking back to her teacher."[1]

Daniel

"Daniel is an 8-year-old second-grader. He and his family arrived in the United States from Mexico two years ago. Daniel has a 14-year-old brother, Julian, who is in middle school. Julian fills a role that is common for children in recently immigrated families, serving as the family's link to the English-speaking world through his ability to translate. Three additional siblings born between Daniel and his brother are still in Mexico. The family's support system includes the father's brothers and their wives, all recent immigrants from Mexico. Daniel's father is a construction worker, and his mother is a housewife.

Daniel's academic performance has been average. He has consistently submitted required assignments, he has perfect attendance, and his interactions with teachers and peers have been good. Recently, Daniel's academic performance has declined, and he has become withdrawn. His teacher, Mrs. Strickland, noted that Daniel has failed several tests, that he has not had his parents sign the required school folder (which includes the tests he failed),

and that he has not had his parents sign permission slips needed for planned field trips. As a result, Daniel has lost recess privileges, he has had to eat by himself at lunch time, and has not been allowed to participate in two field trips. (Although he had earned the right to participate in the field trips, the fact that he did not have written parental permission prevented him from doing so.)

Mrs. Strickland wrote the parents a note on Daniel's folder, explaining that they needed to sign his folder and that Daniel needed to study for his tests. She also telephoned Daniel's home and talked to "someone" there about the situation who said, "OK." Mrs. Strickland had become extremely frustrated because there had been no change. Every morning, she reprimanded Daniel for not bringing the required signed folder and demanded an explanation. Daniel did not respond."[2]

[1] *Source:* Excerpted from Locke, D.C. (1995). Counseling interventions with African American youth. In C. C. Lee (Ed.). *Counseling for Diversity* (pp. 26–27). Boston: Allyn & Bacon, Inc. Reprinted by permission.

[2] *Source:* Excerpted from Zapata, J. T. (1995). Counseling Hispanic children and youth. In C. C. Lee (Ed.). *Counseling for Diversity* (pp. 103–104). Boston: Allyn & Bacon, Inc. Reprinted by permission.

ENISE'S SITUATION in our opening snapshot represents a real test for the education system. Should Denise be labeled as having disabilities, or should someone in the school system be fighting to keep Denise from being labeled? Should she receive special education services? Should she be considered disabled because of her behavioral and academic difficulties? Do her problems reflect stress related to the change in school or cultural stressors? In this chapter, we will examine the very complex issues related to cultural and ethnic diversity and their impact on public education.

Many organizations and service agencies encounter substantial challenge in meeting the broad array of needs in our complex culture. This is certainly true of the education system. Various advocacy groups have emerged when a particular subgroup's educational needs have not been adequately addressed by school systems structured to serve the majority. Discontent surfaces when a segment of students is left out, discriminated against, or treated unfairly, or if the individual potential of such students is not being appropriately developed. When the mainstream activities of a system do not well accommodate diversity, the system must be deemed inadequate, and modifications become necessary.

This rationale played a significant role in the emergence of both multicultural education and special education. **Multicultural education** arose from a belief that the needs of certain children—those with cultural backgrounds that differ from those of the majority—were not being appropriately met. Broad societal unrest related to racial discrimination fueled and augmented this belief. Similarly, **special education** evolved from the failure of general education to meet the needs of youngsters who were not learning as rapidly or in the same way as their age-mates. Reformers believed that two particular groups of students were being mistreated—in one case, because of their cultural or racial background, and in the other, because of their disabilities.

To begin exploring multiculturalism and diversity, we will discuss the basic purpose of general education and the conventional approaches used to achieve this purpose. We will also compare the underlying purposes and approaches of special education and multicultural education and discuss the connections between the two. After building this background, we will examine multicultural and diversity issues in the context of this book's focus: human exceptionality in society, school, and family.

Purposes of and Approaches to Education

The basic purpose of education in the United States is to produce a literate citizenry (Morris & Pai, 1993). According to this perspective, education is presumably intended for everyone; all children should have access to public education through the level of high school. In general terms, this goal is implemented by grouping and teaching students according to chronological age and evaluating their performance based on what society expects children of each age to achieve. Society uses an average of what youngsters of each age typically can learn as its yardstick for assessing their progress. Thus, American education is aimed at the masses, and performance is judged according to an average. Through this system, schools attempt to bring most students to a similar, or at least a minimal, level of knowledge.

focus 1
Identify three ways in which the purposes of and approaches to general education in the United States sometimes differ from those of special education and multicultural education.

■ CULTURAL PLURALISM AND THE ROLE OF EDUCATION

Promoting an understanding of the world's diverse cultures has become a goal of many educators in the United States. Multicultural education values and promotes **cultural pluralism**. It is not aimed at students of cultural or racial minorities, but instead teaches *all* students about cultural diversity and how to function in a multicultural society (Banks, 1997a; Kitano, 1997; Tiedt & Tiedt, 1995). Gollnick and Chinn (1994) have cited six beliefs and assumptions related to multicultural education:

A goal of many educators is promoting an understanding of the world's diverse cultures.

There is strength and value in promoting cultural diversity. Schools should be models for the expression of human rights and respect for cultural differences. Social justice and equality for all people should be of paramount importance in the design and delivery of curricula. Attitudes and values necessary for the continuation of a democratic society can be promoted in schools. Schooling can provide the knowledge and skills for the redistribution of power and income among cultural groups. Educators working with families and communities can create an environment that is supportive of multiculturalism. (p. 29)

Multicultural education opposes the once-prevalent view that schools should minimize cultural differences—that is, rather than seek to homogenize the population, schools should encourage students to gain information about and competence in understanding multiple cultures, both those present in our society and throughout the world (Banks, 1997b; Bennett, 1995).

Multicultural education is intended to teach all students about different cultures. Yet despite some progress, we still largely lack an awareness of how members of different cultural groups have contributed to major developments in our country's history. To illustrate, the recent PBS series on the Civil War, produced by Kenneth Burns, highlighted significant roles played by African Americans that many of us did not learn about in school. Also, during World War II, Native Americans, known as "Code Talkers," served in critical communications roles by transmitting messages in their native tongue, which could not be decoded by Axis forces. And despite the degrading abuse that they received from many sources, Japanese Americans volunteered for critical assignments and served the United States with distinction during World War II. Such stories need to be told.

At school, young people develop attitudes and a knowledge base; their thoughts and feelings about diverse cultures are at least partially shaped by what they learn in the classroom. Incomplete information or stereotypical presentations about different cultures detract from gaining an understanding of the variety of people that characterizes our world. Careless treatment of this important topic perpetuates two problems: a lack of factual information about numerous cultures and a lack of skill in relating to those of different backgrounds. A complete education must include recognition of the roles of many peoples in shaping our country and our world, while fostering attitudes of respect and appreciation.

There are some important differences in the fundamental purposes of general education, special education, and multicultural education. From the outset, the primary purpose of general education runs counter to those of the other two. Aimed at serving the masses, general education attempts to create a leveling effect by bringing everyone to more or less the same level, teaching similar topics in groups, and evaluating achievement based on a norm, or average. Special education, in contrast, tends to focus on the individual. Special education professionals would agree that the basic purpose of special education is to provide an opportunity for each child with a disability to learn and develop to his or her individual potential. Current special education efforts focus on individual needs, strengths, and preferences. This individualized approach is important because many students in special education seem unable to learn well through instruction that is broadly directed at large groups. Thus, special education tends to emphasize individuals and specific skill levels. Evaluation, at least in part, is based on individual growth to a specified mastery level and only partly on **norm-based averages** (average performance scores of agemates).

Contemporary multicultural education promotes recognition and respect for differences and diversity (Kitano, 1997). At a certain level, this is somewhat at odds with the goal of general education to achieve consistency (to bring the population to a comparable level of performance in similar areas of knowledge). Further, general education largely reflects a societal self-portrait of the United States as a "melting pot" for peoples of all backgrounds, emphasizing similarities and downplaying differences. Contemporary multicultural education, on the other hand, sees the school as a powerful tool for appreciating and promoting diversity.

The differences in goals and approaches of general, special, and multicultural education occur not just on a theoretical level, but can create a certain amount of difficulty within school systems and among educators. As one faction (multicultural education) attempts to make inroads into the broader domain of another (general education), an adversarial or competitive situation may result. Yet such misunderstandings may be diminished through thoughtful discussion and examination of the issues.

■ MULTICULTURAL AND DIVERSITY LINKAGES TO SPECIAL EDUCATION

The link between multicultural education and special education has not always been comfortable, largely because of issues concerning racial discrimination and inappropriate educational programming. Multicultural education and special education have been associated in special education's role of serving children who are failing in the general education system. Unfortunately, a disproportionately large number of students placed in special education are from minority backgrounds (Bedell, 1989). This issue continues to surface (MacMillan, Gresham, & Siperstein, 1993), suggesting that special education has been used as a tool of discrimination, a means of separating racial and ethnic minorities from the majority.

The links between special education and multicultural education are numerous. Some of the environmental influences noted earlier that appear to have an impact in special education also seem operative in multicultural education. These influences can cause behavioral or academic difficulties in school. Additionally, certain instructional approaches common to both special and multicultural education can meet a student's academic needs.

As this chapter proceeds, our discussion of how special and multicultural education relate to each other will focus on four major elements of the Individuals with Disabilities Education Act (IDEA) (presented in Chapter 1): nondiscriminatory and multidisciplinary assessment, parental involvement in developing each child's educational program, education in the least restrictive environment, and a free and appropriate public education delivered through an individualized education plan (IEP).

■ PREVALENCE AND OVERREPRESENTATION OF CULTURALLY DIVERSE STUDENTS IN SPECIAL EDUCATION

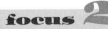

focus 2

Describe the population status of and trends among culturally diverse groups in the United States. How do they have an impact on the educational system?

The term *prevalence* generally refers to the number of people in a given population who exhibit a condition, problem, or particular status (e.g., who have a hearing loss or who have red hair). In general terms, a phenomenon's prevalence is determined by counting how often it occurs. In this section, we will examine prevalence in a somewhat different sense, discussing certain factors relevant to the relationship between human exceptionality and multicultural issues.

In Chapter 1, we identified several factors associated with students at risk for academic failure: diverse cultural backgrounds, limited backgrounds in speaking English, and poverty (Aponte & Crouch, 1995; U.S. Department of Education, 1996). It is important to emphasize that these factors only indicate risk for difficulties in school; they do not necessarily destine a student for a special education placement. Yet a very high percentage—perhaps as high as 41%—of all special education students are from culturally divergent backgrounds (Bedell, 1989). The overrepresentation of students of color in groups labeled as having disabilities is cause for concern (e.g., MacMillan et al., 1993). African American children, for instance, appear more frequently than would be expected in classes for those with serious emotional disturbance and mental retardation, and Hispanic Americans also represent a large and rapidly growing group in special education. At the other end of the spectrum, programs for the gifted and talented seem to have fewer than expected students who are African American, Hispanic American, or Native American (Gollnick & Chinn, 1994).

Unfortunately, misplacement of culturally diverse students into special education classes can happen. Perhaps as many as 41% of all special education students are from culturally divergent backgrounds.

Cultural minority students do not complete school as frequently as their peers from the cultural majority (Aponte & Crouch, 1995). In 1995, 83.2% of the white population between 18 and 24 years of age completed school, whereas the figure for African Americans was 73.6% and that for Hispanic Americans was 55.6% (U.S. Bureau of the Census, 1995). Dropout rates also correlate closely with family income: whereas 7.5% of high school students from low-income families dropped out of school in 1995, only 1.5% of those from middle-income families left high school before graduation (U.S. Bureau of the Census, 1995).

Several culturally or ethnically diverse populations are growing rapidly because of increasing birthrates and immigration levels. For example, African Americans represented approximately 12.7% of the total population in the United States in 1995, but their number is increasing at a rate more than twice that of the Caucasian population (U.S. Bureau of the Census, 1995). Growth of culturally and ethnically diverse groups will affect education, presenting diverse needs that will require a spectrum of educational services (Aponte & Crouch, 1995).

Language differences often contribute to academic difficulties for students from diverse backgrounds who are educated in a system designed by the cultural majority (Reyes, 1992). Baca and Cervantes (1990) found that approximately 7.9 million chil-

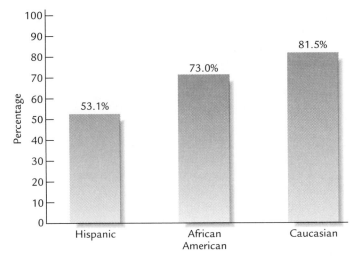

FIGURE 2.1

Percentage of the population 25 years of age and older completing high school in 1995

[*Source:* U.S. Bureau of the Census, 1995]

dren of school age spoke languages other than English in 1980, a growth of nearly 3 million students over 1976 figures. The authors also estimated that 948,000 of these youngsters were both disabled and linguistically different. Census data indicate that, although the overall enrollment of 8- to 15-year-olds decreased from 1979 to 1995, the number of students in this age range speaking a language other than English at home increased (U.S. Bureau of the Census, 1995).

Immigration levels since the Vietnam conflict suggest that Southeast Asian people constitute a rapidly growing sector of the U.S. population. This influx has had a significant impact on the school systems; the number of enrolled 8- to 15-year-olds speaking Asian languages increased significantly from 1979 to 1995 (U.S. Bureau of the Census, 1995). Such growth places a heavy demand on U.S. school systems to provide linguistically appropriate instruction and to exercise vigilance and caution in assessment. And this trend continues—it is anticipated that the number of students with limited English proficiency, known as LEP students, will continue to grow more rapidly than other groups of students (Baca & Almanza, 1991).

The figures reported here broadly represent students who are either bilingual or linguistically diverse. Certainly, many come from backgrounds that permit them to achieve academically in a school system based primarily on the English language. Not all students accounted for here will need special supports or programs. Also, estimates and actual census data are always subject to a certain level of error. However, analyses thus far suggest that such error is relatively small and that, if anything, these data are likely to be somewhat conservative (Kominski, 1989; U.S. Department of Education, 1991). The need for linguistically appropriate instruction is magnified considerably when we consider other multicultural factors such as a careful examination of educational goals and the methods of achieving them.

Nondiscriminatory and Multidisciplinary Assessment

Perhaps nowhere is the link between special and multicultural education more obvious than in issues of **nondiscriminatory assessment**. As mentioned earlier, a disproportionate number of minority

Children tested for potential special education placement must be assessed in their native/primary language.

focus 3

Identify two ways in which assessment may contribute to the overrepresentation of students who are culturally diverse in special education programs.

students is found in special education classes. Decisions regarding referral and placement in these classes are based on psychological assessment, which typically is based on standardized evaluations of intellectual and social functioning. Such assessments often discriminate or are biased against children from ethnically and culturally diverse backgrounds.

In several early cases, courts determined that such evaluations were indeed discriminatory to Hispanic American students (*Diana* v. *State Board of Education*, 1970, 1973) and African American students (*Larry P.* v. *Riles*, 1972, 1979). Additionally, assessment and instruction for Asian American children were addressed in the case of *Lau* v. *Nichols* (1974). These California cases had a national impact and greatly influenced the drafting of IDEA. Two prominent precedents in IDEA, for example, were established in the case of *Diana* v. *State Board of Education*: (1) children tested for potential placement in special education must be assessed in their native or primary language, and (2) children cannot be placed in special classes on the basis of culturally biased tests.

To prevent discriminatory evaluation practices, students must be tested in their native or primary language whenever possible, the evaluation procedures used must be selected and administered in a way that prevents cultural or racial discrimination, and assessment tools must be validated (shown to measure what they purport to measure). Finally, IDEA also mandates that evaluation should involve a multidisciplinary team using several sources of information to make a placement decision. To place these safeguards in context, it is necessary to examine the assessment process and how cultural bias can occur.

■ CULTURAL BIAS AND ASSESSMENT ERROR

Assessment is a powerful tool. Results of tests that assess academic and behavioral differences often determine placement in particular instructional programs—to the student's benefit or detriment. Assessment error constitutes a major controversy in both special education and multicultural education. Many have found that bias exists in the measurement instruments employed in assessment. **Measurement bias** produces error during testing, leading to unfair or inaccurate test results that do not reflect the student's actual mental abilities or skills (Aiken, 1997; McMillan, 1997). Representatives of cultural and ethnic minority groups argue that cultural bias and prejudice are involved in both the construction and development of assessment instruments and in their use. Particularly standardized, norm-referenced instruments, in which minority children's performances are often compared with norms developed from other populations, have been criticized. Under these testing conditions, minority children often appear disadvantaged by cultural differences (Aiken, 1997; Cronbach, 1990; Gregory, 1996; Kaplan & Saccuzzo, 1993).

Bias in psychological assessment has been recognized as a problem for many years (Burt, 1921) and continues to concern professionals (Hoy & Gregg, 1994; MacMillan et al., 1993; Saccuzzo & Johnson, 1995). Some assessment procedures simply fail to document the same level of performance by individuals with diverse cultural backgrounds, even if they have similar abilities. This phenomenon is referred to as **test bias.**

Considerable effort has been expended to develop tests that are culture-free or culture-fair. This effort was rooted in the belief that the test itself was the major element contributing to bias or unfairness. This simplistic perspective was flawed, although over the years it led to some improvements. Revision minimized the most glaring problems by reducing both the amount of culture-specific content in test items and the culture-specific language proficiency required to perform test tasks. However, even these refinements have limited effectiveness when the use of the test and interpretation of results are not appropriate and conceptually sound (Gregory, 1996; Hoy & Gregg, 1994). Recently, attention has focused on procedures as well as the test instrument itself. One of the best ways to ensure fair testing is to prepare those who give tests and interpret the results, so that they understand cultural issues in assessment (Aiken, 1997; Aponte & Clifford, 1995; Stone, 1994). Professionals need training to help them see how easily bias can creep in. Lasting personal impressions can be formed based on a single cue that can in turn trigger bias and incorrect categorization of a student—even in the face of evidence to the contrary (Skowronski & Carlston, 1989).

■ LANGUAGE DIVERSITY

A long-standing major culprit in assessment of culturally diverse students has been language diversity. Assessment of non-English-speaking children has often been biased, providing an inaccurate reflection of abilities (Diaz-Rico & Weed, 1995). If language diversity is not considered as a factor during assessment and educational planning, a child may receive an inappropriate special education placement (McMillan, 1997). As indicated earlier, census data show a substantial and increasing number of children in the American educational system who speak languages other than English (Taverne & Sheridan, 1995). Therefore all teachers, related education personnel, social workers, psychologists, and administrators must become aware of the challenges and possible solutions to making appropriate educational assessments of student with language diversity (Hart, 1993; Trotter, 1992; Wilson & Wood, 1994).

A particularly difficult situation exists for non-English-speaking students with a language disorder, such as delayed language development (Battle, 1993; McMillan, 1997; Pena, Quinn, & Iglesias, 1992). Determining the degree to which each factor contributes to academic deficiency is difficult. It is hard to decide whether such a child should be placed in special education, and if so, whether such placement should occur because the child is linguistically diverse due to culture or linguistically deficient for developmental reasons.

One of the seemingly positive safeguards in IDEA, requiring assessment of a child in his or her native language, also raises new questions. Although this law represents a positive step toward fair treatment of linguistically diverse students, some difficulties have emerged in its implementation. Specifically, the legislation defines *native language* as that used in the home, yet a regulation implementing IDEA defined it as that which is normally used by the youngster in school. This latter definition may present problems for a bilingual student who has achieved a conversational fluency in English, yet whose proficiency may not be adequate to sustain academic work (U.S. Department of Education, 1996). For this child, testing in English is likely to be biased, even though it is considered a proper procedure according to regulations.

■ ASSESSMENT AND THE PREPARATION OF PROFESSIONALS

Psychoeducational assessment professionals, particularly those working with ethnic minority children, must be properly trained to obtain accurate data and minimize the formation of impressions that may lead to bias (Palmer, Hughes, & Juarez, 1991).

focus 4
Identify three ways in which language diversity may contribute to assessment difficulties with students who are from a variety of cultures.

Additionally, professionals must be constantly alert to potential bias due to language differences as well as other factors that may mask students' true abilities. In many cases, information about the child's home life and other environmental matters can provide valuable insight to aid professionals in both administering assessment and interpreting results. That information includes languages spoken in the household and by whom, who the child's caregivers are (parents and others), the amount of time the child spends with caregivers, and the child's out-of-school activities. Uninformed assumptions about family and circumstances can lead to inaccurate assessment, so the evaluator must obtain all information possible about the child and his or her life. It is vitally important to understand the child in the context of his or her family (Ashton, 1992; Sandler, 1994; Speight, Thomas, Kennel, & Anderson, 1995; Watts, 1994). These training challenges are often addressed unsuccessfully in courses in psychology, teacher education, and a number of related areas (e.g., Gergen, Gulerce, Lock, & Misra, 1996; McDiarmid, 1992; Weinstein, 1994).

Assessment is one of several important tools in education, particularly in special and multicultural education. Effective, unbiased assessment requires that instruments be correctly constructed and used. To that end, the purposes of assessment, and education itself, must be considered from the outset: Are we attempting to bring the bulk of citizenry to a similar point in education or knowledge? Are we creating a leveling effect, attempting to make all people alike to some degree? Or are we promoting individual growth and development and encouraging cultural diversity and individual differences?

Parents from Different Cultures and Their Involvement in Special Education

IDEA requires parental involvement in the education of students with disabilities. Parent rights, however, are based on certain assumptions. Perhaps the most fundamental assumption is that parents are consistently proactive and will challenge the school if their child is not being treated properly. Although true of some parents of children in special education, the assumption is not true for all. Many parents are reluctant or afraid to interact with the educational system.

focus 5

Identify three ways in which differing sociocultural mores may affect the manner in which parents become involved in the educational process.

Accepting a child's disability is not easy for any parent, and a family's attitude toward exceptionality can influence how a child's intervention proceeds (Norton & Drew, 1994). People of diverse cultural backgrounds have perspectives and beliefs regarding illness and disability that may differ from those of the majority culture (Aponte & Barnes, 1995). For example, some cultures have great difficulty accepting disabilities because of religious beliefs and values. Views about the family also can affect treatment of children with disabilities.

The extended family structures common in African American and Hispanic American cultures can cause hesitation about accepting care from outside the family and anxieties about special education. Parents of children with disabilities who are poor, have a minority background, and speak a primary language other than English face enormous disadvantages in interacting with the special education system.

Sensitivity in interpersonal communication is of great importance when professionals deliver service to children of families who are culturally diverse. The meanings of certain facial expressions, expression of emotions, manners, behaviors denoting respect, and many other interpersonal matters vary greatly among cultures (Ekman, 1993; Russell, 1994) and affect the interaction between minority family members and educational professionals. Some Asian American families may be reluctant to receive assistance from outside the family. Some Asian parents may feel shame regarding illnesses in general, and the fact that their child has been identified as having disabilities will likely influence their acceptance of the situation and their attitude toward special services (Cummings & DeHart, 1995; Dao, 1991). Moreover, professionals should keep in mind that the immigration status of some families may affect the manner in which they react to attempts to provide services for their children. Although this constitutes a pragmatic consideration rather than a cultural difference, a family residing in the United States illegally or feeling somewhat unsure about its residency status will likely avoid interacting with an educational system.

Families can support multicultural education by working with children on school projects about their cultural heritage.

Public education in the United States predominantly reflects the philosophy of the cultural majority. This is not surprising, since social institutions—in this instance, formal schooling—are typically founded on such mainstream views. In general, when multiple cultures live together, as in the United States, minorities tend to influence public matters less than the cultural majority (Wood et al., 1994). Yet the social mores of the minority subcultures may continue to flourish in private and often emerge in individual interactions and behaviors. Activities or beliefs that are of the utmost importance to one cultural group may be less crucial to another or even viewed with disdain. Such differences surface in discussion of disabilities. For example, although mental retardation is universally recognized by all cultures, its conceptualization, social interpretation, and treatment are culturally specific (Manion & Bersani, 1987). The condition may be considered as negative, such as a punishment on the family, or may be viewed favorably, such as the blessing of knowing an unusual, rare person, depending upon the cultural context. Similarly, certain behaviors that a professional of the majority culture might view as a learning problem may in fact be a product of the acculturation process or considered normal within a child's cultural background.

Most professional educators agree that parental involvement in the educational process is beneficial. This is one reason that legislators included such participation as a major element in IDEA. This perspective, however, overlooks the fact that all parents do not view the educational system in the same way and may not interact effectively with the schools because of their diverse cultural views. A child's educational planning may not be viewed similarly by members of all cultures; these differences affect work in other fields, such as health care (Vaughan, 1993).

Education for Culturally Diverse Students

■ INDIVIDUALIZED EDUCATION

IDEA requires the development of an individualized education plan (IEP) for each student with a disability. Most school districts have considerable experience in this process but face further requirements when addressing the needs of a child with cultural and/or linguistic differences. Depending on background and capabilities, such a student may need remediation for a specific disability, catch-up work in academic subjects, and instruction in English as a second language. The IEP must consider cultural factors, such as language differences, as well as learning and behavior disabilities and perhaps provide for specialized instruction from different professionals for each facet of education. Rarely will a single person have the training and background in culture, language, and the specialized skills needed to remediate disabilities. Baca and Cervantes noted that, with "the potential for larger numbers of highly specialized personnel to be involved in the provision of services, it becomes extremely critical for school districts to recognize that coordination and sequencing of instruction are a primary concern" (1990, pp. 189–190).

An IEP for a student who is culturally diverse and has a disability may address many facets of his or her life. For example, children from different economic levels may have different instructional needs and substantial developmental differences. The IEP should address these matters if it is to be maximally effective for each particular child. Additionally, it may be important to employ facets of the child's cultural background as a strategy in instruction—taking advantage of it as an instructional resource (Moll, 1992).

Stereotypical assumptions about ethnic and cultural background should be discarded. These may involve well-intentioned but misguided efforts to integrate into instruction culturally relevant foods, activities, or holidays. The utmost care should be taken to make sure that such content is specifically correct (not just an uninformed generalization about a religious celebration or folk dance) and actually related to the student's experience—some foods typical to an ethnic group may not be eaten in a particular child's family or neighborhood. Insensitive use of such material may do more to perpetuate an unfortunate stereotype than to enrich a child's understanding of his or her heritage (Baca & Cervantes, 1990). IEPs written for children who are culturally diverse must truly be developed in an individualized fashion, perhaps even more so than for children with disabilities who come from the cultural majority.

■ THE LEAST RESTRICTIVE ENVIRONMENT

Education in the least restrictive environment (LRE) involves a wide variety of placement options (see Chapter 1). The guiding principle is that instruction for students with disabilities should take place in an environment as similar to that of the educational mainstream as possible and in settings with nondisabled peers to the maximum extent appropriate. For the child who is culturally diverse and receiving appropriate special education services, the same is true, although some unique circumstances require additional attention.

focus 6

Identify two areas that require particular attention when developing an individualized education plan (IEP) for a student who is culturally diverse.

focus 7

Identify two considerations that represent particular difficulties in serving children who are culturally diverse in the least restrictive environment.

Culturally diverse children receiving special education services should be taught in settings with nondisabled peers to the maximum extent appropriate.

Exceptional children who have language differences may also receive assistance from bilingual education staff. In some cases, the language instruction may be incorporated into other teaching that focuses on remediation of a learning problem. In situations in which the disability is more severe or the language difference is extreme (perhaps little or no English proficiency), the student may be placed in a separate setting for a portion of instructional time.

Cultural and language instruction may vary as the child grows older, according to the model used in a given school district. Figure 2.2 illustrates how various approaches might be structured into a daily or weekly educational schedule as a student moves from kindergarten to the 12th grade. Each approach differs somewhat in the degree of integration it recommends. Part I, the transition model, moves the

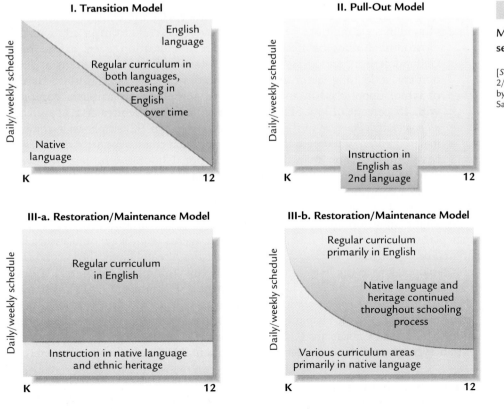

I. Transition Model

Daily/weekly schedule

English language

Regular curriculum in both languages, increasing in English over time

Native language

K   12

II. Pull-Out Model

Daily/weekly schedule

Instruction in English as 2nd language

K   12

III-a. Restoration/Maintenance Model

Daily/weekly schedule

Regular curriculum in English

Instruction in native language and ethnic heritage

K   12

III-b. Restoration/Maintenance Model

Daily/weekly schedule

Regular curriculum primarily in English

Native language and heritage continued throughout schooling process

Various curriculum areas primarily in native language

K   12

FIGURE 2.2

Models of bilingual and bicultural service delivery

[*Source: The Bilingual Special Education Interface,* 2/E by Baca/Cervantes. © 1989. Reprinted by permission of Prentice-Hall, Inc., Upper Saddle River, NJ.]

student into the instructional mainstream as rapidly as possible while addressing issues of linguistic performance and disability remediation. Parts III-a and III-b involve instruction that takes place while the student remains in an integrated setting as much as possible. Part II represents what has long been known as a **pull-out program** and does not reflect integrated instruction. Although some students may require placement in such a setting, pull-out programs have not been viewed favorably in recent years. Baca and Cervantes (1990) have noted that pull-out instructional placements are a particularly sensitive issue in bilingual and bicultural education because they represent segregation. In some cases, placement decisions are based on training limitations of the staff rather than students' needs.

Other Diversity Considerations

Many influences come into play as we consider multicultural and diversity issues in education. In some cases, societal problems contribute to the development of a child's learning difficulties. In other cases, the complications involved in educating people from a variety of cultures who also have differing abilities produce a host of challenges in assessment and instruction. It is important to note that the study of culture and associated variables, such as poverty and migrancy, is complicated by attempts to identify simplistic causal relationships (e.g., a finding of a higher frequency of depression in people of certain ethnic backgrounds may be due to poverty, not culture). Research on race and culture involves complex and interacting variables that defy simple conclusions (Betancourt & Lopez, 1993).

■ CHILDREN LIVING IN POVERTY

Perhaps the most outstanding example of how social and cultural factors interrelate is found in the conditions pertaining to poverty. A child from an impoverished environment may be destined for special education even before birth. Gelfand, Jenson, and Drew (1997) cited statistical data about prenatal development, a defining factor in the child's latter development: "Only 5 percent of white upper-class infants have some complications at birth, compared with 15 percent of low SES [socioeconomic status] whites and *51 percent of all nonwhites who have very low incomes as a group*" (p. 92, emphasis in the original). Children who begin their lives facing such challenges are more likely to have difficulty later than those who do not. Children who live in poverty may be more frail, be sick more often, and exhibit more neurological problems that later contribute to academic difficulties (Drew, Hardman, & Logan, 1996; Gottlieb, Alter, Gottlieb, & Whishner, 1994).

As children develop during the important early years, an impoverished environment places them at risk of malnutrition, toxic agents (e.g., lead), and insufficient parental care (Vaughan, 1993). As with the statistics already cited, these conditions are more prevalent in the lives of cultural and ethnic minorities (Aponte & Crouch, 1995; Hardy & Hazelrigg, 1995; U.S. Department of Education, 1996). Additionally, poverty is associated with ethnic minority status. In 1995, 28.4% of all African Americans and 29.4% of Hispanic Americans lived below the poverty level, compared to 11.2% of Caucasians (U.S. Bureau of the Census, 1997). Census data present an even more disturbing picture for children: 20.5% of all children were con-

focus 8

Identify two ways in which poverty may contribute to the academic difficulties of children from culturally diverse backgrounds, often resulting in their referral to special education.

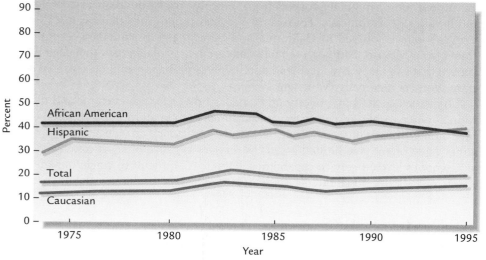

sidered to be living below the poverty level. Analyzed by ethnic origin, over 39.9% of African American children and over 40.3% of Hispanic American children lived below the poverty level; white children represented 16.3% of those living in poverty. Figure 2.3 summarizes these data by ethnicity from 1975 to 1995.

The conditions of poverty often contribute to poor academic performance, place children in at-risk situations, and generate special education referrals (National Research Council, 1997). For example, inadequate access to health care, particularly prenatal care, among cultural minorities can present at-risk circumstances (e.g., Cummings & DeHart, 1995). Conditions of poverty are found more often in populations having multicultural education needs and are associated with homelessness and academic risk (Davis & Wikleby, 1993; Gelfand et al., 1997), contributing to the link between special and multicultural education.

■ CHILDREN IN MIGRANT FAMILIES

Although migrancy is often associated with minority status and poverty, this is not always the case. Frequent mobility sometimes characterizes families of considerable affluence, such as those who move from a summer home to a winter home or take extended trips when it suits parents, rather than school schedules. Similarly, children of military personnel may change schools frequently on a schedule that does not coincide with the academic year.

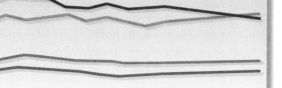

focus 9

Identify two ways in which migrancy among culturally diverse populations may contribute to academic difficulties.

Regardless of reason, forces that interrupt the continuity of schooling have an impact on learning, teacher and peer relationships, and general academic progress. The mobility of wealthy people and others subject to frequent reassignment also has an impact, but it is often offset by other circumstances that contribute to a child's general education (e.g., opportunity for travel, help of tutors). These children are not subject to the same risks as children from families who migrate as a way of life. Unlike military personnel, for example, migrant workers are not assured of employment, housing, or a welcoming sponsor.

In many cases, the circumstances of migrancy are associated with ethnic or cultural diversity as well as economic disadvantage, language differences, and social and physical isolation from much of the larger community (Meister, 1991). Often the proportion of migrant workers from minority backgrounds is extremely high, and it varies geographically. For example, evidence indicates that over 80% of the farm laborers employed in California and other western states are recent immigrants from Mexico. Although reliable data are not available for other regions, it is known that migrancy is widespread and involves perhaps 3 million seasonal or migrant workers nationally (Vaughan, 1993).

The issues created by poverty and language diversity are even more difficult to address when a child moves three or four times each year. Migrant children experience limited continuity and considerable inconsistency in educational programming. They often have limited access to services because of short-term enrollment or a school's limited service capabilities. While it is difficult to single out the exact effects of mobility on children's academic progress, the problem is significant.

■ OTHER FACTORS

A number of other factors link special and multicultural education. Some elicit serious concern regarding the placement of minority children in special education, and others pertain to how such placements might best occur.

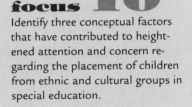

focus 10

Identify three conceptual factors that have contributed to heightened attention and concern regarding the placement of children from ethnic and cultural groups in special education.

Special education focuses on differences. If a young girl has academic difficulty, perhaps failing in reading and math, she is singled out as different. She is different in that her math and reading performances are far below those of her peers, and so she may receive special help in these subjects. Several questions emerge as we consider this example: How do we determine that the student is doing poorly in reading and math? Is the student a candidate for special education? What is the primary reason that the student might be a candidate for special education?

What if the student comes from a culturally different background, as does Denise in the opening snapshot? Is Denise considered disabled because of her academic performance or her culturally different background? This question may not have a clear answer, for contributing factors may be so intertwined that they cannot be separated and weighed in a meaningful manner. Denise may be appropriately considered for special education as long as her performance is not preeminently a cultural matter (merely because she is from a background other than that of the majority). Some might argue that the reason for Denise's receiving special help is irrelevant as long as she gets extra instructional assistance and help with behavioral problems. This perspective may have intuitive appeal, but it is not a satisfactory position for professionals involved in multicultural education. If Denise is receiving special education because of her cultural background and not primarily because she is disabled, she is being labeled and placed inappropriately.

Special education often carries a certain stigma. Many people infer that children in special education are somehow inferior to those who do not require such instruction. Unfortunately, this view persists despite efforts by professionals to change it. Peers may ridicule children who are in special education. Some parents are more comfortable with having their child placed in the general education classes—even if the child might do better in special education. Even parents of children who are gifted and talented are often quick to point out that their children are in an accelerated class so that no one assumes that they are attending a special education class.

This negative perspective on special education is especially harmful to children like Denise if their placement stems from mislabeling or flawed assessment. Multicultural advocates may correctly claim that placing students in special education because of cultural differences is nothing more than means of discrimination and perhaps oppression by the cultural majority. This view explains why multicultural education advocates become concerned, even angry, when culturally diverse children appear to be overrepresented in special education.

An additional problem may occur if a child's special education placement is not multiculturally sensitive and appropriate. The wrong special education intervention can do more harm than good. Even the best instruction will be ineffective if it is provided in English and the student does not comprehend or speak it fluently. As noted earlier, designing appropriate instructional programs for children from culturally different backgrounds is complex and will likely involve a number of different specialists.

Denise's placement in special education may impede her academic progress to the extent that her failure becomes a self-fulfilling prophecy (see Chapter 1). In short,

Cultural considerations relevant to a particular child must be considered when planning specialized instruction for that student with disabilities who comes from a culturally diverse background.

Denise may become what she has been labeled. Her poor academic and social performance may be due to cultural differences, not a disability. If the initial assessment inaccurately construes her cultural differences as showing a low level of ability, Denise may be made into a poor student by the system. The concept of the self-fulfilling prophecy has been discussed for many years. First mentioned directly by Merton (1948), the concept was catapulted to the center of attention by the work of Rosenthal and Jacobson (e.g., 1968a, 1968b), which stimulated controversy that still continues (Dvir, Eden, & Banjo, 1995; Rosenthal, 1987). A great deal remains unknown about the effects of expectations (Merton, 1987). This factor warrants particular attention as we study multicultural issues and specialized instruction.

Multicultural Issues and Specialized Instruction

Specialized instruction for students with disabilities from culturally diverse background must be based on individual need. The IEP must include specific cultural considerations that are relevant for a particular child, addressing language dominance and language proficiency both in terms of conversational and academic skills. The IEP may need to address the type of language intervention needed, which might include enrichment (either in a native tongue or in English) or language development intervention, which may also be in either a native tongue or in English. Instruction may target language enhancement through a strategy integrated with existing curriculum material, such as children's literature (Maldonado-Colon, 1993).

These are only examples of the considerations that may need attention, and they primarily relate to language diversity. Environmental conditions, such as extreme poverty and developmental deprivation, may dictate that services and supports focus on cognitive stimulation that was lacking in the child's early learning. The possible individual strategies are as varied as the factors that make up a child's back-

This checklist provides professionals with points to consider in the process of educating children from culturally diverse backgrounds. These matters should be considered during each of the following: Referral and testing or diagnostic assessment; classification, labeling, or class assignment change; teacher conferences or home communication.

PROCESS	ISSUES	QUESTION TO BE ASKED
Referral, testing, or diagnostic assessment	Language issues	Is the native language different than the language in which the child is being taught and should this be considered in the assessment process? What is the home language? What is the normal conversational language? In what language can the student be successfully taught or assessed—academic language?
	Cultural issues	What are the views toward schooling of the culture from which the child comes? Do differences exist in expectations between the school and family for the child's schooling goals? What are the cultural views toward illness or disability?
	Home issues	What is the family constallation and who are the family members? What is the family's economic status?
Classification, labeling, or class assignment change	Language issues	Does the proposed placement change account for any language differences that are relevant, particularly academic language?
	Cultural issues	Does the proposed placement change consider any unique cultural views regarding schooling?
	Home issues	Does the proposed change consider pertinent family matters?
Teacher conferences or home communication	Language issues	Is the communication to parents or other family members in a language they understand?
	Cultural issues	Do cultural views influence communication between family members and the schools as a formal governmental organization? Is there a cultural reluctance of family members to come to the school? Are home visits a desirable alternative? Is communication from teachers viewed positively?
	Home issues	Is the family constallation such that communication with the schools is possible and positive? Are family members positioned economically and otherwise to respond to communication from the schools in a productive manner? If the family is low SES, is transportation a problem for conferences?

ground. Effective services must be based on the principles of individualized educational planning.

It is also important to note that most children from culturally diverse backgrounds do not require special education. Although the factors discussed here may place such students at risk for such referral, available instruction may meet their needs without special education services. When this is possible, it would be a mistake to label such students as disabled. Table 2.1 outlines points to consider as educators address various elements of the referral process with children from diverse backgrounds.

Case Study

A CASE OF OVERREPRESENTATION, FINANCES, AND SCHOOL REFORM

An associate dean of education, who happens to be African American, was labeled as having mental retardation and placed in special education for a significant portion of his school life. This is just one example of egregious misdiagnoses and possible discrimination in special education placement. Although IDEA is aimed at integrating youngsters with disabilities into the educational mainstream and guarding against ethnic discrimination, overrepresentation still occurs as we approach the 21st century. In fact, a 1993 report by *U.S. News & World Report* suggests that placement of disproportionately high numbers of minorities in special education programs continues at a level far beyond what would be expected based on population demographics. This report indicates that nearly 80% of the states have an overrepresentation of African American students in special education. This information is based on Department of Education survey data provided by the states themselves.

Overrepresentation of students of color in special education has been a continuing concern as indicated throughout this chapter. Concerns regarding misdiagnosis (which occurred in the case of the associate dean) and discriminatory practices have always surfaced in examinations of this problem; sociocultural issues are raised as well as the personal implications for individual children and their families. Other matters also seem notable and relate to serious and broad-based school reform.

Cost factors, for example, cannot be overlooked. The national price tag for special education services has risen *thirtyfold,* to over $30 billion dollars, since 1977. And there is considerable inducement for school districts to expand special education (even in separate rather than integrated programs). First, districts often receive additional funding for special education students over those not receiving such labels. Texas, for example, pays local districts 10 times the normal per-student rate for teaching a youngster in a special education class (the national average is 3 times the normal per-student rate). Second, many states exclude special education scores in the statistical analysis of statewide competency exams. Consequently, their average scores are higher and these districts receive more favorable publicity and have more supportive boards of education. Such circumstances may translate into a better budget once again, to say nothing of enhancing the reputation of the administrator.

So this is a multihorned dilemma. An administrator can increase his or her budget and enhance the prestige of a district by channeling low-achieving students into special education. Such pragmatism, however, runs counter to the fundamental concepts of IDEA and contributes to overrepresentation of minorities in special education. In addition to these serious moral issues, there are also some risks that may capture one's attention. Litigation has been an alternative of continually increasing significance for remedying educational problems, and lawsuits can be very disruptive to the operation of a school district as well as an administrator's personal life. Of five district administrators at a meeting in August 1994 (unrelated to any administrative problems), the one with the *least* crises had *"only one half-million-dollar lawsuit pending."*

■ APPLICATION

How can we balance the various facets of cultural diversity, integrated special services to students with disabilities, and a large public educational system within the context of our general society? How should school finances and other incentives be coordinated with public policy and federal and state legislation? Some vocal critics claim that the educational system should be discarded and a new approach developed from ground zero. However, there is no clear evidence that there would be a financial savings, nor that reforming our existing system would not be an equally effective alternative. What would you do as an administrator? What would you suggest as the parent of a minority child?

Debate Forum

ENGLISH-ONLY OR BILINGUAL EDUCATION?

Declaring English as the official language has had a certain level of support by lawmakers at several levels during the past few years, as recently as 1995. Initiatives to promote such legislation have been evident in nearly 75% of the states as recently as 1987. Yet English is not the primary language for many Americans. Students from culturally diverse backgrounds represent a very large portion of the school enrollment across the country. Critics claim that bilingual education places an unacceptable burden on the educational system, compromising its ability to provide specialized educational services to meet students' needs.

■ **POINT**
Children from different cultures must have certain skills to survive in the world of the cultural majority. They should be taught in English and taught the knowledge base of the cultural majority for their own good. This knowledge will prepare them for success and more efficiently utilize the limited funds available, since specialized culturally sensitive services will not be required.

■ **COUNTERPOINT**
Children from cultures different from that of the majority must have an equal advantage to learn in the most effective manner possible. This may mean teaching them in their native language, at least for some of the time. To do otherwise is a waste of talent, which can ultimately affect the overall progress of our country. To force students who are culturally diverse to use English is also a means of discrimination by the cultural majority.

Review

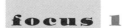 focus 1

Identify three ways in which the purposes of and approaches to general education in the United States sometimes differ from those of special education and multicultural education.

- A major purpose of general education is to provide education for everyone and to bring all students to a similar level of performance.
- Special education focuses on individual differences and often evaluates performance on an individually set or prescribed performance level.
- Multicultural education promotes cultural pluralism and therefore differences.

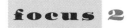 focus 2

Describe the population status of and trends among culturally diverse groups in the United States. How do they have an impact on the educational system?

- Ethnically and culturally diverse groups, such as Hispanic Americans, African Americans, and others, represent substantial portions of the U.S. population.
- Population growth in ethnically and culturally diverse groups is increasing at a phenomenal rate, in some cases at twice that of Caucasians. Both immigration and birthrates contribute to this growth.
- Increased demands for services will be placed on the educational system as culturally diverse populations gradually acquire appropriate services and as significant growth rates continue.

focus 3

Identify two ways in which assessment may contribute to the overrepresentation of students who are culturally diverse in special education programs.

- Through assessment instruments that are designed and constructed with specific language and content favoring the cultural majority.
- Through assessment procedures (and perhaps due to personnel) that are negatively biased, either implicitly or explicitly, toward people who are culturally different.

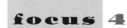 focus 4

Identify three ways in which language diversity may contribute to assessment difficulties with students who are from a variety of cultures.

- Non-English-speaking students may be thought to have speech or language disorders and be referred and tested for special education placement.
- A child's native language may appear to be English because of conversational fluency at school, but he or she may not be proficient enough to engage in academic work or assessment in English.
- A child's academic or psychological assessment may inaccurately portray ability

because of his or her language differences.

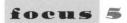

Identify three ways in which differing sociocultural mores may affect the manner in which parents become involved in the educational process.

- Parents from some cultural backgrounds may have a different view of special assistance than the educational institutions.
- Parents from certain cultural backgrounds may be reluctant to take an active role interacting with the educational system.
- Certain behaviors that may suggest a disabling condition needing special education assistance are viewed as normal in some cultures, and parents may not see them as problematic.

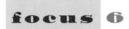

Identify two areas that require particular attention when developing an individualized education plan (IEP) for a

student who is culturally diverse.

- Coordination of different services and professional personnel becomes crucial.
- Cultural stereotypes should not be perpetuated by assumptions that are inappropriate for an IEP.

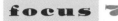

Identify two considerations that represent particular difficulties in serving children who are culturally diverse in the least restrictive environment.

- Cultural or language instruction may be superimposed on other teaching that focuses on remediation of a learning problem, making integration into the educational mainstream more difficult.
- Training limitations of school staff, rather than the child's needs, may influence placement decisions.

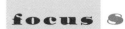

Identify two ways in which poverty may contribute to the academic difficulties of children from culturally diverse backgrounds, often resulting in their referral to special education.

- Circumstances resulting in disadvantaged prenatal development and birth complications occur much more frequently among those of low socioeconomic status and nonwhite populations.
- Environmental circumstances, such as malnutrition and the presence of toxic agents, that place children at risk are found most frequently in impoverished households, and poverty is most frequently evident among ethnic minority populations.

focus 9

Identify two ways in which migrancy among culturally diverse populations may contribute to academic difficulties.

- In many cases, migrant families are characterized by economic disadvantages and language differences.
- Children in migrant households may move and change educational placements several times a year, contributing to limited continuity and inconsistent educational programming.

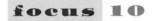

Identify three conceptual factors that have contributed to heightened attention and concern regarding the placement of children from ethnic and cultural groups in special education.

- A stigma is attached to special education.
- Special education placement for children from culturally and ethnically diverse groups may not be educationally effective in meeting their academic problems.
- A self-fulfilling prophecy may be operative, resulting in youngsters' becoming what they are labeled.

Exceptionality and the Family

To begin with . . .

 It was 4:30 A.M. Three hours later, Hillary was born. Ten hours later, we learned that Hillary had Down syndrome. Twelve hours later, I was drunk. Twenty-four hours later, Michelle [my wife] was dealing with two infants, Hillary and me. (Shaw, 1994, p. 44) For a person with a disability, the family will typically be the most important life influence from day-to-day, and the only constant over time. (Berry & Hardman, 1998, p. xx)

 Laura had three friends who were begging their mothers to have her sleep over, and amazingly, three mothers were saying, "Sure no problem." No problem? Excuse me, but are you thinking of the right child? This is Laura Titrud. She spends her nights hooked up to a feeding pump and a bedside two-liter urine drainage bag. . . . And don't forget the nebulizer treatments. Then there's that little problem with bowel incontinence and diarrhea. . . . Much to my surprise, these mothers still answered, "No problem." (Titrud, 1995, p. 28)

 My friends said to me: "Robert, what's with your sister? She's really screwed up! Her eyes are crossed, she drools, she can't talk, she wears diapers and she can't feed herself. She can't do anything." So I told them: "That's not true! She can do a lot! My parents are always trying to keep Traci from going downstairs. They put up gates and all sorts of stuff. And no matter what they put up, she *still* climbs over the top!" (Robert, age 12, about his sister Traci, age 8) (Meyer, 1993, p. 81)

 We helped one family build an outdoor play gym— now the son can play with his siblings and neighborhood children instead of just watching. (CMSU Family Driven Family Support Services, Danville, Pennsylvania) (Covert, 1995, p. 47)

Snapshot

Carlyn

Carlyn is 3 years old. Her brother, Parker, and sister, Rachel, love to laugh and play with Carlyn. They take her sledding; her brother enjoys wrestling with her. They just love being together. In fact, Parker tells his mother that Carlyn is his favorite person in the whole world.

When Carlyn was first born, she wasn't breathing. When the doctors got her breathing, they found other physical dif-

ficulties and diagnosed her as having mental retardation. Her mother, Janna, explains, "It was heartbreaking. I can't explain how you feel inside when you know there's something wrong with your baby."

Carlyn's father is very involved with Carlyn. "Janna and I have had a lot of conversations about Carlyn. One of the things that we have noticed is sometimes people tend to treat Carlyn a little differently when they interact with her. You know, they feel good about it, which is okay and right, but we want Carlyn to have the same things that our other children have. We want people to know that it's normal to talk and interact with children with disabilities, that it should just be an every-

day occurrence. I have a lot of faith and hope that Carlyn will have a bright future to look forward to. And I'm very grateful—I think all of us are—that we have Carlyn. That really sustains us at times, because some times are stressful, and they're very difficult, but nevertheless we're very grateful for Carlyn. That gives us a lot of joy."

When Carlyn first went to the elementary school, she was in preschool. The school seemed quite large and was probably frightening for her. At first she just observed; she didn't interact with the children. But now she loves to play cars with the boys and dolls with the girls. She's learning and enjoys being with the others. She uses all the

children around her to learn; she has good role models.

At school, Carlyn works on her feeding and drinking. Academically, she practices fine motor skills. Her teacher sends notes home when Carlyn passes a milestone—when she walked 10 feet, when she took 5 swallows of a liquid, when she put a puzzle together. Carlyn's teacher hopes that when Carlyn turns 5 she will go to an integrated kindergarten class that will provide any of the services she may need.

According to Carlyn's teacher, "Carlyn's growing leaps and bounds. She's benefiting from us as much as we are from her."

focus 1

Identify five factors that influence the ways in which families respond to infants with birth defects or disabilities.

OWHERE IS THE IMPACT of an individual who is exceptional felt so strongly as in the family. The birth of an infant with disabilities may alter the family as a social unit in a variety of ways. Parents and siblings may react with shock, disappointment, anger, depression, guilt, and confusion. Over time, many parents and siblings develop coping skills that enhance their sense of well-being and their capacity to deal with the stressful demands of caring for a child, youth, or adult with a disability. Additionally, relationships between family members often change.

A child with physical, intellectual, or behavioral disabilities presents unique and diverse challenges to the family unit (Simpson, 1996). In some instances, the child may hurl the family into crisis, resulting in major conflicts among its members. Family relationships may be weakened by the added and unexpected physical, emotional, and financial stress (Falik, 1995; Shelton, Jeppson, & Johnson, 1987). In other instances, this child may be a source of unity that bonds family members together and strengthens their relationships. Many factors influence the reactions of the family, including the emotional stability of each individual, religious values and beliefs, socioeconomic status, and the severity and type of the child's disability (Lian & Aloia, 1994).

This chapter discusses how raising children with disabilities affects parents, other children in the family, and grandparents. We will examine an array of family and parental issues directly related to families with children who are disabled. Additionally, this chapter examines the family as a social system defined by a set of purposes, roles, and expectations (Falik, 1995; Fine, 1992; Gartner, Lipsky, & Turnbull, 1991; Seligman, 1991a). A **social system** approach looks at how each family member fulfills roles consistent with expectations established by discussion, tradition, or other means. In the process, each member functions in an interdependent manner with other members to pursue family goals and to fulfill various expectations. Using a social system framework, it is easy to see how changes in one family member can affect every other member and consequently the entire family system.

Understanding Families

▪ REACTING TO CRISIS

The birth of an infant with significant disabilities has a profound impact on the family. The expected or fantasized child whom the parents and other family members have anticipated does not arrive, and the parents are thrown into an initial state of emotional shock (Seligman & Darling, 1989).

Some conditions, such as spina bifida or **Down syndrome**, are readily apparent at birth, whereas others, such as hearing impairments and learning disabilities, are not detectable until later. Even if attending physicians suspect the presence of a disabling condition, they may be unable to give a confirmed diagnosis without the passage of some time and further testing. When the parents also suspect that something may be wrong, waiting for a diagnosis can be agonizing.

The most immediate and predictable reaction to the birth of a child with a disability is shock, characterized by feelings of confusion, anxiety, anger, and bewilderment. Another reaction is depression, often exhibited in the form of grief or mourning. Some parents describe such emotions as very much like those suffered after the death of a loved one. Many mothers whose babies survive suffer more acute feelings of grief than mothers whose infants die. Additionally, recurrent sorrow and frequent feelings of inadequacy are persistent emotions that many parents experience as they gradually adjust to having an infant with a disability (Peterson, 1987).

Other reactions of family members include uncertainty, disappointment, anger, frustration, guilt, denial, fear, withdrawal, and rejection (Blacher, 1984; Bristor, 1984; Gargiulo, 1985). The level of impact varies, but for most parents such an event creates a family crisis of considerable magnitude.

Parents of children with disabilities experience similar feelings and reactions during certain time intervals. However, the nature of the feelings, their intensity and relationship to specific stages, and the eventual adjustments made individually and collectively by family members vary from one person to

focus 2
What three statements can be made about the stages that parents may experience in responding to infants or young children with disabilities?

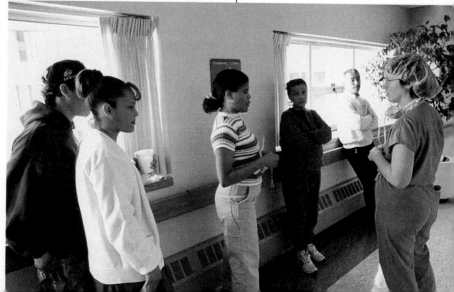

Reactions and feelings of family members upon hearing that a child has a disability may vary. Individuals in each family adjust to the news in different ways.

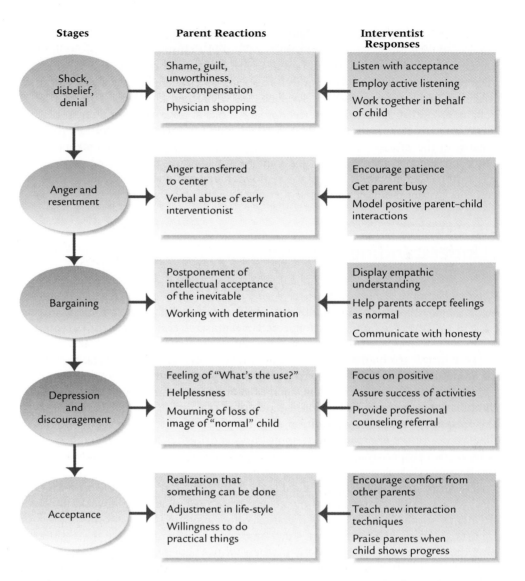

FIGURE 3.1

Potential parent reactions and possible interventions

[*Source: Adapting Early Childhood Curricula for Children*, 4/E. by Cook et al., © 1996. Reprinted by permission of Prentice-Hall, Inc., Upper Saddle River, NJ.]

Stages

Parent Reactions

Interventist Responses

Shock, disbelief, denial

Shame, guilt, unworthiness, overcompensation

Physician shopping

Listen with acceptance

Employ active listening

Work together in behalf of child

Anger and resentment

Anger transferred to center

Verbal abuse of early interventionist

Encourage patience

Get parent busy

Model positive parent–child interactions

Bargaining

Postponement of intellectual acceptance of the inevitable

Working with determination

Display empathic understanding

Help parents accept feelings as normal

Communicate with honesty

Depression and discouragement

Feeling of "What's the use?"

Helplessness

Mourning of loss of image of "normal" child

Focus on positive

Assure success of activities

Provide professional counseling referral

Acceptance

Realization that something can be done

Adjustment in life-style

Willingness to do practical things

Encourage comfort from other parents

Teach new interaction techniques

Praise parents when child shows progress

another (Blacher, 1984; Kroth & Edge, 1997; Simpson, 1996; Turnbull & Turnbull, 1990). Stages associated with various kinds of emotions may overlap one another (see Figure 3.1) and resurface during another period. Some parents may go through distinct periods of adjustment, whereas others may adjust without passing through any sequence of stages. Further research will provide additional information about the very complex, multifaceted relationships among these factors and the responses of parents and other family members during the lifetime of a child with a disability. The process of adjustment for parents is continuous and distinctively individual:

When our son was born my husband and I were told that the parents of a child [with a disability] move through certain stages of reaction: shock, guilt, reaction, and anger, all terminating in the final, blissful stage of adjustment. I do not believe in this pattern. I now know too many parents of children [with disabilities] to be a believer in any set pattern.

I feel we do move through these emotions, and just because we have come to adjustment (which I prefer to call "acceptance" because we spend our whole lives adjusting, although we may at one point accept the situation), that does not mean we never return to other emotions. We may continue to feel any of these emotions at any time, in any order. (West, 1981, p. S10)

Some parents, siblings, and even relatives of children with disabilities employ a kind of cognitive coping that allows them to think about the child, sibling, or grand-child with disabilities in ways that enhance their sense of well-being and capacity for responding positively (Turnbull & Turnbull, 1993). For example, read the following account of one mother and her response to the birth of a child with a disability:

Something like this could tear a marriage apart . . . but instead it has brought us closer.

Right after she was born, I remember this revelation. She was teaching us something . . . how to keep things in perspective . . . to realize what's important. I've learned that every-thing is tentative and that you never know what life will bring.

I've learned that I'm a much stronger person than I had thought. I look back, see how far I've come, and feel very pleased.

The good that's come from this is that I marvel at what a miracle she is . . . it is a miracle that she's alive and that we are going to take her home. (Affleck & Tennen, 1993, p. 136)

This mother was able to interpret the birth and subsequent events in a positive manner. She reduced or successfully managed feelings of shock, distress, and de-pression by thoughtful introspection. Additionally, her positive interpretation of this event aided her adjustment and helped her respond effectively to her child's needs.

In sum, having children with disabilities affects mothers and fathers in diverse ways. The range and sequence of emotions can be highly variable, with some par-ents moving through distinct stages and phases and others not following any spe-cific emotional pattern. The following descriptions of reactions illustrate the vast array of feelings parents may face.

■ SHOCK   The initial response to the birth of an infant with a disability is gener-ally shock, distinguished variously by feelings of anxiety, guilt, numbness, confu-sion, helplessness, anger, disbelief, denial, and despair. Parents sometimes also have feelings of grief, detachment, bewilderment, or bereavement. At this time, when many parents are most in need of assistance, the least amount of help may be avail-able. How long parents deal with these feelings or move through this period de-pends on their psychological makeup, the types of assistance available, and the na-ture and severity of the disabling condition (Lian & Aloia, 1994; Turnbull & Turnbull, 1990). Over time, many parents move from being victims to survivors of trauma (Affleck & Tennen, 1993).

During the initial period of shock, parents may be unable to process or compre-hend information provided by medical and other health care personnel. For this rea-son, information may need to be tactfully repeated to parents until they have fully grasped it. Parents may experience the greatest assaults on their self-worth and value systems during this time. They may blame themselves for their child's disabilities and may seriously question their positive self-perceptions. Likewise, they may be forced to reassess the meaning of life and the reasons for their present challenges. Blacher (1984) has referred to this stage as the *period of emotional disorganization*.

■ REALIZATION   The stage of realization is characterized by several types of behavior. Parents may be anxious or fearful about their ability to cope with the de-mands of caring for a child with unique needs. They may be easily irritated or upset and spend considerable time in self-accusation, self-pity, or self-hate. They may continue to reject or deny information provided by health care professionals.

During this stage, however, parents do come to understand the actual demands and constraints that will come with raising a child with a disability:

When Jessica was diagnosed with cerebral palsy at age 1, I knew something really bad, really terrible, had happened. I was very confused, upset, and scared. I personally did not have to make up the interpretation about the badness or wrongness of the situation. It was something everyone knew, a given: To be disabled or to have a child with a disability is a tragedy. Of course, by the time she was a year old, I was hopelessly in love with her. And, from early in Jessica's infancy, I was committed to having a life of joy with her. (Vohs, 1993, p. 52)

■ DEFENSIVE RETREAT During the stage of defensive retreat, parents attempt to avoid dealing with the anxiety-producing realities of their child's condition. Some try to solve their dilemma by seeking placement for the child in a clinic, institution, or residential setting. Other parents disappear for a while or retreat to a safer and less demanding environment. One mother, on returning home from the hospital with her infant with Down syndrome, quickly packed her suitcase and left with the infant in the family car, not knowing what her destination would be. She simply did not want to face her immediate family or relatives. After driving around for several hours, she decided to return home. Within several months, she adapted very well to her daughter's needs and began to provide the stimulation necessary to her child's growth. Her daughter is now married and works full time in a day-care center for young children.

Jason Kingsley, who was born with Down syndrome, as he appeared at age 3 on *Sesame Street* demonstrating his letter identification skills.

■ ACKNOWLEDGMENT Acknowledgment is the stage in which parents mobilize their strengths to confront the conditions created by having a child with a disability. At this time, parents begin to get involved in the intervention and treatment process. They are also better able to comprehend information or directions provided by a specialist concerning their child's condition and treatment. Some parents become interested in joining an advocacy organization that is suited to their child's condition and the needs of the family. Parents begin to accept the child with the disability. It is during this stage that parents can direct their energies to challenges external to themselves. (See nearby Reflect on This feature.)

When I reflect on what thoughts made the most difference to me in my own growth with Jessica, what stands out the most was the first occurrence of the notion that suffering was not necessary. What that thought allowed me to do was to begin to observe what was actually

Reflect on This

SESAME STREET: MODELING A WORLD THAT RESPECTS EVERY CHILD

In 1970, *Sesame Street* was a very young television program, only in its second season. And I was the show's newest, youngest writer . . .

I became pregnant. In June 1974, my son, Jason, was born—with Down syndrome. Overnight, my academic interest in disability issues became intensely personal. Suddenly, I was struck by the absolute and total *absence* of children like mine in the media. Everyone on television looked so "perfect," so very—the word still catches in my throat—"normal." I looked at television programming, advertising, catalogs, illustrations in magazines; the media was not depicting *my* experience at all!

It was as if my child and I had instantaneously fallen off the face of the earth. We had, in fact, just joined America's largest minority group, but as far as the media was concerned, we were insignificant to the point of invisibility. It was a terrible feeling—a feeling of isolation, of alienation, of hurt and pain at society's total disregard for the integrity and value of my precious son.

Suddenly, the inclusion of children with disabilities—children like *my* child—on *Sesame Street* was an issue of profound personal importance. Fortunately, all the people at *Sesame Street* were being sensitized at the same time.

I am extremely proud to have written many of the "disability segments" for *Sesame Street* during the past 26 years. But it is the real and sincere commitment to those principles shared by all the other writers and, in fact, every member of the show's staff and crew that makes me so grateful and proud to have been associated with *Sesame Street* and Children's Television Workshop for all these years. I am confident that as long as *Sesame Street* exists, it will continue to model a world in which *all* children are understood, accepted, cherished, and respected.[1]

As a young boy, Jason Kingsley, who has Down syndrome, made several appearances on *Sesame Street*, *All My Children*, and other television programs. In 1994, Jason and his friend, Mitchell Levitz, published their book *Count Us In:*

Growing Up with Down Syndrome. The book, published by Harcourt Brace & Company, is currently in its fourth printing.

Jason lived in Chappaqua, New York where he graduated from high school with a full academic diploma in June 1994. He attended the Maplebrook School in Armenia, New York, a post-secondary program for students with learning disabilities. He was the school's first student with Down syndrome and was voted dorm representative.

Kingsley, now 24, enjoys some of the benefits of adulthood—like a nice cold beer in the shade. Jason's dreams for the future include getting a job, living in his own place, getting married, and maybe even being a father.

Currently, Jason is working full time as assistant cultural arts program coordinator for Westchester Arc. He is living independently in his own apartment like Mitchell. Jason explains, "He is a good inspiration for me."[2]

Living independently, Jason proudly opens the door of his new apartment.

[1] *Source:* From "Sesame Street: Modeling a World That Respects Every Child," by E. P. Kingsley, 1996, *Exceptional Parent,* 26(6), pp. 74–76.

[2] *Source:* From "25 Role Models for the Next 25 Years," 1996, *Exceptional Parent,* 26(6), p. 54.

---

going on in the world rather than in my head. While there was not instantaneous change of behaviors or beliefs, I began to view that disability was a natural part of life, that there was nothing inherently wrong with having a disability. (Vohs, 1993, p. 53)

Parents of children with disabilities have important concerns. They want to know what their children's future educational and social needs will be. They want to know what their children will be able to do as adults. They want to know how the child's presence will affect other family members. Moreover, they want to know how to maintain normal family functioning and how to manage the stress associated with having a child with a disability. (See nearby Reflect on This feature.)

Reflect on This

PUBERTY COMES ANYWAY

My daughter, Emily, is 14. Like many teenagers, she is a young woman in some respects, a child in others. We began preparing her for the journey through puberty four years ago, when her body first began to change. The onset of puberty reawakened in us the same fears and uncertainties we felt the day Emily was born, the day we first learned she had Down syndrome. We experience intense feelings when our children enter puberty. It is not an easy time. In fact, it may be very uncomfortable. A father may have to help his daughter with her bra or sanitary napkin. A mother may have to bathe her adolescent son. The child may have questions about his or her sexuality and disability: "Will I be able to marry, to have sex, to have children?" These questions may be difficult to answer. But our feelings of fear, anger, and uncertainty can be worthwhile if they motivate us to prepare our children for this new phase of life.

A TYPICAL REACTION

When her older sister's body began to change, Emily was very interested—much to Stephanie's embarrassment. She wondered when she, too, would get pubic hair and when her breasts would grow. We began to talk about these developments and about menstruation, answering her questions as she examined tampons and sanitary napkins. I realized I would have to lose some of my modesty and desire for privacy in order to help Emily learn what a period looks like, and how we change and dispose of the supplies.

When Emily got her first period, she reacted like many teenage girls "I don't like it. I don't want it anymore." But Emily's teachers helped her see this developmental milestone in a more positive light. They privately congratulated Emily and told her how excited they were that she was growing up.

"SEX AND STUFF"

For two years, we had read books and talked with Emily about how babies are made, using the appropriate terminology to describe sexual intercourse. Then, one day, she came home from school and said, "I know what sex is." When I invited her to explain, she said, "It's when people get married and stuff."

I asked, "Do you mean when the man puts his penis in the woman's vagina?" And suddenly, I saw her face light up with understanding! Discussions with friends at school must have contributed partially to her understanding, but she didn't quite get it until I repeated it again.

A few weeks later, we saw a public service announcement in which a 15-year-old girl talks about how hard it is to be a teenage mother and how she should have said "no" to her boyfriend. When I asked Emily if she knew what the girl was talking about, Emily replied, "Sex and stuff."

Emily has the same expectations for love, marriage, and children as most other teenage girls. We spend a lot of time talking about the responsibilities and realities of all those life choices. I believe it is important to present the facts, to share my values, to talk about the responsibilities of sexual behavior, and to help Emily feel good about herself, so she has the confidence to make good, independent decisions.

Puberty forces us to think about our children's future, which often looks scary. But I've found that sharing these feeling with other parents has been immensely helpful, both for practical tips and reassurance. We may never really be ready for our children to start growing up, but, alas, puberty comes anyway.

Source: From "Puberty Comes Anyway," by J. Noll, 1996, *Exceptional Parent, 26*(12), pp. 61–63.

In spite of this stress and other challenges, parents and family members often interact positively throughout this period. Humor plays a significant role in helping family members gain perspective on their lives and daily experiences (Klein & Schleifer, 1993; Moss, 1995).

■ FAMILY CHARACTERISTICS AND INTERACTIONS

The presence of a child with disabilities strongly influences how family members respond to one another, particularly if the child is severely disabled or has multiple disabilities. In many families, the mother often experiences the greatest amount of trauma and strain. In caring for such a child, she may no longer be able to handle many of the tasks she once performed, and her time with the family may be greatly reduced because of the demands of taking care of the child's unique needs.

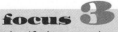

focus 3

Identify three ways in which a newborn child with disabilities influences the family social system.

When the mother is drawn away from the tasks she used to perform, other family members often must assume more responsibility. Adjusting to new roles and routines may be difficult, and family members may need to alter their personal routines. For families that are already experiencing serious emotional, financial, or other problems, the addition of a child with a disability may even break up the family.

As the child with disabilities grows older, the mother frequently faces a unique dilemma: how to strike a balance between activities that nurture the child and those that foster independence. Seeing her child struggle with new tasks, and inevitably experience some failures, can be difficult. Many mothers find the tendency toward overprotectiveness extremely difficult to conquer, but support from those who have already experienced and mastered this problem can help. If the mother or other care providers continue to be overprotective, the child may have difficulty adjusting to each new stage of life and may be unprepared to enter adulthood and semi-independent living.

Each family exhibits a characteristic pattern of conveying information to family members. Communication varies according to the size of the family, its cultural background, and its members' ages (Alper, Schloss, & Schloss, 1994; Misra, 1994; Turnbull & Turnbull, 1990). Generally, the father conveys news of a sibling's disabilities, particularly if the exceptionality is diagnosed at birth, and then the older children clarify the information for the younger ones.

At first, a new closeness may develop in families who discover that one of the children has a disability. During this period, the mother frequently senses this closeness and feels supported by it. Over time, however, this support may wane, and family members may gradually withdraw from the family unit to associate more closely with peers or friends. Questions that children may want to ask parents may be directed to older siblings or may not be asked at all. Such avoidance may occur because children sense the strain on their parents, which is natural when parents must direct a great deal of attention to a child with a disability.

Mothers often develop a strong **dyadic relationship** with a child with a disability, characterized by very close ties. Rather than communicate with all members of the family, a child may use his or her mother as the exclusive conduit for conveying needs and making requests. Dyadic relationships may also develop between other members of the family. Certain siblings may turn to each other for support and nurturing. Older siblings may take on the role of parent substitutes as they take on caregiving responsibilities, and the younger siblings may then develop strong relationships with them.

Every family has a unique power structure. In some families the father holds most of the power, and in others the governance of the family lies with the mother or the family at large. The term *power* refers to amount of control or influence one or more family members exert in managing family decisions, tasks, and activities. Just as families vary greatly in their membership and their organization, the power structure within each family varies according to the characteristics of each member. That power structure is often altered substantially by the arrival of an infant with disabilities. Siblings often assume greater power as they assume more responsibility.

■ HUSBAND–WIFE RELATIONSHIPS The following statements describe one couple's experience in living with a child with a disability:

When I think about having another child, I panic. In fact, I have consumed hours of psychological time thinking about my little boy and our response to him. Actually, my husband and I really haven't dealt successfully with our feelings.

focus 4
Identify three factors in raising a child with a disability that contribute to marital stress.

A successful marital relationship that includes a child with a disability requires mutually satisfactory adaptations by both parents to the responsibilities and life-style changes that caring for the child may involve.

Two years ago, I gave birth to a little boy who is severely disabled. I was about 26 years old and my husband was 27.

We didn't know much about children, let alone children with disabilities, nor did we ever think that we would have a child who would be seriously disabled. When the pediatrician suggested institutionalization for the child, we just nodded our heads. Believe it or not, I had merely looked at him through the observation windows once or twice.

Within several days after the delivery, my husband and I decided to take an extended weekend jaunt to sort things out. Well, the "sorting" didn't really take place. Gradually since that time, I have become less and less interested in things. I sleep a lot more. I don't really look forward to getting up each day. My old friends have stopped coming by, and my husband spends his free time with old friends because I have little energy for any activity outside our home.

Recently, my husband gave me an ultimatum: "Either you decide to have some children, or I'm going to find someone who will." (There are, of course, other things that are bothering him.) Since the birth of this child, I have been absolutely terrified of becoming pregnant again. As a result, my responses to my husband's needs for physical affection have been practically absent—or should I say, nonexistent. I guess you could say we really need some help.

According to Featherstone (1980), "A child's [disability] attacks the fabric of a marriage in four ways. It excites powerful emotions in both parents. It acts as a dispiriting symbol of shared failure. It reshapes the organization of the family. It creates fertile ground for conflict" (p. 91). An infant with disabilities may require more immediate and prolonged attention from the mother for feeding, treatment, and general care, and her attention may become riveted on the child. The balance that once existed between being a mother and a wife disappears. The woman may become so involved with caring for the child that other relationships suffer. The following statements express the feelings that may surface as a result:

"Angela spends so much time with Juan that she has little energy left for me. It is
    as if she has become consumed with his care."

LISA—THAT SPECIAL SOMEONE FOR THE BROWNS

Lisa is a very special member of the Brown family. She was not born into our family but entered it as a Respite Worker because of our son, Aaron, 9 years old.

I remember the first day Lisa came into our house with her eyes huge as she looked at Aaron and saw the extent of his medical and physical needs. I could see she had serious doubts about her abilities. . . .

Lisa supported our family's vision of integration and inclusion for Aaron in all aspects of community life. . . . She was Aaron's resource person at Y-camp, she took him all around the city on walks, on field trips, and honed her sign language so that she could give him additional input about the world around him. Lisa always put on Aaron's hearing aids and glasses when they were reading a story, watching TV, or going for a walk so that Aaron could experience his world more completely. Sometimes she'd suggest a different way she did something that worked well and I was grateful for her thoughtful insights and helpful hints. She even sometimes ran a load of wash, folded laundry, or did a sink of dishes. . . . I didn't expect it but it always made me say "Thanks."

Also because of Lisa's superior abilities, my husband and I were able to go out of town on two occasions for an overnight. These were the first times we had gone away together since having children.

Our son Aaron blossomed whenever Lisa and he did things together. People watching them felt comfortable about joining in the fun and getting to know both of them. She believes in kids and they recognize this and rise to do the best they can, . . . kids with special needs and typical ones, too.

I came in from work one day and, lying on our kitchen table, were Lisa's keys to our van and our home. We had entrusted them to her for two years. And when I saw those keys, I cried. What a gap there is when someone leaves who has filled your life so wonderfully! Boy do we miss her! Lisa and her husband moved to St. Paul, Minnesota, where she is to do an internship in occupational therapy. It's been exciting to have been so involved in HER life, too, her growing and learning during the time she worked for our family. It wasn't all a one-way street. It took patience, flexibility, and give-and-take on all our parts.

Source: From "People in the News, Lisa—That Special Someone for the Browns," *Family Support Bulletin,* pp. 13–14.

"You ask me to pay attention to Juan, but you rarely spend any time with me. When am I going to be a part of your life again?"

"I am developing a resentment toward you and Juan. Who wants to come home when all your time is spent waiting on him?"

Though these feelings are typical of many husbands, others have the opposite reaction. Some may become excessively involved with their disabled children's lives, causing their wives to feel neglected. Wives deeply involved with caregiving may feel overworked, overwhelmed, and in need of a break or reprieve. They may wonder why their husbands are not more helpful and understanding. (See nearby Reflect on This feature.)

Marital partners also have other types of feelings. Fear, anger, guilt, resentment, and related feelings often interfere with communication and finding realistic solutions. Fatigue also profoundly affects how couples function and communicate. As a result, some parents join together to create **respite care** programs, which give them a chance to get away from the demands of child rearing and to relax and renew their relationship.

A number of other factors may also contribute to marital stress: unusually heavy financial burdens for medical treatment or therapy; frequent visits to treatment facilities; lack of shared activities as a couple; lost sleep, particularly in the early years of the child's life; and social isolation from relatives and friends (Beckman-Bell, 1981; Blackard & Barsh, 1982; Fredericks, 1985; Gallagher, Beckman-Bell, & Cross, 1983).

Research related to marital stress and instability is limited and contradictory (Seligman & Darling, 1989; Turnbull & Turnbull, 1990). Some families appear to experience extreme marital turmoil (Gabel, McDowell, & Cerreto, 1983; Schell, 1981), yet others "report no more frequent problems than comparison families" (Seligman & Darling, 1989, p. 93). Still other families report an improvement in the marital relationship following diagnosis of a child with a disability (Turnbull & Turnbull, 1990).

Recent research suggests that husbands who assist regularly with the care and nurture of their children with disabilities contribute support that is genuinely valued by their wives. It also enhances marital satisfaction (Willoughby & Glidden, 1995).

Cleveland (1980) studied how 17 families adapted to a child's traumatic spinal cord injury. She examined the families shortly after the accident and then one year later. As a rule, mothers assumed the major role of caring for the injured child, and husbands reported feelings of anger because of this involvement. Wives also expressed hostility toward their husbands for lacking empathy and understanding. Another source of tension was the husbands' feeling that their spouses were overprotective in caring for the child. Generally, couples reported that their marriages had neither improved nor deteriorated because of the child's injury, but they were concerned about the prolonged period of parenthood they faced.

Counseling may help parents work through feelings such as anger, resentment, and discouragement. Training may help them to develop appropriate expectations for their child's current and future achievement and to acquire skills to respond more effectively and therapeutically to their child's difficulties.

Parent–Child Relationships The relationships between parents and children with disabilities involve many factors. Some of the most crucial include the child's age and gender; the family's socioeconomic status, coping strength, and composition (one-parent family, two-parent family, or blended family); and the nature and seriousness of the disability.

focus 5

Identify four general phases of the developmental cycle that parents go through in rearing a child with a disability.

Families go through a developmental cycle in responding to the needs and nuances of caring for children with disabilities, which includes the following stages: (1) the time at which parents learn about or suspect a disability in their child, (2) the period in which the parents plan the child's education, (3) the point at which the individual with a disability has completed his or her education, and (4) the period when the parents are older and may be unable to care for their adult offspring. The nature and severity of the disability and the willingness of the parents to adapt and to educate themselves in helping the child have an appreciable influence on the parent–child relationship.

Many mothers of children with severe disabilities or serious illnesses have difficulties in finding a baby-sitter. The challenge is far greater than one might imagine, as shown by the following comments:

Marcia's a very mature girl for her age, but she becomes almost terrified when she thinks that she might have to hold our new son, Jeremy. He has multiple disabilities.

I don't dare leave him with our other two children, Amy and Mary Ann. They're much too young to handle Jeremy. But I need to get away from the demands that seem to be ever present in caring for Jeremy. If I could just find one person who could help us, even just once a month, things would be a lot better for me and my family.

Locating a youth or adult who is willing and who is capable of providing quality care for an evening or weekend is extremely difficult. In some areas of the country, however, enterprising teenagers have developed baby-sitting businesses that specialize in tending children with disabilities. Frequently, local disability associations can also be helpful in providing qualified baby-sitters or other respite care providers.

Time away from the child with a disability or serious illness provides parents and siblings with a chance to meet some of their own needs: Parents can recharge themselves for their demanding regimens, and siblings benefit from the exclusive attention of their parents, which reaffirms their importance in the family and their value as individuals (Nisbet, Clark, & Covert, 1991).

Mother–Child Relationships As already mentioned, it is often the mother who becomes primarily responsible for the care of a child with disabilities. If the infant is born prematurely or needs extensive early medical assistance, this relationship may take time to develop. The mother may be prevented from feeding and caregiving if the child needs to spend many weeks in an isolette, supported by sophisticated medical equipment. Some mothers even come to question whether they really had a baby! They experience remoteness because they cannot interact with the infant in a natural, satisfying manner. Many mothers report that they are not given adequate direction on becoming involved with an infant with disabilities.

focus 6

Identify four factors that influence the relationship that develops between infants with disabilities and their mothers.

Mothers are generally concerned about the emotional challenges inherent in caring for children with disabilities and how these children will relate to others. Fathers, on the other hand, are more concerned about the cost of raising and caring for their children, whether the children will be self-supportive in the future, and whether they will be successful in achieving independence (Hornby, 1992; Lamb & Meyer, 1991).

Without support from other adults or professionals, many mothers may feel estranged from their infants and find it difficult to begin the caring process. Physicians, nurses, and other health-related personnel should provide parents with explanations, instructions, and expectations to set the stage for the development of healthy and realistic parent–infant relationships. The mother's expectations are particularly important, because they will shape the way in which she will care for and seek assistance for her infant (Lavelle & Keogh, 1980). Low expectations may result in low involvement.

Reflect on This

NO FATHER'S VOICE

I have a five-year-old daughter and a two-year-old son with cerebral palsy. I work full time, though I need to take time off each week for therapy or doctor's appointments. I am married, but somehow, all the household and child care responsibilities have become mine, and mine alone.

My husband owns his own business. He works day and night and Saturdays, too. On week nights, he usually arrives home around 9 P.M., just as I am tucking the kids into bed. I have griped and complained and cried about him working so late when I need help at home, but nothing ever changes. He has never given our son a bath, and rarely has he fed him. He has never done exercises with our son, nor tried to help him play with a toy. Once, when I asked him to place our son in his standing frame, he complained terribly. He has never offered to take our son to therapy or to a doctor's appointment. . . .

I don't want to make him sound like an awful person—he really isn't. I know he loves all of us very much. Maybe he avoids us so he doesn't have to accept our son's disability and deal with it. But his avoidance is not fair to me; I am tired and I have no help.

I realize we probably need either family or marriage counseling. But I don't know how to get started, or how I would convince my husband to go along with me. And this may sound strange, but I feel like going to counseling would just prove we are failures who can't handle our own problems! I would love to hear from any parent who has been in this situation. Tell me how you've dealt with it.

T.W., Iowa

Source: From "Search, No Father's Voice," 1996, *Exceptional Parent, 26*(2), pp. 12–13.

It is important for the mother of a child with a disability to develop a relationship with her child that does not prevent him or her from ultimately achieving independence.

focus 7
Identify three ways in which fathers may respond to their children with disabilities.

In other cases, a mother may be drawn into a close physical and emotional relationship with her child with a disability or injury. The bond that develops between mother and child can be strong and often impenetrable (Leigh, 1987). The mother becomes, according to Cleveland (1980), the "guardian of affective needs." She assumes primary responsibility for fostering the child's emotional adjustment and becomes the child's personal representative or interpreter. In this role, the mother communicates the child's needs and desires to other family members.

Because of the sheer weight of these responsibilities, other relationships often wane or even disappear. The mother who develops a very close relationship with her offspring with a disability often walks a tightrope. In her desire to protect her child, she often becomes overprotective and thus prevents the child from practicing the skills and participating in the activities that ultimately lead to independence. The mother may also underestimate her child's capacities and so may be reluctant to allow her child to engage in challenging or risky ventures. At the other extreme, some mothers may neglect their children with disabilities and not provide the stimulation so critical to their optimal development.

Father–Child Relationships Not much has been written about fathers and their relationships with children with disabilities. As indicated earlier, the father is often responsible for conveying the news that the mother has given birth to a child with a disability, and for a time, the father may well be responsible for keeping the family aware of the mother's status and the child's condition. The father's reactions to the birth are generally more reserved than those of other family members (Lamb & Meyer, 1991). Fathers are more likely to internalize their feelings and may respond with coping mechanisms such as withdrawal, sublimation, and intellectualization. Fathers of children with mental retardation are typically more concerned than mothers about their children's, particularly their sons', capacity to develop socially adequate behavior and eventual social and educational status. Likewise, they are more affected by the visibility of their children's retardation than are mothers (Lamb & Meyer, 1991).

The relationships that emerge between fathers and children with disabilities reflect the same factors present in mother–child relationships. One important factor may be the gender of the child. If the child is male and the father had idealized the role he would eventually assume in interacting with a son, the adjustment for the father can be very difficult. The father may have had hopes of playing football with the child, having him eventually become a business partner, or participating with his son in a variety of activities. Many of these hopes may not be realized if the child has a severe disability.

Recent research has indicated that, in comparison to mothers, fathers of preschool children with developmental disabilities experience fewer symptoms of

TABLE 3.1	Fathers of children with disabilities

The following questions are those of a concerned father of a child with disabilities. Think about the extent to which professionals address these questions as they work with families and particularly with fathers of children with disabilities.

- Do we encourage fathers to come to appointments if at all possible?

- Are we flexible in our scheduling, setting meetings and appointments early in the morning or late in the afternoon so that men (like mothers who work out of the home) can also attend?

- When we call home and the father answers the phone, do we speak to him or automatically ask for his wife?

- Do we inquire about fathers when the mothers come for weekly appointments?

- If a couple is divorced, do we send information to both parents?

- Have we provided effective support networks for men to gain information, to deal with their grief, and to learn appropriate ways to interact with their children?

Source: "Commentary: What About Fathers?" *Family Support Bulletin,* May, 1991, p. 19.

distress, exhibit higher levels of self-esteem, and demonstrate more internal locus of control in responding to their children with disabilities (Goldberg, Marcovitch, Mac-Gregor, & Lojkasek, 1986). When fathers withdraw or are uninvolved with the child, other family members, particularly mothers, must shoulder more child care responsibilities (Lamb & Meyer, 1991). This withdrawal often creates significant stress for mothers and other family members.

Several advocacy organizations have created support and discussion groups tailored to the needs of fathers (Vadasy, Fewell, Greenberg, Desmond & Meyer, 1986). These groups, often led by a professional and a father of a child with a disability, provide a safe environment in which fathers may express feelings and concerns about their child and other family challenges (see Table 3.1). Participation in these groups yields positive results for fathers as well as other family members (Vadasy et al., 1986), including lower levels of stress and depression, higher satisfaction with social support, increased family cohesion, and increased family unity in dealing with the challenges of rearing a child with a disability.

■ SIBLING RELATIONSHIPS The responses of siblings to a sister or brother with a disability vary (McLoughlin & Senn, 1994; Powell & Gallagher, 1993; Stoneman & Berman, 1993). Upon learning that a brother or sister has a disability, siblings may ask a number of questions:

focus 8
Identify four ways in which siblings respond to a brother or sister with a disability.

"Why did this happen?"
"Is my brother contagious? Can I catch what he has?"
"What am I going to say to my friends?"
"I can't baby-sit him!"
"Am I going to have to take care of him all of my life?"
"Will I have children who are disabled too?"

Like their parents, siblings want to know and understand as much as they can about the condition of their sibling. They want to know how they should respond and how their lives might be different as a result of this event. If these concerns can be adequately addressed, the prognosis for positive sibling involvement with the brother or sister with a disability greatly improves (Seligman, 1991b).

Siblings play a major role in the social and intellectual grow of the sibling with a disability.

Parents' attitudes and behaviors have a significant impact on those of their children toward siblings with disabilities, since children tend to mirror the attitudes and values of their parents (McHale, Sloan, & Simeonsson, 1986). If parents are optimistic and realistic in their views toward the child with a disability, then siblings are likely to share these attitudes. Siblings who are kindly disposed toward assisting the child with a disability can be a real source of support (McHale et al., 1986). In fact, many play a crucial role in fostering the intellectual, social, and affective development of a brother or sister with a disability. Also, siblings of children with disabilities are more likely to assume greater responsibilities for helping, directing, and teaching within the home (Abramovitch, Stanhope, Pepler, & Corter, 1987; Stoneman, Brody, Davis, & Crapps, 1987).

Negative feelings do exist in siblings of children with disabilities (Lobato, 1990; Powell & Gallagher, 1993). Loneliness, anxiety, guilt, and envy are common. Feelings of loneliness may surface in children who wanted a brother or sister with whom they could play. A youth may anxiously wonder who will care for the sibling with a disability when the parents are no longer capable or alive. Guilt may come for many reasons. Believing they are obligated to care for the sibling with a disability, siblings may worry that failure to provide such care would mean they are bad or immoral. Similarly, they may feel guilty about the real thoughts and feelings they have about their sibling, including anger, frustration, resentment, and even hate. Realizing that many parents would not respond positively to the expression of such feelings, some siblings carry them inside for a long time.

With increased inclusion of students with disabilities in neighborhood schools and other general education settings (Berry & Hardman, 1998), siblings are often "called into action." They may be asked to explain their brother's or sister's behavior, to give ongoing support, and to respond to questions that teachers and others might ask. Furthermore, they may be subject to teasing and other related behaviors. Because of these and other factors, some siblings experience a greater risk for behavior problems (Lobato, Faust, & Spirito, 1988).

Many siblings resent the time and attention parents devote to their sister or brother (Therrien, 1993). This resentment may also take the form of jealousy (Forbes, 1987; McHale et al., 1986; Simeonsson & Bailey, 1986). Some siblings feel emotionally neglected, that their parents are not responsive to their needs for attention and emotional support. For some siblings, the predominant feeling is bitter resentment or even rage (Seligman, 1991b). Others have a sense of deprivation, that their social, educational, and recreational pursuits have been seriously limited.

The following statements are examples of such feelings:

"We never went on a family vacation because of my brother, Steven."
"How could I invite a friend over? I never knew how my autistic brother would behave."
"How do you explain to a date that you have a sister who is retarded?"
"Many of my friends stopped coming to my house because they didn't know how to handle my brother, Mike, who is deaf. They simply could not understand him."

"I was always shackled with the responsibilities of tending my little sister. I didn't have time to have fun with my friends."

"I want a real brother, not a retarded one."

Siblings of children with disabilities may also believe they must compensate for their parents' disappointment about having a child with a disability. They may feel undue pressure to excel or to succeed in a particular academic or artistic pursuit. Such perceived pressure can have a profound effect on siblings' physical and mental health, and it increases if the parents express such demands. A pressured child may think, "Why do I always feel as if I have to be the perfect child or the one who always does things right? I'm getting tired of constantly having to win my parents' admiration. Why can't I just be average for once?"

Support groups for siblings of children with disabilities are emerging and can be particularly helpful to adolescents. These groups introduce children and youth to the dynamics of having such a sibling in the family (Atkins, 1987). They establish appropriate expectations and discuss questions that children may be hesitant to ask in a family context. These groups also provide a forum in which individuals can analyze family needs and identify practical solutions.

One of these organizations is the Sibling Information Network. Involvement with this network may be very helpful to children who are experiencing difficulties in relating to a new sibling with a disability. Its members enjoy a quarterly newsletter with quality resource materials, a bibliography of children's literature related to disabling conditions, a list of media on siblings, a list of members and persons who have organized sibling groups, a bibliography of journal articles on siblings, and a collection of articles from the newsletter on various programs and workshops. The headquarters for this new network is located at the University of Connecticut, Department of Educational Psychology, Storrs, Connecticut. Much needless suffering could be eliminated or significantly lessened if parents and professionals would give greater attention to the feelings and experiences of siblings in families with children with disabilities.

Perhaps the best way to help siblings of children with disabilities is to support their parents and families (Berry & Hardman, 1998). Sibling participation in programs that allow them to share information, to express feelings, and to learn how to be meaningfully involved with their sister or brother with a disability contribute much to their well-being.

■ EXTENDED FAMILY RELATIONSHIPS The term **extended family** is frequently used to describe a household in which an immediate (nuclear) family lives with other relatives. For our purposes, the term will identify close relatives with which the immediate family has regular and frequent contact yet who do not necessarily live in the same household. These individuals may include grandparents, uncles, aunts, or cousins.

When a child is born and becomes part of a family, he or she also becomes part of an extended family. Usually, the grandparents make the first official family visit or call to the hospital, which can be extraordinarily taxing and difficult if it entails congratulations and support to a daughter who has given birth to a child with a disability. In a very real fashion, grandparents perceive grandchildren as extensions of themselves. They look forward to babying, bragging about, and showing photographs of their grandchildren, without worrying about the burdens of responsibility that parents must assume. Their responses and corresponding degree of support can be a source of great strength or pronounced pain.

When a grandchild is born with a disability, the joy of the occasion may dissipate. Like parents, grandparents are hurled into a crisis that necessitates reevalua-

tion and reorientation (Seligman & Darling, 1989). They must decide not only how they will respond to their child, who is now a parent, but also how they will relate to the new grandchild. Many grandparents, having grown up in a time when deviation from the norm was barely tolerated, much less understood, enter the crisis process without much understanding. In their day such a birth may have signified the presence of "bad blood" within a family, and so the mother or father of the newborn child may be selected as the scapegoat. Blaming provides only temporary relief, however. It does little to promote the optimal family functioning so necessary in the weeks and months to come.

Often, the initial response of grandparents to the newly born child with a disability may be to provide evidence that they are "pure and not responsible for the present suffering" (McPhee, 1982, p. 14). This is, of course, very counterproductive. Research has indicated that grandparents, particularly during the diagnostic phase, play an influential role in how their children, the new parents, respond to the child with a disability. If the grandparents are understanding and emotionally supportive and provide good role models of effective coping, they may have a positive impact on their own children, the mother and father. If the grandparents are critical or unaccepting, they may add to the present burden and complicate it even further (Seligman & Darling, 1989).

Grandparents and other family members may contribute a great deal to the family's adjustment to life with the child with a disability (Lian & Aloia, 1994). If they live near the family, they may become an integral part of the resource network and may provide support before the energies of their children are so severely depleted that they need additional, costly help. To be of assistance, grandparents must be prepared and informed. They must have an opportunity to voice their questions, feelings, and concerns about the disability and its complications, and they must have means by which they can become informed. Parents can aid in this process by sharing, with their own parents and siblings, pamphlets, materials, and books suggested by health care and educational professionals. They may also encourage their families to become involved in parent and grandparent support groups (Bell & Smith, 1996; Johnson, 1995; Kroth & Edge, 1997). Such informal meetings provide knowledge about the struggles and feelings of their own children and elicit frank and open conversation. To become an important part of the total treatment process, extended family members also need positive feedback on their efforts.

As time passes, three other types of responses may emerge: avoidance, trivialization, and fantasizing (Meyer & Vadasy, 1986). These themes are evident in the statements that follow:

"I don't think those doctors really know what they are talking about. Our grandchild certainly isn't disabled."
"We are not going to worry about this anymore. We're sure he will come out of this."
"There has to be a cure! We'll find a physician who really knows how to handle this condition."

Actually, many grandparents experience many of the same stages and have many of the same needs as the child's parents. And, like parents, grandparents need to receive information when they will best understand it. They need to be informed about the disability and available therapies or treatment approaches, and they need to know about the child's potential over time (Vadasy, Fewell, & Meyer, 1986).

Grandparents may be helpful in several ways (Seligman & Darling, 1989). They may be able to give parents a weekend reprieve from the pressures of maintaining the household and assist with transportation or baby-sitting. Grandparents may often serve as a more objective third party that can help evaluate a situation and provide solutions to seemingly unresolvable problems. The child with a disability profits from the unique attention that only grandparents can provide. This attention can be a natural part of special occasions such as birthdays, vacations, fishing trips, or other traditional family activities.

Yet such assistance and support may be hard to arrange if the child is especially difficult to care for. For instance, few family members freely volunteer to tend a child with an attention deficit disorder. And in gerneral, the child with disabilities is not as likely as others to be invited along for recreational activities such as sleeping overnight at a friend's house, eating dinner with neighbors, or going with another family on a weekend camping trip.

Sometimes relatives and neighbors may be critical of the ways in which parents manage such a child, even if qualified professionals have encouraged such procedures. Social isolation and various forms of punishment may be perceived as abusive, and other types of treatment may also be viewed with a jaundiced eye if they include the use of stimulant drugs, very controlled diets, or point systems. Parents who must administer these home-based treatments often feel that they are completely alone. On the other hand, the support of extended family members, if properly applied, can have a positive effect on the physical, social, and emotional well-being of the primary family.

The role and function of extended family members are often dictated by culture (Misra, 1994). For example, grandparents, aunts, uncles, and older siblings may play significant roles in the care of Hispanic children with disabilities. Similarly, a child with a disability in a Native American family may be cared for primarily by a grandmother or other family members. How various cultures view disabilities differs significantly, so educators and other caregivers must develop an understanding of the families whom they serve and their cultural backgrounds (Simpson, 1996).

■ NONNUCLEAR FAMILIES Although discussion thus far has focused on the traditional nuclear family consisting of a mother, father, and children, there are many types of families. Very few children, fewer than 40%, will live with both biological parents through age 18. Thirty percent of children begin life with married parents who will later divorce. The remaining 30% will be born out of wedlock (Berger, 1994). Some families consist of the father and children, and in others the grandparents serve as primary caregivers for the children, without the mother or father. Other types of families include foster children living with foster parents and gay couples with adopted children.

The nature of families can vary, but the important common factor is the presence of a child with a disability. This child deserves the attention and professionalism of school personnel and other professionals—no matter what type of family unit this child is part of (see the Reflect on This feature on page 88). Primary caregivers or legal guardians of the child, whoever they might be, should be invited to participate fully in all programs and support services.

Family Support

Patterns of family support vary according to the life cycle of the family. Different family members fulfill different roles as the needs of parents, children with disabilities, and their siblings change over

SUGGESTIONS FOR CONFERENCING AND WORKING WITH NONTRADITIONAL FAMILIES

- Be able to suggest resources and services for single-parent, reconstituted, and other nontraditional families.
- Be aware that the priority concerns of single-parent, recombined, and other nontraditional families may differ from those of the educator.

- Be aware that some nontraditional parents may have severe time, energy, and financial restrictions.
- Attempt to include noncustodial parents in conferences and programs.
- Recognize the importance of listening to parents.
- Become familiar with your family-related values.

- Be able to apprise parents and family members of the potential impact of divorce, reconstitution, and other nontraditional factors on the family structure.
- Aid divorced parents, stepparents, adoptive parents, and others to be effective in their respective roles.

- Anticipate atypical behavior in parents and children experiencing turmoil and change.

Source: Adapted with permission from *Working with Parents and Families of Exceptional Children and Youth* by R. L. Simpson, 1996, pp. 109–112, Austin, TX: Pro-Ed.

time (Berry & Hardman, 1998; Lian & Aloia, 1994). During the early childhood years, parents are responsible for many important functions, including seeking out appropriate early intervention programs for the child with a disability, contributing to all their children's self-esteem, teaching daily living skills, and advancing overall development. Early intervention programs focus on achieving certain goals, which are specified in an individualized family service plan (IFSP) (see Chapter 4 for an in-depth discussion of the IFSP). The IFSP addresses child and family needs, details specific services to be provided by multidisciplinary team members, and identifies dates for achieving various goals. Achievements accomplished during this phase of the family cycle lay the foundation for subsequent growth and learning for children with disabilities. Moreover, services and supports provided during this time often prevent the development of other secondary disabling conditions (Peterson, 1987).

Family support during this period focuses on assisting family members to develop an understanding of the child's disability, to learn how to provide home-based services, to become knowledgeable about their legal rights, to learn how to deal with the stress in their lives, and to learn how to communicate effectively with professionals. Many home-based services and supports focus on motor development, speech and language stimulation, and cognitive development. Other assistance may include helping parents deal with specific physical or health conditions that may require specific diets, medications, or therapy regimens. Training programs can sensitize parents to the importance of helping their young child with a disability develop independence, since some parents tend to be overprotective.

During the elementary school years, parents become increasingly concerned about their children's academic achievement and social relationships (Berry & Hardman, 1998). As many school systems move to more inclusive programs, parents may be particularly anxious about how their children are accepted by nondisabled peers (Lian & Aloia, 1994) and the intensity and appropriateness of the instruction given in general education settings. During this period, the individualized education program (IEP) is developed to provide the supports the child will need in order to succeed. Consistent collaboration between parents and various multidisciplinary team members is crucial to achieving IEP goals and objectives (see the Reflect on This feature on page 89).

During the elementary school years, family support involves helping parents sustain their children's academic and social growth. Parents may be trained to assist the

I also remember the first IEP [individualized education plan] meeting we attended. Christopher had been in the program for several weeks and we were feeling pretty proud of his progress. The meeting was attended by his teacher, his three therapists, his mother, and me. Each staff member reviewed their most recent evaluations of Christopher's developmental status and one after the other informed us of just how far behind Christopher was. I sat there listening, feeling sick inside, as I heard that he was 4 months delayed in this skill and 5 months delayed in that skill with skills emerging to only a 3-month delay in another area. One or two staff members made positive comments, but the emphasis was certainly on his deficit. I went home that night and cried to my husband, "Nobody said anything positive about what a wonderful child he is. Nobody mentioned how much he smiles, how well he relates to people. Nobody mentioned how hard he tries to do new things in therapy!" It was truly one of my saddest days!

Source: From "Evolving Attitudes About Family Support" by N. Johnson. Reprinted by permission from *Family Support Bulletin,* 1990, p. 13. Published by United Cerebral Palsy Associations, Inc.

---

child with homework assignments, to support the development of social skills, and to advocate for the child's needs. Parents may also receive instruction in managing or disciplining their children in home and community settings (Kroth & Edge, 1997; Simpson, 1996).

The secondary school years frequently pose significant challenges for adolescents with disabilities, their parents, and their families. Like their peers, adolescents with disabilities experience significant physical and psychological issues, including learning how to deal with their emergent sexuality, developing satisfactory relationships with individuals outside of the home environment, and becoming appropriately independent. Other issues must also be addressed during these years, including preparation for employment, learning how to access adult services, and developing community living skills.

During adolescence, children are likely to comply less with their parents' requests and resist parental authority (Lian & Aloia, 1994). Parents who are attuned to the unique challenges and opportunities of this developmental phase will work closely with educators and other personnel to develop IEPs that address these issues and prepare the adolescent with disabilities for entry into adulthood. Parents may also benefit from training related to dealing with teenage behavior in general and the challenges it presents (Kroth & Edge, 1997; Simpson, 1996).

During their children's adolescence, parents are taught how to "let go," how to access adult services, and how to further their children's independence. Parents need information about setting up trusts and other legal procedures to ensure the welfare of all their children.

The movement from high school to community and adult life can be achieved successfully by adolescents with disabilities if parents and other support personnel have consistently planned for this transition. Transition planning is mandated by IDEA and is achieved primarily through the IEP. IEP goals during this period are related to succeeding in the community and functioning as adults (see Chapter 5).

■ COLLABORATING WITH PROFESSIONALS

The interaction between professionals and parents is too often marked by confusion, dissatisfaction, disappointment, and anger (Powell & Graham, 1996). Several

Transition to adult life can be successful for persons whose parents and support personnel planned for that movement.

focus 10

Identify three types of professional understanding that are essential to establishing positive relationships with parents and families of children with disabilities.

authors have documented these and other negative feelings in parents (Dembo, 1984; Muir-Hutchinson, 1987; Seligman & Darling, 1989). However, researchers believe that relationships between parents and professionals can be significantly improved (Kroth & Edge, 1997; Wisniewski, 1994). Indeed, progress has been made in helping professionals communicate and relate more effectively to parents and others responsible for children and youth with disabilities, especially in the preparation of special educators and other care providers who serve as direct and indirect service providers in family, school, and community-based programs (see the nearby Reflect on This feature). There is now great interest in preparing professionals to be effective collaborators and consultants (Wisniewski, 1994).

Seligman and Seligman (1980) identified three types of professional understanding essential to establishing positive working relationships with families. First, professionals need to understand their impact on parents. Second, they need to understand the impact the individual with a disability has on the family over time. Finally, they need to understand the impact the child and family have on them, the professionals. Developing these kinds of understanding requires open communication, a willingness to learn about others and their cultures, and time for relationship building (Misra, 1994; Wisniewski, 1994).

Quality family support programs provide "whatever it takes" to help families function like families without children with disabilities (Covert, 1995). Excellent family support programs

- focus on the entire family.
- change as the family's needs, roles, and ages change.

"WHAT IS THE MOST HELPFUL THING A PROFESSIONAL EVER SAID TO YOU?"

- It's not your fault. You are not powerful enough to have caused the kinds of problems your child has.
- What do you need for yourself?
- I think your son could be a success story for our agency.
- I value your input.
- Under the circumstances, you are doing the best you can do. Frankly, I don't know what I would do or how I would be able to carry on.
- If you were a perfect parent, your son would still be in this condition.
- I agree with you.
- Your child has made progress and I know he can do more, so we will continue to work with him.
- Why are you taking all of the blame? It takes two to make or break a relationship.
- I don't know. I can't tell you what's wrong with your child or what caused the problem.
- Your child knows right from wrong. She knows most of society's values and that's because you taught them to her.
- There is a lot of love in your family.
- You know, it's okay to take care of yourself too.
- I don't know. I have to give that serious thought.
- I believe in your instincts. You're the expert on your child.
- You're being too hard on yourself.
- Our agency will take your case.
- Thanks so much for your participation in the group [parent support group]. Your intelligence and your calm reasonableness are important influences in the group.

Source: From "What Is the Most Helpful Thing a Professional Ever Said to You?" Spring 1991, p. 20. Reprinted by permission from *Family Support Bulletin.* Published by United Cerebral Palsy Associations, Inc.

- encourage families to express their own needs and direct decisions on how its needs are met.
- treat people with disabilities and their families with dignity by respecting their choices and preferences.
- respect cultural, economic, social, and spiritual differences.
- encourage families to use natural community resources.
- provide convenient and central access to services and resources. (Covert, 1995, p. 56)

Superb family support programs work at keeping families together, enhancing their capacity to meet the needs of the individual with a disability, reducing the need for out-of-home placement, and giving families access to social and recreational activities (Covert, 1995).

■ STRENGTHENING FAMILY SUPPORTS

The primacy of the family in contributing to the well-being of all children is obvious. This is also true for children with disabilities. Research indicates that family members provide one another with the most lasting and often most meaningful support (Turnbull & Turnbull, 1990). Much of what has been done to assist children with disabilities, however, has supplanted, rather than supported, families in their efforts to care and provide for these children (Bradley, Knoll, & Agosta, 1992). Historically, monies and resources have been directed at services and supports outside of the family environment or even beyond the neighborhood or community in which the family resides.

Increasingly, policy makers and program providers are realizing the importance of the family and its crucial role in the development and ongoing care of a child or youth with a disability. This is evidenced in the passage of the Families of Children

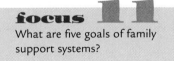

focus 11

What are five goals of family support systems?

TABLE 3.2	Family Support Survey

Feeling welcome and heard	■ Do the program staff acknowledge that you, as a parent, are informed and knowledgeable about your child?
	■ Do they really listen to you?
	■ Do the staff respect your opinions?
	■ Do they honestly care about your child and your family?
	■ Do you feel better after meeting with program staff?
	■ Are you comfortable when you talk with program staff?
Having control	■ Do you have decision-making power over the supports and services that you receive?
	■ Can you change your mind about what types of supports you receive, as your child's and your family's needs change?
	■ Are you invited to participate in the program's policy-making process?
Exchanging information	INFORMATION ABOUT THE PROGRAM
	■ Does information about this program come to you, rather than your having to search for it?
	■ Is the information easy to understand?
	■ Does the information help you make an informed choice, rather than confuse you?
	INFORMATION ABOUT YOUR FAMILY
	■ Do the program staff members ask for information that is unnecessary?
	■ Do they ask questions that make you feel uncomfortable because they are too personal?
	■ Does the process of exchanging information take too long?
Deciding what you need	■ Do the staff members meet with your family individually to discuss and plan for the supports you'll receive (in your preferred language)?
	■ Are you given a choice regarding the time and place at which you meet with program staff?
	■ Do the staff members work together with you to identify your needs?
	■ Do they present you with an array of options to meet your needs?
	■ Do they encourage you to say how you want your needs to be met?
	■ Do they respect your choices and preferences?

with Disabilities Support Act of 1994. This act provides financial assistance to states to develop family-centered, statewide systems to assist families of children with disabilities; promotes development of training activities to empower families to care for children with disabilities; increases interagency coordination in providing family-centered services; and heightens awareness of laws, policies, and organizational structures that impede or facilitate the provision of family-centered support (Covert, 1995).

Services are now being directed at the family as a whole rather than just at the child with the disability. This support is particularly evident in the Individualized Family Service Plan (IFSP) as discussed earlier in this chapter and in Chapter 4 of this text. This orientation honors the distinctive and essential role of parents, siblings, and other extended family members as primary caregivers, nurturers, and teachers. Additionally, these services provide parents and siblings with opportunities to engage in other activities that are important to their physical, emotional, and social well-being.

Family supports enhance the caregiving capacity of the family; give parents and other family members respites from the often tedious and sometimes unrelenting demands of caring for a child with a serious disability; assist the family with per-

TABLE 3.2   *(continued)*

	■ Is an agreement developed that details which supports will be provided (when and by whom), and who will pay?
	■ Is planning for your family's supports a comfortable process?
Getting what you need	■ Do the staff members make a sincere effort to meet your family's needs?
	■ Once supports are agreed upon, do they begin promptly?
	■ Are you satisfied with the delivery of the supports you receive?
	■ Do the supports focus on the family as well as the child with a disability?
	■ Are supports available when your family wants and needs them?
	■ In a crisis, are supports readily available?
	■ If the program cannot fully meet your needs, do the staff members help you get other supports/services in your community (e.g., through schools, child care centers, churches, medical services)?
	■ If the services that you need are not available through any local resource, do the staff members help you to create the supports needed?
Judging the results	■ Does this program offer whatever it takes to meet your family's unique needs?
	■ Does this program work hard to keep your family together?
	■ Does this program better allow you to live as much like other families as possible?
	■ Do the information and supports offered make problem solving easier?
	■ Do these family supports enhance your family's ability to meet the many needs of your child with a disability?
	■ Do the supports you receive from this program help you to feel more in control of your life?
	■ Does this program make a positive difference in the life of your child and your family?
	■ Does this program help your child and family feel more connected to your community?

Source: From *Whatever It Takes! Excellence in Family Support: When Families Experience a Disabilities,* (pp. 54–67), by Susan Covert/HSRI. © 1995 Training Resource Network. Used with permission.

sistent financial demands related to the disability; provide valuable training to families, extended family members, concerned neighbors, and caring friends; and improve the quality of life for all family members (Bradley et al., 1992). Recent research suggests that family support services have reduced family stress, increased the capacity of family members to maintain arduous care routines, improved the actual care delivered by family members, and reduced out-of-home placements (Agosta, 1992; Knoll, 1992). Because of these services, many children and youth with disabilities enjoy the relationships and activities that are a natural part of living in their own homes, neighborhoods, and communities; they truly become active participants in family and the larger community. Covert (1995) has developed a "Family Support Survey" to help parents and other family members assess the quality of services received from family support agencies (see Table 3.2).

■ TRAINING FOR PARENTS, PROFESSIONALS, AND FAMILY MEMBERS

■ TRAINING FOR PARENTS   Parent training is an essential part of most early intervention programs for young children as well as older children with disabilities.

Services and training are directed at the complex and varied needs of each family, and not at the child alone. Much of this training is directed at family empowerment, to help families effectively meet their needs and those of their child. Much of the training is conducted by experienced and skilled parents of children with disabilities who volunteer their time as part of their affiliation with an advocacy or support group. These support groups play an invaluable role in helping parents, other family members, neighbors, and friends effectively respond to the child or youth with a disability. The training may also be directed by one or more professionals invited by the advocacy or support group.

Training may be focused on feeding techniques, language development activities, toilet-training programs, behavior management approaches, motor development activities, or other issues important to parents (Kroth & Edge, 1997; Simpson, 1996). For parents of youth or adults with disabilities, the training may be directed at understanding adult services, accessing recreational programs, finding postsecondary vocational programs, or locating appropriate housing. In some instances, the training informs parents about their legal rights, prepares them to participate effectively in IEP meetings, helps them understand the nature of their child's disability, makes them aware of recreational programs in their communities, or alerts them to funding opportunities (Amlund & Kardash, 1994). Through these training programs, parents learn to solve problems and resolve conflicts and thus are empowered to advocate for their children and themselves.

■ **TRAINING FOR PROFESSIONALS** Training for professionals—educators, social workers, psychologists, medical professionals—focuses primarily on skills in relationship building, communication, and collaboration. Additionally, the training helps professionals understand the complex nature of family cultures, structures, functions, and interactions, and it makes them take a close look at their own attitudes, values, and perceptions about families with children, youth, and adults with disabilities (Darling, 1991; Misra, 1994; Turnbull & Turnbull, 1990). Unfortunately,

The successfully trained professional understands the nature of family cultures and respects the parents as team partners.

professionals often see parents as part of the child's or youth's problem, rather than as partners on a team (Seligman, 1991a). Moreover, they are frequently insensitive to the daily demands inherent in living with a child, youth, or adult who presents persistent challenges. Thus they may use vocabulary that is unfamiliar to parents, may not give parents adequate time to express their feelings and perceptions, and may be insensitive to cultural variations in relating and communicating (Simpson, 1996). Communication and collaboration skills that are stressed include effective communication, problem-solving strategies, negotiation, and conflict resolution (Wisniewski, 1994). Professionals are also trained to understand how parent–professional teams are effectively formed, how they develop positive working relationships, and how these teams optimally function (Amlund & Kardash, 1994).

Will these training efforts make a difference? The answer is not yet clear. Preliminary evidence suggests that training for physicians, particularly pediatric residents, is contributing to more positive perceptions about families and children with disabilities (Darling, 1991; Guralnik, Bennett, Heiser, & Richardson, 1987).

■ TRAINING FOR FAMILY MEMBERS The training of family members is directed at siblings, grandparents, and other relatives. It may even involve close neighbors or caring friends who wish to contribute to the well-being of the family. Often these individuals are tied to the family through religious affiliations or long-standing friendships (Kroth & Edge, 1997).

The first need of siblings is to be informed. Some research suggests that many siblings know very little about their brother's or sister's disability, its manifestations, and its consequences (Seligman, 1991b). Additionally, siblings need to understand that they are not responsible for a particular condition or disability. Other questions also need to be addressed: the inheritability of the disability, the siblings' future role in providing care, the ways in which siblings might explain the disability to their friends, and how the presence of the brother or sister with a disability will affect their family and themselves.

In most instances, the training of siblings occurs through support groups designed for a specific age group. In these groups, siblings can express feelings, vent frustrations, and learn from others. Additionally, they may learn how to deal with situations that will occur again and again. Knowing what to say or how to respond can help build confidence in helping the sibling with disabilities. They may learn sign language, how to complete simple medical procedures, how to manage misbehavior, or how to use certain incentive systems. In some cases, they may be prepared for the eventual death of a brother or sister who has a life-threatening condition.

Training of grandparents, other relatives, neighbors, and friends is crucial. They, like the siblings of children with disabilities, must be informed, have opportunities to express feelings, be able to ask pertinent questions, and receive training that is tailored to their needs. With such preparation and encouragement, they often successfully provide the most consistent respite care that is available to families. Also, they may contribute invaluable help to families in the way of transportation, recreational activities, baby-sitting, and critical emotional support.

Responding to the needs of families with children with disabilities is a multifaceted process. Families need both formal programs and professional services, as well as informal supports available through siblings, extended family members (cousins, aunts, uncles, and grandparents), neighbors, friends, and other community members. Careful orchestration of these programs, services, and social supports enhances the capacity of families to provide quality care to their children with disabilities and to attend to the needs of other family members (Covert, 1995).

SUSAN

Susan and I first met via the telephone over 8 years ago. She called PHP [Parents Helping Parents] in the desperate hope that somehow she, as a single parent, could keep going—keep meeting the needs of her infant daughter with Down syndrome, and keep holding down her job despite weeks of sleepless nights and a child-care situation that she knew was not ideal. As I hung up the phone after listening to and talking with Susan, I felt both emotionally depleted and emotionally energized.

This young mother was at the end of her rope—her limits having been reached by the challenges of infancy, disabil-ity, and single parenthood all rolled into one. Her daughter was on a heart monitor and was having trouble eating; meaning that most of Susan's interactions with her were diffi-cult and filled with anxiety. Susan's own employment situ-ation was precarious due in large part to the many times she had to come in late or missed a day entirely to respond to her daughter's needs. Susan believed that the woman who was providing child care was so nervous about possible medical compli-cations that she was afraid to interact at all with her daugh-ter. Sobbing, she readily admit-ted to the appeal of simply abandoning her daughter in a motel room, so that for once she herself could get some much needed rest and go back to work without the constant interruptions. It was, to say the least, a difficult situation for both Susan and her daughter. And it was an emotionally draining conversation for me.

■APPLICATION

1. What are key issues this PHP support person can address to help Susan deal with her current challenges?
2. What steps should be taken immediately to assist Susan? What steps should be taken during the next six months? Give a rationale for each of your answers.
3. Given your knowledge at this time, what kinds of family support would be appropriate for Susan? How would this support be provided and orchestrated if it were available to her?
4. What ought to be the long-term goals of assistance for Susan?

Source: "Cognitive Coping at Parents Helping Parents" by F. S. Poyadue, 1993. In A. P. Turnbull, J. M. Patterson, S. K. Behr, D. L. Murphy, D. L. Marquis, & M. J. Blue-Banning (Eds.), *Cognitive Coping, Fami-lies, and Disability* (pp. 95–109). Baltimore, Paul H. Brookes. P.O. Box 10624, Baltimore, MD 21285-0624. Reprinted with permission.

Debate Forum

HEALTH CARE INDUSTRY FORCES FAMILY IMPOVERISHMENT

On September 19, 1990, . . . Donald P. of South Bend, Indi-ana, testified before the House Energy and Commerce Sub-committee on Commerce, Consumer Protection and Competitiveness. . . . At a hearing entitled "Access to Health Insurance: Who Is Medically Insurable?" . . . Mr. P. testified about his 8-year-old son Michael who has multiple disabilities.

"My name is Donald P. and I live in South Bend, Indiana, with my wife, Vickie, and our three children, Jeffrey, age 11, Michael, age 8, and Steven, age 4. Michael was born on June 3, 1982. He is a child with multiple disabilities—his diagnosis is colpocephaly (a brain malformation), hypoto-nia, seizure disorder, scoliosis, with a communication disor-der, mental retardation, and multiple developmental de-lays—or in short, cerebral palsy, meaning he cannot walk, talk, dress, toilet, feed, or fend for himself. Michael is physically dependent upon us for his every need, and proba-bly will be dependent upon us and others for physical assis-tance and support throughout his lifetime. . . .

"While my wife was preg-nant with Michael, my em-ployer . . . was taken over in a merger by another company and I was let go. . . . I didn't opt for the [insurance] conver-sion policy when the company policy ended . . . because there seemed to be better coverage by purchasing a private "family" policy for myself, my wife, and my son Jeffrey from Blue Cross–Blue Shield of Indiana, at a premium of $93.60 per month. . . ."

Between June 1982 and April 1986 the following sequence of events forced the P.'s to impoverish themselves to qualify for Medicaid coverage for their son:

- Blue Cross–Blue Shield insurance premiums increased 175 percent in a twelve-month period.
- After being rehired by a prior employer and restored to a prior plan, uncertainty about the future led Mr. P. to retain the Blue Cross–Blue Shield policy as a personal expense.
- Attempts to add Michael to the family plan were ignored by Blue Cross; instead, he was enrolled as an individual policyholder on a separate policy with $1,000 deductible.
- Blue Cross continued the family, minus Michael, in a policy with a $250 deductible.
- After collecting monthly premiums of $50.43 for Michael and $112.31 for the rest of the family for a period of time, Blue Cross canceled both policies, stating in a form letter to all policyholders in Indiana that they could no longer afford to administer the plan.

- The rehire by the previous employer and acceptance into the company's self-insured health benefits followed by a termination created a sense of panic and led to a choice not to purchase a conversion plan for fear the premium would be too high.
- All health insurance coverage lapsed until Mr. P. was employed by a small firm where he was informed that the company health insurance plan would not cover Michael "because of his health conditions." He therefore withheld Michael's name from the application for insurance, in effect denying his son's existence so that the rest of the family could have health insurance coverage.
- Unable to buy insurance for Michael because no one in Indiana was selling it, Mr. P. stated, "The health insurance industry forced me to turn to Medicaid." To qualify, all family assets, savings, individual retirement accounts, and life insurance policies were "spent down," leaving the family impoverished, unprotected, and vulnerable to financial disaster.
- A current employer provides a group plan that covers all of the family, except Michael. Medicaid has paid for Michael's wheelchair and a custom seat insert, a total of $5,400 (or $350 per month since Medicaid covered him). Medicaid denied payment for the lift

necessary to get Michael's wheelchair into the family van, saying it was not "medically necessary." Private charities, other family members, and friends contributed $3,430 for a used wheelchair lift. The family sacrificed Medicaid's respite care allowance for one year so that the $600 allowed could be used instead for the lift.

Mr. P. said they have been stigmatized and excluded, that they have "suffered" and will continue to suffer until the health industry is compelled to modify or eliminate current underwriting principles. Because of their commitment to raise their son with disabilities at home, they "are not very free to pursue economic growth and the American Dream." Instead they are compelled to

- set financial restrictions on their standard of living.
- deny themselves additional education and career advancement.
- forego saving for their children's college educations and their own retirement.
- forsake any inheritance for other family members.

■ POINT

Families with children with disabilities should have access to health insurance that covers reasonable health care for all family members. Insurance companies currently base their coverage on "experience ratings" rather than "community

ratings." Using experience ratings, they identify groups of individuals with whom they can make significant profits given their past health care requirements. They should use community ratings that consider the health needs of *all* individuals in a given area or location and base their pricing and potential profit structures on these community ratings. As a society, we should be willing to share the expense of providing basic medical care to all families and their members. Present insurance policies are patently discriminatory.

■ COUNTERPOINT

Insurance companies are private entities and for-profit businesses. As such, they must operate in ways that allow them to make profits as well as fund the expenses incurred in paying for health care delivered to families and individuals. If insurance companies were to alter their current underwriting standards, their expenses would exceed their incomes and they would not be able to provide health insurance for anyone.

Source: From "Public Testimony, Health Care Industry Forces Family Impoverishment: UCPA Witness Testifies on Access to Health Insurance" by A. I. Bergman and J. Simpson, Fall 1990, Family Support Bulletin, pp. 19–20. Reprinted by permission from Family Support Bulletin. Published by the United Cerebral Palsy Associations, Inc.

Review

focus 1

Identify five factors that influence the ways in which families respond to infants with birth defects or disabilities.

- The emotional stability of each family member
- Religious values and beliefs
- Socioeconomic status
- The severity of the disability
- The type of disability

focus 2

What three statements can be made about the stages that parents may experience in responding to infants or young children with disabilities?

- The stage approach needs further refinement and validation before it can be used accurately to understand, predict, or help parents deal with young infants and children with disabilities.
- Parental responses are highly variable.
- The adjustment process, for most parents, is continuous and distinctively individual.

focus 3

Identify three ways in which a newborn child with disabilities influences the family social system.

- The communication patterns within the family may change.

- The power structure within the family may be altered.
- The roles and responsibilities assumed by various family members may be modified.

focus 4

Identify three factors in raising a child with a disability that contribute to marital stress.

- A decrease in the amount of time available for the couple's activities
- Heavy financial burdens
- Fatigue

focus 5

Identify four general phases of the developmental cycle that parents go through in rearing a child with a disability.

- During the diagnostic period, the presence of a disability is confirmed.
- During the school period (elementary and secondary), parents help the child through many challenges: dealing with teasing and other peer-related behaviors; learning academic, social, and vocational skills; facing the challenges of adolescence.
- During the postschool period, the child makes the transition from school to other educational or vocational activities.
- In the final period, the parents are no longer able to provide direct care and guidance for their son or daughter.

focus 6

Identify four factors that influence the relationship that develops between infants with disabilities and their mothers.

- The mother may be unable to engage in typical feeding and caregiving activities because of the intensive medical care being provided.
- Some mothers may have difficulty bonding to children with whom they have little physical and social interaction.
- Some mothers are given little direction as to how they might become involved with their children. Without minimal involvement, some mothers become estranged from their children and find it difficult to begin the caring and bonding process.
- The expectations that mothers have about their children and their functions in nurturing them play a significant role in the relationship that develops.

focus 7

Identify three ways in which fathers may respond to their children with disabilities.

- Fathers are more likely to internalize their feelings than are mothers.
- Fathers often respond to sons with disabilities differently from how they respond to daughters.
- Fathers may resent the time their wives spend in caring for their children with disabilities.

focus 8

Identify four ways in which siblings respond to a brother or sister with a disability.

- Siblings tend to mirror the attitudes and behaviors of their parents toward a child with disabilities.
- Siblings may play a crucial role in fostering the intellectual, social, and affective development of the child with a disability.
- Some siblings respond with feelings of resentment or deprivation.

focus 9

Identify three types of support grandparents may render to families with children with disabilities.

- They may provide their own children with weekend reprieves from the pressures of the home environment.
- They may assist occasionally with baby-sitting or transportation.
- They may help their children in times of crisis by listening and helping them deal with seemingly unresolvable problems.

focus 10

Identify three types of professional understanding that are essential to establishing positive relationships with parents and families of children with disabilities.

- Professionals need to understand the impact that they have on the family over time.
- Professionals need to understand the impact that the child with disabilities has on the family over time.
- Professionals need to understand the impact that the child with disabilities and his or her family have on them.

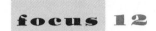

What are five goals of family support systems?

- Enhancing the caregiving capacity of the family
- Giving parents and other family members respites from the demands of caring for a child with a disability
- Assisting the family with persistent financial demands related to the child's disability
- Providing valuable training to families, extended family members, concerned neighbors, and caring friends
- Improving the quality of life for all family members

focus 12

What are five goals of parent training?

- Helping them with specific needs such as feeding their children, teaching them language skills, helping children become toilet trained; accessing adult services; finding appropriate housing; locating appropriate postsecondary vocational training
- Helping them understand their legal rights
- Contributing to their understanding of the nature of the disability or disabilities
- Making them aware of services in the community
- Alerting them to available financial assistance

4
The Early Childhood and Elementary School Years: Special Education, Inclusion, and Collaboration

To begin with . . .

In 1995–96, there were 548,441 children with disabilities between the ages of 3 and 5 receiving special education services. The number of preschool-age children with disabilities in 1995–96 increased by more than 25,000 in one year. Preschool-age children with disabilities now account for nearly 10% of all children with disabilities. (U.S. Department of Education, 1997)

Inclusive education is manifested in many different forms and models in the United States. Political, economic, and pedagogical controversies aside, inclusion is one of the most significant changes in the structure of education in the last decade. (Montgomery, 1994, p. 1)

 As long as there are people with disabilities, there will be a need for special services that goes beyond anything a regular [general] classroom teacher can provide. . . . Regular classroom teachers attempt to meet physical–motor, cognitive–intellectual, and social–emotional needs just as special educators do. Yet, their focus tends to be different. Regular class teachers are given an agenda called the curriculum. They are provided with it prior to seeing any student. They are told that this is what they have to teach, and sometimes what book to use and even how to use it. This more standardized approach to education for the masses generally succeeds. . . . It misses some individual children by a mile, children who may be normal and a little bit different, or who may have a disability and be a lot different. The greater the difference, the greater the chance that the student will fall through the cracks of any standard educational setting. (Lieberman, 1996, p. 24)

 The most recent descriptor for the effort to create greater integration of children with disabilities into school programs is the term *inclusion.* For many educators, the term is viewed as a more positive description of efforts to include children with disabilities in genuine and comprehensive ways in the total life of schools . . . The most effective and needed services that special education can provide must be preserved. At the same time, the education of children with disabilities must be viewed by all educators as a shared responsibility and privilege. Most important, every child must have a place and be made welcome in a regular classroom. (Smith, 1998, pp. 17, 18)

Snapshot

Matt

One day, 4-year-old Matt was playing across the street from his house. As he crossed the street to return home, he was hit by a car. Matt suffered a severe trauma as a result of the accident and was in a coma for more than 2 months. Now he's in school and doing well.

Matt wears a helmet to protect his head, and he uses a walker in his general education kindergarten class in the morning and special education class in the afternoon. The general education kindergarten children sing songs together and work on handwriting, before they work at centers in the classroom. Matt's favorite center is the block area. He spends most of his time there.

Recently, however, he has become interested in the computer and math centers.

He is working on his fine motor skills and speech skills so he can learn to write and use a pencil again. The focus of his academic learning is mastering the alphabet, learning how to count, and recognizing his numbers. He also receives regular speech therapy. He speaks in sentences, but it is very difficult for others to understand what he is saying.

Matt is well liked by his classmates. His teacher enjoys seeing his progress. "Well, it's our hope that he'll be integrated with the other kids eventually, and through the activities we do in the classroom here (in special education) and in the kindergarten, we hope the kids will get to know him and interact with him and that this will help pull up his skills to the level where he can eventually go back to the general education classroom."

Yvonne

■ **THE EARLY CHILDHOOD YEARS**

Anita was elated. She had just learned during an ultrascan that she was going to have twin girls. As the delivery date neared, she thought about how much fun it would be to take them on long summer walks in the new double stroller. Two weeks after her estimated delivery date, she was in the hospital, giving birth to the first of her two twins. The first little girl arrived without a problem. Unfortunately, this was not the case for the second.

There was something different about her; it became obvious almost immediately after the birth. Yvonne just didn't seem to have the same body tone as her sister. Within a couple of days, Yvonne was diagnosed as having cerebral palsy. Her head and the left side of her body seemed to be affected most seriously. The pediatrician calmly told the

family that Yvonne would undoubtedly have learning and physical problems throughout her life. She referred the parents to a division of the state health agency responsible for assisting families with children who have disabilities. Further testing was done, and Yvonne was placed in an early intervention program for infants with developmental disabilities. When she reached the age of 3, Yvonne's parents enrolled her in a preschool program where she would have the opportunity to learn communication and social skills while interacting with children of her own age with and without disabilities. As neither of the parents had any previous direct experience with a child with disabilities, they were uncertain how to help Yvonne. Would this program really help her that much, or should they work with her at home only? It was hard for them to see this little girl go to school so very early in her life.

HIS CHAPTER explores the world of infants, toddlers, preschoolers, and elementary school children with disabilities. For infants, toddlers, and preschool-age children, the world is defined primarily through family and a small, same-age peer group. As the child progresses in age and development, the world expands to include the neighborhood, the school, and eventually, a larger heterogeneous group called the community. For educators, the question is this: How can schools and families work together to individualize a child's instructional program to effectively foster full participation in the home, the school, and eventually the community setting?

The Early Childhood Years

Over the past decade, there has been a growing recognition of the educational, social, and health needs of young children with disabilities. The early experiences of infants and children at risk provide the basis for subsequent learning, growth, and development (Bailey & Wolery, 1992; Noonan & McCormick, 1993; Ramey & Landesman-Ramey, 1992). These first years of life are critical to the overall development of children, including those defined as at risk. Moreover, classic studies in the behavioral sciences from the 1960s and 1970s indicated that early stimulation is critical to the later development of language, intelligence, personality, and a sense of self-worth (Bloom, 1964; Hunt, 1961; Piaget, 1970; White, 1975).

Advocates of **early intervention** services for children at risk believe that intervention should begin as early as possible in an environment free of traditional categorical labels (such as *mentally retarded* or *emotionally disturbed*), particularly if there is any uncertainty about the permanence of the present assessment of the child's condition. Carefully selected services and supports can lessen the long-term impact of the disability and counteract any negative effects of waiting to intervene. The postponement of services may, in fact, undermine a child's overall development as well as his or her acquisition of specific skills.

focus 1

Why is it so important to provide early intervention services as soon as possible to students at risk?

■ BRINGING ABOUT CHANGE FOR YOUNG CHILDREN WITH DISABILITIES

For the better part of the 20th century, comprehensive educational and social services for young children with disabilities were nonexistent or were provided sporadically at best. For families of children with more severe disabilities, often the only option was institutionalization. Harbin (1993) reported that as recently as 1950, many parents were advised to institutionalize a child immediately after birth if he or she had a recognizable physical condition associated with a disability (such as Down syndrome). By doing so, the family would not become attached to the child in the hospital or after returning home.

The efforts of parents and professionals to gain national support to develop and implement community services for young children at risk began in 1968 with the passage of Public Law (PL) 90–538, the Handicapped Children's Early Education Program (HCEEP). A primary purpose of HCEEP was to fund model demonstration programs focused on experimental practices for young children with disabilities. Many of the best practice approaches coming out of these experimental projects were transferred to other early intervention programs through outreach efforts funded through HCEEP.

The documented success of HCEEP eventually culminated in the passage of PL 99–457, in the form of amendments to the Education of the Handicapped Act, passed in 1986 (see Chapter 1). The most important piece of legislation ever enacted on behalf of infants and preschool-age children with disabilities, the act opened up a new era of services for young children with disabilities. It required that all states ensure a free and appropriate public education to every eligible child with a disability between 3 and 5 years of age. For infants and toddlers (birth to 2 years of age), a new program (Part H was changed to Part C in the 1997 Amendments to IDEA) was established to help states develop and implement programs for early intervention services. Every state now provides services for infants and toddlers with disabilities under Part H.

In the next two sections of this chapter, we will discuss the comprehensive services necessary to meet the needs of infants, toddlers, and preschool-age children with disabilities.

■ EARLY INTERVENTION SERVICES FOR INFANTS AND TODDLERS

Early intervention is a term used in myriad ways. For our purposes, it refers to comprehensive services and supports in the areas of education, health care, and social services provided to infants and toddlers. IDEA 97 (PL 105-17), Part C (formerly

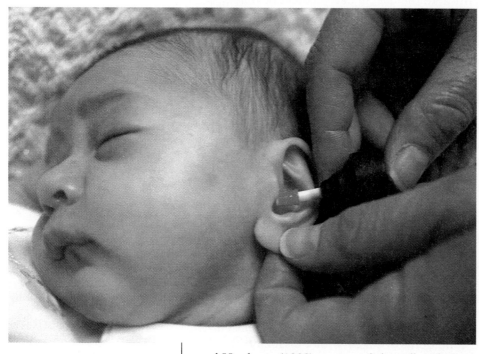

Part H), defines eligible infants and toddlers as those under 3 years of age who need early intervention services for one of two reasons: (1) there is a developmental delay in one or more of the areas of cognitive development, physical development, communication development, social or emotional development, and adaptive development; or (2) there is a diagnosis of a physical or mental condition that has a high probability of resulting in a developmental delay (Sec. 632[1]).

Early intervention services must be directed not only at the young child with a disability, but also at their families. To be effective, early intervention must be focused on the life of the family (Sontag & Schacht, 1994). Berry

Early intervention for infants and toddlers includes early diagnosis and health care.

and Hardman (1998) suggested that all early intervention services must be designed and delivered within the framework of informing and empowering family members.

Advancements in health care have increased the number of at-risk infants who survive birth. **Intensive care specialists,** working with sophisticated medical technologies, are able to save the lives of infants who years ago would have died in the first days or weeks of life. This decrease in mortality is a major reason for the increased demand for trained early intervention specialists.

The intent of intervention programs for infants and toddlers at risk is multifaceted. Goals include diminishing the effects of the disabling condition on the child's growth and development and preventing, as much as possible, deterioration of the at-risk condition. Timing is critical in the delivery of the services. The maxim "the earlier, the better" is very true. Moreover, early intervention may be less costly and more effective than providing services later in the individual's life (Casto & Mastropieri, 1985; Casto & White, 1984; Garber et al., 1991; Reaves & Bums, 1982; Strain, 1984; White, Mastropieri, & Casto, 1984).

Comprehensive intervention services are broad in scope. The Infant and Toddlers Program under IDEA, Part C, specified that programs include the following services:

■ Family training, counseling, and home visits
■ Special instruction

- Speech and language instruction
- Occupational therapy and physical therapy
- Psychological testing and counseling
- Service coordination
- Medical services necessary for diagnostic and evaluation purposes only
- Social work services
- **Assistive technology** devices and services
- Early identification, screening, and assessment services
- Health services necessary to enable the infant or toddler to benefit from the other early intervention services
- Transportation and related costs that are necessary for the infant and toddler and the family to receive service

These services are provided to infants and toddlers on the basis of need as established in the individualized family service plan (IFSP) (see Figure 4.1). The IFSP is structured much like the individualized education program (IEP), but it broadens the focus to include not only the individual, but also all members of the family. The IFSP must contain statements pertaining to the following issues:

- The child's present levels of development (cognitive, speech and language, psychosocial, motor, and self-help)
- The family's concerns, priorities, and resources related to enhancing the child's development
- Major outcomes expected to be achieved for the child and family and the criteria, procedures, and time frames for determining progress
- Specific early intervention services necessary to meet the unique needs of the child and the family
- Projected dates for initiation of services and expected duration
- The service coordinator who will be responsible for implementing the plan
- Procedures for transition from early intervention into a preschool program

■ EARLY INTERVENTION SERVICE DELIVERY

There are essentially three types of delivery models for early intervention programs focusing on the needs of infants and toddlers: center-based, home-based, or a combination of the two (McDonnell, Hardman, McDonnell, & Kiefer-O'Donnell, 1995; Noonan & McCormick, 1993). The center-based model requires that families take their child from the home to a setting where comprehensive services are provided. These sites may be hospitals, churches, schools, or other community facilities. The centers use various instructional approaches, including both developmental and therapeutic models, to meet the needs of infants and toddlers. Noonan and McCormick have suggested that because many center-based programs are heavily furnished with "therapeutic equipment," they tend to look more like "hospital therapy rooms than an early childhood program" (1993, p. 15).

In contrast to the center-based model, and as the name implies, the home-based model provides services to the child and family in their natural living environment. Using the resources of the home, professionals address the needs of the child in terms of individual family values and lifestyles.

Finally, early intervention may be provided through a combination of services at both a center and the home. Infants or toddlers may spend some time in a center-based program, receiving instruction and therapy in individual or group settings,

FIGURE 4.1 A sample individualized family service plan (IFSP)

Background Information		
Child's Name:	Mary	
Family's Name:	Tucker	
Date of Birth: 12-26-96	Age: 20 mo.	
County:		

Family Member's Name	Relationship to Child
Susan	mother
Ann	older sister

Family Support Plan Team

Name	Title	Agency	Date
Susan	Parent		
Jane Jones	Service Coordinator	Home-Based Program	8-1-98
John Johnson	Speech Pathologist	Home-Based Program	8-1-98
Linda Williams	Teacher	Home-Based Program	8-1-98
Don Hunter	Psychologist	Home-Based Program	8-1-98
Pat Bennett	Nurse	Public Health Department	8-1-98

Team Review Dates

30 Days: 9-1-98	3 Months: 11-3-98	6 Months: 2-2-99	9 Months: 5-4-99

[Source: Adapted from *Developing Individualized Family Support Plans* (pp. 168–170) by T. Bennett, B. V. Lingerfelt, and D. E. Nelson, 1990, Cambridge, MA: Brookline Publishing. Copyright 1990 by Brookline Publishing. Reprinted by permission.]

FIGURE 4.1 (continued)

Child's Name: _____ Mary Tucker _____   Family's Name: _____ Tucker _____

Child's Functioning Level

Domain	CA	Age Level/Range	Domain	CA	Age Level/Range	Domain	CA	Age Level/Range
Social Adapt.	20 mo.	14 mo. (10–16)	Fine motor	20 mo.	10 mo. (7–12)			
Gross motor	20 mo.	13 mo. (11–14)	Hearing/Speech	20 mo.	14 mo. (12–16)			
Per-social	20 mo.	11 mo. (9–15)	Performance	20 mo.	10 mo. (8–10)			

Child's Strengths

She is alert, smiles, and interacts a lot with people. She attends to sounds and voices and uses several words (yes, no). She explores her environment through crawling and shows a lot of initiative.

Family's Strengths

Commitment to staying together and helping Mary live as normal a life as possible. Communication between mother and children is good. Has wide informal support network with family and friends, has positive outlook on the situation.

Resources and Support Services	Started	Ended	Resources and Support Services	Started	Ended
Department of Social Services	8-1-98	3-99			
Supplemental Security Income (SSI)	8-1-98				
Home-based services	8-1-98				
Employment Security Commission	9-18-98				

FIGURE 4.1 (continued)

Child's Name: ___Mary___

Family's Name: ___Tucker___

IFSP # ___1512___

FIPP Staff Member: ___Jane Jones___

Date / #	Need/Project Outcome Statement	Source of Support/Resource	Course of Action	Family's Evaluation	
				Date	Rating
9-1-98 / 3	Mary will locate food placed in front of her in order to learn to feed herself.	mom, family, friends Service coordinator—will provide information on feeding strategies.	Adults caring for Mary will place her in her high chair with a cracker on the tray at snacks and mealtimes. During weekly home visits, the service coordinator will present information on feeding and answer questions.	9-1-98 9-18-98 9-29-98	2 3 3
9-1-98 / 4	Mary will make sounds when presented with familiar objects, sounds, and smells to increase her communication abilities.	mom, family, friends Service coordinator—will provide information on teaching strategies.	Adults caring for Mary will talk with her about familiar objects, sounds, and smells during everyday activities and reinforce her sounds, encourage Mary to repeat the name of the object, sound, or smell. During weekly home visits, the service coordinator will present information on encouraging vocalizations.	9-1-98 9-29-98 10-13-98 11-3-98	2 3 3 3
9-1-98 / 5	Mary will find toys placed just out of her reach to begin exploring her environment.	mom, family, friends Service coordinator—will provide information on teaching strategies.	Mom will arrange an area at home for Mary with her toys, and adults caring for Mary will encourage her to find toys within this area. During weekly home visits, the service coordinator will present information on encouraging exploration.	9-1-98 9-18-98 9-29-98 11-3-98	2 2 3 7
9-1-98 / 6	Mary will make transitions from sitting to standing in order to eventually walk.	mom, family, friends Service coordinator—will provide information on teaching strategies.	Adults caring for Mary will place cushions on the floor and use a favorite toy to encourage her to climb on the cushions and pull to standing at the couch. During weekly home visits, the service coordinator will present information on motor development.	9-1-98 9-18-98 9-29-98 10-13-98 11-3-98	2 2 2 3 3

Family's Evaluation:

1...Situation changed, no longer a need

2...Situation unchanged, still a need, goal or project

3...Implementation begun, still a need, goal or project

4...Outcome partially attained or accomplished

5...Outcome accomplished or attained, but not to the family's satisfaction

6...Outcome mostly accomplished or attained to the family's satisfaction

7...Outcome completely accomplished or attained to the family's satisfaction

FIGURE 4.1 *(continued)*

Child's Name: ___Mary___   Family's Name: _____   IFSP # ___1512___

FIPP Staff Member: ___Jane Jones___

Date #	Need/Project Outcome Statement	Source of Support/Resource	Course of Action	Family's Evaluation	
				Date	Rating
9-1-98 / 1	Susan will obtain employment in order to adequately meet her financial responsibilities for herself and her two children.	Service coordinator—support to mom Susan Susan's mother—babysitting Susan's brother—babysitting Employment Security Commission—employment possibilities	Susan will fill out the appropriate forms at Employment Security Commission to start the process of finding a job. She will familiarize herself with their process and be aware of what her responsibilities are. Susan will talk with her mother and brother about babysitting while she interviews for jobs. Susan will also continue to read the classified ads in the paper and follow through on any job leads she feels might pertain to her. During weekly home visits, the service coordinator will check with Susan about progress in looking for a job.	9-1-98 9-18-98 9-29-98 10-13-98 11-3-98	2 3 3 3 7
9-1-98 / 2	Susan will find a day-care center in order to provide adequate supervision of her children enabling her to maintain a full-time job.	Service coordinator—will act as consultant and resource to mom Chamber of Commerce—list of day-care centers Friends—names of day-care centers Church members—names of day-care centers Dept. of Social Services—names of day-care centers Newspapers—names of day-care centers Susan's mother—babysitting Susan's brother—babysitting	Susan will obtain a list of possible day-care centers from friends, the Chamber of Commerce, church members, Department of Social Services (DSS), and the newspaper. Susan will find out information such as types and ages of children served, cost, hours open, and other general information. At weekly home visits, the service coordinator will share information about what to look for in day-care centers. Susan will narrow her list down to her top three choices and visit these programs personally before coming to a final decision. Susan's mother and brother can babysit while Susan visits day-care centers. Susan's children will then be enrolled in the chosen day-care center.	9-1-98 9-18-98 9-29-98 10-13-98 11-3-98	2 3 2 4 7

Family's Evaluation:

1...Situation changed, no longer a need
2...Situation unchanged, still a need, goal or project
3...Implementation begun, still a need, goal or project
4...Outcome partially attained or accomplished
5...Outcome accomplished or attained, but not to the family's satisfaction
6...Outcome mostly accomplished or attained to the family's satisfaction
7...Outcome completely accomplished or attained to the family's satisfaction

and also receive in-home services to promote learning and generalization in their natural environment.

Whether the intervention is delivered at a center or in the home, programs for infants and young children who are at risk or have disabilities must be "intensive, comprehensive, continuous, and focused upon the individual needs of each child" (Peterson, 1987, p. 74). *Intensity* refers to the frequency and amount of time an infant or child is engaged in intervention activities. An intensive approach requires that the child participate in intervention activities that involve two to three hours of contact each day, about four or five times a week. Until the 1980s, this child-centered model of service delivery placed parents in the role of trainers, who provided direct instruction to the child and helped him or her transfer the learning activities from the therapeutic setting to the home environment.

The model of parents as trainers was questioned in the 1980s. Families were dropping out of programs, and many parents did not use the intervention techniques effectively with their children or simply preferred to be parents, not trainers (Bailey & Simeonsson, 1988; Bailey & Wolery, 1992; Benson & Turnbull, 1986; McDonnell et al., 1995). With the passage of PL 99-457 in 1986 (now IDEA), early intervention evolved into a more family-centered approach in which individual family needs and strengths became the basis for determining program goals, supports needed, and services to be provided.

While the needs of the child with disabilities continued to be an important intervention focus, service providers began to realize how inseparable these needs were from those faced by family members or the family unit as a whole. (McDonnell et al., 1995, p. 107)

Providing the breadth of services necessary to meet the individual needs of an infant or toddler within the family constellation requires a multidisciplinary intervention team. It should include professionals with varied experiential backgrounds—such as speech and language therapy, physical therapy, nursing, and education—and also at least one of the child's parents or his or her guardian. The team should review the IFSP at least annually and issue progress updates to the parents every six months. Coordination of early intervention services across disciplines and with the family is crucial if the goals of the program are to be realized.

The traditional academic-year programming (lasting approximately nine months) common to many public school programs is not in the best interests of infants and toddlers who are at risk or have disabilities. Continuity is essential. Services must be provided throughout the early years without lengthy interruptions.

■ EARLY CHILDHOOD SERVICES FOR PRESCHOOL-AGE CHILDREN

focus 2

Identify the critical components of programs for preschool-age children under Public Law 99–457.

Programs for preschool-age children with disabilities have several important components. First, a **child-find** system is set up in each state to locate young children at risk and make referrals to the local education agency for preschool services. Such referrals may come from parents, the family physician, health or social service agencies, or the child's day-care or preschool teacher. Referrals for preschool services may be based on a child's perceived delays in physical development (such as not walking by age 2), speech and language delays (such as nonverbal by age 3), excessive inappropriate behavior (such as frequent temper tantrums, violent behavior, extreme shyness, or excessive crying), or sensory difficulties (unresponsive to sounds, unable to visually track objects in the environment).

Following a referral, a multidisciplinary team initiates an assessment to determine whether the child is eligible for preschool services under IDEA guidelines (see Chapter 1). If the child is eligible for special education services, an individualized education program (IEP) is then developed. Specialists from several disciplines—including physical therapy, occupational therapy, speech and language therapy, pediatrics, social work, and special education—participate in the development and implementation of IEPs for preschool-age children.

The purpose of preschool programs for young children with disabilities is to assist them in living in and adapting to a variety of environmental settings, including home, neighborhood, and school. Depending on individual needs, preschool programs may focus on content areas such as language development, social skills, motor proficiency, and preacademic instruction. Westlake and Kaiser (1991) proposed several principles for guiding early childhood services for students with severe disabilities that have direct relevance for all preschool-age children with disabilities. First, young children with disabilities have the right to services that improve the quality of life and maximize developmental potential. In addition, the earlier the services begin, the more effective they will be in improving quality of life. Finally, services that involve families are more effective than those that do not.

In a review of early childhood program models, Bailey and Wolery (1992) identified three theoretical perspectives that undergird program assessment and intervention: developmental, behavioral, and ecological (see Table 4.1 on page 112). While the developmental and behavioral theories continue as the basis for many early childhood programs, there has been considerable increase in the use of ecological theory. The theory appears to be particularly valid for younger children with severe disabilities. As suggested by McDonnell et al. (1995), ecological theory is "holistic, blends many of the strengths of the other perspectives, and is applicable to children with varying abilities, interests, and family and cultural backgrounds" (p. 146).

Inclusive preschool classrooms staffed by professionals and a special education teacher allow students with disabilities to be educated with their nondisabled peers.

■ HOME- AND CENTER-BASED PRESCHOOL PROGRAMS As for infants and toddlers, programs for preschool-age students with disabilities have been organized using home- and center-based programs or a combination of the two. Home-based programs remain an important option for families who want their preschool-age children to spend most of their time at home. These programs concentrate on ways to teach members of the family to work directly with the child in the natural environment of the home and within the context of daily family routines (Berry & Hardman, 1998).

Beginning at age 3, the use of center-based classes expands considerably to meet the needs of young children with disabilities. These preschool programs may be full- or part-day self-contained special classes or inclusive classes within a general preschool or day-care program. The self-contained preschool special education classroom may be located in a special school housing other educational programs for school-age students with disabilities or in a general education

THEORETICAL PERSPECTIVE	BASIC ASSUMPTIONS ABOUT THE NATURE OF CHILDREN	BASIC ASSUMPTIONS ABOUT LEARNING AND DEVELOPMENT	ASSESSMENT IMPLICATIONS	INTERVENTION IMPLICATIONS
Developmental	Children are born with an intrinsic motivation to explore and master the environment. Skills emerge in a relatively predictable sequence.	Development is primarily a result of physical maturation. Competence is gained through self-initiated exploration and play.	Document the extent to which the child has attained specific developmental milestones.	Arrange the environment and provide materials that are highly interesting to children and are most likely to facilitate competence in developmentally appropriate skills.
Behavioral	Children are born with the capacity to learn. The skills that a child displays emerge as a result of experiences with the environment. Biological and physiological processes also are acknowledged as important.	Antecedents and consequences serve to shape behavior. Children learn behaviors through repeated reinforcing interactions with the environment.	Identify the functional skills needed by the child to increase the likelihood of success in current and future environments.	Provide experiences and support that promote success: Identify and use effective reinforcers to ensure rapid and efficient learning.
Ecological	Children influence and are influenced by the environment. Children inevitably are a part of a family system. Likewise, families are embedded within larger neighborhood, community, and institutional systems.	Development results from the complex interactions or transactions between children and the environment over time. Development cannot be examined in isolation, but rather must be examined over time and in the context of systems within which children and families function.	Determine the child's skills, the characteristics of the caregiving environment, and the family's needs, resources, expectations, and aspirations.	Provide services that support families and children in ways that are congruent with their ecology and are consistent with expressed family goals.

Source: From *Teaching Infants and Preschoolers with Disabilities* (2nd ed.), by D. B. Bailey, Jr., & M. Wolery, 1992, New York: Macmillan.

school building. The students spend most, if not all, of their day alongside other preschool-age students with disabilities with similar needs, as designated in the IEP. Support personnel, such as speech and language therapists and occupational therapists, work directly with the child in the special classroom setting.

■ INCLUSIVE PRESCHOOL CLASSROOMS   In the inclusive classroom setting, preschool-age students with disabilities receive their educational program side by side with nondisabled peers in a regular preschool or day-care program. The programs are staffed by both early childhood professionals and paraprofessionals, with a special education preschool teacher in a co-teaching or consultant role. The child's IEP "specifies the amount and type of special assistance and related services necessary to support implementation of the child's program" (Noonan & McCormick, 1993, p. 17). Strain (1990) identified several reasons for delivering preschool services in inclusive classroom settings:

- It develops friendships between children with disabilities and same-age nondisabled peers.
- Social skill development with nondisabled peers leads to optimal developmental outcomes in future educational and social settings.
- Nondisabled preschool-age children benefit from inclusive experiences with young children who are disabled.
- The type or severity of disability is not correlated with whether or not a preschool-age child with a disability is a good candidate for inclusion.

■ HEAD START Support of **Head Start** programs was enacted as law by Congress in 1965 to provide early enrichment experiences for economically disadvantaged children, to better prepare them for elementary school. Although the original legislation did not include children with disabilities, the law was eventually expanded in 1992 to require that at least 10% of Head Start enrollment be reserved for these children. The U.S. Department of Health and Human Services (1994) reported that, of the 713,943 children in Head Start programs in 1993, children with disabilities accounted for 13.2% of this population. Head Start has been hailed through the years as a major breakthrough in federal support for early childhood education.

In January 1993, federal regulations for children with disabilities under Head Start were expanded to ensure that a disabilities service plan be developed to meet the needs of children with disabilities and their families, that the programs designate a coordinator of services for children with disabilities, and that the necessary special education and related services be provided for children who are designated as disabled under IDEA.

■ TRANSITION FROM PRESCHOOL TO ELEMENTARY SCHOOL

Transitions, although a natural and ongoing part of everyone's life, are often difficult even under the best of circumstances. For preschool-age children with disabilities and their families, the transition from early childhood programs to elementary school can be very stressful. Early childhood programs for preschool-age children with disabilities commonly employ many adults (both professional and paraprofessional) to meet student needs. The environment in preschool programs is usually very structured, offering only limited opportunities for independence. In contrast, elementary school programs, particularly in more inclusive educational settings, promote and support independent functioning on the part of students. As such, it is important for preschool professionals responsible for transition planning to attend not only to the needs and skills of the individual student, but also to how he or she can match the performance demands of the elementary school and classroom setting. Conn-Powers, Ross-Allen, and Holburn (1990, p. 94) summarized the goals that professionals should focus on as they plan for the preschooler's transition to school:

- Promote the speedy adjustment of the child and family to the new educational setting.
- Enhance the child's independent and successful participation in the new educational setting.
- Ensure the uninterrupted provision of appropriate services in the least restrictive school setting.
- Support and empower the family as an equal partner in the transition process.
- Promote collaboration among all constituents in the transition process.

TABLE 4.2	Preschool transitions: Common concerns and intervention goals	
TRANSITION	**EARLY INTERVENTION TO PRESCHOOL**	**PRESCHOOL TO ELEMENTARY SCHOOL (K OR 1)**
Common concerns	■ Child's readiness for classroom program, peer relationships, and bus transportation ■ Changing nature of services from family-centered to child-centered ■ Safety of child with active peers and in playground and bus settings ■ Obtaining desired preschool placement and special services ■ Whether child's individual health and caregiving needs will be met in group setting	■ Child's readiness for more structured school programs and full-day program (when applicable) ■ Whether child will be disruptive, ignored, or rejected in general elementary classes and by typical peers ■ Obtaining desired school placement and special services ■ Safety of child in less closely supervised school settings
Common child goals related to transition	■ Follows directions, rules, and routines ■ Communicates with familiar adults and peers ■ Toilet training ■ Is socially appropriate with peers in a variety of play and preschool activities ■ Transitions between activities at appropriate time ■ Occupies self and sustains attention during caregiving, preschool group, and play activities ■ Completes seat work independently	■ Pays attention and participates without disruption in large and small group activities and instruction ■ Locates and manages own belongings ■ Is socially appropriate with peers in a variety of classroom and school activities ■ Takes care of own toileting, eating, grooming, and dressing needs as required in school setting ■ Demonstrates early academic or "readiness" skills

Source: From *Introduction to Persons with Severe Disabilities* (p. 173), by J. M. McDonnell, M. L. Hardman, A. P. McDonnell, & R. Kiefer-O'Donnell, 1995, Boston: Allyn and Bacon.

■ Increase the satisfaction of all constituents with (1) the outcomes of the transition process, and (2) the transition process itself, including their participation.
■ Increase the likelihood that the child is placed and maintained in the regular kindergarten and elementary school mainstream.

Table 4.2 illustrates some common concerns and goals related to the transition, both from early intervention to preschool programs and from preschool to elementary school.

In summary, early childhood programs for children with disabilities focus on teaching skills that will improve a child's opportunities for living a rich life and on preparing the child to function well in family, school, and neighborhood environments. These children are prepared as early as possible to share meaningful experiences with same-age peers. Additionally, early childhood programs lessen the impact of conditions that may deteriorate or become more severe without timely and adequate treatment and that may prevent children from developing other secondary disabling conditions. The intended outcomes of these programs will not, however, be accomplished without consistent family participation and professional collaboration.

The Elementary School Years

The move from preschool to elementary school raises the issue of whether the child with a disability can adapt (academically, behaviorally, and physically) to the demands of the general education envi-

Yvonne

■ THE ELEMENTARY SCHOOL YEARS

Yvonne left her preschool program at age 5 to attend her neighborhood elementary school. From kindergarten through sixth grade, she divided her day between a general education classroom with her nondisabled friends and a special education class. Her educational program during the elementary years focused on developing basic academic skills, learning to manage her own personal affairs, and participating in social activities with her friends. Yvonne's rate of academic learning was significantly slower than that of other children of her age, and she required extensive specialized instruction in reading and arithmetic. She also needed assistance in developing age-appropriate personal care skills, managing her time, socially interacting with her peers, and participating in recreation and leisure activities.

---

ronment. The degree to which the child can cope with these demands depends on the type and severity of the disability as well as how effectively the school will accommodate his or her needs. A student with a mild disability may manage to function in general education, but may have the negative experience of being viewed as a discipline problem, a slow learner, or a poorly motivated child unless the disability is discovered and addressed. However, the more pronounced differences that characterize students with moderate and severe disabilities rarely go unperceived and, in the school context, require more extensive educational support. The need for ongoing special education services and supports for these individuals span several settings, including home, community, and school.

> **focus 3**
>
> Identify three characteristics of special education that enhance learning opportunities for students with disabilities.

■ CHARACTERISTICS OF SPECIAL EDUCATION

Ensuring an appropriate educational experience for students with disabilities depends upon the provision of effective special education services. Characteristics of special education that enhance learning opportunities for students of all ages and across multiple settings include the following:

- **Individualization**—a student-centered approach to instructional decision making
- **Intensive instruction**—frequent instructional experiences of significant duration
- The explicit teaching of basic, adaptive, and/or functional life skills. (National Research Council, 1997)

■ INDIVIDUALIZATION   The hallmark of special education is decision making based on the individual needs of each student. Research indicates that fundamental differences characterize the ways in which special educators approach instruction, distinguishing them from their general education colleagues. Hocutt suggested that instruction in general education is most often oriented to the masses and centered on the curriculum:

Undifferentiated large-group instruction appears to be the norm in general education. Individual assignments, small group work, and student pairing occur, but much less frequently than whole-class instruction. Teachers typically follow the sequence of lessons outlined in teachers' manuals and focus on content coverage. . . . When surveyed, teachers do not perceive themselves as having the skills for adapting instruction in ways that facilitate individual or small-group instruction. (1996, p. 81)

Special education, on the other hand, is designed to meet the unique needs of every student, regardless of educational need or ability. Using an individually referenced approach to decision making, special education teachers must continually plan and adjust curriculum and instruction in response to the student. Teachers must have at their disposal multiple ways to adapt curriculum, modify their instructional approaches, and motivate their students to learn (National Research Council, 1997). Hardman, McDonnell, and Welch (1997) suggested that the vast majority of teachers, whether in general or special education, do not have expertise in both the subject matter being taught and in adapting curriculum and instruction. Thus, general and special educators need (1) to acquire a core of knowledge and skills that facilitates their ability to teach *all* students and (2) to work collaboratively in meeting the instructional needs of students with disabilities.

■ INTENSIVE INSTRUCTION Intensive instruction involves (1) actively engaging students in their learning by requiring high rates of appropriate response to the material presented, (2) carefully matching instruction to student ability and skill level, (3) providing instructional cues and prompts to support learning and then fading them when appropriate, and (4) providing detailed feedback that is directly focused on the task the student is expected to complete (National Research Council, 1997). Intensive instruction may involve both group and one-to-one learning.

Research suggests that intensive instruction can significantly improve academic achievement and functional skill levels of students with disabilities (Alexander et al., 1991; Billingsley, Liberty, & White, 1994; Glass, Cahen, Smith, & Filby, 1982; Torgesen, 1996; Wasik & Slavin, 1993). In the area of learning disabilities, Lyon (1996) reported that "intensive instruction of appropriate duration provided by trained teachers can remediate the deficient reading skills of many children" (p. 70). This is exemplified in a 1991 study of severely dyslexic children, in which Alexander et al. found that an intensive program of 65 hours of individual instruction in addition to group instruction resulted in significant gains in reading skill. In the area of severe disabilities, Billingsley et al. (1994) found that one-to-one intensive instruction resulted in significant gains in functional skills (such as dressing, money management, sexual behavior, etc.).

■ BASIC SKILLS, ADAPTIVE INSTRUCTION, AND FUNCTIONAL LIFE SKILLS APPROACHES In addition to needing individualized and intensive instruction, students with disabilities require more structured and teacher-directed approaches to learning than students who are not disabled (Brown & Campione, 1990; Dweck & Leggett, 1988; Harris & Graham, 1995; Tarver, 1995). Learning is a continual process of adaptation for students with disabilities as they attempt to cope with the demands of school. These students must adapt to the time constraints placed on them by the educational system. They do not learn as quickly or as efficiently as their classmates and are constantly fighting a battle against failure. They must somehow learn to deal with a system that is often rigid and allows little room for learning or behavior differences. Students with more mild disabilities must also adapt to a teaching process that may be oriented toward the majority of students within a general classroom and not based on individualized assessment of needs or personalized instruction.

focus 4

What is meant by adaptive fit and adaptive instruction for students with disabilities?

Despite these obstacles, however, students with disabilities can learn social and academic skills that will orient them toward striving for success rather than fighting against failure. Success can be achieved only when educators remain flexible, constantly adjusting to meet the needs of these students.

Three general types of instruction may be used when teaching students with disabilities: **basic skills, adaptive instruction,** and **functional life skills.** The basic skills approach stresses that the student must learn a specified set of sequenced

Students with disabilities can learn social skills that will direct them toward success rather than failure.

skills, each a prerequisite to the next. This process, sometimes referred to as the *developmental approach*, can be illustrated by briefly analyzing the teaching of reading.

When learning to read, the student must acquire many individual skills and then be able to link them together as a whole. The student then has the ability to decode abstract information and turn it into meaningful content. When one of the separate skills required for reading is not learned, the entire process may break down. The basic skills approach, whether in reading or any other content area, lays the groundwork for further development and higher levels of functioning.

However, not all children learn basic skills within the time frame dictated by schools. The degree to which a student is able to cope with the requirements of a school setting and the extent to which the school recognizes and accommodates individual diversity are known as **adaptive fit.** This fit is dynamic and constantly changes in the negotiations between the individual and the environment.

For the student who is exceptional, adaptive fit involves his or her attempt to meet the expectations of various learning environments. Such a student may find that the requirements for success within public education are beyond his or her adaptive capabilities and that the system cannot accommodate his or her academic, behavioral, physical, sensory, and communicative differences. As a result, such students develop negative attitudes toward the educational environment. Imagine yourself in a setting that constantly disapproves of how you act and what you do, a place in which activities are difficult and overwhelming, a setting in which your least desirable qualities are emphasized. What would you think about spending more than 1,000 hours a year in such a place?

Over the years, educators have responded in several ways to mismatches between the needs of the student and the demands of the learning environment. One approach has been to move the student from that environment to one more conducive to meeting his or her needs. Another approach has been to leave the student in the negative situation and do nothing until inevitable failure occurs. Still another approach, *adaptive instruction,* has attempted to create a better adaptive fit between the student and the learning environment through instruction. Adaptive instruction *modifies the learning environment to accommodate the unique learning characteristics and needs of individual students, and it provides direct or focused intervention to improve each student's capabilities to successfully acquire subject-matter knowledge and higher-order reasoning and problem-solving skills, to work independently and cooperatively with peers, and to meet the overall intellectual and social demands of schooling. (Wang, 1989, p. 183)*

Adaptive instruction focuses on assessing each student's individual characteristics and capabilities. This approach uses a variety of instructional procedures, materials, and alternative learning sequences in the classroom setting to help students master content at a rate consistent with their abilities and interests. Students are expected to take on increased responsibility for planning and monitoring their learning (Wang, 1989; Wood, 1992; Ysseldyke, Algozzine, & Thurlow, 1992).

For some time, the general classroom teacher has had to work with students who have disabilities without the assistance of any effective support systems. This is no longer the case in many of today's schools. The emergence of inclusive education programs in elementary schools throughout the United States has strengthened collaborative efforts between the general education classroom teacher and the network of supports available in the schools.

When student need and ability make it appropriate, instruction in *functional life skills* can be implemented. Students are taught only those skills that will help them succeed in practical matters related to the natural setting, whether it be the classroom, family, or neighborhood. As described by Brimer (1990), "The skills necessary for a person to control, modify, and interact with the environment receive the highest priority" (p. 364). Content areas taught within a functional approach might include daily living (e.g., self-care, consumer financing, and community travel), personal–social development (e.g., learning socially responsible behaviors), communication skills, recreational and leisure-time activities, and employment skills.

The functional life skills approach is based on the premise that, if these practical skills are not taught through formal instruction, they will not be learned. Most students do not need to be taught these skills because they have already learned them through everyday experience. However, this approach may be suited to students who cannot learn through basic skills or adaptive instruction approaches. This does not mean that students being taught using a functional approach are not also learning basic academic skills. Instruction may occur in these areas, but not in the same sequence as in the basic skills approach. For example, a functional life skills reading approach would initially teach frequently used words that are necessary for survival within the environment (e.g., danger, exit, and rest room signs) and then pair them directly with an environmental cue.

■THE SPECIAL EDUCATION REFERRAL, PLANNING, AND PLACEMENT PROCESS

focus 5

Identify the four steps in referring a child for special education services.

The special education referral, planning, and placement process as mandated in the Individuals with Disabilities Education Act (IDEA) involves four steps: (1) initiating the referral; (2) assessment of student educational need, eligibility, and disability classification; (3) developing the individualized education program (IEP); and (4) determining the least restrictive environment.

■INITIATING THE REFERRAL Referral for special education can occur at different times for different children, depending on type and severity of individual need. Children with more severe disabilities are likely to be referred prior to elementary school and have probably received early intervention and preschool services. For children with mild disabilities, referral is initiated at any time during elementary school as they appear to be having difficulty in academic or social learning. For these children, the general education teacher is the most likely referral source.

The referral begins with a request to the school's **child-study team** or **special services committee** for an assessment to determine the student's qualification for special education services. At a minimum, the child-study team consists of the school principal, the school psychologist, and a special education teacher. It may also include a general education teacher, a speech and language specialist, a school nurse, an occupational therapist, or other support personnel as determined by the child's needs. Once the team receives the referral, it may choose one of two paths: (1) attempt to modify or adapt current instruction in the general education class, or (2) conduct a **formal assessment** to determine the student's eligibility for special education services.

The first alternative, adaptive instruction, is intended to provide additional support services to children who may be at risk for educational failure without inappropriately placing the student in a special education program. Prior to implementing any modifications or adaptations to the child's instruction in the general education classroom, parents are notified that the child is having difficulty and are asked to meet with the school's child-study team. The team and the parents discuss the student's needs and recommend possible changes in instruction. Adaptations vary according to individual need but most often involve modifying curriculum, changing a seating arrangement, changing the length and difficulty of homework or classroom assignments, using peer tutors or volunteer parents to assist with instructional programs, or implementing a behavior management program. It is the responsibility of the general education teacher to implement the modified instruction and to assess the student's progress over a predetermined period of time. If the modifications yield success, there is no need to make a referral for special education. However, if the team determines that the child's educational progress is not satisfactory, the referral process for special education services continues.

If a formal referral for special education services is determined to be the appropriate path, the child-study team (now referred to as the multidisciplinary team, as described in IDEA) reviews the information documented by the classroom teacher and other education professionals, describing the child's needs. Documentation may include results from achievement tests, classroom performance tests, samples of student work, behavioral observations, or anecdotal notes (such as teacher journal entries). The team decides whether additional assessment information is needed in order to determine eligibility for special education. At this time *"a written notice must be provided to parents regarding their child's educational performance indicating that the school proposes to initiate or change the identification, evaluation, or educational placement of the child"* (Federal Register, 1977, p. 42,495). The content of the notice must include all of the following:

- A full explanation of the procedural safeguards available to the parents
- A description of the action proposed or refused by the agency, why the agency proposes or refuses to take the action, and a description of any options the agency considered and the reasons why those options were rejected
- A description of each evaluation procedure, test, record, or report the agency used as a basis for the proposal or refusal
- A description of any other factors relevant to the agency's proposal or refusal

Following a written notice the school must *seek consent in writing from the parents in order to move ahead with the evaluation process.* Informed consent means that parents

- have been fully informed of all information relevant to the activity for which consent is sought, in his or her native language or other mode of communication.
- understand and agree in writing to the carrying out of the activity for which his or her consent is sought, and the consent describes that activity and lists the record (if any) that will be released and to whom.
- understand that the granting of consent is voluntary on the part of the parent and may be revoked at any time.

■ ASSESSING EDUCATIONAL NEED, ELIGIBILITY, AND DISABILITY CLASSIFICATION Once written consent has been obtained from parents, the multidisciplinary team moves ahead to assess the child's educational need. The purpose of this assessment is to evaluate whether the child meets eligibility criteria under IDEA and to determine the need for special education services. The assessment should include the child's performance in both school and home environments. When the assessment process is complete, a decision is made regarding the child's eligibility for special education and his or her disability classification.

Presently, the most common way to classify students for special education services is the categorical approach, in which students are categorized based on individual characteristics. IDEA designates 12 categories of students with disabilities (such as specific learning disabilities, autism, etc.), or their counterparts as mandated in state law, as eligible for special services.

IDEA 97 allows states or LEAs (local education agencies) the option of defining students with disabilities between the ages of 3 and 9 as developmentally delayed. Developmental delays may be in one or more of the following areas: physical development, cognitive development, communication development, social or emotional development, or adaptive development. Proponents for maintaining the categorical approach argue that each of the 12 categories represents unique characteristics and needs. For example, students with behavior disorders have different traits and instructional needs than those with learning disabilities or mental retardation. According to the categorical approach, using a single label to identify all these students will not result in meeting their educational needs (Bryan, Bay, Lopez-Reyna, & Donahue, 1991; Lyon, 1996; Walker & Bullis, 1991).

Other professionals argue that such classification prohibits clearly defining or adequately differentiating the needs of these students in a classroom setting (Gottlieb, Alter, & Gottlieb, 1991; Kliewer & Biklen, 1996; Lilly, 1992; Reynolds, 1991). Kliewer and Biklen (1996) stated, "Labels block the essential agenda of good teaching, namely, inquiry through dialogue and interaction, teacher with student" (p. 93). Jenkins, Pious, and Jewell (1988) concluded, "We can see no justification for separating students by categorical labels" (p. 157). Finally, Reynolds (1991) indicated that the traditional approach to categorization results in unnecessary separation of students and "represents a large and expensive error" (p. 31).

Regardless of the approach to disability classification, once a student's eligibility for special education services is established, the next step is developing the IEP.

■ DEVELOPING THE IEP The cornerstone of a free and appropriate public education as defined in IDEA is the IEP (Schrag, 1996). The first step in IEP development is to determine the appropriate education professionals to be involved in the process and then to appoint someone (such as the special education teacher, school psychologist, or school principal) as the team coordinator. Among other responsibilities, the team coordinator serves as liaison between the school and the family. It is the responsibility of the coordinator to (1) inform parents regarding the process of

Snapshot

Ricardo

Ricardo, a third-grader at Bloomington Hill Elementary School, has recently been referred by his teacher, Ms. Thompson, to the school's special services committee for an evaluation. During the first four months of school, Ricardo has continued to fall further behind in reading and language. He entered third grade with some skills in letter and sound recognition, but had difficulty reading and comprehending material beyond a first-grade level. It was also clear to Ms. Thompson that Ricardo's language development was delayed as well. He had a very limited expressive vocabulary and had some difficulty following directions if more than one or two steps were involved.

Ricardo's mother, Maria Galleghos (a single parent), was contacted by Ms. Thompson to inform her that she would like to refer Ricardo for an in-depth evaluation of his reading and language skills. A representative from the school would be calling her to explain what the evaluation

meant and to get her approval for the necessary testing. The school psychologist, Jean Andreas, made the call to Ms. Galleghos. During the phone conversation Ms. Galleghos reminded the school psychologist that the primary language spoken in the home was Spanish even though Ricardo, his parents, and siblings spoke English as well. Ms. Andreas indicated that the assessment would be conducted in both Spanish and English in order to determine if Ricardo's problems were related to a disability in reading or problems with English as a second language.

Following written approval from Ricardo's mother, the school special services team conducted an evaluation of Ricardo's academic performance. The formal evaluation included achievement tests, classroom performance tests, samples of Ricardo's work, behavioral observations, and anecdotal notes from Ms. Thompson. An interview with Mrs. Galleghos was conducted as part of the process to gain her perceptions of Ricardo's strengths and problem

areas and to give her the opportunity to relate pertinent family history.

The evaluation confirmed his teacher's concerns. Ricardo was more than two years below what was expected for a child his age in both reading and language development. Ricardo's difficulties in these areas did not seem to be primarily related to the fact that he was bilingual, but the issue of English as a second language would need to be carefully taken into consideration in developing an appropriate learning experience.

The team determined that Ricardo qualified for special education services as a student with a specific learning disability. Once again, Ms. Andreas contacted Mrs. Galleghos with the results, indicating that Ricardo qualified for special education services in reading and language. Ms. Andreas pointed out that as a parent of a student with an identified disability, she had some specific legal rights, which would be further explained to her both in writing and orally.

One of those rights is to participate as a partner in the

development of Ricardo's individualized education program (IEP). Ms. Andreas further explained that a meeting would be set up at a mutually convenient time to develop a plan to assist Ricardo over the next year. Prior to that formal meeting, however, Ms. Andreas asked Ms. Galleghos to meet with her and the special education teacher, Mr. Lomas, to talk about how IEP teams work and what everyone needed to do in order to be prepared and work together to help Ricardo. Ms. Galleghos was asked to think about the long-range goals she has for Ricardo. What did she see as important for Ricardo to learn in school? What were her experiences at home that would help the team better understand Ricardo's needs and interests, particularly in the areas of reading and language development?

Source: From *Lifespan Perspectives on the Family and Disability* (p. 184), by J. Berry and M. Hardman, 1998, Boston: Allyn and Bacon.

IEP development, (2) work directly with parents in ascertaining their concerns regarding the IEP process, (3) assist parents in developing specific goals they would like to see their child achieve, (4) schedule IEP meetings that are mutually convenient for both team members and parents, and (5) lead the IEP meetings.

Prior to the IEP meeting, parents should be provided with written copies of all assessment information on their child. Individual conferences with members of the multidisciplinary team or a full team meeting may be necessary prior to developing the IEP in order to assist parents in understanding and interpreting assessment results. Analysis of the assessment information should include a summary of the child's strengths as well as areas in which the child may require special education services beyond his or her current program.

Once there is mutual agreement between educators and parents on the interpretation of the assessment results and the child's specific disability area, the team coordinator organizes and leads the IEP meeting. The purpose of this meeting is for the team (1) to agree upon the annual goals and objectives for the student; (2) to determine the necessary related services, if any, that the student requires; (3) to establish beginning and ending dates for special education services; and (4) to decide the least restrictive environment in which the student should receive special education services (see Figure 4.2).

■ DETERMINING THE LEAST RESTRICTIVE ENVIRONMENT

A student's educational placement is determined only after educators and parents have agreed upon annual goals and short-term objectives. The decision regarding placement rests upon the answers to two questions: First, what is the most appropriate placement for the student, given his or her annual goals? Second, which of the placement alternatives under consideration is consistent with the principle of the least restrictive environment? IDEA stipulates this principle as follows: "The student is to be educated with nondisabled peers to the maximum extent appropriate." (See Chapter 1 for a more in-depth analysis of the least restrictive environment provision in IDEA.)

Again, the IEP process is most successful when parents are viewed as valued and equal members of the team. Parents should be encouraged not only to share their expectations for the child, but also to express approval for or concerns about the goals, objectives, resources, or timelines that are being proposed by educators. The IEP must be the result of a collaborative process that reflects the views of both the school and the family.

Educational Collaboration: Sharing the Responsibility

Collaboration may be defined as

a dynamic framework for educational efforts which endorses collegial, interdependent and co-equal styles of interaction between at least two partners working jointly together to achieve common goals in a decision making process that is influenced by cultural and systemic factors. (Welch & Sheridan, 1995, p. 11)

focus 6

Define collaboration, and distinguish between the roles of the consulting teacher and resource-room teacher.

Several models for partnerships among general educators, special educators, and other support professionals in the public schools have been conceptualized and practiced in an effort to enhance each student's educational experience. We will discuss two of these models: the consulting-teacher model and the resource-room teacher model. Services provided through each collaborative model are intended to support a student in meeting the demands of the general education environment.

FIGURE 4.2   A sample individualized education plan (IEP)

Student's Primary Classification   Serious Emotional Disturbance

Secondary Classification   None

Classroom Observation Done
    Dates   1/15–2/25/98
    Personnel Conducting Observation   School Psychologist, Special Education
        Teacher, General Education Teacher

Present Level of Performance Strengths:
    1) Polite to teachers and peers
    2) Helpful and cooperative in the classroom
    3) Good grooming skills
    4) Good in sports activities

Access to General Education Curriculum

Diane will participate in all content areas within the general education curriculum.
Special education supports and services will be provided in the areas of math and
reading.

Effect of Disability on Access to General Education Curriculum

Emotional disabilities make it difficult for Diane to achieve at expected grade level
performance in general education curriculum in the areas of reading and math. It is
expected that this will further impact her access to the general education curriculum
in other content areas (such as history, biology, English) as she enters junior high
school.

Participation in Statewide or District Assessments

Diane will participate in all state and districtwide assessments of achievement. No
adaptations or modifications required for participation.

Justification for Removal from General Education Classroom:

Diane's objectives require that she be placed in a general education classroom with
support from a special education teacher for the majority of the school day. Based
on adaptive behavior assessment and observations, Diane will receive instruction in
a resource room for approximately one to two hours per day in the areas of social
skill development.

Reports to Parents on Progress toward Annual Goals:

Parents will be informed of Diane's progress through weekly reports of progress on
short-term goals, monthly phone calls from general ed teachers, special education
teachers, and school psychologist, and regularly scheduled report cards at the end of
each term.

Student Name   Diane

Date of Birth   5-3-87

Primary Language:
    HOME   English   Student   English

Date of IEP Meeting   April 27, 1998

Entry Date to Program   April 27, 1998

Projected Duration of Services   One school year

Services Required   Specify amount of time in educational and/or related services per
day or week

General Education Class   4–5 hours p/day

Resource Room   1–2 hours p/day

Special Ed Consultation in General Ed Classroom   Co-teaching and
consultation with general education teacher in the areas of academic and adaptive skills
as indicated in annual goals and short-term objectives.

Self-Contained   none

Related Services   Group counseling sessions twice weekly with guidance counselor.
Counseling to focus on adaptive skill development as described in annual goals and
short-term objectives

P.E. Program   45 min. daily in general ed PE class with support from adapted PE
teacher as necessary

Assessment

Intellectual   WISC-R

Educational   Key Math Woodcock Reading

Behavioral/Adaptive   Burks

Speech/Language

Other

Vision   Within normal limits

Hearing   Within normal limits

FIGURE 4.2 A sample individualized education plan (IEP) *(continued)*

Areas Needing Specialized Instruction and Support Team Signatures IEP Review Date _____

1. Adaptive Skills

LEA Rep. _____

Parent _____

- *Limited interaction skills with peers and adults*

Sp Ed Teacher _____

- *Excessive facial tics and grimaces*

Gen Ed Teacher _____

- *Difficulty staying on task in content subjects, especially reading and math.*

School Psych _____

Student (as appropriate) _____

- *Difficulty expressing feelings, needs, and interests*

Related Services Personnel (as appropriate) _____

2. Academic Skills

Objective Criteria and Evaluation Procedures _____

- *Significantly below grade level in math—3.9*

- *Significantly below grade level in reading—4.3*

Annual Review: Date: _____

Comments/Recommendations

IEP—Annual Goals and Short-Term Objectives	Persons Responsible	Objective Criteria and Evaluation Procedures
#1 ANNUAL GOAL: *Diane will improve her interaction skills with peers and adults.*	*General education teacher and special ed teacher (resource room)*	*Classroom observations and documented data on target behavior*
S.T. OBJ. *Diane will initiate conversation with peers during an unstructured setting twice daily.*	*School psychologist consultation*	
S.T. OBJ. *When in need of assistance, Diane will raise her hand and verbalize her needs to teachers or peers without prompting 80% of the time.*		

FIGURE 4.2 (continued)

IEP—Annual Goals and Short-Term Objectives	Persons Responsible	Objective Criteria and Evaluation Procedures
#2 ANNUAL GOAL: *Diane will increase her ability to control hand and facial movements.* S.T. OBJ. *During academic work, Diane will keep her hands in an appropriate place and use writing materials correctly 80% of the time.* S.T. OBJ. *Diane will maintain a relaxed facial expression with teacher prompt 80% of the time. Teacher prompt will be faded over time.*	General education teacher and special ed teacher (resource room) School psychologist consultation	*Classroom observations and documented data on target behavior*
#3 ANNUAL GOAL: *Diane will improve her ability to remain on task during academic work.* S.T. OBJ. *Diane will work independently on an assigned task with teacher prompt 80% of the time.* S.T. OBJ. *Diane will complete academic work as assigned 90% of the time.*	General education teacher and special ed teacher (resource room) School psychologist consultation	*Classroom observations and documented data on target behavior*
#4 ANNUAL GOAL: *Diane will improve her ability to express her feelings.* S.T. OBJ. *When asked how she feels, Diane will give an adequate verbal description of her feelings or moods with teacher prompting at least 80% of the time.* S.T. OBJ. *Given a conflict or problem situation, Diane will state her feelings to teachers and peers 80% of the time.*	General education teacher and special ed teacher (resource room) School psychologist consultation	*Classroom observations and documented data on target behavior*
#5 ANNUAL GOAL: *Diane will improve math skills one grade level.* S.T. OBJ. *Diane will improve rate and accuracy in oral 1- and 2-digit division facts to 50 problems per minute without errors.* S.T. OBJ. *Diane will improve her ability to solve word problems involving t—x—v.*	Collaboration of general education teacher and special education teacher through co-teaching and consultation	*Precision teaching* *Addison Wesley Math Program Scope and Sequence* *Districtwide Assessment of Academic Achievement*
#6 ANNUAL GOAL: *Diane will improve reading skills one grade level.* S.T. OBJ. *Diane will answer progressively more difficult comprehension questions in designated reading skills program.* S.T. OBJ. *Diane will increase her rate and accuracy of vocabulary words to 80 wpm without errors.*	Collaboration of general education teacher and special education teacher through co-teaching and consultation	*Precision teaching Barnell & Loft Scope and Sequence* *Districtwide Assessment of Academic Achievement*

125

■ THE CONSULTING TEACHER

The general education classroom teacher, particularly at the elementary level, is expected to teach nearly every school-related subject area. The elementary school classroom teacher is responsible for teaching the basic subjects—reading, writing, and arithmetic—as well as developing students' appreciation for the arts, good citizenship, and physical health. This teacher is trained as a generalist, acquiring basic knowledge of every subject area. However, when the general education classroom teacher is confronted with instructional needs beyond his or her experience and training, the result is often frustration for the teacher and failure for the student. Given the present structure of public education (large class size), it is unrealistic and unnecessary for classroom teachers to become specialists in every school subject.

Many school districts offer support to general education classroom teachers through the services of professionals with extensive background in certain areas, such as reading, arithmetic, language, motor development, and behavior and classroom management techniques. Professionals in these areas are usually referred to as **consulting teachers**, although the terms *support teachers, curriculum specialists, master teachers*, and *itinerant teachers* may also be used.

Effective consulting teachers usually have these characteristics: They are professionals with advanced training beyond the basic teacher certification program and are "knowledgeable about a variety of instructional strategies" (Schulz, Carpenter, & Turnbull, 1991). They build mutually trusting relationships through positive interactions with other professionals, are responsive to others, and have a good understanding of the dynamics of social interaction. They view consultation as a learning experience for themselves as well as for the professionals and students they serve. Consulting teachers can make both concrete, specific suggestions to improve students' educational experiences and can look at issues from broad theoretical perspectives. Finally, they are good researchers who know how to locate and use resources effectively (Lipsky & Gartner, 1996).

The consulting-teacher model offers training and support for general classroom teachers and emphasizes modifying the general education environment to accommodate students who are exceptional, rather than move them to separate settings. In a class of 25 to 30 children, 2 or more students are likely to have learning or behavioral needs that require the services of a consulting teacher.

■ THE RESOURCE-ROOM TEACHER

In the resource-room model, the student receives specialized instruction in a classroom that is separate from the general education setting but still within the same school building. Although still receiving the majority of instruction in their general education classroom, students go to the resource room for short periods to supplement their school curricula. The resource room is not intended to be a study hall, where students do their homework or spend time catching up on other classwork; it is under the direction of a qualified special education teacher. The role of the **resource-room teacher** is to provide individualized instruction in academic or behavioral areas that negatively affect each student's chances for success in the general education classroom. The resource-room teacher identifies high-risk skill areas in collaboration with an educational team that includes the student's general education classroom teacher. This team then develops and implements instruction to increase the student's proficiency to a level competitive with classmates in the general education classroom.

TECHNOLOGY AND INCLUSION AT WORK: HERE'S WHAT A FULLY INCLUDED CLASSROOM MIGHT LOOK LIKE

Melissa Graham's fifth grade urban class has 24 children, ranging in ability level from kindergarten to seventh grade, not an atypical situation for many teachers. What's different about Graham's class is that two special education children are fully included. Stephen is severely learning disabled with impaired visual–motor skills. Maria, a bilingual student, is a high-functioning Down syndrome youngster.

Graham believes that technology helps the fully-included students capitalize on their capabilities and helps her create child-centered learning opportunities. Graham teaches with thematic units and she stresses cooperative learning, both of which reinforce the inclusive nature of her classroom.

Stephen works at a Macintosh LC 520 and a laptop that the special education consultant has outfitted with IntelliKeys, a brightly colored alternative keyboard that allows Stephen to use a large arrow in lieu of a mouse. He also has a scanner for all written work, including homework assignments.

Also essential to Stephen's written communication is *Co-Writer*, a word prediction program that reduces the number of key strokes he has to type to create words and sentences. Stephen functions successfully close to grade level by using this technology.

Graham also uses regular technology programs with all her students during their current thematic unit on exploration. For instance, Maria avidly watches the video series *Building a Book with Sparkle* to help her create a dictionary that she uses in a cooperative group project on Christopher Columbus. The children in her group videotape Maria showing a page from her dictionary about Columbus, which they incorporate into a larger multimedia presentation.

Technology in Melissa Graham's class broadens the possibilities for the class as a whole. *Science in Motion: Planets in Motion,* for example, is a package whose videodisc presentation works well with the whole class and whose activity cards lend themselves to small-group activities in which Stephen and Maria can fully participate. There is a second audio track on the videodisc that has a simplified narration that Maria can review with other students.

In a classroom like Graham's, technology, in combination with innovative curriculum practices, enables all students to benefit academically and socially and prepares them to take their place in our diverse society.

*Barbara Hertz is a special education teacher with the Greenwich, Connecticut Public School System. In 1994, she took a leave from her teaching position to research how technology can aid the inclusion of special needs children. She was asked here to describe—both idealistically and realistically—how technology in an inclusive classroom might work. The children and teacher Ms. Hertz portrays are a compilation of the many special education students and teachers she has worked with over the years.

Source: "Here's What a Fully Included Classroom Might Look Like," by B. Hertz. From *Electronic Learning,* March 1994 issue. Copyright © 1994 by Scholastic Inc. Reprinted by permission of Scholastic Inc.

It can be anticipated that approximately 1 or 2 students in a classroom of 25 to 30 will need the additional instructional services offered by the resource-room program. To receive support for resource-room programs through federal and state special education funds, many schools must fulfill a state requirement that all students who receive direct special education services be labeled. In adherence to the concept of the least restrictive environment, therefore, students who receive instruction through resource-room programs, by definition, must have educational needs that require assistance beyond that available in general education classrooms.

The resource-room model has some important features that differ from the traditional self-contained special education classroom. The resource-room model allows students to remain with age-mates for the majority of the school day, eliminating a great deal of the stigma associated with segregated special education classrooms. The resource-room model also provides support to the general education classroom teacher, who, despite realizing that these students have potential for success in the general education classroom, finds it extremely difficult to provide appropriate individualized instruction without some assistance.

■ COLLABORATION THROUGH SCHOOLWIDE ASSISTANCE AND SUPPORT

The movement toward a stronger collaborative relationship among general educators, special educators, and other school support personnel has also emphasized developing schoolwide support or assistance to professionals and students. This essentially means sharing a school's human and material resources to meet the individual needs of students who are at risk or have disabilities. Typically, resources within a school are distributed based on standard staffing patterns: General educators work with "their kids," and special educators work with "their kids." Although this procedure may ensure equitable distribution of resources to students who are at risk or have disabilities, it is not sensitive to their varying needs. Flexibility is a necessary component of accommodating individual diversity.

To meet the challenges posed by student diversity, schools have developed support networks that facilitate collaboration among professionals. **Teacher assistance teams (TATs)**, sometimes referred to as schoolwide assistance teams (SWATs), involve groups of professionals, students, and/or parents working together to solve problems, develop instructional strategies, and support classroom teachers (Vaughn, Bos, & Schumm, 1997). TATs use strategies designed to assist teachers in making appropriate referrals of students who may need special education services as well as those at risk in the general classroom who may not qualify for such services but still need additional support (see the nearby Reflect on This feature).

■ THE ROLE OF THE GENERAL EDUCATION TEACHER

focus 7

Describe the role of the general education classroom teacher in meeting the needs of students with disabilities.

Today's classroom teachers are faced with growing diversity, including increasing numbers of students with disabilities, students from ethnically diverse backgrounds, and students at risk for educational failure due to a number of complex factors in their lives. General education teachers must meet the challenges of achieving increased academic excellence as mandated in the standards-based reform movement as well as responding to students with many different needs coming together in a common environment. The inclusion of students with disabilities in general education schools and classrooms need not be met with teachers' frustration, anger, or refusal. These reactions are merely symptomatic of the confusion surrounding inclusive education.

Inclusive education, in the worst cases, can be synonymous with dumping a student with disabilities, returning him or her to general education without any support service to the classroom teacher or to the student and at the expense of others in the class. As discussed earlier in this chapter, placing students in general education classrooms without needed support services is not in the best interests of either teachers or students.

General education classroom teachers often are responsible for implementing an appropriate educational program for students at risk or with a disability in conjunction with schools' TATs. To meet the needs of these students and to function as informed IEP team members as mandated in IDEA 97, general education classroom teachers should receive expanded training during their initial university preparation and as a component of their ongoing professional development. However, as suggested by Welch (1993), university teacher education programs "have not yet advanced to a similar acceptance of responsibility for students who are at risk of school failure because of learning or behavioral problems or physical disabilities" (p. 17).

Only the rhetoric regarding the importance of including students with disabilities in the teacher education reform discussion has increased dramatically in the past few

Reflect on This

COLLABORATING: WHAT'S MY ROLE AS A TEAM MEMBER?

A team is a group of professionals, parents, and/or students who join together to plan and implement an appropriate educational program for a student at risk or with a disability. Team members may be trained in different areas of study, including education, health services, speech and language, school administration, and so on. In the team approach, these individual people sit down together and coordinate their efforts to help the student, regardless of where or how they were trained. For this approach to work, each team member must clearly understand his or her role and responsibilities as a member of the team. Let's visit with some team members and have them share their perceived role in relationship to working with a student.

■ CONSULTANT OR RESOURCE-ROOM TEACHER

It's my responsibility to coordinate the student's individualized educational plan. I work with each member of the team to assist in selecting, administering, and interpreting appropriate assessment information. I maintain ongoing communication with each team member to ensure that

we are all working together to help the student. It's my responsibility to compile, organize, and maintain good, accurate records on each student. I propose instructional alternatives for the student and work with others in the implementation of the recommended instruction. To carry this out, I locate or develop the necessary materials to meet each student's specific needs. I work directly with the student's parents to ensure that they are familiar with what is being taught at school and can reinforce school learning experiences at home.

■ PARENTS

We work with each team member to ensure that our child is involved in an appropriate educational program. We give information to the team about our child's life outside school and suggest experiences that might be relevant to the home and the community. We also work with our child at home to reinforce what is learned in school. As members of the team, we give our written consent for any evaluations of our child and any changes in our child's educational placement.

■ SCHOOL PSYCHOLOGIST

I select, administer, and interpret appropriate psychological, educational, and behavioral assessment instruments. I consult directly with team members regarding the student's overall educational development. It is also my responsibility to directly observe the student's performance in the classroom and assist in the design of appropriate behavioral management programs in the school and at home.

■ SCHOOL ADMINISTRATOR

As the school district's representative, I work with the team to ensure that the resources of my district are used appropriately in providing services to the student. I am ultimately responsible for ensuring that the team's decisions are implemented properly.

■ GENERAL EDUCATION CLASSROOM TEACHER

I work with the team to develop and implement appropriate educational experiences for the student during the time that he or she spends in my classroom. I ensure that the student's experiences outside my classroom are consistent with the instruction he or she receives from me. In carrying out my responsibilities, I keep an accurate and continuous record of the student's progress. I am also responsible for referring any other students in my classroom who are at risk and may need specialized services to the school district for an evaluation of their needs.

These individuals generally constitute the core members of the team, but the team is not limited to this group. Depending on the needs of the student, many other professionals sometimes serve as team members, including speech and language specialists, social workers, school counselors, school nurses, occupational or physical therapists, adaptive physical education teachers, vocational rehabilitation counselors, juvenile court authorities, physicians, and school media coordinators.

---

years (Goodlad & Lovitt, 1993). In reality, a clear separation between general and special education teacher training programs remains the standard for the vast majority of universities in the United States. In a recent study of six states' implementation of the least restrictive environment clause of IDEA, Hasazi, Johnston, Liggett, and Schattman (1994) found that, in these states, university teacher education programs were not taking any leadership in statewide education reform agendas. On the contrary, they were viewed as barriers to change by state offices of education, school dis-

General education teachers face the challenges of working with a diversity of students that may include students from different ethnic backgrounds and students with disabilities.

tricts, and parents. These authors noted further that many universities are in a strategic position to promote preservice reform in both general and special education because they are receiving considerable funding through state and federal grants to develop in-service training initiatives in model development and innovative practices. Yet, in spite of these initiatives at the doorstep of research institutions, they are not being translated into curricula at the preservice level.

The role of the general education classroom teacher extends not only to working with students with mild differences, but also to involvement with those with more severe disabilities. Success in the general education environment for students with severe disabilities weighs heavily upon the cooperative relationship among the general education classroom teacher, special education teacher, and school support team. The general education classroom teacher works with the team to create opportunities for inclusion of students with disabilities in natural settings. Inclusion may be achieved by having the general education class serve as a homeroom for the student; by developing opportunities for students with severe disabilities to be with their nondisabled peers as often as possible during the day in activities such as recess, lunch, assemblies, and music classes; by developing a peer support program (Giangreco & Putnam, 1991; Sailor, Gerry, & Wilson, 1990; Stainback & Stainback, 1989); and by using multilevel instruction in the classroom setting. In **multilevel instruction,** teachers use different instructional approaches within the same curriculum adapted to individual need and functioning level. The process uses alternative presentation methods to teach key concepts. The teacher must be willing to accept varying types of student activities, evaluation procedures, and multiple outcomes (National Center on Educational Restructuring and Inclusion, 1994). The classroom teacher should also be knowledgeable in the following areas:

■ Understanding how a student's learning, behavior, communication, and physical differences affect his or her ability to acquire academic skills or cope socially in the educational environment
■ Identifying students who may be in need of additional educational support

Regular [General] Class Teachers

- Seek out assistance in your classroom from other professionals, emphasizing a cooperative or team-teaching approach to all children.
- Explore/observe a variety of teaching methods to learn different ways to tailor instruction to the multiple needs and learning styles of your students.
- Accept that not all students will cover the same material at the same time and that a variety of curricula (e.g., functional literacy, community mobility, and college preparation) are equally valid for different students.
- Above all, *be flexible.* This type of change takes time, and every teacher makes mistakes along the way as he or she learns to work with increasingly diverse students.

Special Educators (Teachers and Administrators)

- Recognize that the best service a special educator can provide is to enable a student to function independently in the real world. Each school should model that environment rather than create asylums for children. Special educators should define their role as enriching or supplementing the general education program, through consultation and in-class support, rather than as providing an alternative program.
- Creating an inclusive system will not mean that there will be fewer special educators, but that special educators will do a substantially different job. Discretionary monies should be focused on *joint* special education–general education teacher training efforts that build on the strengths of both fields.
- The school restructuring movement provides a window of opportunity for truly including students with special needs into the general student population. Special educators should be a part of every school governing counsel that has teacher representatives.

Source: From *Winners All: A Call for Inclusive Schools* (p. 29), by National Association of State Boards of Education, 1992, Alexandria, VA: Author. Reprinted with permission.

- Making referrals to the school teacher-assistance team for testing and evaluation of students perceived as being at risk
- Working with other IEP team members to develop and implement individualized instruction in the general education classroom
- Initiating and maintaining ongoing communication with parents

See Table 4.3 for strategies for maintaining successful inclusive classrooms.

■ PEER SUPPORT

One resource that is readily available within the school but often overlooked by classroom teachers is students. Peers can serve as a powerful support system within the classroom in both academic and social areas. They often have more influence on their classmates' behavior than the teacher does. Peer support programs may range from simply creating opportunities in the class for students with disabilities to socially interact with their nondisabled peers on a general education basis to highly structured programs of peer-mediated instruction. **Peer-mediated instruction** involves a structured interaction between two or more students under the direct supervision of a classroom teacher. This instruction generally falls into three areas: group-oriented contingency programs, **peer and cross-age tutoring,** and **cooperative learning.** As described by Zins, Curtis, Graden, and Ponti:

focus 8

Identify three types of peer support programs.

Peer tutoring is one way for a student with a disability to receive support in the general education classroom.

Cross-age and peer tutoring emphasize individual student learning, while cooperative learning emphasizes the simultaneous learning of students as they strive to achieve group goals or group rewards. Group contingencies provide consequences to group members based on group behavior, but they do not directly promote the goals inherent in cooperative learning, such as group collaboration. (1988, p. 114)

Peers are often very reliable and effective in implementing both academic and social programs with their classmates who have disabilities. Vaughn et al. (1997) indicated that "peers may be the most underrated and underused human resource available in general education classrooms" (p. 2360). The effectiveness of peers, however, is dependent on carefully managing the program so that students both with and without disabilities benefit. It is important for teachers to carefully select, train, and monitor the performance of students working as peer tutors (McDonnell et al., 1995; Vaughn et al., 1997).

Inclusive Elementary Schools and Classrooms

Since the publication of *A Nation at Risk* (National Commission on Excellence in Education, 1983), a great deal of effort has been expended to identify characteristics that together would constitute an effective school for *all* students. There seems to be a considerable level of agreement about the key factors that contribute to a student's success both in school and in postschool adjustment. Schools are most successful when they have the following attributes:

- High expectations for success that are linked with a clear and focused mission
- Strong instructional leadership with frequent monitoring of student progress

- Positive relationships with students' families
- Ongoing opportunities to learn for all students

Effective schools are inclusive schools. As suggested by the National Association of State Boards of Education (NASBE) (1992), inclusive schools are "based on the needs of the whole student and not merely the academic achievement of the central band of 'average' students." McDonnell (1993) further suggested that an effective inclusive school is one in which (1) educational programming for all students is individualized, (2) necessary support is provided to all students to ensure their success across learning environments, (3) educational practices have been validated, and (4) the school uses a transdisciplinary model to deliver services. A transdisciplinary model uses a collaborative or team approach to instruction. Team members (such as general educators, special educators, school psychologists, or speech and language therapists) cooperate in developing and implementing a student's instructional program (see the nearby Reflect on This feature).

focus 9
Describe the characteristics of effective inclusive schools and classrooms.

Another major component of the inclusive school is that students are educated in the school they would attend were they not disabled—the **home school** (Giangreco, Cloninger, & Iverson, 1994; Hardman et al., 1997; McLaughlin & Warren, 1992; NASBE, 1992). "All students are educated in their neighborhood school in age-appropriate regular [general] education classrooms and community sites shared by *all* students" (McLaughlin & Warren, 1992, p. 35).

Several factors appear to contribute directly to a school's ability to meet the needs of all students, including those with disabilities. Schools need to establish schoolwide support systems that use both general and special education resources in combination to benefit all students in the school (Bradley & King-Sears, 1997; Shulman & Doughty, 1995). The leadership of the school principal is vital. The principal should openly support the inclusion of all students in the activities of the school, advocate for the necessary resources to meet student needs, and strongly encourage cooperative learning and peer support programs (Gee, 1996; Giangreco et al., 1994; Stainback, Stainback,

& Ayres, 1996; Villa & Thousand, 1992). Inclusive classrooms are characterized by a philosophy that celebrates diversity, rewards collaboration among professionals, and teaches students how to help and support one another.

In the inclusive classroom, there is something for everyone (Bradley & Switlick, 1997; Hunt, Staub, Alwell, & Goetz, 1994; Jorgensen, 1992; Shulman & Doughty, 1995). Teachers and students work together in a problem-solving approach to ensure that the needs of all students are met in the classroom setting. Morsink, Thomas, and Correa (1991) described the process of working together as **interactive teaming**, whereby the team engages in a reciprocal effort to meet a common goal. To do so, members may take on a variety of roles, depending on the need and situation; for example, one member moves into the role of "expert" because he or she has more knowledge or skill in a content area. Through such reciprocity, members share their expertise with one another in "a reciprocal rather than an authoritarian manner" to solve any given problem (Morsink et al., p. 5). Team members will move in and out of the role of expert as a part of the collaboration process. Collaboration should always be viewed as a cooperative, not a competitive, endeavor.

Cooperative learning among students is also an essential element of inclusive classrooms. As with interactive teaming, students may take on various roles in the process. In one situation, the student may be a facilitator or an assistant working with, or providing help to, other students in a particular subject area, such as reading or social skills development. In another situation, the student becomes a learner who benefits from the knowledge or skills of another student (Jorgensen, 1992). Cooperative learning has been successful in teaching both basic academic and social interaction skills to students with and without disabilities (Graves & Bradley, 1997; Hunt et al., 1994; Johnson & Johnson, 1987, 1989). In a summary of the available research, Slavin (1991) reported that cooperative learning is

- most effective when it includes goals for both the group as a whole as well as individual members.
- beneficial for all students, from high achievers to students at risk for school failure.

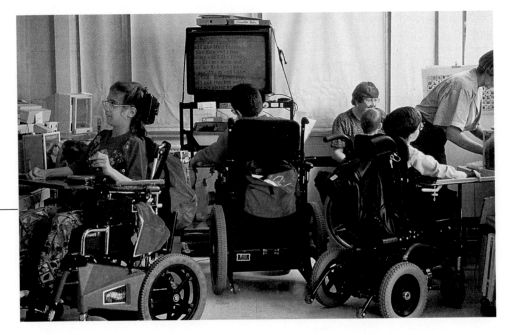

Students in a self-contained special classroom spend most, if not all, of their day working with the special education teacher.

- beneficial to student self-esteem, social relationships among group members, overall acceptance of students with disabilities, and attitudes toward school.

Special Education Classrooms and Schools

Some professionals and parents believe that inclusive education using a collaborative approach with general education may not be beneficial for some students with disabilities. They support a continuum of placements that include self-contained special education classrooms and special schools. In the judgment of these professionals and parents, some students require more intensive and specialized educational services provided in either a self-contained special education classroom or a special school for students with disabilities.

focus **10**
Describe special education classrooms and schools for students with disabilities.

■ THE SELF-CONTAINED SPECIAL EDUCATION CLASSROOM

In the self-contained special education classroom, a qualified special education teacher works with students with disabilities during most, if not all, of the school day. This teacher may still create opportunities for these students to interact with nondisabled peers whenever appropriate, for instance, through academically and nonacademically oriented classes, lunch and playground breaks, school events, peer-tutoring programs, and so forth.

■ THE SPECIAL SCHOOL

Students with disabilities may also be placed in special schools. Proponents of this arrangement have argued that the large numbers of students provide greater homogeneity in grouping and programming and therefore allow teachers to specialize in their subject areas. For example, one individual would teach art, another physical education, and a third math. In small programs, with only one or two teachers, teachers may be required to teach everything from art and home economics to academic subjects. Proponents have also argued that special schools provide for the centralization of supplies, equipment, and special facilities.

Opponents have argued that research on the efficacy of special schools does not support the proponents' rationale. Several authors have contended that, regardless of the severity of their disabling condition, children benefit from placement in a general education facility, where opportunities for inclusion with nondisabled peers are systematically planned and implemented (Ferguson et al., 1992; Gee, 1996; Sailor, Gee, & Karasoff, 1993; Snell, 1991; Stainback, Stainback, & Forest, 1989).

Full Inclusion and the Continuum of Placements

A growing number of both general and special educators have argued that, in spite of certain accomplishments of pull-out programs (removing the student with a disability from the general education classroom for at least part of the day), they have also caused some nega-

focus 11

Identify the arguments for and against the full inclusion of students with disabilities in general education classrooms.

tive effects or obstacles to the appropriate education of students with disabilities (Jenkins et al., 1990; Laski, 1991; Lipsky & Gartner, 1996; Sailor et al., 1993; Stainback & Stainback, 1991; Stainback et al., 1996). The proponents of full inclusion have argued that the current continuum of placements (see Chapter 1) is stigmatizing and fails to serve the individual needs of each student. Such programs result in a fragmented approach to the delivery of special education programs, with little cooperation between general and special educators.

The proponents of full inclusion have argued that general education classrooms that incorporate a partnership between general and special educators result in a diverse and rich learning environment, rather than just a series of discrete programming slots and funding pots. Such a partnership personalizes each student's instructional program and implements it in the least restrictive environment, rather than removing the child to a separate program. Additionally, special educators are more effective in a partnership because they can bring their knowledge and resources to assist general educators in developing intervention strategies that are directly oriented to student needs in the natural setting of the general education classroom. In a study of full-inclusion programs in school districts across four states, Morra (1994) found perceived gains in "the areas of social interaction, language development, appropriate behavior, and self-esteem. Academic progress was also noted. For the nondisabled students, parents and teachers perceived them becoming generally more compassionate, more helpful, and more friendly in relating to . . . students [with disabilities]" (p. 1).

Opponents of full inclusion (Braaten et al., 1988; Fuchs & Fuchs, 1991; Hocutt, 1996; Kauffman, 1991; Lieberman, 1996; Walker & Bullis, 1991) have argued that general education teachers have little expertise in assisting students with learning difficulties and are already overburdened with large class size and inadequate support services. Special educators have been specifically trained to develop instructional strategies and use teaching techniques (e.g., behavior management) that are not part of the training of general education teachers. More specialized academic and social instruction can be realized in a pull-out setting, where students can more effectively prepare to return to the general education classroom. Specialized pull-out settings also allow for centralization of both human and material resources. In the study of inclusive education programs in four states just noted, Morra (1994) found that inclusion programs were viewed by the schools as not being for everyone. School districts indicated that they were struggling with the difficult challenges of "(1) severely emotionally disturbed students who disrupt classrooms and (2) students with learning disabilities who may need a more highly focused, less distracting learning environment than that presented by the general education classroom" (p. 1).

A question appropriate to both supporters and detractors of shared responsibility asks whether professionals in the education system—including school administrators, general class teachers, and special educators—are ready to embrace full inclusion in general education classrooms for students with disabilities. Jenkins et al. (1990, pp. 481–482, 489) have formulated several questions that schools should address in assessing their readiness for full inclusion:

1. To what extent do classroom teachers accept responsibilities for (a) educating all students assigned to them; (b) making and monitoring major instructional decisions for all students in their class; (c) providing instruction that follows a normal developmental curriculum in the basic skills area that is designed to bring students to a level of adult competence; (d) managing instruction for di-

verse populations; and (e) seeking, using, and coordinating assistance for students who require more intense services than those provided to their peers?

2. To what extent do principals have sufficient knowledge about instruction and learning to distribute resources across classrooms so that students with special needs can be accommodated and served effectively?

3. To what extent are "specialists" . . . able to collaborate and communicate with classroom teachers and relinquish to them final authority regarding instructional decision making?

4. To what extent are multidisciplinary teams prepared to require hard evidence that students have received high-quality direct instruction from classroom teachers and support staff?

5. Are multidisciplinary teams prepared to decide that students will not develop competency in basic skills during their school career, and recommend that the students be segregated from their general education classroom peers?

During the elementary years, educational teams are confronted with some difficult decisions about how and what to teach. These decisions must take into account factors such as the student's age, previous learning history, performance demands in the natural setting, and available resources. In addition, educators must consider constraints in making efficient use of limited instructional time. As students with disabilities approach adolescence and eventually the adult years, their life space increases to include a much larger and more heterogeneous environment called "community." In the next chapter, we look at services and supports for adolescents with disabilities during middle school and high school. The chapter includes an exploration of the transition out of school and into life in the community as an adult.

Case Study

JERALD

Jerald will be in the third grade at Robert F. Kennedy Elementary School. Kennedy is a large urban school with a number of students from low economic and culturally diverse backgrounds. Many of its students are described as "disadvantaged" and at significant risk of school failure.

"Jerry is an outgoing kid who loves to talk about anything to anyone at anytime," says his mother. His teacher, Miss Robins, complains that he's "hyperactive, inattentive, and a behavior problem." Both mom and dad and his

teacher agree that Jerald has a great deal of difficulty controlling his emotions.

Mom: I just wish he wasn't so easily frustrated at home when things aren't going his way.

Miss Robins: He's always in a state of fight or flight. When he is in a fighting mode, he hits, teases, and screams at me or the other students. When in a state of "flight," he withdraws and refuses to comply with any requests. He may even put his head on his desk and openly cry to vent his frustrations.

Last year at school, his "fight" behavior increased considerably. Ms. Roberts, his second-grade teacher, reported that "he made very little progress and was uncontrollable—a very disruptive influence on the other children in the class." In the spring, she initiated a referral to assess his eligibility for special education services. His overall assessment indicated that he was falling further behind in reading (word decoding skills at grade level 1.9; reading comprehension at grade level 1.3), and math (grade level 2.1). Behaviorally, he has difficulty expressing his feelings in an

appropriate manner. He is impulsive, easily distracted, and not well liked by his peers.

After determining his eligibility for special education services, the school multidisciplinary team focused his IEP on the following goals:

■ Improving daily interactions with teachers and peers
■ Developing skills to manage his own behavior when faced with difficult or frustrating situations
■ Upgrading reading and math achievement to grade level

The big issue for the team, which includes Jerald's parents, is where he should be placed next year to implement the IEP. Miss Robins and the school principal are concerned that his disruptive behavior will be too difficult to control in a general education classroom. They would like to see him placed in a special class for students who are emotionally disturbed. They are concerned not only for Jerald's education but also the negative effect he has on his classroom peers. Ms. Roberts reported that last year she had to spend a very disproportionate amount of her time dealing with Jerald's inappropriate behavior.

In considering the views of Jerald's teachers and the school principal, the team is considering placement in a self-contained class for students with emotional disturbance. Such a class is not available at his home school, so Jerald would have to be transported to a special education program in another location. The special education resource-room teacher has an alternative point of view, preferring to work on a program of collaborative support for Jerald in the fourth-grade class. She proposes using some cooperative learning techniques, co-teaching, and ongoing support from the school psychologist. Jerald's parents, while recognizing that his disruptive behavior is increasing and that he is falling further behind academically, are reluctant to have him transferred to another school because it would remove him from his family and neighborhood supports. His brother, who is in the fifth grade, also goes to Kennedy Elementary.

■ **APPLICATION**

What do you see as the important issues to consider in deciding what educational setting would be most appropriate to meet Jerald's needs?

In addition to the recommendations made by the special education resource-room teacher, what suggestions would you have relative to the accommodations Jerald would need, should he remain in a third-grade class at his home school?

Debate Forum

PERSPECTIVES ON FULL INCLUSION

Full inclusion: Students are placed in a general education classroom for the entire school day. The necessary support services to ensure an appropriate education come to the student in the general education class setting; the student is *not* "pulled out" into a special education classroom for instruction.

■ **POINT**

We must rethink our current approach to the educational placement of students with disabilities. Pulling these students out of general education classrooms and into separate, segregated settings does not make sense from a standpoint of both values and "what works." From a values standpoint, inclusion is the "right thing to do." Forest (1991) said it best: "All children need to learn with and from other children. . . . All children need to belong and feel wanted and loved. . . . All children need to have fun and enjoy noise and laughter in their lives. . . . All children need to take risks and fall and cry and get hurt. . . . All children need to be in real families and real schools and real neighborhoods" (p. 403).

■ **COUNTERPOINT**

No one is questioning the value of children belonging, of being a part of society. However, it is not necessarily true that placing a child with a disability in a general education classroom means that he or she will "belong." A student with a disability can be as isolated socially in a general education class setting as in a special class 1,000 miles away. How do you translate values into action when the social and academic needs of these students are beyond the expertise of a general education teacher? We must separate the vision from the reality. General education does not have the inclination or the expertise to meet the diverse needs of all students with disabilities. General education is already overburdened with the increasing number of at-risk students, large class sizes, and an inadequate support system.

■ **POINT**

Let's separate reality from vision. The reality is special education has failed; it does not work (Lipsky & Gartner, 1996). Setting the values inherent in the inclusion of all students aside, let's look at the reality (Valdes, Williamson, & Wagner, 1990; Wagner & Blackorby, 1996):

■ Only 56% of students in special education graduate with a diploma.
■ Thirty-eight percent drop out of school.
■ Thirty-one percent receive failing grades in school.

- Only 55% of special education graduates and 40% of the dropouts are employed following their exit from school.
- Only 21% of special education graduates and 5% of the dropouts pursue any type of postsecondary training.

Valdes et al. also pointed out that having positive experiences in school, including interactions with nondisabled peers, puts students with disabilities on a better trajectory toward successful transition into adult life. Several other authors (Lipsky & Gartner, 1996; Reynolds, 1991; Stainback et al., 1996) have noted that there is no evidence that pulling them out of general education classrooms benefits students with disabilities.

■ COUNTERPOINT

There is always a flip side to the research coin. What about the following research findings?
- Ninety-four percent of all educators believe there have been significant improvements in the education of students with disabilities over the past decade.
- Seventy-seven percent of the parents of students with disabilities are satisfied with their special education program (Harris & Associates, 1989).
- Parents of students with disabilities are more satisfied with the public schools than parents of nondis-

abled school-age children (Robert Wood Johnson, 1988).

Additionally, on what basis do you attach blame to special education for low graduation and high dropout rates or for the lack of access to postsecondary education? Because 94% of all students with disabilities are spending at least a portion of their day in general classes, shouldn't we be looking at the system as a whole, not just special education, in trying to deal with student failure? Concerning the high unemployment rate for people with disabilities, shouldn't we look at the failure of adult services to expand opportunities for individuals to receive the necessary training and support to find and succeed in community employment settings?

The conclusions from researchers that special education has failed can be countered by other investigators who reached a very different interpretation (e.g., Hallahan et al., 1988; Hocutt, 1996; Kauffman, 1991). These researchers, while calling for improvements in special education, don't support its abolition.

■ POINT

We could forever argue the point about what the research supports or doesn't support, and still not reach any agreement. Let's come back to the

issue of values and reality. The goal behind full inclusion is to educate students with disabilities with their nondisabled peers in a general education class setting, as a means to increase their access to, and participation in, all natural settings. The general education classroom is a microcosm of the larger society. For the preschool-age child, the world is defined primarily through family and a small same-age peer group. As the child gets older, the world expands to the neighborhood, to the school, and eventually to the larger heterogeneous community. As educators, we must ask how we can educate the child with a disability to foster full participation as the life space of the individual is expanded. What are the barriers to full participation, and how do we work to break them down? A partnership between general and special education is a good beginning to breaking down barriers. Each professional brings his or her knowledge and resources into a single setting in the development of an instructional program that is directly oriented to student need. This unified approach to instruction will provide teachers with the opportunity to work across disciplines and gain a broader understanding of the diversity in all children. Pull-out programs result in a fragmented approach to instruction with lit-

tle cooperation between general and special education.

Finally, students in pull-out programs are much more likely to be stigmatized. Separate education on the basis of a child's learning or behavioral characteristics is inherently unequal.

■ COUNTERPOINT

The value of full inclusion is a laudable goal, but one nevertheless that is misguided as an achievable or even desirable outcome for all students with disabilities. The reality is that specialized academic and social instruction can best be provided, at least for some students, in a pull-out setting. These more restricted settings are the least restrictive environment for some students. Pull-out programs will more effectively prepare the student to return to less restricted settings, such as the general education class. A move to full inclusion will result in the loss of special education personnel who have been trained to work with students who have diverse needs. In spite of the rhetoric about collaboration between general and special education, the responsibilities for the student's education in a full-inclusion classroom will move to the general education class teacher with little or no support. The result will be dumping these students into an environment that will not meet their needs.

Review

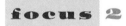focus 1

Why is it so important to provide early intervention services as soon as possible to students at risk?

- The first years of life are important to the overall development of all children—normal, at risk, and disabled.
- Early stimulation is crucial to the later development of language, intelligence, personality, and self-worth.
- Early intervention can prevent and lessen the overall impact of disabilities as well as counteract the negative effects of delayed intervention.
- Early intervention may in the long run be less costly and more effective than providing services later in the individual's life.

focus 2

Identify the critical components of programs for preschool-age children under Public Law 99–457.

- A child-find system must be established in each state to locate young children at risk and make referrals to appropriate agencies for preschool services.
- An individualized education program (IEP) must be developed for each eligible child using a multidisciplinary approach.
- Specialists from several disciplines and at least one of

the parents must participate in the development and implementation of an IEP for each child.

focus 3

Identify three characteristics of special education that enhance learning opportunities for students with disabilities.

- Individualization
- Intensive instruction
- The explicit teaching of basic, adaptive, and/or functional life skills

focus 4

What is meant by adaptive fit and adaptive instruction for students with disabilities?

- The degree to which an individual is able to cope with the requirements of the school setting is described as adaptive fit.
- The purpose of adaptive instruction is to modify the learning environment to accommodate the unique learning characteristics and needs of individual students.
- Adaptive instruction focuses on assessing each student's individual characteristics and capabilities.

focus 5

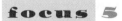
Identify the four steps in referring a child for special education services.

- Initiating the referral

- Assessing the student's educational need and eligibility for special education
- Developing the individual education program
- Determining the least restrictive environment

focus 6

Define collaboration, and distinguish between the roles of the consulting teacher and resource-room teacher.

- Collaboration is a dynamic framework for educational efforts that endorses collegial, interdependent, and co-equal styles of interaction between at least two partners working together to achieve common goals in a decision-making process that is influenced by cultural and systemic factors.
- Consulting teachers work directly with general education classroom teachers on the use of appropriate assessment techniques and intervention strategies. Students who work with consulting teachers are not removed from the general education classroom program but remain with their nondisabled peers while receiving additional instructional assistance.
- Resource-room teachers provide specialized instruction to students with disabilities in a classroom that is separate from the general education room. Under the resource-room program, the student still receives the majority of instruction in

the general education classroom, but is removed from the general education class for short periods to supplement his or her educational experience.

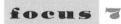focus 7

Describe the role of the general education classroom teacher in meeting the needs of students with disabilities.

- To understand how a student's learning, behavior, communication, and physical differences affect his or her ability to acquire academic skills and cope socially in the educational environment
- To identify students who may be in need of additional educational support
- To make referrals to the team for testing and evaluation of students perceived as being at risk
- To work with team members to develop and implement individualized instruction in the general education classroom
- To initiate and maintain ongoing communication with parents
- To use nondisabled peers effectively as support for students with disabilities

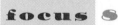focus 8

Identify three types of peer support programs.

- Peer-mediated instruction
- Peer and cross-age tutoring
- Cooperative learning

focus 9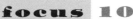

Describe the characteristics of effective inclusive schools and classrooms.

- Educational programming is individualized.
- Support is provided to all students regardless of their instructional needs.
- Effective educational practices have been validated.
- A transdisciplinary model is used to deliver instruction.
- Students with disabilities are educated in the school they would attend, were they not exceptional.
- Strong leadership from the principal is evident.
- Teachers and students work together to tackle difficult challenges.

focus 10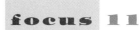

Describe special education classrooms and schools for students with disabilities.

- The self-contained special education classroom employs the expertise of a qualified special education teacher to work with students who have disabilities, for all or part of the school day.
- The self-contained-classroom teacher may still create opportunities for students with disabilities to interact with nondisabled peers whenever appropriate.
- Special schools provide services for large numbers of students with disabilities in a setting away from a general education school and classroom.

focus 11

Identify the arguments for and against the full inclusion of students with disabilities in general education classrooms.

- *Arguments for the full inclusion of students in the general education classroom.* (1) The current system of pulling students out of general education simply does not work; (2) pull-out programs result in a fragmented approach to the delivery of special education, with little cooperation between general and special educators; and (3) students in pull-out programs are stigmatized when segregated from their nondisabled peers.
- *Arguments for removing students to separate environments.* (1) General education teachers have little expertise to assist students with learning difficulties and are already overburdened with large class sizes and inadequate support services; (2) special educators have been specifically trained to develop instructional strategies and use teaching techniques that are not part of the training of general education teachers; (3) more specialized academic and social instruction can be provided in pull-out settings, and such settings can more effectively prepare students to return to the general education classroom; and (4) specialized pull-out settings allow for centralization of both human and material resources.

5

Transition from School and the Adult Years

To begin with . . .

A successful schooling experience will provide the student with the tools and skills necessary to make the transition effectively to the next stage of life. For some, this means going on to college or another educational experience. For others, it means entering the workforce. . . . For students with severe disabilities . . . long-term outcomes (e.g., degree of independence, employment) are designated through the IEP process; instruction then focuses on building skills that will lead to these outcomes in age-appropriate natural settings. . . . For students with mild disabilities, a combination of academic, vocational, and functional outcomes is often selected with the specific mix of components dependent on individual student goals and needs. (National Research Council, 1997, pp. 119, 120)

While the percentage of students completing high school has remained steady for all students, the percentage of students with disabilities completing high school has increased slightly in the past few years. This is especially noteworthy because research shows that fewer dropouts with disabilities return to school for a diploma or GED. Some educational services, such as tutoring, counseling, and enrollment in occupational courses, appear to reduce dropout rates for students with disabilities. (U.S. Department of Education, 1997, pp. iv–16)

The process of transition from youth to adulthood has received considerable attention in recent educational and social science literature. Organized initiatives in special education and vocational rehabilitation support the notion that transition planning is necessary for students with disabilities to ensure that their educational experiences will maximize their independence and self-sufficiency. . . . Unfortunately, the school-to-work transition approach has not yet been fully applied to the transition from public school special education services to institutions of higher education. In that process, students with disabilities often encounter inadequate vocational rehabilitation services and universities and colleges ill-prepared to meet their transition needs. Choosing to attend college rather than going directly to work after high school may place students with disabilities at a disadvantage, because formalized transition policies have not been established to address the higher education option. (Gartin, Rumrill, & Serebreni, 1996, p. 33)

People with disabilities are well aware of the tools they need to achieve independence. Advances in policy, science, and technology are available to support independence as never before. . . . Progress requires a dedicated commitment from all sectors of society—policy makers, people with disabilities and their allies, state and local government officials, non-profit organizations, the private sector, and the media. The achievement of independence for people with disabilities is a test of the very tenets of our democracy. It is a test we can pass. (Dart, cited in National Council on Disability, 1996, p. 7)

Lee

Lee is a high school student with a part-time job stocking shelves at a local store. Lee walks from his high school to catch the bus to work. On his way to the bus, everyone says hello to Lee. He's a great friend to everybody. Everyone makes it a point to stop and ask how he's doing.

At work, his employer gives him a checklist indicating how many cases of each item Lee needs to bring from the backroom to stock on the shelves. Lee can't read, but he can associate the item with the cases in the backroom. Most of Lee's education occurs in the community with the assistance of peer tutors who help him learn to purchase foods, bank, use the bus, and perform various work functions.

In his high school classes, Lee also has access to peer tutors who work with him. They may provide one-on-one tutoring or participate with him in a weight lifting class. They are invaluable to him and his teachers.

Lee has become much more independent because of the skills he has learned in school and practiced in the community. Eventually, he plans to live in an independent living environment.

Albert

From the time he was 16 years old, Albert's high school program had placed a strong emphasis on planning for his transition from school to adult life. During the first two years of high school, Albert spent part of his day in traditional core subjects such as math and science, working with a general education and special education team on academic and adaptive skill development. The remainder of his day was spent outside the classroom in experiences focusing on employment training, recreation, and management of his personal life. As graduation grew nearer, Albert spent more and more of his school day in an on-the-job employment training program. During his high school years, employment training had included sampling various jobs in the local community to match his interests and abilities with the demands of various employment opportunities. Albert was provided on-the-job training and support from teachers and other school staff, vocational education personnel, and vocational rehabilitation counselors. In his final year of high school, Albert was hired to work in housekeeping and laundry at a local hotel, where he continued to receive training and support from school personnel. The transition program also focused on helping Albert learn how to access various community activities, such as parks, theaters, and restaurants. His training also included hygiene, use of a personal schedule, and a time management system.

---

fOR MANY YEARS, the development of appropriate services for people who are exceptional, particularly those with disabilities, has focused primarily on school-age children. As we enter the 21st century, a crucial issue faces students, parents, and professionals: What is the relationship between school instruction and individual needs and preferences during adulthood? There are some substantial reasons why this issue is receiving a great deal of attention.

Research has suggested that many individuals with disabilities are not able to access the services necessary for success in postsecondary education or in the community, either during high school or following graduation (Gartin et al., 1996; Hasazi et al., 1989; Valdes, Williamson, & Wagner, 1990; Wagner & Blackorby, 1996). Sitlington and Frank (1990) surveyed students with learning disabilities one year after their graduation from high school. These researchers found that, although 50% of these students had been enrolled in postsecondary programs, only 6.5% were still in school at the time of the survey.

focus 1
Cite three reasons why it is important to plan for the transition of students with disabilities from school to adult life.

A 1994 Harris poll found that (1) three of ten adults with disabilities were working full- or part-time; (2) 79% of those not working and of working age indicated that they would like to have jobs; and (3) a comparison of working and nonworking individuals with disabilities revealed that those who were working were more satisfied with life, had more money, and were less likely to blame their disability for preventing them from reaching their individual potential (Harris & Associates, 1994).

A study in Vermont directly linked employment following school to an effective transition-planning process that included opportunities for students with disabilities to work while still in school. Researchers at the University of Vermont found that students with disabilities who were employed prior to leaving high school were more likely to be employed as adults and that participation in vocational education was related to eventual employment and higher wages (Hasazi et al., 1989). The U.S. Department of Education's National Longitudinal Transition Study (Valdes et al., 1990; Wagner & Blackorby, 1996) reported that paid employment during high school had become more common, with 42% of students with disabilities being placed in community vocational or employment programs. However, one out of four of these students worked fewer than 10 hours per week and was paid below minimum wage. Additionally, most students were in service and manual labor positions. Five years out of high school, 57% of these students were in competitive employment and 43% of this group was working full-time. The employment rate of individuals with disabilities thus lagged far beyond those of nondisabled adults.

The increasing emphasis on the transition from school to adult life has altered many previously held perceptions about people with disabilities. Without question, the potential of adults with disabilities has been significantly underestimated. In recent years, professionals and parents have begun to address some of the crucial issues facing adolescents with disabilities as they prepare to leave school and face life as adults in their local communities. More than 440,000 students with disabilities exit school each year (U.S. Department of Education, 1997). Since the passage of Public Law 94-142 in 1975 (now IDEA), schools have made significant strides in preparing youth with disabilities for adult life, but much remains to be done. Of the students exiting school, only 28% leave with a high school diploma. Many of the current graduates from special education programs are not adequately prepared for employment and are unable to access further education. They are not able to locate the critical programs and services necessary for success as adults in their local communities (Bursuck & Rose, 1992; Florian & West, 1991; McDonnell, Hardman, McDonnell, & Kiefer-O'Donnell, 1995; Nisbet, 1992). For individuals with more severe disabilities, long waiting lists for employment and housing services prove frustrating. Individuals with disabilities who enroll in postsecondary education will often find that the supports and services necessary for them to find success in college are not available (Gartin et al., 1996).

Transition Planning and Services

The transition from school to adult life is a complex and dynamic process that should begin as early as possible. Transition planning should culminate with the transfer of support from the school to an adult service agency, access to postsecondary education, or life as an independent adult. The planning process involves a series of choices about which experiences would best prepare students with disabilities in their remaining school years for what lies ahead in the adult world. A successful transition from school to the adult years requires both formal (government-sponsored) and natural family supports (McDonnell et al., 1995; Morningstar, Turnbull, & Turnbull, 1996; Szymanski, 1994; Super, 1990; Turnbull et al., 1992). Historically, providing formal supports, such as health care, employment preparation, and supported living, has been emphasized. Only recently has society begun to understand the importance of the family and other natural support networks in preparing the adolescent with disabilities for adult life. Research (Morningstar et al., 1996; Hasazi et al., 1989) suggests that the family unit may be the single most powerful force in preparing the adolescent with disabilities for the adult years.

Legal Requirements for Transition Services

The requirement that every student with a disability receive transition services was enacted as law through the 1990 amendments to the Individuals with Disabilities Education Act (IDEA) and modified by Congress in IDEA 97. Under current law, the term **transition services** means a coordinated set of activities for a student with a disability. These activities

focus 2
How does IDEA define transition services?

- are designed within an outcome-oriented process, which promotes movement from school to postschool activities, including postsecondary education, vocational training, integrated employment (including supported employment), continuing and adult education, adult services, independent living, or community participation.
- are based upon the individual student's needs, taking into account the student's preferences and interests.
- include instruction, related services, community experiences, the development of employment and other postschool adult living objectives, and, when appropriate, acquisition of daily living skills and functional vocational evaluation. (Sec. 602[30])

IDEA requires that beginning at age 14, and updated annually, a student's IEP must include a statement of the transition services that relate to various courses of study (such as participation in advanced placement courses or a vocational education program). Beginning at age 16 (or younger, if determined appropriate by the IEP team), an IEP should include a statement of needed transition services, including, when appropriate, a statement of the responsibilities of other agencies (such as vocational rehabilitation) or any other needed linkages.

Four other pieces of federal legislation are also important in the transition planning process: the Vocational Rehabilitation Act (as amended in 1992), the Carl Perkins Vocational and Applied Technology Education Act of 1990 (PL 98-524), the Americans with Disabilities Act of 1990 (ADA), and the School-to-Work Opportunities Act of 1993. The Vocational Rehabilitation Act provides services through rehabilitation counselors in several areas (such as guidance and counseling, vocational evaluation, vocational training and job placement, transportation, family services, interpreter services, and telecommunication aids and devices). The 1992 amendments to the act encourage stronger collaboration and outreach between the schools and the rehabilitation counselors in transition planning.

focus 3
What information should be included in each student's IEP statement for transition services? Who should be involved in the planning process?

Greater linkages between education and vocational rehabilitation are expected to benefit the student with a disability in moving on to postsecondary education or in obtaining employment. The Carl Perkins Act provides students with disabilities greater access to vocational education services. ADA focuses on equal access to public accommodations, employment, transportation, and telecommunication services following the school transition years. Such services are often directly targeted as a part of the student's transition plan. The School-to-Work Act is intended to provide *all* students in the public schools with education and training to prepare them for first jobs in high-skill, high-wage careers and for further education following high school. Students with disabilities are specifically identified as a target population of the act.

Although educators and others disagree about which programs best bridge the gap between school and adult life, they do agree on the principal components of a transition system. They include the following services:

- Effective school programs that link instruction to community activities and demands
- A cooperative system of transition planning that ensures access to needed postschool services
- An array of adult services to meet the unique educational, employment, residential, and leisure needs of youths with disabilities (McDonnell et al., 1995)

Transition is much more than the mere transfer of administrative responsibility from the school to an adult service agency. It involves many agencies as well as the student and the family in developing activities and services that are appropriate to the individual.

The Individualized Transition Plan (ITP)

The vehicle for identifying and delivering transition services for students with disabilities is the **individualized transition plan (ITP)** (see Figure 5.1). The ITP is a statement within the IEP describing needed transition services. The purpose of the transition statement is to identify the range of services needed by the individual, identify activities that must occur during high school to facilitate the individual's access to adult programs if necessary, and establish timelines and responsibilities for completion of these activities. Wehman (1996) identified seven basic steps in the formulation of a student's ITP: (1) organize ITP teams for all transition-age students; (2) organize a circle of support; (3) identify key activities; (4) hold initial ITP meetings as part of annual IEP meetings; (5) implement the ITP through secondary school and adult services provision; (6) update the ITP annually during the IEP meetings, and implement quarterly follow-up procedure; and (7) hold an exit meeting (see Table 5.1).

McDonnell et al. (1995) suggested that the development of a formal transition plan is important because it establishes a working agreement between the school, the student, parents, and adult service agencies. For one student, the ITP may reflect services and supports necessary for access to postsecondary education; for another, the ITP may focus on employment, supported living, and recreation and leisure.

■ INVOLVING STUDENTS AND PARENTS

In the transition from school to the adult world, many students and parents receive a considerable shock. They realize that the services they were entitled to during the school years are no longer mandated by law. As such, they may experience

FIGURE 5.1   Transition statement in the area of work experience for a student with a severe disability

BACKGROUND INFORMATION	PARTICIPANTS
Student Name: _Lisa O'Neil_	Parents: _Sarah and Gene O'Neil_
Meeting Date: _3/25/98_	School Principal: _Sally Monroe_
Place of Meeting: _Eastridge High School_	Special Education Teacher: _Dennis Cochran_
Proposed Graduation Date: _6/2000_	School Psychologist: _George Rivera_

PLANNING AREA: _Work Experience in Outdoor Recreation_

Transition Goal: _Lisa will initiate a work experience program for a minimum of 10 hours per week through the local parks and recreation program, state fish and game department, and/or national forest service._

SUPPORT ACTIVITIES	RESPONSIBLE PERSON	TIMELINES
Complete application to the appropriate agency for work experience program	Lisa O'Neil w/support from Dennis Cochran	4/15/98
Determine most appropriate work experience site along public transportation route	Team members	5/15/98
Contact vocational rehabilitation and local job service agency to identify personnel to be involved in transition plan	Dennis Cochran	5/15/98
Schedule work experience program into school schedule	Dennis Cochran George Rivera	6/1/98
Meet with director of selected agency to set up logistics for work experience program	Lisa O'Neil Mr. and Mrs. O'Neil Dennis Cochran	9/15/98
Handle logistics for public transportation to and from work experience site (e.g., insurance, backup, etc.); approve off-campus community-based program	Sally Monroe	9/15/98
Obtain public transit bus pass	Mr. and Mrs. O'Neil	9/15/98
Teach bus route to and from work experience site	Dennis Cochran	10/1/98
Develop objectives for Lisa based on work experience requirements on site	Team members and identified agency supervisor	10/1/98
Begin work experience program	School: Dennis Cochran Training site: Identified agency supervisor	10/15/98
Evaluate progress toward identified work experience objectives	Team members	ongoing

[_Source:_ Adapted from _Lifespan Perspectives on the Family and Disability_ (p. 221), by J. Berry and M. L. Hardman, 1998, Boston: Allyn and Bacon.]

TABLE 5.1	Basic steps in the formulation of an ITP
Step 1: Organize ITP teams for all transition-age students.	■ Identify all students who are at transition age. ■ Identify appropriate school service personnel. ■ Identify adult service agencies.
Step 2: Organize a circle of support.	■ Meet with transition-age student and small circle of friends, family members, coworkers, neighbors, church members, and staff to establish individual's needs and preferences for adult life.
Step 3: Identify key activities.	■ Identify those items that are most important to the individual in the transition from school to adult years.
Step 4: Hold initial ITP meetings as part of annual IEP meetings.	■ Schedule the ITP meeting. ■ Conduct the ITP meeting. ■ Develop the ITP.
Step 5: Implement the ITP.	■ Operate according to guidelines defined in local interagency agreements. ■ Use a transdisciplinary and cross-agency approach.
Step 6: Update the ITP annually during the IEP meetings, and implement follow-up procedures.	■ Phase out involvement of school personnel while increasing involvement of adult services personnel. ■ Contact persons responsible for completion of ITP goals to monitor progress.
Step 7: Hold an exit meeting.	■ Ensure most appropriate employment outcome. ■ Ensure most appropriate recreation outcome. ■ Ensure most appropriate community living outcome. ■ Ensure referrals to all appropriate adult agencies and support services.

Source: Adapted from "Individualized Transition Planning," by P. Wehman. In *Life Beyond the Classroom: Transition Strategies for Young People with Disabilities* (2nd ed.), edited by P. Wehman, 1996, pp. 78–98. Baltimore: Paul H. Brookes. Used with permission.

a significant loss in services at a crucial time. In addition, many students and their parents know little, if anything, about adult service systems (see the Reflect on This feature on page 150).

To avoid this problem, during the high school years the student and the parents must be educated about critical components of adult service systems, including the characteristics of agencies, criteria for evaluating programs, and potential as well as current service alternatives. McDonnell, Wilcox, and Hardman (1991) suggested two strategies for getting information to both students and parents. First, school districts need to offer ongoing information seminars to acquaint families with the issues involved in the transition from school to adult life. Second, every school district should develop and use a transition-planning guide to help families complete important planning activities.

■ WORKING WITH ADULT SERVICE AGENCIES

In addition to the student with disabilities, parents, and school personnel, the team developing the ITP may also involve professionals from **adult service agencies** (such

Reflect on This

A recent qualitative study (Gallivan-Fenlon, 1994) examined the transition from school to adult life in one local community in upstate New York. The study looked through the eyes, ears, and voices of 11 young adults with severe disabilities, their families, and the service providers who were providing assistance to them in the transition planning process. Gallivan-Fenlon describes the study as both "disheartening and hopeful." What do you think?

The following are some of the study's findings:

- All the young adults studied held clear aspirations for leading typical, active, . . . lives, which included paid integrated employment, and participation with friends in community activities such as shopping, eating out, traveling, going to concerts, and attending sporting events.

Young adult: "I like to work . . . ain't gonna stay home and sleep."

- The study revealed that young adults with disabilities and their families often do not participate fully in the transition planning process. . . . They may have little to do with developing a job or choosing an adult service provider.

Parent: "It's mostly professionals sharing information and deciding what to do."

- All the young adults were involved, to varying degrees, in community-based training at the high school level.

Parent: "They've taught him all the things he needs to know out in the community."

- There was a lack of knowledge on the part of both families and service providers about what adult services were available in their community. People responsible for coordinating transition at the school level were often unfamiliar with the adult agencies to which they were referring families.

"I know nothing about it. I'm about as green as anything." [Transition coordinator discussing the lack of transition-related knowledge.]

- Young adults experienced a variety of initial transition outcomes during the first six months following their graduation. Unfortunately, the most common outcome . . . was "sitting at home," receiving no services or waiting for another employment opportunity to be developed for them by a particular adult agency after a previous job had fallen through.

Parent: "She needs to be out working, not sitting home watching TV."

- Young adults who worked in the community, even for a brief amount of time following graduation, generally felt very positive about it.

Margie [a young adult with disabilities]: "Did I tell you about my friends at work? . . . Well, there's Mark. He was so nice to me, and there's Sue and Joe. They're my friends."

Source: From "A Closer Look at Transition: How Are We Assisting Young People with Disabilities to Move to Adulthood?" by A. Gallivan-Fenlon, 1994, *TASH Newsletter, 20*(9), 18–21.

---

as vocational rehabilitation counselors, representatives from university or college centers for students with disabilities, the state developmental disability agency, etc.). Adult service agencies focus on providing services to assist individuals with disabilities in accessing postsecondary education, employment, supported living, or leisure activities. Agencies may provide support in vocational rehabilitation, social services, and mental health. Examples of supports include *attendant services, interpreter services,* or *job coaches.*

Adult service agencies should become involved early in the student's secondary school program to begin targeting the services necessary once he or she leaves school. This involvement includes direct participation in the development of the student's transition plan. Adult service professionals should collaborate with the student, parents, and the school in establishing transition goals and identifying appropriate activities for the student during the final school years. Additionally, adult service professionals must be involved in developing information systems that can effectively track students as they leave school programs and monitor the availability and appropriateness of services to be provided during adulthood (Wehman, 1996).

The importance of developing and implementing effective transition services for students with disabilities cannot be overstated. Despite significant federal and state investment in educational services for these students, many remain unemployed, are socially isolated, and depend on the family and community service programs during adulthood. That model transition programs and services have been developed in most areas in the United States demonstrates that students with disabilities can achieve postschool outcomes that will enhance their access and opportunities in nearly every aspect of community life.

Unfortunately, despite the success of model programs, they have not been widely adopted. Concerned by this, **The Association for Persons with Severe Handicaps (TASH)** (1990) has identified several areas of research needed in order to spur the adoption of transition services for students with disabilities:

To prepare a student for transition to the adult world, the parents must join with the student to learn about available adult service agencies.

- The development and validation of strategies to promote inclusion of student values and needs in the transition-planning process
- Identification of factors that contribute to the implementation of successful transition programs
- Examination of the effects of recent educational reform efforts in general education on the design of transition programs
- Longitudinal studies that examine the impact of transition programs on the quality of life achieved by students with disabilities following high school
- Research examining the reasons behind high unemployment and underemployment of people with disabilities

Implementing Transition Services in Secondary Schools

Successful transition begins with a solid foundation, and that foundation is the school. Secondary school programs (middle and high school) must provide activities that will facilitate success for the individual during the adult years. For Lee and Albert, in the opening snapshot, these activities included learning to shop in a neighborhood grocery store and training for a job in the community. For another student with a disability who has different preferences, needs, and abilities, the activities may be more academically based and focus on preparation for postsecondary education.

In this chapter, the term *secondary schools* will encompass both middle school (junior high) and high school. This is not to ignore the important distinctions between middle and high school programs. The purpose of middle school education is to be

focus 4

Identify three outcomes expected for adolescents with disabilities as they enter adulthood.

Strong secondary school programs provide the foundation for a successful transition to the adult world.

"responsive to the special needs of the young adolescent" (Clark & Clark, 1994, p. 5), and that of high school education is to help the older adolescent "move with confidence from school to work and further education" (Boyer, 1983, p. 305). Middle school grade-level configurations vary; some schools encompass sixth through eighth grades and others seventh through ninth grades. Clark and Clark estimated that middle-level schools in the United States number more than 12,000.

IDEA provides that transition services may begin for students with disabilities as early as age 14, when appropriate. As such, middle schools play an important role in the planning process for many of these individuals. The cornerstone of this planning will be an "exploratory curriculum" that provides a direct link between the concepts and skills learned during the elementary years and the knowledge to be acquired during high school that will facilitate transition to adult life. A middle school exploratory curriculum exposes the student to as many programs and activities as possible prior to a more narrow focus during the high school years.

Several outcomes are expected for youth with disabilities as they enter adulthood. First, as adults they should be able to function as independently as possible in their daily lives; their reliance on others to meet their needs should be minimized. As students with disabilities leave school, they should be able to make choices about where they will live, how they will spend their free time, and whether they will immediately begin working in the community or go on to postsecondary education.

Working in the community is of value to the individual with a disability, both for the monetary benefits it offers and for the opportunities for social interaction, personal identity, and contribution to others. All adults should be able to participate in social and leisure-time activities that are an integral part of community life. These activities might include going to the movies, participating in sports (such as skiing, bowling, swimming, etc.), eating out at a restaurant, or just relaxing in a local park.

There are also increasing opportunities for students with disabilities to further their education as they transition from high school to adult life. As suggested by Bursuck and Rose (1992), the primary pathways are vocational education leading to eventual employment and academic programs leading to enrollment in a college or university. These authors further suggest that students with mild disabilities are

TABLE 5.2   Higher education transition model

ESSENTIAL CURRICULAR ELEMENTS	INSTRUCTIONAL OBJECTIVES
Psychosocial adjustment	1. Self-advocacy skill development
	2. Handling frustration
	3. Social problem-solving
	4. College-level social skills
	5. Mentor relationships
Academic development	1. College entrance exam preparation
	2. Test-taking strategies/accommodations
	3. Career awareness
	4. Goal setting
	5. Academic remediation
	6. Career preparation
	7. Learning strategies/study skills
	8. College services
	9. Transition to college
College/community orientation	1. College-level linkage
	2. Buddy systems
	3. College choices
	4. College resources/activities
	5. College orientation program
	6. Campus support groups
	7. Community services assessment

Source: From "The Higher Education Transition Model: Guidelines for Facilitating College Transition Among College-Bound Students with Disabilities," by B. C. Gartin, P. Rumrill, and R. Serebreni, 1996, *Teaching Exceptional Children, 29*(1), p. 31. Copyright 1996 by the Council for Exceptional Children. Reprinted with permission.

more likely to take the academic track and those with moderate to severe disabilities typically select vocational education programs. For students considering college, Table 5.2 shows a model for a student's transition from high school to postsecondary education.

Secondary schools are in the unique position of being able to coordinate activities that enhance student participation in the community and link students such as Lee and Albert with needed programs and services. Schools have many roles in the transition process: assessing individual needs, helping each student develop a transition plan, coordinating transition planning with adult service agencies, and participating with parents in the planning process.

The preferences and needs of adults with disabilities vary according to functioning levels and requirements of each environmental setting. Involvement with community activities may require significant and long-term support for people with severe disabling conditions. Adults with mild disabilities, in contrast, may need only short-term assistance or no support system whatsoever during their adult years.

■ TEACHING SELF-DETERMINATION

A factor that appears to play a critical role in the transition from school to adult life is the teaching of self-determination (personal choice) (McDonnell et al., 1995; Wehmeyer, 1992a, 1992b). **Self-determination** is "the ability of a person to consider options and make appropriate choices regarding residential life, work and leisure time" (Schloss, Alper, & Jayne, 1993, p. 215). That secondary schools need to focus on self-determination is evident from research revealing the reasons why individuals with disabilities fail in employment situations. In a summary of the research in this area, Schloss et al. stated that individuals with disabilities do not fail because they can't do the required tasks of the job. Instead, "failure has been linked to a lack of appropriate *decision making* skills related to the job and inability to adjust to work situations" (p. 216, emphasis added).

focus 5

Why is it important for students with disabilities to receive instruction in self-determination, academics, adaptive and functional life skills, and employment preparation during the secondary school years?

Teaching self-determination skills to students with disabilities helps them to become more efficient in acquiring knowledge and solving problems (Ward, 1991). Students are better able to achieve goals that will facilitate their transition out of school, while making them aware of the specific challenges they will face in the adult years. Ultimately, the student leaves school with a more well developed sense of personal worth and social responsibility (Deci, Vallerand, Pelletier, & Ryan, 1991). Here are five ways in which schools and parents can support the development of self-determination for students with disabilities:

1. Teach skills that promote self-regulation.
2. Emphasize psychosocial skills needed in the workplace.
3. Structure environments to ensure opportunities for students to make choices.
4. Organize instruction to promote self-determination.
5. Use teaching strategies that promote self-determination. (Wehmeyer, 1992a)

Creating opportunities for individual choice and decision making is an important element in the school-to-adult life transition of people with disabilities. Each individual must be able to consider options and make appropriate choices. This means less decision making on the part of service providers and family members and more of a focus on teaching and promoting personal choice (Turnbull et al., 1992). The planning process associated with the development of a student's IEP is an excellent opportunity to promote self-determination. Unfortunately, very few adolescents with disabilities attend their program-planning meetings, and fewer yet *actively* participate (Wehman, 1996).

Although we have discussed self-determination in the context of the secondary school years, it is important to remember that instruction in self-determination must begin early in a child's life. As suggested by Abery (1994), "striving to attain self-determination doesn't begin (or end) during adolescence or early adulthood. Rather it is initiated shortly after birth and continues until we have breathed our last breath" (p. 2).

■ TEACHING ACADEMIC SKILLS

As the emphasis on academic excellence increases as part of the educational reform movement (see Chapter 1), the student with a disability, family members, and the educational team are faced with some difficult curriculum decisions. Should instruction emphasize academic learning in the core content areas such as English, math, or science, or should the focus be on preparation for life (adaptive and functional skills, employment preparation)?

Evidence indicates that students with disabilities are not faring well in the academic content of high school programs or in further postsecondary education (Bursuck & Rose, 1992; Hocutt, 1996; Zigmond & Miller, 1992). These students have high dropout rates and low academic achievement. However, several authors have suggested that students with mild disabilities, particularly those with learning disabilities, are able to achieve in academic content areas beyond current performance indicators (Carnine, Silbert, & Kameenui, 1990; Ellis et al., 1990). Zigmond (1990) suggested that high school programs should reorganize to include not only instruction in survival skills and transition planning, but more "intensive instruction in reading and mathematics" (p. 20) as well as a strong emphasis on successful completion of courses required for graduation. She suggested two service delivery models for students with learning disabilities, one focusing on continued postsecondary education or training and one emphasizing preparation for work. The model promoting postsecondary educational opportunities has five basic components:

1. Students are assigned to general education classes for content subjects required for graduation and for elective courses.
2. One special education teacher is assigned as a support or consulting teacher to work with general education teachers in whose classes students with learning disabilities are placed.
3. Additional special education teachers are responsible for yearly English and reading courses, one survival skills class, and a supervised study hall that students are scheduled to take each year of high school.
4. From the start of grade 9, students interact regularly with a counselor for transition planning.
5. Courses required for graduation are spaced evenly throughout the four years to reduce academic pressures, particularly in grade 9.

For students with more severe disabilities, the purpose of academic learning may be more functional and compensatory. Academic learning is oriented to applied skills in daily living, leisure time, and employment preparation. Functional skills academic programs in the high school concentrate on protection (such as reading street signs, railroad crossings, entrance/exit signs, or product labels) and information (such as reading job application forms, classified ads, maps, telephone directories, or catalogs).

■ TEACHING ADAPTIVE AND FUNCTIONAL LIFE SKILLS

Adaptive and functional life skills training may include accessing socialization activities in and out of school and learning to manage one's personal affairs. A fundamental need of students with disabilities in the secondary school years is access to social activities. It may be important to provide basic instruction on how to develop positive interpersonal relationships and the behaviors that are conducive to successfully participating in community settings (Wehman, 1996). Instructional programs could include the use of nondisabled peer tutors to both model for, and teach, students with disabilities appropriate behaviors in community settings such as restaurants, theaters, or shopping malls.

Adolescence brings on a growing awareness of the requirements of adult life relative to sex-role expectations, personal appearance, and hygiene. Sexual interests are developing, as is conformity to peer opinions, activities, and appearances (Drew, Hardman, & Logan, 1996). Dramatic physical and psychological changes with the onset of puberty can affect the individual's self-esteem. Secondary school programs face the difficult challenge of identifying their role in providing instruction in these areas. However, if these skills are not taught in the home and the school chooses not to include them in an educational program, students with disabilities may be placed at a significant disadvantage as they move from school to life as an adult in the community.

■ EMPLOYMENT PREPARATION

People with disabilities are often characterized as consumers of society's resources rather than as contributors, but employment goes a long way toward dispelling this idea. Paid employment means earning wages through which individuals can obtain material goods and enhance their quality of life; it also contributes to personal identity and status (Drew et al., 1996). Today many adults with disabilities are unemployed or underemployed despite advances in research and development of effective employment practices (Harris, 1994; Valdes et al., 1990; Wagner & Blackorby, 1996).

A study by the National Council on Disability (1989) suggested that high schools have been far too passive in their approach to employment preparation:

Traditionally, many high schools have focused their employment preparation programs on a general assessment of student interests and strengths, and the teaching of vocational readiness skills in a classroom setting. This approach places high schools in a passive role in preparing students for employment. The instruction focuses more on general preparation for employment rather than training for a specific job(s). (p. 42)

More recently, high schools have begun to emphasize employment preparation. Several approaches to training for employment are currently in place: work experience, career education, and community-referenced instruction. In a *work experience program*, the student spends a portion of the school day in classroom settings (which may emphasize academic and/or vocational skills) and the remainder at an off-campus site receiving on-the-job training. The responsibility for the training may be shared among the high school special education teacher, vocational rehabilitation counselor, and vocational education teacher.

Career education includes training in social skills development as well as general occupational skills. Career education programs usually concentrate on developing an awareness of various career choices, exploring occupational opportunities, and developing appropriate attitudes, social skills, and work habits.

Whereas career education is oriented to developing an awareness of various occupations, *community-referenced instruction* involves direct training and ongoing support as necessary in a community employment site. The demands of the work setting and the functioning level, interests, and wishes of each individual determine the goals and objectives of the training. The most notable difference between

Community-referenced instruction places a student in an employment situation and provides him or her with training and ongoing support.

community-referenced instruction and work experience programs is that the former focuses on the activities to be accomplished at the work site rather than on the development of isolated skills in the classroom. An employment training program based on a community-referenced approach includes the following elements:

- A curriculum that reflects the job opportunities available in the local community
- An employment training program that takes place at actual job sites
- Training designed to sample the individual's performance across a variety of economically viable alternatives
- Ongoing opportunities for students to interact with nondisabled peers in a work setting
- Training that culminates in employment placement
- Job placement linked to comprehensive transition planning, which focuses on establishing interagency agreements that support the individual's full participation in the community (Drew et al., 1996; McDonnell, Mathot-Buckner, & Ferguson, 1996)

The Adult Years

Most of the attention given to exceptionality in the past has focused on children and youth. Only recently have professionals begun to address the challenges encountered by adults, altering our overall perspective of exceptionality and broadening the views of many professionals. Would Adolphe's life (see the nearby snapshot) have been better if intervention had occurred when he was younger? What can be done now to ensure that Adolphe has the supports he needs to actively participate in the life of his community?

For most people, reaching adulthood is a time when one leaves home, gets a job, and becomes more self-reliant, no longer dependent on parents or caregivers. For adults with disabilities, living conditions and lifestyles vary greatly. Many people

Snapshot

Adolphe

Adolphe was 31 when he came to what may have been the most startling realization of his life: He was learning disabled! Adolphe was uncertain what this label meant, but at least he now had a term for what had mostly been a difficult life. The label came from a clinical psychologist who had administered a number of tests after Adolphe had been referred by his counselor, whom he had been seeing since his divorce a year ago. The past year had been partic-

ularly rough, although most of Adolphe's life had been troublesome.

As a young child, Adolphe was often left out of group activities. He was not very adept at sports, was uncoordinated, and could not catch or hit a baseball no matter how hard he tried. School was worse. Adolphe had a difficult time completing assignments and often forgot instructions. Paying attention in class was difficult, and it often seemed as though there were more interesting activities than the assignments. Adolphe finally

gave up on school when he was a junior and took a job in a local service station. That employment did not last long, for he was terminated because of frequent billing errors. The owners said they could not afford to lose so much money because of "stupid mistakes on credit card invoices."

The loss of that job did not bother Adolphe much. An enterprising young man, he had already found employment in the post office, which paid much more and seemed to have greater respectability. Sorting letters presented a

problem, however, and loss of that job did trouble Adolphe. He began to doubt his mental ability further and sought comfort in his girlfriend, whom he had met recently at a YMCA dance. They married quickly when she became pregnant, but things did not become easier. After 12 years of marriage, two children, a divorce, and five jobs, Adolphe is finally gaining some understanding of why he has been so challenged throughout his life.

with disabilities lead a somewhat typical existence, living and working in their community, perhaps marrying, and for the most part supporting themselves financially. These adults still need support, however, as do people who are not disabled. That support is most often "time-limited" (such as vocational rehabilitation services) or informal (attention from family members and friends). Those with more severe disabilities reach adulthood still in need of an ongoing formal support system that facilitates their opportunities for paid employment, housing in the community, and access to recreation and leisure experiences.

Next, we look at some of the decisions facing the individual with disabilities and his or her family during the adult years. From there, we move on to discuss what it takes to build a support network for adults with disabilities, concluding with a discussion on issues concerned with aging adults.

■ MAKING CHOICES

Adult status for people with disabilities and their families is often paradoxical. On the one hand, many parents struggle with their child's "right to grow up." On the other hand, they must face the realities of their adult offspring's continuing need for support, further complicated by the issues surrounding what legally or practically constitutes adult status. Just as there is a great deal of variability in the needs and functioning level of people with disabilities, there is also considerable variability in lifestyle during the adult years. Adults with mild disabilities may lead a life similar to those of nondisabled peers, primarily because their challenges while growing up were mostly related to academic performance in school. Some adults with mild disabilities go on to postsecondary education and become self-supporting, eventually working and living independent of their immediate family. As is true for nondisabled people, however, some of these adults may still need assistance, whether it be government-sponsored (such as vocational rehabilitation) or natural (given by family members, friends, and neighbors). Drew et al. (1996) summarized some of the issues surrounding adult life for people with mild disabilities:

What does society expect of an adult? Adults work, earn money, and buy the necessities of life and as many of the pleasures they want or can afford. An adult socializes, often marries, has children, and tries to live as productively and happily as possible. The adult with [mild disabilities] may be unable to find or hold a job, particularly without [some] formal supports in place. If jobs are available, wages may be so low that even the necessities of life may be out of reach. What if the [individual] has no one to socialize with, no one to love or be loved by?

There are many such "what ifs" for adults with [more mild disabilities], who may just exchange the frustrations of earlier life for new and sometimes harsher ones. (p. 283)

For adults with more severe disabilities, ongoing government-funded and natural supports are critical in order to ensure access and participation in employment, supported residential living, and recreation in their local community. Parents and family members of people with severe disabilities often face the stark reality that their caregiving role may not diminish during the adult years and could well extend through a lifetime.

Quality of life during the adult years is most often characterized by (1) employment, useful work, and valued activity; (2) access to further education when desired and appropriate; (3) personal autonomy and independence; (4) social interaction and community participation; and (5) participation within the life of the family. As one reaches the adult years, decisions have to be made relative to each of these areas.

What kind of career or job do I desire? Should I go on to further education to increase my career choices? Where shall I live, and whom shall I live with? How shall I spend my money? Whom do I choose to spend time with? Who will be my friends? Whereas most people face these choices as a natural part of the transition into adult life, the questions facing a person with disabilities and his or her family may be quite different. Issues concerning the competence of the person with a disability to make decisions in his or her best interest, as well as the role of formal and informal support networks to assist in such decision-making, may also arise. (See Reflect on This feature above.)

■ BUILDING A SUPPORT NETWORK FOR ADULTS WITH DISABILITIES

During the adult years, individuals with disabilities and their families must not only come to terms with making choices relative to planning for the future, but also they must deal with the maze of options in adult services. Over the past 30 years, adult services have gone through major reform. The system has evolved from a sole focus on protecting, managing, and caring for persons with disabilities in segregated programs to one of providing the supports necessary for the individual to participate in family and community life. Gerry and Mirsky (1992) suggested that five principles guide adult services as we move into the 21st century:

1. Services for people with disabilities should be based on the needs and wishes of the individuals themselves and, as appropriate, their families.
2. Services for people with disabilities must empower consumers and be flexible enough to reflect the differing and changing needs of people with disabilities.
3. Every person with a disability must have a real opportunity to engage in productive employment.
4. Public and private collaborations must be fostered to ensure that people with disabilities have the opportunities and choices that are available to all Americans.
5. Social inclusion of people with disabilities in their neighborhoods and communities must be a major focus of the overall effort. (See the Reflect on This feature on page 160.)

Reflect on This

In February 1994, the National Organization on Disability in association with Lou Harris and Associates conducted a telephone survey of 1,021 people with disabilities age 16 and older. The survey also included a comparison group of 1,115 adults without disabilities. The purpose of the survey was to gain insights into issues such as employment, lifestyles, political and religious participation, home computer use, and education. The following are just a few of the survey's highlights.

■ WHO ARE AMERICANS WITH DISABILITIES?

- More than half of adults with disabilities report that their disability began in middle age or after the age of 55. Approximately 20% said the onset of disability occurred between birth and adolescence; 26% during young adulthood.
- Half of all adults surveyed said they are so limited by their disability they are completely unable to work, go to school, or take care of their home.
- Adults with disabilities are twice as likely as adults with no disabilities to have less than a high school educa-

tion (25% vs. 12%). Yet, almost half of all adults with disabilities have completed some college, which almost matches the proportion of nondisabled adults who have completed a similar level of education.

- Almost half of all adults with disabilities report that they get at least some of their personal income from benefits and insurance payments.

■ QUALITY OF LIFE

- Adults with disabilities are about equally satisfied with their lives today as they were eight years ago. However, they are markedly less satisfied than are adults without disabilities.
- Insufficient finances are considered the most serious among a number of problems facing adults with disabilities.
- Adults with disabilities engage in social activities with less frequency than do Americans without disabilities. For example, 42% of adults with disabilities have attended movies in the past 12 months compared to 71% of those who are not disabled.
- 30% of adults with disabilities consider negative public

attitude to be a problem in their lives.

■ HEALTH CARE

- While 86% of adults with disabilities indicate they are covered by health insurance, 40% consider inadequate health insurance to be a problem in their lives.
- 75% of adults with disabilities indicate they are satisfied with the health care services they received in the last few years.

■ EMPLOYMENT

- Two in ten adults with disabilities (20%) are working full-time; one in ten works on a part-time basis.
- Nearly 80% of adults with disabilities who were not working would prefer to have a job.
- 47% of adults with disabilities who did not have a job believe that employers are insensitive to people with disabilities; only 26% of those who were working full-time describe employers as uncaring.
- 76% of adults with disabilities who are employed report that they have not encountered physical barriers in the workplace that would prevent them from performing their job effectively.

- 81% of people with disabilities who are not working indicate that it is the severe limitation of their disability or health problem that prevents them from taking a job.

■ FAMILIARITY WITH DISABILITY LAWS

- Only 42% of adults with disabilities have any awareness of laws that have been passed in the last four years [such as the Americans with Disabilities Act] giving protection to people with disabilities; 35% believe that no such laws have been passed.

■ RELIGION

- 50% of adults with disabilities attend church or synagogue at least once a month compared to 58% of adults without disabilities.
- Among those who attend religious services, 60% feel that their congregation tries to make it easy or possible for them to participate in church or synagogue activities.

Source: From *National Organization on Disability/Harris Survey of Americans with Disabilities,* by Harris and Associates, 1994, New York: Author.

In this section, we explore the concept of "supports" for people with disabilities in the context of (1) government-funded programs in the areas of income support, health care, supported residential living, and employment, and (2) natural support networks of family and friends.

■ GOVERNMENT-FUNDED PROGRAMS Two types of adult service programs for people with disabilities are supported by the government: entitlements and eligibility. Under an **entitlement program**, everyone who meets the eligibility criteria must receive the service. **Income support** (such as Supplemental Social Security Income) and medical assistance programs (such as Medicaid and Medicare) are government-supported entitlement programs for adults with disabilities. The Individuals with Disabilities Education Act is an example of an entitlement program for school-age students with disabilities. Entitlement programs require that services be provided to eligible individuals with disabilities without respect to the availability of funds.

focus 6

What are the purposes of government-supported programs for people with disabilities in the areas of income support, health care, residential living, and employment?

Under an eligibility program, in contrast, the person with a disability may meet the eligibility criteria but not receive the service, because there are *not* enough funds to serve everyone. When funds are insufficient, some people with disabilities go on waiting lists for months or even years. Residential services (housing) and many employment programs (such as **supported employment**) are examples of eligibility programs.

Income Support. Government income support programs, enacted through Social Security legislation (Supplemental Security Income [SSI] and Social Security Disability Insurance [SSDI]), provide direct cash payments to people with disabilities and other eligible individuals, thus providing basic economic assistance. Income support programs have been both praised and condemned. They have been praised because an income is provided to people in need who otherwise would have no means to support themselves. They have been condemned because such support programs can make it economically advantageous for people with disabilities to remain unemployed and dependent on society. For many years, an individual who went to work at even 50% of minimum wage would potentially lose income support benefits that far exceeded the amount they would earn on a job. The disincentive to gain employment was somewhat reduced with the passage of the Employment Opportunities for Disabled Americans Act of 1986, Section 1619. This act is not currently operative in every state, however.

Health Care. Government-sponsored health care for people with disabilities comes under two programs: Medicaid and Medicare. **Medicaid**, established in 1965, pays for health care services for individuals receiving SSI cash payments, as well as families receiving welfare payments. Medicaid is an example of a federal–state partnership program that requires participating states to provide matching funds to available federal dollars. The state match can be as low as 22% and as high as 50%, depending on state per capita income.

The Medicaid program can pay for inpatient and outpatient hospital services, laboratory services, and early screening, diagnosis, treatment, and immunization for children. Working within federal regulations, states design their own plans for the delivery of Medicaid services. Thus a service provided in one state may not be provided in another.

Medicare, Title XVIII of the Social Security Act, is a national insurance program for individuals over the age of 65 and for eligible people with disabilities. Medicare has two parts: hospital insurance and supplementary medical insurance. The Hospital Insurance Program pays for short-term hospitalization, related care in skilled nursing facilities, and some home care. The Supplementary Medical Insurance Program covers physician services, outpatient services, ambulance services, some medical supplies, and medical equipment.

People with disabilities living in group homes have access in the home to professional training and support.

Supported Residential Living. For most of the 20th century, federal government support for residential living has been directed to large congregate care settings (institutions, nursing homes). As we enter the next century, however, people with disabilities, their families, and professionals are advocating for smaller community-based residences within local neighborhoods and communities. People with disabilities and their families are also advocating for choice, individualization, and a focus on the abilities of people rather than on their disabilities in making decisions regarding community living.

Three of the most widely used models for residential living are group homes, semi-independent homes and apartments, and foster family care. Group homes may be large (as many as 15 or more people) or small (4 or fewer people). The **group home** model uses professionals to provide ongoing training and support to people with disabilities, emphasizing daily living experiences that are as similar as possible to those of people who are not disabled.

The **semi-independent apartment or home** provides housing for people with disabilities who require less supervision and support. This model for residential living may include apartment clusters (several apartments located close together), a single co-residence home or apartment in which a staff member shares the dwelling, or a single home or apartment occupied by a person with a disability who may or may not receive assistance from a professional.

Foster family care provides a surrogate family for persons with a disability. The goal of foster care is to integrate individuals with disabilities into a family setting where they will learn adaptive skills and work in the community. Foster family care settings may accommodate up to six adults with disabilities.

Employment. Sustained competitive employment for people with disabilities is important for many reasons, as cited earlier (monetary rewards, adult identity, social contacts, and inclusion in a community setting). Yet the reality is that adults with disabilities are significantly underemployed and unemployed when compared to their nondisabled peers (Harris, 1994).

In spite of the bleak data on the unemployment rates of people with disabilities, there is good reason to be optimistic about their future employment opportunities. There is a greater emphasis on employment opportunities for these people than ever before (Rusch, Chadsey-Rusch, & Johnson, 1991; Tines, Rusch, McCaughrin, & Conley, 1990), and the concept of employment for people with disabilities has changed dramatically in recent years (West, Revell, & Wehman, 1992). Competitive employment can now be described in terms of three alternatives: employment with no support services, employment with time-limited support services, and employment with ongoing support services.

An adult with a disability may be able to locate and maintain employment without support from government-sponsored programs. Many find jobs through contacts with family and friends, the local job service, want ads, and the like. For individuals with mild disabilities, the potential for locating and maintaining a job is enhanced greatly if the individual has received employment training and experience during the school years (Hasazi et al., 1989).

An adult with a disability may also have access to several employment services on a time-limited, short-term basis, including vocational rehabilitation, vocational education, and on-the-job training. Time-limited employment services provide intensive, short-term support to people with disabilities who have the potential to make it on their own after receiving government assistance. The most widely known time-limited support service is vocational rehabilitation.

Vocational rehabilitation is intended to help qualified people with disabilities obtain employment. Through the vocational rehabilitation program, federal funds pass to the states to provide services in counseling, training, and job placement. The program, funded under the Vocational Rehabilitation Act, requires that the individual have an employment-related disability.

Vocational rehabilitation has traditionally been viewed as a good investment in returning people with disabilities to the workforce, but more recently its efficacy has

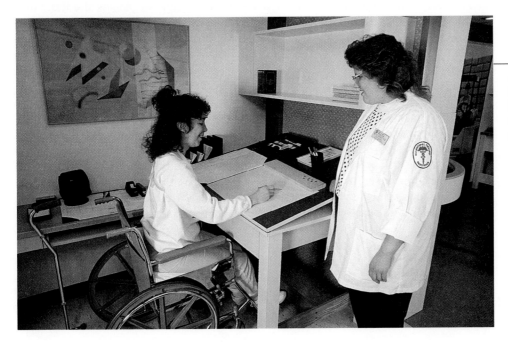

A person with an employment related disability may receive training and job placement assistance through the vocational rehabilitation program.

been questioned (Government Accounting Office [GAO], 1993). The issues raised by the GAO focused on whether vocational rehabilitation is "able to serve all those who are eligible and desire services, whether the services provided are sufficient in scope and suitably targeted to meet the needs of a diverse client, and whether the program's effects persist over the long term" (GAO, 1993, p. 11). Vocational rehabilitation programs throughout the country are attempting to respond directly to the issues raised by the GAO in the area of client diversification and long-term employment. One response is the expansion of a model for ongoing job support for those who need it: the supported employment model.

Supported employment is work in an integrated setting provided for people with disabilities who need some type of continuing support and for whom competitive employment has traditionally not been possible. The criteria for a supported employment placement requires that (1) the job must provide between 20 and 40 hours of work weekly and be consistent with the individual's stamina, (2) the individual must earn a wage at or above minimum wage or at a wage commensurate with production level and based upon the prevailing wage rate for the job, (3) fringe benefits should be similar to those provided for nondisabled workers or with the public as a regular part of working, and (4) work should take place in settings where no more than eight persons with disabilities work together (1986 amendments to the Vocational Rehabilitation Act).

Over the past decade, supported employment has become a viable employment program for people with disabilities in need of long-term support (McDonnell et al., 1995; Rusch et al., 1991; Rusch, Johnson, & Hughes, 1990). The efficacy of supported employment services has been documented through a variety of research studies (Braddock, Hemp, Bachelder, & Fujiura, 1995; Hill et al., 1987; Mank, Rhodes, & Bellamy, 1986; Revell et al., 1994; Rusch et al., 1991; Tines et al., 1990; Vogelsberg, 1986).

Supported employment consists of four main features: wages, social integration with nondisabled peers, ongoing support provided as necessary by a job coach or through natural supports (coworkers), and application of a zero-exclusion principle. A **zero-exclusion principle** veers from the more traditional approach of "getting individuals with disabilities ready for work" to a principle of placing the individual on a job and providing the necessary supports to ensure success. The essential element of a successful supported employment program is establishing a match between the needs, preferences, and abilities of the individual with the demands of a particular job.

■ NATURAL SUPPORTS The importance of natural supports for adults with disabilities, including family, friends, neighbors, and coworkers, cannot be overstated. As is true for all of us, adults with disabilities need a support network that extends beyond government-funded programs. In Chapter 3 of this text, we discussed natural supports in the context of the family. In this section, we emphasize how these supports enhance the individual's opportunities for independence.

Some adults with disabilities may never move away from their primary family. Parents, and in some cases siblings, assume the major responsibilities of ongoing support for a lifetime (Freedman, Krauss, & Seltzer, 1997). In a study of 43 adults with disabilities, Heller and Factor (1993) found that 63% of the persons interviewed indicated that they wanted to remain in the family home. Respondents suggested two reasons for not wanting to leave the primary family: fear of the alternatives and a desire to be near parents and siblings. Seltzer and Krauss (1994) reported that 85% of adults with mental retardation live under the supervision of their parents for most of their lives. Smith, Majeski, and McClenny (1996) characterized this situation as "perpetual parenthood" (p. 172). Perpetual parenthood results from an offspring's continuing dependence through the adult years, either because of a lack of formal resources for the family or because the family simply chooses to keep the individual at home.

Many siblings appear to have attitudes similar to those of their parents. A study by Griffiths and Unger (1994) suggested that most siblings believe that families should be responsible for the care of their adult disabled members. Most indicated that they were "willing to assume future caregiving responsibilities for their brothers/sisters" (p. 225). In a longitudinal study of 140 families who had adults with mental retardation still living at home, Krauss, Seltzer, Gordon, and Friedman (1996) found that many siblings remained very actively involved with their brothers or sisters well into the adult years. These siblings had frequent contact with their brother or sister and were knowledgeable about their lives. In addition, they played a major role in their parents' support network. Interestingly, about one in three of these siblings indicated that they planned to reside with their brother or sister at some point during adult life.

Whether the adult with disabilities continues to live with parents or siblings, in a semi-independent living situation, or independently, extended family members (grandparents, aunts, uncles, etc.) often remain important sources of support. Extended family members may help with transportation, meals, housecleaning, or just "being there" for the individual. Similar support may also come from friends, neighbors, and coworkers. The nature and type of support provided by individuals outside of the family will be unique to the individuals involved and will depend on a mutual level of comfort in both seeking and providing assistance. Clear communication regarding what friends or neighbors are willing to do, and how that matches with the needs and preferences of each individual, is essential.

Issues for Aging Adults with Disabilities

Life expectancy for all adults, including those with disabilities, continues to improve. According to present projections, between the years 2020 and 2030, about 20% of U.S. citizens will be over the age of 65. The fastest-growing age group in the United States is people between the ages of 75 and 85 (Butler, Lewis, & Sunderland, 1991). As life expectancy increases for people with disabilities, concerns have arisen among family members, service providers, and the individuals themselves related to life satisfaction, health care, and living arrangements as they age (Hawkins, 1993). Although

focus 7
Identify two challenges faced by aging people with disabilities.

Snapshot

Roberta

Roberta celebrated her 74th birthday with her dearest friends, Spencer and Josephine. They made a cake in their kitchen and placed a single candle on top.

Roberta's friends seemed like family although none of her actual family were present—they had not visited Roberta for several years. Roberta had lived in a nursing home for people with mental retardation just outside of Bend for the past 10 years, but she was now living in a small group home with Spencer and Josephine. The three friends enjoy their time together, usually chatting, watching movies, or walking through the neighborhood. The support staff present during the day assist them in handling the daily chores of the house, cooking, and doing the laundry. While all three are no longer employed, they spend a day a week volunteering at a local day-care center.

the available information on age-related change in adults has increased as a whole, little is known about aging persons with disabilities (Eklund & Martz, 1993).

Stone and Newcomer (1985) have suggested that although people are living longer, they are not necessarily living better: "Many elderly and disabled persons are not receiving the kind of care they need; others have unmet needs for a variety of noninstitutional services, including home care and supportive living arrangements" (p. 27). These authors have raised several important questions relative to the **long-term health care** and supported living needs of aging people with disabilities:

- How can . . . community care, including self-care and family care, be created, developed, and managed?
- How can the fragmentation among the various funding streams that support long-term care services be reduced?
- How can the level of resources available for long-term community care services be increased?

Statistics concerning aging persons with disabilities are limited, but many elderly people are not receiving the assistance they need.

In the area of health care, more and more researchers are attempting to expand our knowledge about the functional competence and health status of older people with disabilities (Hawkins, 1993). As suggested by Hawkins, "maintaining health and functional status is clearly central to enhancing inclusion, independence, and productivity of adults with disabilities as they grow older" (p. 1).

Similar research is being conducted in the area of community living. Research findings on community living options for older people with disabilities parallel those concerning adults with disabilities in general—a trend toward using smaller community living options. A survey by Martinson and Stone (1993) suggested that although large congregate care facilities (such as nursing homes) remain as a major service provider for older people with disabilities, there is a clear trend toward smaller establishments. These authors note that "older adults with developmental disabilities should have the opportunity to participate in the communities in which they live, instead of being neglected into invisibility" (p. 197).

From the high school transition years through adult life, the issues surrounding delivery of quality services and supports to people with disabilities are varied and complex. With the information in this chapter as background, we now move on to focus on each area of exceptionality. The discussion will continue to highlight multicultural, family, and lifespan issues as well as the nature of educational, medical, and social services. Definitions for each of the areas of exceptionality are presented, along with overviews of prevalence, characteristics, causation, services, and supports.

Case Study

YVONNE

Yvonne is 19 years old and leaving high school to begin her adult life. For most of her high school years, she was in special education classes for reading and math, because she was about three grade levels behind her nondisabled peers. During the last term of high school, she attended a class on exploring possible careers and finding and keeping a job. The class was required for graduation, but it didn't make much sense to Yvonne because she had never had any experience with this area before. It just didn't seem to be related to her other schoolwork.

Although Yvonne wants to get a job in a retail store (such as stocking clothing or shoes), she isn't having much success. She doesn't have a driver's license, and her parents don't have time to run her around to apply for various jobs. The businesses she approached are close by her home and know her well, but they keep telling her she isn't *qualified* for the jobs available. She has never had any on-the-job training in the community. Yvonne's parents are not very enthusiastic about her finding employment because they are afraid she might lose some of her government-funded medical benefits.

■ APPLICATION

In retrospect, what transition planning services would you have recommended for Yvonne during her last years of high school?

How would you help Yvonne now? Do you see the Americans with Disabilities Act playing a role in Yvonne's story?

Whose responsibility is it to work with potential employers to explore "the reasonable accommodations" that would facilitate the opportunity for Yvonne to succeed in a community job?

Debate Forum

STUDENTS WITH DISABILITIES AND THE MEANING OF A HIGH SCHOOL DIPLOMA

Students with disabilities often do not receive the same high school diploma as their nondisabled peers. Many states and local school districts have adopted graduation requirements that specify successful completion of a number of credits in order to receive a diploma. In these areas, students with disabilities must meet the same requirements as their nondisabled peers in order to receive a "regular" high school diploma. If a student with a disability fails to meet graduation requirements, he or she may be awarded a certificate indicating completion (or attendance) of high school. Certificates of completion communicate that a student was unable to meet the requirements to obtain a standard diploma.

Other states, however, award students with disabilities the standard high school diploma based upon a modified criteria that are individually referenced, reflecting the successful completion of IEP goals and objectives as determined by the multidisciplinary team of professionals and the student's parents (National Research Council, 1997).

In 1995, about 28% of students with disabilities exiting school received a standard high school diploma. Students most likely to be awarded a diploma were those with sensory disabilities (vision and hearing loss), orthopedic impairments, and traumatic brain injury. Students least likely to receive a diploma were those with severe multiple disabilities and autism (U.S. Department of Education, 1997).

■ POINT

The purpose of a high school diploma is to communicate to employers, colleges, and society in general that an individual has acquired a specified set of knowledge and skills that prepares him or her to leave school and enter postsecondary education or the world of work. Every student must be held to the same standards, or the diploma has no meaning as a "signal" of competence. The diploma simply becomes a piece of paper that will make no impression on employers or colleges. It will be ignored, as it often is now, as a means to discriminate who is competent and who is not. For those students with disabilities who cannot meet graduation requirements, there is certainly the need to signal what an individual has achieved during high school even though it is not to the same performance level as those who are awarded the diploma. This can be accomplished through a certificate of completion with modified criteria for graduation. What is most important is not to engage in the devaluing of the high school diploma by lowering requirements so that everyone gets the credential. Otherwise, employers and colleges will continue to lose faith in public education as a credible system for preparing students for the future.

■ **COUNTERPOINT**
Although I applaud the move to hold all students to specific requirements (or standards), it is discriminatory to expect every student to meet the "same" standards in order to receive a high school diploma. The purpose of a high school diploma is to communicate that the individual has demonstrated a "personal best" while in school, thus acquiring knowledge and a set of skills consistent with individual ability. I would also support the viewpoint that students with disabilities can achieve at much higher levels than they do now, and expectations should be raised. However, some will never be able to achieve the graduation requirements now in place in many states and school districts. Students with disabilities who cannot perform at the level mandated in graduation requirements should still be awarded a standard diploma based upon requirements consistent with their individual needs and abilities. This is the basis of a free and appropriate public education for students with disabilities. If a standard diploma is not awarded, a student with a disability will be immediately singled out as incompetent and be placed at a major disadvantage with employers, regardless of the skills he or she possesses.

Review

focus 1

Cite three reasons why it is important to plan for the transition of students with disabilities from school to adult life.

- Students with disabilities who leave the public schools are not adequately prepared for postsecondary education or employment.
- Adult service systems do not have the resources to meet the needs of students with disabilities following the school years.
- The capabilities of adults with disabilities have been underestimated.

focus 2

How does IDEA define transition services?

- Transition services are a coordinated set of activities for a student, designed within an outcome-oriented process that promotes movement from school to postschool activities, including postsecondary education, vocational training, integrated employment (including supported employment), continuing and adult education, adult services, independent living, or community participation.
- Activities shall be based upon individual student needs, taking into account preferences and interests.
- Activities shall include instruction, community experiences, development of employment, and other postschool adult-living objectives.

focus 3

What information should be included in each student's IEP statement for transition services? Who should be involved in the planning process?

- The IEP should incorporate a description of interagency responsibilities or linkages prior to the student's departure from school.
- The IEP should identify the range of services needed by the individual in order to participate in the community.
- The IEP should identify activities that must occur during high school to facilitate the individual's access to adult service programs if necessary.
- The IEP should establish timelines and responsibilities for completion of these activities.
- In addition to education personnel, transition planning must include the student with disabilities and his or her parents. Students and parents should be educated about adult service systems, including the characteristics of agencies, criteria for evaluating programs, and potential as well as current service alternatives. Professionals from adult service agencies may also be involved to facilitate the student's access to employment, postsecondary education, supported living, and leisure activities.

focus 4

Identify three outcomes expected for adolescents with disabilities as they enter adulthood.

- Adults with disabilities should be able to function as independently as possible in their daily lives.
- Adults with disabilities should also begin working in the community or go on to postsecondary education.
- Adults with disabilities should be able to participate in social and leisure activities that are an integral part of community life.

focus 5

Why is it important for students with disabilities to receive instruction in self-determination, academics, adaptive and functional life skills, and employment preparation during the secondary school years?

- Self-determination skills help students to solve problems, consider options, and make appropriate choices as they make the transition into adult life.

- Academic skills training is important in meeting school graduation requirements and preparing students with disabilities for further post-secondary education. A functional academic program helps students learn applied skills in daily living, leisure activities, and employment preparation.
- Adaptive and functional life skills help students learn how to socialize with others, maintain personal appearance, and make choices about how to spend free time.
- Employment preparation during high school increases the probability of success on the job during the adult years and places the individual with a disability in the role of a contributor to society.

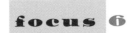

What are the purposes of government-supported programs for people with disabilities in the areas of income support, health care, residential living, and employment?

- Income support programs are direct cash payments to people with disabilities, providing basic economic assistance.
- Medicaid and Medicare are government-supported health care programs. The Medicaid program can pay for inpatient and outpatient hospital services, laboratory services, and early screening, diagnosis, treatment, and immunization for children. Medicare is a national insurance program with two parts: hospital insurance and supplementary medical insurance. The Hospital In-

surance Program pays for short-term hospitalization, related care in skilled nursing facilities, and some home care. The insurance program covers physician services, outpatient services, ambulance services, some medical supplies and medical equipment.

- Residential services show a trend toward smaller, community-based residences located within local neighborhoods and communities. These residences may include group homes, semi-independent homes and apartments, or foster family care. The purpose of residential services is to provide persons with disabilities a variety of options for living in the community.
- There are essentially three alternative approaches to competitive employment for people with disabilities: employment with no support

services, employment with time-limited support services, and employment with ongoing support services. The purpose of all three approaches is to assist people with disabilities obtain a job and maintain it over time.

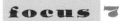

Identify two challenges faced by aging people with disabilities.

- Little research information is available on the effects of aging. We do know that, although people are living longer, they are not necessarily living better.
- Many aging people with disabilities are not able to access adequate health care or receive the ongoing support they need at home.

6

People with Learning Disabilities

To begin with . . .

 The number of children with learning disabilities has grown at a faster pace than many with other disability categories. Between 1987–88 and 1995–96, the number of children ages 6–21 served under IDEA part B grew by 33.91 percent in the United States, the District of Columbia, and Puerto Rico. The growth in children served in all disability areas combined during the same period was 23.26 percent. (U.S. Department of Education, 1997)

 Conventional wisdom has suggested that boys identified with learning disabilities substantially outnumber girls, although some recent research suggests they may be more equal in number. (Lerner, 1997)

 The fastest-growing category of disability is "learning disability," especially the variants of attention-deficit disorder. The number of students requesting accommodations on SAT tests—the great majority involving claims for a learning disability—has doubled in five years. Even so, last year they amounted to less than 2% of all test takers. (Begley, 1998, p. 56)

 More than 90 percent of the prescriptions for psychotropic drugs given children are written by pediatricians, and they are not that knowledgeable about the range of psychotropic drugs for kids. (Youngstrom, 1991)

Snapshot

overall context of Jamaal's world. He fundamentally has a positive outlook and already has plans for attending college—rather long-range planning for a fourth-grader.

Jamaal

Jamaal's difficulties initially became evident in kindergarten, which is somewhat unusual since learning disabilities are more typically identified later in the school years. His parents were frustrated and, like so many parents of children with disabilities, felt that they were not doing something correctly. Jamaal was also aware of some difficulties, mentioning to the teacher that he had trouble concentrating in some cases.

Jamaal expresses himself well verbally and comes up with great ideas; however, he has particular problems with reading and writing. It appears that he falls below his classmates in sight word vocabulary, which influences both academic areas. His fourth-grade teachers are now working very hard to integrate into his instruction the important skills that he will need in order to succeed as he moves on in school. Although he exhibits some disruptive behaviors, they are relatively minor in the

Mathew

Note: The following is a statement prepared by an upper-division psychology undergraduate student who has learning disabilities. Mathew tells his story in his own words, recounting some of his school experiences, his diagnosis, and how his learning disabilities affect his academic efforts.

Imagine having the inability to memorize times tables, not being able to "tell time" until the ninth grade and taking several days to read a simple chapter from a school textbook.

In elementary and high school, I was terrified of math classes for several reasons. First, it did not matter how many times I practiced my times tables or other numerical combinations relating to division, subtraction, and addition, I could not remember them. Second, I dreaded the class time itself for inevitably the teacher would call on me

for an answer to a "simple" problem. Multiplication was the worst! Since I had to count on my fingers to do multiplication, it would take a lot of time and effort. Do you know how long it takes to calculate 9 x 7 or 9 x 9 on your fingers? Suffice it to say too long, especially if the teacher and the rest of the class is waiting.

When I was a sophomore at a junior college I discovered important information about myself. After two days of clinical cognitive testing, I learned that my brain is wired differently than most individuals. That is, I think, perceive, and process information differently. They discovered several "wiring jobs" which are called learning disabilities. First, I have a problem with processing speed. The ability to bring information from long-term memory to conscious (into short-term memory) takes me a long time. Second, I have a deficit with my short-term memory. This means that I cannot hold information there very long. When new information is learned, it must be put into long-term memory. This is an arduous process requiring the information to be rehearsed several times. Third, I have a significant problem with fluid reasoning. Fluid reasoning is the ability to go

from A to G without having to go through B, C, D, E, and F. It also includes drawing inferences, coming up with creative solutions to problems, solving unique problems and the ability to transfer information and generalize. Hence, my math and numerical difficulties.

Perhaps the most unique piece of information I learned was that I have scotopic sensitivity to light. This means that the eyes are overly sensitive to light and glare which tires them rapidly.

With all of this knowledge, I was able to use specific strategies that will help me in compensating for these neurological wiring patterns. Now I tape all lectures rather than trying to keep up taking notes. I take tests in a room by myself and they are not timed. Anytime I need to do mathematical calculations I use a calculator. To compensate for scotopic sensitivity, I use transparent blue-green plastic sheets when I read textbooks and I use green paper when I write assignments, etc.

Source: From *Understanding Child Behavior Disorders* (3rd ed., p. 215), by D. M. Gelfand, W. R. Jenson, and C. J. Drew, 1997, Fort Worth, TX: Harcourt Brace & Co. Used with permission.

LEARNING DISABILITIES comprise a relatively new field of exceptionality that was virtually unrecognized prior to the 1960s. As a disability, it is often thought of as a mild condition because people with learning disabilities usually have average or near-average intelligence, although learning disabilities can occur at all intelligence levels. People with learning disabilities achieve at unexpectedly low levels, particularly in reading and mathematics. Recent thinking suggests that the term *learning disabilities* functions as a generic label representing a very heterogeneous group of conditions, which range from mild to severe in intensity. In many cases, people with learning disabilities have been described as having "poor neurological wiring." Individuals with learning disabilities present a highly variable and complex set of characteristics and needs. As such they represent a substantial challenge to professionals and family members.

Definitions and Classifications

Controversy, confusion, and polarization have long been associated with the field of **learning disabilities.** In the past, many children now identified as having specific learning disabilities would have been labeled as remedial readers, remedial learners, or emotionally disturbed or even mentally retarded children, if they received any special attention or additional instructional support at all. Academic performance represents a major element in the federal definition of learning disabilities (Patrikakou, 1996). Today, services related to learning disabilities represent the largest single program for exceptional children in the United States. Although relatively new, its growth rate has been unparalleled by any other area in special education (U.S. Department of Education, 1997).

focus 1

Identify four reasons why definitions of learning disabilities have varied.

▪ DEFINITIONS

Considerable variation is found in the definitions of learning disabilities. The inconsistency may be due to the field's unique evolution, rapid growth, and strong interdisciplinary nature. The involvement of multiple disciplines (such as medicine, psychology, speech and language, and education) has contributed to the confusing terminology. For example, education coined the phrase "specific learning disabilities"; psychology uses terms such as *perceptual disorders* and *hyperkinetic behavior*; speech and language employ the terms *aphasia* and *dyslexia*; and medicine uses the labels *brain damage, minimal brain dysfunction, brain injury,* and *impairment*. Brain injury, minimal brain dysfunction, and learning disabilities are the most commonly used terms, although all appear in various segments of professional terminology.

A child with a brain injury is described as having an organic impairment resulting in perceptual problems, thinking disorders, and emotional instability. A child with minimal brain dysfunction manifests similar problems but often shows evidence of language, memory, motor, and impulse-control difficulties. Individuals with minimal brain dysfunction are often characterized as average or above average in intelligence, distinguishing the disorder from mental retardation.

■ EARLY HISTORY The term *specific learning disabilities* was first introduced by Samuel Kirk in 1963. His original concept remains largely intact today. The concept is defined by delays, deviations, and performance discrepancies in basic academic subjects (e.g., arithmetic, reading, spelling, and writing) and speech and language problems that cannot be attributed to mental retardation, sensory deficits, or emotional disturbance (Frederickson & Reason, 1995). The common practice in education is to describe individuals with learning disabilities on the basis of what they are not. For example, although they may have a number of problems, they do *not* have mental retardation, emotional disturbance, or hearing loss. Learning disabilities is an umbrella label that includes a variety of conditions and behavioral and performance deficits (Gelfand, Jenson, & Drew, 1997).

■ IDEA DEFINITION A definition developed by the National Advisory Committee on Handicapped Children (1968) of the U.S. Office of Education has been widely used over the years. Similar to Kirk's early concept, this definition was initially incorporated into Public Law (PL) 91-320, the Learning Disabilities Act of 1969, and was also used in the Individuals with Disabilities Education Act (IDEA) of 1990 (Roberts & Mather, 1995):

"Specific learning disability" means a disorder in one or more of the basic psychological processes involved in understanding or in using language, spoken or written, which may manifest itself in an imperfect ability to listen, think, speak, read, write, spell, or to do mathematical calculations. The term includes such conditions as perceptual handicaps, brain injury, minimal brain dysfunction, dyslexia, and developmental aphasia. The term does not include children who have learning problems which are primarily the result of visual, hearing, or motor handicaps, of mental retardation, of emotional disturbance, or of environmental, cultural, or economic disadvantage. (PL 101-476, Sec. 5[b][4])

■ JOINT COMMITTEE DEFINITION The IDEA definition was exclusionary in some ways; it defined conditions that are *not* learning disabilities, but did not offer a substantive explanation of what constitutes a learning disability. The definition was also somewhat ambiguous because it lacked a clear way to measure a learning disability. An earlier definition presented by the National Joint Committee for Learning Disabilities (1988) had certain important elements not stated in IDEA:

Learning disabilities *is a general term that refers to a heterogeneous group of disorders manifested by significant difficulties in the acquisition and use of listening, speaking, writing, reasoning, or mathematical abilities. These disorders are intrinsic to the individual, presumed to be due to central nervous system dysfunction, and may occur across the life span. Problems in self-regulatory behaviors, social perception, and social interaction may exist with learning disabilities but do not by themselves constitute a learning disability. Although learning disabilities may occur concomitantly with other handicapping conditions (for example, sensory impairment, mental retardation, serious emotional disturbance) or with extrinsic influences (such as cultural differences, insufficient or inappropriate instruction), they are not the result of those conditions or influences. (1988, p. 1)*

This definition is important to our discussion for several reasons. First, it describes *learning disabilities* as a generic term that refers to a heterogeneous group of disorders. Second, a person with learning disabilities must manifest significant difficulties. Use of the word *significant* is an effort to remove the connotation that a learning disability constitutes a mild problem. Finally, this definition highlights learning disabilities as lifelong problems and places them in a context of other disabilities and cultural differences. These are important refinements of earlier definitions (Hammill, 1990).

■ OTHER ISSUES IN DEFINING LEARNING DISABILITIES The varying definitions and range of terminology used in the field of learning disabilities have emerged partly because of the different theoretical views of the condition. For example, **perceptual-motor** theories emphasize an interaction between various channels of perception and motor activity. Perceptual-motor theories of learning disabilities focus on contrasts between normal sequential development of motor patterns and the motor development of children with learning disabilities. Children with learning disabilities are seen as having unreliable and unstable perceptual-motor abilities, which present problems when such children encounter activities that require an understanding of time and space.

In contrast, language disability theories concentrate on the child's reception or production of language. Because language is so important in learning, these theories emphasize the relationship between learning disabilities and language deficiencies. On the basis of examining only these two theories, it is clear that very different viewpoints exist regarding these disabilities. This field encompasses many theoretical perspectives regarding the nature of learning problems as well as their causation and treatment.

Yet another view of learning disabilities has emerged in the past few years. Some researchers have suggested that many different, specific disorders have been grouped under one term. They see *learning disabilities* as a general umbrella term that includes a variety of specific problems of both an academic and a behavioral nature. This approach has developed specific terminology to describe particular conditions that fall within the broad category known as learning disabilities. Some of these terms refer to particular areas of functional academic difficulty (e.g., math, spelling, reading), whereas others denote difficulties that are behavioral in nature. This perspective has been adopted by the American Psychiatric Association in the *Diagnostic and Statistical Manual of Mental Disorders* (American Psychiatric Association, 1994). This manual uses the term *learning disorders* to refer specifically to disorders in areas such as reading, mathematics, or written expression. In one sense, this strategy is not surprising. It has long been acknowledged that people with learning disabilities form a very heterogeneous group, yet professionals have continued to describe them as though they were homogeneous. Such characterizations typically reflect the theoretical or disciplinary perspective of the professional, rather than an objective behavioral description of the individual being evaluated. Thus there has been a tendency to focus on defining a particular disorder and then categorizing people according to such definitions, rather than objectively evaluating the individual with problems. This approach inevitably leads to error when evaluating members of a population that represents a wide variety of disorders.

The problems in defining learning disabilities are also reflected in the research on this topic. The wide range of characteristics associated with children having learning disabilities and various methodological problems (such as poor **research design** and measurement error) have caused multiple difficulties in conducting research on learning disabilities (Drew, Hardman, & Hart, 1996; Gelfand et al., 1997). Generalizing research results is questionable, and replication of studies is very difficult. Efforts to standardize and clarify definitions continue, and they are important both for research and intervention purposes (Conte & Andrews, 1993; Ohtsuka, 1993).

The notion of severity has largely been ignored in earlier definitions and concepts related to learning disabilities. To some degree this has changed, although this issue still receives only limited attention (see Jahoda & Cattermole, 1995; Lowe, Felce, & Blackman, 1995; McKinney, Montague, & Hocutt, 1993). Learning disabilities have probably been defined in more ways than any other type of disability. In fact, Hammill (1990) discussed 11 different definitions still being used for this family of disorders. Even those who have learning disabilities offer varying definitions: Reiff, Gerber, and Ginsberg (1993) obtained 57 different definitions from a sample of 60 successful adults with learning disabilities.

In our examination of learning disabilities, we describe behavioral characteristics from different theoretical viewpoints, because the diversity in approaches makes it impossible to select one perspective alone. It is important to know how a person might be classified as having a learning disability according to different perspectives. On the bright side, Hammill (1990) has suggested that consensus regarding definitions in the field of learning disabilities is near, despite the historical controversies. So far, the most broadly agreed-upon characteristics that define learning disabilities include (1) presence of academic problems, especially when characterized by **intraindividual** underachievement; (2) central nervous system dysfunction; (3) presence of learning disabilities throughout a person's life; (4) language problems with listening and speaking; and (5) potential for multiple handicaps (other disorders may coexist with learning disabilities). Additionally, several researchers have defined learning disabilities to include some disruption of psychological processes and conceptual problems (e.g., thinking and reasoning). There is less consensus on these two latter characteristics (Hammill, 1990).

■ LEARNING DISABILITIES AND ATTENTION-DEFICIT/HYPERACTIVITY DISORDER

focus 2

Identify the three major types of ADHD according to the DSM-IV.

One condition often associated with learning disabilities that is not defined in IDEA is **attention-deficit/hyperactivity disorder (ADHD)**. Nonetheless, the essential features of ADHD have long been recognized in many children with learning disabilities. Attention-deficit/hyperactivity disorders, as currently conceived, actually include three subcategories: ADHD, Combined Type; ADHD, Predominantly Inattentive Type; and ADHD, Predominantly Hyperactive–Impulsive Type (APA, 1994). The diagnostic criteria for ADHD outlined in the *Diagnostic and Statistical Manual of Mental Disorders (DSM–IV)* are summarized in Table 6.1. Although many individuals exhibit symptoms that combine inattention, impulsivity, and hyperactivity, some people have a predominant feature that corresponds to one of the three subtypes.

Although ADHD is often associated with learning disabilities, there is not a complete correspondence in characteristics between the two conditions (Denckla, 1996a; Javorsky, 1996). Our discussion of the attributes of learning disabilities in this chapter will show that attention problems, impulsiveness, and hyperactivity have emerged periodically in depictions of learning disabilities. Additionally, perception difficulties and discrimination problems, among others, are often associated with learning disabilities. The distinctions between learning disabilities and ADHD as categories are not at all clear, in part because the definitions have historically overlapped and been applied to very heterogeneous groups of people (Goodyear & Hynd, 1993; Zentall & Ferkis, 1993).

There is great disagreement about the causes of ADHD. Both biological and environmental influences have been implicated (Barkley, Grodzinski, & DuPaul, 1992; Denckla, 1996a; Faraone, Biederman, Lehmman, & Keenan, 1993). Speculation has included genetic inheritance, neurological injury during birth complications, vitamin de-

A. Either (1) or (2):

  1. Six (or more) of the following symptoms of *inattention* have persisted for at least 6 months to a degree that is maladaptive and inconsistent with developmental level:

    Inattention

    a. Often fails to give close attention to details or makes careless mistakes in schoolwork, work, or other activities.

    b. Often has difficulty sustaining attention in tasks or play activities.

    c. Often does not seem to listen when spoken to directly.

    d. Often does not follow through on instructions and fails to finish schoolwork, chores, or duties in the workplace (not due to oppositional behavior or failure to understand instructions).

    e. Often has difficulty organizing tasks and activities.

    f. Often avoids, dislikes, or is reluctant to engage in tasks that require sustained mental effort (such as schoolwork or homework).

    g. Often loses things necessary for tasks or activities (e.g., toys, school assignments, pencils, books, or tools).

    h. Is often easily distracted by extraneous stimuli.

    i. Is often forgetful in daily activities.

  2. Six (or more) of the following symptoms of *hyperactivity-impulsivity* have persisted for at least 6 months to a degree that is maladaptive and inconsistent with developmental level:

    Hyperactivity

    a. Often fidgets with hands or feet or squirms in seat.

    b. Often leaves seat in classroom or in other situations in which remaining seated is expected.

    c. Often runs about or climbs excessively in situations in which it is inappropriate (in adolescents or adults, may be limited to subjective feelings of restlessness).

    d. Often has difficulty playing or engaging in leisure activities quietly.

    e. Is often "on the go" or often acts as if "driven by a motor."

    f. Often talks excessively.

    Impulsivity

    g. Often blurts out answers before questions have been completed.

    h. Often has difficulty awaiting turn.

    i. Often interrupts or intrudes on others (e.g., butts into conversations or games).

B. Some hyperactive–impulsive or inattentive symptoms that caused impairment were presented before age 7 years.

C. Some impairment from the symptoms is present in two or more settings (e.g., at school [or work] and at home).

D. There must be clear evidence of clinically significant impairment in social, academic, or occupational functioning.

E. The symptoms do not occur exclusively during the course of a Pervasive Developmental Disorder, Schizophrenia, or other Psychotic Disorder and are not better accounted for by another mental disorder (e.g., Mood Disorder, Anxiety Disorder, Dissociative Disorder, or a Personality Disorder).

  Code based on type:

  Attention-Deficit/Hyperactivity Disorder, Combined Type: if both Criteria A1 and A2 are met for the past 6 months.

  Attention-Deficit/Hyperactivity Disorder, Predominantly Inattentive Type: if Criterion A1 is met but Criterion A2 is not met for the past 6 months.

  Attention-Deficit/Hyperactivity Disorder, Predominantly Hyperactive-Impulsive Type: if Criterion A2 is met but Criterion A1 is not met for the past 6 months.

  Coding note: For individuals (especially adolescents and adults) who currently have symptoms that no longer meet full criteria, "In Partial Remission" should be specified.

Source: Reprinted with permission from the *Diagnostic and Statistical Manual of Mental Disorders, Fourth Edition* (pp. 83–85). Copyright 1994 American Psychiatric Association.

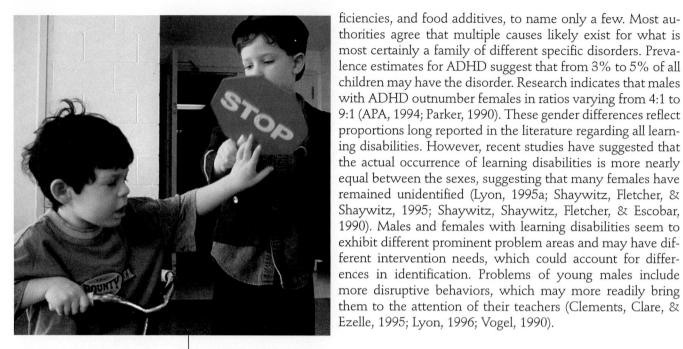

ficiencies, and food additives, to name only a few. Most authorities agree that multiple causes likely exist for what is most certainly a family of different specific disorders. Prevalence estimates for ADHD suggest that from 3% to 5% of all children may have the disorder. Research indicates that males with ADHD outnumber females in ratios varying from 4:1 to 9:1 (APA, 1994; Parker, 1990). These gender differences reflect proportions long reported in the literature regarding all learning disabilities. However, recent studies have suggested that the actual occurrence of learning disabilities is more nearly equal between the sexes, suggesting that many females have remained unidentified (Lyon, 1995a; Shaywitz, Fletcher, & Shaywitz, 1995; Shaywitz, Shaywitz, Fletcher, & Escobar, 1990). Males and females with learning disabilities seem to exhibit different prominent problem areas and may have different intervention needs, which could account for differences in identification. Problems of young males include more disruptive behaviors, which may more readily bring them to the attention of their teachers (Clements, Clare, & Ezelle, 1995; Lyon, 1996; Vogel, 1990).

Although many children may show symptoms of inattention, impulsivity, and hyperactivity, estimates suggest that only 3%–6% have ADHD.

focus 3

Identify two ways in which people with learning disabilities can be classified.

■ CLASSIFICATION

Although learning disabilities represent a complex constellation of behaviors and conditions, they have seldom been formally classified according to severity and have generally been seen as mild disorders. However, reference to severity appears in the literature on learning disabilities, even though it is not accounted for in most definitions (see Jahoda & Cattermole, 1995; Lowe et al., 1995; Raviv & Stone, 1991; Salyer, Holmstrom, & Noshpitz, 1991).

IDEA rules and regulations do address the issue of severity to some extent. They mandate that any criterion for classifying a child as having learning disabilities must be based on preexisting severe discrepancy between capacity and achievement. The determination for placement was related to the following criteria:

1. Whether a child achieves commensurate with his or her age and ability when provided with appropriate educational experiences
2. Whether the child has a severe discrepancy between achievement and intellectual ability in one or more of seven areas relating to communication skills and mathematical abilities

The child's learning disability must be determined on an individual basis, and the severe discrepancy between achievement and intellectual ability must be in one or more of the following areas: oral expression, listening comprehension, written expression, basic reading skill, reading comprehension, mathematical calculation, or mathematical reasoning.

The meaning of the term *severe discrepancy* is debated among professionals (McIntosh & Gridley, 1993; Suresh, 1994; Swanson, 1991, 1992). Although it is stipulated as a classification parameter, there is no broadly accepted way to measure it. What is an acceptable discrepancy between a child's achievement and what is expected at his or her grade level? 25%? 35%? 50%? The idea of severe discrepancy has appeared in the literature for many years, but general agreement regarding its exact definition has never been reached.

A review of the literature on definitions and classifications of learning disabilities, either historical or current, presents a confusing and conflicting array of ideas. Lack of agreement concerning the concepts that relate to the field has caused a number of difficulties in both research and treatment. The people who display characteristics of learning disabilities, however, present some of the most interesting challenges in behavioral science today.

Prevalence

Problems in determining accurate figures related to people with learning disabilities are amplified by differing definitions, theoretical views, and assessment procedures. Prevalence estimates are highly variable, ranging from 1% to 30% of the school-age population (Lerner, 1997). Briefing papers presented in hearings before the National Council on the Handicapped on June 8, 1989, in contrast, indicated that 5% to 10% is a reasonable estimate of the percentage of persons affected by learning disabilities (Stanford Research Institute, 1989) (see Figure 6.1).

Since learning disabilities emerged as a category, its prevalence has been high compared to that of other exceptionalities, a fact that has been controversial for many years. It has been difficult to find one prevalence figure that is agreed on by all involved in the field. In 1995–96, over 5 million children with disabilities (ages 6–21) were being served under IDEA in the United States (including Washington, DC, and Puerto Rico). Of that number, over 2.5 million were classified as having learning disabilities, which represents 51% of the population with disabilities being served (U.S. Department of Education, 1997).

Albert Einstein flunked math in elementary school and showed little ability or interest in school work. His intellectual genius and capability in science and mathematics did not assert itself until his early teens. Einstein represents the discrepancy that can exist in individual students.

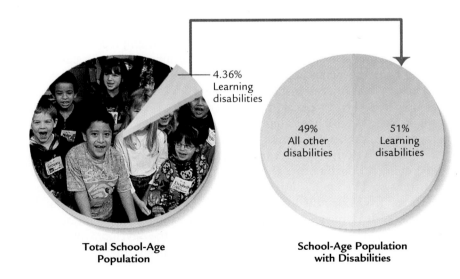

4.36% Learning disabilities

Total School-Age Population

49% All other disabilities

51% Learning disabilities

School-Age Population with Disabilities

FIGURE 6.1

The prevalence of learning disabilities for students 6–21 years of age [U.S. Department of Education, 1997]

PREVALENCE DISTRIBUTION BY DISABILITY

Despite the difficulties involved with defining and classifying learning disabilities, this term describes one of the largest groups served in special education. Use of the *learning disabilities* label for service still continues to grow, as illustrated in Table 6.2. The percentage of change indicated in the table, although substantial, is not as remarkable as the increased *number* of individuals served under the learning disabilities label. The continued growth and high level of service for students with learning disabilities have come under some criticism. Reflect on these questions:

- With definitional problems, does it make much sense to have this group of exceptional individuals represent such a high proportion of those served?

- Do people with learning disabilities really represent such a high proportion of individuals in general?

- Or has this classification become a catchall for those in special education?

focus 4

Identify two current estimated ranges for the prevalence of learning disabilities.

Some professionals and parents who are primarily interested in other disability groups question the high prevalence of learning disabilities. In some cases, they simply feel a sense of competition for the limited funds distributed among groups of people with different disabilities. Others, however, are concerned that the learning disabilities category is being overused to avoid the stigma associated with other labels or because of misdiagnosis, which may result in inappropriate treatment (see the nearby Reflect on This feature and Table 6.2).

Although discrepancies in prevalence occur in all fields of exceptionality, the area of learning disabilities seems more variable than most. Partly this can be attributed to the different descriptions of disabilities and procedures used by the agencies, states, and researchers who do the counting and estimating (Gravestock, 1996; Payette, Clarizio, Phillips, & Bennett, 1995; Swanson, 1996). Another source of discrepancy may be differing or vague definitions of learning disabilities. Prevalence figures gathered through various studies are unlikely to match when different definitions determine what is counted. This situation is common in the field of learning disabilities.

Characteristics

Although many professionals have characterized specific learning disabilities as mild disorders, few have attempted to validate this premise empirically. Identification of subgroups, subtypes, or severity levels in this heterogeneous population has been largely ignored in the past. However, some attempts have been made in the past few years to attend to these issues (Bender & Golden, 1990; Lowe et al., 1995; Payette et al., 1995 ; Raviv & Stone, 1991).

focus 5

Identify seven characteristics attributed to those with learning disabilities, and explain why it is difficult to characterize this group.

For example, McIntosh and Gridley (1993) investigated whether subgroups of children with learning disabilities could be distinguished in a group of 83 children from 6 to 17 years of age. The researchers did identify distinct subgroups, although not all of them displayed the complete array of characteristics associated with current definitions of learning disabilities. Other researchers have identified completely different subgroups (see Bender & Golden, 1990), which is not surprising, given the range of definitional parameters used in the field. Subtype research is important to the development of more effective intervention, geared precisely to the specific needs of distinctive groups within the large, heterogeneous population with learning disabilities (Bender, 1995).

TABLE 6.2 Net change between 1987–1988 and 1995–1996 in number and percentage of individuals ages 6–21 served under IDEA (by disability condition)

DISABILITY	SCHOOL YEAR		NET CHANGE	
	1987–1988	1995–1996	Difference	Percentage
Learning disability	1,937,827	2,595,004	657,177	+33.91
Speech or language difficulty	951,512	1,025,591	74,079	+7.79
Mental retardation	596,928	584,406	–12,522	– 2.10
Emotional disturbance	372,048	438,150	66,102	+17.77
Multiple disabilities	78,588	94,034	15,446	+19.65
Hearing impairments	56,742	67,994	11,252	+19.83
Orthopedic impairments	46,837	63,158	16,321	+34.85
Other health impairments	46,013	133,354	87,341	+189.82
Visual impairments	22,769	25,443	2,674	+11.74
Deafness-blindness	1,426	1,352	–74	–5.19
Autism	*	28,813	N/A	N/A
Traumatic brain injury	*	9,439	N/A	N/A
All disabilities	4,110,690	5,066,738	956,048	+23.26

* Data not available under IDEA service for this disability in 1987–1988.

Source: *19th annual report to Congress on the implementation of IDEA*, 1997, Washington, DC: U.S. Government Printing Office.

The perceptions of teachers and other professionals have also been investigated relative to subgroups and severity (see Gavrilidou, deMesquita, & Mason, 1993; Leviton, Guild-Wilson, Neff, & Gambill, 1993; McConaughy & Achenbach, 1996). Though exhibiting a typical amount of error and variation, ratings are stable enough to make possible some reliable distinctions regarding both subgroups and severity levels among students with learning disabilities. Some research suggests that teacher judgments resemble those made by school psychologists regarding the nature of a disability and its severity in a particular child (Gavrilidou et al., 1993). The perceptions and knowledge of teachers have long been cited as a badly overlooked source of assessment information; their input is vital in designing instructional adaptation for students with learning problems. Also, teachers working with students with learning disabilities quite often encounter youngsters who they firmly believe should *not* be considered learning disabled. In fact, one distinct subgroup commonly noted in studies of students labeled as having learning disabilities has been variously labeled "normal" or "no notable deficits" (Bender & Golden, 1990; McIntosh & Gridley, 1993). Such findings support the belief that many students currently being served as having learning disabilities may have been inappropriately referred. Twenty years ago Larsen (1978) commented on this phenomenon:

It is . . . likely that the large number of students who are referred for mild to moderate underachievement are simply unmotivated, poorly taught, come from home environments where scholastic success is not highly valued, or are dull–normal in intelligence. For all intents and purposes, these students should not automatically be considered as learning disabled, since

Alice

Alice found herself very frustrated with school. She was in the fourth grade, and her grades were very bad. She had worked very hard, but many of the things that were required just didn't seem to make sense.

History was a perfect example. Alice had looked forward to learning more about history; it seemed so fun and interesting when her grandfather told his stories. Alice thought it would have been fun to live back then, when all the kids got to ride horses. But history in school was not

fun, and it didn't make any sense at all. Alice had been reading last night, supposedly about a girl who was her age and was moving West with a wagon train. As she looked at the book, Alice read strange things. One passage said, "Mary pelieveb that things would get detter. What they

hab left Missouri they hab enough foob dut now there was darely enough for one meal a bay. Surely the wagonmaster woulb finb a wet to solve the brodlem." Alice knew that she would fail the test, and she cried quietly in her room as she dressed for school.

there is little evidence that placement in special education will improve their academic functioning. (p. 7)

■ ACADEMIC ACHIEVEMENT

The study of problems and inconsistencies in academic achievement largely prompted the recognition of learning disabilities as an area of exceptionality. Individuals with learning disabilities, while generally of normal or above-average intelligence, seem to have many academic problems. These problems generally persist from the primary grades through the end of formal schooling, including college (Patrikakou, 1996; Wilczenski, 1993; Yanok, 1993).

■ READING   Students with learning disabilities often have reading problems. In fact, the category of learning disabilities itself grew out of the earlier concept known as *remedial reading*. Some estimates have suggested that 80% to 90% of all students

Word recognition, word knowledge, and the use of context to determine meaning are factors in learning to read that present difficulties for students with learning disabilities.

with learning disabilities also have reading disabilities (Bender, 1995; Lyon, 1995b), whereas findings from other studies are as low as 60% (Wong, 1996). The specific reading problems of these students vary as much as the many elements involved in the reading process.

Word knowledge and word recognition, both important parts of reading skill, cause difficulty for people with learning disabilities. When we encounter a word that we know, we recall its meaning from our "mental dictionary." For unfamiliar words, however, we must "sound out" the letters and pronounce them based on our knowledge of typical spelling patterns and pronunciation rules. Skill in this process is particularly important since all words cannot be memorized (there are too many), and students are constantly encountering new ones.

This dimension of word knowledge presents particular problems for students with learning disabilities. To recognize words, students must know the rules of pronunciation, be able to generalize letter patterns, and draw analogies with considerable flexibility. Good readers usually accomplish this task rather easily, fairly quickly, and almost automatically. In

ilities experience great difficulty with this pro-
so only slowly and laboriously. They need spe-
s that will help them succeed at recognizing
993; Lerner, 1997).
ding skill is the use of context to determine
y adept at inferring the general meaning of an
nformation surrounding it. Poor readers have
recognition and reading, although specific in-
h, 1994; Sorrel, 1990). Good and poor readers
have and use background knowledge (Sorrel,
mation is a problem for students with learn-
learning disabilities do not seem to perceive
cusing on minor details (Curran, Kintsch, &
se students learning strategies such as skills
e of mnemonics, problem solving, and rela-
culties and enhance reading performance
Mastropieri, 1993; Vauras, Lehtinen, Olkin-

ing many skills (such as the ability to focus
ects of a task, and the ability to remember)
ject areas. Some difficulties experienced by
in more than one realm of behavior, mak-
nd explain. For example, does a child with
ulties or working memory problems (see
g on the individual, the problem could be
ion of the two. Depending on the severity
of the problem, specific instruction may improve performance. But if the focus of
the training is too limited, the student may not generalize the instruction to other
relevant areas. In cases in which the disability is quite severe (such as dyslexia), it
may be best to teach the person to compensate for the problem, by accessing information through other means and using reading sparingly (Spafford & Grosser, 1996)
(see the Reflect on This feature on page 184).

■WRITING AND SPELLING Children labeled as having learning disabilities
often have markedly different writing performance than their peers without disabilities. This problem affects their academic achievement and frequently persists into
adulthood. Difficulties may occur in handwriting (slow writing, spacing problems,
poor formation of letters), spelling skills, and composition (Gerber & Reiff, 1994;
Graham & Weintraub, 1996). Several such problems are illustrated in Figure 6.2 on
page 185.
   Some children are poor at handwriting because they have not mastered the basic
developmental skills required for the process. Such deficits contribute to the fundamental processes of grasping a pen or pencil and moving it in a fashion that results
in legible writing. In some cases, fine motor development seems delayed in children
with learning disabilities, contributing to physical difficulty in using writing materials. Handwriting also involves an understanding of spatial concepts, such as *up,
down, top,* and *bottom.* These abilities frequently are less well developed in youngsters with learning disabilities than in their age-mates without disabilities (Bender,
1995; Lane & Lewandowski, 1994). The physical actions involved in using pencil or
pen, as well as problems in discerning spatial relationships, can make it difficult to
form letters and use spacing between letters, words, and lines. Some children with

rather mild handwriting problems may be exhibiting slowness in development, which will improve as they grow older, receive instruction, and practice. However, in more severe cases (e.g., the young adult whose writing sample appeared in Figure 6.2), age and practice do not bring about skill mastery (Gerber & Reiff, 1994).

Some researchers view the handwriting, writing, and composition skills of students with learning disabilities as closely related to their reading ability (Hallenbeck, 1996; Richek, Caldwell, Jennings, & Lerner, 1996; Seidenberg, 1989). For example, research does not clearly indicate that children with learning disabilities write more poorly than their normally achieving peers who are reading on a similar level (Grinnell, 1988). Letter reversals and, in severe cases, **mirror writing** have often been used as illustrations of poor handwriting. However, it is also questionable whether children with learning disabilities commit these types of errors more often than their peers without disabilities at the same reading level.

The logic connecting writing and reading abilities has certain intuitive appeal. Most children write to some degree on their own, prior to receiving instruction in school. In general, children who write spontaneously also seem to read spontaneously and tend to have considerable practice at both before they enter school. Their homes (thereby hinting at the influence of parents) tend to have writing materials readily available for experimentation and practice. Likewise, they may often observe their parents writing, and the parents and child may write together. Further research concerning the relationship between reading and handwriting is definitely in order. Instruction in writing for children with learning disabilities has historically been somewhat isolated from the act of reading, focusing instead primarily on the technical skills (Grinnell, 1988).

Poor spelling is often a problem among students with learning disabilities (also evident in Figure 6.2). These children frequently omit letters or add incorrect ones.

FIGURE 6.2

Writing samples of a college
freshman with a learning disability

As I seT hare Thinking abouT This
simiTe I wundr How someone Like Me Cood
posblee make iT thou This cors. BuT some Howl
I muse over come my fers and Wrese So I muse
Be Calfodn in my sef and be NoT aferad To Trie

3 Reasens I Came To College

Reasen#1   To fofel a Drem that my Parens,
Teichers and I hadd — Adrem that I codd
some day by come ArchuTeck.

Reasen#2   To pouv rong those who sed I
codd NoT make iT.

Reasen#3   Becos I am a bulheded.

The text of these samples reads as follows:

As I sit here thinking about this semester, I wonder how someone like me could possibly make it through this course. But somehow I must overcome my fears and worries. So I must be confident in myself and be not afraid to try.

Three Reasons I Came To College

Reason #1. To fulfill a dream that my parents, teachers, and I had—a dream that I could some day become architect.
Reason #2. To prove wrong those who said I could not make it.
Reason #3. Because I am bullheaded.

Their spelling may also show evidence of letter-order confusion and developmentally immature pronunciation (Smith, 1994). Interestingly, relatively little research has been conducted on these spelling difficulties, and teaching methods have been based primarily on individual opinion rather than proven approaches (Grinnell, 1988). Recent literature suggests that spelling skills of students with learning disabilities seem to follow developmental patterns similar to those of their peers without disabilities, but are delayed (Bender, 1995; Lerner, 1997). Characteristics such as visual and auditory memory problems, deficiencies in auditory discrimination, and phonic generalizations have also been implicated in the spelling difficulties with learning disabilities. Further research on spelling is needed to understand this area more clearly.

■ MATHEMATICS Arithmetic is another academic area that causes individuals with learning disabilities considerable difficulty (Deshler, Ellis, & Lenz, 1996). They often have problems with counting, writing numbers, and mastering other simple math concepts (Parmar, Cawley, & Frazita, 1996; Zentall & Ferkis, 1993). Counting objects is perhaps the most fundamental mathematics skill and provides a foundation for the development of the more advanced, yet still basic, skills of addition and subtraction. Some youngsters omit numbers when counting sequences aloud (e.g., 1, 2, 3, 5, 7, 9), and others can count correctly but do not understand the relative value of numbers. Students with arithmetic learning disabilities have additional difficulties when asked to count beyond 9, which requires the use of more than one digit. This skill is somewhat more advanced than single-digit counting and involves knowledge about place value.

Place value is a more complex concept than the counting of objects and is fundamental to understanding addition and subtraction, since it is essential to the processes of carrying and borrowing. Many students with learning disabilities in math have problems understanding place value, particularly the idea that the same digit (e.g., 6) represents different magnitudes when placed in various positions (e.g., 16, 61, 632). Grinnell (1988) stated that the four problems students with learning disabilities encounter include

1. Understanding the grouping process
2. Understanding that each position to the left represents another multiple of ten
3. Understanding the placement of one digit per position
4. Understanding the relationship between the order of the digits and the value of the numeral (p. 349)

These basic mathematics difficulties place major obstacles in the paths of students with learning disabilities, often continuing to cause problems throughout high school (Miller, 1996). Mastery of fundamental quantitative concepts is vital to learning more abstract and complex mathematics, a requirement for youth with learning disabilities seeking to complete high school and attend colleges or universities. These young adults are increasing in number, and it is essential for them to master algebra and geometry during secondary education. These topics have traditionally received minimal or no attention in curriculum designed for students with learning disabilities. Such coursework has tended to emphasize computational skills, though change is occuring as more attention is given to the need for more advanced instruction in mathematics (Lerner, 1997; Wong, 1996). Further research on mathematics difficulties and effective instruction for students encountering such problems grows more important as such young people seek to achieve more challenging educational goals.

■ACHIEVEMENT DISCREPANCY In addition to scoring below their age-mates in overall achievement, students with learning disabilities perform below expectations based on their measured potential. This discrepancy between academic achievement and the student's assessed ability and age has prompted considerable research and theorizing. Attempts to quantify the discrepancy between academic achievement and academic potential for students with learning disabilities have appeared in the literature for some time (Bender, 1995; Payette et al., 1995; Shapiro, Buckhault, & Herod, 1995), but the field still lacks a broadly accepted explanation of the phenomenon. Early in the school years, youngsters with learning disabilities may find themselves 2 to 4 or more years behind their peers in level of academic achievement, and many fall even further behind as they continue in the educational system. This discouraging pattern often results in students' dropping out of high school (U.S. Department of Education, 1996) or graduating without proficiency in basic reading, writing, or math skills.

■ INTELLIGENCE

Certain assumptions about intelligence are being reconsidered in research on learning disabilities. Typically, populations with behavior disorders and learning disabilities are thought to include people generally considered average or near average in intelligence. Differences between students with behavior disorders and those with specific learning disabilities have been defined based on social skill levels and learner characteristics. However, individuals with learning disabilities may also exhibit secondary behavioral disorders, and students with behavior disorders may also have learning difficulties. To further complicate the matter, student classroom performance also suggests that behavior problems are not associated with a particular level of intellectual functioning. It is well known that individuals with intellectual deficits and those with learning disabilities may both exhibit a considerable amount of maladaptive social and interpersonal behavior (Forness & Kavale, 1996; Huntington & Bender, 1993; Symons, Greene, & Symons, 1995). Problems in social adjustment must be viewed as a shared characteristic.

These insights have affected traditional ideas about the distinctions between learning disabilities and mental retardation. High variability between measured intelligence and academic performance has long been viewed as a defining characteristic of people with learning disabilities (Smith, Dowdy, Polloway, & Blalock, 1997; Wong, 1996). Also, descriptions of learning disabilities have often emphasized great intraindividual differences between skill areas; for example, a youngster may have a disability (very low performance) in reading but not in arithmetic. Frequently, this variability in aptitude has been used to distinguish populations with learning disabilities from those with mental retardation. A typical view holds that individuals thought to have mental retardation exhibit a consistent profile of abilities (generally, low performance in all areas), in contrast to the pronounced intraindividual variability associated with learning disabilities. However, intraindividual variability is not limited to students with learning disabilities; it is sometimes evident in students with mental retardation and those with behavior disorders.

■ COGNITION AND INFORMATION PROCESSING

Many other characteristics have been attributed to people with learning disabilities; some fall in the area of **cognition** or **information processing.** Long used in psychology as a model for studying the processes of the mind, the cognitive approach focuses on the way a person acquires, retains, and manipulates information (Hamachek, 1995; Lefrancois, 1995). These processes often emerge as problematic for individuals with learning disabilities. For example, teachers have long complained that such children have poor memory. In many cases, these students seem to learn material one day but cannot recall it the next. Research on the memory skills of these children has been relatively scanty, although it is central to understanding how information is acquired, stored, selected, and recalled. Certain evidence has suggested that children with learning disabilities do not perform as well as normal children on some memory tasks, whereas on other tasks results have shown no differences (Denckla, 1996a;

This teacher is providing several cues to help her students grasp the meaning of the word *cytoplasm.* She has linked a shaded illustration, the whole word cytoplasm, cytoplasm broken syllable-by-syllable, and the actual writing and visualizing of the word and what it represents. A combination of cues is often important for students with learning disabilities.

Male, 1996; Perrig & Perrig, 1995; Swanson, Ashbaker, & Lee, 1996). Additional research is needed to confirm, refute, or clarify clinical impressions gathered so far.

Research also suggests that children with learning disabilities have differing rather than uniformly deficient, cognitive abilities (Denckla, 1996a; Swanson et al., 1996). This finding has led to the development of specific, highly focused instruction for individuals with learning disabilities to replace generic curricula that assume their cognitive skills are generally poor (see Zentall & Ferkis, 1993).

Attention problems have also been associated with learning disabilities. Such problems have often been clinically characterized as **short attention span.** Parents and teachers often note that their children with learning disabilities cannot sustain attention for more than a very short time—in some cases exhibiting considerable daydreaming and high distractibility (Gelfand et al., 1997). Some researchers have observed short attention spans in these children, but others have indicated that they have difficulty in certain types of attention problems and in attending selectively (Richards, Samuels, Turnure, & Ysseldyke, 1990; Zentall & Ferkis, 1993). **Selective attention** problems make it difficult to focus on centrally important tasks or information rather than peripheral or less relevant stimuli. Such problems might emerge when children with learning disabilities are asked to compute simple math problems that are on the chalkboard (which also means they must copy from the board). They may attend to the copying task rather than the math problems. In this situation, the teacher can easily modify the task (e.g., by using worksheets rather than copying from the board) to facilitate completion of an important lesson. Attention problems remain in the spotlight as the information-processing problems of children with learning disabilities is investigated (Reid, 1996; Swanson, 1991, 1992).

■ LEARNING CHARACTERISTICS

Although study of perceptual problems has played a part in the history of learning disabilities, interest in this topic has declined over the years. However, some researchers have continued to view perception difficulties as important.

Perception difficulties in people with learning disabilities represent a constellation of behavior anomalies, rather than a single characteristic. Descriptions of these problems have referred to the visual, auditory, and **haptic** sensory systems. Visual perception difficulty has been closely associated with learning disabilities. It is important to remember that the definitions of learning disabilities exclude impaired vision in the traditional sense—visual perception problems in persons with learning disabilities refer to something distinctly different. This type of abnormality can cause a child to see a visual stimulus as unrelated parts rather than as an integrated pattern; for example, a child may not be able to identify a letter in the alphabet because he or she perceives only unrelated lines, rather than the letter as a meaningful whole. Clearly, such perception causes severe performance problems in school, particularly during the early years (Smith, 1994).

Visual perception problems may also emerge in **figure-ground discrimination,** the process of distinguishing an object from its background. Whereas most of us have little difficulty with figure-ground discrimination, certain children labeled as having learning disabilities may have difficulty focusing on a word or sentence on the page of a textbook because they cannot distinguish it from the rest of the page. This, of course, results in difficulties with schoolwork. This deficit illustrates one of the problems in research on learning disabilities: It could represent a figure-ground discrimination disorder, but it could also reveal an attention deficit or a memory problem. Thus the same abnormal behavior can be accounted for differently by several theories (Bender, 1995).

Other discrimination problems have also appeared in descriptions of people with learning disabilities. Individuals with difficulties in **visual discrimination** may be unable to distinguish one visual stimulus from another (e.g., the difference between words such as *sit* and *sat* or letters such as *V* and *W*); they commonly reverse letters such as *b* and *d*. This type of error is common among young children, causing great concern for parents. Yet most youngsters overcome this problem in the course of normal development and show few reversal or rotation errors with visual images by about 7 or 8 years of age. Children who make frequent errors beyond that age might be viewed as potential problem learners and may need additional instruction specifically aimed at improving such skills.

Auditory perception problems have historically been associated with learning disabilities. Some children have been characterized as unable to distinguish between the sounds of different words or syllables or even to identify certain environmental sounds (e.g., a ringing telephone) and differentiate them from others. Such problems have been termed **auditory discrimination** deficits. People with learning disabilities have also been described as having difficulties in auditory blending, auditory memory, and auditory association. Those with **auditory blending** problems may not be able to blend word parts into an integrated whole as they pronounce the word. **Auditory memory** difficulties may result in an inability to recall information presented orally. **Auditory association** deficiencies may result in an inability to process such information. Clearly, difficulties in these areas can create school performance problems for a child (Taub, Fine, & Cherry, 1994). However, questions have begun to emerge regarding the utility of auditory deficit theories in understanding learning disabilities (see Bender, 1995).

Another area of perceptual difficulty long associated with learning disabilities involves *haptic perception* (touch, body movement, and position sensation). Such difficulties are thought to be relatively uncommon but may be important in some areas of school performance. For example, handwriting requires haptic perception because tactile information about the grasp of a pen or pencil must be transmitted to the brain. In addition, **kinesthetic** information is transmitted regarding hand and arm movements as one writes. Children with learning disabilities have often been described by teachers as having poor handwriting and difficulties in spacing letters and staying on the lines of the paper. Such problems could also be due to visual perception abnormalities, however, so precisely attributing some behaviors to a single factor is difficult. Figure 6.2 on page 185 presents an example of writing by a college freshman with learning disabilities. The two samples in this figure were written on consecutive days, each in a 40-minute period. The note translates what was written.

Not all individuals labeled as having learning disabilities exhibit behaviors that suggest perceptual problems. Patterns of deficiencies vary widely. Also, empirical evidence of perceptual problems in those labeled as having learning disabilities is generally lacking. Overall, the notion of perceptual dysfunction is founded on clinical impressions rather than rigorous research. However, this viewpoint is widespread enough to warrant this brief discussion.

■ HYPERACTIVITY

Hyperactivity is a behavioral characteristic commonly associated with children who are labeled as having learning disabilities. Also termed **hyperkinetic** behavior,

hyperactivity is typically defined as a general excess of activity. Professionals working in the area of learning disabilities, particularly teachers, often mention this behavior first in describing their students, depicting them as fidgeting a great deal and unable to sit still for even a short time (Forness & Kavale, 1996; Lerner, 1997; Symons, Green, & Simons, 1995). Most descriptions portray an overly active child.

Certain points need to be clarified as we discuss hyperactivity in children with learning disabilities. First, not all children with learning disabilities are hyperactive, and vice versa. As many as half the children with learning disabilities may not be hyperactive—certainly it is not a universal characteristic (see Faraone et al., 1993; Zentall & Ferkis, 1993). Currently mixed research results and confusion mark our understanding of how learning disabilities relate to hyperactivity (DuQuiros, Kinsbourne, Palmer, & Rufo, 1994; Javorsky, 1996).

A second point involves the view that hyperkinesis is characterized as a general pattern of excessive activity. This idea may reveal more about stereotypical expectations than about accurate observations. Some research has suggested that it may be more helpful to consider the appropriateness of a child's activity in particular settings rather than make overly broad generalizations about a child's behavior (Bender, 1995). Evidence does indicate that hyperactive children have a higher level of activity than their normal peers in structured settings (such as certain classroom circumstances); however, in relatively unstructured settings (such as play periods), no such differences exist (Smith, 1994).

■ SOCIAL AND EMOTIONAL CHARACTERISTICS

We have discussed the characteristics and behavior of students with learning disabilities as they relate to academic work. Definitions and labels used for these students tend to focus on the academic perspective. Yet children and adolescents with learning disabilities often encounter emotional and interpersonal difficulties that are quite serious and highly resistant to treatment (Farmer & Farmer, 1996; Forness & Kavale, 1996; Symons et al., 1995). Because of their learning problems, they frequently experience low self-esteem and negative emotional consequences that present significant problems (Bender, 1995). They may not be able to interact effectively with others because they misunderstand social cues or cannot discriminate among or interpret the subtleties of typical interpersonal associations.

In some cases the social dimensions of life present greater problems to students with learning disabilities than their specific academic deficits, and yet this dynamic is essentially ignored in the use of definitions and labels related to learning disabilities. Some view the broad category of learning disabilities as less functional than specific terminology that more precisely describes particular problems. Probably little support would be forthcoming for broadening the definition of learning disabilities to incorporate social and emotional dimensions, although it is clear that they are substantial (Huntington & Bender, 1993).

Causation

Researchers have posited a number of possible causes for learning disabilities. Yet in spite of substantial interest and effort related to this field, determining precise causation has been difficult, and the effort to do so still continues. There appear to be many different causes of learning disabilities, and in some cases, a given type of learning disability may have multiple causes (Gelfand et al., 1997). But because it is imperative to assist affected students even before we understand the cause of learning disabilities, frequently the practical issues of assessment and intervention have taken priority in research so that specialized instruction can be offered to such students (Carnine, 1994; Emerson, Reeves, Tompson, & Henderson, 1996).

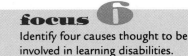

focus 6
Identify four causes thought to be involved in learning disabilities.

■ NEUROLOGICAL FACTORS

For many years, some have viewed the cause of learning disabilities as structural neurological damage or some type of neurological function abnormality. A number of professionals within the field have supported this contention (Bigler, 1992; Seidman, Biederman, Faraone, & Milberger, 1995; Smith, 1994). Neurological factors have been the focus of study and have been specified as an identification criterion in some investigations (Grace & Malloy, 1992; Weinberg & Harper, 1993).

Neurological damage associated with learning disabilities can occur in many ways. Damage may be inflicted on the neurological system at birth by conditions such as abnormal fetal positioning during delivery or anoxia (a lack of oxygen). Infections may also cause neurological damage and learning disabilities, as can certain types of physical injury. As a practical matter, however, neurological damage as a cause of learning disability must be largely inferred, since direct evidence is usually not available (Bender, 1995; Denckla, 1996b; Drew, Hardman, & Logan, 1996) (see also Chapter 8 on the effects of neurological damage as related to mental retardation).

■ MATURATIONAL DELAY

Some theories have suggested that a maturational delay of the neurological system results in the difficulties experienced by some individuals with learning disabilities (Martinius, 1993). In many ways, the behavior and performance of children with learning disabilities resemble those of much younger individuals (Lerner, 1997). They often exhibit delays in skills maturation, such as slower development of language skills, and problems in the visual-motor area and several academic areas, as already noted. Although maturational delay is most likely not a causative factor in all types of learning disabilities, it has received considerable support as one of many.

■ GENETIC FACTORS

Genetic causation has also been implicated in learning disabilities. Genetic abnormalities, which are inherited, are thought to cause or contribute to one or more of the problems categorized as learning disabilities (Dilts, Carey, Kircher, & Hoffman, 1996; Pennington, 1995). This is always a concern for parents, whatever the learning or behavior disorder. Over the years, some research, including studies of **identical twins** and **fraternal twins,** has suggested that such disorders may be inherited (Eme, 1992; Light & DeFries, 1995). These findings must be viewed cautiously because of the well-known problems in separating the influences of heredity and environment, but evidence lends a certain degree of support to the idea that some learning disabilities may be inherited (Faraone et al., 1993; Smith et al., 1997).

■ ENVIRONMENTAL FACTORS

Environmental influences are often suggested as a cause of learning disabilities. Factors such as dietary inadequacies, food additives, radiation stress, fluorescent lighting, unshielded television tubes, smoking, drinking, drug consumption, and inappropriate school instruction are now only beginning to be investigated (see Hallahan, Kauffman, & Lloyd, 1996; Katims, Zapata, & Yin, 1996; Morgane, Austin-LaFrance, Bronzino, & Tonkiss, 1993; Richards, Symons, Greene, & Szuszkiewicz, 1995). Some environmental factors are known to have negative effects on development (e.g., irradiation, lead ingestion, illicit drugs, and family stress). In some cases, these influences appear to be primarily prenatal concerns, and in others, the problems seem limited to the postnatal environment or both (Dyson, 1996; Morgane et al., 1993). Research on the details of environmental causation relating specifically to learning disabilities remains inconclusive, but it is the focus of continuing study.

Assessment

The assessment of individuals with learning disabilities has several purposes. The ultimate goal is to provide appropriate screening, identification, and placement of individuals who require services beyond those needed by most people. This may mean additional help with academic work, social skills, or support related to any aspect of life and involving professionals from any number of human service disciplines. Deciding how to meet a student's individual needs requires a spectrum of different types of information obtained by using a variety of assessment procedures (Aiken, 1997; Payne, 1992; Salvia & Ysseldyke, 1991). This section will examine assessment for learning disabilities in terms of purpose and domain of assessment and will focus on the areas of intelligence, adaptive behavior, and academic achievement.

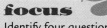 **focus 7**
Identify four questions that are addressed by screening assessment in learning disabilities.

■ FORMAL AND INFORMAL ASSESSMENT

An individual's status in performance, skills, and ability can be evaluated in a number of ways, either formally or informally. Formal and informal assessment have grown to mean standardized tests versus teacher-made tests or techniques. Standardized instruments, such as intelligence tests and achievement tests, are published and distributed on a commercial basis. Teacher-made (or those devised by any professional) techniques or instruments are not commercially available. These may be constructed for specific assessment purposes and are often quite formal, in the sense that great care is taken in the evaluation process. Both formal and informal assessment techniques are effective ways of evaluating students with learning disabilities, and other students as well (Dalton, Tivnan, Riley, & Rawson, 1995). Both are used for evaluation purposes in a number of performance or behavior areas (Gronlund, 1993; McMillan, 1997).

Other distinguishing characteristics can be used to describe assessment instruments. **Norm-referenced assessment** compares an individual's skills or performance with that of others, such as age-mates, usually on the basis of national average scores. Thus, a student's counting performance might be compared with that of his or her classmates, others in the school district of the same age, or state or national average scores. In contrast, **criterion-referenced assessment** compares an individual's skills not with a norm, but with a desired level (criterion) of performance or goal. For example, the goal may involve counting to 100 with no errors by the end of the school year (McMillan, 1997). One particular application of criterion-referenced assessment has received a great deal of attention recently: **Curriculum-**

based assessment uses the objectives in a student's curriculum as the criteria against which progress is evaluated (daFonseca, 1996; Shapiro & Eckert, 1992; Smith et al., 1997). The relationship between evaluation and instructional objectives makes both instruction planning and assessment more efficient. Other terms have also been used for similar procedures (e.g., *objectives-referenced measurement*), but they all involve the concept of assessment referenced to instruction (Worthen, Borg, & White, 1993).

Both norm- and criterion-referenced assessment are useful for working with students with learning disabilities, although the two approaches tend to be used for different purposes. Norm-referenced assessment is often used for administrative purposes, such as compiling census data on how many students are achieving at the state or national average. Criterion-referenced assessment is helpful for specific instructional purposes and planning.

It is very important to note that these two types of assessment do not correspond to two entirely separate types of assessment instruments or procedures. Depending on how a technique, instrument, or procedure is employed, it may be used in a norm-referenced or criterion-referenced manner. Some areas, such as intelligence, are more typically evaluated using norm-referenced procedures. However, even a standardized intelligence test can be scored and used in a criterion-referenced fashion (the test would then function as a source of test items, and a student's performance could not be evaluated exactly as the test developer intended). Assessment should always be undertaken with careful attention to the purpose and future use of the evaluation (Aiken, 1997; Kaplan & Saccuzzo, 1993).

By comparing a student's skill level with a criterion-based assessment, a teacher is able to make a specific instruction plan for the student.

■ SCREENING

Screening of students who seem to have learning disabilities has always been an important facet of assessment. In the process of identifying such students, assessment occurs *prior* to labeling or treatment, although clinicians or others (often parents) in contact with the child often suspect a problem exists (Keim, 1995; Tur-Kaspa & Bryan, 1995). Screening may occur at a rather young age for some individuals and involve assessment to compare the child with others of a similar age. Its role is to "raise a red flag," suggesting that more investigation is needed for one or more reasons.

Four questions are pertinent at this point of the assessment process:

1. Is there a reason to more fully investigate the abilities of the child?
2. Is there a reason to suspect that the child in any way has disabilities?
3. If the child appears to have disabilities, what are the relevant characteristics and what sort of intervention is appropriate?
4. How should we plan for the future of the individual?

Answers to these questions might point to a variety of needs: further classification of the disability, planning of intervention services such as psychological treatment or individualized instruction, or ongoing evaluation of progress. It is important to note that assessment is not a simple, isolated event that results in a single diagnosis (Hewett & Bolen, 1996). It is a complex process involving many different steps. After diagnosis, assessment continues as a dynamic process that undergirds all decision making throughout the time an individual receives services related to learning disabilities (Hoy & Gregg, 1994; Swanson, 1995).

Approaches to assessment, for our purposes, focus on intelligence, adaptive skills, and academic achievement.

■ INTELLIGENCE

Individuals with learning disabilities have long been described as having, for the most part, average or near-average intelligence, although they experience problems in school often typical of students having lower intelligence levels. In many cases, measures of intelligence may be inaccurate due to specific visual, auditory, or other limitations that may affect the student's performance. However, intelligence assessment remains an important matter for individuals with learning disabilities and is often evaluated with a standardized instrument such as an IQ test (Lavin, 1995; Worthen et al., 1993).

The issue of where measured intelligence fits into the definition of learning disabilities is somewhat controversial (Wong, 1996). Some researchers have argued that intelligence quotient (IQ) is irrelevant to the definition of learning disabilities, whereas others see it as important (see Siegel, 1989; Torgesen, 1989). Still others argue that the traditional way of measuring IQ is problematic, but not the concept of intelligence per se (Naglieri & Reardon, 1993). Such difference of opinion is not unusual in the field of learning disabilities.

■ ADAPTIVE SKILLS

People with learning disabilities have frequently been described as exhibiting poor adaptive skills, lacking a sense of what constitutes appropriate behavior within a particular environment. Such descriptions have primarily appeared in clinical reports and have not historically been a routine part of assessment of learning disabilities to the degree they have figured in other areas of exceptionality, such as mental retardation. However, some work has been undertaken to address adaptive skills assessment for individuals with learning disabilities (see Gaskell, Dockrell, & Rehman, 1995; Lowe et al., 1995). Such efforts are based on the assumption that a discrepancy between ability and academic achievement alone is insufficient to fully assess and describe learning disabilities. The study of adaptive skills has contributed to greater understanding of subtypes and severity levels in learning disabilities and is beginning to receive greater attention in the field as researchers focus more on the emotional well-being of students with learning disabilities (see Hallahan et al., 1996; Huntington & Bender, 1993; Lerner, 1997).

■ ACADEMIC ACHIEVEMENT

Academic achievement has always been a major problem for students with learning disabilities. Assessment of academic achievement determines whether there is an overall discrepancy between a student's ability and his or her academic achievement. Such assessment also helps evaluate the student's level of functioning in one or more specific academic areas. Instruments have been developed and used to diagnose specific academic problems (Smith et al., 1997). For example, a number of reading tests, including the Woodcock Reading Mastery Tests, the Diagnostic Reading Scales, and the Stanford Diagnostic Reading Test, are used to determine the nature of reading problems. Likewise, mathematics assessment employs instruments such as the Key Math Diagnostic Arithmetic Test and the Stanford Diagnostic Mathematics Test (Aiken, 1997; Gronlund, 1993).

Academic assessment for students with learning disabilities is very important. For the most part, assessment techniques resemble those used in other areas of exceptionality, because deficits in academic achievement are a common problem among students with a variety of disabilities. Specific skill-deficit diagnosis, however, has a more prominent history in learning disabilities and has prompted the development of focused, skill-oriented academic achievement assessment in other disability areas, as well. As with other exceptionalities, issues of inclusion and collaboration are prominent considerations in choosing the types of assessments employed with regard to instructional placement and implementation in the educational program (Dettmer, Dyck, & Thurston, 1996; Fishbaugh, 1997; Welch & Sheridan, 1995). Assessment with maximum relevance to the setting of application, often termed authentic or alternative assessment, also has attracted growing interest. These methods assess progress or skill using settings and procedures in a context like that in which the student must function in contrast to the sterile, formal style of test administration used in the past (Lee, 1992; McMillan, 1997).

The Elementary School Years

Services and supports for children with learning disabilities have changed over time as professionals have come to view learning disabilities as a constellation of specific individualized needs, rather than a single generic category. Specific disabilities, such as cognitive learning problems, attention deficit and hyperactivity, social and emotional difficulties, and problems with spoken language, reading, writing, and mathematics are receiving research attention (see Lauterbach & Bender, 1995). This approach has resulted in services and supports focused on individual need, rather than general treatment of learning disabilities. Attention is also being paid to social skills instruction for children with learning disabilities and the effective use of peers as tutors (Fuchs, Fuchs, Mathes, & Simmons, 1997; Katims & Pierce, 1995). Recognition that these children learn and develop in a broad context has brought about a shift in the focus of services. Rather than intervening in an isolated problem area and ignoring others, a broad spectrum of issues is addressed (see Beale, 1995; Lerner, 1997). Some services and supports focus on strategic instruction (e.g., teaching the children how to learn), counseling and/or peer and family support (e.g., parent training), and medical treatment, all in the context of a structured educational environment (Katims & Harris, in press; Lerner, 1997).

Services and supports for adolescents or adults with learning disabilities may differ from those for children. Some changes in approach are due to shifting goals as individuals grow older (e.g., the acquisition of basic counting skills versus math instruction in preparation for college) (Denckla, 1993; Yanok, 1993). Educational support requires a broad range of specialized instruction tailored to individual need.

focus 8
Identify three types of intervention or treatment employed with people diagnosed as having learning disabilities.

Interacting in Natural Settings

PEOPLE WITH LEARNING DISABILITIES

■ EARLY YEARS*

TIPS FOR THE FAMILY

- Play verbal direction games, such as finding certain words or sounds, interspersing those that are difficult with those that are easy for the child with learning disabilities.
- Give the child practice in identifying different sounds (e.g., the doorbell and phone).
- Reinforce the child for paying attention.
- Promote family learning about learning disabilities, their child's specific strengths and limitations, and their respect for their child as a person.

TIPS FOR THE PRESCHOOL TEACHER

- Limit verbal instructions to simple sentences, presented briefly, one at a time.
- Determine appropriate content carefully, paying attention to the developmental level of the material.
- Provide multiple examples to clarify points and reinforce meaning.
- Provide more practice than usual, particularly on new material or skills.

TIPS FOR PRESCHOOL PERSONNEL

- Promote a school environment and attitude that encourage respect for children of all abilities.
- Promote the development of instructional programs focusing on preacademic skills, which may be unnecessary for all children but very important for young students with learning disabilities.
- Be alert for students that seem to be of average or higher intelligence but, for reasons that may not be evident, are not performing up to ability.

TIPS FOR NEIGHBORS AND FRIENDS

- Community activities should be arranged to include a broad range of maturational levels so that children with learning disabilities are not shut out or do not experience unnecessary failure at this early age.

■ ELEMENTARY YEARS

TIPS FOR THE FAMILY

- Become involved in the school through parent–teacher organizations and conferences.
- Volunteer as a tutor.
- Learn more about learning disabilities as you begin to understand how they affect your child, perhaps through reading material or enrolling in a short course.

TIPS FOR GENERAL EDUCATION CLASSROOM TEACHER

- Keep verbal instructions simple and brief.
- Have the student with learning disabilities repeat directions back to you, to ensure understanding.
- Use mnemonics in instruction to aid memory.
- Intensify instruction by repeating the main points several times to aid memory.
- Provide additional time to learn material, including repetition or reteaching.

TIPS FOR SCHOOL PERSONNEL

- Encourage individual athletic activities (e.g., swimming) rather than competitive team sports.
- Involve the child in appropriate school activities (e.g., chorus or music) where interests are apparent.
- Develop peer-tutoring programs, in which older students assist children who are having difficulty.

TIPS FOR NEIGHBORS AND FRIENDS

- Learn about advocacy or other groups that can help you learn about and interact with the child with learning disabilities.
- Maintain a relationship with the child's parents, talking with them about the child if and when they feel comfortable doing so.
- As a friend, encourage parents to seek special assistance from agencies that might provide services such as "talking books."
- If you are interested, offer assistance to the child's parents in whatever form they may need, or even volunteer to work with the child as a tutor.

■ SECONDARY AND TRANSITION YEARS

TIPS FOR THE FAMILY

- Provide extra support for your youngster in the family setting, encouraging good school performance despite academic problems that may be occurring.
- Encourage your adolescent to talk about and think about future plans as he or

---

Individuals from varied professions must function as a team and also as unique contributors to create a well-balanced program for the student with learning disabilities (Welch & Sheridan, 1995).

■ ACADEMIC INSTRUCTION AND SUPPORT

A wide variety of approaches to promote the academic learning of children with learning disabilities has been used over the years, including strategies to develop cognition, attention, spoken language, and skill in reading, writing, and mathemat-

she progresses into and through the transition from school to young adult life.

- Try to understand the academic and social difficulties the student may encounter. Encourage impulse control if impulsiveness may be causing some of the problems.
- Do not shy away from the difficult task of encouraging the student to associate with peers who are success oriented rather than those who may be involved in inappropriate behavior.
- Encourage your adolescent to consider and plan for the years after high school, whether those involve continuing on to college or moving into an employment situation.

TIPS FOR THE GENERAL EDUCATION CLASSROOM TEACHER
- Specifically teach self-recording strategies, such as asking: Was I paying attention?
- Relate new material to knowledge the student with learning disabilities already has, making specific connections with familiar information.
- Teach the use of external memory enhancers (e.g., lists and note taking).
- Encourage the use of other devices to improve class performance (e.g., tape recorders).

TIPS FOR SCHOOL PERSONNEL
- Promote involvement in social activities and clubs that will enhance interpersonal interaction.
- Where students with learning disabilities have such interests and abilities, encourage participation in athletics or other extracurricular activities.
- Where interests and abilities are present, involve students in support roles to extracurricular activities (e.g., as team equipment manager).
- Promote the development of functional academic programs that are combined with transitional planning and programs.
- Provide information on college for students with learning disabilities, and encourage them to seek counseling regarding educational options, where appropriate.

TIPS FOR NEIGHBORS AND FRIENDS
- Encourage students to seek assistance from agencies that may provide services (e.g., special newspapers, talking books, and special radio stations).
- Promote involvement in community activities (e.g., scouting, Rotary Club, Chamber of Commerce, or other service organizations for adults).
- Encourage a positive understanding of learning disabilities among neighbors, friends, and community agencies (e.g., law enforcement officials) who may encounter adolescents or adults with disabilities.

■ ADULT YEARS

TIPS FOR THE FAMILY
- Interact with your adult family member with learning disabilities on a level that is consistent with his or her adult status. Despite all the difficulties experienced in school and while maturing, remember that this person is now an adult.
- While recognizing the person's adult status, also remember that your adult family member with learning disabilities will likely continue to experience specific difficulties related to his or her disability. Help the person to devise ways of compensating.

TIPS FOR THERAPISTS OR OTHER PROFESSIONALS
- In adulthood, it is unlikely that basic academic instruction will be the focus of professional intervention. It may be worthwhile to focus on compensatory skills for particularly difficult problem areas.

- Be alert for signs of emotional stress that may require intervention. This person may have a very deep sense of frustration accrued from a lifelong history of difficulties and failure.

TIPS FOR NEIGHBORS AND FRIENDS
- It may be necessary to be more flexible or understanding with adult friends or neighbors with learning disabilities. There may be good explanations for deviations from what is considered normal behavior. However, if certain behaviors are persistent and particularly aggravating to you, you owe it to your friend to discuss the matter rather than letting it interfere with a friendship. You may have numerous friends, but the adult with learning disabilities may have precious few; thus your understanding and honesty are particularly valuable.

*Very young children who may have learning disabilities typically have not been formally diagnosed with the disability, although they may exhibit what appears to be maturational slowness.

ics (Berk & Landau, 1993; Cassel & Reid, 1996; Lavin, 1995). Even within each area, a whole array of instructional procedures has been used to address specific problems. For example, as part of cognitive training, instruction in problem solving, problem-attack strategies, and social competence has been incorporated (Katims & Harris, in press; Lauterbach & Bender, 1995; Welch & Sheridan, 1995).

Just as learning disabilities involve a very heterogeneous population, approaches to cognitive instruction also vary. They are often combined and customized to address individual need; deficits in adaptive skills that interfere with inclusion in general education may also be a focus of instruction (Marston, 1996; Tralli, Colombo,

Deshler, & Schumaker, 1996). Multiple services and supports may make inclusion possible, while also providing a well-defined instructional environment, teaching the child important skills, and addressing interpersonal or social–emotional needs (see Fuchs et al., 1997; Katims & Harris, in press). Orchestrating such an instructional package is not a casual task. Successful inclusion requires determining the intensity and duration of instruction appropriate for the child and choosing supports that will meet the child's needs (Reid, 1996; Tralli et al., 1996). Program design is complex and labor-intensive, but essential to integrating children with learning disabilities into the educational mainstream (Fuchs, Roberts, Fuchs, & Bowers, 1996). Such programs for elementary-level children can build and improve their deficient skills to give them a more promising prognosis for success in later school programs.

■ MATHEMATICS Mathematics instruction for students with learning disabilities exemplifies how building a foundation of basic skills can enhance later learning. Earlier, we noted that children with arithmetic learning difficulties may have problems with basic counting and understanding of place values. For these students, counting may be most effectively taught with manipulative objects. Repetitive experience with counting buttons, marbles, or any such objects provides practice in counting as well as exposure to the concepts of magnitude associated with numbers. Counting and grouping sets of 10 objects can help children begin to grasp rudimentary place-value concepts. For students with learning disabilities, these activities must be quite structured.

Commercial programs of instruction in basic math concepts are also available. Cuisenaire Rods, sets of 291 color-coded rods used for manipulative learning experiences, are an example. These rods, whose differing lengths and colors are associated with numbers, can be used to teach basic arithmetic processes to individual students or groups.

Computer technology has also found its way into math skills instruction for students with learning disabilities (Bender, 1996a, 1996b). Microcomputers are particularly appealing for teaching math because content can be presented in a sequence that is most helpful. Computers can also provide drill and practice exercises for those who need it, an instructional goal that is often difficult for teaching staff to accomplish in a classroom with several children. Concern exists, however, regarding the use of computer technology primarily for drill and practice. Although reinforcement of learning is clearly a strength of many math programs, some focus excessively on drill and practice (Bender & Bender, 1996). Some researchers strongly contend that a broad range of instructional applications is needed, extending beyond elementary skill development to serve a broader range of students (see Drew, 1994; Higgins & Zvi, 1995). To date, computer technology has contributed little to transforming fundamental instruction in mathematics (Mayer, 1997, p. 17). (See the nearby Today's Technology feature).

These points are well taken: Electronic technology can provide some forms of effective instruction for some students with learning disabilities. Students who find the manipulation of objects helpful in understanding math concepts may find microcomputers less useful. Long-term research is needed to study the effectiveness of computer instruction and to determine its most useful application for these children.

■ READING For many years, reading has been widely recognized as a serious problem for students with learning disabilities (see Smith et al., 1997). Consequently, this area of instruction has received a great deal of attention, and many dif-

Today's Technology

SOFTWARE FOR WRITING

riting has long been recognized as an academic area that presents considerable difficulty for children with learning disabilities. Advances in educational applications of technology, especially the development of new computer software, have potential for assisting children with writing problems. An example of such software is Write: OutLoud, a talking word processor. Write: OutLoud cues the user with a beep or a flash on the screen in response to an incorrectly spelled word. This program can also speak! It will read back a sentence or a word so the user can check his or her work for accuracy.

Another software package with a speaking component is the Co: Writer, a word prediction program. It lets users write almost as quickly as they can think by predicting words through a program using artificial intelligence. For example, typing in the first letter or two of a word the user is unsure how to spell will produce a list of possible words from which to choose. It helps those with spelling difficulties and low motor ability; it also helps address grammar and spelling problems.

---

ferent procedures have been used to address this problem. Each procedure has succeeded with certain children but not with all, lending credence to the current belief that many different disabilities may affect students experiencing problems in the same area. Research on specific types of skill instruction, such as prereading activities, guided practice and feedback, and the direct teaching of skills in summarizing, has resulted in significant improvements for students with learning disabilities (see Billingsley & Ferro-Almeida, 1993; Lauterbach & Bender, 1995). Information gained from such research is being incorporated into instructional programs more than ever before. Combined with the realization that one single approach does not fit all students, this trend promises improved instruction and positive outcomes for students with learning disabilities.

Developmental reading instruction programs are often successful for students with learning disabilities (Smith, 1994) and typically introduce controlled sight vocabulary with an analytic phonics emphasis. Perhaps the most widely used developmental approaches involve basal readers such as the Holt Basic Reading; Ginn 720 Series; Scott, Foresman Reading; and Macmillan Series E. Basal readers are most useful for group instruction (often designed for three levels), are well sequenced developmentally, and usually have sufficient detail for use by relatively inexperienced teachers. But their orientation toward group instruction may present some limitations for students with learning disabilities who need heavy doses of individual attention.

Many teachers successfully teach reading to students with learning disabilities using whole-language instruction, which deemphasizes isolated exercises and drills. There are concerns, however, that this population needs a balance between a whole-language approach and focused, intensive, direct instruction related to a student's problem areas (see Hallahan et al., 1996; Lerner, 1997). Individualized reading instruction is often required for a student with serious reading disabilities. This may be accomplished by using many different materials (e.g., trade books), selected to match reading level and to cover topics of high interest to the student. The teacher, who usually is responsible for developing and providing individualized instruction, needs to have considerable knowledge of reading skills and the procedures that will enhance learning of these skills. Effective individualized instruction also requires evaluation of progress, ongoing monitoring, and detailed record keeping. Increasing the student's responsibility for his or her own learning, including self-monitoring skills, appears to enhance instructional effectiveness for students with learning disabilities (Bender, 1995). This self-directed involvement in learning moves students beyond the role of being receivers of content and makes them proactive partners in the instruction–learning process. This idea has led to the development of learning strategies packages that teach students effective skills for being better students. One such program is the GET IT strategy, described by its developers as a cognitive learning strategy for reading comprehension (Welch & Sheridan, 1995). (A brief description of the GET IT strategy is presented in the nearby Reflect on This feature.)

Specific skill-oriented reading instruction may also be found in several commercial diagnostic–prescriptive programs, such as the Fountain Valley Reading Support System, available from Zweig and Associates, and the Ransom Program from Addison-Wesley. Some diagnostic–prescriptive reading programs use computer-assisted instruction, such as the Harcourt Brace CAI Remedial Reading Program and the Stanford University CAI Project. Diagnostic–prescriptive reading programs are individualized, in that they let students work at their own pace. However, these materials are limited to teaching the skills that lend themselves to the particular program's format. But these programs also have considerable strengths: They do not require that the teacher possess a high degree of knowledge and skill, which, as described earlier, is essential for totally individualized, teacher-generated reading instruction. Diagnostic–prescriptive programs generally provide means of ongoing assessment and feedback, and developmental skills are usually well sequenced.

Many approaches and programs are available for reading instruction in addition to those already mentioned, each with strengths and limitations for students with learning disabilities. Other developmentally based approaches include synthetic phonics basals, linguistic phonemic programs, and language experience approaches. In addition, some procedures use multisensory techniques in order to maximize the student's learning. Selection of method and application of instructional technique should be based on a student's particular disability and needs.

Computer software for use in assessment and instruction in reading can assist students with learning disabilities and will likely become more common in the future (Bender & Bender, 1996; Wiig, Jones, & Wiig, 1996). Computer-presented reading instruction offers some particular advantages. It provides individual instruction, as well as never-ending drill and practice, as mentioned earlier. Programs can also combine feedback with corrective instruction. As computer programs advance, reading instruction software will improve (currently, word recognition programs seem to be of higher quality than comprehension software) and become more widely available. However, there is rising concern regarding the appropriate use of software, including enormous needs for long-range planning, faculty training, and other staff development related to technology applications in instruction (see Caftori, 1994; Male, 1997). A broad range of matters require resolution before electronic technology can achieve its potential in educational use.

As children progress into the upper-elementary grades, they may need instruction in compensatory skills or methods to circumvent deficit areas not yet remedied. This instruction may involve tutoring by an outside agency or an individual specializing in the problem or placement in a resource room or even a self-contained class for students with learning disabilities. The chosen approach will reflect the severity of the difficulty, the particular area of deficiency, and, sometimes unfortunately, the resources and attitudes of the decision makers (e.g., families and school districts).

■ BEHAVIORAL INTERVENTIONS

Distinctions between behavioral interventions and academic instruction and support are not always sharp and definitive. Both involve students in learning skills and changing behavior. Behavioral interventions, however, generally use practical applications of learning principles such as reinforcement. Behavioral interventions such as the structured presentation of stimuli (e.g., letters or words), reinforcement for correct responses (e.g., specific praise), and self-monitoring of behavior and performance are used in many instructional approaches (Carpenter & McKee-Higgens, 1996; Reid, 1996). In this section, we briefly discuss some behavioral interventions that are used outside of traditional academic areas.

With certain children, instruction may focus on social skills training. Some students with learning disabilities who experience repeated academic failure, despite their great effort, become frustrated and depressed (Huntington & Bender, 1993; Symons et al., 1995). They may not understand why their classmates without disabilities seem to do little more than they do, yet achieve more success. These students may withdraw or express frustration and anxiety by acting out or becoming aggressive. When this type of behavior emerges, it may be difficult to distinguish these students with learning difficulties from those with behavior disorders as a primary disability, and therefore both diagnosis of the problem and treatment may be quite difficult (Forness & Kavale, 1996; Lowe et al., 1995). In fact, these student groups often manifest many similar behaviors. Social and behavioral difficulties of students with learning disabilities are receiving increasing attention in the literature (Bender, 1995; Farmer & Farmer, 1996).

Behavioral contracts represent one type of intervention often used to change undesirable behavior. Using this approach, a teacher, behavior therapist, or parent establishes a contract with the child that provides him or her with reinforcement for appropriate behavior. Such contracts are either written or spoken, usually focus on a specific behavior (e.g., remaining in his or her seat for a given period of time), and reward the child with something that he or she really likes and considers worth striving for (e.g., going to the library or using the class computer). It is important that the pupil understand clearly what is expected and that the event or consequence be appealing to that child, so that it really does reinforce the appropriate behavior. Behavioral contracts have considerable appeal because they give students some responsibility for their own behavior (Gelfand et al., 1997). They can also be used effectively by parents at home. Contracts in various forms can be applied for students at widely different ages.

Token reinforcement systems represent another behavioral intervention often used with youngsters experiencing learning difficulties. **Token reinforcement systems** allow students to earn tokens for appropriate behavior and evenually exchange them for a reward of value to them (Gelfand et al., 1997; Molineux, 1993; Ross & Braden, 1991). Token systems resemble the work-for-pay lives of most adults, and therefore can be generalized to later life experiences. Although token systems require considerable time and effort to plan and implement, they can be truly effective.

Behavioral interventions are based on fundamental principles of learning largely developed from the early work of experimental psychologists such as B. F. Skinner (1953, 1957, 1971). These principles have been widely applied in many settings for students with learning disabilities as well as other exceptionalities. One of their main strengths is that, once the basic theory is understood, behavioral interventions can be modified to suit a wide variety of needs and circumstances.

The Adolescent Years

Services and supports for adolescents and young adults with learning disabilities differ somewhat from those used for children (Gerber, Reiff, & Ginsberg, 1996; Hallenback, 1996). Age is an important factor to consider when planning services (Denckla, 1993). Even the services and supports used during childhood vary according to age—appropriate assistance for a child of age 6 will not typically work for one who is 12. New issues crop up during the teenage years. Adolescents and young adults with learning disabilities may, like their nondisabled peers, become involved in alcohol or drug use and sexual activity (McCusker, Clare, Cullen, & Reep, 1993; Sigler & Mackelprang, 1993). Certainly they are vulnerable to peer pressure and the possibility of engaging in misconduct (Symons et al., 1995). However, adolescents are also influenced by their parents' expectations, which may be an important positive factor in academic achievement (Patrikakou, 1996). Age-appropriate modifications are essential to effective instruction and services for adolescents with learning disabilities, and most often they must be individually designed.

focus 9

How are services and supports for adolescents and adults with learning disabilities different from those used with children?

■ ACADEMIC INSTRUCTION AND SUPPORT

Academic instruction for adolescents with learning disabilities differs from such programs for younger children. Research suggests that the educational system often fails adolescents with learning disabilities: Only 9.8% of those age 14 and older exited from special education by graduating with a diploma or certificate during 1995–96, and a mere 3.9% returned to general education (U.S. Department of Education, 1997). The goal of secondary education is to prepare individuals for postschool lives and careers, and there is serious doubt that youth with learning disabilities are being adequately supported in meeting this goal. Often these adolescents find that they still need to develop basic academic survival skills (and for some, preparation for college), and they also often lack social skills and comfortable interpersonal relationships (Geisthardt & Munsch, 1996). Even adolescents with learning disabilities who attend college tend to drop out of school at a much higher rate than their nondisabled peers (U.S. Department of Education, 1997; Wilczenski, 1993). Clearly, a comprehensive model, with a variety of components, needs to be developed to address a broad spectrum of needs for adolescents and young adults with learning disabilities.

Relatively speaking, adolescents with learning disabilities have received considerably less attention than their younger counterparts (Clark, 1996; Sitlington, 1996). Academic deficits that first appeared during the younger years tend to grow more marked as students face progressively more challenging work, and by the time many reach secondary school or adolescence (Bender, 1995) they may be further behind academically than they were in the earlier grades. Although academic performance figures prominently in the federal definition of learning disabilities, there still has been relatively little research on factors that influence academic development in adolescents with learning disabilities (Patrikakou, 1996). Problems in motivation, self-reliance, learning strategies, social competence, and skill generalization all emerge repeatedly in investigations on adolescents with learning disabilities (see Billingsley & Ferro-Almeida, 1993; Deci, Hodges, Pierson, & Tomassone, 1992; Lauterbach & Bender, 1995). More often than not, however, these findings appear within individual studies on single components of learning disabilities. Comprehensive instruction is difficult to implement and to investigate.

One continual difficulty facing teachers of adolescents with learning disabilities is time constraints. A limited amount of time is available for instruction, student progress can be slow, and determining what to focus on is difficult. These adolescents and their teachers face a difficult task. In some areas, high school students may not have progressed beyond fifth-grade level academically, and they may have only a rudimentary grasp of some academic topics (Bender, 1995; Curran, Kintsch, & Hedberg, 1996). Yet they are reaching an age at which life grows more complex. A broad array of issues must be addressed, including possible college plans (an increasingly frequent goal for students with learning disabilities), employment goals, and preparation for social and interpersonal life during the adult years. In many areas, instead of building and expanding on a firm foundation of knowledge, many adolescents with learning disabilities are operating on a beginning to intermediate level. They may appear less than fully prepared for the challenges ahead of them, but a well-planned program of supports can do much to smooth the transition to adulthood.

Difficulties in academic learning, combined with limited instructional time, have led researchers to seek alternatives to and supplements for traditional teaching of academic content to students with learning disabilities. One widely used approach emphasizes instructional strategies that foster efficient learning. The student is taught *how to learn* in addition to learning the content (Katims & Harris, in press). Thus the learning-strategies approach essentially promotes self-instruction (Deshler et al., 1996; Lenz, Ellis, & Scanlon, 1996). Learning-strategies programs may involve rather complex academic content, such as writing, and are often employed in the general education classroom, as illustrated in the Reflect on This feature on page 204.

Secondary school instruction for adolescents with learning disabilities may also involve teaching compensatory skills to make up for those not acquired earlier. Compensatory skills often address specific areas of need, such as writing, listening, and social skills. For example, tape recorders may be used in class to offset difficulties in taking notes during lectures and thus compensate for a listening (auditory input) problem. For some individuals, personal problems related to disabilities require counseling or other mental health assistance (Faigel, Doak, Howard, & Sigel, 1992; Forness & Kavale, 1996; Huntington & Bender, 1993). And to further complicate matters during adolescence, hormonal changes come into play; the research is barely beginning to emerge on their effects on adolescents with learning disabilities (see Nass & Baker, 1991; Tallal, 1991). These students tend to have low social status among nearly all the people around them, including peers, teachers, and even parents. Some may become involved in criminal activities, as mentioned periodically in the literature, although the research evidence linking learning disabilities and juvenile delinquency is mixed (Bender, 1995; Smith, 1994; Waldie & Spreen, 1993). Generally, evidence does not suggest that arrests and jail terms for individuals with learning disabilities occur at substantially higher rates than for peers without disabilities.

■ TRANSITION FROM SCHOOL TO ADULT LIFE

Some adolescents and adults with learning disabilities have successfully adapted by themselves to a variety of challenges. However, the difficulties that adolescents with learning disabilities experience do not disappear as they grow older, and specialized services are often needed throughout adolescence, perhaps into adulthood (Denckla, 1993; Gerber et al., 1996; Greasley, 1995). We currently do not understand the factors that contribute to success or lack of it in young adults with learning disabilities. Some of the ingredients that one might think would contribute to success as a young adult (e.g., verbal IQ, length of school enrollment) have not been shown to be accurate predictors (Spekman, Goldberg, & Herman, 1992). This may suggest that truly we do not know what predicts success in young adults such as these, or it may reflect measurement and prediction difficulties that surface in research on

The goals of adolescents with learning disabilities will vary among individuals. Some students may look forward to employment after high school while others might plan some type of continuing education.

adults (Goldstein, Katz, Slomka, & Kelly, 1993). As research accumulates on the transitional years for adolescents with learning disabilities, we may find that unique challenges mark this period of life (this has been the case in studies of other disabilities), differing considerably from the experiences of children with such problems (Clark, 1996; Sitlington, 1996; Wehman, 1992).

Unfortunately, transition services remain rather sparse for adolescents with learning disabilities. However, this area is beginning to receive increased emphasis (Blalock, 1996; Clark, 1996; Sturomski, 1996). We are beginning to learn more about how emotional, interpersonal, and social competence issues affect adults with learning disabilities, and such research will have an impact on transition planning (Bassett & Smith, 1996). Research is emerging on factors such as substance abuse; results suggest an association between alcohol abuse and learning disabilities (Gress & Boss, 1996; Heiligenstein & Keeling, 1995; Rhodes & Jasinski, 1990). Services and supports that address this problem are beginning to be reported (McCusker et al., 1993). Although the picture remains unclear at this point, investigators are also beginning to focus on adults with learning disabilities and matters such as violence and violent crime, with initial results suggesting an at-risk situation for these individuals (Lyall, Holland, & Collins, 1995; Nestor, 1992). Research on interpersonal relationships is also underway, and preliminary findings point to a need for transition services for young adults with learning disabilities in areas of emotional well-being, interpersonal intimacy, and sexuality development (see Huntington & Bender, 1993; Sigler & Mackelprang, 1993). Results suggest that the competence of young adults with learning disabilities in these areas is not notably positive.

Those planning transition programs for adolescents with learning disabilities must consider that their life goals probably approximate those of adolescents without disabilities (Dunn, 1996; Sitlington, 1996). Some students look forward to employment that will not require education beyond high school. Some plan to continue their schooling in vocational and trade schools (Lerner, 1997). As with other areas of exceptionality, schooling should play a significant role in preparing young adults with learning disabilities for the transition from school to work (National Joint Committee on Learning Disabilities, 1994; Stewart & Lillie, 1995). Employment preparation activities such as occupational awareness programs, work experience, career and vocational assessment, development of job-related academic and interpersonal skills, and information about specific employment definitely benefit these students (Evers, 1996). In addition, professionals may need to negotiate with employers to secure some accommodations at work for young adults with learning disabilities (Jacobs & Hendricks, 1992). Limited data are available concerning the employment success of young adults with learning disabilities; most reports combine information on people with a number of disabilities. Most authorities agree, however, that the employment years for these individuals usually are not any easier than their school years, and a definite need exists for transitional programs from school to work (Bender, 1995).

Growing numbers of young people with learning disabilities plan to attend a college or university (see Cox & Klas, 1996; Rojewski, 1996). There is little question that they will encounter difficulties and that careful transition planning is essential for success (Blalock, 1996; Brinkerhoff, 1996). Their dropout rates are higher and their academic performance indicators are lower than those of their counterparts without learning disabilities (Ohler, Levinson, & Barker; 1996; Wilczenski, 1993). It is also clear that, with some additional academic assistance, they not only will survive, but also can be competitive college students (Yanok, 1993). These students need substantial college preparatory counseling before they leave secondary school. There is a considerable difference in the relatively controlled setting of high school and the more unstructured environment of college. To make this significant transition, students profit from focused assistance from their high school counselors (Brinkerhoff, 1996; Skinner & Schenck, 1992).

College-bound students with learning disabilities find that many of their specific needs are related to basic survival skills in higher education. At the college level, it is assumed that students already have adequate ability in taking notes, digesting lecture information auditorily, writing skills, reading, and study habits. Transition programs must strengthen these abilities as much as possible and show the students how to compensate for deficits, using a range of perspectives to plan the student's pursuit of postsecondary education (National Joint Committee on Learning Disabilities, 1994; Stewart & Lillie, 1995). Taped lectures can be replayed many times to help the student understand the information. Students with reading disabilities can obtain the help of readers who tape-record the context of textbooks so that they can listen to the material, rather than make slow progress if reading is difficult and time consuming. College students with learning disabilities must also learn to seek out educational support services and social support networks that will help maximize success (Friehe, Aune, & Leuenberger, 1996).

Perhaps the most helpful survival technique that can be taught to an adolescent with learning disabilities is actually more than a specific skill—it is a way of thinking about survival, an overall attitude of resourcefulness and a confident approach to solving problems. Recall Mathew, the psychology student in this chapter's beginning snapshot. Mathew has an amazing array of techniques that he uses to acquire knowledge while compensating for his specific deficit areas. Students need both proven techniques to deal with problem areas and the ability to generate new ways to tackle challenges that inevitably arise in college. This positive attitude also includes knowing how to seek help and how to advocate for oneself. Transition programs that can instill such a mind-set in students preparing for college have truly served an important purpose.

Students with learning disabilities should also be taught how to establish an interpersonal network of helpers and advocates. In many cases, a faculty member–advocate can be more successful than the student in requesting special testing arrangements or other accommodations (at least to begin with). Faculty in higher education are bombarded with student complaints and requests, most of which are not based on extreme needs, and so are wary of granting special considerations such as extra time. But a request from a faculty colleague may carry more weight. Additionally, many faculty are uninformed about learning disabilities, and overtures from a colleague can enhance the credibility of the student's request.

Concern about the accommodations requested by students who claim to have learning disabilities is genuine and is growing. Because these disabilities are invisible, they are hard to understand and there is great room for abuse in requests for accommodations. Such requests have increased dramatically, and many faculty are skeptical about the legitimacy of many of them (Shea, 1994). Research suggests that some cynicism is understandable; some claims indeed lack a sound justification, and diagnostic documentation provided for many college students claiming to be learning disabled is seriously flawed (see Cooper & Collacott, 1995; McGuire, Madaus, Litt, & Ramirez, 1996). Although the Americans with Disabilities Act clearly mandates accommodation, college students with learning disabilities should be aware that many higher education faculty are skeptical about the merits of this mandate. Some incidents pertaining to this issue have become publicized and politicized, and they may have a detrimental influence on the general higher education environment for those with learning disabilities (see Shapiro, 1997). Providing clear diagnostic evidence of a learning disability will enhance the credibility of a request for accommodation. Even faculty in special education have encountered those who have diagnosed themselves and claimed to have a learning disability; this unprofessional approach is counterproductive to improving the experiences of students with learning disabilities in higher education.

Students with learning disabilities can lead productive, even distinguished, adult lives. But some literature suggests that, even after they complete a college education, adults with learning disabilities have limited career choices (Bender, 1995). A more complete research base is needed in this area. However, we do know that notable individuals have been identified as learning disabled, including scientist and inventor Thomas Edison, president of the United States Woodrow Wilson, scientist Albert Einstein, and governor of New York and vice president of the United States Nelson Rockefeller. We also know that Mathew graduated from college and entered graduate school, and that the young man whose writing we saw in Figure 6.2 did become a successful architect. Such achievements are not accomplished without considerable effort. The outlook for people with learning disabilities can be very promising.

Inclusive Education

Definitions and descriptions of various approaches to inclusive education were introduced in Chapters 1 and 4. Much of the impetus for the inclusive education movement emerged from efforts of parents and advocacy organizations; the concept has been known by various terms such as *mainstreaming, the regular education initiative,* and *integration service models* (see Fuchs & Fuchs, 1995; Kauffman & Hallahan, 1995). A significant portion of students with learning disabilities receives educational services in settings that are either fully or partially inclusive. In 1995–96, 81% of students with learning disabilities from 6 to 21 years of age were served in general education or resource-room settings. Forty-one percent of these students were taught in general education classes (U.S. Department of Education, 1997).

Inclusive education is an important part of the academic landscape for students with learning disabilities, and a variety of specific instructional strategies is employed to enhance success (Fuchs et al., 1997; Katims & Pierce, 1995; Tralli et al., 1996). Inclusive approaches have received increasing attention in the learning disability literature, including debate regarding appropriate formats and the strengths and limitations of placing students with learning disabilities in fully inclusive educational environments (see Mather & Roberts, 1995; McLeskey & Pugach, 1995; Skinner, 1996; Zigmond & Baker, 1995).

Instructing students with learning disabilities in inclusive settings requires significant advance planning. Increasingly, the education of these students is guided by complex, comprehensive plans incorporating instructional services and supports and multiple approaches (Beale, 1995; Katims & Harris, in press). Each student's instructional plan targets specific areas that need more intense or specialized attention. The academic focus may be on a reading problem or difficulties in some other content area (Marston, 1996). Social and behavioral issues may emerge in the inclusive environment, and related interventions may form part of the spectrum of services and supports (see Carpenter & McKee-Higgens, 1996). To be effective, instructional supports must be directly keyed to the student's needs in the context of a general education classroom (Udvari-Solner & Thousand, 1996).

Several factors affect the success of inclusive education for students with learning disabilities. The attitudes of teachers are very influential. Some evidence suggests that general education teachers feel unprepared to teach students with disabilities, to collaborate with special educators, and to make academic adaptations (Schumm & Vaughn, 1995). Adequate teacher preparation is a very important factor in effective inclusive education. Such preparation requires a significant collaborative partnership between general education and special education teacher education programs, which has largely been lacking to date (see McNulty, Connolly, Wilson, & Brewer, 1996; Sindelar, 1995). In addition to curriculum and instructional skills, personal attitudes toward inclusive education are vitally important (Marston, 1996; Stoddard, Hewitt, O'Connor, & Beckner, 1996). General education teachers often have less positive attitudes toward and perceptions of inclusive education than special education teachers do, although such attitudes can be changed (Marston, 1996; Minke, Bear, Deemer, & Griffin, 1996).

Successful inclusion requires much more than merely placing students with learning disabilities in the same classroom with their nondisabled peers. Because these students need supports and adaptations, some have noted that successful inclusion might better be described as supported inclusion rather than mere inclusion. Inclusive education must be undertaken only after careful planning of the instructional approach, services, and supports (Stoddard et al., 1996; Tralli et al., 1996). Such a program can effectively promote academic support, student motivation, and social–emotional skill development for students with learning disabilities (Banerji & Dailey, 1995; Marston, 1996).

Medical Services

Medical professionals are sometimes involved in the diagnosis of learning disabilities and in prescribing medications used in treating conditions that sometimes coexist with learning disabilities. The involvement of physicians varies somewhat according to the age of the person with disabilities.

■ CHILDHOOD

Frequently, physicians diagnose a child's abnormal or delayed development in the areas of language, behavior, and motor functions. Pediatricians often participate in diagnosing physical disabilities that may significantly affect learning and behavior and then interpret medical findings to the family and to other professionals. Physicians may have early involvement with a child with learning disabilities because of the nature of the problem, such as serious developmental delay or hyperactivity. But more often a medical professional sees the young child first because he or she has not entered school yet, and the family physician is the primary adviser for parents (Drew et al., 1996). When other professional expertise is needed, the physician may refer the family to other specialists and then function as a team member in meeting a child's needs.

One example of medical service appropriate for some children with disabilities involves controlling hyperactivity and other challenging behaviors (Javorsky, 1996; Lowe & Felce, 1995a; Willemsen et al., 1996). On the surface, hyperactive behavior may lead one to believe that the child is suffering from greater than normal physiological arousal. Such notions led many researchers to recommend placing such children in environments with few distracting stimuli, known as low-stimulus or stimulus-free settings. However, one treatment often employed with hyperactive children has called into question the overarousal theory. The medication Ritalin (generic name, methylphenidare), which is most often used to control hyperactivity, is from the amphetamine family, which stimulates, rather than suppresses, physiological arousal (see Carlson & Bunner, 1993).

A number of theorists have tried to make sense of the seemingly paradoxical reactions to amphetamines shown by individuals with learning disabilities. It is popularly believed that, although amphetamines increase activity in most people, they decrease activity in children who are hyperactive. Some have suggested that individuals who are hyperactive may be plagued by abnormally low physiological arousal; they are not functioning at an optimal arousal level and are not, contrary to previous assumptions, generally overly aroused (Lerner, 1997).

Although of academic interest, such theories have provided little specific guidance regarding the use of medication to control hyperactivity. On a practical level, psychostimulants appear to result in general improvement for a large portion of children with ADHD, with some estimates as high as 75% (Barkley, 1995). However, some researchers have expressed caution about such treatment. Carlson & Bunner (1993) reviewed a number of investigations on the use of methylphenidate and concluded that it brings about substantial benefit in classroom behavior, but little evidence indicates that it results in long-term improvement in academic performance. Others have echoed the known benefits; some hold that students with hyperactivity do not have an unusual response to the medication and exhibit no significant improvement in long-term academic or social adjustment when taking it (DuPaul, Barkley, & McMurray, 1991; Swanson et al., 1993).

Concerns have been consistently expressed regarding the soundness of research methods used to investigate effects of medication (see Carlson & Bunner, 1993; Swanson et al., 1993). Clearly, too little is known about the effects of medication on hyperactivity. For example, exactly which drug will be effective is seldom known until after treatment has begun. Uncertainty regarding dosage level and the fact that high doses may have toxic effects are adding to the disconcerting confusion (Swanson et al., 1993). Some professionals have seriously questioned the use of medication in light of the evidence on its effectiveness. Concern exists about side effects of the medication as well as possible abuse (Bhaumik, Collacott, Gandhi, & Duggirala, 1995; Deb & Fraser, 1994). The physical side effects of using stimulant medication include insomnia, irritability, decreased appetite, and headaches. However, these side effects seem to be relatively minor and mostly temporary, although they vary greatly among individuals (Swanson et al., 1993). Current thinking suggests that, although there are clear benefits to the use of medication, it may be overprescribed, and expectations that it will produce generalized improvement simply are not supported by research evidence.

▪ ADOLESCENCE

Medical services for adolescents and young adults with learning disabilities differ somewhat from those for children. The literature directly addressing medical services during adolescence is unfortunately scarce, although some have explored specific needs that may require medical attention. For example, stress and serious emotional difficulty, including depression, during the adolescent years are receiving attention (see Geisthardt & Munsch, 1996; Huntington & Bender, 1993; Symons et al., 1995). In some cases, psychiatry may be involved in treatment, either through interactive therapy or the prescribing of antidepressant medication. A larger body of literature related to treating serious emotional difficulty medically will probably emerge, since the need seems to be surfacing. Some efforts are underway to improve assessment of medical, developmental, functional, and growth variables for individuals with learning difficulties, in a variety of settings (see Emerson et al., 1996; Felce & Perry, 1995; Lowe & Felce, 1995b; Perry & Felce, 1995). These efforts too are expanding and hopefully will systematically address individuals with learning disabilities at various age levels.

Some adolescents receiving medication to control hyperactivity may have been taking it for a number of years, since many physician assessments and prescriptions are made during childhood. On the other hand, some treatments are of a rather short duration, and many terminate within two years (Swanson et al., 1993). This finding raises serious questions regarding which type of treatment is most suitable. Other ongoing questions regard problems with side effects and determining which medications are effective in dealing with particular symptoms (Deb & Fraser, 1994; Kiernan, Reeves, & Albortz, 1995). A number of adolescent youth and adults with learning disabilities have struggled through their earlier years and have not received medication until after childhood. In many cases, the medication to assist with behavior and attention problems is again an amphetamine and appears to have the same beneficial results noted earlier (Carlson & Bunner, 1993; Swanson et al., 1993).

The field of learning disabilities and the individuals served within it represent a most interesting array of challenges, perhaps the most perplexing among the high incidence disabilities. In the overall picture of disabilities, these challenges are not trivial, both because they are complex and because they involve such a very large portion of the population that we consider to have disabilities. Progress is evident on many fronts although it is also clear that intense and systematic research efforts are essential if improvement in service is to continue.

Case Study

ALICE REVISITED

Recall Alice, whom we met in the last snapshot. Alice was in the fourth grade when we last saw her and was extremely frustrated with school. Unfortunately, she failed the history test for which she was preparing. She could not obtain enough information from the narrative and consequently could not answer the questions on the test. The exam was a paper-and-pencil test, which, to Alice, looked like the book that she was supposed to read about the family who was moving West with the wagon train. When she received her graded test, Alice broke into tears. This was not the first time she had wept about her schoolwork, but it was the first time that her teacher had observed it.

Alice's teacher, Mr. Dunlap, was worried about her. She was not a troublesome child in class and she seemed attentive. But she could not do the work. On this occasion, Mr.

Dunlap consoled Alice and asked her to stay after school briefly to visit with him about the test. Since it was early in the year, he had no clue what was wrong, except he knew that this charming girl could not answer his test questions. He was astonished when they sat together and he determined that Alice could not even read the questions. If she could not read the questions, he thought, then she undoubtedly can't read the book. But he was fairly certain that she was not lacking in basic intelligence—her conversations simply didn't indicate such a problem.

After further consoling Alice regarding her test, Mr. Dunlap sent her home and then contacted her parents. He knew a little about exceptional children and the referral process. He set the process in motion, meeting with the parents, the school psychologist, and the principal, who also sat in on all the team meetings at this

school. After a diagnostic evaluation, the team met again to examine the psychologist's report. Miss Burns, the psychologist, had tested Alice and found that her scores fell in the average range in intelligence (with a full-scale WISC-III score of 114). She had also assessed Alice's abilities with a comprehensive stuctural analysis of reading skills. This led her to believe that Alice had a rather severe form of dyslexia, which interfered substantially with her ability to read.

Alice's parents expressed a strong desire for her to remain in Mr. Dunlap's class if possible. This was viewed as a desirable choice by each member of the team and the next challenge was to determine how an intervention could be undertaken to work with Alice while she remained in her regular class as much as possible. All team members, the parents included, understand that they have a challenge before them to most effectively

meet Alice's educational and social needs. However, they are all agreed that they are working toward the same objectives, which is a very positive first step.

■ APPLICATION

Placing yourself in the role of Mr. Dunlap and, given the information that you now have regarding Alice, respond to the following questions.
1. How can you facilitate Alice's social needs, particularly focusing on her relationships with her classmates?
2. Should the information regarding Alice's reading difficulties be shared with classmates, or would this be detrimental to their interactions with her?
3. Who should be a part of this broad educational planning?
4. Should you visit with Alice about it?

Debate Forum

IS MEDICATION AN APPROPRIATELY USED TREATMENT FOR CHILDREN WITH LEARNING DISABILITIES?

Concern is growing about the use of medication, particularly psychostimulants, to treat students with learning disabilities. For some children, the utility of medication for treating problems associated with learning disabilities is unquestionable. Some professionals, however, have seriously questioned the administration of medication as currently practiced.

■ POINT
Several points must be raised regarding the administration of medication to children with learning disabilities. The use of medication for treating learning disabilities and ADHD is very widespread and may be overprescribed. Some estimates place the number of children receiving psychostimulant treatment near 1 million. In the context of such wide usage, a basic concern emerges about how little we actually know regarding dosage and effectiveness. Dosages showing improvement in social behavior may range from 50 percent to 400 percent above that recommended as a maximum to improve cognitive abilities. It is unsettling that we know so little about a treatment that is so widely employed.

■ COUNTERPOINT
For some children with learning disabilities and ADHD, medication is the only approach that will bring their hyperactivity under control and thereby allow effective instruction to occur. Without such treatment, these students will be unable to attend to their academic work and will be so disruptive in classroom situations that other students will not be effectively taught. Side effects such as insomnia, irritability, decreased appetite, among others, are relatively minor and temporary for the most part. Research suggests that teachers have reported a substantial proportion of those children receiving medication show an improvement in behavior.

Review

focus 1
Identify four reasons why definitions of learning disabilities have varied.

- *Learning disabilities* is a broad, generic term that encompasses many different specific problems.
- The study of learning disabilities has been undertaken by a variety of different disciplines.
- The field of learning disabilities per se has existed for only a relatively short period of time and is therefore relatively immature with respect to conceptual development and terminology.
- The field of learning disabilities has grown at a very rapid pace.

focus 2
Identify the three major types of ADHD according to the *DSM-IV*.

- Attention-Deficit/Hyperactivity Disorder, Combined Type
- Attention-Deficit/Hyperactivity Disorder, Predominantly Inattentive Type
- Attention-Deficit/Hyperactive Disorder, Predominantly Hyperactive-Impulsive Type

focus 3
Identify two ways in which people with learning disabilities can be classified.

- Whether a child achieves commensurate with his or her age and ability when provided with appropriate educational experiences
- Historically, as a mild disorder but with increasing attention to varying severity

focus 4
Identify two current estimated ranges for the prevalence of learning disabilities.

- From 1% to 30% of the school-age population, depending on the source
- From 5% to 10% is a reasonable current estimate

focus 5
Identify seven characteristics attributed to those with learning disabilities, and explain why it is difficult to characterize this group.

- Typically, average or near-average intelligence
- Uneven skill levels in various areas
- Hyperactivity
- Perceptual problems
- Visual and auditory discrimination problems

- Cognition deficits, such as memory
- Attention problems
- The group of individuals included under the umbrella term *learning disabilities* is so varied that it defies simple characterization denoted by a single concept or term.

focus 6

Identify four causes thought to be involved in learning disabilities.

- Neurological damage or malfunction
- Maturational delay of the neurological system
- Genetic abnormality
- Environmental factors

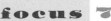

focus 7

Identify four questions that are addressed by screening assessment in learning disabilities.

- Is there reason to investigate the abilities of the child more fully?
- Is there reason to suspect that the child in any way has disabilities?
- If the child appears to have disabilities, what are the characteristics and how should we move to intervention?
- How should we plan for the future of the individual?

focus 8

Identify three types of intervention or treatment employed with people

diagnosed as having learning disabilities.

- Medical treatment, in some circumstances involving medication to control hyperactivity
- Academic instruction and support in a wide variety of areas that are specifically aimed at building particular skill areas
- Behavioral interventions aimed at improving social skills or remediating problems in this area (behavioral procedures may also be a part of academic instruction)

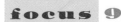

focus 9

How are the services and supports for adolescents and adults with learning disabilities different from those used with children?

- Services and supports for children focus primarily on building the most basic skills.
- Instruction during adolescence may include skill building but also may involve assistance in compensatory skills that permit circumvention of deficit areas.
- Services during adolescence should include instruction and assistance in transition skills that will prepare students for adulthood, employment, and further education, based on their own goals.
- Information for the adult with learning disabilities should include an awareness of how invisible their disability is to others and how requests for accommodation might be viewed with skepticism.

People with Emotional or Behavior Disorders

To begin with . . .

 As adults, we cannot solve young people's problems for them. We can, however, provide them with the knowledge, skills, and encouragement to resolve conflicts in a nonviolent manner, using words instead of fists or weapons. (Attorney General Janet Reno and Secretary of Education Richard W. Riley, cited in Crawford & Bodine, 1996, p. v)

 How did you become a member of the gang? At first they were spreading around that we were going to start one. Everybody just started calling meetings; when it's hot, everybody would be standing around on the corner talking and, you know, people were just calling meetings on certain days. . . . *Was it simply a social group when it first started?* Not at first. It had a point, a purpose. We were getting together for a reason. *What was the reason?* One reason was the slobs [derogatory name for Bloods gang]. You know, Crips and Bloods and stuff. I guess the reason is to take one another out— Crips fighting Bloods, Bloods fighting Crips . . . kill one of them, so they kill one. The goal is to eliminate the Bloods. Another reason is I just be fighting all the time and I needed the back-up. That's all I wanted to do at first. But then people started using knives and weapons and stuff, and I didn't want to get shot. (Benz, 1992, p. 5)

 What is it like to live with a violent and aggressive child?

It means that everyone is looking for a reason for the anger, something that has happened to turn this child into an unpredictable time bomb. By everyone, I mean parents, relatives, neighbors, teachers, siblings, and even the child him or herself. Searching for something to blame, in many cases, turns into just that—a blame game which turns the adults in the child's life against each other.

Our prayers have taken on a dimension of pleading for help and understanding.

I feel like a prisoner in my own home. My child has never been away from me overnight. I can't get away from him.

Everything is unpredictable. Everyone is on edge, including the child. We are always waiting, ready.

The look on my son's face. He asked me, "If you accidentally die, will I get the house?" I'm scared. (Adams, Bosley, & Cooper, 1995, p. 7)

Teacher: How are you today? How are things going?

Student: Not very good but I don't want to talk about it. It's none of your business anyway. It's my life.

Teacher: Why don't you want to talk about it?

Student: What do you care about it anyway? All you teachers are here for is to collect your paychecks. You don't care about us.

Teacher: Try me . . .

Student: I hate math. I hate Mrs. Lewis. She doesn't know how to teach. She doesn't know anything. She doesn't listen. . . . I had my hand up three times to ask a question, and she never called on me. She ignored me all three times. . . . Why do you care anyway? You're just trying to act buddy-buddy with me. When we are done talking, you will go talk with Mrs. Lewis. You will plot against me and sit around and drink your coffee and eat your donuts. All you teachers ever do is sit around and decide how you are going to get rid of students. (Wood, 1996, p. 10)

Eric

Eric is a preschooler. In his mother's words, "He's busy. He's hyper . . . , but he is very intelligent, very perceptive." Eric spends about 4 hours a day at Children's Center, a day treatment center for young children with serious emotional and behavior problems. Professionals at this center are helping Eric develop a variety of behaviors, one of which is learning how to express himself verbally, rather than physically striking out at others.

Eric was referred to Children's Center because of his persistent fighting, biting, hitting, and screaming. Additionally, he had great difficulty in responding to directions and giving sustained attention to various age appropriate tasks. The center's psychologist described him as being the "most extremely hyperactive child that I have tested." Prior to coming to the center, Eric had been ejected from several day-care centers because of his aggressive and noncompliant behaviors.

Eric's mother also experienced great difficulties in managing him. "I feel kind of guilty saying it, but I have to say the truth, I didn't like my son. I couldn't stand him. I couldn't stand being around

him for long, I mean I could take about ten minutes. He would, every day, . . . ruin something in the house."

At Children's Center, Eric has the opportunity to interact with some very talented and caring professionals. He spends most of each day with two child therapists who skillfully respond to his negative as well as his positive behaviors. Moreover, each week Eric has a chance to meet one-on-one with Jim, a child therapist, for individual play therapy. At least once a week, his mother meets with Dorothy, a talented social worker who helps Eric's mother with personal concerns and provides suggestions for dealing with Eric at home.

Eric has made significant progress in the past several months. His attention span has increased so significantly that he now can listen to stories and even wait his turn, something that was virtually impossible for him before he came to Children's Center.

Nick

Nick is a very likable, bright kid. He enjoys athletics and is well above average in his reading performance and other academic skills. During the later part of his fifth grade year, however, he created significant problems for his teacher, whom he saw as being very rude and always picking on him.

The teacher assistance team in the elementary school at-

tempted a variety of prereferral interventions to bring his behavior under control. However, he continued to be noncompliant, problematic during recesses, and generally difficult to manage.

In sixth grade he was placed in a self-contained classroom for students with behavior disorders. He did quite well during this entire year, relating well to his special class teacher, Mrs. Backman, and becoming more self-controlled in his responses to peers and most teachers. The next year he moved on to Northwest, an intermediate school in his neighborhood. Again, he was placed in a self-contained, special education setting with some opportunities for involvement in other classes such as physical education and art.

He made significant progress during his first year at Northwest, partly because of his teacher's social skills program and her expertise in dealing with him. He was now more responsive to verbal redirection and much less reactive to criticism. Because of this progress and other changes in his behavior, he was prepared to spend most of his time outside of the special education classroom. In fact, he now participates for several periods a day in a program for students who are gifted.

His mother sums up his future in this fashion, " I think Nick has a very bright future, but he has to want it." His teachers concur.

Amy

Amy is a very attractive and talented young woman. About midway through the seventh grade, she began to complain about persistent stomachaches, and at the same time, her mother began receiving continual complaints from school personnel about her behavior. In fact, in one year's time, her life went from "beautiful to dismal," as described by her mother. She was not able to eat, was often hostile and suicidal, and did not sleep well. Her behavior at school was "out of control." At this same time, she was prescribed Prozac by one of the physicians with whom her mother was working. Over time, however, her mother took her off this drug, believing that it was not helping her but contributing to her problems in school and at home.

Eventually, Amy was placed in a self-contained classroom at a high school different from the one that she would have attended normally. Her placement in this classroom was based on a number of persistent problems, including a lack of anger control, consistent clashes with authority figures, episodes of inattention, and incomplete school work.

At age 15, after seeing a number of specialists, it was discovered that she had a severe case of endometriosis. She underwent surgery for this condition and gradually things seemed to improve for her.

Amy now spends each morning at a technical training center, where she is learning to become a dental assistant. During the midday hours, she attends several spe-cial classes as well as one regular class of biology at her high school. During the afternoon, she works with a dentist who is contributing to her training as a dental assistant.

Amy's mother describes her as follows: "Right now Amy's a capable, fairly happy, well-adjusted 17-year-old kid. Two years ago she was withdrawn, hostile . . . she was suicidal—I never knew what was going to come out of her next. She couldn't eat, she couldn't sleep, but she's progressed really, really well . . . I'm so proud of her."

We will now explore in some depth emotional and behavior disorders in children and youth. Together, we will examine the ways in which we perceive the behavior of others. We will review factors that give rise to aberrant behaviors. Additionally, you will have opportunities to explore classification systems, to learn about the causes of behavior and emotional problems, to review assessment techniques, and to investigate interventions.

Understanding Emotional or Behavior Disorders

Individuals with **emotional** or **behavior disorders**—such as Eric, Nick, and Amy in the opening snapshots—experience great difficulties in relating appropriately to peers, siblings, parents, and teachers. They also have difficulty responding to academic and social tasks that are essential parts of their schooling. Sometimes, they may exhibit too much behavior. For example, Eric's placement in the Children's Center resulted from his excessively aggressive or noncompliant behaviors. In other cases, individuals with emotional or behavior disorders may not have learned the social skills necessary for successful participation in school settings, as demonstrated by Nick. He, for a variety of reasons, had not learned how to relate well with peers and to accept correction delivered by teachers and others. Amy, as described by her mother, gradually lost her appetite, became suicidal, and dealt with teachers and others in unacceptable ways. However, she is now making great progress with the assistance of her teachers, vocational trainers, and the dentist with whom she works.

■ IDENTIFYING "NORMAL" BEHAVIOR

Many factors influence the ways in which we perceive the behaviors of others (Gelfand, Jenson, & Drew, 1997). Our perceptions of others and their behaviors are significantly influenced by our personal beliefs, standards, and values about what constitutes normal behavior. Our range of tolerance varies greatly, depending on the behavior and situation. Eric's aggressive and oppositional behaviors were not tolerated at the various preschools where he was enrolled for very short periods of time. Moreover, what may be viewed as normal by some may be viewed by others as abnormal. For example, parents may have little foundation for determining what is normal behavior, since their perceptions are often limited by their lack of experience with children in general. They may see their child's behavior as being somewhat challenging, but not abnormal.

focus 1
Identify five factors that influence the ways in which others' behaviors are perceived.

The context in which behaviors occur dramatically influences our views of their appropriateness. For example, teachers and parents expect children to behave reasonably well in settings where they have interesting things to do or where children are doing things they seem to enjoy. Often it is in these settings that children with emotional or behavior disorders misbehave. At times, they seem to be oblivious to the environments in which they find themselves. Some have the social skills to act appropriately but choose not to use them. Sometimes it is the intensity or sheer frequency with which a given behavior or cluster of behaviors occurs that leads us to suspect the presence of behavior or emotional disorders. Eric's mother became perplexed not only with the intensity of his behaviors but also with their frequency. Every day something seemed to be broken or damaged by Eric in their home.

■ FACTORS INFLUENCING EMOTIONAL OR BEHAVIOR DISORDERS

Many factors influence the types of behaviors that individuals with emotional or behavior disorders exhibit or suppress: the parents' and teachers' management styles; the school or home environment; the social and cultural values of the family; the social and economic climate of the community; the responses of peers and siblings; and the biological, academic, intellectual, and social–emotional characteristics of the individuals with the disorders (Kauffman, 1997).

■ EXTERNALIZING AND INTERNALIZING DISORDERS

focus 2

What differentiates externalizing disorders from internalizing disorders?

A number of terms have been used by professionals to describe individuals with emotional, social, and behavior difficulties. These terms include **behavior disorders**, **social maladjustment**, and **emotional disturbance**, among others. Childhood, adolescent, and adult behavior problems can frequently be grouped into two broad but overlapping categories: externalizing and internalizing problems. The latter category refers to behaviors that seem to be directed

Graffiti might be the work of an adolescent who is socially maladjusted and engages in behavior such as defacing property, which directs his feelings and emotions at others.

more at the self than at others. Depressions and phobias are examples of behaviors that are internalized; some clinicians would describe individuals with these conditions as being emotionally disturbed.

Children who exhibit externalizing disorders may be described as engaging in behaviors that are directed more at others than at themselves. These behaviors may have a significant impact on parents, siblings, and teachers. The juvenile offender who chronically engages in crimes involving property damage or injury to others might be identified as being socially maladjusted. The distinction between the two categories is not clear-cut. For example, adolescents who are severely depressed certainly have an impact on their families and others, although the primary locus of the distress is internal or emotional.

Throughout this chapter, the term *behavior disorders* is used to describe persons with both external and internal (emotional) problems. The use of the term reflects our interest in observable behaviors. Our observations and those of others help to determine whether a child or adolescent is depressed, aggressive, suicidal, anxious, delinquent, hyperactive, socially withdrawn, or extremely shy. Keep in mind that behavior disorders may be internal (emotional) and/or external (social) in nature. To discern their presence, we must be able to observe and measure them accurately.

Definitions and Classifications

■ THE IDEA DEFINITION

Several definitions have been used to describe people with behavior disorders. The current definition, used in conjunction with the rules and regulations governing the implementation of the Individuals with Disabilities Education Act (IDEA), is as follows:

focus 3

Identify six essential parts of the definitions describing serious emotional or behavior disorders.

"Seriously emotionally disturbed" is defined as . . . :

(I)   a condition exhibiting one or more of the following characteristics over a long period of time and to a marked degree, which adversely affects educational performance:

   (A)   An inability to learn which cannot be explained by intellectual, sensory or health factors;
   (B)   An inability to build or maintain satisfactory relationships with peers and teachers;
   (C)   Inappropriate types of behavior or feelings under normal circumstances;
   (D)   A general pervasive mood of unhappiness or depression; or
   (E)   A tendency to develop physical symptoms or fears associated with personal or school problems.

(ii)   The term includes children who are schizophrenic or autistic.[1] The term does not include children who are socially maladjusted, unless it is determined that they are seriously disturbed. (Federal Regulations, 1977, p. 42,478)

This description of severe emotional disturbance or behavior disorders was adapted from an earlier definition created by Bower (1959). The IDEA definition for behavior disorders has been criticized because of its lack of clarity, incompleteness, and exclusion of individuals described as socially maladjusted (Council for Children

---

[1] In 1990, the U.S. Department of Education removed autism as a term under the category of serious emotional disturbance. Autism is now a separate category under IDEA.

with Behavior Disorders, 1987, 1989, 1990; Forness, 1996; Forness & Knitzer, 1990). Additionally, this definition mandates that assessment personnel demonstrate that the disorder is adversely affecting students' school performance. In many cases, students with serious behavior disorders—such as eating disorders, depression, suicidal tendencies, and social withdrawal—do not receive appropriate care and treatment, merely because their academic achievement in school appears to be normal or above average. In some cases, these students are gifted (see Chapter 16).

■ THE COUNCIL FOR EXCEPTIONAL CHILDREN DEFINITION

The Council for Exceptional Children has proposed a definition for serious emotional disturbance that goes beyond the language of IDEA (Council for Exceptional Children, 1991; Forness, 1996; Forness & Knitzer, 1990):

Emotional or Behavior Disorders (EBD) refers to a condition in which behavioral or emotional responses of an individual in school are so different from his/her generally accepted, age-appropriate, ethnic, or cultural norms that they adversely affect educational performance in such areas as self-care, social relationships, personal adjustment, academic progress, classroom behavior, or work adjustment.

EBD is more than a transient, expected response to stressors in the child's or youth's environment and would persist even with individualized interventions, such as feedback to the individual, consultation with parents or families, and/or modification of the educational environment.

The eligibility decision must be based on multiple sources of data about the individual's behavioral or emotional functioning. EBD must be exhibited in at least two different settings, at least one of which must be school related.

EBD can coexist with other handicapping conditions as defined elsewhere in this law [IDEA].

This category may include children or youth with schizophrenia, affective disorders, or with other sustained disturbances of conduct, attention, or adjustment. (Council for Exceptional Children, 1991, p. 10)

Features of this definition represent significant advantages over the present IDEA definition, including (1) the inclusion of impairments of adaptive behavior as evidenced in emotional, social, or behavioral differences; (2) the use of normative standards of assessment from multiple sources, including consideration of cultural and/or ethnic factors; (3) the examination of prereferral interventions and other efforts to assist children prior to formally classifying them as disabled; and (4) the potential inclusion of individuals previously labeled as socially maladjusted.

The pressure to include children considered to be socially maladjusted in the federal definition of serious emotional disturbance continues to be a sharply debated issue (Bullock & Gable, 1994; Forness, 1996; McIntyre & Forness, 1996). Proponents for the inclusion of the socially maladjusted have argued that professional practice as well as current research run counter to the exclusionary clause found in the present definition (Center, 1989a, 1989b; Duncan, Forness, & Hartsough, 1995; Kauffman, 1989; Nelson, Rutherford, Center, & Walker, 1991; Wolf, Braukmann, & Ramp, 1987).

Many professionals believe that greater numbers of young children with behavior disorders will receive preventive treatment if the more inclusive definition is adopted, thereby decreasing the need for more intensive and expensive services later in children's lives. Additionally, many clinicians believe that adoption of this definition will lead to greater numbers of children with special needs being served.

■ CLASSIFICATION

Classification systems serve several purposes for human services professionals. First, they provide a means for describing various types of behavior problems in children. Second, they provide a common set of terms for communicating with others. For example, children who are identified as having Down syndrome, a type of mental retardation, share some distinct characteristics, and a set of terminology has evolved to facilitate discussion and research on this condition (see Chapter 8). Third, physicians and other health care specialists use these characteristics and other information as a basis for diagnosing and treating these children.

focus 4

Identify three reasons why classification systems are important to professionals who diagnose, treat, and educate individuals with behavior disorders.

Unfortunately, no standardized set of criteria exists for determining the nature and severity of behavior disorders (Forness, 1988, 1996; Kavale, Forness, & Alper, 1986). Valid eligibility and classification systems would provide educational or psychiatric clinicians with extremely valuable information about the nature of various conditions, effective treatments, and associated complications, but they have not yet been fully developed.

The field of behavior disorders is broad and includes many different types of problems, so it is not surprising that many approaches have been used to classify these individuals. Some classification systems describe individuals according to statistically derived categories, whereby patterns of strongly related behaviors are identified through sophisticated statistical techniques. Other classification systems are clinically oriented; they are derived from the experiences of physicians and social scientists who work directly with children and adults with behavior disorders. Still other classification systems help us understand behavior disorders in terms of their relative severity.

■ STATISTICALLY DERIVED CLASSIFICATION SYSTEMS For a number of years, researchers have collected information about children with behavior disorders. Data collected from parent and teacher questionnaires, interviews, and behavior rating scales have been analyzed using a variety of advanced statistical techniques. Certain clusters or patterns of related behaviors have emerged from these studies. For example, Peterson (1987) found that the behavior disorders exhibited by elementary school children could be accounted for by two dimensions: withdrawal and aggression. Similarly, several researchers have intensively studied child psychiatric patients to develop a valid classification system (Achenbach, 1966; Achenbach, 1991a & 1991b). Statistical analysis of data generated from these studies revealed two broad clusters of behaviors: externalizing symptoms and internalizing symptoms. Externalizing clusters of behaviors included stealing, lying, disobedience, and fighting. Internalizing clusters of behaviors included physical complaints (e.g., stomachaches), phobias, fearfulness, social withdrawal, and worrying.

Other researchers (Quay, 1975, 1979; Von Isser, Quay, & Love, 1980), using similar methodologies, have reliably identified four distinct categories of behavior disorders in children:

1. Conduct disorders involve such characteristics as overt aggression, both verbal and physical; disruptiveness; negativism; irresponsibility; and defiance of au-

thority—all of which are at variance with the behavioral expectations of the school and other social institutions.

2. Anxiety withdrawal stands in considerable contrast to conduct disorders, involving, as it does, overanxiety, social withdrawal, seclusiveness, shyness, sensitivity, and other behaviors implying a retreat from the environment rather than a hostile response to it.

3. Immaturity characteristically involves preoccupation, short attention span, passivity, daydreaming, sluggishness, and other behavior not in accord with developmental expectations.

4. Socialized aggression typically involves gang activities, cooperative stealing, truancy, and other manifestations of participation in a delinquent subculture. (Von Isser et al., 1980, pp. 272–273)

Behaviors related to each of these categories may be very severe to very mild in nature. In thinking about these categories, recall the descriptions of Eric, Nick, and Amy in the opening snapshots. How would they be classified according to these categories? Did Eric have an attention deficit disorder? Was Nick's behavior serious enough to identify him as conduct disordered? And what about Amy's behavior? Does she qualify for placement in any of these categories?

■ CLINICALLY DERIVED CLASSIFICATION SYSTEMS Although several clinically derived classification systems have been developed, the system predominantly used by medical and psychological personnel is the American Psychiatric Association's *Diagnostic and Statistical Manual of Mental Disorders* (4th ed., 1994), or the *DSM-IV*. It was developed and tested by groups and committees of psychiatric, psychological, and health care professionals. Participants in each of these groups included persons who served or worked closely with children, adolescents, and adults with behavior disorders. The categories and subcategories of the *DSM-IV* were developed after years of investigation and field testing. Unfortunately, these psychiatric categories do not serve educational clinicians well as they are not generally considered in identifying children or adolescents for special education services (Duncan et al., 1995).

The current manual identifies seven major groups of disorders that may be exhibited by infants, children, or adolescents. Several of these disorders overlap with other conditions such as mental retardation, autism, and attention deficit disorders:

■ *Pervasive developmental disorders.* Children with these disorders exhibit pervasive and severe deficits in several areas of development. These deficits may include significant problems in relating to parents, siblings, and others; very poor communication skills; and unusual behaviors evidenced in gestures, postures, and facial expressions. Generally these disorders are accompanied by chromosomal abnormalities, structural abnormalities in the nervous system, and congenital infections. Also, these disorders are generally evident at birth or present themselves very early in a child's life. One of these disorders, autism, will be addressed in Chapter 11.

■ *Attention deficit and disruptive behavior disorders.* Children with these disorders manifest a variety of symptoms. For example, they have difficulty responding well to typical academic and social tasks and controlling their physical activity. Often their activity appears to be very random or purposeless in nature. (See Chapter 6 for more information on attention deficit disorders.) Children with disruptive behavior disorders frequently cause physical harm to other individuals or to animals, often destroy property belonging to others, repeatedly participate in theft and deceitful activities, and regularly violate rules and social conventions. In some instances, children with these disorders are highly oppositional. They exhibit a pattern of recurrent negativism, opposition to authority figures, and loss of temper. Other typical behaviors include disobeying, arguing, blaming others for problems and mistakes, and being spiteful. Most students with behavior disorders who are served in special education through IDEA have conduct disorders or oppositional defiant disorders (see Tables 7.1 (on page 224) and 7.2 (on page 225) for diagnostic criteria for these conditions). Think about Nick, who was described in the opening snapshot. How would you classify him?

- *Anxiety disorders.* The category of anxiety disorders that occur during childhood or adolescence is very similar to the anxiety-withdrawal category used in the statistically derived classification system. Children with anxiety disorders have difficulty dealing with anxiety-provoking situations and with separating themselves from parents or other attachment figures (e.g., close friends, teachers, coaches). Unrealistic worries about future events, overconcern about achievement, excessive need for reassurance, and somatic complaints are characteristic of young people who have anxiety disorders.

- *Feeding and eating disorders.* The first of these disorders is called Pica, or the persistent eating of nonnutritive materials for at least one month. Materials consumed may be cloth, string, hair, plaster, or even paint. Often children with pervasive developmental disorders manifest Pica.

    Anorexia and bulimia are common eating disorders evidenced by gross disturbances in eating behavior. These disorders are more prevalent in girls and women. The most distinguishing feature of anorexia nervosa is bodyweight at 15% below the norm. Individuals with this condition are intensely afraid of weight gain and exhibit grossly distorted perceptions of the shapes and sizes of their bodies. Bulimia is characterized by repeated episodes of bingeing, followed by self-induced vomiting or other extreme measures to prevent weight gain. Both of these conditions may result in depressed mood, social withdrawal, irritability, and serious medical conditions.

This young woman with anorexia, a common eating disorder more prevalent in females than in males, eventually died from the disorder.

- *Tic disorders.* Tic disorders involve stereotyped movements or vocalizations that are involuntary, rapid, and recurrent over time. Tics may take the form of eye blinking, facial gestures, sniffing, snorting, repeating certain words or phrases, and grunting. Stress often exacerbates the nature and frequency of tics.

- *Elimination disorders.* Elimination disorders deal with soiling and wetting behaviors in older children. Children who continue to have consistent problems with bowel and bladder control past their fourth or fifth birthday may be diagnosed as having an elimination disorder, particularly if the condition is not a function of any physical disorder.

- *Other disorders of infancy, childhood, or adolescence.* The remaining categories in the *DSM-IV* refer to other disorders that are not easily placed in other categorical areas. Separation anxiety disorder is characterized by inordinate fear about leaving home or being separated from persons to whom the child or adolescent is attached. Behaviors indicative of this disorder include persistent refusal to go to school, excessive worry about personal harm or injury to self or other family

TABLE 7.1   Diagnostic criteria for conduct disorder

A. A repetitive and persistent pattern of behavior in which the basic rights of others or major age-appropriate societal norms or rules are violated, as manifested by the presence of three (or more) of the following criteria in the past 12 months, with at least one criterion present in the past 6 months:

Aggression to people and animals

1. Often bullies, threatens, or intimidates others.
2. Often initiates physical fights.
3. Has used a weapon that can cause serious physical harm to others (e.g., a bat, brick, broken bottle, knife, gun).
4. Has been physically cruel to people.
5. Has been physically cruel to animals.
6. Has stolen while confronting a victim (e.g., mugging, purse snatching, extortion, armed robbery).

Destruction of property

8. Has deliberately engaged in fire setting with the intention of causing serious damage.
9. Has deliberately destroyed others' property (other than by fire setting).

Deceitfulness or theft

10. Has broken into someone else's house, building, or car.
11. Often lies to obtain goods or favors or to avoid obligations (i.e., "cons" others).
12. Has stolen items of nontrivial value without confronting a victim (e.g., shoplifting, but without breaking and entering; forgery).

Serious violations of rules

13. Often stays out at night despite parental prohibitions, beginning before age 13 years.
14. Has run away from home overnight at least twice while living in parental or parental surrogate home (or once without returning for a lengthy period).
15. Is often truant from school, beginning before age 13 years.

B. The disturbance in behavior causes clinically significant impairment in social, academic, or occupational functioning.

C. If the individual is age 18 years or older, criteria are not met for antisocial personality disorder.

Specify type based on age at onset

Childhood-Onset Type: Onset of at least one criterion characteristic of conduct disorder prior to age 10 years.
Adolescent-Onset Type: Absence of any criteria characteristic of conduct disorder prior to age 10 years.

Specify severity

Mild: Few if any conduct problems in excess of those required to make the diagnosis and conduct problems cause only minor harm to others.
Moderate: Number of conduct problems and effect on others intermediate between mild and severe.
Severe: Many conduct problems in excess of those required to make the diagnosis *or* conduct problems cause considerable harm to others.

Source: Reprinted with permission from the *Diagnostic and Statistical Manual of Mental Disorders,* Fourth Edition (pp. 90–91). Copyright 1994 American Psychiatric Association.

Diagnostic criteria for oppositional defiant disorder

A. A pattern of negativistic, hostile, and defiant behavior lasting at least 6 months, during which four (or more) of the following are present:
    1. Often loses temper.
    2. Often argues with adults.
    3. Often actively defies or refuses to comply with adults' requests or rules.
    4. Often deliberately annoys people.
    5. Often blames others for his or her mistakes or misbehavior.
    6. Is often touchy or easily annoyed by others.
    7. Is often angry and resentful.
    8. Is often spiteful or vindictive.

    Note: Consider a criterion met only if the behavior occurs more frequently than is typically observed in individuals of comparable age and developmental level.

B. The disturbance in behavior causes clinically significant impairment in social, academic, or occupational functioning.
C. The behaviors do not occur exclusively during the course of a psychotic or mood disorder.
D. Criteria are not met for conduct disorder, and, if the individual is age 18 years or older, criteria are not met for antisocial personality disorder.

Source: Reprinted with permission from the *Diagnostic and Statistical Manual of Mental Disorders,* Fourth Edition (pp. 93–94). Copyright 1994 American Psychiatric Association.

members, reluctance to go to sleep, and repeated complaints about headaches, stomachaches, and nausea.

The other condition, elective mutism, is a persistent refusal to talk in typical social, school, and work environments. This disorder is really quite rare, representing less than 1% of all psychiatric referrals. This disorder may significantly affect the child's social and educational functioning.

■ CLASSIFICATION ACCORDING TO SEVERITY OF BEHAVIORS
Various researchers have attempted to differentiate mild to moderate disorders from severe ones. As one might expect, the characteristics of individuals with severe behavior disorders are identified more easily than those associated with mild disorders. As illustrated in Table 7.3 on page 226, individuals with severe disorders differ significantly from those with mild disorders in a variety of intellectual, social, academic, and behavioral domains.

Persons who exhibit severe behavior disorders are often described as psychotic. **Psychosis** is a general term. The *DSM-IV* uses more specific terms such as **pervasive developmental disorders** and *schizophrenia,* among others, to refer to infants, children, adolescents, and adults who are psychotic or very seriously disturbed.

Prevalence

Estimates of the prevalence of behavior disorders vary greatly from one source to the next, ranging from 0.05% to 15%. The U.S. Department of Education (1997) reported that 0.74% of all students in U.S. schools are identified as seriously emotionally disturbed. Estimates provided by the Office of Technology Assessment and the National Institute of Medicine suggest that more

TABLE 7.3	Characteristics of individuals with behavior disorders	

GENERAL FACTORS	MILD BEHAVIOR DISORDERS	SEVERE BEHAVIOR DISORDERS
Intelligence	Below average intelligence to gifted; generally below average	Generally in the retarded range
Academic achievement	Academic skills and knowledge well below average; dropout rate exceeds that of individuals with other disabilities	Severe deficits in academic skills; may exhibit rudimentary reading and mathematics abilities
Social relationships	Major problems in developing and maintaining relationships	Few, if any, stable relationships with others; often avoids relationships with other individuals, even peers
Adaptive skills	Generally skilled in daily living skills and caring for self	Major problems in everyday living skills and caring for self
Behaviors problems	Frequently aggressive (verbally and physically), oppositional, noncompliant, and generally obnoxious	Often and consistently violent, assaultive, destructive, or self-injurious
Speech and language problems	Generally normal	Bizarre language, speech problems; sometimes completely lacks functional communication skills
Contact with reality	Contact with reality good; generally aware of environment and other individuals	Out of contact with environment and the persons in it; develops own realities (hallucinates, fantasizes, etc.)
Presence of other disorders	Few, if any, other disorders other than learning problems	Other disorders and disabilities may be present (eating disorders, depression, elimination disorders, etc.)
Employment	Sporadically employed or underemployed, according to abilities	Generally unemployed; not self-sustaining; dependent on others

than 3% of children and adolescents have severe behavior disorders. Other current research indicates that between 7% and 8% of all school-age children may have emotional or behavior disorders sufficiently severe to warrant treatment (Brandenburg, Friedman, & Silver, 1990; Forness, Kavale, & Lopez, 1993).

Kauffman (1997) suggested that 3% to 6% of the school-age population need specialized services because of behavior disorders. Other specialists have suggested that as many as 33% of school-age children experience behavior problems during any given year (Cullinan & Epstein, 1986). Of this number, about one third need assistance provided by personnel outside the typical classroom. Another third of this number need special education and related services.

The fact remains, however, that a significant number of students with behavior disorders do not receive special education (Kauffman, 1997; Knitzer, Steinberg, & Fleisch, 1990; U.S. Department of Education, 1997). Some researchers have suggested that the number of students who receive special education is less than one third of those who actually need this assistance (Brandenburg et al., 1990). The low number of students served is in part due to the lack of standardized criteria, diverse definitions, and meager research about the processes involved in labeling students and related placement decisions (Denny, Gunther, Shores, & Campbell, 1995; Lewitt & Baker, 1996; Kavale et al., 1986; Knitzer et al., 1990; Stephens & Lakin, 1995).

Characteristics

▪ INTELLIGENCE

focus 5

Identify five general characteristics (intellectual, adaptive, and achievement) of children with behavior disorders.

Researchers from a variety of disciplines have studied the intellectual capacity of individuals with behavior disorders. In an early national study of children with behavior disorders enrolled in public school programs, the majority exhibited above-average intelligence (Morse, Cutler, & Fink, 1964). However, recent research has revealed a different picture.

Rubin and Balow (1978) studied three groups of children. The first group comprised students who had been referred and identified as disturbed by medical or psychological personnel but not by their teachers. Their average IQs according to two separate intelligence tests were 109 and 107. The second group of students, who were consistently referred and identified as disturbed by teachers, had IQs of 96 and 92 on the same measures. The last group, who were sporadically identified by teachers as having difficulties had average IQs of 102 on both tests of intelligence. Bower (1982) compared the IQs of children who were disturbed to those of children who were not disturbed. He found that children who were disturbed had average IQs of 92, whereas their nondisturbed peers had average IQs of 103.

Studies dealing with children who have been identified as autistic or schizophrenic reveal still another picture of intellectual functioning. Researchers have found that the majority of these children have IQs in the moderate to severe range of mental retardation (Freeman & Ritvo, 1984; Green, Fein, Joy, & Waterhouse, 1995; Kauffman, 1997). Of course, some of these children did have average or above-average IQs, but they were in the minority.

The preponderance of evidence leads to the conclusion that children with behavior disorders tend to have average to lower-than-average IQs compared to their normal peers (Kauffman, 1997). Additionally, children with severe behavior disorders such as schizophrenia and autism tend to have IQs that fall within the retarded range of functioning.

What impact does intelligence have on the educational and social-adaptive performance of children with behavior disorders? Is the intellectual capacity of a child who is disturbed a good predictor of other types of achievement and social behavior? The answer is yes. Kauffman (1997) asserted that "the IQs of disturbed children appear to be the best single predictor of academic and future social achievement" (p. 245). The below-average IQs of many of these children contribute significantly to the challenges they experience in mastering academic and social tasks in school and other environments.

▪ ADAPTIVE AND SOCIAL BEHAVIOR

Individuals with behavior disorders exhibit a variety of problems in adapting to their homes, schools, and community environments. Furthermore, they have difficulties in relating socially and responsibly to persons such as peers and parents, teachers, and other authority figures (Farmer, Stuart, Lorch, & Fields, 1993; Hundert, 1995).

Listening, asking for teacher assistance, bringing materials to class, following directions, completing assignments, and ignoring distractions are some of the school-related adaptive behaviors that do not come naturally to children with behavior disorders (Walker, 1995). Moreover, such behaviors may not have been successfully taught to these children. Socially, they may have difficulty introducing themselves, beginning and ending conversations, sharing, playing typical age-appropriate games, and apologizing. They may be unable to deal appropriately with situations that produce strong feelings such as anger and frustration.

Social problem solving, accepting consequences of misbehavior, negotiating, expressing affection, and reacting appropriately to failure are not generally part of the behavior repertoire of children with behavior disorders. Because these children have deficits in adaptive social behaviors, they frequently experience difficulties in meeting the demands of the classroom and other environments in which they must participate. Nick, the aggressive boy described in the opening snapshot, experienced many difficulties in accepting the consequences of misbehavior and dealing effectively with criticism. Eric exhibited significant difficulties in attending to tasks, waiting his turn, and using words, rather than his fists, to express himself. Amy, for a variety of reasons, did not deal well with authority figures, particularly her teachers, and consistently chose not to complete school assignments.

In this chapter's section on classification, we reviewed the statistically derived categories of behaviors common to children and adolescents with behavior disorders. These categories included conduct disorder, anxiety withdrawal, immaturity, and socialized aggression. Children and adolescents with conduct disorders engage in verbal and physical aggression. They may threaten other children, extort money from them, or physically hurt them, often without any provocation. In classrooms, these students often defy authority, refuse to follow a teacher's directions, and frequently engage in power struggles with teachers and administrative personnel (Walker, 1995; Walker, Colvin, & Ramsey, 1995).

Children and adolescents who are anxious and withdrawn frequently exhibit behaviors such as seclusiveness and shyness. They may find it extremely difficult to interact with others in normal social events. They tend to avoid contact with others and may be often found daydreaming.

Gang activities, drug abuse, cooperative stealing, truancy, and other delinquent acts characterize children and adolescents who are identified as "undersocialized aggressive" (Kauffman, 1997). These adolescents are often seen as impulsive, hyperactive, irritable, and tenaciously stubborn. Furthermore, they frequently do not get along well with others, engage in behaviors that draw attention to themselves, and are cruel to others.

It is easy to see how the behaviors associated with these categories are maladaptive and interfere with success in school and family (Burnett & Waltz, 1994). Moreover, it is clear that gang activities and cooperative stealing involving adolescents definitely do antagonize and agitate community members.

Children with severe behavior disorders exhibit social and adaptive patterns of behaviors that closely parallel those of children with moderate to severe mental retardation. They may need extensive assistance in developing self-help skills (e.g., toileting, grooming, dressing, and caring for themselves), language competency, and social skills that permit them to interact cooperatively with others in their home environments and elsewhere.

■ ACADEMIC ACHIEVEMENT

Students with behavior disorders experience significant difficulties in academic subject areas (Walker et al., 1995). In comparison to other students with disabilities, they fail more classes and are more frequently unsuccessful in passing minimum competency examinations (Koyangi & Gaines, 1993). Additionally, they are more often retained than other students with disabilities (U.S. Department of Education, 1997). On the high school level, students with behavior disorders have average grade points of 1.7, compared with 2.0 for all high school students with disabilities (Osher, Osher, & Smith, 1994; Wagner et al., 1991).

The dropout and graduation rates for students with behavior disorders are staggering (Osher et al., 1994). Fifty-two to fifty-six percent of these students drop out of school, most before they finish the tenth grade. Forty-two percent actually graduate from high school (Osher & Hanley, 1996; Wagner, 1991). About 17% of students with behavior disorders go on to college.

Studies dealing with post–high school employment rates of students are quite revealing. Only 41% of students with behavior disorders who have exited high school are employed two years later, compared with 59% of typical adolescents. Three to five years later, the contrasts are even stronger: 69% of students without disabilities are employed, compared with 47% of students with behavior disorders (D'Amico & Blackorby, 1992).

Some studies have suggested that many of the programs designed to assist students with behavior disorders overemphasize control and management of behavior rather than the teaching of academic skills or valuable prevocational or vocational training (Cheney, Barringer, Upham, & Manning, 1996; Knitzer et al., 1990; Nichols, 1996; Scheuermann & Webber, 1996). The extent to which poor academic programs contribute to the poor school performance of students with behavior disorders is questionable. Earlier studies of students with behavior disorder reveal a fairly consistent pattern of academic difficulty (Bower, 1981; Graubard, 1964; Stone & Rowley, 1964).

Causation

Throughout history, philosophers, physicians, theologians, and others have attempted to explain why people behave as they do. Historically, people who were mentally disturbed were described as possessed by evil spirits, for which the treatment of choice was religious in nature. Later, Sigmund Freud (1856–1939) and others promoted the notion that behavior could be explained in terms of subconscious phenomena or early traumatic experiences. More recently, some theorists have attributed disordered behaviors to inappropriate learning and complex interactions that take place between individuals and their environments. From a biological perspective, others have suggested that aberrant behaviors are caused by certain biochemical substances, brain abnormalities or injuries, and chromosomal irregularities.

This wealth of etiological explanations offers practitioners many different approaches to treating and preventing various disorders. The variety of theoretical frameworks and perspectives provides a number of choices for explaining the presence of certain behaviors:

1. *The biological approach.* The biological framework explains behavior disorders as a function of inherited or abnormal biological conditions within the body or injury to the central nervous system. Behavior problems presumably surface as a result of some physiological, biochemical, or genetic abnormality or disease.

focus 6
What can be accurately said about the causes of behavior disorders?

2. *The psychoanalytical approach.* Subconscious processes, predispositions or instincts, and early traumatic experiences explain the presence of behavior disorders according to the psychoanalytic perspective. Internal processes occur unobservably in the mind, involving interactions among the id (the person's drives), the ego (the person's orientation to reality), and the superego (the conscience), which are constructs developed by Freud. As individuals gain insight into their psychic conflicts by means of psychotherapy, they may be able to eliminate or solve their behavior problems. The return to normalcy may also be aided by a caring therapist or teacher. According to this theory, this process can be facilitated for children through play therapy, which reveals inner conflicts that can be subsequently resolved through family therapy and therapeutic play experiences provided by understanding adults.

3. *The behavioral approach.* The behavioral approach focuses on aspects of the environment that produce, reward, diminish, or punish certain behaviors. Through treatment, adults and children are given opportunities to learn new adaptive behaviors by identifying realistic goals and receiving reinforcement for attaining these goals. According to this approach, aberrant behaviors can be gradually eliminated or replaced by more appropriate ones.

4. *The phenomenological approach.* From a phenomenological point of view, abnormal behaviors arise from feelings, thoughts, and past events tied to a person's self-perception or self-concept. Faulty perceptions or feelings are thought to cause individuals to behave in ways that are counterproductive to self-fulfillment. Therapy using this approach is centered on helping people develop satisfactory perceptions and behaviors that are consistent with self-selected values.

5. *The sociological–ecological approach.* The sociological–ecological model is by far the most broadly applicable explanation of behavior disorders. Aberrant behaviors are presumed to be caused by a variety of interactions and transactions with other people. For some, the deviant behaviors are taught as part of one's culture. For others, the behaviors result from labeling; individuals labeled as juvenile delinquents, according to this perspective, gradually adopt the patterns of behavior that are associated with the assigned label, and others who are aware of the label treat the individuals as if they were truly delinquent. Theoretically, such treatment promotes the delinquent behavior.

This model also specifies another source of aberrant behavior—*differential association.* This is closely related to the cultural transmission explanation of deviance: People exhibit behavior problems in order to conform to the wishes and expectations of a group so that they can join it or maintain affiliation with it. Finally, the sociological–ecological perspective views aberrant behavior as resulting from a variety of interactions and transactions that occur in a broad array of settings.

Each of these models explains the causes of behavior disorders differently. Unfortunately, clinicians can rarely isolate the exact cause of a child's behavior disorders, but they do understand many conditions and factors that contribute to them. Many professionals concur with the words of Kauffman (1997): "Both the disorder of behavior and [its] causes are usually multidimensional; life seldom refines disorders or their causes into pure unambiguous forms. Children seldom show teachers or researchers a single disorder uncontaminated by elements of other problems, and the cause of a disorder is virtually never found to be a single factor" (p. 159).

Family and home environments play a critical role in the emergence of behavior disorders. Poverty, malnutrition, homelessness, family discord, divorce, childrearing practices, and child abuse have a profound impact on the behaviors observed in children and adolescents (Gelfand et al., 1997).

Children reared in low-income families bear increased risks for wide-ranging challenges including lower intellectual development, deficient school achievement, and high rates of behavior problems. For children whose family poverty is accompanied by other stressors such as homelessness, the death of a parent, child placement in foster care, or persistent child abuse, antisocial behaviors often emerge (Masten et al., 1993).

Family discord and divorce play a role in the development of behavior disorders in some children. The impact of divorce on children is influenced by a variety of factors (e.g., age of the child, financial status of the family, gender of the child, amount of acrimony between the partners), so it is difficult to predict with great precision who will be severely affected. Extended marital conflict and distress are associated with several serious child outcomes, including aggressive behavior, difficulty with schoolwork, depression, health problems, and inferior social competence (Katz & Gottman, 1993; Mattison & Forness, 1995).

Child-management and discipline procedures also play important roles in the development of behavior disorders (Campbell, 1995; Farrington, 1995; Rutter, 1995). However, the way in which child management procedures produce behavior disorders is highly complex (Campbell, 1995; Rutter, 1995). Parents who are extremely permissive, overly restrictive, and/or aggressive often produce children who have conduct disorders. Home environments characterized by inconsistent application of rules and consequences for child misbehavior, lack of parental supervision, reinforcement of aggressive behavior, and parents who model aggression and use aggressive child-management practices can produce children who are very much at risk for developing disruptive behavior disorders or conduct disorders (Campbell, 1995; Farrington, 1995; Rutter, 1995). The same dynamic holds true for behavior problems associated with depression and anxiety. For example, parents of children or adolescents with depression often model negative cognitive styles and may reward and concur with their offspring's self-"put downs" (Dadds, 1995).

Child abuse plays a major role in the development of aggression and other problematic behaviors in children and adolescents (Cicchetti & Toth, 1995; Kendall-Tackett, Williams, & Finkelhor, 1993; Trickett & McBride-Chang, 1995; Wolfe & Burt, 1995). Effects of child abuse on young children include withdrawal, noncompliance, aggression, enuresis, and somatic and physical complaints. Physically abused children exhibit high rates of adjustment problems of all kinds. Neglected children have difficulty in academic subjects and receive below-average grades. Children who have been sexually abused manifest an array of problems, including inappropriate, premature sexual behavior, and poor peer relationships. Similar difficulties are evident in adolescents who have been abused. These include low self-esteem, depression, poor peer and school adjustment, and self-injurious and suicidal behaviors (Kendall-Tackett et al., 1993).

Assessment

■ SCREENING AND REFERRAL

The first step in the assessment process is screening, to identify infants, children, and adolescents most in need of treatment. Screening is important because early identification leads to early treatment, which may lessen the overall impact of the behavior disorders on the individual and family. However, very few school systems or social service agencies engage in truly wide-range screening for behavior disorders, for two reasons. First, such a task is generally very expensive and time consuming, beyond the financial and human resources of most school systems and state social service agencies. Second, many more children might be identified than could be adequately handled by a school system or social agency.

In most school environments, children are considered for screening only after concerned or perplexed teachers have initiated referrals for them. For example, an experienced kindergarten teacher became very concerned about John. He was continually involved in a variety of behaviors atypical for his age—taking off his clothes, crying for prolonged periods, and physically attacking children—all for no obvious reason. These behaviors and others prompted John's kindergarten teacher to take action, discussing the problem not only with his parents but also with the principal.

The actual submission of a referral for a student is generally preceded by a number of parent–teacher conferences. These conferences help teachers and parents determine what action ought to be taken. For example, the student's difficulties may be a symptom of family problems such as an extended parental illness, marital difficulties, or severe financial challenges. If the parents and teacher continue to be perplexed by a child's behavior, a referral may be initiated. Referrals are generally processed by principals, who review them, consult with parents, and then pass them on to a psychologist or assessment team leader.

Once a referral has been appropriately processed and parental or guardian permission for testing and evaluation has been obtained, assessment team members proceed with the tasks of carefully observing and assessing a child's strengths and weaknesses. Their task is to determine whether the child has a behavior disorder and whether he or she qualifies for special education services. Furthermore, the team is responsible for identifying treatment strategies that may be helpful to the parents and teachers.

■ ASSESSMENT FACTORS

focus 7

Identify four factors that need to be assessed carefully in determining whether a child has a behavior disorder.

The severity of behaviors such as those exhibited by the kindergartner John may be examined from several perspectives. First, it is necessary to determine whether any discrepancy exists between his chronological age and the behaviors he consistently displays, so that John's status in relationship to various norms can be scaled. In addition to determining whether John's behaviors are age-appropriate, assessment team members must analyze the frequency of problem behaviors and the circumstances under which they occur. They must also assess whether his inappropriate behaviors are related to specific activities or individuals and whether his problems continue even after someone intervenes.

Assessment includes an evaluation of the influence of John's behaviors on classmates, teachers, and the family. Additionally, team members must assess the teacher's contribution to the present problems. John's interactions with individuals in his school setting and his responses to his home environment significantly influence the recommendations of team members regarding his classification, placement, and eventual treatment.

■ ASSESSMENT TECHNIQUES

A variety of techniques are used to identify children with behavior disorders; all closely parallel the theoretical framework or philosophical perspective held by their evaluators. Usually, an actual diagnosis of the behavioral problems is preceded by a

0 = Not True (as far as you know)
1 = Somewhat or Sometimes True
2 = Very True or Often True

0	1	2	1.	Acts too young for his/her age
0	1	2	5.	Behaves like opposite sex
0	1	2	10.	Can't sit still, restless, or hyperactive
0	1	2	15.	Cruel to animals
0	1	2	20.	Destroys his/her own things
0	1	2	25.	Doesn't get along with other kids
0	1	2	30.	Fears going to school
0	1	2	35.	Feels worthless or inferior
0	1	2	40.	Hears sounds or voices that aren't there (describe):
0	1	2	45.	Nervous, high strung, or tense
0	1	2	50.	Too fearful or anxious

Source: From *Manual for the Child Behavior Checklist/4–18 and 1991 Profile,* by T. M. Achenbach. Burlington: Department of Psychiatry, University of Vermont. Copyright by T. M. Achenbach. Reproduced by permission.

set of screening procedures using behavior checklists or a variety of sociometric devices (e.g., peer ratings) and teacher rating scales.

Typically, parents and teachers are asked to respond to a variety of rating-scale items that describe behaviors that may be classified as behavior disorders. The number of items marked, as well as the rating given to each item, help determine the behavior profiles generated from the ratings. (See Table 7.4, which is drawn from the Child Behavior Checklist for Ages 4-16 [Achenbach, 1991a].) In making their assessments, parents and professionals are asked to consider the child's behavior during the past six months.

Behavioral analysis techniques are also used to compare the behavior of children suspected of exhibiting serious behavioral problems with the behavior of their peers in a given setting. One such technique, direct observation, uses a well-trained observer to count and record a variety of behaviors that may concern a teacher or parent while at the same time monitoring these behaviors in a number of other students. Comparisons drawn from these types of observations can be very helpful in accurately assessing the behavior pattern of a student in contrast to that of his or her peers.

Once the screening process has been concluded, specialists or consultants—including psychologists, special educators, social workers, and psychiatrists—complete in-depth assessments of the child's academic and social–emotional strengths and weaknesses in various environments such as the classroom, the home, and the playground. The assessment team may analyze classroom and playground interactions with peers and teachers using ecological and behavioral analysis techniques (taking frequency counts of various types of behaviors or interactions); administer various tests to evaluate personality, achievement, and intellectual factors; and interview the parents and the child. Additionally, they may observe the child at home and apply an array of other assessment procedures.

EXPERT SYSTEMS AND ARTIFICIAL INTELLIGENCE FOR ASSESSMENT

Researchers are testing the effectiveness of computers in aiding assessment teams to classify students as having behavior disorders, learning disabilities, or mental retardation. Multidisciplinary team members enter assessment data that they have collected and respond to questions that experts have programmed the computer to ask. The so-

called artificial intelligence (AI) that the experts have created examines and processes the data and then makes a reasoned judgment. Additionally, AI systems are also programmed to provide information about interventions that should be applied and the likelihood of their success in treating various learning and behavior problems (Hofmeister & Ferrara, 1986).

Are these expert systems superior to human judgment? This is a difficult question to answer. AI systems represent the best judgment of skilled assessment and intervention specialists. They are much like the expert systems used in medicine that assist physicians in making careful diagnoses and identifying potential treatments.

Imagine having an expert system in your own home for identifying potentially serious behavior problems in your children as well as for ways of dealing with them! You would enter the problem, its duration in time, its average frequency per day, and other salient information, and the computer would provide you with some effective strategies for addressing the problems.

Unfortunately, many assessment devices, particularly **projective inventories** and personality inventories, do not provide information that reliably differentiates individuals who have disorders from those who do not (Gelfand et al., 1997). Likewise, information gained from these devices cannot be readily translated into specific programming for individuals with behavior disorders. Of greatest promise at this point are behavioral analysis techniques and curriculum-based assessment approaches that provide a concrete means for evaluating behavior, determining appropriate instructional approaches, developing appropriate IEP goals, and assessing intervention effects (Kauffman, 1997; Umbreit, 1995; Walker, 1995).

Interventions

Interventions for children and adolescents with behavior disorders include a variety of approaches (Gelfand et al., 1997). Major treatments include insight-oriented therapy, play therapy, group psychotherapy, behavior therapy, marital and family therapy, and drug therapy (see Table 7.5). Unfortunately, many of these therapies are not available to students with behavior disorders (Peacock Hill Working Group, 1990). As a rule, school systems and mental health agencies have not been successful in developing effective collaborative models for serving students with severe behavior disorders (Illback & Nelson, 1996; Osher & Osher, 1995), although there have been some exceptions. Project Wraparound (Eber, 1996) and the Alaska Youth Initiative (Burchard, Burchard, Sewell, & VanDenBerg, 1993) represent unique and comprehensive programs in which schools, families, and mental health agencies have worked effectively together to provide quality education and related services to students with behavior disorders and their families (see the Reflect on This feature on page 236).

focus 8

Identify six major treatment approaches generally used in treating children and adolescents with behavior disorders.

■ INSIGHT-ORIENTED THERAPY

Insight-oriented therapy includes psychoanalytic, nondirective, and client-centered therapy. These approaches assume that children who feel rage, rejection, and

	INTERVENTION APPROACHES					
GENERAL GOALS	Insight-Oriented Therapy	Play Therapy	Group Psychotherapy	Behavior Therapy	Marital and Family Therapy	Drug Therapy
Relieve symptoms	•					•
Treat causes of behavior	•		•		•	
Develop therapeutic relationships	•	•	•		•	
Play out emotional problems		•				
Develop positive peer relationships		•	•	•		
Teach language skills				•		
Teach self-help skills				•		
Teach academic skills				•		
Reduce and/or eliminate behaviors				•		
Teach adaptive behavior				•		
Teach social skills		•		•		
Develop problem-solving skills		•	•		•	
Understand unconscious causes of behavior	•		•			
Control disordered or unusual behavior				•		•
Control aggression				•		•
Control behavior				•		•

guilt can be helped by an understanding and caring therapist. The therapist endeavors to establish a relationship with the child by creating an atmosphere conducive to sharing and expressing feelings. The goal of therapy is to help the child develop insight, or self-understanding, which provides the basis for the relief of symptoms and the development of new, more adaptive behaviors.

■ PLAY THERAPY

Play therapy for young children serves several purposes. It is designed to help them become aware of their own unconscious thoughts and the behaviors that emanate from these thoughts. For children who have been emotionally abused or neglected, another purpose is to provide interaction with a caring, sensitive adult. The vehicle for communication between the therapist and children is free play and other related small-group activities. Through play therapy, children may reveal information about themselves that they cannot talk about, such as the presence of sexual abuse, sibling rivalry, and damaging disciplinary practices. Play therapy can be a valuable source of information for therapists.

Reflect on This

■ INTRODUCTION

Peter was referred for individualized care by the local elementary school basic staffing team. His first-grade teacher reported that he was often aggressive, unable to sit still, and uncompliant. In addition, she complained that his hygiene was very poor and that he often came to school tired. At the time of referral, his parents refused to participate on the school planning team and were openly hostile toward school staff. Despite Peter's above-average intellectual abilities, he was failing in his academic subjects, was disliked by his peers, and spent approximately 70% of his school day in "time-out" situations. Peter's teacher felt that his needs could no longer be met within a mainstream setting. The initial assessments in school indicated that Peter was a child with significant undercontrolled behaviors occurring approximately every five minutes. Some of his more disruptive and dangerous behaviors included running around the classroom, jumping on the desks, hitting, spitting at the other children and the teacher, bolting out of the school, running into the street, and refusing to work and comply with instructions.

Peter's parents were unable to cope with equally problematic behaviors at home. If they placed any limits on his behavior he would destroy things. They reported that he constantly fought with his younger brother, wet the bed every night, hit and kicked his parents, and required constant supervision because he was like a revved-up engine and would get into everything. Their approach to child management was quite punitive and involved yelling, spanking, and locking Peter in his room. An assessment of the home environment revealed a highly punitive and restrictive home situation. Peter's mother and father felt inadequate as parents and rarely interacted with their children. They lacked an understanding of developmental norms and expectations for children, expressed only hostile feelings toward their children, and demanded 100% compliance at all times. Their marital relationship was explosive; during one episode the children were physically hurt and had to be placed in foster care for a short period of time. The child protection agency and school personnel felt that there was considerable potential for further abuse.

Source: Excerpted from J. D. Burchard and R. T. Clarke, "The Role of Individualized Care in a Service Delivery System for Children and Adolescents with Severely Maladjusted Behavior," *Journal of Mental Health Administration, 17*(1), pp. 48–60. Copyright 1990 by *Journal of Mental Health Administration.* Reprinted by permission of Sage Publications, Inc.

■ GROUP PSYCHOTHERAPY

Group psychotherapy and other group-oriented treatment approaches are only occasionally used with children. They are used more frequently with adolescents and young adults. **Activity group therapy** for children is operated much like a club. For example, a mix of aggressive and withdrawn boys meet together weekly for club (therapy) meetings. The therapist's role in the group setting is primarily one of modeling appropriate, healthy behaviors, helping aggressive children become more cooperative, and promoting outgoing behaviors in children who are shy and withdrawn. Group treatment approaches for adolescents are varied and often quite similar to the procedures used with adults. The major difference lies in the concerns and issues that are the focus of therapy sessions. Vorrath's Positive Peer Culture has been used to address a variety of adolescent-related problems, including disruptive classroom behaviors, delinquency, and substance abuse (Sandler, Arnold, Gable, & Strain, 1987; Vorrath & Brendtro, 1985). This treatment approach capitalizes on the power inherent in peer approval and peer-selected rules, contingencies, and solutions. It requires the skill of an experienced therapist, group leader, or teacher.

■ BEHAVIOR THERAPY

Behavioral interventions for children and adolescents focus on developing or improving various self-help, social, language, and academic behaviors. Increasing the rates of desirable behavior is achieved through a variety of approaches. Teachers

Reflect on This

PETER: PART TWO

■ INTERAGENCY CARE AND INTENSIVE FAMILY-BASED SERVICES

Following initial contacts with Peter's family, a multidisciplinary team was formed consisting of the parents and appropriate representatives from mental health, social services, and education. The interdisciplinary team met as needed for three reasons: (1) to plan and coordinate the various services that were provided to the family and child; (2) to provide multiagency ownership with respect to funding services as well as to discuss the utilization of private third-party payments; and (3) to ensure that all efforts were made to provide the least restrictive care prior to any placement of the child into more costly and/or restrictive educational or residential programs. Peter's parents participated in the interagency team to aid in the identification of services.

Due to the necessity to intervene immediately to prevent the child from being placed in a more restrictive environment, the comprehensive ecological assessment was performed as intervention was being applied. As the evaluation process was progressing, services and plans were revised to meet the individual needs of the family, child, and school. For example, an immediate family concern was the parents' lack of appropriate discipline and child management strategies. A family intervention specialist entered the home within seven hours of the referral and initiated interventions designed to assist the parents in developing alternative approaches. As the parents progressed through the training, the ongoing individualized assessment revealed that the parents did not know how to play with their children and felt insecure about interacting with them. Interventions were then applied to educate them about child play situations. At all stages of the assessment process, emphasis was placed on the parents' realistically identifying needs and assisting in the development of services to meet those needs. Although the needs identified by the parents did not always coincide with the priorities of the clinician, involving the parents in this manner ensured more commitment from them to participate and empowered them to be effective advocates for themselves and their children. During a two-year period, the family experienced intensive home-based services, significant respite care, a variety of interventions designed to meet the individual needs of the child such as dry-bed training and conflict resolution training, individual counseling to address alcohol and physical abuse issues, and two summer education programs to assist the children in skill building around safety, social skills, and cooperative play.

Source: Excerpted from J. D. Burchard and R. T. Clarke, "The Role of Individualized Care in a Service Delivery System for Children and Adolescents with Severely Maladjusted Behavior," *Journal of Mental Health Administration, 17*(1), pp. 48–60. Copyright 1990 by *Journal of Mental Health Administration.* Reprinted by permission of Sage Publications, Inc.

---

and special education personnel make extensive use of the principles of behavior modification in this approach. Rewards, point or **token reinforcement systems, behavioral contracts,** and other motivational systems are used to encourage children to engage in normal, adaptive behaviors (see nearby Reflect on This feature).

Behavioral interventions are also employed to reduce or eliminate maladaptive behaviors. Reductions in certain behaviors can be achieved through a variety of means. For instance, a young boy's fighting behavior can be reduced by rewarding his cooperative and problem-solving behaviors and punishing his fighting behaviors. For engaging in fighting, he may lose accumulated tokens (response cost) or be placed in a time-out area where he cannot earn tokens or participate in the ongoing, reinforcing activities of the classroom.

Several researchers and clinicians have experimented with a relatively new behavioral modification approach known as **cognitive–behavioral training** (Gelfand et al., 1997). Some practitioners refer to this training as self-regulation therapy. This approach emphasizes teaching internal verbal strategies to encourage and maintain important social or academic behaviors (Meichenbaum, 1977). For example, a child might be taught the following strategic sequence, which combines thinking with behaving:

Step 1. Motor cue/impulse delay: Stop and think before you act; cue yourself.
Step 2. Problem definition: Say how you feel and exactly what the problem is.

Step 3. Generation of alternatives: Think of as many solutions as you can.
Step 4. Consideration of consequences: Think ahead to what might happen next.
Step 5. Implementation: When you have a really good solution, try it! (Etscheidt, 1991, p. 111)

Results generated from studies using this approach with children and adolescents have been quite promising (Ager & Cole, 1991; Harris & Pressley, 1991).

■ MARITAL AND FAMILY THERAPY

Marital therapy and family therapy are designed to help married individuals and their families enjoy greater success in dealing with problems and relating more effectively with one another. Several types of family therapy have been developed. Some therapists are *psychodynamically oriented*; that is, they are interested in helping family members understand the unconscious dynamics and other factors that may be influencing their interactions. Family therapists who adhere to the *systems orientation* direct their efforts at helping family members understand their roles and functions in the family system. They may determine that a child's disturbance serves some specific family function and is thereby supported by the other family members. *Structural family therapy* emphasizes the assessment of family functioning, or the ways in which family members solve problems and interact with one another. Coalitions within the family may be analyzed, and the views that family members have of themselves and others are evaluated. Therapists using this approach become actively involved with families by assigning homework between sessions and giving participants family-related tasks to complete.

■ DRUG THERAPY

Drug therapy for children is frequently used to treat a variety of conditions and related behaviors (Gelfand et al., 1997). Children who are hyperactive, inattentive, and impulsive are often treated with stimulant drugs. Children with severe behavior disorders may be treated with medications to control disorganized or highly erratic behavior. In other cases, medications may be prescribed for children who have chronic problems with bed-wetting or involuntary urination. Older teenagers or young adults may be prescribed drugs that are ordinarily taken by adults for depression and other psychiatric conditions.

Different service delivery systems are used to make these and other treatments available to children, adolescents, and their families. The type of service delivery and the emphasis of the approach depend on the age of the student, the severity and type of disorder, and the theoretical orientation of the providers. Moreover, the effectiveness of past interventions and input from the family must be considered. For example, a preschooler who is out of control will need an altogether different treatment than an adolescent who is severely depressed.

Self-expression through open-ended art projects can help children with emotional and behavioral disorders. In this inclusive general education elementary classroom every student has a chance to fingerpaint.

EARLY CHILDHOOD SERVICE DELIVERY SYSTEMS	INTERVENTION APPROACHES					
	Insight-Oriented Therapy	Play Therapy	Group Psychotherapy	Behavior Therapy	Marital and Family Therapy	Drug Therapy
Home-based program				•		•
Home-based program followed by specialized center	•	•		•	•	•
Home- and center-based program	•	•	•	•	•	•
Center-based program	•	•	•	•	•	•

The Early Childhood Years

Service delivery systems for young children with behavior disorders are many and varied. However, four systems are generally used to provide these children with appropriate services and supports: (1) the home-based system; (2) the home-based system, followed by involvement with a specialized center; (3) the home- and center-based system; and (4) the center-based system. Personnel in these systems may use a variety of intervention approaches to assist children and families (see Table 7.6).

The *home-based program* approach provides children with specialized services through a home teacher. The teacher trains parents to use behavior modification and other therapeutic procedures to assist their children in learning and mastering new, developmentally appropriate skills.

Referrals for home-based service programs come from physicians, local guidance clinics, public school personnel, and county health nurses. Home teachers assist parents in selecting appropriate goals for their children, which are based on actual performance data of the child as observed firsthand by the parents and home teacher. Using these data and consistent with the child's needs, the home teacher and parents develop a program that involves training related to self-help, language, socialization, and motor skills. Goals are set on a weekly basis, and the teacher visits the family each week to observe both the child and the parents, to be sure that they are encouraging the behaviors associated with the weekly goals. The home teacher discusses any problems in the training process and provides demonstrations and instructions relevant to the goals.

A home-based program may be followed by a specialized center program or a combination of both. These programs provide a carefully conceived, sequential system of interrelated objectives for the home and center programs. In general, children served in this manner receive home-based instruction from birth to approximately 3 years of age. When about $2\frac{1}{2}$ to $3\frac{1}{2}$ years old, a child is phased into a center-based program that builds on the skills developed in the home program. A variation of this

Interacting in Natural Settings

PEOPLE WITH EMOTIONAL OR BEHAVIOR DISORDERS

■ EARLY CHILDHOOD YEARS

TIPS FOR THE FAMILY

- Become involved with parent training and other community mental health services.
- Work closely with family support personnel (e.g., social workers, nurses, and parent group volunteers) in developing effective child-management strategies.
- Use the same intervention strategies at home that are used effectively in the preschool setting.
- Establish family routines, schedules, and incentive systems that reward positive behaviors.
- Join advocacy or parent support groups.

TIPS FOR THE PRESCHOOL TEACHER

- Work closely with the support personnel in your preschool (e.g., director, psychologist, social worker, parent trainers, special educators, etc.) to identify effective and realistic strategies.
- Establish clear schedules, class routines, rules, and positive consequences for all children in your classroom.
- Create a learning and social environment that is nurturing and supportive for everyone.
- Teach specific social behaviors (e.g., following directions, greeting other children, sharing toys, using words to express anger, etc.) to all children.
- Do not be reluctant to ask for help from support per-

sonnel. Remember, collaboration is the key.

TIPS FOR PRESCHOOL PERSONNEL

- Use older, socially competent children to assist with readiness skills and social skills training.
- Help others (e.g., teaching assistants, aides, volunteers, etc.) know what to do in managing children with behavior disorders.
- Make every effort to involve the children in all school-wide activities and special performances.
- Orient and teach the other preschool children about disabling conditions and how they should respond and relate to their peers with behavior problems.
- Collaborate with parents in using the same management systems in your preschool classroom that are used in the home and other specialized settings.

TIPS FOR NEIGHBORS AND FRIENDS

- Become familiar with the things you should do as a neighbor or friend in responding to the positive and negative behaviors of a child with behavior disorders.
- Be patient with parents who are attempting to deal with their child's temper tantrum or other equally challenging behaviors at the grocery store or other like environments.
- Offer parents some time away from their preschooler by watching him or her for a couple of hours.
- Involve the child in your family activities.

- Help parents become aware of advocacy or parent support groups.
- Encourage parents to involve their child in neighborhood and community events (e.g., parades, holiday celebrations, and birthday parties).

■ ELEMENTARY YEARS

TIPS FOR THE FAMILY

- Use the effective management techniques that are being used in your child's classroom in your home environment.
- Help your other children (who are not disturbed) to develop an understanding of behavior disorders.
- Establish rules, routines, and consequences that fit your child's developmental age and interests.
- Take advantage of parent training and support groups that are available in your community.
- Obtain counseling when appropriate for yourself, your other children, and your spouse from a community mental health agency or other public or private source.
- Help your other children and their friends understand the things they can do to assist you in rearing your child with behavior disorders.

TIPS FOR GENERAL EDUCATION CLASSROOM TEACHER

- Provide a structured classroom environment (e.g., clearly stated rules, helpful positive and negative conse-

quences, well-conceived classroom schedules, and carefully taught classroom routines).
- Teach social skills (e.g., dealing with teasing, accepting criticism, etc.) to all of the children with the aid of members of the teacher assistance team.
- Teach self-management skills (e.g., goal selection, self-monitoring, self-reinforcement, etc.) to all children with the aid of members of the teacher assistance team.
- Use cooperative learning strategies to promote the learning of all children and to develop positive relationships among students.
- Do not be reluctant to ask for help from members of your teacher assistance team or the child's parents.

TIPS FOR SCHOOL PERSONNEL

- Use same-age or cross-age peers to provide tutoring, coaching, and other kinds of assistance in developing the academic and social skills of children with behavior disorders.
- Develop a schoolwide management program that reinforces individual and group accomplishments.
- Work closely with the teacher assistance team to create a school environment that is positive and caring.
- Use collaborative problem-solving techniques in dealing with difficult or persistent behavior problems.
- Help all children in the school develop an understanding of how they

should respond to students with behavior problems.

- Involve the child with behavior problems in appropriate afterschool activities (e.g., clubs, specialized tutoring, recreational events, etc.).
- Invite the child to spend time with your family in appropriate recreational events (e.g., swimming, hiking, etc.).
- Teach other children (without behavior problems) how to ignore or support certain behaviors that may occur.
- Catch the child being good rather than looking for "bad" behaviors.
- As a youth leader, coach, or recreational specialist, get to know each child with behavior disorders well so that you can respond with confidence in directing his or her activities.

SECONDARY AND TRANSITION YEARS

TIPS FOR THE FAMILY
- Continue your efforts to focus on the positive behaviors of your child with behavior disorders.
- Assist your child in selecting appropriate postsecondary training, education, and/or employment.
- Give yourself a regular break from the tedium of being a parent, and enjoy a recreational activity that is totally enjoyable for you.
- Ask for help from community mental health services, clergy, or a close friend when you are feeling overwhelmed or stressed.

- Consult regularly with treatment personnel to monitor progress and to obtain ideas for maintaining the behavioral gains made by your child.
- Continue your involvement in advocacy and parent support groups.

TIPS FOR GENERAL EDUCATION CLASSROOM TEACHER
- Create positive relationships within your classroom with cooperative learning teams and group-oriented assignments.
- Use all students in creating standards for conduct as well as consequences for positive and negative behaviors.
- Focus your efforts on developing a positive relationship with the student with behavior disorders by greeting him or her regularly to your class, informally talking with him or her at appropriate times, attending to improvements in his or her performance, and becoming aware of his or her interests.
- Work closely with the members of the teacher assistance team to be aware of teacher behaviors that may adversely or positively affect the student's performance.
- Realize that changes in behavior often occur very gradually, with periods of regression and sometimes tumult.

TIPS FOR SCHOOL PERSONNEL
- Create a school climate that is positive and supportive.
- Provide students with an understanding of their roles and responsibilities in re-

sponding to peers who are disabled.
- Use peers in providing social skills training, job coaching, and academic tutoring, and the like.
- Use members of the teacher assistance team to help you deal with crisis situations and to provide other supportive therapies and interventions.
- Be sure schoolwide procedures are in place for dealing quickly and efficiently with particularly difficult behaviors.

TIPS FOR NEIGHBORS, FRIENDS, AND POTENTIAL EMPLOYERS
- If you have some expertise in a content area (e.g., math, English, history, etc.), offer to provide regular assistance with homework or other related school assignments for students with behavior disorders.
- Provide opportunities for students with behavior disorders to be employed in your business.
- Give parents an occasional reprieve by inviting the youth to join your family for a cook-out, video night, or other family-oriented activities.
- Encourage other children (who are not disordered) to volunteer as peer partners, job coaches, and social skills trainers.
- Do not allow others in your presence to tease, harass, or ridicule a youth with behavior disorders.

ADULT YEARS

TIPS FOR THE FAMILY
- Continue to build on efforts to develop appropriate in-

dependence and interdependence.
- Maintain contact with appropriate medical personnel, particularly if the individual is on some form of medication for his or her condition.
- Make use of appropriate adult service agencies that are required by law to assist with your child's employment, housing, and recreation.
- Prepare your other children or other caregivers as appropriate to assume the responsibilities that you may be unable to assume over time.

TIPS FOR NEIGHBORS, FRIENDS, AND EMPLOYERS
- Be willing to make sensible and reasonable adjustments in the work environments.
- Be aware of adjustments that may need to take place with new medications or treatment regimens.
- Get to know the individual as a person—his or her likes, heroes or heroines, and leisure-time activities.
- Be willing to involve the individual in appropriate holiday and special occasion events such as birthdays, athletic activities, and other social gatherings.
- Be aware of what might be irritating or uncomfortable to the individual.
- Make yourself available to communicate with others who may be responsible for the individual's well-being—a job coach, an independent living specialist, and others.

kind of service delivery system is the Regional Intervention Program (RIP) (Timm, 1993). This program trains parents to serve as the primary therapists for their own children, as principal trainers for other parents, and as care providers for other young children with behavior disorders. This program empowers parents to nurture and care for their children.

The Elementary School Years

Elementary-age children with behavior disorders are likely to have difficulties relating to others, observing class rules, and handling emotional situations. They often exhibit below-average performance in reading and math as well as other areas within the general education curriculum. Academic support may be addressed through specialized instruction and materials provided by a consulting teacher. How and when the special materials are used

Reflect on This

PETER: PART THREE

■ INTENSIVE SCHOOL-BASED SERVICES

Due to pervasive, cross-setting difficulties, a school-based planning team was established consisting of the classroom teacher, a case worker from social services, a special educator, the parent, a school-based integration specialist, and the school nurse. This team met for one hour each week to coordinate a variety of school programs aimed at helping Peter adjust and improve academic skills and to track his progress in school. Again, all services used were child-centered and designed to meet Peter's needs in the various school environments.

The integration specialist assigned to Peter's planning team provided a variety of services including teacher training in behavior management; behavioral analysis of Peter's behaviors in school; technical assistance to the planning team in designing, implement-

ing, and monitoring treatment services within the school; and direct counseling to Peter. The direct counseling Peter received revolved around structured programs to help him gain control of his impulses and manage his own behavior. These programs were supplemented by the school counselor and the classroom teacher through training in social skills and cooperative play behaviors carried out with the entire class. In-school counseling service was provided an average of four times a week.

In addition to individual and group counseling, Peter engaged in a behavior token program with the whole class focusing on improving time on task and work achievement. More structured restitution and time-out procedures were implemented for aggressive behaviors. Over time it was felt that Peter would benefit from more structured positive interactions with other children and the teacher. For this rea-

son, the classroom teacher engaged in scheduled reinforcement of Peter. He was instructed to use a soft voice, work on his assigned task cooperatively, and wait his turn. This reinforcement occurred every five minutes and was decreased by the end of the year to once every half hour.

■ SUMMARY

To date, Peter and his family have received a host of intensive home and school-based treatment services. They have participated in 2 1/2 years of service planning and have been, at one point or another, involved in the mental health, social service, educational and recreational systems of care. The approach of all these services emphasized individual care and incorporated program tracking of services and adjustment. While Peter and his family continue to access services, their needs are less intensive than they were two years ago. His par-

ents are better able to manage his behavior and spend more time interacting with him in positive activities. In addition, both parents are full participants on the school planning team. At present, Peter requires little one-to-one attention, although an intervention is still being provided to foster additional social skills. A major component of Peter's plan at this point in time involves tracking progress and assessing long-term changes. Peter's parents understand that additional services will be provided if they are necessary.

Source: Excerpted from J. D. Burchard and R. T. Clarke, "The Role of Individualized Care in a Service Delivery System for Children and Adolescents with Severely Maladjusted Behavior," *Journal of Mental Health Administration, 17*(1), pp. 48–60. Copyright 1990 by *Journal of Mental Health Administration.* Reprinted by permission of Sage Publications, Inc.

depends on the staffing patterns and resources available in the school. Young children with behavior disorders may be tutored by older, academically capable students. Some children are assisted by aides or general education teachers, with follow-up provided by consultants or special education resource-room teachers (see nearby Reflect on This feature).

Behavioral difficulties may be addressed in a variety of ways. Sometimes, misbehavior reflects a lack of satisfactory rules, routines, and structures within the general education classroom. If this is the case, a consulting teacher may assist the regular class teacher in developing a classroom-management system that benefits not only the child with behavior problems, but other children in the classroom, as well.

Small training groups may be formed by a teacher to assist a child in developing social and problem-solving skills. *Structured Learning* is a program that uses **modeling, role playing, performance feedback,** and **transfer of training** (McGinnis,

Snapshot

JANE

■ STUDENTS AS SOLUTIONS

Jane, a 12-year-old student, started doing strange things at school. The principal, teacher, and resource teacher agreed to call in the "behavior specialists" to design a "compliance training" program.

For a short while Jane stopped being a nuisance and life went on, until she suddenly attacked a schoolmate in the schoolyard, knocking the girl to the ground and touching her breasts and genital area. She had to be physically pulled away. The "attack" frightened the other child involved but did not seriously injure her.

The principal immediately phoned both sets of parents and to his surprise, the mother of the student who was "attacked" did not become hysterical; she realized her daughter was not hurt. Jane's entire family was called in for a serious talk with the principal.

Two months later these responses were gathered from her classroom peers:

Our SWAT (Students Who Are Together) team has a weekly meeting with Mrs. Gill (the resource teacher). Jane comes to every meeting. At the first meeting we told Jane we wanted to help and be her friends. We told her that no matter what she did, we'd be there for her. We apologized for not being around enough before. Sarah invited her to a party and Sue went to visit her at home. Danny, Rose, and Linda call her a lot. Jane's happy now because she's got the SWAT team and because she has friends. We're making new friends, too. Jane's whole attitude has changed and she hasn't hit or attacked anyone since we talked to her. (p. 191)

Jane has changed since her first meeting with the SWAT team. These past couple of weeks she's really opened up. She now feels that she belongs, and she knows we are her friends. She hasn't been acting up or annoying us like she used to. Instead she has been cheery and always talks to us.

She was just recently invited to her first party with boys. She really enjoyed it. I think that Jane has really changed. She used to be so quiet and always kept to herself. Now she is more outgoing and talkative. Like any teenager, Jane needs friends and a social life. (p. 192)

Before SWAT I found Jane moody, babyish, she swore, she spat, and once in a while she would pee in her pants. When SWAT started helping, Jane was overjoyed. Jane would always say that she didn't care about anyone or school. About four days after saying how she didn't care about school she got suspended because she touched a kid in a private spot.

Because of SWAT she is really changing now. I called her at home and she talked to me for 10 minutes on the phone. Jane is trying to act like us. She's becoming like us! (p. 192)

Krystyne Banakiewiczm

A POEM ABOUT JANE
Jane came three years ago
No one did she really know
We tried to teach her wrong
    from right
Tried to make her days sunny
    and bright
Still she walked around so sad
And we knew that we had
To make her feel like one of us
And over her we'd all fuss
Now Jane has many good
    friends
And I hope "our" friendship
    never ends.

Tammi Washnuk

Source: From "Supports for Addressing Severe Maladaptive Behavior" by M. Forest and J. Pearpoint, 1990, Support Networks for Inclusive Schooling: Interdependent Integrated Education, W. Stainback and S. Stainback (Eds.), Baltimore: Paul H. Brookes Publishing Company. Copyright 1990 by Paul H. Brookes Publishing Company. Reprinted with permission.

Jack Pearpoint and Marsha Forest are the Directors and Founders of the Centre for Integrated Education and Community and Inclusion Press. For information, write 24 Thome Crescent, Toronto, Ontario, Canada M6H 255, 416-658-5363.

Goldstein, Sprafkin, & Gershaw, 1984). Prior to the initiation of training, a careful assessment is completed to determine the skills that need to be taught through the structured-learning sequences. The first phase of training consists of modeling activities in which students observe various appropriate social behaviors—for example, a trained peer may model some healthy and effective ways to respond to teasing. Observational learning or modeling activities are followed by role playing, in which students rehearse and practice the behaviors that have been modeled. Students are then given performance feedback directly related to the success with which they have performed the targeted social behavior. After children have demonstrated a solid level of performance in the small-group setting, they are given many opportunities to try their newly learned skills in regular classrooms, during recess periods, and at home.

Unfortunately, studies suggest that social skills training frequently produces mixed results for students with behavior disorders (Kavale & Forness, 1995). Some students are responsive to the training (McMahon, Wacker, Sasso, & Melloy, 1994; Moore, Cartledge, & Heckman, 1995), and others are not. The reasons for these results are not clearly understood. However, progress is being made in constructing and delivering social skills programs that take into account cultural, ethnic, and gender diversity (Cartledge & Milburn, 1996). These programs may be far more effective in achieving the desired changes in social behavior for children and adolescents with behavior disorders.

One of the most comprehensive and successful programs developed for children with behavior disorders was Project Re-Ed (Hobbs, 1965; Weinstein, 1969), which had an ecological focus. Interventions were directed not only at the children, but also at their families, schools, and communities. The program was residential; children attended school at a residential site and went home on weekends. Through teacher–counselors, enrolled children received educational and therapeutic support in special class environments. At the same time, the parents of these children and general school personnel were kept informed of the children's progress by liaison teachers. These liaison teachers were also responsible, in conjunction with other personnel, for helping families and school personnel ready themselves for the reentry of the children into general education classrooms. A variety of treatment approaches were used in helping these children and their families develop the behaviors necessary for successful individual and family living; however, the distinguishing characteristic of this program was its ecological focus. Not only were the children treated, but the major social and education environments of the children were also treated and prepared for their return.

Other programs have been developed that reflect the values of Project Re-Ed. One such program is the Positive Education Program (PEP)(Fecser, 1996). This program fosters specific values and employs certain classroom structures, classroom conditions, and group processes. For example, one of the values fostered by PEP is that each "child should know some joy in each day and look forward to some joyous event for the morrow" (Fecser, 1996, p. 472). Classroom structures include set rules, rituals, routines, and schedules. These structures are designed to give children a sense of safety and predictability at school. Classroom conditions foster a sense of trust and sharing. As trust develops among students, they become involved in group processes that build skills in self-analysis, goal setting, and group problem solving.

Children who exhibit moderate to severe behavior disorders may be served in special classes, located in various kinds of facilities. In some school systems, special classes are found in elementary schools—sometimes, in fact, a small cluster of two to three classes is set up in selected buildings. Other special classes may be found within hospital units, special schools, residential programs, and specialized treatment facilities.

Special classes for children with moderate to severe disorders are characterized by a number of significant features. The first is a high degree of structure; in other words, rules are clear and consistently enforced. The second feature is teacher monitoring of student performance; students receive frequent feedback and reinforcement based on their academic and social behaviors. Often, point systems or token economies are used. These systems award students with a specific number of points or tokens when they achieve specific behaviors; these tokens can be exchanged for various rewards, which may consist of things to eat; school supplies such as pencils, notebooks, or erasers; or activities that students enjoy. Appropriate behaviors are also reinforced by the fact that expected behavioral parameters are well known by all special class members (see Figure 7.1 on page 246).

In addition to these interventions, students may also receive individual counseling or group and family therapy. Many children with behavior disorders may take some form of medication, as well. In these cases, teachers are encouraged to monitor the effectiveness (or ineffectiveness) of the medications carefully and to report signs of negative side effects immediately to parents or guardians.

Programs for children who are seriously disturbed and may be described as schizophrenic or exhibiting pervasive developmental disorders are similar in nature to those already discussed. Such programs, however, may involve a variety of other specialized medical, speech or language, and social services personnel.

The Adolescent Years

Adolescents with behavior disorders represent a significant challenge for educators, mental health specialists, and families. As a group, they have a variety of needs. For example, the high school dropout rate for adolescents with behavior disorders is over 54% (Osher & Hanly, 1996). Of this number, about one third are neither working nor involved in any postsecondary training. As many as 58% of these adolescents have criminal records within 5 years of their leaving or dropping out of school (Wagner et al., 1992).

Adolescents who are chronically delinquent and have been found guilty of felony offenses (e.g., physical assault, armed robbery) present a considerable challenge to school and clinical personnel. Additionally, the proliferation of gangs in many communities poses serious problems for schools, teachers, community members, and gang members themselves (Gelfand et al., 1997). As natural gathering places for gang members, schools provide many opportunities for extortion, drug sales, and other illegal activities. Young people who lack role models and

Over 50% of adolescents with behavior disorders drop out of high school.

FIGURE 7.1   Point card for IEP goals

Name: _____Mike_____   **Date:** _____26 November_____

1. My IEP goal today is: *Raising my hand to get teacher help, to answer questions, or to participate in class discussions.*

Goal "Positives"	Goal "Negative"		Percent "Positives"
ℋℋ ///	//		8/10 = 80%

Points Earned On IEP Goal Today ___8___

2. Returned Daily Home Note: Yes __✓__   No _____   Points Earned On Daily Home Note ___10___

3. Bus Report: Poor __✓__   Good _____   Excellent _____   Points Earned on Bus Report ___3___

POSITIVE CLASSROOM BEHAVIORS	APPROPRIATE LOCATION	ON TASK LISTENED, WORKED CONSISTENTLY, ETC.	APPROPRIATE LANGUAGE	RESPECTFUL OF OTHERS AND THEIR THINGS	APPROPRIATE SOCIAL SKILLS
Time					
8:30 to 9:00	2	0	2	2	0
9:00 to 10:00	2	2	2	2	2
11:00 to 12:00	2	0	2	2	0
12:00 to 1:00	2	2	2	2	0
1:00 to 2:00	2	0	2	2	0
2:00 to 3:00	2	2	2	2	0
3:00 to 3:30	2	2	2	2	0
Points Earned	14	8	14	14	2

Total Positive Classroom Points Earned Today	52
Total Points Earned Today	73
Total Points Spent Today	−10
Total Points Banked Today	63

More than 25,000 Americans are murdered each year (American Psychological Association Commission on Violence and Youth, 1993, p. 13). According to the Los Angeles Police Department's report "Anatomy of a Plague" (1994), which gave statistics on violent crimes that occured during 1993, there were 38,174 robberies, 1,058 murders, 1,808 rapes, and 42,633 aggravated assaults just within the city of Los Angeles. It is no surprise, then, that our prisons and jails are overcrowded. "Today, 2.2% of all Californians over 18 are in jail or prison, or on probation or parole" (Becklund, 1992,

p. B12). Adolescents, particularly boys, commit higher rates of crime than any other age group (U.S. Department of Justice, Federal Bureau of Investigation, 1989). Even more disturbing is the fact that young children are increasingly involved in deadlier crimes. There has been a significant increase in juvenile crime in the most serious categories: murder, rape, robbery, and aggravated assault. For example, in the past a majority of cases in New York City's Family Court were misdemeanors; today more then 90% are felonies (Lacayo, 1994). Homicide by children ages 10 to 14 rose from 194 instances in 1988 to 301 in 1992

(Lacayo, 1994). To further attest to the increasingly violent nature of adolescent behavior, Susan R. Winfield, who presides over the Family Division of the Washington, DC, Superior Court, states, "Youngsters used to shoot each other in the body. Then in the head. Now they shoot each other in the face" (Lacayo, 1994, p. 61). This kind of antisocial behavior is reported to be most acute among urban, lower-class minority adolescents (Elliott & Ageton, 1980).

Source: From Mayer, G. R. (1995). Preventing antisocial behavior in the schools. *Journal of Applied Behavior Analysis, 28*(4), 467. Reprinted by permission.

Additional sources: American Psychological Association Commission on Violence and Youth. (1993). Violence and youth: Psychology's response. Washington, DC: Author. Anatomy of a plague. (1994, May 1). *Los Angeles Times,* p. B1. Becklund, L. (1992, December 11). The city as orphan. *Los Angeles Times,* pp. B1, B12. Elliott, D.S., & Ageton, S.A. (1980). Reconciling race and class differences in self-reported and official estimates of delinquency. *American Sociological Review, 45,* 95–110. Lacayo, R. (1994, September). When kids go bad. *Time, 144* (No. 12), 60–63. U.S. Department of Justice. Federal Bureau of Investigation. (1989). *Uniform Crime Reports,* Washington DC: Author.

---

experience disrupted family structures and economic uncertainty may seek power, friendship, fame, and reputation among their peers through gang membership (Evans & Taylor, 1995; Mathews, 1996). Gangs provide these young people with a sense of family and personal identity. All too often violence and death become everyday realities for gang members, their families, and other innocent bystanders (see the nearby Reflect on This feature).

Programs directed at preventing and treating gang violence are emerging (Brendtro, Brokenleg, & Van Bockern, 1990; Dryfoos, 1991; Eggert, 1994; Goldstein, 1988; Goldstein & Glick, 1987; Hurrelman, 1990; Kuykendall, 1992). Generally these programs center on group support systems, specific skills training, and the development of

These young people are working together on a program to prevent gang violence. Programs like Gang Peace are having success in developing social skills training, anger control instruction, and conflict resolution to replace aggression and violence among adolescence.

healthy relationships with caring adults and other authority figures. Young people are taught how to deal with drug abuse, challenging interpersonal relationships, depression, and situations that often produce uncontrolled anger and violence. Also, these young people are taught how to assess provocations that may lead to aggression, how to analyze and change their self-statements (what they actually say to themselves) in response to these provocations, and how to deal with provocations in healthy and appropriate ways (Eggert, 1994; Goldstein, Harootunian, & Conoley, 1994).

One program that has been developed for adolescents who are severely aggressive and otherwise very difficult to manage is the *Aggression Replacement Training (ART) Program* (Goldstein & Glick, 1987). This program emphasizes social skills training, anger control instruction, and moral education. Adolescents involved in this multielement program learn how to respond to anger appropriately, avoid fights, deal with group pressure, and express affection, as well as other pertinent social skills. Additionally, they learn to engage in self-talk, a self-instructional strategy to control verbally or physically aggressive behaviors. The following is a brief example of self-talk in which the individual talks himself through a situation that, in the past, may have caused him to behave very aggressively: "I am beginning to get very angry. I feel like punchin' this guy, but I need to calm down. If I lose it now, I will get myself in big, f_____ trouble. I need to move away from this f_____ situation—now."

The third component of the ART program, moral development, gives adolescents experiences to improve their reasoning and problem-solving skills as well as other related behaviors. Groups are formed and directed by trained leaders who carefully expose adolescents to moral dilemmas and conflicts. Through ensuing discussions and activities, adolescents develop new ways of thinking and reasoning about moral conflicts and learn how it feels to be someone who has been injured, abused, stolen from, or otherwise hurt. Moreover, adolescents learn how to behave in new, socially appropriate ways when confronted with moral dilemmas.

Another program that is beginning to attract the attention of professionals is *individualized care (IC)* (Burchard & Clarke, 1990). IC is also linked closely to the *Wraparound Approach (WRAP)* (Eber, 1996). WRAP centers on improving the outcomes for children and adolescents with disabilities through coordinated, flexible approaches to integrated, family-centered care. Rather than just providing services to students in school settings or at a mental health agency, services are delivered to children and adolescents, their parents, and families where they are most needed, frequently in their homes. The case study of Peter (see the related Reflect on This features throughout this chapter) provides powerful examples of IC and WRAP in action.

IC is characterized by several principles. The first is directed at the youth: "We will help you reach your potential in spite of the terrible things you have done." Unconditional, family-focused care is directed by a caring individual under the direction of an interdisciplinary team of professionals.

The second principle of IC is called least restrictive care. Adolescents are served within their families and neighborhood schools, and they are moved to other more restrictive environments only if they pose a significant threat to themselves or others. Moreover, they are not placed in other more restrictive environments unless all other less restrictive services have proven to be ineffective.

The third principle is child and family-centered care. Services are precisely designed to meet the needs of the adolescents and his or her family. For example, a person who already has a special relationship with an adolescent may be one of the primary caregivers. This may be a neighbor, a fisherman (in an Alaskan village), a carpenter, an artist, or a friend of the family—anyone who is capable of helping the adolescent, given his or her unique needs at the time.

The fourth and fifth principles of IC are flexible care and flexible funding. Flexible care means that services will be provided when and where they are needed, with sufficient intensity to address the severity of the adolescent's or family's needs. Flexible funding is simply the capacity to use funds in a timely manner to address specific needs. For example, a family in crisis might benefit significantly from the skills of a family intervention specialist who actually lives with them during this time.

The last principle upon which IC is based is interagency, or *wraparound*, care. An intervention plan is created, maintained, and altered from time to time by an interdisciplinary team. This team consists of the adolescent, his or her parents or guardian, and the service providers from mental health, social service, health, vocational, and educational agencies. A major component of interagency care is the proactive client tracking system (PCTS), which provides all team members with weekly assessment of the adolescent's progress. It also promotes the involvement of all parties as well as prevention of potential crises.

Postschool outcomes for adolescents and young adults with behavior disorders are discouraging (Carson, Sitlington, & Frank, 1995; U.S. Department of Education, 1997). Consider the following statistics: Only 15.3% of adolescents with behavior disorders enroll in postsecondary academic programs. Even less enter postsecondary vocational programs. Of the remaining adolescents, only 52% become competitively employed. These percentages are similar to results derived from other studies dealing with individuals with challenging behaviors (Hughes & Rusch, 1996). Moreover, individuals with behavior disorders are not engaged in community events and activities as fully as other individuals with disabilities.

The behaviors that interfere with full participation in work settings and community activities are easily identified. They include aggression, unbecoming social behaviors, temper tantrums, off-task behaviors, and others. However, progress is being made in preparing individuals with behavior disorders and other psychiatric conditions to become employed. Interventions include analyzing environmental events and their relationship to certain aberrant behaviors; intervening directly with inappropriate behaviors in the workplace; providing on-site environmental support for suitable, work-related behaviors; promoting social acceptance and understanding in the workplace; and teaching self-management skills (Hughes & Rusch, 1996). Also, social skills training plays an important role in helping individuals with behavior disorders "earn their way" and interact successfully with their employers, neighbors, family members, and friends.

Inclusive Education

Few issues in recent years have received as much attention in the professional literature as inclusion, particularly the full inclusion of students with behavior disorders (Braaten et al., 1988; Bullock & Gable, 1994; Fuchs & Fuchs, 1994; Kauffman & Lloyd, 1995; Lewis, Chard, & Scott, 1994). The term *full inclusion* is generally defined as the delivery of appropriate, specialized services to children or adolescents with behavior disorders or other disabilities in general education settings. These services are usually directed at improving students' social skills, developing satisfactory relationships with peers and teachers, building targeted academic skills, and improving attitudes of nondisabled peers (Snell, 1990; Stainback & Stainback, 1990).

Another aspect of the full inclusion movement is the recommendation by some professionals that the present delivery systems or placement options be eliminated (Stainback & Stainback, 1992). These systems or options would be replaced by a model in which all students, regardless of their disabling condition, would be educated in their neighborhood schools. These schools would serve all students with disabilities including those with behavior disorders; thus special schools, special classes, and other placements associated with the typical placement continuum would no longer be available.

Critics of this movement have expressed strong concerns about its short- and long-term impact on children and adolescents with behavior disorders and their families. They argue that little research supports the elimination of the current placement and service delivery continuum. They believe that the current continuum provides a range of options and specialized services that are in keeping with the unique needs of many students with behavior disorders and their families (see nearby Reflect on This feature). Additionally, they feel that many general education teachers and related personnel are not adequately prepared to respond to the needs of children and adolescents with behavior disorders in their classes and related school settings (Braaten et al., 1988; Fuchs & Fuchs, 1994; Kauffman, 1993; Kauffman & Lloyd, 1995; Walker & Bullis, 1990).

Recent court decisions and the 1997 amendments to the Individuals with Disabilities Act (IDEA) dealing with the placement of students with disabilities are informative (EDLAW, Inc., 1994; Lewis et al., 1994; Yell, 1995). "The courts have indicated that there are two primary grounds for removing a student from the general education classroom: if the child does not benefit educationally (considering both academic and nonacademic benefits), and if the student disrupts the learning environment or adversely affects the education of other students" (Yell, 1995, p. 188). If a student under consideration poses no significant management problems for the teacher, does not interfere with the safety or learning of other classmates, and can benefit from a parallel or similar curriculum given to other students in general classroom settings, he or she will be placed in these environments.

The 1997 amendments to IDEA authorize school personnel to order a change in placement to an appropriate interim alternative educational setting, another setting, or suspension for not more than 10 school days if the student carries a weapon to school or knowingly possesses or uses illegal drugs or sells or solicits the sale of a controlled substance while at school. During the 10 days the school must conduct a behavior assessment and develop a behavioral intervention plan (if this was not done previously) through the IEP process. Any alternative setting for a student must be determined by the IEP team. Additionally, a hearing officer may order a change in placement to an appropriate interim alternative educational setting for not more than 45 days if the hearing officer determines that the current placement is substantially likely to result in injury to the child or others. In making the decision, the hearing officer must consider whether the school has made reasonable efforts to minimize risks of harm in the current placement and that the interim placement meets the student's needs as described in the IEP (see Chapter 1).

Interestingly, most students with behavior disorders are served in settings separate from general education classrooms (Knitzer et al., 1990; Stephens & Lakin, 1995). In fact, students with behavior disorders are far more likely to be served in special schools and separate facilities than any other group of students with disabil-

Reflect on This

Student's Name: Devi Ante   Grade: Any

Race: Any   Sex: Either

To my administrators: This child will simply not obey!
Here is a referral—now have a nice day!

This child's an adolescent, a hormonally active teen.
This child is very active. This child is very mean.

OFFENSE

He scribbled on my chalkboard. He was "chillin" in the hall.
He won't pull his pants up although they were about to fall.

This child is into junk food. He acts like he's on drugs.
He's socially maladjusted and all his friends are thugs.

He didn't do the classwork. His hands and feet were tappin'.
While I was modeling the lesson, he sat back there nappin'.

This child is noncompliant. This child does not conform.
This child is insubordinate. This child is not the norm!

He wouldn't throw his gum away or take the pick out of his hair.
He didn't do his homework and he doesn't seem to care.

He doesn't seem to want to learn. He doesn't seem to try.
He's really working on my nerves. He really makes me cry!

He scribbled on his desk and tore a page out of a book.
When I said something about it, he just gave me a look.

His vocabulary's excellent but it's all 4-letter words.
Yet he's perfectly descriptive. (I guess that sounds absurd.)

He picks on other people and has instigated fights.
Persecution of his peers is one of his delights.

This child is hyperactive. I think he's A.D.D.
He also might be F.A.S. [fetal alcohol syndrome] or maybe F.A.E. [fetal alcohol effect]

I think offensive touching is another nasty habit.
He thinks, if it is on a girl, he has the right to grab it!

He's somewhat psychopathic and criminally insane.
The saddest thing about him is I know he's not to blame.

He speaks rudely to the staff and comes late to class each day.
This child could give an atheist a true reason to pray!

He's from a dysfunctional family (that's the yuppie alibi).
And he feels he can't progress. His desk looks like a sty.

He was peeking in the Girl's room, then gave me a lame excuse.
I'm really sick and tired of taking all of this abuse.

[Above] are the behaviors that make me write this note. I was going to deal with him compassionately, but he really got my goat.

Source: Rosenblatt, A. (1996). Discipline referral. *Beyond Behavior, 17*(2), 26–27. Published with permission of the Council for Children with Behavioral Disorders and A. Rosenblatt.

---

ities. Additionally, a fifth of all students served in special day schools and half of all students served in residential facilities are children with behavior disorders (Koyangi & Gaines, 1993; Stephens & Lakin, 1995).

Inclusion of students with behavior disorders in general education settings should be determined ultimately by what the child or adolescent with behavior disorders genuinely needs (Kauffman & Smucker, 1995). These needs are generally established through the thoughtful deliberations of parents, professionals, and, as appropriate, the child or adolescent. These deliberations culminate in the creation of an individualized education program (IEP). The IEP sets the stage and creates the basis for determining the services and supports that will address the child's or adolescent's needs, both present and anticipated. If the identified services and supports can be delivered with appropriate intensity and skill in the general education environment without adversely affecting the learning and well-being of other students, placement in this environment should occur. However, if the needs of the student cannot be successfully met in general education settings, other placement alternatives should be selected.

focus 9

Identify nine characteristics of highly effective programs for children and adolescents with behavior disorders.

In summary, effective programs for children and adolescents with behavior disorders are characterized by several important features. These include setting high expectations; interventions that are supported by observational data; ongoing assessment and monitoring of student performance; frequent opportunities for students to practice and use newly learned skills; treatments and strategies that are individually targeted at specific needs identified by a multidisciplinary team and parents; multiple coordinated treatments that are directed at children and adolescents as well as their families; provisions for ensuring that the skills and behaviors learned in treatment settings will be transferred to school, family, neighborhood, and work environments; opportunities, when appropriate, to work with caring peers; and a commitment to sustained intervention for children and adolescents who require long-term support and care (Nelson & Pearson, 1991; Peacock Hill Working Group, 1990). When these features are consistently and effectively applied, children and adolescents with behavior disorders will have a greater chance of reaching their full potential and will participate more meaningfully in their families, neighborhoods, and communities.

Case Study

ENCOUNTER WITH THE DECEPS

Violence was a normal part of our school day. Fights frequently ensued as we passed to classes, and sometimes even during classes. Knives and guns were commonly used to threaten or injure students and teachers. Local gangs periodically came to "visit." I remember that for weeks, "the Deceps" were a constant concern with the frightened pupils in my class. "Who the heck are the Deceps?" I asked the students. Apparently the Deceptions

were a very violent group of adolescents who thought nothing of robbing people and even killing their victims if necessary to get what they desired. I dismissed this talk as mass hysteria until one day I came face-to-face with this frightening gang.

We were in the middle of an intense review for an exam. The room was so hot that I decided to open the door for ventilation. Shortly thereafter, three disheveled boys wearing lavender and blue headbands entered my room. They began

to make sexually suggestive forays toward my female students. One of the boys actually began to fondle a girl's breasts. She cried out to me for help, but I was so scared that I didn't know what to do. Nobody would hear my screams for help because we were far away from the other classes.

I knew I had to do something, and I remembered what my mother always told me: "Girl, you get what you want faster with honey than you do with vinegar." I decided to ap-

proach the boys, and held out my hand to them, indicating that I wanted to make peace rather than promote conflict. They looked at each other and snickered. One said, "Yo, the bitch wants to be friends." I sighed with relief until I felt my hand being crushed by the handshake. Then this punk pulled the rings off my fingers. The other one stole my coat. I had to stand by helplessly for fear that confrontation would turn to violence against me or my students. After they sashayed from the area, I quickly reported the incident to the administration, but was told that there was nothing they could (or would) do.

■ **APPLICATION**

1. In dealing with the Deceps, what other actions could have been taken by the teacher once they arrived in the classroom? Provide a rationale for your suggestions.

2. What steps could have been taken by the school to respond to potential events such as this one? What kinds of obligations do administrators and others have to protect students and teachers from assault and theft?

3. What behaviors are crucial in dealing with an event of this magnitude in a classroom or other similar setting?

Source: Adapted from "Do I Really Want to Teach These Kids?" by T. McIntyre and M. Stefanides, 1993, *Beyond Behavior,* 5(1), p. 18. Published with permission of the Council for Children with Behavioral Disorders.

Debate Forum

SHOULD STUDENTS WITH BEHAVIOR DISORDERS EVER BE EXPELLED FROM SCHOOL?

At the start of his kindergarten year last fall, Jimmy sometimes ran around the classroom and yelled when his teacher tried to present a lesson.

But by the winter, Jimmy P., as he is called in court documents, had become more violent, according to officials at the Ocean View School District in Huntington Beach, California.

School officials said the 6-year-old, who weighs slightly more than 100 pounds, hit and bit his teacher, threw chairs and desks, hit his classmates, and kicked staff members at Circle View Elementary School.

They suspended Jimmy for a few days, but when he returned, his behavior worsened, said James R. Tarwater, the district superintendent.

By the end of the school year, Jimmy's teacher and a classroom aide, both citing severe stress, had taken medical leaves.

Concerned that Jimmy's behavior was endangering his classmates and school personnel, district officials wanted to remove Jimmy from the class and expel him from school.

■ **DOUBLE STANDARD?**

Educators such as Mr. Tarwater say federal laws are tying their hands on disciplining students with disabilities and putting schools at risk for lawsuits from parents of other students who fear for their children's safety.

Educators say the laws create a double standard in the classroom, where students with disabilities are treated one way and students without disabilities another.

Situations such as Jimmy P.'s at Circle View Elementary have brought growing attention to the issue of discipline and students with disabilities—an issue that in many cases is wrapped up in the movement toward "full inclusion" of students with disabilities into regular classrooms in their neighborhood schools.

Proponents of full inclusion say that more inclusive school environments offer students realistic preparation for life and that segregation stigmatizes and isolates students with disabilities.

In many cases, the discipline issue has become a lightning rod for educators who say they are frustrated by special education's cost, litigiousness, and regulation.[1]

■ **POINT**

Students with behavior disorders, particularly those served in general education settings, should be treated like other students in schools. If they come with weapons, distribute drugs, or engage in behaviors dangerous to others, they should be treated like other students in the school who are guilty of similar offenses. They should experience the same disciplinary consequences as students without disabilities. As one judge put it, why should we provide "private tutors at public expense" for youthful offenders "merely because they have a disability."[2] When students with behavior disorders violate school rules as well as state and national laws, they should forfeit their rights as other students do.

■ **COUNTERPOINT**

On the basis of legal and ethical grounds, students with behavior disorders should not be suspended or expelled from schools as other nondisabled students are. Removing students with behavior disorders from the school settings, without giving them appropriate services as determined in their IEPs, merely exacerbates their problems. They need the interventions and services that are targeted to their particular problems and needs. Without these services, they are likely to create even more serious problems for their neighborhoods and for their communities. Suspending or expelling students with behavior disorders without providing appropriate, ongoing education services, roughly speaking, is equivalent to refusing a child with a serious illness appropriate medical care—just because the child is sick.

[1] *Source:* From "Disciplining special education students: A conundrum," by Lynn Schailberg, 1994, *Education Week,* 14(13) (November 30), pp. 14–15. Reprinted with permission from *Education Week,* Vol. 14, #13, November 30, 1994.

[2] *Source:* From "4th circuit upholds expulsion policy," 1996, *The Special Educator,* 12(1), pp. 4–5.

Review

 **focus 1**

Identify five factors that influence the ways in which others' behaviors are perceived.

- Our personal beliefs, standards, and values
- Our tolerance for certain behaviors, which varies according to our standards, values, and levels of emotional fitness at the time the behaviors are exhibited
- Perceptions of normality, which are frequently in the "eye of the beholder" rather than based on an objective standard of normality established by consensus or research
- The context in which a behavior takes place
- The frequency with which the behavior occurs or its intensity

focus 2

What differentiates externalizing disorders from internalizing disorders?

- Externalizing disorders involve behaviors that are directed at others (e.g., fighting, assaulting, stealing, vandalizing)
- Internalizing disorders involve behaviors that are directed inwardly or at oneself more than at others (e.g., fears, phobias, depressions)

 **focus 3**

Identify six essential parts of the definitions describing serious emotional or behavior disorders.

- The behaviors in question must be exhibited to a marked extent.
- Learning problems must not be attributable to intellectual, sensory, or health deficits.
- Satisfactory relationships with parents, teachers, siblings, and others are few.
- Problem behaviors occur in many settings and, under normal circumstances, are considered inappropriate.
- A pervasive mood of unhappiness or depression is frequently displayed by children with behavior disorders.
- Physical symptoms or fears associated with the demands of school are common in some children.

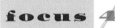 **focus 4**

Identify three reasons why classification systems are important to professionals who diagnose, treat, and educate individuals with behavior disorders.

- They provide a means of describing and identifying various behavior disorders.
- They provide a common language for communicating about various types and subtypes of behavior disorders.

- They sometimes provide a basis for treating a disorder and making predictions about treatment outcomes.

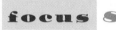 **focus 5**

Identify five general characteristics (intellectual, adaptive, and achievement) of children with behavior disorders.

- Children who are disturbed tend to have average to lower-than-average IQs compared to their normal peers.
- Children with severe behavior disorders tend to have IQs that fall within the retarded range of functioning.
- Children who are disturbed have great difficulty relating socially and responsibly to peers and to parents, teachers, and other authority figures.
- Students who are disturbed perform less well than their ability, as measured by intellectual instruments, would seem to predict.
- Students who are seriously disturbed, particularly those with IQs in the retardation range, are substantially substandard in their academic achievement.

focus 6

What can be accurately said about the causes of behavior disorders?

- Behavior disorders are caused by sets any number

of interacting biological, genetic, cognitive, social, emotional, and cultural variables.

focus 7

Identify four factors that need to be assessed carefully in determining whether a child has a behavior disorder.

- The discrepancy between the child's behavior and expected performance, given his or her age, culture, temperament, and intellectual endowment
- The frequency, intensity, and location of the various problematic behaviors
- The relationship of the behaviors to various events and people
- The influence of family and cultural factors

focus 8

Identify six major treatment approaches used in treating children and adolescents with behavior disorders, and note the service delivery systems through which treatment is given.

- Major approaches to treating behavior disorders include insight-oriented therapy, play therapy, group psychotherapy, behavior therapy, marital and family therapy, and drug therapy.
- The therapies are used in conjunction with various types of service delivery systems, including home-based

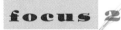

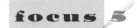

and center-based programs, school-based programs (consulting teacher, resource rooms, self-contained programs, specialized schools), residential programs, hospitals, and one-to-one or family therapy provided by private practitioners.

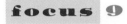

focus 9

Identify nine characteristics of highly effective programs for

children and adolescents with behavior disorders.

- Teachers have appropriately high expectations for student performance.
- Interventions are based on data that affirm their effectiveness.
- Assessment and monitoring procedures are used continuously to document students' progress or lack thereof.
- Many opportunities are provided for students to

practice the skills and behaviors learned.
- Treatments and interventions are carefully selected and matched to problems identified by parents and members of the multidisciplinary team.
- A variety of carefully coordinated treatments is applied simultaneously to children or adolescents and their families.
- Precise steps are taken to ensure that the skills and behaviors learned are

transferred to home, school, community, and work settings.
- Interventions involve caring peers.
- Sustained and coordinated interventions are provided over time for individuals who may require long-term support and treatment.

People with Mental Retardation

To begin with . . .

 People with mental retardation want to be treated equally, and they don't want to be labeled anymore. They want most of all to close down institutions and to be a part of their community. . . . Our challenge now is to consider the ways that each individual with mental retardation can be included rather than excluded, consistent with that person's unique talents, needs, and choices. This approach presumes that there is no single formula for inclusion or definition of inclusion that fits every person with mental retardation. It does presume that no one should be excluded arbitrarily, on the basis of their mental retardation or some other disability label, from being part of their family and community. (President's Committee on Mental Retardation, 1995, p. 2)

 In school, companionship is a natural thing. Once out of school, since most people [with mental retardation] live with their parents, they become more dependent on community contact to have friendships. The most common placement for students with mental retardation is a special class. This means that students with mental retardation are less likely to make friends who come from their neighborhood, as special classes usually draw from a wider area than regular [general] classes. With the addition of traveling on a school bus, the natural network of friends is not readily made, as it is for nondisabled students. (Eidelman, 1994, p. 1)

 When Cyndee was born, people were moping around the hospital because she had Down syndrome. The staff sort of isolated us, leaving us alone. After my husband and I had cried a few tears together, I looked at him and said, "Okay, what are we going to do now?" He said, "Well, we're going to do what we've done with all of our other kids. We'll have the same expectations for her as we have for the others." And to a large extent that's the way we have raised her. Consequently, she is profoundly, severely fifteen, and just happens to have Down syndrome. (Rowley, 1996)

 Future labor shortages and shifting demographics mean employers must look for new sources of labor. Employers are discovering people with mental retardation can help meet the need for workers. Pizza Hut, Incorporated's "Jobs Plus Program" successfully employs 2,600 people with mental retardation. (Joseph P. Kennedy, Jr. Foundation, 1992, p. 2)

257

Lilly

Lilly is an 8-year-old with mental retardation. When she was adopted at the age of 2, her new parents were told she would never talk and might not walk. Through the untiring efforts of her family during the early childhood years, Lilly is able to say some words and use short sentences that are understood by her family and friends. She can now walk without support. Lilly's greatest challenge, according to her mother, is to stay focused. If directed step by step, Lilly is capable of participating in family activities and helping out around the house. Her brother Josh is always there for Lilly, helping her with homework, reading to her, and helping her get dressed in the morning.

At school, Lilly spends part of her day in a classroom with other students who also have mental retardation and part of the day in a general education class with second-grade nondisabled students. While in the special education classroom, Lilly works with peer tutors from the sixth-grade general education class to help her with schoolwork. Her two peer tutors, Nita and Amy, work with Lilly on using the computer to better develop her communication skills. A computer is a wonderful tool for Lilly because all she has to do is learn to hit the right buttons on the Touch Talker program to communicate with family, friends, and teachers. Lilly's second-grade teacher, Mrs. Roberts, describes Lilly as one of the most popular students in her class. The second-grade students love her "neat talking machine." When in the second-grade class, Lilly participates in learning centers where she is paired up with nondisabled students working on a variety of activities.

Lilly's mother and teachers are optimistic about her future. The special education teacher hopes that Lilly will be able to go to her neighborhood school next year and spend even more time with nondisabled students of her own age. "And from there, with her great social skills and her persistence, I see her as being independent in the future, working in a job setting."

Roger

Roger is 19 years old and lives at home with his parents. During the day, he attends high school and works in a local toy company in a small work crew with five other individuals who also have disabilities. Roger and his working colleagues are supervised by a job coach. Roger assembles small toys and is learning how to operate power tools for wood- and metal-cutting tasks. His wages are not enough to allow Roger to be financially independent, so most likely he will always need some financial support from his family or society.

Roger is capable of caring for his own physical needs. He has learned to dress and feed himself and understands the importance of personal care. He can communicate many of his needs and desires verbally but is limited in his ability to participate in social conversations, such as discussing the weather or what's new at the movies. Roger has never learned to read, and his leisure hours are spent watching television, listening to the radio, and visiting with friends.

Becky

Becky is a 6-year-old who has significant delays in intellectual, language, and motor development. These developmental differences have been evident from very early in her life. Her mother experienced a long, unusually difficult labor, and Becky endured severe heart-rate dips; at times, her heart rate was undetectable. During delivery, Becky suffered from birth asphyxiation and epileptic seizures. The attending physician described her as flaccid (soft and limp), with abnormal muscle reflexes. Becky has not yet learned to walk, is not toilet trained, and has no means of communication with others in her environment. She lives at home and attends a local elementary school during the day.

Her education program includes work with therapists to develop her gross motor abilities in order to improve her mobility. Speech and language specialists are examining the possibility of teaching her several alternative forms of communication (e.g., a language board or manual communication system) because Becky has not developed any verbal skills. The special education staff is focusing on decreasing Becky's dependence on others by teaching some basic self-care skills such as eating, toileting, and grooming. The professional staff does not know what the ultimate long-term impact of their intervention will be, but they do know that, although Becky is a child with severe mental retardation, *she is learning.*

HIS CHAPTER focuses on people whose intellectual and social capabilities may differ significantly from the norm. The growth and development of these individuals depend on the educational and social opportunities made available to them. Lilly (see the snapshot) is a child with mental retardation who has a wonderful support network of family, friends, and teachers. As she grows older, she may achieve at least partial independence occupationally and socially within the community. Most likely, Lilly will continue to need some support from family, friends, and government-sponsored programs to assist her in adjusting to adult life in the community.

Roger has completed school and is just beginning life as an adult in his community. Roger is a person with moderate mental retardation. Although he will probably require lifetime support on his job, he is earning wages that contribute to his successful adjustment in the community. Within a few years, he will most likely move away from his family and into a group home or a supervised apartment of his own.

Becky has severe mental retardation. Although the long-term prognosis is unknown, she has many opportunities for learning and development that were not available until recently. Through a positive home environment and an educational program that supports her learning and applying skills at home and at school, Becky can reach a level of development that was once considered impossible.

Lilly, Roger, and Becky are people with mental retardation, but they are not necessarily representative of the range of people who are characterized as having mental retardation. A 6-year-old described as mildly retarded may be no more than one or two years behind in the development of academic and social skills. Many children with mild mental retardation are not identified until they enter school at age 5 or 6, because they may not exhibit physical or learning problems that are readily identifiable during the early childhood years. As these children enter school, developmental delays become more apparent in the classroom environment. During early primary grades, it is not uncommon for the intellectual and social difficulties of children with mild mental retardation to be attributed to immaturity. However, within a few years, school personnel generally recognize the need for specialized services to support the child's development in the natural settings of school, neighborhood, and home.

Individuals with moderate to severe mental retardation have difficulties that transcend the classroom. Many are delayed in nearly every facet of life. Some have significant multiple disabling conditions, including sensory, physical, and emotional problems. Individuals with moderate retardation are capable of developing adaptive skills that allow a degree of independence with ongoing support within their environment. These self-care skills include the abilities to dress and feed themselves, to care for their personal care and health needs, and to develop safety habits that allow them to move safely wherever they go. These individuals have some means of communication. Most can develop spoken language skills, but some may be able to learn only manual communication. Their social interaction skills are limited, however, making it difficult for them to relate spontaneously to others.

Contrast the preceding characteristics with those of individuals who have severe to profound retardation, and the diverse nature of people with mental retardation becomes clear. Individuals with profound retardation often depend on others to maintain even their most basic life functions, including eating, toileting, and dressing. They may not be capable of self-care and often do not develop functional communication skills. These extreme disabilities may require a lifetime of support, whether it be in a special-care setting or at home. In terms of treatment or educational intervention, the only realistic conclusion that can be drawn about this group is that the long-term prognosis for development is unknown.

This does not mean that treatment beyond routine care and maintenance is not beneficial. The extreme nature of these disabilities is the primary reason such individuals were excluded from the public schools for so long. Exclusion was often justified on the basis that schools did not have the resources, facilities, or trained personnel to deal with the needs of lower-functioning students (Drew, Hardman, & Logan, 1996). Given the present emphasis on research and alternative approaches to support people with mental retardation, the future may hold some answers and bring about a more positive outlook.

Definitions and Classification

■ DEFINITION

People with mental retardation have been studied for centuries, by a variety of professional disciplines. The most widely accepted definition of mental retardation is that of the **American Association on Mental Retardation (AAMR),** an organization of professionals of varied backgrounds such as medicine, law, and education. AAMR revised its definition of mental retardation in 1992 for the fourth time in the past 30 years. As defined by AAMR,

> *mental retardation refers to substantial limitations in present functioning. It is characterized by significantly subaverage intellectual functioning, existing concurrently with related limitations in two or more of the following applicable **adaptive skill** areas: communication, self-care, home living, social skills, community use, self-direction, health and safety, functional academics, leisure, and work. Mental retardation manifests itself before age 18. (AAMR Ad Hoc Committee on Terminology and Classification, 1992, p. 5)*

The latest revision of the AAMR definition maintained the basic elements of a definition originally adopted in 1983, which included significantly subaverage general intellectual functioning, impairments in adaptive behavior (skills), and manifestation prior to age 18 (Grossman, 1983). There is, however, an expanded description of adaptive skill areas not found in the 1983 definition. Additionally, the current definition moves away from emphasizing intellectual deficits to focus on the *intensity of supports* needed to assist people with mental retardation in accessing, adapting to, and participating in family, school, and community settings.

■ INTELLIGENCE Significantly subaverage general intellectual functioning is assessed through the use of one or more individually administered standardized intelligence tests. On an intelligence test, a person's score is compared to the statistical average of same-age peers who have taken the same test. The statistical average for an intelligence test is generally set at 100. We state this by saying that the person has an intelligence quotient (IQ) of 100. Psychologists use a mathematical procedure to determine the extent to which an individual's score deviates from this average of 100, to arrive at a measurement called a **standard deviation.** An individual who scores two standard deviations below the average on an intelligence test is in the range that characterizes mental retardation. Depending on the test, this means that individuals with IQs of approximately 70 to 75 and lower would be considered as having mental retardation. AAMR indicates that the information from an intelligence test should be reviewed by a multidisciplinary team and "validated with additional test scores or evaluative information" (AAMR Ad Hoc Committee, 1992, p. 5).

■ ADAPTIVE SKILLS AAMR describes ten primary adaptive skill areas: communication, self-care, home living, social skills, community use, self-direction, health and safety, functional academics, leisure, and work (see Table 8.1). Limitations in adaptive skills, important for overall successful functioning, necessitate the need for *supports* to assist the individual with mental retardation in participating more fully in both family and community life. Consider Becky from the chapter opening snapshot. She has significant limitations in her adaptive skills. She is unable to walk and has a limited repertoire of self-care skills. At 6 years old, she still has no means of communicating with others.

Adaptive skills also may be measured by standardized tests. These tests, most often referred to as *adaptive behavior scales*, generally use structured interviews or direct observations to obtain information. Adaptive behavior scales compare an individual to an established average and measure the ability to take care of personal

TABLE 8.1	1992 AAMR adaptive skill areas

SKILL AREA	PORTRAYAL
Communication	The ability to understand and communicate information by speaking or writing, through symbols, sign language, or nonsymbolic behaviors such as facial expressions, touch, or gestures
Self-care	Skills in such areas as toileting, eating, dressing, hygiene, and grooming
Home living	Functioning in the home, including clothing care, housekeeping, property maintenance, cooking, shopping, home safety, and daily scheduling
Social	Social interchange with others, including initiating and terminating interactions, responding to social cues, recognizing feelings, regulating own behavior, assisting others, and fostering friendships
Community use	Appropriate use of community resources, including traveling in the community, shopping at stores, obtaining services such as at gas stations, receiving medical and dental services, using public transportation and facilities
Self-direction	Making choices, following a schedule, initiating contextually appropriate activities, completing required tasks, seeking assistance, resolving problems, demonstrating appropriate self-advocacy
Health and safety	Maintaining own health, including eating; identifying, treating, and preventing illness; basic first aid; sexuality; physical fitness; and basic safety
Functional academics	Abilities and skills related to learning in school that also have direct application in life
Leisure	Developing a variety of leisure and recreational interests that are age- and culturally appropriate
Work	Abilities that pertain to maintaining part- or full-time employment in the community, including appropriate social and related work skills

Source: Adapted from *Mental Retardation: Definition, Classification, and Systems of Supports* (9th ed., pp. 40–41), Washington, DC: American Association on Mental Retardation. Copyright 1992 by the American Association on Mental Retardation, by permission.

For people with mental retardation, adaptive skills such as home living may be assessed by standardized tests or by informal appraisal. The informal appraisal can be observations made by someone familiar with the individual.

needs (such as hygiene) and to relate appropriately to others in social situations. Adaptive skills may also be assessed through informal appraisal, such as observations by people who are familiar with the individual or through anecdotal records.

■ AGE OF ONSET The AAMR defines the age of onset for mental retardation as prior to 18 years. The reasons for choosing this cutoff point are that society views this age as the point at which individuals usually assume adult roles and that this criterion prevents adults with no history of mental retardation from ever receiving the label. The AAMR also suggests, however, that other societies may view a different age criterion as more appropriate.

■ APPLICATION OF THE DEFINITION The AAMR has developed four assumptions that are viewed as essential as professionals and consumers begin to use the new definition in practice (1992, p. 1):

1. Valid assessment considers cultural and linguistic diversity and differences in communication and behavioral factors.
2. The existence of limitations in adaptive skills occurs within the context of community environments typical of the individual's age peers and is indexed to the person's individualized needs for support.
3. Specific adaptive limitations often coexist with strengths in other adaptive skills or other personal capabilities.
4. With appropriate supports over a sustained period, the life functioning of the person with mental retardation will generally improve.

■ AN EVOLUTION OF DEFINITIONS The 1992 AAMR definition of mental retardation has evolved through years of effort to define the condition clearly and to reflect the ever-changing perceptions of mental retardation. Historically, definitions of mental retardation were based solely on the measurement of intelligence, emphasizing routine care and maintenance rather than treatment and education. Adaptive behavior, as a component of the definition of mental retardation, was first used in 1959 (Heber, 1959). It was defined as the degree to which an individual was able to meet the standards of personal independence and social responsibility expected of the person's age and cultural group. Over the past 35 years, the concept of adaptive behavior has played an increasingly important role in defining and classifying people with mental retardation. Its importance is evident in the 1992 AAMR definition that now includes ten primary adaptive skill areas that must be addressed in considering the overall functioning level of a person with mental retardation. Additionally, legislation (such as the Americans with Disabilities Act and the Individuals with Disabilities Education Act, IDEA) has opened new doors for people with mental retardation and put pressure on professionals to develop and use definitions aimed at assisting individuals in receiving the appropriate supports necessary to improve the quality of their lives (see nearby Reflect on This feature).

Not long after John Kennedy entered the White House in 1961, his sister Eunice Kennedy Shriver began one of the most heartfelt campaigns any Kennedy ever undertook. She argued to family members that it would be immensely helpful if they revealed one of their most closely guarded secrets: that one of their own, the president's sister Rosemary, was mentally retarded. . . . In the spring of 1962, Eunice told JFK she wanted to write a piece for the *Saturday Evening Post* about Rosemary. . . . The article appeared in the September 22 issue, and it was one of the biggest moments and perhaps the most important contribution the Kennedys made to the nation.

What is stunning about the Kennedys'—and most particularly Eunice Shriver's—role in changing the way the world treated mentally retarded people is how little noticed it has been. It is difficult to recall today the life such people faced in the generation before Kennedy's administration. Scores of thousands were warehoused in institutions located in the most remote sites available. That was especially true of women because it was thought to be important to

keep them from getting pregnant and creating another generation of "idiots."

Families like the Kennedys that kept retarded family members at home as they grew up were the objects of considerable scorn. Rosemary was born at the height of the worldwide flu epidemic in 1918 and, though no one was ever sure what caused her relatively mild retardation, it became a difficult fact of life by the time she reached school age. Though the family tried to make things as normal as possible for her, she fell far behind in the hypercompetitive environment as she got older. As she became a young woman, her problems grew and she began to lash out violently on occasion.

The lobotomy. Eventually, Joseph Kennedy was told that there was a "miracle" surgical procedure called a prefrontal lobotomy that could help Rosemary. . . . The surgery was supposed to leave her mental functions relatively intact while eliminating her aggressive behavior. Instead, it rendered her zombie like and she was moved to St. Coletta's in Jefferson, Wis., where she still resides.

Joseph Kennedy was tormented by the fate of his

daughter. In 1946, he created the Joseph P. Kennedy, Jr. Foundation (named after his deceased war hero son) to help retarded people, and in the mid-1950s, he asked Eunice to determine how the foundation's grants could best be used. . . . As JFK entered the presidency, he responded by setting up a task force headed by eminent educator Leonard Mayo to devise a legislative program to attack mental retardation. . . .

Eunice Shriver was clearly the commander of the administration effort. When her friend and panel member Robert E. Cooke suggested the creation of new university-affiliated research centers, she stuck it in the final plan. (More than 70 percent of its 112 recommendations were eventually implemented.)

. . . As Eunice Shriver predicted, the change in public and scientific attitudes prompted by the article and the work of the presidential panel was striking. Over the next generation, the Kennedys' goal—to bring the retarded into the mainstream of American life—has been largely realized. Research breakthroughs on the causes of retardation and beneficial educational programs have proliferated,

thanks to the funding launched in the Kennedy administration. American life and the lives of the retarded have been incalculably enriched by the drive to bring the retarded into full participation in communities, schools, and workplaces.

The spinoffs from these first efforts are equally impressive. The family campaign to bring the retarded out of the closet, including the Shrivers' creation of the widely hailed Special Olympics, was a precursor of the larger disability rights movement. And Sargent Shriver says his inspiration to create the much admired Head Start program for disadvantaged children came from his familiarity with research that early-intervention educational efforts could raise the IQs of the retarded.

When the full judgment of the Kennedy legacy is made— the changes wrought by Eunice Shriver may well be seen as the most consequential.

Source: From "The Most Lasting Kennedy Legacy" by M. Barone and K. Hetter. Copyright, Nov. 15, 1993, *U.S. News and World Report.* Pp. 44–47.

CLASSIFICATION

Classification systems provide a frame of reference for studying, understanding, and providing supports and services to people with mental retardation. Such people are often stereotyped as a homogeneous group of individuals—"the retarded"— with similar physical characteristics and learning capabilities. Actually, mental retardation encompasses a broad range of functioning levels and characteristics. To more clearly understand the diversity of people labeled as such, several classification systems have been developed over the years. We discuss four methods of classifying individuals with mental retardation: the severity of the condition, educability expectations, medical descriptors, and type and extent of needed support. Each classification method reflects an attempt by a particular discipline (such as medicine) to better understand and respond to the needs of individuals with mental retardation.

■ SEVERITY OF THE CONDITION   The extent to which a person's intellectual capabilities and adaptive skills deviate from what is considered "normal" can be described by using terms such as *mild, moderate, severe,* or *profound. Mild* describes the highest level of performance; *profound* describes the lowest level of performance for this population.

Distinctions between severity levels associated with mental retardation are determined primarily by scores on intelligence tests as well as indicators of maladaptive behavior. Historically, professionals have mainly used four levels of intellectual functioning to group individuals with mental retardation according to the severity approach: (1) mild, IQ 55 to 70; (2) moderate, IQ 40 to 55; (3) severe, IQ 25 to 40; and (4) profound, IQ 25 or lower (IQ scores based on standard deviations of the Wechsler Intelligence Scales).

A person's adaptive skills, or the ability to cope with environmental demands, can also be categorized by severity. Like intellectual functioning delays, adaptive skill delays can be described in terms of the degree to which an individual's performance differs from what is expected for his or her chronological age. For example, in the area of independent functioning, average 3-year-olds are expected to feed themselves unassisted with the proper eating utensils, take care of their own personal hygiene, and be fully toilet trained. A child with mild adaptive delays may be able to use eating utensils, but with considerable spilling. This child can dress and take care of personal needs, but only with help. The child may be partially toilet trained; toileting accidents are common. The level of independence for each of these skill areas decreases for individuals with moderate, severe, and profound adaptive skill delays. A 3-year-old with profound adaptive behavior delays generally must be fed by another individual, drinks from a cup with help, cannot take care of personal needs, and has no effective speech.

To better understand adaptive skills, let's look at Lilly, Roger, and Becky from our opening snapshot. As an 8-year-old, Lilly has learned some of the required self-care skills for a child of her age, and although her socialization and communication skills are below what is expected, she is able to successfully interact with others in her environment through the use of **assistive technology.** Roger, at age 19, has developed many skills that allow him to successfully live in his own community with some supervision and support. It took longer for Roger to learn to dress and feed himself than it did for Lilly, but he has learned these skills. Although his verbal communication skills are somewhat rudimentary, he is capable of communicating basic needs and desires. Becky is a child with severe to profound mental retardation. At age 6, her development is significantly delayed in nearly every area. However, it is clear that with appropriate intervention, she is learning.

■ EDUCABILITY EXPECTATIONS   To distinguish among the diverse needs of children with mental retardation, the field of education developed its own classification system. As the word *expectations* implies, children with mental retardation have been classified according to expected achievement in a classroom situation. The specific categories used vary greatly from state to state, depending on the locale and source consulted. Frequently, this type of system specifies a label, an approximate IQ range, and a statement of predicted achievement:

- *Educable (IQ 55 to about 70)*. Second- to fifth-grade achievement in school academic areas. Social adjustment skills will result in independence with intermittent or limited support in the community. Partial or total self-support in a paid community job is a strong possibility.
- *Trainable (IQ 40 to 55)*. Learning primarily in the area of self-care skills; some achievement in areas considered academic. A range of more extensive support will be needed to assist the individual to adapt to community environments. Opportunities for paid work include supported employment in a community job.

Historically, the schools have also used the term *custodial* to describe individuals with IQs below 40, who may be unable to care for even their most basic needs. The custodial category described children who could be maintained or cared for only in a specialized setting. Inherent within this category was the assumption that learning experiences in a public school would be fruitless. We have learned that such an assumption is entirely false, for many of the children labeled custodial only a few years ago are now receiving educational experiences that are increasing their adaptive skills and creating opportunities for successful living in family and community settings. *Custodial* is seldom used in today's public schools, having been replaced in most states with the symptom-severity descriptors *severely retarded* and *profoundly retarded*.

The classification criterion for educability expectation was originally developed to determine for whom the schools would be responsible. As indicated by the terminology, *educable* implied that the child could cope with at least some of the academic demands of the classroom, meaning that the child could learn basic reading, writing, and arithmetic skills. The term *trainable* indicated that the student was noneducable and only capable of being trained in noneducational settings. In fact, until the passage of PL 94–142 in 1975 (now IDEA), many children who were labeled trainable could not get a free public education. IDEA redefined education to include the development of adaptive skills (e.g., self-care, motor, communication) that are not necessarily academic in nature. In some school systems, the terms *educable* and *trainable* have now been replaced by symptom-severity classifications (mild through severe mental retardation).

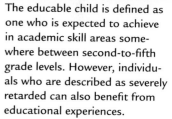

The educable child is defined as one who is expected to achieve in academic skill areas somewhere between second-to-fifth grade levels. However, individuals who are described as severely retarded can also benefit from educational experiences.

■ MEDICAL DESCRIPTORS Mental retardation may be classified on the basis of the origin of the condition rather than the severity or educational expectations associated with it. A classification system that uses the cause of the condition to differentiate individuals with mental retardation is often referred to as a medical classification system because it emerged primarily from the field of medicine. Common medical descriptors include fetal alcohol syndrome, **chromosomal abnormalities** (e.g., Down syndrome), **metabolic disorders** (e.g., phenylketonuria, thyroid dysfunction), and infections (e.g., syphilis, rubella). These medical conditions will be discussed more thoroughly in the section on causation.

■ CLASSIFICATION BASED ON TYPE AND EXTENT OF NEEDED SUPPORT When the AAMR revised its definition of mental retardation in 1992, it also recommended a different way to classify these individuals. Instead of the more traditional classification approaches based on intelligence quotient, educability expectations, or medical origin, the AAMR recommended classifying persons with mental retardation on the basis of the type and extent of the support they would need to function in the natural settings of their home and community. The AAMR recommended four classification levels:

- *Intermittent*. Supports are provided on an "as-needed basis" and characterized as episodic (i.e., person does not always need supports) or short-term during life-span transitions (e.g., job loss or acute medical crisis). Intermittent supports may be of high or low intensity when provided.
- *Limited*. Supports are characterized by consistency; time required may be limited but not intermittent. Fewer staff may be required, and costs may be lower than those associated with more intensive levels of support (e.g., time-limited employment training or transitional supports during school-to-adult provider period).
- *Extensive*. Supports are characterized by regular involvement (e.g., daily) in at least some environments, such as work or home; supports are not time limited (e.g., long-term job and home-living support).
- *Pervasive*. Supports are characterized by constancy and high intensity and are provided across environments; they may be life-sustaining in nature. Pervasive supports typically involve more staff and are more intrusive than extensive or time-limited supports.

The AAMR's emphasis on classifying people with mental retardation on this basis is an important departure from the more restrictive perspectives of the traditional classification approaches. Supports may be described not only in terms of the level of assistance needed, but also by type: formal and natural support systems. Formal supports may be funded through government programs, such as income maintenance, health care, education, housing, or employment. Another type of formal support is the advocacy organization (e.g., the **Arc, A National Organization on Mental Retardation**) that lobbies on behalf of people with mental retardation for improved and expanded services as well as provides family members a place to interact and support one another. **Natural supports** differ from formal supports in that they are not provided by agencies or organizations, but by the nuclear and extended family members, friends, or neighbors. Natural supports are often more effective than formal supports in helping people with mental retardation access and participate in a community setting. Hasazi et al., (1989) suggested that adults with mental retardation who are successfully employed following school find more jobs through their natural support network of friends and family than through formal support systems.

Prevalence

The U.S. Department of Education (1997) reported that 598,770 students between the ages of 6 and 21 were labeled as having mental retardation and receiving service under IDEA during 1995–96. Approxi-

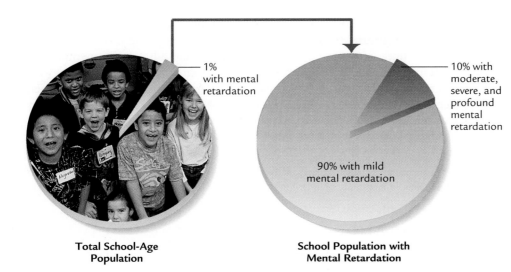

1%
with mental
retardation

10% with
moderate,
severe, and
profound
mental
retardation

90% with mild
mental retardation

**Total School-Age
Population**

**School Population with
Mental Retardation**

FIGURE 8.1

Prevalence of mental retardation

[*Source:* From the *19th Annual Report to Congress,* 1997, Washington, DC: U.S. Government Printing Office.]

mately 14% of all students with disabilities between the ages of 6 and 21 have mental retardation. Overall, students with mental retardation constitute about 1% of the total school population (see Figure 8.1).

Beyond the school years, there is little reliable information regarding the prevalence of mental retardation. The estimates available suggest that from 1% to 3% of the total population has mental retardation. Individuals with mild mental retardation (IQs 55–70) comprise approximately 90% of the estimated prevalence. Based on a 3% prevalence estimate, approximately 2.5% of the general population would be classified as mildly retarded, or about 6.6 million people in the United States (U.S. Census Bureau, 1998).

Individuals with moderate, severe, and profound retardation constitute a much smaller percentage of the general population. Even if we consider the multitude of conditions, prevalence estimates generally range from no more than 0.1 to 1%. Using an estimated prevalence of 0.5%, over 1 million people would fall into the category of moderate to profound mental retardation.

Characteristics

▪ LEARNING AND MEMORY

Intelligence is the ability to acquire, remember, and use knowledge. The primary characteristic of mental retardation is an intellectual deficit that translates to a difference in the rate at and efficiency with which the person acquires, remembers, and uses new knowledge in comparison to the general population (Benson et al., 1993).

Identify four intellectual and adaptive skills characteristics of individuals with mental retardation.

The learning and memory capabilities of people with mental retardation are below average in comparison to their nondisabled peers. Children with mental retardation, as a group, are less able to grasp abstract, as opposed to concrete, concepts. As such, they benefit from instruction that is meaningful and useful, and they learn more from contact with real objects than they do from representations or symbols.

Intelligence is also associated with learning how to learn and with the ability to apply what is learned to new experiences. This process is known as establishing learning sets and generalizing them to new situations. As described by Cipani and Spooner (1994), **generalization** occurs "when a learned response is seen to occur in the presence of 'untaught' stimuli" (p. 157). Children and adults with mental retardation develop learning sets at a slower rate than nonretarded peers, and they are deficient in relating information to new situations (Agran, Salzberg, & Stowitchek, 1987; Hughes, 1992; Turner, Dofny, & Dutka, 1994). The greater the severity of intellectual deficit, the greater the difficulties with memory. Memory problems in children with mental retardation have been attributed to several factors. Individuals with mental retardation have difficulty in focusing on relevant stimuli in learning situations, often attending to the wrong things (Borkowski & Day, 1987; Brooks & McCauley, 1984).

■ SELF-REGULATION

Individuals with mental retardation do not appear to develop efficient learning strategies, such as the ability to rehearse a task (to practice a new concept, either out loud or to themselves, over and over). The ability to rehearse a task is related to a broad concept known as **self-regulation**, or the ability to regulate one's own behavior (Whitman, 1990). Whereas most people will rehearse to try to remember, it does not appear that individuals with retardation are able to apply this skill.

Another factor associated with self-regulation in people with mental retardation is the underdevelopment of metacognitive processes. As described by Sternberg and Spear (1985), **metacognitive processes** are "used to plan how to solve a problem, to monitor one's solution strategy as it is being executed, and to evaluate the results of this strategy once it has been implemented" (p. 303). Children with mental retardation appear to be unable to find, monitor, or evaluate the best strategy to use when confronted with a new learning situation. However, research suggests that they can be taught to change their control processes (Borkowski, Peck, & Damberg, 1983; Glidden, 1985).

■ ADAPTIVE SKILLS

The abilities to adapt to the demands of the environment, relate to others, and take care of personal needs are all important aspects of an independent lifestyle. For people with mental retardation, these social and personal competence skills are often not comparable to those of their nondisabled peers. In the school setting, adaptive behavior is defined as the ability to apply skills learned in a classroom to daily activities.

The child with mental retardation may have difficulty in both learning and applying skills for a number of reasons, including a higher level of distractibility, inattentiveness, failure to read social cues, and impulsive behavior. (Benavidez & Matson, 1993; Bergen & Mosley, 1994; McAlpine, Kendall, & Singh, 1991; Merrill & Peacock, 1994). As such, these children will need to be taught appropriate reasoning, judgment, and social skills that lead to more positive social relationships and personal competence. Some researchers have also suggested that adaptive skill differences for people with mental retardation may also be associated with a lower self-image and a greater expectancy for failure in both academic and social situations (Westling, 1986; Zigler & Balla, 1981). In a study of 764 children in regular education classrooms, Siperstein and Leffert (1997) identified the characteristics of 20 socially accepted and 20 socially rejected students with mental retardation. Characteristics of socially accepted children included a higher level of social skills. These

BEST BUDDIES: "THE ONLY WAY TO HAVE A FRIEND IS TO BE ONE"

American poet and philosopher Ralph Waldo Emerson wrote: "The only way to have a friend is to be one." However, for people with mental retardation few avenues exist by which these individuals can find and keep friendships over time. The reality for most people with mental retardation is that opportunities to establish relationships are often limited to immediate family members and paid service workers. What people with mental retardation want to have is friends outside the immediate family who are not paid to be there.

Best Buddies, founded by Anthony Shriver [son of Eunice Kennedy Shriver] in 1989, is a national service program intended to fill the need by providing an opportunity for people who are not disabled to get to know persons with mental retardation and possibly become friends. People without disabilities are recruited to share their lives by participating in various activities with a person with mental retardation. Activities are selected based on mutual interests, needs, and abilities and can range from going to a movie or sharing a meal to "hanging out" with friends.

- Best Buddies High Schools, a promising new program, began in October 1994. In today's schools, students with mental retardation often enter the same building and walk the same hallways as their peers, but they are left out of social activities. By introducing Best Buddies as a service program in local high schools, the invisible line is crossed that too often separates those with disabilities from those without.

- Best Buddies Colleges is a highly successful program on college and university campuses throughout the United States, England, Canada, and Greece. Best Buddies Colleges has grown from only two campuses in 1989 to over 200 in 1997, thanks to the participation of thousands of college students.

- Best Buddies Citizens takes friendship from the campus to the community by pairing corporate employees, church members, and others in one-to-one friendships with people with mental retardation. The Citizens program is creating friendships in Florida, Utah, Connecticut, Pennsylvania, and Maryland.

Historically, the United States has a strong tradition of community participation—Americans vote, pay taxes, join the PTA, serve on the school board, and so on. Unfortunately, people with mental retardation tend to be left out of community activities because of the general public's misunderstanding of and inexperience with people with differences.

In becoming friends with a person with mental retardation, High School Buddies, College Buddies, and Citizen Buddies learn to appreciate the person first. Such an awareness opens doors for people with mental retardation to more fully enter community workplaces and neighborhoods. Kathy Koski, a former Best Buddies student leader, expressed the importance of Best Buddies this way:

You will never know the impact you are making on your Buddy's [person with mental retardation's] life, or, for that matter, the impact you are making on the community. Everytime you and your Buddy go out, someone realizes that your Buddy is a capable and contributing member of society.

This impact on the community includes parents, siblings, and other family members of those persons with mental retardation who are frustrated at the lack of social opportunities available for a family member with special needs. Beverly Clark, mother of a person with mental retardation matched in a Texas Chapter, said it this way:

A few weeks ago, when I arrived home from work, [my daughter] Pamela greeted me at the door. Pamela told me that her Best Buddy, Erica, had called and asked if she could go to a football game, that they would also eat dinner out, and could she go. I held back my tears of joy until she left for the evening, acting as though it was a normal occurrence. I felt the joy most parents take for granted! (I know, because with my daughter Laura, I take this sort of everyday activity for granted.)

For more information on Best Buddies, call 1-800-89-BUDDY or write Best Buddies, International, 100 S.E. 2nd Street, Suite 1990, Miami, Florida 33131.

children were not perceived by their nondisabled peers as aggressive in their behavior. The authors suggested that there is value in recognizing and teaching the skills that distinguish between those children who are accepted and those who are not (see nearby Reflect on This feature).

▪ ACADEMIC ACHIEVEMENT

Research on the educational achievement of children with mild to moderate mental retardation has suggested that they will experience significant deficits in the areas

focus 4

Identify the academic, motivational, speech and language, and physical characteristics of children with mental retardation.

of reading and mathematics. Westling (1986), in a review of the literature on reading and mental retardation, suggested that "reading is generally considered the weakest area of learning, especially reading comprehension" (p. 127). In general, students with mild retardation are better at decoding words than comprehending their meaning and read below their own mental-age level. Arithmetic skills are also deficient for these children, although their performance may be closer to what is typical for their mental age. These children may be able to learn basic computations but be unable to apply concepts appropriately (Patton, Beirne-Smith, & Payne, 1990).

A growing body of research has indicated that children with moderate and severe mental retardation can be taught to read at least enough to develop a protective or survival vocabulary that will facilitate their inclusion in school and community settings (Browder & Snell, 1993). These children may be able to recognize their names and those of significant others in their lives, as well as common survival words, including *help*, *hurt*, *danger*, and *stop*.

■ MOTIVATION

People with mental retardation are often described as lacking motivation or *outer-directed behavior.* Such individuals may seem unwilling or unable to complete tasks, take responsibility, and be self-directed. Although people with mental retardation may appear to be less motivated than their nondisabled peers, such behavior may be more attributable to the way they have learned to avoid certain situations because of a fear of failure. A child with mental retardation may have a history of failure, particularly in school, and may be afraid to take risks or participate in new situations. The result of failure is often **learned helplessness**—"No matter what I do or how hard I try, I will not succeed." To overcome such children's feelings of learned helplessness, it is important for professionals and family members to focus on providing experiences that have high probabilities for success. The opportunity to strive for success, rather than to avoid failure, is a very important learning experience for these children.

■ SPEECH AND LANGUAGE CHARACTERISTICS

One of the most serious and obvious characteristics of individuals with mental retardation is delayed speech and language development (Warren & Abbeduto, 1992). The most common speech difficulties involve **articulation problems, voice problems,** and **stuttering.** Language problems are generally associated with delays in language development rather than a bizarre use of language (Patton et al., 1990). Kaiser (1993) emphasized that "the overriding goal of language intervention always is to increase the functional communication of students" (p. 348).

The severity of the speech and language problems is positively correlated with the severity of the mental retardation: The milder the mental retardation, the less pervasive the language difficulty. Speech and language difficulties may range from minor speech defects, such as articulation problems, to the complete absence of expressive language. Speech and language difficulties can be corrected for most students with mental retardation when additional support is provided (Cole & Cole, 1989).

Mental retardation may cause speech problems, but speech problems (such as **echolalia)** may also directly contribute to the severity of the mental retardation. Table 8.2 describes the range of speech and language skills for individuals with moderate to profound mental retardation.

TABLE 8.2	Speech and language skills for individuals with moderate to profound mental retardation		

SEVERITY OF MENTAL RETARDATION		
Moderate	Severe	Profound
Most individuals have delays or deviations in speech and language skills, but many develop language abilities that allow them some level of communication with others.	Individuals exhibit significant speech and language delays and deviations (such as lack of expressive and receptive language, articulation difficulties, and little, if any, spontaneous interaction).	Individuals do not exhibit spontaneous communication patterns. Echolalic speech, speech out of context, and purposeless speech may be evident.

■ PHYSICAL CHARACTERISTICS

The physical appearance of most children with mental retardation does not differ from that of same-age children who are not disabled. However, there is a relationship between the severity of the mental retardation and the extent of physical problems for the individual (Drew et al., 1996; Patton et al., 1990). For the person with severe mental retardation, there is a significant probability of related physical problems; genetic factors are likely behind both disabilities. The individual with mild retardation, in contrast, may exhibit no physical differences, because the retardation may be associated with environmental, not genetic, factors. Table 8.3 describes the range of physical characteristics associated with individuals who have moderate to profound mental retardation.

Research has also suggested that there is a higher prevalence of vision and hearing loss (Bensberg & Siegelman, 1976; Fink, 1981) and motor difficulties (Drew et al., 1996) among children with retardation. The majority of children with severe and profound retardation have multiple disabilities that affect nearly every aspect of intellectual and physical development.

Increasing health problems for children with mental retardation may be associated with genetic or environmental factors. For example, individuals with Down syndrome have a higher incidence of congenital heart defects and respiratory problems directly linked to their genetic condition (Marino & Pueschel, 1996). On the other hand, some children with mental retardation experience health problems because of their living conditions. A significantly higher percentage of children with mental retardation come from low socioeconomic backgrounds in comparison to nondisabled peers. Children who do not receive proper nutrition and are exposed to

TABLE 8.3	Physical characteristics of individuals with moderate to profound mental retardation		

SEVERITY OF MENTAL RETARDATION		
Moderate	Severe	Profound
Gross and fine motor coordination is usually delayed. However, the individual is often ambulatory and capable of independent mobility. Perceptual-motor skills exist (e.g., body awareness, sense of touch, eye–hand coordination) but are often delayed in comparison to the norm.	As many as 80% have significant motor difficulties (i.e., poor or nonambulatory skills). Gross or fine motor skills may be present, but the individual may lack control, resulting in awkward or uncontrolled motor movement.	Some gross motor development is evident, but fine motor skills are delayed. The individual is usually nonambulatory and not capable of independent mobility within the environment. The individual may lack perceptual–motor skills.

The physical characteristics of individuals with mental retardation span from no difference when compared to people who are not disabled to significant physical problems.

inadequate sanitation have a greater susceptibility to infections (Drew et al., 1996). Health services for families in these situations may be minimal or nonexistent, depending on whether they are able to access government medical support. As such, children with mental retardation may become ill more often than those who are not retarded. Consequently, children with retardation may miss more school.

Causation

ental retardation is the result of multiple causes, some known, many unknown. Possible causes of mental retardation include sociocultural differences, biomedical factors, behavioral factors, and unknown prenatal influences.

■ SOCIOCULTURAL INFLUENCES

For individuals with mild retardation, the cause of the problem is not generally apparent. A significant number of these individuals come from families of low socioeconomic status and diverse cultural backgrounds; their home situations often offer few opportunities for learning, which only further contributes to their challenges at school. Additionally, because these high-risk children live in such adverse economic conditions, they generally do not receive proper nutritional care. In addition to poor nutrition, high-risk groups are in greater jeopardy of receiving poor medical care and living in unstable families (Davis & McCaul, 1991; Manning & Baruth, 1995).

An important question to be addressed concerning individuals who have grown up in adverse sociocultural situations is this: How much of the person's ability is related to sociocultural influences and how much to genetic factors? This issue is referred to as the **nature-versus-nurture** controversy. Numerous studies over the

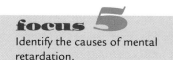

focus 5

Identify the causes of mental retardation.

years have focused on the degree to which heredity and environment contribute to intelligence. These studies show that, although we are reaching a better understanding of the interactive effects of both heredity and environment, the exact contribution of each to intellectual growth remains unknown.

The term used to describe retardation that may be attributable to both sociocultural and genetic factors is **cultural–familial retardation.** Individuals with this condition are often described as (1) being mildly retarded, (2) having no known biological cause for the condition, (3) having at least one parent or sibling who is also mildly retarded, and (4) growing up in a low socioeconomic home environment.

For the majority of people with moderate, severe, and profound mental retardation, problems are evident at birth. To differentiate among the diversity of causes associated with moderate through profound levels of mental retardation, we will briefly review the biomedical and behavioral factors associated with this condition. As defined by the AAMR, **biomedical factors** "relate to biologic processes, such as genetic disorders or nutrition" and **behavioral factors** relate to "potentially causal behaviors, such as dangerous (injurious) activities or maternal substance abuse" (AAMR Ad Hoc Committee, 1992, p. 71).

■ BIOMEDICAL FACTORS

■ CHROMOSOMAL ABNORMALITIES Chromosomes are threadlike bodies that carry the genes that play the critical role in determining inherited characteristics. Defects resulting from chromosomal abnormalities are typically severe and accompanied by visually evident abnormalities. Fortunately, genetically caused defects are relatively rare. The vast majority of humans have normal cell structures (46 chromosomes arranged in 23 pairs) and develop without accident. Aberrations in chromosomal arrangement, either before fertilization or during early cell division, can result in a variety of abnormal characteristics.

One of the most widely recognized types of mental retardation, Down syndrome, results from chromosomal abnormality. A person with Down syndrome is characterized by facial and physical characteristics that are visibly distinctive. Facial features are marked by distinctive epicanthic eyefolds, prominent cheekbones, and a small, somewhat flattened nose. About 5% of individuals with mental retardation have Down syndrome (Patton et al., 1990).

Down syndrome has received widespread attention in the literature and has been a favored topic in both medical and special education textbooks for many years. Part of this attention is due to the ability to identify a cause with some degree of certainty. The cause of such genetic errors has become increasingly associated with the ages of both the mother and the father. The National Information Center for Children and Youth with Disabilities (1991) estimated that about 4,000 infants with Down syndrome are born each year in the United States, or about 1 in every 1,000 live births. MacMillan (1982) reported that, for mothers between the ages of 20 and 30, the chance of having a child with Down syndrome is 1 in 1,200. The probabilities increase significantly (1 in 20) for mothers older than 45 years of age. Abroms and Bennett (1983) indicated that, in about 25% of the cases associated with **trisomy 21** (one type of Down Syndrome), the age of the father (particularly when over 55 years old) is also a factor (see the Reflect on This feature on page 274).

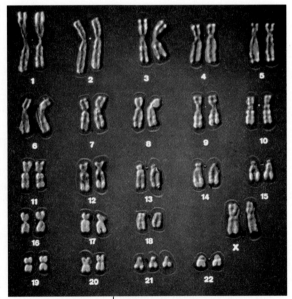

The most common cause of Down syndrome is a chromosomal abnormality known as trisomy 21, in which the twenty-first chromosomal pair carries an extra chromosome.

Reflect on This

MYTHS AND TRUTHS ABOUT DOWN SYNDROME

Myth: Down syndrome is a rare genetic disorder.

Truth: Down syndrome is the most commonly occurring genetic condition. One in every 800 to 1,000 live births is a child with Down syndrome, representing approximately 5,000 births per year in the United States alone. Today, Down syndrome affects more than 350,000 people in the United States.

Myth: Most children with Down syndrome are born to older parents.

Truth: Eighty percent of children born with Down syndrome are born to women younger than 35 years old. However, the incidence of births of children with Down syndrome increases with the age of the mother.

Myth: People with Down syndrome are severely retarded.

Truth: Most people with Down syndrome have IQs that fall in the mild to moderate range of retardation. Children with Down syndrome are definitely educable, and educators and researchers are still discovering the full educational potential of people with Down syndrome.

Myth: Most people with Down syndrome are institutionalized.

Truth: Today people with Down syndrome live at home with their families and are active participants in the educational, vocational, social, and recreational activities of the community. They are integrated into the regular education system and take part in sports, camping, music, art programs, and all the other activities of their communities. In addition, they are socializing with people with and without disabilities, and as adults they are obtaining employment and living in group homes and other independent housing arrangements.

Myth: Parents will not find community support in bringing up their child with Down syndrome.

Truth: In almost every community of the United States there are parent support groups and other community organizations directly involved in providing services to families of individuals with Down syndrome.

Myth: Children with Down syndrome must be placed in segregated special education programs.

Truth: Children with Down syndrome have been included in regular academic classrooms in schools across the country. In some instances they are integrated into specific courses, while in other situations students are fully included in the regular classroom for all subjects. The degree of mainstreaming is based on the abilities of the individual; but the trend is for full inclusion in the social and educational life of the community.

Myth: Adults with Down syndrome are unemployable.

Truth: Businesses are seeking young adults with Down syndrome for a variety of positions. They are being employed in small and medium-sized offices: by banks, corporations, nursing homes, hotels, and restaurants. They work in the music and entertainment industry, in clerical positions, and in the computer industry. People with Down syndrome bring to their jobs enthusiasm, reliability, and dedication.

Myth: People with Down syndrome are always happy.

Truth: People with Down syndrome have feelings just like everyone else in the population. They respond to positive expressions of friendship, and they are hurt and upset by inconsiderate behavior.

Myth: Adults with Down syndrome are unable to form close interpersonal relationships leading to marriage.

Truth: People with Down syndrome date, socialize, and form ongoing relationships. Some are beginning to marry. Women with Down syndrome can and do have children, but there is a 50% chance that their child will have Down syndrome. Men with Down syndrome are believed to be sterile, with only one documented instance of a male with Down syndrome who has fathered a child.

Myth: Down syndrome can never be cured.

Truth: Research on Down syndrome is making great strides in identifying the genes on chromosome 21 that cause the characteristics of Down syndrome. Scientists now feel strongly that it will be possible to improve, correct, or prevent many of the problems associated with Down syndrome in the future.

Source: From *Down Syndrome: Myths and Truths,* 1997, New York: National Down Syndrome Society. (http://www.ndss.org/) Reprinted with permission.

■ METABOLISM AND NUTRITION Metabolic problems are characterized by the body's inability to process (metabolize) certain substances that can then become poisonous and damage tissue in the central nervous system. With **phenylketonuria (PKU),** one such inherited metabolic disorder, the baby is not able to process phenylalanine, a substance found in many foods, including the milk ingested by infants. The inability to process phenylalanine results in an accumulation of poisonous substances in the body. If untreated or not treated promptly (mostly through dietary restrictions), PKU causes varying degrees of mental retardation, ranging from moderate to severe deficits. If treatment is promptly instituted, however, damage may be largely prevented or at least reduced. For this reason, most states now require mandatory screening for all infants in order to treat the condition as early as possible and prevent lifelong problems.

Milk also presents a problem for infants affected by another metabolic disorder. With **galactosemia,** the child is unable to properly process lactose, which is the primary sugar in milk and is also found in other foods. If galactosemia remains untreated, serious damage results, such as cataracts, heightened susceptibility to infection, and reduced intellectual functioning. Dietary controls must be undertaken, eliminating milk and other foods containing lactose.

■ POSTNATAL BRAIN DISEASE

Some disorders are associated with gross postnatal brain disease. **Neurofibromatosis** is an inherited disorder that results in multiple tumors in the skin, peripheral nerve tissue, and other areas such as the brain. Mental retardation does not occur in all cases, although it may be evident in a small percentage of patients. The severity of mental retardation and other problems resulting from neurofibromatosis seems to relate to the location of the tumors (e.g., in the cerebral tissue) and their size and growth. Severe disorders due to postnatal brain disease occur with a variety of other conditions, including **tuberous sclerosis,** which also involves tumors in the central nervous system tissue and degeneration of cerebral white matter.

■ BEHAVIORAL FACTORS

■ INFECTION AND INTOXICATION

Several types of **maternal infections** may result in difficulties for the unborn child. In some cases, the outcome is spontaneous abortion of the fetus; in others, it may be a severe birth defect. The probability of damage is particularly high if the infection occurs during the first three months of pregnancy. **Congenital rubella** (German measles) causes a variety of problems, including mental retardation, deafness, blindness, cerebral palsy, cardiac problems, seizures, and a variety of other neurological problems. The widespread administration of a rubella vaccine is one major reason that mental retardation as an outcome of rubella has declined significantly in recent years.

Another infection associated with mental retardation is the **human immuno-deficiency virus (HIV).** When transmitted from the mother to the unborn child, HIV can result in significant intellectual deficits. The virus actually crosses the placenta and infects the fetus, damaging the infant's immune system. HIV is the single largest cause of preventable infectious mental retardation in the world (Cohen, 1991).

Several prenatal infections can result in other severe disorders. **Toxoplasmosis,** an infection carried by raw meat and fecal material, can result in mental retardation and other problems such as blindness and convulsions. Toxoplasmosis is primarily a threat if the mother is exposed during pregnancy, whereas infection prior to conception seems to cause minimal danger to the unborn child.

Intoxication refers to cerebral damage that occurs due to an excessive level of some toxic agent in the mother–fetus system. Excessive maternal use of alcohol or drugs or exposure to certain environmental hazards such as x-rays or insecticides can cause damage to the child. Damage to the fetus from maternal alcohol consumption, or **fetal alcohol syndrome (FAS),** is characterized by facial abnormalities, heart problems, low birthweight, small brain size, and mental retardation. FAS is recognized as a leading cause of preventable mental retardation throughout the world (Phelps & Grabowski, 1992). It is estimated that more than 50,000 babies are born with alcohol-related problems each year in the United States (National Association, 1991). Similarly, pregnant women who smoke are at greater risk of having a premature baby with complicating developmental problems such as mental retardation (Carta et al., 1994). The use of drugs during pregnancy has varying effects on the infant, depending on frequency, usage, and drug type. Drugs known to produce serious fetal damage include LSD, heroin, morphine, and cocaine. Prescription drugs such as **anticonvulsants** and antibiotics have also been associated with infant malformations (Batshaw & Perret, 1986).

Maternal substance abuse is also associated with gestation disorders involving prematurity and low birthweight. **Prematurity** refers to infants delivered before 35 weeks from the first day of the last menstrual period. **Low birthweight** characterizes babies that weigh 2,500 grams (5.5 pounds) or less at birth. Prematurity and low birthweight significantly increase the risk of serious problems at birth, including mental retardation.

Another factor that can seriously affect the unborn baby is an incompatible blood type between the mother and the fetus. The most widely known form of this problem occurs when the mother's blood is Rh-negative, whereas the fetus has Rh-positive blood. In this situation, the mother's system may become sensitized to the incompatible blood type and produce defensive antibodies that damage the fetus. Medical technology can now prevent this condition through the use of a drug known as Rhogam.

Mental retardation can also occur as a result of postnatal infections and toxic excesses. For example, **encephalitis** may damage the central nervous system following certain types of childhood infections (e.g., measles or mumps). Reactions to certain toxic substances—such as lead, carbon monoxide, and drugs—can also cause central nervous system damage.

■TRAUMAS OR PHYSICAL ACCIDENTS Traumas or physical accidents can occur either prior to birth (e.g., exposure to excessive radiation), during delivery, or after the baby is born. Consider Becky from the chapter opening snapshot: The cause of her mental retardation was trauma during delivery. She suffered from birth asphyxiation as well as epileptic seizures.

The continuing supply of oxygen and nutrients to the baby is a critical factor during delivery. One threat to these processes involves the position of the fetus. Normal fetal position places the baby with the head toward the cervix and the face toward the mother's back. Certain other positions may result in fetal damage as delivery proceeds. One of these, breech presentation, occurs when the buttocks of the fetus, rather than the head, are positioned toward the cervix. The head exits last, rather than first, and can be subjected to several types of stress that would not occur in a normal delivery. The head passes through the birth canal under stress, and the pressure of the contractions has a direct impact on the fetal skull rather than on the buttocks, as in a normal position. In a breech presentation, the umbilical cord may not be long enough to remain attached while the head is expelled, or it may become pinched between the baby's body and the pelvic girdle. In either case, the baby's oxygen supply may be reduced for a period of time until the head is expelled and the lungs begin to function. The baby's lack of oxygen may result in damage to the brain. Such a condition is known as **anoxia** (oxygen deprivation).

Other abnormal positions can also result in delivery problems and damage to the fetus. The fetus may be across the birth canal in what is known as a *transverse position,* which either prevents the baby from exiting through the birth canal or causes such stress during exit that severe damage may occur. In other cases, labor and delivery proceed so rapidly that the fetal skull does not have time to mold properly or in a sufficiently gentle fashion. Rapid births (generally less than two hours) are known as **precipitous births** and may result in mental retardation as well as other problems.

■ UNKNOWN PRENATAL INFLUENCES

Several conditions associated with unknown prenatal influences can result in severe disorders. One such condition involves malformations of cerebral tissue. The most dramatic of these malformations is known as **anencephaly,** a condition in which the individual has a partial or even complete absence of cerebral tissue. In some cases, portions of the brain appear to develop and then degenerate. In **hydrocephalus,** also resulting from unknown origins, an excess of cerebrospinal fluid accumulates in the skull and results in potentially damaging pressure on cerebral tissue. Hydrocephalus may involve an enlarged head and result in decreased intellectual functioning. If surgical intervention occurs early, the damage may be slight because the pressure will not have been serious or prolonged.

Although we have presented a number of possible causal factors associated with mental retardation, cause is often unknown and undeterminable in many cases. Additionally, many conditions associated with mental retardation are due to the interaction of both hereditary and environmental factors. Although we are unable to always identify the causes of mental retardation, measures can be taken to prevent its occurrence.

Prevention

Preventing mental retardation is a laudable goal and has for many years been the focus of professionals in the field of medicine. Over the years, prevention has taken many forms, including the sterilization of people with mental retardation. More recently, preventive measures have focused on immunization against disease, improvement of maternal nutritional habits during pregnancy, addressing maternal substance abuse, appropriate prenatal care, and screening for genetic disorders prior to and at birth.

focus 6

Identify four measures that may prevent mental retardation.

Immunization can protect family members from contracting serious illness and guard against the mother's becoming ill during pregnancy. Diseases such as rubella, which may result in severe mental retardation, heart disease, or blindness, can be controlled through routine immunization programs.

Poor nutritional habits and substance abuse during pregnancy may also contribute to fetal problems and are part of a much larger social problem: the lack of appropriate prenatal care. Delays in prenatal care can have significant consequences for the health of the baby and the mother. Many conditions that are amenable to timely medical treatment can develop serious complications if neglected.

A medical history can alert the attending physician to potential dangers for the mother or the unborn infant that may result from family genetics, prior trauma, or illness. The physician will be able to monitor the health of the fetus, including heart rate, physical size, and position in the uterus. At the time of birth, several factors relevant to the infant's health can be assessed. A procedure known as **Apgar scoring** evaluates the infant's heart rate, respiratory condition, muscle tone, reflex irritability, and color. This screening procedure alerts the medical staff to infants who may warrant closer monitoring and more in-depth assessments. Other screening procedures conducted in the medical laboratory within the first few days of life can detect anomalies that, if not treated, will eventually lead to mental retardation, psychological disorders, physical disabilities, or even death.

Other methods of prevention involve issues of morality and ethics. These include genetic screening and counseling and therapeutic abortion. Genetic screening is a search for certain genes that are predisposed to disease, are already diseased, or can lead to disease in future generations of the same family. Genetic screening may be conducted at various times in the family-planning process or during pregnancy. Screening prior to conception seeks parental predisposition to genetic anomalies that could be inherited by their offspring. Screening after conception seeks any genetic abnormalities in the fetus and can be accomplished through one of several medical procedures, including **amniocentesis, fetoscopy,** and **ultrasound.**

Once genetic screening has been completed, it is the responsibility of a counselor to inform parents of the test results, potential outcomes, and options. The genetic counselor does not make decisions for the parents regarding family planning, but he or she does prepare the parents to exercise their rights. The primary outcome of genetic counseling can be viewed in terms of informing parents concerning decisions they have to make about (1) whether to have children based on the probability of a genetic anomaly occurring or (2) whether to abort a pregnancy if prenatal assessment indicates that the developing fetus has a genetic anomaly.

The abortion option involves a moral controversy that society has been debating for years. For example, if it is detected that a fetus has Down syndrome, what intervention options are available? Certainly, one option involves continuing the pregnancy and making mental, physical, and financial preparations for the additional care that may be required for the child. The other option is to terminate the pregnancy through what is often termed **therapeutic abortion.** This is abortion, nonetheless, and presents ethical dilemmas for many people.

The time immediately following birth, known as the *neonatal period*, may present some of the most difficult ethical dilemmas for parents and professionals. During the neonatal period, the issue is usually whether to withhold medical treatment from a defective newborn. This raises a number of ethical and moral questions: Who makes these decisions? Under what circumstances are such decisions made? What criteria are used to determine whether treatment is to be withheld?

Assessment

Just as a physician assesses an individual with mental retardation to determine the extent of needed medical intervention, professionals from several disciplines assess the individual's need for special education services. This group of professionals joins with the child's parents to assess needs and plan for intervention. Often referred to as the multidisciplinary team, this group usually includes the school psychologist, classroom teachers, and a school administrator. Depending on the needs of the child, other professionals may be involved as well, including a social worker, a speech or language specialist, an occupational or physical therapist, an adaptive physical education teacher, a school counselor, and a school nurse.

The multidisciplinary team has two crucial functions in the assessment of a child: to determine whether the child meets the criteria of mental retardation before placing him or her in a special education program, and to assess the educational needs of the child so that an appropriate educational program can be developed and implemented.

An intelligence test and a measure of adaptive skills must be completed to determine whether the child meets criteria. The most commonly used scales for measuring intelligence in school-age children are the Wechsler Intelligence Scales and the Stanford-Binet Intelligence Scale.

Adaptive skills may be measured by both formal and informal appraisals. Informal appraisals include **ecological assessments** (either through direct observations of the child in the environment or asking people in regular contact with the child, such as parents and classroom teachers, about his or her ability to cope with the demands of the environment). Formal appraisals include the use of standardized adaptive behavior scales such as the Vineland Social Maturity Scale, the Scales of Independent Behavior, and the AAMR Adaptive Behavior Scale.

Once the child has been determined to meet the criteria for mental retardation, the team sets in place specific assessment procedures to determine the nature of an appropriate educational experience for this particular child. The team members' areas of expertise build a broad base for determining the child's needs. The psychologist and the classroom teacher select, administer, and interpret appropriate psychological, educational, and behavioral assessment instruments. In addition, they observe the child's performance in an educational setting and consult with parents and other team members regarding the child's overall development. Parents provide the team with information regarding the child's performance outside of the school setting. They must provide written consent for testing the child in order to change his or her educational placement. Physical therapists, occupational therapists, and adaptive physical education specialists assess the motor development of the child. The speech or language specialist assesses the child's communication abilities. The social worker may collect pertinent information from the home setting as well as other background data relevant to the child's needs. The school nurse assists in the interpretation of information regarding the child's health (e.g., screening of hearing and vision, conferring with physicians, and monitoring medications).

Although each team member has specific responsibilities in assessing the educational needs of the child, it is important that the members work together as a unit. Each member of the team has the responsibility to maintain ongoing communication with other members, to actively participate in problem-solving situations, and to follow through with assigned tasks.

The Early Childhood Years

The provision of appropriate services and supports for people with mental retardation is a lifelong process. For people who have severe retardation, interventions should begin at birth and continue through the adult years. The importance of early intervention cannot be overstated. Significant advances have been made in the area of early intervention, including improved assessment, curricular, and instructional technologies; increasing numbers of children receiving services; and appreciation of the need to individualize services for families as well as children (McDermott & Altrekruse,

focus 7
Why is the need for early intervention services for children with mental retardation so crucial?

1994: McDonnell, Hardman, McDonnell, & Kiefer-O'Donnell, 1995; Noonan & Mc-Cormick, 1993). McDonnell and Hardman (1988), in a review of the literature in early intervention, suggested that "best-practice" indicators include programs that are integrated with students who are not disabled, as well as comprehensive, normalized, adaptable, peer and family referenced, and outcome based.

Early intervention techniques, such as **infant stimulation** programs, focus on the acquisition of sensorimotor functions and intellectual development. This involves learning simple reflex activity and equilibrium reactions. Subsequent intervention then expands into all areas of human growth and development. Intervention based on normal patterns of growth is often referred to as the *developmental milestones approach* (Bailey & Wolery, 1992) because it seeks to develop, remedy, or adapt learner skills based on the child's variation from what is considered normal. This progression of skills continues as the child ages chronologically; rate of progress depends on the severity of condition. Some children who are profoundly retarded may never exceed a developmental age of 6 months. Those with moderate retardation may develop to a level that will enable them to have fulfilled lives as adults, with varying levels of societal support and supervision.

The preschool-age child with mild retardation may exhibit subtle developmental discrepancies in comparison to age-mates, but parents may not identify these discrepancies as significant enough to seek intervention. Even if parents are concerned and seek help for their child prior to school age, they are often confronted with professionals who are apathetic toward early childhood education. Some professionals believe that early childhood services may actually create rather than remedy problems, since the child may not be mature enough to cope with the pressures of structured learning in an educational environment. This maturation philosophy has been ingrained in educators and parents. Simply stated, it means that prior to entering school, a child should reach a point of maturation at which he or she is ready to learn certain skills. Unfortunately, this philosophy has kept many children out of the public schools for years.

The antithesis of the maturation philosophy is the prevention of further learning and behavior problems through intervention. **Head Start,** initially funded as a federal preschool program for disadvantaged students, is a prevention program that attempts to identify and instruct high-risk children prior to their entering public school. Although Head Start did not generate the results that were initially anticipated (the virtual elimination of school-adjustment problems for the disadvantaged student), it has represented a significant move forward and continues to receive widespread support from parents and professionals alike. The rationale for early education is widely accepted in the field of special education and is an important part of the mandate of IDEA (see Chapters 1 and 4).

The Elementary School Years

Education is a relatively new concept as it relates to students with mental retardation, particularly those with more severe characteristics. Historically, many of these students were defined as noneducable by the public schools because they did not fit the programs offered by general education. Because such programs were built on a foundation of academic learning that emphasized reading, writing, and arithmetic, students with mental retardation could not meet the academic standards set by the schools, and as such were excluded. Schools were not expected to adapt to the needs of students with retardation; rather, the students were expected to adapt to the schools.

Through both state and federal mandates (such as IDEA), the schools that excluded these children for so long are facing the challenge of providing an appropriate education for all children with mental retardation. Based on a new set of values, education has been redefined. Educational instruction and support for elementary school-age children with mental retardation focus on decreasing dependence on others while concurrently teaching adaptation to the environment. Therefore, instruction must concentrate on those skills that facilitate the child's interaction with others and emphasize independence in the community. Programs for children with mental retardation generally include development of motor skills, self-care skills, social skills, communication skills, and functional academic skills.

focus 8

Identify five skill areas that should be addressed in programs for elementary-age children with mental retardation.

■ MOTOR SKILLS

The acquisition of motor skills is a fundamental component of the developmental process and a prerequisite to successful learning in other content areas, including self-care and social skills. Gross motor development involves general mobility, including the interaction of the body with the environment. Gross motor skills are developed in a sequence, ranging from movements that make balance possible to higher-order locomotor patterns. Locomotor patterns are intended to move the person freely through the environment. Gross motor movements include controlling the head and neck, rolling, body righting, sitting, creeping, crawling, standing, walking, running, jumping, and skipping.

Fine motor development requires more precision and steadiness than the skills developed in the gross motor area. The development of fine motor skills, including reaching, grasping, and manipulating objects, is initially dependent on the ability of the child to visually fix on an object and visually track a moving target. Coordination of the eye and hand is an integral factor in many skill areas as well as in fine motor development. Eye–hand coordination is the basis of social and leisure-time activities and is essential to the development of the object-control skills required in employment.

Fine motor development and eye-hand coordination are the basis of many leisure activities.

■ SELF-CARE SKILLS

The development of self-care skills is another important content area related to independence. Self-care skills include eating, dressing, and maintaining personal hygiene. Eating skills range from finger feeding, drinking from a cup, and using proper table behaviors, such as employing utensils and napkins, serving food, and following etiquette. Dressing skills include buttoning, zipping, buckling, lacing, and tying. Personal hygiene skills also range on a continuum from rather basic developmental skills to high-level skills relevant to adult behavior. Basic skills include toileting, face and hand washing, bathing, tooth brushing, hair combing, and shampooing. Skills associated with adolescent and adult years include skin care, shaving, hair setting, use of deodorants and cosmetics, and menstrual hygiene.

■ SOCIAL SKILLS

Social skills training is closely aligned with the self-care area in that it relates many of the self-care concepts to the development of good interpersonal relationships. Social skills training emphasizes the importance of physical appearance, proper manners, appropriate use of leisure time, and appropriate sexual behavior. The area of social skills may also focus on the development of personality characteristics conducive to successful integration into society (see nearby Interacting in Natural Settings feature).

■ EARLY CHILDHOOD YEARS

TIPS FOR THE FAMILY

■ Promote family learning about the diversity of all people in the context of understanding the child with intellectual differences.

■ Create opportunities for friendships to develop between your child and children without disabilities, both in family and neighborhood settings.

■ Help facilitate your child's opportunities and access to neighborhood preschools by actively participating in the education planning process. Become familiar with the individualized family service plan (IFSP) and how it can serve as a planning tool to support the inclusion of your child in preschool programs that involve students without disabilities.

TIPS FOR THE GENERAL EDUCATION PRESCHOOL TEACHER

■ Focus on the child's individual abilities first. Whatever labels have been placed on the child (e.g., "mentally retarded") will have little to do with instructional needs.

■ When teaching the child, focus on presenting each component of a task clearly, while reducing outside stimuli that may distract learning.

■ Begin with simple tasks, and move to more complex ones as the child masters skills.

■ Verbally label stimuli, such as objects or people, as often as possible to provide the child with both auditory and visual input.

■ Provide a lot of practice in initial learning phases, using short but frequent sessions to ensure that the child has mastered the skill before moving on to more complex tasks.

■ Create success experiences by rewarding correct responses to tasks as well as appropriate behavior with peers who are not disabled.

■ It is important for the young child with mental retardation to be able to transfer learning from school to the home and neighborhood. Facilitate such transfer by providing information that is meaningful to the child and noting how the initial and transfer tasks are similar.

TIPS FOR PRESCHOOL PERSONNEL

■ Support the inclusion of young children with mental retardation in classrooms and programs.

■ Support teachers, staff, and volunteers as they attempt to create success experiences for the child in the preschool setting.

■ Integrate families into the preschool programs as well as children. Offer parents as many opportunities as possible to be part of the program (e.g., advisory boards, volunteer experiences).

TIPS FOR NEIGHBORS AND FRIENDS

■ Look for opportunities for young neighborhood children who are not disabled to interact during play times with the child who is mentally retarded.

■ Provide a supportive community environment for the family of a young child who is mentally retarded. Encourage the family, including the child, to participate in neighborhood activities (e.g., outings, barbecues, outdoor yard and street cleanups, crime watches).

■ Try to understand how the young child with mental retardation is similar to other children in the neighborhood rather than different. Focus on those similarities in your interactions with other neighbors and children in your community.

■ ELEMENTARY YEARS

TIPS FOR THE FAMILY

■ Actively participate in the development of your son or daughter's individualized education program (IEP). Through active participation, fight for the goals that you would like to see on the IEP that will focus on your child's developing social interaction and communication skills in natural settings (e.g., the general education classroom).

■ To help facilitate your son or daughter's inclusion in the neighborhood elementary school, help educators and administrators understand the importance of inclusion with peers who are not disabled (e.g., riding on the same school bus, going to recess and lunch at the same time, participating in schoolwide assemblies).

■ Participate in as many school functions for parents (e.g., PTA, parent advisory groups, volunteering) as is reasonable, to connect your family to the mainstream of the general education school.

■ Create opportunities for your child to make friends with same-age children without disabilities, both within the family and neighborhood.

TIPS FOR THE GENERAL EDUCATION CLASSROOM TEACHER

■ View children with mental retardation as children, first and foremost. Focus on their similarities with other children rather than their differences.

■ Recognize children with mental retardation for their own accomplishments within the classroom rather than comparing them to those of peers without disabilities.

■ Employ cooperative learning strategies wherever possible to promote effective learning by all students. Try to use peers without disabilities as support for students with mental retardation. This may include establishing peer-buddy programs or peer and cross-age tutoring.

■ Consider all members of the classroom when you organize the physical environment. Find ways to meet the individual needs of each child (e.g., establishing aisles that will accommodate a wheelchair, and organizing desks to facilitate tutoring on assigned tasks.

TIPS FOR SCHOOL PERSONNEL

■ Integrate school resources as well as children. Wherever

possible, help general classroom teachers access the human and material resources necessary to meet the needs of students with mental retardation. Instructional materials and programs should be made available to whoever needs them, not just those identified as being in special education.

- Assist general and special education teachers to develop nondisabled peer-partner and support networks for students with mental retardation.
- Promote the heterogeneous grouping of students. Try to avoid clustering large numbers of students with mental retardation in a single general education classroom. Integrate no more than one or two in each elementary education classroom.
- Maintain the same schedules for students with mental retardation as for all other students in the building. Recess, lunch, school assemblies, and bus arrival and departure schedules should be identical for all students, with and without disabilities.
- Create opportunities for all school personnel to collaborate in the development and implementation of instructional programs for individual children.

TIPS FOR NEIGHBORS AND FRIENDS
- Support families who are seeking to have their child with mental retardation educated in their local school with children who are not disabled. This will help children with mental retardation have more opportunities for interacting with children who are not disabled, both in school and in the local community.

■SECONDARY AND TRANSITION YEARS

TIPS FOR THE FAMILY
- Create opportunities for your son or daughter to participate in activities that are of interest to him or her beyond the school day with their same-age peers who are not disabled, including high school clubs, sports, or just hanging out in the local mall.
- Promote opportunities for students from your son's or daughter's high school to visit your home. Help arrange get-togethers or parties involving students from the neighborhood and/or school.
- Become actively involved in the development of the individualized education and transition program. Explore with the high school their views on what should be done to assist your son or daughter in the transition from school to adult life.

TIPS FOR THE GENERAL EDUCATION CLASSROOM TEACHER
- Collaborate with special education teachers and other specialists to adapt subject matter in your classroom (e.g., science, math, or physical education) to the individual needs of students with mental retardation.
- Let students without disabilities know that the student with mental retardation belongs in their classroom. The goals and activities of this student may be different from those of other students, but with support, the student with mental retardation will ben-

efit from working with you and the other students in the class.
- Support the student with mental retardation in becoming involved in extracurricular high school activities. If you are the faculty sponsor of a club or organization, explore whether this student is interested and how he or she could get involved.

TIPS FOR SCHOOL PERSONNEL
- Advocate for parents of high-school-age students with mental retardation to participate in the activities of the school (e.g., committees and PTA).
- Help facilitate parental involvement in the IEP process during the high school years by valuing parental input that focuses on a desire for including their child in the mainstream of the school. Parents will be more active when school personnel have general and positive contact with the family.
- Provide human and material support to high school special education or vocational teachers seeking to develop community-based instruction programs that focus on students learning and applying skills in actual community settings (e.g., grocery stores, malls, theaters, parks, work sites).

TIPS FOR NEIGHBORS, FRIENDS, AND POTENTIAL EMPLOYERS
- Work with the family and school personnel to create opportunities for students with mental retardation to participate in community activities (such as going to the movies, "hanging out" with nondisabled peers in the neighborhood mall,

going to high school sports events) as often as possible.
- As a potential employer, work with the high school to locate and establish community-based employment training sites for students with mental retardation.

■ADULT YEARS

TIPS FOR THE FAMILY
- Become aware of what life will be like for your son or daughter in the local community during the adult years. What are the formal (government-funded, advocacy organizations) and informal supports available in your community? What are the characteristics of adult service programs? Explore adult support systems in the local community in the areas of supported living, employment, and recreation and leisure.

TIPS FOR NEIGHBORS, FRIENDS, AND POTENTIAL EMPLOYERS
- Seek ways to become part of the community support network for the individual with mental retardation. Be alert to ways that this individual can become and remain actively involved in community employment, neighborhood recreational activities, and local church functions.
- As potential employers in the community, seek information on employment of people with mental retardation. Find out about programs (e.g., supported employment) that focus on establishing work for people with mental retardation while meeting your needs as an employer.

■ COMMUNICATION SKILLS

The ability to communicate with others is an essential component of growth and development. Without communication, there can be no interaction. Communication systems for children with mental retardation take three general forms: verbal language, augmentative communication (including sign language and language boards), and a combination of the verbal and augmentative approaches. The approach used depends on the child's capability. A child who can develop the requisite skills for spoken language will have greatly enhanced everyday interactive skills. For a child unable to develop verbal skills as an effective means of communication, manual communication must be considered. What is important is that the individual develop some form of communication.

Some students with mental retardation will benefit from the use of augmentative communication. Augmentative communication refers to

the variety of communication approaches that are used to assist persons who are limited in their ability to communicate messages through natural modes of communication. These approaches may be unaided (e.g., manual sign and adapted gestures) or aided (utilization of communication boards or electronic devices). Regardless of the communication mode employed, the goals of augmented communicators are similar to those of natural speakers, that is, to express wants and needs, to share information, to engage in social closeness, and to manage social etiquette (Franklin & Beukelman, 1991, p. 321)

■ FUNCTIONAL ACADEMIC SKILLS

A functional academic curriculum is intended to expand the child's knowledge in daily living, recreation, and employment. When teaching functional academic skills, the classroom teacher uses instructional materials that are realistic and part of the

Today's Technology

CHILDREN WITH DOWN SYNDROME LEARN LANGUAGE THROUGH SYNTHESIZED SPEECH

Children with Down syndrome often have significant delays in language development. They may not even be able to speak single words until they are 2 years old and may not be able to string words together until at least 3 or 4 years of age. Even as these children get older and are able to master more language skills, they often apply their vocabulary or new language structure in an inconsistent fashion. Speech is expressed in such a complex and rapid auditory stream that the child with Down syndrome often finds it extremely difficult to comprehend meaning.

Laura Meyers, a specialist in speech and language disabilities, found a way to slow down speech through the use of a computer and assist students with Down syndrome to become more proficient at language acquisition. Two software programs, Exploratory Play and Representational Play,* are designed to help children express and receive speech through computer instruction. Using a computer keyboard, a child may ask for, label, or describe a toy or action by touching a picture on the keyboard. The picture then appears on the screen, and a speech synthesizer says the descriptive word written below it. Using the speech output, the child can then create and describe imaginary play scenes and carry on meaningful conversations with others.

Since synthesized speech can occur at a rate much slower than that of human speech, the child is able to hear more efficiently what is being said. Additionally, through the synthesized speech output the child can generate as many repetitions of exactly the same signal as needed to learn the sound pattern of words, sentences, and phrases.

*Both are available from PEAL software.

Source: From *Computer-Enhanced Language Interventions*, by L. Meyers, n.d., Calabasas, CA: PEAL Software. Copyright PEAL Software. Adapted by permission.

child's environment. Browder and Snell (1993) reported that students with mental retardation, including those with moderate to severe difficulties, can learn "specific academic skills in the context of daily routines, rather than a broad sequence of skills" (p. 476). For example, a functional reading program contains words that are frequently encountered in the environment, such as those used on labels or signs in public places; words that warn of possible risks; and symbols such as the skull and crossbones that denotes poisonous substances. A functional math program involves activities such as learning to use a checkbook, shop in a grocery store, or operate a vending machine.

The Adolescent Years

The goals of an educational program for adolescents with mental retardation are to increase personal independence, enhance opportunities for participation in the local community, prepare for employment, and facilitate a successful transition to the adult years.

focus 9
Identify four educational goals for adolescents with mental retardation.

■ PERSONAL INDEPENDENCE AND PARTICIPATION IN THE COMMUNITY

Independence refers to the development and application of skills that lead to greater self-sufficiency in daily personal life, including personal hygiene, self-care, and appropriate leisure-time activities. Participation in the community includes access to those programs, facilities, and services that those without disabilities often take for granted: grocery stores, shopping malls, restaurants, theaters, parks. Adolescents with mental retardation should have opportunities for contact with nondisabled peers other than caregivers, access to community events, sustained social relationships, and involvement in choices that affect their lives. Work is a crucial measure of any person's success during adulthood, providing the primary opportunity for social interaction, a basis for personal identity and status, and a chance to contribute to the community. These needs are basic to adults who have mental retardation, just as they are to their nondisabled peers.

■ EMPLOYMENT PREPARATION

Employment preparation for adolescents with mental retardation was historically fraught with problems because professionals and the general public held a pessimistic attitude about its effectiveness. Today, that negative philosophy has largely been replaced by a commitment to the development of relevant employment-training programs, particularly in competitive employment settings (McDonnell, Mathot-Buckner, & Ferguson, 1996; Wehman 1996).

Employment training during the high school years is shifting from the isolation and "getting-ready" orientation of a **sheltered workshop** to activities accomplished in community employment. Goals and objectives are developed according to the demands of the community work setting and the functioning level of the individual. The focus is on assisting the individual to learn and apply skills in a job setting while receiving the necessary support to succeed. Providing ongoing assistance to the individual on the job is the basis of an approach known as **supported employment.** Supported employment is defined as work in an integrated setting for

WHAT'S INVOLVED FOR EMPLOYERS IN PROVIDING "REASONABLE ACCOMMODATIONS" FOR PERSONS WITH MENTAL RETARDATION?

People with mental retardation can be effective and successful on the job. Employers describe them as dependable employees who genuinely want to work. Boeing Corporation, in Seattle, reports a strong work ethic and above-average safety among its workers with disabilities. The company also finds improved coworker morale.

Roger Beach of Beach Brothers Printing in Rockville, Maryland, has employed two men with developmental disabilities in the bindery for over ten years. "They are extremely valuable employees who are good at what they do. In fact, they have a talent for the job! Typically, their hourly rate is higher than other workers in the same job, and they have

brought a stability to the job that didn't exist before."

Marriott Hotels' "Bridges . . . From School to Work" Project has placed 75 students with mental retardation in paid internships during the past two years. Seventy percent of the interns were later hired for permanent positions by their host employers.

Thermo King in Hastings, Nebraska, has six employees with mental retardation. Although all were initially supported by job coaches in specially created jobs, some of these employees have moved into competitive-wage jobs.

The keys to employing workers with mental retardation successfully are good communication and a positive attitude. Effective employers look beyond a person's disability

and create a climate of inclusion, respect, and acceptance.

The Americans with Disabilities Act uses specific terms to describe the rights of a person with disabilities, including a person with mental retardation. Employers have to provide "reasonable accommodations" for a "qualified" person with a "disability," as long as that person can perform "essential job functions" without causing the employer "undue hardship."

The following explanations should help employers understand the key terms of the law:

- *Disability.* Mental retardation is a disability under ADA because it substantially limits major life activities. Unless mental retardation is readily apparent, a job applicant must identify

his or her disability before requesting accommodations from an employer.

- *Qualified.* A job applicant has to meet the advertised requirements for a job, including education, licenses, experience, and training. If any of the qualifications do not relate to "essential job functions," the applicant can request that those qualifications be waived. For example, individuals with mental retardation may have earned a certificate of attendance rather than a standard high school diploma. If they can perform "essential job functions," they can ask to have the diploma requirement waived.
- *Essential job functions.* These, unlike "marginal functions," may require specialized

individuals with severe disabilities (including those with mental retardation) who are expected to need continuous support services and for whom competitive employment has traditionally not been possible (see Chapter 5).

Research indicates that individuals with mental retardation, including those with moderate and severe differences, can work in community employment if provided adequate training and support (Hasazi et al., 1989; McDonnell et al., 1996; Tines, Rusch, McCaughrin, & Conley, 1990; Wehman, 1996). Effectively preparing these adolescents for community work settings requires a comprehensive employment-training program during the high school years. Adherence to the following guidelines will help enable the student to access and succeed in a community job following school:

1. The student should receive employment training in community settings prior to graduation from high school.
2. Employment training should focus on work opportunities present in the local area where the individual currently lives.
3. The focus of the employment training should be on specific job training as the student approaches graduation.
4. Collaboration between the school and adult service agencies must be part of the employment-training program. (Hasazi et al., 1989; McDonnell et al., 1996) (See nearby Reflect on This feature.)

skills, training, licenses, or degrees. "Essential job functions" are central and cannot be eliminated without substantially changing the nature of the job. They may include a stated "rate of productivity," but only if a specific rate is critical, such as on an assembly line.

- *Marginal job functions.* These duties could be transferred to another position without causing dramatic changes to either job. An inability to perform "marginal functions" cannot keep a person from being hired if he or she is "qualified" to perform the "essential job functions," with or without "reasonable accommodation."
- *Undue hardship.* When deciding whether an accommodation causes "undue hardship," employers should consider the cost of accommodations, the number of employees in the company, the total business receipts,

and available outside resources. They should also evaluate the impact of accommodations on business operations and productivity. In general, the more employees and the more resources available, the more "reasonable accommodations" an employer is expected to make.

■ EXAMPLES OF "REASONABLE ACCOMMODATIONS"

Making "reasonable accommodations" for an employee with mental retardation is an ongoing process. As the employee's needs or job circumstances change, the number and types of accommodations also change. The examples here show the kinds of accommodations employers may be asked to make:

- *Restructuring jobs.* Employers can reassign "marginal job functions" to other workers.

They can change the order in which work is done or allow more time for an employee to complete tasks.

- *Modifying work schedules.* To accommodate the transportation needs or stamina of a worker, employers can change the beginning and ending times of a shift or the number of hours worked.
- *Using aids or assists.* Employers can use picture cards, color codes, or special equipment to help an employee learn, remember, and perform "essential job functions."
- *Retraining after on-the-job changes.* An employee may need time for retraining and reorientation after any work-related change. This includes changes in supervisors, workouts, equipment, or tasks. Employers should allow a period of adjustment as a "reasonable accommodation." They

should also train any new supervisors to work with individuals with mental retardation.

- *Modifying management strategies.* Supervisors and coworkers should be respectful. They should clearly explain and demonstrate all tasks and talk openly about problems that occur. They should also offer praise and frequent, constructive feedback and include the employee in all social gatherings.

Source: From *The Untapped Resource: The Employee with Mental Retardation,* 1994, developed by the Institute for the Study of Exceptional Children and Youth at the University of Maryland at College Park, under a grant from the Joseph P. Kennedy, Jr. Foundation. Reprinted with permission

Inclusive Education

The educational placement of students with mental retardation has been a critical concern for school personnel and parents for many years. Prior to the late 1960s, special education for students with mental retardation meant segregated education. Since then, much of the focus on educational placement has been concerned with including these students with their nondisabled age-mates. Inclusive education may be defined as the placement of students with mental retardation in general education classrooms with nondisabled peers, consistent with an established individualized education program for each student. Some students with mental retardation may be only partially included for a small part of the school day and attend only those general education classes that their individualized education program (IEP) teams consider consistent with their needs and functioning levels (such as physical education,

Students with mental retardation can participate with their nondisabled peers in many school activities such as field trips.

focus

Why is the inclusion of students with mental retardation with their nondisabled peers important to an appropriate educational experience?

industrial arts, home economics). Other students with mental retardation may attend general education classes for all or the majority of the school day. For these students, special education consists primarily of services and supports intended to facilitate their opportunities and success in the general education classroom. Current placement information from the U.S. Department of Education (1997) indicates that in 1995–96, approximately 9.5% of students with mental retardation between the ages of 6 and 21 were placed in a regular classroom for the entire school day. Approximately 27% of students with mental retardation were served in general education classes with resource room support, and 56% attended separate classes in a general education school building.

Another placement option for students with disabilities is the special school. Special schools are defined as facilities exclusively for students with mental retardation or other disabilities. Approximately 5% of students with mental retardation attended public special schools in 1995–96, and another 1% attended private special schools.

Medical and Social Services

The diverse needs of people with mental retardation require the intervention of several professionals. Because most individuals with moderate to profound mental retardation exhibit problems evident at birth, a physician is usually the first professional to come in contact with these children.

focus 11

Identify the roles of medicine and social services in meeting the diverse needs of people with mental retardation.

The physician's primary roles are as diagnostician, counselor, and caregiver. As a diagnostician, the physician analyzes the nature and cause of the child's condition and then, based on the medical information available, counsels the family concerning the medical prognosis. The physician's role as a family counselor has been challenged by some professionals in the behavioral sciences and by parents because such counseling often exceeds the medical domain. This concern reflects the opinion that medical personnel should counsel families only on medical matters and recommend other resources—educators, psychologists, social workers, clergy, or parent groups—when dealing with issues other than the child's medical needs.

The appropriate social services for a person with mental retardation extend into many realms of life: the primary family, the extended family, the neighborhood, the educational environment, and the community at large. Thus appropriate social services may be classified into five general categories: family support services, community support services, supported living arrangements, leisure-time services, and employment services. Figure 8.2 illustrates some of the supports included within each of these general categories.

Social services provide individuals with mental retardation a greater opportunity to achieve what is commonly referred to as normalization. The principle of **normalization** emphasizes the need to make available to the individual "the patterns and conditions of everyday life which are as close to the norms and patterns of mainstream society" as possible (Nirje, 1970, p. 181). Normalization goes far beyond the mere physical inclusion of the individual into a community. In addition, it promotes the availability of needed supports, such as training and supervision, without which the individual with mental retardation may not be prepared to cope with the demands of community life.

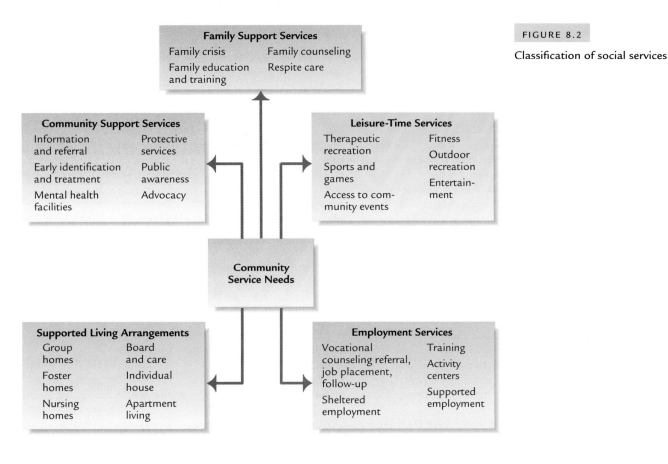

FIGURE 8.2

Classification of social services

Family Support Services

Family crisis   Family counseling

Family education   Respite care
and training

Community Support Services

Information   Protective
and referral   services

Early identification   Public
and treatment   awareness

Mental health   Advocacy
facilities

Leisure-Time Services

Therapeutic   Fitness
recreation
    Outdoor
Sports and   recreation
games
    Entertain-
Access to com-   ment
munity events

**Community
Service Needs**

Supported Living Arrangements

Group   Board
homes   and care

Foster   Individual
homes   house

Nursing   Apartment
homes   living

Employment Services

Vocational   Training
counseling referral,
job placement,   Activity
follow-up   centers

Sheltered   Supported
employment   employment

Case Study

LARA

Lara Clark has two jobs, which is quite an achievement for someone who, according to the records, couldn't walk or talk until age 12. Today, at age 51, Lara works at a medical center and at the local sheltered workshop. She also volunteers at the public library. Her days are full, which as she says, "Is better than doin' nothin'. Nothing is what I used to do." It is hard to imagine how this situation came about until you begin to examine her history.

In a world full of records and files, details about her past are hard to find. From her records, it appears that she lived at home until she was 22 years old, at which time her mother died and Lara was placed in an institution. In 1966, at age 30, Lara went to live in a community care home, where she remained for 11 years even though rumors of physical abuse surrounded the home. After moving to yet another group home, she moved to a rural community where Lara now lives with Carrie and Bob Hanson, their 2-year-old daughter, and two other women with disabilities.

Lara talks about the things she did when she lived with her mother and about her new job and her new friends. She doesn't mention the time that has elapsed between living with her mother and her current life.

Her life of "doin' nothin'" has changed to one bustling from place to place. On Mondays and Tuesdays she goes to the sheltered workshop. On Wednesdays and Fridays she works at the medical center where she places stickers on EKG equipment. On Thursdays she volunteers at the public library where she cleans and stacks books:

I like what I do at the library and the hospital. It's more serious than the workshop. I also like being home most afternoons by 1:30 p.m. I take a nap or work on my afghan.

Although it is hard work, she likes working at the medical center. Her only complaint concerns the times when she worked half-days "because I got home too early." She's happy that she has made friends outside the workshop. However, as suggested by Lara, "The best part of my job at the hospital is that I get paid."

Lara's social activities have also increased since she began work at the medical center. She now goes out to eat with her boyfriend and other friends. She is able to buy her own yarn for her afghans. "Shopping for clothes" is one of the most important benefits of the money, she says.

If the staff at the workshop and the medical center have anything to say about it, Lara's time and pocketbook may fill up even more. Plans are being made for Lara to work five days a week at the medical center instead of splitting her time between the two employment sites.

Working has provided Lara with activities that keep her life busy. However, it would appear that the most important byproduct of her experiences is a change of attitude. Carrie Hanson thinks that the job has provided Lara an independence that she didn't have before:

Lara feels rewarded by what she does at the hospital. She feels she is doing something worthwhile, and getting paid for it. As a result she pays more attention to having money and works harder to get it.

Whether it was the new job, the increased income, or her friends, it is evident to those that meet her that Lara Clark is proud of the work she does, the friends she has, and the life she leads. She no longer thinks she's "doin' nothin'."

■ **APPLICATION**
In the past few years, Lara has been moving from a sheltered workshop to more paid work in a community setting. Brainstorm and list some of the ongoing support that Lara will need as she makes the transition to full-time integrated employment.

Beyond monetary rewards, what are some other benefits that will exist for Lara as a result of her job at the medical center?

Lara is 51 years old. How might life have been different for her had she been born 30 years later?

Source: Adapted from *Stories of Work,* by B. Guy, J. Scott, S. Hasazi, and A. Patten, (n.d.), (unpublished manuscript), Burlington: University of Vermont.

Debate Forum

CAN SPECIAL SCHOOLS FOR STUDENTS WITH MENTAL RETARDATION BE JUSTIFIED?

■ **POINT**
There will always be a need for a special school. Although inclusion may be appropriate for many students with mental retardation, special schools are the least restrictive environment for a small number of children who require intensive instruction and support that cannot be provided in a general education school or classroom. Special schools provide for greater homogeneity in grouping and programming. Teachers can specialize in particular areas such as art, language, physical education, and music. Teaching materials can be centralized and, thus, used more effectively with larger numbers of students. A special school more efficiently uses

available resources. In addition, some parents of students with severe mental retardation believe that their children will be happier in a special school that "protects" them.

■ **COUNTERPOINT**
Research on the efficacy of special schools does not support the contention that such a placement is ever the least restrictive environment (Gee, 1996; Halvorsen & Sailor, 1990; McDonnell et al., 1995; Stainback, Stainback, & Ayres, 1996). On the contrary, investigations over the past 10 years have strongly indicated that students with mental retardation, regardless of the severity of their condition, benefit from placement in general educa-

tion environments where opportunities for interaction with students who are not disabled are systematically planned and implemented (Brimer, 1990; Halvorsen & Sailor, 1990; Hunt, Staub, Alwell, & Goetz, 1994; Meyer, Peck, & Brown, 1991). As stated by Halvorsen and Sailor, "The overwhelming majority of research studies conducted over the past 10 years provides clear support for integrated, less restrictive environments" (1990, p. 152). Inclusion for students with mental retardation embodies a variety of opportunities, both within the general education classroom and throughout the school. Besides interaction in a classroom setting, ongoing inclusion may be found in the

halls, on the playground, in the cafeteria, and at school assemblies.

Stainback et al. (1996) also reported that general education teachers who have the opportunity for interaction with children with mental retardation are not fearful of or intimidated by their presence in the school building. Special schools generally offer little, if any, opportunity for interaction with normal peers and deprive the child of valuable learning and socialization experiences. Special schools cannot be financially or ideologically justified. Public school administrators must now plan to include children with retardation in existing general education schools and classes.

Review

focus 1

Identify the three components of the AAMR definition of mental retardation.

■ Significantly subaverage intellectual functioning is de-

fined as two standard deviations below the mean on an individual test of intelligence.

■ Adaptive skill limitations may occur in communication, self-care, home living, social skills, community use, self-direction, health and safety, functional academics, leisure, and work.

■ The condition is manifested before 18 years of age.

focus 2

Identify four approaches to classifying people with mental retardation.

■ Severity of the condition may

be described in terms of mild, moderate, severe, and profound mental retardation.

■ Educability expectations are designated for groups of children who are educable, trainable, and custodial.

■ Medical descriptors classify mental retardation on the basis of the origin of the condition (e.g., infection, intoxication, trauma, chromosomal abnormality).

- Classification based on the type and extent of support needed categorize people with mental retardation according to intermittent, limited, extensive, or pervasive needs for support in order to function in natural settings.

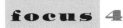

focus 3

Identify four intellectual and adaptive skills characteristics of individuals with mental retardation.

- Intellectual characteristics may include learning and memory deficiencies, difficulties in establishing learning sets, and inefficient rehearsal strategies.
- Adaptive skills characteristics may include difficulties in coping with the demands of school, developing interpersonal relationships, developing language skills, and taking care of personal needs.

focus 4

Identify the academic, motivational, speech and language, and physical characteristics of children with mental retardation.

- Students with mental retardation exhibit significant deficits in the areas of reading and mathematics.
- School-age students with mild mental retardation have poor reading mechanics and comprehension,

compared to their same-age peers.

- Motivational difficulties may reflect learned helplessness—"No matter what I do or how hard I try, I will not succeed."
- The most common speech difficulties involve articulation problems, voice problems, and stuttering.
- Language differences are generally associated with delays in language development rather than the bizarre use of language.
- Physical differences generally are not evident for individuals with mild mental retardation because the retardation is usually not associated with genetic factors.
- The more severe the mental retardation, the greater the probability of genetic causation and compounding physiological problems.

focus 5

Identify the causes of mental retardation.

- The cause of mental retardation is generally not known for the individual who is mildly retarded.
- Causes associated with moderate to profound mental retardation include sociocultural influences, biomedical factors, behavioral factors, and unknown prenatal influences.

focus 6

Identify four measures that may prevent mental retardation.

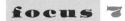

- Immunizations against disease
- Appropriate nutrition for the mother during pregnancy
- Appropriate prenatal care
- Screening for genetic disorders at birth

focus 7

Why is the need for early intervention services for children with mental retardation so crucial?

- Early intervention services are needed to provide a stimulating environment for the child to enhance growth and development.
- Early intervention programs focus on the development of communication skills, social interaction, and readiness for formal instruction.

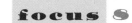

focus 8

Identify five skill areas that should be addressed in programs for elementary-age children with mental retardation.

- Motor development skills
- Self-care skills
- Social skills
- Communication skills
- Functional academic skills

focus 9

Identify four educational goals for adolescents with mental retardation.

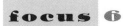

- To increase the individual's personal independence
- To enhance opportunities for participation in the local community

- To prepare for employment
- To facilitate a successful transition to the adult years

focus 10

Why is the inclusion of students with mental retardation with their nondisabled peers important to an appropriate educational experience?

- Regardless of the severity of their condition, students with mental retardation benefit from placement in general education environments where opportunities for inclusion with nondisabled peers are systematically planned and implemented.

focus 11

Identify the roles of medicine and social services in meeting the diverse needs of people with mental retardation.

- The physician's roles include diagnostician, counselor, and caregiver.
- Appropriate social services include community support services, family support services, alternative living arrangements, employment services, and leisure-time services.

People with Communication Disorders

To begin with . . .

 Twenty percent of the children (6–21 years old) with disabilities who were served under federal law during 1995–96 had speech or language impairments. (U.S. Department of Education, 1997)

Language is crucial to all social and educational functioning. Parents are most concerned that their children acquire language because they recognize that a language deficiency may have a serious effect on future educational, social, and vocational opportunities. (Bernstein, 1997, p. 4)

 Using advanced technology it is possible to measure the electrical activity of the brain and see that people process visual, phonological, and grammatical information about words separately. (Azar, 1994)

It is what [the philosopher] Wittgenstein meant when, in referring to our most fundamental technology, he said that language is not merely a vehicle of thought but also the driver. (Postman, 1993, p. 14)

293

Meghan

Meghan is 12 years old. She is a respected member of her sixth-grade class in a school that has become a powerful inclusive community for her. People are drawn to Meghan because of her courage, humor, and her belief in living for her dreams.

Meghan has a strong circle of friends who pay attention to who she is as a person and know how to be with her and share in many different mutual experiences. Meghan enjoys skiing, playing tennis, swimming, music, and movies. Meghan's friends call her on the phone and talk to her—even if she chooses only to listen. If they could just see her smile over the telephone! She goes to birthday parties and has slumber parties. Her friends have given her the opportunity to be a typical sixth-grader.

When Meghan was born, we knew she had cerebral palsy. We saw that she had a projected motor delay and cognitive delay, but how much was uncertain. As parents, we wanted a language-based environment, not a life skills environment for Meghan. We wanted her to have a childhood in which her strengths were recognized, and her hopes for learning encouraged. Meghan may never tell us on demand the 26 letters of the alphabet, a readiness requirement in the developmental center program, but she was able to return to an inclusive fourth-grade community, where she learned the history of California. She knew the people who built the railroad and could tell us this through an adapted curriculum and picture cues, and she was accurate.

Meghan is apraxic. It is hard for her to come up with words—it is hard for her to retrieve them and it is hard for her to summon the motor skills to utter them. But she is driven to talk and to get her messages out. We use many forms of communication with her: verbal modeling, singing because it builds vocabulary (music uses another part of the brain), sign language for a visual way to focus, and a DynaVox. The DynaVox is touch-activated and creates verbal speech. We can program information on its screen to increase practical language skills as well as link up with the curriculum she is being taught in school. Meghan just completed an oral presentation on the Alaskan oil spill. We created a page on the DynaVox with picture cues that had verbal messages sequencing the key topics of her report.

One of Meghan's friends helped her program, "I'm having a bad hair day," into her DynaVox diary. She uses sassy sixth-grade language now, and we think of it as an increase in language skills. We can be the great Mom, Dad, teachers in her life, but it is her peers who are the most valuable resources for they see Meghan as a person first and her disability second. They will make the difference in her tomorrows for they pay attention to what they have in common and not what makes them different.

focus 1
Identify four ways in which speech, language, and communication are interrelated.

We communicate with others many times each day: to order food in a restaurant, thank a friend for doing a favor, ask a question in class, call for help in an emergency, follow instructions regarding the assembly of a gift received by mail, or give directions to someone who is lost. Communication is central to our lives. Although it is one of the most complicated and vital processes people undertake, we seldom think much about communication unless there is a problem.

Speech and language are two highly interrelated components of communication. Problems in either can significantly affect a person's daily life. Because of their complexity, determining the cause of a problem is often perplexing.

Communication is the exchange of ideas, opinions, or facts between senders and receivers. It requires that a sender (an individual or group) compose and transmit a message and that a receiver decode and understand the message (Bernstein,

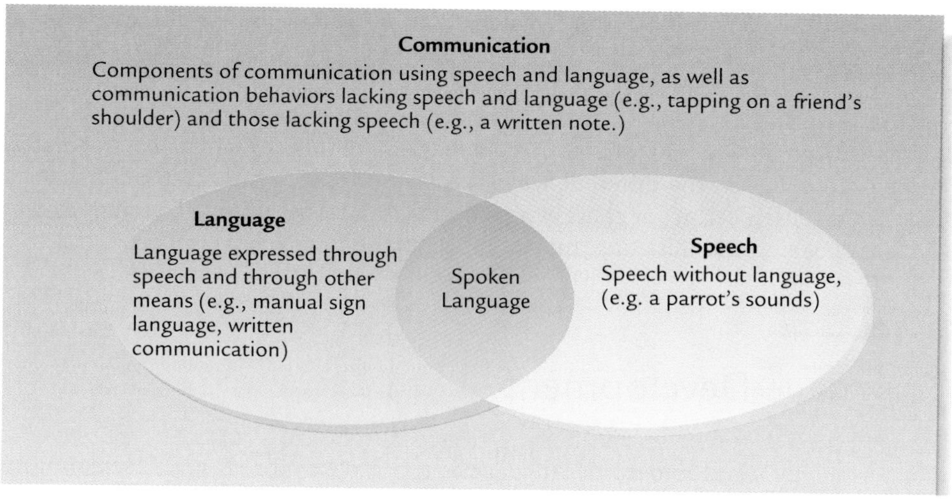

Communication
Components of communication using speech and language, as well as communication behaviors lacking speech and language (e.g., tapping on a friend's shoulder) and those lacking speech (e.g., a written note.)

Language
Language expressed through speech and through other means (e.g., manual sign language, written communication)

Spoken Language

Speech
Speech without language, (e.g. a parrot's sounds)

FIGURE 9.1

A conceptual model of communication, language, and speech

1997a). In this manner, the sender and receiver are partners in the communication process. Communication is an extremely important tool that we use to interact with our environment. Part of this tool involves the use of speech and language.

Although related, speech and language are not synonymous. **Speech** is the audible representation of language. It is one means of expressing language but not the only means. **Language** represents the message contained in speech. It is possible to have language without speech, such as sign language used by people who are deaf, and speech without language, which is uttered by birds that are trained to talk. Communication is the broadest concept. Language is a part of communication. Speech is often thought of as a part of language, although language may exist without speech. Figure 9.1 illustrates the interrelationship of speech, language, and communication.

The Structure of Language

Language consists of several major components including phonology, syntax, morphology, semantics, and pragmatics. **Phonology** refers to the system of speech sounds that an individual utters, that is, rules regarding how sounds can be used and combined. For example, the word *cat* has three phonemes—*C, A, T.* **Syntax** involves the rules governing sentence structure, the way sequences of words are combined into phrases and sentences (Silverman, 1995). For example, the sentence *Will you help Linda?* changes in meaning when the order of words is changed to *You will help Linda.* **Morphology** is concerned with the form and internal structure of words, that is, the transformations of words in terms of such areas as tense and number—such as present to past tense, singular to plural. When we add an *-s* to *cat,* we have produced the plural form, *cats,* consisting of two morphemes, or meaning units—the concept of cat and the concept of plural. Such transformations involve prefixes, suffixes, and inflections. Grammar combines syntax and morphology. **Semantics** represents the understanding of language, the component most concerned with meaning. Semantics addresses whether the "meanings of the words and their combinations convey the speaker's message in a manner appropriate for someone of his or her age" (Silverman, 1995, p. 109). It involves the meaning of a word to an individual, which may be unique in each of our personal "mental dictionaries" (e.g., the meaning of the adjective *nice* in the phrase "nice house").

Pragmatics is a component of language that has received increased attention in recent literature. It is concerned with "the rules that govern the reason(s) for communicating (called communicative functions or intentions) as well as the rules that govern the choice of codes to be used when communicating" (Bernstein, 1997a, p. 9). Basically, pragmatics represents the rules governing the use of language. Pragmatics can be exemplified in the different ways a professor talks when lecturing, makes a point in a faculty meeting, or chats at a party. Pragmatics includes such things as taking turns speaking and initiating, maintaining, and ending a conversation.

Language Development

The development of language is a complex process and fascinating to observe, as parents of infants know well. Young children normally advance through several stages in acquiring language, from a preverbal stage to being able to use words in sentences. A baby's initial verbal communication is primarily limited to crying, which is usually associated with discomfort (e.g., from hunger, pain, or being soiled or wet). Before long (at around 2 months), babies begin to coo as well as cry, verbally expressing reactions to pleasure as well as discomfort. They begin to babble at about 3 to 6 months of age, which involves making some consonant and vowel sounds. At this point, babies often make sounds repeatedly when they are alone, seemingly experimenting with making sounds and not necessarily trying to communicate with anyone. They may also babble when their parents or others are with them, playing or otherwise handling them.

A baby's first word is a momentous, long-anticipated event. In fact, eager parents often attach words to sounds that stretch the imagination of more objective observers and likely have no meaning to the child. Usually the baby begins to string together sounds that occasionally resemble words. To the parents' delight, these sounds frequently include utterances such as "Da-Da" and "Ma-Ma" which, of course, are echoed, repeated, and reinforced greatly by Father and Mother. As the baby actually begins to listen to the speech of adults, exchanges or "conversations" seem to occur, in which the youngster responds by saying "Da-Da" after a parent says it. Although this type of interchange sounds like a conversation, the child's vocal productions may be understood only by those close to him or her (e.g., parents or siblings); people other than immediate family members may not be able to interpret meaning at all. The baby also begins to use different tones and vocal intensity, which makes the vocalization vaguely resemble adult speech. The interactions between babies and their parents can do much to enhance their developing language at this time. Parents often provide a great deal of reinforcement for word approximations, such as praise given in excited tones or hugs. They also provide stimulus sounds and words for the baby to mimic, giving the youngster considerable directed practice.

Within a broad range of 4 to 8 years of age, children with normal language development can correctly articulate most speech sounds in context.

The timing of a baby's actual first word production is open to interpretation although it usually happens between 9 and 14 months. These words often involve echoing (repeating what has been heard) or mimicking, based on verbalizations by those around him or her. At first the words may have little or no meaning, although they soon become attached to people or objects in the child's immediate environment, such as Daddy, Mommy, or milk. Before long these words begin to have more perceptible intent, as the child uses them for requests and an apparent means of pleasing parents. Strings of two and three words that resemble sentences typically begin between 18 and 24 months. At this stage, the meaning of the communication is usually clear, and the child can clearly indicate that he or she wants something. The child uses fairly accurate syntax, usually with the word order subject–verb–object.

Most children with normally developing language are able to use all the basic syntactical structures by 3 to 4 years of age. By 5 years, they have progressed to using six-word sentences, on the average. A child with normal language development articulates nearly all speech sounds correctly and in context somewhere between 4 and 8 years of age. These illustrations are couched in terms of when children produce language, that is, expressive language development. Observations suggest that children develop receptive skills before developing expressive skills. In other words, they are able to understand a great deal more than they can express. Silverman (1995) indicated that most children show some understanding of language as early as 6 to 9 months, often responding first to commands such as "no-no" and to their names.

As we outlined the process of normal language development, variable age ranges were noted for each milestone, some of them rather broad. Several factors contribute to this variability. For one thing, children vary considerably in their rates of development, even those considered normal. Some differences are due to general health and vitality, others are due to inheritance, and still others relate to environmental influences, such as the amount and type of interaction with parents and siblings (Hancock & Kaiser, 1996; Plumert & Nichols-Whitehead, 1996). Note also that age ranges broaden at stages of more advanced development (e.g., 3 to 6 months for babbling; 18 to 24 months for two- and three-word strings), partially because advanced developmental events occur across a wider range of time than earlier stages do. These advanced developments are also more complex, some involving subtleties that are not as blatantly obvious as, say, the first "Da-Da." Thus they may be more difficult to discern, and observation of when they first occur is perhaps less accurate. Table 9.1 on page 298 summarizes general milestones of normal language and prelanguage development.

We will also see considerable variability in abnormal language and speaking ability. In some cases, factors contributing to variability in normal language are also considered to be disorders if they result in extreme performance deviations. We will also find that definitions of speech and language difficulties vary, as do the unique way that such problems are manifested in different individuals.

Language Disorders

Over the course of human history, language has taken many forms. Some early Native Americans communicated using systems of clucking or clicking sounds made with the tongue and teeth. Such sounds were also used in combination with hand signs and spoken language that

TABLE 9.1	Normal language and prelanguage development
AGE	**BEHAVIOR**
Birth	Crying and making other physiological sounds
1 to 2 months	Cooing as well as crying
3 to 6 months	Babbling as well as cooing
9 to 14 months	Speaking first words as well as babbling
18 to 24 months	Speaking first sentences as well as words
3 to 4 years	Using all basic syntactical structures
4 to 8 years	Articulating correctly all speech sounds in context

Source: Mental Retardation: A Life Cycle Approach, 6/E. Drew/Hardman/Logan, © 1996. Reprinted by permission of Prentice-Hall, Inc., Upper Saddle River, NJ.

often differed greatly between tribes. These language systems have been described extensively in a variety of historical documents.

Current definitions of language are broad enough to account for very diverse communication systems. For the most part, these definitions refer to the systems of rules and symbols people use to communicate, including matters of phonology, syntax, morphology, and semantics. Considerable attention is given to meaning and understanding in definitions of language. For example, Bernstein (1997a) defined language as encompassing the "complex rules that govern sounds, words, sentences, meaning, and use. These rules underlie an individual's ability to understand language (language comprehension) and his or her ability to formulate language (language production)" (p. 6).

Speech disorders include problems related to verbal production, that is, vocal expression. Language disorders represent serious difficulties in the ability to understand or express ideas in the communication system being used. The distinction between speech and language disorders is like the difference between the sound of a word and the meaning of a word. As we examine language disorders, we will discuss difficulties in meaning, both in expressing it and receiving it. Table 9.2 lists a number of behaviors that might emerge for a child with a language disorder.

■ DEFINITION

Language disorders occur when there is a serious disruption of the language acquisition process, an irregular development involving comprehension (understanding) or expression that may pertain to written or spoken language (Bernstein, 1997a; Kolk, 1995). Such malfunctions may occur in one or more of the components of language. Because language use is one of the most complex sets of behaviors exhibited by humans, language disorders are complex and present perplexing assessment problems. Language involves memory, learning, message reception and processing, and expressive skills. An individual with a language disorder may have deficits in any of these areas, and it may be difficult to identify the exact nature of the problem. In addition, language problems may arise in the form of language delays or language disorders.

Language delay occurs when the normal rate of development is interrupted, but the systematic sequence of development remains essentially intact. For young-

focus 2

Identify two ways in which language delay and language disorder are different.

TABLE 9.2   Behaviors resulting in teacher referral of children with possible language impairments

The following behaviors may indicate that a child in your classroom has a language impairment that is in need of clinical intervention. Please check the appropriate items.

_____ Child mispronounces sounds and words.

_____ Child omits word endings, such as plural *-s* and past tense *-ed*.

_____ Child omits small unemphasized words, such as auxiliary verbs or prepositions.

_____ Child uses an immature vocabulary, overuses empty words, such as *one* and *thing,* or seems to have difficulty recalling or finding the right word.

_____ Child has difficulty comprehending new words and concepts.

_____ Child's sentence structure seems immature or overreliant on forms, such as subject–verb–object. It's unoriginal, dull.

_____ Child's question and/or negative sentence style is immature.

_____ Child has difficulty with one of the following:

_____ Verb tensing	_____ Articles	_____ Auxiliary verbs
_____ Pronouns	_____ Irreg. verbs	_____ Prepositions
_____ Word order	_____ Irreg. plurals	_____ Conjunctions

_____ Child has difficulty relating sequential events.

_____ Child has difficulty following directions.

_____ Child's questions often inaccurate or vague.

_____ Child's questions often poorly formed.

_____ Child has difficulty answering questions.

_____ Child's comments often off topic or inappropriate for the conversation.

_____ There are long pauses between a remark and the child's reply or between successive remarks by the child. It's as if the child is searching for a response or is confused.

_____ Child appears to be attending to communication but remembers little of what is said.

_____ Child has difficulty using language socially for the following purposes:

_____ Request needs	_____ Pretend/imagine	_____ Protest
_____ Greet	_____ Request information	_____ Gain attention
_____ Respond/reply	_____ Share ideas, feelings	_____ Clarify
_____ Relate events	_____ Entertain	_____ Reason

_____ Child has difficulty interpreting the following:

_____ Figurative language	_____ Humor	_____ Gestures
	_____ Emotions	_____ Body language

_____ Child does not alter production for different audiences and locations.

_____ Child does not seem to consider the effect of language on the listener.

_____ Child often has verbal misunderstandings with others.

_____ Child has difficulty with reading and writing.

_____ Child's language skills seem to be much lower than other areas, such as mechanical, artistic, or social skills.

Source: From R. E. Owens, *Language Disorders: A Functional Approach to Assessment and Intervention* (2nd ed., p. 392). Copyright 1995. All rights reserved. Reprinted by permission of Allyn and Bacon.

sters with a language delay, development follows a normal pattern or course of growth but is substantially slower than in most children of the same age; in other words, they use the language rules typical of a younger child. The term *language disorder* refers to circumstances in which language acquisition is not systematic or sequential; a child with language disorders is not progressing in a sequential acquisition of rule-governed linguistic behavior (Nelson, 1993). We will use the term *language disorder* in a general sense to discuss several types of behaviors. Where evidence suggests that delay may be a major contributor, we will discuss it as such.

■ CLASSIFICATION

Terminology varies widely for both language processes in general and the disorders in those processes. In many cases, language disorders are classified according to their causes, which may be known or only suspected. In other cases, specific labels tend to be employed, such as aphasia. There is some uncertainty in the literature regarding classification of language disorders, although one approach views them in terms of receptive and expressive problems (Silverman, 1995). Here we examine both of these categories as well as aphasia, a problem that may occur in both children and adults.

■ RECEPTIVE LANGUAGE DISORDERS Persons with **receptive language disorders** have difficulty in comprehending what others say. In many cases, receptive language problems in children are noticed when they do not follow an adult's instructions. These children may seem inattentive, as though they do not listen to directions, or they may be very slow to respond (Kuder, 1997). Individuals with receptive language disorders have great difficulty understanding other people's messages and may process only part (or none) of what is being said to them (Silverman, 1995). They have a problem in language processing, which is basically half of the function of language (the other half is language production). Language processing consists of listening to and interpreting spoken language.

Some of this behavior relates to the discussion of learning disabilities in Chapter 6. It is not uncommon for receptive language problems to appear in students with learning disabilities. Such language deficits contribute significantly to academic performance problems and difficulties in social interactions for these students (Lerner, 1997: Smith, Dowdy, Polloway, & Blalock, 1997).

■ EXPRESSIVE LANGUAGE DISORDERS Individuals with **expressive language disorders** have difficulty in language production or formulating and using spoken or written language (Silverman, 1995). Those with expressive language disorders may have limited vocabularies and may use the same array of words, regardless of the situation. Expressive language disorders may appear as immature speech, often resulting in interaction difficulties (Kuder, 1997). People with expressive disorders also use hand signals and facial expressions to communicate.

■ APHASIA Definitions of aphasia have varied over time but still employ strikingly consistent themes. Aphasia refers to a loss of the ability to speak or to comprehend language due to an injury or developmental abnormality in the brain. According to Nelson (1993), aphasia is a language disorder resulting from the effects of brain lesion and marked by impairment of language comprehension, formulation, and use. Thus, definitions of aphasia commonly link the disorder to brain injury brought about by a physical accident or other damage, such as that caused by a stroke. Over the years, many types of aphasia and conditions associated with aphasia have been identified and labeled, such as paraphrasia (marked by disorderly arrangement of spoken words) and dysprosody (a disturbance of stress, pitch, and rhythm of speech). Aphasic language disturbances have also been classified in terms of receptive and expressive problems.

Aphasia may be found both during childhood and the adult years. The term *developmental aphasia* has been widely used in reference to affected children, despite the long-standing association of such problems with neurological damage. Children with aphasia often begin to use words at age 2 or later, and phrases at age 4. The link between aphasia and neurological abnormalities in children has been of continuing interest to researchers, and some evidence has suggested a connection. Despite theories and assumptions, in many cases of aphasia in children, objective evidence of neurological dysfunction has been difficult to acquire.

Adult aphasia typically can be linked to accidents or injuries likely to occur during this part of the lifespan, such as gunshot wounds, motorcycle or auto accidents, and strokes. Some researchers studying this group coined the term *acquired language disorder* to describe aphasia, since it accurately reflects onset of the condition due to injury. Current research suggests that varying symptoms result from damage to different parts of the brain (Kempler, Andersen, & Henderson, 1995; LeDorze & Brassard, 1995). Those with injury to the front part of the brain often can comprehend better than they can speak; they also have considerable difficulty finding words, poor articulation resulting in slow, labored speech, a tendency to omit small words such as *of* and *the*, and generally reduced verbal production. Individuals with aphasia resulting from injury to the posterior (back part) of the brain seem to have more fluent speech, but expressing content is a problem. Speech may also be characterized by use of an unnecessarily large number of words to express an idea or use of unusual or meaningless terms. The speech of these individuals appears to reflect impaired comprehension.

■ CAUSATION

Accurately determining the causes of different language disorders can be difficult. We certainly do not have precise answers regarding what contributes to normal language acquisition, exactly how those contributions occur, and how malfunctions influence language disorders. We do know that certain sensory and other physiological systems must be intact and developing normally if language processes are to develop normally. For example, if hearing is seriously impaired, a language deficit may result (Lonigan, Fischel, Whitehurst, & Arnold, 1992; Radziewicz & Antonellis, 1997). Likewise, serious brain damage might deter normal language functioning. Learning must also progress in a systematic, sequential fashion for language to develop appropriately. For example, children must attend to communication before they can mimic it or build meaning from it. Language learning is like other learning: It must be stimulated and reinforced to be acquired and mastered (Bernstein, 1997b).

In discussing other disabilities, we have encountered many of the physiological problems that may also cause language difficulties. Neurological damage that may affect language functioning can occur prenatally, during birth, or anytime throughout life. For example, oxygen deprivation before or during birth or an accident later in life can cause language problems (e.g., Silverman, 1995). Serious emotional disorders may be accompanied by language disturbances if an individual's perception of the world is substantially distorted (Anand & Wales, 1994; Ward-Lonergan, Liles, & Owen, 1996).

Language disorders may result if learning opportunities are seriously deficient or disrupted. As with speech, children may not learn language if the environment is not conducive to such learning. Modeling in the home may be so infrequent that a

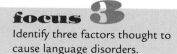

focus 3

Identify three factors thought to cause language disorders.

child cannot learn language in a normal fashion. This might be the case for a family in which no speaking occurs because the parents are deaf, even when the children have normal hearing. Such circumstances are rare, but when they do occur, a language delay is likely. The parents cannot model language for their children, nor can they respond to and reinforce such behavior.

It is important to remember that learning outcomes vary a great deal and are sometimes difficult to explain. In situations that seem normal, we may find a child with serious language difficulty. In circumstances that seem dismal, we may find a child whose language facility is normal. The nearby snapshot presents an example involving four brothers with normal hearing who were born to and raised by parents who were both deaf and had no spoken language facility. The boys seemed to develop language quite normally, although they could not explain that development. Their impressive accomplishments include earning Ph.D's and M.D's (one holds both degrees) and becoming a millionaire through patenting inventions. This illustration represents a rare set of circumstances, but it clearly shows how variable and poorly understood language learning is.

It has long been assumed that language-deprived environments place children at risk for exhibiting language delays or disorders. For example, it has been thought that language acquisition may be delayed when parents use baby talk in communicating with their young children. This view is based on a fundamental principle of learning theory: Children learn what is modeled for and taught to them. There is little question that this tenet is sound, concerning most skill acquisition. Many clinical reports of language problems uphold this notion, and research has also supported certain relationships between parental verbalizations and child language development (Dale, Crain-Thoreson, Notari-Syverson, & Cole 1996; Weiss, 1997). But although some questions have been raised regarding the presumed effects of baby talk, the general influence of parent modeling on child language development is positive.

Typically, brain damage is associated with aphasia that begins during adulthood. The causes of such brain damage are diverse, including physical traumas such as automobile and industrial accidents or shooting incidents. Other factors (e.g., strokes,

Snapshot

Cy

■ **LANGUAGE DIFFERENCES: WE DIDN'T KNOW THEY WERE DIFFERENT**

My name is Cy, and I am one of the four brothers mentioned. Both of my parents were deaf from a very early age; they never learned to speak. When you ask me how we learned speech, I can't really answer, knowing what I now know about how those very early years are so impor-

tant in this area. When we were really young, we didn't even know they were deaf or different (except for Dad's active sense of humor). Naturally, we didn't talk; we just signed. We lived way out in the country and didn't have other playmates. Grandma and Grandpa lived close by, and I spent a lot of time with them. That is when I began to know something was different. We probably began learning to talk there.

When we were about ready to start school, we moved

into town. My first memory related to school is sitting in a sandbox, I guess on the playground. We had some troubles in school, but they were fairly minor as I recall. I couldn't talk or pronounce words very well. I was tested on an IQ test in the third grade and had an IQ of 67. Both Mom and Dad worked, and so we were all sort of out on our own with friends, which probably helped language, but now I wonder why those kids didn't stay away from us because we were a bit different.

Probably the saving grace is that all four of us seem to have pretty well-developed social intelligence or skills. We did get in some fights with kids, and people sometimes called us the "dummy's kids." I would guess that all four of us pretty much caught up with our peers by the eighth grade. One thing is for certain: I would not trade those parents for any other in the world. Whatever they did, they certainly did right.

Cy, Ph.D.

tumors, and diseases) that affect brain tissue may have the same result. In most cases, aphasic trauma seems to be associated with damage to the left hemisphere of the brain.

Distinctions between speech problems and language problems are blurred because they overlap as much as the functions of speech and language overlap. Thus, receptive and expressive language disorders are as intertwined as speech and language themselves. When an individual does not express language well, does he or she have a receptive problem or an expressive problem? These disorders cannot be clearly separated, nor can causation be definitively categorized.

focus 4

Describe two ways in which treatment approaches for language disorders generally differ for children and for adults.

■ INTERVENTION

Any treatment for a language disorder must take into account the nature of the problem and the manner in which an individual is affected. It is also important to consider cultural and linguistic background as an intervention is being planned (de-Montfort-Supple, 1996). Intervention is an individualized undertaking, just as it is for other disorders (Robinson & Robb, 1997; Silverman, 1995). Some causes are rather easily identified and may or may not be remedied by mechanical or medical intervention. Other types of treatment basically involve instruction, or language training.

This student uses a computer that prints in large type that he can easily read. An individual using a computer to communicate probably has a severe physical or cognitive disability that affects communication.

■ INDIVIDUALIZED LANGUAGE PLANS A number of steps are involved in effective language training, including identification, assessment, development of instructional objectives, development of language intervention program, implementation of the intervention program, reassessment of the child, and reteaching, if necessary (Nelson, 1997). These steps are similar to the general stages of special education interventions for other disorders. Thus, the customary approach to language disorder intervention follows the basic steps for treatment, as outlined in IDEA. Specific programs of intervention may involve other activities aimed at individualized intervention (e.g., see Robinson & Robb, 1997).

Programs of language training are tailored to an individual's strengths and limitations. In fact, current terminology labels these individualized language plans (ILPs), similar in concept to the individualized education plans (IEPs) mandated by IDEA. These intervention plans include long-range goals (annual), more short-range and specific behavioral objectives, a statement of the resources to be used in achieving the objectives, a description of evaluation methods, program beginning and ending dates, and an evaluation of the individual's generalization of skills. For young children, interventions often focus on beginning language stimulation. Treatment is intended to mirror the conditions under which children normally learn language, but the conditions may be intensified and taught more systematically. In many cases, parents are trained and involved in the intervention (Eiserman, Weber, & McCoun, 1995; Nelson, 1997; Weiss, 1997).

Many different approaches have been used to remediate aphasia, although consistent and verifiable results have been slow to emerge. Intervention typically involves the development of an individual's profile of strengths, limitations, age, and developmental level, as well as considerations regarding temperament that may affect therapy (Prasad, Sitholey, Dutt, & Srivastava, 1992; Weiss, 1997). From such a profile, an individualized treatment plan can be designed. Several questions immediately surface, including what to teach or remediate first and whether teaching should focus on an individual's strong or weak areas. These questions have been raised from time to time with respect to many disorders. Nearly all clinicians have their own opinions and favored methods for creating a balanced program. Teaching exclusively to a child's weak areas may result in too many failure experiences, which may undermine progress—the child receives so little success and reinforcement that he or she becomes discouraged about the whole process. Good clinical judgment needs to be exercised in balancing remediation attention to the aphasic child's strengths and weaknesses. Intervention programs include collaboration with parents, other family members, and the professionals involved with the overall treatment of the youngster (Nelson, 1997; Weiss, 1997).

Treatment of adults who have acquired aphasia involves relearning or reacquiring language function. Views on treatment have varied over the years. Early approaches included the expectation that adult aphasics would exhibit spontaneous recovery. This approach has largely been replaced by the view that patients are more likely to progress if direct therapeutic instruction is implemented.

The nature of therapy for adults with aphasia has some predictable similarities to treatment for children. Areas of strength and limitation must receive attention during the planning of an individualized remediation program. However, this profile of strengths and deficits will include categories not generally present in such profiles of children. Adults typically need to make readjustment in social, linguistic, and vocational areas, and the notion of readjustment differs substantially from the initial skill acquisition that characterizes treatment for children. The planning of language learning treatment (relearning) for adults focuses on the individual's needs and the most practical methods of service delivery (Springer, Willmes, & Haag, 1993; Thompson, Shapiro, & Roberts, 1993). In some cases individuals with aphasia can be effectively treated in group settings, and in others individual therapy works well (Bollinger,

Today's Technology

AUGMENTATIVE COMMUNICATION AID

DynaVox is a voice-output communication aid that is activated by a touch screen, such as shown here. This technology is particularly exciting because the communication options can be designed and created by the therapist to meet the particular needs of an individual client. The touch screen changes, depending on the communication underway. For example, if the person selects *food* in a main display, the screen changes instantly to present a variety of choices related to food. DynaVox provides for voice output, with choices of 10 different voices (male, female, child) and even has the ability to customize a unique voice for the individual, should that be desirable.

Selections can be made in a number of fashions, such as touching with a finger or touchstick or using a joystick, such as that used with electronic games. This battery-operated device (rechargeable, with up to 14 hours of operation on a charge) represents one type of technology application being used for augmentative communication.

Musson, & Holland, 1993; Hough, 1993). Advances in technology are continually being integrated into treatment (Iacono & Duncum, 1995; Todman, Elder, & Alm, 1995), such as that illustrated in the Today's Technology feature on page 304.

An individualized treatment plan for adult aphasics also involves evaluation, profile development, and teaching and therapy in specific areas within each of the broad domains of language (Hough, 1993). Such training should begin as soon as possible, depending on the patient's condition. Some spontaneous recovery often occurs during the first 6 months after an incident resulting in aphasia (Silverman, 1995), but waiting beyond 2 months to begin treatment may not only be unnecessary, but also seriously delay recovery to whatever degree may be possible.

■ AUGMENTATIVE COMMUNICATION   Some individuals require intervention using means of communication other than oral language. In some cases, the person may be incapable of speaking because of a severe physical or cognitive disability and so will require that a nonspeech means of communication be designed and implemented. Known as **assistive, alternative,** or **augmentative communication,** these strategies may involve a wide variety of approaches, some employing new technological developments. Augmentative communication strategies have received increasing attention in the past few years. They are used to assist people with a variety of disabilities, including mental retardation, autism, and multiple disabilities; they often are employed by those with severe disability (Beukelman & Mirenda, 1992; Owens, 1997; Reichle, York, & Sigafoos, 1991). These strategies must also be individualized to meet specific needs and to fit a person's strengths and limitations. The person must be capable of operating the technology (McNaughton & Lindsay, 1995; Todman et al., 1995). Augmentative communication strategies are providing therapists with important new alternatives for intervention with individuals having language disorders. Research is increasing in this area and indicates considerable effectiveness when techniques and devices are carefully chosen to match an individual's capacities and preferences (e.g., Iacono & Duncum, 1995; Robinson & Owens, 1995).

Today's Technology

COMPUTERS: A LANGUAGE TUTORIAL PROGRAM

Computer technology has made inroads in many areas of human disability in the past few years and will become increasingly important in the future. Language disability intervention is one area where technology is being used with increasing frequency. Advances in both hardware and software have had an impact on language training and have substantial potential for future development.

First Words is a language tutorial program that may have a number of applications for teaching those who are developing or reacquiring language functions. This program uses graphic presentations combined with synthesized speech to teach and test a student's acquisition of high-frequency nouns. The student is presented with two pictures of an object and asked to decide which one represents the word being taught. Students can select an answer using a computer keyboard or a special selection switch or by touching the object on the screen. First Words is a relatively inexpensive program, costing about $200. The voice synthesizer and the touch screen options must be added to the basic package but may be essential elements to effective intervention, depending on the student's capability.

Speech Disorders

Definitions of speech disorders vary greatly; some are quite detailed, and others are more general. However, all of them agree that speech disorders represent deviations of sufficient magnitude to interfere with communication (e.g., Silverman, 1995). Such speaking patterns are so divergent from normal and accepted patterns that they draw attention to the speaking act, thereby distracting the recipient from the meaning of the speaker's message. The detrimental effect of a deviant speaking behavior can have an impact on the listener, the speaker, or both.

Speech is extremely important in contemporary society. Speaking ability can influence a person's success or failure in both the personal–social and professional arenas. Most people have about average speaking ability, and they may envy those who are unusually articulate and pity those who have a difficult time with speech. What is it like to have a serious deficit in speaking ability? Certainly, it is different for each individual, depending on the person's circumstances and the severity of the deficit.

For many individuals, speaking difficulties seriously affect their lives. Strong emotional reactions to their speech may significantly alter their behavior. It is not difficult to imagine the impact that stuttering, for example, may have on classroom settings or social encounters. Speech is so central to functioning in society that speech disorders often significantly affect the quality of life experienced by individuals with this condition. Children may be ridiculed by peers, begin to feel inadequate, and suffer emotional stress.

There are many different speech disorders, and considerable diversity exists in terms of theoretical perspectives regarding causes and treatment. Volumes much longer than this book have focused solely on the topic. In this section, we will discuss several speech disorders that represent major communication disorders, including fluency disorders, delayed speech, articulation disorders, and voice disorders.

Fluency Disorders

In normal speech, we are accustomed to a reasonably smooth flow of words and sentences. For the most part, rhythm and timing are steady, regular, and rapid. Most of us also, at times, pause to think about what we are saying, either because we have made a mistake or want to mentally edit what we are about to say. However, these interruptions are generally infrequent and do not constitute an ongoing speech flow disturbance. In general, our speech is considered fluent with respect to speed and continuity.

Fluency of speech is a significant problem for some people; they have a **fluency disorder.** Their speech is characterized by repeated interruptions, hesitations, or repetitions that seriously interfere with the flow of communication. Some people have a fluency disorder known as cluttered speech, or **cluttering,** which is characterized by speech that is overly rapid, disorganized, and occasionally filled with unnecessary words (Daly, 1993; Silverman, 1995). Stuttering is by far the most well-known type of fluency disorder and has fascinated researchers for years.

■ DEFINITION OF STUTTERING

Stuttering occurs when the flow of speech is abnormally interrupted by repetitions, blocking, or prolongations of sounds, syllables, words, or phrases. Although familiar to most of us, stuttering occurs rather infrequently, in about 1 in 100 people, and it has one of the lower prevalence rates among all speech disorders (Van Riper & Erickson, 1996). For example, articulation disorders (e.g., omitting, adding, or distorting certain sounds) occur in the United States much more often than do stuttering problems.

Laypeople's high awareness of stuttering partly comes from the nature of the behavior. Stuttering is a disturbance in the rhythm and fluency of speech. It may only involve certain sounds, syllables, words, or phrases, and the problem elements may differ among individuals. Such interruptions in speech flow are very evident to both speaker and listener and are perhaps more disruptive to communication than any other type of speech disorder. Listeners often become uncomfortable and may try to assist the stuttering speaker, providing missing or incomplete words. The speaker's discomfort is often magnified by peculiar physical movements, gestures, or facial distortions. Such communication experiences tend to be vividly and easily remembered.

Parents often become concerned about stuttering as their children learn to talk. This apprehension is usually unnecessary, however, since most children exhibit some normal nonfluencies that diminish and cease with maturation. However, these normal nonfluencies have historically played a role in some theories regarding the causes of stuttering.

The way in which parents speak greatly affects their child's speech patterns.

■ CAUSATION OF STUTTERING

Behavioral scientists have looked in many directions to search for a cause of stuttering. One difficulty has been the tendency to search for a single cause. Current thinking suggests that stuttering may instead have a variety of causes (Cooper, 1993; Silverman, 1995). Causation theories regard stuttering from three basic perspectives: as a symptom of an emotional disturbance, as a result of one's biological makeup or neurological problem, and as a learned behavior.

Many professionals have become less interested in both the emotional and biological causation theories of stuttering. Investigation of this perspective is scarce, and the topic is difficult to study due to research methodology problems. Some investigations of emotional problems have explored psychosocial factors emerging from the parent–child interaction (Kelly, 1995), although this work is somewhat fragmentary. Emotional factors have been described as contributors to stuttering, including speculation that stuttering may be a reflection of an individual's capacity being exceeded by demands. But such theories also consider a person's cognitive, linguistic, and motor capacities as other contributors, viewing emotional factors as one of several possible culprits. Research and theoretical literature relating stuttering to emotion continues, but at a relatively sporadic level (Treon, 1995).

Some research has addressed theories of biological causation. Limited evidence indicates that the brains or neurological structures of some who stutter may be organized or function differently from those of their fluent counterparts, although the nature of such differences remains unclear and a matter for speculation (Abe, Yokoyama,

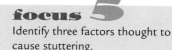

focus 5

Identify three factors thought to cause stuttering.

& Yorifuji, 1993; Costa & Kroll, 1995). Some suggest that individuals who stutter may process information with different sections of the brain than those used by their counterparts with fluent speech. A few authors hypothesize that people who stutter may have brain-hemisphere dominance problems to a greater degree than those who are fluent; that is, the hemispheres of the brain may compete with each other in processing information (Barinaga, 1995). Other research has suggested that a variety of problems may disrupt the person's precise timing ability, which is important in speech production (Wieneke, Janssen, & Brutten, 1995). Some speculate that control mechanisms for speech production may be out of synchronization in people who stutter, or they may result in elevated activity of the muscles involved in speech production (Kuniszyk-Jozkowiak, 1995; Perkins, Kent, & Curlee, 1991; Starkweather, 1995). Thus some research continues on biological causation, but the results are varied.

One theory that has persisted over the years holds that stuttering is a learned behavior emerging from the normal nonfluency of early speech development. The onset of stuttering most often occurs between 3 to 5 years of age, the years when children are still developing language (Yairi & Ambrose, 1992; Yairi, Ambrose, & Niermann, 1993). From a learning causation point of view, a typical child may become a stuttering child if considerable attention is focused on normal nonfluencies at that stage of development. The nonfluency of early stuttering may be further magnified by negative feelings about the self as well as anxiety. Interest in this theory persists (e.g., Ryan & Ryan, 1995; Stewart, 1996), although it also has its critics (e.g., Silverman, 1992).

The influence of heredity on stuttering has been approached from several perspectives. One theory holds that stuttering may be related to gender, since males outnumber females about four to one, but this hypothesis is difficult to test and remains only speculative. Heredity has also been of interest because of the high incidence of stuttering and other speech disorders within certain families as well as with twins (Felsenfeld, 1996; Yairi, Ambrose, Paden, & Throneburg, 1996). However, there is great difficulty in separating hereditary and environmental influences, a problem long evident in human development and behavior disorders research (Drew, Hardman, & Hart, 1996).

In reviewing the research on stuttering, it becomes clear that causation has been an elusive and perplexing matter for workers in speech pathology. Some recent literature has even questioned definition and assessment mechanisms for stuttering (e.g., Cordes & Ingham, 1995, 1996; Yairi, 1996). Researchers and clinicians continue to search for a cause, with the hope of identifying more effective treatment and prevention measures. Some researchers are combining elements of previous theoretical models where evidence suggests a logical connection. For example, Kuniszyk-Jozkowiak (1995) noted that stuttering may be due to a lack of coordination between laryngeal functioning and vocalization. Although this might be viewed as a physical dysfunction, it could also be seen as a result of learning or a combination of the two. Likewise research related to the "demands versus capacity" model mentioned earlier examines cognitive, emotional, linguistic, and motor-related aspects of stuttering (Treon, 1995). Thus, while some cling to the idea a single cause, an emerging trend favors exploring a spectrum of possible dynamics contributing to this condition.

■ INTERVENTION

Many treatment approaches have been applied to stuttering over the years, with mixed results. Techniques such as play therapy, creative dramatics, parental counseling, and involvement of parents, teachers, and classmates have been useful in working with children who stutter (Cooper & Cooper, 1992; Kelly, 1995; Zebrowski & Schum, 1993). Hypnosis has been used to treat some cases of stuttering, but its success has been limited. Speech rhythm has been the focus of some therapy, in some cases using a metronome to establish a speaking pattern (Van Riper & Erickson, 1996). Relaxation therapy and biofeedback have also been used, since tenseness is often observed in people who stutter. In all the techniques noted, outcomes are mixed, and it is common for those who stutter to repeat treatments using several approaches. The inability of any one treatment or cluster of treatments to consistently help people who stutter demonstrates the ongoing need for research in this area. There is also need for research investigating the most effective timing of intervention. Some have favored postponing intervention (Yairi & Carrico, 1992), and others have argued that early intervention is essential (e.g., Onslow, Andrews, & Lincoln, 1994). Early intervention, although it carries a certain risk of labeling, has long been popular in many areas of exceptionality.

Clearly, a complete understanding of stuttering remains elusive. However, treatment approaches have increasingly focused on direct behavioral therapy that attempts to teach individuals who stutter to use fluent speech patterns (e.g., Ryan & Ryan, 1995; Stewart, 1996). In some cases, children are taught to monitor and manage their stuttering (e.g., by speaking more slowly or rhythmically) and to reward themselves for increasing periods of fluency. Some behavioral therapies include information regarding physical factors (e.g., regulating breathing) and direct instruction about correct speaking behaviors. Therapy involves a variety of techniques and procedures, such as an interview to discuss the inconvenience of stuttering, behavior modification training, and follow-up. Because stuttering is a complex problem, effective interventions are likely to be equally complex.

Spoken communication is seriously disturbed by fluency disorders because they interrupt the flow of ideas. For people who stutter, the stream of communication is broken by severe rhythm irregularities. For people with cluttered speech, the flow of ideas is interrupted by extraneous words and disorganization. However, other people with speech disorders do not lack fluency, but are delayed in their speaking ability.

Delayed Speech

■ DEFINITION

Delayed speech refers to a deficit in communication ability that causes a person to speak like someone who is much younger. From a developmental point of view, this difficulty involves a delayed beginning of speech and language. Very young children are generally able to communicate, at least to some degree, before they learn verbal behaviors. They use gestures, gazing or eye contact, facial expressions, other physical movements, and nonspeech vocalizations, such as grunts or squeals (Tiegerman-Farber, 1997a, 1997b). This early development illustrates how communication, language, and speech are interrelated. Especially in very early childhood, it can be difficult to make distinctions between these three elements of a child's behavior (Nelson, 1993).

Delayed speech is considered a failure of speech to develop at the expected age, is often associated with other maturation delays, and may relate to hearing impairment, mental retardation, emotional disturbance, or brain injury. Delayed speech

focus 6

Identify two ways in which learning theory and home environment relate to delayed speech.

Preschool teachers should use all occasions possible to increase the vocabulary of a child with delayed speech. This child may be more comfortable using a puppet to interact with his teacher or other children.

may occur for many reasons and in various forms, and treatment differs accordingly.

Children with delayed speech often make few or no verbalizations that can be interpreted as conventional speech. Some communicate solely through physical gestures. Others may combine gestures and vocal sounds that are not even close approximations of words. Still others may speak, but in a very limited manner, perhaps using single words (typically nouns without auxiliary words, such as *ball* instead of *my ball*) or primitive sentences that are short or incomplete (e.g., *get ball* rather than *would you get the ball*). Such communication is normal for infants and very young children (Tiegerman-Farber, 1997b), but children with delayed speech continue to use these patterns well beyond the age at which most children speak in at least a partially fluent fashion.

Differences between stuttering and delayed speech are obvious, but the distinctions between delayed speech and articulation disorders are not as clear. In fact, children with delayed speech usually make many articulation errors in their speaking patterns. However, their major problems lie in grammatical and vocabulary deficits, which are considered matters of developmental delay. The current prevalence of delayed speech is very unclear, and government estimates do not even provide data regarding provision of services for delayed speech on a continuing basis (U.S. Department of Education, 1997). Such data problems, plus definitional differences among studies, have led many to place little faith in the precision of existing prevalence figures.

■ CAUSATION

Delayed speech may take a number of forms, so it is not surprising that causes of these problems also vary greatly. Several types of environmental deprivation contribute to delayed speech. For example, partial or complete hearing loss may cause an individual to experience serious delay (or absence) of speech development (Radziewicz & Antonellis, 1997). The environment may also be a factor in delayed speech for those with normal hearing. For example, some children's homes provide little opportunity to learn speech; in some families there is minimal conversation or little chance for the child to speak. Other problems may contribute to delayed speech, such as cerebral palsy and emotional disturbances (Ledesma, Ortiz, Gonzaga, & Lee, 1991; Schonweiler, 1994).

Sometimes a conflict exists between parents' expectations and a child's ability to perform. This negative dynamic often occurs as children develop speech. Considerable pressure is placed on children during the period when they normally develop their speaking skills: to go to bed when told, to control urination and defecation properly, and to learn appropriate eating skills, among other things. The demands are great, and they may exceed a child's performance ability. Children react in many ways when more is demanded than they are able to produce. They may refuse. They may simply not talk, withdraw from family interactions, and remain silent. In normal development, children occasionally refuse to follow the directions of adults. One very effective refusal is silence. Parents have few response options, and they may be ineffective. For parents, it is relatively simple to punish misbehaviors such as refusing to go to bed or to clean one's room, but it is a different matter when parents encounter the refusal to talk. It is not easy to force a child to talk by using conventional punishment techniques. In another negative situation, children may be punished for talking. Parents may be irritated by a child's attempt to communicate. A child may speak too loudly or at inappropriate times, such as when adults are reading, watching television, resting, or talking with other adults (even more rules to learn at such a tender age). Prolonged negativism related to talking may result in delayed speech (Gelfand, Jenson, & Drew, 1997).

Thus some children might have delayed speech as a result of environmentally controlled learning. Not speaking may be rewarded in some instances, and in others, not speaking may be a way of refusing to comply with a parent, without receiving punishment. Therefore, in some cases, children may not learn to speak, and in others, they may learn *not* to speak. Imagine the effect on a baby who is yelled at for practicing his or her babbling (perhaps loudly) while Mother is on the telephone. Frightened, the child begins to cry, which further angers Mother, who screams, "Shut up!" Of course, the baby does not understand, and this episode escalates in intensity and becomes even more frightening to the child. Such situations may be alternated with more calm periods, during which the mother hugs the baby and talks in soothing tones. A baby in this type of environment is likely to become very confused about the reaction to vocal output; sometimes it is punished, and other times it is rewarded. If such circumstances exist at the time when a child normally develops speech and persist for a substantial length of time, seriously delayed speech may result.

Delayed speech may emerge from experience deprivation, in which the environment either limits or hinders the opportunity to learn speech. Basic principles of learning suggest that, when one is first learning a skill, the stimulus and reward circumstances are important. A skill that is just beginning to develop is fragile. Stimuli and reinforcement must be reasonably consistent, appropriate, and properly timed. If such conditions do not exist, the skill development may be retarded or even negated. A child left alone for many hours each day, perhaps with only a single light bulb and four walls as stimuli, will not be rewarded for cooing, babbling, or approximating the first word. Over an extended period, this baby will fall behind his or her peers who are being hugged for each sound and hearing adults talk as models. This does not mean that the home environment must be an orchestrated language development program. Most households involve adequate circumstances to promote speech learning.

Although very complex, learning to speak differs little from learning other skills. In some homes, conversation is abnormally infrequent, and parents may rarely speak to either each other or to the children. In such cases, a child may have infrequent speech modeling and little reinforcement for speaking, so delayed speech may result. It is also possible that verbal interchanges between parents reflect a strained relationship or emotional problems, involving threats, arguments, and shouting. A child learning to speak in this setting may learn that speech is associated with unpleasant feelings or even punishment. Seriously delayed speech may result from these environmental circumstances as well. When negative outbursts punctuate long silences, the learning—whether learning not to speak or not learning to speak—may be particularly potent.

Such unpleasant circumstances may impair speech learning. The possible lack of love and caring in such a situation may reveal that emotional health plays a role in learning to speak. But delayed speech can also occur in families that exhibit great love and caring. In some such environments, a child may have little need to learn speech. Most parents are concerned about satisfying their child's needs or desires. However, carrying this ambition to the extreme, a "superparent" may anticipate the child's wants (e.g., toys, water, or food) and provide them even before the child makes a verbal re-

Interacting in Natural Settings

■ EARLY CHILDHOOD YEARS

TIPS FOR THE FAMILY

- Model speech and language to your infant by talking to him or her in normal tones from a very early age, even though he or she may not yet be intentionally communicating directly with you.
- Respond to babbling and other noises the young child makes with conversation, reinforcing early verbal output.
- Do not overreact if your child is not developing speech at the same rate as someone else's infant; great variation is found between children.
- If you are concerned about your child's speech development, have his or her hearing tested to determine whether that source of stimulation is normal.
- Observe other areas of development to assure yourself that your child is progress-ing within the broad boundaries of normal variation.
- If you are seeking day care or a preschool program, search carefully for one that will provide a rich, systematic communication environment.

TIPS FOR THE PRESCHOOL TEACHER

- Encourage parental involvement in all dimensions of the program, including systematic speech and language stimulation at home.
- Consider all situations and events as opportunities to teach speech and language, perhaps focusing initially on concrete objects and later moving to the more abstract, depending on the individual child's functioning level.
- Ask "wh" questions, such as *what, who, when,* and so on, giving the child many opportunities to practice speaking as well as thinking.
- Practice with the child the use of prepositions *in, on, out,* and so on.
- Use all occasions possible to increase the child's vocabulary.

TIPS FOR PRESCHOOL PERSONNEL

- Preschool and day-care staff communicate with the young child and can be involved in either direct or indirect communication instruction.

TIPS FOR NEIGHBORS AND FRIENDS

- Interact with young children with communication disorders as you would with any others, speaking to them and directly modeling appropriate communication.
- Intervene if you encounter other children ridiculing the speech and language of these youngsters; attempt to encourage sensitivity to individual differences among your own and other neighborhood children.

■ ELEMENTARY YEARS

TIPS FOR THE FAMILY

- Stay involved in your child's educational program through active participation with the school.
- Work in collaboration with the child's teacher on speaking practice, blending it naturally into family and individual activities.
- Communicate naturally with the child; avoid "talking down" and thereby modeling the use of simpler language.

TIPS FOR THE GENERAL EDUCATION CLASSROOM TEACHER

- Continue promoting parental involvement in their child's intervention program in whatever manner they can participate.
- Encourage the child with communication disorders to talk about events and things in his or her environment, describing experi-

---

quest. Some parents immediately respond to the child's simplest gesture, thereby rewarding gestures and not promoting the development of speech skills. Learning to speak is much more complex and demanding than making simple movements or facial grimaces. If gesturing is rewarded, speaking is less likely to be learned properly.

Delayed speech is a complex phenomenon, and its causation is equally complicated—as complicated as the speech development process itself. If you are a new parent or anticipating parenthood, you should know that the vast majority of children learn to speak normally. Certainly, parents should not become so self-conscious that they see a problem before one exists.

■ INTERVENTION

Delayed speech treatment approaches are as varied as its causes. Whatever the cause, an effective treatment will teach the child appropriate speaking proficiency for

ences in as much detail as possible.

- Use all situations possible to provide practice for the child's development of speech and language skills.
- Continue to promote the enhancement of vocabulary for the child in a broad array of topic areas.

TIPS FOR SCHOOL PERSONNEL

- Promote an environment where all who are available and in contact with the child are involved in communication instruction, if not directly then indirectly through interaction and modeling.
- Begin encouraging student involvement in a wide array of activities that can also be used to promote speech and language development.

TIPS FOR NEIGHBORS AND FRIENDS

- Interact with children with communication disorders normally; do not focus on the speaking difficulties that may be evident.
- As a neighbor or friend, provide support for the child's parents, who may be struggling with difficult feelings about their child's communication skills.

■ SECONDARY AND TRANSITION YEARS

TIPS FOR THE FAMILY

- Children who still exhibit communication problems at this level are likely to perform on a lower level, suggesting that communication may focus on functional matters such as grooming, feeding, and so on.
- For some children, communication may involve limited verbalization, and consideration should be given to other means of interacting.
- To the degree possible, continue to interact with your child as much and as normally as possible.

TIPS FOR THE GENERAL EDUCATION CLASSROOM TEACHER

- Communication instruction should be embedded in the context of functional areas (e.g., social interactions, request for assistance, choice making).
- Augmented communication devices or procedures may be added to the student's curriculum.

TIPS FOR SCHOOL PERSONNEL

- Develop school activities that will encourage use of a broad variety of skill levels in speaking (i.e., not just the debate club).
- Promote the development of school activities that permit participation through alternative communication modes other than speaking (although with caution, keeping consistent with therapy goals).

TIPS FOR NEIGHBORS AND FRIENDS

- To the degree that you are comfortable, interact with children using alternative communication approaches (e.g., signs, gesturing, pantomiming).

■ ADULT YEARS

TIPS FOR THE FAMILY

- Interact with the adult having communication disorders on a level that is functionally appropriate for his or her developmental level. For some adults with communication disorders, the developmental level may vary depending on the topic (e.g, individuals also having mental retardation). For others, the communication disorder is an inconvenience rather than another disability.

TIPS FOR THERAPISTS OR OTHER PROFESSIONALS

- Remain cognizant of the maturity level of the person with whom you are working. Do not assume interests or inclinations of younger clients simply because the individual has a communication difficulty.
- Be aware of the lifestyle context of the adult when suggesting augmentative devices. Some techniques may not serve a person well who is employed or otherwise engaged in adult activities.

TIPS FOR NEIGHBORS AND FRIENDS

- Communicate in as normal a fashion as possible, given the severity and type of disorder. If the person uses alternative communication methods, consider learning them to the degree that you feel comfortable with such an approach.

his or her age group. In some cases, additional matters, such as hearing impairments, must be considered in the treatment procedures (Radziewicz & Antonellis, 1997). These cases may involve surgery and the use of prosthetic appliances such as hearing aids, as well as specially designed instructional techniques aimed at teaching speech.

If defective learning is the primary cause of the delayed speech, treatment may focus on the basic principles of learned behavior. The stimulus and reinforcement patterns contributing to the delayed speech must be changed, so that appropriate speaking behaviors can be learned. This process sounds simple, but the identification and control of such contingencies may be complex (Gierut, 1996; Kaiser & Hester, 1994). There has been some success over the years in using direct instruction as well as other procedures for increasing spontaneous speech (Owens, 1995). Such instruction emphasizes positive reinforcement of speaking to modify the child's behavior and to develop more normal speech. Other interventions involve collaborative efforts among speech clinicians, teachers, and parents (Nelson, 1993, 1997), which focus on modifying not only the child's speech but also the family environment that contributed to the problem. Because in each case different elements have caused the delay, therapies must be individually tailored to fit the situation.

Articulation Disorders

■ DEFINITION

The largest category of all speech problems is articulation disorders, also known as phonological disorders in the *DSM-IV* (American Psychiatric Association, 1994). For most of those affected, the label **functional articulation disorders** is used. This term refers to articulation problems that are not due to structural physiological defects, such as **cleft palate** or neurological problems, but are likely a result of environmental or psychological influences.

Articulation disorders refer to abnormalities in the speech-sound production process, resulting in inaccurate or otherwise inappropriate execution of speaking. Typical problems include omissions, substitutions, additions, and distortions of certain sounds. Omissions most often involve dropping consonants from the ends of words (e.g., *los* for *lost*), although omissions may occur in any position in a word. Substitutions frequently include saying *w* for *r* (e.g., *wight* for *right*), *w* for *l* (e.g., *fowo* for *follow*), and *th* for *s* (e.g., *thtop* for *stop, thoup* for *soup*). Articulation errors may also involve transitional lisps, in which a *th* sound precedes or follows an *s* (e.g., *sthoup* or *yeths* for *soup* or *yes*). Articulation difficulties come in many forms.

The category of articulation disorders is a rather prevalent type of speech problem (American Psychiatric Association, 1994). Research indicates that most of the speech problems seen by speech clinicians involve articulation disorders, with the vast majority being functional (Patton, Kauffman, Blackbourn, & Brown, 1991; Van Riper & Erickson, 1996). Some estimates suggest that articulation problems represent about 80% of the speech disorders encountered by such professionals (Gelfand et al., 1997). Although most of these difficulties are functional disorders, some articulation problems may be attributed to physiological abnormalities.

The treatment of articulation disorders has been somewhat controversial, due in part to the large number that are functional in nature. A predictable developmental progression occurs in a substantial number of functional articulation disorders. In such cases, articulation problems diminish and may even cease to exist as the child matures. For instance, the *r, s,* or *th* problems disappear for many children after the age of 5. This phenomenon makes many school administrators reluctant to treat functional articulation disorders in younger students, typically because of limited school resources. In other words, if a significant number of articulation disorders are likely to correct themselves as the child continues to develop, why expend precious resources to treat them early on? This logic has a certain amount of appeal, but it can be applied only with caution. In general, improvement of articulation performance continues until a child is about 9 or 10 years of age. If articulation problems persist beyond this age, they are unlikely to improve unless intense intervention occurs. Furthermore, the longer such difficulties are allowed to continue, the more difficult treatment will become and the less likely it will be successful. Although some suggest that the impact of articulation difficulties is ultimately minimal (Silverman, 1995), there is limited evidence that affected individuals may still have residual indications of the disorder many years later (Felsenfeld, Broen, & McGue, 1992).

The decision whether to treat articulation problems in young children is not an easy one and interventions can be quite complex (Van Riper & Erickson, 1996). One option

focus 7

Identify two reasons why some professionals are reluctant to treat functional articulation disorders in young schoolchildren.

Timothy

■ I THINK I TALK OKAY, DON' YOU?

My name is Timothy. I am almost 7½ years old. Mondays after school, I go to the university where I meet "wif a lady who help me talk betto. It was my teacha's idea 'cause she said I don say "l" and "r" good an some othos too. I kinda like it [coming here] but I think I talk okay, don' you? I can say "l" good now all the time and "r" when I reeealy think about it. I have lots of friends, fow, no—five. I don' talk to them about comin hea, guess I'm jus not in the mood. Hey, you witing this down, is that good? You know the caw got hit by a semi this mowning and the doow hanle came off. I'm a little dizzy 'cause we wecked."

Timothy, age 7½

---

is to combine articulation training with other instruction for all very young children. This approach may serve as an interim measure for those who have continuing problems, facilitate the growth of articulation for others, and not overly tax school resources. It does, however, require some training for teachers of young children.

■ CAUSATION

Articulation disorders develop for many reasons. Some are caused by physical malformations, such as abnormal mouth, jaw, or teeth structures, and others result from nerve injury or brain damage (Love, 1992). Functional articulation disorders are often seen as caused by defective learning of the speaking act, in one form or another (Silverman, 1995). However, such categories of causation appear less clear-cut in the practice of working with people with articulation disorders. Function and structure, although related, are not perfectly correlated, as illustrated by the fact that some people with physical malformations that should result in articulation problems do not have problems, and vice versa. Despite this qualifying note, we will examine causation of articulation performance deficits in two general categories: those due to physical oral malformations and those that are clearly defined as functional because there is no physical deformity.

Before we discuss physical abnormalities of the oral cavity, it is important to note that other types of physical defects can affect articulation performances, such as an abnormal or absent **larynx.** Speech formulation involves many different physical structures that must be interfaced with learned muscle and tissue movements, auditory feedback, and a multitude of other factors. Although these functions are almost never perfectly coordinated, most people master them in an unbelievably successful manner. Malformed oral structures alter the manner in which coordinated movements must take place and sometimes make normal or accurate production of sounds extremely difficult, if not impossible.

One well-known faulty oral formation is the cleft palate, often referred to by speech pathologists as clefts of the lip or palate or both. The cleft palate is a gap in the soft palate and roof of the mouth, sometimes extending through the upper lip. The roof of the mouth serves an important function in accurate sound production. A cleft palate reduces the division of the nasal and mouth cavities, influencing the movement of air so important to articulation performance. Clefts are **congenital** defects that occur in about 1 of every 700 births and may take any of several forms (Leck & Lancashire, 1995; Silverman, 1995). Figure 9.2 shows a normal palate in part (a) and unilateral and bilateral cleft palates in parts (b) and (c), respectively; it is easy to see they might impair articulation. These problems are caused by developmental difficulties **in utero** and are often corrected by surgery.

Articulation performance is also significantly influenced by a person's dental structure. Because the tongue and lips work together with the teeth in an intricate

FIGURE 9.2

Normal and cleft palate
configurations:
(a) normal palate configuration;
(b) unilateral cleft palate;
(c) bilateral cleft palate;
(d) repaired cleft palate

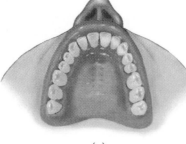

(a)

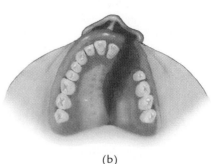

(b)

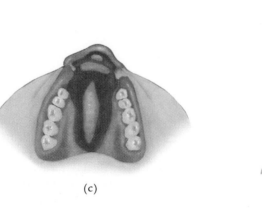

(c)

(d)

manner to form many sounds, dental abnormalities may result in serious articulation disorders. Some dental malformations occur as side effects of cleft palates, as portrayed in parts (b) and (c) of Figure 9.2, but other dental deformities not associated with clefts also cause articulation difficulties.

The natural way in which teeth in the upper and lower jaws meet together is important to speech production. The general term used for the closure and fitting together of dental structures is **occlusion,** or *dental occlusion.* When the fit is abnormal, the condition is known as **malocclusion.** Occlusion involves several factors, including the biting height of the teeth when the jaws are closed, the alignment of teeth in the upper and lower jaws, the nature of curves in upper and lower jaws, and teeth positioning. A normal adult occlusion is portrayed in part (a) of Figure 9.3. The upper teeth normally extend slightly beyond those of the lower jaw, and the bite overlap of those on the bottom is about one third for the front teeth (incisors) when closed.

Occlusion abnormalities take many forms, although we will discuss only two here. When the overbite of the top teeth is unusually large, the normal difference between the lower and upper dental structure is exaggerated. Such conditions may be due to the positioning of the upper and lower jaws, as illustrated in part (b) of Figure 9.3. In other cases, nearly the opposite situation occurs, as illustrated in part (c) of Figure 9.3, and is once again a jaw misalignment. Both exaggerated overbites and underbites may also be the result of abnormal teeth positioning or angles, as well as jaw misalignment. All can result in articulation difficulties.

Faulty learning is thought to be the cause of many functional articulation disorders. In many cases, the sources of defective speech learning are unknown or difficult to identify (Van Riper & Erickson, 1996). Like other articulation problems, those of a functional nature have many specific causes (Silverman, 1995). For example, interactions

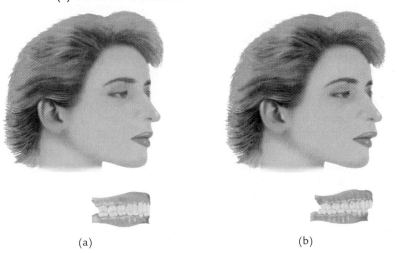
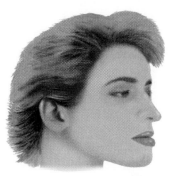

(a)   (b)   (c)

between children with articulation disorders and their mothers tend to be quite different from those of children without such problems, resembling interchanges more typical of younger children (Owens, 1995). In some cases, the existing stimulus and reinforcement patterns may not be appropriate for developing accurate articulation. Parents may not adequately and consistently reward and encourage accurate articulation. Parents are often preoccupied with their daily routines, and encouraging their children to speak properly may not be high on their priority list. However, such encouragement is important, particularly if misarticulation begins to emerge as a problem.

Also, adults may unwittingly view inaccuracies of speech in young children as cute or amusing. Consequently, "baby talk" may be reinforced in a powerful manner, as when asking the young child to say a particular word in the presence of grandparents or other guests and rewarding him or her with laughter and hugs and kisses. Such potent rewards can result in misarticulations that linger long beyond the time when normal maturation would diminish or eliminate them. Related defective learning may come from modeling. Modeling by parents or other adults can result in articulation disorders when they imitate the baby talk of young children. If parents, grandparents, or friends realized the potential results of such behavior, they would probably speak differently with young children. Modeling is a potent tool in shaping learned behavior. Although the influence of baby talk between parents and children has been questioned, modeling and imitation are used in interventions and are thought to influence natural verbal development (Weiss, 1997).

■ INTERVENTION

There are many types of treatment for articulation disorders. Clearly, the treatment for disorders due to physical abnormalities differs from that for disorders that are functional. In many cases, however, treatment may include a combination of procedures.

Considerable progress has been made over the years in various types of surgical repair for cleft palates. Such techniques may involve several different procedures because of the dramatic nature of the structural defect (Bradbury & Hewison, 1994; Van Staden & Gerhardt, 1995). Some procedures include placing Teflon implants in the hard portion of the palate, as well as stretching and stitching together the fleshy tissue. As suggested by Figure 9.2, surgery is often necessary to restructure the upper lip and nose, and corrective dental work may be undertaken as well. It may also be necessary to train or retrain articulation in the individual, depending on age at the time of surgery. A child's continued development may result in later problems; for example, the physical growth of the jaw or mouth may create difficulties for someone who underwent surgery at a very young age. Although early correction has resulted in successful healing and speech for a very high percentage of treated cases, later growth spurts may cause problems.

Cleft-palate treatment may also involve the use of prosthetic appliances (Turner & Williams, 1991). For example, a prosthesis that basically serves as the upper palate or at least covers the fissures may be employed. Such an appliance may be attached to the teeth to hold it in position and resembles the palate portion of artificial dentures.

Dental malformations other than those associated with clefts can also often be treated. Surgery can alter jaw structure and alignment. In some cases, orthodontic treatment may reposition the teeth through extractions and use of braces. Prosthetic appliances, such as full or partial artificial dentures, may also be used. As in other types of problems, the patient who has had orthodontic treatment often requires speech therapy to learn proper speech performance.

Treatment of people who have functional articulation disorders most often focuses on relearning the speaking act and in some cases, learning muscle control and usage (Gibbon, Hardcastle, & Dent, 1995; Van Riper & Erickson, 1996). Although the specific cause of the defective learning is difficult to identify precisely, it is typically assumed that an inappropriate configuration of stimulus and reinforcement characterized the child's environment during speech development (e.g., inappropriate modeling by parents). Treatment attempts to correct that configuration. Several behavior modification procedures have been employed successfully in treating functional articulation disorders (Silverman, 1995). In all cases, treatment techniques are complex: they must teach proper articulation and then assist the individual in generalizing that learning to a variety of word configurations and environments (Elbert, Powell, & Swartzlander, 1991; Gray & Shelton, 1992). Further research on the treatment of articulation disorders is seriously needed, particularly in view of its prevalence. Additionally, some advocate improving the quality of research methods employed in this and other areas of communication disorders (Schoonen, 1991; Sommers, Logsdon, & Wright, 1992).

It should also be noted that differences in dialect can raise interesting issues regarding treatment of articulation problems (Van Riper & Erickson, 1996). When a child's first language is not English, that youngster may use verbal constructions resembling those of his or her first language. These turns of phrase, unusual pronunciations, or use of idiom might make his or her speech distinctive and perhaps difficult to understand. Does this require an intervention similar to those used for articulation disorders? Such a question involves cultural, social, and political implications far beyond those typically considered by professionals working with speech disorders.

Voice Disorders

▪ DEFINITION

Voice disorders involve unusual or abnormal acoustical qualities in the sounds made when a person speaks. All voices differ significantly in pitch, loudness, and other qualities from those belonging to others of the same gender, cultural group, and age. All people have varying acoustical qualities in their voices. However, the characteristics of voice disorders are habitually and sufficiently different from the norm and may divert a listener's attention from the content of a message.

Relatively little attention has been paid to voice disorders in the research literature, for several reasons. First, determining what constitutes voice normalcy involves a great deal of subjective judgment. Moreover, what is considered normal varies according to circumstances (e.g., football games, barroom conversation, or seminar discussion) and geographical location (e.g., the West, a rural area, New England, the Deep South), as well as family environments, personality, and physical structure of the speech mechanism. Another reason for the lack of attention to voice disorders pertains to the acceptable ranges of normal voice.

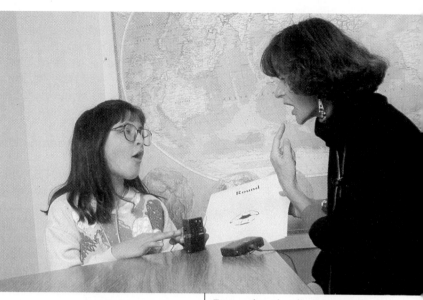

Factors in voice disorders that interfere with communication are pitch, loudness, and quality. A voice disorder exists when these factors, singly or in combination, cause the listener to focus on the sounds being made rather than the message to be communicated.

Most individuals' voices fall within acceptable tolerance ranges. Because of this limited attention, children with voice disorders are often not referred for help, and their problems become persistent when not treated (Leeper, 1992; Van Riper & Erickson, 1996).

Children with voice disorders often speak with an unusual nasality, hoarseness, or breathiness. Nasality involves either too little resonance from the nasal passages (**hyponasality** or **denasality**), which sounds as if the child has a continual cold or stuffy nose, or too much sound coming through the nose (**hypernasality**), which causes a twang in the speech. People with voice disorders of hoarseness have a constant husky sound to their speech, as though they had strained their voices by yelling. Breathiness is a voice disorder with very low volume, like a whisper; it sounds as though not enough air is flowing through the vocal cords. Other voice disorders include overly loud or soft speaking and pitch abnormalities (e.g., monotone speech).

Like so many speech problems, the nature of voice disorders varies greatly. Our description provides considerable latitude, but it also outlines the general parameters of voice disorders often dismissed in the literature: pitch, loudness, and quality. An individual with a voice disorder may exhibit one or more of these factors, significantly interfering with communication (i.e., the listener focuses on the sound, rather than the message).

■ CAUSATION

An appropriate voice pitch is efficient and suited to the situation and the speech content, as well as the speaker's **laryngeal structure.** Correct voice pitch permits inflection without voice breaks or excessive strain. Appropriate pitch varies as emotion and meaning change and should not attract attention. Acoustic characteristics of voice quality include degree of nasality, breathy speech, and hoarse-sounding speech. Like the other parameters of voice, the appropriateness of loudness is based on subjective judgment. The normal voice is not habitually characterized by excessive loudness or unusual softness. Loudness depends greatly on circumstances.

Pitch disorders take several forms. The person's voice may have an abnormally high or low pitch, may be characterized by pitch breaks or a restricted pitch range, or may be monotonal or monopitched. Many individuals experience pitch breaks as they progress through adolescence. Although more commonly associated with young males, pitch breaks also occur in females. Such pitch breaks are a normal part of development, but if they persist much beyond adolescence, they may signal laryngeal difficulties. Abnormally high- or low-pitched voices may be due to a variety of problems. They may be learned through imitation, as when a young boy attempts to sound like his older brother or father. They may also be learned from certain circumstances, such as when an individual placed in a position of authority believes a lower voice pitch is necessary to suggest the image of power. Organic conditions, such as a hormone imbalance, may also result in abnormally high- or low-pitched voices.

Voice disorders involving volume may also have varied causes. Voices that are excessively loud or soft may be learned either through imitation or through perceptions of the environment, much like those mentioned for pitch disorders. An example is mimicking the soft speaking of a female movie star. Other cases of abnormal vocal intensity occur because an individual has not learned to monitor loudness. Beyond learning difficulties, however, some intensity voice disorders occur because of organic problems. For example, abnormally low vocal intensity may result from problems such as paralysis of vocal cords, laryngeal trauma (e.g., larynx surgery for cancer, damage through accident or disease), and pulmonary diseases such as **asthma** or **emphysema** (Love, 1992). Excessively loud speech may occur because of hearing impairments and brain damage.

Voice disorders relating to the quality of speech include vocal production deviances such as abnormal nasality as well as the hoarse and breathy speech noted earlier. Abnormal nasality may take the form of an overly nasal voice (hypernasality) or a voice with reduced acoustic sound (denasality or hyponasality) that dulls the resonance of consonants. Hypernasality occurs essentially because the soft palate does not move upward and back to properly close off the airstream through the nose. Such conditions can be due to improper tissue movement in the speech mechanism, or they may result from organic defects such as an imperfectly repaired cleft palate. Excessive hypernasality may also be learned (think of some country-western singers you have heard) and also characterizes certain regional dialects. Denasality is the type of voice quality produced by having a severe head cold or hay fever. The sounds are congested or dulled, with reduced acoustic resonance. In some cases, however, denasality occurs as the result of learning or abnormal physical structures rather than these more common problems.

■ INTERVENTION

The approach to voice disorder treatment depends on causation. In some cases, when abnormal tissue development or dental structures result in unusual voice production, surgical intervention may be necessary (e.g., Casper & Colton, 1993). In other situations, treatment may involve direct instruction to help the affected individual learn or relearn acceptable voice production. Such interventions often include counseling in regard to how unusual voice sounds affect other people and behavior modification procedures aimed at retraining the person's speaking. These efforts are more difficult if the behavior is long-standing and deeply ingrained. We have already discussed typical speech-related interventions under other speech disorders.

Voice disorders are seldom the focus of referral and treatment in the United States, although they receive some attention in other countries (Harris, 1992; Leeper, 1992; Mans, 1994). Some researchers have argued strongly, however, that voice disorders should be treated more aggressively (Andrews & Summers, 1993; McNamara & Perry, 1994). One important element in planning interventions with voice disorders is clear and open communication with the person seeking treatment (Kreiman et al., 1993). It is important to avoid setting unrealistic expectations about outcomes and to remember that those being treated are the ultimate evaluators of success. Interested readers may wish to consult other sources for additional information regarding voice disorder interventions (e.g., Case, 1991; Pannbacker, 1992).

Prevalence

We have already noted the difficulties involved in estimating the prevalence of other disorders, due to differences in definitions and data-collection procedures. The field of speech disorders is also vulnerable to these problems, and so prevalence estimates vary considerably.

The most typical prevalence figures cited for speech disorders indicate that between 7% and 10% of the population is affected. Approximately 20% of all children (ages 6 to 21) served in programs for those with disabilities were categorized as having speech or language impairments in 1995–1996 (U.S. Department of Education, 1997). These figures do not deviate greatly from other estimates over the years, although some data have suggested substantial differences between geographic locales (e.g., significantly higher percentages in some areas of California than in parts of the Midwest). To some degree, these figures present difficulties when we consider the overall 12% ceiling for services to all students with disabilities, as specified in the Individuals with Disabilities Education Act (IDEA). Obviously, individuals with speech disorders of a mild nature cannot be eligible for federally funded services. However, *The 19th Annual Report to Congress on the Implementation of IDEA* cited speech or language impairments as the second most frequent disability (the first was learning disabilities) receiving special services during the 1995–1996 school year (U.S. Department of Education, 1997).

The frequency with which speech problems occur diminishes in the population as age increases. Speech disorders are identified in about 12% to 15% of children in kindergarten through grade 4. For children in grades 5 through 8, the figure declines to about 4% to 5%. The 5% rate remains somewhat constant after grade 8 unless treatment intervenes. Thus, age and development diminish speech disorders considerably, more so with certain types of problems (e.g., articulation difficulties) than others.

Case Study

RICKY

The following is a statement by Ricky Creech, a person with a serious communication disorder due to cerebral palsy. Ricky communicates by using a computer-controlled electronic augmentative communication device. He provides some insights regarding assumptions people make about individuals who cannot communicate. This is a portion of a presentation made at the National Institutes of Health.

"There is a great need for educating the public on how to treat physically limited people. People are still under the misconception that somehow the ability to speak, hear, see, feel, smell, and reason are tied together. That is, if a person loses one, he has lost the others.

"The number one question people ask my parents is, 'Can he hear?' When I reply that I can, they bend down where their lips are not two feet away from my eyes and say very loudly, 'How—are—you? Do—you—like—that—talking—machine?' Now, I don't mind when that person is a pretty, young girl. But when it is an older or married woman, it is a little embarrassing. When the person is a man, I'm tempted to say something not very nice. . . .

"I would make a great spy. When I am around, people just keep talking—because I can't speak, they think I can't hear or understand what is being said. I have listened to more private conversations than there are on the Watergate tapes. It is a good thing that I am not a blackmailer. If people knew that I hear and understand everything they say, some would die of embarrassment.

"There is another conclusion which people make when first seeing me, which I don't kid about; I don't find it a bit humorous. That is, that I am mentally retarded.

"The idea that if a person can't speak something must be wrong with his mind is the prevalent belief in every class, among the educated as well as the not-so-educated. I have a very good friend who is a nuclear scientist, the most intelligent person I have ever known, but he admitted that when he first saw me his first conclusion was that I was mentally retarded. This was in spite of my parents' assertions that I was not.

"However, this man had a special quality—when he was wrong he could admit it with his mind and his heart—most people can't do both. There are people who know me who know with their minds that I am not mentally retarded, but they treat me as a child because in their hearts they have not really accepted that I have the mentality of an adult. I am an adult and I want to be treated as an adult. I have a tremendous amount of respect for anyone who does."

■ APPLICATION

Have you ever made the same error as the nuclear scientist in the case study? Explain what you felt and how you acted. Having read Ricky Creech's description, how would you react now?

As a professional, how would you explain to people Ricky's communication disorder so they would understand his abilities?

Source: From "Consumers Speak Out on the Life of the Nonspeaker," by R. Creech and J. Viggiano, 1981, *ASHA, 23,* pp. 550–552. Reprinted by permission of the American Speech-Language-Hearing Association.

Debate Forum

TO TREAT OR NOT TO TREAT?

Articulation problems represent about 80% of all speech disorders encountered by speech clinicians, making this type of difficulty the most prevalent of all communication disorders. It is also well-known that young children normally make a number of articulation errors during the process of maturation as they are learning to talk. A substantial portion do not conquer all the rules of language and produce all the speech sounds correctly until they are 8 or 9 years old, yet they eventually develop normal speech and articulate properly. In lay terminology, they seem to "grow out of" early articulation problems. Because of this maturation outcome and the prevalence of articulation problems, serious questions are asked regarding treatment in the early years.

■ POINT

Some school administrators are reluctant to treat young children who display articulation errors, because the resources of school districts are in very short supply and budgets are extremely tight. If a substantial proportion of young children's articulation problems will correct themselves through maturation, then shouldn't the precious resources of school districts be directed to other more pressing problems? Articulation problems should not be treated unless they persist beyond the age of 10 or 11.

■ COUNTERPOINT

Although articulation does improve with maturation, delaying intervention is a mistake. The longer such problems persist, the more difficult treatment will be. Even the issue of financial savings is a false one. If all articulation difficulties are allowed to continue, those children who do not outgrow such problems will be more difficult to treat later, requiring more intense and expensive intervention than if treated early. Early intervention for articulation problems is vitally important.

Review

focus 1

Identify four ways in which speech, language, and communication are interrelated.

- Both speech and language form part, but not all, of communication.
- Some components of communication involve language but not speech.
- Some speech does not involve language.
- The development of communication, language, and speech overlap to some degree.

focus 2

Identify two ways in which language delay and language disorder are different.

- In language delay, the sequence of development is intact but the rate is interrupted.

- In language disorder, the sequence of development is interrupted.

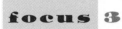

focus 3

Identify three factors thought to cause language disorders.

- Defective or deficient sensory systems
- Neurological damage occurring through physical trauma or accident
- Deficient or disrupted learning opportunities during language development

focus 4

Describe two ways in which treatment approaches for language disorders generally differ for children and for adults.

- Treatment for children generally addresses initial acquisition or learning of language.

- Treatment for adults involves relearning or reacquiring language function.

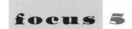

focus 5

Identify three factors thought to cause stuttering.

- Learned behavior, emotional problems, and neurological problems can contribute to stuttering.
- Some research has suggested that people who stutter have a different brain organization from those who do not.
- People who stutter may learn their speech patterns as an outgrowth of the normal nonfluency evident when speech development first occurs.

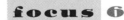

focus 6

Identify two ways in which learning theory and home environment relate to delayed speech.

- The home environment may provide little opportunity to learn speech.
- The home environment may interfere with speech development when speaking is punished.

focus 7

Identify two reasons why some professionals are reluctant to treat functional articulation disorders in young schoolchildren.

- Many articulation problems evident in young children are developmental in nature, and so speech may improve with age.
- Articulation problems are quite frequent among young children, and treatment resources are limited.

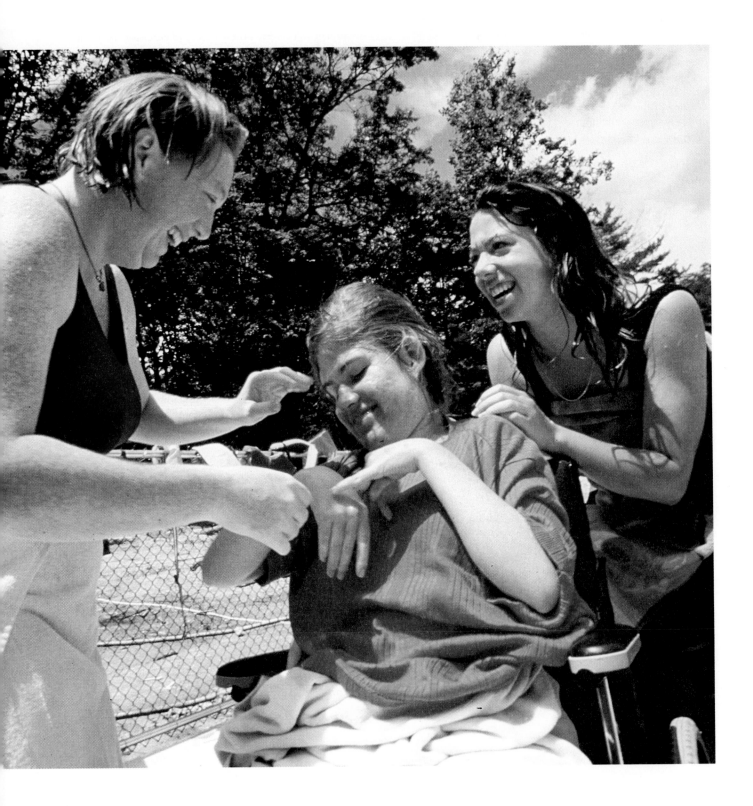

10

People with Severe and Multiple Disabilities

To begin with . . .

 When the court ordered the institution closed, my husband and I led the opposition. We were told that her disability was too severe for her to stay at home. Now all of a sudden, it was "inappropriate." We were all confused, surprised, and many of us were angry. Then as we saw people leaving one-by-one, we started to investigate a little further. Then we began to understand. Living in the community allows Judy to grow more than she could ever grow in the institution. (Beth Atkin, cited in Records, 1994)

 Parents have reminded us that the educational outcomes sought for their children with severe disabilities parallel those for their children without disabilities, although the ways they are operationalized, the path to their attainment, and the supports they require may be different. (Giangreco & Snell, 1996, p. 97)

 Remarkable progress has been made during the past 10 years in using technology to meet the needs of students with disabilities. In particular, researchers have customized technology to meet the needs of students with severe cognitive and physical disabilities . . . Students with severe impairments [disabilities] have increased independence levels through "low tech" solutions such as specially designed pencils, scissors, and silverware and "high tech" advances such as voice recognition systems, word prediction systems, and virtual reality. (U.S. Department of Education, 1997, p. xii)

 Twenty-five years ago, for every three children born with severe handicaps [disabilities], one would be alive at the age of 21. Today, for every three children born with a severe defect, two are alive at the age of 21, and the prediction is that it will be two and one-half out of three by the year 2000 due to advances in medical technology. (National Association of State Directors, 1991, p. 1)

Kevin

Kevin never had the opportunity to go to preschool, and didn't begin his formal education in the public schools until the age of 6. He is now 15 years old and goes to Eastmont Junior High—his neighborhood school. Kevin does not verbally speak, walk, hear, or see. Professionals have used several labels to describe him, including severely disabled, severely multiply handicapped, deaf–blind, and profoundly mentally retarded. His teenage classmates at Eastmont call him Kevin. Throughout the day, Kevin has a support team of administrators, teachers, paraprofessionals, and peers that work together to meet his instructional, physical, and medical needs. And he has many, many needs. Kevin requires some level of support in everything he does, ranging from eating and taking care of personal hygiene to communicating with others. In the last few years, he has learned to express himself through the use of assistive technology. Kevin has a personal communication board with picture symbols that keeps him in constant contact with teachers, friends, and family. Through the use of an electronic wheelchair and his ability to use various switches, Kevin is able to maneuver his way through just about any obstacle in his environment. He is also learning to feed himself independently.

Kevin lives at home with his family, which includes three older brothers. His parents, siblings, and grandparents are very supportive, always looking for ways to help facilitate Kevin's participation in school, family, and community activities. What he loves to do most is go shopping with his mom at the local mall, eat with friends at a fast-food restaurant, relax on the lawn in the neighborhood park, and play miniature golf at Mulligan's Pitch and Putt.

KEVIN, in the opening snapshot, is an individual with **severe and multiple disabilities**. In one way or another, he will require services and support in nearly every facet of his life. Some people with severe disabilities have significant intellectual, learning, and behavioral differences; others are physically disabled with vision and hearing loss. Most have significant, multiple disabilities. Kevin certainly has multiple needs, one of which is communication. Yet, although he is unable to communicate verbally, he is able to express himself through the use of a communication board. Thus, in many circumstances, a disability may be described as severe, but through today's technology and our understanding of how to adapt the environment, the impact on the individual may be diminished.

Definitions

The needs of people with severe and multiple disabilities cannot be met by one profession. The nature of their disabilities extends equally into the fields of education, medicine, psychology, and social services. Since these individuals present such diverse characteristics and require the attention of several professions, it is not surprising that numerous definitions have been used to describe them.

HISTORICAL DESCRIPTIONS OF SEVERE DISABILITIES

Historically, terminology associated with severe disabilities communicated a sense of hopelessness and despair. The condition was described as extremely debilitating, inflexibly incapacitating, or uncompromisingly crippling. Abt Associates (1974) described individuals with severe handicaps as unable "to attend to even the most pronounced social stimuli, including failure to respond to invitations from peers or adults, or loss of contact with reality" (p. v). The definition went on to use terms such as self-mutilation (e.g., head banging, body scratching, and hair pulling), ritualistic behaviors (e.g., rocking and pacing), and self-stimulation (e.g., masturbation, stroking, and patting). The Abt definition focused almost exclusively on the individual's deficits and negative behavioral characteristics.

In 1976, Justen proposed a definition that moved away from negative terminology to descriptions of the individual's developmental characteristics. "The 'severely handicapped' refers to those individuals . . . who are functioning at a general development level of half or less than the level which would be expected on the basis of chronological age and who manifest learning and/or behavior problems of such magnitude and significance that they require extensive structure in learning situations" (p. 5).

Whereas Justen emphasized a discrepancy between normal and atypical development, Sailor and Haring (1977) proposed a definition that was oriented to the educational needs of each individual:

A child should be assigned to a program for the severely/multiply handicapped according to whether the primary service needs of the child are basic or academic. . . . If the diagnosis and assessment process determines that a child with multiple handicaps needs academic instruction, the child should not be referred to the severely handicapped program. If the child's service need is basic skill development, the referral to the severely/multiply handicapped program is appropriate. (p. 68)

In 1991, Snell further elaborated on the importance of defining severe disabilities on the basis of educational need, suggesting that the emphasis be on supporting the individual in inclusive classroom settings. The Association for Severe Handicaps (Meyer, Peck, & Brown, 1991a), while agreeing in principle with Snell, proposed a definition that focused on inclusion in all natural settings: family, community, and school (see the Reflect on This feature on page 328).

THE TASH DEFINITION OF SEVERE DISABILITIES

The Association for Persons with Severe Handicaps (TASH) proposed the following definition of severe disabilities:

focus 1

What are the three components of the TASH definition of severe disabilities?

These people include individuals of all ages who require extensive ongoing support in more than one major life activity in order to participate in integrated community settings and to enjoy a quality of life that is available to citizens with fewer or no disabilities. Support may be required for life activities such as mobility, communication, self-care, and learning as necessary for independent living, employment, and self-sufficiency. (Meyer, Peck, & Brown, 1991a, p. 19)

The TASH definition focused on the relationship of the individual with the environment (adaptive fit), the need to include people of all ages, and "extensive ongoing support" in life activities. The adaptive fit between the individual and the environment

If you have a severe disability, the very first thing that others would most likely be told about you would be a summary of your "deficits." Chances are, whatever you were, there would be a file containing a lengthy description of your intellectual shortcomings, your physical impairments, and your behavior problems. Even the most rudimentary personal information included on a driver's license—your eye color, hair color, height, and weight—remains a mystery throughout hundreds of pages of written records. Nowhere would someone learn that you had a lovely smile, a strong sense of identity, and a family that cared about you. Instead, we might read about your "inappropriate affect," your "noncompliance," and the "overprotectiveness" of your "difficult" parents. And although you might like to think of yourself as an active teenager interested in the "top 40" hits and the latest fashion in dress, hairstyle, and makeup, you may find yourself listening to nursery rhymes, dressed in a shapeless sweatsuit, your hair cropped short and straight, and with no access to even acne medication, much less makeup. Why? Because an assumption has been made that your *disability* tells all there is to know about you, and from the moment you were diagnosed (or even *dually* diagnosed), you ceased being regarded as a person and became a "subject," a "client," or—worse yet—a "case." Your personality, your identity, and your lifestyle have become minor and even hidden details in a clinical history that tells the world about your weaknesses, faults, and deficits.

Source: From "Definition of the People TASH Serves," by L. H. Meyer, C. A. Peck, and L. Brown. In *Critical Issues in the Lives of People with Disabilities,* edited by L. H. Meyer, C. A. Peck, and L. Brown, 1991, p. 17. Paul H. Brookes Publishing Company, PO Box 10624, Baltimore, MD, 21285-0624. Reprinted with permission.

is a two-way street. First, it is important to determine the capability of the individual to cope with the requirements of family, school, and community environment. Second, how do these various environments recognize and accommodate the need of the individual with severe disabilities? The adaptive fit of the individual with the environment is a dynamic process requiring continuous adjustment that fosters a mutually supportive coexistence. The TASH definition of severe disabilities suggests that an adaptive fit can be created only when there is extensive ongoing support (formal and/or natural) for each individual as he or she moves through various life activities, including social interactions, taking care of personal needs, making choices about lifestyle, working, and moving from place to place.

■ THE IDEA DEFINITIONS OF SEVERE AND MULTIPLE DISABILITIES

focus 2

Define the terms *multiple disabilities* and *deafness–blindness* as described in IDEA.

The Individuals with Disabilities Education Act (IDEA) does not include the term "severe disabilities" as one of the 12 categorical definitions of disability identified in federal regulation. The law does, however, describe children with severe disabilities and their need for intensive educational services:

"Children with severe disabilities" refers to children with disabilities who, because of the intensity of their physical, mental, or emotional problems, need highly specialized education, social, psychological, and medical services in order to maximize their full potential for useful and meaningful participation in society and for self-fulfillment. (34C.F.R., Part 300, Sec.315.4[d])

The law goes on to indicate that individuals with severe disabilities may be subsumed under any one of IDEA's categories, such as mental retardation, autism, serious emotional disturbance, speech and language impairments, and so on. (These disability conditions are discussed in other chapters in this text.) IDEA does include multiple disabilities and deafness–blindness as specific disability categories.

■ MULTIPLE DISABILITIES Multiple disabilities as defined in the IDEA federal regulations means

concomitant impairments (such as mental retardation–orthopedic impairments, etc.), the combination of which causes such severe educational problems that they cannot be accommodated in special education programs solely for one of the impairments. The term does not include children who are deaf–blind. (Federal Register, 1977 [August 23]42[63], pp. 42,478–42,479)

This definition includes multiple conditions that can occur in any of several combinations. One such combination, described by the term **dual diagnosis**, is receiving a great deal of attention.

Dual diagnosis involves persons who have serious emotional problems (behavior disorders) in conjunction with mental retardation. Estimates of people with mental retardation also having serious emotional problems range from 25% to 90% (Reiss, 1990; Senatore, Matson, & Kazdin, 1985). The expanding use of this term has raised apprehension among some professional groups, particularly TASH. TASH suggests that the term may be misapplied as a rationale for the use of aversive behavioral procedures, psychotropic medications, and punishment through the judicial system. To deal with the confusion surrounding the use of this label more effectively, TASH recommended the following:

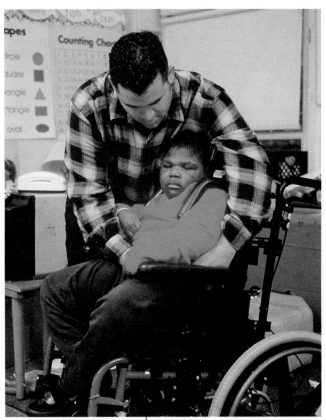

In addition to other services and supports, a child with severe disabilities needs a highly specialized education.

■ Programs for people described as having a dual diagnosis must include individualized, personalized services and nonaversive methods.
■ Additional research must be undertaken to determine the influence of environmental factors affecting the increase in behaviors associated with mental illness.
■ Support and assistance must be based on individual need rather than labels. (Meyer, Peck, & Brown, 1991b)

The relationship between severe retardation and emotional disturbance is not understood as clearly as that between retardation and physical disabilities. In fact, there is a great deal of confusion concerning the overlapping characteristics of these supposedly different populations. The characteristics of individuals with serious emotional disturbances appear to be closely related to those of individuals with severe retardation, but, by definition, individuals with emotional disturbances are not truly retarded (see the Reflect on This feature on page 330).

■ DEAFNESS–BLINDNESS For some multiple disabilities, mental retardation may not be a primary symptom. One such condition is deafness–blindness, a **dual sensory impairment**. The concomitant vision and hearing difficulties exhibited by people who are **deaf–blind** result in severe communication deficits as well as

THE DUAL DIAGNOSED DILEMMA OF MORRIS MASON

The state of Virginia electrocuted 32-year-old Morris Mason on June 25, 1985, in spite of his dual diagnosis of mental retardation and mental illness. Mason grew up on the sparsely populated Eastern Shore. Folks knew him as a school dropout, a loner, and the butt of other kids' pranks.

He spent time in three mental hospitals, where he was diagnosed as having an "IQ of 66, and schizophrenic reactions." At age 22, he lost control, committed an act of arson, and went to prison.

Two and a half years later, he left the prison, but he couldn't adjust to the outside world. Feeling himself rapidly losing control, he called his parole officer twice, asking for help. On May 12, 1978, he called again, asking that he be placed in a "halfway house" or

some kind of supervised environment. The parole officer set a meeting for later that week.

That appointment was never kept because the next day Mason went on an alcoholic rampage, killing a 72-year-old woman and burning her house. On May 14, he attacked two girls, ages 12 and 13, leaving one with paraplegia.

He pleaded guilty and waived his right to a trial. Sentenced to death, he left the courtroom "talking crazy" about being "the killer for the Eastern Shore" and making "the Eastern Shore popular."

The Eastern Shore's demand for revenge, understandably, never ceased. On the other hand, the judges never stopped the legal machinery long enough to determine whether it was proper to electrocute a person so retarded and mentally ill. Virginia law

requires the transfer of any prisoner diagnosed as insane to a mental health facility. The prison warden, however, is solely responsible for initiating a sanity hearing in the case of a condemned prisoner. As for the man's mental retardation, it was ignored. . . .

After Mason's execution, Joseph Giarratano, a fellow inmate on death row, wrote a touching memoir:

When they executed Morris, they didn't kill a consciously responsible individual: they executed a child in a man's body. To this day I do not believe that Morris knew right from wrong, or left from right for that matter. He just didn't want anyone to be angry with him. That includes the guards who worked the unit. The guards were always his best listeners: they had to be here for eight hours a shift anyway. And Morris would stand there and

babble for as long as they would sit and listen. Back then conditions on the row were pretty harsh, but nothing seemed to faze him. No one here, prisoner or guard, saw Morris as a threat. If he were here today he would still be chattering on about sports, and trying to please people in his own out-of-touch-with-reality way. *

*From *Last Rights* by Joseph B. Ingle. Copyright 1990 by Joseph B. Ingle. Used by permission of the publisher, Abingdon Press.

Source: From *Unequal Justice?* by Robert Perske. Copyright 1991 by Robert Perske and Martha Perske. Used by permission of the publisher, Abingdon Press.

developmental and educational difficulties that require extensive support across several professional disciplines.

IDEA defines deafness–blindness as:

concomitant hearing and visual impairments, the combination of which causes such severe communication and other developmental and educational problems that they cannot be accommodated in special education programs solely for children who are deaf or blind. (Federal Register, 1977 [August 23]42[63], pp. 42,478–42,479)

The impact of both vision and hearing loss on the educational needs of the student is a matter of debate among professionals. One view of deaf–blindness holds that these individuals are severely retarded "to the extent that sensory function in vision and hearing was also severely impaired" (Hammer, 1989, p. 177). Another view is that they are average in intelligence and lost their hearing and sight after having acquired language. Downing and Eichinger (1990) suggested that intellectual functioning for persons who are deaf–blind may range from normal or gifted to severe mental retardation. These individuals may also have physical and behavioral disabilities. These authors define people who are deaf–blind as lacking in the ability to initiate or respond to "appropriate interactions with others and often [exhibiting] behavior that is considered socially inappropriate" (p. 99).

Prevalence

Individuals with severe and multiple disabilities constitute a very small percentage of the general population. Even if we consider the multitude of conditions, prevalence estimates generally range from no more than 0.1% to 1.0%. Brown (1991) suggested that this group of people constitutes the lowest 1% of the general population. Approximately 4 out of every 1,000 persons are severely disabled where the primary symptom is mental retardation. The U.S. Department of Education (1997) estimated that about 94,034 students between the ages of 6 and 21 were served in the public schools under the label multiple disabilities during the 1995–1996 school year. These students account for 1.9% of the over 5 million students considered eligible for services under IDEA. The Department of Education also reported that there were 1,352 students between the ages of 6 and 21 labeled as deaf–blind. These students account for 0.0002% of students with disabilities served under IDEA. Overall, about 14,000 individuals in the United States are identified as deaf–blind.

focus 3

Identify the estimated prevalence and causes of severe and multiple disabilities.

Causation

Multiple disabilities result from multiple causes. For the vast majority of individuals with severe and multiple disabilities, the differences are evident at birth. Birth defects may be the result of genetic or metabolic disorders, including chromosomal abnormalities, phenylketonuria, or Rh incompatibility. Poor maternal health during pregnancy may also cause birth defects. The abuse of drugs, tobacco, and alcohol; poor maternal nutrition; infectious diseases (e.g., HIV); radiation exposure; venereal disease; and advanced maternal age are all factors. Severe and multiple disabilities can also result from incidents or conditions that occur late in life, such as poisoning, accidents, malnutrition, physical and emotional neglect, and disease. (See Chapter 8 for a more in-depth discussion of genetic and behavioral factors.)

Characteristics

The multitude of characteristics exhibited by people with severe and multiple disabilities is mirrored by the numerous definitions associated with these conditions. A close analysis of these definitions reveals a consistent focus on people whose life needs cannot be met without substantial assistance from others, including family, friends, and society. With this support, however, individuals with severe and multiple disabilities have a much greater probability of escaping the stereotype that depicts them solely as consumers

focus **4**

What are the characteristics of persons with severe and multiple disabilities?

of societal resources and becoming contributing members of families and communities.

School-age students with severe and multiple disabilities may be characterized according to their instructional needs. Snell (1991) suggested that professionals concentrate more on the instructional needs and placement of these individuals in inclusive educational settings and less on general, often stereotyped population characteristics. For Kevin (see the opening snapshot), this would mean concentrating on educational outcomes that will decrease his dependence on others in his environment and create opportunities to enhance his inclusion at home, at school, and in the community. Instruction would be developed with these outcomes in mind, rather than on the basis of a set of general characteristics associated with the label *severely disabled*. As proposed by Snell and Brown (1993), educators need to build upon three assumptions regarding the learning characteristics of students with severe/multiple disabilities:

1. Learning is not only possible but probable.
2. There are more similarities between these students and their typical peers than differences.
3. With the proper supports, life functioning improves. (p. 99)

■ INTELLIGENCE AND ACADEMIC ACHIEVEMENT

Most individuals with severe and multiple disabilities have mental retardation as a primary condition. As such, their learning and memory capabilities are diminished. The greater the intellectual deficit, the more difficulty the individual will have in learning, retaining, and applying information. Individuals with severe and multiple disabilities will require specialized and intensive instruction in order to acquire and use new skills across a number of settings.

Given the diminished intellectual capability of many individuals with severe and multiple disabilities, academic learning is often a low instructional priority. The vast majority of students with severe disabilities are unable to learn from basic academic programs in reading, writing, and mathematics. Instruction in functional skills is the most effective approach to academic learning. Basic academic subjects are taught

This student uses a mirror to improve his functional skills at mealtime. The skill will be more useful if taught in a natural setting such as the home or in the school cafeteria.

only in the context of daily living. A functional program in reading focuses on those words that facilitate a child's access to the environment (*rest room, danger, exit,* etc.). Functional math skill development relates more to developing strategies for telling time or the consumer's use of money. As suggested by Drew, Hardman, & Logan (1996), a functional approach teaches academic skills in the context of environmental cues. The learning of new skills is always paired directly with environmental stimuli. Snell and Brown (1993) stressed that the teacher must use instructional materials that are realistic. Traditional materials, such as workbooks, basal readers, flash cards, and so on, do not work for students with severe disabilities because they are unable to relate the materials to the natural setting of home or community.

■ ADAPTIVE SKILLS

The learning of adaptive skills is critical to success in natural settings. These skills involve both personal independence and social interaction. Personal independence skills range from the ability to take care of one's basic needs, such as eating, dressing, and hygiene, to living on one's own in the community (including getting and keeping a job, managing money, or finding ways to get around in the environment). Social interaction skills involve being able to communicate one's needs and preferences, as well as listening and appropriately responding to others. People with severe and multiple disabilities often do not have age-appropriate adaptive skills and need ongoing services and supports to facilitate learning and application in this area. We do know that when given the opportunity to learn adaptive skills through participation in settings with nondisabled peers, individuals with severe disabilities have a higher probability of maintaining and meaningfully applying this learning over time (Brown et al., 1991).

■ SPEECH AND LANGUAGE SKILLS

People with severe and multiple disabilities generally have significant deficits and delays in speech and language skills, ranging from articulation and fluency disorders to an absence of any expressive oral language (Cole & Cole, 1989). Speech and language deficits and delays are positively correlated with the severity of mental retardation (McLean, Brady, & McLean, 1996). As is true for adaptive skill learning, individuals with severe and multiple disabilities will acquire and use appropriate speech and language if these skills are taught and applied in natural settings. It is also important that functional communication systems (such as signing, picture cards, communication boards, gesturing) are an integral part of instruction. Regardless of the communication system(s) used to teach speech and language skills, they must be applied across multiple settings. For example, if picture cards are used in the classroom, they must also be a part of the communication system used at home and in other environments.

■ PHYSICAL AND HEALTH CHARACTERISTICS

People with severe and multiple disabilities have significant physical and health care needs. For instance, these individuals have a higher incidence of congenital heart disease, **epilepsy**, respiratory problems, diabetes, and metabolic disorders. They also exhibit poor muscle tone and often have conditions such as **spasticity**, **athetosis**, and **hypotonia.** Such conditions require that professionals in the schools and other service agencies know how to administer medications, **catheterization**, **gastronomy tube feeding,** and **respiratory ventilation** (Sobsey & Cox, 1991).

■ VISION AND HEARING CHARACTERISTICS

Vision and hearing loss are common among individuals with severe and multiple disabilities. Sobsey and Wolf-Schein (1991) suggest that approximately 40% of these individuals will have a substantial vision and/or hearing loss. Some individuals, particularly those described as deaf–blind, have significant vision *and* hearing disorders that require services and supports beyond those for a person who is blind *or* deaf.

Assessment

raditionally, there has been a heavy reliance on standardized measurements, particularly the IQ test, in identifying people with severe and multiple disabilities, particularly when the primary symptom is mental retardation. For example, the American Association on Mental Retardation (AAMR) defined mental retardation as "significantly subaverage general intellectual functioning" as determined by the results of an intelligence (IQ) test (AAMR Ad Hoc Committee, 1992). Some professionals (Evans, 1991; Meyer et al., 1991b) have suggested that standardized testing, particularly the IQ test, has no place in identifying people with severe and multiple disabilities. Others (Wehman & Parent, 1997) believe that IQ tests may be appropriate for diagnosis but provide no "meaningful information for making curriculum decisions such as what to teach and how to teach it" (p. 158).

focus 5

Describe the functional (ecological) approach to assessing the needs of people with severe and multiple disabilities.

A proposed alternative to standardized tests is a **functional** or **ecological assessment approach**, which has the following characteristics:

■ It focuses on practical *independent living skills* that enable the person to survive and succeed in the real world.
■ It has an *ecological* emphasis that looks at the individual functioning in his or her surrounding environment.
■ It examines the *process* of learning and performance.
■ It suggests *intervention* techniques that may be successful.
■ It specifies ongoing monitoring procedures that can evaluate treatment progress. (Gaylord-Ross & Browder, 1991, p. 45)

As described in the TASH definition of severe disabilities, functional assessment is concerned with the match between the needs of the individual and the demands of the environment (adaptive fit). The purpose of the assessment is to determine what supports are necessary to achieve the intended outcomes of access and participation in natural settings.

Skills are never taught in isolation from actual performance demands. Additionally, the individual does not "get ready" to participate in the community through a sequence of readiness stages as in the developmental model, but learns and uses skills in the setting where the behavior is expected to occur. (McDonnell, Wilcox, & Hardman, 1991, p. 23)

The Early Childhood Years

The axiom "the earlier the better" is certainly applicable to early intervention services and supports for young children with severe and multiple disabilities. There is no question of whether or when services or supports should begin for young children with severe and multiple disabilities. They must begin at birth. Effective early intervention services that begin when the child is born are critical to the prevention and amelioration of social, medical, and educational problems that can occur throughout the life of the individual (Bailey & Wolery, 1992; Ramey & Landesman-Ramey, 1992).

During the early childhood years, services and supports are concentrated on two age groups: infants and toddlers, and preschool-age children.

■ SERVICES AND SUPPORTS FOR INFANTS AND TODDLERS

Effective programs for infants and toddlers with severe and multiple disabilities are both child- and family-centered. A child-centered approach is focused on identifying and meeting individual needs. Services begin with infant stimulation programs intended to elicit sensory, cognitive, and physical responses in newborns that will connect them with their environment. As the child develops, health care, physical therapy, occupational therapy, and speech and language services may become integral components of a child-centered program.

Family-centered programs are characterized by a holistic approach that involves the child as a member of the family unit. The needs, structure, and preferences of the family drive the delivery of services and supports (Eiserman, Weber, & McCoun, 1995). The overall purpose of family-centered intervention is to enable family members to initially cope with the birth of a child with a severe disability and eventually become empowered to grow together and support one another. Berry and Hardman (1997) suggested that family-centered approaches build on and increase family strengths, address the needs of every family member, and support mutually enjoyable family relationships. Supports for families may include parent-training programs, counseling, and **respite care** (see the Reflect on This feature on page 336).

■ SERVICES AND SUPPORTS FOR PRESCHOOL-AGE CHILDREN

Preschool programs for young children with severe and multiple disabilities continue the emphasis on family involvement while extending the life space of the child to a school setting. McDonnell, Hardman, McDonnell, & Kiefer-O'Donnell (1995) suggested four goals for preschool programs serving children with severe disabilities:

1. Maximize the child's development in a variety of important developmental areas. These include social communication, motor skills, cognitive skills, pre-academic skills, self-care, play, and personal management.
2. Develop the child's social interaction and classroom participation skills. Focus on developing peer relationships and teaching the child to follow adult direc-

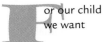

Reflect on This

WHAT FAMILIES WANT

For our child we want

- Independence
- Personal happiness
- Feelings of accomplishment
- Respect
- Ability to walk
- Ability to communicate
- Good friends
- Understanding that he/she is loved

- Employment
- Skills to feed him/herself
- Skills to dress him/herself
- Being comfortable enough to sleep through the night
- Skills to drive a car
- The experience of having a loving relationship with a member of the opposite sex
- To know and love God

For our family we want

- Social outings (especially restaurants)
- Sleep-filled nights
- Enjoyment of an evening out (as a couple)
- Normal sibling relationships
- Relatives and friends to understand the nature of our child's disabilities

- Help with planning some adaptations to our home

Source: From *Into Our Lives* by M. Hunt, P. Cornelius, P. Leventhal, P. Miller, T. Murray, & G. Stoner, 1990, Akron, OH: Children's Hospital Medical Center. Reprinted by permission.

tions, respond to classroom routines, and become self-directed (complete classroom activities without constant adult supervision).

3. Increase community participation through support to family members and other caregivers. Work to identify alternative caregivers so that the family has a broader base of support and more flexibility to pursue other interests. Help the family to identify activities within the neighborhood that their preschooler would enjoy to provide the child with opportunities to interact with same-age

For children with severe disabilities, some educators recommend a preschool program that blends the elements of special education, multicultural education, and developmentally appropriate practices.

peers. Activities may involve swimming or dancing lessons, joining a soccer team, going to church, and so on.

4. Prepare the child for inclusive school placements, and provide support for the transition to elementary school. The transition out of preschool will be facilitated if educators from the receiving elementary school work collaboratively with family and preschool personnel.

To meet these goals, Grenot-Scheyer, Schwartz, and Meyer (1997) proposed that preschool programs for children with severe disabilities blend the principles and elements of **developmentally appropriate practices (DAP),** multicultural education, and special education. DAP was developed by the National Association for the Education of Young Children as an alternative to an academic curricula for preschoolers. It emphasizes age-appropriate child exploration and play activities that are consistent with individual need. Multicultural education emphasizes acceptance of people from different cultural and ethnic backgrounds within and across the preschool curriculum. Successful culturally inclusive programs blend principles and practices that guide special education, inclusive education, and multicultural education (Grenot-Scheyer et al., 1997). Special education focuses on assessing individual needs, providing intensive instruction, and teaching explicit skills within the context of an individualized education program (IEP).

The combination of DAP, multicultural education, and special education work together to provide a quality experience for preschool-age children with severe disabilities. The following factors characterize an effective and inclusive preschool program using the three practices in combination:

- The program has a holistic view of child development. Teachers have a thorough understanding of child development and support the inclusion of diverse learners in the classroom.
- The classroom is viewed as a community of learners. Students have opportunities to enhance feelings of self-worth, social responsibility, and belonging.
- The program is based on a collaborative ethic. Colleagues view each other as equals, sharing their knowledge and skills.
- Educators use authentic assessment. **Authentic assessment** consists of a variety of performance-based assessments that require children to demonstrate a response in a real-life context.
- The classroom is heterogeneous. Children must have the opportunity to work and play in diverse and heterogeneous groups that attend to individual strengths and needs.
- A range of individualized supports and services are available. Teachers and therapists provide support in the natural setting of the classroom in the context of ongoing activities.
- The program engages children and uses an active learning model. Learning by doing is emphasized in meaningful contexts.
- The program emphasizes reflective teaching. Teachers are good observers of their own behavior as well as the behavior of the children.
- The program emphasizes multiple ways of teaching and learning. Children are encouraged to use multiple methods to solve problems. Teaching approaches are selected for a "goodness of fit" between the teacher and the learner. (Grenot-Scheyer et al., 1997)

BENJAMIN'S SCHOOL

Kipps Elementary School is one of 13 elementary schools in the Montgomery County Public School Division in the southwestern part of Virginia. Kipps is a new school which opened in the fall of 1994. At Kipps, like other schools in the system, students with disabilities attend general education classes in their neighborhood schools with their peers who do not have disability labels. Principals and staff in each school are involved in shared decision-making teams whereby decisions about the school's resources are made cooperatively with staff and with the input of parents; these decisions are consistent with the schools' and district's philosophy of providing special education services in the

least restrictive environment within the neighborhood school. The special education services and supports needed for each student are planned collaboratively by the student's educational team to address the individual student's strengths and needs; supports are implemented, evaluated, and revised by the team on an individual basis, not prescribed by a disability category. Collaboration between the special education teachers, classroom teachers, parents, and other team members (e.g., related services personnel) provides the essential mechanism for planning and problem-solving.

At Kipps, Benjamin is one of 10 students with severe disabilities, each of whom is enrolled full-time in a general

education classroom. These students range from 5 to 11 years old and are placed in kindergarten through grade 5. These students have special education labels such as "multi-handicapped," "developmental delay," "autism," and "mental retardation" and have one or more of the following conditions or characteristics: cerebral palsy, visual impairment, Down syndrome, challenging behavior, and nonsymbolic communication.

Benjamin's first year of inclusive education was in preschool within Head Start. He is now 7 years old and in Tricia William's second-grade classroom with others of his age. Benjamin has cerebral palsy, moves about with a walker, and has a special education label of multiple handi-

caps. He has developmental delays, visual impairments, and speech and language impairments, and hydrocephalus. He communicates primarily by words and phrases, gestures, and facial expressions. Benjamin, who is well known for being highly social, is described by some of his classmates as being "a very popular kid."

Benjamin's classroom has the same number of students as other classrooms in the school but is assigned one teaching assistant in the morning, who alternates with another in the afternoon. Both assistants attend to special needs presented by Benjamin, assist with general classroom activities, and also support educational needs of other students who do not

The Elementary School Years

Historically, services and supports for students with severe and multiple disabilities have been oriented to protection and care. The objective was to protect the individual from society, and society from the individual. This philosophy resulted in programs that isolated the individual and provided physical care rather than preparation for life in a heterogeneous world. Today, educators working in tandem with parents are concentrating their efforts on preparing students with severe and multiple disabilities to participate actively in the life of the family, school, and community (see the nearby Reflect on This feature).

Given the emphasis on lifelong learning and living in natural settings, educators have identified several features that characterize quality programs for elementary-age students with severe and multiple disabilities:

focus 7
Identify the features of effective services and supports for children with severe and multiple disabilities during the elementary school years.

- Self-determination—student preferences and needs are taken into account in developing educational objectives.

have disability labels. By dividing their time across two different classrooms, these assistants develop more versatile skills, and capacity is created within the school that minimizes the disruption caused by the inevitable absence of the teachers or assistants. Benjamin's special education teacher, Kenna Colley, distributes her time among the classrooms at Kipps where the 10 students with severe disabilities on her "caseload" are placed by working with the classroom teachers, teaching assistants, related services personnel, and peers. Through this collaboration, Benjamin participates in the same educational activities as his classmates although at times he may be pursuing different learning outcomes than they are and/or he may need individualized adaptations to ensure that his involvement is meaningful (e.g., enlarged print materials, specialized seating, peer assistance).

Benjamin's educational program is oriented toward his participation in school routines with an emphasis on skills needed for communication, peer relationships, mobility, and self-care. Though these represent the focus of his individualized curriculum, he is exposed to a broad array of curricular content in general education areas such as physical education, music, art, science, social studies, and language arts. The related services providers work with classroom staff to provide educationally relevant input that is required to support Benjamin's program in general class and school activities.

Mr. Van Dyke established twice-monthly "inclusion meetings" devoted to collaborative problem-solving. Teachers share their successes and concerns in a round-robin fashion, and the group makes decisions about solutions, determines who is responsible, and sets timelines. When complex problems arise, Mr. Van Dyke meets with a smaller group of teachers and facilitates solution finding. "Whole school" strategies also result from collaborative problem solving at Kipps. For Benjamin, who is very social and is learning to move more quickly through the school, a whole school strategy was put in place this year by requesting that everyone reduce their socialization with him in the hall, and instead, wait for times when he is not moving through the schools on a schedule. Teachers in turn advised their classes with sensitive explanations of the reasons.

Peer support is central to the inclusive school program in Montgomery County and takes several forms. For example, peers' questions are answered in respectful ways; teachers model appropriate interactions and help to students with disabilities as needed; teachers work with peers to problem-solve and discuss issues of concern (e.g., "How can we help Benjamin participate?"); and cooperative groups and activity-based instruction are frequently used within classroom activities. All staff members at Kipps Elementary School share responsibility for welcoming, including, and educating *all* the students in the school including those with severe disabilities.

Source: From "Severe and Multiple Disabilities," by M. F. Giangreco & M. E. Snell. In *Improving the Implementation of the Individuals with Disabilities Education Act: Making Schools Work for All of America's Children (Supplement)*, 1996, pp. 97–132. Washington, DC: National Council on Disability. Reprinted with permission.

- The school values and supports parental involvement.
- Instruction focuses on frequently used functional skills related to everyday life activities.
- Assistive technology is available to maintain or increase the functional capabilities of the student with severe and multiple disabilities.

SELF-DETERMINATION

People with severe and multiple disabilities, like everyone else, must be in a position to make their own life choices as much as possible. School programs that promote self-determination enhance each child's opportunity to become more independent in the life of the family and in the larger community setting. Providing students with severe disabilities the opportunity to communicate their needs and preferences enhances self-esteem and the ability to solve problems (Ward, 1991).

PARENTAL INVOLVEMENT

Schools are more successful in meeting the needs of students when they establish positive relationships with the family (Newton & Tarrant, 1992). The important role that parents play during the early childhood years must continue and be supported during elementary school. Parents who actively participate in their child's educational program exert more influence on the development and implementation of instruction that is consistent with individual needs and preferences. Parental involvement can be a powerful predictor of postschool adjustment for students with severe and multiple disabilities.

A strong home–school partnership requires that parents and educators

- acknowledge and respect each other's differences in values and culture.
- listen openly and attentively to each other's concerns.
- value varying opinions and ideas.
- discuss issues openly and in an atmosphere of trust.
- share in the responsibility and consequences of making a decision. (Berry & Hardman, 1997)

■ TEACHING FUNCTIONAL SKILLS

Effective educational programs focus on the functional skills necessary for students with severe and multiple disabilities to live successfully in the natural settings of family, school, and community. A functional skill is one that will have immediate use for the individual. If the student with severe disabilities is to learn how to

Today's Technology

MEET JOEY

Identified as having cerebral palsy and also being "deaf–blind with cognitive disabilities," Joey spent the first four years of his school career in a special day class, where he spent a great deal of time lying in a beanbag chair. He had no consistent method of communication other than screaming and crying, which he used when staff attempted to engage him in an activity. Even the peer helpers from general education classes avoided contact with Joey. The majority of interactions that students or staff had with Joey were to provide personal care services, such as feeding and changing his diaper. About the time that Joey turned 8, his life changed significantly as assistive tech-

nology was introduced into his range of supports and services.

Four years ago, when he was 8 years old and still attending a special day class, Joey began to learn about cause and effect through the use of a set of adapted switches connected to a Bart Simpson toy. The standard remote control switch for the toy featured one button to move Bart forward and a second to move him backward. The remote control was rewired so that Joey could hit either a large plate for forward motion or a large pillow switch to reverse the movement. Due to Joey's limited vision, the toy was placed on a table so that, at the very least, he could feel the vibration of the toy moving across the

table's surface. As soon as Joey became engaged in the activity, exciting things happened. First, he clearly began to follow the movement of Bart's yellow head as it moved across his field of vision. Second, peers in the room saw this activity as a way to interact with Joey. Finally, as his peers helped him to press the switches, Joey began to associate the operation of the switch with the movement of the toy. As a result, his peers began to consider many more activities in which Joey could participate. The classroom teacher set up a variety of appliances that could be switch controlled so that Joey could practice throughout the day. It became obvious that Joey could perform these same ac-

tivities in general education classes.

Over the next couple of years, Joey began spending more time in general education classes where he participated in activities instead of simply observing them. He became more proficient at switch use and was able to operate a number of individualized devices. One device was used for climate control. Because the school operated on a year-round schedule, the children had to acclimate to warm classrooms. Some teachers permitted students to take turns "misting" the classroom. Joey participated by using a switch-operated spray bottle which was modified from a sports bottle. While a classmate pointed the sprayer

cross a street safely, shop in a grocery store, play a video game, or eat in a local restaurant, the necessary skills should be taught in the actual setting where the behavior is to be performed. It should not be assumed that a skill learned in a classroom will transfer to a setting outside of the school. Instruction in a more natural environment can ensure that the skill will be useful and maintained over time. This instruction should involve the following elements:

- Many different people
- A variety of settings within the community
- Varied materials that will interest the learner and match performance demands

■ ASSISTIVE TECHNOLOGY

Assistive technology, as defined in federal law, means any item, piece of equipment, or product system that can be used to increase, maintain, or improve the functional capabilities of students with disabilities (The Technology-Related Assistance for Individuals with Disabilities Act, PL 100-407). Wehman (1997) identified several categories of assistive technology:

- Mobility (wheelchairs, lifts, adaptive driving controls, scooters, laser canes)
- Seating and positioning (assistance in choosing and using a wheelchair)
- Computers (environmental control units, word processors, software, keyboards)

in different directions, Joey operated the water flow. Other adaptations included a Plexiglas display board that was used for communication, and a variety of appliances that he controlled with his switches.

By the time Joey entered fifth grade, he made the transition from being a "visitor from Room #5" to being a full-time member of the class. New situations required new adaptations. Joey's classmates had been responsible for raising Joey's hand to summon the teacher, but they felt that Joey needed his own method. A "low-tech" light switch was mounted on Joey's laptray so that he could attract the teacher's attention. His ability to use a switch increased so that he could use several of them, coded with Picture Communication Symbols to operate a Speakeasy commu-

nication device with messages recorded by a student whom he chose. He used another switch to turn on a tape recorder to play the same book on tape that the other students were reading during "silent reading" time. Consistent use of switches helped to increase his motivation and dexterity for accessing the computer through the Ke:nx program. These abilities would be essential for participating at his neighborhood middle school.

Joey's seating and positioning needs were adjusted, including time scheduled to be out of his wheelchair and sitting at a desk. His therapy needs were met during the regular physical education periods, as coordinated by his teacher, with consultative support from the school district's physical therapist and adaptive physical education specialist.

The special education teacher worked closely with the fifth-grade teacher to adapt the curriculum and make accommodations as necessary. Joey's classmates were an invaluable source of creativity who thought of innovative strategies to increase Joey's participation. As they became more familiar with Joey and the way in which he responded, they were key players in identifying new goals based on their keen insights and perceptions of Joey's needs and desires. The entire range of services and supports that were listed on his IEP were designed and implemented through effective collaboration of all of the professionals involved. People learned to perform their roles in new settings and under different circumstances. By the end of the school year, everyone agreed that Joey had surpassed all earlier expectations. Eventually it was determined

that Joey no longer required services from the vision and hearing specialists, as he was obviously using both of these sensory modes adequately in all of his daily activities. His transition plan for moving to the middle school included a discussion of scheduling him into classes where he would remain with a number of his fifth-grade classmates. The possibilities for Joey are endless, and as luck would have it, his new school is a technology magnet, a perfect place for him to continue to build his skills in using all kinds of technology.

Source: Adapted from Sax, C., Pumpian, I., & Fisher, D. (1997, March). *Assistive Technology and Inclusion.* Issue Brief. Pittsburgh, PA: Consortium on Inclusive Schooling Practices, Allegheny University of the Health Sciences, pp. 1–5. Reprinted with permission.

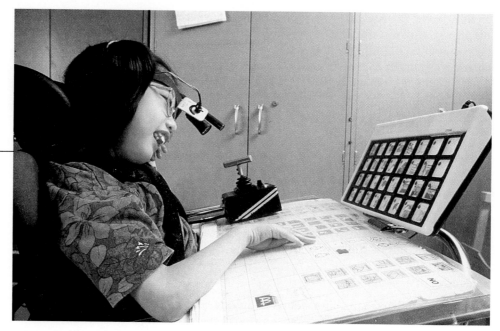

By using an electric communication board with picture and symbol cues, this student with multiple disabilities is able to create and respond to language. Augmentative communication through assistive devices is an integral part of this student's IEP.

- Toys and games (software, switch-operated toys)
- Activities of daily living (feeders, lifts, watch alarms, memory books)
- Communication (touch talkers, reading systems, talking keyboards (p. 475)

Students with severe and multiple disabilities will benefit from any one or more of these assistive devices or activities. Given that communication deficits and delays are primary characteristics of these students, **augmentative communication** will nearly always be an integral component of an individualized education program. Mirenda, Iacono, and Williams (1990) suggested that augmentative communication may include (1) adapting existing vocal or gestural abilities into meaningful communication; (2) teaching manual signing (such as American Sign Language), static symbols, or icons (such as **Blissymbols**); and (3) using manual or electronic communication devices (such as electric communication boards, picture cues, or synthetic speech).

The Adolescent Years

Societal perceptions about the capabilities of people with severe and multiple disabilities have been significantly altered over the past several years. There is little question that until very recently the potential of these individuals to learn, live, and work in community settings was significantly underestimated. Giangreco and Snell (1996) indicated that there is now strong evidence that people with severe and multiple disabilities can become active participants in the lives of their community and family. This realization has prompted professionals and parents to seek significant changes in the ways that schools prepare students for the transition into adult life.

In a review of the research on successful community living for people with severe disabilities, McDonnell, Mathot-Buckner, and Ferguson (1996) have pointed out four outcomes that are important in planning for the transition to adult life: (1) establishing a network of friends and acquaintances, (2) developing the ability to use community resources on a regular basis, (3) securing a paid job that supports the use of community resources and interaction with peers, and (4) establishing independence and autonomy in making lifestyle choices (p. 9).

Describe four outcomes that are important in planning for the transition from school to adult life for adolescents with severe and multiple disabilities.

Inclusive Education

Many professionals argue that the provision of services and supports in an inclusive educational setting is a critical factor in delivering a quality program for students with severe and multiple disabilities (Gee, 1996; Giangreco & Snell, 1996; Putnam, 1994; Sailor, Gee, & Karasoff, 1993; Thousand, Villa, & Nevin, 1994). Effective educational programs for these students include continual opportunities for interaction between students with severe disabilities and their nondisabled peers. Frequent and age-appropriate interactions between students with disabilities and their nondisabled peers can enhance opportunities for successful participation in the community during the adult years. Social interaction can be enhanced by creating opportunities for these students to associate both during and after the school day. Successful inclusion efforts are characterized by the following features:

focus 9

Describe four features that characterize successful inclusive education for students with severe and multiple disabilities.

- Physical placement of students with severe and multiple disabilities in general education schools and classes
- Systematic organization of opportunities for interaction between students with severe and multiple disabilities and students without disabilities
- Specific instruction to increase the competence of students with severe and multiple disabilities in interacting with students who are not disabled
- Highly trained teachers competent in the necessary instructional and assistive technology that facilitates social interaction between students with and without disabilities

One of the most important characteristics of the postschool environments in which students ultimately must function is the need for frequent interaction with people who are not disabled. Consequently, it is logical to plan educational programs that duplicate this feature of the environment and actively build skills required for successful interaction.

As students with severe and multiple disabilities are included in general education schools and classrooms, it is important to find ways to encourage social interactions between these students and students who are not disabled. Planned opportunities for interaction may include the use of in-class peer supports (tutors, circles of friends) as well as access to everyday school activities such as assemblies, recess, lunch, or field trips.

Interacting in Natural Settings

PEOPLE WITH SEVERE AND MULTIPLE DISABILITIES

■ EARLY CHILDHOOD YEARS

TIPS FOR THE FAMILY

- During the infant and toddler years, seek out family-oriented programs that focus on communication and the building of positive relationships among all individual members.
- Seek supports and services for your preschool-age child that promote communication and play activities with same-age nondisabled peers.
- Seek opportunities for friendships to develop between your child and children without disabilities in family and neighborhood settings.
- Use the individualized family service plan (IFSP) and the individualized education plan (IEP) as a means to establish goals that develop your child's social interaction and classroom participation skills.

TIPS FOR THE GENERAL EDUCATION PRESCHOOL TEACHER

- Establish a classroom environment that promotes and supports diversity.
- Use a child-centered approach to instruction that acknowledges and values every child's strengths, preferences, and individual needs.
- Ignore whatever labels have been used to describe the child with severe and multiple disabilities. There is no relationship between the label and the instruction

needed by the child to succeed in natural settings.
- Create opportunities for ongoing communication and play activities among children with severe disabilities and their same-age nondisabled peers. Nurture interactive peer relationships across a variety of instructional areas and settings.

TIPS FOR PRESCHOOL PERSONNEL

- Support the inclusion of young children with severe and multiple disabilities in all preschool classrooms and programs.
- Always refer to children by name, not by label. If you must label, use child-first language—"children with severe disabilities."
- Communicate genuine respect and support for all teachers, staff, and volunteers who look for ways to include children with severe disabilities in preschool classrooms and schoolwide activities.
- Welcome families into the preschool programs. Listen to what parents have to say about the importance of, or concerns about, including their child in school programs and activities. Create opportunities for parents to become involved in their child's program through volunteering, school governance, and so on.

TIPS FOR NEIGHBORS AND FRIENDS

- First and foremost, see the child with severe disabilities as an individual who has needs, preferences,

strengths, and weaknesses. Avoid the pitfalls of stereotyping and "self-fulfilling prophecies."
- Support opportunities for your children and those of friends and neighbors to interact and play with a child with severe and multiple disabilities.
- Help children without disabilities build friendships rather than caregiving roles with children who have severe and multiple disabilities.
- Provide a supportive community environment for the family of a young child with severe and multiple disabilities. Encourage the family, including the child, to participate in neighborhood activities.

■ ELEMENTARY YEARS

TIPS FOR THE FAMILY

- Actively participate in the development of your son's or daughter's IEP. Write down the priorities and educational goals that you see as important to allow your child to participate in the natural settings of home, school, and community.
- Follow up at home on activities that the school suggests are important to help your child generalize skills learned at school to other natural settings.
- Actively participate as a volunteer in the school whether it be in your child's classroom or in another situation. Show your appreciation and support for administrators, teachers, and

staff who openly value and support the inclusion of your child in the school and classroom.
- Continually communicate with administrators and teachers how important it is to include children with severe disabilities in classroom and schoolwide activities (such as riding on the same school bus, going to recess and lunch at the same time, participating in schoolwide assemblies).

TIPS FOR THE GENERAL EDUCATION CLASSROOM TEACHER

- See children with severe and multiple disabilities as individuals, not labels. Focus on their similarities with other children rather than their differences.
- Openly value and support diversity in your classroom. Set individualized goals and objectives for all children.
- Develop a classroom environment and instructional program that recognize multiple needs and abilities.
- Become part of a team that works together to meet the needs of all children in your classroom. View the special education teacher as a resource that can assist you in developing an effective instructional program for the child with severe and multiple disabilities.

TIPS FOR SCHOOL PERSONNEL

- Communicate that diversity is a strength in your school. Openly value diversity by providing the resources necessary for teachers to work with students who have a range of needs and come from heterogeneous backgrounds.

- Integrate school resources as well as children. Develop schoolwide teacher-assistance or teacher-support teams that use a collaborative ethic to meet the needs of every student.
- Support general and special education teachers in the development of peer-partner and support networks for students with severe and multiple disabilities.
- Include all students in the programs and activities of the school.

TIPS FOR NEIGHBORS AND FRIENDS

- Openly communicate to school personnel, friends, and neighbors your support of families who are seeking to have their child with severe and multiple disabilities be a part of an inclusive school setting.
- Communicate to your children and those of friends and neighbors the value of inclusion. Demonstrate this value by creating opportunities for children with severe disabilities and their families to play an active role in the life of the community.

■ SECONDARY AND TRANSITION YEARS

TIPS FOR THE FAMILY

- Seek opportunities for students from your son's or daughter's high school to visit your home. Help arrange get-togethers or par-

ties involving students from the neighborhood or school.

- Communicate to the school what you see as priorities for your son or daughter in the transition from school to adult life. Suggest goals and objectives that promote and support social interaction and community-based activities with nondisabled peers. Work with the school to translate your goals into an individualized transition plan (ITP).

TIPS FOR THE GENERAL EDUCATION CLASSROOM TEACHER

- Become part of a schoolwide team that works together to meet the needs of all students in high school. Value the role of the special educator as teacher, collaborator, and consultant who can serve as a valuable resource in planning for the instructional needs of students with severe disabilities. Collaborate with special education teachers and other specialists to adapt subject matter in your classroom (e.g., science, math, or physical education) to the individual needs of students with severe and multiple disabilities.
- Communicate the importance of students with severe disabilities being included in school programs and activities. Although the goals and activities of this student may differ from those of other students, with support they will benefit from working with you and other students in the class.

- Support the student with severe disabilities becoming involved in extracurricular high school activities. If you are the faculty sponsor of a club or organization, explore whether this student is interested and how he or she could get involved.

TIPS FOR SCHOOL PERSONNEL

- Advocate for parents of high-school-age students with severe and multiple disabilities to participate in the activities and governance of the school.
- Support parental involvement in the transition-planning process during the high school years by listening to parents.
- Support high school special education or vocational teachers seeking to develop community-based instruction programs that focus on students learning and applying skills in actual community settings (e.g., grocery stores, malls, theaters, parks, work sites).

TIPS FOR NEIGHBORS, FRIENDS, AND POTENTIAL EMPLOYERS

- Work with the family and school personnel to create opportunities for students with severe and multiple disabilities to participate in community activities (such as going to the movies, "hanging out" with nondisabled peers in the neighborhood mall, going to high school sporting events) as often as possible.
- As a potential employer, work with the high school to locate and establish

community-based employment training sites for students with severe and multiple disabilities.

■ ADULT YEARS

TIPS FOR THE FAMILY

- Develop an understanding of life after school for your son or daughter during the adult years. What are the formal (government-funded, parent organizations) and informal supports (family and friends) available in your community? What are the characteristics of adult service programs? Explore adult support systems in the local community in the areas of supported living, employment, and recreation and leisure.

TIPS FOR NEIGHBORS, FRIENDS, AND POTENTIAL EMPLOYERS

- Become part of the community support network for the individual with severe and multiple disabilities. Be alert to ways that this individual can become and remain actively involved in community employment, neighborhood recreational activities, and local church functions.
- As potential employers in the community, seek information on employment of people with severe and multiple disabilities. Find out about programs (such as supported employment) that focus on establishing work for people with mental retardation while meeting your needs as an employer.

Severe Disabilities and Biomedical Dilemmas

apid advances in medical technology have resulted in the survival of an increasing number of infants with severe and multiple disabilities. Today, many such infants who would have died at birth only five to ten years ago now often live well into their adult years. However, this decrease in infant mortality and increase in lifespan have raised a number of serious ethical issues regarding decisions about prevention, care, and selective nontreatment of infants with severe disabilities. In recent years, there has been an increasing awareness and interest in **bioethics**, particularly as it relates to serious illness and severe disabilities. Bioethical issues include concerns about the purpose and use of genetic engineering, screening for genetic diseases, abortion, and the withholding of life-sustaining medical treatment. A number of questions have been raised by both professionals and parents. When do individual rights begin? Who should live, and who should die? What is personhood? Who defines quality of life? What are the rights of the individual with severe disabilities in relationship to the obligations of a society? Who shall make the difficult decisions?

focus 10

Describe four bioethical dilemmas that can have an impact on people with severe disabilities and their families.

■ GENETIC ENGINEERING

The purpose of genetic engineering is to conquer disease. Through the identification of a faulty gene that causes a disease, such as cystic fibrosis, we are able to prevent future occurrence and treat those who have the condition. There is, however, a dilemma. Although genetic engineering may be seen as holding considerable promise for reducing human suffering in the future, it can also be viewed as a means to enhance or perfect human beings. The potential impact of genetic engineering on human suffering was described by Choppin (1991, p. 1):

A leading human geneticist told this story recently. On a Friday morning he was called by a colleague, a neurologist, who said that a woman was in his office with her young son, who appeared to have a fatal inherited disease. In addition, she was pregnant—and the neurologist said he urgently needed advanced laboratory help to make a diagnosis. By Friday afternoon it was determined that the young boy did have the disease—but by Monday it was clear that, fortunately, the baby the mother was carrying did not. In the 21st century, such stories will probably be told many times, but with an added line: "By Tuesday we started effective therapy for the disease in the young boy."

■ GENETIC SCREENING AND COUNSELING

Genetic screening is a search for genes in the human body that are predisposed to disease, are already diseased, or may lead to disease in future generations of the same family. Genetic screening has become widespread throughout the world but is not without controversy (Cohen, 1990). According to one view, screening must be restricted to very limited circumstances or society will not accept or be willing to care for children born with severe and multiple disabilities. Hauerwas (1986) suggested that "it has become common in our society to assume that certain children

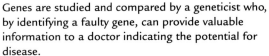
Genes are studied and compared by a geneticist who, by identifying a faulty gene, can provide valuable information to a doctor indicating the potential for disease.

born with severe birth defects who also happen to be retarded should not be kept alive in order to spare them a lifetime of suffering" (p. 54).

The next logical step following genetic screening is counseling for family members to understand the results and implications of the screening. The concerns surrounding genetic counseling focus on the neutrality of the counselor. The role of the genetic counselor is one of giving information and not becoming a "moral adviser" or psychotherapist for the family. Drew et al. (1996) noted that it is difficult for genetic counselors to maintain neutrality when they have personal beliefs and strong feelings about what should be done. A Presidential Commission for the Study of Ethical Problems in Medicine (1983) found that counselors can become directive to family members in their attempts to help them make the "right" decision in regard to future pregnancies or ongoing treatment of a condition. The commission's findings are particularly relevant today in light of society's reliance on physicians as family advisers and authority figures.

■ SELECTIVE ABORTION AND WITHHOLDING MEDICAL TREATMENT

No other issue polarizes society like the unborn child's right to life versus a woman's right to choose. Rapidly advancing medical technology makes the issue of abortion even more complex. A number of chromosomal and metabolic disorders that may result in severe and multiple disabilities can now be identified in utero. Thus, parents and physicians are placed in the untenable position of deciding whether or not to abort a fetus diagnosed with severe anomalies. On one side are those who argue that the quality of life for the child born with severe disabilities may be so diminished that, if given the choice, they would choose not to live under such circumstances. Additionally, the family may not be able to cope with a child who is severely disabled. On the other side are those who point out that no one has the right to decide for someone else whether a life is "worth living." For people with severe disabilities, there have been major strides in education, medical care, technology, and social inclusion that have enhanced their quality of life.

Controversy also surrounds the issue of denying routine medical treatment to an infant with a disability (Drew et al., 1996). The application of one standard for a child who was not disabled and another for a child with a severe disability has resulted in some difficult questions that are not easily addressed:

Does every living newborn have the right to the treatment that is most likely to preserve life, or is it permissible to sometimes let such an infant die, or even take active steps to end the life of the infant?

Who has the responsibility, or the right, to make decisions on these matters, either for the individual infant or for such infants in general?

How should the scarce and expensive resources required for neonatal intensive care be allocated, both at the individual and general level? (Neal, 1990, p. 92)

Several national organizations (The Association for Persons with Severe Handicaps, the Arc—A National Organization on Mental Retardation, the American Association on Mental Retardation) have taken strong positions opposing the withholding of medical treatment when any decision is based on the individual being disabled. These organizations hold that everyone is entitled to the right to life, and it is the obligation of society to protect people from the ignorance and prejudices that may be associated with disability.

Case Study

THE BEGINNING OF A NEW CIRCLE OF FRIENDS

Joanne and Jennifer are new students in the fifth grade homeroom. It's midafternoon of their first day at the new school, and time for recess. The special education aide has break now, so Tom and Maria, two students in the homeroom, volunteer to help Jennifer outside to the playground. Halfway down the hall, Jennifer begins to wheel her chair—slowly, but by herself. Tom lights up.

"Hey, I didn't know that you could do that. Why didn't you tell me before?"

Jennifer first smiles and then lets out a full laugh. The two other fifth-graders join in. They continue slowly outside,

where Tom leaves to play softball. Joanne, the other new student, has been invited to join an impromptu soccer game, serving, because of her height, as goalie. Maria, not wanting to leave Jennifer simply to sit by herself during recess, asks, "Do you want to play jump rope?"

Again, Jennifer smiles, and looks toward the group of girls next to the building who have already begun to play jump rope. Maria understands and helps Jennifer over a curb, as the two girls move on to the game.

Once there, Maria asks, "Do you know how to twirl?"

Jennifer shakes her head no, so Maria places the end of the

rope in her hand, and holding it together, says, "Okay, hold it like this, and go round this way," guiding her movements with her hand.

Soon, Jennifer gets the hang of it, and Maria is able to let go. It's her turn to jump, so she leaves Jennifer's side, and begins her routine. She is able to jump longer than any of the other girls. As she spins around to complete a maneuver, she faces Jennifer as she jumps. Seeing her twirl, Maria sticks out her tongue and both girls laugh. Unfortunately, the twirling stops, ending Maria's turn. It doesn't really matter, because a new game will start again tomorrow and Maria usually wins anyway.

In a moment Ms. Nelson calls to the students to return to class, and Maria and Jennifer come in together. As they enter the room, Ms. Nelson asks the classmates to take out their library books and use the remaining time to read silently. Marsha, who had been playing soccer with Joanne, asks her teacher if she could loan her one of her books to read. Ms. Nelson approves, and the girls go to the reading corner of the room to choose among Marsha's three books.

The special education aide, in seeing Jennifer enter the class, takes her chair and moves her to the side of the room to work on her communication board. Maria asks her teacher, "Ms. Nelson, is it okay if I give Jennifer one of my books to look at?"

The special education aide hearing the request interrupts, saying, "Honey, Jennifer really can't read your books. But thanks anyway."

"Well, what if we read together?"

Both her teacher and the aide think for a second, and simultaneously give their approval. Together, Maria and Jennifer spend the remainder of class reading her two books, one on raising tropical fish and the other about a girl on a ranch and her pet horse.

Class ends, and the special education aide helps Jennifer place her papers in her backpack and go out to the special education bus.

From a young child's perspective, establishing friends is one of the more important activities of school. Taking advantage of natural opportunities that occur at school is crucial for all students, including those with severe disabilities. Learning to communicate, including new ways to listen, is all part of the process of building bonds. With positive experiences come new opportunities.

Often, the best action on the part of team members is to not act and to let the natural events and efforts of peers begin to evolve.

■ APPLICATION
■ Could this experience have as easily occurred in a special school or if Jennifer had to be served solely in a self-contained classroom?
■ How can this relationship be continued outside of school?
■ Under what conditions is it appropriate to change scheduled instruction (such

as working on a communication board) for more spontaneous opportunities?
■ Why is being a "member" of the homeroom so important to establishing friendships for children with severe disabilities?

Source: Adapted from _Introduction to Persons with Severe Disabilities_ (p. 194), by J. M. McDonnell, M. L. Hardman, A. P. McDonnell, R. Kiefer-O'Donnell, 1995, Boston: Allyn and Bacon. Reprinted with permission.

Debate Forum

DO PARENTS ALWAYS HAVE THE RIGHT TO DECIDE?

The family setting:

Mother, 34 years old, hospital nurse
Father, 35 years old, lawyer
Two normal children in the family

In late fall of 1963, Mr. and Mrs. A gave birth to a premature baby boy. Soon after birth, the child was diagnosed as a "mongoloid"[1] (Down syndrome), with the added complication of an intestinal blockage (duodenal atresia). The latter condition could be corrected with an operation of quite nominal risk. Without the operation, the child could not be fed and would die.

At the time of birth Mrs. A overheard the doctor express his belief that the child was a mongol. She immediately indicated she did not want the child. The next day, in consultation with a physician, she maintained this position, refusing to give permission for the corrective operation on the intestinal blockage. Her husband supported her in this position, saying that his wife knew more about these things (i.e., mongoloid children) than he. The reason the mother gave for her position—"It would be unfair to the other children of the household to raise them with a mongoloid."

The physician explained to the parents that the degree of mental retardation cannot be predicted at birth—running from very low mentality to borderline subnormal. As he said: "Mongolism, it should be stressed, is one of the

milder forms of mental retardation. That is, mongols' I.Q.s are generally in the 50–80 range, and sometimes a little higher. That is, they're almost always trainable. They can hold simple jobs. And they're famous for being happy children. They're perennially happy and usually a great joy." Without other complications, they can anticipate a long life.

Given the parents' decision, the hospital staff did not seek a court order to override the decision. The child was put in a side room and, over an 11-day period, allowed to starve to death.

Following this episode, the parents undertook genetic counseling (chromosome studies) with regard to future possible pregnancies.

■ POINT
The right to decide whether this baby has the operation to remove the intestinal blockage must ultimately rest with the parents. Their reasons for this decision should not be questioned, since the ultimate responsibility for raising this child or deciding to let him die will rest with them. Only they can weigh all the factors that will affect their family, including impact on the other children, emotional issues, and financial burdens. No one should attempt to step into the shoes of these parents in what may be the most difficult decision of their lives.

■ COUNTERPOINT
It is the responsibility of the physician to override the parents' decision in this case. The

[1]The term _mongoloid_ was in common use in 1963 when this baby was born. It is no longer an acceptable descriptor for a person with Down syndrome.

rights of the baby must not be weighed against the "greater good" for the family or society. This child is going to be denied an operation that, were he not disabled, would have been done on a routine basis. Allowing this infant to starve to death because he has a disability can only be described as child abuse, if not murder.

Source: From *Selective Nontreatment of Handicapped Newborns*, by R. Weir, 1984, New York: Oxford University Press, pp. 50–51; *Introduction to Persons with Severe Disabilities*, by J. McDonnell, M. Hardman, A. P. McDonnell, and R. Kiefer-O'Donnell, 1995, Boston: Allyn and Bacon, p. 94.

Review

What are the three components of the TASH definition of severe disabilities?

- The relationship of the individual with the environment (adaptive fit)
- The inclusion of people of all ages
- The necessity of extensive ongoing support in life activities

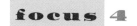

Define the terms *multiple disabilities* and *deafness– blindness* as described in IDEA.

- Multiple disabilities refers to concomitant impairments (such as mental retardation–orthopedic impairments, etc.). The combination causes educational problems so severe that they cannot be accommodated in special education programs solely for one impairment.
- Deafness–blindness involves concomitant hearing and visual impairments. The combination causes communication and other de-velopmental and educational problems so severe that they cannot be accommodated in special education programs solely for children who are deaf or blind.

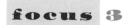

Identify the estimated prevalence and causes of severe and multiple disabilities.

- Prevalence estimates generally range from 0.1% to 1% of the general population.
- In 1994, students with multiple disabilities accounted for about 1.8% of the 5 million students with disabilities served in the public schools. Approximately 0.0003% of students with disabilities were labeled deaf–blind.
- There are many possible causes of severe and multiple disabilities. Most severe and multiple disabilities are evident at birth.
- Birth defects may be the result of genetic or metabolic problems. Factors associated with poisoning, accidents, malnutrition, physical and emotional neglect, and disease are also known causes.

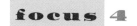

What are the characteristics of persons with severe and multiple disabilities?

- Mental retardation is a primary condition.
- Most children will be unable to learn basic academics. Instruction in functional academics is the most effective approach to learning academic skills.
- These individuals often do not have age-appropriate adaptive skills.
- Significant speech and language deficits and delays are a primary characteristic.
- Physical and health problems are common, involving conditions such as congenital heart disease, epilepsy, respiratory problems, spasticity, athetosis, and hypotonia. Vision and hearing loss are also common.

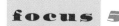

Describe the functional (ecological) approach to assessing the needs of people with severe and multiple disabilities.

- It focuses on independent living skills that enable the person to survive and succeed in the real world.
- It emphasizes ecology and looks at the individual functioning in his or her surrounding environment.
- It examines the process involved in learning and performance.
- It suggests intervention techniques that may be successful.
- It specifies ongoing monitoring procedures that can evaluate treatment progress.

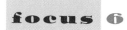

Identify the features of effective services and supports for children with severe and multiple disabilities during the early childhood years.

- Services and supports must begin at birth.
- Programs for infants and toddlers are both child- and family-centered.
- The goals for preschool programs are to maximize development across several developmental areas, to develop social interaction and classroom participation skills, to increase community participation through support to family and caregivers, and to prepare the

child for inclusive school placement.

■ Effective and inclusive preschool programs have a holistic view of the child, see the classroom as community of learners, base the program on a collaborative ethic, use authentic assessment, create a heterogeneous environment, make available a range of individualized supports and services, engage educators in reflective teaching, and emphasize multiple ways of teaching and learning.

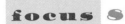 **7**

Identify the features of effective services and supports for children with severe and multiple disabilities during the elementary school years.

■ Self-determination—student preferences and needs are taken into account in developing educational objectives.
■ The school values and supports parental involvement.
■ Instruction focuses on frequently used functional

skills related to everyday life activities.

■ Assistive technology is available to maintain or increase the functional capabilities of the student with severe and multiple disabilities.

 **8**

Describe four outcomes that are important in planning for the transition from school to adult life for adolescents with severe and multiple disabilities.

■ Establishing a network of friends and acquaintances
■ Developing the ability to use community resources on a regular basis
■ Securing a paid job that supports the use of community resources and interaction with peers
■ Establishing independence and autonomy in making lifestyle choices

 **9**

Describe four features that characterize successful inclusive education for

students with severe and multiple disabilities.

■ Physical placement of students with severe and multiple disabilities in general education schools and classes.
■ Systematic organization of opportunities for interaction between students with severe and multiple disabilities and students without disabilities.
■ Specific instruction to increase the competence of students with severe and multiple disabilities in interacting with students who are not disabled.
■ Highly trained teachers competent in the necessary instructional and assistive technology that facilitates social interaction between students with and without disabilities.

focus 10

Describe four bioethical dilemmas that can have an impact on people with severe disabilities and their families.

■ Genetic engineering may be used to conquer disease or as a means to enhance or perfect human beings.
■ Genetic screening may be effective in preventing disease but can also have an effect on society's willingness to accept or take care of children born with severe and multiple disabilities.
■ Genetic counselors can provide important information to families but may also lose neutrality and give their own personal beliefs about what the family should do.
■ Selective abortion and options for the withholding of medical treatment may allow parents to make the very personal decision about whether the quality of life for their unborn child may be so diminished that life would not be worth living. However, it can also be argued that no one has the right to decide for someone else whether a life is worth living.

People with Autism

To begin with . . .

 His way of walking on the balls of his feet was akin to prancing. . . . Both boys relied heavily on peripheral vision. Even when spoken to, I felt like they listened to me "sideways." (Biklen, 1990, p. 291)

 I had begun to feel something was missing but I did not know what it was. I had a doll and wanted very much to cut it open to see if it had any feelings inside. I took a knife and tried to pry it open but became afraid of the consequences of breaking the doll and simply went on wondering for the next few years. (Williams, 1992, p. 46)

On average, about three of every four students with disabilities spend their day in a general education classroom or resource room setting. However, only about 20% of students with autism spend their day in these settings. In fact, 25% of students with autism are educated in separate buildings or residential facilities in comparison to 4% of other students with disabilities. (U.S. Department of Education, 1997)

 Temple Grandin, Ph.D. in animal science and a faculty member at Colorado State University, has published over 100 articles on topics including animal behavior, facilities management, and autism. Temple Grandin has autism. (Sacks, 1993)

Josh

Josh is in a general education class at his elementary school. His friend Marshall, who has learning disabilities, is a close friend to Josh. Marshall says, "Josh likes to dribble the basketball. Other people help Josh, but I help him a lot, too."

When Josh was born, his parents thought he was deaf, but tests showed he could hear. At age 30 months, Josh

was diagnosed with autism. His parents couldn't afford a specialized clinic or treatment facility and felt at a loss for what to do. They visited a school with a separate unit for children with autism, mental retardation, and other disabilities. During the visit, Josh mingled with other children and mimicked their behavior—shouts, some violent movements. Josh's parents decided not to place Josh in that school.

Josh entered a general education class. The special education teacher at the school was concerned at first because Josh would bite his nails, scratch his legs. He wasn't interacting with the other stu-

dents. Gradually, he started to talk and interact with the other students. His special education teacher says, "I think this wouldn't have happened if he were only interacting with other autistic children."

Josh's dad feels strongly about including students with disabilities in the general education classroom: "When wheelchairs come in (to school) in the morning and the Down syndrome (students) come in in the morning, and Josh comes in in the morning, they are the students. They are not the special education students. It's a long process and it's just becoming comfortable."

Billy

Billy is a blue-eyed, blond little boy of striking beauty; he is almost too perfect physically. His parents first became aware that Billy was different and had special problems when he was 5 years old but had not yet begun to talk. Some of his other behaviors also bothered Billy's parents a great deal. Billy didn't seem to play like other children. He would rock for long periods of time in his crib, and he had little interest in toys. At best, Billy would just spin the wheels of his trucks and stare as they turned. Most disturbing to Billy's parents was the fact that he showed little af-

focus 1
Identify four areas of functional challenge often found in children with autism.

A UTISM FIRST became a recognized disability category in the Individuals with Disabilities Education Act of 1990 (IDEA). Although newly acknowledged in federal law, autism began to appear in the research literature in the first half of the 20th century and is thought to have been described as early as the early 1800s (Carrey, 1995). The word *autism* is taken from the Greek *autos,* meaning "self," to indicate the extreme sense of isolation and detachment from the world around them that characterizes individuals with autism.

Symptoms of autism tend to appear very early. Most cases emerge before the age of 2½, and few are diagnosed after the age of 5. Autism is one of the most seriously disruptive of all childhood disabilities, resulting in varying degrees of deficiencies in language, interpersonal skills, emotional or affective behavior, and intellectual functioning (Klinger & Dawson, 1996; Teeter & Semrud-Clikeman, 1997). It is a disability that impairs the normal development of many areas of functioning.

Increased attention has been paid to autism in the past several years by both researchers and the media. Examples of public visibility are found in the story of Temple Grandin, mentioned in the chapter opening, and in the autobiography of Donna

fection. Billy was not a warm baby. When his mother picked him up to cuddle, Billy would start to cry and arch his back until he was put back in his crib. Billy treated other children and adults as objects of no consequence in his life. He didn't care about people; he would rather be left alone.

Since Billy's behavior was recognized as different from normal, other changes have occurred. Billy developed language very slowly and in a strange way. His language is what specialists call "echolalic" in nature. When asked a question, Billy simply responds by echoing the question. Billy also has a great deal of trouble using pronouns and prepositions correctly when trying to talk. He will commonly reverse pronouns and refer to himself as "you" or refer to another person as "I." The correct use of prepositions also causes Billy

a great deal of difficulty. Up or down, on or under, or a yes-or-no answer to a question are very confusing concepts for Billy. He simply answers yes or no at random. When viewed as a whole, Billy's language is not just delayed; it is also disturbed in some fundamental way. He simply does not learn. Over and over he makes the same language mistakes.

Aside from Billy's atypical language development, he now spends a great deal of time in repetitive, non-goal-oriented behavior, called *self-stimulatory* or *stereotypic* behavior. He has progressed from simple rocking and spinning the wheels on his toys to flapping his hands and twirling in circles until he falls from dizziness. If made to stop this behavior, Billy will throw ferocious temper tantrums that include screaming, biting, and often head-banging. This self-destructive

behavior is very disconcerting because, in his tantrums, Billy not only breaks things but hurts himself as well.

Billy also has a tremendous need to protect himself against any sort of change, including changes in his daily routine or his physical environment. Billy's mother recently rearranged the furniture in the living room while he was napping. When Billy awoke and entered the rearranged room, he immediately started to cry and whine; then he had a tantrum until the furniture was returned to its original position. Changes in his daily schedule also produce near-panic reactions that end up in tantrums. It seems as though Billy has memorized his environment and daily schedule, and any change produces the unknown for Billy. Adjustment and relearning are very difficult for him.

Billy's behavior cripples his family as well as himself. The furniture arrangement episode is only one of many incidents in which Billy requires his parents' constant attention. If left alone for even short periods of time, Billy can hurt himself or break something. After claiming all the attention his parents and older brother can give, Billy returns little. He is not affectionate and will not even look his brother in the eye, nor does he seek his mother's affection. Billy suffers from a rare childhood developmental disorder known as infantile autism.

Source: Adapted from *Understanding Child Behavior Disorders* (2nd ed., p. 288), by D. M. Gelfand, W. R. Jenson, and C. J. Drew, 1988, New York: Holt, Rinehart and Winston.

Williams, entitled *Nobody, Nowhere* (1992). Although these cases are perhaps not typical of autism, they educate and capture the interest of a considerable segment of the public.

Definition

The federal regulations for IDEA employ the following definition of autism:

Autism means a developmental disability significantly affecting verbal and nonverbal communication and social interaction, generally evident before age 3, that adversely affects educational performance. Characteristics of autism include irregularities and impairments in communication, engagement in repetitive activities and stereotyped movements, resistance to environmental change or change in daily routines, and unusual responses to sensory experiences. (U.S. Department of Education, 1991, p. 41,271)

This definition specifically states that evidence of autism typically emerges before 3 years of age, reflecting a commonly held view. The definition does not intend, however, to preclude a diagnosis of autism if a child shows evidence of the condition after age 3. Additionally, the federal regulations clearly distinguish autism from serious emotional disturbance, a condition that is addressed elsewhere in the law (U.S. Department of Education, 1991, p. 41,266). Such specific attention to autism is very recent. During the 1991–1992 school year, data were first collected regarding the number of children identified as having autism and served in the public schools (U.S. Department of Education, 1997).

TABLE 11.1   Diagnostic criteria for autism

A. A total of six (or more) items from (1), (2), and (3), with at least two from (1), and one each from (2) and (3):

1. Qualitative impairment in social interaction, as manifested by at least two of the following:
    a. Marked impairment in the use of multiple nonverbal behaviors such as eye-to-eye gaze, facial expression, body postures, and gestures to regulate social interaction.
    b. Failure to develop peer relationships appropriate to developmental level.
    c. A lack of spontaneous seeking to share enjoyment, interests, or achievements with other people (e.g., by a lack of showing, bringing, or pointing out objects of interest).
    d. Lack of social or emotional reciprocity.

2. Qualitative impairments in communication as manifested by at least one of the following:
    a. Delay in, or total lack of, the development of spoken language (not accompanied by an attempt to compensate through alternative modes of communication such as gestures or mime).
    b. In individuals with adequate speech, marked impairment in the ability to initiate or sustain a conversation with others.
    c. Stereotyped and repetitive use of language or idiosyncratic language.
    d. Lack of varied, spontaneous make-believe play or social imitative play appropriate to developmental level.

3. Restricted repetitive and stereotyped patterns of behavior, interests, and activities, as manifested by at least one of the following:
    a. Encompassing preoccupation with one or more stereotypic and restricted patterns of interest that is abnormal either in intensity or focus.
    b. Apparently inflexible adherence to specific, nonfunctional routines or rituals.
    c. Stereotypic and repetitive motor mannerisms (e.g., hand or finger flapping or twisting, or complex whole-body movements).
    d. Persistent preoccupation with parts of objects.

B. Delays or abnormal functioning in at least one of the following areas, with onset prior to age 3 years: (1) social interaction, (2) language as used in social communication, or (3) symbolic or imaginative play.

C. The disturbance is not better accounted for by Rett's Disorder or Childhood Disintegrative Disorder.

Source: Reprinted with permission from the *Diagnostic and Statistical Manual of Mental Disorders,* Fourth Edition (pp. 70–71). Copyright 1994. American Psychiatric Association.

Definitional statements provide a partial picture of autism, although most professionals are reluctant to make broad generalizations regarding people with this condition. All people with autism are certainly not alike and it is much more accurate to speak of a range of characteristics than to create a single typical profile. The diagnostic criteria outlined for autism by the American Psychiatric Association are listed in Table 11.1 (APA, 1994).

Prevalence

Autism is a relatively rare condition. The American Psychiatric Association has estimated that the prevalence is about 2 to 5 cases per 10,000 (APA, 1994). Although this is the commonly accepted prevalence range (Rosenberg, Wilson, Maheady, & Sindelar, 1997; Wolf-Schein, 1996), some research has shown considerably higher figures of 9 to 14 per 10,000 (Deb & Prasad, 1994; Ohtaki, Kawano, Urabe, & Komori, 1992; Wing, 1993). The wide variation in prevalence is likely due to differences in definition and diagnostic criteria employed. This disparity in figures may diminish over time as greater consensus about what constitutes autism is achieved. Gender differences are evident in prevalence of autism, with males outnumbering females substantially. Estimates of these prevalence differences range from 2.1 to 1, to 4 to 1 (Deb & Prasad, 1994; Fombonne & du Mazaubrun, 1992).

The U.S. Department of Education (1997) reported that 28,813 students with autism between the ages of 6 and 21 received special education and related services in the public schools during the 1995–1996 year. This was an increase of more than 6,000 students from the previous year. Autism accounts for about .005% of all students with disabilities.

focus 2
What are the two general ranges of prevalence estimated for autism?

Characteristics

Children with autism exhibit a number of rather unusual behaviors and characteristics, some very early in life. For example, significant impairment in interpersonal interaction may be observed by parents of infants with autism. These babies may be notably unresponsive to physical contact or affection (Gelfand, Jenson, & Drew, 1997). Parents often report that such infants become rigid when picked up and are "not cuddly"; they avoid eye contact, averting their gaze rather than looking directly at another person. Such behavior may continue in older children, as evident in Biklen's description of 11- and 12-year-olds quoted in the chapter opener. In many cases, children with autism rely heavily on peripheral vision and avoid direct, face-to-face visual contact.

Children with autism are frequently described in terms of social impairments, social unresponsiveness, and extreme difficulty in relating to other people (Cohen, Volkmar, Anderson, & Klin, 1993; O'Neill, 1997). Often, these children seem to prefer interacting with inanimate objects, forming attachments to objects rather than to people. They appear to be insensitive to the feelings of others and in many cases treat other people as objects, even physically pushing or pulling others around to suit their needs (Sue, Sue, & Sue, 1990). Clearly, children with autism interact with

focus 3
Identify six characteristics of children with autism.

their environment in ways that are not typical, as though they have difficulty making sense of the world around them.

■ IMPAIRED OR DELAYED LANGUAGE

Impaired or delayed language development is routinely found in children with autism (Davis, Fennoy, Laraque, & Kanem, 1992; Teeter & Semrud-Clikeman, 1997). Approximately half do not develop speech, and those who do often engage in strange language and speaking behavior, such as **echolalia** (repeating back only what has been said to them) (Kuder, 1997; Nientimp & Cole, 1992; Tirosh & Canby, 1993). In many cases, children with autism who speak will reproduce parts of conversations that they have heard but do so in a very mechanical fashion, with no sign that they attach meaning to what was said. This echolalic behavior is sometimes misinterpreted as an indicator of high intellectual abilities. Children with autism who develop language often have a limited speaking repertoire, exhibit an uneven level of development in various language skill areas, and fail to use pronouns in speech directed at other people (Tiegerman-Farber, 1997). The speech of these children differs from their peers in grammatical complexity and makes little use of semantics in sentence structure (Scarborough, Rescorla, Tager-Flusberg, & Fowler, 1991). Additionally, the tonal quality of their speech is often unusual or flat, and in some cases, their speech appears to serve the purpose of self-stimulation rather than communication.

■ SELF-STIMULATION

A person with autism often has difficulty forming attachments with other people.

Self-stimulating behavior is frequently associated with autism, although it does not characterize everyone with the condition. Children with autism often engage in physical forms of **self-stimulation,** such as flicking their hands in front of their faces repeatedly (Rosenberg et al., 1997). They also tend to manipulate objects in a repetitive fashion, suggesting self-stimulation (Stahmer & Schreibman, 1992). Behavior such as spinning objects, rocking, or hand flapping may continue for hours. Some behaviors that seem to start as harmless self-stimulation may worsen or take more exaggerated forms, potentially injuring the child. These behaviors include face slapping, biting, and head banging. Behavior that becomes self-injurious is more often found in low-functioning children and can understandably cause concern and stress for parents and others around them.

■ RESISTANCE TO CHANGE IN ROUTINE

Intense resistance to change or rigidity is often mentioned in discussions of children with autism. Familiar routines—for example, during meals or at bedtime—obsessively concern them, and any deviation from the set pattern may upset them greatly. Youngsters affected in this manner may insist on a particular furniture arrangement or one type of food for a given meal (e.g., specific cereal for breakfast); they may even wash themselves in a particular pattern, somewhat approximating obsessive–compulsive or stereotypic behaviors (Gordon, State, Nelson, & Hamburger, 1993; Levinson & Reid, 1993). Often, items must be arranged in a symmetrical fashion to satisfy the child with autism. Some reports note that obsessive preoccupations with sex and public masturbation characterize some people with autism and are resistant to change (van Son-Schoones & van Bilsen, 1995).

Such obsessive, ritualistic behaviors create numerous problems, as one might expect, in any effort to integrate the child into daily life activities. For example, most people pay little attention to the exact route they take when driving to the grocery store or to the precise pattern of moving through the store once they arrive. For parents attempting to take their child with autism along, however, minor deviations may cause serious crisis situations (Norton & Drew, 1994).

■ INTELLIGENCE

Lower intellectual functioning is found in most children with autism; about 75% have measured IQs below 70 (Kauffmann, 1993; O'Neill, 1997). These children have particular difficulty with verbal and reasoning skills in intelligence-testing situations. Although it has long been thought that they have difficulty in learning by imitating the behaviors of others, recent thinking suggests that this problem is more appropriately seen as one or more specific information-processing deficiencies (Scott & Baron-Cohen, 1996; Smith & Bryson, 1994). Intellectual ability varies among children having autism; high-functioning individuals test at a normal or near-normal level (Piven, Harper, Palmer, & Arndt, 1996; Siegel, Minshew, & Goldstein, 1996). High-functioning individuals may have rather substantial vocabularies, but they do not always appropriately use the words that they can spell and define. In some cases, very high-functioning people with autism appear to use language quite well, although there may still be clues that something is different. Such is the case with the description of Temple Grandin by Oliver Sacks in the nearby Reflect on This feature.

Reflect on This

COMPLETE DIRECTIONS—WITH HUMOR

I phoned Temple from the Denver airport to reconfirm our meeting—it was conceivable, I thought, that she might be somewhat inflexible about arrangements, so time and place should be set as definitely as possible. It was an hour and a quarter's drive to Fort Collins, Temple said, and she provided minute directions for finding her office at Colorado State University, where she is an assistant pro-

fessor in the Animal Sciences Department. At one point, I missed a detail, and asked Temple to repeat it, and was startled when she repeated the entire directional litany— several minutes' worth—in virtually the same words. It seemed as if the directions had to be given as they were held in Temple's mind, entirely—that they had fused into a fixed association or program and could no longer be separated into their components.

One instruction, however, had to be modified. She told me at first that I should turn right onto College Street at a particular intersection marked by a Taco Bell restaurant. In her second set of directions, Temple added an aside here, said the Taco Bell had recently had a facelift and been housed in a fake cottage, and no longer looked in the least "bellish." I was struck by the charming, whimsical adjective "bellish"— autistic people are often

called humorless, unimaginative, and "bellish" was surely an original concoction, a spontaneous and delightful image.

Source: From *An Anthropologist on Mars* by Oliver Sacks. Copyright © 1995 by Oliver Sacks. Reprinted by permission of Alfred A. Knopf Inc. Originally appeared in *The New Yorker.*

Snapshot

Steven

■ REFLECTIONS OF A PARENT

Steven was 2½ years old when our daughter, Katherine, was born. This was the time when I seriously began to search for help. I knew something was wrong shortly after Steve's birth, but when I tried to describe the problem, no one seemed to understand what I was saying. In spite of chronic ear infections, Steve looked very healthy. He was slow in developing language, but that could easily be attributed to his ear trouble. Since he was our first baby, I thought that maybe we just weren't very good parents.

When he was 2½, we enrolled Steven in a diagnostic nursery school. He did not seem to understand us when we spoke. I wondered whether he was retarded or had some other developmental problem. The nursery school gave us their opinion when he was 4. They said Steve seemed to have normal intelligence, but he perseverated, was behind socially, and did not seem to process verbs. The school said he had some signs of autism and some signs of a learning disability.

When Steve was 4½, he did some amazing things. He began to talk, read, write, and play the piano. I was taking beginning adult piano lessons at the time, and Steve could play everything I did. In fact, he could play any song he heard and even added chords with his left hand. Relatives and friends began to tell us that he was a genius and that this accounted for his odd behavior. I really wanted to believe this genius theory.

I enrolled Steven in a public kindergarten at age 5. This teacher had another theory about Steve's strange behavior. She believed that we were not firm enough with him. She also sent the social worker to our home to see what we were doing with him.

I often wondered if we were just very poor parents. I certainly had enough people tell us so! Whenever I went to anyone for help, I was likely to begin crying. Then the doctor or whoever would start to watch my behavior closely. I could just see each of them forming a theory in his or her mind: The child is okay, but the mother is a mess. I wondered if I was a very cold mother. Maybe I was subtly rejecting my son. Then again, maybe it was his father. My mother always said he didn't spend enough time with Steve.

I didn't understand when the psychiatrist told me Steve had a *pervasive developmental disorder*. I began to get the picture when the other terms were used. I had heard of autism before. Something was terribly wrong, but it had a physical basis. It was not my fault at all. This was a relief but also a tremendous blow. It has really helped to have a name for the problem. We used to wonder whether Steve was lying awake nights, dreaming up new ways to get our attention. We lived from crisis to crisis. We would finally handle one problem, only to have a new one develop in its place. Steve still does unusual things, but it doesn't send us into a panic anymore.

Sheri, Steve's Mother

Approximately 10% to 15% of those with autism exhibit what are known as splinter skills, areas of ability in which performance levels are unexpectedly high compared to other skills. For instance, a student with autism may perform unusually well at memory tasks or drawing, but have serious deficiencies in language skills and abstract reasoning. For parents of such students, these splinter skills create enormous confusion. Although most parents realize early on that their child with autism is exceptional, they also hope that he or she will be healthy and come to function at a high level. These hopes may be fueled by the child's demonstration of unusual skills.

In some cases, the parents may believe that whatever is wrong with the child is their fault, as portrayed in the nearby snapshot about Steven. A great deal remains unknown about autism. For example, are the savant characteristics portrayed in the movie *Rain Man* simply extremes of splinter skills? Can splinter skills be effectively exploited in a functional way to facilitate school or work activity? Some preliminary evidence suggests it is possible, and research continues in this fascinating area (Mottron & Belleville, 1995; Pring, Hermelin, & Heavey, 1995; Shields-Wolfe & Gallagher, 1992).

The challenging behavior patterns found in children with autism often cause a variety of difficulties. Restricted behavioral repertoires, communication limitations, stereotypic self-stimulation, resistance to changes in routine, and unusual responses to the environment pose problems and may limit integration options for some individuals with autism (Smith & Bryson, 1994). Although many have the ability and the skills necessary to participate in community jobs or living arrangements, the presence of a challenging behavior may lead to placement in a more restricted setting. Continued research on behavior management, social interactions, and program development is essential if these individuals are to achieve maximum integration into the community.

■ LEARNING CHARACTERISTICS

Learning characteristics of children with autism frequently differ from those of their normally developing peers and may present significant educational challenges. Some of the characteristics described earlier have a significant effect on learning. For example, students who resist change may perseverate (repeatedly focus) on a specific item to be learned and find it hard to direct their attention to the next topic or problem in an instructional sequence (Berger, Van Spaendonck, & Horstink, 1993). Because of problems with understanding social cues and relating to people, students with autism may experience difficulty in interacting with teachers and other students in a school setting (Cohen et al., 1993; O'Neill, 1997).

The abilities of children with autism frequently develop unevenly, both within and among skill areas. These children may not generalize learned skills to other settings or topics. They are often impulsive and inconsistent in their responses, presenting a challenge to teachers. Children with autism frequently have difficulty with processing information and abstract ideas, and they may focus on one or more select stimuli while failing to understand the general concept being presented (Minshew & Goldstein, 1993; Schopler & Mesibov, 1995).

Some children with autism possess qualities that can form a helpful focus for instruction. For example, individuals with autism are sometimes noted as enjoying routine. If a child shows this tendency, teachers can employ it when practice or drill is warranted to learn a skill. In certain cases, teachers can capitalize on splinter skills to achieve educational goals (Shields-Wolfe & Gallagher, 1992). Additionally, some

The teacher who works with a child with autism should be prepared to use different teaching strategies that compensate for the uneven skills development of the child.

individuals with autism seem to have relatively strong long-term memory skills, particularly for factual information such as names, numbers, and dates (Mottron, Belleville, & Stip, 1996). Once these students have learned a piece of information, they will not forget it. Their long-term memory skills may equal those of their normally developing peers.

Generalizations regarding the characteristics of children with autism are difficult to make. Despite the many stereotypes that exist about these individuals, their traits are highly variable. Learning characteristics, both limitations and strengths, must be individually assessed and considered in educational programming.

Causation

focus 4

Identify the two broad theoretical views regarding the causes of autism.

Historically, two broad theories about the causes of autism have been most prominent: biological and psychodynamic. The **psychodynamic** perspective implicates family interactions as causal factors in autism. Theorists subscribing to this view have speculated that the child withdraws from rejection and erects defenses against psychological pain. In so doing, he or she retreats to an inner world and essentially does not interact with the outside environment, and therefore withdraws from other people. Psychodynamic theories have largely fallen out of favor because research has failed to support this position. However, some researchers continue to explore this area, addressing topics such as fears, the newborn's anxieties, and the meaning of the child's autistic symptoms (Roser, 1996; Roser & Buchholz, 1996).

A substantial amount of the current research on causation in autism has explored biological factors, particularly genetics (Bailey, LeCouteur, Gottesman, & Bolton, 1995). For example, in the late 1960s a condition involving damage to the chromosome structure, known as **fragile X syndrome,** emerged in the literature as a potential cause of autism. Researchers found that this condition appeared in a certain percentage of males with autism. It now appears that fragile X syndrome is not a major cause of autism; only a small percentage of those with autism have the condition (Simonoff, Bolton, & Rutter, 1996; Wolf-Schein, 1996).

Research has not yet established a solid information base related to the nature of genetic causation of autism—the current body of data and its interpretation are not yet adequate to explain the causes of this condition (Cammisa & Hobbs, 1993; Cuccaro, Wright, Abramson, & Marstellar, 1993). One problem in this research is the relative infrequency with which autism appears in the population at large. Although some research on twins has suggested a genetic link (Bailey et al., 1995), additional evidence is clearly needed.

Abnormal development and damage to the central nervous system have received attention recently as a possible cause of autism. Neurological problems, such as brain cell differences, absence of specialization in the brain hemispheres, and neurological chemical imbalances, are also being investigated (Murray, 1996; Teeter & Semrud-Clikeman, 1997). Developments in technology have enabled research once possible only through autopsy, if at all. For example, through such technology-assisted research, it has been found that some people with autism appear to have an abnormality in a portion of the brain (Siegel, Asarnow, Tanguay, & Call, 1992). One abnormal area, known as the **vermis** and located in the cerebellum, may be related to the cognitive malfunctions found in autism. Further research is needed to confirm this finding as well as other theories related to neurological problems. Some researchers find them to be less likely than genetic causation (Bailey, 1993).

Neurological damage may be caused by a number of problems during prenatal development as well as early infancy. Maternal infections, alcohol abuse, and other problems during pregnancy have great potential of damaging the developing fetus and have been associated with autism and other disabilities involving the central nervous system (Harris, MacKay, & Osborn, 1995). In particular, viral infections such as rubella have been implicated, although a great deal of research is still needed to explore this area (Drew, Hardman, & Logan, 1996). Problems during the birth process—such as unusual hemorrhaging, difficult deliveries, and anoxia—are also known causes of neurological injuries in babies. Children with autism seem more often to have histories of delivery problems than do children without disabilities. Despite the multitude of potential neurological causes, no single type of trauma has been consistently identified as related to autism (Cammisa & Hobbs, 1993).

Causes of autism remain unsolved puzzles; research and interest in the condition continue (Murray, 1996). Accumulated evidence strongly implicates biological factors, although some biological malfunctions clearly may be related to environmental influences (Reichelt, Knivsberg, Lind, & Nodland, 1991; Teeter & Semrud-Clikeman, 1997). Many current researchers have viewed autism as a behavioral syndrome with multiple biological causes (Bailey, 1993; Cammisa & Hobbs, 1993; Gillberg, 1990a, 1990b). To date, researchers have not identified any single specific factor that causes autism. Rather, the condition appears to consist of an assortment of symptoms and is hard to pin down as a specific disease, which is why it is often called a syndrome. As with many areas of disability, a greater understanding of causation should help improve treatment. Better research methodology is vital for further progress in the investigation of the causes of autism (Lenzenweger & Haugaard, 1996; Prior, 1992).

Services and Supports

Identifying the causation of autism is closely linked to discovering effective treatments. A number of different approaches have been used to treat autism, some based on a particular theory of causation, others focusing on specific observable behaviors, and some appearing to be rather trendy and controversial (Carr & Carlson, 1993; Reichelt et al., 1991; Simpson, 1993). Significant progress has been made in successful interventions for those with autism although some writers emphasize the importance of continued investigation regarding their effectiveness (Campbell, Schopler, Cueva, & Hallin, 1996).

focus 5

Identify four major approaches to the treatment of autism.

▪ EDUCATION

A wide variety of instructional options are required to effectively educate children with autism. Such alternatives range from specialized individual programs to integrated placement accompanied by support services. The unusual maladaptive behaviors mentioned earlier have unfortunately resulted in stereotypes about youngsters with autism, leading to undue segregation. However, current studies emphasize the benefits of integration for educational purposes to the maximum degree possible, with placement and programming tailored to the student's age and

The IEP of a child with autism should focus on developing functional communication skills and social skills.

functioning level (Kamps, Leonard, & Potucek, 1995; Mesibov & Shea, 1996). The ultimate goal is to prepare individuals with autism to live in their home community and in the least restrictive setting. Under IDEA, students with autism are entitled to a free and appropriate education in the least restrictive environment.

Children with autism require an individualized educational plan (IEP), including statements of short- and long-term goals. For most students with autism, a central component of the IEP should focus on developing functional communication skills, social skills, and the maximum amount of independence possible. Needs will vary among individuals. Some students will benefit from intensive language training, augmentative communication, and an emphasis on developing social, self-help, and self-protection skills (Chapman, Fisher, Piazza, & Kurtz, 1993; Handlan & Bloom, 1993; Koegel & Koegel, 1996). For others, traditional academic subjects will be the focus of instruction. Some will need to deal with topics not always covered in general education curricula, such as sexual awareness, sexual behavior, and sex education; others should address additional areas that concern the children's parents (Strain, Kohler, & Goldstein, 1996; van Son-Schoones & van Bilsen, 1995; Zanolli, Daggett, & Adams, 1996). Educational interventions for children with autism increasingly use technological enhancements, such as virtual reality and multimedia (Heimann, Nelson, & Tjus, 1995; Strickland, Marcus, & Mesibov, 1996). Additional research on the effectiveness of such applications is essential.

Creative, innovative, and positive teachers are particularly important in providing effective education for students with autism (Moreno & Donellan, 1991). As noted earlier, these children present unique challenges. Some seemingly insignificant actions by teachers can create great difficulties for students who have autism—difficulties that can easily be avoided by informed teachers. For example, many high-functioning individuals with autism who have language skills interpret speech very literally, so it is important to avoid using slang, idiom, and sarcasm. Such phrases might be translated by the individual with autism to mean something other than their intended message.

Parental participation in preparing children with autism for school and other segments of life can be of great assistance (Koegel, Bimbela, & Schreibman, 1996; Norton & Drew, 1994; Schreibman & Koegel, 1996). This preparation can include instilling a positive attitude in the child, helping him or her with scheduling, and teaching him or her the physical layout of the school (e.g., drawing a map of where to go, based on the daily schedule) (Krantz, MacDuff, & McClannahan, 1993). Identifying and introducing the child to a "safe place" and a "safe person" will help him or her cope, should the child become confused or encounter a particularly upsetting event (Moreno & Donellan, 1991). The case study at the end of this chapter illustrates parental involvement as we revisit Billy, the youngster we met in the chapter opening snapshot.

■ PSYCHOLOGICAL AND MEDICAL SERVICES

Interventions based on the psychodynamic theory of causation historically focused on repairing emotional damage and resolving inner conflict. This approach aims to remedy the presumably faulty relationship between the child with autism and his or her parents; this theory assumes that parental rejection or absence resulted in withdrawal by the child (deBenedetti-Gaddini, 1993; Weininger, 1993). This treatment model has been criticized because solid empirical evidence supporting its effectiveness is lacking. The internal psychological nature of the problem, as seen by this approach, makes it very difficult to evaluate the treatment's effectiveness.

A variety of medical treatments have been used for children with autism. Some early medical therapies (e.g., electroconvulsive shock and psychosurgery) have been discarded because they appeared to have questionable results and harmful side effects. Likewise, certain medications used in the past had doubtful therapeutic value and were very controversial (e.g., D-lysergic acid, more commonly known as LSD). Other medications used for people with autism have included antipsychotic drugs, anticonvulsants, serotonergic drugs, and dopamine medication (Aman, Van Bourgondien, & Wolford, 1995). Specific symptoms have been addressed with specific medication, such as obsessive–compulsive behaviors with clomipramine (Gordon et al., 1993); other antipsychotic drugs seem to help reduce unusual speech patterns and self-injurious behaviors, particularly with older patients. Decreasing self-injury and social withdrawal have also been evident in some research on responses to other drugs (Menage, Thibault, Berthelemy, & Lelord, 1992; Nelson & Pribor, 1993; Osman & Loschen, 1992; Rothenberger, 1993). However, other research on drug therapy has recorded mixed results or no improvement in the condition (Komori, Matsuishi, Yamada, & Yamashita, 1995; Oades, Stern, Walker, & Clark, 1990).

Overall, medication has shown some promising, but mixed, results in the treatment of autism. It appears to have potential that can be further maximized as research continues. But any drug treatment should be used thoughtfully and always in conjunction with a multicomponent, comprehensive treatment plan (Campbell et al., 1996; Rothenberger, 1993). Most authorities agree that autism represents such a heterogeneous set of symptoms that no single medication will effectively treat all children so affected (Klinger & Dawson, 1996; Teeter & Semrud-Clikeman, 1997).

■ BEHAVIORAL INTERVENTION

Behavioral treatment for children with autism is undertaken without concern about the underlying cause of the disability. Such interventions attempt to enhance appropriate behaviors and decrease inappropriate or unadaptive ones (Charlop-Christy & Haymes, 1996; Kauffman, 1993) . The goals of behavior management for individuals with autism are achieved by first precisely defining the behavior to be developed or phased out, observing such behavior over the course of instruction, and recording data on appropriate and inappropriate behaviors. Accurate and reliable data collection is a cornerstone of behavioral intervention, a process greatly enhanced by new technology, as indicated in the Today's Technology feature on page 368.

Behavioral interventions may focus on conduct such as self-stimulation, tantrum episodes, or self-inflicted injury (Belcher, 1995; Early, 1995). Such therapy has substantially reduced or eliminated these problem behaviors in many cases (Kauffman, 1993; Trevarthen, Aitken, Papoudi, & Robarts, 1996). Behavioral treatment has also been effective in remediating deficiencies in fundamental social skills and language development in children with autism (Davis, Brady, Williams, & Hamilton, 1992; Durand & Carr, 1992). Parental involvement in behavioral treatment has shown promising results (Estrada & Pinsof, 1995; Koegel et al., 1996; Simpson, 1995). Research has also demonstrated that certain students with autism can be effectively taught to employ self-directed behavior management, which further enhances efficiency (Koegel & Koegel, 1996; Schreibman & Koegel, 1996).

Interacting in Natural Settings

■ EARLY CHILDHOOD YEARS

TIPS FOR THE FAMILY

■ Seek out and read information regarding autism, and become as knowledgeable about the disability as possible. Be an active partner in the treatment of your child; take parent training classes (e.g., behavior management workshops).

■ When working with the child with autism, concentrate on one behavior at a time as the target for change; emphasize the positive, increasing appropriate behavior rather than focusing solely on inappropriate behavior.

■ Involve all family members in learning about your child's disability and working with him or her when appropriate.

■ Protect your own health by obtaining respite care when needed to get rest or to get a break. You may need to devise a family schedule that allows adequate time for sleep. Plan ahead for respite; otherwise, when you need it most, you will be too exhausted to find it.

■ Help prepare your child for school by instilling a positive attitude about it, helping him or her with the idea of a school schedule and how to find a "safe place" and "safe person" at school.

TIPS FOR THE PRESCHOOL TEACHER

■ Depending on the child's level of functioning, you may have to use physical cues or clear visual modeling to persuade him or her to do something; children with autism may not respond to social cues.

■ Pair physical cues with verbal cues to begin teaching verbal compliance.

■ Limit instruction to one thing at a time; focus on what is concrete rather than abstract.

■ Avoid verbal overload by using short, directive sentences.

TIPS FOR PRESCHOOL PERSONNEL

■ Encourage the development of programs in which older children model good behavior and interact intensely with children with autism.

■ Promote ongoing relationships between the preschool and medical personnel who can provide advice and assistance for children with autism.

■ Promote the initiation of parent–school relationships to assist both parents and preschool personnel in working together to meet the child's needs and offer mutual support.

■ Promote the appropriate involvement of nonteaching staff through workshops that provide information and awareness. Consistent interaction and expectations are important.

NEIGHBORS AND FRIENDS

■ Be supportive of the parents and siblings of a child with autism. They may be under a great deal of stress and need moral support.

■ Be positive with the parents. They may receive information that places blame on them, which should not be magnified by their friends.

■ Offer parents a respite to the degree that you're comfortable; you may only give them a short time away to go to the store, but the break will be very helpful to them.

■ ELEMENTARY YEARS

TIPS FOR THE FAMILY

■ Be active in community efforts for children with autism; join local or national parent groups.

■ Use your knowledge and resources to identify a good program for your child; participate in this program in whatever arrangement might be available to parents.

■ Consistently follow through with the basic principles of your child's treatment program at home. This may mean taking more workshops or training on various topics.

■ Continue family involvement; be sensitive to the feelings of siblings who may be feeling left out or embarrassed by the child with autism.

■ It may be necessary to take safety precautions in the home (e.g., installing locks on all doors).

TIPS FOR THE GENERAL EDUCATION CLASSROOM TEACHER

■ Help with organizational strategies, assisting the student with autism with matters that are difficult for him or her (e.g., remembering how to use an eraser). Keep instruction as unrestrictive as possible, perhaps placing a prompting note or picture somewhere.

■ Avoid abstract ideas unless they are necessary in instruction. Be as concrete as possible.

■ Communicate with specific directions or questions, not vague or open-ended statements.

■ If the child becomes upset, he or she may need to change activities or go to a place in the room that is "safe" for a period of time.

■ Use rules and schedules that are written with accompanying pictures so students clearly understand what is expected of them.

■ If the child is not learning a particular task, it may need to be broken down into smaller steps or presented through more than one medium (e.g., visual and verbal).

■ Begin preparing the child with autism for a more variable environment by programming and teaching adaption to changes in routine. Involve the child in planning for the changes, mapping out what they might be.

TIPS FOR SCHOOL PERSONNEL

■ Promote an all-school environment where children model appropriate behavior and receive reinforcement for it.

■ Develop peer-assistance programs, in which older students can help tutor and model appropriate behavior for children with autism.

■ Encourage the development of strong, ongoing school–parent relationships and support groups working together to meet the child's needs. Consistent expectations are important.

- Do not depend on the child with autism to take messages home to parents for anything unless you are trying this out as a skill for him or her to learn; communication is a major problem, and even a note may be lost.

TIPS FOR NEIGHBORS AND FRIENDS

- If you interact with the child with autism, be positive and praise him or her for appropriate behavior.
- To the degree possible, ignore trivial disruptions or misbehaviors; focus on positive behaviors.
- Don't take misbehaviors personally; the child is not trying to make your life difficult or manipulate you.
- Avoid using nicknames or cute names such as "buddy" or "pal."
- Avoid sarcasm and idiom, such as "beating around the bush." These children may not understand and may interpret what you say literally.

■ SECONDARY AND TRANSITION YEARS

TIPS FOR THE FAMILY

- Be alert to developmental and behavioral changes as the child grows older, watching for changing effects of any medication that may occur.
- Continue as an active partner in your child's educational and treatment program, planning for the transition to adulthood.
- Begin acquainting yourself with the adult services that will be available when your child leaves school. If he or she is high functioning, consider or plan for adult living out of the family home.

TIPS FOR THE GENERAL EDUCATION CLASSROOM TEACHER

- Gradually increase the level of abstraction in teaching, remaining aware of the individual limitations the child with autism has.
- Continue preparing the student for an increasingly variable environment through instruction and example.
- Focus increasingly on matters of vital importance to the student as he or she matures (e.g., social awareness and interpersonal issues between the sexes).
- Teach the student with an eye toward postschool community participation, including matters such as navigating the community physically, activities, and employment. Teach the student about interacting with police in the community, since they require responses different from those appropriate for other strangers.*

TIPS FOR SCHOOL PERSONNEL

- To the degree possible for children with autism, promote involvement in social activities and clubs that enhance interpersonal interaction.
- Encourage the development of functional academic programs for students with autism that are combined with transition planning and programs.
- Promote a continuing working relationship with school staff and other agency personnel that might be involved in the student's overall treatment program (e.g., health care providers, social service agencies, and others).
- Work with other agencies that may encounter the child in the community

(e.g., law enforcement). Provide workshops if possible to inform officers regarding behavioral characteristics of people with autism that might be misinterpreted.

TIPS FOR NEIGHBORS AND FRIENDS

- Encourage a positive understanding of people with autism by other neighbors and friends who may be in contact with the child and able to provide environmentally appropriate interaction.
- Promote the positive understanding of people with autism by community agencies that may encounter these individuals at this stage of life (e.g., law enforcement officials, fire department personnel).
- Support the parents as they consider the issues of adulthood for their child. Topics such as guardianship and community living may be difficult for parents to discuss.

■ ADULT YEARS

TIPS FOR THE FAMILY

- Be alert for behavioral or developmental changes that may occur as the individual matures. Maturation may require medication adjustments.
- Continue to seek out adult services that are available to individuals with disabilities.
- Seek legal advice regarding plans for the future when you are no longer able to care for the family member with autism. Plan for financial arrangements and other needs, such as naming an advocate. Backup plans should be made; do not always count on the youngster's siblings. Consider

guardianship by other persons or agencies.

TIPS FOR THERAPISTS OR OTHER PROFESSIONALS

- Remain cognizant of the maturity level of the individual with whom you are working. Despite the presence of autism, some individuals have mature interests and inclinations. Do not treat the person as a child.
- Promote collaboration between appropriate adult service agencies to provide the most comprehensive services possible.

TIPS FOR NEIGHBORS AND FRIENDS

- Encourage a positive understanding of people with autism by other neighbors and friends who may be in contact with the adult having autism.
- Promote the positive understanding of people with autism by community agencies that may encounter these individuals at this stage of life (e.g., law enforcement officials, fire department personnel).
- Support the family members as they consider the issues of adulthood for the individual. Topics such as guardianship and community living may be difficult for parents and siblings to discuss.

*A portion of this material is adapted from *High-Functioning Individuals with Autism: Advice and Information for Parents and Others Who Care* by S. J. Moreno and A. M. Donellan, 1991, Crown Point, IN: Maap Services.

In a general education elementary school classroom, a young boy with autism receives help in language through verbalizing to a teacher's aide what he has drawn.

It is important to emphasize that behavioral therapy does not claim to cure autism. Its procedures specifically focus on improving certain behaviors. This approach seems effective for many children with autism, prompting decreases in problem behaviors and improvement of survival skills (Carr & Carlson, 1993; Chapman et al., 1993). For both children and their families, such gains constitute a significant step toward living a more normal life (Nientimp & Cole, 1992).

Today's Technology

COLLECTING DATA: THE VIDEX TIMEWAND

Most of us are familiar with the bar-code scanners used at checkout stands in many stores. The clerk passes the code symbol over a scanner, the price is instantly entered into the cash register, and a record of the sale is made for inventory control. This same technology is now being applied to coding and recording data on behavioral observations.

Known as the *Videx Time-Wand,* this device simplifies reliable data collection for behavioral interventions with a variety of conditions, such as autism. Appropriate and inappropriate behaviors are defined very specifically and then given a code, which is translated into a bar-code symbol much like we see at the market. These bar codes are then placed on an observation sheet to be used by the observer. The observer also carries a small, portable bar-code reader with a wand that is passed over the relevant code symbol when that particular behavior is observed. Data on behavioral occurrences are recorded as well as clock-time stamped to indicate when the behavior occurred. These data are stored electronically (the unit will hold up to 16,000 characters of information) and transferred to a portable computer at the end of an observation session, for analysis and graphing.

Use of the TimeWand reduces the strain on therapists who were previously required to physically write down behavioral codes while attempting to continue observation. Use of this technology thereby improves the accuracy of data collection and also expedites data processing and translation into treatment action. Information regarding this automated data-collection method is available from Walter Nelson and Gordon Defalco at the Fircrest School in Seattle, Washington, or Richard Saunders at the Parson Research Center, University of Kansas.

In the early 1990s, Biklen (1990, 1992) reported on a treatment being used for people with autism in Australia that specifically focuses on remedying their communication problems. Known as *facilitative communication*, in this procedure the person with autism uses typing as a means of communicating. A therapist–facilitator provides physical support by touching and putting light pressure on the student's arm or shoulder as well as interpersonal support through positive attitudes and interactions. Facilitative communication as a treatment for the communication problems associated with autism has been controversial enough to prompt a number of special programs on national television news shows, featuring both proponents and critics. Although advocates of this treatment are emphatic in their support, other researchers have been unable to obtain results supporting its effectiveness, raising serious questions regarding its soundness (Beck & Pirovano, 1996; Biklen, 1996; Bomba, O'Donnell, Markowitz, & Holmes, 1996). Because of the facilitator's participation through touching the arm of the person, some question whether the facilitator is doing the communicating or the person with autism (Fried-Oken, Paul, & Fay, 1995). Further objective research is clearly needed to clarify the role of facilitated communication with individuals having autism (Silliman, 1995).

Impact on the Family

The impact of a child with autism on his or her family members is enormous (Schreibman & Koegel, 1996; Singer & Powers, 1993). Living with such a child is exhausting and presents many challenges, including strained relationships, vastly and permanently increased financial burdens, social isolation, grief, and considerable physical and emotional fatigue (Kasari & Sigman, 1997; Norton & Drew, 1994). The youngster with autism may sleep only a few hours each night and spend many waking hours engaged in self-abusive or disruptive behavior. It is easy to see how parents may feel as if they are running a marathon, 24 hours a day, 7 days per week, with no respite. Not only is the normal

Reflect on This

SYLVESTER STALLONE AND SEARGEOH

Stallone, one of the world's most successful movie actors, won stardom with *Rocky*, a small-budget film that received the Academy Award for Best Picture of 1976 and earned him Academy nominations for Best Actor and Best Original Screenplay. . . . By June of 1982, Sylvester Stallone was a successful and rich movie star.

He was 35 and had a huge hit with his film *Rocky III*. And then his world was turned upside down when his second son, Seargeoh, then 3, was diagnosed with autism, a psychological disorder.

"When I heard, I was violently angry," Stallone said. "I didn't understand why this would happen to my boy. I felt betrayed. If you have a bad hand to deal, give it to me, not to an innocent child. What purpose did it serve? Was my life too good? Is it something I did, some word I said?" Stallone hesitated a moment and then said, "Seargeoh has no idea who I am. I'm just another person to him. You have to accept his love on his terms. There is nothing I can offer or buy or give my son that can help him. I feel I let my child down. I feel helpless, and I have to accept that."

Source: From "A Chance to Go the Distance," by D. Rader, 1997, *Parade Magazine*, July 6, pp. 4–5.

Reflect on This

EXTRAORDINARY TALENTS OF INDIVIDUALS WITH AUTISM

One of the many mysteries surrounding the phenomenon of autism is the extraordinary talents and abilities demonstrated by some individuals. . . . In the past, such individuals were referred to as *idiot savants*. *Idiot i*s an antiquated term for someone with mental retardation, and *savant* means "knower" in French. Some professionals now prefer the term *savant syndrome* to describe a condition in which persons with serious mental limitations demonstrate spectacular "islands of brilliance in a sea of mental disability."

Given the scope of talents in the human repertoire, these "islands" are confined to a narrow range of abilities: a flair for music or visual arts, mathematical aptitude, mechanical wizardry, or mnemonic skills such as calendar calculation (being able to report instantly on what day of the week a particular date will fall in a given year, past or future). The trait that binds these unique abilities is superior memory skills that are idiosyncratic, emotionless, and enigmatic. Indeed, savants often seem to accomplish feats of brilliance as if by rote. No emotion shades their performance.

How are savants able to do what they do? While no conclusive findings exist, theories abound. For example, one theory has suggested that the sensory deprivation and social isolation experienced by many individuals with autism causes them to be bored and thus they adopt trivial preoccupations. Another theory has suggested that autism is associated with deficits in the left hemisphere of the brain, which governs the use of language and other logical, conceptual, and abstract skills. Savants' skills are usually associated with right-brain functions—spatial perception, visu-

alization, mechanical dexterity, and movement—suggesting that the right hemisphere is dominant.

Clearly, much remains unknown about both autism and the savant syndrome. Certainly, little is understood about how they exist in the same person. Increased understanding will hopefully benefit those who struggle with autism.

Source: Reprinted by permission of Omni, copyright 1989, Omni Publications International, Ltd.

---

family routine interrupted, but also the constant demands are physically and emotionally draining, resulting in a number of problems for family members such as high stress levels, depression, and some affective disorders among mothers (Bristol, Gallagher, & Holt, 1993; Donenberg & Baker, 1993; Schreibman & Koegel, 1996;

Temple Grandin, an assistant professor of animal science at Colorado State University, is a high-functioning person with autism. In addition to writing several hundred papers on autism, she has revolutionized the treatment of animals and barn design for animals who are being raised for consumption.

Trevarthen et al., 1996). This situation grows even more confusing if the child with autism also has savant-like skills in some areas, such as those examined in the nearby Reflect on This feature.

Siblings of children with autism may experience a number of problems, particularly during the early years. They may have difficulty understanding their parents' distress regarding their brother or sister and the level of attention afforded this child, and they may manifest symptoms of stress or depression (Gold, 1993; Senel & Akkok, 1995). Siblings may also have difficulty accepting the emotional detachment of the youngster, who might seem not to care for them at all. Like the siblings of children with other disabilities, brothers and sisters of a child with autism may be embarrassed by him or her and therefore reluctant to bring friends home. However, if they become informed about the condition and overcome their sense of social embarrassment, siblings can be a significant resource in assisting parents (Norton & Drew, 1994).

The arrival of a child with autism will present a significant challenge to parents and other family members. Parents usually have to turn to multiple sources for assistance and information, and relations between professionals and parents are not simple or easy (Gray, 1993). Groups such as the Autism Society of America can provide a great deal of help and support from an understanding perspective not always available elsewhere. Parents may have to become aggressive and vocal as they search for services from various agencies. They must also preserve their own health and vitality, since their ability to cope will be significantly diminished if they neglect their personal well-being. This requires that respite time and care be provided from a number of sources, including the extended family and outside agencies. Perhaps the most difficult issue for parents is the realization that no clear-cut answers exist to address many of the questions they have. Intervention must be tailored to meet specific needs and to suit the unique circumstances of each family and affected individual (O'Neill, 1997).

Case Study

BILLY

What happens to a boy like Billy, who was discussed in the chapter opening snapshot? His parents are exhausted from years of caring for their son, who seems oblivious to their efforts. Placing him in the state hospital would be an easy answer, but Billy's parents sense that this would be disastrous for his development and later adjustment. If admitted to the state hospital, he could spend the rest of his life there.

This family was lucky. When Billy was ready to start school, the school district and the local mental health center arranged to place him in a special classroom within a regular public school. The classroom was well staffed, so that he had individual instruction and treatment from a teacher who was trained to manage children with behavior disorders. Billy's disruptive self-stimulation and tantrums were decreased through the use of time-out procedures (seclusion for short periods of time). Intense language training was implemented, and slowly he has learned more appropriate language. His echolalia has begun to disappear. When his appropriate behavior becomes stabilized in the classroom, he will begin an academic program and learn reading and writing.

There have also been changes for Billy's family. The mental health center offered a series of child management classes that taught the family, including Billy's brother, how to handle his disruptive behavior. The classes also gave Billy's family a chance to see that they were not alone and that other families had similar problems with their children who had disturbances. When the course was officially finished, the parents decided to continue meeting and planning for their children. The group members supported one another in times of need and worked actively to keep their children out of large institutions.

Although Billy is now making progress both behaviorally and academically, he will probably always have autism and be in need of special help. But great things are beginning to happen. The other day, just before the bus came to get Billy, he hugged his mother and kissed her good-bye for the first time, just like a normal boy.

■APPLICATION

1. What impact do you think Billy's parents had on his ultimate prognosis as a child with autism?
2. How might the outcome have been different if they had placed him in the state hospital?
3. Is it realistic for his mother to expect him to "grow out" of his autistic behaviors?

Source: Adapted from *Understanding Child Behavior Disorders* (2nd ed., p. 312), by D. M. Gelfand, W. R. Jenson, and C. J. Drew, 1988, New York: Holt, Rinehart and Winston.

Debate Forum

SELF-STIMULATION AS A REINFORCER?

Reinforcers as behavioral treatments are sometimes difficult to find for some children having autism. Teachers must often take what the client gives them to work with and remain flexible in designing an intervention program. Many individuals with autism do not respond to the same types of rewards that others do, and social rewards may not provide reinforcement or have any effect at all on these youngsters, at least in the initial stages of a treatment program. Research has also shown that, in some cases, tangible reinforcers may produce desired results, but they often seem to lose their power for individuals with autism. Given these circumstances, some researchers have suggested that self-stimulation, which appears to be a powerful and durable reinforcer, should be used to assist in teaching appropriate behavior. Self-stimulation is very different for each child and may involve manipulation of items such as coins, keys, and twigs.

■ POINT

Because reinforcers are often difficult to identify for children with autism, it is important to use whatever is available and practical in teaching these youngsters. Self-stimulation has been recognized as providing strong reinforcement for those who engage in it. Although typically viewed as an inappropriate behavior, self-stimulation may be very useful in teaching the beginning phases of more adaptive behavior and other skill acquisition. For some children with autism, it may be the most efficient reinforcer available, so why not use it, at least initially?

■ COUNTERPOINT

Using inappropriate behavior as a reinforcer carries with it certain serious problems and in fact may be unethical. The use of self-stimulation as a reinforcer may cause an increase in this behavior, making it an even more pronounced part of the child's inappropriate demeanor. Should this occur, it may make self-stimulation more difficult to eliminate later.

Review

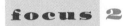

focus 1

Identify four areas of functional challenge often found in children with autism.

- Language
- Interpersonal skills
- Emotional or affective behaviors
- Intellectual functioning

focus 2

What are the two general ranges of prevalence estimated for autism?

- Approximately 2 to 5 cases per 10,000
- From 9 to 14 cases per 10,000

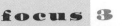

focus 3

Identify six characteristics of children with autism.

- As infants, they are often unresponsive to physical contact or affection from their parents and later have extreme difficulty relating to other people.
- Most have impaired or delayed language skills, with about half not developing speech at all.
- Those who have speech often engage in echolalia and other inappropriate behavior.
- They frequently engage in self-stimulatory behavior.
- They meet changes in their routine with intense resistance.
- Most have a reduced level of intellectual functioning.

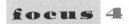

focus 4

Identify the two broad theoretical views regarding the causes of autism.

- The psychodynamic view places a great deal of emphasis on the interaction between the family and the child.
- The biological view has included neurological damage and genetics as possible causes.

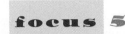

focus 5

Identify four major approaches to the treatment of autism.

- Psychodynamic-based therapy focuses on repairing the emotional damage presumed to have resulted from faulty family relationships.
- Medically based treatment often involves the use of medication.
- Behavioral interventions focus on enhancing specific appropriate behaviors or on reducing inappropriate behaviors.
- Educational interventions employ the full range of educational placements.

People with Traumatic and Acquired Brain Injury

To begin with . . .

 In the United States, acquired brain injury—not AIDS, not cancer, not disease—is the largest killer and disabler of our children. Each year thousands of children and adolescents are rushed to emergency rooms with some type of acquired brain injury. Fortunately, the medical care system is able to save the lives of most of these children. Unfortunately, many who sustain acquired brain injuries end up with problems that change the course of their entire lives. The impact of an acquired brain injury on a child does not occur merely at a point in time, but rather as lifelong experience. It can affect the way the student thinks, feels, behaves, moves, learns, and participates in the world. (p. xiii)[1]

 When I got my head injured I was riding my bike. I was leaving school. It was 3 o'clock. A man in a truck hit me on Walker Street next to the church. I was in the hospital and I was in a rehabilitation place for ½ year. I missed lots of school. . . . They thought I wasn't right. I got messed up all the time in class. There was too much going on. I cried and the kids picked on me. Now it is 2½ years later. I am in Grade 6 now. I feel a lot better but my work isn't that good. My mom says I have to be "patient." I just want to be OK. Thank you to my teachers. (Maria, age 12, struck by drunk driver, p. xi)[1]

 The doctors told me in rehabilitation that I almost died. Now I'm not sure if it was that great for me to live. Since my traumatic brain injury, life has been hell. Everyone says I made a terrific comeback, but I ask "come back" to what? My old friends don't speak to me except to say "hi" and I'm in lower classes than I was before. They asked me to write about why this book is important to teachers. Easy. For me, and probably other kids my age, we made great progress. I walk, I talk, I eat, but that's it. My life has been trashed. When people say "Hey, get a life" they really should think about having a traumatic brain injury. Somebody stole my life. (Robert, age 16, survivor of head-on collision without seatbelt, p. xi)[1]

When I almost drowned, I was only 5 years old, but the damage to my brain has followed me all my life. Elementary and high school were a struggle; college still is. But people never gave up on me. I had one of the first computers the school ever purchased. My classes were adjusted to "fit" what I needed. Today I'm studying to be a social worker or counselor. My teachers cared. They reached out to me in every way possible even though we were in a tiny school system. I know that to succeed in this world you need to value yourself as a real person. All the special things they will tell you in this book are certainly important, but I feel the most important thing is to not be afraid of "me"—and to care about me. I can succeed. It just may take a little longer then usual. But I will succeed. (Maggie, age 20, near-drowning survivor, pp. xi–xii)[1]

---

[1] *Source:* In *Educational Dimensions of Acquired Brain Injury* edited by R. C. Savage & G. F. Wolcott, pp. xi–xiii. Copyright 1994, Austin, TX: PRO-ED, Inc. Reprinted by permission.

Ashley

Ashley was a very normal child, inquisitive and active. One of her great pleasures was having her picture taken at the local mall. Additionally, she loved to run and to blow bubbles. Her favorite activity was visiting the local pet and fish store. There she would move from aquarium to aquarium, pointing with great delight at her favorite fish. Her vocalizations were exuberant and elaborate even though they were not well understood. Nevertheless, it was clear that she delighted in seeing the fish and being with her mom in the store.

When Ashley was about 18 months old, her life changed in a matter of seconds. She and her mother had just attended a family party. On the way home, Ashley's mom decided to visit a friend and just say hi. After leaving the friend's home, they approached an intersection with the usual stoplight. The light was red and they stopped. Their car's left signal lights indicated their intention to turn, and they waited for traffic opposite them to clear. Ashley was comfortably placed in her car seat. As soon as the oncoming traffic cleared, they appropriately began the left turn.

Her mother relates the remainder of the story as follows: "As I looked out the left side, I saw this van coming toward us. I don't remember him hitting us. We know he did. Then the next thing I remember is being in the emergency room and thinking that everything was okay. If I'm fine, I knew Ashley was on the other side of the car in her car seat, in the back, strapped in, and I figured if I was okay, she was."

Several days passed before Ashley's mom was able to see her. "I went down and saw her a couple of days later. I was released from the hospital and that was the first time I was able to see her. And it was kind of hard to go down there and see your child hooked up to all these machines and just not move, just lie there."

Ashley spent the next 24 days in the intensive care unit (ICU) at Primary Children's Medical Center. She was then moved to a rehabilitation unit where she spent the next 4 months.

"During the time in rehab she went in and out of surgery. She had two internal shunts and two external shunt surgeries to relieve the pressure that had built up inside her head from the accident. When we brought her home she couldn't see. She was diagnosed cortically blind. She couldn't talk. It was just as if she was a newborn child. She had just barely learned to hold her head up before we left Primary, so it was like having this 30-pound newborn. One thing we missed the most was her smile. It's so nice to see it back."

Definition

focus 1
Identify three key elements of traumatic and acquired brain injury.

Traumatic brain injury (TBI) results from "rapid acceleration and deceleration of the brain, including shearing (tearing) of nerve fibers, contusion (bruising) of the brain tissue against the skull, brain stem injuries, and edema (swelling)" (Lehr, 1990, p. 15). Injuries that do not involve penetration of the skull are referred to as closed-head or generalized head injuries. Head injuries in children are usually of this type. Focal or open-head injuries, such as gunshot wounds, are not common for children.

Two types of brain damage, primary and secondary, have been described by medical professionals. *Primary damage* is a direct outcome of the initial impact to the brain. *Secondary damage* develops over time as the brain responds to the initial trauma. For instance, an adolescent who is hit accidentally with a baseball bat may develop a hematoma, an area of internal bleeding within the brain. This may be the primary damage. However, with the passage of time, the brain's response to the initial injury may be pervasive swelling, which may cause additional insult to the brain. This is referred to as secondary damage.

The Individuals with Disabilities Act (IDEA) defines traumatic brain injury as

an acquired injury to the brain caused by an external force, resulting in total or partial functional disability or psychosocial impairment, or both, that adversely affects a student's educational performance. The term applies to open and closed head injuries resulting in impairments in one or more areas, such as cognition, language, memory, attention, reasoning, abstract thinking, judgment, problem-solving, sensory, perceptual, and motor abilities; psychosocial behavior, physical functions, information processing, and speech. The term does not apply to brain injuries that are congenital or degenerative or brain injuries induced by birth trauma. (Federal Register, vol. 57, no. 189, p. 44,802)

A student must have an injury that significantly influences educational performance in order to receive special education services.

Another term, **acquired brain injury (ABI),** is also emerging in the professional literature. It "refers to both traumatic brain injuries, such as open or closed head injuries, and nontraumatic brain injuries, such as strokes and other vascular accidents, infectious diseases (e.g., encephalitis, meningitis), anoxic injuries (e.g., hanging, near-drowning, choking, accidents . . . [involving anesthesia], severe blood loss), metabolic disorders (e.g., insulin shock, liver and kidney disease), and toxic products taken into the body through inhalation or ingestion. The term does not refer to brain injuries that are congenital or brain injuries induced by birth trauma" (Savage & Wolcott, 1994b, pp. 3–4). These traumatic and acquired brain injuries result in disabilities that may adversely affect individuals' information processing, social behaviors, memory capacities, reasoning and thinking, speech and language skills, and sensory and motor abilities (Ponsford, 1995b).

Presently, classification systems of TBI or ABI do not provide much direction to educators or parents who are attempting to respond to an individual's needs (Savage & Wolcott, 1994a). If parents or teachers understood the disabilities related to certain kinds of head injuries, they could respond with greater precision in applying and using various interventions for cognitive, behavioral, and neuromotor–physical problems.

Prevalence

Each year nearly 5 million children experience head injuries. Of this number, about 200,000 are hospitalized (Rosman, 1994). About 2% to 5% of these children develop severe neurological complications (Jaffe et al., 1992; Rudoph & Kamei, 1994). Most of these injuries could be prevented with proper use of seat belts, child restraints, helmets, and other educational and preventive measures. Twenty percent of the high school students who play football in the United States each year experience minor head injuries (Feenick & Judd, 1994). Unfortunately, many of these adolescents do not receive medical attention.

Newly emerging definitions of acquired and traumatic brain injury make it difficult to precisely identify the number of children who are functionally affected by brain injuries. To further complicate matters, children do not access health care systems in the same manner as adolescents and adults, and children's head injuries frequently remain undiagnosed. Nevertheless, there is some general information available regarding prevalence. About 0.18% to 2.5% of the general population experience acquired or traumatic brain injuries (Graham & McIntosh, 1996; Savage & Wolcott, 1994a).

There is a dramatic increase in the frequency of acquired brain injuries during the adolescent years. The number of injuries that occur between the ages of 15 and 19

Most of the head injuries 5 million children experience annually could be prevented with the proper use of such preventative aids as helmets, seat belts, and child restraints.

years usually equals the total number of injuries sustained during the first 14 years of life. This increase in injuries is attributable to several factors, including increased participation in contact sports, greater access to and use of automobiles, more frequent use of racing and mountain bikes, and injuries sustained from firearms.

The number of head injuries in boys exceeds that in girls. As a rule, boys are two to four times more likely to sustain serious head injuries (Savage & Wolcott, 1994a), particularly during adolescence.

Characteristics

Individuals with traumatic or acquired brain injury present a variety of challenges to families and professionals (Krych & Ashley, 1995; Ponsford, Sloan, & Snow, 1995; Russell, 1993; Williams, 1994). The injuries may affect every aspect of an individual's life. Additionally, the resulting disabilities have a profound effect on the individual's family.

Generally, the individual will need services and supports in four areas: cognition, speech and language, social and behavioral skills, and neuromotor and physical functioning (Ponsford, 1995a). Cognitive problems have an impact on thinking and perception. For example, individuals with a brain injury may be unable to remember or retrieve newly learned information. They may be able to attend or concentrate only for brief periods of time. Another serious problem may be an inability to adjust or respond flexibly to changes in home or school environments (Savage & Wolcott, 1994a).

A person with TBI may also struggle with speech, producing unintelligible sounds or indistinguishable words. Speech may be slurred and labored. The individual may know what he or she wants to say, but be unable to express it. Profes-

focus 2

Identify four general characteristics of individuals with traumatic or acquired brain injuries.

sionals often use the term aphasia to describe this condition. **Expressive aphasia** refers to an inability to express one's own thoughts and desires. Language problems may also be evident. For example, a school-age student may be unable to retrieve a desired word or expression, particularly when in a "high demand" instructional setting or anxiety-producing social situation. These difficulties with word retrieval may cause individuals to limit their use of speech and language or to use repetitive expressions or word substitutions. Interestingly, many children with brain injuries have similar experiences of great frustration in knowing an answer or response to a question, but being unable to retrieve it when called on by teachers (Ylvisaker et al., 1994). (See Chapter 10 for additional information on expressive aphasia.)

Social and behavior problems may present the most challenging aspects of TBI and ABI. For many individuals, the injury produces significant changes in their personalities, their temperaments, their dispositions related to certain activities, and their behaviors. In fact, the social and behavior problems may worsen over time, depending on the nature of the injury, the preinjury adjustment of the individual, and other factors such as the age at time of the injury. Behavior effects include increased irritability and emotionality, compromised motivation and judgment, an inability to restrict socially inappropriate behaviors, insensitivity to others, and low tolerance for frustration and inconvenience (Deaton & Waaland, 1994; Rivera et al., 1994).

Neuromotor and physical disabilities also characterize individuals with brain injuries (see the Reflect on This feature on page 380). Neuromotor problems may involve poor eye–hand coordination. For example, an adolescent may be able to pick up a ball but be unable to produce the motions and efforts necessary to throw it to someone else. Additional problems may include impaired balance, an inability to walk unassisted, significantly reduced stamina, or paralysis. Impaired vision and hearing may also be present. The array and depth of the challenges faced by individuals with brain injuries and their families can be overwhelming and disheartening. However, with appropriate support and coordinated, multidisciplinary treatment, the individual and family can move forward with their lives and develop effective coping skills (Savage & Wolcott, 1994a).

Causation

Certain causes of brain injury are most prevalent for particular age groups. The most common source of injury across all age groups is automobile-related accidents (see Table 12.1 on page 381). For small children, the most common cause is a "fall from a short distance" (Haslam, 1996, p. 325). Another major cause of injury in young children is physical abuse. These injuries generally occur when infants are shaken or struck. These actions may cause shearing of brain matter or severe bleeding (Haslam, 1996). Other common causes of head injuries in older children include falls from playground equipment, bicycles, and trees; blows to the head from baseball bats, balls, or other sports equipment; and pedestrian accidents. Children with learning disabilities and attention deficit disorders are more likely to experience head injuries than are other children in the general population.

The first sign that the brain has sustained injury often is a coma. The severity and nature of complications and the eventual outcomes of the trauma are directly related

focus **3**
Identify the most common causes of brain injury in children, youth, and adults.

TABLE 12.1	Common causes of traumatic and acquired brain injury
AGE	MOST COMMON CAUSES
Infants	Abuse and neglect
Toddlers	Abuse and falls
Early elementary	Falls and pedestrian–motor vehicle accidents
Late elementary and middle school	Pedestrian–bicycle accidents, pedestrian–motor vehicle accidents, and sports
High school	Motor vehicle accidents

to the location and degree of injury to the brain. Jennett & Teasdale (1974) developed a scale to assess the potential impact of head injuries on children and to predict the level of functioning they might eventually reach (see Table 12.2). Scores of 3 to 5 generally indicate poor outcomes in children over time (Haslam, 1996).

The number of children and others who experience serious head trauma would be significantly reduced if seat belts and other child-restraint devices were consistently used. A significant decrease in accidents due to driving under the influence of alcohol and other mind-altering substances would also spare many from experiencing injuries to the brain.

Programs that attack the problem of driving under the influence of alcohol or other substances should be vigorously supported. Likewise, guidelines to prevent accidents, and to minimize damage should they occur, should form part of a child's

TABLE 12.2	Scoring of activities by the Glasgow Coma Scale		
ACTIVITY	BEST RESPONSE	SCORE	
Eye opening	Spontaneous	4	
	To speech	3	
	To pain	2	✓
	None	1	
Verbal	Oriented	5	
	Confused	4	
	Inappropriate words	3	
	Nonspecific sounds	2	✓
	None	1	
Motor	Follows commands	6	
	Localizes pain	5	
	Withdraws to pain	4	
	Abnormal flexion	3	✓
	Extends	2	
	None	1	
Total		7	

Reflect on This

NEGLECTED COMMUNICATION

Hi! My name is Carol J., "CJ" for short. I'm in the tenth grade and I had a head injury last year. This is my story. I hope it helps you understand what happens when you get a head trauma injury.

I was with my boyfriend in his three-wheeler. We were riding around the fields and didn't have any helmets on. Yes, I know how stupid that sounds. Anyway, we were trying to get "air" over some jumps when the three-wheeler I guess hit a rock and it bounced me off some other rocks. My boyfriend (except he is not my boyfriend now) flipped the bike and it came down on top of both of us. . . . I was knocked out.

My boyfriend went and got his father who put me in his truck and took me to the medical center. I guess my parents met us there but I don't remember because I ended up in a coma for 1 week. I remember my mom and dad being near me when I was in a coma. . . .

I was in the hospital for 1 month. I had to go over to another hospital after I got out of the medical center for some speech therapy, some physical therapy, and occupational therapy. My therapists were really great and made me work hard. I owe them a lot. The trouble started when I got back to school.

When I got back to school (the ninth grade) my teachers had a meeting about me. My mom and dad went to the meeting and I went, too. I don't remember much of what was said but I sure remember all the work they piled on me to take home. I had a whole month of schoolwork to make up and there were only 2 months of school left!

Everything in school was hard. I kept forgetting my locker number. I went to some wrong classes. And my friends were saying I was trying to get attention with my head injury. I even had one teacher tell me that I had better get my work in soon or I would fail for the year. Pretty soon I started getting really depressed and didn't want to go to school or talk to my friends. I hated everything. I hated school, I hated my friends, I hated some of my teachers, and I hated having a traumatic brain injury. I really hated taking the Dilantin. It was like I was retarded or something. I don't mean that in a mean way. I just felt horrible.

My biggest mistake was at the beginning of my tenth grade year. I had made it through ninth grade thanks to two teachers who helped me after school. But over the summer I started hanging around some different kids. We didn't do anything, we just went around. I didn't see many of my old friends, not

even Elaine. When school started again I was really different. My parents were fighting all the time and I heard them talk about divorce. My two younger brothers by my dad's first marriage were doing really great in school. And I still felt like I had a head injury. One day at school one of my friends from the summer gave me some liquor to drink. . . .

Pretty soon I was taking my own "hair spray" [liquor] to school every day. The teachers didn't know a thing. My grades were failures and none of my friends cared because they had the same grades. One day I stopped taking my Dilantin. I figured, what the hell, I'm not taking this crap anymore nor am I going to take any other crap from anyone. My parents only yelled at me and the teachers didn't know I was alive. On the day before my third-period study hall I went into the girls' room. One of the girls in there had a bottle of vodka and was drinking from it with another girl. They said, "Here—want some," and I took the bottle and drank half of it down. I don't know what ever made me do it. The two girls started to laugh and said drink the rest so I did. Two hours later I was in the hospital.

After I drank the vodka I had a seizure. The two girls took off and somebody told the principal. He got the

school nurse and she called an ambulance. I'm not sure what they did in the hospital and I really don't care to know. I guess I was violent and they had to drug me up.

I'm back in school again and I see my guidance counselor every day. She also helps me with some of my classes, especially algebra. I'm trying to stay calm and take my medication. My parents have separated and they think this is the best thing for right now. I still think I caused them to split up but my mom says no. I am also trying to make some new friends. Elaine is still nice to me and I think that school is going better. I'm also getting some help two times a week from Dr. S. who is a head injury doctor. He says many of my problems were due to my head injury and not being able to handle things like I could before. I'm not sure but he says you've got nowhere to go but up.

I hope you or anyone you know never has a head injury.

Source: From "A neuroeducational model for teaching students with acquired brain injuries," by Savage, R. C. & Mishkin, L. In *Educational Dimensions of Acquired Brain Injury,* edited by R. C. Savage and G. F. Wolcott, pp. 393–411. Copyright 1994, Austin, TX: PRO-ED, Inc. Reprinted by permission.

education both at home and at school. The importance of wearing protective devices such as helmets and obeying safety rules cannot be stressed enough.

Educational Supports and Services

Educational supports focus on the environmental changes and transition issues that characterize the child's return to school. Specific teaching techniques should be informed by current research about learning, the brain, and acquired brain injuries. It is essential that educators and health care providers work together in effectively blending clinical, educational, and family interventions (DePompei & Williams, 1994). Unfortunately, many children with brain injuries leave hospitals or rehabilitation settings without adequate preparation to adapt to the school environment. They are not ready to return to school. Many teachers who receive these students are not adequately prepared to respond to their cognitive, academic, and behavioral needs (Savage & Mishkin, 1994).

Stuart and Goodsitt (1996) recommended that a discharge planning model be followed, in which a transition liaison works directly with the family, hospital personnel, and community agencies. This individual should have "a working knowledge of medical terminology . . . , a thorough awareness and understanding of community and school services, and empathy for family needs" (Stuart & Goodsitt, 1996, p. 59). This liaison works in conjunction with other medical and health personnel to make certain that the child or youth is safe and sufficiently healthy to leave the health care facility. Additionally, the transition liaison ensures that parents and teachers are adequately prepared to receive and care for the child (Stuart & Goodsitt, 1996).

Students with traumatic or acquired brain injuries may return to one of several school placements, depending on their needs. Appropriate teaching activities include establishing high expectations for the child, providing precise feedback, giving students strategies for organizing information, and providing many opportunities for practice (Blosser & DePompei, 1994; Gillis, 1996).

Educational services must be tailored to a student's specific needs. Effort should be directed at improving broadly applicable skills, such as problem solving, planning, and developing insight. Teaching may also focus on building appropriate social behaviors (performing in stressful situations, taking initiative, working with others, etc.), expressive and receptive language skills (word retrieval, event description, understanding instructions, reading nonverbal cues, etc.), and writing skills (sentence development, legibility, etc.) (see Table 12.3).

The initial individualized education programs (IEPs) for students with brain injuries should be written for short periods of time, perhaps lasting from 6 to 8 weeks. Moreover, these IEPs should be reviewed often to make adjustments, depending on the progress and growth of students. It is not uncommon for some students to improve dramatically in the first year following their injuries (Savage & Mishkin, 1994). Flexibility and responsiveness on the part of teachers and other support staff are essential to the well-being of students with traumatic and acquired brain injuries (Savage & Mishkin, 1994).

focus 4
Describe the focus of educational interventions for individuals with traumatic or acquired brain injuries.

IMPAIRMENT	CLASSROOM BEHAVIORS	SKILLS AND TEACHING STRATEGIES
General Behaviors		
Decreased judgment	Is impulsive	Establish a system of verbal or nonverbal signals to cue the student to alter behavior (e.g., call the student's name, touch the student, use a written sign or hand signal).
Poor problem-solving skills	Does not carefully think through solutions to situations	To help develop problem-solving skills, ask questions designed to help the student identify the problem. Plan and organize implementation of a solution together.
Social Behaviors		
Subtle noncompliance with classroom rules and activities	Is withdrawn and unwilling to participate in group activities (e.g., work on a science project, small group discussion) Refuses to recite in class even when called upon	Help the student strengthen his or her self-concept. Begin to elicit responses from the student during individual activities and seat work when you can be assured that the student can answer correctly; gradually request occasional responses in front of the student's friends, then in small groups; repeat until the student feels comfortable participating in a large group.
Rudeness, silliness, immaturity	Makes nasty or inappropriate comments to fellow students and teachers Laughs aloud during serious discussions or quiet seat work	Help the student develop better judgment by presenting "what if" situations and choices. Discuss the student's responses together. Give the student opportunities to verbally express judgment and decision making regarding appropriate behavior as well as opportunities to role-play such behaviors.
Expressive Language		
Tangential (rambling) communication	Tends to ramble without acknowledging the listener's interest or attention May discuss the appropriate topic, but not focus on the key concept (e.g., when asked to name the major food groups, the student might begin a discussion about growing crops)	When the student begins to digress from the topic, either provide a nonverbal cue or stop the student from continuing in front of classmates. Teach the student to recognize nonverbal behaviors indicating lack of interest or desire to make a comment. (Work with this skill during private conversations with the student.) Teach about the beginning, middle, and ending of stories. Stop the student's response and restate the original question, focusing the student's attention on the key issues.

continued next page

IMPAIRMENT	CLASSROOM BEHAVIORS	SKILLS AND TEACHING STRATEGIES
Expressive Language		
Word retrieval errors	Answers using many vague terms ("this," "that," "those things," "whatchamacallits")	To improve word recall, teach the student to use association skills and to give definitions of words he cannot recall.
	Has difficulty providing answers in fill-in-the-blank tests	Teach memory strategies (rehearsal, association, visualization, etc.).
Receptive Language		
Inability to determine salient features of questions asked, information presented, or assignments read	Completes the wrong assignment (e.g., teacher requested that the class complete problems 9–12; this student completed problems 1–12)	Encourage the student to write assignments in a daily log.
Inability to read nonverbal cues	Is unaware that the teacher or other classmates do not want to be bothered while they are working	To raise social awareness, use preestablished nonverbal cues to alert the student that behavior is inappropriate. Explain what was wrong with the behavior and what would have been appropriate.
Written Language		
Simplistic sentence structure and syntactic disorganization	Uses sentences and chooses topics that are simplistic compared with expectations for age and grade; writes themes that are short and dry	Provide the student with worksheets that focus on vocabulary, grammar, and proofreading skills.
Decreased speed and accuracy; poor legibility	Is slower on timed tests than classmates	Accept that the student will take longer to complete assignments; reduce and alter the requirements.

Source: Blosser, J. L. & DePompei, R. (1994). Creating an effective classroom environment. In R. C. Savage & G. F. Wolcott (Eds.), *Educational dimensions of acquired brain injury* (pp. 413–451). Austin, TX: PRO-ED. Reprinted by permission

Services for the person with brain injury do not stop as he or she becomes an adult. Family and care providers should be aware of the services available. They can also create opportunities for the adult with disabilities to be involved in leisure and recreational events.

TABLE 12.4	Checklist for transition to postsecondary education for students with TBI

Physical Accessibility
- To what degree are buildings, dormitories, and activities accessible?
- Are transportation alternatives and mobility assistance available?
- Are health and medical care available, and are personnel knowledgeable about traumatic brain injury (TBI)?
- Are living arrangements accessible, safe, and modifiable to needs?
- Are fatigue, endurance, stress, and energy parameters known?

Academic Programs and Support Services
- Have campus support services and informed resources been identified?
- Have student information processing skills and deficits been identified?
- What accommodations are made for admissions, registration, and changes?
- Are faculty, advisors, and staff trained or knowledgeable about TBI?
- Are syllabuses, texts, and instructional formats available prior to class?
- Are alternative assignments and testing formats or compensatory aids allowed?

Social and Personal Support Systems
- Have social functioning and at-risk situations been assessed?
- How well are student disability-related needs and concerns articulated?
- How well does the student accept and manage assistance?
- Are accessible social networks and leisure and recreation activities present?

Vocational Training and Job Placement
- Are career counselors experienced in working with students with disabilities?
- Are Division of Rehabilitation Services or other agencies involved?
- Are apprentice, intern, or supported employment opportunities known? (Bergland & Haffbauer, 1996, p. 55)

Source: From "New Opportunities for Students with Traumatic Brain Injury: Transition to Postsecondary Education,"
by M. Bergland & D. Hoffbauer. *Teaching Exceptional Children,* (1996, Winter), vol. 28, no. 2, p. 55. Copyright 1996 by
The Council for Exceptional Children. Reprinted by permission.

For students who want to move on to postsecondary education, multidisciplinary team members may contribute significantly to the transition process. Critical factors include the physical accessibility of the campus, living arrangements, academic program and support, social and personal support systems, and career and vocational training and placement (Bergland & Hoffbauer, 1996). (See Table 12.4.)

Collaboration and cooperation are the key factors in achieving success with individuals with traumatic and acquired brain injuries. A great deal can be accomplished when families, students, and care providers come together, engage in appropriate planning, and work collaboratively.

Medical and Psychological Services

New medical technologies have revolutionized the treatment of traumatic and acquired brain injuries. In previous decades, the vast majority of individuals with such injuries died within a short time of their accidents. With the development of **computed tomography (CT)** scans, intracranial pressure monitors, **magnetic resonance imaging (MRI),** and the capacity to control bleeding and swelling of the brain, many individuals with traumatic brain injury survive (Savage & Wolcott, 1994a).

focus 5
Identify four common types of head injuries.

Interacting in Natural Settings

■ EARLY CHILDHOOD YEARS

TIPS FOR THE FAMILY

- Become fully informed about your child's condition.
- Become familiar with special services available in your school and with health care systems.
- Develop positive relationships with care providers.
- Seek out appropriate assistance through advocacy and support groups.
- Pursue family or individual counseling for persistent relationship-centered problems.
- Develop sensible routines and schedules for the child.
- Communicate with siblings, friends, and relatives; help them become informed about the injury and their role in the treatment process.

TIPS FOR THE PRESCHOOL TEACHER

- Communicate with parents, special education personnel, and health care providers to develop appropriate expectations, management, and instruction.
- Interact frequently with parents, special education personnel, and health care providers.

- Watch for abrupt changes in the child's behavior. If they occur, notify parents and other professionals immediately.
- Involve socially sophisticated peers and other older children in working with the preschooler with TBI.
- Become familiar with events that "set the child off."
- Use management procedures that promote appropriate independence and foster learning.

TIPS FOR PRESCHOOL PERSONNEL

- Participate in orientation and team meetings with the preschool teacher.
- Develop an understanding of the child and the condition.
- Communicate frequently with the preschool teacher and parents about concerns and promising developments.
- Employ the same management strategies used by the parents and preschool teacher.
- Be patient with the rate of progress behaviorally, socially, and academically.
- Help other children understand the child.

TIPS FOR NEIGHBORS AND FRIENDS

- Offer to become educated about the condition and its impact on the child.
- Become familiar with recommended management procedures for directing the child.
- Inform your own children about the dynamics of the condition; help them understand how to react and respond to variations in behavior.
- Involve the child in appropriate family activities.

■ ELEMENTARY YEARS

TIPS FOR THE FAMILY

- Remember that the transition back to the school and family environment requires explicit planning and preparation.
- Prepare siblings, peers, and neighbors for the child's return to the home and community.
- Learn about and use management procedures that promote the child's well-being.
- Carefully plan with school personnel the child's reentry into school.

TIPS FOR THE GENERAL EDUCATION CLASSROOM TEACHER

- Become fully familiar with the child's condition.
- Communicate with medical and other personnel about expectations, management strategies, and approaches for dealing with persisting problems.
- Use appropriate routines and schedules to foster learning and good behavior.
- Help other children understand how they can contribute to the child's growth and healing within the classroom setting.
- Let peers and older youngsters work with the student on academic and social tasks.
- Do not be reluctant to communicate with other professionals and parents when problems occur.
- Remember that teamwork among caring professionals and parents is essential to the child's success.

TIPS FOR SCHOOL PERSONNEL

- Become informed; seek to understand the unique characteristics of TBI.
- Behave as if the child were your own.

- Seek to understand and use instructional and management approaches that are well suited to the child.
- Use the expertise that is present in the school and school system; collaborate with other specialists.

- Adopt an inclusive attitude about family and neighborhood events; invite the child or youth to join in family-centered activities, picnics, appropriate recreational and sports activities, and holiday events.
- Learn how to respond effectively and confidently to the common problems that the child or youth may present.
- Communicate concerns and problems immediately in a compassionate fashion.

SECONDARY AND TRANSITION YEARS

TIPS FOR THE FAMILY
- Prepare and plan for the secondary, transitional, and adult years.
- Work closely with school and adult services personnel in developing a transition plan.
- Develop a thoughtful and comprehensive transition plan that includes education, employment, housing, and use of leisure time.
- Become aware of all the services and resources that are available through state and national funding.
- Begin to develop plans for the individual's care and support over the lifespan.

TIPS FOR THE GENERAL EDUCATION CLASSROOM TEACHER
- Be sure that appropriate steps have been taken to prepare the youth to return to school and related activities.
- Realize that there will be significant changes in the youth's functioning, academically, socially, and behaviorally.
- Work closely with members of the multidisciplinary team in developing appropriate schooling and employment experiences.
- Report any changes in behavior immediately to parents and other specialists within the school.

TIPS FOR SCHOOL PERSONNEL
- Determine what environmental changes need to be made.
- Employ teaching procedures that best fit the youth's current cognitive status and academic functioning.

- Consider having the youth gradually phased into a complete school day.
- Be prepared for emotions of anger, depression, and rebellion.
- Focus on the youth's current strengths.
- Help the youth develop appropriate compensatory skills.

TIPS FOR NEIGHBORS, FRIENDS, AND POTENTIAL EMPLOYERS
- Remember that the injury will significantly alter the youth's personality and functioning in many areas.
- Involve the youth in appropriate family, neighborhood, and community activities, particularly youth activities and parties.
- Use successful management procedures employed in the home and school settings.
- Become informed about the youth's capacities and interests.
- Work with vocational and special education personnel in providing employment explorations and part-time employment.

ADULT YEARS

TIPS FOR THE FAMILY
- Begin developing appropriate independence skills throughout the school years.

- Determine early what steps can be taken to prepare the youth for meaningful part-time or full-time employment.
- Become thoroughly familiar with postsecondary education opportunities and adult services for individuals with disabilities.
- Explore various living and housing options early in the youth's secondary school years.
- Provide opportunities for the young adult to experience different kinds of living arrangements.

TIPS FOR NEIGHBORS, FRIENDS, AND EMPLOYERS
- Keep up a spirit of neighborliness.
- Create opportunities for the adult to be involved in age-relevant activities, including movies, sports events, going out to dinner, and so on.
- Work closely with educational and adult support services personnel in creating employment opportunities, monitoring performance on the job, and making appropriate adjustments.

The medical and psychological services available to Russian skater Elena Berezhnaya enabled her to successfully return to skating after receiving a traumatic head injury in practice. After months of care and rehabilitation, she and her partner were bronze medal winners in the XVIII Winter Olympics.

Head injuries may be described in different ways, according to the nature of the injury (Rizzo & Tranel, 1996). Types of injuries include concussions, contusions, skull fractures, and epidural and subdural hematomas (masses of blood, usually clotted).

- *Concussions.* **Concussions** are the most common closed-head injuries. They occur most frequently in children and adolescents through contact sports such as football, hockey, and martial arts. Children who display weakness on one side of the body or a dilated pupil may have a concussion and should be examined immediately by a physician (Haslam, 1996).
- *Contusions.* **Contusions** are characterized by extensive damage to the brain, including laceration of the brain, bleeding, swelling, and bruising. The resulting effect of this kind of injury is intense stupor or coma. Individuals with contusions should be hospitalized immediately (Haslam, 1996).
- *Skull fractures.* The consequences of **skull fractures** depend on the location, nature, and seriousness of the fracture. Unfortunately, some fractures are not easily detectable through radiological examination. Injuries to the lower back part of the head are particularly troublesome and difficult to detect. These basilar skull (base of the skull) fractures may set the stage for serious infections of the central nervous system. Immediate medical care is essential for fractures in order to determine the extent of the damage and to develop appropriate interventions (Haslam, 1996).

■ *Epidural and subdural hematomas.* Hemorrhaging or bleeding is the central feature of epidural and subdural hematomas. An **epidural hematoma** is caused by damage to an artery (a thick-walled blood vessel carrying blood from the heart) between the brain and the skull (see Figure 12.1). If this injury is not treated promptly and appropriately, the affected individual will die. A **subdural hematoma** is caused by damage to tiny veins that draw blood from the outer layer of the brain (cerebral cortex) to the heart. The aggregation of blood between the brain and its outer covering (dura) produces pressure that adversely affects the brain and its functioning (see Figure 12.2 on page 390). If the subdural bleeding is left untreated, the result can be death (Haslam, 1996).

Medical treatment of traumatic and acquired brain injury proceeds in stages. At the onset of the injury, medical personnel focus on maintaining the child's life, treating the swelling and bleeding, minimizing complications, reducing the level of coma, and completing the initial neurologic examination (Gelber, 1995; Haslam, 1996). This stage of the treatment is often characterized by strained interactions between physicians and parents. Many physicians are unable to respond satisfactorily to the overwhelming psychological needs of parents and family members because of the complex medical demands

focus 6

Describe four important elements of medical treatment for individuals with traumatic or acquired brain injuries.

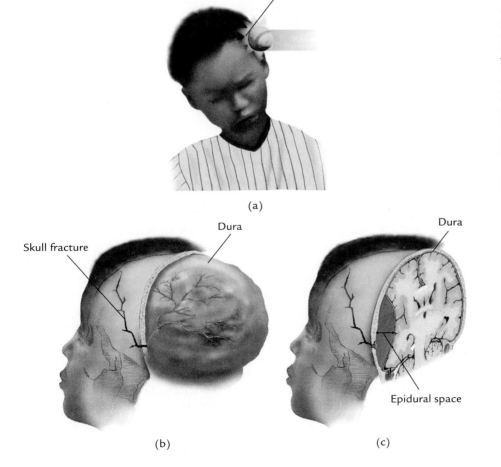

(a)

(b)   (c)

Skull fracture

Dura

Dura

Epidural space

Temporal area

FIGURE 12.1

An epidural hematoma. (a) A forceful injury occurs in the temporal area of the brain. (b) The injury may result in a fractured skull causing bleeding in the middle meningeal artery. Blood collects between the skull and the dura—a tough membrane covering the brain. (c) As the blood collects, pressure builds on vital structures within the brain.

[*Source:* Adapted from Common Neurological Disorders in Children by Robert H. A. Haslam (p. 330) in R. H. A. Haslam & P. J. Valletutti (eds.) *Medical Problems in the Classroom,* Copyright 1996, Austin, TX: PRO-ED, Inc. Reprinted by permission.]

FIGURE 12.2

A subdural hematoma. (a) Violent
shaking or hitting a child may
cause damage to the cerebral cortex. (b) Trauma to the brain results in the rupturing of small
veins. (c) Blood gathers between
the dura and the brain, resulting
in pressure on vital brain
structures.

[*Source:* Adapted from Common
Neurological Disorders in Children by
Robert H. A. Haslam (p. 332) in
R. H. A. Haslam & P. J. Valletutti (eds.)
Medical Problems in the Classroom, Copyright
1996, Austin, TX: PRO-ED, Inc. Reprinted
by permission.]

(a)

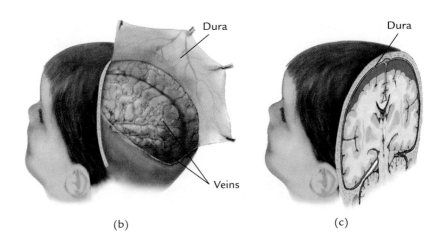

(b)   (c)

presented by the injured child. Other trained personnel—including social workers, psychologists, and clergy—should address the parents' and family's needs.

If the child remains in a coma, physical or occupational therapists may use specialized stimulation techniques to reduce the depth of the coma. If the child becomes agitated by stimuli in the hospital unit, such as conversations of visitors, noises produced by housecleaning staff, obtrusive light, or touching, steps may be taken to control or reduce the problem. As the injured individual comes out of the coma, personnel will focus on orienting him or her to the environment. This may include talking about where the person is located, introducing the care providers who are delivering the intensive care, indicating where loved ones are, sharing what has transpired since entering the hospital, and responding to other questions that he or she may have. Many persons who have been injured do not remember their accidents or the resulting medical interventions.

The next stage of treatment focuses on relearning and performing skills and behaviors that the person had mastered before the injury. This treatment may take time and considerable effort. Gradually, children are prepared for return to their homes and appropriate school environments. Their families prepare as well, receiving ongoing support and counseling. Additionally, arrangements are made for appropriate speech and language, physical, and occupational therapies, and specialized teaching as necessary (Gillis, 1996).

Many individuals return to their homes, schools, or employment settings as vastly different people. These differences are often exhibited in emotional excesses that are unpredictable and extreme. Furthermore, these individuals may have difficulties recognizing and accepting their postinjury challenges and deficits (Stevens, 1994). The last stages of intervention focus on providing counseling and therapy to help the individual cope with the injury and its residual effects, assisting the family in maintaining the gains that the individual has achieved, terminating specific head injury services; and referring the person to community agencies and educational programs for additional services as needed.

Case Study

DARIN

Darin was 27 months old when he was riding in his parents' jeep while sitting on his mother's lap. A car abruptly stopped, and Darin's father hit the brakes, propelling his son and wife into the dashboard of the jeep. Darin struck the hand-grip bar on the dashboard with his forehead, receiving a moderate gash.

Darin's parents immediately took him to the emergency room at the local medical center. On the way to the hospital, Darin was vomiting and lost consciousness for 30 to 45 minutes. The physician who saw Darin closed the laceration on his forehead and admitted him overnight. The next day, Darin was very disoriented and confused. Testing revealed that Darin had a small bleed in his left frontal lobe that needed to be removed by surgery. The operation was successful, and Darin went home in 1 week.

Over the next 6 months, Darin had uncontrollable crying spells, was very impulsive, and was inattentive. When he was 4 years old, his parents enrolled him in a preschool. His teacher reported that Darin had five to six tantrums every day and that he needed to be isolated in a time-out area for his own safety and the safety of his schoolmates.

By the time Darin started kindergarten, his impulsivity and outbursts were so severe that the teacher recommended counseling with the school psychologist. Darin was retained in kindergarten and again retained in first grade. He spent most of his time outside the classroom in counseling or one-on-one tutoring sessions because of his distractibility and behavioral outbursts. At midyear, his parents

were asked to have Darin evaluated by a child psychiatrist. Although a psychiatrist interviewed Darin and his parents, nobody noted Darin's prior brain injury. The psychiatrist recommended that the parents receive counseling and behavior modification training in order to work with their child.

When Darin turned 10 years old, he was hospitalized for severe behavioral outbursts and depression. He was placed in a private psychiatric facility for 2 years and has shown little if any progress to date. Darin's medical records still do not note his traumatic brain injury.[1]

■ APPLICATION

1. What essential mistakes were made over time in the treatment of Darin's medical and educational problems?

2. What specific, serious behaviors would have alerted you as an educator, health care provider, or parent that new steps and actions needed to be taken to assist Darin?

3. Ideally, what steps and actions should have been pursued by the medical and educational personnel to address Darin's problems?

4. Provide a rationale for the steps or actions you have identified.

[1]Source: Adapted from "A neuroeducational model for teaching students with acquired brain injury," by R. C. Savage & L. Mishkin. In *Educational Dimensions of Acquired Brain Injury*, edited by R. C. Savage and G. F. Wolcott, p. 397, Copyright 1994, Austin, TX: PRO-ED, Inc. Reprinted by permission.

Debate Forum

WHOSE PROBLEM IS THIS? WHO IS RESPONSIBLE FOR BEHAVIOR CHANGE?

Sarah is a 12-year-old who sustained a severe brain injury in a bicycle–car collision 4 years ago. She has been in school for the past 3 years but refuses to do assigned tasks she does not like. Sarah's school and her family tend to blame each other for Sarah's problems. Her school notes that her family brings her to school late each morning, in time for a preferred activity (art) but missing disliked classes (math and social sciences). Her school also notes the family's failure to carry out behavior programs, particularly regarding eating and homework completion, in the home.

Sarah's parents still blame themselves for their daughter's injury because they did not require her to wear a bike helmet. They feel that Sarah has special needs and that the school does not recognize Sarah's needs and is too strict. They note that they do not have behavioral problems at home; they simply allow Sarah to do what Sarah enjoys doing. Due to the school's and family's blaming one another, little cooperation or collaboration exists between them. Sarah continues to refuse activities, have tantrums, and steal food at school, and the school staff acknowledges that they often end up punishing her, which is against the program developed for her. The family is able to avoid these behaviors in the home by not allowing her to be frustrated—or to be challenged.[1]

■ POINT

School personnel may exercise only so much control in promoting and implementing behavior change programs with students. The ultimate responsibility for this problem lies with Sarah's parents. They are responsible for advancing their child's growth and development. Their inaction in the long run will only hurt them and their daughter.

■ COUNTERPOINT

Parents and school personnel should join together in promoting appropriate behavioral changes in Sarah. Blaming each other only worsens the problems in the short run and ensures their continuance and amplification in the future. For the sake of the family, the school, and society in general, the parents and educators should come together to begin resolving the problems that Sarah presents.

[1]*Source:* Adapted from "Changing the Behaviors of Students with Acquired Brain Injuries" by A. V. Deaton. In *Educational Dimensions of Acquired Brain Injury,* edited by R. C. Savage & G. F. Wolcott, p. 263, Copyright 1994, Austin, TX: PRO-ED, Inc. Copyright, 1994. Reprinted by permission.

These students with traumatic brain injury attend a resource classroom in addition to their general education classes. TBI is the largest disabler of children, and adolescent boys between the ages of 15 and 19 are the most vulnerable group.

Review

focus 1

Identify three key elements of traumatic and acquired brain injury.

- The brain is damaged by external forces that cause tearing, bruising, or swelling.
- The injuries, open and/or closed head, dramatically influence the individual's functioning in several areas, including psychosocial behavior, speech and language, cognitive performance, vision and hearing, and motor abilities.
- The brain injury often results in permanent disabilities.

focus 2

Identify four general characteristics of individuals with traumatic or acquired brain injuries.

- Individuals with traumatic or acquired brain injuries often exhibit cognitive deficits, including problems with memory, concentration, attention, and problem solving.

- Speech and language problems are frequently evident, including word retrieval problems, slurred or unintelligible speech, and aphasia.
- These individuals may also present social and behavioral problems, including increased irritability, inability to suppress or manage socially inappropriate behaviors, low thresholds for frustration, and insensitivity to others.
- Neuromotor and physical problems may also be present, including eye–hand coordination impairments, vision and hearing deficits, and paralysis.

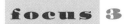

focus 3

Identify the most common causes of brain injury in children, youth, and adults.

- The most common causes of brain injury in young children are falls, neglect, and physical abuse.
- For children in the elementary grades, the most common causes are falls, accidents in which a car hits a bicyclist or pedestrian, and sports.
- For high school students and adults, the most common causes are motor vehi-

cle accidents and sports-related injuries.

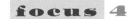

focus 4

Describe the focus of educational interventions for individuals with traumatic or acquired brain injuries.

- Educational interventions are directed at improving the general behaviors of the individual, including problem solving, planning, and developing insight; building appropriate social behaviors; and developing expressive and receptive language skills as well as writing skills.
- Other academic skills that are relevant to a student's needs and developmental level are also taught.
- Transition planning for postsecondary education and training is also essential to the well-being of the individual with traumatic or acquired brain injury.

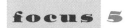

focus 5

Identify four common types of head injuries.

- Common head injuries include concussions, contusions, skull fractures, and

epidural and subdural hematomas.

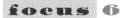

focus 6

Describe four important elements of medical treatment for individuals with traumatic or acquired brain injuries.

- The first stage of treatment is directed at preserving the individual's life, addressing swelling and bleeding, and minimizing complications.
- Once the individual regains consciousness or can benefit from more active therapies, the learning and relearning of pre-injury skills begin.
- The last stage focuses on preparing the individual to return to home, school, or work settings, and readying the individual to work with other health care and training providers.
- The last stage is also characterized by the provision of psychological services directed at helping individuals and their families cope with the injuries and their effects.
- Throughout all the stages of treatment, multidisciplinary collaboration and cooperation are essential to the individual's success.

13 People with Hearing Loss

To begin with . . .

 Tamara stands farther along the counter . . . "Look at these," she tells them, surveying rows of bookmarks, ink, stamps, key chains, all cut with the same ASL hand shapes. Displayed on a lower shelf are flashers that can be attached to a doorbell or telephone ringer, and the latest, sleekest, portable TTYs (or telecommunication devices for the deaf, TDDs, as these trimmer models are properly called). There are travel alarm clocks that vibrate instead of beep and can be slipped beneath a pillow. (A long time ago . . . deaf people depended on a more organic alarm clock: if they wanted to rise at a particular hour, they simply drank the commensurate amount of water before retiring.) There are even baby criers, which are attached to a crib and trigger a light in the parents' room when the infant wails. (Not very long ago, deaf parents rigged string from crib slats to their own toes and relied on the transmitted vibrations to know when their babies were stirring.) (Cohen, 1994, p. 243)

 Poverty has been associated with an increased risk of children being born with a lower than average birth weight. Low birth weight babies are at a higher risk of developing . . . *hearing impairments.* When poverty and low weight occur together, the number of students who need special education services is greater than would be predicted for those factors independently. (U.S. Department of Education, 1997, p. ii)

 Hearing loss is often not understood. Loss of hearing is not accompanied by outward, easily recognizable characteristics. A person with a hearing impairment can pass other people on the street without their knowing that this person has a disability. At other times, a hearing loss may be mistaken for an emotional disorder or mental retardation. Some people argue that hearing loss (particularly deafness) is not a disability at all but a cultural difference. (Smith, 1998, p. 219)

Despite having a profound hearing loss that began before starting elementary school, I attended regular [general education] classes in the local public school system at a time when mainstreaming [inclusion] was not the norm. Although there is probably nothing in my academic record that might indicate that time spent in the regular public school system was different than [that of] a student with normal hearing, there are many incidents that occurred because of my hearing problem. Many of these incidents would have occurred even if my teachers had been fully aware of my hearing problem and knew how to deal with it. Some of the incidents, however, were problems that should have been avoided if teachers and other school officials had been better trained in how to deal with hearing problems. (Thomas R. Clouser, cited in Maxon & Brackett, 1992, p. xiii)

Shelley

Shelley is the third oldest in a family of six children. At the age of 18 months, she was diagnosed with a severe hearing

loss and immediately fitted with hearing aids for both ears. Although her parents have no hearing problems, Shelley has an older brother and a younger sister who are profoundly deaf and a younger brother with a severe hearing loss. She and her non-hearing siblings were all born deaf or hard of hearing. While growing up, Shelley's parents worked diligently to ensure that she had every chance

possible to develop and use speech. Through the support of her family, the use of hearing aids, and the combination of speech and signing skills, Shelley grew up in a hearing world where she successfully completed public school and went on to receive a graduate degree with an emphasis in teaching children who are deaf or hard of hearing. She is now a university faculty member in early childhood special

education and the mother of two young children, Matthew and Molly. Matthew and Molly, ages 2½ and 16 months, are both hearing children. Shelley describes herself as the kind of person who clearly wants to be perceived as an individual first. She likes to say, "I've got a desire or a drive in me that I just wanted to be the same as everyone else. So basically, I just have broken ears."

LTHOUGH SHELLEY is unable to hear most sounds, her life is one of independence and fulfillment (see the opening snapshot). In Shelley's case, as well as those of many people who are deaf or hard of hearing, the obstacles presented by the loss of hearing are not insurmountable.

In a world often controlled by sound, the ability to hear and speak is a critical link in the development of human communication. Children who can hear learn to talk by listening to those around them. Our everyday communication systems would make little sense without sound. Telephones, loudspeakers, car horns, musical instruments, alarm clocks, fire alarms, radios, stereos, and intercoms would be useless in a world without sound. Our sense of hearing is an important factor in the way we learn to perceive our world and in the way the world perceives us.

How difficult is it, then, for the person who cannot hear to adjust to a hearing world? Most people with hearing loss, such as Shelley, can and do adjust successfully to life within their local communities. Unfortunately, others feel shunned by their own families and neighbors. Feeling like outsiders, they may deal with their stigma in a number of ways. Some may try to adjust as much as possible to the demands of the hearing world. Others may live a life of isolation, avoiding those who can hear. Still others may become part of organized groups whose members share the common bond of hearing loss.

The Hearing Process

Audition is the act or sense of hearing. The auditory process involves the transmission of sound through the vibration of an object to a receiver. The process originates with a vibrator—such as a string, reed, membrane, or column of air—that causes displacement of air particles.

To become sound, a vibration must have a medium to carry it. Air is the most common carrier, but vibrations can also be carried by metal, water, and other substances. The displacement of air particles by the vibrator produces a pattern of circular waves that move away from the source.

This movement, referred to as a sound wave, can be illustrated by imagining the ripples resulting from a pebble dropped in a pool of water. Sound waves are patterns of pressure that alternately push together and pull apart in a spherical expansion. Sound waves are carried through a medium (e.g., air) to a receiver. The human ear is one of the most sensitive receivers there is, capable of being activated by incredibly small amounts of pressure and able to distinguish more than half a million different sounds.

The ear is the mechanism through which sound is collected, processed, and transmitted to a specific area in the brain that decodes the sensations into meaningful language. The anatomy of the hearing mechanism is discussed in terms of the external, middle, and inner ears. These structures are illustrated in Figure 13.1.

focus 1

Describe how sound is transmitted through the human ear.

■ THE EXTERNAL EAR

The external ear consists of a cartilage structure on the side of the head called the auricle, or pinna, and an external ear canal referred to as the meatus. The only outwardly visible part of the ear, the auricle, is attached to the skull by three ligaments. Its purpose is to collect sound waves and funnel them into the meatus. The meatus secretes a wax called cerumen, which protects the inner structures of the ear by trapping foreign materials and lubricating the canal and eardrum. The eardrum, or tympanic membrane, is located at the inner end of the canal between the external and middle ear. The concave membrane is positioned in such a manner that, when struck by sound waves, it can vibrate freely.

FIGURE 13.1   Structure of the ear

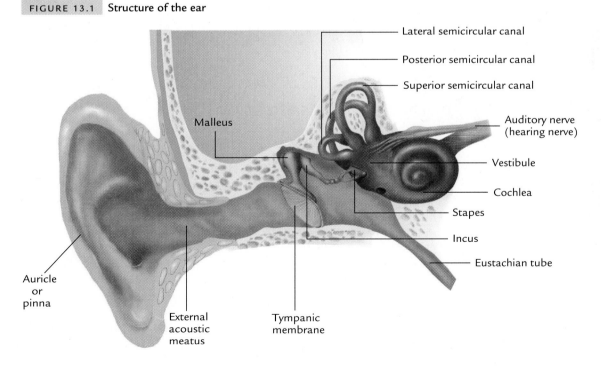

Lateral semicircular canal

Posterior semicircular canal

Superior semicircular canal

Auditory nerve (hearing nerve)

Vestibule

Cochlea

Stapes

Incus

Eustachian tube

Malleus

Auricle or pinna

External acoustic meatus

Tympanic membrane

■ THE MIDDLE EAR

The inner surface of the eardrum is located in the air-filled cavity of the middle ear. This surface consists of three small bones that form the ossicular chain: the malleus, incus, and stapes, often referred to as the hammer, anvil, and stirrup because of similarities in shape to these common objects. The three bones transmit the vibrations from the external ear through the cavity of the middle ear to the inner ear.

The eustachian tube, extending from the throat to the middle-ear cavity, equalizes the air pressure on the eardrum with that of the outside by controlling the flow of air into the middle-ear cavity. Although air conduction is the primary avenue through which sound reaches the inner ear, conduction can also occur through the bones of the skull. Bone conduction appears comparable to air conduction in that the patterns of displacement produced in the inner ear are similar.

■ THE INNER EAR

The inner ear consists of a multitude of intricate passageways. The cochlea lies horizontally in front of the vestibule (a central cavity where sound enters directly from the middle ear), where it can be activated by movement in the ossicular chain. The cochlea is filled with fluid similar in composition to cerebral spinal fluid. Within the cochlea is Corti's organ, a structure of highly specialized cells that translate vibrations into nerve impulses that are sent directly to the brain.

The other major structure within the inner ear is the vestibular mechanism, containing the semicircular canals that control balance. The semicircular canals have enlarged portions at one end and are filled with fluid that responds to head movement. The vestibular mechanism integrates sensory input passing to the brain and assists the body in maintaining equilibrium. Motion and gravity are detected through this mechanism, allowing the individual to differentiate between sensory input associated with body movement and input coming from the external environment. Whenever the basic functions of the vestibular mechanism or any of the structures in the external, middle, and inner ear are interrupted, hearing loss may occur.

Definitions and Classification

■ DEFINITIONS

Deafness and hearing loss may be defined according to the degree of hearing impairment, which is determined by assessing a person's sensitivity to loudness (sound intensity) and pitch (sound frequency). The unit used to measure sound intensity is the decibel (db); the range of human hearing is approximately 0 to 130 db. Sounds louder than 130 db (such as those made by jet aircraft at 140 db) are extremely painful to the ear. Conversational speech registers at 40 to 60 db, loud thunder at about 120 db, and a rock concert at about 110 db.

The frequency of sound is determined by measuring the number of cycles that vibrating molecules complete per second. The unit used to measure cycles per second is the hertz (Hz). The higher the frequency, the higher the hertz. The human ear can hear sounds ranging from 20 to approximately 15,000 Hz. The pitch of speech sounds ranges from 300 to 4,000 Hz, whereas the pitches made by a piano keyboard range from 27.5 to 4,186 Hz. Although the human ear can hear sounds at the 15,000-Hz level, the vast majority of sounds in our environment range from 300 to 4,000 Hz.

focus 2
Distinguish between the terms *deaf* and *hard of hearing.*

■ DEAFNESS AND HARD OF HEARING   Two terms, *deaf* and *hard of hearing* (or *partial hearing*), are commonly used to distinguish the severity of a person's hearing loss. *Deaf* is often overused and misunderstood, commonly applied to describe a wide variety of hearing loss; however, the term should be used in a more precise fashion. It describes specifically those individuals whose hearing loss is in the extreme—90 db or greater. Even with the use of hearing aids or other forms of amplification, for people who are deaf the primary means for developing language and communication is through the visual channel. Deafness, as defined by the Individuals with Disabilities Education Act (IDEA), means

a hearing impairment which is so severe that the child is impaired in processing linguistic information through hearing, with or without amplification, which adversely affects educational performance. (IDEA 97, 34 C.F.R. 300.7)

A person who is deaf is most often described as someone who cannot hear sound. As such, the individual is unable to understand human speech. However, many people who are deaf have enough residual hearing to recognize sound at certain frequencies, but still may be unable to determine the meaning of the sound pressure waves.

For persons defined as hard of hearing, audition is deficient but remains somewhat functional. Individuals who are hard of hearing have enough residual hearing that, with the use of a hearing aid, they are able to process human speech auditorily.

The distinction between deaf and hard of hearing, based on the functional use of residual hearing, is not as clear as many traditional definitions imply. New breakthroughs in the development of hearing aids as well as improved diagnostic procedures have enabled many children labeled as deaf to use their hearing functionally under limited circumstances.

focus 3
Why is it important to consider age of onset and anatomical site when defining a hearing loss?

In addition to measuring a person's sensitivity to loudness and pitch, two other factors are involved in defining deafness and hard of hearing: the age of onset and the anatomical site of the loss.

■ AGE OF ONSET   Hearing loss may be present at birth (congenital) or acquired at any time during life. **Prelingual disorders** occur prior to the age of 2, or before speech development. **Postlingual disorders** occur at any age following speech acquisition. About 90% of deafness in children occurs at birth or prior to the child's learning to speak (Dolnick, 1993). The distinction between a congenital and an acquired hearing loss is important. The age of onset will be a critical variable in determining the type and extent of interventions necessary to minimize the effect of the individual's disability (Greenberg & Kusche, 1989; Talbott & Wehman, 1996). This is particularly true in relation to speech and language development. A person who is born with hearing loss has significantly more challenges, particularly in the areas of communication and social adaptation (Quigley & Paul, 1989).

■ ANATOMICAL SITE OF THE LOSS   The two primary types of hearing loss based on anatomical location are peripheral problems and central auditory problems. There are three types of peripheral hearing loss: conductive, sensorineural, and mixed. A **conductive hearing loss** results from poor conduction of sound along the passages leading to the sense organ (inner ear). The loss may result from a blockage in the external canal, as well as from an obstruction interfering with the movement of the eardrum or ossicle. The overall effect is a reduction or loss of loudness. A conductive loss can be offset by amplification (hearing aids) and medical intervention. Surgery has proved to be effective in reducing or even restoring a conductive loss.

Sensorineural hearing losses are a result of an abnormal sense organ and a damaged auditory nerve. A sensorineural loss may distort sound, affecting the clarity of human speech, and cannot presently be treated adequately through medical intervention. A sensorineural loss is generally more severe than a conductive loss and is permanent. Losses of greater than 70 db are usually sensorineural and involve severe damage to the inner ear. One common way to determine whether a loss is conductive or sensorineural is to administer an air and bone conduction test. An individual with a conductive loss would be unable to hear a vibrating tuning fork held close to the ear, because of blocked air passages to the inner ear, but may be able to hear the same fork applied to the skull as well as someone with normal hearing would. An individual with a sensorineural loss would not be able to hear the vibrating fork, regardless of its placement. This test is not always accurate, however, and must therefore be used with caution in distinguishing between conductive and sensorineural losses. **Mixed hearing loss**, a combination of conductive and sensorineural problems, can also be assessed through the use of an air and bone conduction test. In the case of a mixed loss, abnormalities are evident in both tests.

Although most hearing losses are peripheral, such as conductive and sensorineural problems, some occur where there is no measurable peripheral loss. This type of loss, referred to as a central auditory disorder, occurs when there is a dysfunction in the cerebral cortex. The cerebral cortex, the outer layer of gray matter of the brain, governs thought, reasoning, memory, sensation, and voluntary movement. Consequently, a central auditory problem is not a loss in the ability to hear sound but a disorder of symbolic processes, including auditory perception, discrimination, comprehension of sound, and language development (expressive and receptive).

■ CLASSIFICATION

Hearing loss, like other disabilities, may be classified according to the severity of the condition. Table 13.1 illustrates a symptom severity classification system and presents information relative to a child's ability to understand speech patterns at the various severity levels.

Classification systems based solely on a person's degree of hearing loss should be used with a great deal of caution when determining appropriate services and supports. These systems do not reflect the individual's capabilities, background, or experience; they merely suggest parameters for measuring a physical defect in auditory function. As a young child, for example, Shelley from our opening snapshot was diagnosed as having a severe hearing loss in both ears, yet throughout her life she successfully adjusted to both school and community experiences. She went on to college and now has a successful career as a university faculty member. Consequently, many factors beyond the severity of the hearing loss must be assessed when determining the potential of an individual. In addition to severity of loss, factors such as

TABLE 13.1	Classification of hearing loss	

AVERAGE HEARING LOSS IN BEST EAR AS MEASURED IN DECIBELS (DB) (ISO*) AT 500–2,000 HERTZ (HZ)	SEVERITY LEVEL	EFFECT ON ABILITY TO UNDERSTAND SPEECH
0–25 db	Insignificant	No significant difficulty with faint or normal speech
25–40 db	Mild (hard of hearing)	Frequent difficulty with faint sounds; some difficulty with normal speech (conversations, groups)
40–60 db	Moderate (hard of hearing)	Frequent difficulty with normal speech (conversations, groups); some difficulty with loud speech
60–80 db	Severe (range includes hard of hearing and deaf)	Frequent difficulty with even loud speech; may have difficulty understanding even shouted or amplified speech
80 db or more	Profound (deaf)	Usually cannot understand even amplified speech

Source: *International Standards Organization.

general intelligence, emotional stability, scope and quality of early education and training, the family environment, and the occurrence of other disabilities must also be considered.

Prevalence

The prevalence of hearing loss has been extremely difficult to determine. Approximately 1 in every 1,000 babies is born deaf, but 50% of these children aren't identified as having hearing loss until about three years of age (Goldberg, 1993). Estimates of hearing loss in the United States go as high as 28 million people, or 11% of the total population (Toufexis, 1991). LaPlante (1991) has estimated that 813,000 people with hearing loss need specialized services in the United States.

The difficulty in determining prevalence is due to two factors: inconsistent definitional criteria and methodological problems in the surveys. Varying criteria have

focus 4
What are the estimated prevalence and causes of hearing loss?

For people who are deaf, the visual channel is the primary means for developing language. A student who is deaf in this general education classroom is assisted by an interpreter using signs to explain what other students can hear.

been used to define and classify hearing loss. For instance, the differentiation between unilateral (one ear) and bilateral (two ears) losses may not have been taken into consideration. Finally, there are questions related to the age of the individuals, since most surveys focus exclusively on school-age children.

The most accurate data source on children with a hearing loss is the U.S. Department of Education's *19th Annual Report to Congress* (1997). This report indicated that 68,070 students defined as having a hearing impairment between the ages of 6 and 21 were receiving at least some specialized services in U.S. schools in 1995–1996. These students account for approximately 1.3% of the more than 5 million students labeled as having a disability. It is important to note that these figures represent only those students who receive special services and that a number of students with hearing loss who would benefit from additional services do not receive them. About 35% of the students with hearing loss are being served in general education classrooms full time, 19% in general education classes with resource-room support, 29% in separate special education classes, 7% in separate public or private day schools for students with hearing loss, and 10% in public or private residential living facilities or homebound hospital programs (U.S. Department of Education, 1997).

Causation

A number of conditions, generally classified as congenital (existing at birth) or acquired factors, may result in a hearing loss. The American Speech-Language-Hearing Association has listed several conditions that place an individual in the high-risk category for hearing loss:

1. Family history of childhood hearing loss
2. Congenital or perinatal infection

3. Anatomical malformations involving the head and neck
4. Birthweight of less than 1,500 grams
5. Bacterial meningitis
6. Severe asphyxia at birth

Our discussion focuses on some of these factors while highlighting causal factors related to anatomical site of loss (external, middle, or inner ear).

■ CONGENITAL FACTORS

■ HEREDITY Although more than 200 types of deafness have been related to hereditary factors, the cause of 50% of all hearing loss remains unknown (National Information Center, 1984; Schildroth, 1994). Trybus (1985) sampled 55,000 school-age students with hearing losses and found that approximately 11% of all cases were associated with hereditary factors.

One of the most common diseases affecting the sense of hearing is otosclerosis. The cause of this disease is unknown, but it is generally believed to be hereditary and is manifested most often in early adulthood. Otosclerosis is characterized by destruction of the capsular bone in the middle ear and the growth of weblike bone that attaches to the stapes. As a result, the stapes is restricted and unable to function properly. Hearing loss results in about 15% of all cases of otosclerosis and at twice the rate for females as for males. Victims of otosclerosis suffer from high-pitched throbbing or ringing sounds known as tinnitus, a condition associated with disease of the inner ear.

■ PRENATAL DISEASE Several conditions, although not inherited, can result in sensorineural loss. The major cause of congenital deafness is infection, of which rubella, cytomegalovirus (CMV), and toxoplasmosis are the most common.

The rubella epidemic of 1963–1965 dramatically increased the incidence of deafness in the United States. During the 1960s, approximately 10% of all congenital deafness was associated with women contracting rubella during pregnancy. For about 40% of the individuals who are deaf, the cause is rubella. About 50% of all children with rubella acquire a severe hearing loss. Most hearing losses caused by rubella are sensorineural, although a small percentage may be mixed. In addition to hearing loss, children who have had rubella sometimes acquire heart disease (50%) cataracts or glaucoma (40%), and mental retardation (40%). Since the advent of the rubella vaccine, the elimination of this disease has become a nationwide campaign and the incidence of rubella has dramatically decreased.

Congenital cytomegalovirus (CMV) is a viral infection. The most frequently occurring virus among newborns, it is characterized by jaundice, microcephaly, hemolytic anemia, mental retardation, hepatosplenomegaly (enlargement of liver and spleen), and hearing loss. There are some significant barriers to prevention of this virus because it is difficult to diagnose (Schildroth & Hotto, 1991). Although no vaccine is currently available to treat CMV, some preventive measures can be taken, such as ensuring safe blood transfusions and good hygiene and avoiding contact with persons who have the virus (Pueschel & Mulick, 1990). CMV is detectable in utero through amniocentesis. However, there is considerable debate regarding the accuracy of amniocentesis in identifying the condition (Moaven, Gilbert, Cunningham, & Rawlinson, 1995).

Congenital toxoplasmosis infection is characterized by jaundice and anemia, but frequently the disease also results in central nervous system disorders (e.g., seizures, hydrocephalus, microcephaly). Approximately 15% of infants born with this disease are deaf.

Other factors associated with congenital sensorineural hearing loss include maternal Rh-factor incompatibility and the use of ototoxic drugs. Maternal Rh-factor incompatibility does not generally affect a firstborn child, but as antibodies are produced during subsequent pregnancies, multiple problems can result, including deafness. Fortunately, deafness as a result of Rh-factor problems is no longer common. With the advent of an anti-Rh gamma globulin (RhoGAM) in 1968, the incidence of Rh-factor incompatibility has significantly decreased. If injected into the mother within the first 72 hours after the birth of the first child, she does not produce antibodies that harm future unborn infants.

Ototoxic drugs are so labeled because of their harmful effects on the sense of hearing. If taken during pregnancy, these drugs can result in a serious hearing loss in the infant. Although rare, congenital sensorineural loss can also be caused by congenital syphilis, maternal chicken pox, anoxia, and birth trauma.

A condition known as **atresia** is a major cause of congenital conductive loss. Congenital aural atresia results when the external auditory canal is either malformed or completely absent at birth. A congenital malformation may lead to a blockage of the ear canal through an accumulation of cerumen, which is a wax that hardens and blocks incoming sound waves from being transmitted to the middle ear.

■ ACQUIRED FACTORS

■ POSTNATAL DISEASE One of the most common causes of hearing loss in the postnatal period is infection. Postnatal infections—such as measles, mumps, influenza, typhoid fever, and scarlet fever—are all associated with hearing loss. Meningitis is an inflammation of the membranes that cover the brain and spinal cord and is a cause of severe hearing loss in school-age children. Sight loss, paralysis, and brain damage are further complications of this disease. The incidence of meningitis has declined, however, because of the development of antibiotics and chemotherapy.

Another common problem that may result from postnatal infection is known as **otitis media**, an inflammation of the middle ear. This condition, resulting from severe colds that spread from the eustachian tube to the middle ear, is the most common caused of conductive hearing loss in younger children. It is difficult to diagnose, especially in infancy, at which time symptoms are often absent. Otitis media has been found to be highly correlated with hearing problems (Giebink, 1990; Martin, 1986).

■ ENVIRONMENTAL FACTORS Environmental factors—including extreme changes in air pressure caused by explosions, physical abuse of the cranial area, impact from foreign objects during an accident, and loud music—also contribute to acquired hearing loss. Loud noise is rapidly becoming one of the major causes of hearing problems. All of us are subjected to hazardous noise, such as noise from jet engines and loud music, more often than ever before. With the increasing use of headphones, such as those on portable compact disk players, many people (particularly adolescents) are subjected to damaging noise levels. Occupational noise (e.g., from jackhammers, tractors, and sirens) is now the leading cause of sensorineural hearing loss. Other factors associated with acquired hearing loss include degenerative processes in the ear that may come with aging, cerebral hemorrhages, allergies, and intercranial tumors.

Characteristics

The effects of hearing loss on the learning or social adjustment of individuals are extremely varied, ranging from far reaching, as in the case of prelingual sensorineural deafness, or quite minimal, as in the case of a mild postlingual conductive loss. Fortunately, prevention, early detection, and intervention have recently been emphasized, resulting in a much improved prognosis for individuals who are deaf and hard of hearing.

■ INTELLIGENCE

Over the past 20 years, reviews of the research on the intellectual characteristics of children with hearing loss have suggested that the distribution of IQ scores for these individuals is similar to that of hearing children (Braden, 1992; Greenberg & Kusche, 1989; Paul & Quigley, 1990). Findings suggested that intellectual development for people with hearing loss is more a function of language development than cognitive ability. Any difficulties in performance appear to be closely associated with speaking, reading, and writing the English language, but are not related to level of intelligence. For example, Wood (1991) suggested that children using sign language have to divide their attention between the signs and the instructional materials. Although the child may seem slower in learning, the reality may be that the child is carrying an additional cognitive load and simply needs more time to process the information. Rodda, Cumming, and Fewer (1993) suggested that a hearing loss does make it difficult for the individual to process auditory information. However, these authors emphasize that, when people with a hearing loss have compensated for this barrier, they appear to use cognitive strategies similar to those employed by hearing people.

focus 5

Describe the basic intelligence, speech and language skills, educational achievement, and social development associated with people who are deaf or hard of hearing.

■ SPEECH AND ENGLISH LANGUAGE SKILLS

Speech and English language skills are the areas of development most severely affected for those with a hearing loss, particularly for children who are born deaf. These children have a very difficult time learning to speak (Cole, 1992). Numerous papers published within the past 50 years on the speech skills of children with a hearing loss (Levitt, 1989) have clearly suggested that the effects of a hearing loss on English language development vary considerably. For people with mild and moderate hearing losses, the effect may be minimal. Even for individuals born with moderate losses, effective communication skills are possible because the voiced sounds of conversational speech remain audible. Although individuals with moderate losses cannot hear unvoiced sounds and distant speech, English language delays can be prevented if the hearing loss is diagnosed and treated early (Luetke-Stahlman & Luckner, 1991). The majority of people with hearing loss are able to use speech as the primary mode for English language acquisition.

In some general or special education classes signing may be used as a means of communication and instruction with students who do not communicate easily through spoken language. Although this child with Down syndrome is not deaf, she is learning math through signing.

For the person who is congenitally deaf, most loud speech is inaudible, even with the use of the most sophisticated hearing aids. These people are unable to receive information through speech unless they have learned to lip-read. Sounds produced by the person who is deaf are extremely difficult to understand (low in intelligibility). Children who are deaf exhibit significant articulation, voice quality, and tone discrimination problems. Researchers have found that, even as early as 8 months of age, babies who are deaf appear to babble less than their hearing peers (Stoel-Gammon & Otomo, 1986).

Persons who are congenitally deaf have a great deal of difficulty adequately communicating with the hearing world. For any chance of overcoming this severe disability, they must have access to early and extensive training in English language production and comprehension. A hearing loss is a serious barrier to verbal learning. "The sense of hearing plays a crucial role not only in the understanding of speech, but also in providing the cues needed for the acquisition of speech and language in the normal, developing child" (Levitt, 1989, p. 23).

■ EDUCATIONAL ACHIEVEMENT

The educational achievement of students with a hearing loss may be significantly delayed in comparison to that of their hearing peers. Students who are deaf or have a partial hearing loss have considerable difficulty succeeding in an educational system that depends primarily on the spoken word and written language to transmit knowledge. Low achievement is characteristic of students who are deaf (Greenberg & Kusche, 1989; Gustason, 1990; Paul & Quigley, 1990); they average 3 to 4 years below their age-appropriate grade levels. However, even students with mild to moderate losses achieve below expectations based on their performance on tests of cognitive ability (Greenberg & Kusche, 1989). Reading is the academic area most negatively affected for students with a hearing loss. Any hearing loss, whether mild or profound, appears to have detrimental effects on reading performance (Gallaudet Research Institute, 1994; Leybaert, 1993). Students who are deaf obtain their highest achievement scores in reading during the first three years of school, but by third grade, reading performance is surpassed by both arithmetic and spelling performance. By the time students who are deaf reach adolescence (age 13), their reading performance is equivalent to that of about a third-grade child with normal hearing (Gallaudet Research Institute, 1994).

To counteract the difficulty with conventional reading materials, specialized instructional programs have been developed for students with a hearing loss. One such program is the Reading Milestones series (Quigley & King, 1984), which uses content that focuses on the interests and experiences of children with a hearing loss while incorporating linguistic controls: the careful pacing of new vocabulary, the clear identification of syntactic structures, and the movement from simple to complex in introducing new concepts (e.g., idioms, inferences). Reading Milestones has become the most widely used reading program for students who are deaf.

Spelling performance is also below average for students with a hearing loss, but less so than reading performance. Quigley and Kretschmer (1982) reported that students who are deaf leave school with about a seventh-grade spelling ability. Interestingly, these students make far fewer phonetic spelling errors than their hearing counterparts (Hanson, Shankweiler, & Fischer, 1983).

The written language of students who are deaf is simple and limited in comparison to that of their hearing counterparts (Paul & Quigley, 1990). The sentences written by students with a hearing loss are generally short and rudimentary, resembling sentences written by less mature students without hearing impairments.

The available research on math achievement suggests that arithmetic computation skills are deficient for students with a hearing loss, in comparison to their hearing peers. Karchmer (1985) reported that the average adolescent who is deaf leaves school with about a seventh-grade mathematical ability. Researchers have found that these students are not very proficient in number conservation, questioning skills, and word-problem solving (Quigley & Paul, 1989).

■ SOCIAL DEVELOPMENT

A hearing loss modifies the individual's capacity to receive and process auditory stimuli. People who are deaf or have a partial hearing loss receive a reduced amount of auditory information; that information is also distorted, compared to the input received by those with normal hearing. Consequently, the perceptions of auditory information by people with a hearing loss, particularly those who are deaf, will differ from the norm. As stated by Marschark (1993), "Deaf children will experience a somewhat different world than hearing children and these differences undoubtedly will have implications for their psychological development" (p. 9). (See the Reflect on This feature on page 408.)

Reviews of the literature on social and psychological development in children who are deaf have suggested that there are differences in development when compared to hearing peers (Charlson, Strong, & Gold, 1992; Greenberg & Kusche, 1989; Marschark, 1993). Different or delayed language acquisition may lead to more limited opportunities for social interaction. Children who are deaf may have more adjustment problems when attempting to communicate with their hearing counterparts but appear to be more secure when conversing with nonhearing peers (Stinson & Whitmire, 1992; Vernon & Andrews, 1990).

Social adjustment patterns are also positively correlated with the severity of the hearing loss. The more severe the loss, the greater the potential for social isolation. However, it is important to note that most individuals with severe hearing losses, such as Shelley in the chapter opening snapshot, are socially well adjusted.

Educational Services and Supports

In the United States, educational programs for children who are deaf or hard of hearing emerged in the early 19th century. The residential school for the deaf was the primary model for educational service delivery; it was a live-in facility where students were segregated from the family environment. In the latter half of the 19th century, day schools were established in which students lived with their families while receiving an education in a special school for students identified as deaf. As the century drew to a close, some public schools established special classes within general education schools for children with a hearing loss.

focus 6

Why are educational services for students who are deaf or hard of hearing described as being in the process of change?

The residential school continued to be a model for educational services well into the 20th century. However, with the introduction of electrical amplification, advances in medical treatment, and improved educational technology, more options became available within public school systems. Today, educational programs for students who are deaf or hard of hearing range from the residential school to inclusive education in a general education classroom with support services.

The delivery of educational services to students with a hearing loss is in the process of change. Since 1986, with the advent of early childhood amendments in Public Law 99-457, an expanding emphasis has been placed on early intervention. Luetke-Stahlman and Luckner (1991) suggested that children with a hearing loss must

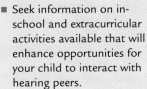

PEOPLE WITH HEARING LOSS

■ EARLY CHILDHOOD YEARS

TIPS FOR THE FAMILY

- Promote family learning about diversity in all people in the context of understanding the child with a hearing loss.
- Keep informed about organizations and civic groups that can provide support to the young child with a hearing loss and also the family.
- Get in touch with your local health, social services, and education agencies about infant, toddler, and preschool programs for children with a hearing loss. Become familiar with the individualized family service plan (IFSP) and how it can serve as a planning tool to support the inclusion of your child in early intervention programs.
- Focus on the development of communication for your child. Work with professionals to determine what mode of communication (oral, manual, and/or total communication) will be most effective in developing early language skills.
- Label stimuli (e.g., objects and people) both visually and verbally as often as possible to provide the child with multiple sources of input.

TIPS FOR THE PRESCHOOL TEACHER

- Language deficits are a fundamental problem for young children with a hearing loss. Focus on developing some form of expressive and receptive communication in the classroom as early as possible. Help young children with a hearing loss to understand words that are abstract, have multiple meanings, and are part of idiomatic expressions (e.g., *run down the street* versus *run for president*).
- Help hearing classmates interact with the child with a hearing loss. Help hearing children be both verbal and visual with the student who is deaf or hard of hearing. If the child with a hearing loss doesn't respond to sound, have the hearing children learn to stand in the line of sight. Teach them to gain the attention of the child with a hearing loss without physical prompting.
- Work closely with parents so that early communication and skill development for the young child with a hearing loss is consistent across school and home environments.
- Become very familiar with acoustical devices (e.g., hearing aids) that may be used by the young child with a hearing loss. Make sure that these devices are worn properly and work in the classroom environment.

TIPS FOR PRESCHOOL PERSONNEL

- Support the inclusion of young children with a hearing loss in your classrooms and programs.
- Support teachers, staff, and volunteers as they attempt to create successful experiences for the young child with a hearing loss in the preschool setting.
- Work very closely with families to keep them informed and active members of the school community.

TIPS FOR NEIGHBORS AND FRIENDS

- Work with the family of a young child with a hearing loss to seek opportunities for interactions with hearing children in neighborhood play settings.
- Focus on the capabilities of the young child with a hearing loss, rather than the disabilities. Understand how the child communicates: orally? manually? or both? If the child uses sign language, take the time to learn fundamental signs that will enhance your communication with him or her.

■ ELEMENTARY YEARS

TIPS FOR THE FAMILY

- Learn about your rights as parents of a child with a hearing loss. Actively participate in the development of your child's individualized education plan (IEP). Through active participation, fight for goals on the IEP that will focus on your child's developing social interaction and communication skills in natural settings.
- Participate in as many school functions for parents as is reasonable (e.g., PTA, parent advisory groups, volunteering) to connect your family to the school.

- Seek information on in-school and extracurricular activities available that will enhance opportunities for your child to interact with hearing peers.
- Keep the school informed about the medical needs of your child. If he or she needs or uses acoustical devices to enhance hearing capability, help school personnel understand how these devices work.

TIPS FOR THE GENERAL EDUCATION CLASSROOM TEACHER

- Outline schoolwork (e.g., the schedule for the day) on paper or the blackboard so the student with a hearing loss can see it.
- As much as possible, require classroom work to be answered in complete sentences to provide the necessary practice for students with a hearing loss.
- Remember that students with hearing loss don't always know how words fit together to make understandable sentences. Help them develop skills by always writing in complete sentences.
- Have the student with a hearing loss sit where he or she can see the rest of the class as easily as possible. Choose a buddy to sit by and keep him or her aware of what is going on in class.
- When lecturing, have the student with a hearing loss sit as close to you as possible.
- Don't be surprised to see gaps in learning. Demonstrations of disgust or

amazement will make the student feel he or she is at fault.

- Be sure to help the student with a hearing loss know what is going on at all times (e.g., pass on announcements made over the intercom).
- Always give short, concise instructions and then make sure the student with a hearing loss understood them by having him or her repeat the information before performing the task.
- Type scripts (or outlines of scripts) for movies and video-tapes used in class. Let the student read the script for the movie.
- When working with an interpreter, remember to:
  - Introduce the interpreter to the class at the beginning of the year, and explain his or her role.
  - Always speak directly to the student, not the interpreter.
  - Pause when necessary to allow the interpreter to catch up, since he or she

may often be a few words behind.
- Face the class when speaking. (When using a blackboard, write on the board first, then turn to face the class to speak.)
- Include students who are deaf in class activities and encourage these students to participate in answering questions.

TIPS FOR SCHOOL PERSONNEL
- Integrate school resources as well as children. Wherever possible, help general education classroom teachers access the human and material resources necessary to meet the needs of students with a hearing loss. For example:
  - *The audiologist.* Keep in close contact with this professional, and seek advice on the student's hearing and the acoustical devices being used.
  - *The special education teacher trained in deafness or hard of hearing.* This professional is necessary as both a

teacher of students with a hearing loss and as a consultant to general educators. Activities can range from working on the development of effective communication skills to dealing with behavioral difficulties. The general education teacher may even decide to work with the special education teacher on learning sign language, if appropriate.
- *Speech and language specialists.* Many students with a hearing loss will need help with speech acquisition and application in the school setting.
- Assist general and special education teachers to develop peer partner and support networks for students with a hearing loss. Peer partners may help by serving as tutors or just by reviewing for tests and class assignments.
- Work to help the student with a hearing loss strive for independence. Assistance

from peers is sometimes helpful, but it should never reach the point where other students are doing work for the student with a hearing loss.

TIPS FOR NEIGHBORS AND FRIENDS
- Help families with a child who is deaf or hard of hearing to be an integral part of neighborhood and friendship networks. Seek ways to include the family and the child wherever possible in neighborhood activities (e.g., outings, barbecues, outdoor yard and street cleanups, crime watches).

■ SECONDARY AND TRANSITION YEARS

TIPS FOR THE FAMILY
- Become familiar with adult services systems (e.g., rehabilitation services, social security, health care) while your son or daughter is still in high school. Understand the type of vocational or employment training that

receive early intervention as soon as possible if they are to learn the language skills necessary for reading and other academic subjects. There is little disagreement that the education of the child with a hearing loss must begin at the time of the diagnosis.

Educational goals for students with a hearing loss are comparable to those for their hearing peers. The student with a hearing loss brings many of the same strengths and weaknesses to the classroom as the hearing student. Adjustment to learning experiences is often comparable for both groups, as well. Students with a hearing loss, however, face the formidable problems associated with being unable to communicate effectively with hearing teachers and peers (see Interacting in Natural Settings, which begins on page 409).

■ TEACHING COMMUNICATION SKILLS

Four approaches are commonly used in teaching communication skills to students with a hearing loss: auditory, oral, manual, and total communication. There is

he or she will need prior to graduation. Find out the school's view on what a high school should be doing to assist someone who is deaf or hard of hearing make the transition from school to adult life.

■ Create opportunities out of school for your son or daughter to participate in activities with same-age hearing peers.

TIPS FOR THE GENERAL EDUCATION CLASSROOM TEACHER

■ Collaborate with specialists in hearing loss and other school personnel to help students adapt to subject matter in your classroom (e.g., science, math, physical education).

■ Become aware of the needs of and resources available for students with a hearing loss in your classroom. Facilitate student learning by establishing peer-support systems (e.g., note takers) to help students with a hearing loss be successful.

■ Use diagrams, graphs, and visual representations whenever possible when presenting new concepts.

■ Help the student with a hearing loss become involved in extracurricular high school activities. If you are the faculty sponsor of a club or organization, explore whether the student is interested and how he or she could get involved.

TIPS FOR SCHOOL PERSONNEL

■ Advocate for parents of high-school-age students with a hearing loss to participate in school activities (such as committees, PTA).

■ Parents will be more active when school personnel have general and positive contact with the family.

TIPS FOR NEIGHBORS, FRIENDS, AND POTENTIAL EMPLOYERS

■ Work with family and school personnel to create opportunities for students with a hearing loss to par-

ticipate in community activities as much as possible with individuals who are deaf or hard of hearing, as well as those who are not.

■ As a potential employer for people with a hearing loss, work with the high school and vocational rehabilitation counselors to locate and establish employment training sites.

■ADULT YEARS

TIPS FOR THE FAMILY

■ Become aware of the supports and services available for your son or daughter in the local community in which they will live as adults. What formal supports are available in the community through government-funded programs or advocacy organizations for people with a hearing loss? through informal supports (family and friends)? What are the characteristics of quality adult services for people with a hearing loss?

Explore adult services in the local community in the areas of postsecondary education, employment, and recreation.

TIPS FOR NEIGHBORS, FRIENDS, AND POTENTIAL EMPLOYERS

■ Seek ways to become part of a community support network for individuals with a hearing loss. Be alert to ways that these individuals can become and remain actively involved in community employment, neighborhood recreational activities, and local church functions.

■ As potential employers in the community, seek out information on employment of people with a hearing loss. Find out about programs that focus on establishing employment opportunities for people with a hearing loss, while meeting your needs as an employer.

---

a long history of controversy regarding which approach is the most appropriate (Moores, 1990). As we move into the next century, however, it is clear that no single method or collection of methods can meet the individual needs of all children with a hearing loss. It is not our purpose to enter into the controversy regarding these approaches but to present a brief description of each approach.

focus 7

Identify four approaches to teaching communication skills to persons with a hearing loss.

■THE AUDITORY APPROACH The auditory approach emphasizes the use of amplified sound and residual hearing to develop oral communication skills. The auditory channel is considered the primary avenue for language development, regardless of the severity or type of hearing loss. As such, the use of hearing aids is recommended as early as possible. Children are strongly encouraged to learn normal speech production, and the use of manual communication (other than natural gestures) is discouraged. The auditory approach uses a variety of electroacoustic

Reflect on This

COMMUNICATING THROUGH AN INTERPRETER

Interpreters can help facilitate communication during lectures, meetings, or other group situations. Before hiring an interpreter, keep in mind that an interpreter is a trained professional bound by a code of ethics. Knowing sign language does not qualify a person to act as an interpreter. It is best to use a professional interpreter.

Before requesting an interpreter, ask the person who is deaf if he or she has any interpreter preferences. Some may prefer an interpreter skilled in signed English or American Sign Language (ASL); others may rely on speech reading and thus need an oral interpreter. If the person who is deaf will be doing most of the talking, an interpreter who is skilled in voicing what is signed will be needed. Here are some tips to keep in mind when scheduling interpreting services:

- Inform the interpreting service of the needs of the person who is deaf and in what setting the interpreting will occur.
- Discuss fees and privileges with the interpreter beforehand.

Speak directly to the person who is deaf, not the interpreter. The interpreter is not part of the conversation and is not permitted to voice personal opinions or enter the conversation.

Remember that the interpreter is a few words behind the speaker. Give the interpreter time to finish before you ask questions so that the person who is deaf can ask questions or join in the discussion.

Treat the interpreter as a professional. It is courteous to introduce the interpreter to the group and explain why he or she is attending. The interpreter should be given the same privileges as the other group members.

If a meeting will last more than 2 hours, it is preferable to have two interpreters. It is difficult to interpret for more than an hour and a half.

Schedule breaks about every hour. Following a manual or oral interpreter for a long time is tiring for a person who is deaf.

Provide good lighting for the interpreter. If the situation requires darkening the room to view slides, for example, auxiliary lighting is necessary so that the person who is deaf can see the interpreter.

Permit only one person to speak at a time during group discussions. It is difficult for an interpreter to follow several people speaking at once. Ask for a brief pause between speakers to permit the interpreter to finish before the next speaker starts.

Speak clearly and in a normal tone when using an interpreter. Do not rush through a speech.

Allow time for people to study handouts, charts, or overheads. A person who is deaf cannot watch the interpreter and study written information at the same time.

When facilitating discussions, call on individual speakers rather than waiting for people to speak up. Because the interpreter needs to be a few words behind, people who are deaf don't always have an opportunity to become involved in discussions. Also, they sometimes don't realize that other people are starting to speak—often their contributions are passed over.

As a final courtesy, thank the interpreter after the service has been performed. If there have been any problems or misunderstandings, let the interpreter or referral service know. Also ask the person who is deaf if the service was satisfactory.

Source: Adapted from Seattle Community College, Regional Education Program for Deaf Students, Seattle, WA.

---

devices to enhance residual hearing. One such device employs a behind-the-ear hearing aid connected to a high-powered frequency-modulated radio-frequency (FM-RF) system. These units use a one-way wireless system on radio-frequency bands. The receiver unit (about the size of a deck of cards) is worn by the student, and a wireless microphone-transmitter-antenna unit is worn by the teacher. One advantage of using an FM-RF system is that the teacher can be connected to several students at a time.

■ THE ORAL APPROACH The oral approach to teaching communication skills also emphasizes the use of amplified sound and residual hearing to develop oral language. This approach emphasizes the need for individuals with a hearing loss to function in the hearing world. Individuals are encouraged to speak and be spoken to. In addition to electroacoustic amplification, the teacher may employ speech reading, reading and writing, and motokinesthetic speech training (feeling an individual's face and reproducing breath and voice patterns). Speech reading (sometimes referred to as lipreading) is the process of understanding another person's speech by watching lip movement and facial and body gestures. This skill is difficult to master, especially for the person who has been deaf since an early age and thus never acquired speech. Problems with speech reading include that many sounds are not distinguishable on the lips and that the reader must attend carefully to every word spoken, a difficult task for preschool and primary-age children. Additionally, the speech reader must be able to see the speaker's mouth at all times (see the Reflect on This feature on page 412).

■ THE MANUAL APPROACH The manual approach to teaching communication skills stresses the use of signs in teaching children who are deaf to communicate. The use of signs is based on the premise that many such children are unable to develop oral language and consequently must have some other means of communication. Manual communication systems are divided into two main categories: sign languages and sign systems.

Sign languages are a systematic and complex combination of hand movements that communicate whole words and complete thoughts rather than the individual letters of the alphabet. One of the most common sign languages is the **American Sign Language (ASL)**, with a vocabulary of more than 6,000 signs. Examples of ASL signs are shown in Figure 13.2. ASL is currently the most widely used sign language among many adults who are deaf because it is easy to master and has historically been the preferred mode of communication. It is a language, but it is not English. Its signs represent concepts rather than single words. The use of ASL in a school setting has been strongly recommended by some advocates for people who are deaf, because it is considered their natural language (Lane, 1992). In fact, two stud-

Alabama, Hawaii

Arkansas, Florida, Maine, Kentucky, Louisiana, Virginia, North Carolina, South Carolina

California, Illinois, Utah

Colorado, Texas (1 of 2)

Massachusetts

Michigan, Ohio

FIGURE 13.2

Examples of one concept (Faint) expressed in American Sign Language

Faint: My mother fainted from the ammonia fumes.

[*Source:* Reprinted by permission of the publisher, from E. Shroyer and S. Shroyer, *Signs Across America,* (1984): 79–80. Washington, DC: Gallaudet University Press. Copyright © 1984 by Gallaudet University.]

FIGURE 13.3

The American manual alphabet

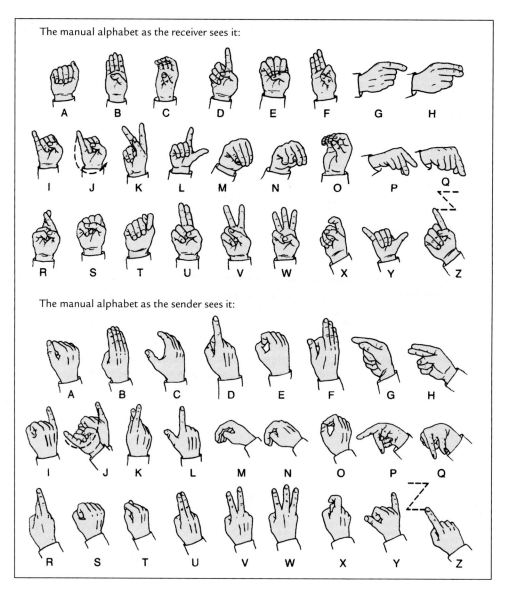

The manual alphabet as the receiver sees it:

A B C D E F G H
I J K L M N O P Q
R S T U V W X Y Z

The manual alphabet as the sender sees it:

A B C D E F G H
I J K L M N O P Q
R S T U V W X Y Z

ies by Bonvillian and Folven (1993) suggested that "sign language acquisition provides support for the view that ASL acquisition in young children [who are deaf] closely resembles that of spoken language development. . . . The general order of language emergence in sign was quite similar to that previously reported for spoken language development" (p. 241).

Sign systems differ from sign languages in that they attempt to create visual equivalents of oral language through manual gestures. With finger spelling, a form of manual communication that incorporates all 26 letters of the English alphabet, each letter is signed independently on one hand to form words. Figure 13.3 illustrates the manual alphabet. In recent years, finger spelling has become a supplement to ASL. It is not uncommon to see a person who is deaf using finger spelling when there is no ASL sign for a word. The four sign systems used in the United States are Seeing Essential English, Signing Exact English, Linguistics of Visual English, and Signed English. Few educators rely solely on the manual system to teach communication skills. This system is in common use as a component of the fourth—the combined approach to teaching communication skills known as total communication.

■ TOTAL COMMUNICATION **Total communication** has roots traceable to the 16th century. Over the past four centuries, many professionals advocated for an instructional system that employed every method possible to teach communication skills. This approach was known as the combined system or simultaneous method. The methodology of the early combined system was imprecise; essentially, any recognized approach to teaching communication was used as long as it included a manual component. The concept of total communication differs from the older combined system in that it is not used only when the oral method fails or when critical learning periods have long since passed. In fact, total communication is not a system at all, but a philosophy (Lowenbraun & Thompson, 1989).

[handwritten note: most commoly used today]

The philosophy of total communication holds that the simultaneous presentation of signs and speech will enhance each person's opportunity to understand and use both systems more effectively. Total communication programs use residual hearing, amplification, speech reading, speech training, reading, and writing in combination with manual systems. A method that may be used as an aid to total communication but is not a necessary component of the approach is cued speech. **Cued speech** is intended to facilitate the development of oral communication by combining hand signals with speech reading. Gestures provide additional information concerning sounds not identifiable by lipreading. The result is that an individual has access to all sounds in the English language through either the lips or the hands.

Total communication relies on both speech and simultaneous presentation of signs. In this class, the teacher uses amplification and signing to help her students.

■ TECHNOLOGY

focus 8
Describe the uses of closed-caption television and computer-assisted instruction for people with a hearing loss.

■ CLOSED CAPTIONING   Educational and leisure-time opportunities for people with a hearing loss have been greatly expanded through technological advances such as **closed-caption television** and computer-assisted instruction. The closed-caption TV process translates dialogue from a television program into captions, or subtitles. These captions are then converted to electronic codes that can be inserted into the television picture on sets specially adapted with decoding devices. The process is called the line-21 system, because the caption is inserted into blank line 21 of the picture.

Captioning is not a new idea. In fact, it was first used on motion picture film in 1958. Most libraries in the United States distribute captioned films for individuals with a hearing loss. Available only since 1980, closed captioning on television has experienced steady growth over the past 15 years. In its first year of operation, national closed-caption programming was available about 30 hours per week. By 1987, more than 200 hours per week of national programming were captioned in a wide range of topics, from news and information to entertainment and commercials. The Commission on the Education of the Deaf (1988) estimated that by 1987 more than 50,000 people in 150,000 homes were watching captioned TV. By 1993, all major broadcast networks were captioning 100% of their prime-time broadcasts, national news, and children's programming. More than 400 hours of captioned television programs are now available along with numerous videos of major motion pictures. (Alexander Graham Bell Association, 1993; Withrow, 1994). With the passage of the Television Decoder Circuitry Act in 1993, it is expected that the numbers of viewers watching captioned TV will expand even more dramatically. This act requires that all television sets sold in the United States be equipped with a decoder that allows captions to be placed anywhere on the television screen. This prevents captions from interfering with on-screen titles or other information displayed on the TV broadcast.

This student can work at his own pace and level using computer-assisted instruction.

Reflect on This

DEFIANTLY DEAF

How to reconcile this Deaf experience with the rest of the world? Should it be reconciled at all? M. J. Bienuenu has been one of the most vocal and articulate opponents of the language of disability. "I am Deaf," she says to me in Knoxville, drawing out the sign for "Deaf," the index finger moving from chin to ear, as though she is tracing a broad smile. "To see myself as Deaf is as much of a choice as it is for me to be a lesbian. I have identified with my culture, taken a public stand, made myself a figure within this community." Considerably gentler now than in her extremist heyday in the early 1980s, she acknowledges that "for some deaf people, being deaf is a disability. Those who learn forced English while being denied sign emerge semilingual rather than bilingual, and they are disabled people. But for the rest of us, it is no more a disability than being Japanese would be."

This is tricky territory. If being deaf is not a disability, then people who are deaf should not be protected under the Americans with Disabilities Act. It should not be legally required (as it is) that interpreters be provided in hospitals and other public service venues, that a relay operator be available on all telephone exchanges, that all televisions include the chip for caption access. It should not be necessary for the state to provide for separate schools. Deaf people should not be eligible for Social Security Disability Insurance (which they often claim). Those who say that being deaf is not a disability open themselves up to a lot of trouble. . . . It is tempting, in the end, to say there is no such thing as a disability. Equally, one might admit that almost everything is a disability. There are as many arguments for correcting everything as there are for correcting nothing.

Perhaps it would be most accurate to say that "disability" and "culture" are really matters of degree. Being deaf is a disability and a culture in modern America; so is being gay; so is being African American; so is being female; so even, increasingly, is being a straight white male; so is being paraplegic, or having Down syndrome. What is at issue is which things are so "cultural" that you wouldn't think of "curing" them, and which things are so "disabling" that you must "cure" them—and the reality is that for some people each of these experiences is primarily a disability experience while for others it is primarily a cultural one. Some African Americans are handicapped by blackness; some who are gay are handicapped by gayness; some paraplegics thrive on the care they receive and would be lost if their mobility were returned. Some people who are deaf are better off deaf and some would be better off hearing. Some could perhaps be both.

Source: Adapted from "Defiantly Deaf," by A. Solomon, August 28, 1994, *The New York Times Magazine,* Section 6, pp. 1–7, xx.

■ COMPUTER-ASSISTED INSTRUCTION Computer-assisted instruction offers an exciting dimension to learning for persons with a hearing loss. The microcomputer places the individual in an interactive setting with the subject matter. It is a powerful motivator. Most people find microcomputers fun and interesting to work with on a variety of tasks. Additionally, computer-assisted instruction can be individualized so that students can gain independence by working at their own pace and level.

Microcomputer programs are now available for instructional support in a variety of academic subject areas, from reading and writing to learning basic sign language. A recent innovation is a software program that will display an individual's speech in visual form on the screen to assist in the development of articulation skills. Another innovative microcomputer system is called C-print. Using a laptop computer equipped with a computer shorthand system and commercially available software packages, C-print provides real-time translations of the spoken word. A trained operator is required to listen to speech, then type special codes representing words into the computer. These codes are transcribed into words that are shown almost simultaneously on a screen sitting atop an overhead projector. A printout of the transcription can be obtained as well (Wilson, 1992). C-print will provide a major service to students with a hearing loss attending college classes or oral lectures; they

Today's Technology

Despite her teaching experience, Michele Cournoyer realized she needed new skills to reach the 14-year-old boy who had just enrolled at Willie Ross School for the Deaf.

"When you have a student looking at you who can't read or write but is intelligent and has a full language system, you have to do something," she said.

Cournoyer's new student was fluent in American Sign Language, with its rich vocabulary and its own syntax. He could say whatever he wanted, but only in sign.

The youngster did not have enough command of written English to use an ordinary dictionary or even an ASL dictionary. Cournoyer turned to

Smith College psychology professor Peter de Villiers, who has a special interest in how people with hearing loss acquire language.

They decided to use the youngster's existing knowledge of ASL and a computer.

"He could express concepts," recalled Cournoyer. "He had a fully working vocabulary, but it was not English."

Aided by Becky Haines, his research assistant, and Hampshire College student Nat Sims, they turned to hypercard software. Such software enables a user to flip through a stack of cards on the computer screen. A teacher types as much of a story as he or she wishes on a card, underlining the words that will be unfamiliar to the student.

Using an ASL dictionary and a scanner, the teacher transfers the sign for each underlined word to a separate card.

"They read a story. When they come to an unfamiliar word, they click the mouse and up pops a card with a sign," de Villiers said.

"Getting information about the meaning online as you are reading is much more effective in learning than looking it up in a dictionary or learning a list of words," de Villiers said. "They are better able to learn English words if they see them in sign rather than English."

"I already have data to show these students learn English words better if they get sign feedback than if they see an English definition."

"We are not teaching a new concept, we are giving them a label for a pre-existing concept," Cournoyer said. "It is so motivating, such a tremendous incentive when they see a sign which is their language. They have pride that is really remarkable."

Before using the computer, Cournoyer said, it was a chore for children to read three pages in a book; now, they read three or four whole stories.

"It makes them feel good," she said. "They hit a button and see their language right there for them."

Source: Adapted from "First the Word, Then—Click!—the Sign," by J. Caldwell, October 2, 1994, *Boston Sunday Globe,* pp. B23–B24.

---

typically find note taking an extremely difficult activity, even when an oral interpreter is available.

The interactive video disc is another important innovation in computer-assisted instruction. The video disc, a recordlike platter, is placed in a video disc player that is connected to a microcomputer and television monitor. The laser-driven disc is interactive, allowing the individual to move through instruction at his or her own pace. Instant repetitions of subject matter are available to the learner at the touch of a button (see the nearby Today's Technology feature).

■ TELECOMMUNICATION DEVICES A major advance in communication technology for people with a hearing loss is the telecommunication device (TDD). In 1990, the Americans with Disabilities Act renamed them **text telephones (TTs).** TTs send, receive, and print messages through thousands of stations across the United States. People with a hearing loss can now dial an 800 number to set up conference calls, make apointments, or order merchandise or fast food. Anyone wanting to speak with a person using a TT can do so through the use of a standard telephone.

The teletypewriter and printer (TTY) is another effective use of technology for people who are deaf. It allows them to communicate by phone via a typewriter that converts typed letters into electric signals through a modem. These signals are sent through the phone lines and then translated into typed messages and printed on a typewriter connected to a phone on the other end.

Medical and Social Services

■ MEDICAL SERVICES

focus 9
Why is the early detection of hearing loss so important?

Medicine plays a major role in the prevention, early detection, and remediation of a hearing loss. Integrally involved in the medical assessment and intervention process are several specialists, including the genetics specialist, the pediatrician, the family practitioner, the otologist, the neurosurgeon, and the audiologist.

■ **THE GENETICS SPECIALIST** Prevention of a hearing loss is a primary concern of the genetics specialist. A significant number of hearing losses are inherited or occur during prenatal, perinatal, and postnatal development. Consequently, the genetics specialist plays an important role in preventing disabilities through family counseling and prenatal screening.

■ **THE PEDIATRICIAN AND FAMILY PRACTITIONER** Early detection of a hearing loss can prevent or at least minimize the impact of the disability on the overall development of an individual. Generally, it is the responsibility of the pediatrician or family practitioner to be aware of a problem and to refer the family to an appropriate hearing specialist. These responsibilities require that the physician be familiar with family history and conduct a thorough physical examination of the child. The physician must be alert to any symptoms (e.g., delayed language development) that indicate potential sensory loss.

■ **THE OTOLOGIST** The otologist is the medical specialist who is most concerned with the hearing organ and its diseases. Otology is a component of the larger specialty of diseases of the ear, nose, and throat. The otologist, like the pediatrician, screens for potential hearing problems, but the process is much more specialized and exhaustive. The otologist also conducts an extensive physical examination of the ear to identify syndromes that are associated with conductive or sensorineural loss. This information, in conjunction with family history, provides data regarding appropriate medical treatment.

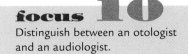
focus 10
Distinguish between an otologist and an audiologist.

Treatment may involve medical therapy or surgical intervention. Common therapeutic procedures include monitoring aural hygiene (e.g., keeping the external ear free from wax), blowing out the ear (e.g., a process to remove mucus blocking the eustachian tube), and administering antibiotics to treat infections. Surgical techniques may involve the cosmetic and functional restructuring of congenital malformations such as a deformed external ear or closed external canal (atresia). Fenestration refers to the surgical creation of a new opening in the labyrinth of the ear to restore hearing. A stapedectomy is a surgical process conducted under a microscope whereby a fixed stapes is replaced with a prosthetic device capable of vibrating, thus permitting the transmission of sound waves. A myringoplasty is the surgical reconstruction of a perforated tympanic membrane (eardrum).

Cochlear implant surgical procedures have proved to be highly successful. These implants, consisting of a receiver code, electrodes (internal), a microphone, a transducer, and a transmitter (external), restore hearing through electronic stimulation of the auditory nerve. Cochlear implants are becoming more widely used with both adults and children, with more than 2,500 individuals in the United States and

Canada receiving these implants prior to 1994 (Barringer, 1993). Some adults who were deafened in their later years reported nearly full recovery in their hearing following the implant, and others still needed lipreading to understand the spoken word (Tye-Murray, 1993). Cochlear implants may not be appropriate for some children. The learning of speech and language following a cochlear implant remains difficult for young prelingual deaf children (Geers & Tobey, 1992). Additionally, caution should be exercised because of the risk of possible damage to an ear that has some residual hearing and the risk of infection from the implant.

■THE AUDIOLOGIST   The degree of hearing loss, measured in decibel and hertz units, is ascertained by an audiologist using a process known as audiometric evaluation. The listener receives tones that are relatively free of external noise (puretone audiometry) or spoken words, in which speech perception is measured (speech audiometry). An electronic device (audiometer) detects the person's response to sound stimuli, and a record (audiogram) is obtained from the audiometer that graphs the individual's threshold for hearing at various sound frequencies.

Whereas an otologist presents a biological perspective on hearing loss, an audiologist emphasizes the functional impact of losing one's hearing. The audiologist first screens the individual for a hearing loss, then determines both the nature and severity of the condition. Social, educational, and vocational implications of the hearing loss are then discussed and explored.

Although audiologists are not specifically trained in the field of medicine, these professionals interact constantly with otologists to provide a comprehensive assessment of hearing. The audiologist is trained in the measurement of hearing. Patrick (1987) addressed the goals of audiometry: "(1) to identify those individuals who have sufficient hearing loss to compromise communication and/or learning in the typical classroom; (2) to find and send for medical management of those students who have middle ear pathologies; and (3) to perform these tasks in the most cost-effective and efficient manner" (p. 402).

Another important function served by audiologists and otologists is to provide assistance regarding the selection and use of hearing aids. At one time or another, most people with a hearing loss will probably wear hearing aids. Hearing aids amplify sound, but they do not correct hearing. Hearing aids have been used for centuries. Early acoustic aids included cupping one's hand behind the ear as well as the ear trumpet. Modern electroacoustic aids do not depend on the loudness of the human voice to amplify sound but utilize batteries to increase volume. Electroacoustic aids come in three main types: body worn, behind-the-ear aids, and in-the-ear aids. Which hearing aid is best for a particular person depends on the degree of hearing loss, the age of the individual, and the physical condition of the individual (Maxon & Brackett, 1992). The common components of hearing aids are given in Table 13.2.

Body-worn hearing aids are typically worn on the chest, using a harness to secure the unit. The hearing aid is connected by a wire to a transducer, which is worn at ear level and delivers a signal to the ear via an earmold. Body-worn aids are becoming less common because of the disadvantages of being chest-mounted, the location of the microphone, and inadequate high-frequency response. The behind-the-ear aid (also referred to as an ear-level aid) is the most common electroacoustical device for children with a hearing loss (Maxon & Brackett, 1992). All components of the behind-the-ear aid are fitted in one case behind the outer ear. The case then connects to an earmold that delivers the signal directly to the ear. In addition to their portability, behind-the-ear aids have the advantage of producing the greatest

TABLE 13.2 Common hearing aid components and their functions

COMPONENT	OPTIONS	FUNCTION
Microphone	Directional, omnidirectional	Pick up acoustic signal and change it into an electrical signal
Amplifier	Low–high gain	Increase signal intensity
Transducer	Air conduction	Change electrical signal to acoustic signal
	Bone conduction	Change electrical signal to vibratory signal
Battery	Various disposable, rechargeable	Provide a power supply for the hearing aid

Source: From *The Hearing Impaired Child: Infancy Through High School Years,* by A. B. Maxon and D. Brackett, 1992, Boston: Andover Medical Publishers, p. 7. Reprinted by permission.

amount of electroacoustic flexibility (amount of amplification across all frequencies). The primary disadvantage is problems with acoustic feedback. As discussed earlier in this chapter, the behind-the-ear aid may be used with an FM-RF system. These aids may be fitted monaurally (on one ear) or binaurally (on both ears).

The in-the-ear aid fits within the ear canal. All major components (microphone, amplifier, transducer, and battery) are housed in a single case that has been custom made for the individual user. The advantage of the in-the-ear aid is the close positioning of the microphone to the natural reception of auditory signals in the ear canal. In-the-ear aids are recommended for individuals with mild hearing losses who do not need frequent changes in earmolds. As such, these aids are not usually recommended for young children. Additionally, in-the-ear aids have more problems with feedback because of the close proximity of the microphone to the transducer (Maxon & Brackett, 1992).

Although the quality of commercially available aids has improved dramatically in recent years, they do have distinct limitations. For example, hearing-aid use has been found to be positively related to speech use but appears to have little effect on reading ability (Mertens, 1990). The criteria for effectiveness must be measured against wearability, the individual's communication skills, and educational achievement.

The stimulation of residual hearing through a hearing aid enables most people with a hearing loss to function as hard of hearing. However, the use of a hearing aid must be implemented as early as possible, before sensory deprivation takes its toll on the child. It is the audiologist's responsibility to weigh all the factors involved (e.g., convenience, size, weight) in the selection and use of an aid for the individual. The individual should then be directed to a reputable hearing-aid dealer.

■ SOCIAL SERVICES

The social consequences of being deaf or hard of hearing are highly correlated with the severity of the loss. For the individual who is deaf, social integration may be extremely difficult because societal views of deafness have reinforced social isolation. The belief that such a person is incompetent has

focus 11
Identify factors that may impede the social integration of people who are deaf into the hearing world.

The arts including theater are an important part of the curriculum for students with disabilities. A teacher who is deaf is instructing a class of students who are also deaf.

been predominant from the time of the early Hebrews and Romans, who deprived these people of their civil rights, to 20th-century America, where, in some areas, it is still difficult for adults who are deaf to obtain driver's licenses or adequate insurance coverage or to be gainfully employed. Individuals with the greatest difficulty are those born with congenital deafness. The inability to hear and understand speech has often isolated these people from their hearing peers. For example, people who are deaf tend to marry other people who are deaf (Woodward, 1982). Solomon (1994) reported that when people who are deaf do marry people who can hear, the marriage ends in divorce about 90% of the time.

A segment of individuals who are deaf are actively involved in organizations and communities specifically intended to meet their needs. The National Association for the Deaf (NAD) was organized in 1880. The philosophy of the NAD is that every person who is deaf has the same rights as those in the hearing world—the right to life, liberty, and the pursuit of happiness. NAD emphasizes that the exercise of these rights must be to the satisfaction of those who are deaf and not to their teachers and parents who do not have the condition.

NAD serves individuals who are deaf in many capacities. Among its many contributions, NAD publishes books on deafness, sponsors cultural activities, and lobbies throughout the United States for legislation promoting the rights of persons who are deaf.

Another prominent organization is the Alexander Graham Bell Association for the Deaf, which advocates the integration of persons with a hearing loss into the social mainstream. The major thrust of this approach is the improvement of proficiency in speech communications. As a clearinghouse for information for people who are deaf and their advocates, the association publishes widely in the areas of parent counseling, teaching methodology, speech reading, and auditory training. In addition, it sponsors national and regional conferences that focus on a variety of issues pertinent to the social adjustment of people who are deaf.

Because of the unique communication problems of persons with a hearing loss, many are unable to benefit from mental health services in their communities. Mental health professionals may be unaware of the communication barriers that prevent people with a hearing loss from obtaining services. Such professionals must be trained to address the unique needs of these people. Mental health professionals should work with parents as early as possible to assist young children in adjusting to their sensory limitation. As these children become older, counselors must be available to help them explore their feelings regarding the disability and to cope with the reactions of parents, family, and peers.

As we approach the next century, it is clear that the advances in education, medicine, social services, and technology are opening opportunities never thought possible for people with a hearing loss. This is not to ignore the many challenges that still face individuals with a hearing loss (such as underemployment, social isolation). But certainly, much has been accomplished. As suggested by Stokoe (1993):

Perspectives on deafness are changing in a radical way. . . . A first generation of deaf people are at last breaking down the prejudicial barriers to professional education. Deaf psychologists, linguists, and anthropologists are beginning to show the world new landscapes of the country they live in. (p. 374)

Case Study

MARIO AND SAMANTHA

■ MARIO

It's a Monday in May, near the end of the school year. The classroom door is open, and the hearing students are pouring in, greeting their friends and talking excitedly about their weekend experiences. Mario, who is deaf, slips in silently, sits down alone, and buries his head in a book as he waits for class to begin. He cannot hear the buzz of activity and conversation around him. He was not a part of the weekend activities. No one speaks to him. He looks up as a girl he likes comes up the row to her seat and drops her books down on the desk. He ventures to speak softly to her, not noticing that she is already talking and joking with a guy across the room. Mario finally captures her glance and asks his question, but the girl doesn't understand what he says. (His speech is slightly impaired, and the room is noisy.) After two more repetitions of "How was your weekend?" he is rewarded with a perfunctory "Oh, fine!" before she turns around and gets wrapped up in a detailed, secret exchange with her best girlfriend, who sits right behind her. They giggle and talk, glancing up once in a while to catch the eye of the boy across the room. Mario rearranges the papers on his desk.

Finally, the teacher begins to lecture, and the lively conversational exchanges become subdued. The hearing students settle into pseudo-attentive postures, reverting to subtle, subversive communications with those around them. Mario, in his front row, corner seat, turns his eyes on the interpreter. He keeps his focus there, working to grasp visually what the other students are effortlessly half-listening to. The teacher questions a student in the back of the room. Her hearing friends whisper help. Their encouragement boosts her confidence and she boldly answers the teacher. Satisfied, the teacher moves on to question someone else. The first student joins those whispering to the boy who's now on the spot. He picks up the quiet cues and impresses the instructor with his evident mastery of the subject. A peer support system of companionable cooperation helps keep everyone afloat.

However, only those with sensitive hearing and social support can tap into this interwoven network of surreptitious assistance. When a pointed question is directed to Mario, he is on his own. No student schemes bring him into the "we" of class camaraderie. Instead, when he speaks, the students suddenly stop talking and stare. But he is oblivious to the awkward silence in the room. He is verbally stumbling, searching for an answer that will pacify the teacher, and yet not be too specific. He strains to minimize the risk of opening himself up for embarrassment of saying something that misses the mark entirely. While he is still speaking, the bell rings and the other students pack up and start moving out the back door. Mario, his eyes on the teacher, doesn't notice the interpreter's signal that the bell has already sounded. The teacher smiles uncomfortably and cuts him off to give last-minute instructions as the students pour out the door.[1]

■ SAMANTHA

It is a crisp autumn morning, the kind that some people breathe in deeply as they look forward to the challenges of the day. School has begun an hour ago. Mrs. Jones' algebra class is examining some equations. Puzzled by Mrs. Jones' explanation, Samantha raises her hand and questions her teacher about an equation. While Samantha signs her question, Mrs. Jones watches Samantha (pleased that she understands much of what Samantha is signing) and listens to Samantha's interpreter. Several of Samantha's classmates watch her signing, nodding in agreement that the explanation was not clear. Later, as the students work some math problems, Samantha and a hearing friend exchange suggestions through signs. As Samantha and her classmates leave for their next class, Mrs. Jones calls out to the class and signs to Samantha, "Have a nice day."

Samantha and two of her hearing friends hurry to their next class. On the way, they animatedly sign to each other about the upcoming school dance. Samantha's planning to go with one of her friends who is deaf from the mainstream program, Jason. As they reach their next class, they meet Mike and Ernestine, two other students in the mainstream program who are deaf. Samantha and her two friends greet Mike and Ernestine and they enter the class together. During the civics class the students and teachers have a lively exchange about the responsibility of citizens when faced with a law they feel is immoral. (Occasionally the teacher reminds the students not to interrupt one another or talk so fast so that all of the students, deaf and hearing, can catch what is being said.) Samantha, Mike, and Ernestine join in through sign language, and several of the hearing students sign as they speak. An interpreter speaks and signs as needed.

After civics, Samantha and Ernestine head to an English class and Mike to a physical education class. The English class is taught by Mr. Roberts, a deaf education teacher in the mainstream program. Being deaf, Mr. Roberts signs gracefully and eloquently. The class is alive as they discuss poetry by hearing and deaf poets. Tony, Margaret, and Lee, three hearing students, are in the class with Samantha and her deaf classmates. They will attend for two weeks as the class discusses and dramatizes poetry. Mr. Roberts uses his voice to help them understand, though they sign quite well. At the end of the two weeks, the class will dramatize and sign several poems for other deaf and hearing students.[2]

■ APPLICATION

1. Compare and contrast the social and educational isolation of Mario in a general education setting with the inclusive nature of Samantha's school experiences.
2. Are the two case studies of Mario and Samantha representative of your experiences with students who are deaf in general education classroom settings? Why or why not?
3. How is a school like Samantha's organized? What is needed to support and include students who are deaf in the social and academic life of the school?

[1] *Source:* Adapted from "Alone in the Crowd," by C. Wixtrom, 1988, *The Deaf American,* 38(12), pp. 14–15.

[2] *Source:* Adapted from "The Challenges of Educating Together Deaf and Hearing Youth: Making Mainstreaming Work," by P. C. Higgins, 1990, Springfield, IL: Charles C. Thomas.

Debate Forum

LIVING IN A DEAF COMMUNITY

Deaf Community: a cultural group comprised of persons who share similar attitudes toward deafness. The "core Deaf Community" is comprised of those persons who have a hearing loss, share a common language, values, and experiences and a common way of interacting with each other, with non-core members of the Deaf Community, and with the Hearing Community. The wider Deaf Community is comprised of individuals (both deaf and hearing) who have positive, accepting attitudes toward deafness which can be seen in their linguistic, social, and political behaviors. (SMI & Madonna University, 1991)

The inability to hear and understand speech may lead an individual to seek community ties and social relationships primarily with other individuals who are deaf. These individuals may choose to isolate themselves from hearing peers and live, learn, work, and play in a social subculture known as "a deaf community." An example of this strong sense of community occurred in 1988, when the appointment of a hearing person as president of Gallaudet University, a university for people who are deaf, resulted in widespread student protest and the eventual appointment of the university's first president who is deaf.

■ POINT

The deaf community is a necessary and important component of life for many individuals who are deaf. The individual who is deaf has a great deal of difficulty adjusting to life in a hearing world. Through the deaf community, this person can find other individuals with similar problems, common interests, a common language (e.g., sign language), and a common culture. Membership in the deaf community is an achieved status that must be earned by the individual who is deaf. The individual must demonstrate a strong identification with the deaf world, understand and share experiences that come with being deaf, and be willing to actively participate in the deaf community's activities. The deaf community gives the individual an identity that can't be found among their hearing peers.

■ COUNTERPOINT

Participation in the deaf community only further isolates individuals who are deaf from those who hear. A separate subculture unnecessarily accentuates the differences between people who can and cannot hear. The life of the individual who is deaf need be no different from that of anyone else. Individuals who are deaf can live side by side with their hearing peers in local communities, sharing common bonds and interests. There is no reason why they can't participate together in the arts, enjoy sports, and share leisure-time and recreational interests. Membership in the deaf community may only further reinforce the idea that people who have disabilities should grow up and live in a culture away from those who do not. The fact is, the majority of people who are deaf do not seek membership in the deaf community. These individuals are concerned that the existence of such a community makes it all the more difficult for them to assimilate into society at large.

Review

focus 1

Describe how sound is transmitted through the human ear.

- A vibrator—such as a string, reed, or column of air—causes displacement of air particles.
- Vibrations are carried by air, metal, water, or other substances.
- Sound waves are displaced air particles that produce a pattern of auricular waves that move away from the source to a receiver.
- The human ear collects, processes, and transmits sounds to the brain, where they are decoded into meaningful language.

focus 2

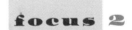

Distinguish between the terms *deaf* and *hard of hearing*.

- A person who is deaf typically has profound or total loss of auditory sensitivity and very little, if any, auditory perception.
- For the person who is deaf, the primary means of information input is through vision; speech received through the ears is not understood.
- A person who is hard of hearing (partially hearing) generally has residual hearing through the use of a hearing aid, which is sufficient to process language through the ear successfully.

focus 3

Why is it important to consider age of onset and anatomical site when defining a hearing loss?

- Age of onset is critical in determining the type and extent of intervention necessary to minimize the effect of the hearing loss.
- Three types of peripheral hearing loss are associated with anatomical site: conductive, sensorineural, and mixed.
- Central auditory hearing loss occurs when there is a dysfunction in the cerebral cortex (outer layer of gray matter in the brain).

focus 4

What are the estimated prevalence and causes of hearing loss?

- It has been extremely difficult to determine the prevalence of hearing loss. Estimates of hearing loss in the United States go as high as 28 million people, or 11% of the total population.
- The most accurate estimates of prevalence are for school-age children. Approximately 1% of the 4.4 million students with disabilities have a hearing loss.
- There are more than 60 types of hereditary-related hearing losses.
- A common hereditary disorder is otosclerosis (bone destruction in the middle ear).

- Nonhereditary hearing problems evident at birth may be associated with maternal health problems: infections (e.g., rubella), anemia, jaundice, central nervous system disorders, the use of drugs, venereal disease, chicken pox, anoxia, and birth trauma.
- Acquired hearing losses are associated with postnatal infections, such as measles, mumps, influenza, typhoid fever, and scarlet fever.
- Environmental factors associated with hearing loss include extreme changes in air pressure caused by explosions, head trauma, foreign objects in the ear, and loud noise.

focus 5

Describe the basic intelligence, speech and language skills, educational achievement, and social development associated with people who are deaf or hard of hearing.

- The distribution of IQ scores of individuals with a hearing loss is similar to that of hearing children.
- On performance subtests of IQ batteries, the scores of children who are deaf fall in the average range for nonverbal intelligence.
- For people with mild and moderate losses, the effects on speech and language may be minimal. Although individuals with moderate losses cannot hear unvoiced

sounds and distant speech, language delays can be prevented if the hearing loss is diagnosed and treated early.
- The majority of people with a hearing loss are able to use speech as the primary mode for language acquisition. People who are congenitally deaf are unable to receive information through the speech process unless they have learned to lip-read (speech read). Sounds produced by the person who is deaf are extremely low in intelligibility.
- Reading is the academic area most adversely affected for students with a hearing loss.
- Arithmetic computation skills are deficient for students with a hearing loss in comparison to those of their hearing peers.
- Research has lent support to the notion that some individuals with a hearing loss may have social deficiencies and differences when contrasted to their hearing peers. There is little agreement as to why this may be, but a relationship exists between the severity and type of hearing loss and social problems.

focus 6

Why are educational services for students who are deaf or hard of hearing described as being in the process of change?

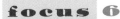

- The availability of educational services for students with a hearing loss, from preschool through adolescence, continues to increase.
- Educational programming is becoming more individualized in order to meet the needs of each student.

focus 7

Identify four approaches to teaching communication skills to persons with a hearing loss.

- The auditory approach to communication emphasizes the use of amplified sound and residual hearing to develop oral communication skills.
- The oral approach to communication emphasizes the use of amplified sound and residual hearing but may also employ speech reading, reading and writing, and motokinesthetic speech training.
- The manual approach stresses the use of signs in teaching children who are deaf to communicate.
- The total communication approach employs the use of residual hearing, amplification, speech reading, speech training, reading, and writing in combination with manual systems to teach communication skills to children with a hearing loss.

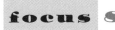 **focus 8**

Describe the uses of closed-caption television and computer-assisted instruction for people with a hearing loss.

- Closed-caption television translates dialogue from a television program into captions (subtitles) that are broadcast on the television screen.
- Closed-caption television provides the person with a hearing loss greater access to information and entertainment than was previously thought possible.
- Microcomputers are powerful motivators that place

people with a hearing loss in interactive settings with access to vast amounts of information.
- TT systems provide efficient ways for people who are deaf to communicate over long distances.
- TTY devices allow people who are deaf to use a typewriter, modem, and printer to communicate over the phone.

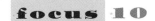 **focus 9**

Why is the early detection of hearing loss so important?

- Early detection of hearing loss can prevent or minimize the impact of the dis-

ability on the overall development of an individual.

 **focus 10**

Distinguish between an otologist and an audiologist.

- An otologist is a medical specialist who is concerned with the hearing organ and its diseases.
- An audiologist is concerned with the sociological and educational impact of hearing loss on an individual.
- Both the audiologist and otologist assist in the process of selecting and using a hearing aid.

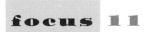 **focus 11**

Identify factors that may impede the social integration of people who are deaf into the hearing world.

- The inability to hear and understand speech has isolated some people who are deaf from their hearing peers.
- Societal views of deafness may reinforce isolation.

14

People with Vision Loss

 In Ann Arbor, Michigan, Phillip Jones, a 78-year-old widower [who is blind], delights in his Personal Reader's ability to inject excitement into its intonation when it sees an exclamation point. He also likes how it can read a page of German or Italian with a pronounced American accent. "It's easy for me to understand because the machine reads those languages the same way I would read them." (Ziegler, 1991, p. 119)

 Jorge Luis Borges (1899–1986) was one of the most original and influential of modern writers. Borges regarded his progressive blindness, the result of an inherited eye disease, not as entirely tragic but as an opportunity. "Blindness has not been for me a total misfortune; it should not be seen in a pathetic way. It should be seen as a way of life; one of the styles of living. . . . The world of the blind is not the night that people imagine."(Borges, cited in Lopate, 1994)

 Since it has been clearly demonstrated that blind children benefit from interacting with disabled and nondisabled children, both interaction opportunities should be fully encouraged in whatever setting that is considered appropriate. We believe that the mandate in IDEA which states that, "to the maximum extent appropriate, children with disabilities [should be] educated with children who are nondisabled," does not intend that blind children avoid interaction with each other. (Joint Organizational Committee, 1993, p. 1)

 A daily frustration of blindness: Not being able to scope out the shortest checkout line at the grocery store. (Susan, personal communication)

Snapshot

John

Born prematurely and weighing only 1 pound 13 ounces, John is a child with vision loss. Now 9 years old, John lives with his parents and brother Michael, none of whom have any visual problems. John loves technology and has a CB radio, several TVs, a computer, and a tape recorder. He doesn't care for outdoor activities and isn't into sports. He uses braille to read, and has a cane to help him find his way through the world.

John: "I really like to be blind, it's a whole lot of fun. The reason I like to be blind is because I can learn my way around real fast and I have a real fast thinking memory. I can hear things that some people can't hear and smell. Actually, my sense of hearing is the best. . . . I have a CB radio that [I] talk to different people on and sometimes I can talk to people in different places around the world."

John's parents: "John can do anything he wants to do if he puts his mind to it. He's smart enough, he loves all kinds of radio communications. He talks about being on the radio, on TV, and there's no reason why he can't do that as long as he studies hard in school."

Michael: "I didn't want a blind brother."

John: "Sometimes my brother gets along good and sometimes he comes here in my room and under my desk there's a little power switch that controls all my TVs, scanner, CB, tape recorder. He'll flip that then he'll laugh about it, run and go somewhere and I'll have to turn it back on, lock my door, and go tell mom. So that's how he handles it and she puts him in time out."

John's third-grade teacher: "John is very well adjusted. He has a wonderful, delightful personality. He's intelligent.

We were a little worried about his braille until this year. Probably because of his prematurity, [he has] a little trouble with the tactual. Of course, braille is all tactual . . . But he's pulling out of that and that was his last problem with education. He's very bright. He could do many things. He loves computers."

John: "I'd like to be a few different things, and I'll tell you a few of them. I'd like to be a newscaster, an astronaut, or something down at NASA and a dispatcher. So, that's three of the things out of a whole million or thousand things I'd like to be."

THROUGH THE VISUAL PROCESS, we observe the world around us and develop an appreciation for and a greater understanding of the physical environment. Vision is one of our most important sources for the acquisition and assimilation of knowledge, but we often take it for granted. From the moment we wake up in the morning, our dependence on sight is obvious. We rely on our eyes to guide us around our surroundings, inform us through the written word, and give us pleasure and relaxation.

What if this precious sight was lost or impaired? How would our perceptions of the world change? Losing sight is ranked right behind cancer and AIDS as our greatest fear (Jernigan, 1992). This fear is often nurtured by the misconception that persons with vision loss are helpless and unable to lead satisfying or productive lives. It is not uncommon for people with sight to have little understanding of those with vision loss. People who are sighted may believe that most adults who are blind are likely to live a deprived socioeconomic and cultural existence. Children who have sight may believe that their peers who are blind are incapable of learning many basic skills, such as telling time or using a computer, or enjoying leisure-time and recreational activities such as swimming or watching television. Another attitudinal barrier is the religious belief that blindness is a punishment for sins (Bishop, 1987). As the chapter opening snapshot about John strongly suggests, these negative perceptions of people with vision loss are often inaccurate. John is an active child who has not allowed his vision loss to keep him from the activities that he values. To understand more clearly the nature of vision loss within the context of normal sight, we begin our discussion with an overview of the visual process. Since vision is basically defined as the act of seeing with the eye, we first review the physical components of the visual system.

The Visual Process

The physical components of the visual system include the eye, the **visual cortex** in the brain, and the **optic nerve,** which connects the eye to the visual cortex. The basic anatomy of the human eye is illustrated in Figure 14.1. The **cornea** is the external covering of the eye, and in the presence of light, it bends or refracts visual stimuli. These light rays pass through the **pupil,** which is an opening in the **iris.** The

focus 1

Why is it important to understand the visual process as well as know the physical components of the eye?

FIGURE 14.1

The parts of the human eye   [*Source: The Salt Lake Tribune,* February 8, 1996, p. C1.]

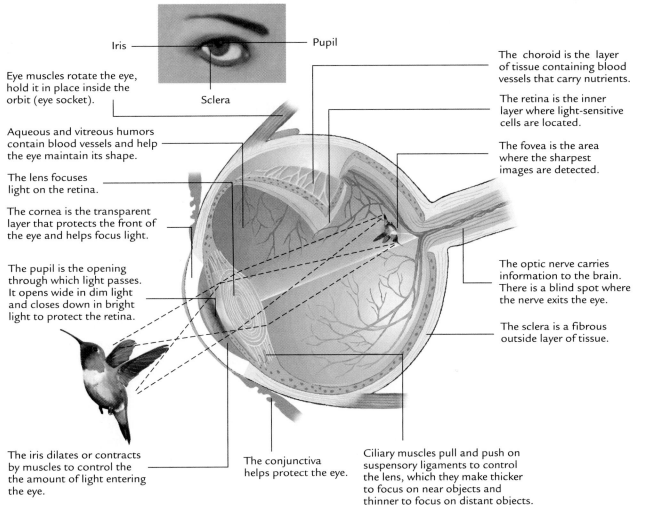

Iris — Pupil

Sclera

Eye muscles rotate the eye, hold it in place inside the orbit (eye socket).

Aqueous and vitreous humors contain blood vessels and help the eye maintain its shape.

The lens focuses light on the retina.

The cornea is the transparent layer that protects the front of the eye and helps focus light.

The pupil is the opening through which light passes. It opens wide in dim light and closes down in bright light to protect the retina.

The choroid is the layer of tissue containing blood vessels that carry nutrients.

The retina is the inner layer where light-sensitive cells are located.

The fovea is the area where the sharpest images are detected.

The optic nerve carries information to the brain. There is a blind spot where the nerve exits the eye.

The sclera is a fibrous outside layer of tissue.

The iris dilates or contracts by muscles to control the the amount of light entering the eye.

The conjunctiva helps protect the eye.

Ciliary muscles pull and push on suspensory ligaments to control the lens, which they make thicker to focus on near objects and thinner to focus on distant objects.

431

pupil dilates or constricts to control the amount of light entering the eye. The iris is the colored portion of the eye and consists of membranous tissue and muscles whose function is to adjust the size of the pupil. The lens, like the cornea, bends light rays so they strike the **retina** directly. As in a camera lens, the lens of the eye reverses the images. The retina consists of light-sensitive cells that transmit the image to the brain by means of the optic nerve. Images from the retina remain upside down until they are flipped over in the visual cortex occipital lobe of the brain.

The visual process is a much more complex phenomenon than suggested by a description of the physical components involved. The process is an important link to the physical world, helping us to gain information beyond the range of other senses, while also helping us to integrate the information acquired primarily through hearing, touch, smell, and taste. For example, our sense of touch can tell us that what we are feeling is furry, soft, and warm, but only our eyes can tell that it is a brown rabbit with a white tail and pink eyes. Our nose may perceive something with yeast and spices cooking, but our eyes can confirm that it is a large pepperoni pizza with bubbling mozzarella and green peppers. Our hearing can tell us that a friend sounds angry and upset, but only our vision can perceive the scowl, clenched jaw, and stiff posture. The way we perceive visual stimuli shapes our interactions with and reactions to the environment while providing a foundation for the development of a more complex learning structure.

Contrary to what some people who are sighted may believe, children and adults who are blind can lead productive lives. This elementary school principal is only one of many successful professionals.

Definitions and Classification

■ DEFINITIONS

The term *vision loss* describes a condition experienced by people with a wide range of educational, social, and medical needs directly related to a partial or complete loss of sight. This definition encompasses people who

have never had any visual function, those who had normal vision for some years before becoming gradually or suddenly partially or totally blind, those with [disabilities] in addition to the visual loss, those with selective impairments of parts of the visual field, and those with a general degradation of acuity across the visual field. (Warren, 1989, p. 155)

focus 2

Distinguish between the *terms blind* and *partially sighted*.

A variety of terms are used to describe levels of vision loss, a diversity that has created some confusion among professionals in various fields of study. The rationale for the development of various definitions is directly related to their intended use. For example, eligibility for income-tax exemptions or special assistance from the American Printing House for the Blind requires that individuals with vision loss qualify under one of two general subcategories: blind or partially sighted (low vision).

■ BLINDNESS The word *blindness* has many meanings. In fact, there are over 150 citations for **blind** in an unabridged dictionary. **Legal blindness,** as defined by the Social Security Administration, is visual acuity of 20/200 or worse in the best

FIGURE 14.2

The field of vision

(a) Normal field of vision is about 180°.
(b) A person with a field of vision of 20° or less is considered blind.

(a) 180°   (b) 20°

eye with best correction, as measured on the **Snellen test**, or a visual field of 20% or less. The definition of legal blindness includes a wide range of visual ability that involves both acuity and field of vision (Corn & Koenig, 1996).

Visual acuity is determined by the use of an index that refers to the distance from which an object can be recognized. The person with normal eyesight is defined as having 20/20 vision. However, if an individual is able to read at 20 feet what a person with normal vision can read at 200 feet, then his or her visual acuity would be described as 20/200. Most people consider those who are legally blind to have some light perception; only about 20% are totally without sight.

A person is also considered blind if his or her field of vision is limited at its widest angle to 20 degrees or less (see Figure 14.2). A restricted field is also referred to as **tunnel vision,** pinhole vision, or tubular vision. A restricted field of vision severely limits a person's ability to participate in athletics, read, or drive a car.

Blindness can also be characterized as an educational disability. Educational definitions of blindness focus primarily on students' ability to use vision as an avenue for learning. Children who are unable to use their sight and rely on other senses, such as hearing and touch, are described as educationally blind. **Educational blindness,** in its simplest form, may be defined by whether vision is used as a primary channel of learning. Regardless of the definition used, the purpose of labeling a child as educationally blind is to ensure that he or she receives an appropriate instructional program. This program must assist the student who is blind in utilizing other senses as a means to succeed in a classroom setting and in the future as an independent and productive adult.

■PARTIAL SIGHT (LOW VISION) People with partial sight or low vision have a visual acuity greater than 20/200 but not greater than 20/70 in the best eye after correction. The field of education also distinguishes between being blind and partially sighted when determining the level and extent of additional support services required by a student. The term **partially sighted** describes people who are able to use vision as a primary source of learning.

A vision specialist often works with students with vision loss to make the best possible use of remaining sight. This includes the elimination of unnecessary glare in the work area, removal of obstacles that could impede mobility, use of large-print books, and use of special lighting to enhance visual opportunities. Although many children with low vision do use printed materials and special lighting in learning activities, some use **braille** because they can see only shadows and limited movement. These children require the use of tactile or other sensory channels to gain maximum benefit from learning opportunities (Barraga & Erin, 1992).

Two very distinct positions have been formed regarding individuals who are partially sighted and their use of residual vision. The first suggests that such individuals should make maximal use of their functional residual vision through the use of magnification, illumination, and specialized teaching aids (e.g., large-print books and posters), as well as any exercises that will increase the efficiency of remaining vision. This position is contrary to the more traditional philosophy of sight conservation or sight saving, which advocates restricted use of the eye. It was once believed that students with vision loss could keep what sight they had much longer if it was used sparingly. However, extended reliance on residual vision in conjunction with visual stimulation training now appears to actually improve a person's ability to use sight as an avenue for learning.

■ CLASSIFICATION

focus 3

What are the distinctive features of refractive eye problems, muscle disorders of the eye, and receptive eye problems?

Vision loss may be classified according to the anatomical site of the problem. Anatomical disorders include impairment of the refractive structures of the eye, muscle anomalies in the visual system, and problems of the receptive structures of the eye.

■ REFRACTIVE EYE PROBLEMS **Refractive problems** are the most common type of vision loss and occur when the refractive structures of the eye (cornea or **lens**) fail to focus light rays properly on the retina. The four types of refractive problems are hyperopia, or farsightedness; myopia, or nearsightedness; astigmatism, or blurred vision; and cataracts.

Hyperopia occurs when the eyeball is excessively short from front to back (has a flat corneal structure), forcing light rays to focus behind the retina. The person with hyperopia can clearly visualize objects at a distance but cannot see them at close range. This individual may require convex lenses so that a clear focus will occur on the retina.

Myopia occurs when the eyeball is excessively long (has increased curvature of the corneal surface), forcing light rays to focus in front of the retina. The person with myopia can view objects at close range clearly but cannot see them from a distance (e.g., 100 feet). This individual requires eyeglasses to assist in focusing on distant objects. Figure 14.3 illustrates the myopic and hyperopic eyeballs and compares them to the normal human eye.

Astigmatism occurs when the curvature or surface of the cornea is uneven, preventing light rays from converging at one point. The rays of light are refracted in different directions, and the visual images are unclear and distorted. Astigmatism may occur independently of or in conjunction with myopia or hyperopia.

Cataracts occur when the lens becomes opaque, resulting in severely distorted vision or total blindness. Surgical treatment for cataracts (such as lens implants) has advanced rapidly in recent years, returning to the individual most of the vision that was lost.

■ MUSCLE DISORDERS Muscular defects of the visual system occur when one or more of the major muscles within the eye are weakened in function, resulting in a loss of control and an inability to maintain tension. People with muscle disorders cannot maintain their focus on a given object for even short periods of time. The three types of muscle disorders are nystagmus (uncontrolled rapid eye movement), strabismus (crossed eyes), and amblyopia (an eye that appears normal but does not

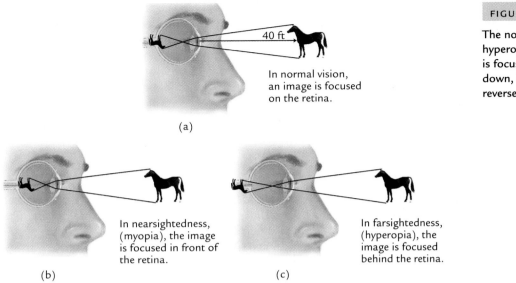

FIGURE 14.3

In normal vision, an image is focused on the retina.

(a)

In nearsightedness, (myopia), the image is focused in front of the retina.

(b)

In farsightedness, (hyperopia), the image is focused behind the retina.

(c)

The normal (a), myopic (b), and hyperopic (c) eyeballs. The image is focused on the retina upside down, but the brain immediately reverses it.

function properly). **Nystagmus** is a continuous, involuntary, rapid movement of the eyeballs in either a circular or side-to-side pattern. **Strabismus** occurs when the muscles of the eyes are unable to pull equally, thus preventing the eyes from focusing together on the same object. Internal strabismus **(esotropia)** occurs when the eyes are pulled inward toward the nose; external strabismus **(exotropia)** occurs when the eyes are pulled out toward the ears. The eyes may also shift on a vertical plane (up or down), but this condition is rare. Strabismus can be corrected through surgical intervention. Persons with strabismus often experience a phenomenon known as double vision, since the deviating eye causes two very different pictures coming to the brain. To correct the double vision and reduce visual confusion, the brain attempts to suppress the image in one eye. As a result, the unused eye loses its ability to see. This condition, known as **amblyopia,** can also be corrected by surgery or by forcing the affected eye into focus by covering the unaffected eye with a patch.

■RECEPTIVE EYE PROBLEMS Disorders associated with the receptive structures of the eye occur when there is a degeneration of or damage to the retina and the optic nerve. These disorders include optic atrophy, retinitis pigmentosa, retinal detachment, retrolental fibroplasia, and glaucoma. **Optic atrophy** is a degenerative disease that results from the deterioration of nerve fibers connecting the retina to the brain. **Retinitis pigmentosa,** the most common hereditary condition associated with loss of vision, appears initially as night blindness and gradually degenerates the retina. Eventually, it results in total blindness.

Retinal detachment occurs when the retina separates from the choroid and the sclera. This detachment may result from disorders such as glaucoma, retinal degeneration, or extreme myopia. It can also be caused by trauma to the eye, such as a boxer's receiving a hard right hook to the face.

Retinopathy of prematurity (ROP), formerly known as *retrolental fibroplasia,* is one of the most devastating eye disorders in young children. It occurs when too much oxygen is administered to premature infants, resulting in the formation of scar tissue behind the lens of the eye, which prevents light rays from reaching the retina. ROP gained attention in the early 1940s, with the advent of improved incubators for premature infants. These incubators substantially improved the concentration of oxygen available to the infant but resulted in a drastic increase in the number of children with vision loss. The disorder has also been associated with neurological, speech, and behavior problems in children and adolescents. Now that a relationship has been established between increased oxygen levels and blindness, premature infants can be protected by careful control of the amount of oxygen received in the early months of life.

Prevalence

The prevalence of vision loss is often difficult to determine. For example, although about 20% of the population have some visual problems, most of these defects can be corrected to a level where they do not interfere with learning. Nelson and Dimitrova (1993) suggested that about 1.5% of school-age children have severe vision loss and thus require significant specialized support in their educational program. Based on the U.S. Department of Education's *19th Annual Report to Congress* (1997), 25,484 school-age children with vision loss between the ages of 6 and 21 receive specialized services in U.S. public schools in 1995–1996.

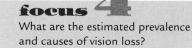

focus 4
What are the estimated prevalence and causes of vision loss?

Thousands of children born blind during the maternal rubella epidemic in 1963 and 1964 constituted a significant percentage of the enrollment in special education and residential schools for the blind in the 1970s and 1980s. Maternal rubella is now essentially under control, since the introduction of a rubella vaccine. Retrolental fibroplasia (now known as retinopathy of prematurity) has been a major cause of blindness in infants since the 1960s and continues to be a factor. (See the nearby Reflect on This feature). In spite of the multiple known causes of blindness, however, a large percentage of the cases have unknown causes.

We have focused on prevalence figures as they relate to school-age children. Blindness, however, is also a function of increasing age. Approximately 75% of all people who are blind are over 45 years old.

Causation

■ GENETICALLY DETERMINED DISORDERS

A number of genetic conditions can result in vision loss, including **albinism** (resulting in **photophobia** due to lack of pigmentation in eyes, skin, and hair), retinitis pigmentosa (degeneration of the retina), **retinoblastoma** (malignant tumor in the retina), optic atrophy (loss of function of optic nerve fibers), cataracts, severe myopia associated with retinal detachment, lesions of the cornea, abnormalities of the iris (coloboma or aniridia), **microphthalmia** (abnormally small eyeball), hydrocephalus (excess cerebrospinal fluid in the brain) leading to optic atrophy, **anophthalmia** (absence of the eyeball), and **buphthalmos** or glaucoma (abnormal distention and enlargement of the eyeball) (Chapman & Stone, 1989).

Glaucoma results from an increased pressure in the eye, which can damage the optic nerve if left untreated. The incidence of glaucoma is highest in persons over

Reflect on This

INFANT BLINDNESS

Advances in neonatal medicine over the past decade have allowed doctors to save growing numbers of very premature infants. But some of those surviving babies are part of a far less publicized trend: an alarming rise in the numbers of blind children. Doctors say retinopathy of prematurity (ROP)—a condition in which abnormal blood vessels and scar tissue grow over the retina of a very premature and tiny infant—is the primary cause of the increase.

Blindness in infancy and childhood is still a relatively rare disability. According to the American Printing House for the Blind, 53,576 American children under age 18 are legally blind. That figure is growing by about 3% per year, says Tuck Tinsley, president of the printing house, a government-funded institution that supplies virtually all educational materials for the blind.

Previous decades have brought about temporary surges in childhood blindness, Tinsley notes—including a swell of premature babies born in the late 1940s and early 1950s who were overtreated with oxygen in incubators. In the '80s, the crack cocaine epidemic led to another wave of blind children.

But, Tinsley says, "Retinopathy of prematurity is the thing today causing the increase. These are children who wouldn't even have survived a few years ago."

Directors of blind children's centers in Phoenix, San Francisco, Boston, Los Angeles, and other cities report increased enrollments because of ROP and cortical visual impairment, but there is no official tracking or registry of blind children nationwide, so the increase cannot be officially verified.

"The scientific studies that actually prove the increase haven't been done," says Dennak L. Murphy, executive director of San Francisco's Blind Babies Foundation, which has maintained one of the most accurate and long-running registries of blind children in the nation.

"Blindness is a low-incidence disability," he says, "so no one studies it."

Retinopathy of prematurity usually occurs in babies born at 26 weeks gestation—more than three months premature—and weighing less than two pounds. About 40% of infants weighing less than two pounds will develop ROP, compared to 5% of babies born at three pounds, according to the American Academy of Ophthalmology.

ROP often clears up by itself. But in some babies laser surgery or cryosurgery is attempted to reverse the abnormal growth. If that is unsuccessful, ROP can lead to detached retinas. In these cases, surgery can sometimes restore limited vision, but many children are left legally blind.

Experts estimate that 2% of all very low birthweight babies develop ROP-related blindness or severe vision impairment.

"And since [neonatologists] are saving so many more babies at low birthweights, the total number of blind babies is going up," says Kay Ferrell, a professor of special education at the University of Northern Colorado who is directing one of the largest U.S. studies of blind children.

Source: From "Infant Blindness," by S. Roan, August 17, 1995, *Salt Lake Tribune,* pp. C1, C8. Reprinted by permission.

---

the age of 40 who have a family history of the disease. Glaucoma is treatable, either through surgery to drain fluids from the eye or through the use of medicated eye drops to reduce pressure (Isenberg, 1992).

■ ACQUIRED DISORDERS

Acquired disorders can occur prior to, during, or after birth. Several factors present prior to birth, such as radiation or the introduction of drugs into the fetal system, may result in vision loss. A major cause of blindness in the fetus is infection, which may be due to diseases such as rubella and syphilis. Other diseases that can result in blindness include influenza, mumps, and measles.

The leading cause of blindness in children is retinopathy of prematurity. As noted earlier, ROP results from administering of oxygen over prolonged periods of time to low-birthweight infants. Almost 80% of preschool-age blind children lost their sight as a result of ROP during the peak years of the disease (1940s through 1960s).

Vision loss after birth may be due to several factors. Trauma, infections, inflammations, and tumors are all related to loss of sight. **Cortical visual impairment (CVI)** is a leading cause of acquired blindness. CVI, which involves damage to the occipital lobes and/or the visual pathways to the brain, can result from severe trauma, asphyxia, seizures, infections of the central nervous system, drugs, poisons, or other neurological conditions.

Characteristics

A vision loss present at birth will have a more significant effect on individual development than one that occurs later in life. Useful visual imagery may disappear if sight is lost prior to the age of 5. If sight is lost after the age of 5, it is possible for the person to retain "some visual memories which may help in imagining and understanding many concepts" (Best, 1992, p. 3). These visual memories can be maintained over a period of years. Total blindness that occurs prior to age 5 has the greatest negative influence on overall functioning. However, many people who are blind from birth or early childhood are able to function at a level consistent with sighted persons of equal ability.

■ INTELLIGENCE

Children with vision loss sometimes base their perceptions of the world on input from senses other than vision. This is particularly true of the child who is congenitally blind, whose learning experiences are significantly restricted by the lack of vision. Consequently, everyday learning opportunities that people with sight take for granted, such as reading the morning newspaper or watching television news coverage, may be substantially altered.

Reviews of the literature on intellectual development suggest that children with vision loss differ from their sighted peers in some areas of intelligence, ranging from understanding spatial concepts to a general knowledge of the world (Parsons & Sabornie, 1987; Warren, 1989). However, comparing the performances of individuals with and without sight may not be appropriate if those with sight have an advantage. The only valid way to compare the intellectual capabilities of these children must be based on tasks in which vision loss does not interfere with performance. Hull (1990) suggested that persons who are blind rely much more on their tactile and auditory senses than their sighted peers. He describes the phenomena as "seeing with one's fingers."

■ SPEECH AND LANGUAGE SKILLS

For children with sight, speech and language development occurs primarily through the integration of visual experiences and the symbols of the spoken word. Depending on the degree of loss, children with vision loss are at a distinct disadvantage in developing speech and language skills because they are unable to visually associate words with objects. Because of this, such children must rely on hearing or touch for input, and their speech may develop at a slower rate. Once these children have learned speech, however, it is typically fluent.

focus 5

Describe how a vision loss can affect intelligence, speech and language skills, educational achievement, social development, physical orientation and mobility, and perceptual-motor development.

There is some conflicting evidence regarding the differences in overall language development between children with vision loss and their sighted peers (Chapman & Stone, 1989; Kekelis, 1992; Warren, 1989). Warren suggested that

while there are some differences in language usage and word meaning, most of these have clear explanations in the experiential base of visually [disabled] children. . . . Visually [disabled] children should be exposed to a full range of age-appropriate vocabulary, and should be provided with concrete physical experience as well as verbal explanations of referents for the development of meaning. (1989, p. 164)

Parsons and Sabornie (1987), in contrast, reported that preschool-age children with limited vision performed significantly lower than their sighted peers on a language scale in the areas of auditory comprehension, verbal ability, and overall language. Preschool-age and school-age children with vision loss may develop a phenomenon known as **verbalism,** or the excessive use of speech (wordiness), in which individuals use words that have little meaning to them. Finally, Anderson, Dunlea, and Kekelis (1984) reported that the language development of six children who were blind, as studied over a 3-year period, appeared to be comparable to that of their sighted peers. However, the investigators were concerned that, in terms of quality, children who were blind seemed to have more difficulty understanding words as symbolic vehicles and formed hypotheses about word meaning much more slowly than their sighted peers.

■ EDUCATIONAL ACHIEVEMENT

The educational achievement of students with vision loss may be significantly delayed when compared to that of sighted peers. In the area of reading, for example, a study of school-age students in the public schools indicated that 31% of students who are blind could not read; an additional 22% were at a reading readiness level (American Printing House for the Blind, 1992).

Numerous variables influence educational achievement for students with vision loss. Possible reasons for delays in educational achievement range from excessive school absences due to the need for eye surgery or treatment as well as years of failure in programs that did not meet each student's specialized needs.

On the average, children with vision loss are 2 years behind sighted children in grade level. Thus, any direct comparisons of students with vision loss to those with sight would indicate significantly delayed academic growth. However, this age phenomenon may have resulted from entering school at a later age, absence due to medical problems, or lack of appropriate school resources and facilities.

■ SOCIAL DEVELOPMENT

The ability of children with vision loss to adapt to the social environment depends on a number of factors, both hereditary and experiential. It is true that each of us experiences the world in his or her own way, but there are common bonds that provide a foundation on which to build perceptions of the world around us. One such bond is vision. Without vision, perceptions about ourselves and those around us can be drastically different.

For the person with vision loss, these differences in perception may produce some social–emotional challenges. For example, Crocker and Orr (1996) found that although preschool-age children with significant vision loss were capable of interacting with same-age nondisabled peers, there were some differences between the two groups of children. Children with vision loss were less likely to initiate a social interaction and had fewer opportunities to socialize with other children. These authors pointed out that the success of an inclusive preschool is dependent upon the "presence of specialized programs [supports] to encourage and reinforce interactions between children with visual impairments and their peers with full sight" (p. 461).

Kekelis (1992) found that school-age children with severe vision loss have difficulty in "play" situations, seek attention inappropriately, and ask a lot of irrelevant questions. People with vision loss are unable to imitate the physical mannerisms of others and therefore do not develop one very important component of social communication: body language. Because the subtleties of nonverbal communication can significantly alter the intended meaning of spoken words, a person's inability to learn and use visual cues (e.g., facial expressions, hand gestures) has profound consequences for interpersonal interactions. The person with vision loss can neither see the visual cues that accompany the messages received from others nor sense the messages that he or she may be conveying through body language.

Social problems may also result from the exclusion of persons with vision loss from social activities that are integrally related to the use of sight (e.g., sports, movies). Individuals with vision loss are often excluded from such activities without a second thought, simply because they cannot see. This reinforces the mistaken notion that they do not want to participate and would not enjoy these activities. The important point to remember is that social skills can be learned and effectively used by a person with vision loss (MacCuspie, 1992). Excluding them from social experiences more often stems from negative public attitudes than from the individuals' lack of social adjustment skills.

■ ORIENTATION AND MOBILITY

A unique limitation facing people with vision loss is the basic problem of getting from place to place. Such individuals may be unable to orient themselves to other people or objects in the environment simply because they cannot see them, and therefore they will not understand their own relative position in space. Consequently, they may be unable to move in the right direction and may fear getting injured, and so attempt to restrict their movements in order to protect themselves. In addition, parents and professionals may contribute to such fears by overprotecting the person who has vision loss from the everyday risks of life. Shielding the individual in this way will hinder acquisition of independent mobility skills and create an atmosphere promoting lifelong overdependence on caregivers (see nearby Reflect on This feature).

Vision loss can affect fine motor coordination and interfere with the ability to manipulate objects. Poor eye–hand coordination interferes with learning how to use tools related to job skills and daily living skills (e.g., using eating utensils, a toothbrush, a screwdriver). Prevention or remediation of fine motor problems may require training in the use of visual aid magnifiers and improvement of basic fine motor skills. This training must begin early and focus directly on experiences that will enhance opportunities for independent living (Best, 1992).

■ PERCEPTUAL-MOTOR DEVELOPMENT

Perceptual-motor development is essential in the development of locomotion skills, but it is also important in the development of cognition, language, socializa-

Reflect on This

BLEEDING HEARTS

I was the only person who was blind attending a birthday party at a friend's house. Though I had been in the company of this friend, along with others, countless times in the past 2 years, I had not been to her house before, and I appreciated being given a tour. My favorite place—the area that attracted all of us—was the deck. This friend has a wonderful, spacious deck upon which we found beautiful, comfortable outdoor furniture. At one end I observed a wooden stairway going down into the yard. As I approached the stairs, this friend panicked, admonishing me to "Watch out!" Before I could utter a word, Barbara, another friend, spoke. She had also seen me approach the stairs, but she has spent much time with me and is very aware of the fearful behavior of those who do not or will not understand that it is all right for me to move around on my own.

Accurately observing the situation from her more enlightened perspective, she said, "Don't worry about it, that's what her cane is for." I assumed that was the end of the incident. During the course of the meal and the frivolity, Barbara and several others remarked on how beautiful the bleeding heart flowers were. She said, "You and I can go down and look at them before we leave." I agreed that this would be a pleasant experience, and I looked forward to it.

I have often been the only person who is blind in a group of sighted people and have desired to marvel as much as they do at our natural surroundings. I have always known I could do so, albeit at times in a different way. However, quite often, due to fear and apparent lack of information, many of those attending such gatherings seem reluctant to allow me the opportunity to "see for myself." Through the years I have come to realize that, if I want to look at something in my own way, I would do well simply to do it, regardless of the possible consternation around me. I am not usually one to upset the apple cart, but when the apples would benefit from a good stirring up, I'm likely to do it. I do this because of my belief that the world is as much mine as anyone else's, and the beauty and grandeur of nature beckon me no less. I am a part of nature, and nature is a part of me. I also believe that, though we learn from other humans, our learning is not limited to this source. Nature teaches us as well. In fact, this broader teaching and bonding of hearts is exactly what occurred during this birthday party in May.

After the party had ended and most of the guests had departed, I remembered the bleeding hearts. Since Barbara was busy inside the house and since she and I both knew I was perfectly capable of looking at the flowers without waiting for her, I approached the stairs and began to descend. The owner of the house and another woman named Ruth were observing me. The owner scolded Ruth: "Watch her; don't let her go down there; it's weird out in the yard." Ruth ignored the admonition, commenting that she'd like to see the flowers too. She quietly followed me down the stairs. I attempted to reassure anyone listening that I was okay. As I finished my descent, what I found at the bottom of the stairs was some uneven terrain, certainly nothing particularly dangerous or weird. Ruth walked over to the flowers, and I met her there. We knelt down to examine them—their dainty little hearts with strands of bloom dangling from them. How delicate and vulnerable they seemed. Yet they showed no sign of worry or fear as I touched their beauty, and their beauty touched me.

At that moment I felt such an awareness of the bleeding hearts—the human one above me on the deck, bleeding worry and fear, and the blossoms bleeding only beauty. I am deeply grateful for the power in me to take steps beyond such worry and fear and to receive nature's beauty. I am also grateful for the two women, Barbara and Ruth, whose loving and respectful responses to the situation enhanced that beauty for us all. I am also grateful for the woman who invited me to the party at which this event occurred—and just think of the opportunity she had to learn something new about people who are blind and to participate also in nature's beauty.

Could it be, after all, that these were not bleeding hearts, but bonding hearts?

Source: Adapted from "Bleeding Hearts," by L. L. Eckery (1994, November), *The Braille Monitor*, pp. 649–650. © National Federation of the Blind.

tion, and personality. In a comprehensive review of the literature, Warren (1984) reported that perceptual discrimination abilities (e.g., discriminating texture, weight, and sound) of children with vision loss are comparable to those of sighted peers. Obviously, children with vision loss do not perform as well on more complex tasks of perception, including form identification, spatial relations, and perceptual-motor integration. In fact, Ochaita and Huertas (1993) suggested that people who are blind are delayed in the development of spatial abilities in comparison with sighted peers and will not reach full development until well into their teen years. An early visual experience prior to the onset of blindness or partial loss of sight may provide a child with some advantage in developing manipulatory and locomotor skills.

A popular misconception regarding the perceptual abilities of persons with vision loss is that, because of their diminished sight, they develop greater capacity in other sensory areas. For example, people who are blind are supposedly able to hear or smell some things that people with normal vision cannot perceive. This notion has never been empirically validated.

Educational Supports and Services

■ ASSESSMENT

In the area of education, the assessment process is no different for students with vision loss than for students who are sighted. The educational team assesses the cognitive ability, academic achievement, language skills, motor performance, and social–emotional functioning of the student. Assessment must also focus specifically on how the student utilizes any remaining vision (visual efficiency) in conjunction with other senses. *The Visual Efficient Scale*, developed by Barraga and Erin (1992), assesses the overall visual functioning of the individual to determine how he or she uses sight to acquire information.

A functional approach to assessment goes beyond determining visual acuity and focuses on capacity, attention, and processing (Blanksby & Langford, 1993). Visual capacity includes both acuity and field of vision, but also encompasses the response of the individual to visual information. The assessment of visual attention involves observing the individual's sensitivity to visual stimuli (alertness), ability to use vision to select information from a variety of sources, attention to a visual stimulus, and ability to process visual information. Visual-processing assessment determines which, if any, of the components of normal visual functioning are impaired.

The nature and severity of the visual problem determine the assessment instruments to be used. Some assessment instruments have been developed specifically for students with vision loss, and others are intended for sighted students but have been adapted to students with vision loss. Some instruments developed for sighted students are used in their original form with students with vision loss. Regardless of the instruments employed, educational assessment, in conjunction with medical and psychological data, must provide the diagnostic information that will ensure that an appropriate educational experience is developed for the student with vision loss.

■ MOBILITY TRAINING AND DAILY LIVING SKILLS

focus 6

Identify two content areas that should be included in educational programs for students with vision loss.

The educational needs of students with vision loss are comparable to those of their sighted counterparts. In addition, many instructional methods currently used with students who are sighted are appropriate for students with vision loss. However, the educator must be aware that certain content areas usually unneccessary for sighted students are essential to the success of students with vision loss in the educational environment. These areas include mobility and orientation training as well as acquisition of daily living skills.

The ability to move safely, efficiently, and independently through the environment enhances the individual's opportunities to learn more about the world and thus be less dependent on others for survival. Lack of mobility restricts individuals with vision loss in nearly every aspect of educational life. Such students may be unable to orient themselves to physical structures in the classroom (e.g., desks, chairs, and aisles), hallways, rest rooms, library, or cafeteria. Whereas a person with sight can automatically establish a relative position in space, the individual with vision loss must be taught some means of compensating for a lack of visual input. This may be accomplished in a number of ways. It is important that students with vision loss not only learn the physical structure of their school but also develop specific techniques to orient them to unfamiliar surroundings.

These orientation techniques involve using the other senses. For example, the senses of touch and hearing can help identify cues that designate where the bathroom is in the school. Although it is not true that people who are blind have superior hearing abilities, they may learn to use their hearing more effectively by focusing on subtle auditory cues that often go unnoticed. The efficient use of hearing, in conjunction with the other senses (including any remaining vision), is the key to independent travel for people with vision loss.

This student with significant vision loss is receiving mobility training to help him achieve greater independence.

Independent travel with a sighted companion but without the use of a cane, guide dog, or electronic device is the most common form of travel for young school-age children. However, with the increasing emphasis on instructing young children in orientation at an earlier age, the introduction of the long cane (Kiddy Cane) for young children has become more common (Pogrund, Fazzi, & Schreier, 1993) (see the Reflect on This feature on page 446). As these children grow older, they may be instructed in the use of a Mowat Sensor. The **Mowat Sensor**, approximately the size of a flashlight, is a hand-held ultrasound travel aid that vibrates at different rates to warn of obstacles in front of the individual.

Guide dogs or electronic mobility devices may be appropriate for the adolescent or adult, since the need to travel independently significantly increases with age. A variety of electronic mobility devices is currently being used for everything from enhancing hearing efficiency to detecting obstacles. The **Laser cane** converts infrared light into sound as light beams strike objects in the path of the person who is blind. The **Sonicguide**, worn on the head, emits ultrasound and converts reflections from objects into audible noise in such a way that the individual can learn about the structure of objects. For example, loudness indicates size: The louder the noise, the larger the object.

The acquisition of daily living skills is another curriculum area important to success in the classroom and independence in society. Most people take for granted many routine events of the day, such as eating, dressing, bathing, and toileting. An individual with sight learns very early in life the tasks associated with perceptual-motor development, including grasping, lifting, balancing, pouring, and manipulating objects. These daily living tasks become more complex during the school years as a child learns personal hygiene, grooming, and social etiquette. Eventually, individuals with sight acquire many complex daily living skills that later contribute to

■ EARLY CHILDHOOD YEARS

TIPS FOR THE FAMILY

■ Assist your child with vision loss in learning how to get around in the home environment. Then give him or her the freedom to move freely about.

■ Help your child orient to the environment by removing all unnecessary obstacles around the home (e.g., shoes left on the floor, partially opened doors, a vacuum cleaner left out). Keep him or her informed of any changes in room arrangements.

■ Instruction in special mobility techniques should begin as early as possible with the young child who has vision loss.

■ Keep informed about organizations and civic groups that can provide support to the child and the family.

■ Get in touch with your local health, social services, and education agencies about infant, toddler, and preschool programs for children with vision loss. Become familiar with the individualized family service plan (IFSP) and how it can serve as a planning tool to include your child in early intervention programs.

TIPS FOR THE PRESCHOOL TEACHER

■ Mobility is a fundamental part of early intervention programs for children with vision loss. Help them learn to explore the environment in the classroom, school, and local neighborhood.

■ Work with the child on developing a sense of touch and using hearing to acquire information. The young child may also need assistance in learning to smile and make eye contact.

■ Work closely with the family to develop orientation and mobility strategies that can be learned and applied in both home and school settings.

■ Help other sighted children in the classroom interact with the young child with vision loss by teaching them to speak directly to him or her in a normal tone of voice so as not to raise the noise level.

■ Become very familiar with both tactile (e.g., braille) and auditory aids (e.g., personal readers) that may be used by the young child to acquire information.

TIPS FOR PRESCHOOL PERSONNEL

■ Support the inclusion of young children with vision loss in your classrooms and programs.

■ Support teachers, staff, and volunteers as they attempt to create successful experiences for the young child with vision loss in the preschool setting.

■ Work very closely with families to keep them informed and active members of the school community.

TIPS FOR NEIGHBORS AND FRIENDS

■ Never assume that, because a young child has a vision loss, he or she cannot or should not participate in family and neighborhood activities that are associated with sight (e.g., board games, sports, hide-and-seek).

■ Work with the young child's family to seek opportunities for interaction with sighted children in neighborhood play settings.

■ ELEMENTARY YEARS

TIPS FOR THE FAMILY

■ Learn about the programs and services available during the school years for your child with vision loss. Learn about your child's right to an appropriate education, and actively participate in the development of your child's individual education plan (IEP).

■ Participate in as many school functions for parents as is reasonable to connect your family to the school (e.g., PTA, parent advisory groups, volunteering).

■ Seek information on in-school and extracurricular activities that will enhance opportunities for your child

to interact with sighted peers.

■ Keep the school informed about the medical needs of your child.

■ If your child needs or uses specialized mobility devices to enhance access to the environment, help school personnel to understand how these devices work.

TIPS FOR THE GENERAL EDUCATION CLASSROOM TEACHER

■ Remove obstacles in the classroom that may interfere with the mobility of students with vision loss, including small things like litter on the floor, to desks that are blocking aisles.

■ Place the child's desk as close as necessary to you during group instruction. He or she should also sit as close as possible to visual objects associated with instruction (e.g., blackboard, video monitor, or classroom bulletin board).

■ Be consistent in where you place classroom materials so that the child with vision loss can locate them independently.

■ When providing instruction, always try to stand with your back to the windows. It is very difficult for a person with vision loss to look directly into a light source.

■ Work closely with a vision specialist to determine any specialized mobility or lighting needs for the student with vision loss (e.g., special desk lamp, cassette recorder, largeprint books, personal reader).

■ Help the student gain confidence in you by letting him or her know where you are in the classroom. It is especially helpful to let the student know when you are planning to leave the classroom.

TIPS FOR SCHOOL PERSONNEL

■ Integrate school resources as well as children. Wherever possible, help general education classroom teachers access the human and material resources necessary to meet the needs of students with vision loss. For example:

• *A vision specialist.* A professional trained in the education of students with vision loss can serve as an effective consultant to you and the children in several areas (e.g., mobility training, use of special equipment, communication media, instructional strategies).

• *An ophthalmologist.* Students with a vision loss often have associated medical problems. It is helpful for the teacher to understand any related medical needs that can affect the child's educational experience.

• *Peer-buddy and support systems.* Peer support can be an effective tool for learning in a classroom setting. Peer-buddy systems can be established in the school to help the child with initial mobility needs and/or any tutoring that would help him or her succeed in the general education classroom.

■ Support keeping the school as barrier free as possible; this includes providing adequate lighting in classrooms and hallways.

■ It is critical that children with vision loss have access to appropriate reading materials (e.g., braille books, large-print books, cassette recordings of books) in the school library and media center.

TIPS FOR NEIGHBORS AND FRIENDS

■ Help the family of a child who is visually impaired be an integral part of the neighborhood and friendship networks. Seek ways to include the family and child wherever possible in neighborhood activities.

■ **SECONDARY AND TRANSITION YEARS**

TIPS FOR THE FAMILY

■ Become familiar with the adult services system (e.g., rehabilitation services, Social Security, health care) while your son or daughter is still in high school. Understand the type of vocational or employment training that he or she will need prior to graduation.

■ Find out the school's view on what it should do to assist students with vision loss in making the transition from school to adult life.

■ Create opportunities for your son or daughter to participate in out-of-school activities with same-age sighted peers.

TIPS FOR THE GENERAL EDUCATION CLASSROOM TEACHER

■ Assist students with vision loss to adapt to subject matter in your classroom while you adapt the classroom to meet their needs (e.g., in terms of seating, oral instruction, mobility, large-print or braille textbooks).

■ Access to auditory devices (e.g., cassette recorders for lectures) can facilitate students' learning.

■ Support the student with vision loss in becoming involved in extracurricular activities. If you are the faculty sponsor of a club or organization, explore whether the student is interested and how he or she could get involved.

TIPS FOR SCHOOL PERSONNEL

■ Assist parents of students with vision loss to actively participate in school activities (e.g., parent/ teacher groups and advisory committees).

■ Maintain positive and ongoing contact with the family.

TIPS FOR NEIGHBORS, FRIENDS, AND POTENTIAL EMPLOYERS

■ Seek ways of becoming part of a community support network for the individuals with a vision loss. Be alert to ways that individuals can become and remain actively involved in community employment, neighborhood recreational activities, and local church functions.

■ As potential employers in the local community, seek information on employment of people with a vision loss.

■ **ADULT YEARS**

■ Become aware of the support and services available for your son and daughter in the local community in which they will live as adults. Identify the government-supported programs available to assist people with vision loss in the areas of post-secondary education opportunities, employment, and recreation/leisure. Identify informal supports, such as family and friends, to assist your son or daughter.

■ Work with the person who has vision loss and the family to become part of a community support network for individuals with vision loss. Help the individual with vision loss to become and remain involved in community employment, neighborhood recreational activities, and local church functions.

■ As an employer in the community, seek out information on the employment of people with vision loss. Find out about the programs that focus on establishing employment opportunities for people with a vision loss, while meeting your needs as an employer.

How strange it is for sighted people to recognize that there is a human being who is using a stick as an extension of his perception! It is not easy for sighted people to realize the implications of the fact that the blind person's perception of the world, sound apart, is confined to the reach of his body, and to any extension of his body which he can set up, such as a cane. This is illustrated, I think, by the great difficulty which most sighted people have in helping a lost blind person to reorient himself. The indications of place that sighted people provide are usually too general, or they presuppose that the blind person has a greater knowledge of his environment than he may actually have.

It is so easy and normal for people to assume that your head is what you use to see with. If you met a creature from Mars, it would not take you long to work out that it was seeing you with a particular feeler, which was in your direction, or that it was seeing you through its bottom, which was always pointed towards you whichever way you moved. When sighted people approach a blind person, beginning with the natural expectation that they are dealing with a fellow creature, the implication that they are dealing with a fellow creature, the implications of the fact that this person is actually "seeing" through his white cane are difficult to absorb. Sometimes when I was being led by a sighted person, he or she would lift up my arm, so that my cane did not quite reach the ground. I have managed to avoid this problem by using a longer cane since December 1982. It is more common for people to guide me by grabbing the cane itself, and pointing to things with it, tapping and saying, "There."

People tend to stab at approaching steps with the white cane. I point out gently that, unless I myself am holding the cane, I cannot receive from it the information I need. "Please let go of the cane," I say, "just let me hold your arm."

It is natural for people to regard the white cane as a sort of walking stick. It is looked upon as something that gives support. It is not immediately thought of as an instrument of sense perception, as a way of gathering information about the world.

Source: Adapted from *Touching the Rock* by John Hull. Copyright © 1990 by John M. Hull. Reprinted by permission of Pantheon Books, a division of Random House, Inc.

their independence as adults. Money management, grocery shopping, doing laundry, cooking, cleaning, household repairs, sewing, mowing the lawn, and gardening are all daily tasks associated with adult life and are learned from experiences that are not usually a part of an individual's formal educational program.

For someone with vision loss, however, routine daily living skills are not learned through everyday experiences. In fact, such children may be discouraged from developing self-help skills and may be overprotected from the challenges and risks of everyday life by their parents, siblings, or other family members and friends.

▪ INSTRUCTIONAL CONTENT

Mobility training and daily living skills are components of an educational program that must also include an academic curriculum. Corn et al. (1995) suggested that "educational and developmental goals, including instruction, will reflect the assessed needs of each student [with a visual impairment] in all areas of academic and disability-specific core curricula" (p. 5). Particular emphasis must be placed on developing receptive and expressive language skills. Students with vision loss must learn to listen in order to understand the auditory world more clearly. Finely tuned receptive skills contribute to the development of expressive language, which allows these children to orally describe their perceptions of the world. Oral expression can then be expanded to include handwriting as a means of communication. The acquisition of social and instructional language skills opens the door to many areas, including mathematics and reading.

Abstract mathematical concepts may be difficult for students who are blind. These students will probably require additional practice in learning to master symbols, number facts, and higher-level calculations. As concepts become more complex, additional aids may be necessary to facilitate learning. Specially designed talking microcomputers, calculators, rulers, compasses, and the Crammer abacus have been developed to assist students in this area.

Reading is another activity that can greatly expand the information base for individuals with vision loss. For people who are partially sighted, various optical aids are available: video systems that magnify print, hand-held magnifiers, magnifiers attached to eyeglasses, and other telescopic aids. Another means to facilitate reading for partially sighted students is the use of large-print books, generally available through the American Printing House for the Blind in several print sizes. Other factors that must be considered in teaching reading to students who are partially sighted include adequate illumination and the reduction of glare.

Lenz (1989) recommended the use of advance organizers when working with students with vision loss. Advance organizers prepare students by previewing the instructional approach and materials to be used in a lesson. These organizers essentially identify the topics or tasks to be learned, give the student an organizational framework, indicate the concepts to be introduced, list new vocabulary, and state the intended outcomes for the student.

■ COMMUNICATION MEDIA

For students who are partially sighted, their limited vision remains a means of obtaining information. The use of optical aids in conjunction with auditory and tactile stimuli allows these individuals an integrated sensory approach to learning. However, this approach is not possible for students who are blind. Because they do not have access to visual stimuli, they may have to compensate through the use of tactile and auditory media. Through these media, children who are blind develop an understanding of themselves and the world around them. One facet of this development process is the acquisition of language, and one facet of language acquisition is learning to read.

For the student who is blind, the tactile sense represents entry into the symbolic world of reading. Currently, the most widely used tactile medium for teaching reading is the braille system (see the Reflect on This feature on page 448). This system, which originated with the work of Louis Braille in 1829, is a code that utilizes a six-dot cell to form 63 different alphabetical, numerical, and grammatical characters. To become a proficient braille reader, an individual must learn 263 different configurations, including alphabet letters, punctuation marks, short-form words, and contractions. As illustrated in Figure 14.4, braille is not a tactile reproduction of the standard English alphabet but a separate code for reading and writing.

Although used by only about 10% of students who are blind (American Printing House for the Blind, 1992), braille is still considered to be an efficient means for teaching reading and writing. Critics of the system argue that most readers who use braille are much slower than those who read from print and that braille materials are bulky and tedious. It can be argued, however, that, without braille, people who are blind would be much less independent. Some individuals who are unable to read braille (such as people with diabetes who have decreased tactual sensitivity) are more dependent on sight readers and recordings. Simple tasks—such as labeling cans, boxes, or cartons in a bathroom or kitchen—become nearly impossible to complete.

focus 7

How can communication media facilitate learning for people with vision loss?

Reflect on This

BRAILLE READERS FOUND TO USE VISUAL CORTEX

When blind people "read" Braille with their fingertips, they are somehow able to use the same part of the brain—called the visual cortex—that sighted persons use to interpret things they see. That's the conclusion of new experiments that challenge traditional ideas about how sensory information is processed in the brain.

According to orthodox neuroscience, tactile stimuli are processed in a region of the brain's convoluted outer layer called the somatosensory cortex. Visual information goes by a completely different route to an area at the back of the brain called the visual cortex. Eventually, the twain may meet and be integrated into a single perception—but only after each has been separately processed. There are no known nerve pathways that would permit tactile signals to get to the visual cortex directly.

But in the journal *Nature*, researchers from the National Institute of Neurological Disorders and Stroke here report that persons who are blind from an early age seem to have rearranged their neural wiring so that sensory information from a forefinger running over patterns of raised Braille dots prompts a flurry of action in the brain's visual processing centers. Norihiro Sadato and colleagues at NINDS monitored the cerebral activity of eight adept Braille readers, six other blind subjects, and 10 sighted subjects, using a technique called positron emission tomography. PET scans show which areas of the brain are most active (that is, which cells are consuming the most blood-borne nutrients) during a given task.

In this case, the eight blind subjects were scanned while they read raised dot patterns in Braille. The other subjects were monitored while performing various analogous tasks: running their fingers over a uniform grid of Braille dots; feeling the size and angle of grooves in an array of dots; and detecting dot patterns of English letters. When sighted subjects performed those tasks, their scans showed diminished activity in the visual cortex and the expected levels of action in somatosensory areas that normally process tactile information. But when any of the 14 blind subjects read Braille or interpreted dot patterns, they exhibited substantial increases in the visual cortex. Neither group showed any visual cortex activity during the "non-discriminatory" task of merely sweeping their fingers over the uniform dot grid, which involved purely tactile sensation.

Recent research has shown that when people create imaginary mental images of objects, brain activity increases in the same parts of the visual cortex that are used when actually viewing an object. But none of the NINDS subjects was asked to form mental pictures during any of the tasks, and none reported doing so. Moreover, some of the subjects were blind from birth and presumably had no way to form imagined visual images.

So how did the Braille readers use the visual cortex, and what mechanism might make that possible? "That's the million-dollar question," said NINDS neuropsychologist Jordan Grafman, a co-author of the *Nature* paper. "One hypothesis is that there are certain properties of cells in the visual cortex that resemble properties of cells in the somatosensory cortex"—especially in their ability to discriminate geometrical information about a stimulus.

"If that's true," he said, "then it might be possible under special conditions that cells in either . . . cortex could adapt to sensory input coming from the other area."

It is conceivable, the NINDS team suspects, that information can travel from region to region through some unknown "indirect preexisting pathway." In normal circumstances, in which a sighted person is touching something, that pathway would be shut down to focus attention on tactile stimuli and avoid confusing the brain.

But that pathway might be opened "in an emergency of unusual situation" such as blindness, Grafman said.

Once the phenomenon is better understood, he said, it might be possible to concoct drugs that would encourage this kind of compensatory rerouting, known as neural plasticity.

Source: From "Braille Readers Found to Use Visual Cortex: Results Defy Traditional Ideas of Brain Function," by C. Suplee, April 11, 1996, *Washington Post*, p. A4. © 1996 The Washington Post. Reprinted with permission.

Braille writing is accomplished through the use of a slate and stylus. Using this procedure, a student writes a mirror image of the reading code, moving from right to left. The writing process may be facilitated by using a braille writer, a hand-operated machine with six keys that correspond to each dot in the braille cell.

Innovations for braille readers that reduce some of the problems associated with the medium include the Mountbat Brailler and the Braille 'n Speak. The Mountbat Brailler is electronic, thus making it easier to operate than a manual unit. The

FIGURE 14.4

The braille alphabet

a	b	c	d	e	f	g	h	i	j

k	l	m	n	o	p	q	r	s	t

u	v	w	x	y	z

w	h	a	t	i	s

y	o	u	r	n	a	m	e

Mountbat Brailler weighs about 15 pounds and can be hooked up to a computer keyboard attachment to input information. The Braille 'n Speak is a device designed to enable users to input information through a braille keyboard. The Braille 'n Speak can translate braille into synthesized speech or print. The device has accessories for entering or reading text for a host computer, for reading computer disks, and for sending or receiving a fax.

One tactile device that does not use the braille system is the **Optacon Scanner.** This machine exposes printed material to a camera and then reproduces it on a

Special computers such as Power-Braille are designed for people who read and write braille. Such electronic aids are faster and easier to use than a braille writer.

Today's Technology

THE MAGIC MACHINES OF RAY KURZWEIL

Lawyer Melea Rodgers has just arrived for work at the Decatur, Alabama, City Hall. The petite young woman with shoulder-length blond hair sits down at her desk and picks up her stack of morning mail. She opens the first letter and presses a switch on a brief-case-size machine on her desk.

"Hello, this is Perfect Paul," says a resonant male voice coming from the device. "I am ready." Rodgers picks up a palm-size scanner and slowly begins to slide it back and forth on the letter. In a moment, Perfect Paul continues. "Dear Miss Rodgers," he says, as he begins reading the entire letter.

Melea Rodgers went blind as a result of diabetes several years ago. Until she received this Kurzweil Personal Reader, she depended on office-mates and her mother to read not only her daily mail, but thousands of pages of regulations and court documents.

Now she can have any page read aloud to her in any of nine distinct voice-styles—from the resonant bass of Huge Harry to the breathy tones of Whispering Wendy. "Ever since I got my Kurzweil last year, I've been on my own. It's a wonderful feeling," says Rodgers.

The Kurzweil whose name adorns the machine is Ray-mond Kurzweil, one of the most remarkable inventors alive. A soft-spoken business-man–scientist in Waltham, Massachusetts, Kurzweil has repeatedly astonished colleagues and competitors with his "smart machines" that are transforming the lives of millions.

- Paul Scher, rehabilitation-services consultant for Sears in Chicago, can now enjoy his evenings instead of using them to keep up with office paperwork. "I used to depend on a device that converts written material into a tactile pattern," says Scher. "It took forever. The Kurzweil is a fantastic breakthrough."

- Judge Craig Alston of Bay City, Michigan, suffers from a degenerative eye disease. Now legally blind, Alston often addresses students and community groups on the dangers of drinking and driving. To add dramatic impact, he sometimes brings along his Personal Reader and has Perfect Paul read from medical, scientific and accident reports.

Few things give Ray Kurzweil more of a sense of fulfillment than hearing such stories. "I've received hundreds of letters from blind people who say they couldn't have gotten their college degree or couldn't hold their current job if it hadn't been for the Reader. It's a great feeling."

As a small boy growing up in Queens, New York, Kurzweil was an accomplished magician. Then in 1960, at age 12, he discovered the computer. Within three years he had written a program that saved so much time in doing statistical analyses that IBM later distributed it to customers throughout the country.

"I was already interested in how we recognize things—how we pick up patterns. That, to me, is the key to intelligence. And I began dreaming of making pattern recognition the area where I would concentrate," says Kurzweil.

On a freezing January morning in 1976, the young inventor staged a demonstration for the press that caused a sensation. That evening the robot-like voice of his prototype reading machine delivered Walter Cronkite's sign-off on the "CBS Evening News."

The following day, singer Stevie Wonder heard Kurzweil demonstrating his reader on the "Today Show" and traveled to Cambridge to meet the inventor. "He wanted one right away," Kurzweil recalls. "The first machine weighed about 350 pounds and cost $50,000, but we loaded it right into his car." Wonder stayed up all that night reading. In the years since, the Kurzweil machine has been "a brother and a friend," he says.

The Personal Reader is also used in schools to aid students with reading disabilities. Researchers have discovered that these students can sometimes overcome their [impairment] if they scan a page of a book, then follow along with Perfect Paul as he pronounces each word, like an infinitely patient teacher.

Ray Kurzweil is now devoting much of his time to new and different machines. The Kurzweil music synthesizer has become the standard for such stars as Stevie Wonder, Kenny Rogers and Neil Diamond. Kurzweil has also created a voice-recognition mechanism that permits a busy doctor to speak into a hand-held device after completing an examination and receive a typed report in minutes.

Source: From "The Magic Machines of Ray Kurzweil," by E. Ziegler, February 1991, *Reader's Digest*, pp. 119–122. Copyright 1991 by *Reader's Digest*. Reprinted with permission.

fingerpad using a series of vibrating pins that are tactile reproductions of the printed material. Developed by J. C. Bliss and available commercially since 1971, thousands of Optacons are currently in use worldwide. Although the Optacon greatly expands access to the printed word, it has drawbacks, as well. It requires tactile sensitivity; as such, reading remains a slow, laborious process. Additionally, the Optacon requires considerable training for the individual to become a skilled user. These drawbacks, along with the development of reading machines, have resulted in the declining use and production of the Optacon Scanner in the 1990s.

Many of the newer communication systems do not make use of the tactile sense because it is not functional for all individuals who are blind (many do not have tactile sensitivity, including some elderly people). Such individuals must rely solely on the auditory sense to acquire information. Specialized auditory media for people who are blind are becoming increasingly available. One example is the reading machine, hailed as a major breakthrough in technology for persons with a vision loss (Dixon & Mandelbaum, 1990). Reading machines, manufactured by Kurzweil, IBM, and Arenstone, convert printed matter into synthetic speech at a rate of about 400 words per minute. They can also convert print to braille. The costs associated with reading machines have decreased substantially in the past few years, and most can be purchased with computer accessories for under $5,000. Several advocacy organizations for those with blindness and many banks throughout America currently provide low-interest loans for people with vision loss so they can purchase the device (Ziegler, 1991).

Other auditory aids that assist people who are blind include talking calculators, talking-book machines, compact disk players, and audiotape recorders. For example, the Note Teller is a small compact machine that can identify denominations of U.S. currency using a voice synthesizer that communicates in either English or Spanish (*Journal of Visual Impairments*, 1992).

Communication media that facilitate participation of people with vision loss in the community include specialized library and newspaper services that offer books in large print, on cassette, and in braille. The New York Times, for example, publishes a weekly special edition with type three times the size of its regular type. McDowell (1990) reported that the sale of large-print books increased by 30% from 1989 to 1990 in bookstores throughout the United States. Books are also available on computer disk (electronic books) and can be converted to large print through the use of a personal computer. A reader can change the size of print from an electronic book, or even change from print to voice (Rogers, 1992).

Responding to a human voice, another device known as the **Personal Companion** can look up a telephone number and dial it. Using a synthesized voice, the Personal Companion is able to read a newspaper delivered over telephone lines, balance a checkbook, turn on and off home appliances, and maintain a daily appointment book.

Closed-circuit television (CCTV) systems are another means to enlarge the print from books and other written documents. Initially explored in the 1950s, the design of CCTV systems became more practical in the 1970s and are now in wider use than ever before. The components of the newer CCTV systems include a small television camera with variable zoom lens and focusing capacity, TV monitor, and a sliding platform table for the printed materials (Miller-Wood, Efron, & Wood, 1990). An individual sits in front of the television monitor to view printed material that can be enhanced up to 60 times its original size through the use of the TV camera and zoom lens. Some CCTVs are also available with split-screen capability to allow near and distant objects to be viewed together. These machines can also accept input directly from a computer as well as printed material (Best, 1992).

Miller-Wood et al., identified several advantages and disadvantages of CCTV systems for people with vision loss. Advantages include greater efficiency and magnification capabilities. "In addition to such features as reversed polarity, brightness, and light intensity, the contrast of the image can be adjusted independently to accommodate various [visual] conditions" (p. 559). Primary disadvantages include cost, greater physical size, lack of portability, and poor availability of maintenance services. The authors suggested, however, that over time CCTV systems are cost-effective when compared to the production and overall cost of large-print books, the time involved in enlarging or adapting materials, and the cost of employing personal readers.

■ EDUCATIONAL PLACEMENT

Historically, education for individuals with vision loss—specifically, blindness—was provided through specialized residential facilities. These segregated centers have traditionally been referred to as asylums, institutions, or schools. One of the first such facilities in the United States was the New England Asylum for the Blind, later named the Perkins School. This facility opened its doors in 1832 and was one of several eastern U.S. schools that used treatment models borrowed from well-established European institutions. For the most part, the early U.S. institutions operated as closed schools, where a person who was blind would live and learn in an environment that was essentially separate from the outside world. The philosophy was to get the person who was blind "ready for the outside world," even though this approach provided little real exposure to it.

More recently, some residential schools have advocated an open system of intervention. These programs are based on the philosophy that children who are blind should have every opportunity to gain the same experiences that would be available if they were growing up in their own communities.

Both open and closed residential facilities exist today as alternative intervention modes, but they are no longer the primary social or educational systems available to people who are blind. As was true for John in the chapter opening snapshot, the vast majority of individuals who are blind or partially sighted now live at home, attend local public schools, and interact within the community.

Educational programs for students with vision loss are based on the principle of flexible placement. As suggested by Corn et al. (1995), local education agencies are

focus 8

What range of educational services is available to students with vision loss?

responsible for ensuring that every student with a visual impairment has access to a full array of placement options. As such, a wide variety of services must be available to these students in the public schools, ranging from general education class placement, with little or no assistance from specialists, to separate residential schools. Between these extremes, the public schools generally offer several alternative classroom structures, including the use of consulting teachers, resource rooms, part-time special classes, or full-time special classes. Placement of a student in one of these programs depends on the extent to which the loss of vision affects his or her overall educational achievement. Many students with vision loss are able to function successfully within general education settings if the learning environment is adapted to meet their needs.

Some organizations advocating for students who are blind strongly support the concept of flexible placements within a continuum ranging from general education classroom to residential school (Joint Organizational Committee, 1993). The report of the Joint Organizational Committee, which represented eight national organizations, opposed the "full inclusion" of students who are blind as the only educational option in the public schools. They recommended a full continuum of alternative placements, emphasizing caution concerning the social isolation, lower self-esteem, and poor performance of students who are blind in inclusive settings when support is not made available. Some professionals have also indicated that graduates of inclusive programs in general education classrooms lack the skills needed for independent functioning during the adult years (Sacks, Kekelis, & Gaylord-Ross, 1992).

Whether the student is to be included into the general education classroom or taught in a special class, a vision specialist must be available, either to support the general education classroom teacher or to provide direct instruction to the student. A vision specialist has received concentrated training in the education of students with vision loss. This specialist and the rest of the educational support team have knowledge of appropriate educational assessment techniques, specialized curriculum materials and teaching approaches, and the use of various communication media. Specialized instruction for students who have vision loss may include a major modification in curricula, including teaching concepts that children who are sighted learn incidentally (e.g., walking down the street, getting from one room to the next in the school building, getting meals in the cafeteria, and using public transportation).

Medical and Social Services

■ MEDICAL SERVICES

Initial screenings for vision loss are usually based on the individual's visual acuity. Visual acuity may be measured through the use of the Snellen test, developed in 1862 by Dutch ophthalmologist Herman Snellen. This visual screening test is used primarily to measure central distance vision. The subject stands 20 feet from a letter chart, or E-chart (the standard eye-test chart), and reads each symbol, beginning with the top row. The different sizes of each row or symbol represent what a person with normal vision would see at the various distances indicated on the chart. As indicated earlier in this chapter, a person's visual acuity is then determined by the use of an index that refers to the distance at which an object can be recognized. The person with normal eyesight is defined as having 20/20 vision.

focus 9
What steps can be taken to prevent and medically treat vision loss?

Since the Snellen test measures only visual acuity, it must be used primarily as an initial screening device that is supplemented by more in-depth assessments, such as a thorough ophthalmological examination. Parents, physicians, school nurses, and educators must also carefully observe the child's behavior, and a complete history of possible symptoms of a vision loss should be documented. These observable symptoms fall into three categories: appearance, behavior, and complaints. Table 14.1 on page 454 describes some warning signs of vision loss. The existence of symptoms does not necessarily mean a person has a significant vision loss, but it does indicate that an appropriate specialist should be consulted for further examination.

■ PREVENTION Prevention of vision loss is one of the major goals of the field of medicine. Prevention measures can be grouped into three categories: genetic screening and counseling, appropriate prenatal care, and early developmental assessment.

TABLE 14.1   Warning signs of visual problems

PHYSICAL SYMPTOMS	OBSERVABLE BEHAVIOR	COMPLAINTS
Eyes are crossed	Blinks constantly	Frequent dizziness
Eyes are not functioning in unison	Trips or stumbles frequently	Frequent headaches
Eyelids are swollen and crusted with red rims	Covers one eye when reading	Pain in the eyes
Eyes are overly sensitive to light	Holds reading material either very close or very far away	Itching or burning of the eyes or eyelids
Frequent sties	Distorts the face or frowns when concentrating on something in the distance	Double vision
Eyes are frequently bloodshot		
Pupils are of different sizes	Walks cautiously	
Eyes are constantly in motion	Fails to see objects that are to one side or the other	

Since some causes of blindness are hereditary, it is important for the family to be aware of genetic services. One purpose of genetic screening is to identify those who are planning for a family and who may possess certain detrimental genotypes (such as albinism or retinoblastoma) that can be passed on to their descendants. Screening may also be conducted after conception to determine whether the unborn fetus possesses any genetic abnormalities. Following screening, a genetic counselor informs the parents of the test results so that the family can make an informed decision about conceiving a child or carrying a fetus to term.

Adequate prenatal care is another means of preventing problems. Parents must be made aware of the potential hazards associated with poor nutritional habits, the use of drugs, and exposure to radiation (e.g., x-rays) during pregnancy. One example of preventive care during this period is the use of antibiotics to treat various infections (e.g., influenza, measles, syphilis), thus reducing the risk of infection to the unborn fetus.

Developmental screening is also a widely recognized means of prevention. (It was through early developmental screening that a medical specialist confirmed that John—in the chapter opening snapshot—had a serious vision loss and would require the assistance of a trained vision specialist.) Early screening of developmental problems enables the family physician to analyze several treatment alternatives and, when necessary, to refer the child to an appropriate specialist for a more thorough evaluation of developmental delays.

This screening—which also includes examination of hearing, speech, motor, and psychological development—includes attention to vision as well. Early screening involves a medical examination at birth, examining the physical condition of the newborn and also obtaining a complete family medical history. The eyes should be carefully examined for any abnormalities, such as infection or trauma.

At 6 weeks of age, visual screening forms part of another general developmental assessment. This examination should include input from the parents concerning how their child is responding (e.g., smiling and looking at objects or faces). The physician should check eye movement and search for infection, crusting on the eyes, or **epiphora** (an overflow of tears resulting from obstruction of the lacrimal ducts).

The next examination should occur at about 6 months of age. A defensive blink should be present at this age, and eye movement should be full and coordinated. If any imbalance in eye movements is noted, a more thorough examination should be conducted. Family history is extremely important, since in many cases there is a familial pattern of vision problems.

Between the ages of 1 and 5, visual evaluation should be conducted at regular intervals. An important period occurs just prior to the child's entering school. Visual problems must not go undetected as children attempt to cope with the new and complex demands of the educational environment.

■ TREATMENT In addition to medicine's emphasis on prevention of vision loss, significant strides have also been made in the treatment of these problems. The nature of medical interventions depends on the type and severity of the loss. For individuals who are partially sighted, use of an optical aid can vastly improve access to the visual world. Most of these aids take the form of corrective glasses or contact lenses, which are designed to magnify the image on the retina. Some aids magnify the retinal image within the eye, and others clarify the retinal image. Appropriate use of optical aids, in conjunction with regular medical examinations, not only helps correct existing visual problems but may also prevent further deterioration of existing vision.

Surgery, muscle exercises, and drug therapy have also played important roles in treating persons with vision loss. Treatment may range from complex laser surgical procedures and corneal transplants to the process known as atropinization. **Atropinization** is the treatment for cataracts that involves washing out the eye with the alkaloid drug atropine, which permanently dilates the pupil.

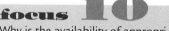

focus **10**

Why is the availability of appropriate mental health services important for people with vision loss?

■ SOCIAL SERVICES

Some individuals with vision loss may have social adjustment difficulties, including poor self-esteem and general feelings of inferiority. To minimize these

Despite advancements in electronic mobility devices, the guide dog continues to be an important source of support for people who are blind. The dog's intelligence and companionship contribute to its popularity.

problems, mental health services should be made available as early as possible in the person's life. These services can begin with infant stimulation programs and counseling for the family. As the child grows older, group counseling can assist in coping with feelings concerning blindness and provide guidance in the area of human sexuality (limited vision may distort perception of the physical body). Counseling eventually extends into matters focusing on marriage, family, and adult relationships. For the adult with vision loss, special guidance may be necessary in preparation for employment and independent living.

Mobility of the person with vision loss can be enhanced in large cities by the use of auditory pedestrian signals at crosswalks known as audible traffic signals (ATS). The *walk* and *don't walk* signals are indicated by auditory cues, such as actual verbal messages (e.g., "Please do not cross yet"), different bird chirps for each signal, or a sonalert buzzer (Peck & Uslan, 1990). ATS is somewhat controversial among people who are blind and professionals in the field. Those not supporting the use of ATS have two basic concerns. First, the devices promote negative public attitudes, indicating a presumption that such assistance is necessary for a person who is blind to be mobile. Second, the devices may actually contribute to unsafe conditions because they mask traffic noise for the person who is blind.

Restaurant menus, elevator floor buttons, and signs in buildings (such as rest rooms) can be produced in braille. Additionally, telephone credit cards, personal checks, ATM cards, special mailing tubes, and panels for household appliances are also available in braille. Future access to community services may be greatly enhanced by the development of devices that use synthesized speech for purchasing subway and rail tickets or obtaining money from automatic teller machines (Schreier, 1990).

Case Study

MICHAEL

Clasping a cane in his right hand and book bag in the other, Michael Harris is darting though Kearns High School on his way to his next class. Peer tutor Rebecca Hale is helping this student, who is blind, negotiate the crowd.

"Hi, Mike!" blurt passers-by.

Suddenly, in a rich baritone voice, Michael belts out the first chorus of "I'll Be Home for Christmas."

No one marvels. The voice is familiar and pleasant. Frequently, the 17-year-old stays after school, where he sits cross-legged, propped against a locker, and sings. He even takes requests.

"The most important thing is these kids are just like any other kids," says Deanne Graves, teacher for those with visual impairments in Granite School District. "They have ups and downs. We need to treat them just like everybody else. Just because they have a disability does not mean they cannot aspire to whatever they want."

Michael has been part of the inclusion movement since he was a fifth-grader at Western Hills Elementary. He prefers it to his time at the Utah Schools for the Deaf and the Blind.

"One of the things I like about mainstreaming [is that there are kids from my neighborhood]. When I went to the School for the Blind, there were kids from all over the valley," he says. "So basically there was nobody from my neighborhood."

During his third-period college prep English course, the class is reading *Cyrano de Bergerac* aloud. Since Michael has fallen slightly behind, he sits outside the room with his tutor, Rebecca, listening to *Cyrano* on tape.

Unexpectedly, the fire alarm sounds. It is a routine fire drill. Rebecca, who gets credit for helping Michael, leads him out of the building in the mass student exodus.

About three minutes later, Michael is swarmed by a crowd as they listen to his jokes.

"What do you call twins before they are born?" he asks. "Womb mates." The crowd laughs; Michael loves it.

■ APPLICATION
1. Are Michael's experiences similar to or different from those of other students with vision loss that you have known in high school?
2. Describe any accommodations or supports that Michael is probably receiving that help him function so well in a general education classroom.

Source: Adapted from *Disabled Students Making It in the Mainstream,* by S. A. Autman (October 31, 1994), *Salt Lake Tribune,* pp. B1, B2. Reprinted by permission of S. A. Autman and The Salt Lake Tribune.

Debate Forum

GENERAL EDUCATION SCHOOLS VERSUS SPECIAL SCHOOLS: WHERE SHOULD CHILDREN WHO ARE BLIND BE EDUCATED?

In 1900, the first class for students who were blind opened in the Chicago public schools. Prior to this, such children were educated in state residential schools, where they lived away from their families. Until 1950, the ratio of students attending schools for the blind to those in general education public schools was about 10 to 1. In that year, however, the incidence of children with retrolental fibroplasia (now known as retinopathy of prematurity) increased, resulting in significant numbers of children who were blind attending public schools. By 1960, more children with blindness were being educated with their nondisabled peers in general education public schools than in schools for the blind. Nonetheless, the issue of what is the most appropriate educational environment for children who are blind continues to be debated internationally.

■ POINT
Children who are blind should be educated in public schools and classrooms alongside their seeing peers. Inclusion allows children who are blind to remain at home with their family and live in a local neighborhood, which is just as important for these children as it is for their sighted friends. It also allows children who are blind to have greater opportunities for appropriate modeling of acceptable behaviors.

Schools for children who are blind have endeavored over the years to offer the best education possible, one intended to be equivalent to that offered to children who can see. However, these schools cannot duplicate the experiences of living at home and being part of the local community. Although it can be argued that the special school is geared entirely to the needs of the child who is blind, there is much more to education than a segregated educational environment can provide. During the growing years, the child must be directly involved in the seeing world in order to have the opportunity to adjust and become a part of society.

■ COUNTERPOINT
The special school for children who are blind provides a complete education that is oriented entirely to the unique needs of these individuals. The teachers in these schools have years of experience in working exclusively with children who are blind and are well aware of what educational experiences are needed to help them reach their fullest potential. Additionally, special schools are equipped with a multitude of educational resources developed for children who are blind. General education schools and classrooms cannot offer the intensive, individualized programs in areas such as music, physical education, and arts and crafts that are available through schools for the blind. The strength of the special school is that it is entirely geared to the specialized needs of the child who is blind. Thus, it can more effectively teach him or her the skills necessary to adapt to life experiences.

Review

focus 1

Why is it important to understand the visual process as well as know the physical components of the eye?

■ The visual process is an important link to the physical world, helping people to gain information beyond that provided by the other senses and also helping to integrate the information acquired primarily through sound, touch, smell, and taste.

■ Our interactions with the environment are shaped by the way we perceive visual stimuli.

focus 2

Distinguish between the terms *blind* and *partially sighted*.

■ Legal blindness is visual acuity of 20/200 or worse in the best eye with best correction, or a field of vision of 20% or less.

■ Educational definitions of blindness focus primarily on the individual's inability to use vision as an avenue for learning.

■ A person who is partially sighted has a visual acuity greater than 20/200 but not greater than 20/70 in the best eye after correction.

■ A person who is partially sighted can still use vision as a primary means of learning.

focus 3

What are the distinctive features of refractive eye problems, muscle disorders of the eye, and receptive eye problems?

■ Refractive eye problems occur when the refractive structures of the eye (cornea or lens) fail to focus light rays properly on the retina. Refractive problems include hyperopia (farsightedness), myopia (nearsightedness), astigmatism (blurred vision), and cataracts.

■ Muscle disorders occur when the major muscles within the eye are inadequately developed or atrophic, resulting in a loss of control and an inability to maintain tension. Muscle disorders include nystagmus (uncontrolled rapid eye movement), strabismus (crossed eyes), and amblyopia (loss of vision due to muscle imbalance).

■ Receptive eye problems occur when the receptive structures of the eye (retina and optic nerve) degenerate or become damaged. Receptive eye problems include optic atrophy, retinitis pigmentosa, retinal detachment, retrolental fibroplasia, and glaucoma.

focus 4

What are the estimated prevalence and causes of vision loss?

■ At least 20% of the general population have some vision loss.

■ About .04% of all school-age children meet the IDEA definition of being blind or partially sighted. Over 25,000 students have visual impairments and received specialized services in the U.S. public schools in 1995–1996.

■ Approximately 75% of all people who are blind are over 45 years of age.

focus 5

Describe how a vision loss can affect intelligence, speech and language skills, educational achievement, social development, physical orientation and mobility, and perceptual-motor development.

■ Performance on tests of intelligence may be negatively affected by a vision loss in areas ranging from spatial concepts to general knowledge of the world.

■ Children with vision loss are at a distinct disadvantage in developing speech and language skills because they are unable to visually associate words with objects.

■ Children with vision loss cannot learn speech by visual imitation but must rely on hearing or touch for input.

■ Factors that may influence the educational achievement of a student with vision loss include (1) late entry to school; (2) failure in inappropriate school programs; (3) loss of time in school due to illness, treatment, or surgery; (4) lack of opportunity; and (5) slow rate of acquiring information.

■ People with vision loss are unable to imitate the physical mannerisms of sighted peers and thus do not develop body language, an important form of social communication.

■ A person with sight may misinterpret what is said by a person with a vision loss because his or her visual cues may not be consistent with the spoken word.

■ People with vision loss are often excluded from social activities that are integrally related to the use of vision, thus reinforcing the mistaken idea that they do not want to participate.

■ Lack of sight may prevent a person with vision loss from understanding his or her own relative position in space.

■ A vision loss may affect fine motor coordination and interfere with a person's ability to manipulate objects.

■ The perceptual discrimination abilities of people with vision loss in the areas of texture, weight, and sound are comparable to those of sighted peers.

■ People who are blind do not perform as well as people with sight on complex tasks of perception, including form identification, spatial relations, and perceptual-motor integration.

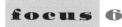 **focus 6**

Identify two content areas that should be included in educational programs for students with vision loss.

- Mobility and orientation training
- The acquisition of daily living skills

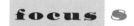 **focus 7**

How can communication media facilitate learning for people with vision loss?

- Through communication media—such as optical aids in conjunction with auditory and tactile stimuli—individuals with vision loss can better develop an understanding of themselves and the world around them.
- Tactile media—including the raised-dot braille system

and the Optacon Scanner—can greatly enhance the individual's access to information.

- Specialized media—including the Kurzweil Personal Readers, closed-circuit TV systems, talking calculators, talking-book machines, CD players, and audiotape recorders—provide opportunities for people with vision loss that were not thought possible only a few years ago.

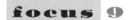 **focus 8**

What range of educational services is available to students with vision loss?

- Residential facilities provide children who are blind with opportunities for the same kinds of experiences that would be available if they were growing up in their own communities.

- The vast majority of individuals with vision loss live at home, attend public schools, and interact within their own communities.
- Services available within the public schools range from general education class placement, with little or no assistance, to special day schools.

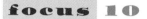 **focus 9**

What steps can be taken to prevent and medically treat vision loss?

- Vision loss can be prevented through genetic screening and counseling, appropriate prenatal care, and early developmental assessment.
- The development of optical aids, including corrective glasses and contact lenses, has greatly improved access to the sighted world for people with vision loss.

- Medical treatment may range from complex laser surgical procedures and corneal transplants to drug therapy (e.g., atropinization).

focus 10

Why is the availability of appropriate mental health services important for people with vision loss?

- Mental health services address individual problems with self-concept and feelings of inferiority that often stem from having a vision loss.
- Mental health services include infant stimulation programs, family counseling, and individual counseling relative to preparation for employment and independent living.

People with Physical and Health Disabilities

To begin with . . .

 Two-thirds of Americans with disabilities of working age are not employed and say they want to work. (United Cerebral Palsy, 1997b, p. 1)

 Over a lifetime, the average individual with Type I [juvenile onset] diabetes will spend close to 60,000 hours doing self-treatment. (Juvenile Diabetes Foundation, 1997a, p. 1)

 AIDS is the leading cause of death among children 2–5 years old in many cities of the eastern United States. (Parks, 1996, p. 916)

 Mr. [Christopher] Reeves,

I just wanted to say thank you for all the inspiration that you give to the World in your fight. You are truly someone that many of us look up to. Keep fighting, keep trying, and keep striving. One day very soon they'll find a way to beat spinal cord injury and we'll be able to see a true Super Man walk again.

Bill Boxler (Boxler, 1997)

Linda

I just turned twenty-one. I never thought I would actually reach the official age of adulthood, but it has come and gone; and I am, at least according to law, a little more responsible for my behavior. Actually, I've been responsible for a lot of my behavior since I was a young child. For reasons that I don't completely understand, I've always had a personal resilience that helped me deal with the challenges that have been an integral part of my life.

My mother, who is an exquisitely beautiful woman, was very excited about my birth. I was her first child. The expectations she had for me were wonderful. But, within moments of my delivery, it was discovered that I had a serious birth defect known as spina bifida. This discovery altered many of my mom's expectations for me. Although my parents didn't know a great deal about spina bifida at the time, they shortly became specialists.

Their major concern at the time of my birth was not my physical appearance, even though the sac on my spine was quite gross, but the prevention of infection, my intellectual capacity, and the degree of paralysis.

The sac and related nerve tissue were surgically cared for very early in my life through several operations. Fortunately, the infection that was an ever-present threat during the first days and months of my existence was successfully prevented. Because of the location of the sac with neural tissue, I'm paralyzed from the waist down. I walk with the aid of crutches now.

As for my intellectual capacity, I've just completed my second year of college. I'm not an academic superstar, but I do hold my own in my major, which is fashion merchandising.

To be frank with you, my greatest challenge hasn't been my paralysis per se, but my lack of bowel control. I'd love to have the facility that most normal people have, but I don't. I'm working on my attitude about this particular problem. I'm not nearly as sensitive about it as I once was.

PHYSICAL DISABILITIES can affect a person's ability to move about, to use arms and legs effectively, to swallow food, and to breathe independently. They may also affect other capacities such as vision, cognition, speech, language, hearing, and bowel control. The Individuals with Disabilities Education Act (IDEA) uses the term **orthopedically impaired** to describe students with physical disabilities and the term **other health impaired** to describe students with health disabilities.

As described in IDEA, **health disabilities** cause individuals to have "limited strength, vitality or alertness, due to chronic or acute health problems such as a heart condition, tuberculosis, rheumatic fever, nephritis, asthma, sickle cell anemia, hemophilia, epilepsy, lead poisoning, leukemia, or diabetes which adversely affect . . . educational performance" (23 Code of Federal Regulations, Sec. 300.5 [7]). For example, children and youth with sickle cell anemia often experience periods of persistent pain in their arms, legs, abdomen, or back that often interfere with their school performance and also prevent them from participating in activities that are important to their social and emotional well-being.

In recent years, new subgroups have emerged within the health disabilities area. They are often referred to as **medically fragile** or **technologically dependent.** These individuals are at risk for medical emergencies and often require specialized support in the form of ventilators or nutritional supplements. Often children or youth who are medically fragile have progressive diseases such as cancer or AIDS. Other children have episodic conditions that lessen their attentiveness, stamina, or energy. Sickle cell anemia is a good example of a condition that is episodic in nature.

Technologically dependent or technology-assisted individuals use devices such as ventilators for breathing, urinary catheters and colostomy bags for bowel and bladder care, tracheostomy tubes for supplying oxygen-enriched air to congested lungs, or suctioning equipment for the removal of mucus from airways. Some of these devices will be discussed in greater detail later in the chapter.

Physical and health disabilities also affect how individuals with various conditions or diseases view themselves and how they are seen by others—parents, brothers and sisters, peers, teachers, neighbors, and employers. The impact of these disabilities is also felt on a number of social, educational, and psychological fronts. For example, children and youth who must spend significant periods of time away from their homes, neighborhoods, or schools for medical care or support may have limited opportunities to develop friendships with neighborhood and school peers, to attend special social events, and to develop certain social skills. The degree to which individuals with physical and health disabilities become integral participants in their neighborhoods and communities is directly related to the quality and timeliness of treatment received from various professionals, the nurturing provided by parents, siblings, and teachers, and the support and acceptance supplied by neighbors and other community members. In this regard, significant progress has been made in civil rights legislation, particularly with the passage of the Americans with Disabilities Act (ADA) (see Chapter 1). The intent of this act is to give men, women, and children with disabilities full access to public services, transportation, telecommunications, public accommodations, and employment. It attempts to put persons with disabilities on the same team and playing field as those without disabilities; also, it is designed to make environments and services deficit-free for individuals with disabilities.

One of the first provisions of ADA deals with employment. It prohibits employers from discriminating against qualified persons with disabilities in the workplace. Additionally, it requires employers to make reasonable accommodations so that these persons can fully use their skills and truly contribute to the success of the business, industry, or enterprise. Other provisions in the act ensure that children, youth, and adults with disabilities have access to and the ability to participate in integrated recreational programs. These programs might include "open plunge" swimming, regular participation in community center aerobics classes, membership in a neighborhood bowling league, and involvement in summer camping programs for youth.

ADA also addresses transportation, public accommodations and services, and telecommunication assistance. All new buses and at least one car on every passenger train must be wheelchair accessible, and public and private accommodations and services will be readily accessible to persons with disabilities. For example, hair salons, dentist's offices, fitting rooms, fast-food restaurants, locker rooms, video arcades, and playgrounds must be designed with persons with disabilities in mind. No longer should children, youth, or adults with disabilities and their families worry about accessibility of bathroom facilities or whether they can enter and participate in certain social or recreational environments. The community should truly be open to them for employment experiences, for recreation, and for other commonplace services that many without disabilities take for granted.

Individuals with physical and health disabilities often require highly specialized interventions to realize their maximum potential. Moreover, the range of medical services, educational placements, and therapies is extremely diverse and highly specific to the person and his or her needs. Students with physical and health disabilities may be served in general education, special education, hospital, home, or residential settings.

This chapter concludes with a discussion of several pressing social and health-related problems. Although not typically included in a chapter dealing with physical or health disabilities, these problems are of vital importance to many families, neighborhoods, schools, as well as local and state governments. They include child abuse and neglect, adolescent pregnancy, suicide in youth, and parental drug and alcohol abuse. Each problem will be discussed in some depth, with emphasis on current interventions or prevention strategies.

PHYSICAL DISABILITIES

The discussion of physical disabilities will be limited to a representative sample of physically disabling conditions: cerebral palsy, spina bifida, spinal cord injuries, and muscular dystrophy.

Cerebral Palsy

■ DEFINITIONS AND CONCEPTS

erebral palsy (CP) is a disability resulting from damage to the brain either before, during, or after birth. Evidenced by motor problems, general physical weakness, lack of coordination, and speech disorders, the syndrome is not contagious, progressive, or remittent. Its seriousness and overall impact can range from very mild to very severe. Individuals with cerebral palsy have poor coordination, irregular movement patterns, and poor balance, or a blend of these characteristics (Miller & Bachrach, 1995). There are three major types of CP: "spastic—stiff and difficult movement; athetoid—involuntary and uncontrolled movement; ataxic—disturbed sense of balance and depth perception" (United Cerebral Palsy, 1997a, p. 2).

CP is a complicated and perplexing condition. Individuals with CP are likely to have mild to severe problems in nonmotor areas of functioning, including hearing impairments, speech and language disorders, intellectual deficits, visual impairments, and general perceptual problems. Because of the multifaceted nature of this condition, many individuals with CP are considered to be multidisabled. Thus, CP cannot be characterized by a set of homogeneous symptoms; it is a condition in which a variety of problems may be present in differing degrees of severity.

focus 1
Why are many individuals with cerebral palsy considered multidisabled?

■ PREVALENCE AND CAUSATION

In the United States, 500,000 children and adults present one or more of the features of CP (United Cerebral Palsy, 1997a). The prevalence of CP is about 4 to 5 per 2,000 live births (Miller et al., 1995). These figures fluctuate according to several variables. For example, some children born with severe forms of CP do not survive, and the birth prevalence rate does not include these children who die. Other children may be diagnosed with CP several months or years after their births.

The causes of CP are varied (see Table 15.1). Any condition that can adversely affect the brain can cause CP. Chronic disease, premature birth, maternal infection, birth trauma, blood incompatibility, fetal infection, and postbirth infection may all be sources of this neurological–motor disorder (United Cerebral Palsy, 1997a).

TABLE 15.1   Factors influencing the occurrence of cerebral palsy

PERIOD OF TIME	FACTORS
Preconception (parental background)	■ Biological aging (parent or parents over age 35) ■ Biological immaturity (very young parent or parents) ■ Environmental toxins ■ Genetic background and genetic disorders ■ Malnutrition ■ Radiation damage
First trimester of pregnancy (0 to 3 months)	*Early weeks:* ■ Nutrition: malnutrition, vitamin deficiencies, amino acid intolerance ■ Toxins: alcohol, drugs, poisons, toxins from smoking *Late weeks:* ■ Maternal disease: thyrotoxicosis (abrupt over secretion of thyroid hormone, resulting in elevated heart rate and potential coma), genetic disorders ■ Nutrition: malnutrition, amino acid intolerance
Second trimester of pregnancy (3+ to 6 months)	*Early weeks:* ■ Infection: CM (cytomegalo) virus, rubella, HIV, syphilis, chicken pox, uterine infection *Late weeks:* ■ Placental abnormalities, vascular blockages, fetal malnutrition, chronic hypoxia, growth factor deficiencies
Third trimester of pregnancy (6+ to 9 months)	*Early weeks:* ■ Prematurity and low birthweight ■ Blood factors: Rh incompatibility, jaundice ■ Cytokines: neurological tissue destruction ■ Inflammation and infection of the uterine lining *Late weeks:* ■ Prematurity and low birthweight ■ Hypoxia: insufficient blood flow to the placenta, perinatal hypoxia ■ Infection: listeria, meningitis, streptococcus group B (bacterial infection), septicemia (bacteria growing in the blood stream), inflammation and infection of the uterine lining
Perinatal period and infancy (first 2 postnatal years)	■ Endocrine: hypoglycemia, hypothyroidism ■ Hypoxia: perinatal hypoxia, respiratory distress syndrome ■ Infection: meningitis, encephalitis ■ Multiple births: death of a twin or triplet ■ Stroke: hemorrhagic or embolic stroke ■ Trauma: abuse, accidents

Source: Adapted from "Cerebral Palsy: Contributing Risk Factors and Causes," Research Fact Sheets; September 1995; by United Cerebral Palsy Research and Education Foundation, Copyright 1995. Reprinted by permission.

■ INTERVENTIONS

Rather than treat CP, professionals and parents work at managing the condition and its various manifestations. It is essential that the management and interventions begin as early as the CP is diagnosed. The interventions center on the child's movement, social and emotional development, learning, speech, and hearing (United Cerebral Palsy, 1997a).

Effective interventions for the various forms of CP are based on accurate and continuous assessments. Motor deficits and other related challenges associated with CP are not unchanging, but evolve over time. Continuous assessment allows care providers to adjust treatment programs and select placement options in accordance with the emerging needs of the child or youth.

Treatment of CP involves many medical and human service specialties aggregated in *multidisciplinary* and *transdisciplinary teams* (Miller et al., 1995). These teams, composed of medical experts, physical and occupational therapists, teachers, social workers, volunteers, and family members join together to help children, youth, and adults with CP realize their full potential.

The thrust of treatment efforts depends on the nature of the problems and strengths presented by the individual child or youth. Generally, treatments are directed at preventing additional physical deformities; developing useful posture and movements; providing appropriate orthopedic surgery when needed to lengthen heel cords, hamstrings, or tendons; dealing with feeding and swallowing problems; securing suitable augmentative communication and other assistive devices; prescribing appropriate medications, and developing mobility and independence (Miller et al., 1995). Because of the multifaceted nature of CP, other specialists may also be involved, including ophthalmologists, audiologists, speech and language clinicians, and vocational and rehabilitation specialists.

Physical and occupational therapists play very significant roles in the lives of children and youth with CP. These individuals provide essentially three types of crucial services: assessments to detect deformities and deficits in movement quality; pro-

This man with cerebral palsy operates a computer using a mouth stick to press the computer keys.

gram planning such as assisting with the writing of IEPs, selection of adaptive equipment and assistive devices, and development of home programs for parents and other family members; and delivery of therapy services (Miller et al., 1995). School-centered services may include indirect treatment provided in the form of consultation, in-service training, and informal monitoring of student performance; direct service through regular treatment sessions in out-of-class settings; and in-class or multisite service delivery to students in general education classrooms, on playgrounds, in their homes, or at other community sites (Miller et al., 1995).

Recent developments in augmentative communication have a tremendous impact on children, youth, and adults with CP and other conditions that impair speech and language production. Many augmentative communication devices are electronic in nature or computer based. Once such device is the *Touch Talker* with *Minispeak*. This device provides children with symbols or icons that, when pressed in certain sequences, produce audio output such as "I'd like a quarter pounder with fries, and a large Coke, please." "I need to go to the bathroom." "Do you know what we are having for lunch?" Selecting augmentative communication devices for a child or youth is a team effort. Teachers, parents, speech and language specialists, physical and occupational therapists, and rehabilitation engineers play important roles in providing pertinent information (Miller et al., 1995).

As persons with CP move into adulthood, they may require various kinds of support, including continuing therapy, personal assistance services, independent living services, vocational training, and counseling. These kinds of support help individuals with CP realize their full potential in employment, relationships with others, and participation in their own neighborhoods and communities (United Cerebral Palsy, 1997a).

Spina Bifida

■ DEFINITIONS AND CONCEPTS

focus 2
What is spina bifida myelomeningocele?

Spina bifida is a birth defect characterized by an abnormal opening in the spinal column. It originates in the first days of pregnancy, often before a mother even knows that she is expecting a child. Through the process of cell division and differentiation, a neural tube forms in the developing fetus. At about 26–27 days this neural tube fails to completely close, for reasons not fully understood. This failure results in various forms of spina bifida, frequently involving some paralysis of various portions of the body, depending on the location of the opening (Sujansky, Stewart, & Manchester, 1997). It may or may not influence intellectual functioning. Spina bifida is usually classified as either spina bifida occulta or spina bifida cystica.

Spina bifida occulta is a very mild condition in which a small slit is present in one or more of the vertebral structures. Most people with spina bifida occulta are unaware of its presence unless they have had a spinal x-ray for diagnosis of some other condition. Spina bifida occulta has little, if any, impact on a developing infant.

Spina bifida cystica is a malformation of the spinal column in which a tumor-like sac herniates out through an opening or cleft on the infant's back (see Figure 15.1). Spina bifida cystica exists in many forms; however, two prominent forms will receive attention in this discussion: **spina bifida meningocele** and **spina bifida myelomeningocele.** In the meningocele type, the sac contains spinal fluid but no nerve tissue. In the myelomeningocele type, the sac does contain nerve tissue.

FIGURE 15.1

Side views of a normal spine (a) and spines affected by spina bifida occulta (b) and spina bifida cystica (c)

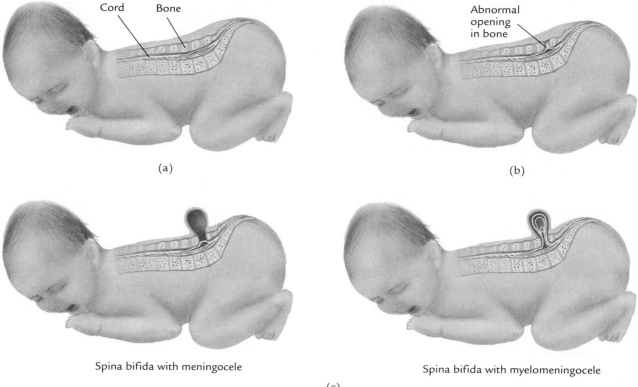

Cord   Bone

(a)

Abnormal opening in bone

(b)

Spina bifida with meningocele

Spina bifida with myelomeningocele

(c)

Spina bifida myelomeningocele is the most serious form of spina bifida. It generally results in weakness or paralysis in the legs and lower body, an inability to voluntarily control the bladder or bowel, and the presence of other orthopedic problems (club feet, dislocated hip, etc.). There are two types of myelomeningocele: one in which the tumorlike sac is open, revealing the neural tissue, and one in which the sac is closed or covered with a combination of skin and membrane.

Children with spina bifida occulta exhibit the normal range of intelligence. Most children with myelomeningocele also have normal IQs. For children whose learning capacity is normal or above average, no special educational programming is required.

■ PREVALENCE AND CAUSATION

Prevalence figures for spina bifida, both myelomeningocele and meningocele, vary. Spina bifida affects about 1 out of every 1,000 newborns in the United States (Spina Bifida Association of America, 1997).

The exact cause of spina bifida is unknown, although there is a slight tendency for the condition to run in families. In fact, myelomeningocele appears to be transmitted genetically, probably as a function of certain prenatal factors interacting with genetic predispositions. It is also possible that certain harmful agents taken by the mother prior to or at the time of conception, or during the first few days of pregnancy, may be responsible for the defect. **Teratogens** that may induce malformations in the spine include radiation, maternal hyperthermia (high fever), and excess glucose. Other causative factors include congenital rubella and chromosome abnormalities (Sujansky et al., 1997).

Folic acid deficiencies have been implicated strongly in the cause of spina bifida (Kelly, 1996; Spina Bifida Association of America, 1996b). Pregnant mothers should take particular care to augment their diets with 0.4 mg of folic acid each day. Folic acid is a common water-soluble B vitamin. Intake of this vitamin reduces the probability of neural tube defects in developing infants.

■ INTERVENTIONS

Several tests are now available to identify babies with myelomeningocele before they are born. One such test involves the analysis of the mother's blood for the presence of a specific fetal protein (alfa-fetoprotein, AFT). This protein leaks from the developing child's spine into the amniotic fluid of the uterus and subsequently enters the mother's bloodstream. If blood tests prove to be positive for this AFT, ultrasonic scanning of the fetus may be performed to confirm the diagnosis.

Confirmation of the myelomeningocele creates intense feelings in parents. If the diagnosis is early in the child's interuterine development, parents are faced with the decision of continuing or discontinuing the pregnancy. If parents decide to continue the pregnancy, they have time to process their intense feelings and to prepare for the child's birth and care. If they decide to discontinue the pregnancy, they must deal with the feelings produced by this action as well. If the condition is discovered at the time of the child's birth, it also produces powerful and penetrating feelings, the first of which is generally shock. All members of the health team (physicians, nurses, social workers, etc.) as well as other persons (religious advisers, siblings, parents, and close friends) assist in dealing with the feelings that are experienced in these situations and the decisions that must be made.

Immediate action is often called for when the child with myelomeningocele is born, depending on the nature of the lesion, its position on the spine, and the presence of other related conditions. Decisions regarding medical interventions are extremely difficult to make, for they often entail problems and issues that are not easily or quickly resolved. For example, in 80% of children with myelomeningocele, a portion of the spinal cord is exposed, placing them at great risk for developing bacterial meningitis and a subsequent mortality rate of over 50%.

The decision to undertake surgery is often made quickly if the tissue sac is located very low on the infant's back. The purpose of the surgery is to close the spinal opening and lessen the potential for infection. Another condition that often accompanies myelomeningocele is hydrocephalus, a condition characterized by excessive accumulations of cerebral fluid within the brain. More than 25% of children with myelomeningocele evidence this condition at birth. Moreover, 80% to 90% of all children with myelomeningocele develop it after they are born. Surgery may also be

Children with spina bifida have normal intelligence. The vast majority of students with spina bifida are in general education classes. This student with a serious form of spina bifida is also able to enjoy the experience of summer camp.

FIGURE 15.2

Ventriculoperitoneal shunt

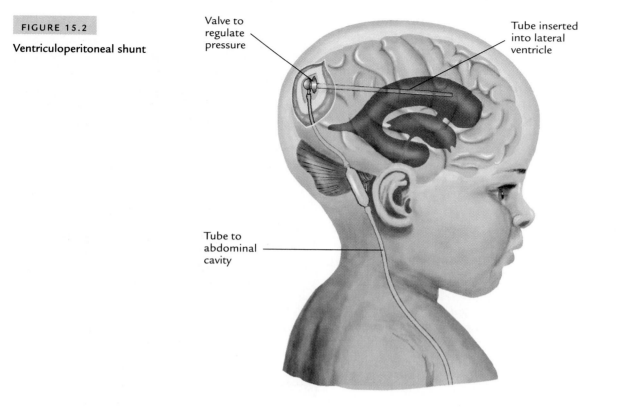

Valve to regulate pressure

Tube inserted into lateral ventricle

Tube to abdominal cavity

performed for this condition in the first days of life. The operation includes insert-ing a small silastic tube between the ventricles of the brain and connecting this tube with an absorption site in the abdomen. The excessive spinal fluid is diverted from the ventricles of the brain to a thin layer of tissue, the peritoneum that lines the ab-dominal cavity in the body (see Figure 15.2).

Children with spina bifida myelomeningocele may have little if any voluntary bowel or bladder control. This condition is directly attributable to the paralysis caused by malformation of the spinal cord and removal of the herniated sac con-taining nerve tissues. Very early on, however, children as young as 4 years old can be taught effective procedures to manage bladder problems (see the nearby Reflect on This feature). As they mature, they can develop effective regimens and proce-dures for bowel management.

Physical therapists play a critical role in helping children as they learn to cope with the paralysis caused by myelomeningocele. Paralysis obviously limits the chil-dren's exploratory activities so critical to later learning and perceptual motor per-formance. With this in mind, many such children are fitted with modified skate-boards, which allow them to explore their surroundings. Utilizing the strength in their arms and hands, they may become quite adept at exploring their home envi-ronments. Gradually, they move to leg braces, crutches, a wheelchair, or a combi-nation of the three. Some children are ambulatory and do not require the use of a wheelchair.

Education programs for students with serious forms of spina bifida vary accord-ing to the needs of each student. The vast majority of students with myelomeningo-cele are served in general education settings. School personnel can contribute to the

MANAGEMENT OF URINARY PROBLEMS

Various methods of emptying the bladder are used for students who have partial or complete loss of bladder control. A number of external urinary collection devices (condoms) have been devised for the male. For the female, a catheter is often used.

External urinary collection devices come in several styles. Usually a soft rubber sheath, or condom, is placed over the penis, and the urine is collected in an external urinary collection bag. The bag may be attached to the leg under clothing. Collection bags are suspended from a waistband; some have straps that encircle the hips for extra support. Collected urine is emptied from a conveniently placed outlet.

One method of maintaining continence is through the use of a catheter, or small rubber tube, inserted through the urethra (hollow tube carrying urine from the bladder to the outside of the body) to drain urine from the bladder into a collection bag which can be worn on the leg. Such an indwelling catheter can be changed by the individual or by the caretaker. Both males and females can be fitted with catheters. Insertion of indwelling catheters should not be considered an automatic solution to loss of control. The permanent presence of a catheter increases the likelihood of urinary infection and bladder stones. When an indwelling catheter is used, a high fluid intake is advisable. Very few students have indwelling catheters.

Another method of maintaining continence and keeping bladder infections at a minimum is clean intermittent catheterization (CIC). Catheters can be carried inconspicuously in a purse or in a small container. Clean intermittent catheterization employs nonsterile (clean) techniques. This procedure emphasizes frequency and de-emphasizes sterile techniques. Students may catheterize themselves if they can stand or sit unassisted on a toilet. Some students can also catheterize themselves in a wheelchair. Self-catheterization can be learned by children as young as 4 years old. The catheterization procedure is carried out by inserting a small plastic or rubber catheter into the bladder to drain urine every 3 to 4 hours. Some students use disposable diapers and protective pants until they achieve dryness between catheterizations.

Source: Teaching Individuals with Physical and Multiple Disabilities, by Bigge, © 1991. Reprinted by permission of Prentice-Hall, Inc., Upper Saddle River, NJ.

well-being of these students in several ways: making sure class layouts permit students to move effectively through classrooms and other settings with their crutches or wheelchairs; supporting students' efforts in using various bladder and bowel management procedures and ensuring appropriate privacy in using them; requiring these students to be as responsible as anyone else in the class for customary assignments; involving them fully in field trips, physical education, and other school-related activities; and communicating regularly with parents. Additionally, if the student has a shunt, teachers should be alert to signs of its malfunctioning, including irritability, neck pain, headache, vomiting, reduced alertness, and decline in school performance. As with all physical disabilities, collaboration and cooperation among all caregivers are critical to the well-being of each child or youth.

Spinal Cord Injury

■ DEFINITIONS AND CONCEPTS

Spinal cord injury (SCI) occurs when the spinal cord is traumatized or severed. Trauma can result through extreme extension or flexing from a fall, an automobile accident, or a sports injury. The cord can also be severed through the same types of accidents, although such occurrences are extremely rare. Usually in such cases, the cord is bruised or otherwise injured, after

Although some activities are limited, this mother with a spinal cord injury participates in playtime with her children.

which swelling and, within hours, bleeding often occur. Gradually, a self-destructive process ensues, in which the affected area slowly deteriorates and the damage becomes irreversible (Baskin, 1996).

The overall impact of injury on an individual depends on the site and nature of the insult. If the injury occurs in the neck or upper back, the resulting paralysis and effects are usually quite extensive. If the injury occurs in the lower back, paralysis is confined to the lower extremities. Like individuals with spina bifida, loss of voluntary bowel and bladder function may result from the injuries sustained in a SCI. For a brief review of the areas affected by different paralytic conditions, see Table 15.2.

Spinal cord injuries usually occur in situations that inflict other serious damage to the individual. Accompanying injuries include head trauma (15%), fractures of some portion of the trunk (20%), and significant chest injuries (15%) (Gutierrez, Vulpe, & Young, 1994).

The physical characteristics of spinal cord injuries are similar to those of spina bifida myelomeningocele except that hydrocephalus does not tend to develop. The three main types of spinal cord injuries are: **paraplegia, quadriplegia,** and **hemiplegia.** Note, however, that these terms are broad descriptions of functioning and are not precise enough to accurately convey an individual's actual level of motor functioning.

■ PREVALENCE AND CAUSATION

Spinal cord injuries are primarily a male phenomenon. Young men between the ages of 16 and 30 represent from 85% to 90% of patients treated for spinal cord injuries (Baskin, 1996). The incidence of spinal cord injuries increases during the summer months. These injuries generally occur in the early hours of the morning. Twenty-five percent of the injuries are alcohol related (Baskin, 1996). An estimated 10,000 spinal cord injuries occur each year in the United States (National Spinal Cord Injury Statistical Center, 1997).

TABLE 15.2	Topographical descriptions of paralytic conditions
DESCRIPTION	**AFFECTED AREA**
Monoplegia	One limb
Paraplegia	Lower body and both legs
Hemiplegia	One side of the body
Triplegia	Three appendages or limbs, usually both legs and one arm
Quadriplegia	All four extremities and usually the trunk
Diplegia	Legs more affected than arms
Double hemiplegia	Both halves of the body, with one side more affected than the other

Most spinal cord injuries (35.9%) result from motor vehicle crashes. The next largest cause is violent acts (26.1%), primarily gunshot wounds. The next most frequent causes of SCI are recreational sporting activities (6.9%) and falls (23.6%) (National Spinal Cord Injury Statistical Center, 1997).

■ INTERVENTIONS

The immediate care rendered to a person with an SCI is crucial. The impact of the injury can be magnified if proper procedures are not employed soon after the accident or onset of the condition.

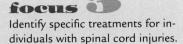

focus 3
Identify specific treatments for individuals with spinal cord injuries.

The first phase of treatment provided by a receiving hospital is the management of shock. Quickly thereafter, the individual is immobilized to prevent movement and possible further damage. As a rule, surgical procedures are not undertaken immediately. The major goal of medical treatment at this point is to stabilize the spine, manage swelling, and prevent further complications. Pharmacological interventions are critical during this phase of treatment. Recent studies support the use of high and frequent doses of methylprednisolone, an anti-inflammatory agent. This medication often reduces the severity of the injury and improves the functional outcome for the affected individual (Baskin, 1996).

Catheterization may be employed to control urine flow, and steps may be taken to reduce swelling and bleeding at the injury site. Traction may be used to stabilize certain portions of the spinal column and cord. Medical treatment of spinal cord injuries is long-term and often tedious.

Once physicians have successfully stabilized the spine and treated other medical conditions, the rehabilitation process promptly proceeds. The individual is taught to use new muscle combinations and take advantage of any and all residual muscle strength. He or she is also taught to use orthopedic equipment, such as handsplints, braces, reachers, headsticks (for typing), and plateguards. Together with an orthopedic specialist, occupational and physical therapists become responsible for the physical reeducation and training process.

Psychiatric and other support personnel also engage in rehabilitation activities (Baskin, 1996). Psychological adjustment to a spinal cord injury can take a great deal of time. The goal of all treatment is to help the injured individual become as independent as possible (see nearby Today's Technology feature).

Today's Technology

ENVIRONMENTAL CONTROL SYSTEMS

In the future, biomedical engineers, in conjunction with other health professionals, will have a profound effect on the lives of individuals with physical disabilities. Presently, a variety of environmental control systems allow those with physical disabilities to operate home appliances and other devices. These systems typically have several important components, including a visual display, a central processing unit (CPU), and a transducer (control switch). In some cases, a transducer allows individuals to activate various devices in their home environments without using their hands. The transducer can be activated by a dual control, a "sip-puff" switch, an input controller from a powered wheelchair, a computer, an electronic communication aid, or a voice-recognition component. Using these switching devices, individuals with physical disabilities can operate telephones, radios, CD players, televisions, video equipment, electronic beds, call signals for requesting assistance, intercoms, and even page turners. The visual display allows the individual to check whether the outside doors are locked, the lights are on in the kitchen, or the alarm clock has been set. If the kitchen lights have been left on, the individual can turn them off with a voiced command.

As the individual masters self-care skills, other educational and career objectives can be pursued with the assistance of the rehabilitation team. The members of this team change constantly, according to the skills and needs of the individual.

Education for individuals with spinal cord injuries is similar to that for uninjured children or adults. Teachers must be aware, however, that some individuals with spinal cord injuries will be unable to feel pressure and pain in the lower extremities, so pressure sores and skin breakdown may occur in response to prolonged sitting. Repositioning and movement will help prevent these problems. Parents and teachers should be aware of signs of depression that may accompany the school reentry process, including loss of appetite, excessive sleeping or irregular sleep patterns, reduced energy, avoidance of interaction with others, and loss of interest in daily school or work-related activities.

Muscular Dystrophy

■ DEFINITIONS AND CONCEPTS

Muscular dystrophy is a progressive disorder that affects the muscles of the hips, legs, shoulders, and arms, which over time causes individuals with this disease to lose their ability to walk and to use their arms and hands effectively. The loss of ability occurs as fatty tissue gradually replaces muscle tissue. Heart muscle may also be affected, resulting in symptoms of heart failure. There are different forms of muscular dystrophy. The seriousness of the various dystrophies is influenced by heredity, age of onset, the physical location and nature of onset, and the rate at which the condition progresses.

focus 4
Describe the physical limitations associated with muscular dystrophy.

Duchenne type muscular dystrophy (DMD) is the most severe form of dystrophy. DMD generally manifests itself between the ages of 2 and 5. Early in the second decade of life, individuals with DMD must use wheelchairs to move from place to place. By the second or early in the third decade of life, young adults with DMD die from respiratory insufficiency or cardiac failure (Kelly, 1996).

DMD is first evidenced in the pelvic girdle, although it sometimes begins in the shoulder girdle muscles. With the passage of time, individuals begin to experience a loss of respiratory function and are unable to cough up secretions that may result in pneumonias. Also, severe spinal curvature develops over time with wheelchair use; this condition can be prevented through spinal fusion.

■ PREVALENCE AND CAUSATION

About 200,000 people are affected by muscular dystrophies and related disorders. About 1 in every 3,000 to 3,500 males is affected by DMD. Mothers who are carriers transmit this condition to 50% of their male offspring. One third of the cases of DMD arise by mutation in families with no history of the disease.

Molecular genetics has contributed greatly to our understanding of neuromuscular diseases and their causes. In some cases, the specific genetic locus of the dystrophy can be identified. Such is the case with DMD (Kelly, 1996), which is tied to a sex-linked recessive gene. Additionally, the biochemical defects associated with various dystrophies can now be recognized.

■ INTERVENTIONS

There is no known cure for muscular dystrophy. The focus of treatment is maintaining or improving the individual's functioning and preserving his or her ambulatory independence for as long as possible. The first phases of maintenance and prevention are handled by a physical therapist, who works to prevent or correct contractures (a permanent shortening and thickening of muscle fibers). As the condition becomes more serious, treatment generally includes prescribing supportive devices, such as walkers, braces, nightsplints, surgical corsets, and hospital beds. Eventually, the person with muscular dystrophy will need to use a wheelchair.

People with muscular dystrophy are frequently given some type of medication in hopes of increasing muscle strength and counteracting the disease's effect on the heart. If a child receives medication, parents and teachers play important roles in observing any peculiar reactions that may occur and reporting these to parents and physicians.

The terminal nature of DMD poses challenging problems to affected individuals, their families, and caregivers. Fortunately, significant progress has been made in helping individuals with terminal illnesses deal with death. Programs developed for families who have a terminally ill child, youth, or adult serve several purposes. They give children with terminal illnesses opportunities to ask questions about death, to express their concerns, and to work through their feelings about death. Programs for parents are designed to help them understand their children's conceptions about death, to suggest ways in which they might respond to certain questions or concerns, and to relate the steps they might take in successfully preparing for and responding to the child's death and related events (Stevens & Dunsmore, 1996).

HEALTH DISABILITIES

Health disabilities affect children, youth, and adults in a variety of ways. For example, a child with juvenile diabetes who has engaged in a vigorous game of volleyball with classmates may need to drink a little fruit juice or soda pop just before or after the activity to regulate blood sugar levels. An adult with diabetes may need to follow a special diet regimen and regularly receive appropriate doses of insulin. By way of review, IDEA describes persons with health disabilities as individuals with "limited strength, vitality or alertness, due to chronic or acute health problems such as a heart condition, tuberculosis, rheumatic fever, nephritis, asthma, sickle cell anemia, hemophilia, epilepsy, lead poisoning, leukemia, or diabetes which adversely affect . . . educational performance" (23 Code of Federal Regulations, Sec. 300.5 [7]).

Not all of these health conditions will be discussed in this portion of the chapter. Acquired immune deficiency syndrome (AIDS), seizure disorders (epilepsy), diabetes, cystic fibrosis (CF), and sickle cell anemia (SCA) will be reviewed in some depth.

Acquired Immune Deficiency Syndrome (AIDS)

■ DEFINITIONS AND CONCEPTS

AIDS in children and youth is defined by the following characteristics: (1) the presence of the **human immunodeficiency virus (HIV)**, a virus that attacks specialized white cells within the body,

focus 5

What steps should be taken to assist infants and children with AIDS?

and/or the presence of antibodies to HIV in the blood or tissues, as well as (2) recurrent bacterial diseases. The first reports regarding some of the features of AIDS, received by the Centers for Disease Control in the spring of 1981, dealt exclusively with young men who had a rare form of pneumonia. Reports were received simultaneously by the Centers for Disease Control regarding an increased incidence of a rare skin tumor, Kaposi's sarcoma. Individuals who had developed these conditions were homosexual men in their 30s and 40s. Many died or were severely debilitated within 12 months of diagnosis.

Prior to the spring of 1981, primary-care physicians in New York, San Francisco, and other large cities had seen many cases of swollen lymph nodes in homosexual men. Many of these individuals exhibited this condition for months or even years after their initial diagnosis, without suffering serious side effects. However, those who developed **opportunistic infections** often experienced severe side effects or even death. Eventually, these opportunistic infections were linked to a breakdown in the functioning of the **immune system.** People with these infections exhibit pronounced depletions of a particular subset of white blood cells, T lymphocytes. White blood cells fight infections; without sufficient numbers and kinds of them, the body is rendered defenseless. Individuals with this condition become subject to a wide range of opportunistic infections and tumors affecting the gastrointestinal system, central nervous system, and skin.

Individuals with AIDS move through a series of disease stages (Bellinir & Dresser, 1995; Kalichman, 1995). The first stage is the exposure stage, the period during which the transmission of the HIV occurs. The second stage is characterized by the production of antibodies in infected individuals. These antibodies appear about 2 to 12 weeks after the initial transmission of the virus. About 30% of individuals experience flu-like symptoms for a few days to several weeks. During stage three, the immune system declines, and the virus begins to destroy cells of the immune system. However, many individuals with HIV show few if any symptoms at all during this stage. This asymptomatic phase may continue for 3 to 10 years. About half of all individuals with HIV develop AIDS within 10 years. For children, the onset of AIDS ranges from 1 to 3 years. At stage four, individuals begin to manifest symptoms of a damaged immune system, including weight loss, fatigue, skin rashes, and night sweats. In more severe cases, opportunistic diseases begin to evidence themselves in individuals with AIDS. At stage five, recurrent and chronic diseases begin to take their toll. Gradually the immune system fails and death occurs. (See Table 15.3 for psychological stages of terminally ill persons.)

Children with AIDS are generally diagnosed between 2 months and 3 years of age. Presenting problems include diarrhea, failure to thrive, and acute signs such as respiratory failure or life-threatening bacterial infections (Parks, 1996).

■ PREVALENCE AND CAUSATION

Lafferty and Hopkins (1996) suggested that 800,000 to 1 million individuals in the United States are infected with HIV. About 1 of every 250 Americans—about 1 of every 100 men and about 1 of every 800 women—is infected with this virus (Bellinir & Dresser, 1995).

Information regarding the prevalence of AIDS among children and youth is far less accurate and complete than that for adults. About 1% of the recognized cases of AIDS involve children and youth (Sigel, 1997). Recent studies suggest that about 0.17% of childbearing women in the United States test positive for HIV. These mothers give

| TABLE 15.3 | Psychological "stages" encountered by persons who are terminally ill |

1. *Denial.* Patients totally reject the reality or even the remote possibility that they will die soon.

2. *Anger.* This stage indicates the first real step toward acceptance and marks the end of the difficult period of denial. It is characterized by the question, "Why me?" Rage and resentment are most often ventilated against healthy people who represent those things that the dying person will lose.

3. *Bargaining.* The patient promises something in exchange for prolongation of life. The promise is often religious, for example, "If You (God) give me one more year to live, I will attend church [or synagogue] regularly." Such compromise marks the beginning of the person's recognition of his limited time.

4. *Depression.* When no longer able to deny the illness, when forced to undergo more surgery or hospitalization, or when thinner and weaker, the person can no longer deny the impending death. Depression may be preparatory for the total loss of everything and everyone the person loves. The person should be allowed to express grief and mourning, encouraging completion of this stage more quickly and easily.

5. *Acceptance.* If given enough time and help in adjusting, the person may reach a stage where he or she is neither depressed nor angry about his fate. Granted, the person is not joyfully happy; but the struggle is over, and the person accepts reality. In this stage, the person who is dying begins to separate from interpersonal relationships and may prefer the company of only one loved one. The fear, bitterness, anguish, and concern about unfinished business is gone. Comfort consists of having someone there who is quietly reassuring.

Source: Teaching Individuals with Physical and Multiple Disabilities, by Bigge, © 1991. Reprinted by permission of Prentice-Hall, Inc., Upper Saddle River, NJ.

birth to about 7,000 children each year (Lafferty & Hopkins, 1996). Adolescents account for less than 1% of the individuals with AIDS in the United States.

The cause of AIDS is the human immunodeficiency virus (HIV). This virus is passed from one person to another through sexual contact that includes the exchange of bodily fluids, usually semen or vaginal secretions; blood exchange through injection drug use (IDU) and transfusions; perinatal contact; and breast milk (Bellenir & Dresser, 1995; Lafferty & Hopkins, 1996).

Eighty percent of adolescents develop AIDS through sexual activity or intravenous drug use. Adolescent males acquire the HIV infection primarily through homosexual activity. Young females generally acquire the infection through heterosexual activity. In most cases, the transmission of HIV to adolescents occurs through relations with older men who have been sexually active for long periods of time.

Several factors will influence the prevalence figures and deaths related to AIDS in the United States and the world. These include (1) the success or failure of various education and prevention programs, (2) the emergence of new treatments for AIDS, and (3) the appearance of new, related viruses such as HIV-2 (Lafferty & Hopkins, 1996).

■ INTERVENTIONS

To date, there is no known cure for AIDS, although much work is being done to test new drugs (e.g., didanosine, zalcitabine, and nevirapine). Progress is being made, and certain agents are now ready for testing or have been tested in human beings. Despite this progress, 10% to 15% of children born with HIV develop AIDS in the first months of life and die shortly thereafter, and another 15% to 20% develop AIDS following the infancy period. From 65% to 75% of children who test positive for HIV thrive.

Early diagnosis of infants with HIV is crucial. Early antiviral therapy and prophylactic treatment of opportunistic diseases can contribute significantly to the infected child's well-being and positive prognosis over time. The frequency and nature of treatment depend on the age of onset and the age at which the child develops the first opportunistic infection (Bellenir & Dresser, 1995).

Providing appropriate interventions for infants with AIDS can be challenging. These infants, like those without AIDS, are totally dependent on others for their care. Many mothers who pass the AIDS virus on to their children are not prepared to care effectively for their infants. Typically, these mothers come from impoverished environments with little access to health care and other appropriate support services. Additionally, these mothers are often intravenous drug users and as such are not reliable caregivers (Briere et al., 1996).

The Centers for Disease Control developed a number of recommendations in responding to children and youth with AIDS in day-care centers and schools. Placement for education and care should be based on "the behavior, neurologic development, and physical condition of the child and the expected type of interaction" (Hanlon, 1991, p. 695). The only children or youth who should be excluded from these settings are those "who lack control of body secretions, or who display behavior, such as biting, and those children who have uncoverable, oozing lesions" (Hanlon, 1991, p. 695).

Treating adolescents with HIV and AIDS can be very challenging. For example, ensuring that they comply with medical regimens is difficult. Those who have HIV yet show no obvious symptoms may neglect keeping regular medical appointments and taking antiviral medications because they wish to avoid these constant re-

If prevention is the most effective means of controlling the spread of AIDS, adolescents must be fully informed about the nature and cause of the disease.

minders that they have contracted a potentially fatal disease. Youth with HIV and AIDS need to learn how to make medical regimens a regular part of their lives in order to maintain good health and longevity. They also need assistance in dealing with the psychological reactions of anxiety and depression that often accompany the discovery that they have HIV. Finally, they and others benefit significantly from instruction directed at helping them understand AIDS, making wise decisions about their sexual behavior, using assertiveness skills, and effectively communicating with others (Parks, 1996).

At this point, prevention is the single most effective means of controlling the spread of AIDS (McFarland, 1997). At the heart of prevention is informed choice and individual empowerment to make responsible decisions regarding one's own health, as well as that of others. Current health education programs emphasize health enhancement and an understanding of the personal, social, environmental, and economic factors that influence behavior, rather than merely distributing information about the causes and effects of AIDS.

Seizure Disorders (Epilepsy)

▪ DEFINITIONS AND CONCEPTS

Seizure disorders or epilepsies "are a group of conditions marked by recurrent seizures, which are clinical manifestations of abnormal discharges in the brain" (Lerner, 1995, p. 133). A **seizure** is a cluster of behaviors that occurs in response to abnormal neurochemical activity in the brain. It typically has the effect of altering the individual's level of consciousness while simultaneously resulting in certain characteristic motor patterns (Haslam, 1996). Several classification schemes have been employed to describe the various types of seizure disorders (see Table 15.4 on page 480). We will briefly discuss two types of seizures: tonic/clonic and absence.

Generalized **tonic-clonic seizures,** formerly called *grand mal seizures,* affect the entire brain. The **tonic** phase of these seizures is characterized by a stiffening of the body, the **clonic** phase by repeated muscle contractions and relaxations. Tonic/clonic seizures are often preceded by a warning signal known as an **aura,** in which the individual senses a unique sound, odor, or physical sensation just prior to the onset of the seizure. In some instances, the seizure is also signaled by a cry or other similar sound. The tonic phase of the seizure begins with a loss of consciousness, after which the individual falls to the ground. Initially, the trunk and head of the body become rigid during the tonic phase. The clonic phase follows and consists of involuntary muscle contractions (violent shaking) of the extremities. Irregular breathing, blueness in the lips and face, increased salivation, loss of bladder and bowel control, and perspiration may occur to some degree.

The nature, scope, frequency, and duration of tonic/clonic seizures vary greatly from person to person. Such seizures may last as long as 20 minutes or less than 1 minute. One of the most dangerous aspects of tonic/clonic seizures is potential injury from falling and striking objects in the environment. In responding to this type of seizure, it is best to ease the person to the floor, if possible; remove any dangerous objects from the immediate vicinity; place a soft pad under his or her head, such

focus 6

Describe immediate treatment for a person who is experiencing a tonic/clonic seizure.

TABLE 15.4 Types of seizures

SEIZURE TYPE	CHARACTERISTICS
Partial Seizures	
■ Simple partial (retain consciousness)	■ Tonic/clonic movements, involving the face, neck, or extremities; head and eyes may turn to one side; aura may precede the seizure; may persist for 10–20 minutes; consciousness is maintained
■ Complex partial (lose consciousness)	■ Altered consciousness; blank or glazed look; automatisms (lip smacking, continual swallowing movements, and chewing); semipurposeful movements (buttoning, repetitive rubbing, or pulling clothing)
Generalized Seizures	
■ Absence seizures	■ Formerly known as petit mal seizures; brief periods of staring, inattention, and loss of concentration; usually lasting less than 30 seconds; interruptions of speech; brief fluttering of the eyelids; reception and retention of instruction may be compromised
■ Generalized tonic/clonic seizures	■ Sudden loss of consciousness; may result in falling; eyes roll upward; respirations may momentarily cease; rhythmic synchronous movements of the body and face may occur (clonic); arms and legs may become rigid (tonic); usually followed by relaxed posture, moans, drowsiness, and sleep
■ Myclonic seizures	■ Brief symmetrical muscular contractions with loss of body tone; may result in falling and thereby trauma to face and mouth; may present developmental delays in functioning; may be accompanied by tonic/clonic seizures; may present learning and behavioral problems

Source: Adapted from "Common Neurological Disorders in Children," by R. H. A. Haslam. In *Medical Problems in the Classroom*, by R. H. A. Haslam & O. J. Valletutti, 1996, pp. 314–320. Austin, TX: Pro-Ed, Inc. Reprinted by permission.

as a coat or blanket; and allow him or her to rest after the seizure has terminated. Nothing should be placed in the person's mouth.

A period of sleepiness and confusion usually follows a tonic/clonic seizure. The individual may exhibit drowsiness, nausea, headache, or a combination of these symptoms. Such symptoms should be treated with appropriate rest, medication, or other therapeutic remedies. Seizure characteristics and after effects vary and should be treated with this in mind.

Absence seizures, formerly identified as *petit mal seizures,* are characterized by brief periods (moments or seconds) of inattention that may be accompanied by rapid eye blinking and head twitching. During these seizures, the brain ceases to function as it normally would. The individual's consciousness is altered in an almost imperceptible manner. People with this type of seizure disorder may experience these seizures as often as 100 times a day. Such inattentive behavior may be viewed as daydreaming by a teacher or work supervisor, but the episode is really due to a momentary burst of abnormal brain activity that the individual does not consciously control. The lapses in attention caused by this form of epilepsy can greatly hamper the individual's ability to respond properly to or profit from a teacher's presentation or a supervisor's instruction. Treatment and control of absence seizures are generally achieved through prescribed medication.

■ PREVALENCE AND CAUSATION

Prevalence figures for seizure disorders vary, in part because of the social stigma associated with them. Seizure disorders or epilepsies occur in about 0.5% to 0.7% of the population (Haslam, 1996; Zimmerman & Kingsley, 1997). Seventy-five percent of all individuals who have seizures experience their first one prior to their 18th birthday (Dreifuss, 1988).

The causes of seizure disorders are many, including perinatal factors, tumors of the brain, complications of head trauma, infections of the central nervous system, vascular diseases, and genetic factors. Also, some seizures are caused by ingestion of street drugs, toxic chemicals, and poison (Haslam, 1996).

■ INTERVENTIONS

The treatment of seizure disorders begins with a careful medical investigation in which the physician develops a detailed health history of the individual and completes an in-depth physical examination. Moreover, it is essential that the physician receive a thorough description of the actual seizure itself. These preliminary treatment steps may be followed by other diagnostic procedures, including blood tests, CT scans or MRIs, and spinal fluid taps to determine if the individual has meningitis. EEGs may also be performed to confirm clinical impressions of the physician. However, it should be noted that many seizure disorders are not detectable through electroencephalographic measures.

Many types of seizures can be treated successfully with a carefully managed regimen of drug therapy. Significant headway has been made with the discovery of effective drugs, particularly for children with tonic/clonic, complex partial, and absence seizures. Anticonvulsant drugs must be chosen very carefully, however. The potential risk and benefit of each medication must be balanced. Once a drug has been prescribed, families should be educated in its use to be aware of any side effects and the necessity for consistent administration (Haslam, 1996). Maintaining a regular medication regimen can be very challenging for children and their parents. In some instances, medication may be discontinued after several years of seizure-free behavior. This is particularly true for young children who do not have some form of underlying brain pathology.

Other treatments for seizure disorders include surgery, stress management, and diet modifications. The goal of surgery is to remove that precise part of the brain that is damaged and causing the seizures (Zimmerman & Kingsley, 1997). Surgery is considered for individuals with uncontrollable seizures, essentially those who have not responded well to anticonvulsant medications. Using a variety of sophisticated scanning procedures, physicians attempt to isolate the damaged area of the brain that corresponds with the seizure activity. The outcomes of surgery for children and youth with well-defined foci of seizure activity are excellent (Haslam, 1996). Obviously the surgery must be done with great care. Brain tissue, once removed, is gone forever. Additionally, the function that the tissue performed will be entirely eliminated or can be only marginally restored (Zimmerman & Kingsley, 1997).

Stress management is designed to improve the child's or youth's general functioning. Because seizures are often associated with illnesses, inadequate rest, and other stressors, parents and other care providers work at helping children, youth, and adults understand the importance of attending consistently to their medication routines, developing emotional resilience, and maintaining healthful patterns of behavior.

Diet modifications alter the way in which the body uses energy from food. Typically, our bodies convert the carbohydrates we consume into glucose (sugar). Several types of seizures can be controlled by instituting a ketogenic diet. When following this diet, individuals consume fats rather than carbohydrates. Instead of producing glucose, they produce ketones, a special kind of molecule. This change in food consumption changes the metabolism of the brain, which normally uses sugars to "fire" its functions. For reasons that are not completely understood, the brain is less receptive to certain kinds of seizures under this diet. However, the diet is extraordinarily difficult to maintain on a long-term basis (Zimmerman & Kingsley, 1997).

Individuals with seizure disorders need calm and supportive responses from others. Treatment efforts of various professionals and family members must be carefully orchestrated to provide these individuals with opportunities to use their abilities and talents. Educators should be aware of the basic fundamentals of seizure disorders and their management. Also, they should be aware of their critical role in observing seizures that may occur at school. The astute observations of a teacher may be invaluable to a health care team in developing appropriate medical interventions for the child or youth.

Diabetes

■ DEFINITIONS AND CONCEPTS

Diabetes mellitus is a developmental or hereditary disorder characterized by inadequate secretion or use of **insulin,** which is produced by the pancreas to process carbohydrates. There are basically two types of diabetes mellitus: insulin-dependent diabetes mellitus (IDDM), commonly known as Type I or juvenile onset, and noninsulin-dependent diabetes mellitus (NIDDM), referred to as Type II or adult onset (Bellenir & Dresser, 1994; Daneman & Frank, 1996).

Glucose—a sugar that is one of the end products of digesting carbohydrates—is used by the body for energy. Some glucose is used quickly, while some is stored in the liver and muscles for later use. However, muscle and liver cells cannot absorb and store glucose without insulin, a hormone produced by the pancreas that converts glucose into energy for use in body cells to perform their various functions. Without insulin, glucose accumulates in the blood, causing a condition known as hyperglycemia. Left untreated, this condition can cause serious, immediate problems for people with IDDM, leading to loss of consciousness or diabetic coma (Children with Diabetes, 1997a).

Typical symptoms associated with glucose buildup in the blood are extreme hunger, thirst, and frequent urination. Although progress has been made in regulating insulin levels, the prevention and treatment of the complications that accompany diabetes—including blindness, cardiovascular disease, and kidney disease—still pose tremendous challenges for health care specialists.

IDDM, or juvenile onset diabetes, is particularly troublesome. Compared to the adult form, this disease tends to be more severe and progresses more quickly. Generally, the symptoms are easily recognized. The child develops an unusual thirst for water and other liquids. His or her appetite also increases substantially, but listlessness and fatigue occur despite increased food and liquid intake (Daneman & Frank, 1996).

focus 7

Identify three problems that individuals with diabetes may eventually experience.

NIDDM is the most common form of diabetes and is often associated with obesity in individuals over age 40. Individuals with this form of diabetes are at less risk for diabetic coma, and most individuals can manage the disorder through exercise and dietary restrictions. If these actions fail, insulin therapy may be necessary (Bellenir & Dresser, 1994).

■ PREVALENCE AND CAUSATION

It is estimated that 5% of the U.S. population has diabetes. The prevalence rate for children with insulin-dependent (i.e., must administer insulin) diabetes is approximately 10 to 15 per 100,000 children and youth under age 20. About 800,000 individuals have Type I or juvenile onset diabetes. Also, an additional 30,000 individuals in the United States develop the condition each year (Children with Diabetes, 1997a).

The causes of diabetes remain obscure, although considerable research has been conducted on the biochemical mechanisms responsible for it (Daneman & Frank, 1996). Diabetes develops gradually in individuals. Individuals with Type I diabetes have a genetic predisposition for the disease (Children with Diabetes, 1997a). A youngster's environment and heredity interact in determining the severity and the long-term nature of the condition. However, even in identical twins, when one twin develops Type I diabetes, the other twin is affected only 50% of the time. There must be an environmental trigger that activates the onset of the disease. Some researchers believe that to be a particular virus, *Coxsachie B*. Progressively, the body's immune system is affected and the destruction of beta cells occurs. These are the cells in the pancreas that produce and regulate insulin production. Without insulin the youngster develops the classic symptoms of Type I diabetes: excessive thirst, urination, and hunger; weight loss; fatigue; blurred vision; and high blood sugar levels (Children with Diabetes, 1997a).

■ INTERVENTIONS

Medical treatment centers on the regular administration of insulin, which is essential for children and youth with juvenile diabetes. Several exciting advances have been made in recent years to monitor blood sugar levels and deliver insulin to people with diabetes. Recent success with pancreas transplants has virtually eliminated the disease for some individuals. Also, significant progress is being made with the development of the bioartificial pancreas (Children with Diabetes, 1997b) and gene therapy (Cable News Network, 1997). Interestingly, Type I diabetes in animals has been delayed or even prevented with injection of insulin and specific enzymes (Children with Diabetes, 1997b).

Maintaining normal levels of glucose is now achieved in many instances with an insulin infusion pump, which is worn by persons with diabetes and powered by small batteries. The infusion pump operates continuously and delivers the dose of insulin determined by the physician and the patient. This form of treatment is effective only if used in combination with carefully followed diet and exercise programs.

Juvenile diabetes is a lifelong condition that can have a pronounced effect on the child in a number of areas. Possible complications for children with long-standing diabetes include blindness, heart attacks, and kidney problems. Many of these problems can be delayed or prevented by maintaining adequate blood sugar levels with appropriate food intake and insulin injections.

Cystic Fibrosis

■ DEFINITIONS AND CONCEPTS

Cystic fibrosis (CF) is an inherited, systemic, generalized disease that begins at conception. Although the lifespan of persons with CF has been lengthened through new treatments, death within the early adult years is often inevitable. CF is a disorder of the secretion glands, which produce abnormal amounts of mucus, sweat, and saliva. Three major organ systems are affected: the lungs, pancreas, and sweat glands. The gluelike mucus in the lungs obstructs their functioning and increases the likelihood of infection, gradually destroying the lungs after repeated infections (Kelly, 1996; Minty, 1996). Lung deterioration places a burden on the heart, and heart failure may result. The pancreas is affected in a similar fashion; excessive amounts of mucus prevent critical digestive enzymes from reaching the small intestine. Without these enzymes, proteins and fats consumed by the individual with CF are lost in frequent, greasy, flatulent stools.

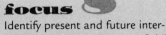

focus 8

Identify present and future interventions for the treatment of children and youth with cystic fibrosis.

■ PREVALENCE AND CAUSATION

Cystic fibrosis is primarily a Caucasian phenomenon. It affects 1 in 3,300 live births among Caucasian children living in North America, England, Europe, and Australia. Among African Americans, the prevalence rate is about 1 in 17,000. CF is virtually absent in the countries of Japan and China. Males and females appear to be influenced in about equal numbers (Hill & Lebenthal, 1995). The median survival age for individuals with CF is 30.1 years (Cystic Fibrosis Foundation, 1996a).

CF is a genetically transmitted disease. The gene for the CF transfer regulator (CFTR) is very large, and some 2,000 mutations have already been identified (Rudolph & Kamei, 1994). CFTR, a protein, produces improper transportation of sodium and salt (chloride) within cells that line organs such as the lungs and pancreas (Cystic Fibrosis Foundation, 1996a; Minty, 1996). CFTR prevents chloride from exiting these cells. This blockage affects a broad range of organs and systems in the body, including reproductive organs in men and women, the lungs, sweat glands, and the digestive system (Cystic Fibrosis Foundation, 1996a; Kelly, 1996; Minty, 1996).

■ INTERVENTIONS

The prognosis for an individual with CF depends on a number of factors. The two most critical are early diagnosis of the condition and the quality of care provided after diagnosis. If diagnosis occurs late, irreversible damage may be present. With early diagnosis and appropriate medical care, most individuals with CF can achieve weight and growth gains similar to those of their normal peers. Early diagnosis and improved treatment strategies have lengthened the average lifespan of children with CF; more than half now live beyond their 30th year (Minty, 1996).

The best and most comprehensive treatment is provided through CF centers located throughout the United States. These centers provide experienced medical and support staff (respiratory care personnel, social workers, dieticians, genetic counselors, and psychologists). Moreover, they maintain diagnostic laboratories especially equipped to perform pulmonary function testing and sweat testing. Sweat of children with CF has abnormal concentrations of sodium or chloride; in fact, sweat tests provide the definitive data for a diagnosis of CF in infants and young children (Hill & Lebenthal, 1995).

Interventions for CF are varied and complex, with treatment continuing throughout the person's lifetime. Consistent and appropriate application of medical, social, educational, and psychological components of treatment allows these individuals to live longer and with less discomfort and fewer complications than in years past.

Treatment of CF is designed to accomplish a number of goals. The first is to diagnose the condition before any severe symptoms are exhibited. Other goals include control of chest infection, maintenance of adequate nutrition, education of the family regarding the condition, and provision of a suitable education for the child.

Management of respiratory disease caused by CF is critical. If respiratory insufficiency can be prevented or minimized, the individual's life will be greatly enhanced and prolonged. Antibiotic drugs, postural drainage (chest physical therapy), and medicated vapors play important roles in the medical management of CF (Cystic Fibrosis Foundation, 1996a; Kelly, 1996).

Diet management is also essential for the child with CF. Generally, the child with this condition requires more caloric intake than his or her normal peers. The diet should be high in protein and adjusted appropriately if the child fails to grow and make appropriate weight gains. Individuals with CF benefit significantly from the use of replacement enzymes that assist with food absorption (Kelly, 1996). Also, the intake of vitamins is very important to individuals with digestive system problems.

The major social and psychological problems of children with CF relate to chronic coughing, small stature, offensive stools, gas, delayed onset of puberty and secondary sex characteristics, and unsatisfying social relationships. Also, these children and youth may spend a significant amount of time away from school settings. Thus teachers, counselors, and other support personnel play essential roles in helping these students feel at home in school settings, making up past work, and forming friendships with others. Moreover, support groups play important roles in helping students with CF understand themselves and their disease, while developing personal resilience and ongoing friendships.

Exciting new interventions for CF are being explored, including gene therapy, lung transplants, mucus-thinning drugs, and the use of high doses of ibuprofen with young children. Gene therapy is particularly promising as it addresses the root cause of CF. Researchers are experimenting with a modified cold virus and other mechanisms (nose drops, flexible tube, and fat capsules) to deliver normal genes to damaged airways in individuals with CF. These normal genes promote the repair of defective CF cells (Cystic Fibrosis Foundation, 1996b).

Sickle Cell Anemia

■ DEFINITIONS AND CONCEPTS

Sickle cell anemia (SCA) is an inherited disorder that profoundly affects the function and structure of red blood cells. The hemoglobin molecule in the red blood cells of individuals with SCA is abnormal, in that it is vulnerable to structural collapse when the blood-oxygen level is significantly diminished. As the blood-oxygen level declines,

focus 9

Describe the impact of the sickling of cells on body tissues.

these blood cells become distorted and form bizarre shapes. This process, known as *sickling*, distorts the normal donutlike shapes of cells to resemble microscopic sickle blades. Obstructions in vessels of affected individuals can lead to stroke and damage of other organs in the body.

People affected by sickle cell anemia experience unrelenting **anemia.** In some cases, it is tolerated well; in others, the condition is quite debilitating. Another aspect of SCA involves frequent infections; periodic vascular blockage, which occurs as the sickled cells obstruct microvascular channels, can often cause severe and chronic pain in the extremities, abdomen, or back. In addition, the disease may affect any organ system of the body. SCA also has a significant negative effect on the physical growth and development of infants and children (Med Access, 1996a).

■ PREVALENCE AND CAUSATION

Approximately 1 in 400 African American infants has SCA (Med Access, 1996a). Moreover, about 7% to 10% of African Americans carry the sickle cell gene (Ezekowitz & First, 1994). Sickle cell disease is most prevalent in areas of the world in which malaria is widespread. "If a parasite infects a red cell that contains sickle hemoglobin, the cell automatically undergoes sickling, sequesters the parasite, destroys it along with its cell" (Ezekowitz & First, 1994, p. 570). Thus, the protective effect of this hemoglobin performs some important functions in certain parts of the world in combating potentially fatal malarial infections (Kelly, 1996; Med Access, 1996b).

Sickle cell anemia is caused by various combinations of genes. A child who receives a mutant S-hemoglobin gene from each parent exhibits SCA to one degree or another. The disease usually presents itself at 6 months of age and continues throughout the individual's lifetime.

■ INTERVENTIONS

A number of treatments may be employed to deal with the problems caused by sickle cell anemia; however, the first step is early diagnosis. Babies should be screened at birth, particularly infants who are at risk for this disease. Early diagnosis lays the groundwork for the prophylactic use of antibiotics to prevent infections in the first 5 years of life. This treatment, coupled with appropriate immunizations and nutrition, prevents further complications of the disease (Med Access, 1996a). Moreover, these treatments significantly reduce the death rate associated with SCA. In recent years, as many as 40% of the children with SCA died from infections.

Children, youth, and adults usually learn to adapt to their anemia and lead relatively normal lives. When their lives are interrupted by crises, a variety of treatment approaches can be used. For children, comprehensive and timely care is crucial. For example, children with SCA who develop fevers should be treated aggressively. In fact, parents of these children may be taught how to palpate the spleen and recognize early signs of potentially serious problems. Hydration is also an important component of treatment. Lastly, pain management may be addressed with narcotic and nonnarcotic drugs.

Several factors predispose individuals to SCA crises: dehydration from fever, reduced liquid intake, and hypoxia (air that is poor in oxygen content). Stress, fatigue, and exposure to cold temperatures should be avoided by those who have a history of SCA crises.

Treatment of crises is generally directed at keeping the individual warm, increasing liquid intake, ensuring good blood oxygenation, and administering medication for infection. Assistance can also be provided during crisis periods by partial-exchange blood transfusions with fresh, normal red cells. Transfusions may also be necessary for individuals with SCA who are preparing for surgery or are pregnant.

SOCIAL AND HEALTH-RELATED PROBLEMS

In this section we review child abuse and neglect, adolescent pregnancy, suicide in youth, and parental drug and alcohol abuse. Although these conditions are not typically thought of as physical and health disabilities, they do influence significant numbers of families and place children and youth at risk for problems in their schools and communities.

Child Abuse and Neglect

■ DEFINITIONS AND CONCEPTS

*C*hild abuse involves every segment of society and crosses all social, religious, and professional lines. The definition of child abuse can range from a narrow focus, limited to intentional inflicted injury, to a broad scope, covering any act that impairs the developmental potential of a child. Included in the definition are neglect (acts of omission) and physical, psychological, or sexual injury (act of commission) by a parent or caretaker. (Monteleone & Brodeur, 1994, p. 2)

Child abuse and neglect occur among all ethnic groups and at all socioeconomic levels. Educators must be aware of its existence and be willing to address it.

Look closely and you can see the scars.

There are no bruises.
And no broken bones.
She seems the picture of the perfect child.
But if you look closely, you can see how rejection, fear and constant humiliation have left scars that have tragically affected her childhood.

So now only a shattered spirit remains.
And the light of laughter has gone out.
Remember that words hit as hard as a fist.
So watch what you say.
You don't have to lift a hand to hurt your child.

Take time out. Don't take it out on your kid.

Write National Committee for Prevention of Child Abuse, Box 2866E, Chicago, IL 60680.

Children believe what their parents tell them.

"You disgust me!"

"You're pathetic. You can't do anything right!"

"You can't be my kid."

"Hey stupid! Don't you know how to listen."

"I wish you were never born!"

Words hit as hard as a fist.
Next time, stop and listen to what you're saying.
You might not believe your ears.

Take time out. Don't take it out on your kid.
Write National Committee for Prevention of Child Abuse, Box 2866E, Chicago, IL 60680.

Interacting in Natural Settings

PEOPLE WITH PHYSICAL AND HEALTH DISABILITIES

■ EARLY CHILDHOOD YEARS

TIPS FOR THE FAMILY

■ Work closely with medical personnel to lessen the overall impact of the disorder over time. This may include using prophylactic medications, monitoring the impact of certain medications, asking for reading materials, following dietary routines, communicating honest concerns, and asking questions about instructions not well understood.

■ Provide the child with physical or health disabilities opportunities to freely explore his or her environment to the maximum degree possible. This may require some adaptations or specialized equipment (e.g., custom-made wheelchairs, prosthetic devices).

■ Involve the child with other children as time and energy permit. Only children can teach one another certain things. This may include inviting one or several children to your home for informal play activities, celebration of social events, and other age-appropriate activities.

■ Join advocacy and support groups that provide the information and assistance you need.

TIPS FOR THE PRESCHOOL TEACHER

■ Be sure that the physical environment in the classroom lends itself to the needs of children who may have physical or health disorders (e.g., aisles in the classroom are sufficiently large for free movement in a wheelchair). Like any other children, these children benefit from moving around and fully exploring every inch of every environment. Also, it readies them in a gradual way to become appropriately independent.

■ Become aware of specific needs of the child by consulting with parents. For example, the child may need to refrain from highly physical activities.

TIPS FOR PRESCHOOL PERSONNEL

■ Be sure that other key personnel in the school who interact directly with the child are informed of his or her needs.

■ Orient all the children in your classroom to the needs of the child with physical or health disabilities. This could be done by you, the parents or siblings, or other educational personnel in the school. Remember, your behavior toward the child will say more than words will ever convey.

■ Be sure that arrangements have been made for emergency situations. For example, peers may know exactly what to do if a fellow class member begins to have a seizure. Additionally, classmates should know how they may be helpful in directing and assisting the child during a fire drill or other emergency procedure.

TIPS FOR NEIGHBORS AND FRIENDS

■ Involve the child with physical or health disabilities and his or her family in holiday gatherings. Be sensitive to dietary regimens, opportunities for repositioning, and alternative means for communicating.

■ Become aware of the things that you may need to do. For example, you may need to learn what to do if a child with insulin-dependent diabetes shows signs of glucose buildup.

■ ELEMENTARY YEARS

TIPS FOR THE FAMILY

■ Maintain a healthy and ongoing relationship with the care providers that are part of your child's life. Acknowledge their efforts and reinforce behaviors and actions that are particularly helpful to you and your child.

■ Continue to be involved with advocacy and support groups.

■ Stay informed by subscribing to newsletters that are produced and disseminated by advocacy organizations.

■ Develop and maintain good relationships with the persons who teach and serve your child within the school setting.

TIPS FOR THE GENERAL EDUCATION SCHOOL TEACHER

■ Be informed and willing to learn about the unique needs of the child with physical or health disorders in your classroom. For example, schedule a conference with the child's parents before the year begins to talk about medications, prosthetic devices, levels of desired physical activities, and so on.

■ Inform the other children in the class. Help them become aware of their crucial role in contributing to the well-being of the child with physical or health disorders.

■ Use socially competent and mature peers to assist you (e.g., providing tutoring, physical assistance, social support in recess activities).

■ Be sure that plans have been made and practiced for dealing with emergency situations (e.g., some children may need to be carried out of a building or room).

■ If the child's condition is progressive and life threatening, begin to discuss the ramifications of death and loss. Many excellent books about this topic are available for children.

TIPS FOR SCHOOL PERSONNEL

- Be sure that all key personnel in the school setting who interact with the child on a regular basis are informed about treatment regimens, dietary requirements, and signs of potentially problematic conditions such as fevers and irritability.
- Meet periodically as professionals to deal with emergent problems, brainstorm for solutions, and identify suitable actions.
- Children can be involved periodically in brainstorming activities that focus on involving the child with physical or health disorders to the maximum degree possible.
- Institute cross-age tutoring and support. When possible, have the child with a physical or health condition become a tutor.

TIPS FOR NEIGHBORS AND FRIENDS

- Involve the child with physical or health disorders in your family activities.
- Provide parents with some respite care. They will appreciate the time to themselves.
- Be informed! Be aware of the needs of the child by regularly talking to his or her parents. They will sin-

cerely appreciate your concern.

SECONDARY AND TRANSITION YEARS

TIPS FOR THE FAMILY

- Remember that, for some individuals with physical or health disabilities, the secondary or young adult years may be the most trying, particularly if the conditions are progressive in nature.
- Begin planning early in the secondary school years for the youth's transition from the public school to the adult world. Incorporate goals related to independent living in the IEP.
- Be sure that you are well informed about the adult services offered in your community and state.

TIPS FOR THE GENERAL EDUCATION SCHOOL TEACHER

- Continue to be aware of the potential needs for accommodation and adjustment.
- Treat the individual as an adult.
- Realize that the youth's studies may be interrupted from time to time with medical treatments or other important health care services.

TIPS FOR SCHOOL PERSONNEL

- Acknowledge individuals by name, become familiar with their interests and hobbies, joke with them occasionally, and involve them in

meaningful activities such as fund raisers, community service projects, and decorating for various school events.
- Provide opportunities for all students to receive recognition and be involved in school-related activities.
- Realize that peer assistance and tutoring may be particularly helpful to certain students. Social involvement outside the school setting should be encouraged (e.g., going to movies, attending concerts).
- Use members of teacher assistance teams to help with unique problems that surface from time to time. For example, you may want to talk with special educators about management ideas that may improve a given child's behavior in your classroom.

TIPS FOR NEIGHBORS, FRIENDS, AND POTENTIAL EMPLOYERS

- Continue to be involved in the individual's life.
- Be aware of assistance that you might provide in the event of a youth's gradual deterioration or death.
- Involve the individual in age-appropriate activities (e.g., cookouts, video nights, or community events).
- Encourage your own teens to volunteer as peer tutors or volunteers.
- If you are an employer, provide opportunities for job sampling, on-the-job training, or actual employment.

■ ADULT YEARS

TIPS FOR THE FAMILY

- Make provisions for independent living away from home. Work with adult service personnel and advocacy organizations in lining up appropriate housing and related support services.
- Provide support for appropriate employment opportunities.
- Work closely with local and state adult services personnel. Know what your rights are and how you can qualify your son or daughter for educational or other support services.

TIPS FOR NEIGHBORS, FRIENDS, AND EMPLOYERS

- Provide appropriate accommodations for leisure and work activities.
- Adopt an adult for regular recreational and social activities.
- Provide regular opportunities for recognition and informative feedback. When persons with disabilities are hired, be sure that they regularly receive specific information about their work performance. Feedback may include candid comments about their punctuality, rate of work completion, and social interaction with others. Withholding information, not making reasonable adjustments, and not expecting these individuals to be responsible for their behaviors is a great disservice to them.

Child abuse can be regarded as a means of maladaptive coping by parents. Abusive parents and caregivers are confronted with personal and family challenges that influence their responses to children. Some parents are able to cope with these challenges with adaptive behaviors that are helpful to their children; other parents, unfortunately, respond with maladaptive, harmful behaviors.

Many factors contribute to the neglect of children (Finkelhor, 1996). Many parents living in poverty cannot provide the necessary shelter, food, clothing, and health care required for the well-being of their children. Often the stress experienced by these parents is overwhelming, and little is available in the way of support systems and services to help them. Many parents who neglect their children simply do not understand their children's behaviors and their important roles in caring for them. Moreover, many parents who neglect their children have very serious problems themselves, including substance abuse and serious psychiatric problems (Erickson & Egeland, 1996).

Child neglect results when parents abandon their children or fail to care for them in healthy ways. In short, children who are not adequately cared for are considered neglected. These children are often malnourished, infrequently bathed or changed, left without suitable supervision, and rarely held or appropriately stimulated.

Neglect is evidenced in many ways. Some of these children are grossly underweight for their age. They often fail to thrive yet display no medical problems. Some may exhibit persistent and severe diaper rashes because of inconsistent care (Erickson & Egeland, 1996).

Physical abuse of children generally results in serious physical harm or injury to the affected child and sometimes even death. Abusive parents often exhibit inconsistent childrearing practices. Furthermore, their child management approaches are often hostile and aggressive in nature. These parents may also experience stress-eliciting problems arising from unemployment, youthful parenthood, limited incomes, and other related factors (Kolko, 1996).

Another form of child mistreatment is **sexual abuse**—incest, assault, or sexual exploitation. "Sexual abuse involves any sexual activity with a child where consent is not or cannot be given" (Berliner & Elliott, 1996, p. 51). Girls are at greater risk for sexual abuse than are boys. Additionally, children and youth with disabilities are 1.75 times more likely than children without disabilities to be sexually abused (Berliner & Elliott, 1996).

Behavioral indicators of sexual abuse include anxiety, depression, age-inappropriate knowledge about sex, running away from home, suicide attempts, substance abuse problems, and fantasies with sexual connotations. However, many children who have been sexually abused show no signs. Manifestations of their maltreatment may not surface until the adult years and are often evidenced in interpersonal relationship problems (Berliner & Elliott, 1996).

Emotional abuse or psychological maltreatment is often the result of "acts of rejecting, terrorizing, isolating, exploiting, and missocializing" (Hart, Brassard, & Karlson, 1996, p. 75) (see Table 15.5). Outcomes of this kind of abuse are many and varied. Children who have been severely ignored are often lethargic and apathetic. Often they are developmentally delayed in physical development, language acquisition, and cognitive development.

Children who have been psychologically or physically rejected have impaired self-esteem, are often hostile and aggressive, and view themselves as having few if any strengths or skills. Programs directed at helping abused children develop positive coping behaviors are beginning to emerge.

TABLE 15.5	Categories of emotional abuse

Ignoring the child and failing to provide necessary stimulation, responsiveness, and validation of the child's worth in normal family routine.

Rejecting the child's value, needs, and requests for adult validation and nurturance.

Isolating the child from the family and community; denying the child normal human contact.

Terrorizing the child with continual verbal assaults, creating a climate of fear, hostility, and anxiety, thus preventing the child from gaining feelings of safety and security.

Corrupting the child by encouraging and reinforcing destructive, antisocial behavior until the child is so impaired in socioemotional development that interaction in normal social environments is not possible.

Verbally assaulting the child with constant name-calling, harsh threats, and sarcastic put-downs that continually "beat down" the child's self-esteem with humiliation.

Overpressuring the child with subtle but consistent pressure to grow up fast and to achieve too early in the areas of academics, physical/motor skills, and social interaction, which leaves the child feeling that he or she is never quite good enough.

Source: From "Emotional Abuse" by P. S. Pearl. In *Child Maltreatment: A Clinical Guide and Reference,* edited by J. A. Monteleone and A. E. Brodeur, 1994, pp. 261–269. St. Louis: G. W. Medical Publishing. Reprinted by permission.

■ PREVALENCE AND CAUSATION

Establishing accurate and precise prevalence estimates for child abuse is very difficult. In addition to the problem of underreporting, much of the difficulty is attributable to the lack of consistent criteria for child abuse and sundry reporting procedures used in various states. Current estimates for child neglect, physical abuse, and sexual exploitation of children and youth range between ages 13 to 17 and ages 30 to 39 per 1,000 children. The first estimate relates to substantiated abuse and the second estimate relates to calculated abuse (Mian, 1996).

Several factors may cause a parent or caregiver to be abusive. These include crises caused by unemployment, poverty, unwanted pregnancy, serious health problems, substance abuse, high levels of mobility, isolation from natural and community support networks, marital problems, death of a significant other, inadequate intellectual and moral development, and economic difficulties (Baumrind, 1995; Buchanan, 1996; Mian, 1996; Thompson, 1995). Other potential factors include the withdrawal of spousal support, having a child at a very young age, having a particularly challenging infant (one with severe disabilities), or caring for a nonbiologically related child (Baumrind, 1995). Several personality traits frequently characterize abusive parents, including poor impulse control, deficits in role-taking and empathy, and low self-esteem (Baumrind, 1995).

Interestingly, research suggests that parents who were abused as children are at risk of engaging in child abuse themselves. However, most children who were abused do not grow up to be abusive parents (Buchanan, 1996).

Child abuse and neglect occur among all ethnic groups and at all socioeconomic levels. Thus, all educators of children and youth must be aware of its existence and be willing to address it. State laws designate educators and other professionals who work with children (e.g., health care providers, police officers, social workers,

focus 10
Identify five factors that may contribute to child abuse and neglect.

clergy) as mandated reporters, which means they have a legal responsibility to report suspected abuse or neglect to administrators or appropriate law enforcement or child protection agencies. Laws vary from state to state; thus, educators must become familiar with the definition of abuse used in their jurisdiction, as well as what their responsibilities are in reporting.

Clearly, reporting child abuse or neglect is a serious undertaking; however, the responsibility need not be intimidating (Monteleone, 1996). Although the reporter should have ample reason to suspect that abuse or neglect has occurred, he or she is not responsible for proving that it has. Moreover, laws often protect individuals who report abuse and neglect by ensuring some level of confidentiality. The reporter's primary consideration should be the welfare of the child. Unfortunately, many educators are not adequately prepared "to identify, report, and intervene in cases of suspected child abuse and neglect" (Mian, 1996, p. 587).

■ INTERVENTIONS

Treatment of child abuse and neglect is a multifaceted process (Baumrind, 1995; Briere, 1996; Buchanan, 1996; Chaffin, Bonner, Worley, & Lawson, 1996; Friedrich, 1996). The entire family must be involved. The first goal is to treat the abused or neglected child for any serious injuries and simultaneously prevent further harm or neglect (Buchanan, 1996). Hospitalization may be necessary to deal with immediate physical injuries or other complications, during which the child protection and treatment team, in conjunction with the family, develops a comprehensive treatment plan (Jenny, 1996; Johnson, 1996). Once the child's immediate medical needs have been met, a variety of treatment options may be employed: individual play therapy, therapeutic play school, regular preschool, foster care, residential care, hospitalization, or group treatment.

Treatment programs for parents and families of abused and neglected children are directed at helping parents and other family members function more appropriately in responding to their children's needs as well as their own. These programs focus on personal impulse control, alternative methods of disciplining, and anger management. Neglectful parents may receive one-on-one assistance with practical child-care tasks such as feeding and diapering an infant, managing a challenging 2-year-old, and effectively dealing with various kinds of crying. Additionally, resources may be provided to assist with obtaining adequate and nutritious food, suitable clothing, regular medical and dental care, and appropriate housing (Briere et al., 1996).

Some programs are directed at reducing economic and emotional stress by providing affordable day care, helping parents become employable and employed, and providing opportunities for additional education and training (Buchanan, 1996; Thompson, 1995). Also, collaboration among service providers is beginning to emerge. Such collaboration makes it possible for families to receive services that are tailored to their specific needs (Thompson, 1995).

Adolescent Pregnancy

■ DEFINITIONS AND CONCEPTS

dolescent pregnancy is the outcome of conception in girls 19 years old or younger. The impact of adolescent pregnancy is highly variable, depending on age, class, and race (Johnson, 1995). More than

Adolescent pregnancies occur in more than 30% of the cases involving sexually active females between the ages of 15 to 19 years old. Rarely do adolescent fathers provide care and support for the mother and child.

80% of the pregnancies that occur during the adolescent years are unwanted (Kaplan & Mammel, 1997). Many adolescent mothers remain unmarried, leave school, experience severe financial problems, and frequently become reliant on welfare (Johnson, 1995); however, some successfully negotiate the challenges associated with adolescent pregnancy, complete their schooling, and eventually enter the workforce without welfare services.

Teens undergo a number of developmental changes during adolescence: the construction of an identity, development of personal relationships and responsibilities, gradual preparation for vocational or professional work through education, emancipation from their parents, and various adjustments to a complex society. Many if not all of these developmental changes are significantly affected by pregnancy (Johnson, 1995).

The risks and consequences associated with adolescent pregnancy are substantial, particularly if the young mother is 15 years of age or younger. Children born to these mothers experience higher rates of infant mortality, birth defects, mental retardation, central nervous system problems, and intelligence deficits (Carson & Carson, 1996; Kaplan & Mammel, 1997). Additionally, adolescent fathers are often fathers in absentia; few truly assume the role of parent. It is the adolescent mother and her immediate family who shoulder the burdens of caring for and supporting the child (Kaplan & Mammel, 1997).

■ PREVALENCE AND CAUSATION

The prevalence of adolescent pregnancy is staggering. More than 1 million girls become pregnant each year in the United States. Additionally, 39% of these pregnancies are terminated by induced abortions (Johnson, 1995).

"About 45 percent of 15- to 19-year-old females are sexually active, and more than one-third of these become pregnant within 2 years after the onset of sexual activity" (Kaplan & Mammel, 1997, p. 153). Furthermore, most ado-

focus 11

Identify factors that may contribute to the increased prevalence of adolescent pregnancy.

lescents do not employ any contraception measures until after they have been sexually active for about 15 months (Johnson, 1995).

Adolescent girls become pregnant for a number of varied and complex reasons. Contributing factors include a lack of knowledge about conception and sexuality, lack of access to or misuse of contraceptives, desires to escape family control, need to be more adult, aspirations to have someone to love, means of gaining attention and care, and inability to make sound decisions. Societal factors also play a role in the increased number of adolescents who become pregnant: greater permissiveness and freedom, social pressure from peers, and continual exposure to sex through the media (Johnson, 1995).

Other factors that contribute to adolescent pregnancy include a lack of understanding about fertility and contraception, an inability to communicate with those who can help young women make informed decisions (their parents, sexual partners, and health care providers), and the inherent penchant of many teens for risk-taking and impulse behaviors. Also, these young women may be fearful about explaining their behavior to parents and accepting the consequences of their sexual activity. Denial on a number of levels keeps them from behaving responsibly (Johnson, 1995).

■ INTERVENTIONS

The goals of treatment for the pregnant adolescent are varied. The first goal is to help the prospective mother cope with the discovery of being pregnant. What emerges from this discovery is a crisis—for her, for the father, and for the families of both individuals, although responses vary among various ethnic and socioeconomic groups (Johnson, 1995). Some adolescents may respond with denial, disbelief, bitterness, disillusionment, or a variety of other feelings. Parents often react to the announcement with anger, then shame and guilt.

Treatment during this period focuses on reducing interpersonal and intrapersonal strain and tension. A wise counselor involves the family in crisis intervention, which is achieved through careful mediation and problem solving. For many adolescents, this period involves some very intense decision making: Should I keep the baby? Should I have the baby and then put it up for adoption? Should I have an abortion? Should I get married? If the adolescent chooses to have the baby, nutritional support for the developing infant, quality prenatal and perinatal care, and training for eventual child care, education, and employment skills become the focus of the intervention efforts (Johnson, 1995).

Group processes have been used extensively in the rehabilitation and treatment of pregnant adolescents. Groups provide adolescents with opportunities to develop friendships based on mutual needs. The communication in such group settings is often uniquely suited to the needs and perspectives of the adolescents involved, with members providing psychological support for one another. As relationships and friendships grow, other types of support also emerge.

Unfortunately, many services rendered to pregnant adolescents fade after delivery of the child. One of the major problems for these mothers is becoming pregnant again (Kaplan & Mammel, 1997). Steps should be taken to help these mothers explore options and approaches that significantly reduce the potential for repeating their past behavior. Problems do not cease with delivery; the development of functional life skills for independent living is a long-term educational and rehabilitation process. If adolescents are not assisted in developing these survival skills, they are likely to return to the decision-making processes and behaviors of the past (Johnson, 1995).

Suicide in Youth

■ DEFINITIONS AND CONCEPTS

Suicide in youth is generally a premeditated act that culminates in the taking of one's life. Several other terms have been developed to describe suicide, including *completed suicide, attempted suicide,* and *suicidal ideation.* Completed suicide refers to death caused by a set of acts leading to loss of life. Attempted suicide is characterized by self-harming behaviors that could end in death. Suicidal ideation refers to the thoughts one has about suicide and the frequency of these thoughts during a set period of time.

Suicide is a means of satisfying needs, alleviating pain, and coping with the challenges and stressors inherent in being a youth in today's society (Jurich & Collins, 1996). Suicide is now the third most common form of death in young people of 15 to 24 years of age in the United States (Clark, 1997). "Over 50% of suicides occur in young people who are sad, despairing, or depressed; another 20% are described as angry, with the suicidal attempt occurring rather impulsively. Substance abuse is implicated in at least 20% of the suicides" (Clark, 1997, p. 197).

■ PREVALENCE AND CAUSATION

The prevalence of suicide among young people of ages 15–24 is 11.3 per 100,000. The prevalence rate for children of 14 years and younger is 0.8 to 1.7 (Clark, 1997). Many professionals believe that these figures represent only a small portion of the actual number of youth suicides, particularly if one considers the number of youth whose deaths are described as accidental (Jurich & Collins, 1996). Far more young males than females commit suicide. However, females are three times more likely to attempt suicide. In contrast to males, females use far less violent and lethal means.

focus 12

Identify the major causes of youth suicide.

The causes of suicide are multidimensional and are best viewed as a collection of interacting elements (Jurich & Collins, 1996; Stillion & McDowell, 1996), including biological, personal, family, peer, and community factors. For example, some studies suggest that alterations in brain chemistry place some youth at risk for suicide (Jurich & Collins, 1996). Personal factors associated with suicide include clinical depression and other psychiatric conditions. In fact, many clinicians believe that depression is the most powerful discriminant for suicidal behavior (Jurich & Collins, 1996).

Families of suicidal youth may present several problems. These include a lack of warmth or connectedness with their children, extreme rigidity or chaos, severe marital discord, and parental death or suicide.

Peers strongly influence the views adolescents have about themselves and how they behave. The youth who feels rejected or isolated is at risk for suicide. This is also true of youth whose romantic relationships are problematic or highly unstable. Another factor related to suicide in youth is sexual identity. Youth who struggle with their sexual identity and experience extreme peer rejection are vulnerable to suicide.

Communities play a key role in the prevention of suicide. If the community is youth-friendly, provides social supports for youth development, and encourages productive youth activities, its rate of suicide will be lower. On the other hand, if the community is transient, insensitive to the needs of youth, and lacking in recreational and employment options, suicide in youth will be more likely.

Reflect on This

■ TO WHOM IT MAY CONCERN:

Why? Because my life has been nothing but misery and sorrow for 20¾ years! Going backwards: I thought Susan loved me, but I suppose not. "I love you Jason" was only a lie. I base my happiness on relationships with girls—when I'm "going steady," I'm happy. When a girl dumps me (which is always the case) I'm terribly depressed. In fact, over the last three years I've been in love at least four times seriously, but only to have my heart shattered—like so many icicles falling from a roof. But I've tried to go out with at least 30–40 girls in the last few years—none of them ever fell in love with me. My fate was: "To love, but not be loved."

My mother threw me out of the house in March. I guess she must really hate me; she doesn't even write me letters. I think she always hated me.

In high school, and even before that, nobody liked me. They all made fun of me and no girl would ever go to the proms with me.

I haven't anything to live for. Hope? Five years ago I wanted to end my life—I've been hoping for five years! Susan was just the straw that broke the camel's back. I simply cannot take it anymore! I only wanted someone to love; someone who would love me back as much as I loved her.

Yeah, I had pretty good grades, but the way my luck runs, I wouldn't have gotten a job anyway. I got fired over the summer 'cause the boss said, "Jason, you don't have any common sense." Gee, that really made my day.

I walk down the streets of Madison and people call out of dorm windows: "Hey Asshole!" What did I do to them? I don't even know them!

I've been pretty miserable lately . . . , so I think I will change the scenery. What's the big deal! I was gonna die in 40 or 50 years anyway. (Maybe sooner: when George [Bush] decides to push the button in Washington, D.C.!)

Good-bye Susan, Sean, Wendy, Joe, Mr. Montgomery, Dr. Johnston, Jack, and everyone else who made my life a little more bearable while it lasted.

Jason

P.S. You might want to print this in the newspaper. It would make excellent reading!

■ LAST WILL

(Only will. I never made one before.)

I probably am wasting my time, because you need a lawyer or a witness for a will to be legal, but here goes:

To Sean—go my records, tapes, cassette player, clock/radio, and my camera (in the doctor's bag in closet).

To Wendy—I leave my car (if you want it, if not, give it to ET), my big black coat and my military school uniform—you said you wanted them.

To Joe and Wendy—all my posters, if you want them.

To Jack—miscellaneous items left over (that's still a lot, so don't complain).

To Susan—I leave memories of nice times we had. Also my airbrush (in doctor bag w/camera), and all my love; I'll miss you forever.

If I've forgotten anyone—I'm sorry.

Jason

Please: No autopsy.

Source: Adapted from *Suicide Across the Lifespan* (pp. 110–111), by J. M. Stillion & E. E. McDowell, 1996, Washington, DC: Taylor and Francis. Copyright, 1996. Reprinted by permission.

Generally, suicide is the culmination of serious, numerous, and long-standing problems. As a child moves into adolescence, these problems often become more serious. Findings from psychological autopsy studies suggest that 93% to 95% of adults who die by suicide met objective criteria for a mental disorder in the weeks preceding their deaths, most commonly major depression, substance abuse, and schizophrenia. Similar studies have been conducted with populations of youth. Findings suggest that drug abuse is the most common problem, followed closely by depression (Davis & Tolan, 1993).

Substance abuse of all forms also contributes to suicide. Due to the effects of drugs or alcohol, a young person's effectiveness in dealing with the primary problems of adolescence will be reduced, and numerous secondary problems may result as well.

INTERVENTIONS

Treatment of suicidal youth is directed at protecting them from further harm, decreasing acute suicidal tendencies, decreasing suicide risk factors, and treating mental disorders (Clark, 1997). Interventions are also aimed at enhancing factors that protect against suicidal tendencies and decrease vulnerability to repeated suicidal behavior. These interventions may include "sterilizing" the home of pills, guns, knives, razor blades, and other dangerous items. Also, driving restrictions may be included as one of the interventions.

Hospitalization may be the first step. Any physical injuries or complications that the youth may have suffered are addressed first. Then, a variety of professionals, together with parents, begin the planning process and implementation of treatment. Therapies directed at decreasing the problems manifested by suicide attempters include individual, peer-group, and family therapy (Clark, 1997).

Multiple levels and kinds of prevention may be implemented for youth who are suicidal. For example, crisis intervention is directed at moving youth away from imminent suicide and making referrals for appropriate treatment. In contrast, prevention programs are designed to provide early intervention, assist children and youth in developing coping skills, teach them how to manage stress, and provide counseling and other therapeutic services for children and adolescents throughout their school years (Obiakor, Mehring, & Schwenn, 1997). Prevention is a community endeavor in many ways, aimed at developing a network of social connections that give adolescents meaningful experiences with peers and other individuals. These connections may avert problems associated with loneliness and alienation.

Maternal Drug and Alcohol Abuse

DEFINITION AND CONCEPTS

Expectant mothers who use drugs place themselves and their children at risk for a variety of problems (Bellenir, 1996). Table 15.6 on pages 498 and 499 outlines the short-term effects of various drugs on their users. Each drug listed has the potential for creating physical or psychological addiction. Moreover, the effects of these drugs may last from 1 hour to 24 hours. Some drugs may produce flashbacks days or weeks later (Watkins & Durant, 1996).

focus 13

Identify the potential effects of maternal substance abuse on the developing child.

Substance-exposed infants are affected in several ways (Watkins & Durant, 1996). For example, infants exposed prenatally to cocaine exhibit low birthweights, sleeping and eating disorders, and increased irritability. Other known effects for young infants are presented in Table 15.7 on page 500.

Drug abuse in parents produces other problems that affect young children. Caring for infants and young children requires a great deal of selflessness and patience. If the children's parents are primarily concerned about obtaining and using drugs, they are not able to provide the essential nurturing, stimulation, and care necessary for normal development and attachment (Watkins & Durant, 1996).

PREVALENCE AND CAUSATION

The actual prevalence of babies directly affected by substance abuse is difficult to determine. Many expectant mothers are reluctant to reveal their substance abuse for fear that they will be prosecuted for child abuse.

TABLE 15.6   Key substances of abuse and their effects

TYPE OF DRUG	STREET NAME(S)	METHODS OF USE	SHORT-TERM EFFECTS*	DURATION OF ACUTE EFFECTS
Alcohol		Consumed in alcoholic beverages	Euphoria, drowsiness, dizziness, slurred speech, staggering, stupor	About 1 hour per drink
Cocaine/crack	C, coke, snow, nose, candy, rock, french fries, girl	Sniffed (cocaine); smoked, injected (crack)	Euphoria, energy, rapid heartbeat/breathing, high body temperature, dilated pupils, sweating, pallor	1–2 hours
Opiates (heroin, opium, Demerol, morphine)	H, horse, junk, smack, boy, dope, DO	Injected or sniffed	Pleasure; stupor; vomiting; increased urination; constipation; sweating, itchy skin; slowed breathing	3–6 hours
Marijuana/hashish	Pot, grass, weed, reefer, Colombian, blunts, hash	Smoked or cooked with food and eaten	Relaxation, reduced inhibition, impaired coordination and balance, rapid heartbeat, red eyes, dry mouth and throat, impaired motor skills, concentration, and short-term memory	2–4 hours
Depressants (sleeping pills, tranquilizers, sedating anti-histamines)	Bennies, reds, red birds, red devils, red hearts, downers, blue heavens, purple hearts	Swallowed in tablet or capsule form	Slowed central nervous system activity, relaxation, sense of well-being, slurred speech, staggering, blurred vision, impaired thinking and perception, slowed reflexes and breathing	1–24 hours

*Not to be used to diagnose addiction or drug use

TABLE 15.6   *(continued)*

TYPE OF DRUG	STREET NAME(S)	METHODS OF USE	SHORT-TERM EFFECTS*	DURATION OF ACUTE EFFECTS
Stimulants (amphetamines, methamphetamines)	Uppers, speed, meth, crank, dexies, crystal, ice, white crosses, crystal meth, chalk, glass, go, zip, chris, chrisy	Swallowed in tablet or capsule form	Increased alertness, rapid heartbeat and breathing, dilated pupils, dry mouth, aggressive or bizarre behavior, hallucinations, tremors, severe paranoia	2–4 hours
Hallucinogens (LSD and PCP)	Acid, dust, angel dust	Taken orally as drops, powder, or pellets	Dilated pupils, nausea, dizziness, muscle weakness or stiffness, rapid reflexes, increased body temperature and blood pressure, loss of appetite, altered perceptions, impaired thought processes and short-term memory, extreme mood swings	2–12 hours, with potential for flashbacks
Inhalants (solvents, aerosol nitrates)	Sniffing, huffing	Inhaled from bag or saturated cloth, inhaled directly from can	Lightheadedness, slowed breathing and heartbeat, other slowed functions, slurred speech, ringing in ears	Variable
Anabolic steroids		Taken orally or injected	Feeling of well-being, increased energy, heightened blood pressure, tissue growth, rapid weight gain, water and oil retention, aggressive behavior, increased male sex characteristics	N/A

*Not to be used to diagnose addiction or drug use

Source: From *Working with Children and Families Affected by Substance Abuse* by Kathleen Pullan Watkins and Lucius Durant, Jr. Copyright 1996. Reprinted with permission of Prentice-Hall/Center for Applied Research in Education.

TABLE 15.7   Known effects of prenatal drug and alcohol exposure

	COCAINE	OPIATES	ALCOHOL
At birth	Low birthweight; small head circumference; increased muscle tone; sleeping and eating disorders; resistance to being comforted	Low birthweight; small head circumference; increased muscle tone; sleeping and eating disorders; neonatal abstinence syndrome (decreased attentional and social abilities); social responsiveness; heightened sensitivity to various stimuli; exaggerated reflexes; stuffy/runny nose; rapid respirations; apnea; chest contractions	Low birthweight; small head circumference; craniofacial malformations (small eyes or eye openings; malformed ears; poorly defined philtrum; thin upper lip or nose; flattened midfacial features; crossed eyes); heart murmurs; kidney/liver problems; undescended testicles; hernias; increased muscle tension; sleep problems; hard to comfort; reflex abnormalities; mental retardation
In childhood	*Toddler*: Lower scores on measures of development; less appropriate play; more impulsive; less securely attached *Preschooler*: Most test normally on development, language, and behavior tests; some show expressive language and behavior and organization deficits	*Toddler*: Functions normally on developmental and cognitive tests *Preschooler:* Normal results for most; some show memory, perceptual, and other cognitive deficits	Small for height or weight; alert; talkative; friendly; exhibits fluttering movements; difficulty making transitions; severe tantrums; unable to handle wide range of stimuli; difficulty attending; motor and developmental delays; learning disabilities

Source: From *Working with Children and Families Affected by Substance Abuse* by Kathleen Pullan Watkins and Lucius Durant, Jr. Copyright 1996. Reprinted with permission of Prentice-Hall/Center for Applied Research in Education.

About 15% of women of childbearing age are substance abusers. Research conducted by the National Association of Perinatal Addiction Research and Education suggests that about 11% of pregnant women use illicit drugs, most of whom use cocaine during their pregnancies (Bellenir, 1996).

Cocaine is inexpensive, readily available, easily ingested, and highly addictive. In fact, it is the drug of choice for many substance abusers. Because of the low molecular weight of cocaine, it readily crosses the placenta to the developing fetus. Also, cocaine easily passes through the blood-brain barrier, thereby altering the chemistry and functioning of the brain. Cocaine may also be passed from the mother to the child through her breast milk. The regular presence of cocaine in the developing fetus or child affects its development and functioning in a variety of detrimental ways (see Figure 15.3).

■ INTERVENTIONS

Implementing interventions for mothers and their babies who have been exposed to drugs is a challenging and complex process, particularly if the mother is

FIGURE 15.3

The effects of maternal cocaine use on mothers and fetuses/babies

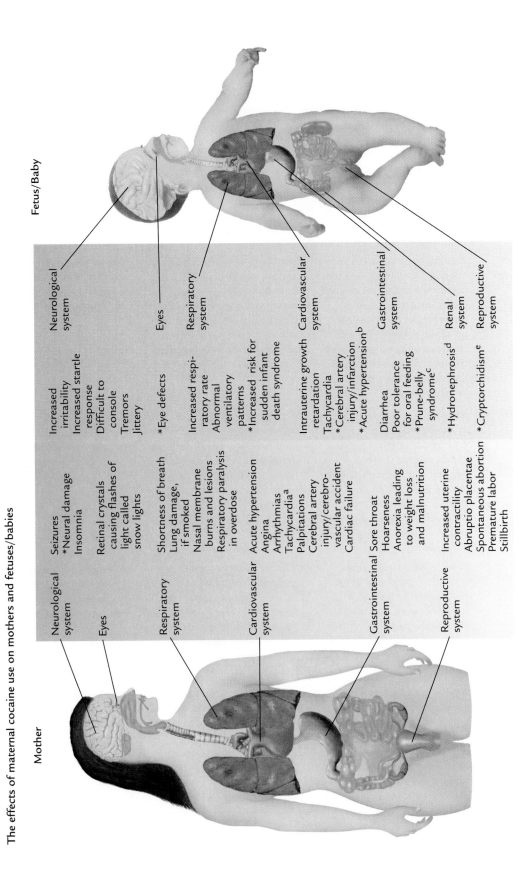

Mother

Neurological system	Seizures *Neural damage Insomnia
Eyes	Retinal crystals causing flashes of light called snow lights
Respiratory system	Shortness of breath Lung damage, if smoked Nasal membrane burns and lesions Respiratory paralysis in overdose
Cardiovascular system	Acute hypertension Angina Arrhythmias Tachycardia[a] Palpitations Cerebral artery injury/cerebrovascular accident Cardiac failure
Gastrointestinal system	Sore throat Hoarseness Anorexia leading to weight loss and malnutrition
Reproductive system	Increased uterine contractility Abruptio placentae Spontaneous abortion Premature labor Stillbirth

Fetus/Baby

Neurological system	Increased irritability Increased startle response Difficult to console Tremors Jittery
Eyes	*Eye defects
Respiratory system	Increased respiratory rate Abnormal ventilatory patterns *Increased risk for sudden infant death syndrome
Cardiovascular system	Intrauterine growth retardation Tachycardia *Cerebral artery injury/infarction[b] *Acute hypertension
Gastrointestinal system	Diarrhea Poor tolerance for oral feeding *Prune-belly syndrome[c]
Renal system	*Hydronephrosis[d]
Reproductive system	*Cryptorchidism[e]

* Suspected but not established
[a] Abnormally high heart rate
[b] An episode of dangerously high blood pressure
[c] Abdominal musculature does not develop, resulting in a stomach that protrudes
[d] Swollen kidney(s)
[e] Testicles remain in the abdominal cavity

[*Source:* From "The Dangers of Prenatal Cocaine Use," by J. Smith, 1988, *American Journal of Maternal Child Nursing, 13*(3), p. 175. Copyright 1988 by *American Journal of Maternal Child Nursing.*]

TABLE 15.8 Stages in the development of parenting competence in the substance-abusing woman

STAGE	CHARACTERISTICS OF THE MOTHER	IMPACT ON THE CHILD	ROLE OF THE PARENT EDUCATOR
1. Drug-abusing mother	Egocentric; focused on own needs, in particular obtaining drugs or alcohol; little structure in daily life; few or no sober support systems; poor impulse control; tendency to repeat abusive or neglectful patterns of own childhood	May be victim of abuse or neglect; lags often apparent in language and social skills development	Usually views others with mistrust, suspicion; difficult to reach; doesn't view parenting as an important issue
2. Short period of sobriety on methadone maintenance	Continuing egocentrism; some impulse-control improvement; developing awareness of need for life structuring; some awareness of child's needs; possibility of enmeshment, strong overidentification with child; child's developmental milestones may be perceived as threatening	May be parentified [child assumes aspects of the parenting role]; develops awareness of own dependence on parent; self-esteem and autonomy are negatively affected; child not viewed as an individual by parent	Growth of trust in relationship with woman; discussion of certain childrearing problems may be possible
3. Relapse period	Behavior regression to stage 1; significant guilt is experienced related to relapse and its effects; shows beginning of understanding of impact of addiction on self, child; may resent attentions to child; feel or express anger and resentment toward parent and educator	Acting-out, regressive, or withdrawn behaviors common; aggression and destructive behavior most obvious in boys; girls may turn emotions inward, withdraw	Discussion of child's needs may be possible; should be approached with caution to avoid overwhelming mother
4. Renewed sobriety	Woman becomes concerned with others' opinions of her child; wants to be seen as sober, not part of community of addicted persons; addiction may still be hidden from children and extended family	May be viewed as "child of addiction" or "child of sobriety" (good vs. bad child); strong guilt feelings may develop as child is unable to meet parental expectations; child at high risk for emotional damage	Attempt to reach parent about dangers to child's psychosocial development; needs to be challenged to change parenting style and behaviors
5. True sobriety	Woman able to deal more honestly with addiction issues; reveals addiction to children, extended family; focuses on change, personal growth; best able to use all appropriate support systems, including parent educator	Child has opportunity to separate from parent, develop own identity; chance to reject patterns set by early parenting; with support may experience catch-up period of development	Respond as needed to maternal overtures for feedback, support

Source: From *Working with Children and Families Affected by Substance Abuse* by Kathleen Pullan Watkins and Lucius Durant, Jr. Copyright 1996. Reprinted with permission of Prentice-Hall/Center for Applied Research in Education.

addicted. Mothers with serious drug abuse histories may need as much treatment as their affected infants. In fact, often mothers may need more assistance. Think for a moment about being a pediatrician, faced with the decision of releasing an infant who is at risk and needs sophisticated care to a mother suspected of drug abuse. What action would you take? Some babies are initially placed with grandparents or other caregivers until their mothers are capable of caring for them.

Educationally oriented treatments for preschoolers affected by substance abuse focus on designing well-structured learning environments, creating small classes (eight children per teacher), and providing developmentally appropriate learning environments that are child-sized, visually interesting, and suitably stimulating. These environments also provide experiential learning activities, rather than paper-and-pencil-type tasks (Watkins & Durant, 1996). Programs for school-age children are beginning to emerge as practitioners and researchers learn more about the effects of substance abuse on the development and performance of young children.

Treatment programs for substance-abusing parents focus on their own problems related to substance abuse and their need for specific, hands-on training in parenting skills (Bellenir, 1996). Many parents move through several stages of treatment (see Table 15.8).

Trainers and therapists help parents explore and develop appropriate skills. These include specific feeding techniques, holding and comforting approaches, positioning for play and exploration, and communicating with their young children (Watkins & Durant, 1996). Additionally, child-care workers or case managers respond quickly to relapses or other related problems that may endanger the infant or young child. Effective treatment and training programs are orchestrated and carried out most effectively by a multidisciplinary team of caring and committed professionals (Bellenir, 1996; Watkins & Durant, 1996).

Case Study

KRISTEN'S EPILEPSY

I will never forget the image of the people who gathered around me and my frail companion. With each sneer from the crowd I hated them more and more. I couldn't understand why our tragedy was their comedy.

After a few minutes, the seizure stopped. My mother picked Kristen up and carried her to the car. When we got home, I asked her why the people laughed.

"They don't understand, Bobby. They don't know about epilepsy."

I thought how odd that seemed. I was 3 when Kristen was diagnosed and by 4 or 5, I knew as much about epilepsy as most adults did. I never realized that most people knew so little about epilepsy.

I used to hate those people who laughed at Kristen. I felt like telling them that they were simply lousy human beings. One day though, I realized that Kristen didn't hate them. When they laugh at Kristen now, I try to explain epilepsy to them. Most people apolo-

gize and walk away. Some even offer help. Others continue to laugh and tease. It still doesn't bother Kristen and I've learned from her to not let it bother me.

■ APPLICATION
1. How should Bobby explain epilepsy to other adults?
2. What appropriate responses ought to be made by adults or others who witness a seizure in process? Give several reasons for your responses.

3. How can a teacher or other caring adult help young children and teenagers respond to their peers with seizure disorders in an appropriate and supportive fashion?

Source: Adapted from *Brothers and Sisters: A Guide for Families of Children with Epilepsy*, by R. Underwood, 1989, Epilepsy Foundation of America, Landover, MD.

AIDS AND THE PUBLIC SCHOOLS

Guillermo is a first-grader. Unless you knew him well, you would assume that he was a very normal kid. He likes cold drinks and pizza and watches cartoons every Saturday morning.

In school, he performs reasonably well. He's not an academic superstar, but he is learning to read and write quite well. His teacher likes him and says that he is quite sociable for his age and size. Guillermo is a little on the small side, but he doesn't let that get in the way of his enjoying most things in life.

Since his foster parents have had him, he has been quite happy. The crying and whining that characterized his first weeks in their home have disappeared. He is now pretty much a part of the family.

His older foster brother, John, likes him a lot. John and Guillermo spend a good deal of time together. They are

about 16 months apart in age. John is a second-grader and a mighty good one at that. He has always excelled in school, and he loves to help Guillermo when he can.

Guillermo, from day one of his placement, has been ill regularly. He has one infection after another. Of course, his foster parents knew that this would be the case, since Guillermo has AIDS. His biological mother could not care for him, as she was a drug addict and has AIDS herself.

Keeping a secret is sometimes very hard, and such was the case for John. From the very beginning of Guillermo's placement in his home, John knew that there was something special about him. His parents have talked to him about Guillermo and his condition. It was a family decision to have Guillermo live in their home. John is often scared, not for himself but for

Guillermo. He wonders how long he will be able to play with his young friend and constant companion. Also, it is often hard to keep the family secret about Guillermo.

Guillermo attends the neighborhood school. Those who are aware of his condition are his classmates, their parents, his teacher, the principal, the school board members, and, of course, John. Just about everyone kept the secret at first, and Guillermo was well received by the overwhelming majority of his classmates. He played with them, enjoyed stories with them, and had a good wrestle now and then with some of the boys in his class.

Over time, other parents and students learned about Guillermo's condition, and a big uproar ensued about his being in school. The PTA was divided. The principal was in favor of Guillermo's continued

attendance, but a few vocal parents began a petition to have Guillermo taught by a teacher for the homebound.

■ **POINT**
Given our current knowledge about the ways in which AIDS is spread in adults and children, there is no reason to remove Guillermo from his neighborhood school. His behavior and physical condition do not place other children at risk for acquiring the HIV virus or developing AIDS.

■ **COUNTERPOINT**
With the limited knowledge we have about AIDS and its transmission, we should not let children with AIDS or the HIV virus attend neighborhood schools. We should wait until we know a great deal more about the disease. The potential risks for other children are too great and far reaching.

Review

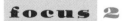 **focus 1**

Why are many individuals with cerebral palsy considered multidisabled?

■ Often, individuals with cerebral palsy have several disabilities, including hearing impairments, speech and language disorders, intellec-

tual deficits, visual impairments, and general perceptual problems.

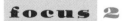 **focus 2**

What is spina bifida myelomeningocele?

■ Spina bifida myelomeningocele is a defect in the spinal column. The myelomeningocele type presents itself in

the form of a tumorlike sac on the back of the infant, which contains spinal fluid and nerve tissue.

■ Myelomeningocele is also the most serious variety of spina bifida in that it generally includes paralysis or partial paralysis of certain body areas, causing lack of bowel and bladder control.

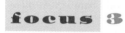 **focus 3**

Identify specific treatments for individuals with spinal cord injuries.

■ Immediate pharmacological interventions are needed, with high and frequent doses of methylprednisolone. These doses reduce the severity of the injury and improve the functional outcome over time.

- Stabilization of the spine is critical to the overall outcome of the injury.
- Once the spine has been stabilized, the rehabilitation process begins. Physical therapy helps the affected individual make full use of any and all residual muscle strength.
- The individual is also taught to use orthopedic devices, such as handsplints, braces, reachers, headsticks, and other augmentative devices.
- Psychological adjustment is aided by psychiatric and psychological personnel.
- Rehabilitation specialists aid the individual in becoming retrained or reeducated; they may also help in securing employment.
- Some individuals will need part-time or full-time attendant care for assistance with daily activities (e.g., bathing, dressing, and shopping).

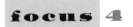

Describe the physical limitations associated with muscular dystrophy.

- Individuals with muscular dystrophy progressively lose their ability to walk and to use their arms and hands effectively because fatty tissue begins to replace muscle tissue.

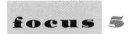

What steps should be taken to assist infants and children with AIDS?

- Infants and children should be provided with the most effective medical care avail-

able, particularly controlling opportunistic infections with appropriate medications.

- Children with AIDS should attend school unless they exhibit behaviors that are dangerous to others or are at risk for developing infectious diseases that would exacerbate their condition.

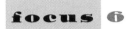

Describe immediate treatment for a person who is experiencing a tonic/clonic seizure.

- Ease the person to the floor.
- Remove any dangerous objects from the immediate vicinity.
- Place a soft pad under the person's head (e.g., a coat or blanket).
- Allow the person to rest after the seizure has ended.

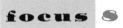

Identify three problems that individuals with diabetes may eventually experience.

- Structural abnormalities that occur over time may result in blindness, cardiovascular disease, and kidney disease.

Identify present and future interventions for the treatment of children and youth with cystic fibrosis.

- Drug therapy for prevention and treatment of chest infections
- Diet management, use of replacement enzymes for food absorption, and vitamin intake

- Family education regarding the condition
- Chest physiotherapy and postural drainage
- Inhalation therapy
- Psychological and psychiatric counseling
- Use of mucus-thinning drugs, gene therapy, and lung or lung/heart transplant

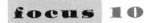

Describe the impact of the sickling of cells on body tissues.

- Sickled cells are more rigid than normal cells; as such, they frequently block microvascular channels. The blockage of channels reduces or terminates circulation in these areas, and tissues robbed of blood nutrients and oxygen die.

Identify five factors that may contribute to child abuse and neglect.

- Unemployment, poverty, and substance abuse
- Isolation from natural and community support networks
- Marital problems
- Having a particularly challenging, needy, or demanding infant
- Poor impulse control

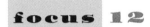

Identify factors that may contribute to the increased prevalence of adolescent pregnancy.

- General factors include a lack of knowledge about conception and sexuality, a

desire to escape family control, an attempt to be more adult, a desire to have someone to love, a means of gaining attention and love, and an inability to make sound decisions.

- Societal factors include greater sexual permissiveness and freedom, social pressure from peers, and continual exposure to sex through the media.

focus 12

Identify the major causes of youth suicide.

- The causes of suicide are multidimensional. They involve biological, personal, family, peer, and community factors.
- Alterations in brain chemistry put some individuals at risk for suicide.
- Often, clinical depression or other psychiatric conditions precede suicide.
- Other causative factors include extreme peer rejection, problems with sexual identity, and substance abuse.

focus 13

Identify the potential effects of maternal substance abuse on the developing child.

- The effects include low birthweight, sleeping and eating disorders, heightened sensitivity, and challenging temperaments.
- Children exposed to cocaine are at greater risk for neurological problems, eye defects, respiratory problems, cardiovascular complications, and other health problems.

16

People Who Are Gifted, Creative, and Talented

To begin with . . .

 The general objects—are to provide an education adapted to the years, the capacity, and the condition of everyone, and directed to their freedom and happiness—We hope to avail the state of those talented which nature has sown as liberally among the poor as the rich, but which perish without use, if not sought for and cultivated. (Thomas Jefferson, *Notes on Virginia*)

 Dear Adam and Eve,

Did you guys feel yourself being created? What did you eat besides the apple you weren't supposed to eat? Tell me, how did you keep fit and trim? Where is the garden now? (Samantha W., age 8, in a class for gifted and talented children)

 Renda F. Subotnik: What role can families play in supporting their talented child?

Vladimir Feltsman: Huge. It's impossible to develop a child's musical talent without the parents' support, especially here in the United States. There has to be a certain understanding of what the child is doing and what he or she needs, like time for concentration and privacy. Families must provide instruments, and certain sacrifices have to be made. It's not great fun to listen to someone practice, especially violin. (Vladimir Feltsman, piano virtuoso and educational innovator, cited in Subotnik, 1997, p. 313)

 As many as 540,000 children and youth with disabilities may be gifted. (Johnson, Karnes, & Carr, 1997)

507

Dwight

Dwight spends most of his time in a variety of creative business endeavors. He is currently president of Broadcast International, a company that specializes in using satellite technologies to deliver information to businesses and consumers throughout the United States.

Dwight is an exceptionally talented musician, composer, and arranger. He plays a number of instruments with great skill, including the bass viol, the fender bass, the guitar, the drums, and the piano. In addition, he has perfect pitch and sings well. During his early 20s, he was the musical director for a popular rock group that performed on television and in concerts around the world. In this capacity, he wrote musical scores, arranged songs and instrumentals, and developed an extensive library of recordings for radio stations.

As a youngster, Dwight's siblings and classmates referred to him as "the little professor" or "Doc." Throughout his school years, Dwight easily mastered the content in his classes, from science to math to creative writing. His interests were broad, and school was a sheer pleasure.

As a senior in high school, Dwight composed and arranged all types of musical scores. One example of his tremendous talent involved an audiotape that he created when he was 17. The tape included 15 contemporary songs, each systematically produced using the instruments he played himself. First, he recorded the piano on one tape track, then drums on another track, and so on. The result was a musical presentation that would have impressed many professional producers.

HE TERMS **gifted, creative,** and **talented** are associated with people who have extraordinary abilities in one or more areas of performance. In many cases, we admire such individuals and occasionally are a little envious of their talents. The ease with which they are able to master diverse and difficult concepts is impressive. Because of their unusual abilities and skills, educators and policy makers frequently assume that these individuals will reach their full potential without any specialized programs or assistance.

For many years, behavioral scientists described children with exceptionally high intelligence as being gifted. Only recently have researchers and practitioners included the adjectives *creative* and *talented* in their descriptions, to suggest domains of performance other than those measured by intelligence tests. Capacities associated with creativity include *elaboration*, the ability to embellish or enrich an idea; *transformation*, the ability to construct new meanings or change an idea into something new and novel; and *visualization*, the capacity to mentally manipulate ideas or images. Individuals who are talented display extraordinary skills in mathematics, sports, music, or other areas. Dwight is one of those individuals who is probably gifted, creative, and talented (see the chapter opening snapshot). Not only did he excel in intellectual (traditional academic) endeavors, but he also exhibited tremendous prowess in producing and performing music. Certainly, the behaviors and traits associated with these terms interact with one another to produce the various constellations of giftedness. Some individuals soar to exceptional heights in the talent domain, others achieve in intellectual areas, and still others excel in creative endeavors. Furthermore, a select few exhibit remarkable levels of behavior and achievement across several domains.

Historical Background

Definitions describing the unusually able in terms of intelligence quotients and creativity measures are recent phenomena. Not until the beginning of the 20th century was there a suitable method for quantifying or measuring the human attribute of intelligence (Clark, 1997). The breakthrough occurred in Europe when Alfred Binet, a French psychologist, constructed the first developmental assessment scale for children in the early 1900s. This scale was created by observing children at various ages in order to identify specific tasks that ordinary children were able to perform at each age. These tasks were then sequenced according to age-appropriate levels. Children who could perform tasks well above that which was normal for their chronological age were identified as being developmentally advanced.

Binet and Simon (1905, 1908) developed the notion of **mental age.** The mental age of a child was derived by matching the tasks (memory, vocabulary, mathematical, comprehension, etc.) the child was able to perform according to the age scale (typical performance of children at various stages). Although this scale was initially developed and used to identify children with mental retardation in the Parisian schools, it eventually became an important means for identifying those who had higher than average mental ages, as well.

Lewis M. Terman, an American educator and psychologist, expanded the concepts and procedures developed by Binet. He was convinced that Binet and Simon had developed an approach for measuring intellectual abilities in all children. This belief prompted him to revise the Binet instrument, adding greater breadth to the scale. In 1916, Terman published the **Stanford-Binet Intelligence Scale** in conjunction with Stanford University. During this period, Terman developed the term

focus 1

Briefly describe several historical developments directly related to the measurement of various types of giftedness.

Snapshot

Eduardo

Eduardo and his family are recent immigrants to the United States. At age 10, he has become quite adept in speaking English. His primary language is Spanish. He is the oldest of seven children.

Eduardo's father is a supervisor on a large farm in southern California. With a lot of effort, he developed sufficient English skills to be of great value to farm owners who now employ him full time. They have hired him to work directly with migrant workers who regularly assist with the harvest of various kinds of produce and fruit. He is also skilled mechanically and, in the off-season, repairs equipment and farm machinery.

Eduardo's schooling has been quite irregular until the past two years. Prior to having a stable residence, he traveled with his family up and down the West Coast of the United States, like many migrant families.

Eduardo's schoolmates really enjoy him. He has lots of friends and is invited frequently to birthday parties and social events. He seems to have a real knack for making friends and having adults like him.

Eduardo's parents view him as being especially alert and bright. He seems to be interested in many topics and is rarely bored. At the moment, he is intrigued with tractors. His mother indicates that he always "questioned her to death." Moreover, he seems to be capable of easily entertaining himself. Recently, he spent an entire afternoon looking through a farm magazine and drawing farm equipment that caught his attention.

Since the beginning of this school year, Eduardo has made phenomenal gains in reading, math, and English. In fact, he has become an avid reader of both Spanish and English books that are available at his school. Although it has been difficult to assess his innate ability, he appears to be a child of some promise, intellectually and socially. However, his parents are worried about providing him with the necessary resources to fully utilize his curiosity and ability. They are also concerned about his late start with consistent schooling.

FIGURE 16.1

Guilford's structure of the intellect model. Each little cube represents a unique combination of one kind of operation, one kind of content, and one kind of product, and hence a distinctly different intellectual ability or function.

[*Source:* From *Way Beyond the IQ: Guide to Improving Intelligence and Creativity* (p. 151) by J. P. Guilford, 1977, Buffalo, NY: Creative Education Foundation. Copyright 1977 by Creative Education Foundation. Reprinted by permission.]

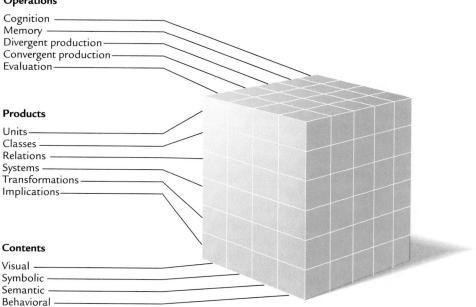

Operations

Cognition
Memory
Divergent production
Convergent production
Evaluation

Products

Units
Classes
Relations
Systems
Transformations
Implications

Contents

Visual
Symbolic
Semantic
Behavioral

intelligence quotient, or **IQ.** The IQ score was obtained by dividing a child's mental age by his or her chronological age and multiplying that figure by 100 (MA/CA × 100 = IQ). For example, a child with a mental age of 12 and a chronological age of 8 would have an IQ of 150 (12/8 × 100 = 150).

Gradually, other researchers became interested in studying the nature and assessment of intelligence. They tended to view intelligence as an underlying ability or capacity that expressed itself in a variety of ways. The unitary IQ scores that were derived from the Stanford-Binet tests were representative of and contributed to this notion.

Over time, however, other researchers came to believe that intellect was represented by a variety of distinct capacities and abilities (Cattell, 1971; Guilford, 1959). This line of thinking suggested that each distinct intellectual capacity could be identified and assessed. Several mental abilities were investigated, including memory capacity, divergent thinking, vocabulary usage, and reasoning ability (see Figure 16.1). Gradually, use of the multiple ability approach outgrew that of the unitary intelligence notion. Its proponents were convinced that the universe of intellectual functions was extensive and that the intelligence assessment instruments utilized at that time measured a very small portion of an individual's true intellectual capacities.

One of the key contributors to the multidimensional theory of intelligence was J. P. Guilford (1950, 1959). He saw intelligence as a diverse range of intellectual and creative abilities. Guilford's work led many researchers to consider intelligence as more than a broad, unitary ability and to focus their scientific efforts on the emerging field of creativity and its various subcomponents, such as divergent thinking, problem solving, and decision making. Gradually, tests or measures of creativity were developed, using the constructs drawn from models created by Guilford and others.

In summary, conceptions of giftedness during the early 1920s were closely tied to the score that an individual obtained on an intelligence test. Thus, a single score, an IQ, was the index by which one was identified as being gifted. Commencing with the work of Guilford (1950, 1959) and Torrance (1961, 1965, 1968), notions re-

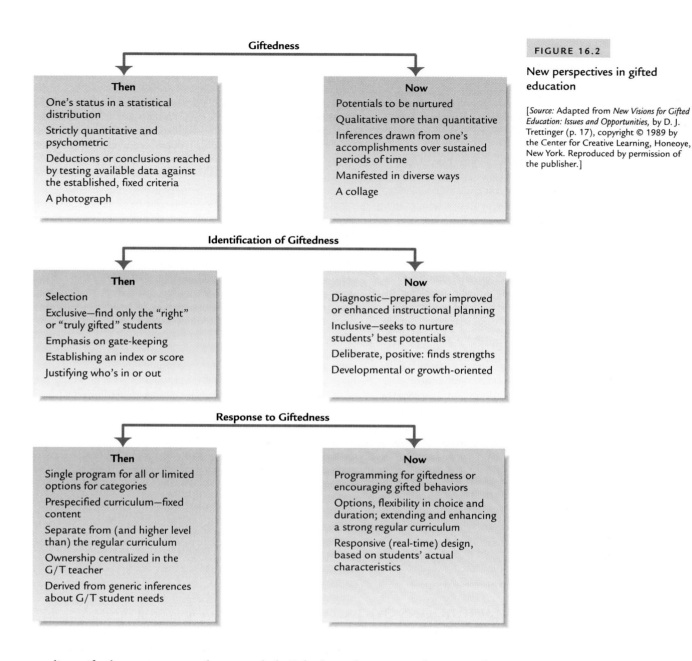

FIGURE 16.2

New perspectives in gifted education

[*Source:* Adapted from *New Visions for Gifted Education: Issues and Opportunities,* by D. J. Trettinger (p. 17), copyright © 1989 by the Center for Creative Learning, Honeoye, New York. Reproduced by permission of the publisher.]

Giftedness

Then
One's status in a statistical distribution

Strictly quantitative and psychometric

Deductions or conclusions reached by testing available data against the established, fixed criteria

A photograph

Now
Potentials to be nurtured

Qualitative more than quantitative

Inferences drawn from one's accomplishments over sustained periods of time

Manifested in diverse ways

A collage

Identification of Giftedness

Then
Selection

Exclusive—find only the "right" or "truly gifted" students

Emphasis on gate-keeping

Establishing an index or score

Justifying who's in or out

Now
Diagnostic—prepares for improved or enhanced instructional planning

Inclusive—seeks to nurture students' best potentials

Deliberate, positive: finds strengths

Developmental or growth-oriented

Response to Giftedness

Then
Single program for all or limited options for categories

Prespecified curriculum—fixed content

Separate from (and higher level than) the regular curriculum

Ownership centralized in the G/T teacher

Derived from generic inferences about G/T student needs

Now
Programming for giftedness or encouraging gifted behaviors

Options, flexibility in choice and duration; extending and enhancing a strong regular curriculum

Responsive (real-time) design, based on students' actual characteristics

garding giftedness were greatly expanded. Giftedness began to refer not only to those with high IQs, but also to those who demonstrated high aptitude on creativity measures such as *Torrance Tests of Creative Thinking* (Torrance, 1966), *PRIDE (Preschool and Primary Interest Descriptor,* Rimm, 1982), *Sternberg Triarchic Abilities Test* (Sternberg, 1993), and *GIFT (Gift Inventory for Finding Talent,* Rim & Davis, 1983). More recently, the term *talented* has been added to the descriptors associated with giftedness. As a result, individuals who demonstrate remarkable skills in the visual or performing arts or who excel in other areas of performance may be designated as gifted. See Figure 16.2.

Currently, no federal mandate in the United States requires that educational services be provided for students identified as gifted, as they are provided for those with other exceptional conditions. Some funding is provided through the federal

John is just a few days away from being 11 years old. On the Washington Pre-College Test (WPC), a test for college-bound high school seniors, he recently scored at the 80th percentile on the verbal portion and at the 10th percentile on the quantitative portion. For the past two years, he has been enrolled at California State University, Los Angeles (CSULA), taking math and other college-level courses. During this time period, he has endeavored to improve his math performance. John has been enrolled in an excellent program for students who are gifted in his junior high; however, he finds his university classes to be more challenging and varied.

John's initial experiences with his university coursework were fraught with problems. His elementary school training had not provided him with any skill in taking notes. His parents, however, were and are very supportive. When they discovered that he was having difficulty in taking notes, his mother obtained permission to attend some of his courses with him. They both took notes and then made comparisons each day after class. Within three weeks, John had mastered the skill and was well on his way to becoming a competent note taker.

When he first began his university work, John viewed himself as being a "mathematical moron" because of his low entry scores on the WPC. The change in his self-perception as a mathematician came when he enrolled in a chemistry course at CSULA. It really captured his attention and interest. He soon discovered that an understanding of algebra was central to succeeding in the course. Motivated by this discovery, he soon became proficient in algebra. In his most recent test, he scored at the 70th percentile on the quantitative portion of the WPC.

John's general feelings about himself and his capacity fluctuated a lot after his early entrance to college. Sometimes he felt overconfident and other times discouraged. Now he has a realistic view of his strengths and weaknesses and is pursuing his university coursework with a balanced perspective on himself.

This fall, John will enroll full time as a college student. He is now 14 and has a full year of college credit under his belt. By the time he is 15 he will be a junior. Today, he is probably thinking about the graduate school he would like to attend after finishing his bachelor's degree.

government through the Jacob K. Javits Gifted and Talented Students Act. This act supports a national research center, demonstration programs, and activities for leadership personnel throughout the United States (Gallagher, 1997). The actual funding of services for individuals who are gifted is a state-by-state challenge, and as such, there is tremendous variability in the quality and types of programs offered to students (see the nearby Reflect on This feature).

Definitions and Concepts

Definitions of giftedness have been influenced by a variety of innovative and knowledgeable individuals. One of the most recent definitions is derived from the Javits Gifted and Talented Education Act:

Children and youth with outstanding talent perform or show the potential for performing at remarkably high levels of accomplishment when compared with others of their age, experience, or environment.

These children and youth exhibit high performance capability in intellectual, creative, and/or artistic areas, possess an unusual leadership capacity, or excel in specific academic fields. They require services or activities not ordinarily provided by the schools.

Outstanding talents are present in children and youth from all cultural groups, across all economic strata, and in all areas of human endeavor. (U.S. Department of Education, 1993, p. 3)

focus 2

Identify five major components of definitions that have been developed to describe giftedness.

TABLE 16.1	The who, what, and how of giftedness	
WHO	WHAT	HOW
Producer	Thoughts	Creativity Proficiency
	Tangibles	Creativity Proficiency
Performer	Staged artistry	Creativity Proficiency
	Human services	Creativity Proficiency

Source: From "The Meaning and Making of Giftedness," by A. Tannenbaum. In *Handbook of Gifted Education*, edited by N. Colangelo & G. Davis, 1997, p. 28. Copyright © 1997 by Allyn and Bacon. Reprinted by permission.

This new definition may help schools and school personnel achieve a variety of important objectives. They include identifying a variety of students across disciplines with diverse talents, using many different kinds of assessment measures to identify gifted students, providing students of all backgrounds with equal access to opportunities to develop their potential, identifying capacities not readily apparent in some students, and taking into account students' drives and passions for achievement in various areas (U.S. Department of Education, 1993).

Tannenbaum (1997), a renowned authority in gifted education, has developed a new definition for giftedness in children. It is as follows:

Keeping in mind that developed talent exists only in adults, I propose a definition of giftedness in children to denote their potential for becoming critically acclaimed performers or exemplary producers of ideas in spheres of activity that enhance the moral, physical, emotional, social, intellectual, or aesthetic life of humanity.

In detailing this proposed definition as it pertains to childhood promise, it is useful to answer three basic questions about giftedness in its maturity, most often in adulthood.

1. *Who qualifies to join the pool of possibly gifted individuals?*
2. *What broad realms of achievement among pool members are judged for signs of excellence?*
3. *How do pool members demonstrate their giftedness in these domains of human accomplishment? (Tannenbaum, 1997, p. 27)*

Tannenbaum (1997) has defined two types of gifted individuals: performers and producers (see Table 16.1). Performers provide "staged artistry" or highly skilled "human services" (p. 27). Producers, on the other hand, generate remarkable "thoughts" and "tangibles" (p. 27). What makes these individuals extraordinary or gifted? Tannenbaum believes that such individuals prove their excellence through "proficiency" and "creativity" (p. 27).

Capturing the essence of any human condition in a definition can be very perplexing. This is certainly the case in defining the human attributes, abilities, and potentialities that constitute giftedness. Definitions do serve a number of important purposes, however. For example, definitions may have a profound influence on the following: the number of students ultimately selected for special programs, the types of instruments and selection procedures utilized, the scores an individual must

Jon

Jon worked with the first- and second-grade class for gifted students for half of his kindergarten time each day. By the end of kindergarten, he was reading at a fourth-grade level and doing math far advanced for his age. The individualized math program in which he participated in first grade enabled him to complete the third-grade book by the end of the year. By fourth grade, he took algebra I at the middle school, and in fifth grade he took advanced geometry at the high school. By the end of eighth grade, he completed advanced placement (AP) calculus and had earned a 5 on the AP test. During high school, he completed three more college-level math courses through a correspondence program.

"I know that without the school's advanced study program, Jon would not have been able to excel at the level he has," his mother said. "The aspect for which I am most grateful is that while he has had the opportunity to work at his own level in most subjects, he has also been with his age-mates in all classes except mathematics."

Alicia

Alicia is a 5-year-old African American who lives in central Harlem. She is one of 11 children under the age of 13. Her mother is addicted to crack, and her absentee father is an alcoholic.

Despite the daily challenges that face Alicia, she is a survivor. Her academic profile is astonishing: She can carry out sophisticated math computations, is teaching herself to read, can weave imaginative stories, and is passionate about playing card games with her teacher in the Project Synergy Summer Program at Teachers College. Her standardized math assessment places her in the 85th percentile, despite her difficult home environment and low-achieving school.

Source: From *National Excellence: A Case for Developing America's Talent,* 1993, the U.S. Department of Education, Office of Education Research and Improvement.

obtain in order to qualify for specialized instruction, the types of education provided, the amount of funding required to provide services, and the types of training individuals need to teach the gifted and talented. Thus, definitions are important from both practical and theoretical perspectives.

New conceptualizations of giftedness and intelligence have recently emerged from theoretical and research literature (Ramos-Ford & Gardner, 1997; Sternberg, 1997). One of the new approaches to intelligence is Sternberg's triarchic theory of human intelligence (Sternberg, 1997), according to which intellectual performance is divided into three parts: analytic, synthetic, and practical. Analytic intelligence is ex-

Creativity in children should always be encouraged. These seats were painted by students and are imitations of paintings by well-known artists.

TABLE 16.2   The seven intelligences

INTELLIGENCE	BRIEF DESCRIPTION	RELATED CHILD AND ADULT ROLES
Linguistic	The capacity to express oneself in spoken or written language with great facility	Superb storyteller, creative writer, or inventive speaker: 　　Novelist, lyricist, lawyer
Logical–mathematical	The ability to reason inductively and deductively, to complete complex computations	Thorough counter, calculator, notation maker, or symbol user: 　　Mathematician, physicist, computer scientist
Spatial	The capacity to create, manipulate, and represent spatial configurations	Creative builder, sculptor, artist, or skilled assembler of models: 　　Architect, talented chess player, mechanic, navigator
Bodily–kinesthetic	The ability to perform various complex tasks or activities with one's body or part of the body	Skilled playground game player, emerging athlete or dancer: 　　Surgeon, dancer, professional athlete
Musical	The capacity to discriminate musical pitches, hear musical themes, sense rhythm, timbre, and texture	Good singer, creator of original songs or musical pieces: 　　Musician, composer, director
Interpersonal	The ability to understand others' actions, emotions, and intents, and to act effectively in response to verbal and nonverbal behaviors of others	Child organizer or orchestrator, child leader, or a very social child: 　　Teacher, therapist, political social leader
Intrapersonal	The capacity to understand well and respond to one's own thoughts, desires, feelings, and emotions	A sensitive child, a resilient child, or an optimistic child: 　　Social worker, therapist, counselor, hospice worker

hibited by people who perform well on aptitude and intelligence tests. Individuals with synthetic giftedness are unconventional thinkers who are creative, intuitive, and insightful. People with practical intelligence are extraordinarily adept in dealing with problems of everyday life and those presented in their work environments.

Another emerging view of giftedness has been developed by Ramos-Ford and Gardner (1997). They have defined intelligence or giftedness as "an ability or set of abilities that permit an individual to solve problems or fashion products that are of consequence in a particular cultural setting" (Ramos-Ford & Gardner, 1991, p. 56). This perspective of giftedness is referred to as the theory of **multiple intelligences.** Intelligence manifests itself in linguistic, logical–mathematical, spatial, musical, bodily–kinesthetic, interpersonal, and intrapersonal behaviors. Table 16.2 provides brief definitions of each area and the child and adult roles associated with each type of intelligence.

Currently developing definitions of giftedness reflect a movement to discard unitary measures of IQ as the major measure of an individual's potential giftedness in favor of multiple measures of creativity, problem-solving ability, talent, and intelligence. However, despite these changes, critics argue that many, if not most, local, district, and state definitions are elitist in nature and favor the "affluent" and "privileged" (Margolin, 1996; Richert, 1997).

Definitions of giftedness are diverse and somewhat controversial. They reveal the complex nature of giftedness and the concerns of the people who create the definitions. In a multicultural, pluralistic society such as that of the United States, different abilities and capacities are encouraged and valued by different parents and teachers. Also, definitions of giftedness often mirror educational, societal, and political priorities at a particular time. For example, the launching of *Sputnik* triggered the development of a variety of programs for gifted students in math and science. The problems of definition and description are not easily resolved, yet such efforts are vital to both research and practice.

Prevalence

Determining the number of children who are gifted is a challenging matter. The complexity of the task is directly related to problems inherent in determining who is gifted and what constitutes giftedness (Richert, 1997). Definitions of giftedness range from being quite restrictive in terms of the number of children to which they apply to being very inclusive and broad. Consequently, the prevalence estimates are highly variable.

Prevalence figures prior to the 1950s were primarily limited to the intellectually gifted: those identified for the most part by intelligence tests. At that time, 2% to 3% of the general population was considered gifted. During the 1950s, when professionals in the field advocated an expanded view of giftedness (Conant, 1959; De-Hann & Havighurst, 1957), the prevalence figures suggested for program planning were substantially affected. Terms such as *academically talented* were used to refer to the upper 15% to 20% of the general school population.

Thus, prevalence estimates have fluctuated, depending on the views of policy makers, researchers, and professionals during past decades. Currently, 3% to 15% of the students in the school population may be identified as gifted, depending on the regulations of a particular state.

Characteristics

Accurately identifying the characteristics of gifted people is an enormous task. Characteristics attributed to those who are gifted have been generated by different types of studies (MacKinnon, 1962; Terman, 1925). Gradually, stereotypical views of giftedness emerged from these studies.

For example, shortly after the publication of the Stanford-Binet Intelligence Scale, Terman (1925) received funding to begin an intriguing work, *Genetic Studies of Genius*. His initial group of subjects included more than 1,500 students, drawn from both elementary and secondary classroom settings, who had obtained IQ scores at or above 140 on the Stanford-Binet. In conjunction with other associates, he investigated their physical characteristics, personality attributes, psychological and marital adjustment, educational at-

focus 3

Identify four problems inherent in accurately describing the characteristics of individuals who are gifted.

TABLE 16.3	Terman's findings in the study of people who are gifted
DOMAINS	DIFFERENTIATING CHARACTERISTICS
Physical characteristics	■ Robust and in good health ■ Above average in physical stature
Personality attributes and aesthetic psychological adjustment	■ Above average in willpower, popularity, perseverance, emotional maturity, aesthetic perceptivity, and moral reasoning ■ Keen sense of humor and high levels of self-confidence ■ Equal to peers in marital adjustment ■ Well adjusted as adults; few problems with substance abuse, suicide, and mental health
Educational attainment	■ Generally read before school entrance ■ Frequently promoted ■ Excelled in reading and mathematical reasoning ■ Consistently scored in the top 10% on achievement tests
Career achievement	■ Mates primarily involved in professional and managerial positions ■ Women primarily teachers or homemakers (probably due to cultural expectations at the time) ■ By age 40 had completed 67 books, 1,400 scientific and professional papers, 700 short stories, and a variety of other creative and scholarly works ■ Adult achievers came primarily from encouraging home environments

tainment, and career achievement at the average ages of 20, 35, and so on (see Table 16.3). Terman's work provided the impetus for the systematic study of individuals who are gifted.

Unfortunately, much of the initial research relating to the characteristics of giftedness was conducted with restricted population samples. Generally, the studies did not include adequate samples of females or individuals from various ethnic and cultural groups; nor did early researchers carefully control for factors directly related to socioeconomic status. Therefore, characteristics generated by these studies may not represent the population of gifted individuals as a whole, but rather may reflect a select group from advantaged environments.

Given the present multifaceted definitions of giftedness and emerging views of intelligence (Gallagher, 1997), we must conclude that gifted people are members of a heterogeneous population. Consequently, research findings of the past and present must be interpreted with great caution by practitioners assessing a particular child's behavior and attributes.

Clark (1997) synthesized the work of past investigators and developed a comprehensive listing of differential characteristics of gifted individuals, their needs, and their possible problems. Table 16.4 presents a representative listing of some of the characteristics of children who are gifted, according to Clark's five domains: cognitive, affective, physical, intuitive, and societal. Again, remember that individuals who are gifted vary greatly in the extent that they exhibit any or all of the characteristics identified by researchers. One of the interesting features of Clark's listing is the delineation of possible concomitant problems that may surface as a result of the individual's characteristics.

TABLE 16.4   Representative characteristics of people who are gifted and potential concomitant problems

DOMAINS	DIFFERENTIATING CHARACTERISTICS	PROBLEMS
Cognitive (thinking)	Extraordinary quantity of information, unusual retentiveness	Boredom with regular curriculum; impatience with waiting for group
	High level of language development	Perceived as showoff by children of the same age
	Persistent, goal-directed behavior	Perceived as stubborn, willful, uncooperative
	Unusual capacity for processing information	Resent being interrupted; perceived as too serious; dislike for routine and drill
Affective (feeling)	Unusual sensitivity to the expectations and feelings of others	Unusually vulnerable to criticism of others; high level of need for success and recognition
	Keen sense of humor—may be gentle or hostile	Use of humor for critical attack on others, resulting in damage to interpersonal relationships
	Unusual emotional depth and intensity	Unusual vulnerability; problem focusing on realistic goals for life's work
	Advanced levels of moral judgment	Intolerance of and lack of understanding from peer group, leading to rejection and possible isolation
Physical (sensation)	Unusual discrepancy between physical and intellectual development	Results in adults who function with a mind/body dichotomy; children are comfortable expressing themselves only in mental activity, resulting in a limited development both physically and mentally
	Low tolerance for lag between standards and athletic skills	Refusal to take part in any activities where they do not excel, limiting experience with otherwise pleasurable, constructive physical activities
Intuitive	Early involvement and concern for intuitive knowing and metaphysical ideas and phenomena	Ridiculed by peers; not taken seriously by elders; considered weird or strange
	Creativity apparent in all areas of endeavor	Seen as deviant; become bored with mundane tasks; may be viewed as troublemaker
Societal	Strongly motivated by self-actualization needs	Frustration of not feeling challenged; loss of unrealized talents
	Leadership	Lack of opportunity to use social ability constructively may result in its disappearance from child's repertoire or its being turned into a negative characteristic (e.g., gang leadership)
	Solutions to social and environmental problems	Loss to society if these traits are not allowed to develop with guidance and opportunity for meaningful involvement

Source: From *Growing Up Gifted* 5/E by Clark, Barbara, © 1979. Adapted by permission of Prentice-Hall, Inc., Upper Saddle River, NJ.

Clark (1997) has also developed a listing of characteristics of children, adolescents, and adults who are described as being extraordinarily creative. Table 16.5 provides a list of behaviors associated with different kinds of creativity.

TABLE 16.5	Characteristics of creative people

Rationally Thinking Creative Individuals
- Self-disciplined, independent, often anti-authoritarian
- Zany sense of humor
- Able to resist group pressure, a strategy developed early
- Greater tolerance for ambiguity and discomfort
- Little tolerance for boredom

Feeling Creative Individuals
- Unfrightened by the unknown, the mysterious, the puzzling; often attracted to it
- More self-accepting; less afraid of what others would say; less need for other people; lack of fear of own emotions, impulses, and thoughts
- Have more of themselves available for use, for enjoyment, for creative purposes; waste less of their time and energy protecting themselves against themselves
- Capacity to be puzzled
- Ability to accept conflict and tension from polarity rather than avoiding them

Physical/Sensing Creative Individuals
- An ability to toy with elements and concepts
- Perceiving freshly
- Ability to defer closure and judgment
- Ability to accept conflict and tension
- Skilled performance of the traditional arts

Intuitive Creative Individuals
- Are able to withstand being thought of as abnormal or eccentric
- Are more sensitive
- Have a richer fantasy life and greater involvement in daydreaming
- When confronted with novelty of design, music, or ideas, get excited and involved (less creative people get suspicious and hostile)

Source: From *Growing Up Gifted* 5/E by Clark, Barbara,. © 1979. Adapted by permission of Prentice-Hall, Inc., Upper Saddle River, NJ.

Origins of Giftedness

Scientists have long been interested in identifying the origins of intelligence. Conclusions have varied greatly. For years, many scientists adhered to a hereditary explanation of intelligence: that people inherit their intellectual capacity at conception. Thus, intelligence was viewed as an innate capacity that remained relatively fixed during an individual's lifetime. The prevailing belief then was that little could be done to enhance intellectual ability.

During the 1920s and 1930s, scientists such as John Watson began to explore the new notion of behavioral psychology, or behaviorism. Like other behaviorists who followed him, Watson believed that the environment played an important role in the development of intelligence as well as personality traits. Initially, Watson largely discounted the role of heredity and its importance in intellectual development.

focus 4
Identify three factors that appear to contribute significantly to the emergence of various forms of giftedness.

Later, however, he moderated his views, moving somewhat toward a theoretical perspective in which both hereditary and environment contributed to an individual's intellectual ability.

During the 1930s, many investigators sought to determine the proportional influence of heredity and environment on intellectual development. Some genetic proponents asserted that as much as 70% to 80% of an individual's capacity is determined by heredity and the remainder by environmental influences. Environmentalists believed otherwise. This controversy, known as the **nature-versus-nurture** controversy, is likely to continue for some time, in part because of the complexity and breadth of the issues involved (Plomin, 1997). However, important progress has been made in teasing out the genetic and environmental contributors to high intelligence. For example, the inherited aspect of intelligence increases in influence with age. "This finding is especially interesting because it is counterintuitive. People usually assume that environmental factors increasingly account for variance in intelligence as experiences accumulate during the course of life" (Plomin, 1997, p. 70). Recent research suggests that the influence of nurture is far more profound in the preadolescent years than thereafter (Plomin, 1997). Additionally, more research is needed to investigate the role of young children in "selecting, modifying, and creating their own environments" for growth and stimulation (Plomin, 1997, p. 72).

Thus far, we have focused on the origins of intelligence rather than giftedness per se. Many of the theories regarding the emergence or essence of giftedness have been derived from the study of general intelligence. Few authors have focused directly on the origins of giftedness. Moreover, the ongoing changes in the definitions of giftedness have further complicated the precise investigation of its origins.

Research continues to provide a range of answers about the inheritability of high intellectual capacity, creativity, and other exceptional talents. Of particular interest is the investigative work currently underway in the field of genetics. In coming decades, investigators will be able to identify precise genes responsible for various manifestations of intelligence (Plomin, 1997). We do know, however, that early environmental factors play important roles in the crystallization of intellectual abilities, and far more attention needs to be devoted to improving early learning environments for young children (Gallagher, 1997).

Thus, the precise origins of the various forms of giftedness are yet to be determined. Current thinking favors an interaction of natural endowment and appropriate environmental stimulation produce giftedness (Gallagher, 1997; Jackson & Klein, 1997; Plomin, 1997).

Assessment

The focus of assessment procedures for identifying potential giftedness is beginning to change (Frasier, 1997; Richert, 1997). Elitist definitions and exclusive approaches are being replaced with more defensible, inclusive methods of assessment. Particular tests for identifying persons with potential for gifted performance are being more carefully matched with the students for which they were designed. Children who were once excluded from programs for the gifted because of formal or standard cut-off scores that favored particular groups of students are now being included as candidates. Multiple sources of information are now collected and reviewed in determining who is potentially gifted (Frasier, 1997; Richert, 1991). The identification process

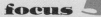

focus 5

Describe the range of assessment devices used to identify the various types of giftedness.

is now closer to meeting the ideals of identifying needs and potentials, rather than merely labeling individuals as gifted.

Young gifted children are identified using several approaches. One of the tasks of parents and other care providers is to be aware of the behaviors that may signal giftedness in their child or children (Jackson & Klein, 1997). Given the heterogeneous nature of giftedness, this can be a challenging task. Children identified as gifted develop in vastly different ways. Some may read, walk, and talk quite early, whereas others may be slow in these areas. Aspects of giftedness may emerge early in a child's development or later on as the child matures. Consequently, the identification process should continue throughout a child's developmental years.

Several approaches have been developed to identify more accurately children who are disadvantaged and also gifted. Some theorists and practitioners have argued for the adoption of a *contextual paradigm.* Rather than use information derived solely from typical intelligence tests or other talent assessments, this approach centers on divergent views of giftedness as valued and determined by community members, parents, grandparents, and competent informants (Frasier, 1997). Other like approaches focus on nontraditional measures of giftedness. These approaches use multiple criteria; broader ranges of scores for inclusion in special programs; peer nomination; assessments by persons other than educational personnel; and information provided by adaptive behavior assessments. Furthermore, these approaches seek to understand students' motivations, interests, capacity for communication, reasoning abilities, capacity for imagination, and humor (Frasier, 1997). For example, if 60% of the students in a given school population come from a certain cultural minority group and only 2% are identified as gifted using traditional measures, the screening committee may want to reexamine and adjust its identification procedures.

Elementary and secondary students who are gifted are identified in a variety of ways. The first step is generally screening. During this phase, teachers, psychologists, and other school personnel attempt to select all students who are potentially gifted. A number of procedures are employed in the screening process. Historically, information obtained from group intelligence tests and teacher nominations has been used to select the initial pool of students. However, many other measures and data-collection techniques have been instituted since giftedness has come to be viewed as a multidimensional, not unidimensional, concept (Richert, 1997). Measures may include developmental inventories, parent and peer nominations, achievement tests, creativity tests, motivation assessments, teacher nominations, and evaluations of student projects (Assouline, 1997; Hunsaker, Finley, & Frank, 1997; Richert, 1997).

Richert (1997) has developed six principles that should be followed in identifying children as gifted (see Table 16.6 on page 522). Using these principles, students from a variety of backgrounds and cultures have an equitable opportunity for being identified as gifted.

■ TEACHER NOMINATION

Teacher nomination has been an integral part of many screening approaches. This approach is fraught with problems, however. Teachers often favor children who are well dressed, cooperative, and task oriented. Students who are bright underachievers as well as those who are bright and disruptive may be overlooked. Moreover, teachers are frequently given few if any specific criteria for nominating students. Also, many teachers are unfamiliar with the general traits, behaviors, and dispositions that underlie giftedness (Hunsaker et al., 1997).

TABLE 16.6	Principles for identifying gifted children and adolescents

1.	Defensibility	■ Procedures should be based on the best available research and recommendations.
2.	Advocacy	■ Identification should be designed in the best interests of all students. Students should not be harmed by the procedures.
3.	Equity	■ Procedures should guarantee that no one is overlooked. Students from all groups should be considered for representation according to their demographic representation in the district.
		■ The civil rights of students should be protected.
		■ Strategies should be specified for identifying the disadvantaged gifted student.
		■ Cutoff scores should be avoided because they are the most common way that disadvantaged students are discriminated against. (High scores should be used to include students, but if students meet other criteria—through self or parent nominations, for example—then a lower test score should not be used to exclude them.)
4.	Pluralism	■ The broadest defensible definition of giftedness should be used.
5.	Comprehensiveness	■ As many learners with gifted potential as possible should be identified and served.
6.	Pragmatism	■ Whenever possible, procedures should allow for the cost-effective modification and use of available instruments and personnel.

Source: From "Excellence with Equity in Identification and Programming," by S. Richert. In *Handbook of Gifted Education,* 2/E edited by N. Colangelo and G. Davis, 1997, p. 79. Copyright © 1997 by Allyn and Bacon. Reprinted by permission.

Fortunately, some of these problems have been addressed. Several scales, approaches, and guidelines are now available to aid teachers and others responsible for making nominations. In fact, several researchers have developed nomination procedures that are highly correlated with success in gifted programs, particularly in areas such as language skills, creativity, and group skills (Hunsaker et al., 1997).

■ INTELLIGENCE AND ACHIEVEMENT TESTS

Intelligence testing continues to be a major source of information for screening and identifying general ability or intellectual giftedness in children and adolescents (Assouline, 1997). Past research related to intelligence assessment, however, reveals some interesting findings. Wallach (1976) analyzed a series of studies on the relationship between future professional achievement and scores obtained earlier on academic aptitude tests or intelligence tests. He found that performance scores in the upper ranges, particularly those frequently used to screen and identify students who are gifted, served as poor criteria for predicting future creative and productive achievement.

Other criticisms have been aimed at intelligence tests and their uses, some of which were discussed earlier in this chapter. One of the major criticisms relates to the restrictiveness of such instruments. Many of the higher mental processes that characterize the functioning of individuals who are gifted are not measured adequately, and some are not assessed at all. Another criticism involves the limitations inherent in using the typical intelligence tests with individuals who are culturally different. Few instruments currently available are suitably designed to assess the abilities of children and adolescents who substantially differ from the core culture.

522   CHAPTER 16   PEOPLE WHO ARE GIFTED, CREATIVE, AND TALENTED

However, some progress is being made in helping educators identify gifted children who are members of minority groups, underachievers, or at risk (Richert, 1997).

Similar problems are inherent in achievement tests. For example, achievement tests are not generally designed to measure the true achievement of children who are academically gifted. Such individuals are often prevented from demonstrating their unusual prowess because of the restricted range of the test items. These **ceiling effects,** as they are known, prevent children who are gifted from demonstrating their achievement at higher levels.

■ CREATIVITY TESTS

Concerns have been raised about the measurement of creativity independent of some talent or performance domain (Davis, 1997; Gallagher, 1997). Because of the nature of creativity and the many forms in which it can be expressed, developing tests to assess its presence and magnitude is a formidable task (Davis, 1997). In spite of these challenges, a number of creativity tests have been formulated (Rimm, 1982; Rimm & Davis, 1983; Torrance, 1966; Williams, 1980). Two main categories of creativity tests are presently in use: (1) tests designed to assess divergent thinking and (2) inventories that provide information about students' personalities and biographical traits. Callahan (1991) has suggested the use of multiple measures of creativity to substantiate prowess in this area of performance. A typical question on a divergent thinking test may read as follows: What would happen if your eyes could be adjusted to see things as small as germs?

Once the screening steps have been completed, the actual identification and selection of students are begun. During this phase, each of the previously screened students is carefully evaluated again, using more individualized procedures and assessment tools. Ideally, these techniques should be closely related to the definition of giftedness used by the district or school system and the nature of the program envisioned for students (see the nearby Reflect on This feature).

Reflect on This

SUGGESTIONS FOR CREATING A CLIMATE OF CREATIVITY

1. Remember that students will be most creative when they enjoy what they are doing.
2. Use tangible rewards as little as possible; instead, encourage students to take pride in what they have accomplished.
3. Avoid competitive situations within the classroom.
4. Downplay your evaluation of students' creative work; instead, help them become more proficient at recognizing their own strengths and weaknesses.
5. Whenever possible, give students choices about what they will do and how they will accomplish their goals.
6. Make intrinsic motivation a regular focus of class discussions; encourage students to become aware of their own special interests, and help them to distance themselves from extrinsic constraints.
7. Encourage students to become active, independent learners, and allow them to take confident control of their own learning process.
8. In any ways that you can, show students that you value creativity—that you not only allow it but also actively engage in it.
9. Show students that you are an intrinsically motivated individual who enjoys thinking creatively.

Source: From "Creativity, Thinking Skills, and Eminence," by B. A. Hennessey. In *Handbook of Gifted Education*, edited by N. Colangelo and G. A. Davis, 1997, p. 290. Boston: Allyn and Bacon.

Services and Supports

■ EARLY CHILDHOOD

Parents can promote the early learning and development of their children in a number of ways. During the first 18 months of life, 90% of all social interactions with children take place during activities such as feeding, bathing, changing diapers, and dressing (Clark, 1997). Parents who are interested in advancing their child's mental and social development use these occasions for talking to him or her; providing varied sensory experiences such as bare-skin cuddling, tickling, and smiling; and conveying a sense of trust.

As children progress through infancy, toddler, and preschool periods, the experiences provided become more varied and uniquely suited to the child's emerging interests. Language and cognitive development are encouraged by means of stories that are read and told. Children are also urged to make up their own stories. Brief periods are also reserved for discussions or spontaneous conversations that arise from events that have momentarily captured their attention. Requests for help in saying or printing a word are promptly fulfilled. Thus, many children who are gifted learn to read before they enter kindergarten or first grade.

During the school years, parents continue to advance their children's development by providing opportunities that correspond to their children's strengths and interests. The simple identification games played during the preschool period now become more complex. Discussions frequently take place with peers and other interesting adults, in addition to parents. The nature of the discussions and the types of questions asked become more sophisticated. Parents assist their children in moving to higher levels of learning by asking questions that involve analysis (comparing and contrasting ideas), synthesis (integrating and combining ideas into new and novel forms), and evaluation (judging and disputing books, newspaper articles, etc.). Other ways parents can help include (1) furnishing books and reading materials on a broad range of topics; (2) providing appropriate equipment as various interests surface (e.g., microscopes, telescopes, chemistry sets); (3) encouraging regular trips to the public library and other learning-resource centers; (4) providing opportunities for participation in cultural events, lectures, and exhibits of various kinds; (5) encouraging participation in extracurricular and community activities outside the home; and (6) fostering relationships with potential mentors and other resource people in the community.

■ PRESCHOOL PROGRAMS A variety of preschool programs have been developed for young children who are gifted. Some children are involved in traditional programs, which focus on activities and curricula devoted primarily to the development of academic skills. Many of the traditional programs emphasize affective and social development, as well. The entry criteria for these programs are varied, but the primary considerations are usually the child's IQ and social maturity. Moreover, the child must be skilled in following directions, attending to tasks of some duration, and controlling impulsive behavior.

Creativity programs are designed to help children develop their natural endowments in a number of artistic and creative domains. Another purpose of such programs is to help the children discover their own areas of promise. Children in these programs are also prepared for eventual involvement in traditional academic areas of schooling.

focus 6

Identify nine strategies that foster the development of children and adolescents who are gifted.

Once a school system determines what areas of giftedness it has to serve, for example, creativity, school personnel must continuously evaluate the effectiveness of the program.

▪ CHILDHOOD AND ADOLESCENCE

Giftedness in elementary and secondary students may be nurtured in a variety of ways (Clark, 1997). Numerous service delivery systems and approaches are used in responding to the needs of students who are gifted. Frequently, the nurturing process has been referred to as **differentiated education,** that is, an education uniquely and predominately suited to the capacities and interests of individuals who are gifted.

▪ INSTRUCTIONAL APPROACHES Instructional approaches are selected based on a variety of factors. First, a school system must determine what types of giftedness it is capable of serving. It must also establish identification criteria and measures that allow it to select qualified students fairly. For example, if the system is primarily interested in advancing creativity, measures and indices of creativity should be utilized. If the focus of the program is accelerating math achievement and understanding, instruments measuring mathematical aptitude and achievement should be employed. With regard to identifying giftedness in students who are culturally diverse, progress in instrumentation and measurement development has been made. A variety of formal and informal approaches have been developed that allow practitioners to measure potential giftedness in culturally diverse students (Richert, 1997). Second, the school system must select the organizational structures through which children who are gifted are to receive their differentiated educations. Third, school personnel must select the instructional approaches to be utilized within each program setting. Fourth, school personnel must select continuous evaluation procedures and techniques that help them assess the overall effectiveness of the program. Data generated from program evaluation efforts can serve as a catalyst for making appropriate changes.

▪ SERVICE DELIVERY SYSTEMS Once the types of giftedness to be emphasized have been selected and procedures to identify students have been established,

Gifted elementary students here are given the opportunity to discuss the message and merits of fine art.

suitable service delivery systems must be chosen. Their structures resemble those used in other areas of special education.

Clark (1997) described several options in developing services for students who are gifted (see Figure 16.3). Each of the learning environments in this model has inherent advantages and disadvantages. For example, students who are enrolled in general education classrooms and are given opportunities to spend time in seminars, resource rooms, special classes, and other novel learning circumstances profit from

FIGURE 16.3

Clark's continuum model for ability grouping.

[*Source:* From *Growing Up Gifted,* 5/E by Clark, Barbara, Copyright © 1979. Adapted by permission of Prentice-Hall, Inc., Upper Saddle River, NJ.]

General education classroom

General education class with cluster

General education class with pullout

General education class with cluster and pullout

Individualized classroom

Individualized classroom with cluster

Individualized classroom with pullout

Individualized classroom with cluster and pullout

Special class with some integrated classes

Special class

Special school

the experiences because they are allowed to work at their own levels of ability (Lando & Schneider, 1997). Furthermore, such pull-out activities provide a means for students to interact with one another and to pursue areas of interest that may not be part of the usual school curriculum. However, the disadvantages of such a program are numerous. The major part of the instructional week is spent doing things that may not be appropriate for students who are gifted, given their abilities and interests. Also, when they return to general education classes, they are frequently required to make up missed assignments.

Another example of Clark's *alternatives for elementary, middle, and high schools* is the special class with opportunities for coursework integrated with regular classes. This approach has many advantages. Students have the best of both worlds, academically and socially. Directed independent studies, seminars, mentorships, and cooperative studies are options that are made possible through this arrangement. Students who are gifted can interact intensively with other able students as well as regular students in their integrated classes. This program also has disadvantages, however. A special class requires a well-trained teacher, and many school systems simply do not have sufficient funds to secure the services of a specially trained teacher. Without a skilled teacher, the special class instruction or other specialized learning activities may just be more of the general education curriculum.

VanTassel-Baska (1997) has generated several beliefs that should be considered in developing curricula for gifted students (see Table 16.7). The beliefs provide a basis for development of the *integrated curriculum model*. This model focuses on advanced content, including sophisticated literature and writing activities; process and product development in the form of scientific research; and issues-oriented themes that tie students' research to specific social, political, or economic problems.

The selection of service delivery systems and curricula for gifted students depends on several factors. These include having sufficient financial and human resources (e.g., trained personnel, specialists in gifted education, mentors), flexibility in determining student placement and progress, and a climate of excellence, characterized by high standards and significant student engagement in learning activities (VanTassel-Baska, 1997). Optimally, delivery systems should facilitate the achievement of curricular goals and should correspond with the types of giftedness being nurtured.

TABLE 16.7   Guiding beliefs for curriculum development for the gifted

1. All learners should be provided curriculum opportunities that allow them to attain optimum levels of learning.

2. Gifted learners have different learning needs compared with typical learners. Therefore, curriculum must be adapted or designed to accommodate these needs.

3. The needs of gifted learners cut across cognitive, affective, social, and aesthetic areas of curriculum experiences.

4. Gifted learners are best served by a confluent approach that allows for both accelerated and enriched learning.

5. Curriculum experiences for gifted learners need to be carefully planned, written down, implemented, and evaluated in order to maximize potential effect.

Source: From "What Matters in Curriculum for Gifted Learners: Reflections on Theory, Research, and Practice," by J. VanTassel-Baska. In *Handbook of Gifted Education,* 2/E edited by N. Colangelo and G. Davis, 1997, p. 126. Copyright © 1997 by Allyn and Bacon. Reprinted by permission.

Successful classrooms and programs for gifted students are led by teachers who have advanced preparation and knowledge specifically related to gifted education, who relish change, and who enjoy working collaboratively with other professionals. Furthermore, these teachers believe in differentiated instruction, can use a variety of strategies to deliver it, and have leadership skills and enjoy having some autonomy in fulfilling their teaching responsibilities (Westberg & Archambault, 1997).

■ ACCELERATION Traditionally, programs for students who are gifted have emphasized the practices of acceleration and enrichment. Schiever & Maker (1997) defined **acceleration** as both a curriculum and program delivery service. Early entrance to kindergarten or college, part-time grade acceleration, and grade skipping are all examples of acceleration as service delivery systems. Acceleration allows students to achieve at rates consonant with their capacities. In the past, grade skipping was a common administrative practice in providing for the needs of learners of high abilities. The decline in this practice is attributed to the conviction of some individuals that grade skipping may heighten a student's likelihood of becoming socially maladjusted. Others believe that accelerated students will experience significant gaps in learning because of grade skipping. Acceleration is generally limited to two years in the typical elementary school program. Unfortunately, acceleration does not provide gifted students with opportunities to receive a differentiated curriculum suited to their specific needs (Schiever & Maker, 1997).

Another practice related to grade skipping is telescoped or condensed schooling, which enables students to progress through the content of several grades in a significantly reduced time span. An allied practice is that of allowing students to progress rapidly through a particular course or content offering. Acceleration of this nature provides students with sequential, basic learning at a pace commensurate with their abilities. School programs that do not employ grade levels are particularly suitable for telescoping. Because of their very nature, students, regardless of their chronological ages, may progress through a learning or curriculum sequence that is not constricted by artificial grade boundaries.

Forms of condensed programming at the high school level include earning credit by examination, enrolling in extra courses for early graduation, reducing or eliminating certain coursework, enrolling in intensive summer programs, and taking approved university courses while completing high school requirements. Many of these options enable students to enter college early or begin bachelor's programs with other advanced students. Dwight, the talented musician and broadcasting entrepreneur described in the chapter opening snapshot, was able to profit from honors courses in high school by earning college credit before his actual enrollment in a university. Many students who are gifted are ready for college-level coursework at age 14, 15, or 16. Some students of unusually high abilities are prepared for college-level experiences prior to age 14.

Research on acceleration and its impact suggests that carefully selected students profit greatly from such experiences (Schiever & Maker, 1997). The major benefits of acceleration, as established by research and effective practice, include improved motivation and confidence and early completion of advanced or professional training.

■ ENRICHMENT Like acceleration, **enrichment** refers to curricular as well as service delivery systems (Schiever & Maker, 1997). Enrichment experiences extend or broaden a person's knowledge. Enrichment refers to courses of study such as music appreciation, foreign languages, and mythology that are added to a student's curriculum and are usually not more difficult than other classes in which the student is involved. Other examples of enrichment involve experiences in which the student develops sophisticated thinking skills (i.e., synthesis, analysis, interpretation, and evaluation) or opportunities to develop and master advanced concepts in a particular subject area. Some forms of enrichment are actually types of acceleration. A student whose enrichment involves having an opportunity to fully pursue mathematical concepts that are well beyond his or her present grade level is experiencing a form of acceleration. Obviously, the two approaches are interrelated. Acceleration and enrichment are essentially complementary curricular and service delivery components (Schiever & Maker, 1997).

The enrichment approach is the most common means of serving students who are gifted. It is also the most abused approach, in that it is often applied in name only and in a sporadic fashion, without well-delineated objectives or rationale. There are also other problems with the enrichment approach. It is often used by school systems in a superficial fashion, as a token response to the demands of parents of children who are gifted. Enrichment activities are viewed by some professionals as periods devoted to educational trivia or instruction heavy in student assignments but light in content. Quality enrichment programs are characterized by carefully selected activities, modules, or units; challenging but not overwhelming assignments; and evaluations that are rigorous yet fair. Additionally, good enrichment programs focus on thoughtful and careful plans for student learning and learning activities that stress higher-order thinking and application skills (Schiever & Maker, 1997).

There is a paucity of systematic experimental research regarding enrichment programs. Despite many of the limitations of current and past research, evidence supports the effectiveness of enrichment approaches, particularly when it is delivered to specific ability groups (Maker & Nielsen, 1995, 1996). However, little long-term experimental research addressing the effectiveness of enrichment programs has been conducted. Nonexperimental evaluations of enrichment programs have indicated that students, teachers, and parents are generally satisfied with their nature and content.

Enrichment activities do not appear to detract from the success students experience on regularly administered achievement tests. Sociometric data regarding students who are pulled out of general education classrooms for enrichment activities are also positive. Students do not appear to suffer socially from involvement in enrichment programs that take place outside their general education classrooms.

■ SPECIAL PROGRAMS AND SCHOOLS Programs designed to advance the talents of individuals in nonacademic areas, such as the visual and performing arts, have grown rapidly in recent years. Students involved in these programs frequently spend half their school day working in academic subjects and half in arts studies. Often the arts instruction is provided by an independent institution, but some school systems maintain their own separate schools. Most programs provide training in the visual and performing arts, but a few emphasize instruction in creative writing, motion picture and television production, and photography.

So-called governor's schools (distinctive summer programs generally held at university sites) and specialized residential or high schools in various states also provide valuable opportunities for students who are talented and academically gifted (Kolloff, 1997). Competitively selected students are provided with curricular experiences that are closely tailored to their individual aptitudes and interests. Faculties for these schools are meticulously selected for competence in various areas and for their ability to stimulate and motivate students. Nevertheless, these schools and special programs are few in number and serve only a small number of the students who would profit from them.

■ CAREER EDUCATION Career education and career guidance are essential components of a comprehensive program for students who are gifted (Perrone, 1997). Ultimately, career education activities and experiences are designed to help students make educational and occupational decisions. Differentiated learning experiences provide elementary and middle school students with opportunities to investigate and explore. Many of these investigations and explorations are career related and designed to help students understand what it might be like to be a zoologist, a neurosurgeon, or a filmmaker. Students also become familiar with the training and effort necessary for work in these fields. In group meetings, they may discuss the factors that influenced a scientist to pursue a given problem or conduct experiments that led to a particular discovery. As students who are gifted grow and mature, both cognitively and physically, the nature and scope of their career education activities become more sophisticated and varied.

■ MENTORING Some students are provided opportunities to work directly with research scientists, artists, musicians, or other professionals who excel in their fields of endeavor. Students may spend as many as two days a week, 3 or 4 working hours a day, in laboratory facilities, mentored by the scientists and professionals with whom they work (Clasen & Clasen, 1997). Other students rely on intensive workshops or summer programs related to specific careers and supplemented with internships and individually tailored instruction (Olszewski-Kubilius, 1997).

The benefits of mentoring to gifted students are numerous. Students receive sophisticated learning experiences that are highly motivating and stimulating. They gain invaluable opportunities to explore careers and confirm their interests and commitments to certain areas of study. Mentoring experiences may uncover potential in underachieving or disabled students, whose abilities may not stand out in conventional

A student works with her mentor, a motivating force who brings experience to the relationship and offers guidance and opportunities to explore career interests.

classroom settings. Mentoring may also promote the development of self-reliance, interpersonal skills, and lifelong, productive friendships (Clasen & Clasen, 1997).

focus 7

Identify six problems that complicate the selection of careers or professional pursuits for adolescents who are gifted.

■ CAREER CHOICES AND CHALLENGES Career interests, values, and dispositions appear to crystallize early in gifted students. In fact their interests are neither broader nor more restricted than those of their classmates (Achter, Benbow, & Lubinski, 1997). Many gifted students know early on what paths they will follow in postsecondary schooling. These paths often fall within the fields of engineering, health professions, and physical sciences.

Appropriate interest and "above-level ability" assessments (Achter, Benbow, & Lubinski, 1997, p. 12), career guidance and exploration (Olszewski-Kubilius, 1997), and other forms of counseling play an important role in helping young people who are gifted utilize their remarkable abilities and talents. These assessments should be made available to these young people in early adolescence. As gifted students come to understand more clearly their individual strengths and weaknesses, they will make better choices in fields of study and professional careers (Achter et al., 1997; Moon, Kelly, & Feldhusen, 1997).

Every gifted program ought to provide differentiated counseling services to help gifted students and their families deal with personal, social, educational, and career problems (Moon et al., 1997). The approaches used by counselors, therapists, and educators will vary according to the nature of the problems and the student's needs. One promising approach is the use of group counseling. Colangelo (1997), a long-time advocate for counseling for gifted individuals, put it this way, "It is my observation that gifted students are considerably smarter about course work than about themselves. They have the ability to be insightful about themselves, but seldom opportunity to articulate and share their insights" (pp. 257–358). Group counseling conducted by a well-trained therapist or counselor would be helpful to many gifted students. Table 16.8 provides some interesting questions that gifted young people might pursue in group counseling sessions.

At age nine this gifted student showed an early interest in finance by investing a cash gift in a company. The value of the investment doubled in three months. By age seventeen, he had a private fund that outperformed many mutual funds.

TABLE 16.8	Useful questions for group counseling discussions

1. What does it mean to be gifted?
2. What do your parents think it means to be gifted?
3. What do your teachers think it means to be gifted?
4. What do other kids in school think it means to be gifted?
5. How is being gifted an advantage for you? How is it a disadvantage?
6. Have you ever deliberately hidden your giftedness? If so, how?

Source: From "Counseling Gifted Students: Issues and Practices," by N. Colangelo. In *Handbook of Gifted Education,* 2/E edited by N. Colangelo & G. A. Davis, 1997, p. 356. Copyright © 1997 by Allyn and Bacon. Reprinted by permission.

Problems caused by excessive or inappropriate parental expectations or other related problems may need to be addressed in a family context. Counselors and therapists may help parents develop realistic expectations that fit their child's abilities, aspirations, and true interests (Silverman, 1997). As with other exceptionalities, the provision of counseling services is best achieved through multidisciplinary efforts (Moon et al., 1997).

■ PROBLEMS AND CHALLENGES OF GIFTEDNESS Students who are gifted must cope with a number of problems (Delisle, 1997; Kerr, 1997; Perrone, 1997). One problem is the expectations they have of themselves and those that have been explicitly and implicitly imposed by parents, teachers, and others. Students who are gifted frequently feel an inordinate amount of pressure to achieve high grades or to select particular professions. They often feel obligated or duty bound to achieve and contribute with excellence in every area, a syndrome called *perfectionism* (Adderholdt-Elliott, 1987). Such pressure often fosters a kind of conformity, preventing students from selecting avenues of endeavor that truly fit them and their personal interests.

VanTassel-Baska (1989) identified a number of social–emotional needs of students who are gifted that differentiate them from their same-age peers:

■ Understanding how they are different from and similar to their peers
■ Appreciating and valuing their own uniqueness as well as that of others
■ Understanding and developing relationship skills
■ Developing and valuing their high-level sensitivity
■ Gaining a realistic understanding of their own abilities and talents
■ Identifying ways of nurturing and developing their own abilities and talents
■ Adequately distinguishing between pursuits of excellence and pursuits of perfection
■ Developing the behaviors associated with negotiation and compromise

Students who are gifted need ongoing and continual access to adult role models who have interests and abilities that parallel theirs; the importance of these role models cannot be overestimated (Clasen & Clasen, 1997). Role models are particularly important for gifted students who grow up and receive their schooling in rural and remote areas. Such students often complete their public schooling without the benefit of having a mentor or professional person with whom they can talk or discuss various educational and career-related issues.

Historically Neglected Groups

■ FEMALES

Silverman (1986, p. 43) posed the question, "What happens to the gifted girl?" The number of girls identified as gifted appears to decline with age. This phenomenon is surprising when we realize that girls tend to walk and talk earlier than their male counterparts; that girls, as a group, read earlier; that girls score higher than boys on IQ tests during the preschool years; and that the grade-point averages of girls during the elementary years are higher than those of boys.

Just exactly what happens to girls? Is the decline in the number of girls identified as gifted related to their socialization? Does some innate physiological or biological

Debate continues on why gender appears to affect whether a gifted child reaches his or her potential. Some suggest that societal values that encourage certain gender behaviors are contributing factors. Some schools are experimenting with gender segregated classes in an effort to reduce the achievement differential between girls and boys.

mechanism account for this decline? Why do some gifted females fail to realize their potential? To what extent do value conflicts about women's roles contribute to mixed achievement in gifted women? The answers to these and other important questions are gradually emerging.

One of the explanations given for this decline is the gender-role socialization that girls receive. Behaviors associated with competitiveness, risk taking, and independence are not generally encouraged in girls. Behaviors that are generally fostered in girls include dependence, cooperation, and nurturing. The elimination of independent behaviors in girls is viewed by Silverman (1986) as being the most damaging aspect of their socialization. More recent research suggests that girls who develop social self-esteem, "the belief that one has the ability to act effectively and to make decisions independently," are more likely to realize their potential (Kerr, 1997). Without independence, the development of high levels of creativity, achievement, and leadership will be severely limited.

Females who are gifted and talented experience unique problems in addition to those already identified. These problems include fear of appearing "unfeminine" or unattractive when competing with males, competition between marital and career aspirations, stress induced by traditional cultural and societal expectations, and self-imposed or culturally imposed restrictions related to educational and occupational choices (Delisle, 1997; Kerr, 1997; Silverman, 1997). Although many of these problems are far from being resolved at this point, some progress is being made. Women in greater numbers are choosing to enter professions traditionally pursued by men (Kerr, 1997).

Fortunately, multiple role assignments are emerging in many families, wherein the usual tasks of mothers are shared by all members of the family or are completed by someone outside the family. Cultural expectations are changing, and as a result, options for women who are gifted are rapidly expanding (see the Reflect on This feature on page 536).

focus 8

Identify some of the problems that girls who are gifted experience in careers and other pursuits.

Interacting in Natural Settings

PEOPLE WHO ARE GIFTED, CREATIVE, AND TALENTED

■ EARLY CHILDHOOD YEARS

TIPS FOR THE FAMILY

- Realize that giftedness is evidenced in many ways (e.g., concentration, memory, pleasure in learning, sense of humor, social knowledge, task orientation, ability to follow and lead, capacity and desire to compete, information capacity).
- Provide toys for children who are gifted that may be used for a variety of activities.
- Take trips to museums, exhibits, fairs, and other places of interest.
- Provide an environment that is appropriately challenging.
- Supply proper visual, auditory, verbal, and kinesthetic stimulation.
- Talk to the child in ways that foster a give-and-take conversation.
- Begin to expose the child to picture books and ask him or her to find certain objects or animals or respond to age-appropriate questions.
- Avoid unnecessary restrictions.
- Provide play materials that are developmentally appro-

priate and may be a little challenging.

TIPS FOR THE PRESCHOOL TEACHER

- Look for ways in which various talents and skills may be expressed (e.g., cognitive, artistic, leadership, socialization, motor ability, memory, special knowledge, imagination).
- Provide opportunities for the child who is gifted to express these talents.
- Capitalize on the child's curiosity. Develop learning activities that relate to his or her passions.
- Allow the child to experiment with all the elements of language—even written language—as he or she is ready.

TIPS FOR PRESCHOOL PERSONNEL

- Remember that conversation is critical to the child's development. Do not be reluctant to spend a great deal of time asking the child various questions as he or she engages in various activities.
- Become a specialist in looking for gifts and talents across a variety of domains (e.g., artistic, social, cognitive).
- Allow for rapid mastery of concepts and then allow the child to move on to

other more challenging activities rather than holding him or her back.

TIPS FOR NEIGHBORS AND FRIENDS

- Recognize that people have a variety of gifts and talents that can be encouraged.
- Provide preschool opportunities for all children who are potentially gifted to have the necessary environmental ingredients to fully use their talents or gifts.
- Enjoy and sometimes endure the neighborhood child who has chosen your home as his or her lab for various experiments in cooking, painting, and building.

■ ELEMENTARY YEARS

TIPS FOR THE FAMILY

- Maintain the search for individual gifts and talents; some qualities may not be evident until the child is older.
- Provide out-of-school experiences that foster talent or skill development (e.g., artistic, physical, academic, leadership).
- Enroll the child who is gifted in summer programs that are offered by universities or colleges.

- Monitor the child's school environment to be sure that adequate steps are being taken to respond to his or her unique skills.
- Join an advocacy group for parents in your community or state.
- Subscribe to child publications that are related to your child's current interests.
- Encourage your child's friendships and associations with other people who have like interests and aptitudes.

TIPS FOR THE GENERAL EDUCATION SCHOOL TEACHER

- Provide opportunities for enrichment as well as acceleration.
- Allow students who are gifted to pursue individual projects that require sophisticated forms of thinking or production.
- Become involved in professional organizations that provide assistance to teachers of students who are gifted.
- Take a course that specifically addresses the instructional strategies that might be used with children who are gifted.
- Encourage children to become active participants in various events that emphasize particular skill or know-

ledge areas (e.g., science fairs, music competitions).

- Develop clubs and programs that allow children who are gifted to pursue their talents.
- Create award programs that encourage talent development across a variety of domains.
- Involve community members in offering enrichment and acceleration activities (e.g., artists, engineers, writers).
- Foster the use of inclusive procedures for identifying students who are potentially gifted from groups that are culturally diverse, disadvantaged, or have disabilities.

TIPS FOR NEIGHBORS AND FRIENDS
- Contribute to organizations that foster talent development.
- Volunteer to serve as judges for competitive events.
- Be willing to share your talents with young, emergent scholars, musicians, athletes, and artists.
- Become a mentor for someone in your community.

SECONDARY AND TRANSITION YEARS

TIPS FOR THE FAMILY
- Continue to provide sources of support for talent development outside of the home.
- Regularly counsel your child about courses that he or she will take.
- Provide access to tools (e.g., computers, video cameras) and resources (e.g., specialists, coaches, mentors) that contribute to the child's performance.
- Expect variations in performance from time to time.
- Provide opportunities for rest and relaxation from demanding schedules.
- Continue to encourage involvement with peers who have similar interests and aptitudes.

TIPS FOR THE GENERAL EDUCATION SCHOOL TEACHER
- Provide a range of activities for students with varying abilities.
- Provide opportunities for students who are gifted to deal with real problems or develop actual products.
- Give opportunities for genuine enrichment activities, not just more work.
- Remember that giftedness manifests itself in many ways. Determine how various types of giftedness may be expressed in your content domain.
- Help eliminate conflicting and confusing signals about career choices and fields of study often given to young women who are gifted.

TIPS FOR SCHOOL PERSONNEL
- Provide, to the degree possible, a variety of curriculum options, activities, clubs, and the like.
- Acknowledge excellence in a variety of performance areas (e.g., leadership, visual and performing arts, academics).
- Continue to use inclusive procedures in identifying individuals who are potentially gifted and talented.
- Encourage participation in competitive activities in which students are able to use their gifts and talents (e.g., science fairs, debate tournaments, music competitions).

TIPS FOR NEIGHBORS, FRIENDS, AND POTENTIAL EMPLOYERS
- Provide opportunities for students to "shadow" talented professionals.
- Volunteer as a professional to work directly with students who are gifted in pursuing a real problem or producing an actual product.
- Become a mentor for a student who is interested in what you do professionally.
- Support the funding of programs for students who are gifted and talented and who come from disadvantaged environments.
- Provide summer internships for students who have a particular interest in your profession.

- Serve as an adviser for a high school club or other organization that gives students additional opportunities to pursue talent areas.

ADULT YEARS

TIPS FOR THE FAMILY
- Continue to nurture appropriate interdependence and independence.
- Assist with the provision of specialized assistance.
- Celebrate the accomplishments and provide support for challenges.
- Let go.

TIPS FOR EDUCATIONAL PERSONNEL
- Exhibit behaviors associated with effective mentoring.
- Provide meaningful ways to deal with pressure.
- Allow the individuals to be themselves.
- Provide adequate time for discussion and interaction.
- Be aware of other demands in the individuals' lives.

TIPS FOR POTENTIAL EMPLOYERS
- Establish appropriately high expectations.
- Provide opportunities for diversion and fun.
- Be sensitive to changing interests and needs.
- Allow employees to be involved with young gifted students on a volunteer basis.

Reflect on This

ENCOURAGING GIFTEDNESS IN GIRLS

■ **SUGGESTIONS FOR THE FAMILY**
- Hold high expectations for daughters.
- Do not purchase gender-role-stereotyped toys.
- Avoid overprotectiveness.
- Encourage high levels of activity.
- Allow girls to get dirty.
- Instill beliefs in their capabilities.
- Support their interests.
- Identify them as gifted during their preschool years.
- Find for them playmates who are gifted to identify with and emulate.
- Foster interests in mathematics outside of school.
- Consider early entrance and other opportunities to accelerate.
- Encourage enrollment in mathematics courses.
- Introduce them to professional women in many occupations.
- Encourage their mothers to acknowledge their own giftedness.

- Encourage their mothers to work at least part time outside the home.
- Encourage fathers to spend time alone with daughters in so-called masculine activities.
- Share household duties equally between the parents.
- Assign chores to siblings on a nonsexist basis.
- Discourage the use of sexist language or teasing in the home.
- Monitor television programs for sexist stereotypes, and discuss these with children of both genders.
- Encourage siblings to treat each other equitably, rather than according to the traditional gender-role stereotypes they may see outside the home.

■ **SUGGESTIONS FOR TEACHERS AND COUNSELORS**
- Believe in girls' logicomathematical abilities, and provide many opportunities for

them to practice mathematical reasoning within other subject areas.
- Accelerate girls through the science and mathematics curriculum whenever possible.
- Have special clubs in mathematics for girls who are high achieving.
- Design coeducational career development classes in which both girls and boys learn about career potentialities for women.
- Expose boys and girls to role models of women in various careers.
- Discuss nontraditional careers for women, including salaries for men and women and schooling requirements.
- Help girls set long-term goals.
- Discuss underachievement among females who are gifted and ask how they can combat it in themselves and others.
- Have girls read biographies of famous women.

- Arrange opportunities for girls to "shadow" a female professional for a few days to see what her work entails.
- Discourage sexist remarks and attitudes in the classroom.
- Boycott sexist classroom materials, and write to the publishers for their immediate correction.
- Discuss sexist messages in the media.
- Advocate special classes and afterschool enrichment opportunities for students who are gifted.
- Form support groups for girls with similar interests.

Source: From "What Happens to the Gifted Girl?" by L. K. Silverman. In *Critical Issues in Gifted Education, Vol. 1: Defensible Programs for the Gifted,* edited by C. J. Maker, 1986, pp. 43–89. Austin, TX: Pro-Ed. (Copyright owned by author.) Adapted by permission.

■ **PERSONS WITH DISABILITIES**

For some time, intellectual giftedness has been largely associated with high IQs and high scores on aptitude tests. These tests, by their very nature and structure, measure a limited range of mental abilities. Because of their limitations, they have not been particularly helpful in identifying persons with disabilities who are intellectually or otherwise gifted. However, persons with disabilities such as cerebral palsy, learning disabilities, and other disabling conditions can be gifted. Helen Keller, Vincent van Gogh, and Ludwig van Beethoven are prime examples of individuals with disabilities who were also gifted. Some theorists and practitioners suggest that as many as 2% of individuals with disabilities are gifted (Johnson et al., 1997). Fortunately, we have begun to look for various kinds of giftedness in children with disabilities.

In this context, the person who is gifted is defined as "one who has exhibited exceptional potential for (a) learning, (b) achieving academic excellence in one or more

Charelle is an African American student in the third grade, on free lunch, homeless for much of the year, and much loved and supported by both parents. Her mother is a housekeeper in a local hospital. Her father "flips burgers" (her words) at a fast-food restaurant. Now in housing in a different school zone, Charelle still attends the school in which she began, because her mother makes the long bus ride with Charelle, continuing on to her own job via public transportation. Charelle is often as much as an hour late for class because of the extended bus ride, but when she arrives in her classroom, she becomes immediately absorbed in her schoolwork. Charelle's teacher feels the long ride seems worthwhile to Charelle's parents because the school has been nurturing to the family, and that Project START "may have been the icing on the cake (that kept them coming)."

Charelle seems to be hungry, not so much for food as for knowledge. She often asks for extra schoolwork to do at home. Her current teacher calls her "a joy. I feel lucky to have her in my class. There are few children intrinsically motivated like Charelle. . . . She's a real big ham. She would act out anything. She's just kind of bright and bubbly and effervescent and gregarious. . . . She writes. She loves to tell stories. She's a good leader in a group. . . . Not as a forceful leader, but she coaches, like, 'Well, maybe we should do this.' She's blown the doors off math in here. I have her well into fourth-grade math." Charelle's second-grade teacher echoes, "She's very talented in writing and reading. She is very creative, good in art, good in all subjects." The teacher points out a piece of Charelle's artwork, which is permanently displayed in the school corridor.

Source: From "Challenging expectations: Case studies of high potential, culturally diverse young children," by C. Tomlinson, C. Callahan, and K. Lelli, 1997, *Gifted Child Quarterly, 41*(2), pp. 5–17.

subject areas, and (c) manifesting superior abilities through language, problem solving, and creative production" (Whitmore & Maker, 1985, p. 10). Although many challenges are still associated with identifying individuals with disabilities who are gifted, much progress has been made.

Successful identification of giftedness is made in environments that elicit signs of mental giftedness and information about the individual's performance gathered from many sources. It is important that the child be given opportunities to perform tasks that are not impeded by his or her disabling condition. Also, if and when tests of mental ability are used, they must be appropriately adapted, both in administration and scoring. Additionally, the identification process should occur at regular intervals. The performance of some children with disabilities changes dramatically with appropriate instruction and related technologies (Johnson et al., 1997).

Differential education for children with disabilities who are gifted is still in its infancy. A great deal of progress has been made, particularly in the adaptive uses of computers and related technologies, but much development work remains to be done. Additionally, a great deal is still unknown about the service delivery systems and materials that are best suited for these individuals (see the Reflect on This feature at the top of this page).

■ CHILDREN FROM DIFFERENT CULTURAL BACKGROUNDS OR LIVING IN POVERTY

Typical identification procedures often fail to identify children as being gifted when they come from minority groups or disadvantaged environments. However, many practitioners are now using multiple criteria to reveal potential and giftedness in children who are diverse or poor (Frasier, 1997).

focus 9

Identify seven essential elements of programs for gifted children who come from diverse backgrounds and who may live in poverty.

Reflect on This

MULTICULTURALISM AND GIFTED STUDENTS

- Among African American students who score at the highest levels on the Scholastic Aptitude Test (those with a combined verbal and math SAT score of 1400 or above), more than 18% leave school because of academic problems. Up to 70% of African American students who enroll in 4-year colleges drop out at some point.
- Graduate school enrollments of American students in mathematics and science have declined substantially in the past 20 years, while the number of foreign-born students enrolled has risen. In 1990, 57% of doctorates granted in the United States in mathematics went to students from other countries.
- Minorities are not entering many important fields in mathematics and science. For example, African Americans make up 12% of the population, yet earn only 5% of the baccalaureate degrees awarded each year in science and mathematics, receive only 1% of the Ph.D.s, and make up only 2% of all employed scientists and engineers in the country. Hispanics make up 9% of the population, but represent only 3% of the baccalaureate degrees in science and mathematics, 2% of the Ph.D.s, and 2% of all employed scientists and engineers in the country.

Therefore, the fastest-growing sectors of our society are seriously underrepresented in leadership positions in science and mathematics.

Source: "National excellence: A case for developing America's talent." U.S. Department of Education (1993, p. 11).

Past research conducted by Van Tassel-Baska and Chepko-Sade (1986) has suggested that as many as 15% of the gifted population may be children who are disadvantaged. In fact, the actual number of students who are disadvantaged and also gifted may be even greater, given the identification criteria used in this study. A great deal of talent and ability remains undeveloped and untapped because so few of these students are identified and provided with appropriate learning experiences (see the nearby Reflect on This feature).

Instructional programs for children and adolescents who are disadvantaged and gifted have several key components. First and foremost, the teachers in these programs are well trained in "differentiating required subject areas" (Richert, 1997, p. 85). They understand learning styles, how to build and capitalize on students' interests, and how to maximize students' affective, cognitive, and ethical capacities (Richert, 1997).

There is a general consensus that programs for these children should begin early and be tailored to the needs and interests of each identified child. These programs should be focused on "individual possibilities rather than norm-defined 'shortcomings'" (Tomlinson, Callahan, & Lelli, 1997, p. 5). Moreover, these programs help parents understand their roles in fostering giftedness and talent development (Tomlinson et al., 1997). Often the emphasis in the early years is on reading instruction, language development, and foundation skills. Other key components include experiential education that provides children with many opportunities for hands-on learning, activities that foster self-expression, plentiful use of mentors and role models who represent the child's cultural or ethnic group, involvement of the community, and counseling throughout the school years that gives serious consideration to the cultural values of the family and the child who is gifted. Lastly, the programs are enhanced by a team approach, or "multiavenue approach," in which mentors, parents, teachers, and other community members work together to meet the needs of these children (Tomlinson et al., 1997).

Case Study

CHARACTERISTICS OF GIFTED CALVIN?

hat follows is a series of cartoon strips from *Calvin and Hobbes*.
They depict in part the relationship Calvin has with his dad.

■ APPLICATION

1. Is Calvin gifted, creative, and talented? Provide a rationale for your answer.
2. If Calvin's dad asked you how to handle Calvin's "giftedness," what recommendations would you make? Give a rationale for your answers.
3. If Calvin's dad were enrolled in your parenting class and asked for your counsel as the group leader, what would you recommend?

WHAT WOULD YOU DO WITH JANE?

Many children who are gifted are prevented from accelerating their growth and learning for fear that they will be hurt emotionally and socially. Parents' comments such as these are common: She's so young. Won't she miss a great deal if she doesn't go through the fourth and fifth grade experiences? What about her friends? Who will her friends be if she goes to college at such a young age? Will she have the social skills to interact with kids that are much older? If she skips these two grades, won't there be gaps in her learning and social development?

On the other hand, the nature of the questions or comments by parents about acceleration may also be positive: She is young in years only! She will adjust extremely well. Maybe she is emotionally mature enough to handle this type of acceleration. The increased opportunities provided through university training will give her greater chances to develop her talents and capacities. Perhaps the older students with whom she will interact are better suited to her intellectual and social needs.

Consider Jane, a child who is gifted. In third grade, she thrived in school, and just about everything associated with her schooling at that time was positive. Her teacher was responsive and allowed her and others to explore well beyond the usual "read-the-text-then-respond-to-the-ditto-sheet" routine. Much self-pacing was possible, and materials galore were presented for both independent studies and queries.

In the fourth and fifth grades, however, things began to change radically. Jane's teachers were simply unable to provide enough interesting and challenging work for her. It was during the latter part of the fourth grade that she began to view herself as different. Not only did she know, but her classmates knew, that learning came exceptionally easily to her. At this same time, Jane was beginning to change dramatically in her cognitive capacity. Unfortunately, her teachers persisted in unnecessary drills and other mundane assignments, and Jane gradually became bored and lapsed into a type of passive learning. Rather than attacking assignments with vigor, she performed them carelessly, often making many stupid errors. Gradually, what ensued was a child who was very unhappy in school. School had been the most interesting place for her to be before she entered fourth grade. Then it became a source of pain and boredom.

Jane's parents decided that they needed to know more about her capacities and talents. Although it was expensive and quite time consuming, they visited a nearby university center for psychological services. Jane was tested, and the results were very revealing. For the first time, Jane's parents had some objective information about her capacities. She was in fact an unusually bright and talented young lady. Jane's parents then began to consider the educational alternatives available to her.

The counselor who provided the interpretation of the results at the university center strongly recommended that Jane be advanced to the seventh grade in a school that provided services to students who were talented and gifted. This meant that Jane would skip one year of elementary school and have an opportunity to move very rapidly through her junior and senior high school studies. Furthermore, she would potentially be able to enter the university well in advance of her peers.

Jane's parents knew that her performance has diminished significantly in the last year. Moreover, her attitude and disposition about school seem to be worsening. What would you do as her parents? What factors would you consider important in making the decision? Or is the decision Jane's and hers alone?

■ POINT

Jane should be allowed to accelerate her educational pace. Moving to the seventh grade will benefit her greatly, intellectually and socially. Most girls develop more rapidly physically and socially than boys do. Skipping one grade will not hinder her social development at all. In fact, she will benefit from the interactions that she will have with other able students, some of whom will also have skipped a grade or two. Additionally, the research regarding the impact of accelerating students is positive, particularly if the students are carefully selected. Jane has been carefully evaluated and deserves to have the opportunity to be excited about learning and achieving again.

■ COUNTERPOINT

There are some inherent risks in having Jane skip her sixth-grade experience and moving on to the seventh grade. Jane is neither socially nor emotionally prepared to deal with the junior high environment. She may be very able intellectually and her achievement may be superior, but this is not the time to move her into junior high. Socially, she is still quite awkward for her age. This awkwardness would be intensified in the junior high setting. Acceleration for Jane should be considered later on, when she has matured more socially.

She should be able to receive the acceleration that she needs in her present elementary school. Certainly, other able students in her school would benefit from joining together for various activities and learning experiences. The acceleration should take place in her own school, with other students who are gifted and of her own age. Maybe all Jane needs is some release time to attend a class or two elsewhere. Using this approach, she could benefit from involvement with her same-age peers and still receive the stimulation that she so desperately needs. Allowing her to skip a grade now would hurt her emotionally and socially in the long run.

Review

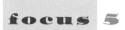

Briefly describe several historical developments directly related to the measurement of various types of giftedness.

- Alfred Binet developed the first developmental scale for children during the early 1900s. Gradually, the notion of mental age emerged, that is, a representation of what the child was capable of doing compared with age-specific developmental tasks.
- Lewis M. Terman translated the Binet scale and made modifications suitable for children in the United States.
- Gradually, the intelligence quotient, or IQ (mental age/chronological age x 100 = IQ), became the gauge for determining giftedness.
- Intelligence was long viewed as a unitary structure or underlying ability. But this view gradually changed, and researchers began to believe that intelligence was represented in a variety of distinct capacities and abilities.
- J. P. Guilford and other social scientists began to develop a multidimensional theory of intelligence, which prompted researchers to develop models and assessment devices for examining creativity.
- Programs were gradually developed to foster and develop creativity in young people.

- More recently V. Ramos-Ford and H. Gardner have developed the multiple intelligences perspective, which designates seven areas of intelligence: linguistic, logical–mathematical, spatial, musical, bodily–kinesthetic, interpersonal, and intrapersonal behaviors.

Identify five major components of definitions that have been developed to describe giftedness.

- Children and adolescents who are gifted perform or show potential for performing at remarkably high levels when compared with others of their age, experience, or environment.
- Children who are gifted exhibit high performance capability in intellectual, creative, and/or artistic areas.
- Such children may possess unusual leadership capacity or excel in specific academic fields.
- Gifted children become extraordinarily proficient performers or creative producers.
- Such children and adolescents need special educational opportunities to realize their full intellectual and creative potential.

Identify four problems inherent in accurately describing the characteristics of individuals who are gifted.

- Individuals who are gifted vary significantly in a variety of characteristics; they are not a homogeneous group.
- Because research regarding the characteristics of people who are gifted has been conducted with different population groups, the characteristics that have surfaced represent the population studied rather than the gifted population as a whole.
- Many early studies of individuals who are gifted led to a stereotypical view of giftedness.
- Historically, studies regarding the characteristics of individuals who are gifted have not included adequate samples of females, minority or ethnic groups, or socioeconomic groups.

focus 4

Identify three factors that appear to contribute significantly to the emergence of various forms of giftedness.

- Genetic endowment certainly contributes to manifestations of giftedness in all of its varieties.
- Environmental stimulation provided by parents, teachers, coaches, tutors, and others contributes significantly to the emergence of giftedness.
- The interaction of innate abilities with environmental influences and encouragement fosters the development and expression of giftedness.

focus 5

Describe the range of assessment devices used to identify the various types of giftedness.

- Developmental checklists and scales
- Parent and teacher inventories
- Intelligence and achievement tests
- Creativity tests
- Other diverse observational information provided by parents, grandparents, and other knowledgeable informants

focus 6

Identify nine strategies that foster the development of children and adolescents who are gifted.

- Environmental stimulation provided by parents from infancy through adolescence
- Differentiated education and specialized service delivery systems that provide enrichment activities and/or possibilities for acceleration
- Early entrance to kindergarten or school
- Grade skipping
- Early admission to college
- Honors programs at the high school and college levels
- Specialized schools in the performing and visual arts, math, and science
- Mentor programs with university professors and other talented individuals
- Specialized counseling facilities

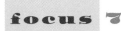

Identify six problems that complicate the selection of careers or professional pursuits for adolescents who are gifted.

- Because individuals who are gifted are often talented, capable, and interested in a broad spectrum of areas, they find it difficult to make an appropriate career or profession choice.
- Women who are gifted may lack adequate models or mentors with whom to identify in pursuing various career and professional options.
- Women may also be influenced by traditional cultural and societal expectations that are restrictive.

- Adolescents who are gifted may be unduly influenced by their parents' expectations, their own expectations, and their preconceived notions as to what people who are gifted ought to do professionally or academically.
- Some adolescents who are gifted are socially isolated in the sense that they do not have access to peers who are gifted and with whom they can discuss their aspirations, interests, and problems.
- Adolescents who are gifted and live in rural or remote areas may have few if any role models with whom they can relate or identify.

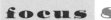

Identify some of the problems that girls who are gifted experience in careers and other pursuits.

- Fear of appearing "unfeminine" or unattractive when competing with males
- Competition between marital and career aspirations
- Stress induced by traditional cultural and societal expectations
- Self-imposed or culturally imposed restrictions related to educational and occupational choices

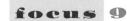

Identify seven essential elements of programs for gifted children who come from diverse backgrounds and who may live in poverty.

- The programs are staffed with skilled and competent teachers and other support personnel.
- The staff members work as teams.
- Teachers and others responsible for developing the learning experience understand learning styles, students' interests, and how to build students' affective, cognitive, and ethical capacities.
- The programs focus on students' strengths, not their deficits.
- The programs involve parents as full partners in the talent development process.
- The programs use mentors and other good role models who represent the diversity in the community.
- The programs begin early in the children's educational lives.

Absence seizures. Seizures characterized by brief lapses of consciousness, usually lasting not more than ten seconds. Eye blinking and twitching of the mouth may accompany these seizures.

Acceleration. A process whereby students are allowed to achieve at a rate that is consistent with their capacity.

Acquired brain injury (ABI). A more global term than *traumatic brain injury (TBI)*. It refers to injuries that may result from strokes and other vascular accidents, infectious diseases, anoxic injuries (hanging, near-drowning), anesthetic accidents, severe blood loss, metabolic disorders, and ingestion of toxic products.

Activity group therapy. A group-oriented approach used to treat youngsters with behavior disorders.

Adaptive fit. Compatibility between demands of a task or setting and a person's needs and abilities.

Adaptive instruction. Instruction that modifies the learning environment to accommodate unique learner characteristics.

Adaptive skills. Skills that facilitate an individual's ability to function in community, family, and school settings. Adaptive skills may include communication, self-care, home living skills, social skills, use of community resources, self-direction, health and safety awareness, functional academic skills, leisure pursuits, and work skills.

Adult service agencies. Agencies that provide services to assist individuals with disabilities to become more independent as adults. Adult agencies include rehabilitation services, social services, mental health services, and so on.

Albinism. Lack of pigmentation in eyes, skin, and hair.

Alternative communication. See *Augmentative communication.*

Amblyopia. Loss of vision due to an imbalance of eye muscles.

American Association on Mental Retardation (AAMR). An organization of professionals from many disciplines involved in the study and treatment of mental retardation.

American Sign Language (ASL). A type of sign language commonly used by people with hearing impairments. ASL signs represent concepts rather than single words.

Americans with Disabilities Act. Civil rights legislation in the United States that provides a mandate to end discrimination against people with disabilities in private sector employment, all public services, public accommodations, transportation, and telecommunications.

Amniocentesis. A prenatal assessment of a fetus, which involves analysis of amniotic fluid to screen for possible abnormalities.

Anemia. A condition in which the blood is deficient in red blood cells.

Anencephaly. A condition in which the person has a partial or complete absence of cerebral tissue.

Anophthalmos. An absence of the eyeball.

Anoxia. A lack of oxygen that may result in permanent damage to the brain.

Anticonvulsants. Medication prescribed to control seizures (convulsions).

Apgar scoring. An evaluation of a newborn that assesses heart rate, respiratory condition, muscle tone, reflexes, and color.

Aphasia. An acquired language disorder caused by brain damage that is characterized by complete or partial impairment of language comprehension, formulation, and use.

Aqueous humor. A fluid that lies between the lens and cornea of the eye.

Arc, The—A National Organization on Mental Retardation. A national organization of people with mental retardation, parents, professionals, and friends that aims to enhance the quality of life for people with mental retardation in family, school, and community settings.

Articulation problems. Speech problems such as omissions, substitutions, additions, and distortions.

Asphyxiation. An impaired or absent exchange of oxygen and carbon dioxide.

Assistive communication. Forms of communication that supplement or take the place of speaking. See also *Augmentative communication.*

Assistive technology. Technological devices that help an individual with disabilities adapt to the natural settings of home, school, and family. The technology may include computers, hearing aids, wheelchairs, and so on.

Association for Persons with Severe Handicaps. An organization of people with severe disabilities, professionals, family members, and friends dedicated to creating opportunities for people with severe disabilities to grow up, live, work, and be educated side-by-side with people who are not disabled.

Asthma. A condition, often of allergic origin, that is characterized by continuous labored breathing, wheezing, a sense of constriction in the chest, and attacks of coughing and gasping.

Astigmatism. A refractive problem that occurs when the surface of the cornea is uneven or structurally defective, preventing the light rays from converging at one point.

Athetosis. A condition characterized by constant contorted, twisting motions in the wrists and fingers.

Atresia. The absence of a normal opening.

Atropinization. Treatment for cataracts that involves washing the eye with atropine, permanently dilating the pupil.

Attention deficit disorder (ADD). See *Attention-deficit/hyperactivity disorder (ADHD)*.

Attention-deficit/hyperactivity disorder (ADHD). A disorder in youngsters characterized by difficulties maintaining attention because of a limited ability to concentrate. Such youngsters typically exhibit impulsive actions and hyperactive behavior. See also *Undifferentiated attention deficit disorder*.

Audiogram. A record obtained from an audiometer that graphs an individual's threshold of hearing at various sound frequencies.

Audiologist. A specialist in the assessment of hearing ability.

Audiometer. An electronic device used to detect a person's response to sound stimuli.

Audition. The act or sense of hearing.

Auditory association. The ability to associate verbally presented ideas or information.

Auditory blending. The act of blending the parts of a word into an integrated whole when speaking.

Auditory discrimination. Ability to distinguish between the sounds of different words, syllables, or environmental noises.

Auditory memory. The ability to recall verbally presented material.

Augmentative communication. Forms of communication that employ nonspeech alternatives.

Aura. A sensation that occurs just before a seizure, which the person is able to remember.

Authentic assessment. An alternative to the traditional use of standardized tests to measure student progress. Assessment is based on student progress in meaningful learning activities.

Autism. A childhood disorder with onset prior to 36 months of age that is characterized by extreme withdrawal, self-stimulation, intellectual deficits, and language disorders.

Bacterial meningitis. An inflammation of the membranes in the brain or spinal cord caused by bacterial infection.

Barrier-free facility. A building or other structure that is designed and constructed so that people with mobility disabilities (such as those in wheelchairs) can move freely, accessing all areas without encountering architectural obstructions.

Behavioral contract. Agreement, written or oral, between people stating that if one party behaves in a certain manner (such as the student completes homework), the other (such as the teacher or parent) will provide a specific reward.

Behavioral factors. Behaviors, such as dangerous activities or maternal substance abuse, that can cause mental retardation or other disabilities.

Behavior disorders. Conditions in which the emotional or behavioral responses of individuals in various environments are significantly different from those of their peer, ethnic, and cultural groups. These responses seriously affect social relationships, personal adjustment, schooling, and employment.

Binet-Simon Scales. An individual test of intelligence developed by Alfred Binet and Theodore Simon in 1905 in France. Later translated into English (1908) and revised and standardized by Lewis Terman. See also *Stanford-Binet Individual Intelligence Scale*.

Bioethics. The study of ethics in medicine.

Biomedical factors. Biologic processes, such as genetic disorders or deficits in nutrition, that can cause mental retardation or other disabilities.

Blind. According to the American Medical Association, a condition characterized by central visual acuity not exceeding 20/200 in the person's better eye with correcting lenses, or visual acuity, if better than 20/200, that is limited in the central field of vision.

Blissymbols. A rebus system developed by C. K. Bliss that ties a specific symbol to a word. There are four types of Blissymbols: pictographic, ideographic, relational, and abstract.

Braille. A system of writing used by many people who are blind, which involves combinations of six raised dots, punched into paper, that can be read with the fingertips.

Buphthalmos. An abnormal distention and enlargement of the eyeball.

Cataract. A clouding of the eye lens, which becomes opaque, resulting in visual problems.

Catheterization. The process of introducing a hollow tube (catheter) into body cavities to drain fluid; for example, introducing a tube into an individual's bladder to drain urine.

Ceiling effects. A restricted range of test questions or problems that does not permit academically gifted students to demonstrate their true capacity of achievement.

Cerebral palsy. A neurological disorder characterized by motor problems, general physical weakness, lack of coordination, and perceptual difficulties.

Child abuse. Inflicted, nonaccidental, sexual, physical, and/or psychological trauma and/or physical injury to a child.

Child find. A system within a state or local area that attempts to identify all children who are disabled or at risk in order to refer them for appropriate support services.

Child neglect. A lack of interaction with a child on the part of other family members, which deprives the youngster of vital opportunities for development.

Child-study team. A term synonymous with multidisciplinary team or special services team. The team required by IDEA to develop an individualized education program for the child with a disability. See also *Multidisciplinary approach*.

Choroido-retinal degeneration. Deterioration of the choroid and retina.

Chromosomal abnormalities. Defects or damage in the chromosomes of an individual. Chromosomes are threadlike material that carry the genes and therefore play a central role in passing along inherited characteristics.

Civil Rights Act of 1964. Legislation passed in the United States that prohibits discrimination against individuals on the basis of race, sex, religion, or national origin.

Cleft palate. A gap in the soft palate and roof of the mouth, sometimes extending through the upper lip.

Clonic. The phase of a seizure in which the muscles of the body contract and relax in rapid sequence.

Closed-caption television. Process by which words spoken on television programs are given subtitles on the screen; also called the "line-21" system, since the caption is inserted into blank line 21 of the picture. This makes television programs accessible to people with hearing impairments.

Closed-circuit television (CCTV). A TV system, which includes a small television camera with zoom lens, TV monitor, and sliding platform table, that allows an individual with vision loss to view printed material enlarged up to 60 times its original size.

Cluttering. A speech disorder characterized by excessively rapid, disorganized speaking, often including words or phrases unrelated to the topic.

Cochlear implant. Surgical implanting of electronic prosthetic components that stimulate the auditory nerve and restore hearing.

Cognition. The act of thinking, knowing, or processing information.

Cognitive–behavioral training. A process in which individuals are taught to internalize speech strategies that will help them respond to problematic situations.

Collaboration. In educational settings, one or more people working together to attain a common goal; sometimes referred to as professional partnerships.

Communication. The process of transmitting or receiving messages and the meaning of those messages.

Computed tomography. A technique of x-ray imaging by which computers create cross-sectional images of very specific body areas or organs.

Computer-assisted instruction. The use of computers to provide instruction, rehearsal, and testing.

Concussion. A condition of impaired brain functioning derived from brutal shaking, violent blows, or other serious impacts to the head.

Conditioning. The process in which new objects or situations elicit responses that were previously elicited by other stimuli.

Conductive hearing loss. A hearing loss resulting from poor conduction of sound along the passages leading to the sense organ.

Congenital. A condition existing at birth.

Congenital defect. An imperfection with which the infant or child is born.

Congenital rubella. German measles contracted by a mother during pregnancy. It can cause a variety of problems, including mental retardation, deafness, blindness, and other neurological problems.

Consulting teacher. Teachers who provide support to general education classroom teachers and their students through specialized training and assistance in modifying curricula and environment to accommodate students with diverse needs.

Contusion. A condition in which the brain is bruised as a result of a severe hit or blow.

Consultive services. Assistance provided by specialists in general education settings to improve the quality of education or other intervention for a student with a disability.

Continuum of placements. A range of educational placements required in the Individuals with Disabilities Education Act to meet the least restrictive environment mandate for students with disabilities. Placements range from general education classrooms with support services to homebound and hospital programs.

Cooperative learning. Learning situation in which students work together to achieve group goals or attain group rewards.

Cornea. The external covering of the eye.

Cortical visual impairment (CVI). A leading cause of acquired blindness, which involves damage to the occipital lobes and/or the visual pathways to the brain. CVI can result from severe trauma, asphyxia, seizures, infections of the central nervous system, ingestion of drugs or poisons, or other neurological conditions.

Corti's organ. A structure of highly specialized cells in the cochlea, which translate vibration into nerve impulses that are sent to the brain.

Criterion-referenced assessment. Type of assessment that compares a person's performance to some specific established level (the criterion); his or her performance is not compared with that of other people.

Cued speech. A communication method used by people with hearing impairments, which combines hand signals with speech reading.

Cultural approach to labeling. An approach that defines what is normal according to the standards established by a given culture.

Cultural–familial retardation. A term applied to people with mental retardation whose condition may be attributable to both sociocultural and genetic factors.

Cultural pluralism. Multiple cultural subgroups living together in a manner that supports and maintains subsocietal differences, thereby continuing each group's cultural or ethnic traditions.

Curriculum-based assessment. A type of assessment that uses the objectives of a student's curriculum as the criterion against which progress is evaluated.

Cystic fibrosis. A hereditary disease that usually appears during early childhood. It involves a generalized disorder of exocrine glands, evidenced by respiratory problems and excessive loss of salt in perspiration.

Cytomegalic virus. A condition in newborns due to infection by cytomegalovirus (CMV).

Deaf. A term used to describe individuals who have hearing losses greater than 75 to 80 dB, use vision as their primary means of input, and cannot understand speech through the ear.

Deafness–blindness. A disorder involving simultaneous vision and hearing deficiencies. See *Dual sensory impairments.*

Delayed speech. A deficit in speaking proficiency in which the individual performs like someone much younger.

Denasality. A voice resonance problem that occurs when too little air passes through the nasal cavity.

Developmental approach to labeling. Labeling approach based on deviations in the course of development from what is considered normal growth.

Developmentally appropriate practices (DAP). Instructional approaches that use curriculum and learning environments consistent with the child's developmental level.

Deviant. A term used to describe the behavior of individuals who are unable to adapt to social roles or to establish appropriate interpersonal relationships.

Diabetes mellitus. A familial constitutional disease characterized by inadequate utilization of insulin, resulting in disordered metabolizing of carbohydrates, fats, and proteins.

Differentiated education. Instruction and learning activities that are uniquely and predominantly suited to the capacities and interests of gifted students.

Disability. Result of a loss of physical functioning or difficulties in learning and social adjustment that significantly interfere with normal growth and development. As defined by the Americans with Disabilities Act, a person with a disability has a physical or mental impairment that substantially limits the person in some major life activity, and this physical or mental impairment has resulted in discrimination.

Disorder. A disturbance in normal functioning (mental, physical, or psychological).

Down syndrome. A condition due to a chromosomal abnormality that results in unique physical characteristics and varying degrees of mental retardation. It has historically been described as "mongolism," a term no longer acceptable because of its negative connotations.

Dual diagnosis. A finding of both serious emotional problems and mental retardation in some persons.

Dual sensory impairments. A condition characterized by both vision and hearing sensory impairments (deafness–blindness). The condition can result in severe communication problems as well as developmental and educational difficulties that require extensive support across several professional disciplines.

Dyadic relationship. Two individuals who develop and maintain a significant affiliation.

Dyslexia. A severe impairment of the ability to read.

Early intervention. Comprehensive services for infants and toddlers who are disabled or at risk for acquiring a disability. Services may include education, health care, social, and/or psychological assistance.

Echolalia. A meaningless repetition or imitation of words that have been spoken, with no real attempt at communication.

Ecological approach. A term used in psychology to describe abnormal behavior resulting more from the interaction of an individual with the environment than from disease within the individual.

Ecological assessments. Assessments, such as direct observation of an individual, that analyze how an individual interacts in a natural environmental setting.

Educational blindness. Condition in which vision is not used as primary channel for learning.

Educational integration. As applied to students with disabilities, the physical placement of students with disabilities in general education classrooms and/or schools alongside their nondisabled peers.

Educationally disadvantaged. See *Students at risk.*

Electroacoustic devices. A general term referring to electronic aids that assist a person to hear.

Emotional disorders. Disorders characterized by behaviors associated with anxiety, fearfulness, phobias, social withdrawal, and depression.

Emotional disturbance. Condition that may result in behavior problems that originate internally. Persons with these problems may have difficulties in expressing or dealing with emotions related to normal family, school, or work-related experiences. See *Behavior disorders.*

Emphysema. A condition in which the lungs are unable to perform properly, causing shortness of breath.

Encephalitis. An inflammation of brain tissue that may damage the central nervous system.

Enrichment. Educational experiences for gifted students that enhance their thinking skills and extend their knowledge.

Entitlement program. A government-funded program in which everyone who meets the eligibility requirements must receive the designated service. The Individuals with Disabilities Education Act is an entitlement program.

Epidural hematoma. A collection of blood between the skull and the covering of the brain, culminating in pressure on vital brain structures.

Epilepsy. A condition characterized by differing types of recurrent seizures.

Epiphora. An overflow of tears due to obstruction of the lacrimal ducts of the eye.

Esotropia. A form of strabismus in which the eyes are pulled inward toward the nose.

Eustachian tube. A structure that extends from the throat to the middle ear cavity and controls air flow into the middle ear cavity.

Exceptional. A term describing any individual whose physical, mental, or behavioral performance deviates so substantially from the average (higher or lower) that additional services are necessary to meet the individual's needs.

Exotropia. A form of strabismus in which the eyes are pulled outward toward the ears.

Expressive aphasia. An inability to express verbally one's own thoughts and desires.

Expressive language disorders. Difficulties in language production.

Extended family. Close relatives to a family who visit or interact with the family on a regular basis.

Feebleminded. A term that appeared in the early literature on mental retardation but is now outdated; roughly means "of weak mind."

Fenestration. The surgical creation of a new opening in the labyrinth of the ear to restore hearing.

Fetal alcohol syndrome. Damage caused to the fetus by the mother's consumption of alcohol.

Fetoscopy. A procedure for examining the fetus, using a needle-like camera inserted into the womb to videoscan the fetus for visible abnormalities.

Figure–ground discrimination. The process of distinguishing an object from its background.

Finger spelling. A sign system of communication that incorporates all letters of the alphabet, signed independently on one hand, to form words.

Fluency disabilities. Speech problems such as repetitions, prolongation of sound, hesitations, and impediments in speech flow.

Fluency disorders. A type of speech disorder where the natural flow and rhythm of speaking is excessively interrupted, often by frequent pauses, prolongation of sounds, repetitions, or unrelated sounds.

Formal assessment. The use of assessment techniques to determine a person's eligibility for special education services. It includes the use of standardized measures, such as intelligence tests, achievement tests, and adaptive behavior scales, which compare a child's performance with that of others.

Formal supports. Supports provided to people with disabilities that are funded through government programs (such as the public schools).

Foster family care. A supported living arrangement for persons with disabilities where an individual lives in a family setting, learns adaptive skills, and works in a community job.

Fragile X syndrome. A condition found in some males with autism and involving damage to the chromosome structure, which appears as a breaking or splitting at the end of the X chromosome.

Fraternal twins. Twins that develop from two fertilized eggs in two placentas. Often such twins do not resemble one another closely.

Free and appropriate public education. Provision within the Individuals with Disabilities Education Act that requires every eligible student with a disability to be included in public education. The Supreme Court declared that an appropriate education consists of "specially designed instruction and related services" that are individually designed to provide "educational benefit."

Full inclusion. Arrangement in which students with disabilities or at risk receive all instruction in the general education classroom setting. Support services come to students. Students do not leave the general education classroom for instructional support.

Functional articulation disorders. Articulation problems that are not due to structural defects or neurological problems, but are more likely the result of environmental or psychological influences.

Functional assessment approach. An approach that emphasizes the relationship between individual functioning and the environment in which the individual lives, learns, and works.

Galactosemia. A metabolic disorder in which the infant has difficulty processing lactose. It may cause mental retardation and other problems.

Gastronomy tube feeding. The process of feeding the individual through a rubber tube that is inserted into the stomach.

Gender identity disorders. Problems related to an individual's perception of his or her biologically assigned sex and his or her gender identity.

Generalization. The process of applying previously learned information to new settings or situations.

Genetic counselor. A specially trained professional who counsels couples regarding their genetic history and chances of producing a handicapped baby.

Geneticist. A professional who specializes in the study of heredity.

Gifted, creative, and talented. Terms applied to those who have extraordinary abilities in one or more areas and are capable of superior performance.

Glaucoma. A disorder of the eye characterized by high pressure inside the eyeball.

Group home. A supported living arrangement for people with disabilities where professionals provide ongoing training and support in a community home setting.

Handicap. A limitation imposed on an individual by the environment and the person's capacity to cope with that limitation.

Haptic. Refers to touch sensation and information transmitted through body movement or position.

Hard-of-hearing. A term used to describe individuals with a sense of hearing that is deficient but somewhat functional.

Head Start. A federally funded preschool program for disadvantaged students to give them "a head start" prior to entering elementary school.

Health disabilities. Disabling conditions characterized by limited stamina, vitality, or alertness due to chronic or acute health problems.

Health disorders. Conditions or diseases that interfere with an individual's functioning but do not necessarily or initially have an impact on their ability to move about independently in various settings.

Hemiplegia. Paralysis that involves one side of the body in a lateral fashion.

Hertz (Hz). A unit used to measure the frequency of sound based on the number of cycles that vibrating molecules complete per second.

Home school placement. Arrangement through which students with disabilities are educated in the school they would attend if they were not labeled as having a disability.

Human immunodeficiency virus (HIV). A virus that reduces the immune system functioning in affected individuals and has been linked to AIDS.

Hydrocephalus. An excess of cerebrospinal fluid, often resulting in enlargement of the head and causing pressure on the brain, which may cause mental retardation.

Hyperactivity. See *Hyperkinetic behavior.*

Hyperkinetic behavior. An excess of behavior that is inappropriate to the given circumstances.

Hypernasality. A voice resonance disorder that occurs when excessive air passes through the nasal cavity, often resulting in an unpleasant twanging sound.

Hyperopia. Farsightedness; a refractive problem wherein the eyeball is excessively short, focusing light rays behind the retina.

Hyponasality. A voice disorder involving resonance where too little air passes through the nasal cavity (denasality).

Hypotonia. Refers to poor muscle tone.

Identical twins. Twins that develop from a single fertilized egg in a single placental sac. Such twins will be of the same sex and usually resemble one another closely.

Immune system. The normally functioning system within a person's body that protects it from disease.

Inclusive education. Emerging terminology describing the education of students with disabilities side by side with their nondisabled peers and friends in general education settings. See also *Full inclusion* and *Partial inclusion.*

Income support. A government-sponsored program in which the individual receives cash payments to support living needs.

Individual approach to labeling. The process of labeling ourselves as a reflection of how we perceive ourselves.

Individualization. A student-centered approach to instructional decision making.

Individualized education program (IEP). Provision in the Individuals with Disabilities Education Act that requires students with disabilities to receive an educational program based on multidisciplinary assessment and designed to meet individual needs. The law requires that the program take into account the student's present level of performance, annual goals, short-term instructional objectives, related services, percent of time in general education, timeline for special education services, and an annual evaluation.

Individualized family service plan (IFSP). A plan of intervention for preschool-age children similar in content to the IEP. It includes statements regarding the child's present development level, the family's strengths and needs, the major outcomes of the plan, a delineation of the specific interventions and delivery systems to accomplish outcomes, dates of initiation and duration of services, and a plan for transition into public schools.

Individualized transition plan. A statement of needed transition services within each student's IEP. It identifies the range of services needed, activities that must occur during high school to facilitate the individual's access to adult programs if necessary, and timelines and assignment of responsibilities for completion of these activities.

Individuals with Disabilities Education Act (IDEA—Public Law 101-476). The new name for Public Law 94-142 (The Education for All Handicapped Children Act) as per the 1990 amendments to the Education of the Handicapped Act. IDEA also added two new categories of disability: autism and traumatic brain injury.

Infant stimulation. Refers to early intervention procedures that emphasize providing an infant with an array of visual, auditory, and physical stimuli to promote development.

Information processing. A model used to study the way in which people acquire, remember, and manipulate information.

Institution. An establishment or facility governed by a collection of fundamental rules.

Insulin. A secretion of the pancreas that assists the body by allowing glucose to enter the body's cells.

Insulin infusion pump. Battery-operated devices that dispense insulin on a continuous basis to diabetic patients.

Integration. As applied to persons with disabilities, the physical placement of individuals with disabilities into the natural settings of community, home, or general education class or school with their nondisabled peers.

Intelligence quotient (IQ). A score obtained from an intelligence test that provides a measure of mental ability in relation to age.

Intensive care specialists. Health care professionals (such as physicians and nurses) trained specifically to provide medical care to newborns who are seriously ill, disabled, or at risk of developing serious medical problems. Also referred to as neonatal specialists.

Intensive instruction. An instructional approach that involves (1) actively engaging students in their learning by requiring high rates of appropriate responding to the material presented; (2) carefully matching instruction to student ability and skill level; (3) providing instructional cues and prompts to support learning and then fading them when appropriate; and (4) providing detailed feedback that is directly focused on the task the student is expected to complete.

Interactive teaming. Teachers, students, and other school professionals working together in a problem-solving approach to ensure that the needs of all students are met in a classroom setting.

Intoxication. An excessive level of some toxic agent in the mother–fetus system, which may cause cerebral damage to the fetus.

Intraindividual. Refers to comparisons of an individual's different areas of performance. A person may be described in terms of his or her own strengths and weaknesses rather than in comparison to other individuals (a norm).

In utero. A term pertaining to child development "in the uterus" or before birth; may refer to abnormalities or accidents that occur during this developmental period, such as in utero infection.

Iris. The colored portion of the eye.

Itinerant teacher. Teacher who moves from place to place (such as school to school or home to home) to provide instruction and support to students. The term can apply to a teacher who regularly visits an incapacitated student in their home or in a hospital setting to provide tutorial instruction. It may also be used to describe a teacher who moves from school to school to provide specialized instructional services.

Kinesthetic. Describes the sensation of body position, presence, or movement resulting chiefly from stimulation of sensory nerve endings in the muscles, tendons, and joints.

Language. The intended messages contained in the speaker's utterances.

Language delay. A delay in the normal rate of language development wherein the developmental sequence remains intact.

Language disorder. A serious disruption in the sequence of language development.

Laryngeal. Pertaining to the larynx.

Larynx. The portion of the throat that contains the vocal mechanism.

Laser cane. A mobility device used by people who are blind, which converts infrared light into sound as light beams strike objects.

Latchkey kids. Children who, because both parents work, must come home to an empty house; children with no after-school support.

Learned helplessness. A condition in which, after repeated failures or control by others in school, family, or community settings, an individual refuses or becomes unwilling to take on new tasks or challenges.

Learning disability. A condition in which one or more of the basic psychological processes in understanding or using language is deficient.

Learning disorders. A condition characterizing people who are significantly below average in learning performance when compared to others of a comparable chronological age.

Least restrictive environment. Provision in the law (IDEA) that requires students with disabilities to be educated with their nondisabled peers to the maximum extent appropriate.

Legal blindness. Visual acuity of 20/200 or worse in the best eye with best correction, as measured on the Snellen Test, or a visual field of 20% or less.

Lens. The clear structure in the eye that focuses light rays on the retina.

Line-21 system. See *Closed-caption television.*

Long-term health care. The nature and extent of the lifelong needs of people with disabilities relative to health care.

Low birthweight. A term applied to babies that weigh 5.5 pounds (2,500 grams) or less at birth.

Magnetic resonance imaging. An imaging technique by which computers create cross-sectional images of specific body areas or organs.

Mainstreaming. The process in education whereby students with disabilities are integrated into general education classes with their nondisabled peers; refers to both instructional and social integration.

Malocclusion. An abnormal fit of the upper and lower dental structures.

Manual communication. Communication that involves sign language.

Master teacher. A highly trained and skilled teacher who serves on a supervisory and consultive basis, assisting other teachers in meeting the diverse needs of students in a classroom setting.

Maternal infection. Infection in a mother during pregnancy, which may threaten potential injury to the unborn child.

Measurement bias. Unfair or inaccurate assessment results due to cultural background, sex, or race. See also *Test bias.*

Medicaid. A government-sponsored health care program for people with disabilities and others that pays for certain medical service, such as early screening, diagnosis, treatment, and immunizations.

Medically fragile. Disability category within the area of health disabilities that describes people who are at risk for medical emergencies and often depend on technological support, such as a ventilator, or nutritional supplements to sustain health or even life.

Medical model. Describes human development having two dimensions: normal and pathological. A normal state is the absence of biological problems; a pathological state is alteration in the organism caused by disease.

Medicare. A government-sponsored national insurance program for retired people and eligible people with disabilities, which provides hospital insurance and supplementary medical insurance. Medicaid may pay for short-term hospitalization, care in nursing facilities, and limited home care. Physician services, outpatient services, ambulance services, medical supplies, and equipment may also be provided under the Medicaid program.

Melting pot. A view, often associated with the United States, that many cultures blend together into one, losing their distinctive and diverse elements.

Meningitis. An inflammation of the membranes covering the brain and spinal cord.

Mental age. A concept used in psychological assessment that relates to the general mental ability typically possessed by a child or youth of a given chronological age.

Mental retardation. Substantial limitations in functioning, characterized by significantly subaverage intellectual functioning concurrent with related limitations into two or more adaptive skill areas (see *Adaptive skills*). Mental retardation manifests itself prior to age 18.

Metabolic disorders. The body's tendency to process (metabolize) substances that can become poisonous and damage the central nervous system.

Metacognitive processes. A term used to describe the process employed by an individual in planning how to solve a problem, monitor the solution strategy as it is being implemented, and evaluate the results of the strategy.

Microphthalmia. An abnormally small eyeball.

Mirror writing. Writing backwards from right to left, the letters appearing like ordinary writing seen in a mirror.

Mixed hearing loss. A hearing loss resulting from a combination of conductive and sensorineural problems.

Modeling. A teaching process wherein the instructor demonstrates the appropriate behavior or skill to be learned as a means of teaching it.

Morphology. Form and internal structure of words; transformation of words related to tense and number.

Mowat sensor. A hand-held travel aid, approximately the size of a flashlight, used by people who are blind. An alternative to the cane for warning about obstacles in front of the individual.

Multicultural education. Education that promotes learning about multiple cultures and their values.

Multidisciplinary approach. An approach in which professionals in several disciplines (such as educators, psychologists, and social workers) work together to achieve a common goal. An example is the multidisciplinary team (including parents) required in IDEA for the development of an individualized education program.

Multilevel instruction. Using different instructional approaches within the same curriculum to achieve student outcomes based on individual need and functioning level.

Multiple intelligences. A term that describes various types of giftedness, namely, linguistic, musical, bodily–kinesthetic, spatial, interpersonal, intrapersonal, and logical–mathematical.

Muscular dystrophy. A group of inherited, chronic disorders that are characterized by gradual wasting and weakening of the voluntary skeletal muscles.

Myopia. Nearsightedness; a refractive problem wherein the eyeball is excessively long, focusing light in front of the retina.

Myringoplasty. A surgical reconstruction of a perforated ear drum.

Natural supports. Supports for people with disabilities that are provided by family, friends, and peers.

Nature versus nurture. Controversy concerning how much of a person's ability is related to sociocultural influences (nurture) as opposed to genetic factors (nature).

Neurofibromatosis. An inherited disorder resulting in tumors of the skin and other tissue (such as the brain).

Neurological. Pertaining to the nervous system.

Neurotic disorders. Behavior characterized by combinations of anxieties, compulsions, obsessions, and phobias.

Nondiscriminatory and multidisciplinary assessment. A provision of IDEA requiring that testing be given in a child's native or primary language, procedures be selected and administered to prevent cultural or racial discrimination, assessment tools be validated for the purpose for which they are being used, and that assessment be conducted by a multidisciplinary team using several pieces of information to formulate a placement decision.

Normalization. Making sure that a person with a disability experiences the patterns and conditions of everyday life and mainstream society as much as possible.

Norm-based averages. See *Norm-referenced assessment.*

Norm-referenced assessment. Assessment in which a person's performance is compared with the average performance of a larger group.

Nystagmus. Uncontrolled rapid eye movements.

Occlusion. The closing and fitting together of upper and lower dental structures.

Occupational therapist. A professional who specializes in designing and delivering instruction to prepare a person for work-related activities.

Occupational therapy. Treatment approach that involves the design and delivery of instruction related to potential work-related activities.

Opportunistic infection. An infection caused by germs that are not usually capable of causing infection in normal people, but can do so if certain changes in the immune system provide such an opportunity.

Optacon Scanner. A tactile scanner used for reading by people who are blind; an alternative to the braille system. The Optacon "reads" printed material and reproduces it on a finger pan through a series of vibrating pins.

Optic atrophy. A degenerative disease that results from deteriorating nerve fibers connecting the retina to the brain.

Optic nerve. The nerve that connects the eye to the visual center of the brain.

Orthopedically impaired. See *Physical disorders.*

Ossicular chain. The three small bones (malleus, incus, and stapes; or hammer, anvil, and stirrup) that transmit vibrations through the middle ear cavity to the inner ear.

Other health impaired. A category of disability under the Individuals with Disabilities Education Act that includes students with limited strength due to health problems. See also *Health disabilities.*

Otitis media. An inflammation of the middle ear.

Otologist. One who is involved in the study of the ear and its diseases.

Otosclerosis. A disease of the ear characterized by destruction of the capsular bone in the middle ear and the growth of a weblike bone that attaches to the stapes. The stapes is thus restricted and unable to function properly.

Ototoxic drugs. Drugs that can be poisonous to or have a deleterious effect on the eighth cranial (auditory) nerve or on the organs of hearing and balance.

Paperless brailler. A device for writing in braille whereby the information is recorded and retrieved without using paper, such as on a standard magnetic tape cassette.

Paraplegia. Paralysis that involves the legs only.

Partial inclusion. Arrangement in which students with disabilities receive most of their instruction in general education settings but are "pulled out" to a special education class or resource room when appropriate.

Partially sighted. Having visual acuity greater than 20/200 but not greater than 20/70 in the better eye after correction.

Pathology. Alterations in an organism, caused by disease.

Peer and cross-age tutoring. A cooperative learning situation in which one or more peers provide instruction to other students to achieve instructional goals. In cross-age tutoring, students of different ages work together.

Peer-mediated instruction. Structured interactions between two or more students that are designed by school personnel to achieve instructional goals.

Perceptual disorders. Disorders related to an inability to use one or more of the senses.

Perceptual-motor skills. The ability to interpret stimuli and then perform appropriate actions in response to them.

Performance feedback. Information given to students by teachers or therapists regarding how well they performed.

Personal companion. A technological device that responds to a human voice and can look up and dial a telephone number, read a newspaper delivered over telephone lines, balance a checkbook, turn appliances on or off, and maintain an appointment book.

Pervasive developmental disorder. A term used by the American Psychiatric Association in *DSM-III-R,* referring to a general class of psychological disorder characterized by impaired development of social interaction abilities and communication skills.

Phenylketonuria (PKU). A genetic disorder that may cause mental retardation if left untreated.

Phonology. The system of speech sounds used by an individual.

Photophobia. An intolerance to light.

Physical disabilities. A category of disability in which problems with a person's physical condition or body characteristics interfere with the ability to function.

Physical disorders. Bodily impairments that interfere with an individual's mobility, coordination, communication, learning, and/or personal adjustment.

Physical therapist. A person who performs physical therapy, a treatment of a physical deficiency by stretching, exercise, or massage.

PKU. See *Phenylketonuria.*

Postlingual disorders. Hearing impairments occurring at any age following speech development.

Postural drainage. Draining of fluids by making a change in posture. This technique is used by persons with cystic fibrosis.

Pragmatics. A component of language that is concerned with the use of language in social contexts, including rules that govern language functions and forms of messages.

Precipitous birth. A delivery wherein the time between the onset of labor and birth is unusually short (generally less than two hours).

Precision teaching. An instructional approach that specifically pinpoints the skills to be taught, measures the initial level of those skills, specifies goals and objectives for improvement, and measures progress on a daily basis. The program design is altered if progress is not sufficient.

Prelingual disorders. Hearing impairments that occur prior to age 2 or the time of speech development.

Prematurity. Condition of infants delivered before 37 weeks from the first day of the mother's last menstrual period.

Projective inventories. Inventories that are generally composed of ambiguous or open-ended stimuli. Children are encouraged to talk about these stimuli, thereby revealing their underlying psychological problems or unconscious conflicts.

Prosthesis. A device that replaces a missing or malfunctioning part of the body, such as an arm, a joint, or teeth. Also called *prosthetic device.*

Psychodynamic approach. An approach that views psychological disorders as originating in unconscious conflicts and anxieties.

Psychosis. A general term for a serious behavior disorder involving a loss of contact with reality and characterized by delusions, hallucinations, or illusions.

Psychotic disorders. See *Psychosis.*

Public Law 94-142 (The Education for All Handicapped Children Act). Part B of the Education of the Handicapped Act passed in 1975, mandating that all eligible students regardless of the extent or type of handicap are to receive at public expense the special education services necessary to meet their individual needs. See also *Individuals with Disabilities Education Act.*

Public Law 99-457. U.S. legislation that extended the rights and protections of IDEA (formerly Public Law 94-142) to preschool-age children (ages 3 through 5). The law also established a program for infants and toddlers with disabilities.

Pull-out programs. Programs that move the student with a disability from the general education classroom to a separate class for at least part of the school day. See also *Partial inclusion.*

Pupil. The opening in the iris of the eye, which expands.

Quadriplegia. A condition characterized by paralysis of all four of the body's extremities and usually the trunk.

Reasonable accommodations. Requirements within the Americans with Disabilities Act to ensure that a person with a disability has an equal chance of participation. The intent of ADA is to create a "fair and level playing field" for the person with a disability. A reasonable accommodation takes into account each person's needs resulting from his or her disability. Accommodations may be provided in the areas of employment, transportation, telecommunications, and so on.

Receptive language disorders. Difficulties in comprehending what others say.

Refractive problems. Visual disorders that occur when the refractive structures of the eye fail to properly focus light rays on the retina.

Related services. Services that ensure that students with disabilities benefit from their educational experience. They include special transportation, speech pathology services, psychological services, physical and occupational therapy, recreation, rehabilitation counseling, social services, and medical services.

Research design. The procedural plan for undertaking a research study.

Resource room. An educational placement option for students with disabilities involving specialized instruction for a specified time period during the day. The majority of the student's day, however, is spent in his or her general education classroom. The specialized assistance provided in the resource room reinforces and supplements general education class instruction.

Resource-room teacher. A teacher providing instruction in a resource room. See also *Resource room.*

Respiratory ventilation. Using a mechanical aid (ventilator) to supply oxygen to an individual with respiratory problems.

Respite care. Assistance provided by individuals outside of the immediate family, giving parents and other family members a break from providing care to the child with a disability (for a recreational event, a vacation, and so on). Some states provide funding to families to secure this kind of care.

Retina. Light-sensitive cells in the interior of the eye that transmit images to the brain via the optic nerve.

Retinal detachment. A condition that occurs when the retina is separated from the choroid and sclera.

Retinitis pigmentosa. A hereditary condition resulting from a break in the choroid.

Retinoblastoma. A malignant tumor in the retina.

Retopathy of prematurity. A term now used for retrolental fibroplasia. See *Retrolental fibroplasia (RLF).*

Retrolental fibroplasia (RLF). Scar tissue formation behind the lens of the eye, preventing light rays from reaching the retina. It is caused by administering excessive oxygen to premature infants.

Rigidity. A condition that is characterized by continuous and diffuse tension as the limbs are extended.

Role playing. The process of letting students rehearse and practice behaviors they are to learn; often used to practice appropriate social behaviors.

Rubella. See *Congenital rubella.*

Schoolwide assistance teams (SWAT). Groups of professionals, students, and parents working together toward the common goal of providing instructional support. SWAT teams assist school personnel in making referrals for students at risk of failure.

Screening. A preliminary assessment process, which may suggest that further evaluation of a child's needs and function-ing level is necessary. The role of screening is to "raise a red flag" if a problem is indicated.

Seizure. A cluster of behaviors (altered consciousness, characteristic motor patterns, and so on) that occur in response to abnormal neurochemical activity in the brain.

Seizure disorders. A cluster of brain disorders that suddenly alter the individual's consciousness, accompanied by uncontrolled jerking and motor activity. See also *Epilepsy.*

Selective attention. Attention that often does not focus on centrally important tasks or information.

Self-determination. The ability of a person to consider options and make appropriate choices regarding residential life, work, and leisure time activities.

Self-regulation. The ability to regulate one's own behavior.

Self-stimulation. Repetitive behavior that has no apparent purpose other than providing the person with some type of stimulation.

Semantics. The component of language most concerned with the meaning and understanding of language.

Semi-independent apartment or home. A model for providing housing for persons with disabilities who require less supervision and support.

Sensorineural hearing loss. A hearing loss resulting from an abnormal sense organ (inner ear) and a damaged auditory nerve.

Sensory disorders. Differences in vision and hearing that affect performance.

Severe and multiple disabilities. A cross-classification of disabilities that involve significant physical, sensory, intellectual, and/or social–interpersonal performance deficits. These deficits are evident in all environmental settings and often involve deficits in several areas of performance. Causes of such disabilities are not always identifiable. Individuals with functional disabilities at this level may require significantly altered environments and extensive care, treatment, and accommodations.

Sexual abuse. A form of maltreatment involving incest, sexual assault, or sexual exploitation.

Sheltered workshop. Segregated vocational training and employment setting for people with disabilities.

Short attention span. An inability to focus attention on a task for a sustained period. Often concentration can be sustained only for a few seconds or minutes.

Sickle cell anemia (SCA). An inherited disease that profoundly disrupts the function and structure of red blood cells.

Sign systems. An approach to communication that differs from sign languages by attempting to produce visual equivalents of oral language through manual and visual means.

Skull fracture. A break, crack, or split of the skull resulting from a violent blow or other serious impact to the head.

Snellen Test. A test of visual acuity.

Social maladjustment. Term used to describe the problem behaviors of individuals, particularly youth, who have difficulty with the law. *Juvenile delinquency* is an associated term.

Social system. An organization that provides structure for human interactions, defining individual and group roles, establishing expectations concerning behavior, and specifying individual and group responsibilities in a social environment. The system is ecological in nature; changes in one individual often create changes for other individuals within the system.

Sonic guide. An electronic mobility device for people who are blind. It is worn on the head, emits ultrasound waves, and produces audible noise to indicate objects in the person's path.

Spasticity. A condition that involves involuntary contractions of various muscle groups.

Special education. As defined in the Individuals with Disabilities Education Act, specially designed instruction provided to students with disabilities in all settings, including the workplace and training centers.

Special education classroom. A classroom setting under the supervision of a qualified special educator that provides specially designed instruction to meet the needs of students with disabilities.

Special day schools. See *Special schools*.

Special schools. A general term applied to segregated educational placements for students with disabilities. Students who are not disabled generally do not attend special schools.

Special services committee. See *Child-study team*.

Speech and language disorders. Difficulties in communicating effectively. Speech disorders are characterized by difficulties in voice quality, production of sounds, or speech rhythm. Language disorders are characterized by an inability to produce or understand messages.

Stanford-Binet Intelligence Scale. A standardized individual intelligence test, originally known as the Binet-Simon Scales, revised and standardized by Lewis Terman at Stanford University.

Stapes (stirrup). One of three bones in the ossicular chain. See also *Ossicular chain*.

Speech. The audible production of language.

Speech and language disorders. Difficulties in communicating effectively.

Spina bifida. A developmental defect of the spinal column.

Spina bifida cystica. A malformation of the spinal column in which a tumor-like sac forms on the infant's back.

Spina bifida meningocele. A cystic swelling or tumor-like sac that contains spinal fluid but no nerve tissue.

Spina bifida myelomeningocele. A cystic swelling or tumor-like sac that contains both spinal fluid and nerve tissue.

Spina bifida occulta. A very mild condition of spina bifida in which an oblique slit is present in one or several of the vertebral structures.

Spinal cord injury. An injury in which the spinal cord is traumatized or transected.

Standard deviation. A statistical measure of the amount an individual score deviates from the average.

Standards-based reform. An educational reform movement that focuses on student achievement as the primary measure of school success. Such academic standards specify the knowledge and skills students should acquire at each grade level. Students must also demonstrate mastery of that knowledge.

Stapedectomy. A surgical process that replaces defective stapes in the ear with a prosthetic device.

Sterilization. The process of making an individual unable to reproduce, usually accomplished surgically.

Strabismus. Crossed eyes (internal) or eyes that look outward (external).

Students at risk. Students described as vulnerable to failure in the public schools, including those who drop out of school, live in poverty, are directly affected by substance abuse, are homeless, have no access to medical care, are latchkey kids, are abused and neglected, come from single-parent families, become pregnant as teenagers, and come from differing cultural backgrounds and may have limited English-speaking abilities. Some definitions of at-risk students include students with disabilities.

Stuttering. A speech problem involving abnormal repetitions, prolongations of sounds, and hesitations as one speaks.

Subdural hematoma. A collection of blood between the covering of the brain and the brain itself, resulting in pressure on vital brain structures.

Suicide. The taking of one's own life.

Supported employment. Paid work in integrated community settings for individuals with severe disabilities who are expected to need continuous support services and for whom competitive employment has traditionally not been possible.

Syntax. The order and way in which words and sequences of words are combined into phrases, clauses, and sentences.

TDD systems. Telecommunication devices for people who are deaf, which send, receive, and print messages.

Teacher assistance teams (TAT). See *Schoolwide assistance teams*.

Technology dependent. See *Medically fragile*.

Teratogens. Substances or conditions that cause physical malformations and illnesses.

Test bias. Unfairness in a testing procedure or test instrument, giving a group a particular advantage or disadvantage because of culture, sex, or race. See also *Measurement bias*.

Text Telephones (TTs). Telephones that send, receive, and print messages through thousands of stations across the United States.

Therapeutic abortion. Termination of a pregnancy when a defect is found in the fetus during prenatal evaluation.

Tic disorders. Stereotypical movements or vocalizations that are involuntary, rapid, and recurrent over time.

Tinnitus. High-pitched throbbing or ringing in the ear, associated with disease of the inner ear.

Token reinforcement system. A system in which students may earn plastic chips, marbles, or other tangible items that may be exchanged for desired activities, food items, special privileges, or other rewards for positive behavior changes.

Tonic. The phase of a seizure in which the entire body becomes very rigid and stiff.

Tonic/clonic seizure. A seizure in which the entire brain is affected. These seizures are characterized by stiffening of the body, followed by a phase of rapid muscle contractions (extreme shaking).

Total communication. A communication philosophy and approach used by people with hearing impairments, which employs various combinations of elements from manual, oral, and other techniques available to facilitate understanding.

Toxoplasmosis. An infection caused by protozoa carried in raw meat and fecal material.

Transducer. A device that receives energy from one system and retransmits it to another, often in a different form. Transducers are used in cochlear implants to alter sound into electric nerve-stimulating signals.

Transfer of training. The process of generalizing behaviors or skills learned in one setting to other settings or circumstances.

Transition from school to adult life. Period of time between leaving school and entering adult life. See also *Transition services* and *Transition plan.*

Transition plan. An individualized plan for each student with a disability, which includes a statement of the services needed to facilitate leaving school and entering adult life.

Transition services. A coordinated set of activities for students with disabilities that are designed to facilitate the move from school to employment, further education, vocational training, independent living, and community participation.

Traumatic brain injury. Direct injuries to the brain such as a tearing of nerve fibers, bruising of the brain tissue against the skull, brain stem trauma, and swelling.

Trisomy 21. Type of Down syndrome in which the chromosomal pairs do not separate properly during the formation of sperm or egg cells, resulting in an extra chromosome on the 21st pair; also called nondisjunction.

Tuberous sclerosis. A birth defect that does not appear until late childhood, is related to mental retardation in about 66% of the cases, and is characterized by tumors on many organs.

Tunnel vision. Refers to a restricted field of vision that is 20 degrees or less at its widest angle.

Type I diabetes. Diabetes caused when the pancreas stops functioning properly. Insulin-producing cells in the pancreas produce little or no insulin.

Type II diabetes. Diabetes in which the pancreas does produce insulin, but insufficiently or ineffectively.

Ultrasound. An evaluation procedure that employs high-frequency sound waves to record tissue densities. Ultrasound may be used as a prenatal assessment to locate fetal abnormalities.

Undifferentiated attention-deficit disorder (UADD). Disorder in youngsters who exhibit difficulties maintaining attention (because of a limited ability to concentrate) and impulsive actions, but who do not exhibit hyperactive behavior. See also *Attention-deficit/hyperactivity disorder (ADHD).*

Verbalism. The excessive use of speech (wordiness), in which individuals use words that have little meaning to them.

Vermis. A portion of the brain in the cerebellum that appears to be underdeveloped in children with autism.

Vestibular mechanism. A structure in the inner ear containing three semicircular canals filled with fluid. It is sensitive to movement and assists the body in maintaining equilibrium.

Visual acuity. Sharpness and clearness of vision.

Visual cortex. The visual center of the brain, located in the occipital lobe.

Visual discrimination. The act of distinguishing one visual stimulus from another.

Visual impairment. The loss of seeing or sight. The term encompasses both partially sight and blindness.

Vitreous fluid. A jelly-like substance that fills most of the interior of the eye.

Vocational rehabilitation. A government-sponsored program to assist people with disabilities to find employment consistent with their needs and abilities.

Voice disorder. A condition in which an individual habitually speaks with a voice that differs in pitch, loudness, or quality from the voices of others of the same sex and age in a given cultural group.

Voice problems. Abnormal acoustical qualities in speech.

Zero-exclusion principle. A principle holding that no person with a disability can be rejected for a service—regardless of the nature, type, or extent of the disabling condition.

■ CHAPTER 1

Baron, R. A., & Byrne, D. (1994). *Social psychology: Understanding human interaction* (7th ed.). Boston: Allyn and Bacon.

Berry, J., & Hardman, M. L. (1998). *Lifespan perspectives on the family and disability.* Boston: Allyn and Bacon.

Binet, A., & Simon, T. (1905). Méthodes nouvelles pour le diagnostic du niveau intellectuel des anormaux [New methods for determining the intellectual capacity of people with mental retardation]. *L'Année Psychologique, 11,* 191–244.

Bradley, V. J., Knoll, J., & Agosta, J. M. (1992). *Emerging issues in family support.* Washington, DC: American Association on Mental Retardation.

Brown v. Topeka, Kansas, Board of Education. (1954). 347 U.S. 483.

Carlson, N. R. (1997). *Psychology: The science of behavior* (5th ed.). Boston: Allyn and Bacon.

Cassidy, V. M., & Stanton, J. E. (1959). An investigation of factors involved in the educational placement of mentally retarded children: A study of differences between children in special and regular classes in Ohio. (U.S. Office of Education Cooperative Research Program, Project No. 043). Columbus, OH: Ohio State University.

Center for Policy Research on the Impact of General and Special Education Reform. (1996, June). *Issues brief: Standards-based reform and students with disabilities.* Alexandria, VA: Author.

Children's Defense Fund. (1991). *Child poverty in America.* Washington, DC: Author.

Danielsen, L. C., & Bellamy, G. T. (1989). State variation in placement of children with handicaps in segregated environments. *Exceptional Children, 55*(5), 448–455.

Davis, W. E., & McCaul, E. J. (1991). The emerging crisis: Current and projected status of children in the United States (Monograph). Orono, ME: Institute for the Study of At-Risk Students.

Dotter, D. L., & Roebuck, J. B. (1988). The labeling approach re-examined: Interactionism and the components of deviance. *Deviant Behavior, 9*(1), 19–32.

Drew, C. J., Hardman, M. L., & Logan, D. R. (1996). *Mental retardation: A life cycle approach* (6th ed.). Columbus, OH: Merrill.

Dunn, L. M. (1968). Special education for the mildly retarded—is much of it justifiable? *Exceptional Children, 35,* 229–237.

Erickson, R. N., Thurlow, M. L., & Thor, K. (1995). *1994 state special education outcomes.* Minneapolis, MN: University of Minnesota, National Center on Educational Outcomes.

Gelb, S. (1995). The best in man: Degenerationism and mental retardation, 1900–1920. *Mental Retardation, 33*(1), 1–9.

Graham, S., & Dwyer, A. (1987). Effects of the learning disability label, quality of writing performance, and examiner's level of expertise on the evaluation of written products. *Journal of Learning Disabilities, 20*(5), 317–318.

Harris, L., & Associates. (1987). *International Center for the Disabled survey II: Employing disabled Americans.* New York: Author.

Harris, L., & Associates. (1989). *International Center for the Disabled survey III: A report card on special education.* New York: Author.

Harris, L., & Associates. (1994). *National Organization on Disability/Harris Survey of Americans with Disability.* New York: Author.

Harris, L., & Associates. (1995). *National Organization on Disability/Harris Survey of Americans with Disability.* New York: Author.

Hastings, R. P. (1994). On "good" terms: Labeling people with mental retardation. *Mental Retardation, 32*(5), 363–365.

Hastings, R. P., & Remington, B. (1993). Connotations of labels for mental handicap and challenging behavior: A review and research evaluation. *Mental Handicap Research, 6,* 237–249.

Hawking, S. (1988). *A brief history of time: From the big bang to black holes.* New York: Bantam Books.

Hehir, T. (1994, Summer). What's going on in the Office of Special Education Programs? *OSERS News Update,* 10.

Hendrick Hudson District Board of Education v. Rowley. (1982). 458 U.S. 176.

House Report No. 485. (1990). 101st Congress, 2d Session. Part 2 at 51; Part 3 at 28.

Inclusion works here. (1993). *Inclusion News: Illinois, 1*(1), 1.

Johnson, G. O. (1961). A comparative study of the personal and social adjustment of mentally handicapped children placed in special classes with mentally handicapped children who remain in regular classes. Syracuse, NY: Syracuse University Research Institute, Office of Research in Special Education and Rehabilitation.

Jordan, T. E., & deCharms, R. (1959). The achievement motive in normal and mentally retarded children. *American Journal of Mental Deficiency, 64,* 80–84.

Jorgensen, C. M. (1992). Natural supports in inclusive schools: Curricular and teaching strategies. In J. Nisbet (Ed.), *Natural supports in school, at work, and in the community for people with disabilities* (pp. 179–215). Baltimore, MD: Brookes.

Kammeyer, K. C. W., Ritzer, G., & Yetman, N. T. (1997). *Sociology: Experiencing changing societies* (7th ed.). Boston: Allyn and Bacon.

Kaufman, M. J., Gotlieb, J., Agard, J. A., & Kukic, M. B. (1975). Mainstreaming: Toward an explication of the concept. In E. L. Meyen, G. A. Vergason, & R. J. Whelan (Eds.), *Alternatives for teaching exceptional children* (pp. 45–54). Denver, CO: Love.

Kukic, S. (1993). From rhetoric to action: Inclusion in the state of Utah. *Special Educator, 14*(1), 2–4.

Landers, M. F., & Weaver, M. F. (1997). *Inclusive education: A process, not a placement.* Swampscott, MA: Watersun Publishing.

Lipsky, D. K., & Gartner, A. (1991). Restructuring to quality. In J. W. Lloyd, N. N. Singh, & A. C. Repp (Eds.), *The regular education initiative: Alternative perspectives on concepts, issues, and models* (pp. 43–56). Sycamore, IL: Sycamore.

Lipsky, D. K., & Gartner, A. (1996). Inclusive education and school restructuring. In W. Stainback & S. Stainback (Eds.), *Controversial issues confronting special education: Divergent perspectives* (pp. 3–15). Boston: Allyn and Bacon.

Manning, M. L., & Baruth, L. G. (1995). *Students at risk.* Boston: Allyn and Bacon.

McCleary, I. D., Hardman, M. L., & Thomas, D. (1990). International special education. In T. Husen & T. N. Postlewaite (Eds.), *International encyclopedia of education: Research and studies* (pp. 608–615). New York: Pergamon.

McLaughlin, M. W., Shepard, L. A., & O'Day, J. A. (1995). *Improving education through standards-based reform: A report by the National Academy of Education Panel on Standards-Based Education Reform.* Stanford, CA: The National Academy of Education.

Mills v. District of Columbia Board of Education. (1972). 348 F. Supp. 866 (D.D.C.).

Minow, M. (1991). *Making all the difference: Inclusion, exclusion, and American law.* Ithaca, NY: Cornell University Press.

Montgomery, A., & Rossi, R. (1994, January). *Educational reforms and students at risk: A review of the current state of the art.* Washington, DC: U.S. Department of Education, Office of Educational Research and Improvement.

National Association of State Boards of Education (NASBE). (1992, October). *Winners all: A call for inclusive schools.* Alexandria, VA: Author.

National Center on Educational Restructuring and Inclusion (NCERI). (1994). National survey on inclusive education. *Bulletin of the National Center on Educational Restructuring and Inclusion, 1,* 1–4.

National Commission on Excellence in Education. (1983). *A nation at risk: The imperative for educational reform.* Washington, DC: Author.

National Council on Disability. (1996). *Achieving independence: The challenge for the 21st century.* Washington, DC: Author.

National Research Council. (1997). *Educating one and all: Students with disabilities and standards-based reform.* Washington, DC: National Academy Press.

National School Boards Association. (1989). *An equal chance: Educating at-risk children to succeed.* Alexandria, VA: Author.

Natriello, G., McDill, E. L., & Pallas, A. M. (1990). *Schooling disadvantaged children: Racing against catastrophe.* New York: Teachers College Press, Columbia University.

Nisbet, J. (1992). Introduction. In J. Nisbet (Ed.), *Natural supports in school, at work, and in the community for people with disabilities* (pp. 1–16). Baltimore, MD: Brookes.

O'Day, J. A., & Smith, M. S. (1993). Systemic reform and educational opportunity. In S. H. Fuhrman (Ed.), *Designing coherent education policy* (pp. 250–313). San Francisco, CA: Jossey-Bass.

Pennsylvania Association for Retarded Citizens v. Commonwealth of Pennsylvania. (1971). 334 F. Supp. 1257 (E.D.Pa. 1971).

Polloway, E. A. (1984). The integration of mildly retarded students in the schools: A historical review. *Remedial and Special Education, 5*(4), 18–28.

Powell, T. H., & Graham, P. L. (1996). Parent-professional participation. In *Improving the implementation of the Individuals with Disabilities Education Act: Making schools work for all of America's children.* (Suppl., pp. 603–628). Washington, DC: National Council on Disability.

Putnam, J. W. (1993). Foreword. In J. W. Putnam (Ed.), *Cooperative learning and strategies for inclusion* (p. xiii). Baltimore, MD: Brookes.

Reynolds, M. C. (1991). Classification and labeling. In J. W. Lloyd, N. N. Singh, & A. C. Repp (Eds.), *The regular education initiative: Alternative perspectives on concepts, issues, and models* (pp. 29–41). Sycamore, IL: Sycamore.

Reynolds, M. C. (1994). A brief history of categorical programs: 1945–1993. In K. Wong & M. C. Wang (Eds.), *Rethinking policy for at-risk students* (pp. 3–24). Berkeley, CA: McCutchan Publishing.

Rosenhan, D. I. (1973). On being sane in insane places. *Science, 179,* 250–258.

Sailor, W., Anderson, J. L., Halvorsen, A. T., Doering, K., Filler, J., & Goetz, L. (1989). *The comprehensive local school.* Baltimore, MD: Brookes.

Sawyer, R. J., McLaughlin, M. J., & Winglee, M. (1994). Is integration of students with disabilities happening? An analysis of national data trends over time. *Remedial and Special Education, 15*(4), 204–215.

Seifert, K. L., & Hoffnung, R. J. (1991). *Child adolescent development* (2nd ed.). Boston: Allyn and Bacon.

Senate Report No. 1165. (1989). 101st Cong. 1st Sess. 21.

Shapiro, J. P. (1994). *No pity.* New York: Random House, Times Books.

Shriner, J. G., & Thurlow, M. L. (1992). *State special education outcomes 1991.* Minneapolis, MN: University of Minnesota, National Center on Educational Outcomes.

Smith, R. W., Osborne, L. T., Crim, D., & Rho, A. H. (1986). Labeling theory as applied to learning disabilities. *Journal of Learning Disabilities, 19*(4), 195–202.

Stainback, S., Stainback, W., & Ayres, B. (1996). Schools as inclusive communities. In W. Stainback & S. Stainback (Eds.), *Controversial issues confronting special education: Divergent perspectives* (pp. 31–43). Boston: Allyn and Bacon.

Thurstone, T. G. (1959). An evaluation of educating mentally handicapped children in special classes and regular classes (U.S. Office of Education, Cooperative Research Project No. OE-SAE 6452). Chapel Hill, NC: University of North Carolina.

U.S. Department of Education. (1997). To assure the free appropriate public education of all children with disabilities. *19th annual report to Congress on the implementation of the Education for All Handicapped Children Act.* Washington, DC: U.S. Government Printing Office.

Van Bourgondien, M. E. (1987). Children's responses to retarded peers as a function of social behaviors, labeling and age. *Exceptional Children, 53*(5), 432–439.

Watson, J. B., & Rayner, R. (1920). Conditioned emotional reactions. *Journal of Experimental Psychology, 3,* 1–14.

West, J. (1991). Implementing the act: Where do we begin? In L. West (Ed.), *The Americans with Disabilities Act: From policy to practice* (pp. xi–xxxi). New York: Millbank Memorial Fund.

■ CHAPTER 2

Aiken, L. R. (1997). *Psychological testing and assessment* (9th ed.). Boston: Allyn and Bacon.

Aponte, J. F., & Barnes, J. M. (1995). Impact of acculturation and moderator variables on the intervention and treatment of ethnic groups. In J. F. Aponte, R. Y. Rivers, & J. Wohl (Eds.), *Psychological interventions and cultural diversity* (pp. 19–39). Boston: Allyn and Bacon.

Aponte, J. F., & Clifford, J. (1995). Education and training issues for intervention with ethnic groups. In J. F. Aponte, R. Y. Rivers, &

J. Wohl (Eds.), *Psychological interventions and cultural diversity* (pp. 283–300). Boston: Allyn and Bacon.

Aponte, J. F., & Crouch, R. T. (1995). The changing ethnic profile of the United States. In J. F. Aponte, R. Y. Rivers, & J. Wohl (Eds.), *Psychological interventions and cultural diversity* (pp. 1–18). Boston: Allyn and Bacon.

Ashton, P. T. (1992). Editorial. *Journal of Teacher Education, 43,* 82.

Baca, L. M., & Almanza, E. (1991). *Language minority students with disabilities.* Reston, VA: Council for Exceptional Children.

Baca, L. M., & Cervantes, H. T. (1990). *The bilingual special education interface* (2nd ed.). Columbus, OH: Merrill/Macmillan.

Banks, J. A. (1997a). Multicultural education: Characteristics and goals. In J. A. Banks & C. A. M. Banks (Eds.), *Multicultural education: Issues and perspectives* (3rd ed.) (pp. 3–31). Boston: Allyn and Bacon.

Banks, J. A. (1997b). *Teaching strategies for ethnic studies* (6th ed.). Boston: Allyn and Bacon.

Battle, D. E. (1993). *Communication disorders in multicultural populations.* Stoneham, MA: Andover Medical Publishers.

Bedell, F. D. (1989, June 8–9). Testimony delivered at hearings conducted by the National Council on the Handicapped, Washington, DC.

Bennett, C. (1995). *Comprehensive multicultural education: Theory and practice* (3rd ed.). Boston: Allyn and Bacon.

Betancourt, H., & Lopez, S. R. (1993). The study of culture, ethnicity, and race in American psychology. *American Psychologist, 48,* 629–637.

Burt, C. (1921). *Mental and scholastic tests.* London: King.

Cronbach, L. J. (1990). *Essentials of psychological testing* (5th ed.). New York: Harper & Row.

Cummings, C. M., & DeHart, D. D. (1995). Ethnic minority physical health: Issues and interventions. In J. F. Aponte, R. Y. Rivers, & J. Wohl (Eds.), *Psychological interventions and cultural diversity* (pp. 234–249). Boston: Allyn and Bacon.

Dao, M. (1991). Designing assessment procedures for educationally at-risk Southeast Asian–American students. *Journal of Learning Disabilities, 24,* 594–601.

Davis, L. A., & Wikleby, M. A. (1993). Sociodemographic and health-related risk factors among African-American, Caucasian and Hispanic homeless men: A comparative study. *Journal of Social Distress and the Homeless, 2*(2), 83–101.

Diana v. State Board of Education. (1970, 1973). C-70, 37 RFP (N.D. Cal., 1970, 1973).

Diaz-Rico, L. T., & Weed, K. Z. (1995). *The crosscultural, language, and academic development handbook.* Boston: Allyn and Bacon.

Drew, C. J., Hardman, M. L., & Logan, D. R. (1996). *Mental retardation: A life cycle approach* (6th ed.). Columbus, OH: Merrill.

Dvir, T., Eden, D., & Banjo, M. L. (1995). Self-fulfilling prophecy and gender: Can women be Pygmalion and Galatea? *Journal of Applied Psychology, 80,* 253–270.

Ekman, P. (1993). Facial expression and emotion. *American Psychologist, 48,* 384–392.

Gelfand, D. M., Jenson, W. R., & Drew, C. J. (1997). *Understanding child behavior disorders* (3rd ed.). Fort Worth, TX: Harcourt Brace & Co.

Gergen, K. J., Gulerce, A., Lock, A., & Misra, G. (1996). Psychological science in cultural context. *American Psychologist, 51,* 496-503.

Gollnick, D. M., & Chinn, P. C. (1994). *Multicultural education in a pluralistic society* (4th ed.). Columbus, OH: Merrill.

Gottlieb, J., Alter, M., Gottlieb, B. W., & Wishner, J. (1994). Special education in urban America: It's not justifiable for many. *Journal of Special Education, 27,* 453–465.

Gregory, R. J. (1996). *Psychological testing: History, principles, and applications* (2nd ed.). Boston: Allyn and Bacon.

Hardy, M. A., & Hazelrigg, L. E. (1995). Gender, race/ethnicity, and poverty in later life. *Journal of Aging Studies, 9,* 43–64.

Hart, A. W. (1993). *Principal succession: Establishing leadership in schools.* Albany, NY: State University of New York Press.

Hoy, C., & Gregg, N. (1994). *Assessment: The special educator's role.* Pacific Grove, CA: Brooks/Cole.

Kaplan, R. M., & Saccuzzo, D. T. (1993). *Psychological testing.* Pacific Grove, CA: Brooks/Cole.

Kitano, M. K. (1997). A rationale and framework for course change. In A. I. Morey and M. K. Kitano (Eds.), *Multicultural course transformation in higher education: A broader truth* (pp. 1–17). Boston: Allyn and Bacon.

Kominski, R. (1989). How good is "How well"? An examination of the census English-speaking ability question. Paper presented at the Annual Meeting of the American Statistical Association, Washington, DC.

Larry P. v. Riles. (1972). C-71-2270 US.C, 343 F. Supp. 1306 (N.D. Cal. 1972).

Larry P. v. Riles. (1979). 343 F. Supp. 1306, 502 F. 2d 963 (N.D. Cal. 1979).

Lau v. Nichols. (1974, January 21). 414, U.S., 563–572.

Locke, D. C. (1995). Counseling interventions with African American youth. In C. C. Lee (Ed.), *Counseling for diversity* (pp. 21–40). Boston: Allyn and Bacon.

MacMillan, D. L., Gresham, F. M., & Siperstein, G. N. (1993). Conceptual and psychometric concerns about the 1992 AAMR definition of mental retardation. *American Journal on Mental Retardation, 98,* 325–335.

Maldonado-Colon, E. (1993). Cultural integration of children's literature. In J. V. Tinajero and A. F. Ada (Eds.), *The power of two languages: Literacy and biliteracy for Spanish-speaking students.* New York: Macmillan/McGraw-Hill.

Manion, M. L., & Bersani, H. A. (1987). Mental retardation as a Western sociological construct: A cross-cultural analysis. *Disability, Handicap, and Society, 2,* 231–245.

McDiarmid, G. W. (1992). What to do about differences? A study of multicultural education for teacher trainees in the Los Angeles Unified School District. *Journal of Teacher Education, 43,* 83–93.

McMillan, J. H. (1997). *Classroom assessment: Principles and practice for effective instruction.* Boston: Allyn and Bacon.

Meister, J. S. (1991). The health of migrant farm workers. *Journal of Occupational Medicine, 6,* 503–513.

Merton, R. K. (1948). The self-fulfilling prophecy. *Antioch Review, 8,* 193–210.

Merton, R. K. (1987). Three fragments from a sociologist's notebooks: Establishing the phenomenon, specified ignorance, and strategic research materials. *Annual Review of Sociology, 13,* 1–28.

Moll, L. C. (1992). Bilingual classroom studies in community analysis: Some recent trends. *Educational Researcher, 21*(2), 20–24.

Morris, Van C., & Pai, Y. (1993). *Philosophy and the American school: An introduction to the philosophy of education* (2nd ed.). Lanham, MD: University Press of America.

National Research Council. (1997). *Educating one and all: Students with disabilities and standards-based reform*. Washington, DC: National Academy Press.

Norton, P., & Drew, C. J. (1994). Autism and potential family stressors. *American Journal of Family Therapy, 22*, 68–77.

Palmer, D. J., Hughes, J. N., & Juarez, L. (1991). School psychology training and the education of minority at-risk youth: The Texas A&M University program emphasis on handicapped Hispanic children and youth. *School Psychology Review, 20*, 472–484.

Pena, E., Quinn, R., & Iglesias, A. (1992). The application of dynamic methods to language assessment: A nonbiased procedure. *Journal of Special Education, 26*, 269–280.

Reyes, M. (1992). Challenging venerable assumptions: Literacy instruction for linguistically different students. *Harvard Educational Review, 62*, 427–446.

Rosenthal, R., & Jacobson, L. (1968a). *Pygmalion in the classroom: Teacher expectation and pupils' intellectual development*. New York: Holt, Rinehart & Winston.

Rosenthal, R., & Jacobson, L. (1968b). Self-fulfilling prophecies in the classroom: Teachers' expectations as unintended determinants of pupils' intellectual competence. In M. Deutsch, I. Katz, & A. R. Jensen (Eds.), *Social class, race, and psychological development* (pp. 219–253). New York: Holt, Rinehart & Winston.

Russell, J. A. (1994). Is there universal recognition of emotion from facial expression? A review of the cross-cultural studies. *Psychological Bulletin, 115*, 102–141.

Saccuzzo, D. P., & Johnson, N. E. (1995). Traditional psychometric tests and proportionate representation: An intervention and program evaluation study. *Psychological Assessment, 7*(2), 183–194.

Sandler, I. (1994). In search of proficiency in multicultural training in community psychology. *American Journal of Community Psychology, 22*, 803–806.

Skowronski, J. J., & Carlston, D. E. (1989). Negativity and extremity biases in impression formation: A review of explanations. *Psychological Bulletin, 105*, 131–142.

Speight, S. L., Thomas, A. J., Kennel, R. G., & Anderson, M. E. (1995). Operationalizing multicultural training in doctoral programs and internships. *Professional Psychology: Research and Practice, 26*, 401–406.

Stone, B. J. (1994). Group ability test versus teachers' ratings for predicting achievement. *Psychological Reports, 73*(3, Pt. 2), 1487–1490.

Taverne, A., & Sheridan, S. (1995). Parent training in interactive book reading: An investigation of its effects with families at risk. *School Psychology Quarterly, 10*, 41–64.

Tiedt, P. L., & Tiedt, I. M. (1995). *Multicultural teaching: A handbook of activities, information, and resources* (4th ed.). Boston: Allyn and Bacon.

Trotter, A. (1992). When principals gather. *Executive Educator, 14*(6), 27–29.

U.S. Bureau of the Census. (1993). *Current population reports* (Series P-60, No. 181). Education Statistics on Disk. Washington, DC: U.S. Department of Education, Office of Educational Research and Improvement, National Center for Education Statistics.

U.S. Bureau of the Census. (1995). Census Population Profile of the United States (P23-189). Washington, DC: U.S. Government Printing Office.

U. S. Department of Education. (1991). The condition of bilingual education in the nation: A report to the Congress and the President. Washington, DC: U. S. Government Printing Office.

U. S. Department of Education. (1996). To assure the free appropriate public education of all children with disabilities. *18th annual report to Congress on the implementation of the Individuals with Disabilities Education Act*. Washington, DC: U.S. Government Printing Office.

Vaughan, E. (1993). Individual and cultural differences in adaptation to environmental risks. *American Psychologist, 48*, 673–680.

Watts, R. J. (1994). Graduate training for a diverse world. *American Journal of Community Psychology, 22*, 807–809.

Weinstein, R. S. (1994). Pushing the frontiers of multicultural training in community psychology. *American Journal of Community Psychology, 22*, 811–820.

Wilson, B., & Wood, J. (1994). Why counselors need training in cultural sensitivity. *TCA Journal, 22*(2), 52–56.

Wood, W., Lundgren, S., Ouellette, J., Busceme, S., & Blackstone, T. (1994). Minority influence: A meta-analytic review of social influence processes. *Psychological Bulletin, 115*, 323–345.

Zapata, J. T. (1995). Counseling Hispanic children and youth. In C. C. Lee (Ed.), *Counseling for Diversity* (pp. 85–108). Boston: Allyn and Bacon.

■ CHAPTER 3

Abramovitch, R., Stanhope, L., Pepler, D. J., & Corter, C. (1987). Patterns of sibling interaction among preschool-age children. In M. E. Lamb & B. Sutton-Smith (Eds.), *Sibling relationships* (pp. 61–68). Hillsdale, NJ: Erlbaum.

Affleck, G., & Tennen, H. (1993). Cognitive adaptation to adversity: Insights from parents of medically fragile infants. In A. P. Turnbull, J. M. Patterson, S. K. Behr, D. L. Murphy, D. L. Marguis, & M. J. Blue-Banning (Eds.), *Cognitive coping, families, and disability* (pp. 135–150). Baltimore, MD: Brookes.

Agosta, J. (1992). Evaluating family support services: Two quantitative case studies. In V. J. Bradley, J. Knoll, & J. M. Agosta (Eds.), *Emerging issues in family support* (pp. 99–150). Washington, DC: The American Association on Mental Retardation.

Alper, S. K., Schloss, P. J., & Schloss, C. N. (1994). *Families of students with disabilities*. Boston: Allyn and Bacon.

Amlund, J. T., & Kardash, C. M. (1994). Group approaches to consultation and advocacy. In S. K. Alper, P. J. Schloss, & C. N. Schloss (Eds.), *Families of students with disabilities* (pp. 181–204). Boston: Allyn and Bacon.

Atkins, D. V. (1987). Siblings of the hearing-impaired: Perspectives for parents. *Volta Review, 89*(5), 32–45.

Beckman-Bell, P. (1981). Child-related stress in families of handicapped children. *Topics in Early Childhood Special Education, 1*(3), 45–54.

Bell, M. L., & Smith, B. R. (1996). Grandparents as primary caregivers: Lessons in love. *Teaching Exceptional Children, 28,* 18–19.

Berger, K. S. (1994). *The developing person through the lifespan*. New York: Worth.

Berry, J., & Hardman, M. L. (1998). *Lifespan perspectives on family and disability*. Boston: Allyn and Bacon.

Blacher, J. (1984). Sequential stages of parental adjustment to the birth of a child with handicaps: Fact or artifact? *Mental Retardation, 22*(2), 55–68.

Blackard, M. K., & Barsh, E. T. (1982). Parents' and professionals' perceptions of the handicapped child's impact on the family. *Journal of the Association for the Severely Handicapped, 7,* 62–70.

Bradley, V. J., Knoll, J., & Agosta, J. M. (1992). *Emerging issues in family support.* Washington, DC: The American Association on Mental Retardation.

Bristor, M. W. (1984). The birth of a handicapped child—A holistic model for grieving. *Family Relations, 33,* 25–32.

Cheers! *Exceptional Parent, 26*(6), 54.

Cleveland, M. (1980). Family adaptation to traumatic spinal-cord injury: Response to crisis. *Family Therapy, 29*(4), 558–565.

Covert, S. B. (1995). *Whatever it takes: Excellence in family support: When families experience a disability.* St. Augustine, FL: Training Resource Network.

Darling, R. B. (1991). Parent–professional interaction. In M. Seligman (Ed.), *The family with a handicapped child* (2nd ed., pp. 119–150). Boston: Allyn and Bacon.

Dembo, T. (1984). Sensitivity of one person to another. *Rehabilitation Literature, 45,* 90–95.

Falik, L. H. (1995). Family patterns of reaction to a child with a learning disability: A meditational approach. *Journal of Learning Disabilities, 28*(6), 335–341.

Featherstone, H. (1980). *A difference in the family: Living with a disabled child.* New York: Penguin.

Fine, M. J. (1992). A systems–ecological perspective on home–school intervention. In M. J. Fine & C. Carlson (Eds.), *Family–school intervention* (pp. 1–17). Boston: Allyn and Bacon.

Forbes, E. (1987). My brother, Warren. *Exceptional Parent, 17*(5), 50–52.

Fredericks, B. (1985). Parents/families of persons with severe mental retardation. In D. Bricker & J. Filler (Eds.), *Severe mental retardation: From theory to practice.* Reston, VA: Council for Exceptional Children.

Gabel, H., McDowell, J., & Cerreto, M. C. (1983). Family adaptation to the handicapped infant. In S. G. Garwood & R. R. Fewell (Eds.), *Educating handicapped infants* (pp. 455–493). Rockville, MD: Aspen.

Gallagher, J. R., Beckman-Bell, P., & Cross, A. H. (1983). Families of handicapped children: Sources of stress and its amelioration. *Exceptional Children, 50,* 10–19.

Gargiulo, R. M. (1985). *Working with parents of exceptional children: A guide for professionals.* Boston: Houghton Mifflin.

Gartner, A., Lipsky, D. K., & Turnbull, A. P. (1991). *Supporting families with a child with disabilities.* Baltimore, MD: Brookes.

Goldberg, S., Marcovitch, S., MacGregor, D., & Lojkasek, M. (1986). Family responses to developmentally delayed preschoolers: Etiology and the father's role. *American Journal of Mental Deficiency, 90*(6), 610–617.

Guralnik, M. J., Bennett, F. C., Heiser, K. E., & Richardson, H. B., Jr. (1987). Training future primary care pediatricians to serve handicapped children and their families. *Topics in Early Childhood Special Education, 6,* 1–11.

Hornby, G. (1992). A review of fathers' accounts of their experiences parenting children with disabilities. *Journal of Child and Family Studies, 7,* 363–374.

Johnson, J. (1995). Grandparents have special needs, too. *Exceptional Parent, 25*(12), 30–31.

Klein, S. D., & Schleifer, M. J. (1993). *It isn't fair!* Westport, CT: Bergin & Garvey.

Knoll, J. (1992). Being a family: The experience of raising a child with a disability or chronic illness. In V. J. Bradley, J. Knoll, & J. M. Agosta (Eds.), *Emerging issues in family support* (pp. 9–56). Washington, DC: American Association on Mental Retardation.

Kroth, R. L., & Edge, D. (1997). *Strategies for communicating with parents and families of exceptional children.* Denver, CO: Love.

Lamb, M. E., & Meyer, D. J. (1991). Fathers of children with special needs. In M. Seligman (Ed.), *The family with a handicapped child* (2nd ed.) (pp. 151–180). Boston: Allyn and Bacon.

Lavelle, N., & Keogh, B. K. (1980). Expectations and attributions of parents of handicapped children. In J. J. Gallagher (Ed.), *New directions for exceptional children, parents, and families of handicapped children.* San Francisco, CA: Jossey-Bass.

Leigh, J. (1987). Parenting and the hearing-impaired. *Volta Review, 89*(5), 11–21.

Lian, M. J., & Aloia, G. (1994). Parental responses, roles, and responsibilities. In S. K. Alper, P. J. Schloss, & C. N. Schloss (Eds.), *Families of students with disabilities* (pp. 51–94). Boston: Allyn and Bacon.

Lobato, D. J. (1990). *Brothers, sisters, and special needs: Information and activities for helping young siblings of children with chronic illness and developmental disabilities.* Baltimore, MD: Brookes.

Lobato, D. J., Faust, D., & Spirito, A. (1988). Examining the effects of chronic disease and disability on children's sibling relationships. *Journal of Pediatric Psychology, 13,* 389–407.

McHale, S. M., Sloan, J., & Simeonsson, R. J. (1986). Sibling relationships and adjustment of children with disabled brothers and sisters. *Journal of Children in Contemporary Society, 16,* 131–158.

McLoughlin, J. A., & Senn, C. (1994). Parental responses, roles, and responsibilities. In S. K. Alper, P. J. Schloss, & C. N. Schloss (Eds.), *Families of students with disabilities* (pp. 51–94). Boston: Allyn and Bacon.

McPhee, N. (1982). A very special magic: A grandparent's delight. *Exceptional Parent, 12*(3), 13–16.

Meyer, D. J. (1993). Lesson learned: Cognitive coping strategies of overlooked family members. In A. P. Turnbull, J. M. Patterson, S. K. Behr, D. L. Murphy, D. L. Marguis, & M. J. Blue-Banning (Eds.), *Cognitive coping, families, and disability* (pp. 81–94). Baltimore, MD: Brookes.

Meyer, D. J., & Vadasy, P. F. (1986). *Grandparent workshops: How to organize workshops for grandparents of children with handicaps.* Seattle, WA: University of Washington Press.

Misra, A. (1994). Partnership with multicultural families. In S. K. Alper, P. J. Schloss, & C. N. Schloss (Eds.), *Families of students with disabilities* (pp. 143–180). Boston: Allyn and Bacon.

Moss, J. (1995). Learning the "ability words." *Exceptional Parent, 25*(6), 96.

Muir-Hutchinson, L. (1987). Working with professionals. *Exceptional Parent, 17*(5), 8–10.

Nisbet, J., Clark, M., & Covert, S. (1991). Living it up! An analysis of research on community living. In L. H. Meyer, C. A. Peck, & L. Brown (Eds.), *Critical issues in the lives of people with severe disabilities* (pp. 115–144). Baltimore, MD: Brookes.

Peterson, N. L. (1987). *Early intervention for handicapped and at-risk children: An introduction to early-childhood special education.* Denver, CO: Love.

Powell, T. H., & Gallagher, P. H. (1993). *Brothers and sisters: A special part of exceptional families.* Baltimore, MD: Brookes.

Powell, T. H., & Graham, P. L. (1996). Parent–professional participation. In *Improving the implementation of the Individuals with Disabilities Education Act: Making schools work for all of America's children* (Suppl., pp. 603–628). Washington, DC: National Council on Disability.

Schell, G. C. (1981). The young handicapped child: A family perspective. *Topics in Early Childhood Special Education, 1*(3), 21–28.

Seligman, M. (1991a). *The family with a handicapped child* (2nd ed.). Boston: Allyn and Bacon.

Seligman, M. (1991b). Siblings of disabled brothers and sisters. In M. Seligman (Ed.), *The family with a handicapped child* (2nd ed., pp. 181–202). Boston: Allyn and Bacon.

Seligman, M., & Darling, R. B. (1989). *Ordinary families, special children.* New York: Guilford.

Seligman, M., & Seligman, D. A. (1980). The professional's dilemma: Learning to work with parents. *Exceptional Parent, 10*(5), 511–513.

Shaw, L. (1994). Honor thy son. *Exceptional Parent, 24*(7), 44–45.

Shelton, T. L., Jeppson, E. S., & Johnson, B. H. (1987). *Family-centered care for children with special health-care needs.* Washington, DC: Association for the Care of Children's Health.

Simeonsson, R. J., & Bailey, D. B. (1986). Siblings of the handicapped child. In J. J. Gallagher & W. Vietze (Eds.), *Families of handicapped persons* (pp. 67–77). Baltimore, MD: Brookes.

Simpson, R. L. (1996). *Parents working with parents and families of exceptional children: Techniques for successful conferencing and collaboration* (3rd ed.). Austin, TX: Pro-Ed.

Stoneman, Z., & Berman, P. W. (1993). *The effects of mental retardation, disability, and illness on sibling relationships.* Baltimore, MD: Brookes.

Stoneman, Z., Brody, G. H., Davis, C. H., & Crapps, J. M. (1987). Mentally retarded children and their older same-sex siblings: Naturalistic in-home observations. *American Journal of Mental Retardation, 92,* 290–298.

Therrien, V. L. (1993). For the love of Wes. In S. D. Klein and M. J. Schlerfer (Eds.), *It isn't fair!* Westport, CT: Bergin & Garvey.

Titrud, J. (1995). The first sleepover. *Exceptional Parent, 25*(11), 28–29.

Turnbull, A. P., & Turnbull, H. R., III. (1990). *Families, professionals, and exceptionality* (2nd ed.). Columbus, OH: Merrill.

Turnbull, A. P., & Turnbull, H. R., III. (1993). Participatory research on cognitive coping: From concepts to research planning. In A. P. Turnbull, J. M. Patterson, S. K. Behr, D. L. Murphy, D. L. Marguis, & M. J. Blue-Banning (Eds.), *Cognitive coping, families, and disability* (pp. 1–14). Baltimore, MD: Brookes.

Vadasy, P. F., Fewell, R. R., Greenberg, M. T., Desmond, M. L., & Meyer, D. J. (1986). Follow-up evaluation of the effects of involvement in the fathers program. *Topics in Early Childhood Education, 6,* 16–31.

Vadasy, P. F., Fewell, R. R., & Meyer, D. J. (1986). Grandparents of children with special needs: Insight into their experiences and concerns. *Journal of the Division for Early Childhood, 10*(1), 36–44.

Vohs, J. (1993). On belonging: A place to stand, a gift to give. In A. P. Turnbull, J. M. Patterson, S. K. Behr, D. L. Murphy, D. L. Marguis, & M. J. Blue-Banning (Eds.), *Cognitive coping, families, and disability* (pp. 51–66). Baltimore, MD: Brookes.

West, E. (1981). My child is blind—thoughts on family life. *Exceptional Parent, 1*(1), S9–S12.

Willoughby, J. C., & Glidden, L. M. (1995). Father helping out: Shared child care and marital satisfaction of parents and children with disabilities. *American Journal on Mental Retardation, 99*(4), 399–406.

Wisniewski, L. (1994). Interpersonal effectiveness in consultation and advocacy. In S. K. Alper, P. J. Schloss, & C. N. Schloss (Eds.), *Families of students with disabilities* (pp. 205–228). Boston: Allyn and Bacon.

■ CHAPTER 4

Alexander, A., Anderson, H., Heilman, P. C., et al. (1991). Phonological awareness training and remediation of analytic decoding deficits in a group of severe dyslexics. *Annals of Dyslexia, 41,* 193–206.

Bailey, D. B., & Simeonsson, R. J. (1988). Home-based early intervention. In S. L. Odom & M. B. Karnes (Eds.), *Early intervention for infants and children with handicaps: An empirical base* (pp. 199–215). Baltimore, MD: Brookes.

Bailey, D. B., Jr., & Wolery, M. (1992). *Teaching infants and preschoolers with disabilities* (2nd ed.). Columbus, OH: Merrill.

Benson, H. A., & Turnbull, A. P. (1986). Approaching families from an individualized perspective. In R. H. Horner, L. H. Meyer, & H. D. Fredericks (Eds.), *Education of learners with severe handicaps: Exemplary service strategies* (pp. 127–157). Baltimore, MD: Brookes.

Berry, J., & Hardman, M. L. (1998). *Lifespan perspectives on family and disability.* Boston: Allyn and Bacon.

Billingsley, F. F., Liberty, K. A., & White, O. R. (1994). The chronology of instruction. In E. C. Cipani & F. Spooner (Eds.), *Curricular and instructional approaches for persons with severe disabilities* (pp. 81–116). Boston: Allyn and Bacon.

Bloom, B. S. (1964). *Stability and change in human characteristics.* New York: Wiley.

Braaten, S., Kauffman, J., Braaten, B., Polsgrove, L., & Nelson, C. M. (1988). The regular education initiative: Patent medicine for behavioral disorders. *Exceptional Children, 55*(1), 21–27.

Bradley, D. F., & King-Sears, M. E. (1997). The change process: Change for people and schools. In D. F. Bradley, M. E. King-Sears, & D. Tessier-Switlick (Eds.), *Teaching students in inclusive settings: From theory to practice* (pp. 56–82). Boston: Allyn and Bacon.

Bradley, D. F., & Switlick, D. M. (1997). From isolation to cooperation in teaching. In D. F. Bradley, M. E. King-Sears, & D. Tessier-Switlick (Eds.), *Teaching students in inclusive settings: From theory to practice* (pp. 109–128). Boston: Allyn and Bacon.

Brimer, R. W. (1990). *Students with severe disabilities: Current perspectives and practices.* Mountain View, CA: Mayfield.

Brown, A. L., & Campione, J. C. (1990). Interactive learning environments and the teaching of science and mathematics. In M. Gardner, J. Greens, F. Reif, A. Schoenfeld, A. DiSessa, & E. Stage (Eds.), *Toward a scientific practice of science education* (pp. 111–139). Hillsdale, NJ: Erlbaum.

Bryan, T., Bay, M., Lopez-Reyna, T., & Donahue, M. (1991). Characteristics of students with learning disabilities: The extant database and its implications for educational programs. In J.

Lloyd, N. N. Singh, & A. C. Repp (Eds.), *The regular education initiative: Alternative perspectives on concepts, issues, and models* (pp. 113–132). Sycamore, IL: Sycamore.

Casto, G., & Mastropieri, M. A. (1985). The efficacy of early intervention programs for handicapped children: A meta-analysis. Logan, UT: Early Intervention Research Institute.

Casto, G., & White, K. R. (1984). The efficacy of early intervention programs with environmentally at-risk infants. *Journal of Children in Contemporary Society, 17,* 37–48.

Conn-Powers, M. C., Ross-Allen, J., & Holburn, S. (1990, Winter). Transition of young children into the elementary education mainstream. *Topics in Early Childhood Special Education, 9*(4), 91–105.

Dweck, C. J., & Leggett, E. (1988). A social–cognitive approach to motivation and personability. *Psychological Review, 95,* 256–273.

Federal Register (1977). *Federal Code of Regulations, Public Law 94-142,* p. 42,495.

Ferguson, D., Meyer, G., Jeanchild, L., Juniper, L., & Zingo, J. (1992). Figuring out what to do with the grownups: How teachers make inclusion "work" for students with disabilities. *Journal of the Association for Persons with Severe Handicaps, 17*(4), 218–226.

Forest, M. (1991). It's about relationships. In L. H. Meyer, C. A. Peck, & L. Brown (Eds.), *Critical issues in the lives of people with severe disabilities* (pp. 399–408). Baltimore, MD: Brookes.

Fuchs, D., & Fuchs, L. (1991). Framing the REI debate: Abolitionists versus conservationists. In J. W. Lloyd, N. N. Singh, & A. C. Repp (Eds.), *Regular education initiative: Alternative perspectives on concepts, issues, and models* (pp. 241–255). Sycamore, IL: Sycamore.

Garber, H. L., Hodge, J. D., Rynders, J., Dever, R., & Velu, R. (1991). The Milwaukee Project: Setting the record straight. *American Journal on Mental Retardation, 95*(5), 493–525.

Gee, K. (1996). Least restrictive environment: Elementary and middle school. In *Improving the implementation of the Individuals with Disabilities Education Act: Making schools work for all of America's children* (Suppl., pp. 395–425). Washington, DC: National Council on Disability.

Giangreco, M. F., & Putnam, J. W. (1991). Supporting the education of students with severe disabilities in regular education environments. In L. H. Meyer, C. A. Peck, & L. Brown (Eds.), *Critical issues in the lives of people with severe disabilities* (pp. 245–270). Baltimore, MD: Brookes.

Glass, G., Cahen, L., Smith, M. L., & Filby, N. (1982). *School class size.* Beverly Hills, CA: Sage.

Goodlad, J. I., & Lovitt, T. C. (1993). *Integrating general and special education.* Columbus, OH: Merrill.

Gottlieb, J., Alter, M., & Gottlieb, B. W. (1991). Mainstreaming academically handicapped children in urban schools. In J. W. Lloyd, N. N. Singh, & A. C. Repp (Eds.), *The regular education initiative: Alternative perspectives on concepts, issues, and models* (pp. 95–112). Sycamore, IL: Sycamore.

Graves, D. K., & Bradley, D. F. (1997). Establishing the classroom as a community. In D. F. Bradley, M. E. King-Sears, & D. Tessier-Switlick (Eds.), *Teaching students in inclusive settings: From theory to practice* (pp. 365–383). Boston: Allyn and Bacon.

Hallahan, D. P., Keller, C. E., McKinney, J. D., Lloyd, J. W., & Bryan, T. (1988). Examining the research base of the regular education initiative: Efficacy studies and the adaptive learning environments model. *Journal of Learning Disabilities, 21,* 29–35.

Harbin, G. L. (1993). Family issues of children with disabilities: How research and theory have modified practice in intervention. In N. J. Anastasiow & S. Harel (Eds.), *At risk infants: Interventions, families, and research* (pp. 101–114). Baltimore, MD: Brookes.

Hardman, M. L., McDonnell, J., & Welch, M. (1997). *Preparing special education teachers in an era of school reform.* Washington, DC: The Federal Resource Center, Academy for Educational Development.

Harris, L., & Associates. (1989, June). *The ICD survey III: A report card on special education.* New York: Louis Harris & Associates.

Harris, K. R., & Graham, S. (1995). Constructivism: Principles, paradigms, and integration. *The Journal of Special Education, 28,* 233–247.

Hasazi, S. B., Johnston, A. P., Liggett, A., & Schattman, R. A. (1994). A qualitative policy study of the least restrictive environment provision of the Individuals with Disabilities Education Act. *Exceptional Children, 60*(5), 1–18.

Hocutt, A. M. (1996). Effectiveness of special education: Is placement the critical factor? In *Special education for students with disabilities, 6*(1), 77–102. Los Angeles, CA: The Center for the Future of Children.

Hunt, J. M. (1961). *Intelligence and experience.* New York: Ronald Press.

Hunt, P., Staub, D., Alwell, M., & Goetz, L. (1994). Achievement by all students within the context of cooperative learning groups. *Journal of the Association for Persons with Severe Handicaps, 19*(4), 290–301.

Jenkins, J. R., Pious, C. G., & Jewell, M. (1990). Special education and the regular education initiative: Basic assumptions. *Exceptional Children, 56*(6), 479–491.

Johnson, D. W., & Johnson, R. (1987). Research shows the benefit of adult cooperation. *Educational Leadership, 45*(3), 27–30.

Johnson, D. W., & Johnson, R. (1989). *Cooperation and competition: Theory and research.* Edina, MN: Interaction Book Co.

Jorgensen, C. M. (1992). Natural supports in inclusive schools: Curricular and teaching strategies. In J. Nisbet (Ed.), *Natural supports in school, at work, and in the community for people with disabilities* (pp. 179–215). Baltimore, MD: Brookes.

Kauffman, J. M. (1991). Restructuring in sociopolitical context. Reservations about the effects of current reform proposals on students with disabilities. In J. W. Lloyd, N. N. Singh, & A. C. Repp (Eds.), *The regular education initiative: Alternative perspectives on concepts, issues, and models* (pp. 57–66). Sycamore, IL: Sycamore.

Kliewer, C., & Biklen, D. (1996). Labeling: Who wants to be retarded? In W. Stainback & S. Stainback (Eds.), *Controversial issues confronting special education: Divergent perspectives* (pp. 83–95). Boston: Allyn and Bacon.

Laski, F. J. (1991). Achieving integration during the second revolution. In L. H. Meyer, C. A. Peck, & L. Brown (Eds.), *Critical issues in the lives of people with severe disabilities* (pp. 409–421). Baltimore, MD: Brookes.

Lieberman, L. M. (1996). Preserving special education . . . for those who need it. In W. Stainback & S. Stainback (Eds.), *Controversial issues confronting special education: Divergent perspectives* (2nd ed., pp. 16–27). Boston: Allyn and Bacon.

Lilly, M. S. (1992). Labeling: A tired, overworked, yet unresolved issue in special education. In W. Stainback & S. Stainback (Eds.), *Controversial issues confronting special education: Divergent perspectives* (pp. 85–95). Boston: Allyn and Bacon.

Lipsky, D. K., & Gartner, A. (1996). Inclusive education and school restructuring. In W. Stainback & S. Stainback (Eds.), *Controversial issues confronting special education: Divergent perspectives* (2nd ed., pp. 3–15). Boston: Allyn and Bacon.

Lyon, G. R. (1996). Learning disabilities. In *Special education for students with disabilities, 6*(1), 54–76. Los Angeles, CA: The Center for the Future of Children.

McDonnell, J. M. (1993). Reflections on supported inclusion programs for students with severe disabilities. *Special Educator, 14*(1), 9–12.

McDonnell, J. M., Hardman, M. L., McDonnell, A. P., & Kiefer-O'Donnell, R. (1995). *Introduction to persons with severe disabilities.* Boston: Allyn and Bacon.

McLaughlin, M. J., & Warren, S. H. (1992). *Issues and options in restructuring schools and special education programs.* College Park, MD: University of Maryland at College Park.

Montgomery, J. (1994, July). Selected strategies for inclusive classrooms. Paper presented at the Anglo-American Symposium on Educational Reform and Students with Special Needs. Cambridge, UK: University of Cambridge Institute of Education.

Morra, L. G. (1994, April 28). Districts grapple with inclusion programs. Testimony before the U.S. House of Representatives on Special Education Reform. Washington, DC: U.S. General Accounting Office.

Morsink, C. V., Thomas, C. C., & Correa, V. I. (1991). *Interactive learning: Consultation and collaboration in special programs.* New York: Macmillan.

National Association of State Boards of Education. (1992, October). *Winners all: A call for inclusive schools.* Alexandria, VA: Author.

National Center on Educational Restructuring and Inclusion. (1994, Spring). National survey on inclusive education. *NCERI Bulletin* (1), 3.

National Commission on Excellence in Education. (1983). *A nation at risk: The imperative for educational reform.* Washington, DC: Author.

National Research Council. (1997). *Educating one and all: Students with disabilities and standards-based reform.* Washington, DC: National Academy Press.

Noonan, M. J., & McCormick, L. (1993). *Early intervention in natural environments: Methods and procedures.* Pacific Grove, CA: Brooks/Cole.

Peterson, N. L. (1987). *Early intervention for handicapped and at-risk children.* Denver, CO: Love.

Piaget, J. (1970). Piaget's theory. In P. H. Mussen (Ed.), *Carmichael's manual of child psychology* (3rd ed., vol. 1). New York: Wiley.

Ramey, C., & Landesman-Ramey, S. (1992). Early educational intervention with disadvantaged children—to what effect? *Applied and Preventive Psychology, 1,* 130–140.

Reaves, J., & Bums, J. (1982). An analysis of the impact of the handicapped children's early education program (Final Report No. 2 for Special Education Programs, U.S. Department of Education, Contract No. 300-81-0661). Washington, DC: Roy Littlejohn Associates.

Reynolds, M. C. (1991). Classification and labeling. In J. W. Lloyd, N. N. Singh, & A. C. Repp (Eds.), *The regular education initiative: Alternative perspectives on concepts, issues, and models* (pp. 43–56). Sycamore, IL: Sycamore.

Robert Wood Johnson. (1988). *Serving handicapped children: A special report.* Princeton, NJ: Author.

Sailor, W., Gee, K., & Karasoff, P. (1993). School restructuring and full inclusion. In M. Snell (Ed.), *Systematic instruction of persons with severe handicaps* (4th ed., pp. 1–30). Columbus, OH: Merrill.

Sailor, W., Gerry, M., & Wilson, W. C. (1990). Disability and school integration. In T. Husen & T. N. Postlewaite (Eds.), *International encyclopedia of education: Research and studies* (2nd suppl., pp. 158–163). New York: Pergamon.

Schrag, J. (1996). *The IEP: Benefits, challenges, and future directions.* Alexandria, VA: The National Association of State Directors of Special Education.

Schulz, J. B., Carpenter, C. D., & Turnbull, A. P. (1991). *Mainstreaming exceptional students: A guide for classroom teachers.* Boston: Allyn and Bacon.

Shulman, M. S., & Doughty, J. F. (1995, December). The difficult dichotomy: One school district's response. *Phi Delta Kappan,* 292–294.

Slavin, R. (1991). Synthesis of research on cooperative learning. *Educational Leadership, 48,* 71–82.

Smith, D. J. (1998). *Inclusion: Schools for all students.* Belmont, CA: Wadsworth.

Snell, M. E. (1991). Schools are for all kids: The importance of integration for students with severe disabilities and their peers. In J. W. Lloyd, N. N. Singh, & A. C. Repp (Eds.), *The regular education initiative: Alternative perspectives on concepts, issues, and models* (pp. 133–148). Sycamore, IL: Sycamore.

Sontag, J., & Schacht, R. (1994). An ethnic comparison of parent participation and information needs in early intervention. *Exceptional Children, 16*(5), 422–431.

Stainback, W., & Stainback, S. (1989). Practical organizational strategies. In S. Stainback, W. Stainback, & M. Forest (Eds.), *Educating all students in the mainstream of education* (pp. 71–87). Baltimore, MD: Brookes.

Stainback, W., & Stainback, S. (1991). Rationale for integration and restructuring: A synopsis. In J. W. Lloyd, N. N. Singh, & A. C. Repp (Eds.), *The regular education initiative: Alternative perspectives on concepts, issues, and models* (pp. 225–240). Sycamore, IL: Sycamore.

Stainback, S., Stainback, W., & Ayres, B. (1996). Schools as inclusive communities. In W. Stainback & S. Stainback (Eds.), *Controversial issues confronting special education: Divergent perspectives* (pp. 31–43). Boston: Allyn and Bacon.

Stainback, S., Stainback, W., & Forest, M. (Eds.). (1989). *Educating all students in the mainstream of regular education.* Baltimore, MD: Brookes.

Strain, P. (1984). Efficacy research with young handicapped children: A critique of the status quo. *Journal of the Division for Early Childhood, 9,* 4–10.

Tarver, S. (1995). Direct instruction. In W. Stainback & S. Stainback (Eds.), *Controversial issues confronting special education: Divergent perspectives* (2nd ed., pp. 143–152). Boston: Allyn and Bacon.

Torgesen, J. K. (1996, January). *The prevention and remediation of reading disabilities.* John F. Kennedy Center Distinguished Lecture Series. Nashville, TN: Vanderbilt University.

U.S. Department of Education. (1997). To assure the free appropriate public education of all children with disabilities. *19th annual report to Congress on the implementation of the Education of the Handicapped Act.* Washington, DC: U.S. Government Printing Office.

U.S. Department of Health and Human Services. (1994, March). Office of Human Development Services. *Fact Sheet.* Washington, DC: Author.

Valdes, K. A., Williamson, C. L., & Wagner, M. M. (1990). *The national longitudinal transition study of special education students, statistical almanac: Vol. 5. Youth categorized as mentally retarded.* Menlo Park, CA: SRI International.

Vaughn, S., Bos, C. S., & Schumm, J. S. (1997). *Teaching mainstreamed, diverse, and at-risk students in the general education classroom.* Boston: Allyn and Bacon.

Villa, R., & Thousand, J. (1992). *Restructuring for caring and effective education.* Baltimore, MD: Brookes.

Wagner, M., & Blackorby, J. (1996). Transition from high school to work or college: How special education students fare. In *Special education for students with disabilities, 6*(1), 103–120. Los Angeles, CA: The Center for the Future of Children.

Walker, H. M., & Bullis, M. (1991). Behavior disorders and the social context of regular class integration: A conceptual dilemma? In J. W. Lloyd, N. N. Singh, & A. C. Repp (Eds.), *The regular education initiative: Alternative perspectives on concepts, issues, and models* (pp. 75–93). Sycamore, IL: Sycamore.

Wang, M. C. (1989). Accommodating student diversity through adaptive instruction. In S. Stainback, W. Stainback, & M. Forest (Eds.), *Educating all students in the mainstream of education* (pp. 183–197). Baltimore, MD: Brookes.

Wasik, B. A., & Slavin, R. E. (1993). Preventing early reading failure with one-to-one tutoring: A review of five programs. *Reading Research Quarterly, 28,* 179–200.

Welch, M. (1993). Commentary: Faculty partnerships can make special ed part of the mainstream. *The Holmes Group Forum, 7*(6), 17–18.

Welch, M., & Sheridan, S. (1995). *Educational partnerships: Serving students at-risk.* San Francisco, CA: Harcourt Brace Jovanovich.

Westlake, C. R., & Kaiser, A. P. (1991). Early childhood services for children with severe disabilities. In L. H. Meyer, C. A. Peck, & L. Brown (Eds.), *Critical issues in the lives of people with severe disabilities* (pp. 429–458). Baltimore, MD: Brookes.

White, B. L. (1975). *The first three years of life.* Englewood Cliffs, NJ: Prentice Hall.

White, K. R., Mastropieri, M. A., & Casto, G. (1984). An analysis of special education early-childhood education projects approved by the joint dissemination review panel. *Journal of the Division for Early Childhood Education, 9,* 11–26.

Wood, J. W. (1992). *Adapting instruction for mainstreamed and at-risk students.* New York: Macmillan.

Ysseldyke, J. E., Algozzine, B., & Thurlow, M. L. (1992). *Critical issues in special education.* Boston: Houghton Mifflin.

Zins, J. E., Curtis, M. J., Graden, J. L., & Ponti, C. R. (1988). *Helping students succeed in the regular classroom.* San Francisco, CA: Jossey-Bass.

■ **CHAPTER 5**

Abery, B. (1994). Self-determination: It's not just for adults. *IMPACT, 6*(4), 2. ERIC Document Reproduction Service, No. ED 368 109.

Boyer, E. L. (1983). *High school: A report on secondary education in America.* New York: Harper & Row.

Braddock, D., Hemp, R., Bachelder, L., & Fujiura, G. (1995). *The state of the states in developmental disabilities.* Washington, DC: American Association on Mental Retardation.

Bursuck, W. D., & Rose, E. (1992). Community college options for students with mild disabilities. In F. R. Rusch, L. DeStefano, J. Chadsey-Rusch, L. A. Phelps, & E. Syzmanski (Eds.), *Transition from school to adult life* (pp. 71–91). Sycamore, IL: Sycamore.

Butler, R. N., Lewis, M., & Sunderland, T. (1991). *Aging and mental health.* New York: Merrill.

Carnine, D., Silbert, J., & Kameenui, E. J. (1990). *Direct instruction reading* (2nd ed.). Columbus, OH: Merrill.

Clark, S. N., & Clark, D. C. (1994). *Restructuring the middle level school: Implications for school leaders.* New York: State University of New York Press.

Deci, E. L., Vallerand, R. J., Pelletier, L. G., & Ryan, R. M. (1991). Motivation and education: The self-determination perspective. *Educational Psychologist, 26,* 325–346.

Drew, C. J., Hardman, M. L., & Logan, D. R. (1996). *Mental retardation: A life cycle approach (6th ed.).* Columbus, OH: Merrill.

Eklund, S. J., & Martz, W. L. (1993). Maintaining optimal functioning. In E. Sutton, A. R. Factor, B. A. Hawkins, T. Heller, & G. B. Seltzer (Eds.), *Older adults with developmental disabilities* (p. 1). Baltimore, MD: Brookes.

Ellis, E. S., Deshler, D. D., Schumaker, J. B., Lenz, B. K., & Clark, F. (1990). An instructional model for teaching learning strategies. *Focus on Exceptional Children, 23,* 1–24.

Florian, L., & West, J. (1991). Beyond access: Special education in America. *European Journal of Special Needs Education, 6*(2), 124–132.

Freedman, R. I., Krauss, M. W., & Seltzer, M. (1997). Aging parents' residential plans for adult children with mental retardation. *Mental Retardation, 35*(2), 114–123.

Gartin, B. C., Rumrill, P., & Serebreni, R. (1996). The higher education transition model: Guidelines for facilitating college transition among college-bound students with disabilities. *Teaching Exceptional Children, 29*(1), 30–33.

Gerry, M. H., & Mirsky, A. J. (1992). Guiding principles for public policy on natural supports. In J. Nisbet (Ed.), *Natural supports in school, at work, and in the community for people with severe disabilities* (pp. 341–346). Baltimore, MD: Brookes.

Government Accounting Office (GAO). (1993, August). *Vocational rehabilitation: Evidence of federal program's effectiveness is mixed.* Washington, DC: Author.

Griffiths, D. L., & Unger, D. G. (1994, April). Views about planning for the future among parents and siblings of adults with mental retardation. *Family Relations, 43,* 221–227.

Harris, L., and Associates. (1994). *National Organization on Disability/Harris survey of Americans with disabilities.* New York: Author.

Hasazi, S. B., Johnson, R. E., Hasazi, J., Gordon, L. R., & Hull, M. (1989). A statewide follow-up survey of high school exiters: A comparison of former students with and without handicaps. *Journal of Special Education, 23,* 243–255.

Hawkins, B. A. (1993). Health and medical issues. In E. Sutton, A. R. Factor, B. A. Hawkins, T. Heller, & G. B. Seltzer (Eds.), *Older adults with developmental disabilities* (p. 1). Baltimore, MD: Brookes.

Heller, T., & Factor, A. R. (1993). Support systems, well-being, and placement decision-making among older parents and their adult children with developmental disabilities. In E. Sutton, A.

R. Factor, B. A. Hawkins, T. Heller, & G. B. Seltzer (Eds.), *Older adults with developmental disabilities* (pp. 107–122). Baltimore, MD: Brookes.

Hill, M. L., Wehman, P. H., Kregel, J., Banks, P. D., & Metzler, H. M. D. (1987). Employment outcomes for people with moderate and severe disabilities: An eight-year longitudinal analysis of supported competitive employment. *The Journal of the Association for Persons with Severe Handicaps, 12*, 182–189.

Hocutt, A. M. (1996). Effectiveness of special education: Is placement the critical factor? In *Special education for students with disabilities, 6*(1), 77–102. Los Angeles, CA: The Center for the Future of Children.

Klein, J. (1994). Supported living: Not just another "rung" on the continuum. *TASH Newsletter, 20*(7), 16–18.

Krauss, M. W., Seltzer, M. M., Gordon, R., & Friedman, D. H. (1996, April). Binding ties: The roles of adult siblings of persons with mental retardation. *Mental Retardation, 34*(2), 83–93.

Mank, D. M., Rhodes, L. E., & Bellamy, G. T. (1986). Four supported employment alternatives. In W. E. Kiernan & J. A. Stark (Eds.), *Pathways to employment for adults with developmental disabilities* (pp. 139–154). Baltimore, MD: Brookes.

Martinson, M. C., & Stone, J. A. (1993). Small-scale community living options serving three or fewer adults with developmental disabilities. In E. Sutton, A. R. Factor, B. A. Hawkins, T. Heller, & G. B. Seltzer (Eds.), *Older adults with developmental disabilities* (pp. 199–221). Baltimore, MD: Brookes.

McDonnell, J. M., Hardman, M. L., McDonnell, A. P., & Kiefer-O'Donnell, R. (1995). *Introduction to persons with severe disabilities.* Boston: Allyn and Bacon.

McDonnell, J., Mathot-Buckner, C., & Ferguson, B. (1996). *Transition programs for students with moderate/severe disabilities.* Pacific Grove, CA: Brooks/Cole.

McDonnell, J., Wilcox, B., & Hardman, M. L. (1991). *Secondary programs for students with developmental disabilities.* Boston: Allyn and Bacon.

Morningstar, M. E., Turnbull, A. P., & Turnbull, H. R. (1996). What do students with disabilities tell us about the importance of family involvement in the transition from school to adult life? *Exceptional Children, 62,* 249–260.

National Council on Disability. (1996). Disability demographics. In *Achieving independence: The challenge for the 21st century* (pp. 13–16). Washington, DC: Author.

National Council on Disability. (1989). *The education of students with disabilities: Where do we stand?* Washington, DC: Author.

National Research Council. (1997). *Educating one and all: Students with disabilities and standards-based reform* (pp. 119–120). Washington, DC: National Academy Press.

Nisbet, J. (1992). Introduction. In J. Nisbet (Ed.), *Natural supports in school, at work, and in the community for people with disabilities* (pp. 1–16). Baltimore, MD: Brookes.

Revell, W. G., Wehman, P., Kregel, J., West, M., & Rayfield, R. (1994). Supported employment for persons with severe disabilities: Positive trends in wages, models, and funding. *Education and Training in Mental Retardation and Developmental Disabilities, 29*(4), 256–264.

Rusch, F. R., Chadsey-Rusch, J., & Johnson, J. R. (1991). Supported employment: Emerging opportunities for employment integration. In L. H. Meyer, C. A. Peck, & L. Brown (Eds.), *Critical is-*

sues in the lives of people with severe disabilities (pp. 145–170). Baltimore, MD: Brookes.

Rusch, F. R., Johnson, J. R., & Hughes, C. (1990). Analysis of co-worker involvement in relation to level of disability versus placement approach among supported employees. *The Journal of the Association for Persons with Severe Handicaps, 15*, 32–39.

Schloss, P. J., Alper, S., & Jayne, D. (1993). Self-determination for persons with disabilities: Choice, risk, and dignity. *Exceptional Children, 60*(3), 215–225.

Seltzer, M. M., & Krauss, M. W. (1994). Aging parents with resident adult children: The impact of lifelong caregiving. In M. M. Seltzer, M. W. Krauss, & M. P. Janicki (Eds.), *Life course perspectives on adulthood and old age* (pp. 3–18). Washington, DC: The American Association on Mental Retardation.

Sitlington, P., & Frank, A. (1990). Are adolescents with learning disabilities successfully crossing the bridge to adult life? *Learning Disability Quarterly, 13*, 97–111.

Smith, G. C., Majeski, R. A., & McClenny, B. (1996). Psycho-educational support groups for aging parents: Development and preliminary outcomes. *Mental Retardation, 34*(3), 172–181.

Stone, R., & Newcomer, R. (1985). Health and social services policy and the disabled who have become old. In M. P. Janicki & H. Wisniewski (Eds.), *Aging and developmental disabilities* (pp. 27–39). Baltimore, MD: Brookes.

Szymanski, E. (1994). Transitions: Life-span and life-space considerations for empowerment. *Exceptional Children, 60,* 402–410.

The Association for Persons with Severe Handicaps (TASH). (1990, November). Testimony on future directions for research presented to the U.S. Department of Education, National Institute on Disability and Rehabilitation Research. Washington, DC: Author.

Tines, J., Rusch, F. R., McCaughrin, W., & Conley, R.W. (1990). Benefit–cost analysis of supported employment in Illinois: A statewide evaluation. *American Journal on Mental Retardation, 95,* 55–67.

Turnbull, A. P., Turnbull, H. R., Bronicki, G. J., Summers, J. A., & Roeder-Gordon, C. (1992). *Disability and the family: A guide to decisions for adulthood.* Baltimore, MD: Brookes.

U.S. Department of Education. (1996). To assure the free appropriate public education of all handicapped children. *18th annual report to Congress on the implementation of the Education of the Handicapped Act.* Washington, DC: U.S. Government Printing Office.

U.S. Department of Education. (1997). To assure the free appropriate public education of all children with disabilities. *19th annual report to Congress on the implementation of the Education for All Handicapped Children Act.* Washington, DC: U.S. Government Printing Office.

Valdes, K. A., Williamson, C. L., & Wagner, M. M. (1990). *The national longitudinal transition study of special education students, statistical almanac: Vol. 5. Youth categorized as mentally retarded.* Menlo Park, CA: SRI International.

Vogelsberg, R. T. (1986). Competitive employment in Vermont. In F. R. Rusch (Ed.), *Competitive employment issues and strategies* (pp. 35–50). Baltimore, MD: Brookes.

Wagner, M., & Blackorby, J. (1996). Transition from high school to work or college: How special education students fare. In *Special education for students with disabilities, 6*(1), 103–120. Los Angeles, CA: The Center for the Future of Children.

Ward, M. J. (1991). Self-determination revisited: Going beyond expectations. In C. Valdisision (Dir.), *Transition summary, no. 7: Options after high school for youth with disabilities.* Washington, DC: NICHCY. ERIC Document Reproduction Service, No. ED 340 170.

Wehman, P. (1996). *Life beyond the classroom: Transition strategies for young people with disabilities* (2nd ed.). Baltimore, MD: Brookes.

Wehmeyer, M. (1992a). Self-determination: Critical skills for outcome-oriented transition services: Steps in transition that lead to self-determination. *Journal for Vocational Special Needs Education, 16*(1), 3–7.

Wehmeyer, M. (1992b). Self-determination and the education of students with mental retardation. *Education and Training in Mental Retardation, 27,* 302–314.

West, M., Revell, W. G., & Wehman, P. (1992). Achievement and challenges—I: A five-year report on consumer and system outcomes from the supported employment initiative. *The Journal of the Association for Persons with Severe Handicaps, 17,* 227–235.

Zigmond, N. (1990). Rethinking secondary school programs for students with learning disabilities. *Focus on Exceptional Children, 23,* 1–22.

Zigmond, N., & Miller, S. (1992). Improving high school programs. In F. R. Rusch, L. DeStefano, J. Chadsey-Rusch, L. A. Phelps, & E. Syzmanski, *Transition from school to adult life* (pp. 17–31). Sycamore, IL: Sycamore.

■ CHAPTER 6

Aiken, L. R. (1997). *Psychological testing and assessment* (9th ed.). Boston: Allyn and Bacon.

American Psychiatric Association. (1994). *Diagnostic and statistical manual of mental disorders* (4th ed.). Washington, DC: Author.

Banerji, M., & Dailey, R. A. (1995). A study of the effects of an inclusion model on students with specific learning disabilities. *Journal of Learning Disabilities, 28,* 511–522.

Barkley, R. (1995). *Taking charge of ADHD: The complete authoritative guide for parents.* New York: Guilford.

Barkley, R. A., Grodzinsky, G., & DuPaul, G. J. (1992). Frontal lobe functions in attention deficit disorder with and without hyperactivity: A review and research report. *Journal of Abnormal Child Psychology, 20,* 163–188.

Bassett, D. S., & Smith, T. E. C. (1996). Transition in an era of reform. *Journal of Learning Disabilities, 29*(2), 161–166.

Beale, I. L. (1995). Learning disabilities: Current status and future prospects. *Journal of Child and Family Studies, 4*(3), 267–277.

Begley, S. (1988, January 26). My brain made me do it. *Newsweek,* p. 56.

Bender, R. L. (1996a). Buying the right software. In R. L. Bender & W. N. Bender (Eds.), *Computer-assisted instruction for students at risk for ADHD, mild disabilities, or academic problems* (pp. 33–58). Boston: Allyn & Bacon.

Bender, R. L. (1996b). Students and computers. In R. L. Bender & W. N. Bender (Eds.), *Computer-assisted instruction for students at risk for ADHD, mild disabilities, or academic problems* (pp. 59–84). Boston: Allyn and Bacon.

Bender, R. L., & Bender, W. N. (1996). What computers can do. In R. L. Bender & W. N. Bender (Eds.), *Computer-assisted instruction for students at risk for ADHD, mild disabilities, or academic problems* (pp. 4–32). Boston: Allyn and Bacon.

Bender, W. N. (1995). *Learning disabilities: Characteristics, identification, and teaching strategies* (2nd ed.). Boston: Allyn and Bacon.

Bender, W. N., & Golden, L. B. (1990). Subtypes of students with learning disabilities as derived from cognitive, academic, behavioral, and self-concept measures. *Learning Disability Quarterly, 13*(3), 183–194.

Berk, L. E., & Landau, S. (1993). Private speech of learning disabled and normally achieving children in classroom and laboratory contexts. *Child Development, 64,* 556–571.

Bhaumik, S., Collacott, R. A., Gandhi, D., & Duggirala, C. (1995). A naturalistic study in the use of antidepressants in adults with learning disabilities and affective disorders. *Human Psychopharmacology: Clinical and Experimental, 10*(4), 283–288.

Bigler, E. D. (1992). The neurobiology and neuropsychology of adult learning disorders. *Journal of Learning Disabilities, 25,* 488–506.

Billingsley, B. S., & Ferro-Almeida, S. C. (1993). Strategies to facilitate reading comprehension in students with learning disabilities. *Reading and Writing Quarterly: Overcoming Learning Difficulties, 9*(3), 263–278.

Blalock, G. (1996). Community transition teams as the foundation for transition services for youth with learning disabilties. *Journal of Learning Disabilties, 29*(2), 148–159.

Brinckerhoff, L. C. (1996). Making the transition to higher education: Opportunities for student empowerment. *Journal of Learning Disabilities, 29,* 118–136.

Caftori, N. (1994). Educational effectiveness of computer software. *Technological Horizons in Education, 22*(1), 62–65.

Carlson, C. L., & Bunner, M. R. (1993). Effects of methyl-phenidate on the academic performance of children with attention-deficit hyperactivity disorder and learning disabilities. *School Psychology Review, 22,* 184–198.

Carnine, D. S. (1994). Introduction to the mini-series: Diverse learners and prevailing, emerging, and research-based educational approaches and their tools. Special Section: Educational tools for diverse learners. *School Psychology Review, 23,* 341–350.

Carpenter, S. L., & McKee-Higgens, E. (1996). Behavior management in inclusive classrooms. *Remedial and Special Education, 17*(4), 195–203.

Cassel, J., & Reid, R. (1996). Use of self-regulated strategy intervention to improve word problem-solving skills of students with mild disabilities. *Journal of Behavioral Education, 6*(2), 153–172.

Clark, G. M. (1996). Transition planning assessment for secondary-level students with learning disabilities. *Journal of Learning Disabilities, 29,* 79–92.

Clements, J., Clare, I., & Ezelle, L. A. (1995). Real men, real women, real lives? Gender issues in learning disabilities and challenging behaviour. *Disability and Society, 10,* 425–435.

Conte, R., & Andrews, J. (1993). Social skills in the context of learning disability definitions: A reply to Greshamm and Elliott in directions for the future. *Journal of Learning Disabilities, 26,* 146–153.

Cooper, S. A., & Collacott, R. A. (1995). Histrionic personality disorder as pseudo-learning disability. *Journal of Intellectual Disability Research, 39,* 450–453.

Cox, D. H., & Klas, L. D. (1996). Students with learning disabilities in Canadian colleges and universities: A primer for service provision. *Journal of Learning Disabilities, 29,* 93–97.

Curran, C. E., Kintsch, E., & Hedberg, N. (1996). Learning disabled adolescents' comprehension of naturalistic narratives. *Journal of Educational Psychology, 88*, 494–507.

DaFonseca, V. (1996). Assessment and treatment of learning disabilities in Portugal. *Journal of Learning Disabilities, 29(2)*, 114–117.

Dalton, B., Tivnan, T., Riley, M. K., & Rawson, P. (1995). Revealing competence: Fourth-grade students with and without learning disabilities show what they know on paper-and-pencil and hands-on performance assessments. *Learning Disabilities Research and Practice, 10(4)*, 198–214.

Deb, S., & Fraser, W. (1994). The use of psychotropic medication in people with learning disability: Towards rational prescribing. *Human Psychopharmacology: Clinical and Experimental, 9(4)*, 259–272.

Deci, E. L., Hodges, R., Pierson, L. H., & Tomassone, J. (1992). Autonomy and competence as motivational factors in students with learning disabilities and emotional handicaps. *Journal of Learning Disabilities, 25*, 457–471.

Denckla, M. B. (1993). The child with developmental disabilities grown up: Adult residua of childhood disorders. *Neurologic Clinics, 11*, 105–125.

Denckla, M. B. (1996a). Biological correlates of learning and attention: What is relevant to learning disability and attention-deficit hyperactivity disorder? *Journal of Developmental and Behavioral Pediatrics, 17(2)* 114–119.

Denckla, M. B. (1996b). Research on executive function in a neurodevelopmental context: Application of clinical measures. *Developmental Neuropsychology, 12*, 5–15.

Deshler, D. D., Ellis, E. S., & Lenz, B. K. (1996). *Teaching adolescents with learning disabilities: Strategies and methods*. Denver, CO: Love.

Dettmer, P. A., Dyck, N. J., & Thurston, L. P. (1996). *Consultation, collaboration, and teamwork for students with special needs* (2nd ed.). Boston: Allyn and Bacon.

Dilts, C. V., Carey, J. C., Kircher, J. C., & Hoffman, R. O. (1996). Children and adolescents with neurofibromatosis1: A behavioral phenotype. *Journal of Developmental and Behavioral Pediatrics, 17(4)*, 229–239.

Drew, C. J. (1994). *Technology in teacher education: Theoretical, research, and administrative issues*. Paper presented at the Annual Meeting of the American Educational Research Association, New Orleans, LA.

Drew, C. J., Hardman, M. L., & Hart, A. W. (1996). *Designing and conducting behavioral research*. Boston: Allyn and Bacon.

Drew, C. J., Hardman, M. L., & Logan, D. R. (1996). *Mental retardation: A life cycle approach* (6th ed.). Columbus, OH: Merrill.

Dunn, C. (1996). Status report on transition planning for individuals with learning disabilities. *Journal of Learning Disabilities, 29(1)*, 17–30.

DuPaul, G., Barkley, R., & McMurray, M. (1991). Therapeutic effects of medication on ADHD: Implications for school psychologists. *School Psychology Review, 20*, 203–219.

DuQuiros, G. B., Kinsbourne, M., Palmer, R. L., & Rufo, D. T. (1994). Attention deficit disorder in children: Three clinical variants. *Journal of Developmental and Behavioral Pediatrics, 15(5)*, 311–319.

Dyson, L. L. (1996). The experiences of families of children with learning disabilities: Parental stress, family functioning, and sibling self-concept. *Journal of Learning Disabilities, 29*, 280–286.

Eme, R. F. (1992). Selective female affliction in the developmental disorders of childhood: A literature review. *Journal of Clinical Child Psychology, 21*, 354–364.

Emerson, E., Reeves, D., Thompson, S., & Henderson, D. (1996). Time-based lag sequential analysis and the functional assessment of challenging behaviour. *Journal of Intellectual Disability Research, 40*, 260–274.

Evers, R. B. (1996). The positive force of vocational education: Transition outcomes for youth with learning disabilities. *Journal of Learning Disabilities, 29*, 17–30.

Faigel, H. C., Doak, E., Howard, S. D., & Sigel, M. L. (1992). Emotional disorders in learning disabled adolescents. *Child Psychiatry and Human Development, 23*, 31–40.

Faraone, S. V., Biederman, J., Lehmman, B. K., & Keenan, K. (1993). Evidence for the independent familial transmission of attention deficit hyperactivity disorder and learning disabilities: Results from a family genetic study. *American Journal of Psychiatry, 150*, 891–895.

Farmer, T. W., & Farmer, E. M. Z. (1996). Social relationships of students with exceptionalities in mainstream classrooms: Social networks and homophily. *Exceptional Children, 62*, 431–450.

Felce, D., & Perry, J. (1995). Quality of life: Its definition and measurement. *Research in Developmental Disabilities, 16(1)*, 51–74.

Fishbaugh, M. S. E. (1997). *Models of collaboration*. Boston: Allyn and Bacon.

Forness, S. R., & Kavale, K. A. (1996). Treating social skill deficits in children with learning disabilities: A meta-analysis of the research. *Learning Disability Quarterly, 19*, 2–13.

Frederickson, N., & Reason, R. (1995). Discrepancy definitions of specific learning difficulties. *Educational Psychology in Practice, 10(4)*, 195–205.

Friehe, M., Aune, B., & Leuenberger, J. (1996). Career service needs of college students with disabilities. *Career Development Quarterly, 44*, 289–300.

Fuchs, D., & Fuchs, L. (1995). Inclusive schools movement and the radicalization of special education reform. In J. Kauffman & D. Hallahan (Eds.), *The illusion of full inclusion* (pp. 213–242). Austin, TX: Pro-Ed.

Fuchs, D., Fuchs, L. S., Mathes, P. G., & Simmons, D. C. (1997). Peer-assisted learning strategies: Making classrooms more responsive to diversity. *American Educational Research Journal, 34*, 174–206.

Gaskell, G., Dockrell, J., & Rehman, H. (1995). Community care for people with challenging behaviors and mild learning disability: An evaluation of an assessment and treatment unit. *British Journal of Clinical Psychology, 34*, 383–395.

Gavrilidou, M., deMesquita, P. B., & Mason, E. J. (1993). Greek teachers' judgments about the nature and severity of classroom problems. *School Psychology International, 14*, 169–180.

Geisthardt, C., & Munsch, J. (1996). Coping with school stress: A comparison of adolescents with and without learning disabilities. *Journal of Learning Disabilities, 29*, 287–296.

Gelfand, D. M., Jenson, W. R., & Drew, C. J. (1997). *Understanding child behavior disorders* (3rd ed.). Fort Worth, TX: Harcourt Brace & Co.

Gerber, P., & Reiff, H. B. (Eds.). (1994). *Learning disabilities in adulthood: Persisting problems and evolving issues*. Boston: Andover Medical Publishers.

Gerber, P., Reiff, H., & Ginsberg, R. (1996). Reframing the learning disabilities experience. *Journal of Learning Disabilities, 29,* 98–101.

Goldstein, G., Katz, L., Slomka, G. T., & Kelly, M. A. (1993). Relationships among academic, neuropsychological, and intellectual status in subtypes of adults with learning disability. *Archives of Clinical Neuropsychology, 8,* 41–53.

Goodyear, P., & Hynd, G. W. (1993). Attention-deficit disorder with (ADD/H) and without (ADD/WO) hyperactivity: Behavioral and neuropsychological differentiation. *Journal of Clinical Child Psychology, 21,* 273–305.

Grace, J., & Malloy, P. (1992). Neuropsychiatric aspects of right hemisphere learning disability. *Neuropsychiatry, Neuropsychology, and Behavioral Neurology, 5*(3), 194–204.

Gravestock, S. (1996). Depot neuroleptic usage in adults with learning disabilities. *Journal of Intellectual Disability Research, 40*(1), 17–23.

Greasley, P. (1995). Individual planning with adults who have learning difficulties: Key issues—key sources. *Disability and Society, 10,* 353–363.

Gress, J. R., & Boss, M. S. (1996). Substance abuse differences among students receiving special education school services. *Child Psychiatry and Human Development, 26*(4), 235–246.

Grinnell, P. C. (1988). Teaching handwriting and spelling. In D. K. Reid (Ed.), *Teaching the learning disabled: A cognitive developmental approach* (pp. 245–278). Boston: Allyn and Bacon.

Gronlund, N. E. (1993). *How to make achievement tests and assessments* (5th rev. ed.). Boston: Allyn and Bacon.

Hallahan, D. P., Kauffman, J. M., & Lloyd, J. W. (1996). *Introduction to learning disabilities.* Boston: Allyn and Bacon.

Hallenbeck, M. J. (1996). The cognitive strategy in writing: Welcome relief for adolescents with learning disabilities. *Learning Disabilities Research and Practice, 11*(2), 107–119.

Hamachek, D. (1995). *Psychology in teaching, learning, and growth* (5th ed.). Boston: Allyn and Bacon.

Hammill, D. D. (1990). On defining learning disabilities: An emerging consensus. *Journal of Learning Disabilities, 23,* 74–84.

Heiligenstein, E., & Keeling, R. P. (1995). Presentation of unrecognized attention deficit hyperactivity disorder in college students. *Journal of American College Health, 43*(5), 226–228.

Hewett, J. B., & Bolen, L. M. (1996). Performance changes on the K-TEA: Brief Form for learning-disabled students. *Psychology in the Schools, 33*(2), 97–102.

Higgins, E. L., & Zvi, J. C. (1995). Assistive technology for postsecondary students with learning disabilities: From research to practice. *Annals of Dyslexia, 45,* 123–142.

Hoy, C., & Gregg, N. (1994). *Assessment: The special educator's role.* Pacific Grove, CA: Brooks/Cole.

Huntington, D. D., & Bender, W. N. (1993). Adolescents with learning disabilities at risk. Emotional well-being, depression, suicide. *Journal of Learning Disabilities, 26,* 159–166.

Jacobs, A. E., & Hendricks, D. J. (1992). Job accommodations for adults with learning disabilities: Brilliantly disguised opportunities. *Learning Disability Quarterly, 15,* 274–285.

Jahoda, A., & Cattermole, M. (1995). Activities of people with moderate to severe learning difficulties: Living with purpose or just killing time? *Disability and Society, 10,* 203–219.

Javorsky, J. (1996). An examination of youth with attention-deficit/hyperactivity disorder and language learning disabilities: A clinical study. *Journal of Learning Disabilities, 29,* 247–258.

Kaplan, R. M., & Saccuzzo, D. T. (1993). *Psychological testing.* Pacific Grove, CA: Brooks/Cole.

Katims, D. S., & Harris, S. (in press). Improving the reading comprehension of middle school students in inclusive classrooms. *Journal of Adolescent and Adult Literacy.*

Katims, D. S., & Pierce, P. L. (1995). Literacy-rich environments and the transition of young children with special needs. *Topics in Early Childhood Special Education, 15,* 219–234.

Katims, D. S., Zapata, J., & Yin, Z. (1996). Risk factors for substance use by Mexican American youth with and without learning disabilities. *Journal of Learning Disabilities, 29,* 213–219.

Kauffman, J., & Hallahan, D. (1995). *The illusion of full inclusion.* Austin, TX: Pro-Ed.

Keim, J. (1995). Screening students for potential learning disabilities. *Journal of College Student Psychotherapy, 9*(3), 71–79.

Kiernan, C., Reeves, D., & Alborz, A. (1995). The use of anti-psychotic drugs with adults with learning disabilities and challenging behaviour. *Journal of Intellectual Disability Research, 39*(4), 263–274.

Lane, S. E., & Lewandowski, L. J. (1994). Oral and written compositions of students with and without learning disabilities. *Journal of Psychoeducational Assessment, 12*(2), 142–153.

Larsen, S. (1978). Learning disabilities and the professional educator. *Learning Disability Quarterly, 1*(1), 5–12.

Lauterbach, S. L., & Bender, W. N. (1995). Cognitive strategy instruction for reading comprehension: A success for high school freshmen. *High School Journal, 79,* 58–64.

Lavin, C. (1995). Clinical applications of the Stanford-Binet Intelligence Scale: Fourth Edition to reading instruction of children with learning disabilities. *Psychology in the Schools, 32,* 255–263.

Lee, F. Y. (1992). Alternative assessments. *Childhood Education, 69*(2), 72–73.

Lefrancois, G. R. (1995). *Of children: An introduction to child development* (8th ed.). Belmont, CA: Wadsworth.

Lenz, B. K., Ellis, E. S., & Scanlon, D. (1996). *Teaching learning strategies to adolescents and adults with learning disabilities.* Austin, TX: Pro-Ed.

Lerner, J. (1997). Learning disabilities: Theories, diagnosis, and teaching strategies (7th ed.). Boston: Houghton Mifflin.

Leviton, A., Guild-Wilson, M., Neff, R. K., & Gambill, P. (1993). The Boston teacher questionnaire: I. Definition of syndromes. *Journal of Child Neurology, 8,* 43–53.

Light, J. G., & DeFries, J. C. (1995). Comorbidity of reading and mathematics disabilities: Genetic and environmental etiologies. *Journal of Learning Disabilities, 28*(2), 96–106.

Lowe K., & Felce, D. (1995a). The definition of challenging behavior in practice. *British Journal of Learning Disabilities, 23*(3), 118–123.

Lowe, K., & Felce, D. (1995b). How do carers assess the severity of challenging behavior? A total population study. *Journal of Intellectual Disability Research, 39*(2), 117–127.

Lowe, K., Felce, D., & Blackman, D. (1995). People with learning disabilities and challenging behaviour: The characteristics of those referred and not referred to specialist teams. *Psychological Medicine, 25,* 595–603.

Lyall, I., Holland, A. J., & Collins, S. (1995). Offending by adults with learning disabilities: Identifying need in one health district. *Mental Handicap Research, 8*(2), 99–109.

Lyon, G. R. (1995a). Toward a definition of dyslexia. *Annals of Dyslexia, 45,* 13–30.

Lyon, G. R. (1995b). Research initiatives in learning disabilities: Contributions from scientists supported by the National Institute of Child Health and Human Development. *Journal of Child Neurology, 10* (Suppl. 1), S120–S126.

Lyon, G. R. (1996). Learning disabilities. *The Future of Children, 6*(1), 54–76.

Male, D. B. (1996). Metamemorial functioning of children with moderate learning difficulties. *British Journal of Educational Psychology, 66,* 145–157.

Marston, D. (1996). A comparison of inclusion only, pull-out only, and combined service models for students with mild disabilities. *Journal of Special Education, 30*(2), 121–132.

Martinius, J. (1993). The developmental approach to psychopathology in childhood and adolescence. *Early Human Development, 34*(1–2), 163–168.

Mather, N., & Roberts, R. (1995). Sold out? A response to McLeskey and Pugach. *Learning Disabilities Research and Practice, 10*(4), 239–249.

McConaughy, S. H., & Achenbach, T. M. (1996). Contributions of a child interview to multimethod assessment of children with EBD and LD. *School Psychology Review, 25,* 24–39.

McCusker, C. G., Clare, I. C., Cullen, C., & Reep, J. (1993). Alcohol-related knowledge and attitudes in people with a mild learning disability: The effects of a "sensible drinking" group. *Journal of Community and Applied Social Psychology, 3,* 29–40.

McGuire, J. M., Madaus, J. W., Litt, A. V., & Ramirez, M. O. (1996). An investigation of documentation submitted by university students to verify their learning disabilities. *Journal of Learning Disabilities, 29,* 297–304.

McIntosh, D. E., & Gridley, B. E. (1993). Differential ability scales: Profiles of learning-disabled subtypes. *Psychology in the Schools, 30,* 11–24.

McKinney, J. D., Montague, M., & Hocutt, A. M. (1993). Educational assessment of students with attention deficit disorder. *Exceptional Children, 60,* 125–131.

McLeskey, J., & Pugach, M. C. (1995). The real sellout: Failing to give inclusion a chance: A response to Roberts and Mather. *Learning Disabilities Research and Practice, 10*(4), 233–238.

McMillan, J. H. (1997). *Classroom assessment: Principles and practice for effective instruction.* Boston: Allyn and Bacon.

McNulty, B. A., Connolly, T. R., Wilson, P. G., & Brewer, R. D. (1996). LRE policy: The leadership challenge. *Remedial and Special Education, 17*(3), 158–167.

Minke, K. M., Bear, G. G., Deemer, S. A., & Griffin, S. M. (1996). Teachers' experiences with inclusive classrooms: Implications for special education reform. *Journal of Special Education, 30,* 152–186.

Molineux, M. (1993). Improving home programme compliance of children with learning disabilities. *Australian Occupational Therapy Journal, 40,* 23–32.

Morgane, P. J., Austin-LaFrance, R., Bronzino, J. D., & Tonkiss, J. (1993). Prenatal malnutrition and development of the brain. *Neuroscience and Biobehavioral Reviews, 17,* 91–128.

Naglieri, J. A., & Reardon, S. M. (1993). Traditional IQ is irrelevant to learning disabilities—intelligence is not. *Journal of Learning Disabilities, 26,* 127–133.

Nass, R., & Baker, S. (1991). Androgen effects on cognition: Congenital adrenal hyperplasia. *Psychoneuroendocrinology, 16,* 189–201.

National Advisory Committee on Handicapped Children. (1968). *Special education for handicapped children: First annual report.* Washington, DC: Department of Health, Education, and Welfare.

National Joint Committee on Learning Disabilities. (1988). [Letter to NJCLD member organizations.]

National Joint Committee on Learning Disabilities. (1994). *Secondary to postsecondary education transition planning for students with learning disabilities.* Austin, TX: Pro-Ed.

Nestor, P. G. (1992). Neuropsychological and clinical correlates of murder and other forms of extreme violence in a forensic psychiatric population. *Journal of Nervous and Mental Disease, 180,* 418–423.

Ohler, D. L., Levinson, E. M., & Barker, W. F. (1996). Career maturity in college students with learning disabilities. *Career Development Quarterly, 44,* 278–288.

Ohtsuka, A. (1993). Current and future issues in the definition of learning disabilities. *Japanese Journal of Special Education, 30*(5), 29–40.

Parker, H. C. (1990). *C.H.A.D.D.: Children with attention deficit disorders: Parents supporting parents.* Education position paper, Plantation, FL.

Parmar, R. S., Cawley, J. F., & Frazita, R. R. (1996). Word problem-solving by students with and without mild disabilities. *Exceptional Children, 62,* 415–429.

Patrikakou, E. N. (1996). Investigating the academic achievement of adolescents with learning disabilities: A structural modeling approach. *Journal of Educational Psychology, 88,* 435–450.

Payette, K. A., Clarizio, H. F., Phillips, S. E., & Bennett, D. E. (1995). Effects of simple and regressed discrepancy models and cutoffs on severe determination. *Psychology in the Schools, 32*(2), 93–102.

Payne, D. A. (1992). *Measuring and evaluating educational outcomes.* New York: Macmillan.

Pennington, B. F. (1995). Genetics of learning disabilities. *Journal of Child Neurology, 10* (Suppl. 1), S69–S77.

Perrig, P., & Perrig, W. J. (1995). Implicit and explicit memory in mentally retarded, learning disabled and normal children. *Swiss Journal of Psychology, 54*(2), 77–86.

Perry, J., & Felce, D. (1995). Objective assessments of quality of life: How much do they agree with each other? *Journal of Community and Applied Social Psychology, 5*(1), 1–19.

Raviv, D., & Stone, C. A. (1991). Individual differences in the self-image of adolescents with learning disabilities: The roles of severity, time of diagnosis, and parental perceptions. *Journal of Learning Disabilities, 24,* 602–611, 629.

Reid, R. (1996). Research in self-monitoring with students with learning disabilities: The present, the prospects, the pitfalls. *Journal of Learning Disabilities, 29,* 317–331.

Reiff, H. B., Gerber, P. J., & Ginsberg, R. (1993). Definitions of learning disabilities: The insiders' perspectives. *Learning Disability Quarterly, 16,* 114–125.

Rhodes, S. S., & Jasinski, D. R. (1990). Learning disabilities in alcohol-dependent adults: A preliminary study. *Journal of Learning Disabilities, 23,* 551–556.

Richards, C. M., Symons, D. K., Greene, C. A., & Szuszkiewicz, T. (1995). The bidirectional relationship between achievement and externalizing behavior problems of students with learning disabilities. *Journal of Learning Disabilities, 28,* 8–17.

Richards, G. P., Samuels, S. J., Turnure, J. E., & Ysseldyke, J. E. (1990). Sustained and selective attention in children with learning disabilities. *Journal of Learning Disabilities, 23*, 129–136.

Richek, M., Caldwell, J., Jennings, J., & Lerner, J. (1996). *Reading problems: Assessment and teaching strategies.* Boston: Allyn and Bacon.

Roberts, R., & Mather, N. (1995). Legal protections for individuals with learning disabilities: The IDEA, Section 504, and the ADA. *Learning Disabilities Research and Practice, 10*(3), 160–168.

Rojewski, J. W. (1996). Educational and occupational aspirations of high school seniors with learning disabilities. *Exceptional Children, 62*, 463–476.

Ross, P. A., & Braden, J. P. (1991). The effects of token reinforcement versus cognitive behavior modification on learning-disabled students' math skills. *Psychology in the Schools, 28*, 247–256.

Salvia, J., & Ysseldyke, J. E. (1991). *Assessment* (5th ed.). Boston: Houghton Mifflin.

Salyer, K. M., Holmstrom, R. W., & Noshpitz, J. D. (1991). Learning disabilities as a childhood manifestation of severe psychopathology. *American Journal of Orthopsychiatry, 61*, 230–240.

Schumm, J. S., & Vaughn, S. (1995). Getting ready for inclusion: Is the stage set? *Learning Disabilities Research and Practice, 10*(3), 169–179.

Seidenberg, P. L. (1989). Relating text-processing research to reading and writing instruction for learning disabled students. *Learning Disabilities Focus, 5*, 4–12.

Seidman, L. J., Biederman, J., Faraone, S. V., & Milberger, S. (1995). Effects of family history and comorbidity on the neuropsychological performance of children with ADHD: Preliminary findings. *Journal of the American Academy of Child and Adolescent Psychiatry, 34*, 1015–1024.

Shapiro, E. S., & Eckert, T. L. (1992). *Acceptability of curriculum-based assessment by school psychologists.* Paper presented at the 100th Annual Convention of the American Psychological Association. Washington, DC.

Shapiro, J. P. (1997). The strange case of somnolent Samantha: Do the learning disabled get too much help? *U.S. News and World Report, 122*(14), 31.

Shaywitz, B., Fletcher, J., & Shaywitz, S. (1995). Defining and classifying learning disabilities and attention deficit hyperactivity disorder. *Journal of Child Neurology, 10* (Suppl. 1), S50–S57.

Shaywitz, S. E., Shaywitz, B. A., Fletcher, J. M., & Escobar, M. D. (1990). Prevalence of reading disability in boys and girls: Results of the Connecticut longitudinal study. *Journal of the American Medical Association, 264*, 998–1002.

Shea, C. (1994). "Invisible" maladies: Students who say they have learning disabilities encounter skepticism. *The Chronicle of Higher Education, 41*(2), 53, 55.

Siegel, L. S. (1989). IQ is irrelevant to the definition of learning disabilities. *Journal of Learning Disabilities, 22*, 469–479, 496.

Sigler, G., & Mackelprang, R. W. (1993). Cognitive impairments: Psychosocial and sexual implications and strategies for social work intervention. *Journal of Social Work and Human Sexuality, 8*(2), 89–106.

Sindelar, P. T. (1995). Full inclusion of students with learning disabilities and its implications for teacher education. *Journal of Special Education, 29*, 234–244.

Sitlington, P. L. (1996). Transition to living: The neglected component of transition programming for individuals with learning disabilities. *Journal of Learning Disabilities, 29*, 31–39.

Skinner, B. F. (1953). *Science and human behavior.* New York: Free Press.

Skinner, B. F. (1957). *Verbal behavior.* New York: Appleton-Century-Crofts.

Skinner, B. F. (1971). *Beyond freedom and dignity.* New York: Knopf.

Skinner, M. E., & Schenck, S. J. (1992). Counseling the college-bound student with a learning disability. *School Counselor, 39*, 369–376.

Skinner, M. F. (1996). Full inclusion and students with disabilities: One size fits all? *Reading and Writing Quarterly: Overcoming Learning Difficulties, 12*(2), 241–244.

Smith, C. R. (1994). *Learning disabilities: The interaction of learner, task, and setting* (3rd ed.). Boston: Allyn and Bacon.

Smith, T. E. C., Dowdy, C. A., Polloway, E. A., & Blalock, G. E. (1997). *Children and adults with learning disabilities.* Boston: Allyn and Bacon.

Sorrel, A. L. (1990). Three reading comprehension strategies: TELLS, story mapping, and QARS. *Academic Therapy, 25*, 359–368.

Spafford, C. S., & Grosser, G. S. (1996). *Dyslexia: Research and resource guide.* Boston: Allyn and Bacon.

Spekman, N. J., Goldberg, R. J., & Herman, K. L. (1992). Learning disabled children grow up: A search for factors related to success in the young adult years. *Learning Disabilities Research and Practice, 7*(3), 161–170.

Stanford Research Institute. (1989, June 7–8). *National longitudinal transition study of special education students: The education of students with disabilities: Where do we stand?* Briefing paper for testimony given at hearings conducted by the National Council on the Handicapped, Washington, DC.

Stewart, A., & Lillie, P. (1995). Transition plan. In *Secondary education and beyond: Providing opportunities for students with learning disabilities* (pp. 58–81). Pittsburgh, PA: Learning Disabilities Association of America.

Stoddard, K., Hewitt, M., O'Connor, D., & Beckner, J. (1996). Inclusive practices through teacher research. *Remedial and Special Education, 17*(4), 237–244.

Sturomski, N. (1996). The transition of individuals with learning disabilities into the work setting. *Topics in Language Disorders, 16*(3), 37–51.

Suresh, T. (1994). Anorexia nervosa and learning disability. *British Journal of Learning Disabilities, 22*(4), 155.

Swanson, H. L. (1991). Operational definitions and learning disabilities: An overview. *Learning Disability Quarterly, 14*(4), 242–254.

Swanson, H. L. (1992). Operational definitions and learning disabilities: An overview: Erratum. *Learning Disability Quarterly, 15*(1), 19.

Swanson, H. L. (1995). Effects of dynamic testing on the classification of learning disabilities: The predictive and discriminant validity of the Swanson Cognitive Processing Test. *Journal of Psychoeducational Assessment, 13*(3), 204–229.

Swanson, H. L. (1996). Meta-analysis, replication, social skills, and learning disabilities. *Journal of Special Education, 30*, 213–221.

Swanson, H. L., Ashbaker, M. H., & Lee, C. (1996). Learning disabled readers' working memory as a function of processing demands. *Journal of Experimental Child Psychology, 61*, 242–275.

Swanson, H. L., & Berninger, V. (1995). The role of working memory in skilled and less skilled readers' comprehension. *Intelligence, 21*, 83–108.

Swanson, J. M., McBurnett, K., Wigal, T., Pfiffner, L. J., Lerner, M. A., Williams, L., Christian, D. L., Tamm, L., Wilcutt, E., Crowley, K., Clevenger, W., Khouzam, N., Woo, C., Crinella, F. M., & Fisher, T. D. (1993). Effect of stimulant medication on children with attention deficit disorder: A "review of reviews." *Exceptional Children, 60,* 154–162.

Symons, D., Green, C., & Symons, S. (1995). Using multiple reporters of problem behavior to predict clinical referral of adolescents with learning disabilities. *Canadian Journal of School Psychology, 11*(2), 178–190.

Tallal, P. (1991). Hormonal influences in developmental learning disabilities. *Psychoneuroendocrinology, 16,* 203–211.

Torgesen, J. K. (1989). Why IQ is relevant to the definition of learning disabilities. *Journal of Learning Disabilities, 22,* 484–486.

Tralli, R., Colombo, B., Deshler, D. D., & Schumaker, J. B. (1996). The strategies intervention model: A model for supported inclusion at the secondary level. *Remedial and Special Education, 17*(4), 204–216.

Tur-Kaspa, H., & Bryan, T. (1995). Teachers' ratings of the social competence and school adjustment of students with LD in elementary and junior high school. *Journal of Learning Disabilities, 28,* 44–52.

Udvari-Solner, A., & Thousand, J. S. (1996). Creating a responsive curriculum for inclusive schools. *Remedial and Special Education, 17,* 182–192.

U.S. Department of Education. (1997). To assure the free appropriate public education of all children with disabilities. *19th annual report to Congress on the implementation of the Individuals with Disabilities Education Act.* Washington, DC: U. S. Government Printing Office.

Vauras, M., Lehtinen, E., Olkinuora, E., & Salonen, P. (1993). Devices and desires: Integrative strategy instruction from a motivational perspective. *Journal of Learning Disabilities, 26,* 384–391.

Vogel, S. A. (1990). Gender differences in intelligence, language, visual-motor abilities, and academic achievement in students with learning disabilities: A review of the literature. *Journal of Learning Disabilities, 23,* 44–52.

Waldie, K., & Spreen, O. (1993). The relationship between learning disabilities and persisting delinquency. *Journal of Learning Disabilities, 26,* 417–423.

Willemsen, S., Sophie, H. N., Buitelaar, J. K., Weijnen, F. G., & Thijssen, J. H. H. (1996). Plasma beta-endorphin concentration in people with learning disability and self-injurious and/or autistic behaviour. *British Journal of Psychiatry, 168,* 105–109.

Wehman, P. (1992). Transition for young people with disabilities: Challenges for the 1990s. *Education and Training in Mental Retardation, 27,* 112–118.

Weinberg, W. A., & Harper, C. R. (1993). Vigilance and its disorders. *Neurologic Clinics, 11,* 59–78.

Welch, M., & Sheridan, S. M. (1995). *Educational partnerships: An ecological approach to serving students at risk.* San Francisco, CA: Harcourt Brace Jovanovich.

Wiig, E. S., Jones, S. S., & Wiig, E. D. (1996). Computer-based assessment of word knowledge in teens with learning disabilities. *Language, Speech, and Hearing Services in Schools, 27,* 21–28.

Wilczenski, F. L. (1993). Comparison of academic performances, graduation rates, and timing of drop out for LD and nonLD college students. *College Student Journal, 27*(2), 184–194.

Wong, B. Y. (1993). Pursuing an elusive goal: Molding strategic teachers and learners. *Journal of Learning Disabilities, 26,* 354–357.

Wong, B. Y. L. (1996). *The ABCs of learning disabilities.* San Diego, CA: Academic Press.

Worthen, B. R., Borg, W. R., & White, K. R. (1993). *Measurement and evaluation in the schools.* White Plains, NY: Longman.

Yanok, J. (1993). College students with learning disabilities enrolled in developmental education programs. *College Student Journal, 27*(2), 166–174.

Youngstrom, N. (1991). Most child clinicians support prescribing. *APA Monitor, 22*(3), 21.

Zentall, S. S., & Ferkis, M. A. (1993). Mathematical problem solving for youth with ADHD, with and without learning disabilities. *Learning Disability Quarterly, 16,* 6–18.

Zigmond, N., & Baker, J. M. (1995). Concluding comments: Current and future practices in inclusive schooling. *Journal of Special Education, 29,* 245–250.

■ CHAPTER 7

Achenbach, T. M. (1966). The classification of children's psychiatric symptoms: A factor analytic study. *Psychological Monographs: General and Applied, 615,* 1–37.

Achenbach, T. M. (1991a). *Manual for the child behavior checklist/4–18 and 1991 profile.* Burlington, VT: University of Vermont, Department of Psychiatry.

Achenbach, T. M. (1991b). *Manual for the teacher's report form and 1991 profile.* Burlington, VT: University of Vermont, Department of Psychiatry.

Adams, J., Bosley, P., & Cooper, R. (1995). Families who love violent children. *Journal of Emotional and Behavioral Problems, 4*(1), 6–10.

Ager, C. L., & Cole, C. L. (1991). A review of cognitive–behavioral interventions for children and adolescents with behavior disorders. *Behavioral Disorders, 16*(4), 276–287.

American Psychiatric Association. (1994). *Diagnostic and statistical manual of mental disorders,* (4th ed.). Washington, DC: Author.

Benz, M. (1992). Voices of youth. *Journal of Emotional and Behavioral Problems, 1*(1), 5–8.

Bower, E. M. (1959). The emotionally handicapped child and the school. *Exceptional Children, 26,* 6–11.

Bower, E. M. (1981). *Early identification of emotionally handicapped children in the school* (3rd ed.). Springfield, IL: Thomas.

Bower, E. M. (1982). Defining emotional disturbance: Public policy and research. *Psychology in the Schools, 19*(1), 55–60.

Braaten, S., Kauffman, J. M., Braaten, B., Polsgrove, L., & Nelson, C. M. (1988). The regular education initiative: Patent medicine for behavioral disorders. *Exceptional Children, 55*(1), 21–27.

Brandenburg, N. A., Friedman, R. M., & Silver, S. E. (1990). The epidemiology of childhood psychiatric disorders: Recent prevalence findings and methodologic issues. *Journal of the American Academy of Child and Adolescent Psychiatry, 29,* 76–83.

Brendtro, L. K., Brokenleg, M., & Van Bockern, S. (1990). *Reclaiming youth at risk.* Bloomington, IN: National Education Service.

Bullock, L. M., & Gable, R. A. (1994). Monongraph on inclusion: Ensuring appropriate services to children and youth with emotional and behavioral disorders. Reston, VA: Council for Exceptional Children.

Burchard, J., Burchard, S., Sewell, C., & VanDenBerg, J. (1993). *One kid at a time: Evaluative case studies and description of the Alaska Youth Initiative Demonstration Project.* Juneau, AK: State of Alaska Division of Mental Health and Mental Retardation.

Burchard, J. D., & Clark, R. T. (1990). The role of individualized care in a service delivery system for children and adolescents with severely maladjusted behavior. *Journal of Mental Health Administration, 17*(1), 48–60.

Burnett, G., & Walz, G. (1994). Gangs in these schools. *ERIC Clearing House on Urban Education.* Washington, DC: Office of Education Research and Improvement.

Campbell, S. B. (1995). Behavior problems in preschool children: A review of recent research. *Journal of Child Psychology and Psychiatry, 36,* 113–149.

Carson, R. R., Sitlington, P. L., & Frank, A. R. (1995). Young adulthood for individuals with behavior disorders: What does it hold? *Behavior Disorders, 20*(2), 127–135.

Cartledge, G., & Milburn, J. F. (1996). *Cultural diversity and social skills instruction: Understanding ethnic and gender differences.* Champaign, IL: McNaughton & Gunn.

Center, D. B. (1989a). *Social maladjustment: An interpretation.* Paper presented at the 67th Annual International Conference of the Council for Exceptional Children, San Francisco, CA.

Center, D. B. (1989b). Social maladjustment: Definition, identification and programming. *Focus on Exceptional Children, 22*(1), 1–12.

Cheney, D., Barringer, C., Upham, D., & Manning, B. (1996). Project destiny: A model for developing educational support teams through interagency networks for youth with emotional or behavioral disorders. In R. J. Illback & C. M. Nelson (Eds.), *Emerging school-based approaches for children with emotional and behavioral problems: Research and practice in service integration* (pp. 57–76). Binghamton, NY: The Haworth Press.

Cicchetti, D., & Toth, S. L. (1995). A developmental psychopathology perspective on child abuse and neglect. *Journal of the American Academy of Child and Adolescent Psychiatry, 34,* 541–565.

Council for Children with Behavior Disorders. (1987). Position paper on definition and identification of students with behavior disorders. *Behavioral Disorders, 13*(1), 9–19.

Council for Children with Behavior Disorders. (1989). *A new proposed definition and terminology to replace "serious emotional disturbance" in Education of the Handicapped Act.* Reston, VA: Author.

Council for Children with Behavior Disorders. (1990). *Position paper on the exclusion of children with conduct disorders and behavior disorders.* Reston, VA: Author.

Council for Exceptional Children. (1991). *Report of the CEC advocacy and governmental relations committee regarding the new proposed U.S. federal definition of serious emotional disturbance.* Reston, VA: Author.

Crawford, D., & Bodine, R. (1996). *Conflict resolution education: A guide to implementing programs in schools, youth-serving organizations, and community and juvenile justice settings.* Washington, DC: U.S. Department of Justice, U.S. Department of Education.

Cullinan, D., & Epstein, M. H. (1986). Behavior disorders. In N. Haring (Ed.), *Exceptional children and youth* (4th ed.). Columbus, OH: Merrill.

Dadds, M. R. (1995). *Families, children, and the development of dysfunction.* Thousand Oaks, CA: Sage.

D'Amico, R., & Blackorby, J. (1992). Trends in employment among out-of-school youth with disabilities. In M. Wagner, L. Newman, C. Marder, R. D'Amico, & J. Blackorby, (Eds.), *What happens next?* Menlo Park, CA: SRI International.

Denny, R. K., Gunther, P. L., Shores, R. E., & Campbell, C. R. (1995). Educational placements of students with emotional and behavioral disorders: What do they indicate? In J. M. Kauffman, J. W. Lloyd, D. P. Hallahan, & T. A. Astuto (Eds.), *Issues in educational placement: Students with emotional and behavioral disorders* (pp. 119–144). Hillsdale, NJ: Erlbaum.

Dryfoos, J. (1991). Preventing high risk behavior. *American Journal of Public Health, 81*(2), 157–158.

Duncan, B. D., Forness, S. R., & Hartsough, C. (1995). Students identified as seriously emotionally disturbed in school-based day treatment: Cognitive, psychiatric, and special education characteristics. *Behavior Disorders, 20*(4), 238–252.

Eber, L. (1996). Restructuring schools through the wraparound approach: The LADSE experience. In R. J. Illback & C. M. Nelson (Eds.), *Emerging school-based approaches for children with emotional and behavioral problems: Research and practice in service integration* (pp. 135–149). Binghamton, NY: The Haworth Press.

EDLAW, Inc. (1994). *EDLAW's 6th annual Utah special education law institute.* Potomac, MD: EDLAW, Inc.

Eggert, L. L. (1994). *Anger management for youth: Stemming aggression and violence.* Bloomington, IN: National Education Service.

Etscheidt, S. E. (1991). Reducing aggressive behavior and improving self-control: A cognitive–behavioral treatment program for behaviorally disordered adolescents. *Behavioral Disorders, 16*(2), 107–115.

Evans, J. P., & Taylor, J. (1995, February). Understanding violence in contemporary and earlier gangs: An exploratory application of the theory of reasoned action. *Journal of Black Psychology, 21*(1), 71–81.

Farmer, T. W., Stuart, C. B., Lorch, N. H., & Fields, E. (1993). The social behavior and peer relations of emotionally and behaviorally disturbed students in residential treatment: A pilot study. *Journal of Emotional and Behavioral Disorders, 1,* 223–234.

Farrington, D. P. (1995). The development of offending and antisocial behaviour from childhood: Key findings from the Cambridge Study in Delinquent Development. *Journal of Child Psychology and Psychiatry, 36,* 929–964.

Fecser, F. A. (1996). A model re-ED classroom for troubled students. In N. J. Long, W. C. Morse, & R. G. Newman (Comp.), *Conflict in the classroom: The education of at-risk and troubled students* (5th ed., pp. 471–481). Austin, TX: Pro-Ed.

Forest, M., & Pearpoint, J. (1990). Supports for addressing severe maladaptive behavior. In W. Stainback & S. Stainback (Eds.), *Support networks for inclusive schooling: Interdependent integrated education.* Baltimore: Paul H. Brookes.

Forness, S. R. (1988). Planning for the needs of children with serious emotional disturbance: The National Special Education and Mental Health Coalition. *Behavioral Disorders, 13*(2), 127–133.

Forness, S. R. (1996). Schoolchildren with emotional or behavioral disorders: Perspectives on definition, diagnosis, and treatment. In B. Brooks & D. Sabatino (Eds.), *Personal perspectives on emotional disturbance/behavioral disorders* (pp. 84–95). Austin, TX: Pro-Ed.

Forness, S. R., Kavale, K. A., & Lopez, M. (1993). Conduct disorders in school: Special education eligibility and comorbidity. *Journal of Emotional and Behavioral Disorders, 1*(2), 101–108.

Forness, S. R., & Knitzer, J. K. (1990). *A new proposed definition and terminology to replace "serious emotional disturbance" in the Education of the Handicapped Act.* Alexandria, VA: National Mental Health Association.

Freeman, B. M., & Ritvo, E. R. (1984). The syndrome of autism: Establishing the diagnosis and principles of management. *Pediatric Annals, 13,* 284–296.

Fuchs, D., & Fuchs, L. S. (1994). Inclusive schools movement and the radicalization of special education reform. *Exceptional Children, 60*(4), 294–309.

Gelfand, D. M., Jenson, W. R., & Drew, C. J. (1997). *Understanding child behavior disorders* (3rd ed.). New York: Holt.

Goldstein, A. P. (1988). *The prepared curriculum: Teaching prosocial competencies.* Champaign, IL: Research Press.

Goldstein, A. P., & Glick, B. (1987). *Aggression replacement training: A comprehensive intervention for aggressive youth.* Champaign, IL: Research Press.

Goldstein, A. P., Harootunian, B., & Conoley, J. C. (1994). *Student aggression: Prevention, control, replacement.* New York: Guilford.

Graubard, S. (1964). The extent of academic retardation in a residential treatment center. *Journal of Education Research, 58,* 78–80.

Green, L., Fein, D., Joy, S., & Waterhouse, L. (1995). Cognitive functioning in autism. In E. Schopler & G. B. Mesibov (Eds.), *Learning and cognition in autism* (pp. 13–31). New York: Plenum.

Harris, K. R., & Pressley, M. (1991). The nature of cognitive strategy instruction: Interactive strategy construction. *Exceptional Children, 57*(5), 392–404.

Hobbs, N. (1965). How the Re-ED plan developed. In N. J. Long, W. C. Morse, & R. G. Newman (Eds.), *Conflict in the classroom.* Belmont, CA: Wadsworth.

Hofmeister, A. M., & Ferrara, J. M. (1986). *Artificial intelligence application in special education: How feasible?* (Final Report). Logan, UT: Utah State University.

Hughes, C., & Rusch, F. R. (1996). People with challenging behavior in integrated work environments. In D. H. Lehr & F. Brown (Eds.), *People with disabilities who challenge the system* (pp. 307–331). Baltimore, MD: Brookes.

Hundert, J. (1995). *Enhancing social competence in young students: School-based approaches.* Austin, TX: Pro-Ed.

Hurrelman, K. (1990). Health promotion for adolescents: Preventative and corrective strategies against problem behaviors. *Journal of Adolescence, 13*(3), 231–250.

Illback, R. J., & Nelson, C. M. (Eds.). (1996). *Emerging school-based approaches for children with emotional and behavioral problems: Research and practice in service integration.* Binghamton, NY: The Haworth Press.

Katz, L. F., & Gottman, J. M. (1993). Patterns of marital conflict predict children's internalizing and externalizing behaviors. *Developmental Psychology, 29*(6), 940–950.

Kauffman, J. M. (1989). *Characteristics of behavior disorders of children and youth* (4th ed.). Columbus, OH: Merrill.

Kauffman, J. M. (1993). How might we achieve the radical reform of special education? *Exceptional Children, 60*(1), 6–16.

Kauffman, J. M. (1997). *Characteristics of emotional and behavioral disorders of children and youth.* Upper Saddle River, NJ: Prentice-Hall.

Kauffman, J. M., & Lloyd, J. W. (1995). A sense of place: The importance of placement issues in contemporary special education. In J. M. Kauffman, J. W. Lloyd, D. P. Hallahan, & T. A. As-

tuto (Eds.), *Issues in educational placement: Students with emotional and behavioral disorders* (pp. 3–19). Hillsdale, NJ: Erlbaum.

Kauffman, J. M., & Smucker, K. (1995). The legacies of placement: A brief history of placement options and issues with commentary on their evolution. In J. M. Kauffman, J. W. Lloyd, D. P. Hallahan, & T. A. Astuto (Eds.), *Issues in educational placement: Students with emotional and behavioral disorders* (pp. 21–44). Hillsdale, NJ: Erlbaum.

Kavale, K. A., & Forness, S. R. (1995). Social skill deficits and training: A meta-analysis of the research in learning disabilities. In T. E. Scruggs & M. A. Mastropieri (Eds.), *Advances in learning and behavioral disabilities* (pp. 119–160). Greenwich, CT: JAI Press.

Kavale, K. A., Forness, S. R., & Alper, A. E. (1986). Research in behavioral disorders/emotional disturbance: A survey of subject identification criteria. *Behavioral Disorders, 11*(3), 159–167.

Kendall-Tackett, K. A., Williams, L. M., & Finkelhor, D. (1993). Impact of sexual abuse on children: A review and synthesis of recent empirical studies. *Psychological Bulletin, 113,* 164–180.

Knitzer, J., Steinberg, Z., & Fleish, B. (1990). *At the schoolhouse door: An examination of programs and policies for children with behavioral and emotional problems.* New York: Bank Street College of Education.

Koyangi, C., & Gaines, S. (1993). *All systems failure: An examination of the results of neglecting the needs of children with serious emotional disturbance.* Washington, DC: National Mental Health Association.

Kuykendall, C. (1992). *From rage to hope: Strategies for reclaiming Black and Hispanic youth.* Bloomington, IN: National Education Service.

Lewis, T. J., Chard, D., & Scott, T. M. (1994). Full inclusion and the education of children and youth with behavioral disorders. *Behavioral Disorders, 19*(4), 277–293.

Lewitt, E. M., & Baker, L. S. (1996). Children in special education. *The Future of Children, 6*(1),139–151.

Masten, A. S., Miliotis, D., Graham-Bermann, S. A., Ramirez, M., & Neemann, J. (1993). Children in homeless families: Risks to mental health and development. *Journal of Consulting and Clinical Psychology, 61,* 355–343.

Mathews, F. (1996). Re-framing gang violence: A pro-youth strategy. In N. J. Long, W. C. Morse, & R. G. Newman (Comp.), *Conflict in the classroom: The education of at-risk and troubled students* (5th ed., pp. 217–226). Austin, TX: Pro-Ed.

Mattison, R. E., & Forness, S. R. (1995). Mental health system involvement and SED placement decisions. In J. M. Kauffman, J. W. Lloyd, D. P. Hallahan, & T. A. Astuto (Eds.), *Issues in educational placement: Students with emotional and behavioral disorders* (pp. 197–211). Hillsdale, NJ: Erlbaum.

McGinnis, E., Goldstein, A. P., Sprafkin, R. P., & Gershaw, N. J. (1984). *Skillstreaming the elementary school child: A guide for teaching prosocial skills.* Champaign, IL: Research Press.

McIntyre, T., & Forness, S. R. (1996). Is there a new definition yet, or are our kids still seriously emotionally disturbed? *Beyond Behavior: A Magazine Exploring Behavior in Our Schools, 7*(3), 4–9.

McMahon, C. M., Wacker, D. P., Sasso, G. M., & Melloy, K. J. (1994). Evaluation of the multiple effects of social skill intervention. *Behavior Disorders, 20*(1), 35–50.

Meichenbaum, D. H. (1977). *Cognitive-behavior modification: An integrative approach.* New York: Plenum.

Moore, R. J., Cartledge, G., & Heckman, K. (1995). The effects of social skill instruction and self-monitoring on game-related behaviors of adolescents with emotional or behavioral disorders. *Behavior Disorders, 20*(4), 253–266.

Morse, W. C., Cutler, R. L., & Fink, A. H. (1964). *Public school classes for emotionally handicapped: A research analysis.* Washington, DC: Council for Exceptional Children.

Nelson, C. M., & Pearson, C. A. (1991). *Integrating services for children and youth with emotional and behavioral disorders.* Reston, VA: The Council for Exceptional Children.

Nelson, C. M., Rutherford, R. B., Center, D. B., & Walker, H. M. (1991). Do public schools have an obligation to serve troubled children and youth? *Exceptional Children, 57*(5), 406–415.

Nichols, P. (1996). The curriculum of control: Twelve reasons for it, some arguments against it. In N. J. Long, W. C. Morse, & R. G. Newman (Comp.), *Conflict in the classroom: The education of at-risk and troubled students* (5th ed., pp. 82–94). Austin, TX: Pro-Ed.

Osher, D., & Hanley, T. V. (1996). Implications of the national agenda to improve results for children and youth with or at risk of serious emotional disturbance. In R. J. Illback & C. M. Nelson (Eds.), *Emerging school-based approaches for children with emotional and behavioral problems: Research and practice in service integration* (pp. 7–36). Binghamton, NY: The Haworth Press.

Osher, D. M., & Osher, T. W. (1995). Comprehensive and collaborative systems that work: A national agenda. In C. M. Nelson, R. Rutherford, & B. I. Wolford (Eds.), *Developing comprehensive systems that work for troubled youth.* Richmond, KY: National Coalition for Juvenile Justice Services.

Osher, D., Osher, T., & Smith, C. (1994). Toward a national perspective in emotional and behavioral disorders: A developmental perspective. *Beyond Behavior, 6*(1), 6–17.

Peacock Hill Working Group. (1990). *Problems and promises in special education and related services for children and youth with emotional and behavioral disorders.* Charlottesville, VA: Author.

Peterson, N. L. (1987). *Early intervention for handicapped and at-risk children: An introduction to early childhood–special education.* Denver, CO: Love.

Quay, H. C. (1975). Classification in the treatment of delinquency and antisocial behavior. In N. Hobbs (Ed.), *Issues in the classification of children* (Vol. 1, pp. 377–392). San Francisco, CA: Jossey-Bass.

Quay, H. C. (1979). Classification. In H. C. Quay & J. S. Werry (Eds.), *Psychopathological disorders of childhood* (2nd ed., pp. 1–41). New York: Wiley.

Rosenblatt, A. (1996). Discipline referral. *Beyond Behavior 7*(2), 26–27.

Rubin, R. A., & Balow, B. (1978). Prevalence of teacher identified behavior problems: A longitudinal study. *Exceptional Children, 45*(2), 102–111.

Rutter, M. (1995). Clinical implications of attachment concepts: Retrospect and prospect. *Journal of Child Psychology and Psychiatry, 36,* 549–571.

Sandler, A. G., Arnold, L. B., Gable, R. A., & Strain, P. S. (1987). Effects of peer pressure on disruptive behavior of behaviorally disordered classmates. *Behavioral Disorders, 12*(2), 104–110.

Schailberg, L. (1994, November 30). Disciplining special education students: A conundrum. *Education Week, 1,* 14–15.

Scheuermann, B., & Webber, J. (1996). Level systems: Problems and solutions. *Beyond Behavior, 7*(2), 18–21.

Snell, M. E. (1990). Schools are for all kids: The importance of integration for students with severe disabilities and their peers.

In J. W. Lloyd, A. C. Repp, & N. N. Singh (Eds.), *The regular education initiative: Alternative perspectives on concepts, issues, and models* (pp. 133–148). Sycamore, IL: Sycamore.

Special Educator (1996, August). 4th Circuit upholds expulsion policy. *The Special Educator, 12*(1), 4–5.

Stainback, W., & Stainback, S. (1990). *Supportive networks for inclusive schooling.* Baltimore, MD: Brookes.

Stainback, W., & Stainback, S. (1992). *Curriculum considerations in inclusive classrooms: Facilitating learning for all students.* Baltimore, MD: Brookes.

Stephens, S. A., & Lakin, K. C. (1995). Where students with emotional or behavioral disorders go to school. In J. M. Kauffman, J. W. Lloyd, D. P. Hallahan, & T. A. Astuto (Eds.), *Issues in educational placement: Students with emotional and behavioral disorders* (pp. 47–74). Hillsdale, NJ: Erlbaum.

Stone, F., & Rowley, V. N. (1964). Educational disability in emotionally disturbed children. *Exceptional Children, 30*(9), 423–426.

Timm, M. A. (1993). The Regional Intervention Program: Family treatment by family members. *Behavioral Disorders, 19*(1), 34–43.

Trickett, P. K., & McBride-Chang, C. (1995). The developmental impact of different forms of child abuse and neglect. *Developmental Review, 15,* 311–337.

Umbreit, J. (1995). Functional assessment and intervention in a regular classroom setting for the disruptive behavior of a student with attention deficit hyperactivity disorder. *Behavioral Disorders, 20,* 267–278.

U.S. Department of Education. (1997). To assure the free appropriate public education of all children with disabilities. *19th annual report to Congress on the implementation of the Individuals with Disabilities Act.* Washington, DC: U.S. Government Printing Office.

Von Isser, A., Quay, H. C., & Love, C. T. (1980). Interrelationships among three measures of deviant behavior. *Exceptional Children, 46*(4), 272–276.

Vorrath, H. H., & Brendtro, L. K. (1985). *Positive peer culture* (2nd ed.). New York: Aldine.

Wagner, M. (1991). *Dropouts with disabilities: What do we know? What can we do?* Menlo Park, CA: SRI International.

Wagner, M., D'Amico, R., Marder, C., Newman, L., & Blackorby, J. (1992). *What happens next? Trends in postschool outcomes of youth with disabilities: The second comprehensive report from the National Longitudinal Transition Study of special education students.* Menlo Park, CA: SRI International.

Wagner, M., Newman, L., D'Amico, R., Jay, E. D., Bulter-Nalin, P., Marder, C., & Cox, R. (1991). *Youth with disabilities: How are they doing? The first comprehensive report from the National Longitudinal Study of special education students.* Menlo Park, CA: SRI International.

Walker, H. M. (1995). *The acting-out child: Coping with classroom disruption* (2nd ed.). Longmont, CO: Sopris West.

Walker, H. M., & Bullis, M. (1990). Behavior disorders and the social context of regular class integration: A conceptual dilemma? In J. W. Lloyd, A. C. Repp, & N. N. Singh (Eds.), *The regular education initiative: Alternative perspectives on concepts, issues, and models* (pp. 133–148). Sycamore, IL: Sycamore.

Walker, H. M., Colvin, G., & Ramsey, E. (1995). *Antisocial behavior in school: Strategies and best practices.* Pacific Grove, CA: Brooks/Cole.

Weinstein, L. (1969). Project, Re-ED schools for emotionally disturbed children: Effectiveness as viewed by referring agencies, parents, and teachers. *Exceptional Children, 35,* 703–711.

Wolf, M. M., Braukmann, C. J., & Ramp, K. A. (1987). Serious delinquent behavior as part of a significantly handicapping condition: Cures and supportive environments. *Journal of Applied Behavior Analysis, 20*(4), 347–359.

Wolfe, V., & Birt, J. (1995). The psychological sequel of child sexual abuse. In T. H. Ollendick & R. J. Prinz (Eds.), *Advances in clinical child psychology* (Vol. 17, pp. 233–263). New York: Plenum.

Wood, F. H. (1996). Life stories and behavior change. *Beyond Behavior, 7*(1), 8–14.

Yell, M. L. (1995). *Clyde K. & Sheila K. v. Puyallup School District:* The courts, inclusion, and students with behavior disorders. *Behavior Disorders, 20*(3), 179–189.

■ CHAPTER 8

AAMR Ad Hoc Committee on Terminology and Classification. (1992). *Classification in mental retardation* (9th ed.). Washington, DC: American Association on Mental Retardation.

Agran, M., Salzberg, C. L., & Stowitchek, J. (1987). An analysis of the effects of a social-skills training program using self-instructions on the acquisition and generalization of two social behaviors in a work setting. *Journal of the Association for Persons with Severe Handicaps, 12*(2), 131–139.

Bailey, D. B., Jr., & Wolery, M. (1992). *Teaching infants and preschoolers with disabilities* (2nd ed.). Columbus, OH: Merrill.

Batshaw, M. L., & Perret, Y. M. (1986). *Children with handicaps: A medical primer* (2nd ed.). Baltimore, MD: Brookes.

Benavidez, D., & Matson, J. L., (1993). Assessment of depression in mentally retarded adolescents. *Research in Developmental Disabilities, 14,* 179–188.

Bensberg, G., & Siegelman, C. (1976). Definitions and prevalence. In L. Lloyd (Ed.), *Communication, assessment, and intervention strategies.* Baltimore, MD: University Park Press.

Benson, G., Aberdanto, L., Short, K., Nuccio, J. B., & Mans, F. (1993). Development of a theory of mind in individuals with mental retardation. *American Journal on Mental Retardation, 98*(6), 427–433.

Bergen, A. E., & Mosley, J. L. (1994). Attention and attention shift efficiency in individuals with and without mental retardation. *American Journal on Mental Retardation, 98*(6), 732–743.

Borkowski, J. G., & Day, J. (1987). *Cognition in special children: Comparative approaches to retardation, learning disabilities, and giftedness.* Norwood, NJ: Ablex.

Borkowski, J. G., Peck, V. A., & Damberg, P. R. (1983). Attention, memory, and cognition. In J. L. Matson & J. A. Mulich (Eds.), *Handbook of mental retardation* (pp. 479–497). New York: Pergamon.

Brimer, R. W. (1990). *Students with severe disabilities: Current perspectives and practices.* Mountain View, CA: Mayfield.

Brooks, P. H., & McCauley, C. (1984). Cognitive research in mental retardation. *American Journal of Mental Deficiency, 88,* 479–486.

Browder, D. M., & Snell, M. E. (1993). Functional academics. In M. E. Snell (Ed.), *Instruction of persons with severe disabilities* (pp. 432–479). New York: Merrill.

Carta, J. J., Sideridis, G., Rinkel, P., Guimaraes, S., Greenwood, C., Baggett, K., Peterson, P., Atwater, J., McEvoy, M., & McConnel, S. (1994). Behavioral outcomes of young children pre-natally exposed to illicit drugs: Review and analysis of experimental literature. *Topics in Early Childhood Special Education, 14*(2), 184–209.

Cipani, E., & Spooner, F. (1994). *Curricular and instructional approaches for persons with severe disabilities.* Boston: Allyn and Bacon.

Cohen, H. J. (1991). The rehabilitation needs of children with HIV infections and associated developmental disabilities. *Physical Medicine and Rehabilitation State-of-the-Art Reviews, 5*(2), 313.

Cole, M., & Cole, J. (1989). *Effective intervention with the language impaired child* (2nd ed.). Rockville, MD: Aspen.

Davis, W. E., & McCaul, E. J. (1991). The emerging crisis: Current and projected status of children in the United States (Monograph). Orono, ME: Institute for the Study of At-Risk Students.

Drew, C. J., Hardman, M. L., & Logan, D. R. (1996). *Mental retardation: A life cycle approach* (6th ed.). Columbus, OH: Merrill.

Eidelman, S. (1994). Did you know? *Byline: The Official Newsletter of Best Buddies International, 6*(1), 1.

Fink, W. (1981). The distribution of clients and their characteristics in programs for the mentally retarded and other developmentally disabled throughout Oregon. Unpublished manuscript, Oregon Mental Health Division, Eugene, OR.

Franklin, K., & Beukelman, D. R. (1991). Augmentative communication: Directions for future research. In J. F. Miller (Ed.), *Research on child language disorders: A decade of progress* (pp. 321–337). Austin, TX: Pro-Ed.

Gee, K. Least restrictive environment: Elementary and middle school. (1996). In *Improving the implementation of the Individuals with Disabilities Education Act: Making schools work for all of America's children* (Suppl., pp. 395–425). Washington, DC: The National Council on Disability.

Glidden, I. M. (1985). Semantic processing, semantic memory, and recall. In N. R. Ellis (Ed.), *International review of research in mental retardation* (Vol. 13, pp. 247–278). New York: Academic Press.

Grossman, J. J. (Ed.). (1983). *Manual on terminology and classification in mental retardation.* Washington, DC: American Association on Mental Deficiency.

Halvorsen, A. T., & Sailor, W. (1990). Integration of students with severe and profound disabilities: A review of research. In R. Gaylord-Ross (Ed.), *Issues and research in special education* (pp. 110–172). New York: Teachers College Press.

Hasazi, S., Johnson, R. E., Hasazi, J., Gordon, L. R., & Hull, M. (1989). Employment of youth with and without handicaps following school: Outcomes and correlates. *Journal of Special Education, 23,* 243–245.

Heber, R. F. (1959). A manual on terminology and classification in mental retardation. *American Journal of Mental Deficiency, 64,* Monograph Supplement (Rev. ed.), 1961.

Hughes, C. (1992). Teaching self-instruction utilizing multiple exemplars to produce generalized problem solving among individuals with severe mental retardation. *American Journal on Mental Retardation, 97*(3), 302–314.

Hunt, P., Staub, D., Alwell, M., & Goetz, L. (1994). Achievement by all students within the context of cooperative learning groups. *Journal of the Association for Persons with Severe Handicaps, 19*(4), 290–301.

Joseph P. Kennedy, Jr. Foundation and the Institute for the Study of Exceptional Children and Youth at the University of Maryland at College Park. (1992). *The untapped resource: The employee with mental retardation.* Washington, DC: Author.

Kaiser, A. P. (1993). Functional language. In M. E. Snell (Ed.), *Instruction of persons with severe disabilities* (pp. 347–379). Columbus, OH: Merrill.

Kirk, S. (1958). *Early education of the mentally retarded: An experimental study.* Urbana, IL: University of Illinois Press.

MacMillan, D. L. (1982). *Mental retardation in school and society* (2nd ed.). Boston: Little, Brown.

Manning, M. L., & Baruth, L. G. (1995). *Students at risk.* Boston: Allyn and Bacon.

Marino, B. R., & Pueschel, S. M. (1996). *Heart disease in persons with Down syndrome.* Baltimore, MD: Brookes.

McAlpine, C., Kendall, K. A., & Singh, N. N. (1991). Recognition of facial expressions of emotion by persons with mental retardation. *American Journal on Mental Retardation, 96,* 29–36.

McDermott, S., & Altrekruse, J. (1994). Dynamic model for preventing mental retardation: The importance of poverty and deprivation. *Research on Developmental Disabilities, 15*(1), 49–65.

McDonnell, A., & Hardman, M. L. (1988). A synthesis of best practice guidelines for early childhood services. *Journal of the Division for Early Childhood Education, 12*(8), 328–391.

McDonnell, J., Mathot-Buckner, C., & Ferguson, B. (1996). *Transition programs for students with moderate/severe disabilities.* Pacific Grove, CA: Brooks/Cole.

McDonnell, J., Hardman, M. L., McDonnell, A. P., & Kiefer-O'-Donnell, R. (1995). *Introduction to persons with severe disabilities.* Boston: Allyn and Bacon.

Merrill, E. C., & Peacock, M. (1994). Allocation of attention and task difficulty. *American Journal on Mental Retardation, 98*(5), 588–593.

Meyer, L. H., Peck, C. A., & Brown, L. (Eds.). (1991). *Critical issues in the lives of people with severe disabilities.* Baltimore, MD: Brookes.

National Association of State Directors of Special Education. (1991). Reference notes for understanding the forces at work which are driving social policy. Washington, DC: Author.

National Information Center for Children and Youth with Disabilities. (1991). *General information about Down syndrome.* Fact Sheet no. 4 (FS4). Washington, DC: Author.

Nirje, B. (1970). The normalization principle and its human management implications. *Journal of Mental Subnormality, 16,* 62–70.

Noonan, M. J., & McCormick, L. (1993). *Early intervention in natural environments: Methods and procedures.* Pacific Grove, CA: Brooks/Cole.

Patton, J. R., Beirne-Smith, J., & Payne, J. S. (1990). *Mental retardation* (3rd ed.). Columbus, OH: Merrill.

President's Committee on Mental Retardation. (1995). *The journey to inclusion: A resource for state policy makers.* Washington, DC: Author.

Rowley, S. (1996). It takes a village to raise a child. In S. Wade (Ed.), *Casebook on inclusive education: Parent, student, and general education teacher perspectives.* Boston: Allyn and Bacon.

Siperstein, G. N., & Leffert, J. S. (1997). Comparison of socially accepted and rejected children with mental retardation. *Mental Retardation, 101*(4), 339–351.

Stainback, S., Stainback, W., & Ayres, B. (1996). Schools as inclusive communities. In W. Stainback & S. Stainback (Eds.), *Con-

troversial issues confronting special education: Divergent perspectives* (pp. 31–43). Boston: Allyn and Bacon.

Sternberg, R. J., & Spear, I. C. (1985). A triarchic theory of mental retardation. In N. R. Ellis (Ed.), *International review of research in mental retardation* (Vol. 13, pp. 301–326). New York: Academic Press.

Tines, J., Rusch, F. R., McCaughrin, W., & Conley, R. W. (1990). Benefit-cost analysis of supported employment in Illinois: A statewide evaluation. *American Journal on Mental Retardation, 95,* 55–67.

Turner, L., Dofny, E., & Dutka, S. (1994). Effective strategy and attribution training on strategy maintenance and transfer. *American Journal on Mental Retardation, 98*(4), 445–454.

U.S. Bureau of the Census (1998). The official statistics. Internet: http://www.census.gov/mp/www/index2.html.

U.S. Department of Education. (1997). To assure the free appropriate public education of all children with disabilities. *19th annual report to Congress on the implementation of the Education of the Handicapped Act.* Washington, DC: U.S. Government Printing Office.

Wehman, P. (1996). *Life beyond the classroom: Transition strategies for young people with disabilities* (2nd ed.). Baltimore, MD: Brookes.

Westling, D. (1986). *Introduction to mental retardation.* Englewood Cliffs, NJ: Prentice Hall.

Whitman, T. L. (1990). Self-regulation and mental retardation. *American Journal on Mental Retardation, 94*(4), 347–362.

Zigler, E., & Balla, D. (1981). Issues in personality and motivation of mentally retarded persons. In M. J. Begab, H. C. Haywood, & H. L. Garber (Eds.), *Psychosocial influences in retarded performance: Vol. 1. Issues and theories in development.* Baltimore, MD: University Park Press.

■ CHAPTER 9

Abe, K., Yokoyama, R., & Yorifuji, S. (1993). Repetitive speech disorder resulting from infarcts in the paramedian thalami and midbrain. *Journal of Neurology, Neurosurgery and Psychiatry, 56,* 1024–1026.

American Psychiatric Association. (1994). *Diagnostic and statistical manual of mental disorders* (4th ed.). Washington, DC: Author.

Anand, A., & Wales, R. J. (1994). Psychotic speech: A neurolinguistic perspective. *Australian and New Zealand Journal of Psychiatry, 28,* 229–238.

Andrews, M. L., & Summers, A. C. (1993). A voice stimulation program for preschoolers: Theory and practice. *Language, Speech, and Hearing Services in Schools, 24*(3), 140–145.

Azar, B. (1994). Brain imaging raises, answers questions. *APA Monitor, 25*(8), 14.

Barinaga, M. (1995). Brain researchers speak a common language. *Science, 270*(5241), 1437–1438.

Bernstein, D. K. (1997a). The nature of language and its disorders. In D. K. Bernstein and E. Tiegerman-Farber (Eds.), *Language and communication disorders in children* (4th ed., pp. 1–25). Boston: Allyn and Bacon.

Bernstein, D. K. (1997b). Language development: The preschool years. In D. K. Bernstein and E. Tiegerman-Farber (Eds.), *Language and communication disorders in children* (4th ed., pp. 97–126). Boston: Allyn and Bacon.

Beukelman, D. R., & Mirenda, P. (1992). *Augmentative and alternative communication: Management of severe communication disorders in children and adults.* Baltimore, MD: Brookes.

Bollinger, R. L., Musson, N. D., & Holland, A. L. (1993). A study of group communication intervention with chronically aphasic persons. *Aphasiology, 7,* 301–313.

Bradbury, E. T., & Hewison, J. (1994). Early parental adjustment to visible congenital disfigurement. *Child Care, Health and Development, 20*(4), 251–266.

Case, J. L. (1991). *Clinical management of voice disorders* (2nd ed.). Austin, TX: Pro-Ed.

Casper, J. K., & Colton, R. H. (1993). *Clinical manual for laryngectomy and head and neck cancer rehabilitation.* San Diego, CA: Singular Press.

Cooper, E. B. (1993). Red herrings, dead horses, straw men, and blind alleys: Escaping the stuttering conundrum. *Journal of Fluency Disorders, 18*(4), 375–387.

Cooper, E. B., & Cooper, C. S. (1992). A fluency disorders prevention program for preschoolers and children in the primary grades. *American Journal of Speech–Language Pathology, 1*(1), 28–31.

Cordes, A. K., & Ingham, R. J. (1995). Stuttering includes both within-word and between-word disfluencies. *Journal of Speech and Hearing Research, 38,* 382–386.

Cordes, A. K., & Ingham, R. J. (1996). Disfluency types and stuttering measurement: A necessary connection? *Journal of Speech and Hearing Research, 39,* 404–405.

Costa, A. D., & Kroll, R. M. (1995). Sertraline in stuttering. *Journal of Clinical Psychopharmacology, 15,* 443–444.

Dale, P. S., Crain-Thoreson, C., & Notari-Syverson, A., & Cole, K. (1996). Parent–child book reading as an intervention technique for young children with language delays. *Topics in Early Childhood Special Education, 16,* 213–235.

Daly, D. A. (1993). Cluttering: The orphan of speech–language pathology. *American Journal of Speech–Language Pathology, 2*(2), 6–8.

DeMontfort-Supple, M. (1996). Prologue: Beyond bilingualism. *Topics in Language Disorders, 16*(4), 1–8.

Drew, C. J., Hardman, M. L., & Hart, A. W. (1996). *Designing and conducting behavioral research.* Boston: Allyn and Bacon.

Eiserman, W. D., Weber, C., & McCoun, M. (1995). Parent and professional roles in early intervention: A longitudinal comparison of the effects of two intervention configurations. *Journal of Special Education, 29,* 20–44.

Elbert, M., Powell, T. W., & Swartzlander, P. (1991). Toward a technology of generalization: How many exemplars are sufficient? *Journal of Speech and Hearing Research, 34,* 81–87.

Felsenfeld, S. (1996). Progress and needs in the genetics of stuttering. *Journal of Fluency Disorders, 21*(2), 77–103.

Felsenfeld, S., Broen, P. A., & McGue, M. (1992). A 28-year follow-up of adults with a history of moderate phonological disorder: Linguistic and personality results. *Journal of Speech and Hearing Research, 35,* 1114–1125.

Gelfand, D. M., Jenson, W. R., & Drew, C. J. (1997). *Understanding child behavior disorders* (3rd ed.). Fort Worth, TX: Harcourt Brace & Co.

Gibbon, F., Hardcastle, B., & Dent, H. (1995). A study of obstruent sounds in school-age children with speech disorders using elec-

tropalatography. *European Journal of Disorders of Communication, 30*(2), 213–225.

Gierut, J. A. (1996). An experimental test of phonemic cyclicity. *Journal of Child Language, 23,* 81–102.

Gray, S. I., & Shelton, R. L. (1992). Self-monitoring effects on articulation carryover in school-age children. *Language, Speech, and Hearing Services in the Schools, 23,* 334–342.

Hancock, T. B., & Kaiser, A. P. (1996). Siblings' use of milieu teaching at home. *Topics in Early Childhood Special Education, 16,* 168–190.

Harris, T. M. (1992). The pharmacological treatment of voice disorders. *Folia Phoniatrica, 44*(3–4), 143–154.

Hough, M. S. (1993). Treatment of Wernicke's aphasia with jargon: A case study. *Journal of Communication Disorders, 26*(2), 101–111.

Iacono, T., & Duncum, J. E. (1995). Comparison of sign alone and in combination with an electronic communication device in early language intervention: Case study. *Augmentative and Alternative Communication, 11*(4), 249–254.

Kaiser, A. P., & Hester, P. P. (1994). Generalized effects of enhanced milieu teaching. *Journal of Speech and Hearing Research, 37,* 1320–1340.

Kelly, E. M. (1995). Parents as partners: Including mothers and fathers in the treatment of children who stutter. *Journal of Communication Disorders, 28*(2), 93–105.

Kempler, D., Andersen, E. S., & Henderson, V. W. (1995). Linguistic and attentional contributions to anomia in Alzheimer's disease. *Neuropsychiatry, Neuropsychology, and Behavioral Neurology, 8,* 33–37.

Kolk, H. (1995). A time-based approach to agrammatic production. *Brain and Language, 50,* 282–303.

Kreiman, J., Gerratt, B. R., Kempster, G. B., Erman, A., & Berke, G. S. (1993). Perceptual evaluation of voice quality: Review, tutorial, and a framework for future research. *Journal of Speech and Hearing Research, 36,* 21–40.

Kuder, S. J. (1997). *Teaching students with communication and language disabilities.* Boston: Allyn and Bacon.

Kuniszyk-Jozkowiak, W. (1995). The statistical analysis of speech envelopes in stutters and non-stutterers. *Journal of Fluency Disorders, 20,* 11–23.

Leck, I., & Lancashire, R. J. (1995). Birth prevalence of malformations in members of different ethnic groups and in the offspring of matings between them, in Birmingham, England. *Journal of Epidemiology and Community Health, 49*(2), 171–179.

Ledesma, L. K., Ortiz, M. H., Gonzaga, F. C., & Lee, L. V. (1991). Speech delay in Filipino children: A clinical profile. *Philippine Journal of Psychology, 24*(2), 20–25.

LeDorze, G., & Brassard, C. (1995). A description of the consequences of aphasia on aphasic persons and their relatives and friends, based on the WHO model of chronic diseases. *Aphasiology, 9,* 239–255.

Leeper, L. H. (1992). Diagnostic examination of children with voice disorders: A low-cost solution. *Language, Speech, and Hearing Services in Schools, 23,* 353–360.

Lerner, J. (1997). *Learning disabilities: Theories, diagnosis, and teaching strategies* (7th ed.). Boston: Houghton Mifflin.

Lonigan, C. J., Fischel, J. E., Whitehurst, G. J., & Arnold, D. S. (1992). The role of otitis media in the development of expressive language disorder. *Developmental Psychology, 28,* 430–440.

Love, R. J. (1992). *Childhood motor speech disability*. New York: Macmillan.

Mans, E. J. (1994). Psychotherapeutic treatment of patients with functional voice disorders. *Folia Phoniatrica et Logopaedica, 46,* 1–8.

McNamara, A. P., & Perry, C. K. (1994). Vocal abuse prevention practices: A national survey of school-based speech–language pathologists. *Language, Speech, and Hearing Services in Schools, 25*(2), 105–111.

McNaughton, S., & Lindsay, P. (1995). Approaching literacy with AAC graphics. *Augmentative and Alternative Communication, 11*(4), 212–228.

Nelson, N. W. (1993). *Childhood language disorders in context: Infancy through adolescence*. New York: Macmillan.

Nelson, N. W. (1997). Language intervention in school settings. In D. K. Bernstein and E. Tiegerman-Farber (Eds.), *Language and communication disorders in children* (4th ed., pp. 325–381). Boston: Allyn and Bacon.

Onslow, M., Andrews, C., & Lincoln, M. (1994). A control/experimental trial of an operant treatment for early stuttering. *Journal of Speech and Hearing Research, 37,* 1244–1259.

Owens, R. E., Jr. (1995). *Language disorders: A functional approach to assessment and intervention* (2nd ed.). Boston: Allyn and Bacon.

Owens, R. E., Jr. (1997). Mental retardation: Difference and delay. In D. K. Bernstein and E. Tiegerman-Farber (Eds.), *Language and communication disorders in children* (4th ed., pp. 457–523). Boston: Allyn and Bacon.

Pannbacker, M. (1992). Some common myths about voice therapy. *Language, Speech, and Hearing Services in Schools, 23,* 12–19.

Patton, J. R., Kauffman, J. M., Blackbourn, J. M., & Brown, G. B. (1991). *Exceptional children in focus* (5th ed.). New York: Macmillan.

Perkins, W. H., Kent, R. D., & Curlee, R. F. (1991). A theory of neuropsycholinguistic function in stuttering. *Journal of Speech and Hearing Research, 34,* 734–752.

Plumert, J. M., & Nichols-Whitehead, P. (1996). Parental scaffolding of young children's spatial communication. *Developmental Psychology, 32,* 523–532.

Postman, N. (1993). *Technopoly: The surrender of culture to technology*. New York: Vintage Books.

Prasad, M., Sitholey, P., Dutt, K., & Srivastava, R. P. (1992). ADL (activity of daily living) training and treatment of temper-tantrums in a severely retarded aphasic child. *Indian Journal of Clinical Psychology, 19,* 37–39.

Radziewicz, C., & Antonellis, S. (1997). Considerations and implications for habilitation of hearing impaired children. In D. K. Bernstein and E. Tiegerman-Farber (Eds.), *Language and communication disorders in children* (4th ed., pp. 574–603). Boston: Allyn and Bacon.

Reichle, J., York, J., & Sigafoos, J. (1991). *Implementing augmentative and alternative communication: Strategies for learners with severe disabilities*. Baltimore, MD: Brookes.

Robinson, L. A., & Owens, R. E. (1995). Functional augmentative communication and positive behavior change. *Augmentative and Alternative Communication, 11*(4), 207–211.

Robinson, N. B., & Robb, M. P. (1997). Early communication assessment and intervention: An interactive process. In D. K. Bernstein and E. Tiegerman-Farber (Eds.), *Language and commu-nication disorders in children* (4th ed., pp. 155–196). Boston: Allyn and Bacon.

Ryan, B. P., & Ryan, B. V. K. (1995). Programmed stuttering treatment for children: Comparison of two establishment programs through transfer, maintenance, and follow-up. *Journal of Speech and Hearing Research, 38,* 61–72.

Schonweiler, R. (1994). Synopsis of results on 1,300 children with delayed speech development from an etiopathogenetic, audiologic, and phenomenologic viewpoint. *Folia Phoniatrica et Logopaedica, 46,* 18–26.

Schoonen, R. (1991). The internal validity of efficacy studies: Design and statistical power in studies of language therapy for aphasics. *Brain and Language, 41,* 446–464.

Silverman, F. H. (1992). *Stuttering and other fluency disorders*. Englewood Cliffs, NJ: Prentice Hall.

Silverman, F. H. (1995). *Speech, language, and hearing disorders*. Boston: Allyn and Bacon.

Smith, T. E. C., Dowdy, C. A., Polloway, E. A., & Blalock, G. E. (1997). *Children and adults with learning disabilities*. Boston: Allyn and Bacon.

Sommers, R. K., Logsdon, B. S., & Wright, J. M. (1992). A review and critical analysis of treatment research related to articulation and phonological disorders. *Journal of Communication Disorders, 25,* 3–22.

Springer, L., Willmes, K., & Haag, E. (1993). Training in the use of wh-questions and prepositions in dialogues: A comparison of two different approaches in aphasia therapy. *Aphasiology, 7,* 251–270.

Starkweather, C. W. (1995). A simple theory of stuttering. *Journal of Fluency Disorders, 10,* 91–116.

Stewart, T. (1996). Good maintainers and poor maintainers: A personal construct approach to an old problem. *Journal of Fluency Disorders, 21,* 33–48.

Thompson, C. K., Shapiro, L. P., & Roberts, M. M. (1993). Treatment of sentence production deficits in aphasia: A linguistic-specific approach to wh-interrogative training and generalization. *Aphasiology, 7,* 111–133.

Tiegerman-Farber, E. (1997a). Social cognition: The communication imperative. In D. K. Bernstein and E. Tiegerman-Farber (Eds.), *Language and communication disorders in children* (4th ed., pp. 26–59). Boston: Allyn and Bacon.

Tiegerman-Farber, E. (1997b). The ecology of the family: The language imperative. In D. K. Bernstein and E. Tiegerman-Farber (Eds.), *Language and communication disorders in children* (4th ed., pp. 60–96). Boston: Allyn & Bacon.

Todman, J., Elder, L., & Alm, N. (1995). Evaluation of the content of computer-aided conversations. *Augmentative and Alternative Communication, 11*(4), 229–234.

Treon, M. (1995). A bi-polar etiologic stuttering threshold hypothesis and related proposed treatment approach. *Psychology: A Journal of Human Behavior, 32*(3–4), 35–51.

Turner, G. E., & Williams, W. N. (1991). Fluoroscopy and nasendoscopy in designing palatal lift prostheses. *Journal of Prosthetic Dentistry, 66,* 63–71.

U.S. Department of Education. (1997). To assure the free appropriate public education of all children with disabilities. *19th annual report to Congress on the implementation of the Individuals with*

Disabilities Education Act. Washington, DC: U.S. Government Printing Office.

Van Riper, C., & Erickson, R. L. (1996). Speech correction: An introduction to speech pathology and audiology (9th ed.). Boston: Allyn and Bacon.

Van Staden, F., & Gerhardt, C. (1995). Mothers of children with facial cleft deformities: Reactions and effects. *South African Journal of Psychology, 25,* 39–46.

Ward-Lonergan, J. M., Liles, B. Z., & Owen, S. V. (1996). Contextual strategy instruction: Socially/emotionally maladjusted adolescents with language impairments. *Journal of Communication Disorders, 29*(2), 107–124.

Weiss, A. L. (1997). Planning language intervention for young children. In D. K. Bernstein and E. Tiegerman-Farber (Eds.), *Language and communication disorders in children* (4th ed., pp. 272–323). Boston: Allyn and Bacon.

Wieneke, G. H., Janssen, P., & Brutten, G. J. (1995). Variance of central timing of voiced and voiceless periods among stutterers and nonstutterers. *Journal of Fluency Disorders, 20,* 171–189.

Yairi, E. (1996). Applications of disfluencies in measurements of stuttering. *Journal of Speech and Hearing Research, 39,* 402–404.

Yairi, E., & Ambrose, N. (1992). Onset of stuttering in preschool children: Selected factors. *Journal of Speech and Hearing Research, 35,* 782–788.

Yairi, E., Ambrose, N., & Niermann, R. (1993). The early months of stuttering: A developmental study. *Journal of Speech and Hearing Research, 36,* 521–528.

Yairi, E., Ambrose, N. G., Paden, E. P., & Throneburg, R. N. (1996). Predictive factors of persistence and recovery: Pathways of childhood stuttering. *Journal of Communication Disorders, 29,* 51–77.

Yairi, E., & Carrico, D. M. (1992). Early childhood stuttering: Pediatricians' attitudes and practices. *American Journal of Speech–Language Pathology, 1*(3), 54–62.

Zebrowski, P. M., & Schum, R. L. (1993). Counseling parents of children who stutter. *American Journal of Speech–Language Pathology, 2*(2), 65–73.

■ CHAPTER 10

AAMR Ad Hoc Committee on Terminology and Classification. (1992). *Classification in mental retardation* (9th ed.). Washington, DC: American Association on Mental Retardation.

Abt Associates. (1974). *Assessments of selected resources for severely handicapped children and youth: Vol. 1. A state-of-the-art paper.* Cambridge, MA: Author. ERIC Document Reproduction Service, No. ED 134 614.

Bailey, D. B., Jr., & Wolery, M. (1992). *Teaching infants and preschoolers with disabilities* (2nd ed.). Columbus, OH: Merrill.

Berry, J., & Hardman, M. L. (1998). *Lifespan perspectives on family and disability.* Boston: Allyn and Bacon.

Brown, L. (1991). Who are they and what do they want? In L. H. Meyer, C. A. Peck, & L. Brown (Eds.), *Critical issues in the lives of people with severe disabilities* (p. xxv). Baltimore, MD: Brookes.

Brown, L., Schwarz, P., Udvari-Solner, A., Rattura Kampschroer, E., Johnson, F., Jorgensen, J., & Gruenewald, I. (1991). How much time should students with severe intellectual disabilities spend in regular education classrooms and elsewhere? *The Journal of the Association for Persons with Severe Handicaps, 16*(a), 39–47.

Choppin, P. W. (1991). Foreword. In *Blazing a genetic trail: A report from the Howard Hughes Medical Institute* (p. 1). Bethesda, MD: Howard Hughes Medical Institute.

Cohen, L. G. (1990). *Before their time: Fetuses and infants at-risk.* AAMR Monographs, edited by Michael J. Begab. Washington, DC: American Association on Mental Retardation.

Cole, M., & Cole, J. (1989). *Effective intervention with the language impaired child* (2nd ed.). Rockville, MD: Aspen.

Downing, J., & Eichinger, J. (1990). Instructional strategies for learners with dual sensory impairments in integrated settings. *The Journal of the Association for Persons with Severe Handicaps, 15,* 98–105.

Drew, C. J., Hardman, M. L., & Logan, D. R. (1996). *Mental retardation: A life cycle approach* (6th ed.). Columbus, OH: Merrill.

Eiserman, W. D., Weber, C., & McCoun, M. (1995). Parent and professional roles in early intervention: A longitudinal comparison of the effects of two intervention configurations. *Journal of Special Education, 29*(1), 20–44.

Evans, I. M. (1991). Testing and diagnosis: A review and evaluation. In L. H. Meyer, C. A. Peck, & L. Brown (Eds.), *Critical issues in the lives of people with severe disabilities* (pp. 25–44). Baltimore, MD: Brookes.

Gaylord-Ross, R., & Browder, D. (1991). Functional assessment: Dynamic and domain properties. In L. H. Meyer, C. A. Peck, & L. Brown (Eds.), *Critical issues in the lives of people with severe disabilities* (pp. 45–66). Baltimore, MD: Brookes.

Gee, K. (1996). Least restrictive environment: Elementary and middle school. In *Improving the implementation of the Individuals with Disabilities Education Act: Making schools work for all of America's children* (Suppl., pp. 395–425). Washington, DC: The National Council on Disability.

Giangreco, M. E., & Snell, M. E. (1996). Severe and multiple disabilities. In *Improving the implementation of the Individuals with Disabilities Education Act: Making schools work for all of America's children* (Suppl., pp. 97–132). Washington, DC: National Council on Disability.

Grenot-Scheyer, M., Schwartz, I. S., & Meyer, L. H. (1997, April). Blending best practices for young children: Inclusive early childhood programs. *TASH Newsletter,* 8–11.

Hammer, E. K. (1989). Research issues in educating visually handicapped persons with multiple impairments. In M. C. Wang, M. C. Reynolds, & H. J. Walberg (Eds.), *Handbook of special education: Research and practice: Vol. 3. Low incidence conditions* (pp. 173–188). Oxford, UK: Pergamon.

Hauerwas, S. (1986). Suffering the retarded. Should we prevent retardation? In P. R. Dokecki & R. M. Zaner (Eds.), *Ethics of dealing with persons with severe handicaps* (pp. 53–70). Baltimore, MD: Brookes.

Hunt, P., Staub, D., Alwell, M., & Goetz, L. (1994). Achievement by all students within the context of cooperative learning groups. *Journal of the Association for Persons with Severe Handicaps, 19*(4), 290–301.

Justen, J. (1976). Who are the severely handicapped? A problem in definition. *AAESPH Review, 1*(5), 1–11.

McDonnell, A., & Hardman, M. L. (1988). A synthesis of best practice guidelines for early childhood services. *Journal of the Division for Early Childhood Education, 12*(8), 328–341.

McDonnell, J., Hardman, M., McDonnell, A. P., & Kiefer-O'Donnell, R. (1995). *Introduction to persons with severe disabilities.* Boston: Allyn and Bacon.

McDonnell, J., Mathot-Buckner, C., & Ferguson, B. (1996). *Transition programs for students with moderate/severe disabilities.* Pacific Grove, CA: Brooks/Cole.

McDonnell, J., Wilcox, B., & Hardman, M. (1991). *Secondary programs for students with developmental disabilities.* Boston: Allyn and Bacon.

McLean, L., Brady, N., & McLean, J. (1996). Reported communication abilities of individuals with severe mental retardation. *American Journal of Mental Retardation, 100*(6), 580–591.

Meyer, L. H., Peck, C. A., & Brown, L. (1991a). Definition of the people TASH serves. In L. H. Meyer, C. A. Peck, & L. Brown (Eds.), *Critical issues in the lives of people with disabilities* (p. 19). Baltimore, MD: Brookes.

Meyer, L. H., Peck, C. A., & Brown, L. (1991b). Definitions and diagnosis. In L. H. Meyer, C. A. Peck, & L. Brown (Eds.), *Critical issues in the lives of people with disabilities* (p. 17). Baltimore, MD: Brookes.

Mirenda, P., Iacono, T., & Williams, R. (1990). Communication options for persons with severe and profound disabilities: State of the art and future directions. *Journal of the Association for Persons with Severe Disabilities, 15,* 3–21.

National Association of State Directors of Special Education. (1991). *Reference notes for speechmaking or understanding the forces at work which are driving social policy.* Washington, DC: Author.

Neal, B. W. (1990). Ethical aspects in the care of very low birth weight infants. *Pediatrician, 17,* 92–99.

Newton, C., & Tarrant, T. (1992). *Managing change in America's schools.* London: Routledge.

President's Commission for the Study of Ethical Problems in Medicine and Biomedical and Behavioral Research. (1983). *Screening and counseling for genetic conditions.* Washington, DC: Author.

Putnam, J. (1994). *Cooperative learning and strategies for inclusion: Celebrating diversity in the classroom.* Baltimore, MD: Brookes.

Ramey, C., & Landesman-Ramey, S. (1992). Early educational intervention with disadvantaged children—to what effect? *Applied and Preventive Psychology, 1,* 130–140.

Records, T. (1994). *Deinstitutionalization—from theory to practice.* Washington, DC: National Association of Developmental Disabilities Councils.

Reiss, S. (1990). Prevalence of dual diagnosis in community-based day programs in the Chicago metropolitan area. *American Journal on Mental Retardation, 94*(6), 578–585.

Sailor, W., Gee, K., & Karasoff, P. (1993). School restructuring and full inclusion. In M. Snell (Ed.), *Systematic instruction of persons with severe handicaps* (4th ed., pp. 1–30). Columbus, OH: Merrill.

Sailor, W., & Haring, N. (1977). Some current directions in the education of the severely/multiple handicapped. *AAESPH Review, 2,* 67–86.

Senatore, V., Matson, J., & Kazdin, A. (1985). An inventory to assess psychopathology of mentally retarded adults. *American Journal of Mental Deficiency, 82,* 459–466.

Snell, M. E. (1991). Schools are for all kids: The importance of integration for students with severe disabilities and their peers. In J. Lloyd, N. N. Singh, & A. C. Repp (Eds.), *The regular education initiative: Alternative perspectives on concepts, issues, and models* (pp. 133–148). Sycamore, IL: Sycamore.

Snell, M. E., & Brown, F. (1993). Instructional planning and implementation. In M. E. Snell (Ed.), *Instruction of students with severe disabilities* (pp. 99–151). New York: Merrill.

Sobsey, D., & Cox, A. W. (1991). Integrating health care and educational programs. In F. P. Orelove & D. Sobsey (Eds.), *Educating children with multiple disabilities: A transdisciplinary approach* (2nd ed, pp. 155–186). Baltimore, MD: Brookes.

Sobsey, D., & Wolf-Schein, E. G. (1991). Sensory impairments. In F. P. Orelove & D. Sobsey (Eds.), *Educating children with multiple disabilities: A transdisciplinary approach* (2nd ed., pp. 119–154). Baltimore, MD: Brookes.

Thousand, J., Villa, R., & Nevin, A. (1994). *Creativity and collaborative learning: A practical guide to empowering students with severe disabilities.* Baltimore, MD: Brookes.

U.S. Department of Education. (1997). To assure the free appropriate public education of all children with disabilities. *19th annual report to Congress on the implementation of the Individuals with Disabilities Education Act.* Washington, DC: U.S. Government Printing Office.

Ward, M. J. (1991). Self-determination revisited: Going beyond expectations. In C. Valdisision (Dir.), Transition summary, no. 7: Options after high school for youth with disabilities. Washington, DC: NICHCY. ERIC Document Reproduction Service, No. ED 340 170.

Wehman, P. (1997). Traumatic brain injury. In P. Wehman (Ed.), *Exceptional individuals in school, community, and work* (pp. 451–485). Austin, TX: Pro-Ed.

Wehman, P., & Parent, W. (1997). Severe mental retardation. In P. Wehman (Ed.), *Exceptional individuals in school, community, and work* (pp. 145–173). Austin, TX: Pro-Ed.

▪ CHAPTER 11

Aman, M. G., Van Bourgondien, M. E., & Wolford, P. L. (1995). Psychotropic and anticonvulsant drugs in subjects with autism: Prevalence and patterns of use. *Journal of the American Academy of Child and Adolescent Psychiatry, 34,* 1672–1681.

American Psychiatric Association. (1994). *Diagnostic and statistical manual of mental disorders* (4th ed.). Washington, DC: Author.

Bailey, A. J. (1993). The biology of autism. *Psychological Medicine, 23,* 7–11.

Bailey, A., LeCouteur, A., Gottesman, I., & Bolton, P. (1995). Autism as a strongly genetic disorder: Evidence from a British twin study. *Psychological Medicine, 25,* 63–77.

Beck, A. R., & Pirovano, C. M. (1996). Facilitated communicators' performance on a task of receptive language. *Journal of Autism and Developmental Disorders, 26,* 497–512.

Belcher, T. L. (1996). Behavioral treatment vs. behavioral control: A case study. *Journal of Developmental and Physical Disabilities, 7,* 235–241.

Berger, H. J., Van Spaendonck, K. P., & Horstink, M. W. (1993). Cognitive shifting as a predictor of progress in social understandings in high-functioning adolescents with autism: A prospective study. *Journal of Autism and Developmental Disorders, 23,* 341–359.

Biklen, D. (1990). Communication unbound: Autism and praxis. *Harvard Educational Review, 60,* 291–314.

Biklen, D. (1992). Typing to talk: Facilitated communication. *American Journal of Speech–Language Pathology, 1*(2), 15–17.

Biklen, D. (1996). Learning from the experiences of people with disabilities. *American Psychologist, 51,* 985–986.

Bomba, C., O'Donnell, L., Markowitz, C., & Holmes, D. L. (1996). Evaluating the impact of facilitated communication on the communicative competence of fourteen students with autism. *Journal of Autism and Developmental Disorders, 26,* 43–58.

Bristol, M. M., Gallagher, J. J., & Holt, K. D. (1993). Maternal depressive symptoms in autism: Response to psychoeducational intervention. *Rehabilitation Psychology, 38,* 3–10.

Cammisa, K. M., & Hobbs, S. H. (1993). Etiology of autism: A review of recent biogenic theories and research. *Occupational Therapy in Mental Health, 12*(2), 39–67.

Campbell, M., Schopler, E., Cueva, J., & Hallin, A. (1996). Treatment of autistic disorder. *Journal of the American Academy of Child and Adolescent Psychiatry, 35,* 134–143.

Carr, E. G., & Carlson, J. I. (1993). Reduction of severe behavior problems in the community using a multicomponent treatment approach. *Journal of Applied Behavior Analysis, 26,* 157–172.

Carrey, N. J. (1995). Itard's 1828 memoir on "Mutism caused by a lesion of the intellectual functions": A historical analysis. *Journal of the American Academy of Child and Adolescent Psychiatry, 34,* 1655–1661.

Chapman, S., Fisher, W., Piazza, C. C., & Kurtz, P. F. (1993). Functional assessment and treatment of life-threatening drug ingestion in a dually diagnosed youth. *Journal of Applied Behavior Analysis, 26,* 255–256.

Charlop-Christy, M. H., & Haymes, L. K. (1996). Using obsessions as reinforcers with and without mild reductive procedures to decrease inappropriate behaviors of children with autism. *Journal of Autism and Developmental Disorders, 26,* 527–546.

Cohen, D. J., Volkmar, F., Anderson, G. M., & Klin, A. (1993). Integrating biological and behavioral perspectives in the study and care of autistic individuals: The future. *Israel Journal of Psychiatry and Related Sciences, 30,* 15–32.

Cuccaro, M. L., Wright, H. H., Abramson, R. K., & Marstellar, F. A. (1993). Whole-blood serotonin and cognitive functioning in autistic individuals and their first-degree relatives. *Journal of Neuropsychiatry and Clinical Neurosciences, 5*(1), 94–101.

Davis, C. A., Brady, M. P., Williams, R. E., & Hamilton, R. (1992). Effects of high-probability requests on the acquisition and generalization of responses to requests in young children with behavior disorders. *Journal of Applied Behavior Analysis, 25,* 905–916.

Davis, E., Fennoy, I., Laraque, D., & Kanem, N. (1992). Autism and developmental abnormalities in children with perinatal cocaine exposure. *Journal of the National Medical Association, 84,* 315–319.

Deb, S., & Prasad, K. B. G. (1994). The prevalence of autistic disorder among children with a learning disability. *British Journal of Psychiatry, 165,* 395–399.

deBenedetti-Gaddini, R. (1993). On autism. *Psychoanalytic Inquiry, 13,* 134–143.

Donenberg, G., & Baker, B. L. (1993). The impact of young children with externalizing behaviors on their families. *Journal of Abnormal Child Psychology, 21,* 179–198.

Drew, C. J., Hardman, M. L., & Logan, D. R. (1996). *Mental retardation: A life cycle approach* (6th ed.). Columbus, OH: Merrill.

Durand, V. M., & Carr, E. G. (1992). An analysis of maintenance following functional communication training. *Journal of Applied Behavior Analysis, 25,* 777–794.

Early, B. P. (1995). Decelerating self-stimulating and self-injurious behaviors of a student with autism: Behavioral intervention in the classroom. *Social Work in Education, 17,* 244–255.

Estrada, A. U., & Pinsof, W. M. (1995). The effectiveness of family therapies for selected behavioral disorders of childhood. *Journal of Marital and Family Therapy, 21,* 403–440.

Fombonne, E., & du Mazaubrun, C. (1992). Prevalence of infantile autism in four French regions. *Social Psychiatry and Psychiatric Epidemiology, 27*(4), 203–210.

Fried-Oken, M., Paul, R., & Fay, W. (1995). Issues raised by facilitated communication for theorizing and research on autism: Comment. *Journal of Speech and Hearing Research, 38,* 200–202.

Gelfand, D. M., Jenson, W. R., & Drew, C. J. (1997). *Understanding child behavior disorders* (3rd ed.). Fort Worth, TX: Harcourt Brace & Co.

Gillberg, C. (1990a). Autism and pervasive developmental disorders. *Journal of Child Psychology and Psychiatry and Allied Disciplines, 31,* 99–119.

Gillberg, C. (1990b). Infantile autism: Diagnosis and treatment. *Acta Psychiatrica Scandinavica, 81,* 209–215.

Gold, N. (1993). Depression and social adjustment in siblings of boys with autism. *Journal of Autism and Developmental Disorders, 23,* 147–163.

Gordon, C. T., State, R. C., Nelson, J. E., & Hamburger, S. D. (1993). A double-blind comparison of clomipramine, desipramine, and placebo in the treatment of autistic disorder. *Archives of General Psychiatry, 50,* 441–447.

Gray, D. E. (1993). Negotiating autism: Relations between parents and treatment staff. *Social Science and Medicine, 36,* 1037–1046.

Handlan, S., & Bloom, L. A. (1993). The effect of educational curricula and modeling/coaching on the interactions of kindergarten children with their peers with autism. *Focus on Autistic Behavior, 8*(2), 1–11.

Harris, S. R., MacKay, L. L. J., & Osborn, J. A. (1995). Autistic behaviors in offspring of mothers abusing alcohol and other drugs: A series of case reports. *Alcoholism Clinical and Experimental Research, 19,* 660–665.

Heimann, M., Nelson, K. E., & Tjus, T. (1995). Increasing reading and communications skills in children with autism through an interactive multimedia program. *Journal of Autism and Developmental Disorders, 25,* 459–480.

Kamps, D. M., Leonard, B. R., & Potucek, J. (1995). Cooperative learning groups in reading: An integration strategy for students with autism and general classroom peers. *Behavior Disorders, 21,* 89–109.

Kasari, C., & Sigman, M. (1997). Linking parental perceptions to interactions in young children with autism. *Journal of Autism and Developmental Disorders, 27,* 39–57.

Kauffman, J. M. (1993). *Characteristics of emotional and behavioral disorders of children and youth* (5th ed.). New York: Macmillan.

Klinger, L. G., & Dawson, G. (1996). Autistic disorder. In E. J. Mash and R. A. Barkley (Eds.), *Child Psychopathology* (pp. 311–339). New York: Guilford.

Koegel, L. L., & Koegel, R. L. (1996). The child with autism as an active communicative partner: Child-initiated strategies for improving communication and reducing behavior problems. In E. D. Hibbs and P. S. Jensen (Eds.), *Psychosocial treatments for child and adolescent disorders: Empirically based strategies for clinical practice* (pp. 553–572). Washington, DC: American Psychological Association.

Koegel, R. L., Bimbela, A., & Schreibman, L. (1996). Collateral effects of parent training on family interactions. *Journal of Autism and Developmental Disorders, 26,* 347–359.

Komori, H., Matsuishi, T., Yamada, S., & Yamashita, Y. (1995). Cerebrospinal fluid biopterin and biogenic amine metabolites during oral R-THBP therapy for infantile autism. *Journal of Autism and Developmental Disorders, 25,* 183–193.

Krantz, P. J., MacDuff, M. T., & McClannahan, L. E. (1993). Programming participation in family activities for children with autism: Parents' use of photographic activity schedules. *Journal of Applied Behavior Analysis, 26,* 137–138.

Kuder, S. J. (1997). *Teaching students with language and communication disabilities.* Boston: Allyn and Bacon.

Lenzenweger, M. F., & Haugaard, J. J. (1996). *Frontiers of developmental psychopathology.* New York: Oxford University Press.

Levinson, L. L., & Reid, G. (1993). The effects of exercise intensity on the stereotypic behaviors of individuals with autism. *Adapted Physical Activity Quarterly, 10,* 255–268.

Menage, P., Thibault, G., Berthelemy, C., & Lelord, G. (1992). CD4 1 CD45RA 1 T lymphocyte deficiency in autistic children: Effect of a pyridoxine–magnesium treatment. *Brain Dysfunction, 5,* 326–333.

Mesibov, G. B., & Shea, V. (1996). Full inclusion and students with autism. *Journal of Autism and Developmental Disorders, 26,* 337–346.

Minshew, N. J., & Goldstein, G. (1993). Is autism an amnesic disorder? Evidence from the California Verbal Learning Test. *Neuropsychology, 7,* 209–216.

Moreno, S. J., & Donellan, A. M. (1991). *High-functioning individuals with autism: Advice and information for parents and others who care.* Crown Point, IN: Maap Services.

Mottron, L., & Belleville, S. (1995). Perspective production in a savant autistic draughtsman. *Psychological Medicine, 25,* 639–648.

Mottron, L., Belleville, S., & Stip, E. (1996). Proper name hyperamnesia in an autistic subject. *Brain and Language, 53,* 326–350.

Murray, J. B. (1996). Psychophysiological aspects of autistic disorders: Overview. *Journal of Psychology, 130,* 145–158.

Nelson, E. C., & Pribor, E. F. (1993). A calendar savant with autism and Tourette syndrome: Response to treatment and thoughts on the interrelationships of these conditions. *Annals of Clinical Psychiatry, 5,* 135–140.

Nientimp, E. G., & Cole, C. L. (1992). Teaching socially valid social interaction responses to students with severe disabilities in an integrated school setting. *Journal of School Psychology, 30,* 343–354.

Norton, P., & Drew, C. J. (1994). Autism and potential family stressors. *American Journal of Family Therapy, 22,* 68–77.

Oades, R. D., Stern, L. M., Walker, M. K., & Clark, C. R. (1990). Event-related potentials and monoamines in autistic children on a clinical trial of fenfluramine. *International Journal of Psychophysiology, 8,* 197–212.

Ohtaki, E., Kawano, Y., Urabe, F., & Komori, H. (1992). The prevalence of Rett syndrome and infantile autism in Chikugo district, the southwestern area of Fukuoka prefecture, Japan. *Journal of Autism and Developmental Disorders, 22,* 452–454.

O'Neill, R. (1997). Autism. In J. W. Wood & A. M. Lazzari (Eds.), *Exceeding the boundaries: Understanding exceptional lives* (pp. 462–502). Fort Worth, TX: Harcourt Brace College Publishers.

Osman, O. T., & Loschen, E. L. (1992). Self-injurious behavior in the developmentally disabled: Pharmacologic treatment. *Psychopharmacology Bulletin, 28,* 439–449.

Piven, J., Harper, J., Palmer, P., & Arndt, S. (1996). Course of behavioral change in autism: A retrospective study of high-IQ adolescents and adults. *Journal of the American Academy of Child and Adolescent Psychiatry, 35,* 523–529.

Pring, L., Hermelin, B., & Heavey, L. (1995). Savants, segments, art and autism. *Journal of Child Psychology and Psychiatry and Allied Disciplines, 36,* 1065–1076.

Prior, M. R. (1992). Childhood autism: What do we know and where should we go? *Behaviour Change, 9*(2), 96–103.

Reichelt, K. L., Knivsberg, A. M., Lind, G., & Nodland, M. (1991). Probable etiology and possible treatment of childhood autism. *Brain Dysfunction, 4*(6), 308–319.

Rosenberg, M. S., Wilson, R., Maheady, L., & Sindelar, P. T. (1997). *Educating students with behavior disorders* (2nd ed.). Boston: Allyn and Bacon.

Roser, K. (1996). A review of psychoanalytic theory and treatment of childhood autism. *Psychoanalytic Review, 83,* 325–341.

Roser, K., & Buchholz, E. S. (1996). Autism from an intersubjective perspective. *Psychoanalytic Review, 83,* 305–323.

Rothenberger, A. (1993). Psychopharmacological treatment of self-injurious behavior in individuals with autism. *Acta Paedopsychiatrica: International Journal of Child and Adolescent Psychiatry, 56*(2), 99–104.

Sacks, O. (1993). A neurologist's notebook: An anthropologist on Mars. *The New Yorker,* December 27, 1993/January 3, 1994, pp. 106–125.

Scarborough, H. S., Rescorla, L., Tager-Flusberg, H., & Fowler, A. E. (1991). The relation of utterance length to grammatical complexity in normal and language-disordered groups. *Applied Psycholinguistics, 12,* 23–45.

Schopler, E., & Mesibov, G. B. (Eds.). (1995). *Learning and cognition in autism.* New York: Plenum.

Schreibman, L., & Koegel, R. L. (1996). Fostering self-management: Parent-delivered pivotal response training for children with autistic disorder. In E. D. Hibbs and P. S. Jensen (Eds.), *Psychosocial treatments for child and adolescent disorders: Empirically based strategies for clinical practice* (pp. 525–552). Washington, DC: American Psychological Association.

Scott, F. J., & Baron-Cohen, S. (1996). Logical, analogical, and psychological reasoning in autism: A test of the Cosmides theory. *Development and Psychopathology, 8,* 235–245.

Senel, H. G., & Akkok, F. (1995). Stress levels and attitudes of normal siblings of children with disabilities. *International Journal for the Advancement of Counseling, 18*(2), 61–68.

Shields-Wolfe, J., & Gallagher, P. A. (1992). Functional utilization of splinter skills for the employment of a young adult with autism. *Focus on Autistic Behavior, 7*(4), 1–16.

Siegel, B. V., Asarnow, R., Tanguay, P., & Call, J. D. (1992). Regional cerebral glucose metabolism and attention in adults with a history of childhood autism. *Journal of Neuropsychiatry and Clinical Neurosciences, 4*(4), 406–414.

Siegel, D. J., Minshew, N. J., & Goldstein, G. (1996). Wechsler IQ profiles in diagnosis of high-functioning autism. *Journal of Autism and Developmental Disorders, 26,* 389–406.

Silliman, E. R. (1995). Issues raised by facilitated communication for theorizing and research on autism: Comment. *Journal of Speech and Hearing Research, 38,* 204–206.

Simonoff, E., Bolton, P., & Rutter, M. (1996). Mental retardation: Genetic findings, clinical implications and research. *Journal of Child Psychology and Psychiatry and Allied Disciplines, 37,* 259–280.

Simpson, R. L. (1993). What about this facilitated communication? Or, to paraphrase George Bush and Bill Clinton, Is this another matter of trust? *Focus on Autistic Behavior, 8*(2), 12–15.

Simpson, R. L. (1995). Individualized education programs for students with autism: Including parents in the process. *Focus on Autistic Behavior,10*(4), 11–15.

Singer, G. H. S., & Powers, L. E. (Eds.). (1993). *Families, disability, and empowerment: Active coping skills and strategies for family interventions.* Baltimore, MD: Brookes.

Smith, I. M., & Bryson, S. E. (1994). Imitation and action in autism: A critical review. *Psychological Bulletin, 116,* 259–273.

Stahmer, A. C., & Schreibman, L. (1992). Teaching children with autism appropriate play in unsupervised environments using a self-management treatment package. *Journal of Applied Behavior Analysis, 25,* 447–459.

Strain, P., Kohler, F. W., & Goldstein, H. (1996). Learning experiences, an alternative program: Peer-mediated interventions for young children with autism. In E. D. Hibbs and P. S. Jensen (Eds.), *Psychosocial treatments for child and adolescent disorders: Empirically based strategies for clinical practice* (pp. 573–587). Washington, DC: American Psychological Association.

Strickland, D., Marcus, L. M., & Mesibov, G. B. (1996). Brief report: Two case studies using virtual reality as a learning tool for autistic children. *Journal of Autism and Developmental Disorders, 26,* 651–659.

Sue, D., Sue, D., & Sue, S. (1990). *Understanding abnormal behavior* (3rd ed.). Boston: Houghton Mifflin.

Teeter, P. A., & Semrud-Clikeman, M. (1997). *Child neuropsychology: Assessment and interventions for neurodevelopmental disorders.* Boston: Allyn and Bacon.

Tiegerman-Farber, E. (1997). Autism: Learning to communicate. In D. K. Bernstein and E. Tiegerman-Farber (Eds.), *Language and communication disorders in children* (4th ed., pp. 524–573). Boston: Allyn and Bacon.

Tirosh, E., & Canby, J. (1993). Autism with hyperlexia: A distinct syndrome? *American Journal on Mental Retardation, 98,* 84–92.

Trevarthen, C., Aitken, K., Papoudi, D., & Robarts, J. (1996). *Children with autism: Diagnosis and interventions to meet their needs.* London: Jessica Kingsley Publishers.

U.S. Department of Education. (1991, August 19). Notice of proposed rulemaking. *Federal Register, 56*(160), 41,271.

U.S. Department of Education. (1997). To assure the free appropriate public education of all children with disabilities. *19th annual report to Congress on the implementation of the Individuals with Disabilities Education Act.* Washington, DC: U.S. Government Printing Office.

van Son-Schoones, N., & van Bilsen, P. (1995). Sexuality and autism: A pilot study of parents, health care workers and autistic persons. *International Journal of Adolescent Medicine and Health, 8*(2), 87–101.

Weininger, O. (1993). Attachment, affective contact, and autism. *Psychoanalytic Inquiry, 13,* 49–62.

Williams, D. (1992). *Nobody nowhere: The extraordinary autobiography of an autistic.* New York: Avon Books.

Wing, L. (1993). The definition and prevalence of autism: A review. *European Child and Adolescent Psychiatry, 2*(2), 61–74.

Wolf-Schein, E. G. (1996). The autistic spectrum disorder: A current review. *Developmental Disabilities Bulletin, 24,* 33–55.

Zanolli, K., Daggett, J., & Adams, T. (1996). Teaching preschool age autistic children to make spontaneous initiations to peers using priming. *Journal of Autism and Developmental Disorders, 26,* 407–422.

■ CHAPTER 12

Bergland M., & Hoffbauer, D. (1996, Winter). New opportunities for students with traumatic brain injuries: Transition to post-secondary education. *Teaching Exceptional Children, 28*(2), 54–56.

Blosser, J. L., & DePompei, R. (1994). Creating an effective classroom environment. In R. C. Savage & G. F. Wolcott (Eds.), *Educational dimensions of acquired brain injury* (pp. 413–451). Austin, TX: Pro-Ed.

Deaton, A. V., & Waaland P. (1994). Psychosocial effects of acquired brain injury. In R. C. Savage & G. F. Wolcott (Eds.), *Educational dimensions of acquired brain injury* (pp. 239–255). Austin, TX: Pro-Ed.

DePompei, R., & Williams, J. (1994). Working with families after TBI: A family-centered approach. *Topics in Language Disorders: Collaboration in Assessment and Intervention After TBI, 15*(1), 68–81.

Feenick, J. J., & Judd, D. (1994). Physical interventions and accommodations. In R. C. Savage & G. F. Wolcott (Eds.), *Educational dimensions of acquired brain injury* (pp. 367–390). Austin, TX: Pro-Ed.

Gelber, D. A. (1995). The neurologic examination of the traumatically brain-injured patient. In M. J. Ashley & D. K. Krych (Eds.), *Traumatic brain injury rehabilitation* (pp. 23–41). New York: CRC Press.

Gillis, R. J. (1996). *Traumatic brain injury rehabilitation for speech–language pathologists.* Boston: Butterworth-Heinemann.

Graham, D. I., & McIntosh, T. K. (1996). Neuropathology of brain injury. In R. W. Evans (Ed.), *Neurology and trauma* (pp. 53–90). Philadelphia, PA: Saunders.

Haslam, R. H. (1996). Common neurological disorders in children. In R. H. A. Haslam & P. J. Valletutti (Eds.), *Medical problems in the classroom: The teacher's role in diagnosis and management* (3rd ed., pp. 301–339). Austin, TX: Pro-Ed.

Jaffe, K. M., Fay, G. C., Polissar, N. L., Martin, K. M., Shurtleff, H., Rivara, J. B., & Winn, H. R. (1992). Severity of pediatric traumatic brain injury and early neurobehavioral outcome: A cohort study. *Archives of Physical Medicine and Rehabilitation,* 73(6), 540–547.

Jennett, B., & Teasdale, G. (1974). Assessment of coma and impaired consciousness. *Lancet, 2,* 81–84.

Krych, D. K., & Ashley, M. J. (1995). An overview of traumatic brain injury rehabilitation: The field evaluation. In M. J. Ashley & D. K. Krych (Eds.), *Traumatic brain injury rehabilitation* (pp. 1–21). New York: CRC Press.

Lehr, E. (1990). *Psychological management of traumatic brain injuries in children and adolescents.* Rockville, MD: Aspen.

Ponsford, J. (1995a). Mechanisms, recovery and sequelae of traumatic brain injury: A foundation for the REAL approach. In J. Ponsford, S. Sloan, & P. Snow, *Traumatic brain injury: Rehabilitation for everyday adaptive living* (pp. 1–31). Hillsdale, NJ: Erlbaum.

Ponsford, J. (1995b). Traumatic brain injury in children. In J. Ponsford, S. Sloan, & P. Snow, *Traumatic brain injury: Rehabilitation for everyday adaptive living* (pp. 295–325). Hillsdale, NJ: Erlbaum.

Ponsford, J., Sloan, S., & Snow, P. (1995). *Traumatic brain injury: Rehabilitation for everyday adaptive living.* Hillsdale, NJ: Erlbaum.

Rivera, J. B., Jaffe, K. M., Polissar, N. L., Fay, G. C., Martin, K. M., Shurtleff, H. A., & Liao, S. (1994). Family functioning and children's academic performance and behavior problems in the year following traumatic brain injury. *Archives of Physical Medicine and Rehabilitation, 75,* 369–379.

Rizzo, M., & Tranel, E. (1996). Overview of head injury and postconcussive syndrome. In M. Rizzo & D. Tranel (Eds.), *Head injury and postconcussive syndrome* (pp. 1–18). New York: Churchill Livingstone Inc.

Rosman, N. P. (1994). Acute head trauma. In F. A. Oski, C. D. DeAngelis, R. D. Feigin, J. A. McMillan, & J. B. Warshaw (Eds.), *Principles and practices of pediatrics* (2nd ed., pp. 2038–2048). Philadelphia, PA: Lippincott.

Rudolph, A. M., & Kamei, R. K. (1994). *Rudolph's fundamentals of pediatrics.* Norwalk, CT: Appleton & Lange.

Russell, N. K. (1993). Educational considerations in traumatic brain injury: The role of the speech-language pathologist. *Language, Speech, and Hearing Services in Schools, 24,* 67–75.

Savage, R. C., & Wolcott, G. F. (Eds.). (1994a). *Educational dimensions of acquired brain injury.* Austin, TX: Pro-Ed.

Savage, R. C., & Wolcott, G. F. (1994b). Overview of acquired brain injury. In R. C. Savage & G. F. Wolcott (Eds.), *Educational dimensions of acquired brain injury* (pp. 3–12). Austin, TX: Pro-Ed.

Savage, R. C., & Mishkin, L. (1994). A neuroeducational model for teaching students with acquired brain injuries. In R. C. Savage & G. F. Wolcott (Eds.), *Educational dimensions of acquired brain injury* (pp. 393–411). Austin, TX: Pro-Ed.

Stevens, A. M. (1994). Traumatic brain injury and special education: An information resource guide. ERIC Document Reproduction Service, No. EC 377 613.

Stuart, J. L., & Goodsitt, J. L. (1996, Winter). From hospital to school: How a transition liaison can help. *Teaching Exceptional Children, 28*(2), 58–62.

Williams, D. (1994). *Traumatic brain injury: When children return to school.* ERIC Document Reproduction Service, No. EC 303 243.

Ylvisaker, M., Szekeres, S. F., Haarbauer-Krupa, J., Urbanczyk, B., & Feeney, T. (1994). Speech and language intervention. In R. C. Savage & G. F. Wolcott (Eds.), *Educational dimensions of acquired brain injury* (pp. 185–235). Austin, TX: Pro-Ed.

■ CHAPTER 13

Alexander Graham Bell Association. (1993, August). July 1, 1993 marks history in advancement of TV captioning. *Newsounds, 18,* 1.

Barringer, F. (1993, May 16). Pride in a soundless world: Deaf oppose a hearing aid. *New York Times,* A1, A14.

Berg, F. S. (1987). *Facilitating classroom listening.* Austin, TX: Pro-Ed.

Bonvillian, J. D., & Folven, R. J. (1993). Sign language acquisition: Developmental aspects. In M. Marschark & M. D. Clark (Eds.), *Psychological perspectives on deafness* (pp. 229–265). Hillsdale, NJ: Erlbaum.

Braden, J. P. (1992). Intellectual assessment of deaf and hard-of-hearing people: A quantitative and qualitative research synthesis. *School Psychology Review, 21,* 82–94.

Charlson, E., Strong, M., & Gold, R. (1992). How successful deaf teenagers experience and cope with isolation. *American Annals of the Deaf, 137*(3), 261–270.

Cohen, L. H. (1994). *Train go sorry: Inside a deaf world.* Boston: Houghton Mifflin.

Cole, E. B. (1992). Promoting emerging speech in birth to 3-year-old hearing-impaired children. *The Volta Review, 94,* 63–77.

Commission on the Education of the Deaf. (1988). *Toward equality: Education of the deaf.* Washington, DC: U.S. Government Printing Office.

Dolnick, E. (1993). Deafness as culture. *The Atlantic Monthly, 272*(3), 37–53.

Gallaudet Research Institute. (1994). Gallaudet Research Institute Working Papers 89–3. Washington, DC: Author.

Geers, A. E., & Tobey, E. (1992). Effects of cochlear implants and tactile aids on the development of speech production skills in children with profound hearing impairment. *The Volta Review, 94,* 135–163.

Giebink, G. S. (1990). Medical issues in hearing impairment: The otitis media spectrum. In J. Davis (Ed.), *Our forgotten children: Hard-of-hearing pupils in the schools* (pp. 49–55). Bethesda, MD: Self-Help for Hard of Hearing People.

Goldberg, B. (1993). Universal hearing screening of newborns: An idea whose time has come. *ASHA, 35,* 63–64.

Greenberg, M. T., & Kusche, C. A. (1989). Cognitive, personal, and social development of deaf children and adolescents. In M. C. Wang, M. C. Reynolds, & H. J. Walberg (Eds.), *Handbook of special education: Research and practice: Vol. 3. Low incidence conditions* (pp. 95–129). Oxford, UK: Pergamon.

Gustason, G. (1990). Signing exact English. In H. Bornstein (Ed.), *Manual communication: Implications for education.* Washington, DC: Gallaudet University Press.

Hanson, V. L., Shankweiler, D., & Fischer, F. W. (1983). Determinants of spelling ability in deaf and hearing adults: Access to linguistic structure. *Cognition, 14,* 323–344.

Karchmer, M. A. (1985). Demographics and deaf adolescence. In G. B. Anderson & D. Watson (Eds.), *The habilitation and rehabilitation of deaf adolescents* (pp. 28–47). Washington, DC: Gallaudet College Press.

Lane, H. (1992). *The mask of benevolence: Disabling the deaf community.* New York: Knopf.

LaPlante, M. P. (1991). The demographics of disability. In J. West (Ed.), *The Americans with Disabilities Act: From policy to practice* (pp. 55–80). New York: Milbank Memorial Fund.

Levitt, H. (1989). Speech and hearing in communication. In M. C. Wang, M. C. Reynolds, & H. J. Walberg (Eds.), *Handbook of special education: Research and practice: Vol. 3. Low incidence conditions* (pp. 23–45). Oxford, UK: Pergamon.

Leybaert, J. (1993). Reading in the deaf: The roles of phonological codes. In M. Marschark & M. D. Clark (Eds.), *Psychological perspectives on deafness* (pp. 269–309). Hillsdale, NJ: Erlbaum.

Lowenbraun, S., & Thompson, M. (1989). Environments and strategies for learning and teaching. In M. C. Wang, M. C.

Reynolds, & H. J. Walberg (Eds.), *Handbook of special education: Research and practice: Vol. 3. Low incidence conditions* (pp. 47–69). Oxford, UK: Pergamon.

Luetke-Stahlman, B., & Luckner, J. (1991). *Effectively educating students with hearing impairments.* White Plains, NY: Longman.

Marschark, M. (1993). Origins and interactions in the social, cognitive, and language development of deaf children. In M. Marschark & M. D. Clark (Eds.), *Psychological perspectives on deafness* (pp. 7–26). Hillsdale, NJ: Erlbaum.

Martin, F. N. (1986). *Introduction to audiology* (3rd ed.). Englewood Cliffs, NJ: Prentice Hall.

Maxon, A. B., & Brackett, D. (1992). *The hearing impaired child: Infancy through high school years.* Boston: Andover Medical Publishers.

Mertens, D. M. (1990). A conceptual model for academic achievement: Deaf student outcomes. In D. F. Moores & K. P. Meadow-Orlands (Eds.), *Educational and developmental aspects of deafness* (pp. 25–72). Washington, DC: Gallaudet University Press.

Moaven, L. D., Gilbert, G. L., Cunningham, A. L., & Rawlinson, W. D. (1995). Amniocentesis to diagnose congenital cyomegalovirus infection. *Medical Journal of Australia, 162,* 334–335.

Moores, D. F. (1990). Research in educational aspects of deafness. In D. F. Moores & K. P. Meadow-Orlands (Eds.), *Educational and developmental aspects of deafness* (pp. 11–24). Washington, DC: Gallaudet University Press.

National Information Center on Deafness and the National Association of the Deaf. (1984). *Deafness: A fact sheet.* Washington, DC: Gallaudet College.

Patrick, P. E. (1987). Identification audiometry. In F. N. Martin (Ed.), *Hearing disorders in children* (pp. 402–425). Austin, TX: Pro-Ed.

Paul, P. V., & Quigley, S. P. (1990). *Education and deafness.* White Plains, NY: Longman.

Pueschel, S. M., & Mulick, J. A. (1990). *Prevention of developmental disabilities.* Baltimore, MD: Brookes.

Quigley, S. P., & King, C. (Eds.). (1984). *Reading milestones.* Beaverton, OR: Dormac.

Quigley, S. P., & Kretschmer, R. E. (1982). *The education of deaf children: Issues, theory and practice.* Baltimore, MD: University Park Press.

Quigley, S. P., & Paul, P. V. (1989). English language development. In M. C. Wang, M. C. Reynolds, & H. J. Walberg (Eds.), *Handbook of special education: Research and practice: Vol. 3. Low incidence conditions* (pp. 3–22). Oxford, UK: Pergamon.

Rodda, M., Cumming, C., & Fewer, D. (1993). Memory, learning, and language: Implications for deaf education. In M. Marschark & M. D. Clark (Eds.), *Psychological perspectives on deafness* (pp. 339–352). Hillsdale, NJ: Erlbaum.

Schildroth, A. N. (1994). *Annual survey of hearing-impaired childen and youth: 1992–1993 school year.* Washington, DC: Gallaudet University, Center for Assessment and Demographic Studies.

Schildroth, A. N., & Hotto, S. A. (1991). Annual survey of hearing impaired children and youth: 1989–1990 school year. *American Annals of the Deaf, 137*(2), 63–69.

SMI & Madonna University. (1991). Terminology and definitions. Detroit, MI: Author.

Smith, J. D. (1998). *Inclusion: Schools for all students.* Belmont, CA: Wadsworth.

Solomon, A. (1994, August 28). Defiantly deaf. *The New York Times Magazine,* Section 6, 1–7, xx.

Stinson, M. S., & Whitmire, K. (1992). Students' views of their social relationships. In T. N. Kluwin, D. F. Moores, & M. G. Gaustad (Eds.), *Toward effective public school programs for deaf students: Context, process, and outcomes* (pp. 149–174). New York: Teachers College Press.

Stoel-Gammon, C., & Otomo, K. (1986). Babbling development of hearing-impaired and normally hearing subjects. *Journal of Speech and Hearing Disorders, 51,* 33–41.

Stokoe, W. C. (1993). The broadening and sharpening of psychological perspectives on deafness. In M. Marschark & M. D. Clark (Eds.), *Psychological perspectives on deafness* (pp. 365–376). Hillsdale, NJ: Erlbaum.

Talbott, R. F., & Wehman, P. (1996). Hearing disorders. In P. Wehman (Ed.), *Exceptional individuals in school, community, and work* (pp. 321–356). Austin, TX: Pro-Ed.

Toufexis, A. (1991, August 5). Now hear this—if you can. *Time,* pp. 50–51.

Trybus, R. J. (1985). *Today's hearing-impaired children and youth: A demographic profile.* Washington, DC: Gallaudet Research Institute.

Tye-Murray, N. (1993). Vowel and diphthong production by young users of cochlear implants and the relationship between the phonetic level evaluation and spontaneous speech. *Journal of Speech and Hearing Research, 36,* 488–502.

U.S. Department of Education. (1997). To assure the free appropriate public education of all children with disabilities. *19th annual report to Congress on the implementation of the Education of the Handicapped Act.* Washington, DC: U.S. Government Printing Office.

Vernon, M., & Andrews, J. F. (1990). *The psychology of deafness: Understanding peopole who are deaf and hard-of-hearing.* White Plains, NY: Longman.

Wilson, D. L. (1992, July 15). Dramatic breakthroughs for deaf students: New technologies offer greater participation. *The Chronicle of Higher Education,* A16–A17.

Withrow, F. B. (1994). Jericho: The walls come tumbling down! *American Annals of the Deaf, 139,* 18–21.

Wood, D. (1991). Communication and cognition: How the communication styles of hearing adults may hinder—rather than help—deaf learners. *American Annals of the Deaf, 136*(3), 247–251.

Woodward, J. (1982). *How you gonna get to heaven if you can't talk to Jesus¿* Silver Spring, MD: T. J. Publishers.

■ CHAPTER 14

American Printing House for the Blind. (1992). *Annual report.* Louisville, KY: Author.

Anderson, E., Dunlea, A., & Kekelis, L. (1984). Blind children's language: Resolving some differences. *Journal of Child Language, 11*(3), 645–664.

Barraga, N. C., & Erin, J. N. (1992). *Visual handicaps and learning* (3rd ed.). Austin, TX: Pro-Ed.

Best, A. B. (1992). *Teaching children with visual impairments.* Philadelphia, PA: Open University Press.

Bishop, V. E. (1987). Religion and blindness: From inheritance to opportunity. *Journal of Visual Impairment and Blindness, 1*(6), 256–259.

Blanksby, D. C., & Langford, P. E. (1993). VAP-CAP: A procedure to assess the visual functioning of young visually impaired children. *Journal of Visual Impairment and Blindness, 86,* 46–49.

Chapman, E. K., & Stone, J. M. (1989). *The visually handicapped child in your classroom.* London: Cassell.

Corn, A. L., Hatlen, P., Huebner, K. M., Ryan, F., & Siller, M. A. (1995). *The national agenda for the education of children and youth with visual impairments, including those with multiple disabilities.* New York: American Foundation for the Blind.

Corn, A. L., & Koenig, A. J. (1996). Perspectives on low vision. In *Foundations of low vision: Clinical and functional perspectives* (pp. 1–21). New York: American Foundation for the Blind.

Crocker, A. D., & Orr, R. R. (1996). Social behaviors of children with visual impairments enrolled in preschool programs. *Exceptional Children, 62*(5), 451–462.

Dixon, J. M., & Mandelbaum, J. B. (1990, December). Reading through technology: Evolving methods and opportunities for print-handicapped individuals. *Journal of Visual Impairment and Blindness,* 493–496.

Hull, J. M. (1990). *Touching the rock.* New York: Pantheon.

Isenberg, S. J. (1992). Vision focus: Understanding the medical and functional implications of vision loss in young blind and visually impaired children. In R. L. Pogrun, D. L. Fazzi, & J. S. Lampert (Eds.), *Early focus: Working with young blind and visually impaired children and their families* (pp. 13–35). New York: American Foundation for the Blind.

Jernigan, K. (1992, June). Equality, disability, and empowerment. *The Braille Monitor,* pp. 292–298.

Joint Organizational Committee. (1993). *Full inclusion of students who are blind or visually impaired: A position statement.* Washington, DC: Author.

Journal of Visual Impairments. (1992). Talking wallet, *86,* 411.

Kekelis, L. S. (1992). Peer interactions in childhood: The impact of visual impairment. In S. Z. Sacks, L. S. Kekelis, & R. J. Gaylord-Ross (Eds.), *The development of social skills by blind and visually impaired students* (pp. 13–35). New York: American Foundation for the Blind.

Lenz, B. K. (1989). Set the stage for learning—use advance organizers, *Strategram, 1,* 1–4.

Lopate, P. (Ed.). (1994). *The art of the personal essay: An anthology from the classical era to the present.* New York: Anchor Books.

MacCuspie, P. S. (1992). The social acceptance and interaction of visually impaired children in integrated settings. In S. Z. Sacks, L. S. Kekelis, & R. J. Gaylord-Ross (Eds.), *The development of social skills by blind and visually impaired students* (pp. 83–102). New York: American Foundation for the Blind.

McDowell, E. (1990, January 8). New markets are found for large-print books. *New York Times,* p. C7.

Miller-Wood, D. J., Efron, M., & Wood, T. A. (1990, December). Use of closed circuit television with a severely visually impaired child. *Journal of Visual Impairment and Blindness,* 559–565.

Nelson, K. A., & Dimitrova, E. (1993). Severe visual impairment in the United States and in each state. *Journal of Visual Impairments and Blindness, 87,* 80–85.

Ochaita, E., & Huertas, J. A. (1993). Spatial representation by persons who are blind: A study of the effects of learning and development. *Journal of Visual Impairment and Blindness, 85,* 37–41.

Parsons, A. S., & Sabornie, E. J. (1987). Language skills of young low-vision children: Performance on the preschool language scale. *Journal of the Division for Early Childhood, 11*(3), 217–225.

Peck, A. F., & Uslan, M. (1990, December). The use of audible traffic signals in the United States. *Journal of Visual Impairment and Blindness,* 547–551.

Pogrund, R. L., Fazzi, D. L., & Schreier, E. M. (1993). Development of a preschool "Kiddy Cane." *Journal of Visual Impairment and Blindness, 86,* 52–54.

Rogers, M. (1992, June 20). The literary circuitry. *Newsweek,* pp. 66–67.

Sacks, S. Z., Kekelis, L. S., & Gaylord-Ross, R. J. (1992). *The development of social skills by blind and visually impaired students.* New York: American Foundation for the Blind.

Schreier, E. M. (1990, December). The future of access technology for blind and visually impaired people. *Journal of Visual Impairment and Blindness,* 520–523.

U.S. Department of Education. (1997). To assure the free appropriate public education of all children with disabilities. *19th annual report to Congress on the implementation of the Education of the Handicapped Act.* Washington, DC: U.S. Government Printing Office.

Warren, D. H. (1984). *Blindness and early childhood development.* New York: American Foundation for the Blind.

Warren, D. H. (1989). Implications of visual impairments for child development. In M. C. Wang, M. C. Reynolds, & H. J. Walberg (Eds.), *Handbook of special education: Research and practice: Vol. 3. Low incidence conditions* (pp. 155–172). Oxford, UK: Pergamon.

Ziegler, E. (1991, February). The magic machines of Ray Kurzweil. *Reader's Digest,* pp. 119–122.

■ CHAPTER 15

Baskin, D. S. (1996). Spinal cord injury. In R. W. Evans (Ed.), *Neurology and trauma* (pp. 276–299). Philadelphia, PA: Saunders.

Baumrind, D. (1995). *Child maltreatment and optimal caregiving in social contexts.* New York: Garland.

Bellenir, K. (1996). *Substance abuse sourcebook.* Detroit, MI: Omingraphics.

Bellenir, K., & Dresser, P. (Eds.). (1994). *Diabetes sourcebook.* Detroit, MI: Omnigraphics.

Bellenir, K., & Dresser, P. (Eds.). (1995). *AIDS sourcebook.* Detroit, MI: Omnigraphics.

Berliner, L., & Elliott, D. M. (1996). Sexual abuse of children. In J. Briere, L. Berliner, J. A. Bulkley, C. Jenny, & T. Reid (Eds.), *The APSAC handbook on child maltreatment* (pp. 51–71). Thousand Oaks, CA: Sage.

Bigge, J. L. (1991). *Teaching individuals with physical and multiple disabilities.* New York: Macmillan.

Boxler, B. (1997). Untitled. Available: http://www.circleoffriends.org/chris/postings/0004.html.

Briere, J. (1996). A self-trauma model for treating adult survivors of severe child abuse. In J. Briere, L. Berliner, J. A. Bulkley, C. Jenny, & T. Reid (Eds.), *The APSAC handbook on child maltreatment* (pp. 140–157). Thousand Oaks, CA: Sage.

Briere, J., Berliner, L., Bulkley, J. A., Jenny, C., & Reid, T. (Eds.). (1996). *The APSAC handbook on child maltreatment.* Thousand Oaks, CA: Sage.

Buchanan, A. (1996). *Cycles of child maltreatment: Facts, fallacies and interventions.* Chichester, UK: Wiley.

Cable News Network. (1997). *Experimental gene therapy offers hope to diabetics.* Available: http://cnn.com/HEALTH/9704/30/nfm.diabetes.gene/index.html.

Carson, G., & Carson, S. (1996). Sexual development, function, and consequences. In R. H. A. Haslam & P. J. Valletutti (Eds.), *Medical problems in the classroom* (pp. 539–573). Austin, TX: Pro-Ed.

Chaffin, M., Bonner, B. L., Worley, K. B., & Lawson, L. (1996). Treating abused adolescents. In J. Briere, L. Berliner, J. A. Bulkley, C. Jenny, & T. Reid (Eds.), *The APSAC handbook on child maltreatment* (pp. 119–139). Thousand Oaks, CA: Sage.

Children with DIABETES. (1997a). *What is Type I diabetes?* Available: http://www.casleweb.com/diabetes/d_0n_100.htm.

Children with DIABETES. (1997b). *Research news and information.* Available: http://www.castleweb.com/diabetes/d_0j_106.htm.

Clark, R. B. (1997). Suicide in children and adolescents. In W. W. Hay, Jr., J. R. Groothuis, A. R. Hayward, & M. J. Levin (Eds.), *Current pediatric diagnosis and treatment* (pp. 197–198). Norwalk, CT: Appleton & Lange.

Cystic Fibrosis Foundation. (1996a). *Facts about cystic fibrosis.* Available: http://www.cff.org/factsabo.htm.

Cystic Fibrosis Foundation. (1996b). *Gene therapy.* Available: http://www.cff.org/genether.htm.

Daneman, D., & Frank, M. (1996). The student with diabetes mellitus. In R. H. A. Haslam & P. J. Valletutti (Eds.), *The teacher's role in diagnosis and management* (3rd ed., pp. 97–113). Austin, TX: Pro-Ed.

Davis, L., & Tolan, P. H. (1993). Alternative and preventative interventions. In P. H. Tolan & B. J. Cohler (Eds.), *Handbook of clinical research and practice with adolescents* (pp. 427–452). New York: Wiley.

Dreifuss, F. E. (1988). What is epilepsy? In H. Reisner (Ed.), *Children with epilepsy.* Kensington, MD: Woodbine House.

Erickson, M. F. & Egeland, B. (1996). Child neglect. In J. Briere, L. Berliner, J. A. Bulkley, C. Jenny, & T. Reid (Eds.), *The APSAC handbook on child maltreatment* (pp. 4–20). Thousand Oaks, CA: Sage.

Ezekowitz, R. A., & First, L. R. (1994). Hematology. In M. E. Avery & L. R. First (Eds.), *Pediatric medicine* (2nd ed., pp. 53–606). Baltimore, MD: Williams & Wilkins.

Finkelhor, D. (1996). Introduction. In J. Briere, L. Berliner, J. A. Bulkley, C. Jenny, & T. Reid (Eds.), *The APSAC handbook on child maltreatment* (pp. ix–xiii). Thousand Oaks, CA: Sage.

Friedrich, W. N. (1996). An integrated model of psychotherapy for abused children. In J. Briere, L. Berliner, J. A. Bulkley, C. Jenny, & T. Reid (Eds.), *The APSAC handbook on child maltreatment* (pp. 104–118). Thousand Oaks, CA: Sage.

Gutierrez, P. A., Vulpe, M., & Young, R. R. (1994). Spinal cord injury. In J. H. Stein (Ed.), *Internal medicine* (pp. 1134–1144). St. Louis, MO: Mosby.

Hanlon, S. F. (1991). School and day care issues: The legal perspective. In P. A. Pizzo & C. M. Wilfert (Eds.), *Pediatric AIDS: The challenges of HIV infection in infants, children, and adolescents* (pp. 693–703). Baltimore, MD: Williams & Wilkins.

Hart, S. N., Brassard, M. R., & Karlson, H. C. (1996). Psychological maltreatment. In J. Briere, L. Berliner, J. A. Bulkley, C. Jenny, & T. Reid (Eds.), *The APSAC handbook on child maltreatment* (pp. 72–89). Thousand Oaks, CA: Sage.

Haslam, R. (1996). Common neurological disorders in children. In R. H. A. Haslam & P. J. Valletutti (Eds.), *Medical problems in the classroom* (pp. 301–336). Austin, TX: Pro-Ed.

Hill, I. D., & Lebenthal, E. (1995). Cystic fibrosis. In W. S. Haubrich, F. Schaffner, & J. E. Berk (Eds.), *Gastroenterology* (5th ed., pp. 3035–3052). Philadelphia, PA: Saunders.

Jenny, C. (1996). Medical issues in sexual abuse. In J. Briere, L. Berliner, J. A. Bulkley, C. Jenny, & T. Reid (Eds.), *The APSAC handbook on child maltreatment* (pp. 195–205). Thousand Oaks, CA: Sage.

Johnson, C. F. (1996). Physical abuse: Accidental versus intentional trauma in children. In J. Briere, L. Berliner, J. A. Bulkley, C. Jenny, & T. Reid (Eds.), *The APSAC handbook on child maltreatment* (pp. 206–226). Thousand Oaks, CA: Sage.

Johnson, P. A. (1995). Adolescent sexuality, pregnancy, and parenthood. In I. M. Bobak, D. L. Lowdermilk, & M. D. Jensen (Eds.), *Maternity nursing* (4th ed., pp. 722–747). St. Louis, MO: Mosby.

Jurich, A. P. & Collins, O. P. (1996). Adolescents, suicide, and death. In C. A. Corr & D. E. Balk (Eds.), *Handbook of adolescent death and bereavement* (pp. 65–84). New York: Springer.

Juvenile Diabetes Foundation International. (1997). Diabetes fact sheet. Available: http://www.jdfcure.com/facts.htm.

Kalichman, S. C. (1995). *Understanding AIDS: A guide for mental health professionals.* Washington, DC: American Psychological Association.

Kaplan, D. W., & Mammel, K. A. (1997). Gynecologic disorders in adolescence. In W. W. Hay, Jr., J. R. Groothuis, A. R. Hayward, & M. J. Levin (Eds.), *Current pediatric diagnosis and treatment* (pp. 153–157). Norwalk, CT: Appleton & Lange.

Kelly, T. E. (1996). The role of genetic mechanisms in childhood disabilities. In R. H. A. Haslam & P. J. Valletutti (Eds.), *Medical problems in the classroom* (pp. 125–159). Austin, TX: Pro-Ed.

Kolko, D. J. (1996). Child physical abuse. In J. Briere, L. Berliner, J. A. Bulkley, C. Jenny, & T. Reid (Eds.), *The APSAC handbook on child maltreatment* (pp. 21–50). Thousand Oaks, CA: Sage.

Lafferty, W. E., & Hopkins, S. G. (1996). Epidemiology. In H. Spach & T. M. Hooton (Eds.), *The HIV manual: A guide to diagnosis and treatment* (pp. 14–19). New York: Oxford University Press.

Lerner, A. J. (Ed.). (1995). *The little black book of neurology.* (3rd ed.). St. Louis, MO: Mosby.

McFarland, E. J. (1997). Human immunodeficiency virus (HIV) infections: Acquired immunodeficiency syndrome (AIDS). In W. W. Hay, Jr., J. R. Groothuis, A. R. Hayward, & M. J. Levin (Eds.), *Current pediatric diagnosis and treatment* (pp. 992–1002). Norwalk, CT: Appleton & Lange.

Med Access. (1996a). Sickle cell anemia. Available: http://www.medaccess.com/h_child/sickle/sca_02.htm.

Med Access. (1996b). Sickle cell anemia. Available: http://www.medaccess.com/h_child/sickle/sca_01.htm.

Mian, M. (1996). Child abuse. In R. H. A. Haslam & P. J. Valletutti (Eds.), *Medical problems in the classroom* (pp. 585–600). Austin, TX: Pro-Ed.

Miller, F., & Bachrach, S. (1995). *Cerebral palsy: A complete guide for caregiving.* Baltimore, MD: The Johns Hopkins University Press.

Minty, G. D. (1996, July). What is CF? Available: http://www2.cal.ca/distsite/frank/cf-basic.html.

Monteleone, J. A. (1996). *Recognition of child abuse for the mandated reporter* (2nd ed.). St. Louis, MO: G. W. Medical Publishing.

Monteleone, J. A., & Brodeur, A. E. (1994). *Child maltreatment: A clinical perspective.* St. Louis, MO: G. W. Medical Publishing.

National Spinal Cord Injury Statistical Center (NSCISC). (1997). FAQ data. Available: http://www.sci.rehabm.uab.edu/shared/faq.data.html.

Obiakor, F. E., Mehring, T. A., & Schwenn, J. O. (1997). *Disruption, disaster, and death: Helping students with crises.* Reston, VA: The Council for Exceptional Children.

Parks, W. (1996). Human immunodeficiency virus. In W. E. Nelson, R. E. Behrman, R. M. Kliegman, & A. M. Arvin (Eds.), *Textbook of pediatrics* (15th ed., pp. 916–919). Philadelphia, PA: Saunders.

Pearl, P. S. (1994). Emotional abuse. In J. A. Monteleone & A. E. Brodeur (Eds.), *Child maltreatment: A clinical guide and reference* (pp. 259–279). St. Louis: G. W. Medical Publishing.

Rudolph, A. M., & Kamei, R. K. (1994). *Rudolph's fundamentals of pediatrics.* Norwalk, CT: Appleton & Lange.

Sigel, E. J. (1997). Sexually transmitted diseases. In W. W. Hay, Jr., J. R. Groothuis, A. R. Hayward, & M. J. Levin (Eds.), *Current pediatric diagnosis and treatment* (pp. 1095–1105). Norwalk, CT: Appleton & Lange.

Smith, J. (1988). The dangers of prenatal cocaine use. *American Journal of Maternal Child Nursing, 13*(3), 174–179.

Spina Bifida Association of America. (1996). Spina bifida association of america (SBAA) information about folic acid. Available: http://ww.infohiway.com/spinabifida/folic.html.

Spina Bifida Association of America. (1997). Facts about spina bifida. Available: http://ww.infohiway.com/spinabifida/facts.html.

Stevens, M. M., & Dunsmore, J. C. (1996). Helping adolescents who are coping with a life-threatening illness, along with their siblings, parents, and peers. In C. A. Corr & D. E. Balk (Eds.), *Handbook of adolescent death and bereavement* (pp. 329–353). New York: Springer.

Stillion, J. M., & McDowell, E. E. (1996). *Suicide across the life span: Premature exits* (2nd ed.). Washington, DC: Taylor & Francis.

Sujansky, E., Stewart, J. M., & Manchester, D. K. (1997). Polygenic disease (multifactorial inheritance). In W. W. Hay, Jr., J. R. Groothuis, A. R. Hayward, & M. J. Levin (Eds.), *Current pediatric diagnosis and treatment* (pp. 904–908). Norwalk, CT: Appleton & Lange.

Thompson, R. A. (1995). *Preventing child maltreatment through social support.* Thousand Oaks, CA: Sage.

Underwood, R. (1989). Untitled. In Epilepsy Foundation of America, *Brothers and sisters: A guide for families of children with epilepsy (1994).* Lanover, MD: Epilepsy Foundation of America.

United Cerebral Palsy Research & Educational Foundation. (1995, September). Cerebral palsy: Contributing risk factors and causes. Available: http://www.ucpa.org/html/research/riskupdate.html.

United Cerebral Palsy Resource Center. (1997a, May). Cerebral palsy—facts and figures. Available: http://www.ucpa.org/html/esearch/factsfigs.html.

United Cerebral Palsy Resource Center. (1997b, May). Fast facts sheet on UCP's 1996 ADA snapshot on America. Available: http://www.ucpa.org/html/resources/1996_fastfacts.html.

Watkins, K. P. & Durant, L., Jr. (1996). *Working with children and families affected by substance abuse: A guide for early childhood education and human service staff.* West Nyack, NY: The Center for Applied Research in Education.

Zimmerman, D. D., & Kingsley, R. E. (1997, June). General information about epilepsy. Available: http://www.iupui.edu/~epilepsy/general.htm.

■ CHAPTER 16

Achter, J. A., Benbow, C. P., & Lubinski, D. (1997). Rethinking multipotentiality among the intellectually gifted: A critical review and recommendations. *Gifted Child Quarterly, 41*(1), 5–15.

Adderholdt-Elliott, M. (1987). *Perfectionism: What's bad about feeling too good?* Minneapolis, MN: Free Spirit.

Assouline, S. G. (1997). Assessment of gifted children. In N. Colangelo & A. D. Davis (Eds.), *Handbook of gifted education* (2nd ed., pp. 89–108). Boston: Allyn and Bacon.

Binet, A., & Simon, T. (1905). Mèthodes nouvelles pour le diagnostique du mivea intellectual des anomaux. *L'Année Psychologique, 11,* 196–198.

Binet, A., & Simon, T. (1908). Le dévelopment de l'intelligence chez les enfants. *L'Année Psychologique, 14,* 1–94.

Callahan, C. M. (1991). Superior abilities. In J. M. Kauffman & D. P. Hallahan (Eds.), *Handbook of special education.* Englewood Cliffs, NJ: Prentice Hall.

Cattell, R. B. (1971). *Abilities: Their structure, growth, and action.* Boston: Houghton Mifflin.

Clark, B. (1992). *Growing up gifted* (4th ed.). Columbus, OH: Merrill.

Clark, B. (1997). *Growing up gifted* (5th ed.). Columbus, OH: Merrill.

Clasen, D. R. & Clasen, R. E. (1997). Mentoring: A time-honored option for education of the gifted and talented. In N. Colangelo & A. D. Davis (Eds.), *Handbook of gifted education* (2nd ed., pp. 218–229). Boston: Allyn and Bacon.

Colangelo, N. (1997). Counseling gifted students: Issues and practices. In N. Colangelo & A. D. Davis (Eds.), *Handbook of gifted education* (2nd ed., pp. 353–365). Boston: Allyn and Bacon.

Conant, J. B. (1959). *The American high school today.* New York: McGraw-Hill.

Davis, G. A. (1997). Identifying creative students and measuring creativity. In N. Colangelo & A. D. Davis (Eds.), *Handbook of gifted education* (2nd ed., pp. 269–281). Boston: Allyn and Bacon.

DeHann, R., & Havighurst, R. J. (1957). *Educating gifted children.* Chicago, IL: University of Chicago Press.

Delisle, J. R. (1997). Gifted adolescents: Five steps toward understanding and acceptance. In N. Colangelo & A. D. Davis (Eds.), *Handbook of gifted education* (2nd ed., pp. 475–482). Boston: Allyn and Bacon.

Frasier, M. M. (1997). Gifted minority students: Reframing approaches to their identification and education. In N. Colangelo & A. D. Davis (Eds.), *Handbook of gifted education* (2nd ed., pp. 498–515). Boston: Allyn and Bacon.

Gallagher, J. J. (1997). Issues in the education of gifted students. In N. Colangelo & A. D. Davis (Eds.), *Handbook of gifted education* (2nd ed., pp. 27–42). Boston: Allyn and Bacon.

Guilford, J. P. (1950). Creativity. *American Psychologist, 5,* 444–454.

Guilford, J. P. (1959). Three faces of intellect. *American Psychologist, 14,* 469–479.

Hennessey, B. A. (1997). Teaching for creative development: A social-psychological approach. In N. Colangelo & A. D. Davis (Eds.),

Handbook of Gifted Education (2nd ed.) (pp. 282–291). Boston: Allyn and Bacon.

Hunsaker, S. L., Finley, V. S., & Frank, E. L. (1997). An analysis of teacher nominations and student performance in gifted programs. *Gifted Child Quarterly, 4*(2), 19–24.

Jackson, N. E., & Klein, E. J. (1997). Gifted performance in young children. In N. Colangelo & A. D. Davis (Eds.), *Handbook of gifted education* (2nd ed., pp. 460–474). Boston: Allyn and Bacon.

Johnson, L. J., Karnes, M. B., & Carr, V. W. (1997). Providing services to children with gifts and disabilities: A critical need. In N. Colangelo & A. D. Davis (Eds.), *Handbook of gifted education* (2nd ed., pp. 516–527). Boston: Allyn and Bacon.

Kerr, B. (1997). Developing talents in girls and young women. In N. Colangelo & A. D. Davis (Eds.), *Handbook of gifted education* (2nd ed., pp. 483–497). Boston: Allyn and Bacon.

Kolloff, P. B. (1997). Special residential high schools. In N. Colangelo & A. D. Davis (Eds.), *Handbook of gifted education* (2nd ed., pp. 198–206). Boston: Allyn and Bacon.

Lando, B. Z., & Schneider, B. H. (1997). Intellectual contributions and mutual support among developmentally advanced children in homogeneous and heterogeneous work/discussion groups. *Gifted Child Quarterly, 4*(2), 44–57.

MacKinnon, D. W. (1962). The nature and nurture of creative talent. *American Psychologist, 17*(7), 484–495.

Maker., C. J., & Nielsen, A. B. (1995). *Teaching models in the education of the gifted.* Austin, TX: Pro-Ed.

Maker, C. J., & Nielson, A. B. (1996). *Curriculum development and teaching strategies for gifted learners.* Austin, TX: Pro-Ed.

Margolin, L. (1996). A pedagogy of privilege. *Journal for the Education of the Gifted, 19*(2), 164–180.

Moon, S. M., Kelly, K. R., & Feldhusen, J. F. (1997). Specialized counseling services for gifted youth and their families: A needs assessment. *Gifted Child Quarterly, 41*(1), 16–25.

Olszewski-Kubilius, P. (1997). Special summer and Saturday programs for gifted students. In N. Colangelo & A. D. Davis (Eds.), *Handbook of gifted education* (2nd ed., pp. 180–188). Boston: Allyn and Bacon.

Perrone, P. A. (1997). Gifted individuals' career development. In N. Colangelo & A. D. Davis (Eds.), *Handbook of gifted education* (2nd ed., pp. 398–407). Boston: Allyn and Bacon.

Plomin, R. (1997). Genetics and intelligence. In N. Colangelo & A. D. Davis (Eds.), *Handbook of gifted education* (2nd ed., pp. 67–74). Boston: Allyn and Bacon.

Ramos-Ford, V., & Gardner, H. (1991). Giftedness from a multiple intelligences perspective. In N. Colangelo & G. A. Davis (Eds.), *Handbook of gifted education* (pp. 55–64). Boston: Allyn and Bacon.

Ramos-Ford, V., & Gardner, H. (1997). Giftedness from a multiple intelligences perspective. In N. Colangelo & A. D. Davis (Eds.), *Handbook of gifted education* (2nd ed., pp. 54–66). Boston: Allyn and Bacon.

Richert, E. S. (1991). Rampant problems and promising practices in identification. In N. Colangelo & G. A. Davis (Eds.), *Handbook of gifted education* (pp. 81–96). Boston: Allyn and Bacon.

Richert, E. S. (1997). Excellence with Equity ™ in identification and programming. In N. Colangelo & A. D. Davis (Eds.), *Handbook of gifted education* (2nd ed., pp. 75–88). Boston: Allyn and Bacon.

Rimm, S. B. (1982). *PRIDE: Preschool and primary interest descriptor.* Watertown, WI: Educational Assessment Service.

Rimm, S. B., & Davis, G. A. (1983, September/October). Identifying creativity, Part II. *G/C/T*, 19–23.

Schiever, S. W., & Maker, C. J. (1997). Enrichment and acceleration: An overview and new directions. In N. Colangelo & A. D. Davis (Eds.), *Handbook of gifted education* (2nd ed., pp. 113–125). Boston: Allyn and Bacon.

Silverman, L. K. (1986). What happens to the gifted girl? In C. J. Maker (Ed.), *Critical issues in gifted education: Defensible programs for the gifted,* Vol. 1 (pp. 43–89). Austin, TX: Pro-Ed.

Silverman, L. K. (1997). Family counseling for the gifted. In N. Colangelo & A. D. Davis (Eds.), *Handbook of gifted education* (2nd ed., pp. 382–397). Boston: Allyn and Bacon.

Sternberg, R. J. (1993). Sternberg triarchic abilities test. Unpublished test.

Sternberg, R. J. (1997). A triarchic view of giftedness: Theory and practice. In N. Colangelo & A. D. Davis (Eds.), *Handbook of gifted education* (2nd ed., pp. 43–53). Boston: Allyn and Bacon.

Subotnik, R. (1997). Talent developed: Conversations with masters in the arts and sciences. *Journal for the Education of the Gifted, 20*(3), 306–317.

Tannenbaum, A. J. (1997). The meaning and making of giftedness. In N. Colangelo & A. D. Davis (Eds.), *Handbook of gifted education* (2nd ed., pp. 27–42). Bsoton: Allyn and Bacon.

Terman, L. M. (1925). *Genetic studies of genius: Vol. 1. Mental and physical traits of a thousand gifted children.* Stanford, CA: Stanford University Press.

Tomlinson, C. A., Callahan, C. M., & Lelli, K. M. (1997). Challenging expectations: Case studies of high-potential, culturally diverse young children. *Gifted Child Quarterly, 4*(2), 5–17.

Torrance, E. P. (1961). Problems of highly creative children. *Gifted Child Quarterly, 5*, 31–34.

Torrance, E. P. (1965). *Gifted children in the classroom.* New York: Macmillan.

Torrance, E. P. (1966). *Torrance tests of creative thinking.* Bensenville, IL: Scholastic Testing Service.

Torrance, E. P. (1968). Finding hidden talent among disadvantaged children. *Gifted and Talented Quarterly, 12*, 131–137.

U.S. Department of Education. (1993). *National excellence: A case for developing America's talent.* Washington, DC: Office of Education Research and Improvement, U.S. Department of Education.

Van Tassel-Baska, J. (1989). Counseling the gifted. In J. Feldhusen, J. Van Tassel-Baska, & K. Seeley (Eds.), *Excellence in educating the gifted.* Denver, CO: Love.

VanTassel-Baska, J. (1997). What matters in curriculum for gifted learners: Reflections on theory, research, and practice. In N. Colangelo & A. D. Davis (Eds.), *Handbook of gifted education* (2nd ed., pp. 126–135). Boston: Allyn and Bacon.

Van Tassel-Baska, J., & Chepko-Sade, D. (1986). *An incidence study of disadvantaged gifted students in the Midwest.* Evanston, IL: Center for Talent Development, Northwestern University.

Wallach, M. A. (1976). Tests tell us little about talent. *American Scientist, 64*, 57.

Westberg, K. L., & Archambault, F. X., Jr. (1997). A multi-site case study of successful classroom practices for high ability students. *Gifted Child Quarterly, 41*(1), 42–51.

Whitmore, J. R., & Maker, C. J. (1985). *Intellectual giftedness in disabled persons.* Rockville, MD: Aspen.

Williams, F. E. (1980). Creativity assessment packet. East Aurora, NY: DOK.

Crain-Thoreson, C., 302
Crapps, J. M., 84
Crawford, D., 215
Crim, D., 6–7
Crinella, F. M. *See* Swanson, J. M.
Crocker, A. D., 439–440
Cronbach, L. J., 54
Cross, A. H., 79
Crouch, R. T., 52, 60
Crowley, K. *See* Swanson, J. M.
Cuccaro, M. L., 362
Cueva, J., 363. *See also* Campbell, M.
Cullen, C., 202. *See also* McCusker, C. G.
Cullinan, D., 226
Cumming, C., 405
Cummings, C. M., 57, 61
Cunningham, A. L., 403
Curlee, R. F., 308
Curran, C. E., 183, 203
Curtis, M. J., 131–132
Cutler, R. L., 227
Cystic Fibrosis Foundation, 484–485

Dadds, M. R., 231
DaFonseca, V., 192–193
Daggett, J., 364
Dailey, R. A., 208
Dale, P. S., 302
Dalton, B., 192
Daly, D. A., 306
Damberg, P. R., 268
D'Amico, R., 229. *See also* Wagner, M.
Daneman, D., 482–483
Danielsen, L. C., 29
Dao, M., 57
Darling, R. B., 71, 79–80, 85–86, 90, 94, 95
Dart, 1
Davis, C. A., 365
Davis, C. H., 84
Davis, E., 358
Davis, G. A., 511, 523
Davis, L. A., 61
Davis, L., 496
Davis, W. E., 40, 41–42, 272
Dawson, G., 354, 365
Day, J., 268
Deaton, A. V., 379
Deb, S., 210, 357
DeBenedetti-Gaddini, R., 364–365
DeCharms, R., 19
Deci, E. L., 154, 203
Deemer, S. A., 208
DeFries, J. C., 191
DeHann, R., 516
DeHart, D. D., 57, 61
Delisle, J. R., 532, 533
Dembo, T., 89–90
DeMesquita, P. B., 181
DeMontfort-Supple, M., 303
Denckla, M. B., 176, 187, 188, 191, 195, 202, 204
Denny, R. K., 226
Dent, H., 318
DePompei, R., 382
Deshler, D. D., 185, 197–198, 203. *See also* Ellis, E. S.; Tralli, R.
Desmond, M. L., 83

Dettmer, P. A., 195
Dever, R. *See* Garber, H. L.
Diana v. *State Board of Education,* 54
Diaz-Rico, L. T., 55
Dilts, C. V., 191
Dimitrova, E., 436
Dixon, J. M., 451
Doak, E., 204
Dockrell, J., 194
Doering, K. *See* Sailor, W.
Dofny, E., 268
Dolnick, E., 399
Donahue, M., 120
Donellan, A. M., 364
Donenberg, G., 370
Dotter, D. L., 6
Doughty, J. F., 133, 134
Dowdy, C. A., 187, 300. *See also* Smith, T. E. C.
Downing, J., 330–331
Dreifuss, F. E., 481
Dresser, P., 476–478, 482–483
Drew, C. J., 15, 56, 60, 61, 156, 157, 158, 174, 175, 191, 198, 209, 217, 260, 271, 272, 308, 311, 333, 347, 348, 357, 359, 363, 364, 369, 371. *See also* Gelfand, D. M.
Dryfoos, J., 247
Duggirala, C., 210
Du Mazaubrun, C., 357
Duncan, B. D., 220, 222
Duncum, J. E., 305
Dunlea, A., 439
Dunn, C., 205
Dunn, L. M., 36–37
Dunsmore, J. C., 475
DuPaul, G., 176, 209–210
DuQuiros, G. B., 190
Durand, V. M., 365
Durant, L., Jr., 497, 503
Dutka, S., 268
Dutt, K., 304
Dvir, T., 63
Dweck, C. J., 116
Dwyer, A., 6
Dyck, N. J., 195
Dyson, L. L., 192

Early, B. P., 365
Eber, L., 234, 248
Eckert, T. L., 192–193
Eden, D., 63
Edge, D., 71–72, 86, 89, 90, 94, 95
EDLAW, Inc., 250
Efron, M., 451–452
Egeland, B., 490
Eggert, L. L., 247, 248
Eichinger, J., 330–331
Eidelman, S., 257
Eiserman, W. D., 303, 335
Eklund, S. J., 165–166
Ekman, P., 56–57
Elbert, M., 318
Elder, L., 305
Elliott, D. M., 490
Ellis, E. S., 155, 185, 203. *See also* Deshler, D. D.

Eme, R. F., 191
Emerson, E., 191, 210
Epstein, M. H., 226
Erickson, M. F., 490
Erickson, R. L., 307, 309, 314, 316, 318, 319
Erickson, R. N., 33–34
Erin, J. N., 433, 442
Erman, A. *See* Kreiman, J.
Escobar, M. D., 178
Estrada, A. U., 365
Etscheidt, S. E., 238
Evans, I. M., 334
Evans, J. P., 247
Evers, R. B., 206
Ezekowitz, R. A., 486
Ezelle, L. A., 178

Factor, A. R., 164
Faigel, H. C., 204
Falik, L. H., 70, 71
Faraone, S. V., 176, 190, 191
Farmer, E. M. Z., 190, 201
Farmer, T. W., 190, 201, 227
Farrington, D. P., 231
Faust, D., 84
Fay, G. C. *See* Jaffe, K. M.; Rivera, J. B.
Fay, W., 369
Fazzi, D. L., 443
Featherstone, H., 78
Fecser, F. A., 244
Feeney, T. *See* Ylvisaker, M.
Feenick, J. J., 377
Fein, D., 227
Felce, D., 175–176, 209, 210. *See also* Lowe, K.
Feldhusen, J. F., 531. *See also* Moon, S. M.
Felsenfeld, S., 308, 315
Fennoy, I., 358
Ferguson, B., 157, 285, 343. *See also* McDonnell, J.
Ferguson, D., 135
Ferkis, M. A., 176, 185, 188, 190
Ferrara, J. M., 234
Ferro-Almeida, S. C., 183, 199, 203
Fewell, R. R., 83, 86
Fewer, D., 405
Fields, E., 227
Filby, N., 116
Filler, J. *See* Sailor, W.
Fine, M. J., 71
Fine, E., 189
Fink, A. H., 227
Fink, W., 271
Finkelhor, D., 231, 490
Finley, V. S., 521. *See also* Hunsaker, S. L.
First, L. R., 486
Fischel, J. E., 301
Fischer, F. W., 407
Fishbaugh, M. S. E., 195
Fisher, T. D. *See* Swanson, J. M.
Fisher, W., 364. *See also* Chapman, S.
Fleisch, B., 226. *See also* Knitzer, J.
Fletcher, J., 178
Florian, L., 145
Folven, R. J., 413–414
Fombonne, E., 357
Forbes, E., 84

McKee-Higgens, E., 201, 208
McKinney, J. D., 175–176. *See also* Hallahan, D. P.
McLaughlin, M. J., 29, 133
McLaughlin, M. W., 18
McLean, J., 333
McLean, L., 333
McLeskey, J., 208
McLoughlin, J. A., 83
McMahon, C. M., 244
McMillan, J. H., 54, 55, 192, 195
McMurray, M., 209–210
McNamara, A. P., 321
McNaughton, S., 305
McNulty, B. A., 208
McPhee, N., 86
Med Access, 486
Mehring, T. A., 497
Meichenbaum, D. H., 238
Meister, J. S., 61
Melloy, K. J., 244
Menage, P., 365
Merrill, E. C., 268
Mertens, D. M., 421
Merton, R. K., 63
Mesibov, G. B., 361, 363–364, 364
Metzler, H. M. D. *See* Hill, M. L.
Meyer, D. J., 69, 81, 82, 83, 86
Meyer, G. *See* Ferguson, D.
Meyer, L. H., 290, 327, 329, 334, 337
Mian, M., 491, 492
Milberger, S., 191
Milburn, J. F., 244
Miliotis, D. *See* Masten, A. S.
Miller, F., 464, 466–467
Miller, S., 155, 186
Miller-Wood, D. J., 451–452
Mills v. *District of Columbia Board of Education,* 20–21
Minke, K. M., 208
Minow, M., 4
Minshew, N. J., 359, 361
Minty, G. D., 484
Mirenda, P., 305, 342
Mirsky, A. J., 159
Mishkin, L., 382, 383
Misra, A., 77, 87, 90, 94
Misra, G., 56
Moaven, L. D., 403
Molineux, M., 202
Moll, L. C., 58
Montague, M., 175–176
Montgomery, A., 40, 42
Montgomery, J., 101
Moon, S. M., 531, 532
Moore, R. J., 244
Moores, D. F., 410–411
Moreno, S. J., 364
Morgane, P. J., 191–192
Morningstar, M. E., 146
Morra, L. G., 136
Morris, V. C., 49
Morse, W. C., 227
Morsink, C. V., 134
Mosley, J. L., 268
Moss, J., 76

Mottron, L., 360, 361–362
Muir-Hutchinson, L., 90
Mulick, J. A., 403
Munsch, J., 203, 210
Murray, J. B., 362, 363
Musson, N. D., 304–305

Naglieri, J. A., 194
Nass, R., 204
National Advisory Committee on Handicapped Children, 174
National Association of State Boards of Education, 39, 133
National Association of State Directors of Special Education, 276, 325
National Center on Educational Restructuring and Inclusion, 39, 130
National Commission on Excellence in Education, 33, 132
National Council on Disability, 11, 143, 156
National Information Center for Children and Youth with Disabilities, 273
National Information Center on Deafness and the National Association of the Deaf, 403
National Joint Committee on Learning Disabilities, 174–175, 206
National Research Council, 33, 34, 61, 115, 116, 143, 167
National School Boards Association, 41
National Spinal Cord Injury Statistical Center, 472–473
Natriello, G., 41
Neal, B. W., 348
Neemann, J. *See* Masten, A. S.
Neff, R. K., 181
Nelson, C. M., 220, 234, 252. *See also* Braaten, S.
Nelson, E. C., 365
Nelson, J. E., 358–359. *See also* Gordon, C. T.
Nelson, K. A., 436
Nelson, K. E., 364
Nelson, N. W., 299, 300, 303, 304, 309, 313
Nestor, P. G., 205
Nevin, A., 343
Newcomer, R., 166
Newman, L. *See* Wagner, M.
Newton, C., 339
Nichols, P., 229
Nichols-Whitehead, P., 297
Nielsen, A. B., 529
Nientimp, E. G., 358, 368
Niermann, R., 308
Nirje, B., 288
Nisbet, J., 39, 81, 145
Nodland, M., 363
Noonan, M. J., 103, 105, 112, 279–280
Norton, P., 56, 359, 364, 369, 371
Noshpitz, J. D., 178
Notari-Syverson, A., 302
Nuccio, J. B. *See* Benson, G.

Oades, R. D., 365
Obiakor, F. E., 497
Ochaita, E., 441–442
O'Connor, D., 208
O'Day, J. A., 18, 33

O'Donnell, L., 369
Ohler, D. L., 206
Ohtaki, E., 357
Ohtsuka, A., 175
Olkinuora, E., 183
Olszewski-Kubilius, P., 530–531
O'Neill, R., 357, 359, 361, 371
Onslow, M., 309
Orr, R. R., 439–440
Ortiz, M. H., 310
Osborn, J. A., 363
Osborne, L. T., 6–7
Osher, D. M., 234
Osher, D., 229, 245
Osher, T. W., 234
Osher, T., 229
Osman, O. T., 365
Otomo, K., 406
Ouellette, J. *See* Wood, W.
Owen, S. V., 301
Owens, R. E., 305
Owens, R. E., Jr., 305, 313, 317

Paden, E. P., 308
Pai, Y., 49
Pallas, A. M., 41
Palmer, D. J., 55
Palmer, P., 359
Palmer, R. L., 190
Pannbacker, M., 321
Papoudi, D., 365. *See also* Trevarthen, C.
Parent, W., 334
Parker, H. C., 178
Parks, W., 461, 476, 479
Parmar, R. S., 185
Parsons, A. S., 438, 439
Patrick, P. E., 420
Patrikakou, E. N., 173, 182, 202, 203
Patton, J. R., 270, 271, 273, 314
Paul, P. V., 399, 405, 406, 407
Paul, R., 369
Payette, K. A., 180–181, 186
Payne, D. A., 192
Payne, J. S., 270. *See also* Patton, J. R.
Peacock, M., 268
Peacock Hill Working Group, 234, 252
Pearson, C. A., 252
Peck, A. F., 456
Peck, C. A., 290, 327, 329. *See also* Meyer, L. H.
Peck, V. A., 268
Pelletier, L. G., 154
Pena, E., 55
Pennington, B. F., 191
Pennsylvania Association for Retarded Citizens v. *Commonwealth of Pennsylvania,* 20–21
Pepler, D. J., 84
Perkins, W. H., 308
Perret, Y. M., 276
Perrig, P., 187–188
Perrig, W. J., 187–188
Perrone, P. A., 530, 532
Perry, C. K., 321
Perry, J., 210
Peterson, N. L., 71, 88, 110, 221
Peterson, P. *See* Carta, J. J.
Pfiffner, L. J. *See* Swanson, J. M.

Amblyopia, 434–435
American Association on Mental Deficiency, 9
American Association on Mental Retardation, 9n, 260–262, 334
American Federation for the Blind, 9
American Printing House for the Blind, 447
American Psychiatric Association, 8, 175, 222–225
American Sign Language, 413f, 413–414
Americans with Disabilities Act (1990), 10–12, 23t, 146–147, 207, 463
  definition of disability, 11
  purpose of, 10
  reasonable accommodations, 11–12, 286–287, 463
  and students with disabilities, 32
Amniocentesis, 278
Amphetamines, 209–210, 499t
Anabolic steroids, 499t
Analytic intelligence, 514–515
Anemia, 486
Anencephaly, 277
Anger, in terminal illness, 477t
Anophthalmia, 436
Anorexia nervosa, 223
Anoxia, 276, 363
Anthropology, 5
Antibiotics
  and birth defects, 276
  in sickle cell anemia, 486
Anticonvulsants, 276, 365, 481
Antihistamines, sedating, 498t
Anti-inflammatory drugs, 473
Antipsychotics, 365
Anti-Rh gamma globulin, 276, 404
Anti-viral therapy, 478
Anxiety disorders, 223
Anxiety withdrawal, 222, 228
Apartment, semi-independent, 162
Apgar scoring, 277–278
Aphasia, 173, 300–301
  causation, 302–303
  developmental, 301
  expressive, 379
  intervention, 303–305
  in traumatic brain injury, 378–379
Arc—A National Organization on Mental Retardation, 8n, 266, 348
ART. See Aggression Replacement Training Program
Articulation disorders, 270, 314–318
  causation, 314–317
  definition of, 314
  functional, 314–318
  intervention, 317–318, 322–323
  physical abnormalities and, 314–318
Artificial intelligence, for assessment, 234
Asian Americans, parents, and special education, 57
Assessment, 18–19, 27, 34. See also Specific disorders
  authentic, 337
  computers and artificial intelligence in, 234
  criterion-referenced, 192–193
  curriculum-based, 192–193, 234

in early childhood years, theoretical perspectives and, 111, 112t
  early developmental, 453–455
  ecological, 279, 334
  error, cultural bias and, 54–55
  formal, for special education, 119
  functional, 334
  language diversity and, 54–55
  in native/primary language, 22t, 25, 54–55
  nondiscriminatory and multidisciplinary, 24–25
    multicultural issues in, 53–56
  norm-referenced, 192–193
  preparation of professionals, and bias, 55–56
Assistive communication, 305
Assistive listening systems, 408
Assistive technology, 105, 264, 339–342
Association for Children with Learning Disabilities, 9
Association for Persons with Severe Handicaps, The, 151, 327–328, 329, 348
Association for Retarded Citizens, 8n
Asthma, 320
Astigmatism, 434
Asylums, 452
Ataxic cerebral palsy, 464
Athetoid cerebral palsy, 464
Athetosis, 333
Atresia, 404
Atropinization, 455
Attempted suicide, 495
Attendant services, 150
Attention
  in ADHD, 176, 177t
  learning disabilities and, 188
Attention deficit disorders, 222
  and head injury risk, 379
Attention-deficit/hyperactivity disorder
  causes, 176–178
  diagnostic criteria for, 177t
  learning disabilities and, 176–178
  medication for, 209–210
  prevalence, 178
  sex and, 178
  subcategories, 176
Audible traffic signals, 456
Audiologist, 420–421
Audition, 396
Auditory approach, in hearing loss, 411–412
Auditory association, 189
Auditory blending, 189
Auditory discrimination, 189
Auditory media, in vision loss, 450–451
Auditory memory, 189
Auditory perception, learning disabilities and, 188–189
Augmentative communication, 284, 304–305, 322, 342, 467
Aura, 479
Authentic assessment, 337
Autism, 353–373
  in adults, 367
  behavioral intervention in, 365–369
  biological factors in, 362–363

causation, 362–363
  challenging behavior in, 360–361
  characteristics of, 357–362
  definition of, 355–357
  diagnostic criteria for, 356t
  in early childhood, 366
  and education, 363–364
  in elementary school, 366–367
  facilitative communication in, 369
  and family, 366–367, 369–371
  in IDEA, 219, 219n, 354–356, 364
  impaired or delayed language in, 356t, 358
  and intelligence, 227, 359–361
  and interacting in natural settings, 366–367
  learning characteristics of, 361–362
  prevalence, 357
  psychodynamic theory of, 362–363, 364–365
  psychological and medical services in, 364–365
  resistance to change in routine, 358–359
  savant syndrome in, 370
  in secondary school, 367
  self-stimulation in, 355, 358, 371
    as reinforcer, 372
  services and supports in, 363–369
  sex differences in, 357
  social interaction in, 356t, 357–358
Autism Society of America, 371
Automobile-related accidents, 379, 380t, 471, 473
Avoidance, 86

Baby-sitters, 80–81
Bargaining, in terminal illness, 477t
Barrier-free access, 13
Basal readers, 199
Basic skills approach, to special education, 115–117
BEH. See Bureau of Education for the Handicapped
Behavior
  abnormal, 16–17
  adaptive, behavior disorders and, 227–228
  challenging, in autism, 360–361
  normal, identifying, 217–218
  social, behavior disorders and, 227–228
Behavioral analysis techniques, 233–234
Behavioral contracts, 201–202, 237
Behavioral intervention plan, 31, 250
Behavioral psychology, 519–520
Behavioral theory, and early childhood programs, 111, 112t
Behavior disorders, 3, 215–255
  and academic achievement, 228–229
  adaptive and social behavior in, 227–228
  in adolescence, 245–249
  assessment, 231–234
    factors, 232
    screening and referral, 231–232
    techniques, 232–234, 233t
  causation, 229–231
    behavioral approach, 230
    biological approach, 229–230

Diplomas, for students with disabilities, 167–168
Direct observation, 233
Disabilities
 definition of, 3
  in IDEA 97, 23–24, 23t, 120
  in Section 504 and ADA, 11, 32
 and giftedness, 536–537
 as label, 2–3
 medical model, 14–16
 prevalence distribution by, 179–180, 180t
 psychological understanding of, 16
 severe and multiple, 325–551
 sociological understanding of, 17–18
 understandings of, 13–18
Discharge planning model, in traumatic brain injury, 382
Discipline
 and IDEA 97, 23t, 30–32, 250
 procedures, and behavior disorders, 231
 referral, 251
Discrimination. See also Americans with Disabilities Act (1990)
 history of, 7–8
 labeling and, 4
Disease model, of exceptionality, 14
Disorder(s). See also specific disorders
 definition of, 3
 as label, 2–3
Disruptive behavior disorders, 222–223
Divergent thinking, 510, 523
Diversity, 47–67. See also Multicultural issues
Divorce, and behavior disorders, 230–231
DMD. See Duchenne muscular dystrophy; Muscular dystrophy
Dopamine drugs, 365
Double hemiplegia, 472t
Double vision, 435
Down syndrome, 71, 271, 273
 myths and truths about, 274
 synthesized speech in, 284
Driving under the influence, 380
Dropout rates, 53f
 behavior disorders and, 229, 245
 for culturally diverse students, 52
 income and, 52
 for students at risk, 40
 for students with disabilities, 143
Drugs, illicit, student discipline for, 30–32, 250
Drug therapy
 for ADHD, 209–210
 for AIDS, 477–478
 for autism, 365
 for behavior disorders, 235t, 238, 239t, 245
 for learning disabilities, 209–210, 212
 for seizure disorders, 481
 in spinal cord injury, 473
Drug use/abuse
 intravenous, and AIDS, 477
 key substances and effects, 497, 498t–499t
 maternal, 497–503
 during pregnancy, 276, 497–500, 500t, 501f

of students at risk, 40
and youth suicide, 495–496
Drunken driving, 380
DSM-IV. See Diagnostic and Statistical Manual of Mental Disorders
Dual diagnosis, 329–330
Dual sensory impairment, 329
Duchenne muscular dystrophy, 474–475. See also Muscular dystrophy
Due process, in education, 25, 35t
Dyadic relationship, 77
DynaVox, 304
Dyslexia, 116, 173, 184

Ear
 external, 397
 inner, 398
 middle, 398
 structures of, 397f, 397–398
Early childhood, 103–114
 autism in, 366
 behavior disorders in, 239–242
 changes for, 103–104
 giftedness in, 524, 534
 hearing loss in, 409
 infants and toddlers
  early intervention for, 104–110
  service delivery, 105–110
  transition to preschool, 114t
 learning disabilities in, 196
 mental retardation in, 279–280, 282
 physical and health disabilities in, 488
 preschool children
  home- and center-based programs, 111–112, 239t, 239–242
  inclusive classrooms for, 112–113
  services for, 110–111
  transition to elementary school, 113–114, 114t
 severe and multiple disabilities in, 335–337
 theoretical perspectives of, 111, 112t
 traumatic brain injury in, 386
 vision loss in, 435–437, 439, 440, 444
Early intervention, 103
 center-based model, 105
 combination of services, 105–110
 eligibility, 104
 in hearing loss, 408–410
 home-based model, 105
 and IDEA 97, 104–105
 for infants and toddlers, 104–110
 intensity of, 110
 in mental retardation, 279–280
 service delivery, 105–110
 in severe and multiple disabilities, 335
 for stuttering, 309
 theoretical perspectives and, 111, 112t
 transition to preschool, 114t
Eating disorders, 223
EBD. See Emotional or behavior disorders
Echolalia, 270, 358
Ecological approach, to abnormal behavior, 16–17
Ecological assessment, 279, 334
Ecological theory, and early childhood programs, 111, 112t

Edison, Thomas, 5–6
Educability expectations, in mental retardation, 264–265
Education. See also Inclusion, educational; Special education
 access to, 18
 changes in, 18–21
 comparison of general, special and multi-cultural, 50–51
 cultural pluralism and, 50–51
 language diversity and, 52–53
 legal precedents in, 20–21, 21t–22t
 purposes of and approaches to, 49–53
 successful schools, attributes of, 132–133
Education, differentiated, 525, 528, 530, 537
Educational achievement. See Achievement
Educational Amendments Acts (1974), 22t
Educational blindness, 433
Educational collaboration. See Collaboration, educational
Educational integration, 36t, 38
Educationally disadvantaged, 41
Education of the Handicapped Act (1975), 23t
Education of the Handicapped Act amendments (1986), 21–22, 23t, 103, 408
Elaboration, 508
Elective mutism, 225
Electronic mobility devices, 443
Elementary school, 114–122
 autism in, 366–367
 behavior disorders in, 240–245
 communication disorders in, 312–313
 educational collaboration in, 122–132
 family supports in, 88–89
 giftedness in, 525–532, 534–535
 hearing loss in, 409–410
 inclusion in, 132–135
  full, and continuum of placement, 135–137
 learning disabilities in, 195–202
  academic instruction and support, 196–201
  behavioral interventions, 201–202
  medical services/medication, 209–210
 mental retardation in, 280–285
 physical and health disabilities in, 488–489
 severe and multiple disabilities in, 338–342, 344–345
  assistive technology and, 339–342
  parental involvement and, 339–340
  and self-determination, 338–339
  teaching functional skills, 339–341
 traumatic brain injury in, 380t, 386–387
 vision loss in, 439–440, 444–445
Eligibility
 for early intervention, 104
 for special education, 23–24, 34t, 120
Eligibility programs, 160–161
Elimination disorders, 223
Emotional abuse, 490, 491t
Emotional disorders
 in dual diagnosis, 329–330
 and language disorders, 301
Emotional disorganization, 73

Emotional disturbance, 218
Emotional or behavior disorders, 215–255.
    See also Behavior disorders
    externalizing and internalizing disorders,
        218–219, 221
    factors influencing, 218
    and interacting in natural settings,
        240–241
    understanding, 217–219
Emphysema, 320
Employment, 160
    ADA and, 12, 286–287, 463
    behavior disorders and, 229, 241, 249
    community-referenced instruction,
        156–157
    giftedness and, 535
    government supports for, 162–164
    hearing loss and, 411
    learning disabilities and, 205–206
    mental retardation and, 283, 286–287
        preparation, 285–286
    physical and health disabilities and, 489
    reasonable accommodations, 286–287,
        463
    severe and multiple disabilities and, 345
    supported, 161, 164, 285–286
        zero-exclusion principle in, 164
    transition from school, 145, 156–157,
        205–206, 285–286
    traumatic brain injury and, 387
    vision loss and, 445
    work experience program, 156–157
Employment Opportunities for Disabled
        Americans Act (1986), 161
Encephalitis, 276
English language skills, hearing loss and,
        405–406
English-only education, 65
Enrichment, 528–529
Entitlement programs, 160–161
Environmental bias, 7
Environmental control systems, 473
Epidural hematoma, 389, 389f
Epilepsy, 333, 479–482, 503. *See also* Seizure
        disorders
Epiphora, 454
Esotropia, 435
Exceptional
    definition of, 3
    as label, 7
Exceptionality
    medical model of, 14–16
    multidisciplinary view of, 1–45
    psychological understanding of, 16–17
    sociological understanding of, 17–18
    terminology, 14f
    understandings of, 13–18
Exclusion, labeling and, 4
Exotropia, 435
Experience deprivation, and delayed speech,
        311
Expressive aphasia, 379
Expressive language, vision loss and, 446
Expressive language disorders, 300
    in traumatic brain injury, 379, 383t–384t
Expressive skills, 297
Expulsion, 253

Extended family
    of adults with disabilities, 165
    of exceptional children, 85–87
External ear, 397
Externalizing disorders, 218–219, 221
Eye(s)
    muscle disorders of, 434–435
    receptive problems in, 435–436
    refractive problems in, 434, 435f
    structure of, 431f, 431–432
Eye-hand coordination, 281, 379, 440

Facilitative communication, 369
Failure to thrive, 476
Falls, 379, 380t
Families of Children with Disabilities
        Support Act (1994), 91–92
Family, 69–99
    of adults with disabilities, 164–165
    autism and, 366–367, 369–371
    behavior disorders and, 240–241
    characteristics and interactions, 76–77
    and child abuse, treatment programs in,
        492
    communication disorders and, 312–313
    crisis reaction, 71–76, 72f, 469
        acknowledgement, 74–76
        defensive retreat, 74
        realization, 73–74
        shock, 73, 469
    dyadic relationships, 77
    early intervention and, 104
    extended family relationships, 85–87,
        165
    father-child relationships, 82–83, 83t
    financial issues, 96–97
    giftedness and, 534–535, 536
    grandparents, 85–87, 95
    hearing loss and, 409–411
    husband-wife relationships, 77–83
    inclusion in, historical perspective on,
        8–9
    learning disabilities and, 196–197
    mental retardation and, 282–283
    mother-child relationships, 81–82
    nonnuclear, 87–88
    parent-child relationships, 80–83
    physical and health disabilities and,
        488–489
    power structure, 77
    severe and multiple disabilities and,
        335–336, 344–345
    sibling relationships, 83–85, 165
    social system approach to, 71
    traumatic brain injury and, 378, 386–387,
        389–391
    vision loss and, 444–445
    and youth suicide, 495
Family-centered care, 248–249, 335
Family practitioner, in hearing loss, 419
Family support, 87–96, 335
    attributes of quality, excellent and su-
        perb, 90–91
    collaboration with professionals, 89–91
    strengthening, 91–93
    survey, 92t–93t
    training, 93–95

Family therapy, 17, 235t, 238, 239t
Fantasizing, as response to disability, 86
FAPE. *See* Free and appropriate public
        education
Farsightedness, 434
Fathers, 82–83, 83t
    adolescent, 493
Feeding disorders, 223
Females, gifted, 532–533
    encouraging, 536
Fenestration, 419
Fetal alcohol syndrome, 265, 275–276
Fetoscopy, 278
Figure-ground discrimination, 188–189
Finger spelling, 414f, 414–415
First Words, 305
Flexible care, 249
Flexible funding, 249
Flexible placement, 452–453
Fluency disorders, 306–309
Fluid reasoning, 172
Folic acid, 469
Formal supports
    in inclusive education, 39
    in mental retardation, 266
Foster family care, 162
Fragile X syndrome, 362
Fraternal twins, studies of, 191
Free and appropriate public education, 24,
        25–26, 34t
Frequency, 398–399
Freud, Sigmund, 229–230
Full inclusion, 39, 249–250
    definition of, 36t
    perspectives on, 135–137, 138–139
Functional academic skills
    in mental retardation, 284–285
    in severe and multiple disabilities,
        332–333
Functional articulation disorders, 314–318
Functional assessment, 334
Functional life skills, 155–156
    in adolescent pregnancy, 494
    in severe and multiple disabilities,
        340–341
    in special education, 115–116, 118

Galactosemia, 275
Gangs, 40, 215, 228, 245–247, 252–253
Gastronomy tube feeding, 333–334
General education teacher
    and educational inclusion, 128–131, 131t,
        208
    and IDEA 97, 26, 128
    and gifted students, 534–535
    and students with autism, 366–367
    and students with behavior disorders,
        240–241
    and students with communication disor-
        ders, 312–313
    and students with hearing loss, 409–411
    and students with learning disabilities,
        196–197
    and students with mental retardation,
        282–283
    and students with physical and health
        disabilities, 488–489

and students with severe and multiple disabilities, 344–345
and students with traumatic brain injury, 386–387
and students with vision loss, 444–445
training for, 128–130
Generalization, 267–268
Gene therapy, 485
Genetic counselors, 16
Genetic engineering, 346
Geneticists, 16
Genetic screening and counseling, 278, 346–347, 453–454
Genetics specialist, in hearing loss, 419
Genetic Studies of Genius, 516–517
GET IT strategy, 200
GIFT (Gift Inventory for Finding Talent), 511
Gifted, 508
Giftedness, 507–542, 508
and acceleration, 528, 540–541
assessment, 520–523
creativity tests, 523
intelligence and achievement tests, 522–523
principles of, 521, 522t
teacher nomination, 521–522
career choices and challenges in, 531–532
and career education, 530
characteristics of, 516–518, 517t, 518t
continuum model for ability grouping, 526f, 526–527
creativity and, 508, 510–511, 513, 513t
curriculum in, 527, 527t
definitions and concepts, 512–516
differentiated education in, 525, 528, 530, 537
and enrichment, 528–529
group counseling in, 531t, 531–532
historical background of, 509–512
historically neglected groups in, 532–538
children living in poverty, 537–538
culturally diverse children, 522, 537–538
females, 532–533, 536
persons with disabilities, 536–537
instructional approaches in, 525
intelligence and, 508–511, 514–516
multiple intelligences, 515, 515t
triarchic theory of, 514–515
and interacting in natural settings, 534–535
as label, 2
mentoring in, 530–531
multicultural issues in, 538
new perspectives of, 511f
origins of, 519–520
in performers, 513, 513t
prevalence, 516
problems and challenges of, 518t, 532
in producers, 513, 513t
service delivery systems in, 525–526
services and supports, 524–532
in childhood and adolescence, 525–532, 534–535
in early childhood, 524, 534
funding, 511–512
preschool programs, 525, 534
special programs and schools in, 529–530

talents and, 508, 511
Gifts and talents, 3
Girls, gifted, 532–533
encouraging, 536
Glasgow Coma Scale, 380t
Glaucoma, 435, 436–437
Glucose, 482–483
Goodness of fit, 337
Government, ADA and, 12
Government-funded programs, 160–164
Governor's schools, 529–530
Grade skipping, 528, 540–541
Grammar, 295
Grand mal seizures, 479
Grandparents, 85–87, 95
Group home, 162
Grouping, mathematical, learning disabilities and, 186, 198
Group-oriented contingency programs, 131–132
Group psychotherapy, 17
for behavior disorders, 235t, 236, 239t
in giftedness, 531t, 531–532
Guardianship, 367
Guide dogs, 443
Guilford, J.P., 510–511

Hallucinogens, 499t
Handicap, definition of, 3
Handicapped, as label, 2–3
Handicapped Children's Early Education Program, 103
Handicapped Children's Protection Act (1986), 23t
Handwriting, learning disabilities and, 183–185, 185f
Haptic perception, learning disabilities and, 188–189
Hard of hearing, 399
Hashish, 498t
Hate crimes, 40
Hawking, Stephen, 2–3
HCEEP. *See* Handicapped Children's Early Education Program
Head injury, 375–393. *See also* Traumatic brain injury
with spinal cord injury, 472
types of injury, 388–389, 389f, 390f
Head Start, 113
Health care, 96–97, 160
government-sponsored, 161
long-term, for aging people with disabilities, 166
Health disabilities, 461–464, 475–487. *See also Specific disabilities*
in adolescence, 488–489
in adults, 489
in early childhood, 488
in elementary school, 488–489
and interacting in natural settings, 488–489
Health disorders, 3
Health insurance, 96–97, 160
Hearing aids, 400, 411–412, 420–421, 421t
Hearing-assist devices, 408
Hearing loss, 395–427
in adolescence, 410–411

age of onset, 399
anatomical sites of loss, 399–400
causation, 402–405
acquired factors in, 404
congenital factors in, 403–404
environmental factors in, 404–405
heredity, 403
prenatal disease, 403–404
central auditory disorder, 399–400
characteristics of, 405–408
classification, 400, 401t
conductive, 399–400, 404
definitions of, 398–400
in early childhood, 409
and educational achievement, 406–407
educational services and supports in, 402, 408–418
in elementary school, 409–410
high-risk categories for, 402–403
and intelligence, 405
and interacting in natural settings, 409–411
medical services in, 419–421
in mental retardation, 271
mixed, 399–400
peripheral, 399–400
postlingual disorders, 399
prelingual disorders, 399
prevalence, 401–402
sensorineural, 399–400, 404
in severe and multiple disabilities, 334
and social development, 407–408
social services in, 421–423
speech and language skills in, 301, 310, 405–406
teaching communication skills in, 410–415
auditory approach, 411–412
manual approach, 413–415
oral approach, 412–413
total communication, 415
technology and, 416–418
closed captioning, 416
computer-assisted instruction, 416–418
telecommunication devices, 418
in traumatic brain injury, 379
treatment of, 419–420
hearing aids, 400, 411–412, 420–421, 421t
surgery, 400, 419–420
Hearing process, 396–398
Heart disease, congenital, 333
Helmets, 377, 382
Hematoma(s)
epidural, 389, 389f
subdural, 389, 390f
Hemiplegia, 472, 472t
Hendrick Hudson District Board of Education v. *Rowley* (1982), 23t, 25–26
Heredity
and hearing loss, 403
in intelligence and giftedness, 519–520
Heroin, 498t
Hertz, 398–399
Higher education
learning disabilities in, 206–207

Higher education *(continued)*
 transition to, 153, 153*t,* 206
  traumatic brain injury and, 385, 385*t*
High school. *See also* Secondary school
 diplomas, for students with disabilities, 167–168
 purpose of, 151–152
Hispanic Americans
 dropout rates, 52
 family and disability, 87
 in gifted programs, 52
 living in poverty, 60–61
 parents, and special education, 56
 in science and mathematics studies, 538
 in special education, 52–53
HIV. *See* Human immunodeficiency virus
HIV-2, 477
Hoarseness, 319–320
Hobsen v. *Hansen* (1969), 22*t*
Home(s)
 group, 162
 semi-independent, 162
Home-based programs
 in behavior disorders, 239*t,* 239–242
 for infants and toddlers, 105
 for preschool children, 111, 239*t,* 239–242
Homebound programs, 27, 28, 29
Home school placement, 39, 133
Homosexuality, and AIDS, 476–477
Hospital education programs, 27, 28, 29
Hospital Insurance Program, 161
Human immunodeficiency virus, 275, 475–479. *See also* Acquired immune deficiency syndrome
 prevalence, 476–477
 transmission, 477
Husband-wife relationships, 77–83
Hydration, and sickle cell anemia, 486
Hydrocephalus, 277, 436
 in spina bifida, 469–470
Hyperactivity
 in ADHD, 176, 177*t*
 learning disabilities and, 189–190
 medication for, 209–210
Hyperglycemia, 482
Hyperkinetic behavior, 173, 189–190
Hypernasality, 319–320
Hyperopia, 434, 435*f*
Hypnosis, 309
Hyponasality, 319–320
Hypotonia, 333

IC. *See* Individualized care
IDDM. *See* Insulin-dependent diabetes mellitus
IDEA. *See* Individuals with Disabilities Education Act
IDEA 97. *See* Individuals with Disabilities Education Act amendments
Ideation, suicidal, 495
Identical twins, studies of, 191
Idiot savant, 370
IEP. *See* Individualized education plan
IFSP. *See* Individualized family service plan
ILP. *See* Individualized language plans
Immaturity, 222, 228

Immune system, 476
Immunization, 277
Impairment, 173
Impulsiveness, in ADHD, 176, 177*t*
Inclusion
 history of, 8–9
 social, 159
Inclusion, educational, 38–39, 101
 behavior disorders and, 249–252
 collaboration and, 122–132
 continuum of placement, 135–137
 definition of, 36*t*
 elementary schools and classrooms, 132–135
 evolving terminology, 36*t*
 formal supports in, 39
 full, 36*t,* 39, 135–137, 138–139, 249–250
 home school placement, 39, 133
 interactive teaming in, 134
 learning disabilities and, 198, 207–208
 mental retardation and, 287–288, 290
 natural supports in, 39
 partial, 36*t,* 39
 preschool, 112–113, 337
  effective, characteristics of, 337
 readiness of schools, 136–137
 school reform and, 33–39
 severe and multiple disabilities and, 332, 337, 343
 spina bifida and, 470–471
 strategies for general and special educators, 131*t*
 teacher perceptions of, 208
 technology and, 127
 vision loss and, 452–453, 456–457
Income, and dropout rates, 52
Income support, 161
Independence, personal
 mental retardation and, 285
 in severe and multiple disabilities, 333
Individual approach, to labeling, 5–6
Individualization, in special education, 115–116
Individualized care, 248–249
Individualized education plan, 24, 26–27, 88–89, 250, 252
 in autism, 364
 for culturally diverse students, 58
 development of, 120–122
 and language diversity, 63
 point card for goals, 246*f*
 for preschool children, 111–112
 requirements, 26–27, 34
 sample form, 123*f*–125*f*
 team, 26, 120–122
 transition planning in, 146
 in traumatic brain injury, 383
Individualized family service plan, 21–22, 88, 92, 105, 110
 sample, 106*f*–109*f*
Individualized language plans, 303–304
Individualized transition plan, 147–151, 148*f*
 formulation of, steps in, 147, 149*t*
Individuals with Disabilities Education Act (1990), 21–32, 23*t,* 43, 250
 autism in, 219, 219*n,* 354–356, 364
 behavior disorders in, 219–220, 250

 children served under, by disability, 179, 180*t*
 comparison with Section 504, 32, 34*t*–35*t*
 deafness-blindness in, 330–331
 deafness in, 399
 enforcement, 35*t*
 free and appropriate public education, 24, 25–26, 34*t*
 funding, 34*t*
 health disabilities in, 462, 475
 individualized education plan, 24, 26–27, 34
 learning disabilities in, 174, 178
 least restrictive environment, 24, 27–29, 28*f*
 mediation between parents and schools, 25
 nondiscriminatory and multidisciplinary assessment, 24–25
 parental safeguards and involvement, 24, 25, 35*t*
 physical disabilities in, 462
 related services, 22–23
 severe and multiple disabilities in, 328–331
 special education eligibility, 23–24, 34*t,* 120
 special education referral, planning and placement, 118–122
 speech disorders in, 321
 transition services, 146
 traumatic brain injury in, 377
 zero-exclusion principle, 31
Individuals with Disabilities Education Act amendments (1997)
 and disability definition, 23*t,* 23–24, 120
 and discipline, 23*t,* 30–32, 250
 early intervention, 104–105
 and general education teacher, 26, 128
 individual education program (IEP), 23*t,* 26–27
  sample form, 123*f*–125*f*
  and team, 26, 31–32
 mediation between parents and schools, 25
Infant(s), with disabilities
 AIDS, 476–478
 autism, 357
 early intervention for, 104–110, 335
 legal precedents affecting, 21–22, 103
 service delivery, 105–110
 severe and multiple disabilities in, 335, 344
 substance-exposed, 497
 traumatic brain injury, 379, 380*t*
 vision loss, 435–436, 437
 withholding medical treatment for, 348–350
Infant stimulation, 280, 335, 456
Infections
 and autism, 363
 and hearing loss, 403–404
 HIV, 475–479
 and mental retardation, 265, 275
 opportunistic, in AIDS, 476, 478
 in sickle cell anemia, 486–487
 in spina bifida, 469

Teacher(s) *(continued)*
    and students with mental retardation, 282–283
    and students with physical and health disabilities, 488–489
    and students with severe and multiple disabilities, 337, 344–345
    and students with traumatic brain injury, 382–383, 383*t*–384*t*, 386–387
    and students with vision loss, 444–445
    support, 126
Teacher assistance teams, 128
Teacher nomination, in gifted assessment, 521–522
Team(s)
    child-study, 119
    in educational collaboration, 126–132
    in IEP process, 26, 120–122
    interactive, 134
    multidisciplinary, 24, 119, 278–279, 466
    schoolwide assistance, 128
    teacher assistance, 128
    transdisciplinary, 466
Technologically dependent, 462–463
Technology
    for assessment, 234
    assistive, 105, 264, 339–342
    and communication, 284, 304–305
    and educational inclusion, 127
    in hearing loss, 416–418
    and students with autism, 364
    and students with learning disabilities, 198
Technology-Related Assistance for Individuals with Disabilities Act, 341
Teenagers. *See* Adolescent(s)
Telecommunication assistance, 12, 463
Telecommunication devices, in hearing loss, 418
Telescoped schooling, 528
Teletypewriter and printer, 418
Television
    closed-caption, 416
    closed-circuit, 451–452
Television Decoder Circuitry Act (1993), 416
Teratogens, 469
Terman, Lewis M., 509–510, 516–517
Terminal illness, 475
    psychological stages in, 477*t*
Test bias, 54
Text telephones, 418
Therapeutic abortion, 278
Therapeutic recreation, 13
Tic disorders, 223
Tinnitus, 403
T lymphocytes, 476
Tobacco use, 40, 276
Toddlers, with disabilities
    early intervention for, 104–110, 335
    legal precedents affecting, 21–22, 103
    prenatal drug and alcohol exposure and, 500*t*
    service delivery, 105–110
    severe and multiple disabilities, 335, 344
    transition to preschool, 114*t*
Token reinforcement systems, 202, 237
Tonic/clonic seizures, 479–480, 480*t*, 481

Torrance Tests for Creative Thinking, 511
Total communication, 415
Touch Talker, 467
Toxoplasmosis, 275, 403–404
Training
    for family members, 95
    for general education teachers, 128–130
    for parents, 93–94
    for physicians, 15–16, 94
    for professionals, 94–95
    social skills, 243–244
    transfer of, in behavior disorders, 243–244
Training schools, 8
Tranquilizers, 498*t*
Transdisciplinary teams, 466
Transfer of training, 243–244
Transformation, 508
Transition services, 89, 145–146
    adult service agencies and, 149–151
    autism and, 367
    behavior disorders and, 241, 249
    communication disorders and, 313
    components of, 147
    definition of, 146
    giftedness and, 535
    hearing loss and, 410–411
    individualized transition plan, 147–151, 148*f*, 149*t*
    learning disabilities and, 196–197, 204–207
    legal requirements for, 146–147
    mental retardation and, 283, 285–286
    parent and student involvement, 147–149
    physical and health disabilities and, 489
    in secondary schools, 151–157
    severe and multiple disabilities and, 342–343, 345
    traumatic brain injury and, 382, 387
    vision loss and, 445
Transportation, 12, 463
Transverse position, 276–277
Trauma
    and aphasia, 302–303
    during birth, 276–277, 301, 363
    and spinal cord injury, 471–473
Traumatic brain injury, 23–24, 375–393
    in adolescence, 377–378, 387
    in adults, 387
    causation, 379–382, 380*t*
    characteristics of, 378–379
    and cognition, 378
    definition of, 376–377
    developing cognitive-communicative skills in, 383*t*–384*t*
    in early childhood, 386
    educational supports and services in, 382–385
    in elementary school, 386–387
    and interacting in natural settings, 386–387
    medical and psychological services in, 385–391
    neuromotor and physical functioning in, 378–379
    potential effect, assessment of, 379–380, 380*t*

    prevalence of, 377–378
    primary and secondary damage in, 376
    sex differences in, 378
    social and behavioral skills in, 378–379, 383*t*
    speech and language disorders in, 378–379, 383*t*–384*t*
    and transition to postsecondary education, 385, 385*t*
    types of injury, 388–389, 389*f*, 390*f*
Trephining, 17
Triarchic theory, of intelligence, 514–515
Triplegia, 472*t*
Trisomy 21, 273
Trivialization, 86
TTs, 418
TTY, 418
Tuberous sclerosis, 275
Tubular vision, 433
Tunnel vision, 433
Twin studies, 191
    in autism, 362
    in diabetes, 483

UCP. *See* United Cerebral Palsy Organization
Ultrasound, 278
Undersocialized aggression, 228
United Cerebral Palsy Organization, 8–9
Urinary management, 470–471

Ventilators, 462–463
Ventriculoperitoneal shunt, 469–470, 470*f*
Verbalism, 439
Verbal language, 284
Vermis, 362–363
Video disc, 418
Videx TimeWand, 368
Violence
    adolescents and, 228, 245–248, 252–253
    behavior disorders and, 215, 228, 245–248
    learning disabilities and, 205
    and students at risk, 40
    of students with disabilities, and discipline, 30–32, 250, 253
Virtual reality, 364
Vision loss, 429–459
    in adolescence, 445
    assessment, 442, 453–454
    causation, 436–438
        acquired disorders, 437–438
        genetically determined disorders, 436–437
    characteristics of, 438–442
    classification, 434–436
    communication media in, 447–452
    daily living skills in, 442–446
    definitions of, 432–434
    in early childhood, 435–437, 439–440, 444
    and educational achievement, 439
    and educational placement, 452–453, 456–457
    educational supports and services in, 442–453

in elementary school, 439–440, 444–445
and instructional content, 446–447
and intelligence, 438
and interacting in natural settings, 444–445
medical services in, 453–455
in mental retardation, 271
and mobility, 440, 456
mobility training in, 442–443
muscle disorders and, 434–435
and orientation, 440
and perceptual-motor development, 440–441
prevalence, 436
prevention, 453–455
receptive eye problems and, 435–436
refractive eye problems and, 434, 435f
screening for, 453–455
in severe and multiple disabilities, 334
and social development, 439–440
social services in, 455–456
speech and language skills in, 438–439
subcategories, 432–434

in traumatic brain injury, 379
treatment of, 455
warning signs of, 453, 454t
Visual acuity, 433, 442, 453
Visual attention, 442
Visual capacity, 442
Visual contact, in autism, 353, 357
Visual cortex, 431–432, 448
Visual discrimination, 189
Visual Efficient Scale, 442
Visual field, 433, 433f, 442
Visualization, 508
Visual perception, learning disabilities and, 188–189
Visual process, 431f, 431–432
Visual processing, 442
Vocational education, 152–153
Vocational rehabilitation, 163–164
Vocational Rehabilitation Act, 10, 146, 163.
    See also Section 504
Voice disorders, 318–321
    definition of, 318–319

intervention, 320–321
Volume, 398–399
    voice, 319–320

Watson, John, 519–520
Watson, John B., 16
Whole-language instruction, 199
Word knowledge, 182–183
Word recognition, 182–183
Work experience program, 156–157
Wraparound Approach, 248
Wraparound care, 249
Writing, learning disabilities and, 183–185, 185f
Written language
    hearing loss and, 407
    in traumatic brain injury, 384t
Wundt, Wilhelm, 16

Zalcitabine, 477
Zero-exclusion principle, 31
    in supported employment, 164

The following photo credits constitute an extension of the copyright page.